CUBA

CHRISTOPHER P. BAKER

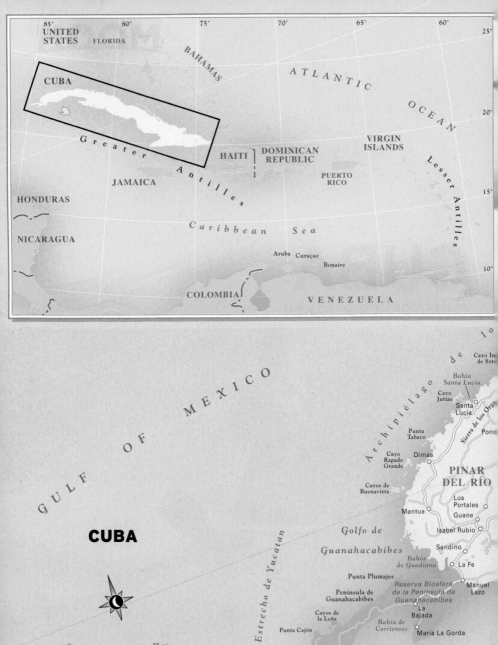

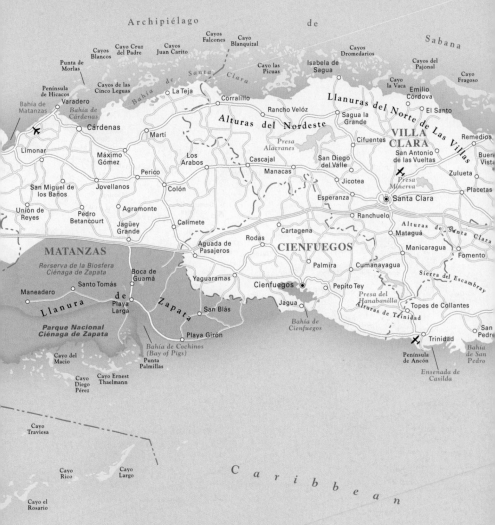

Archipiélago de Sabana

Cayos Falcones
Cayo Blanquizal
Cayos Cruz del Padre
Cayos Blancos
Cayos Juan Carito
Cayos Dromedarios
Cayos del Pajonal
Punta de Morlas
Cayo Fragoso
Cayo las Picuas
Isabela de Sagua
Cayo la Vaca
Emilio Córdova
Cayos de las Cinco Leguas
Península de Hicacos
La Teja
Corrillo
El Santo
Bahía de Santa Clara
Llanuras del Norte de Las Villas
Varadero
Bahía de Matanzas
Rancho Velóz
Sagua la Grande
Bahía de Cárdenas
Cárdenas
Martí
Alturas del Nordeste
Cifuentes
VILLA CLARA
Remedios
Buena Vista
Limonar
Máximo Gómez
Presa Alacranes
San Diego del Valle
San Antonio de las Vueltas
Zulueta
Los Arabos
Cascajal
Perico
Manacas
San Diego del Valle
Presa Minerva
Placetas
San Miguel de los Baños
Jovellanos
Colón
Jicotea
Santa Clara
Esperanza
Unión de Reyes
Pedro Betancourt
Agramonte
Calímete
Ranchuelo
Alturas de Santa Clara
Jagüey Grande
Cartagena
Mataguá
Manicaragua
Fomento
MATANZAS
Aguada de Pasajeros
Rodas
CIENFUEGOS
Palmira
Cumanayagua
Reserva de la Biosfera Ciénaga de Zapata
Boca de Guamá
Yaguaramas
Sierra del Escambray
Santo Tomás
Pepito Tey
Maneadero
Llanura de Zapata
Playa Larga
Cienfuegos
Presa del Hanabanilla
Alturas de Trinidad
Topes de Collantes
San Blás
Jagua
San Pedro
Parque Nacional Ciénaga de Zapata
Playa Girón
Bahía de Cienfuegos
Cayo del Macio
Bahía de Cochinos (Bay of Pigs)
Trinidad
Bahía de San Pedro
Punta Palmillas
Península de Ancón
Cayo Diego Pérez
Cayo Ernest Thaelmann
Ensenada de Casilda

Cayo Traviesa

Caribbean

Cayo Rico
Cayo Largo

Cayo el Rosario

CUBA (CONTINUED)

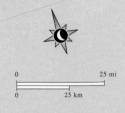

| 0 | 25 mi |
| 0 | 25 km |

Archipiélago de Camagüey

Cayos de Villa Clara
Cayo Santa María
Cayo francés
Bahía Buena Vista

Cayo Guillermo
Cayo Coco
Cayo Botella
Punta San Juan
Bahía de Perros
Comunidad Celia Sánchez

Cayo Paredón Grande
Cayo Judas
Cayo Mégano Grande
Cayo Cruz
Cayo Romano
Bahía de Jigüey
Cayo Guajaba

Llanuras del Nordeste de Las Villas

Yaguajay
Meneses
Mayajigua
Laguna de la Leche
Morón
Bolivia
Llanura Septentrional
Bahía de la Gloria

Jarahueca
Peres
Florencia
Ciro Redondo
Primero de Enero
Miraflores
Velazco
Esmeralda
Sola

A l t u r a s Embalse Lebrije
Taguasco
d e l
Jicotea
N o r d e s t e
Sierra de Cubitas
Senado

Abaiguán
Jatibónico
Majagua
Orlando González
Colorado
Ciego de Ávila
Gaspar
Presa Caonao
Presa Amistad Cubano-Búlgara
CAMAGÜEY
Minas
Crucero de Lugareno

Sancti Spiritus
Embalse Zaza
La Ferrolana
Sanguily
Piedrecitas
Camagüey

SANCTI SPÍRITUS
Jíbaro
Júcaro
Florida
Jimaguayú
Siboney

anao
Pojabo
Romero
Cayos Ana María
Vertientes
Concordia
Contramaestre
Sierra del Chorillo

Golfo de Ana María
Cayo Algodón Grande
Laguna Lamar
Santa Cruz del Sur

Cayo Cuervo

Cayo Bretón
Cayos Cinco Balas
Cayo Grande
Parque Nacional Jardines de la Reina
Cayo Chocolate
Cayo Punta Macho
Cayes Pingues
Cayos Pilón
Cayos Mate
Cayo Media Luna

Cayo Caballones
Cayo Anclitas
Cayo Granada
Cayo Culebra

Archipiélago de los Jardines de la Reina
Cayo Cabeza del Este

S e a

© AVALON TRAVEL

CIEGO DE ÁVILA

Llanura de Jucaro Morón

Llanura Meridional

O C E A N

Paso de los Vientos

Bahía de Banes

El
nón

Bahía de
Levisa

Bahía Sagua
de Tánamo

Cayo
Saetía

Cayo
Nicaro

Levisa

Cayo Mambí

Sierra de Cristal

Sagua de
Tánamo

Mayarí
Arriba

ANTIAGO
DE CUBA

La
ueba

Los
Reynaldos

La Maya

Alto Songo

minos

El Caney

Cayo Moa
Grande

Moa

Punta
Gorda

Cuchillas de Moa

Punta
Guarico

Cuchillas de Toa

Bernardo

GUANTÁNAMO

Bayate

Honduras

El Salvador

Costa
Rica

Niceto
Pérez

Cainamera

Reserva de la
Biosfera Baconao

Siboney

Baconao

Bahía de
Guantánamo

Santiago
de Cuba

Bahía de
antiago
e Cuba

Puriales de
Caujeri

Manuel Tames

Héctor Infante

Guantánamo

Boquerón

US NAVAL
STATION

Punta
Barlovento

Bahía de
Miel

Baracoa

Reserva de la
Biosfera Cuchillas
de Toa

Cuchillas de Baracoa

Jamal

Mesa Abajo

Punta del
Fraile

Maisí

Punta de
Quemado

La Maquina

Punta Caleta

Sierra de Purial

Cajobabo

San Antonio Del Sur

S e a

C a r i b b e a n

CUBA (CONTINUED)

0   25 mi

0   25 km

Contents

DISCOVER
Cuba

The time to visit Cuba is now! With the renewal of diplomatic relations between the United States and Cuba, it is easier to travel to this Caribbean island of eccentricity and enigma than it's been in decades.

With all the media attention on politics, it's easy to overlook the sheer beauty of this relentlessly photogenic isle: diamond-dust beaches and bathtub-warm seas the color of peacock feathers; bottle-green mountains and jade valleys full of dramatic formations; colonial cities with cobbled plazas and cathedrals; and, above all, the sultriness and spontaneity of the people in a place called the most emotionally involving in the Western Hemisphere.

Divers are delirious over Cuba's deep-sea treasures. Birding is the best in the Caribbean. There are crocodiles, too, lurking leery-eyed in well-preserved everglades. Horseback-riding options abound. Cuba is a prime destination for fishing and bicycle touring. Motorcycle tours are available. In the Sierra Maestra, hikers can follow revolutionary trails trod by Fidel Castro and Che Guevara. There is salsa, *mojitos,* and *cuba libres* to enjoy, and the world's finest cigars, fresh from the factory.

Clockwise from top left: 1950s Chevrolet; Cuban cigars; musician; student at the Escuela Nacional de Ballet; Castillo el Morro, Santiago de Cuba.

Cuba's most enigmatic appeal, however, is the sense that you are living inside a romantic thriller. Cuba is intoxicating, laced with the sharp edges and sinister shadows that made Ernest Hemingway wish that he could stay forever. No other Western nation offers such sensual and surreal sensations, made more romantic by Cuba's caught-in-a-time-warp setting.

Cuba is a special place at a special time, quickly fading to myth. The rush is on as the rest of the world tries to get there before it changes and before the nature of Cuban society is transformed as commercialism creeps in and prices soar.

Now is the time to go….

Clockwise from top left: a young Cuban celebrates her Quinceañera; Cuban flag on a patriotic car in Havana; musician at the Casa de la Trova el Guyabero; 1920s mansion in Havana.

Planning Your Trip

Where to Go

Havana

Habana Vieja (Old Havana) is the colonial core, full of plazas, cathedrals, museums, and bars. **Parque Histórico Militar Morro-Cabaña** preserves the largest castle in the Americas. The **Vedado** district teems with beaux-arts, art nouveau, and art deco mansions; a magnificent **cemetery;** and the one-of-a-kind **Plaza de la Revolución.** There are even gorgeous **beaches** nearby.

Artemisa and Pinar del Río

These valleys are where the world's finest tobacco is grown. **Viñales** has magnificent scenery, plus preeminent **climbing** and **caving.** Scuba divers rave about **Cayo Levisa** and **María la Gorda. Península de Guanahacabibes** has birding and hiking trails, as does **Las Terrazas,** Cuba's

most developed eco-resort. Head to **Finca El Pinar San Luis** for Tobacco 101.

Isla de la Juventud Special Municipality

Slung beneath Cuba, this archipelago draws few visitors. The exception is **Cayo Largo,** a coral jewel with stupendous beaches. **Isla de la Juventud** boasts **Presidio Modelo,** the prison where Fidel was held; **Refugio Ecológico Los Indios,** great for birding; and Cuba's finest **diving** off **Punta Francés.** Two days is all that's required to explore Isla de la Juventud, plus two days more for Cayo Largo.

Mayabeque and Matanzas

Cuba's premier beach resort, **Varadero,** has the lion's share of hotels, plus Cuba's only 18-hole

a 1958 Edsel Corsair, Havana

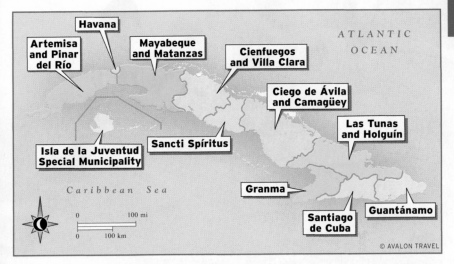

© AVALON TRAVEL

golf course and exceptional **diving.** Colonial-era **Matanzas** is a center for **Afro-Cuban music and dance.** The Caribbean's largest swamp, the **Ciénaga de Zapata,** offers fantastic **birding** and **fishing.** Nearby, **Playa Girón,** site of the 1961 Bay of Pigs invasion, has an engaging **museum.**

Cienfuegos and Villa Clara

Bird-watchers and hikers are enamored of the **Sierra Escambray,** where **forest trails** lead to **waterfalls. Santa Clara** draws visitors to the **mausoleum and museum of Che Guevara.** Sleepy **Remedios** explodes with fireworks during the year-end *parranda* and is gateway to the **beaches** of **Cayos de Villa Clara. Cienfuegos** offers French-inspired colonial architecture and a world-class botanical garden, the **Jardín Botánico Soledad.**

Sancti Spíritus

Sancti Spíritus is a charming hill town that is a crown jewel of **colonial architecture.** It's a great base for hiking at **Gran Parque Natural Topes de Collantes,** lazing at **Playa Ancón,** or riding a **steam train** into the **Valle de los Ingenios.** The provincial capital, **Sancti Spíritus,** also has a colonial core worth exploring, and anglers

are lured to **Embalse Zaza** for world-class bass fishing.

Ciego de Ávila and Camagüey

Tiny Ciego de Ávila Province is the setting for **Cayo Coco,** the most developed isle of the **Jardines del Rey archipelago.** Come here for magnificent **beaches** and to view **flamingos. Playa Santa Lucía** has some of Cuba's best **diving.** The less developed **Jardines de la Reina archipelago** is a new frontier for anglers and divers. **Camagüey** city has quaint **cobbled plazas** and **colonial architecture.**

Las Tunas and Holguín

For travelers, Las Tunas Province is a place to pass through en route to history-packed **Holguín,** with its intriguing **plazas** and lively artistic **culture.** Nearby are the beaches of **Guardalavaca,** an archaeological site at **Museo Aborigen Chorro de Maíta,** the alpine setting of **Pinares de Mayarí,** and Fidel Castro's birthplace at the **Museo Conjunto Histórico Birán.**

Granma

Off-the-beaten-path Granma Province is dominated by the **Sierra Maestra,** the mountainous base for Fidel Castro's guerrilla war. You can

Cuba's musical heritage is evident on the streets of Havana.

hike to his headquarters, **La Comandancia de la Plata,** and to the summit of **Pico Turquino,** Cuba's highest peak. Independence was launched in **Bayamo,** which touts a vibrant **colonial plaza.** For scenery, the lonesome coast road east of the ho-hum beach resort of **Marea del Portillo** can't be beat.

Santiago de Cuba

The city of **Santiago de Cuba,** founded in 1514, predates Havana and has strong Haitian and Jamaican influences. Much of Cuba's **musical heritage** was birthed here. The **Moncada barracks, museums,** and **mausoleums** recall the city's revolutionary fervor. In 2016, Fidel Castro's remains were interred at **Cementerio Santa Ifigenia.** At sunset, visitors flock to **Castillo de San Pedro del Morro** for a **cannon-firing** ceremony. In July the city hosts Cuba's preeminent **Carnaval.** Visitors can explore the eclectic attractions of nearby **Reserva de la Biosfera Baconao** and the basilica at **Cobre.**

Guantánamo

This mountainous province is synonymous with the **U.S. naval base,** which can be viewed from a hilltop restaurant at Glorieta. The town of **Guantánamo** has a lovely colonial plaza and is alive with **traditional music.** Near the **Zoológico de Piedra**—literally a stone zoo—fascinates. The **La Farola** mountain road leads to **Baracoa,** Cuba's oldest city, full of vernacular charm and boasting the island's most dramatic physical setting. Some of the nation's best birding and hiking can be enjoyed at **El Yunque** and **Parque Nacional Alejandro de Humboldt.**

Know Before You Go

When to Go

Cuba has fairly distinct seasons: a relatively dry and mild **winter** (November-April) and a hot and wet **summer** (May-October). Early **spring** is the ideal time to travel, especially in the Oriente (the eastern provinces), which can be insufferably hot in summer. Christmas and New Year's are the busiest periods; many accommodations and car rental agencies sell out then, and finding a domestic flight is nearly impossible. Hotel prices are usually lower in summer—the low season (*temporada baja*)— when hurricanes are a slim possibility. Tropical storms can lash the island even in winter, however.

You might want to time your visit to coincide with a major festival, such as **Carnaval** in Santiago de Cuba or the **Festival del Nuevo Cine Latinoamericano** (Festival of New Latin American Cinema) in Havana.

Before You Go
PASSPORTS AND VISAS

Visitors to Cuba need a **passport** valid for at least six months beyond their intended length of stay; a **ticket** for onward travel; and a **tourist visa,** typically issued when you check make your plane reservation to Cuba or sign up for a people-to-people educational program. Stays of up to 30 days are permitted (90 days for Canadians), extendable one time.

TRANSPORTATION

Most international visitors fly into either Havana's **José Martí International Airport** or Varadero's **Juan Gualberto Gómez International Airport.** Cuba is a large island (more than 1,000 kilometers east-west). In Havana, getting around is simple thanks to an efficient **taxi** system. Traveling between cities by public transportation, however, can be a challenge. **Víazul tourist buses** connect major cities and resorts, as do domestic flights. Renting a car is recommended for serendipitous travelers, but cars are in short supply and roads are full of hazards.

U.S. CITIZENS

U.S. law bans travel by individuals who don't fit into one of the 12 license categories of allowable travel. However, every U.S. citizen qualifies for travel under the "people-to-people" license category, as long as it's with a licensed academic institution or tour company. Since June 2017, solo travel is no longer allowed for people-to-people travel. "Tourism" (i.e., purely recreational travel and beach vacations) is not allowed. For more details, see page 545.

The Best of Cuba

Cuba is a large island, and exploring the isle fully would take at least a month. This fast-paced itinerary provides a sampling of the top scenery, beaches, and cities for those intent on seeing the best of the island in two weeks. Rent a car and plan to spend at least three days touring Havana before heading out to the provinces (don't underestimate how much there is to see in the capital city).

Day 1

Arrive at José Martí International Airport in **Havana;** transfer to a hotel or *casa particular* in Habana Vieja or the Vedado district.

Day 2

Take a self-guided walking tour of **Habana Vieja,** including the **Plaza de Armas, Plaza de la Catedral,** and **Plaza Vieja,** as well as the key museums, galleries, and shops along the surrounding streets. Return at night to savor the plazas lit by traditional gas lanterns. Don't fail to sip a *mojito* at **La Bodeguita del Medio.**

Day 3

This morning, concentrate your time around **Parque Central** and **Paseo de Martí.** You'll want to visit the **Capitolio Nacional, Fábrica de Tabaco Partagás,** the **Museo Nacional de Bellas Artes,** and the **Museo de la Revolución.** A daiquiri at **El Floridita** is a must. At dusk, walk the **Malecón.**

Day 4

Spend the morning exploring the streets of **Vedado,** being sure to call in at the **Hotel Nacional,** the **Hotel Habana Libre Tryp,** and **Universidad de la Habana.** After cooling off with an ice cream at **Coppelia** (with pesos in hand, stand in line with the Cubans), hail a taxi to take you to **Cementerio Colón** and **Plaza de la Revolución.**

mural of Che Guevara, Plaza de la Revolucion, Havana

Day 5

Rent a car and tour **suburban Havana,** calling in at the **Museo Ernest Hemingway.** Then head west along the Autopista Habana-Pinar to **Las Terrazas,** an eco-resort and rural community in the heart of the Sierra del Rosario. Hike the trails and visit the artists' studios. Overnight at Hotel Moka.

Day 6

Continue west to **Valle de Viñales.** Spend the afternoon exploring **Viñales** village, the **Cuevas del Indio,** and the tobacco fields. Overnight either in a *casa particular* or at the Horizontes La Ermita.

Day 7

This morning, head to the town of Pinar del Río and **Finca El Pinar San Luis,** then take the Autopista east to Havana and onward to **Santa Clara.** Visit the mausoleum and museum of Che Guevara and spend the night in town.

Days 8-9

Continue east to the historic town of **Remedios.**

tobacco field, Valle de Viñales

During Christmas week, you'll want to overnight in Remedios to enjoy the local fireworks battles called *parrandas.* Once done, follow the coast road east via Morón to **Cayo Coco,** arriving midafternoon. Spend day 9 relaxing on the beach and enjoying water sports.

Day 10

Depart Cayo Coco and head south via the provincial capital, **Ciego de Ávila,** and then turn west and follow the Carretera Central for **Sancti Spíritus.** After strolling downtown, continue through the **Valle de los Ingenios,** stopping at Hacienda Iznaga. Arriving in **Trinidad,** spend the rest of the afternoon perambulating the ancient plazas.

Day 11

After further walking the cobbled colonial heart of Trinidad, visit the **studio of artist Lázaro Niebla,** then check in with "horse whisperer" Julio Muñoz and go **horseback riding** in the countryside. Tonight, check out an Afro-Cuban performance before heading to the **Disco Ayala,** set in a cave.

Cuba boasts glorious beaches. Most are scattered along the north shore, with concentrations immediately east of Havana, in Varadero, on Cayo Largo, on the Jardines del Rey (Ciego de Ávila and Camagüey Provinces), and in Holguín. The south coast has relatively few noteworthy beaches. Swimming requires caution, as many beaches are known for riptides. Arrive with plenty of mosquito repellent, and avoid most beaches at dusk, when minuscule but ferocious no-see-ums are active.

- **Playas del Este:** This series of lovely beaches is within a 30-minute drive of Havana; they get lively with *habaneros* on weekends. The best sections are Tarará and Playa Mégano.

- **Playa El Francés:** Tucked at the southwestern extreme of Isla de la Juventud, there's a reason this white-sand beach draws big cruise ships. It's a beauty, with turquoise waters for snorkeling. You'll need to hire an obligatory EcoTur guide in Nueva Gerona to get here.

- **Playa Sirena:** Reached by a sandy unpaved road, this stunning beach is the best that Cayo Largo (and Cuba) can offer. The turquoise waters must be seen to be believed—but the waters shelve deeply and are not safe for children.

- **Playa Mayor:** Varadero's main beach has silvery sands that run unbroken for five miles or more. Although it's lined with hotels and thatched restaurants the whole way, you can still find quiet spots all to your lonesome.

- **Playa Ancón:** If you tire of wandering the cobbled streets of Trinidad, explore this beach just a few minutes away. The scuba diving here is superb, and there's a dive shop at the Hotel Playa Ancón; you can use the recreational services for a fee.

Playas del Este

- **Playa Flamenco:** The miles-long, palm-shaded, white-sand beach at Cayo Coco is lined with all-inclusive resorts, all with water sports.

- **Playa Pilar:** The high point of Cayo Guillermo, this beach is backed by sand dunes and has a rustic seafood restaurant.

- **Playa Los Pinos:** Sugar-white sand dissolves into turquoise shallows that stretch as far as the eye can see. It's just you and whatever day-trippers call in on excursions from Playa Santa Lucía. Bring your snorkeling gear to explore the coral reefs farther out.

Day 12

Get up early again to follow the long and winding road over the **Sierra Escambray** to **Gran Parque Natural Topes de Collantes.** Descend to **El Nicho** to bathe in mineral pools at the base of the waterfall before continuing to the lovely bayside city of **Cienfuegos,** with time to stroll the pedestrian boulevard and explore **Parque Martí.**

Days 13-14

Drive west to **Playa Girón,** the landing site for the 1961 Bay of Pigs invasion. Visit the museum before continuing west to **Cueva de los Peces** to snorkel in the blue hole and turquoise Caribbean. At **La Boca de Guamá** stop to visit the **crocodile farm.** Head back to Havana via the Autopista. This evening, visit the **Tropicana** cabaret, being sure to have made reservations. On day 14, fly home.

¡Viva la Revolución!

Thousands of visitors arrive every year to pay homage to, or at least learn about, the *Revolución.* Whatever your politics, a pilgrimage along the revolutionary trail following the footsteps of Fidel Castro & Co. makes for a fascinating historical journey.

Day 1
Arrive at José Martí International Airport in **Havana;** transfer to a hotel or *casa particular* in Habana Vieja or the Vedado district.

Day 2
Start the day with a visit to the **Museo de la Revolución,** housed in the former presidential palace of dictator Fulgencio Batista, whom the Revolution overthrew. Spend some time viewing the fascinating sites nearby. In the afternoon,

tour **Habana Vieja**. Visit the **Museo Casa Natal de José Martí,** birthplace of the national hero whom Fidel Castro called the "intellectual author" of the Revolution, and **Casa-Museo del Che,** near the Fortaleza de San Carlos de la Cabaña.

Day 3
Today, concentrate your sightseeing around **Vedado.** Must-see sights include the **Casa Museo Abel Santamaría,** a former apartment that was the secret headquarters for Castro's 26th of July Movement; the **Universidad de la Habana,** where the **Escalinata** (staircase) was a venue for clashes with Batista's police; **Galería 23 y 12,** where Castro first announced that Cuba was socialist; and **Plaza de la Revolución,** the seat of Communist government.

revolutionary slogans on La Rampa, Havana

Music and dance form the pulsing undercurrent of Cuban life. Spanning the spectrum from traditional *son* to high culture, here are key venues and experiences not to miss in Havana.

SOULFUL TRADITIONS

The **Tablao de Pancho** hosts a supper show with old-time crooners belting out songs from *The Buena Vista Social Club*.

For *bolero* head to **Café Concierto Gato Tuerto,** a 1950s-era lounge where you expect the Rat Pack to stroll in any moment.

The **Conjunto Folklórico Nacional** will wow you with traditional Afro-Cuban dance to the beat of the drums.

Salsa is at its sizzling best at the **Casa de la Música,** where salsa dance lessons are also hosted.

No visit to Havana is complete without a trip to the **Tropicana** for a sexy cabaret show like no other.

Tropicana cabaret, Havana

HIGH CULTURE

Cubans astound with their appreciation of ballet, theater, and classical and choral music, and Havana is replete with venues.

The **Basilica de San Francisco de Asís** hosts classical and chamber ensembles most Saturday evenings. Nearby, the intimate **Iglesia de San Francisco de Paula** is *the* venue to hear choral groups.

The acclaimed **Ballet Nacional de Cuba** typically performs at the **Gran Teatro de la Habana.** The Teatro Nacional hosts the Orquesta Sinfónica Nacional de Cuba. The Gran Teatro's chic **Adagio Barconcert** lounge bar hosts live classical and jazz ensembles.

Havana boasts several jazz venues, including the snazzy **Café Miramar** and intimate **Privé.**

Day 4

Head west from Havana to Pinar del Río Province to visit **Cuevas de los Portales,** used as Che Guevara's command center during the Cuban Missile Crisis. Continue to **Viñales** to visit the tobacco fields and overnight.

Day 5

Depart Pinar del Río along the Autopista for the town of **Santa Clara,** the setting for the battle that toppled the Batista regime. Your tour should include the **Tren Blindado** (a troop train destroyed by Che Guevara's troops) and the **Complejo Escultórico Memorial Comandante Ernesto Che Guevara,** with an excellent museum devoted to the Argentinian revolutionary.

Day 6

It's a long day's drive along the Carretera Central to reach **Holguín,** with time for exploring the colonial heart of the city. Check out the **Plaza de la Revolución.**

Day 7

Leaving the city, take **Avenida Simón Bolívar,** lined with monuments to nationalist and revolutionary heroes, including a pop-art rendition of Che. Your destination is **Museo Conjunto Histórico Birán,** Fidel Castro's birthplace and home into adolescence. Afterwards, continue via Palma Soriano, arriving in **Santiago de Cuba** in the afternoon with time to visit **Cementerio Santa Ifigenia,** where Fidel Castro's remains are interred.

Day 8

The first stop is **Cuartel Moncada,** the site of the 1953 attack that launched the Revolution; today the former barracks holds the Museo Histórico 26 de Julio. Nearby is the **Museo Abel Santamaría,** named for a prominent revolutionary tortured to death following the failed attack. Tour the historic town center, including **Parque Céspedes** (where Fidel Castro gave his victory speech after Batista was toppled); the **Colegio Jesuita Dolores,** where Fidel attended school; and the **Museo Lucha Clandestina,** recalling the clandestine war in the cities.

Day 9

Head to **Siboney** to visit the farmhouse from where Castro and his revolutionaries set out to attack the Moncada barracks. The route is lined with monuments to those who died in the attack. Afterwards, head into the mountains to **Mayarí Arriba** and the **Complejo Histórico de Museos del Segundo Frente** and the nearby mausoleum, recalling the "Second Front" led by Raúl Castro. Return to Santiago for the evening.

Day 10

Head west along the coast via Chivírico—a stupendous drive. Beyond Ocujal, visit **La Comandancia de la Plata,** with exhibits detailing the revolutionary war in the mountains. Continue to the **Parque Nacional Desembarco del Granma,** site of the landing of Fidel's army in 1956. Overnight in **Niquero.**

Day 11

Call in at **Media Luna** to view the **Museo Celia Sánchez,** birthplace of the revolutionary heroine who ran the secret supply line to Fidel's

Valle de Viñales

Cuba is a visual delight, and anyone who enjoys driving (and can handle the daunting obstacles that line the way) will thrill to these scenic drives.

- **Mariel to Valle de Viñales via Circuito Norte:** This winding ridge-top drive between mountain and sea begins one hour west of Havana and offers lovely views of the *mogotes* of the Sierra del Rosario.

- **Chambas to Caibarién via Circuito Norte:** This route offers quintessentially Cuban rural scenery: tobacco fields tended by ox-drawn plows and shaded by royal palms, with rustic *bohíos* in the lee of mountains.

- **Trinidad to Sancti Spíritus via Circuito Sur:** A roller-coaster ride travels through swathes of lime-green sugarcane in the Valle de los Ingenios. Farther east, you'll pass the rugged Alturas de Banao.

- **Trinidad to Santa Clara via Manicaragua:** This mountain drive with steep climbs and hairpin turns winds through forests and rolling tobacco country. Drive cautiously on the switchback ascent to Topes de Collantes.

- **Bartolomé Masó to Marea del Portillo:** On this four-wheel-drive challenge via the Sierra Maestra, the staggering mountain vistas are topped by views over the coast and sea, but the steep, looping road is in awful condition.

- **Marea del Portillo to Santiago de Cuba:** Massive copper-colored cliffs loom out

cruising Havana in classic American cars

of the sea on this lonesome drive, which features awesome coastal scenery. Cuba's highest peaks are within fingertip distance beyond the stark low-desert plains.

- **Cajobabo to Baracoa via La Farola:** The road ascends steeply through the pine-clad Sierra Cristal, with snaking bends and occasional pullouts for savoring the vistas.

army in the Sierra Maestra. In **Manzanillo,** visit the **Monumento Celia Sánchez,** then continue via Bartolomé Masó to **Santo Domingo,** where a small museum features a 3-D map of the war in the Sierra Maestra. Overnight in Santo Domingo.

Day 12

This morning hike to **La Comandancia de la Plata,** Fidel's headquarters deep in the Sierra Maestra. In the afternoon, continue via Bayamo, arriving in **Las Tunas** in early evening.

Day 13

Prepare for the long drive back to Havana today via the Carretera Central and Autopista. In the morning, transfer to the airport for your departure flight.

Cars, Cigars, and Cabarets

Cuba is a mother lode for anyone who loves classic American autos, fine cigars, quality rums, and Las Vegas-style cabaret revues. Before 1959, Havana was the hottest spot in the Caribbean, notorious for its glittering cabarets, smooth rum, and chrome-laden Cadillacs. The good news is that the tail fins of '57 Eldorados still glint beneath the floodlit mango trees of nightclubs such as the Tropicana, the open-air extravaganza now in its seventh decade of stiletto-heeled hedonism.

Day 1
Arrive at José Martí International Airport in **Havana**; transfer to a hotel or *casa particular* in Habana Vieja or Vedado.

Day 2
This morning, concentrate your time around **Parque Central,** where the highlight will be the shop at **Fábrica de Tabaco Partagás.** After buying some premium smokes, head to the **Fábrica de Tabaco H. Upmann** (formerly Romeo y Julieta) for a guided tour of this cigar factory. Then rent a classic 1950s auto and set out for a tour of the city. In the evening, enjoy dinner at **La Guarida** restaurant and then thrill to the sexy spectacle of the Hotel Nacional's **Cabaret Parisien.**

Day 3
Today, follow Hemingway's ghost. Drive out to the village of San Miguel del Padrón and the **Museo Ernest Hemingway,** in the author's former home. Afterwards, head to **Cojímar** for a seafood lunch at **La Terraza** restaurant, once popular with Papa and his former skipper, the late local resident Gregorio Fuentes. Return to Havana for a *mojito* and stogie at **La Bodeguita del Medio.** Explore **Plaza de la Catedral** and **Plaza de Armas,** being sure to stop in at the **Hotel Ambos Mundos** (Room 511, where Hemingway was a longtime guest, is a

sorting tobacco leaves

Dive into Cuba

Cuba has some of the Caribbean's most spectacular diving. The coral formations rival those of anywhere else in the region, and the wreck diving is varied and fascinating. These are the major venues worth planning a trip around:

- **The "Blue Circuit":** You don't have to leave Havana to dive. Wrecks litter the Atlantic seabed, with dive sites extending 10 kilometers east of the city, beginning at Bacuranao.

- **Playa María la Gorda:** This is the place to dive with whale sharks. El Valle de Coral Negro (Black Coral Valley) is another highlight, and there are Spanish wrecks in the bay.

- **Cayo Levisa:** This tiny, coral-fringed cay off the north coast of Pinar del Río Province is a dedicated dive resort.

- **Punta Francés:** Spanish galleons and coral formations await divers a short distance off the south shore of Isla de la Juventud.

- **Ciénaga de Zapata:** The Club Octopus International Dive Center, at Playa Larga, will take you diving in *cenotes,* water-filled limestone sinkholes. You can even dive wrecks of landing craft that grounded during the Bay of Pigs invasion.

- **Playa Santa Lucía:** Although the hotels here aren't much to speak of, the diving is sensational. A big draw is shark feeding, performed by the dive master.

Cayo Levisa

- **Jardines de la Reina:** Never mind shark feeding. How about *riding* a shark? The "Gardens of the Queen," south of Camagüey, are virgin territory, with stupendous coral reefs, colorful fishes, marine turtles, moray eels, and other stars of the show.

museum) and the **Museo del Ron,** a splendid museum giving insight into production of Cuba's fine rums. This evening, sample the daiquiris at **El Floridita.**

Day 4

Rent a car or hire a taxi for a day trip to **Pinar del Río.** Set out early to visit the tobacco fields of **Valle de Viñales** and the **Finca El Pinar San Luis,** *finca* (farm) of the late Alejandro Robaina, a legend after whom the Cuban state named a brand of cigar. Return to Havana in the evening for dinner at **El Aljibe.**

Share fine cigars and *añejo* rums with the connoisseurs at the **La Casa del Habano** in Miramar.

Day 5

Head out to **Marina Hemingway** for a full day of sportfishing for blue marlin in Hemingway's "great blue river." This evening, enjoy dinner at **La Fontana,** one of Havana's chicest restaurants.

Days 6-7

This morning, head to **Club Habana,** a chic

Eco-Adventures

Eastern Cuba receives relatively few visitors despite boasting many of Cuba's eminent national parks and historic sites. For an eco-adventure, exploring the Sierra Maestra and its adjacent mountain ranges can't be beaten.

ECOTOURS

- Hike to the summit of **El Yunque,** a fantastic mountain formation dominating the landscape around Baracoa.

- Drive **La Farola,** a switchbacked mountain road that takes you through several ecosystems, including pine forest at higher elevations.

- Head to **Punta Maisí** via coffee country, with time to explore a private coffee farm. Then explore the cactus-studded landscapes of **Reserva Ecológica Maisí-Caleta.**

- Hire a guide to look for *Polymita pictas* snails and go birding in **Parque Nacional Alejandro de Humboldt,** then take a boat ride up the Río Toa. Look for manatees in the river estuary.

El Yunque at dawn, Baracoa

CULTURAL IMMERSION

Baracoa is the oldest town in the Americas and retains a distinct culture that owes much to the legacy of the pre-Columbian Taíno, while Santiago and Guantánamo are infused with Haitian and Jamaican influences.

- For an immersion in Taíno culture head to the **Museo Arqueológico Cueva del Paraíso,** with pre-Columbian skeletons in situ.

- Descendants of the Taíno keep their traditions alive at the village of **El Güirito.**

- Baracoa is Cuba's ground zero for cacao and chocolate production. For Cacao 101 visit **Finca Duaba,** then head to Baracoa's **Casa de Cacao** for a tasting at this artisanal chocolate "factory."

- In Guantánamo and Santiago de Cuba, the **Tumba Francesa** keeps alive the Haitian music, dance, and dress traditions.

- *Son* (Cuba's quintessential sound) is said to have been birthed at Santiago de Cuba's **Casa de la Trova,** where you can still hear traditional Cuban music at its best.

private club (open to nonmembers for a fee) where you can relax on the fine beach, partake of water sports, and sample cocktails and fine cigars. After dinner at **El Cocinero** *paladar,* head to the **Tropicana** nightclub for the sauciest cabaret in Cuba.

Havana

Havana is the political, cultural, and industrial heart of the nation.

It lies 150 kilometers (93 miles) due south of Florida on Cuba's northwest coast. It is built on the west side of the sweeping Bahía de la Habana and extends west 12 kilometers to the Río Jaimanitas and south for an equal distance.

Countless writers have commented on the exhilarating sensation that engulfs visitors to this most beautiful and beguiling of Caribbean cities. Set foot one time in Havana and you can only succumb to its enigmatic allure. It is impossible to resist the city's mysteries and contradictions.

Havana (pop. 2.2 million) has a flavor all its own, a merging of colonialism, capitalism, and Communism into one. One of the great historical cities of the New World, Havana is a far cry from the Caribbean backwaters that call themselves capitals elsewhere in the Antilles. Havana is a city, notes architect Jorge Rigau, "upholstered in columns, cushioned by colonnaded arcades." The buildings come in a spectacular amalgam of styles—from the academic classicism of aristocratic homes, rococo residential exteriors, Moorish interiors, and art deco and art nouveau to stunning exemplars of 1950s moderne.

At the heart of the city is enchanting Habana Vieja (Old Havana), a living museum inhabited by 60,000 people and containing perhaps the finest collection of Spanish-colonial buildings in all the Americas. Baroque churches, convents, and castles that could have been transposed from Madrid or Cádiz still reign majestically over squares embraced by the former palaces of Cuba's ruling gentry and cobbled streets still haunted by Ernest Hemingway's ghost. Hemingway's house, Finca Vigía, is one of dozens of museums dedicated to the memory of great men and women. And although older monuments of politically incorrect heroes were pulled down, they were replaced by dozens of monuments to those on the correct side of history.

The heart of Habana Vieja has been restored, and most of the important structures have been given facelifts, or better, by the City Historian's office. Some have even metamorphosed into boutique hotels. Nor is there a shortage of 1950s-era modernist hotels steeped in Mafia associations. And hundreds of *casas particulares* provide an opportunity to live life alongside the *habaneros* themselves. As for food, Havana is in the midst of a gastro-revolution. A dynamic new breed of

---

Previous: 1959 Cadillac outside Hotel Nacional; Plaza Vieja, Habana Vieja. **Above:** Capitolio, Habana Vieja.

Look for ★ to find recommended
sights, activities, dining, and lodging.

Highlights

★ **Museo Nacional de Bellas Artes:** Divided into national and international sections, this art gallery is among the world's finest (pages 42 and 47).

★ **Capitolio Nacional:** Cuba's former congressional building is an architectural glory reminiscent of Washington's own capitol (page 43).

★ **Plaza de la Catedral:** This small, atmospheric plaza is hemmed in by colonial mansions and a baroque cathedral (page 49).

★ **Plaza de Armas:** The restored cobbled plaza at the heart of Old Havana features tons of charm; don't miss the Castillo de la Real Fuerza and Palacio de los Capitanes Generales (page 54).

★ **Plaza Vieja:** Undergoing restoration, this antique plaza offers offbeat museums, Havana's only brewpub, flashy boutiques, and heaps of ambience (page 61).

★ **Hotel Nacional:** A splendid landmark with magnificent architecture and oodles of history, this hotel is a great place to relax with a *mojito* and cigar while soaking in the heady atmosphere of the past (page 78).

★ **Necrópolis Cristóbal Colón:** This is one of the New World's great cemeteries, with dramatic tombstones that comprise a who's who of Cuban history (page 84).

★ **Parque Histórico Militar Morro-Cabaña:** An imposing castle complex contains the Castillo de los Tres Reyes del Morro and massive Fortaleza de San Carlos de la Cabaña, with cannons in situ and soldiers in period costume (page 96).

★ **Tropicana:** Havana at its most sensual, the Tropicana hosts a spectacular cabaret with more than 200 performers and dancers (page 106).

★ **Museo Ernest Hemingway:** "Papa's" former home is preserved as it was on the day he died. His sportfishing boat, the *Pilar*, stands on the grounds (page 159).

paladar (private restaurant) owner is now offering world-class cuisine in spectacular settings. Streets from Habana Vieja to Vedado resound with the sound of jackhammers. Pockets of gentrification—an inconceivable word for Cuba until now—are emerging as the rapprochement with the United States and the tourism boom it has fostered are translating into money, money, money and a surge of private investment in boutique bars, boutiques, and chic *casas particulares* billed as boutique "hotels."

Nonetheless, it's increasingly hard to find a vacant hotel room: Havana is jam-packed with *yanqui* visitors making the most of the heretofore forbidden fruit. A series finale of *House of Lies*, plus segments of *Fast & Furious 8*, have been filmed in Havana as Hollywood, too, has cottoned on. In 2017, U.S. cruise ships arrived, flooding the plazas with tour groups. The arts scene remains unrivaled in Latin America, with first-rate museums and galleries—not only formal galleries, but informal ones where contemporary artists produce unique works of amazing profundity and appeal. There are tremendous crafts markets and boutique stores. Afro-Caribbean music is everywhere, quite literally on the streets. Lovers of sizzling salsa have dozens of venues from which to choose. Havana even has a hot jazz scene. Classical music and ballet are world class. And neither Las Vegas nor Rio de Janeiro can compare with Havana for sexy cabarets, with top billing now, as back in the day, belonging to the Tropicana.

PLANNING YOUR TIME

Havana is so large, and the sights to be seen so many, that one week is the bare minimum needed. Metropolitan Havana sprawls over 740 square kilometers (286 square miles) and incorporates 15 *municipios* (municipalities). Havana is a collection of neighborhoods, each with its own distinct character. Because the city is so spread out, it is best to explore Havana in sections, concentrating your time on the three main districts of touristic interest—Habana Vieja, Vedado, and Miramar—in that order.

If you have only one or two days in Havana, book a get-your-bearings trip by HabanaBusTour or hop on an organized city tour offered by Havanatur or a similar agency. This will provide an overview of the major sights. Concentrate the balance of your time around Parque Central, Plaza de la Catedral, and Plaza de Armas. Your checklist of must-sees should include the **Capitolio Nacional, Museo de la Revolución, Museo Nacional de Bellas Artes, Catedral de la Habana, Museo de la Ciudad de la Habana,** and **Parque Histórico Militar Morro-Cabaña,** featuring two restored castles attended by soldiers in period costume.

Habana Vieja, the original colonial city within the 17th-century city walls (now demolished), will require at least three days to fully explore. You can base yourself in one of the charming historic hotel conversions close to the main sights of interest.

Centro Habana has many *casas particulares* and fine restaurants but few sites of interest, and its rubble-strewn, dimly lit streets aren't the safest. Skip Centro for **Vedado,** the modern heart of the city that evolved in the early 20th century, with many ornate mansions in beaux-arts and art nouveau style. Its leafy streets make for great walking. Many of the city's best *casas particulares* are here, as are most businesses, *paladares,* and nightclubs. The **Hotel Nacional, Universidad de la Habana, Cementerio Colón,** and **Plaza de la Revolución** are sights not to miss.

If you're interested in beaux-arts or art deco architecture, then the once-glamorous **Miramar, Cubanacán,** and **Siboney** regions, west of Vedado, are worth exploring. Miramar also has excellent restaurants, deluxe hotels, and some of my favorite nightspots.

Most other sections of Havana are run-down residential districts of little interest to tourists. A few exceptions lie on the east side of Havana harbor. **Regla** and neighboring **Guanabacoa** are together a center of Santería and Afro-Cuban music. The 18th-century

Havana

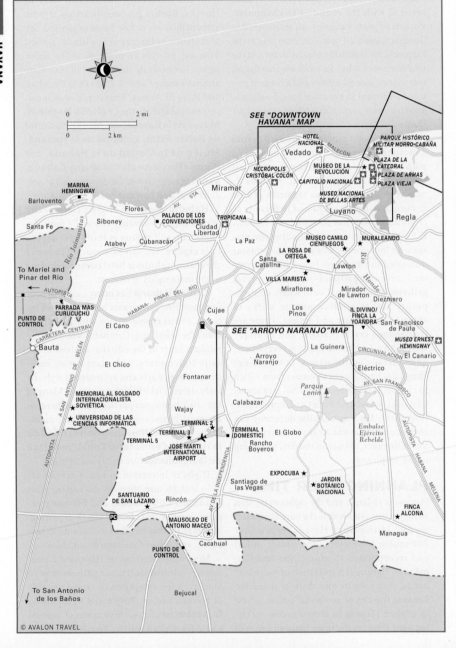

SEE "DOWNTOWN HAVANA" MAP

HOTEL NACIONAL

PARQUE HISTÓRICO MILITAR MORRO-CABAÑA

MALECÓN

Vedado

PLAZA DE LA CATEDRAL

PLAZA DE ARMAS

NECRÓPOLIS CRISTÓBAL COLÓN

MUSEO DE LA REVOLUCIÓN

PLAZA VIEJA

CAPITOLIO NACIONAL

Miramar

MUSEO NACIONAL DE BELLAS ARTES

MARINA HEMINGWAY

Luyano

Regla

Barlovento

Florés

PALACIO DE LOS CONVENCIONES

TROPICANA

Santa Fe

Siboney

Ciudad Libertad

Río Jaimanitas

Atabey

Cubanacán

La Paz

MUSEO CAMILO CIENFUEGOS

MURALEANDO

LA ROSA DE ORTEGA

Río Hondo

Santa Catalina

Lawton

To Mariel and Pinar del Río

AUTOPISTA

HABANA - PINAR DEL RÍO

VILLA MARISTA

Miraflores

Mirador de Lawton

Diezmero

PARRADA MAS CURUCUCHÚ

Cujae

Los Pinos

IL DIVINO/ FINCA LA YOANDRA

San Francisco de Paula

PUNTO DE CONTROL

El Cano

SEE "ARROYO NARANJO" MAP

CARRETERA CENTRAL

MUSEO ERNEST HEMINGWAY

Bauta

La Guinera

CIRCUNVALACIÓN

El Canario

A SAN ANTONIO DE BELEN

El Chico

Arroyo Naranjo

Eléctrico

Fontanar

AV. SAN FRANCISCO

MEMORIAL AL SOLDADO INTERNACIONALISTA SOVIÉTICA

Parque Lenin

Embalse Ejército Rebelde

UNIVERSIDAD DE LAS CIENCIAS INFORMÁTICA

Wajay

Calabazar

AUTOPISTA

AUTOPISTA HABANA MELENA

TERMINAL 2

TERMINAL 3

TERMINAL 1 (DOMESTIC)

El Globo

TERMINAL 5

JOSÉ MARTI INTERNATIONAL AIRPORT

Rancho Boyeros

EXPOCUBA

AV. DE LA INDEPENDENCIA

JARDIN BOTÁNICO NACIONAL

SANTUARIO DE SAN LÁZARO

Rincón

Santiago de las Vegas

PC

MAUSOLEO DE ANTONIO MACEO

FINCA ALCONA

PUNTO DE CONTROL

Cacahual

Managua

To San Antonio de los Baños

Bejucal

© AVALON TRAVEL

0   2 mi

0   2 km

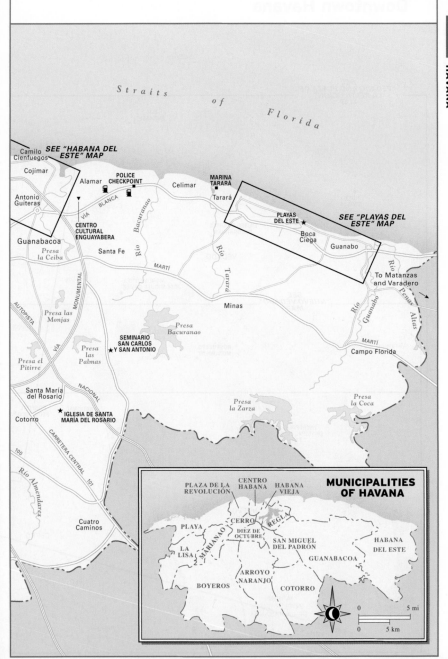

Straits of Florida

SEE "HABANA DEL ESTE" MAP

Camilo Cienfuegos
Cojímar
Antonio Guiteras
Guanabacoa
Alamar
POLICE CHECKPOINT
Celimar
MARINA TARARÁ
Tarará
PLAYAS DEL ESTE ★
SEE "PLAYAS DEL ESTE" MAP
Boca Ciega
Guanabo
CENTRO CULTURAL ENGUAYABERA
Santa Fe
Presa la Ceiba
VÍA BLANCA
Río Bacuranao
MARTÍ
Río Tarará
To Matanzas and Varadero
Peñas Altas
Río Guanabo
MONUMENTAL
AUTOPISTA
Presa las Monjas
Presa las Palmas
Presa Bacuranao
Minas
SEMINARIO SAN CARLOS Y SAN ANTONIO ★
VÍA
MARTÍ
Campo Florida
Presa el Pitirre
NACIONAL
Santa María del Rosario
Presa la Zarza
Presa la Coca
Cotorro
★ IGLESIA DE SANTA MARÍA DEL ROSARIO
CARRETERA CENTRAL
100
101
Río Almendares
Cuatro Caminos

MUNICIPALITIES OF HAVANA

PLAZA DE LA REVOLUCIÓN
CENTRO HABANA
HABANA VIEJA
CERRO
REGLA
PLAYA
MARIANAO
DIEZ DE OCTUBRE
SAN MIGUEL DEL PADRÓN
HABANA DEL ESTE
LA LISA
GUANABACOA
ARROYO NARANJO
BOYEROS
COTORRO

0   5 mi
0   5 km

Downtown Havana

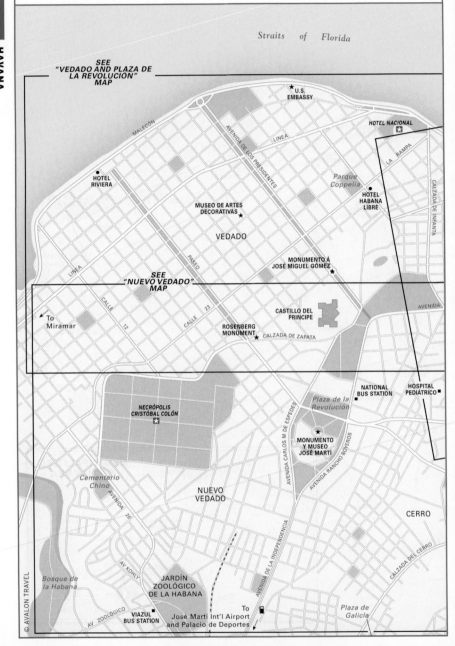

Straits of Florida

SEE "VEDADO AND PLAZA DE LA REVOLUCIÓN" MAP

★ U.S. EMBASSY

HOTEL NACIONAL ★

MALECÓN

AVENIDA DE LOS PRESIDENTES

LINEA

LA RAMPA

CALZADA DE INFANTA

● HOTEL RIVIERA

Parque Coppelia

● HOTEL HABANA LIBRE

MUSEO DE ARTES DECORATIVAS ★

VEDADO

PASEO

MONUMENTO Á JOSÉ MIGUEL GÓMEZ ★

SEE "NUEVO VEDADO" MAP

LINEA

CALLE

← To Miramar

12

CALLE 23

CASTILLO DEL PRINCIPE

AVENIDA

ROSENBERG MONUMENT ★

CALZADA DE ZAPATA

NATIONAL BUS STATION ■

HOSPITAL PEDIÁTRICO ■

NECRÓPOLIS CRISTÓBAL COLÓN ✪

AVENIDA CARLOS M DE ESPEDES

Plaza de la Revolución

★ MONUMENTO Y MUSEO JOSÉ MARTÍ

AVENIDA RANCHO BOYEROS

Cementerio Chino

AVENIDA 26

NUEVO VEDADO

CERRO

CALZADA DEL CERRO

AVENIDA DE LA INDEPENDENCIA

Bosque de la Habana

AV KOHLY

JARDÍN ZOOLÓGICO DE LA HABANA

VIAZUL BUS STATION ■

To José Martí Int'l Airport and Palacio de Deportes →

Plaza de Galicia

AV. ZOOLÓGICO

© AVALON TRAVEL

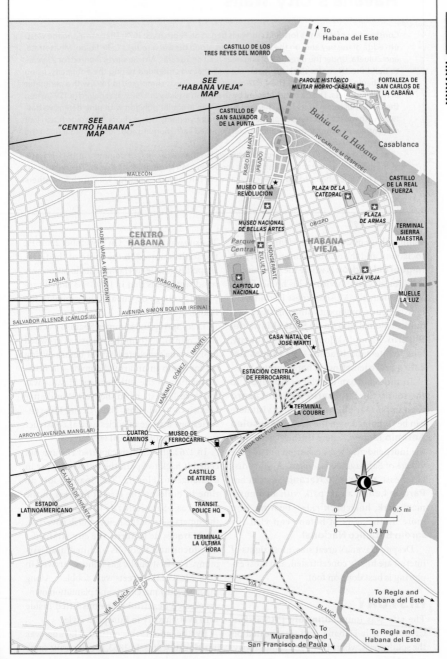

To
Habana del Este

CASTILLO DE LOS
TRES REYES DEL MORRO

SEE
"HABANA VIEJA"
MAP

PARQUE HISTÓRICO
MILITAR MORRO-CABAÑA

FORTALEZA DE
SAN CARLOS DE
LA CABAÑA

SEE
"CENTRO HABANA"
MAP

CASTILLO DE
SAN SALVADOR
DE LA PUNTA

Bahía de la Habana

Casablanca

MALECÓN

AV CARLOS M CESPEDES

PASEO DE MARTÍ

PRADO

MUSEO DE LA
REVOLUCIÓN

PLAZA DE LA
CATEDRAL

CASTILLO
DE LA REAL
FUERZA

CENTRO
HABANA

MUSEO NACIONAL
DE BELLAS ARTES

OBISPO

PLAZA
DE ARMAS

TERMINAL
SIERRA
MAESTRA

ZANJA

DRAGONES

PADRE VARELA (BELASCOAIN)

Parque
Central

ZULUETA

MONSERRATE

HABANA
VIEJA

CAPITOLIO
NACIONAL

PLAZA VIEJA

MUELLE
LA LUZ

SALVADOR ALLENDE (CARLOS III)

AVENIDA SIMON BOLIVAR (REINA)

EGIDO

CASA NATAL DE
JOSÉ MARTÍ

MAXIMO GOMEZ (MONTE)

ESTACIÓN CENTRAL
DE FERROCARRIL

ARROYO (AVENIDA MANGLAR)

CUATRO
CAMINOS

MUSEO DE
FERROCARRIL

TERMINAL
LA COUBRE

AVENIDA DEL PUERTO

CALZADA DE INFANTA

CASTILLO
DE ATERÉS

TRANSIT
POLICE HQ

ESTADIO
LATINOAMERICANO

TERMINAL
LA ÚLTIMA
HORA

0   0.5 mi

0   0.5 km

VIA
BLANCA

VIA BLANCA

To Regla and
Habana del Este

To
Muraleando and
San Francisco de Paula

To Regla and
Habana del Este

Havana's City Walls

Construction of Havana's fortified city walls began on February 3, 1674. They ran along the western edge of the bay and, on the landward side, stood between today's Calle Egido, Monserrate, and Zulueta. Under the direction of engineer Juan de Siscaras, African slaves labored for 23 years to build the 1.4-meter-thick, 10-meter-tall wall that was intended to ring the entire city, using rocks hauled from the coast. The 4,892-meter-long wall was completed in 1697, with a perimeter of five kilometers. The damage inflicted by the British artillery in 1762 was repaired in 1797, when the thick wall attained its final shape. It formed an irregular polygon with nine defensive bastions with moats and steep drops to delay assault by enemy troops. In its first stage it had just two entrances (nine more were added later), opened each morning and closed at night upon the sound of a single cannon.

As time went on, the *intramuros* (the city within the walls) burst its confines. In 1841, Havana authorities petitioned the Spanish crown for permission to demolish the walls. The demolition began in 1863, when African slave-convicts were put to work to destroy what their forefathers had built.

fishing village of **Cojímar** has Hemingway associations, and the nearby community of **San Miguel del Padrón** is where the great author lived for 20 years. A visit to his home, **Finca Vigía,** today the Museo Ernest Hemingway, is de rigueur. Combine it with a visit to the exquisite colonial **Iglesia de Santa María del Rosario.** About 15 kilometers east of the city, long, white-sand beaches—the **Playas del Este**—prove tempting on hot summer days.

In the suburban district of **Boyeros,** to the south, the **Santuario de San Lázaro** is an important pilgrimage site. A visit here can be combined with the nearby **Mausoleo Antonio Maceo,** where the hero general of the independence wars is buried outside the village of Santiago de las Vegas. A short distance east, the **Arroyo Naranjo** district has **Parque Lenin,** a vast park with an amusement park, horseback rides, boating, and more. Enthusiasts of botany can visit the **Jardín Botánico Nacional.**

Despite Havana's great size, most sights of interest are highly concentrated, and most exploring is best done on foot.

HISTORY

The city was founded in July 1515 as San Cristóbal de la Habana, and was located on the south coast, where Batabanó stands today.

The site was a disaster. On November 25, 1519, the settlers moved to the shore of the flask-shaped Bahía de la Habana. Its location was so advantageous that in July 1553 the city replaced Santiago de Cuba as the capital of the island.

Every spring and summer, Spanish treasure ships returning from the Americas crowded into Havana's sheltered harbor before setting off for Spain in an armed convoy—*la flota.* By the turn of the 18th century, Havana was the third-largest city in the New World after Mexico City and Lima. The 17th and 18th centuries saw a surge of ecclesiastical construction and a perimeter wall was built.

In 1762, the English captured Havana but ceded it back to Spain the following year in exchange for Florida. The Spanish lost no time in building the largest fortress in the Americas—San Carlos de la Cabaña. Under the supervision of the new Spanish governor, the Marqués de la Torre, the city attained a new focus and rigorous architectural harmony. The first public gas lighting arrived in 1768. Most of the streets were cobbled. Along them, wealthy merchants and plantation owners erected beautiful mansions fitted inside with every luxury in European style.

By the mid-19th century, Havana was bursting its seams. In 1863, the city walls came tumbling down. New districts went up westward, and graceful boulevards pushed into the surrounding countryside, lined with a parade of *quintas* (summer homes) fronted by classical columns. By the mid-1800s, Havana had achieved a level of modernity that surpassed that of Madrid.

Following the Spanish-Cuban-American War, Havana entered a new era of prosperity. The city spread out, its perimeter enlarged by parks, boulevards, and dwellings in eclectic, neoclassical, and revivalist styles, while older residential areas settled into an era of decay.

By the 1950s Havana was a wealthy and thoroughly modern city with a large and prospering middle class, and had acquired skyscrapers such as the Focsa building and the Hilton (now the Habana Libre). Ministries were being moved to a new center of construction (today the Plaza de la Revolución), inland from Vedado. Gambling found new life, and casinos flourished.

Following the Revolution in 1959, a mass exodus of the wealthy and the middle class began, inexorably changing the face of Havana. Tourists also forsook the city, dooming Havana's hotels, restaurants, and other businesses to bankruptcy. Festering slums and shantytowns marred the suburbs. The government ordered them razed. Concrete apartment blocks were erected on the outskirts. That accomplished, the Revolution turned its back on the city. Havana's aged housing and infrastructure, much of it already decayed, have ever since suffered neglect.

Tens of thousands of poor peasant migrants poured into Havana from Oriente. The settlers changed the city's demographic profile: Most of the immigrants were black; today, as many as 400,000 *"palestinos,"* immigrants from Santiago and the eastern provinces, live in Havana.

Finally, in the 1980s, the revolutionary government established a preservation program for Habana Vieja, and the Centro Nacional de Conservación, Restauración, y Museología was created to inventory Havana's historic sites and implement a restoration program that would return the ancient city to pristine splendor. Much of the original city core now gleams afresh with confections in stone, while the rest is left to crumble.

Sights

HABANA VIEJA

Habana Vieja (4.5 square km) is defined by the limits of the early colonial settlement that lay within fortified walls. The legal boundary of Habana Vieja includes the Paseo de Martí (Prado) and everything east of it.

Habana Vieja is roughly shaped like a diamond, with the Castillo de la Punta its northerly point. The Prado runs south at a gradual gradient from the Castillo de la Punta to Parque Central and, beyond, Parque de la Fraternidad. Two blocks east, Avenida de Bélgica parallels the Prado, tracing the old city wall to the harborfront at the west end of Desamparados. East of Castillo de la Punta, Avenida Carlos Manuel de Céspedes (Avenida del Puerto) runs along the harbor channel and curls south to Desamparados.

The major sites of interest are centered on Plaza de Armas, Plaza de la Catedral, Plaza Vieja, and Parque Central. Each square has its own flavor. The plazas and surrounding streets shine after a complete restoration that now extends to the area east of Avenida de Bélgica and southwest of Plaza Vieja, between Calles Brasil and Merced. This was the great ecclesiastical center of colonial Havana and is replete with churches and convents.

Habana Vieja is a living museum—as many as 60,000 people live within the confines of the old city wall—and suffers from inevitable ruination brought on by the tropical climate,

Habana Vieja

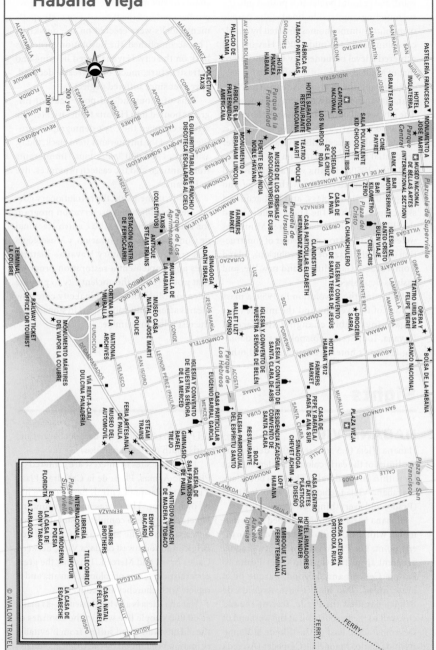

© AVALON TRAVEL

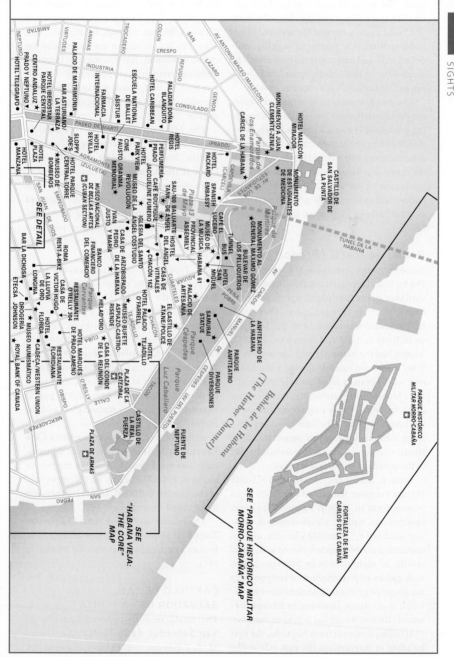

hastened since the Revolution by years of neglect. The grime of centuries has been soldered by tropical heat into the chipped cement and faded pastels. Beyond the restored areas, Habana Vieja is a quarter of sagging, mildewed walls and half-collapsed balconies. The much-deteriorated (mostly residential) southern half of Habana Vieja requires caution.

The past few years have witnessed a spectacular tourist boom. Gentrification is sweeping pockets of Habana Vieja. Suddenly every third building in this overcrowded, once sclerotic northern extreme of Habana Vieja is in the throes of a remake as a boutique B&B, hip restaurant, or—what's this?—a gourmet *heladería* selling homemade gelato. You'll want to avoid Habana Vieja when the cruise ships are in.

Paseo de Martí (Prado)

Paseo de Martí, colloquially known as the Prado, is a kilometer-long tree-lined boulevard that slopes southward, uphill, from the harbor mouth to Parque Central. The beautiful boulevard was initiated by the Marqués de la Torre in 1772 and completed in 1852, when it had the name Alameda de Isabella II. It lay *extramura* (outside the old walled city) and was Havana's most notable thoroughfare. Mansions of aristocratic families rose on each side and it was a sign of distinction to live here. The *paseo*—the daily carriage ride—along the boulevard was an important social ritual, with bands at regular intervals to play to the parade of *volantas* (carriages).

French landscape artist Jean-Claude Nicolas Forestier remodeled the Prado to its present form in 1929. It's guarded by eight bronze lions, with an elevated central walkway bordered by an ornate wall with alcoves containing marble benches carved with scroll motifs. At night, it is lit by brass gas lamps with globes atop wrought-iron lampposts in the shape of griffins. Schoolchildren sit beneath shade trees, listening to lessons presented alfresco. An art fair is held on Sundays.

Heading downhill from Neptuno, the first building of interest, on the east side at the corner of Virtudes, is the former **American Club**—U.S. expat headquarters before the Revolution. The **Palacio de Matrimonio** (Prado #306, esq. Ánimas, tel. 07/866-0661, Tues.-Fri. 8am-6pm), on the west side at the corner of Ánimas, is where many of Havana's wedding ceremonies are performed. The palace, built in 1914, boasts a magnificent neo-baroque facade and spectacularly ornate interior.

The Moorish-inspired **Hotel Sevilla** (Trocadero #55) is like entering a Moroccan medina. It was inspired by the Patio of the Lions at the Alhambra in Granada, Spain. The hotel opened in 1908. The gallery walls are festooned with black-and-white photos of famous figures who have stayed here, from singer Josephine Baker and boxer Joe Louis to Al Capone, who took the entire sixth floor (Capone occupied room 615).

At Trocadero, budding dancers train for potential ballet careers in the **Escuela Nacional de Ballet** (National School of Ballet, Prado #207, e/ Colón y Trocadero, tel. 07/861-6629, cuballet@cubarte.cult.cu; entry by permission only). On the west side, the **Casa de los Científicos** (Prado #212, esq. Trocadero, tel. 07/862-1607), the former home of President José Miguel Gómez, first president of the republic, is now a hotel; pop in to admire the fabulous stained glass and the chapel.

At Prado and Colón, note the art deco **Cine Fausto,** an ornamental band on its upper facade; two blocks north, examine the mosaic mural of a Nubian beauty on the upper wall of the **Centro Cultural de Árabe** (between Refugio and Trocadero).

The bronze **statue of Juan Clemente-Zenea** (1832-1871), at the base of the Prado, honors a nationalist poet shot for treason in 1871.

CASTILLO DE SAN SALVADOR DE LA PUNTA

The small, recently restored **Castillo de San Salvador de la Punta** (Av. Carlos M. de Céspedes, esq. Prado y Malecón, tel.

07/860-3195, Wed.-Sun. 10am-6pm, CUC1) guards the entrance to Havana's harbor channel at the base of the Prado. It was built in 1589 directly across from the Morro castle so that the two fortresses could catch invaders in a crossfire. A great chain was slung between them each night to secure Havana harbor.

Gazing over the plaza on the west side of the castle is a life-size statue of Venezuelan general Francisco de Miranda Rodríguez (1750-1816), while 100 meters east of the castle is a statue of Pierre D'Iberville (1661-1706), a Canadian explorer who died in Havana.

PARQUE DE MÁRTIRES AND PARQUE DE LOS ENAMORADOS

The park immediately south of the Castillo de San Salvador, on the south side of Avenida Carlos Manuel de Céspedes, at the base (and east) of the Prado, is divided in two by Avenida de los Estudiantes. **Parque de los Enamorados** (Park of the Lovers), on the north side of Avenida de los Estudiantes, features a statue of an Indian couple, plus the **Monumento de Estudiantes de Medicina,** a small Grecian-style temple shading the remains of a wall used by Spanish firing squads. On November 27, 1871, eight medical students met their deaths after being falsely accused of desecrating the tomb of a prominent loyalist. A trial found them innocent, but enraged loyalist troops held their own trial and shot the students, who are commemorated each November 27.

Parque de Mártires (Martyrs' Park), on the south side of Avenida de los Estudiantes, occupies the ground of the former Tacón prison, built in 1838. Nationalist hero José Martí was imprisoned here 1869-1870. The **Carcel de la Habana** prison was demolished in 1939. Preserved are two of the punishment cells and the chapel used by condemned prisoners before being marched to the firing wall.

Parque Central

Spacious Parque Central is the social epicenter of Habana Vieja. The park—bounded by the Prado, Neptuno, Zulueta, and San Martín—is presided over by stately royal palms shading a marble **statue of José Martí**. It was sculpted by José Vilalta de Saavedra and inaugurated in 1905. Adjacent, baseball fanatics gather at a point called *"esquina caliente"* ("hot corner") to argue the intricacies of *pelota* (baseball).

The park is surrounded by historic hotels, including the triangular **Hotel Plaza** (Zulueta #267), built in 1909, on the northeast face of the square. In 1920, baseball legend

dancers at the Escuela Nacional de Ballet

Babe Ruth stayed in room 216, preserved as a museum with his signed bat and ball in a case. Much of the social action happens in front of the **Hotel Inglaterra** (Paseo de Martí #416), opened in 1856 and today the oldest Cuban hotel still extant. The sidewalk, known in colonial days as the Acera del Louvre, was a focal point for rebellion against Spanish rule. A plaque outside the hotel entrance honors the "lads of the Louvre sidewalk" who died for Cuban independence. Inside, the hotel boasts elaborate wrought-ironwork and exquisite Mudejar-style detailing, including arabesque archways and *azulejos* (patterned tile). A highlight is the sensuous life-size bronze statue of a Spanish dancer—*La Sevillana*—in the main bar. Hopefully the fin de siècle charm will survive the 2016 remake initiated by U.S. hotel company Starwood.

GRAN TEATRO DE LA HABANA ALICIA ALONSO

Immediately south of the Inglaterra, the **Gran Teatro** (Paseo de Martí #452, e/ San Rafael y Neptuno, tel. 07/862-9473, guided tours Tue.-Sat. 9am-5pm, CUC2) originated in 1837 as the Teatro Tacón, drawing operatic luminaries such as Enrico Caruso and Sarah Bernhardt. The current neobaroque structure dates

from 1915, when a social club—the Centro Gallego—was built around the old Teatro Tacón for the Galician community.

The building's exorbitantly baroque facade drips with caryatids and has four towers, each tipped by a white marble angel reaching gracefully for heaven. It functions as a theater for the Ballet Nacional and Ópera Nacional de Cuba. The main auditorium, the exquisitely decorated 2,000-seat Teatro García Lorca, features a painted dome and huge chandelier. Smaller performances are hosted in the 500-seat Sala Alejo Carpentier and the 120-seat Sala Artaud. After a two-year restoration, it reopened in 2016 (in time for President Obama's speech here) and is spectacularly illuminated at night.

★ MUSEO NACIONAL DE BELLAS ARTES (INTERNATIONAL SECTION)

The international section of the **Museo Nacional de Bellas Artes** (National Fine Arts Museum, San Rafael, e/ Zulueta y Monserrate, tel. 07/863-9484 or 07/862-0140, www.bellasartes.cult.cu, Tues.-Sat. 9am-5pm, Sun. 10am-2pm, entrance CUC5, or CUC8 for both sections, guided tour CUC2) occupies the former Centro Asturiano, on the southeast

Parque Central, Habana Vieja

side of the square. The building, lavishly decorated with neoclassical motifs, was erected in 1885 but rebuilt in Renaissance style in 1927 following a fire and housed the postrevolutionary People's Supreme Court. A stained glass window above the main staircase shows Columbus's three caravels.

The art collection is displayed on five floors covering 4,800 square meters. The works span the United States, Latin America, Asia, and Europe—including masters such as Gainsborough, Goya, Murillo, Rubens, Velásquez, and various Impressionists. The museum also boasts Latin America's richest trove of Roman, Greek, and Egyptian antiquities. It has a top-floor restaurant.

★ **CAPITOLIO NACIONAL**

The statuesque **Capitolio Nacional** (Capitol, Paseo de Martí, e/ San Martín y Dragones), one block south of Parque Central, dominates Havana's skyline. It was built between 1926 and 1929 as Cuba's Chamber of Representatives and Senate and designed after the U.S. Capitol. The 692-foot-long edifice is supported by colonnades of Doric columns, with semicircular pavilions at each end of the building. The lofty stone cupola rises 62 meters, topped by a replica of 16th-century Florentine sculptor Giambologna's famous bronze *Mercury*.

A massive stairway—flanked by neoclassical figures in bronze by Italian sculptor Angelo Zanelli that represent Labor and Virtue—leads to an entrance portico with three tall bronze doors sculpted with 30 bas-reliefs that depict important events of Cuban history. Inside, facing the door is the *Estatua de la República* (Statue of the Republic), a massive bronze sculpture (also by Zanelli) of Cuba's Indian maiden of liberty. At 17.5 meters (57 feet) tall, she is the world's third-largest indoor statue (the other two are the gold Buddha in Nava, Japan, and the Lincoln Memorial in Washington, DC). In the center of the floor a replica of a 24-carat diamond marks Kilometer 0, the point from which all distances on the island are calculated.

The 394-foot-long **Salón de los Pasos Perdidos** (Great Hall of the Lost Steps), so named because of its acoustics, is inlaid with patterned marble motifs and features bronze bas-reliefs, green marble pilasters, and massive lamps on carved pedestals of glittering copper. Renaissance-style candelabras dangle from the frescoed ceiling. The semicircular Senate chamber and Chamber of Representatives are at each end.

At press time the building remained closed for a three-year restoration and will supposedly reopen as the home of the Asemblea Nacional.

Parque de la Fraternidad and Vicinity

Paseo de Martí (Prado) runs south from Parque Central three blocks, where it ends at the junction with Avenida Máximo Gómez (Monte). Here rises the **Fuente de la India Noble Habana** in the middle of the Prado. Erected in 1837, the fountain is surmounted by a Carrara marble statue of the legendary Indian queen. In one hand she bears a cornucopia, in the other a shield with the arms of Havana. Four fish at her feet occasionally spout water.

The **Asociación Cultural Yoruba de Cuba** (Prado #615, e/ Dragones y Monte, tel. 07/863-5953, www.yorubacuba.org, daily 9am-5pm) has a rather prosaic upstairs **Museo de los Orishas** (CUC10, students CUC3) dedicated to the *orishas* of Santería; no photos are permitted. The constitution for the republic was signed in 1901 in the restored **Teatro Martí** (Dragones, esq. Zulueta), one block west of the Prado.

PARQUE DE LA FRATERNIDAD

The **Parque de la Fraternidad** (Friendship Park) was laid out in 1892 on an old military drill square, the Campo de Marte, to commemorate the fourth centennial of Columbus's discovery of America. The current layout by Jean-Claude Nicolas Forestier dates from 1928. The **Árbol de la Fraternidad Americana** (Friendship

Restoring Old Havana

Old Havana has been called the "finest urban ensemble in the Americas." The fortress colonial town that burst its walls when Washington, DC, was still a swamp is a 140-hectare repository of antique buildings. More than 900 of Habana Vieja's 3,157 structures are of historical importance. Of these, only 101 were built in the 20th century. Almost 500 are from the 19th; 200 are from the 18th; and 144 are from the 16th and 17th. Alas, many buildings are crumbling into ruins.

In 1977, the Cuban government named Habana Vieja a National Monument. In 1982, UNESCO named Habana Vieja a World Heritage Site worthy of international protection. Cuba formalized a plan to rescue much of the old city from decades of neglect under the guidance of Eusebio Leal Spengler, the official city historian, who runs the **Oficina del Historiador de la Ciudad de La Habana** (Av. del Puerto, esq. Obrapí, Habana Vieja, tel. 07/861-5001, www.ohch.cu). Leal, who grew up in Habana Vieja, is a member of Cuba's National Assembly, the Central Committee of the Communist Party, and the all-important Council of State.

The ambitious plan stretches into the future and has concentrated on four squares: Plaza de Armas, Plaza de la Catedral, Plaza Vieja, and Plaza de San Francisco. The most important buildings have received major renovations; others have been given facelifts. Priority is given to edifices with income-generating tourist value. Structures are ranked into one of four levels according to historical and physical value. The top level is reserved for museums; the second level is for hotels, restaurants, offices, and schools; and the bottom levels are for housing.

Until 2016, **Habaguanex** (Calle Oficios 52, e/ Obrapía y Lamparilla, Plaza de San Francisco, Havana, tel. 07/204-9201, www.habaguanex.ohc.cu) was responsible for opening and operating commercial entities such as hotels, restaurants, cafés, and shops. The profits helped finance further infrastructural improvements; 33 percent of revenues are supposedly devoted to social projects such as theaters, schools, and medical facilities. In 2016, the military's Business Administration Group, GAESA, took control of Habaguanex. Word is that the businesses will be dispersed to subsidiaries of GAESA: the hotels to Gaviota, the restaurants to CIMEX, and the shops to TRD Caribe.

Still, there is little evidence of actual homes being restored. In southern Habana Vieja, where there are relatively few structures of touristic interest, talk of restoration raises hollow laughs from the inhabitants occupying overcrowded *solares* (slums).

Tree) was planted at its center on February 24, 1928, to cement goodwill between the nations of the Americas. Busts and statues of outstanding American leaders such as Simón Bolívar and Abraham Lincoln watch over.

The **Palacio de Aldama** (Amistad #510, e/ Reina y Estrella), on the park's far southwest corner, is a grandiose mansion built in neoclassical style in 1844 for a wealthy Basque, Don Domingo Aldama y Arrechaga. Its facade is lined by Ionic columns and the interior features murals of scenes from Pompeii. It is not open to the public.

To the park's northeast side, a former graveyard for rusting antique steam trains has been cleared to make way for a new hotel, **Pancea Havana Cuba.**

FÁBRICA DE TABACO PARTAGÁS

The original **Partagás Cigar Factory** (Industria #520, e/ Dragones y Barcelona), on the west side of the Capitolio, features a four-story classical Spanish-style facade capped by a roofline of baroque curves topped by lions. It closed in 2010 for repair and remained so at press time, with little sign of progress. The cigar-making facility moved to the former **El Rey del Mundo factory** (Luceña #816, esq. Penalver, Centro Habana) and is open for tours. The factory specialized in full-bodied Partagás cigars, started in 1843 by Catalan immigrant Don Jaime Partagás Ravelo. Partagás was murdered in 1868—some say by a rival who discovered that Partagás was having an affair with his wife—and his ghost is said to haunt the building. A tobacco shop and cigar

Visiting Havana's Cigar Factories

cigar factories produce for export

You'll forever remember the pungent aroma of a cigar factory. The factories, housed in colonial buildings, remain much as they were in the mid-19th century. Though now officially known by ideologically sound names, they're still commonly referred to by their prerevolutionary names. (Note that the factory names switch between factories with annoying regularity when one or more close for repair.) Each specializes in cigar brands of a particular flavor—the government assigns to certain factories the job of producing particular brands.

You must book in advance through a state tour desk or agency (CUC10). No cameras or bags are permitted.

Fábrica Corona (20 de Mayo #520, e/ Marta Abreu y Línea, Cerro, tel. 07/873-0131, Mon.-Fri. 9am-11am and 1pm-3pm) is a modern cigar factory producing Hoyo de Monterey, Punch, and other labels.

Fábrica de Tabaco H. Upmann (Padre Varela, e/ Desagüe y Peñal Verno, Centro Habana, tel. 07/878-1059 or 07/879-3927, 9am-1pm), formerly the Fábrica de Tabaco Romeo y Julieta, makes about a dozen brand names and is the best factory to visit.

Fábrica de Tabaco Partagás (Luceña, esq. Penalver, Centro Habana), formerly the El Rey del Mundo factory, opened in 2011 to house the Partagás workers. Cramped and noisy, it is not as rewarding to visit.

lounge remain open on the ground floor (tel. 07/863-5766).

Zulueta (Calle Agramonte)

Calle Agramonte, more commonly referred to by its colonial name of Zulueta, parallels the Prado and slopes gently upward from Avenida de los Estudiantes to the northeast side of Parque Central. Traffic runs one-way uphill.

At its north end is the **Monumento al** **General Máximo Gómez.** This massive monument of white marble by sculptor Aldo Gamba was erected in 1935 to honor the Dominican-born hero of the Cuban wars of independence who led the Liberation Army as commander-in-chief. Gómez (1836-1905) is cast in bronze, reining in his horse.

One block north of Parque Central, at the corner of Zulueta and Ánimas, is **Sloppy Joe's,** commemorated as Freddy's Bar in

Hemingway's *To Have and Have Not*. Restored in 2013, it reopened its doors after decades lying shuttered and near-derelict.

The old Cuartel de Bomberos fire station houses the tiny **Museo de Bomberos** (Museum of Firemen, Zulueta #257, e/ Neptuno y Ánimas, tel. 07/863-4826, Tues.-Fri. 9:30am-5pm, free), displaying a Merryweather engine from 1894 and antique firefighting memorabilia.

Immediately beyond the Museo Nacional de Bellas Artes and Museo de la Revolución is **Plaza 13 de Marzo,** a grassy park named to commemorate the ill-fated attack of the presidential palace by student martyrs on March 13, 1957. At the base of Zulueta, at the junction with Cárcel, note the flamboyant art nouveau building housing the **Spanish Embassy.**

MUSEO DE LA REVOLUCIÓN

The ornate building facing north over Plaza 13 de Marzo was initiated in 1913 to house the provincial government. Before it could be finished (in 1920), it was earmarked as the Palacio Presidencial (Presidential Palace), and Tiffany's of New York was entrusted with its interior decoration. It was designed by Belgian Paul Belau and Cuban Carlos Maruri in an eclectic style, with a lofty dome.

Following the Revolution, the three-story palace was converted into the dour **Museo de la Revolución** (Museum of the Revolution, Refugio #1, e/ Zulueta y Monserrate, tel. 07/862-4091, daily 9am-5pm, CUC8, cameras CUC2, guide CUC2). It is fronted by a SAU-100 Stalin tank used during the Bay of Pigs invasion in 1961 and a semi-derelict watchtower, **Baluarte de Ángel,** erected in 1680.

The marble staircase leads to the Salón de los Espejos (the Mirror Room), a replica of that in Versailles (replete with paintings by Armando Menocal); and Salón Dorado (the Gold Room), decorated with gold leaf and highlighted by its magnificent dome.

Rooms are divided chronologically. Maps describe the progress of the revolutionary war. Guns and rifles are displayed alongside grisly photos of dead and tortured heroes. The Rincón de los Cretinos (Corner of Cretins) pokes fun at Batista, Ronald Reagan, and George Bush. There's a café to the rear.

At the rear, in the former palace gardens, is the **Granma Memorial,** preserving the vessel that brought Castro and his revolutionaries from Mexico to Cuba in 1956. The *Granma* is encased in a massive glass structure. It's surrounded by vehicles used in the revolutionary war: armored vehicles, the bullet-riddled "Fast

Museo de la Revolución

Delivery" truck used in the student commandos' assault on the palace on March 13, 1957 (Batista escaped through a secret door), and Castro's Toyota jeep from the Sierra Maestra. There's also a turbine from the U-2 spy plane downed during the missile crisis in 1962, plus a Sea Fury aircraft and a T-34 tank.

★ MUSEO NACIONAL DE BELLAS ARTES (CUBAN SECTION)

The Cuban section of the **Museo Nacional de Bellas Artes** (National Fine Arts Museum, Trocadero, e/ Zulueta y Monserrate, tel. 07/863-9484 or 07/862-0140, www.bellasartes.cult.cu, Tues.-Sat. 9am-5pm, Sun. 10am-2pm, entrance CUC5, or CUC8 for both sections, guided tour CUC2) is housed in the soberly classical Palacio de Bellas Artes. The museum features an atrium garden from which ramps lead to two floors exhibiting a complete spectrum of Cuban paintings, engravings, sketches, and sculptures. Works representing the vision of early 16th- and 17th-century travelers merge into colonial-era pieces, early 20th-century Cuban interpretations of Impressionism, Surrealism, and works spawned by the Revolution.

Monserrate (Avenida de los Misiones)

Avenida de los Misiones, or Monserrate as everyone knows it, parallels Zulueta one block to the east (traffic is one-way, downhill) and follows the space left by the ancient city walls. At the base of Monserrate, at its junction with Calle Tacón, is the once lovely **Casa de Pérez de la Riva** (Capdevila #1), built in Italian Renaissance style in 1905. It was closed for restoration at press time and is due to reopen as the Museo de la Música.

Immediately north is a narrow pedestrian alley (Calle Aguiar e/ Peña Pobre y Capdevila) known as **Callejón de los Peluqueros** (Hairdressers' Alley). Adorned with colorful murals, it's the venue for the community **ArteCorte** project—the inspiration of local stylist Gilberto "Papito" Valladares—and features barber shops, art galleries, and cafés.

Papito (Calle Aguiar #10, tel. 07/861-0202) runs a hairdressers' school and salon that doubles as a barbers' museum.

IGLESIA DEL SANTO ÁNGEL CUSTODIO

The Gothic **Iglesia del Santo Ángel Custodio** (Monserrate y Cuarteles, tel. 07/861-8873), immediately east of the Palacio Presidencial, sits atop a rock known as Angel Hill. The church was founded in 1687 by builder-bishop Diego de Compostela. The tower dates from 1846, when a hurricane toppled the original, while the facade was reworked in neo-Gothic style in the mid-19th century. Cuba's national hero, José Martí, was baptized here on February 12, 1853.

The church was the setting for the tragic marriage scene that ends in the violent denouement on the steps of the church in the 19th-century novel *Cecilia Valdés* by Cirilo Villaverde. A bust of the author and a statue of Cecilia grace the **Plazuela de Santo Ángel** outside the main entrance (the corner of Calles Compostela and Cuarteles). This colorful little plaza is a popular venue for music-video and film shoots.

EDIFICIO BACARDÍ

The **Edificio Bacardí** (Bacardí Building, Monserrate #261, esq. San Juan de Dios), former headquarters of the Bacardí rum empire, is a stunning exemplar of art deco design. Designed by Cuban architect Esteban Rodríguez and finished in December 1929, it is clad in Swedish granite and local limestone. Terra-cotta of varying hues accents the building, with motifs showing Grecian nymphs and floral patterns. It's crowned by a Lego-like pyramidal bell tower topped with a brass bat—the famous Bacardí motif. The building now houses various offices. The **Café Barrita** bar (daily 9am-6pm), a true gem of art deco design, is to the right of the lobby, up the stairs.

EL FLORIDITA

The famous restaurant and bar **El Floridita** (corner of Monserrate and Calle Obispo, tel.

07/867-1299, www.floridita-cuba.com, daily 11:30am-midnight) has been serving food since 1819, when it was called Pina de Plata. You expect a spotlight to come on and Desi Arnaz to appear conducting a dance band, and Hemingway to stroll in as he would every morning when he lived in Havana and drank with Honest Lil, the Worst Politician, and other real-life characters from his novels. A life-size bronze statue of Hemingway, by sculptor José Villa, leans on the dark mahogany bar where Constante Ribailagua once served frozen daiquiris to the great writer (Hemingway immortalized both the drink and the venue in his novel *Islands in the Stream*) and such illustrious guests as Gary Cooper, Tennessee Williams, Marlene Dietrich, and Jean-Paul Sartre.

El Floridita has been spruced up for tourist consumption with a 1930s art deco polish. They've overpriced the place, but sipping a daiquiri here is a must. Depsite the restaurant's fantastic fin de siècle ambience, dining is subpar.

PLAZA DEL CRISTO

Plaza del Cristo lies at the west end of Amargura, between Lamparilla and Brasil, one block east of Monserrate. It was here that Wormold, the vacuum-cleaner salesman turned secret agent, was "swallowed up among the pimps and lottery sellers of the Havana noon" in Graham Greene's *Our Man in Havana*. Wormold and his daughter, Millie, lived at the fictional 37 Lamparilla.

The plaza is dominated by the tiny **Iglesia de Santo Cristo Buen Vieja** (Villegas, e/ Amargura y Lamparilla, tel. 07/863-1767, daily 9am-noon), dating from 1732, but with a Franciscan hermitage dating from 1640. Buen Viaje was the final point of the Vía Crucis (the Procession of the Cross) held each Lenten Friday and beginning at the Iglesia de San Francisco de Asís. The church, named for its popularity among sailors, who pray here for safe voyages, has an impressive cross-beamed wooden ceiling and exquisite altars, including one to the Virgen de la Caridad showing three boatmen being saved from a tempest.

The handsome **Iglesia y Convento de Santa Teresa de Jesús** (Brasil, esq. Compostela, tel. 07/861-1445), two blocks east of Plaza del Cristo, was built by the Carmelites in 1705. The church is still in use, although the convent ceased to operate as such in 1929, when the nuns were moved out and the building was converted into a series of homes.

Across the road is the **Drogería Sarrá** (Brasil, e/ Compostela y Habana, tel. 07/866-7554, daily 9am-5pm, free), a fascinating apothecary that is now the **Museo de la Farmacia Habanera.** Its paneled cabinets are still stocked with herbs and pharmaceuticals in colorful old bottles and ceramic jars.

The Harbor Channel

Throughout most of the colonial era, sea waves washed up on a beach that lined the southern shore of the harbor channel and bordered what is today Calle Cuba and, eastward, Calle Tacón, which runs along the site of the old city walls forming the original waterfront. In the early 19th century, the area was extended with landfill, and a broad boulevard—**Avenida Carlos Manuel de Céspedes** (Avenida del Puerto)—was laid out along the new harborfront. **Parque Luz Caballero,** between the *avenida* and Calle Tacón, is pinned by a statue of José de la Luz Caballero (1800-1862), a philosopher and nationalist. In 2014, a statue of feudal samurai Hasekura Tsunenaga (the first Japanese to visit Cuba, in 1614) was erected.

Overlooking the harborfront at the foot of Empedrado is the **Fuente de Neptuno** (Neptune Fountain), erected in 1838.

The giant and beautiful modernist glass cube at the Avenida del Puerto and Calle Narciso López, by Plaza de Armas, is the **Cámara de Rejas,** the new sewer gate. Educational panels tell the history of Havana's sewer system.

CALLES CUBA AND TACÓN

Calle Cuba extends east from the foot of Monserrate. At the foot of Calle Cuarteles is the Palacio de Mateo Pedroso y Florencia, known today as the **Palacio de Artesanía** (Artisans Palace, Cuba #64, e/ Tacón y Peña Pobre, Mon.-Sat. 9am-8pm, Sat. 9am-2pm, free), built in Moorish style for nobleman Don Mateo Pedroso around 1780. Pedroso's home displays the typical architectural layout of period houses, with stores on the ground floor, slave quarters on the mezzanine, and the owner's dwellings above. Today it houses craft shops, boutiques, and folkloric music.

Immediately east is **Plazuela de la Maestranza,** where a remnant of the old city wall is preserved. On its east side, in the triangle formed by the junction of Calles Cuba, Tacón, and Chacón, is a medieval-style fortress, **El Castillo de Atane,** a police headquarters built in 1941 as a pseudo-colonial confection.

The Seminario de San Carlos y San Ambrosio, a massive seminary running the length of Tacón east of El Castillo de Atane, was established by the Jesuits in 1721 and is now the **Centro Cultural Félix Varela** (e/ Chacón y Empedrado, tel. 07/862-8790, www.cfv.org.cu, Mon.-Sat. 9am-4pm, free). The downstairs cloister is open to the public.

The entrance to the seminary overlooks an excavated site showing the foundations of the original seafront section of the city walls, here called the **Cortina de Valdés.**

Tacón opens to a tiny *plazuela* at the junction with Empedrado, where horse-drawn cabs called *calezas* offer guided tours. The **Museo de Arqueología** (Tacón #12, e/ O'Reilly y Empedrado, tel. 07/861-4469, Tues.-Sat. 9am-2pm, CUC1) displays pre-Columbian artifacts, plus ceramics and items from the early colonial years. The museum occupies Casa de Juana Carvajal, a mansion first mentioned in documents in 1644, and features floor-to-ceiling murals depicting 18th-century life.

★ Plaza de la Catedral

The exquisite cobbled **Plaza de la Catedral** (Cathedral Square) was the last square to be laid out in Habana Vieja. It occupied a lowly quarter where rainwater and refuse collected (it was originally known as the Plazuela de la Ciénaga—Little Square of the Swamp). A cistern was built in 1587, and only in the following century was the area drained. Its present texture dates from the 18th century. The

Plaza de la Catedral

square is Habana Vieja at its most quintessential, the atmosphere enhanced by women in traditional costume who will pose for your camera for a small fee.

CATEDRAL SAN CRISTÓBAL DE LA HABANA

On the north side of the plaza and known colloquially as Catedral Colón (Columbus Cathedral) is the **Catedral San Cristóbal de la Habana** (St. Christopher's Cathedral, tel. 07/861-7771, Mon.-Fri. 9am-5pm, Sat.-Sun. 9am-noon, tower tour CUC1), initiated by the Jesuits in 1748. The order was kicked out of Cuba by Carlos III in 1767, but the building was eventually completed in 1777 and altered again in the early 19th century. The original baroque interior (including the altar) is gone, replaced in 1814 by a classical interior.

The baroque facade is adorned with clinging columns and ripples like a great swelling sea; Cuban novelist Alejo Carpentier thought it "music turned to stone." A royal decree of December 1793 elevated the church to a cathedral. A second bell tower, narrower than the first, was added. Columns divide the rectangular church into three naves. The neoclassical main altar is made of wood; the murals above are by Italian painter Guiseppe Perovani. The chapel immediately to the left has several altars. Note the wooden image of Saint Christopher, patron saint of Havana, dating to 1633.

The Spanish believed that a casket brought to Havana from Santo Domingo in 1796 and that resided in the cathedral for more than a century held the ashes of Christopher Columbus. It was returned to Spain in 1899. All but the partisan *habaneros* now believe that the ashes were those of Columbus's son Diego.

CASA DE LOS MARQUESES DE AGUAS CLARAS

This splendid mansion, on the northwest side of the plaza, was built during the 16th century by Governor General Gonzalo Pérez de

Angulo and has since been added to by subsequent owners. Today a café occupies the portico; the inner courtyard, with its fountain, houses the Restaurante El Patio. The upstairs restaurant offers splendid views over the plaza. Sunlight pouring in through stained glass *mediopuntos* saturates the floors with shifting colors.

CASA DEL CONDE DE BAYONA

This simple two-story structure, on the south side of the square, is a perfect example of the traditional Havana merchant's house of the period, with side stairs and an *entresuelo* (mezzanine of half-story proportions). It was built in the 1720s for Governor General Don Luis Chacón. Today it houses the **Museo de Arte Colonial** (Colonial Art Museum, San Ignacio #61, tel. 07/862-6440, daily 9:30am-5pm, entrance CUC2, cameras CUC5, guides CUC1), which re-creates the lavish interior of an aristocratic colonial home. One room is devoted to colorful stained glass *vitrales*.

CALLEJÓN DEL CHORRO

At the southwest corner of the plaza, this short cul-de-sac is where a cistern was built to supply water to ships in the harbor. The *aljibe* (cistern) marked the terminus of the Zanja Real (the "royal ditch," or *chorro*), a covered aqueduct that brought water from the Río Almendares some 10 kilometers away.

The **Casa de Baños,** which faces onto the square, looks quite ancient but was built in the 20th century in colonial style on the site of a bathhouse erected over the *aljibe*. Today the building contains the **Galería Victor Manuel** (San Ignacio #56, tel. 07/861-2955, daily 9am-8pm), selling quality arts.

At the far end of Callejón del Chorro is the not-to-be-missed **Taller Experimental de la Gráfica** (tel. 07/864-7622, tgrafica@cubarte. cult.cu, Mon.-Fri. 9am-4pm), a graphics cooperative where you can watch artists make prints for sale using antique presses and lithographic stones.

CASA DE CONDE DE LOMBILLO

On the plaza's east side is the **Casa de Conde de Lombillo** (tel. 07/860-4311, Mon.-Fri. 9am-5pm, Sat. 9am-1pm, free). Built in 1741, this former home of a slave trader houses a small post office (Cuba's first), as it has since 1821. The building now holds historical lithographs. The mansion adjoins the **Casa del Marqués de Arcos,** built in the 1740s for the royal treasurer. What you see is the rear of the mansion; the entrance is on Calle Mercaderes, where the building facing the entrance is graced by the *Mural Artístico-Histórico,* by Cuban artist Andrés Carrillo. A restoration of the mansion was completed in 2017; the venue now hosts the **Café Literario Marque de Arcos** café, library, and exhibition space.

The two houses are fronted by a wide portico supported by thick columns. Note the mailbox set into the wall, a grotesque face of a tragic Greek mask carved in stone, with a scowling mouth as its slit. A life-size bronze statue of Spanish flamenco dancer Antonio Gades (1936-2004) leans against one of the columns.

CENTRO WILFREDO LAM

The **Centro Wilfredo Lam** (San Ignacio #22, esq. Empedrado, tel. 07/864-6282, www.wlam.cult.cu, Tues.-Sat. 10am-5pm), on cobbled Empedrado, on the northwest corner of the plaza, occupies the former mansion of the counts of Peñalver. This art center displays works by the eponymous Cuban artist as well as artists from Latin America. The institution studies and promotes contemporary art from around the world.

LA BODEGUITA DEL MEDIO

No visit to Havana is complete without popping into **La Bodeguita del Medio** (Empedrado #207, tel. 07/866-8857, daily 10am-midnight), half a block west of the cathedral. This neighborhood hangout was originally the coach house of the mansion next door. Later it was a bodega, a mom-and-pop grocery store where Spanish immigrant Ángel Martínez served food and drinks.

Today troubadours move among thirsty *turistas* and the house drink is the somewhat weak *mojito.* Adorning the walls are posters, paintings, and faded photos of Ernest Hemingway, Carmen Miranda, and other famous visitors. The walls were once decorated with the signatures and scrawls of visitors dating back decades. Alas, a renovation wiped away much of the original charm; the artwork was erased and replaced in ersatz style, with visitors being handed blue pens (famous visitors now sign a chalkboard). The most famous graffiti is credited to Hemingway: *"Mi mojito en La Bodeguita, mi daiquirí en El Floridita,"* he supposedly scrawled on the sky-blue walls. According to Tom Miller in *Trading with the Enemy,* Martínez concocted the phrase as a marketing gimmick after the writer's death. Errol Flynn thought it "A Great Place to Get Drunk."

CASA DEL CONDE DE LA REUNIÓN

Built in the 1820s, at the peak of the baroque era, this home has a trefoil-arched doorway opening onto a *zaguán* (courtyard). Exquisite *azulejos* (painted tiles) decorate the walls. Famed novelist Alejo Carpentier used the house as the main setting for his novel *El Siglo de las Luces* (The Enlightenment). A portion of the home, which houses the Centro de Promoción Cultural, is dedicated to his memory as the **Fundación Alejo Carpentier** (Empedrado #215, tel. 07/861-5506, www.fundacioncarpentier.cult.cu, Mon.-Fri. 8:30am-4:30pm, free).

One block west, tiny **Plazuela de San Juan de Dios** (Empedrado, e/ Habana y Aguiar) is pinned by a white marble facsimile of *Don Quixote* author Miguel de Cervantes sitting in a chair, pen in hand, lending the plaza its colloquial name: Parque Cervantes. Visitors on the revolutionary trail should continue one block north up Aguiar to Calle Tejadillo. To the right is the **Museo Bufete Aspiazo-Castro-Risende** (Tejadillo #57; tel. 07/861-5001, by appointment), the office where Fidel Castro worked as a lawyer 1950-1952. The **Arzobispado de la Habana,**

Habana Vieja: The Historic Core

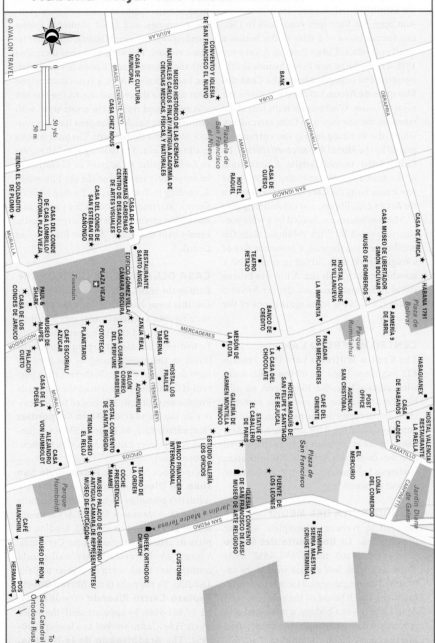

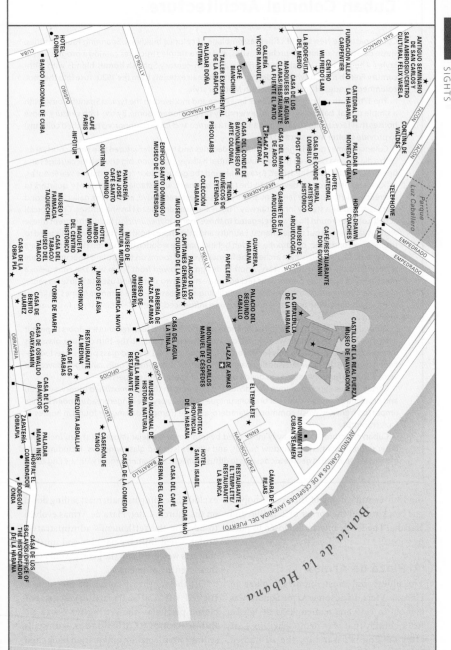

Cuban Colonial Architecture

Cuba boasts the New World's finest assemblage of colonial buildings. Spanning four centuries, these palaces, mansions, churches, castles, and more simple structures catalog a progression of styles. The academic classicism of aristocratic 18th-century Spanish homes blends with 19th-century French rococo, while art deco and art nouveau exteriors from the 1920s fuse into the cool, columned arcades of ancient palaces in Mudejar style.

The 17th-century home was made of limestone and modeled on the typical Spanish house, with a simple portal, balconies, and tall, generously proportioned rooms. By the 18th century, those houses that faced onto squares had adopted a *portico* and *loggia* (supported by arched columns) to provide shelter from sun and rain.

Colonial homes grew larger with ensuing decades and typically featured two small courtyards, with a dining area between the two, and a central hallway, or *zaguán*, big enough for carriages and opening directly from the street. Arrayed around the ground floor courtyard were warehouses, offices, and other rooms devoted to the family business, with stables and servants' quarters to the rear, while the private family quarters were sequestered above, around the galleried second story reached by a stately inner stairway. The design was unique to Havana houses. Commercial activity on the ground floor was relegated to those rooms (*dependencias*) facing the street (these were usually rented out to merchants). Laundry and other household functions were relegated to the inner, second patio, or *traspatio*, hidden behind massive wooden doors often flanked by pillars that in time developed ornate arches. The formal layout of rooms on the ground floor was usually repeated on the main, upper story. Another design borrowed from Spain was the *entresuelo*, a mezzanine of half-story proportions tucked between the two stories and used to house servants.

By the 19th century, the wealthy were building neoclassical-style summer homes (*quintas*) in Havana's hilly suburbs. Many, however, were influenced by the Palladian style, fashionable in Europe.

Ground-floor windows were full height from ground level and featured shutter-doors to permit a free flow of air. Later windows acquired ornate grilled *rejas* (bars). In the 19th century, glass was introduced, though usually only for decoration in multicolored stained glass panes inserted between or above the louvered wooden panels. Meanwhile, ornate metal grills called *guardavecinos* were adopted for upper stories to divide balconies of contiguous properties.

Certain styles evolved unique to individual cities, as with the *arco mixtilíneo* (doorway lintel) and projecting turned-wood roof brackets unique to Camagüey; the gingerbread wooden homes (imported from Key West) common in Varadero; and the trompe l'oeil murals found in homes of Sancti Spíritus.

Cuban structures were heavily influenced by traditional Mudejar (Moorish) styles, including inner patios, ornamented window guards, and *vitrales* (stained glass windows, including half-moon *mediopuntos*) in geometric designs to diffuse sunlight, saturating a room with shifting color.

the 18th-century home of the archbishop, is one block west at the corner of Tejadillo and Habana. The lovely interior is closed to public view.

★ Plaza de Armas

The oldest and most important plaza in Habana Vieja, handsome Arms Square was laid out in 1519 and named Plaza de Iglesia for a church that was demolished in 1741 after an English warship, the ill-named HMS *Invincible*, was struck by lightning and

exploded, sending its main mast sailing down on the church. Later, Plaza de Armas evolved to become the settlement's administrative center, when military parades and musical concerts were held and the gentry would take their evening promenade.

Off the southeast corner of the square, tucked off Calle Baratillo, is an enclosed plazuela—the setting for **Feria de Publicaciones y Curiosidades,** with stalls selling tatterdemalion antiquarian books and small antiquities.

A Walk Down Calle Mercaderes

Cobbled Calle Mercaderes between Obispo and Plaza Vieja, four blocks south, is full of attractions. Setting out toward Plaza Vieja from the Hotel Ambos Mundos, after 20 meters you'll pass the charming **Casa de Ásia** (Mercaderes #111, tel. 07/863-9740, Tues.-Sat. 9:15am-4:45pm, Sun. 9:15am-12:45pm, entrance CUC1, cameras CUC2, videos CUC10) on your left, containing an array of carved ivory, silverware, mother-of-pearl furniture, kimonos, and Asian armaments. Opposite, call in to the **Maqueta de Centro Histórico** (Model of the Historic Center, Calle 28 #113, e/ 1ra y 3ra, tel. 07/206-1268, maqueta@gdic.cu, Tues.-Sat. 9:30am-6:30pm, adults CUC3, students, seniors, and children CUC1, guided tour CUC1, cameras CUC2); this 1:500 scale model of Habana Vieja measures eight by four meters, with every building delineated and color coded by use. Guides give a spiel.

On the west side, 20 meters farther south, the **Casa del Tabaco** houses the **Museo del Tabaco** (Mercaderes #120, tel. 07/861-5795, Tues.-Sat. 10am-5pm, Sun. 9am-1pm, free), a cigar museum upstairs.

At the end of the block, at the corner of Obrapía, the **Casa de Benito Juárez** (also called Casa de México, Mercaderes #116, tel. 07/861-8166, Tues.-Sat. 9:30am-4:45pm, Sun. 9:30am-1pm, entrance by donation) displays artwork and costumes from Mexico, including priceless Aztec jewelry.

Turn west onto Obrapía to visit the **Casa de la Obra Pía** (House of Charitable Works, Obrapía #158, tel. 07/861-3097, Tues.-Sat. 9:30am-5pm, Sun. 9:30am-noon, free), 20 meters west of Mercaderes. This splendid mansion was built in 1665 by Capitán Martín Calvo de la Puerta y Arrieta, the Cuban solicitor general. (The house and street are named for his *obra pía,* or pious act, of devoting a portion of his wealth to sponsoring five orphan girls every year.) The family coat of arms, surrounded by exuberant baroque stonework, is emblazoned above the massive portal, brought from Cádiz in 1686. The mansion features art galleries. Across the street, the **Casa de África** (Obrapía #157, e/ Mercaderes y San Ignacio, tel. 07/861-5798, africa@patrimonio.ohc.cu, Tues.-Sat. 9:30am-5pm, Sun. 9:30am-noon, CUC2) celebrates African culture and is full of African art and artifacts. On the third floor is a collection of paraphernalia used in Santería.

One block east, between Mercaderes and Oficios, is the **Casa de Oswaldo Guayasamín** (Obrapía #112, tel. 07/861-3843, Tues.-Sat. 9am-5:30pm, Sun. 9am-1:30pm, free), housing a museum of art by the Ecuadorian painter, who lived and worked here for many years. Next door is the **Casa de los Abanicos** (Obrapía #107, tel. 07/863-4452, Mon.-Sat. 10am-7pm, Sun. 10am-1pm, free), where traditional Spanish fans (*abanicos*) are made by hand.

Return to Mercaderes and pop into **Habana 1791** (Mercaderes #176, tel. 07/861-3525, Mon.-Sat. 10am-7pm, Sun. 10am-1pm), on the southwest corner of Obrapía, where traditional fragrances are made and sold. Continue south half a block past the small **Plaza de Bolívar** to the **Armería 9 de Abril** (Mercaderes #157, tel. 07/861-8080, Mon.-Sat. 9am-5pm, CUC1), a museum that commemorates four members of Castro's 26th July Movement killed in an assault on the armory on April 9, 1958.

One block south, the corner of Mercaderes and Armagura is known as the Cruz Verde (Green Cross) because it was the first stop on the annual Vía Crucis pilgrimage. Here is the **Museo de Chocolate** (tel. 07/866-4431, daily 9am-11pm), selling sweets and featuring a museum relating the history of chocolate.

PALACIO DE LOS CAPITANES GENERALES

The somber yet stately **Palacio de los Capitanes Generales** (Palace of the Captains-Generals) was completed in 1791 and became home to 65 governors of Cuba between 1791 and 1898. After that, it was the U.S. governor's residence, the early seat of the Cuban government (1902-1920), and Havana's city hall (1920-1967).

The palace is fronted by a loggia supported by Ionic columns and by "cobblewood," laid instead of stone to soften the noise of carriages and thereby lessen the disturbance of the governor's sleep. The three-story structure surrounds a courtyard that contains a statue of Christopher Columbus by Italian sculptor Cucchiari. Arched colonnades rise on all sides. In the southeast corner, a hole containing the coffin of a nobleman is one of several graves from the old Cementerio de Espada. To the north end of the loggia is a marble **statue of Fernando VII.**

Today, the palace houses the **Museo de la Ciudad de la Habana** (City of Havana Museum, Tacón #1, e/ Obispo y O'Reilly, tel. 07/861-5001, Tues.-Sun. 9:30am-5pm, last entry at 4pm, entrance CUC3, cameras CUC5, guide CUC5). The stairs lead up to palatially furnished rooms. The Salón del Trono (Throne Room), made for the king of Spain but never used, is of breathtaking splendor. The museum also features the Salón de las Banderas (Hall of Flags), with magnificent artwork that includes *The Death of Antonio Maceo* by Menocal, plus exquisite collections illustrating the story of the city's (and Cuba's) development and the 19th-century struggles for independence.

PALACIO DEL SEGUNDO CABO

On the park's northwest corner, the austere **Palacio del Segundo Cabo** (Palace of the Second Lieutenant, O'Reilly #14, tel. 07/862-8091, Mon.-Fri. 6am-midnight) dates from 1770, when it was designed as the city post office. Later it became the home of the vice governor-general and, after independence, the seat of the Senate. Today it is a cultural center.

CASTILLO DE LA REAL FUERZA

The pocket-size **Castillo de la Real Fuerza** (Royal Power Castle, O'Reilly #2, tel. 07/864-4490, Tues.-Sun. 9:30am-5pm, entrance CUC3, cameras CUC5), on the northeast corner of the plaza, was begun in 1558 and completed in 1577. It's the oldest of the four forts that guarded the New World's most precious harbor. Built in medieval fashion, with walls 6 meters wide and 10 meters tall, the castle forms a square with enormous triangular bulwarks at the corners, their sharp angles slicing the dark waters of the moat. It was almost useless from a strategic point of view, being landlocked far from the mouth of the harbor channel and hemmed in by surrounding buildings that would have formed a great impediment to its cannons in any attack. The governors of Cuba lived here until 1762.

Cuban man painting in Plaza de Armas

El Caballero de París

Many myths surround the enigmatic real-life character known as the "Gentleman of Paris." Born in 1899 to a humble family in Vilaseca, Galicia, Spain, José María López Lledín migrated to Cuba at the age of 13. He worked in various menial jobs until some time in the late 1920s, when he was imprisoned, supposedly for a crime he did not commit. The event unhinged him. By the time of his release he'd gone mad.

His hair long and curly, with pointed beard, and wearing a dark suit and cape, José took to the streets as a likable tramp. For five decades he roamed Havana's streets as El Caballero de París. He never begged for alms but offered gallant words to the ladies, pens and pencils to kids, or perhaps a leaf or a verse in reward for favors. *Habaneros* regarded him with affection.

Eventually his health declined and with it his ragged appearance. He was admitted to the psychiatric hospital, where he died in 1985. He was buried in the Santiago de las Vegas cemetery. In 1999, his body was exhumed and relocated to the crypt of the **Iglesia y Convento de San Francisco de Asís.**

Visitors enter via a courtyard full of cannons and mortars. Note the royal coat of arms carved in stone above the massive gateway as you cross the moat by a drawbridge.

The castle houses the not-to-be-missed **Museo de Navegación** (Naval Museum), displaying treasures from the golden age when the riches of the Americas flowed to Spain. The air-conditioned Sala de Tesoro gleams with gold bars and coins, plus precious jewels, bronze astrolabes, and silver *reales* ("pieces of eight"). The jewel in the crown is a four-meter interactive scale model of the *Santisima Trinidad* galleon, built in Havana 1767-1770 and destroyed at the Battle of Trafalgar.

A cylindrical bell tower rising from the northwest corner is topped by a bronze weathervane called **La Giraldilla de la Habana** showing a voluptuous figure with hair braided in thick ropes; in her right hand is a palm tree and in her left a cross. This figure is the official symbol of Havana. The vane is a copy; the original, which now resides in the foyer, was cast in 1631 in honor of Isabel de Bobadilla, the wife of Governor Hernando de Soto, the tireless explorer who fruitlessly searched for the fountain of youth in Florida. De Soto named his wife governor in his absence—the only female governor ever to serve in Cuba. For four years she scanned the horizon in vain for his return.

Immediately east of the castle, at the junction of Avenida del Puerto and O'Reilly, is an obelisk to the 77 Cuban seamen killed during World War II by German submarines.

EL TEMPLETE

A charming copy of a Doric temple, **El Templete** (The Pavilion, daily 9:30am-5pm, CUC1.50 including guide) stands on the northeast corner of the Plaza de Armas. It was inaugurated on March 19, 1828, on the site where the first mass and town council meeting were held in 1519, beside a massive ceiba tree. The original ceiba was felled by a hurricane in 1828 and replaced by a column fronted by a small bust of Christopher Columbus. A ceiba has since been replanted and today shades the tiny temple; its interior features a wall-to-ceiling triptych depicting the first mass, the council meeting, and El Templete's inauguration. In the center of the room sits a bust of the artist, Jean-Baptiste Vermay (1786-1833).

PALACIO DEL CONDE DE SANTOVENIA

Immediately south of El Templete is the former **Palacio del Conde de Santovenia** (Baratillo, e/ Narciso López y Baratillo y Obispo). Its quintessentially Cuban-colonial facade is graced by a becolumned portico and, above, wrought-iron railings on balconies whose windows boast stained glass *mediopuntos*. The *conde* (count) in question was famous for hosting elaborate parties, most notoriously a three-day bash in 1833 to celebrate the accession to the throne of Isabel II that climaxed with the ascent of a gaily decorated gas-filled balloon. Later that century the building served as a hotel. Today it's the Hotel Santa Isabel. President Carter stayed here during his visit to Havana in 2002.

MUSEO NACIONAL DE HISTORIA NATURAL

On the south side of the plaza, the **Museo Nacional de Historia Natural** (Natural History Museum, Obispo #61, e/ Oficios y Baratillo, tel. 07/863-9361, museo@mnhnc.inf.cu, Tues.-Sun. 9:30pm-5pm, CUC3) covers evolution in a well-conceived display. The museum houses collections of Cuban flora and fauna—many in clever reproductions of their natural environments—plus stuffed tigers, apes, and other beasts from around the world. Children will appreciate the interactive displays.

Immediately east, the **Biblioteca Provincial de la Habana** (Havana Provincial Library, tel. 07/862-9035, Mon.-Fri. 8:15am-7pm, Sat. 8:15am-4:30pm, Sun. 8:15am-1pm) once served as the U.S. Embassy.

One block south along Calle Oficios, at the corner of Justiz, the former Depósito del Automóvil has been beautifully restored as **Mezquita Abdallah** (Oficios #18, no tel.)—a mosque and the only place in Havana where Muslims can practice the Islamic faith. The prayer hall is decorated with hardwoods inlaid with mother-of-pearl. Only Muslims may enter, but you can peer in at the beautiful Mughal architecture through glass-panel doors.

Across the street, the **Casa de los Árabes** (Arabs' House, Oficios #12, tel. 07/861-5868, Tues.-Sat. 9am-4:30pm, Sun. 9am-1pm, free) comprises two Moorish-inspired 17th-century mansions that house a small yet impressive

museum dedicated to a Levantine and Islamic theme.

Plaza de San Francisco

Cobbled Plaza de San Francisco, two blocks south of Plaza de Armas, at Oficios and the foot of Amargura, faces onto Avenida del Puerto. During the 16th century this area was the waterfront. Iberian emigrants disembarked, slaves were unloaded, and galleons were replenished and treasure fleets loaded for the passage to Spain. A market developed on the plaza, which became the focus of the annual Fiesta de San Francisco each October 3, when a gambling fair was established. At its heart is the **Fuente de los Leones** (Fountain of the Lions) by Giuseppe Gaggini, erected in 1836.

The five-story neoclassical building on the north side is the **Lonja del Comercio** (Goods Exchange, Amargura #2, esq. Oficios, tel. 07/866-9588, Mon.-Sat. 9am-6pm), dating from 1907, when it was built as a center for commodities trading. Restored, it houses offices of international corporations, news bureaus, and tour companies. The dome is crowned by a bronze figure of the god Mercury.

Behind the Lonja del Comercio, entered by a wrought-iron archway topped by a most-uncommunist fairytale crown, is the **Jardín Diana de Gales** (Baratillo, esq. Carpinetti, daily 9am-6pm), a park unveiled in 2000 in memory of Diana, Princess of Wales. The three-meter-tall column is by acclaimed Cuban artist Alfredo Sosabravo. There's also an engraved Welsh slate and stone plaque from Althorp, Diana's childhood home, donated by the British Embassy.

The garden backs onto the **Casa de los Esclavos** (Obrapía, esq. Av. del Puerto), a slave-merchant's home that now serves as the principal office of the city historian.

IGLESIA Y CONVENTO DE SAN FRANCISCO DE ASÍS

Dominating the plaza on the south side, the **Iglesia y Convento de San Francisco**

A Walk Along Calle Obispo

Pedestrians-only Calle Obispo links Plaza de Armas with Parque Central and is Habana Vieja's busiest shopping street.

Begin at Plaza Albear and walk east. Fifty meters on your left you'll pass the Infotur office. Crossing Calle Havana, five blocks east of Plaza Albear, you arrive at Havana's erstwhile "Wall Street," centered on Calles Obispo, Cuba, and Aguiar, where the main banks were concentrated prior to the Revolution. The **Museo Numismático** (Coin Museum, Obispo, e/ Habana y Aguiar, tel. 07/861-5811, Tues.-Sat. 9am-5pm, Sun. 9:30am-12:45pm, CUC1) displays a broad-ranging collection of coins and banknotes spanning the Greco, Roman, and Phoenician epochs, as well as Spanish coins plus Cuban money from the republican era. Across the street is the **Museo 28 de Septiembre** (Obispo #310, tel. 07/864-3253, daily 9am-5:30pm, CUC2), a dour museum telling the history of the Committees for the Defense of the Revolution.

Continue one block to **Drogería Johnson** (Obispo #361, tel. 07/862-3057, daily 9am-5pm), an ancient apothecary that still operates as a pharmacy.

At the corner of Calle Cuba you reach the former **Banco Nacional de Cuba** (Obispo #211, esq. Cuba), in a splendid neoclassical building fronted by fluted Corinthian columns; it is occupied by the Ministerio de Finanzas y Precios (Ministry of Finance and Prices). Beyond, don't miss the **Museo y Farmacia Taquechel** (Obispo #155, esq. Aguiar, tel. 07/862-9286, daily 9am-6pm, free), another fascinating and dusty old apothecary with mixing vases, mortars and pestles, and colorful ceramic jars.

Across the street, on the north side of Obispo, is the **Edificio Santo Domingo,** a looming contemporary building occupying the site of the Convento de Santo Domingo, which between 1727 and 1902 housed the original University of Havana. The building has been remodeled with a replica of the original baroque doorway and campanile containing the original bell. Today it houses the university's school of restoration. On the north side is the **Museo de la Universidad** (Calle O'Reilly, no tel., Tues.-Sat. 9:30am-5pm, Sun. 9:30am-1pm), displaying miscellany related to the early university.

Fifty meters beyond Museo y Farmacia Taquechel you'll arrive at the rose-pink **Hotel Ambos Mundos** (Obispo #153, esq. Mercaderes, tel. 07/860-9530), dating from 1925. Off and on throughout the 1930s, Hemingway laid his head in room 511, where he wrote *The Green Hills of Africa* and *Death in the Afternoon*. The room is today a museum (daily 10am-5pm, CUC2). Hemingway's quarters have been preserved, with furnishings from his home, Finca Vigía, including his typewriter.

One block farther brings you to a 50-meter-long cobbled pedestrian section and the oldest mansion in Havana: The **Casa del Agua la Tinaja** (Obispo #111) sells mineral water (CUC0.25 a glass). The **Museo de la Orfebrería** (Museum of Silverwork, Obispo #113, tel. 07/863-9861, Tues.-Sat. 9:30am-5pm, Sun. 9:30am-1pm, free) is crammed with silver and gold ornaments from the colonial era, including a splendid collection of swords and firearms. Next door, the **Museo de Pintura Mural** (Painted Mural Museum, Obispo #119, tel. 07/864-2354, Tues.-Sat. 9:30am-5pm, Sun. 9:30am-1pm) displays colonial murals, plus a *quitrin*, the traditional low-slung, horse-drawn cart of the colonial nobility.

Another 50 meters brings you to Plaza de Armas.

de Asís (Oficios, e/ Amargura y Brasil, tel. 07/862-9683, daily 9am-5:30pm, entrance CUC2, guide CUC1, cameras CUC2, videos CUC10) was completed in 1730 in baroque style with a 40-meter bell tower. The church was eventually proclaimed a basilica, serving as Havana's main church. It was from here that the processions of the Vía Crucis (Procession of the Cross) departed every Lenten Friday, ending at the Iglesia del Santo Cristo del Buen Vieja. The devout passed down Calle Amargura (Street of Bitterness), where stations of the cross were set up at street corners. After the Protestant English worshiped here in 1762, the Catholic Spanish considered it desecrated and it was never again used for religious purposes.

The main nave, with its towering roof supported by 12 columns, each topped by an apostle, features a trompe l'oeil that extends the perspective of the nave. The sumptuously adorned altars are gone, replaced by a huge crucifix suspended above a grand piano. (The cathedral serves as a concert hall, with classical music performances hosted 6pm Sat. and 11am Sun. Sept.-June.) Aristocrats were buried in the crypt; some skeletons can be seen through clear plastic set into the floor. Climb the campanile (CUC1) for a panoramic view. A side nave contains the **Museo de Arte Sacro,** featuring religious icons.

A life-size bronze statue (by José Villa Soberón) of an erstwhile and once-renowned tramp known as **El Caballero de París** (Gentleman of Paris) graces the sidewalk in front of the cathedral entrance. Many Cubans believe that touching his beard will bring good luck.

On the basilica's north side is **Jardín Madre Teresa de Calcuta,** a garden dedicated to Mother Teresa. It contains the small **Iglesia Ortodoxa Griega,** a Greek Orthodox church opened in 2004.

CALLE OFICIOS

Facing the cathedral, cobbled Calle Oficios is lined with 17th-century colonial buildings that possess a marked Mudejar style, exemplified by their wooden balconies. Many of the buildings have been converted into art galleries, including **Galería de Carmen Montilla Tinoco** (Oficios #162, tel. 07/866-8768, Mon.-Sat. 9am-5pm, free); only the front of the house remains, but the architects have made creative use of the empty shell. Next door, **Estudio Galería Los Oficios** (Oficios #166, tel. 07/863-0497, Mon.-Sat. 9:30am-5pm, Sun. 9am-1pm, free) displays works by renowned artist Nelson Domínguez.

Midway down the block, cobbled Calle Brasil extends west about 80 meters to Plaza Vieja. Portions of the original colonial-era aqueduct (the Zanja Real) are exposed. Detour

to visit the **Aqvarium** (Brasil #9, tel. 07/863-9493, Tues.-Sat. 9am-5pm, Sun. 9am-1pm, CUC1, children free), displaying tropical fish. Next door, **La Casa Cubana del Perfume** (Brasil #13, tel. 07/866-3759, Mon.-Sat. 10am-7pm, Sun. 10am-1pm) displays colonial-era distilleries, has aromatherapy demos, and sells handmade perfumes made on-site.

Back on Oficios, the former Casa de Don Lorenzo Montalvo houses a convent and the **Hostal Convento de Santa Brígida.** To its side, the **Coche Presidencial Mambí** railway carriage (Mon.-Fri. 8:30am-4:45pm, CUC1) stands on rails at Oficios and Churruca. It served as the official presidential carriage of five presidents, beginning in 1902 with Tomás Estrada Palma. Its polished hardwood interior gleams with brass fittings.

The door inset in the wall behind the carriage opens to the Salón Blanco, housing **El Genio de Leonardi da Vinci Exhibición Permanente** (no tel., Tues.-Sat. 9:30am-4pm, CUC2), dedicated to the Renaissance genius. It displays copies (and contemporary reinterpretations) of his artwork, plus magnificent 3-D models of his inventions—from bicycles, gliders, and helicopters to a diving suit—all labeled in various languages. Da Vinci (1452-1519) died the year of Havana's founding.

Immediately east of the Coche is the **Museo Palacio de Gobierno** (Government Palace Museum, Oficios #211, esq. Muralla, tel. 07/863-4358, Tues.-Sat. 9:30am-5pm, Sun. 9:30am-1pm). This 19th-century neoclassical building housed the Cámara de Representantes (Chamber of Representatives) during the early republic. Later it served as the Ministerio de Educación (1929-1960) and, following the Revolution, housed the Poder Popular Municipal (Havana's local government office). Today it has uniforms, documents, and other items relating to its past use, and the office of the President of the Senate is maintained with period furniture. The interior lobby is striking for its magnificent stained glass skylight.

The **Tienda Museo el Reloj** (Watch Museum, Oficios, esq. Muralla, tel.

07/864-9515, Mon.-Sat. 10am-7pm, Sun. 10am-1pm) doubles as a watch and clock museum, and a deluxe store selling watches and pens made by Cuervo y Sobrinos, a Swiss-Italian company that began life in Cuba in 1882.

On the southeast side of Oficios and Muralla is **Casa Alejandro Von Humboldt** (Oficios #254, tel. 07/863-9850, Tues.-Sat. 9am-5pm, Sun. 9am-noon, CUC1), a museum dedicated to the German explorer (1769-1854) who lived here while investigating Cuba in 1800-1801.

★ Plaza Vieja

The last of the four main squares to be laid out in Habana Vieja, **Plaza Vieja** (Old Square, bounded by Calles Mercaderes, San Ignacio, Brasil, and Muralla) originally hosted a covered market. It is surrounded by mansions and apartment blocks where, in colonial times, residents looked down on executions and bullfights.

In the 20th century the square sank into disrepair. Today it is in the final stages of restoration. Even the white Carrara marble fountain—an exact replica of the original by Italian sculptor Giorgio Massari—has reappeared. Two decades ago, most buildings were squalid tenements; the tenants have since moved out as the buildings metamorphosed into boutiques, restaurants, museums, and luxury apartments for foreign residents.

Various modern sculptures grace the park. At the southeast corner is *Viaje Fantástico,* by Roberto Fabelo—a bronze figure of a bald, naked woman riding a rooster.

EAST SIDE

The tallest building is the **Edificio Gómez Villa,** on the square's northeast corner. Take the elevator to the top for views over the plaza and to visit the **Cámara Oscura** (tel. 07/866-4461, daily 9am-5:30pm, CUC2). The optical reflection camera revolves 360 degrees, projecting a real-time picture of Havana at 30 times the magnification onto a two-meter-wide parabola housed in a completely darkened room.

The shaded arcade along the plaza's east side leads past the Casa de Juan Rico de Mata, today the headquarters of **Fototeca** (Mercaderes #307, tel. 07/862-2530, fototeca@cubarte.cult.cu, Tues.-Sat. 10am-5pm), the state-run agency that promotes the work of Cuban photographers. It hosts photo exhibitions.

Next door, the **Planetario Habana**

Plaza Vieja at night

(Mercaderes #309, tel. 07/864-9544, shows Wed.-Sat. 9:30am-5pm, Sun. 9:30am-12:30pm, CUC10 adults, children under 12 free) delights visitors with its high-tech interactive exhibitions on space science and technology. A scale model of the solar system spirals around the sun in the 66-seat theater.

The old **Palacio Cueto,** on the southeast corner of Plaza Vieja, is a phenomenal piece of Gaudí-esque art nouveau architecture dating from 1906. It awaits restoration as a hotel.

SOUTH SIDE

On the southeast corner, the Casa de Marqués de Prado Amero today houses the **Museo de Naipes** (Museum of Playing Cards, Muralla #101, tel. 07/860-1534, Tues.-Sat. 9:30am-5pm, Sun. 9am-2:30pm, entrance by donation), displaying playing cards through the ages.

The 18th-century **Casa de los Condes de Jaruco** (House of the Counts of Jaruco, Muralla #107), or "La Casona," on the southeast corner, was built between 1733 and 1737. It is highlighted by mammoth doors that open into a cavernous courtyard surrounded by lofty archways festooned with hanging vines. Art galleries (Tues.-Sat. 9am-5pm) occupy the downstairs.

WEST SIDE

On the plaza's southwest corner, cool off with a chilled beer brewed on-site in the **Factoría de Plaza Vieja** (San Ignacio #364, tel. 07/866-4453, daily 11am-1am), in the former Casa del Conde de Casa Lombillo. The copper stills are displayed in the main bar, where a 1913 Ford delivery truck now sits amid artworks by such famous Cuban artists as Kcho and Nelson Domínguez. Accessed via a door next to the brewpub is the **Taller de Luthiería** (tel. 07/801-8339), a workshop run by Habaguanex that repairs string instruments.

The **Casa del Conde de San Estéban de Cañongo** (San Ignacio #356, tel. 07/868-3561, Mon.-Fri. 9:30am-5:30pm, Sat. 9:30am-1pm) is today a cultural center. Adjoining, on the northwest corner of the plaza, is the Casa de las Hermanas Cárdenas, housing the

Centro de Desarollo de Artes Visuales (San Ignacio #352, tel. 07/862-2611, Tues.-Sat. 10am-6pm). The inner courtyard is dominated by an intriguing sculpture by Alfredo Sosabravo. Art education classes are given on the second floor. The top story has an art gallery.

Well worth the side trip is **Hotel Raquel** (San Ignacio, esq. Amargura, tel. 07/860-8280), one block north of the plaza. This former 1908 bank and warehouse is an architectural jewel with a stunning stained glass atrium ceiling and art nouveau facade. The hotel is themed to honor the city's former Jewish community.

MUSEO HISTÓRICO DE LAS CIENCIAS NATURALES CARLOS FINLAY

One block west and one north of the plaza is the **Museo Histórico de las Ciencias Naturales Carlos Finlay** (Museum of Natural History, Cuba #460, e/ Amargura y Brasil, tel. 07/863-4824, Mon.-Fri. 9am-5pm, Sat. 9am-1pm, CUC2). Dating from 1868 and once the headquarters of the Academy of Medical, Physical, and Natural Sciences, today it contains a pharmaceutical collection and tells the tales of Cuban scientists' discoveries and innovations. The Cuban scientist Dr. Finlay is honored, of course; it was he who on August 14, 1881, discovered that yellow fever is transmitted by the *Aedes aegipti* mosquito. The museum also contains, on the third floor, a reconstructed period pharmacy.

Adjoining the museum to the north, the **Convento y Iglesia de San Francisco el Nuevo** (Cuba, esq. Amargura, tel. 07/861-8490, free) was completed in 1633 for the Augustine friars. It was consecrated anew in 1842, when it was given to the Franciscans, who then rebuilt it in renaissance style in 1847. The church has a marvelous domed altar and nave.

Southern Habana Vieja

The mostly residential and dilapidated southern half of Habana Vieja, south of Calle Brasil,

Jews in Cuba

Today, Havana's Jewish community (La Comunidad Hebrea) numbers only about 1,500, about 5 percent of its prerevolutionary size, when it supported five synagogues and a college.

The first Jew in Cuba, Luis de Torres, arrived with Columbus in 1492 as the explorer's translator. He was followed in the 16th century by Jews escaping persecution at the hands of the Spanish Inquisition. Later, Jews emigrating from Eastern Europe passed through Cuba en route to the United States in significant numbers until the United States slammed its doors in 1924, after which they settled in Cuba.

By the 1950s, about 20,000 Jews lived in Havana, concentrated around Calle Belén and Calle Acosta, which bustled with kosher bakeries, cafés, and clothes stores. Following the Revolution they became part of the Cuban diaspora. About 95 percent of them fled.

Although the Castro government discouraged Jews from practicing their faith, Jewish religious schools were the only parochial schools allowed to remain open after the Revolution. The government has always made matzo available and even authorized a kosher butcher shop to supply meat for observant Jews.

JEWISH HERITAGE SITES

Habana Vieja's Jewish quarter features the **Sinagoga Adath Israel** (Picota #52, esq. Acosta, tel. 07/861-3495, adath@ip.etecsa.cu, by appointment), with a wooden altar carved with scenes from Jerusalem and historic Havana. Nearby is the **Parque de Los Hebreos** (Calle Acosta esq. Damas), with a giant menorah. **Chevet Achim** (Inquisidor, e/ Luz y Santa Clara, tel. 07/832-6623, by appointment) was built in 1914 and is the oldest synagogue in Cuba. The building is owned and maintained by the Centro Sefardi but is not used.

In Vedado, the **Casa de la Comunidad Hebrea de Cuba** (Calle I #253, e/ 13 y 15, tel. 07/832-8953, patronato.ort@enet.uc, Mon.-Fri. 9:30am-5pm), or Patronato, is the Jewish community headquarters. Services at the adjacent **Bet Shalon Sinagogo** are Friday at 7:30pm (May-Sept.) or 6pm (Oct.-Apr.) and Saturday at 10am (year-round). Nearby, the **Centro Sefardí** (Calle 17 #462, esq. E, tel. 07/832-6623, judiosefarad@yahoo.com) hosts a Holocaust museum.

Guanabacoa, on the east side of Havana harbor, has two Jewish cemeteries. The **Cementerio de la Comunidad Religiosa Ashkenazi** (Av. de la Independencia Este, e/ Obelisco y Puente, Mon.-Fri. 8am-11am and 2pm-5pm), also known as the United Hebrew Congregation Cemetery, is for Ashkenazim. It is entered by an ocher-colored Spanish-colonial frontispiece with a Star of David. A **Holocaust memorial** immediately to the left of the gate stands in memory of the millions who lost their lives to the Nazis. Behind the Ashkenazi cemetery is the **Cementerio de la Unión Sefardi** (Calle G, e/ 5ta y Final, daily 7am-5pm), for Sephardic Jews. It too has a memorial to Holocaust victims.

JEWISH AID ORGANIZATIONS

The following organizations send humanitarian aid to Cuba and/or offer organized trips: the **B'nai B'rith International** (tel. 877/222-9590, www.bnaibrith.org/cuba-missions.html), the **Cuba-America Jewish Mission** (www.cajm.org), and **Jewish Solidarity** (tel. 305/642-1600, http://jewishcuba.org/solidarity).

was the ecclesiastical center of Havana during the colonial era and is studded with churches and convents. This was also Havana's Jewish quarter.

Southern Habana Vieja is enclosed by Avenida del Puerto, which swings along the harborfront and becomes Avenida San Pedro, then Avenida Leonor Pérez, then Avenida Desamparados as it curves around to Avenida de Bélgica (colloquially called Egido). The waterfront boulevard is overshadowed by warehouses. Here were the old P&O docks where the ships from Miami and Key West used to land and where Pan American World Airways had its terminal when it was still operating the old clipper flying boats.

CALLE EGIDO

Egido follows the hollow once occupied by Habana Vieja's ancient walls. It is a continuation of Monserrate and flows downhill to the harbor. The **Puerta de la Tenaza** (Egido, esq. Fundición) is the only ancient city gate still standing; a plaque inset in the wall shows a map of the city walls as they once were. About 100 meters south, on Avenida de Puerto, the **Monumento Mártires del Vapor La Coubre** is made of twisted metal fragments of *La Coubre,* the French cargo ship that exploded in Havana harbor on March 4, 1960 (the vessel was carrying armaments for the Castro government). The monument honors the seamen who died in the explosion.

Egido's masterpiece is the **Estación Central de Ferrocarril** (esq. Arsenal), or Terminal de Trenes, Havana's railway station. Designed in 1910, it blends Spanish Revival and Italian Renaissance styles and features twin towers displaying the shields of Havana and Cuba (and a clock permanently frozen at 5:20). It is built atop the former Spanish naval shipyard. It closed in 2015 for a long restoration that will incorporate contemporary architecture.

On the station's north side, the small, shady **Parque de los Agrimensores** (Park of the Surveyors) features a remnant of the **Cortina de la Habana,** the old city wall. The park is now populated by steam trains retired from hauling sugarcane; the oldest dates from 1878.

Two blocks north of the park, do not miss the **Mercado Agropecuario Egido** (e/ Apodaca y Corrales), Havana's most colorful farmers market. Take (and hold on to) your camera! Head two blocks west, then turn left onto **Cárdenas.** The two blocks between Misión y Apodaca feature some astounding examples of Gaudi-style art nouveau architecture (especially noteworthy are #103, #107, and #161).

MUSEO CASA NATAL DE JOSÉ MARTÍ

The birthplace of Cuba's preeminent national hero, **Museo Casa Natal de José Martí** (Leonor Pérez #314, esq. Av. de Bélgica, tel. 07/861-3778, Tues.-Sat. 9am-5pm, entrance CUC1, guide CUC1, cameras CUC2, videos CUC10) sits one block south of the railway station at the end of a street named after Martí's mother. The leader of the independence movement was born on January 28, 1853, in this simple house with terra-cotta tile floors. The house displays many of his personal effects, including an *escritorio* (writing desk) and even a lock of Martí's hair.

IGLESIA Y CONVENTO DE NUESTRA SEÑORA DE BELÉN

The **Iglesia y Convento de Nuestra Señora de Belén** (Church and Convent of Our Lady of Bethlehem, Compostela y Luz, tel. 07/860-3150, Mon.-Sat. 10am-4pm, Sun. 9am-1pm, free; visits only with a prearranged guide with Agencia San Cristóbal), the city's largest religious complex, occupies an entire block. The convent, completed in 1718, was built to house the first nuns to arrive in Havana and later served as a refuge for convalescents. In 1842, Spanish authorities ejected the religious order and turned the complex over to the Jesuits, who established a college for the sons of the aristocracy. As the nation's official weather forecasters, they erected the Observatorio Real (Royal Observatory) atop the tower in 1858; it was in use until 1925. The church and convent are linked to contiguous buildings across the street by an arched walkway—the **Arco de Belén** (Arch of Bethlehem)—spanning Acosta.

IGLESIA Y CONVENTO DE SANTA CLARA DE ASÍS

Partially restored, the **Iglesia y Convento de Santa Clara de Asís** (Convent of Saint Clair of Assisi, Cuba #610, e/ Luz y Sol, tel. 07/761-3335), two blocks east of Belén, is a massive former nunnery completed in 1644. The nuns moved out in 1922. It is a remarkable

José Martí

José Martí, the "Apostle of the Nation," is the most revered figure in Cuban history: the canonical avatar of Cuba's independece movement and the "ideological architect" of the Cuban Revolution, according to Fidel Castro. There is hardly a quadrant in Havana that does not have a street, square, or major building named in his honor.

José Julian Martí de Pérez was born in 1853 in Habana Vieja. His father was from Valencia, Spain, and became a policeman in Cuba; his mother came from the Canary Islands. When the Ten Years War erupted in 1868, Martí was 15 years old. Already he sympathized with the nationalist cause. At the age of 16, he published his first newspaper, *La Patria Libre* (Free Fatherland). Martí was sentenced to six years' imprisonment, including hard labor. Martí suffered a hernia and gained permanent scars from his shackles. In 1871, his sentence was commuted to exile on the Isla de Pinos, and briefly thereafter he was exiled to Spain, where he earned a degree in law and philosophy. Later, he settled in Mexico, where he became a journalist, and in Guatemala, where he taught. In 1878, as part of a general amnesty, he was allowed to return to Cuba but was then deported again. He traveled through France and Venezuela and, in 1881, to the United States, where he settled in New York for the next 14 years. He worked as a reporter and acted as a consul for Argentina, Paraguay, and Uruguay.

THE PEN AND THE SWORD

Dressed in his trademark black frock coat and bow tie, with his thick moustache waxed into pointy tips, Martí devoted his time to winning independence for Cuba. He wrote poetry wedding the rhetoric of nationalism to calls for social justice. He was one of the most prolific and accomplished Latin American writers of his day.

He admired the liberty of America but became a staunch anticolonialist, and his voluminous writings are littered with astute critiques of U.S. culture and politics. He despised the expansionist nature of the United States. "It is my duty...to prevent, through the independence of Cuba, the U.S.A. from spreading over the West Indies and falling with added weight upon other lands of Our America. All I have done up to now and shall do hereafter is to that end."

Prophetically, Martí's writings are full of invocations to death. It was he who coined the phrase *"La Victoria o el Sepulcro"* (Victory or the Tomb), which Fidel Castro has turned into a call for *"Patria o Muerte"* (Patriotism or Death).

THEORY INTO ACTION

Having established himself as the acknowledged political leader of the independence cause, he melded the various exile factions together and integrated the cause of Cuban exiled workers into the crusade—they contributed 10 percent of their earnings to his cause. He also founded La Liga de Instrucción, which trained revolutionary fighters.

In 1895, Martí was named major general of the Armies of Liberation; General Máximo Gómez was named supreme commander. On April 11, 1895, Martí, Gómez, and four followers landed at Cajobabo, in a remote part of eastern Cuba. Moving through the mountains, they finally linked up with Antonio Maceo and his army of 6,000. The first skirmish with the Spanish occurred at Dos Ríos on May 19, 1895. Martí was the first casualty. He had determined on martyrdom and committed sacrificial suicide by riding headlong into the enemy line.

The **Centro de Estudios Martiana** (Calzada #807 e/ Calles 2 y 4, Vedado, Havana, tel. 07/836-4966, www.josemarti.cu) studies his life and works.

building, with a lobby full of beautiful period pieces. The cloistered courtyard is surrounded by columns. Note the 17th-century fountain of a Samaritan woman, and the beautiful cloister roof carved with geometric designs—a classic *alfarje*—in the Salón Plenario, a marble-floored hall of imposing stature. Wooden carvings abound. The second cloister contains the so-called Sailor's House, built by a wealthy ship owner for his daughter, whom he failed to dissuade from a life of asceticism.

IGLESIA PARROQUIAL DEL ESPÍRITU SANTO

The **Iglesia Parroquial del Espíritu Santo** (Parish Church of the Holy Ghost, Acosta #161, esq. Cuba, tel. 07/862-3410, Mon.-Fri. 8am-noon and 3pm-6pm), two blocks south of Santa Clara de Asís, is Havana's oldest church, dating from 1638 (the circa-1674 central nave and facade, as well as the circa-1720 Gothic vault, are later additions), when it was a hermitage for the devotions of free blacks. Later, King Charles III granted the right of asylum here to anyone hunted by the authorities.

The church's many surprises include a gilded, carved wooden pelican in a niche in the baptistry. The sacristy, where parish archives dating back through the 17th century are preserved, boasts an enormous cupboard full of baroque silver staffs and incense holders. Catacombs to the left of the nave are held up by subterranean tree trunks. You can explore the eerie vault that runs under the chapel, with the niches still containing the odd bone. Steps lead up to the bell tower.

IGLESIA Y CONVENTO DE NUESTRA SEÑORA DE LA MERCED

Iglesia y Convento de Nuestra Señora de la Merced (Our Lady of Mercy, Cuba #806, esq. Merced, tel. 07/863-8873, daily 8am-noon and 3pm-6pm) is Havana's most impressive church, thanks to its ornate interior multiple dome paintings and walls entirely painted in early-20th-century religious frescoes. The church, begun in 1755, has strong Afro-Cuban connections (the Virgin of Mercy is also Obatalá, goddess of earth and purity), drawing devotees of Santería. Each September 24, scores of worshippers cram in for the Virgen de la Merced's feast day. More modest celebrations are held on the 24th of every other month.

Boxing fans might nip across the street to **Gimnasio Rafael Trejo** (Cuba #815, tel. 07/862-0266, Fri. 7pm), where young boxers train in a tumbledown open-air facility.

ALAMEDA DE PAULA

The 100-meter-long Alameda de Paula promenade runs alongside the waterfront boulevard between Luz and Leonor Pérez. Lined with marble and iron street lamps, the promenade is the midst of a two-decades-long remodeling project. In 2016, it gained a new ferry terminal and statues.

The raised central median that is the Alameda proper begins on the south side of **Parque Aracelio Iglesias** (Av. del Puerto y Luz), where passengers alight ferries at Emboque de Luz terminal. Two blocks south at Calle Jesús María stands a carved column with a fountain at its base, erected in 1847 in homage to the Spanish navy. It bears an unlikely Irish name: **Columna O'Donnell,** for the Capitán-General of Cuba, Leopoldo O'Donnell, who dedicated the monument. It is covered in relief work on a military theme and crowned by a lion with the arms of Spain in its claws.

At the southern end of the Alameda, **Iglesia de San Francisco de Paula** (San Ignacio y Leonor Pérez, tel. 07/860-4210, daily 9am-5pm) highlights the circular Plazuela de Paula. The quaint, restored church features marvelous artworks including stained glass pieces. It is used for baroque and chamber concerts. To its east, occupying a waterfront wharf, is the **Antiguo Almacén de Madera y el Tabaco** (daily noon-midnight), a beer hall with an on-site brewery.

A stone's throw south, the **Centro Cultural Almacenes de San José** (Av. Desamparados at San Ignacio, tel. 07/864-7793, daily 10am-6pm), or Feria de la

Artesanía—the city's main arts and crafts market—also occupies a former waterfront warehouse. Several antique steam trains sit on rails outside. Immediately to the south is the **Museo de Automóviles** (Automobile Museum, Desemparados esq. Damas, tel. 07/863-9942, automovil@ bp.patrimonio.ohc.cu, Tues.-Sat. 9:30am-5pm, Sun. 9am-1pm, entrance CUC1.50, cameras CUC2, videos CUC10), displaying an eclectic range of 30 antique automobiles—from a 1905 Cadillac to singer Benny More's 1953 MGA and revolutionary leader Camilo Cienfuegos's 1959 mint Oldsmobile. Classic Harley-Davidson motorcycles are also exhibited.

MUSEO DEL RON

Two blocks north of Luz is the Fundación Destilería Havana Club, or **Museo del Ron** (Museum of Rum, Av. San Pedro #262, e/ Muralla y Sol, tel. 07/861-8051, daily 9:30am-5:30pm, CUC7 including guide and drink). Occupying the former colonial mansion of the Conde de la Mortera, it's a must-see introduction to the manufacture of Cuban rum. Tours begin with an audiovisual presentation and include exhibits such as a mini-cooperage,

pailes (sugar boiling pots), wooden *trapiches* (sugarcane presses), *salas* dedicated to an exposition on sugarcane, and the colonial sugar mills where the cane was pressed and the liquid processed. An operating production unit replete with bubbling vats and copper demonstrates the process. The highlight is a model of an early-20th-century sugar plantation at 1:22.5 scale, complete with working steam locomotives.

Hemingway once favored **Dos Hermanos** (Av. San Pedro #304, esq. Sol, tel. 07/861-3514), a simple bar immediately south of the museum.

SACRA CATEDRAL ORTODOXA RUSA

Immediately south of Dos Hermanos bar is the beautiful, gleaming white **Sacra Catedral Ortodoxa Rusa** (Russian Orthodox Cathedral, Av. del Puerto and Calle San Pedro, daily 9am-5:45pm), a 21st-century construction. Officially called the **Iglesia Virgen de María de Kazan,** it whisks you allegorically to Moscow with its bulbous, golden minarets. No photos are allowed inside, where a gold altar and chandeliers hang above gray marble floors.

Sacra Catedral Ortodoxa Rusa

CENTRO HABANA

Laid out in a near-perfect grid, mostly residential Centro Habana (Central Havana, pop. 175,000) lies west of the Paseo de Martí and south of the Malecón. The region evolved following demolition of the city walls in 1863. Prior, it had served as a glacis. The buildings are deep and tall, of four or five stories, built mostly as apartment units. Many houses are in a tumbledown state, and barely a month goes by without at least one building collapse.

The major west-east thoroughfares are the Malecón to the north and Zanja and Avenida Salvador Allende through the center, plus Calles Neptuno and San Rafael between the Malecón and Zanja. Three major thoroughfares run perpendicular, north-south: Calzada de Infanta, forming the western boundary; Padre Varela, down the center; and Avenida de Italia (Galiano), farther east.

In prerevolutionary days, Centro Habana hosted Havana's red-light district, and prostitutes roamed such streets as the ill-named Calle Virtudes (Virtues). Neptuno and San Rafael formed the retail heart of the city. The famous department stores of prerevolutionary days still bear neon signs promoting U.S. brand names from yesteryear.

Caution is required, as snatch-and-grabs and muggings are common.

The Malecón (Centro)

Officially known as Avenida Antonio Maceo, and more properly the Muro de Malecón (literally "embankment," or "seawall"), Havana's seafront boulevard winds dramatically along the Atlantic shoreline between the Castillo de San Salvador de la Punta and the Río Almendares. The six-lane seafront boulevard was designed as a jetty wall in 1857 by Cuban engineer Francisco de Albear but not laid out until 1902, by U.S. governor General Leonard Wood. It took 50 years to reach the Río Almendares, almost five miles to the west.

The Malecón is lined with once-glorious high-rise houses, each exuberantly distinct from the next. Unprotected by seaworthy paint, they have proven incapable of withstanding the salt spray that crashes over the seawall. Many buildings have already collapsed, and an ongoing restoration has made little headway against the elements.

All along the shore are the worn remains of square baths—known as the "Elysian Fields"—hewn from the rocks below the seawall, originally with separate areas for men, women, and blacks. These **Baños del Mar** preceded construction of the Malecón. Each is about four meters square and two meters deep, with rock steps for access and a couple of portholes through which the waves wash in and out.

The Malecón offers a microcosm of Havana life: the elderly walking their dogs; the shiftless selling cigars and cheap sex to tourists; the young passing rum among friends; fishers tending their lines and casting off on giant inner tubes (*neumáticos*); and always, scores of couples courting and necking. The Malecón is known as "Havana's sofa" and acts, wrote Claudia Lightfoot, as "the city's drawing room, office, study, and often bedroom."

Every October 26, schoolchildren throw flowers over the seawall in memory of revolutionary leader Camilo Cienfuegos, killed in an air crash on that day in 1959.

The most intriguing site is *Primavera* (esq. Galiano), a fantastical bronze bust by sculptor Rafael San Juan. A tribute to Cuban women, with mariopas (the national flower) for hair, it went up for the 2015 Havana Biennial.

PARQUE MACEO

Dominating the Malecón to the west, at the foot of Avenida Padre Varela, is the massive bronze **Monumento Antonio Maceo,** atop a marble base in a plaza with a fountain. The classical monument was erected in 1916 in honor of the mulatto general and hero of the wars of independence who was known as the "Bronze Titan." The motley tower that stands at the west end of the plaza is the 17th-century **Torreón de San Lázaro.** Although it looks modern, it was built in 1665 to guard the former cove of San Lázaro.

To the south, the **Hospital Hermanos Almeijeiras** looms over the park; its basement forms Cuba's "Fort Knox." The **Convento y Capilla de la Inmaculada Concepción** (San Lázaro #805, e/ Oquendo y Lucena, tel. 07/878-8404, Mon.-Fri. 8am-5pm, Sat. 5pm-7pm, Sun. 8am-11am) is immediately west of the hospital. This beautiful church and convent was built in Gothic style in 1874 and features notable stained glass windows and a painted altar.

Barrio Cayo Hueso

Immediately west of the Plaza Antonio Maceo, a triangular area bordered roughly by the Malecón, San Lázaro, and Calzada de Infanta forms the northwest corner of Centro Habana. Known as Barrio Cayo Hueso, the region dates from the early 20th century, when tenement homes were erected atop what had been the Espada cemetery (hence the name, Cay of Bones). Its several art deco inspirations include the **Edificio Solimar** (Soledad #205, e/ San Lázaro y Ánimas) apartment complex, built in 1944.

The pseudo-castle at the corner of Calle 25 and the Malecón was before the Revolution the **Casa Marina,** Havana's most palatial brothel.

Hallowed ground to Cubans, the tiny **Museo Fragua Martiana** (Museum of Martí's Forging, Principe #108, esq. Hospital, tel. 07/870-7338, fragua@comuh.uh.cu, Mon.-Fri. 9am-4pm, Sat. 9am-noon, free) occupies the site of the former San Lázaro quarry, where national hero José Martí and fellow prisoners were forced to break rocks. The museum displays manuscripts and shackles. To its rear, the quarry has been turned into a garden, with a life-size bronze statue of Martí.

Every January 27 the nighttime **La Marcha de las Antorchas** (March of the Torches) takes place to celebrate Martí's birthday. Thousands of students walk with lit torches from the university (which oversees the site) to the Fragua Martiana.

"SALVADOR'S ALLEY"

Almost every dance enthusiast in the know gravitates to **Callejón de Hamel** (e/ Aramburu y Hospital) on Sunday for Afro-Cuban rumbas in an alley adorned by local artist Salvador González Escalona with evocative murals in sun-drenched yellow, burnt orange, and blazing reds, inspired by Santería. The alley features a Santería shrine and fantastical totemic sculptures. González, a bearded artist with an eye for self-promotion, has an eclectic gallery, **Estudio-Galería Fambá** (Callejón de Hamel #1054, tel. 07/878-1661, eliasasef@yahoo.es, daily 9:30am-6pm). Alas, *jineteros* abound.

The area has several other sites associated with *santería*, including **Parque del Trillo** (Calle San Miguel y Hospital), four blocks south. Note the sacred ceiba trees on each corner; the plastic bags at their base contain offerings. *Santero* **Abel Hierrezuelo Nolasco** (Calle Espada #268 Apt. 9 bajos, e/ San Lázaro y Concordia, no tel., by donation) displays an amazing collection of effigies.

Parque de los Mártires Universitarios (Infanta, e/ Calles Jovellar y San Lázaro), one block west of Callejón de Hamel, honors students who lost their lives during the fights against the Machado and Batista regimes.

Soaring over Calzada de Infanta, about 100 meters south of San Lázaro, **Convento y Iglesia del Carmen** (Infanta, e/ Neptuno y Concordia, tel. 07/878-5168, Tues.-Sun. 7:30am-noon and 3pm-7pm) is one of Havana's largest and most impressive churches. Built in baroque fashion, the church is capped by a 60.5-meter-tall tower topped by a sculpture of Our Lady of Carmen.

Galiano

This boulevard, lined with arcaded porticos, runs south from the Malecón to Avenida Salvador Allende and is Centro's main north-south artery. The **Hotel Lincoln** (Galiano, e/ Ánimas y Virtudes) was where Argentina's world-champion race-car driver Juan Manuel Fangio was kidnapped by Castro's revolutionaries in 1958 during the Cuban Grand

Centro Habana

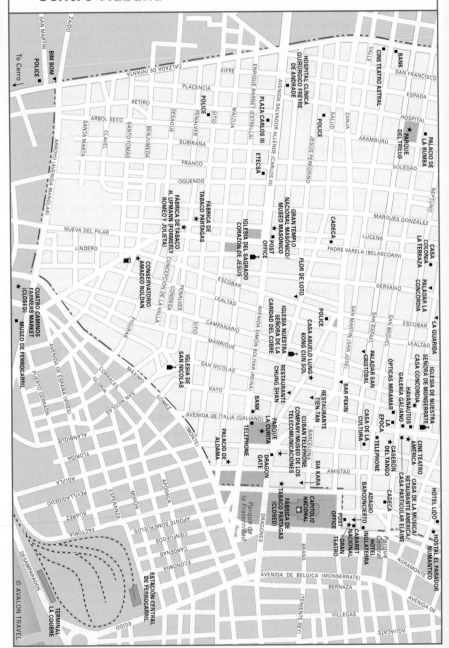

© AVALON TRAVEL

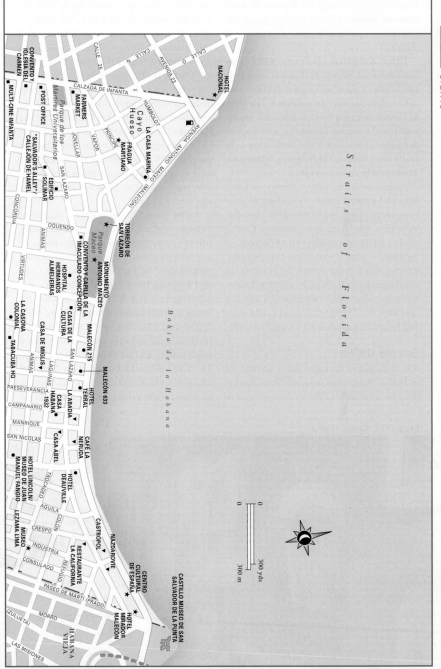

Straits of Florida

Bahia de la Habana

CALLE 25
CALLE N
CALLE O
AVENIDA 23
HOTEL NACIONAL
CONVENTO Y IGLESIA DEL CARMEN
CALZADA DE INFANTA
MULTI-CINE INFANTA
FARMERS MARKET
HUMBOLDT
Cayo Hueso
LA CASA MARINA
AVENIDA ANTONIO MACEO (MALECÓN)
POST OFFICE
Parque de los Mártires Universitarios
JOVELLAR
PRÍNCIPE
VAPOR
FRAGUA MARTIANO
"SALVADOR'S ALLEY" CALLEJÓN DE HAMEL
SAN LÁZARO
EDIFICIO SOLIMAR
CONCORDIA
OQUENDO
ANIMAS
TORREÓN DE SAN LÁZARO
Parque Maceo
MONUMENTO ANTONIO MACEO
CONVENTO Y CAPILLA DE LA IMACULADA CONCEPCIÓN
VIRTUDES
HOSPITAL HERMANOS ALMEIJEIRAS
CASA DE LA CULTURA
MALECÓN 215
SAN LÁZARO
LA CASONA COLONIAL
CASA DE MIGUIS
TABACUBA HQ
ANIMAS
LAGUNAS
MALECÓN 633
PRESEVERANCIA
CASA HABANA 1932
HOTEL TERRAL
CAMPANARIO
MANRIQUE
CASA ABEL
SAN NICOLÁS
LA ABADÍA
CAFÉ LA NERUDA
HOTEL LINCOLN/ MUSEO DE JUAN MANUEL FANGIO
HOTEL DEAUVILLE
TROCADERO
AGUILA
COLÓN
MUSEO LEZAMA LIMA
CRESPO
CASTROPOL
INDUSTRIA
CONSULADO
RESTAURANTE LA CALIFORNIA
REFUGIO
NAZDAROVIE
PASEO DE MARTÍ (PRADO)
(ZULUETA)
MORRO
LAS MISIONES
CENTRO CULTURAL DE ESPAÑA
CASTILLO MUSEO DE SAN SALVADOR DE LA PUNTA
HOTEL MIRADOR MALECÓN
HABANA VIEJA

0   300 yds
0   300 m

Prix. Room 810 is today the **Museo de Juan Manuel Fangio** (open when not occupied), presenting a predictably one-sided version of the affair.

Cine América (Galiano #253, esq. Concordia, tel. 07/862-5416) dates from 1941 and is one of the world's great art deco theaters, albeit severely deteriorated. The foyer features a terrazzo floor inlaid with zodiac motifs and a map of the world, with Cuba at the center in polished brass. Kitty-corner, the rarely open **Iglesia de Nuestra Señora de Monserrate** dates from 1843.

Literature buffs might detour to **Casa Museo Lezama Lima** (Trocadero #162, e/ Crespo y Industria, tel. 07/863-4161, Tues.-Sat. 9am-5pm, Sun. 9am-1pm, entrance CUC2, guide CUC1), four blocks east of Galiano, in the former home of writer José Lezama Lima. The novelist is most famous for *Paradiso,* an autobiographical, sexually explicit, homoerotic baroque novel that viewed Cuba as a "paradise lost." Lima fell afoul of Fidel Castro and became a recluse until his death in 1975.

Barrio Chino

The first Chinese immigrants to Cuba arrived in 1847 as indentured laborers. Over ensuing decades, as many as 150,000 arrived to work the fields. They were contracted to labor for miserable wages insufficient to buy their return. Most stayed, and many intermarried with blacks. The Sino-Cuban descendants of those who worked off their indenture gravitated to Centro Habana, where they settled in the zones bordering the Zanza Real, the aqueduct that channeled water to the city. They were later joined by other Chinese. In time Havana's Chinese quarter, Barrio Chino, became the largest in Latin America. The vast majority of Chinese left Cuba immediately following the Revolution; those who stayed were encouraged to become "less Chinese and more Cuban."

Today, Barrio Chino is a mere shadow of its former self, with about 2,000 descendants still resident. Approximately a dozen social associations (*casinos*) attempt to keep Chinese culture alive. In 1995, the city fathers initiated Proyecto Integral Barrio Chino to revitalize the area and its culture. The **Casa de Artes y Tradiciones Chinas** (Salud #313, e/ Gervasio y Escobar, tel. 07/860-9976, barriochino@patrimonio.ohc.cu) features a small gallery and tai chi and dance classes. The **Casa Abuelo Lung Kong Cun Sol** (Dragones #364, e/ Manrique y San Nicolás, tel. 07/862-5388) exists to support elders in the

Barrio Chino, Centro Habana

Chinese community; on the third floor, the **Templo San Fan Kong** has an exquisitely carved gold-plated altar.

In 1995, the government of China funded a **Pórtico Chino** (Dragon Gate, or *paifang*) across Calle Dragones, between Amistad and Aguila, announcing visitors' entry from the east. The highlight is pedestrian-only **Callejón Cuchillo** (Knife Alley), lined with Chinese restaurants and aglow at night with Chinese lanterns.

Two blocks to the southwest, the **Iglesia Nuestra Señora de la Caridad del Cobre** (Manrique #570, esq. Salud, tel. 07/861-0945), erected in 1802, features exquisite statuary, stained glass, and a gilded altar. A shrine to the Virgen del Cobre draws worshippers (both Catholics and believers in santería come to worship her avatar, Ochún), who bring sunflowers to adorn the shrine.

Soaring over Barrio Chino is the eclectic-style former headquarters of the Cuban Telephone Company, inaugurated in 1927 and at the time the tallest building in Havana. Today utilized by Etecsa, the Cuban state-owned telephone company, it hosts the impressive **Museo de las Telecomunicaciones** (tel. 07/860-7574, Mon.-Fri. 10am-4pm), telling the history of the telephone in Cuba and with a functional and interactive antique telephone exchange.

Avenidas Simón Bolívar and Salvador Allende

Avenida Simón Bolívar (formerly Avenida Reina) runs west from Parque de la Fraternidad. It is lined with once-impressive colonial-era structures gone to ruin. Beyond Avenida Padre Varela (Belascoain), the street broadens into a wide boulevard called Avenida Salvador Allende, laid out in the early 19th century (when it was known as Carlos III) by Governor Tacón.

The **Gran Templo Nacional Masónico** (Grand Masonic Temple, Av. Salvador Allende, e/ Padre Varela y Lucena) was established in 1951. Though no longer a

Freemasons' lodge, it retains a mural in the lobby depicting the history of Masonry in Cuba. Upstairs, reached by a marble staircase, the **Museo Nacional Masónico** (tel. 07/878-4795, www.granlogiacuba.org/museo, Mon.-Fri. 2pm-6pm) has eclectic exhibits—from ceremonial swords to an antique steam-powered fire engine, plus busts honoring great American Masons (including George Washington, Abraham Lincoln, and Simón Bolívar).

One of the few structures not seemingly on its last legs, the **Iglesia del Sagrado Corazón de Jesús** (Church of the Sacred Heart of Jesus, Simón Bolívar, e/ Padre Varela y Gervasio, tel. 07/862-4979, daily 8am-noon and 3pm-6pm) is a Gothic inspiration that could have been transported from medieval England. It was built in 1922 with a beamed ceiling held aloft by great marbled columns. Gargoyles and Christian allegories adorn the exterior.

Cuatros Caminos

South of Avenidas Simón Bolívar and Salvador Allende, the down-at-the-heels neighborhoods of southern Centro Habana extend to Cuatros Caminos, an all-important junction where the **Mercado Agropecuario Cuatros Caminos** (Four Roads Farmers Market) takes up an entire block between Máximo Gómez and Cristina (also called Avenida de la México), and Manglar Arroyo and Matadero. The dilapidated 19th-century market hall closed in 2015 for restoration.

On the east side of Cristina, facing the market, is the **Museo de Ferrocarril** (Railway Museum, tel. 07/879-4414, Tues.-Sat. 9:30am-5pm, Sun. 9:30am-1pm, entrance CUC2, camera CUC5), housed in the former Estación Cristina. The exhibits include model trains, bells, signals, and even telegraph equipment that tell the history of rail in Cuba. Sitting on rails in its lobby is an 1843 steam locomotive (Cuba's first) called *La Junta*. Three other antique steam trains are displayed, along with various diesel locomotives.

FÁBRICA DE TABACO H. UPMANN

The most rewarding cigar factory tour in Havana is offered at **Fábrica de Tabaco H. Upmann** (H. Upmann Tobacco Factory, Padre Varela #852, e/ Desagüe y Peñal Verno, tel. 07/878-1059 or 07/879-3927, 9am-1pm, CUC10), five blocks northwest of Cuatro Caminos. The factory was founded in 1875 by Inocencia Álvarez and later became the Romeo y Julieta factory, making the famous brand of that name. At press time, it had become the temporary home of the H. Upmann brand, whose name it now bears. The facade, however, is topped by a scroll with the original name: "Cuesta Rey & Co."

To the rear is the old Fábrica El Rey del Mundo, decorated with Ionic columns. Today it operates as the temporary **Fábrica de Tabaco Partagás** (Luceña esq. Penalver, Centro Habana). A visit here is not as rewarding due to the cramped conditions. One block south is the **Conservatorio Amaeo Roldán** (Padre Varela, esq. Carmen), a music conservatory boasting a well-preserved classical facade.

CERRO AND DIEZ DE OCTUBRE

South of Habana Vieja and Centro the land rises gently to Cerro, which developed during the 19th century as the place to retire for the torrid midsummer months. Many wealthy families maintained two homes in Havana—one in town, another on the cooler *cerro* (hill). The area is replete with once-stately *quintas* (summer homes) in neoclassical, beaux-arts, and art nouveau styles. Alas, the region is terribly deteriorated and the majority of buildings transcend sordid.

Cerro merges east into the less-crowded municipality of Diez de Octubre, a relatively leafy and attractive residential area laid out during the 20th century comprising the district of Santo Suárez and, to its east, Luyanó.

Avenida Máximo Gómez and Calzada de Cerro

Avenida Máximo Gómez (popularly called Monte; the name changes to Calzada de Cerro west of Infanta) snakes southwest from Parque de la Fraternidad and south of Arroyo (Avenida Manglar), connecting Habana Vieja with Cerro. During the 19th century, scores of summer homes in classical style were erected. It has been described by writer Paul Goldberger as "one of the most remarkable streets in the world: three unbroken kilometers of 19th-century neoclassical villas, with colonnaded arcades making an urban vista of heartbreaking beauty." The avenue ascends southward, marching backward into the past like a classical ruin, with once-stunning arcades and houses collapsing behind decaying facades.

One of the most splendid mansions is the palatial **Quinta del Conde de Santovenia,** erected in 1845 in subdued neoclassical style with a 1929 neo-Gothic chapel addition. Today housing the **Hogar de Ancianos Santovenia** (Calzada de Cerro #1424, e/ Patria y Auditor, tel. 07/879-6072, visits by appointment Tues., Thurs., and Sat. 4pm-5pm and Sun. 10am-noon), it has served as a home for the elderly (*hogar de ancianos*) for more than a century. It's run by Spanish nuns.

Rising over the south of Cerro is **Estadio Latinoamericano** (Consejero Aranjo y Pedro Pérez, Cerro, tel. 07/870-6526), Havana's main baseball stadium. To its northwest is **Fábrica de Tabaco Corona** (20 de Mayo #520, e/ Marta Abreu y Línea, Cerro, tel. 07/873-0131, Mon.-Fri. 9am-11am and 1pm-3pm, CUC10 guided tours), a modern cigar factory producing Hoyo de Monterey, Punch, and other labels.

Proyecto Comunitario Muraleando

Founded in 2001, this art-focused community project spans roughly four blocks along Calle Aguilera southeast of Porvenir. Fourteen core residents have cleaned up their once trash-strewn neighborhood and turned the metal garbage pieces into fanciful art, such as the **Arco de Triunfo**—an arch made of old wheel rims. Walls have been brightened with colorful murals, including an international wall with murals by non-Cuban painters.

The headquarters is **El Tanque** (Aguilera, esq. 9 de Abril, Luyanó), a converted water tank that now holds a performance art space and art gallery. On weekends, it hosts free art workshops for adults and kids, plus a children's street party every month. A highlight is **Obelisko Amistad** (Friendship Obelisk), with plaques representing differing countries; visitors are invited to circle the column and ask for peace for the world.

About 1.5 km southwest, off Avenida Porvenir, is **Museo Casa Natal Camilo Cienfuegos** (Calle Pocito #228, esq. Lawton, tel. 07/698-3509, Tues.-Sat. 9:30am-3:30pm, Sun. 9:30am-noon, free), occupying a small house built in eclectic style in 1920 and where on February 6, 1932, was born Camilo Cienfuegos Gorriarán, who rose to be Fidel's chief of staff before dying in a mysterious plane crash in 1959. Furnished with original pieces, it has five rooms dedicated to his life as a child and, later, revolutionary commander.

VEDADO AND PLAZA DE LA REVOLUCIÓN

The *municipio* of Plaza de la Revolución (pop. 165,000), west of Centro Habana, comprises the leafy residential streets of Vedado and, to the southwest, the modern enclave of Nuevo Vedado and Plaza de la Revolución.

Vedado—the commercial heart of "modern" Havana—has been described as "Havana at its middle-class best." The University of Havana is here. So are many of the city's prime hotels and restaurants, virtually all its main commercial buildings, and block after block of handsome mansions and apartment houses in art deco, eclectic, beaux-arts, and neoclassical styles—luxurious and humble alike lining streets shaded by stately jagüeyes dropping their aerial roots to the ground.

Formerly a vast open space between Centro Habana and the Río Almendares, Vedado (which means "forbidden") served as a buffer zone in case of attack from the west; construction was prohibited. In 1859, however, plans were drawn up for urban expansion. Strict building regulations called for 15 feet of gardens between building and street, and more in wider *avenidas*. Regularly spaced parks were mandated. The conclusion of the Spanish-Cuban-American War in 1898 brought U.S. money rushing in. Civic structures, hotels, casinos, department stores, and restaurants sprouted alongside nightclubs.

The sprawling region is hemmed to the north by the Malecón, to the east by Calzada de Infanta, to the west by the Río Almendares, and to the southeast by the Calzada de Ayestaran and Avenida de la Independencia. Vedado follows a grid pattern laid out in quadrants. Odd-numbered streets (*calles*) run east-west, parallel to the shore. Even-numbered *calles* run perpendicular. (To confuse things, west of Paseo, *calles* are even-numbered; east of Paseo, *calles* run from A to P.) The basic grid is overlaid by a larger grid of broad boulevards (*avenidas*) an average of six blocks apart: Calle L to the east, and Avenida de los Presidentes, Paseo, and Avenida 12 farther west.

Dividing the quadrants east-west is Calle 23, which rises (colloquially) as La Rampa from the Malecón at its junction with Calzada de Infanta. La Rampa runs uphill to Calle L and continues on the flat as Calle 23. Paralleling it to the north is a second major east-west thoroughfare, Línea (Calle 9), five blocks inland of the Malecón, which it meets to the northeast.

Vedado slopes gently upward from the shore to Calle 23 and then gently downward toward Plaza de la Revolución.

The Malecón (Vedado)

Extending west from Centro Habana, the Malecón runs along the bulging, wave-battered shorefront of northern Vedado, curling from La Rampa in the east to the Río Almendares in the west, a distance of three miles. The sidewalk is pitted underfoot, but a stroll makes for good exercise while taking in such sights as the **Monumento Calixto García** (Malecón y Av. de los Presidentes),

Vedado and Plaza de la Revolución

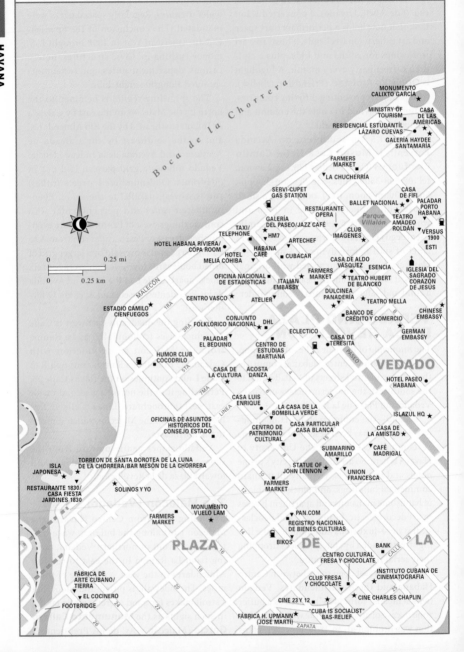

Boca de la Chorrera

MONUMENTO CALIXTO GARCÍA

MINISTRY OF TOURISM
CASA DE LAS AMÉRICAS
RESIDENCIAL ESTUDANTIL LÁZARO CUEVAS
GALERÍA HAYDEE SANTAMARÍA

FARMERS MARKET
▼ LA CHUCHERRÍA

SERVI-CUPET GAS STATION
CASA DE FIFI
PALADAR PORTO HABANA
BALLET NACIONAL
RESTAURANTE OPERA
Parque Villalón
TEATRO AMADEO ROLDAN
▼ VERSUS 1900
GALERÍA DEL PASEO/JAZZ CAFÉ
CLUB IMÁGENES
ESTI
TAXI/ TELEPHONE
HM7
ARTECHEF
HOTEL HABANA RIVIERA/ COPA ROOM
HABANA CAFÉ
CUBACAR
CASA DE ALDO VASQUEZ
ESENCIA
IGLESIA DEL SAGRADO CORAZON DE JESUS
HOTEL MELIÁ COHIBA
OFICINA NACIONAL DE ESTADÍSTICAS
ITALIAN EMBASSY
FARMERS MARKET
TEATRO HUBERT DE BLANCKO
DULCINEA PANADERÍA
TEATRO MELLA
CENTRO VASCO
ATELIER
BANCO DE CRÉDITO Y COMERCIO
CHINESE EMBASSY
ESTADIO CAMILO CIENFUEGOS
CONJUNTO FOLKLÓRICO NACIONAL
DHL
GERMAN EMBASSY
PALADAR EL BEDUINO
ECLECTICO
CASA DE TERESITA
CENTRO DE ESTUDIAS MARTIANA
HUMOR CLUB COCODRILO
VEDADO
CASA DE LA CULTURA
ACOSTA DANZA
HOTEL PASEO HABANA
CASA LUIS ENRIQUE
LA CASA DE LA BOMBILLA VERDE
OFICINAS DE ASUNTOS HISTÓRICOS DEL CONSEJO ESTADO
ISLAZUL HQ
CENTRO DE PATRIMONIO CULTURAL
CASA PARTICULAR CASA BLANCA
CASA DE LA AMISTAD
ISLA JAPONESA
TORREON DE SANTA DOROTEA DE LA LUNA DE LA CHORRERA/BAR MESÓN DE LA CHORRERA
SUBMARINO AMARILLO
CAFÉ MADRIGAL
STATUE OF JOHN LENNON
UNION FRANCESCA
RESTAURANTE 1830/ CASA FIESTA JARDINES 1830
SOLINOS Y YO
FARMERS MARKET
MONUMENTO VUELO LAM
PAN.COM
FARMERS MARKET
REGISTRO NACIONAL DE BIENES CULTURAS
PLAZA
BIKOS
DE
BANK
LA
CENTRO CULTURAL FRESA Y CHOCOLATE
FÁBRICA DE ARTE CUBANO/ TIERRA
INSTITUTO CUBANA DE CINEMATOGRAFIA
EL COCINERO
CLUB FRESA Y CHOCOLATE
CINE CHARLES CHAPLIN
FOOTBRIDGE
CINE 23 Y 12
"CUBA IS SOCIALIST" BAS-RELIEF
FÁBRICA H. UPMANN (JOSÉ MARTI)
ZAPATA

MALECÓN
1RA
3RA
5TA
7MA
LINEA
PASEO
CALLE 23

0   0.25 mi
0   0.25 km

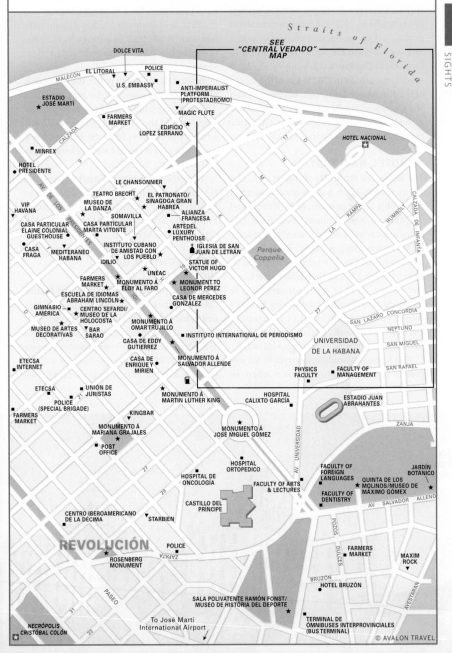

Straits of Florida

SEE "CENTRAL VEDADO" MAP

DOLCE VITA
EL LITORAL
POLICE
MALECÓN
U.S. EMBASSY
ANTI-IMPERIALIST PLATFORM (PROTESTADROMO)
ESTADIO JOSÉ MARTÍ
MAGIC FLUTE
CALZADA
FARMERS MARKET
EDIFICIO LOPEZ SERRANO
17
O
N
HOTEL NACIONAL
MINREX
9
HOTEL PRESIDENTE
M
AV DE LOS PRESIDENTES
LE CHANSONNIER
L
LA RAMPA
CALZADA DE INFANTA
HUMBOLT
TEATRO BRECHT
MUSEO DE LA DANZA
EL PATRONATO/ SINAGOGA GRAN HABREA
VIP HAVANA
SOMAVILLA
K
ALIANZA FRANCESA
CASA PARTICULAR ELAINE COLONIAL GUESTHOUSE
CASA PARTICULAR MARTA VITONTE
ARTEDEL LUXURY PENTHOUSE
CASA FRAGA
MEDITERANEO HABANA
INSTITUTO CUBANO DE AMISTAD CON LOS PUEBLO
IGLESIA DE SAN JUAN DE LETRAN
Parque Coppelia
F
IDILIO
STATUE OF VICTOR HUGO
J
27
FARMERS MARKET
UNEAC
MONUMENTO Á ELOY AL FARO
MONUMENTTO LEONOR PÉREZ
ESCUELA DE IDIOMAS ABRAHAM LINCOLN
CASA DE MERCEDES GONZÁLEZ
GIMNASIO AMÉRICA
CENTRO SEFARDI/ MUSEO DE LA HOLOCOSTA
D
MONUMENTO Á OMAR TRUJILLO
SAN LAZARO CONCORDIA
MUSEO DE ARTES DECORATIVAS
BAR SARAO
NEPTUNO
CASA DE EDDY GUTIERREZ
INSTITUTO INTERNATIONAL DE PERIODISMO
UNIVERSIDAD DE LA HABANA
SAN MIGUEL
ETECSA INTERNET
CASA DE ENRIQUE Y MIRIEN
MONUMENTO Á SALVADOR ALLENDE
SAN RAFAEL
PHYSICS FACULTY
FACULTY OF MANAGEMENT
ETECSA
UNIÓN DE JURISTAS
MONUMENTO Á MARTIN LUTHER KING
HOSPITAL CALIXTO GARCÍA
ESTADIO JUAN ABRAHANTES
POLICE (SPECIAL BRIGADE)
KINGBAR
FARMERS MARKET
MONUMENTO Á MARIANA GRAJALES
MONUMENTO Á JOSÉ MIGUEL GÓMEZ
AV UNIVERSIDAD
ZANJA
POST OFFICE
27
29
HOSPITAL ORTOPEDICO
HOSPITAL DE ONCOLOGÍA
FACULTY OF FOREIGN LANGUAGES
FACULTY OF DENTISTRY
JARDÍN BOTÁNICO
QUINTA DE LOS MOLINOS/MUSEO DE MÁXIMO GÓMEX
FACULTY OF ARTS & LECTURES
AV SALVADOR ALLEND
CASTILLO DEL PRÍNCIPE
CENTRO IBEROAMERICANO DE LA DÉCIMA
STARBIEN
POZOS
REVOLUCIÓN
POLICE
ZAPATA
FARMERS MARKET
DULCES
MAXIM ROCK
ROSENBERG MONUMENT
BRUZÓN
HOTEL BRUZÓN
AYESTARAN
PASEO
31
33
NECRÓPOLIS CRISTÓBAL COLÓN
SALA POLIVATENTE RAMÓN FONST/ MUSEO DE HISTÓRIA DEL DEPORTE
TERMINAL DE ÓMNIBUSES INTERPROVINCIALES (BUS TERMINAL)
To José Martí International Airport
© AVALON TRAVEL

featuring a bronze figure of the 19th-century rebel general on horseback; the **Hotel Habana Riviera** (Malecón y Paseo), opened by the Mafia in 1958 and recently remodeled to show off its spectacular modernist lobby; and the **Torreón de Santa Dorotea de la Luna de la Chorrera** (Malecón y Calle 20), a small fortress built in 1762 to guard the mouth of the Río Almendares. Immediately beyond "La Chorrera," the Restaurante 1830 features a Gaudí-esque garden that includes a dramatic cupola and a tiny island in Japanese style.

★ HOTEL NACIONAL

The landmark **Hotel Nacional** (Calles O y 21, tel. 07/836-3564) is dramatically perched atop a cliff at the junction of La Rampa and the Malecón. Now a national monument, this grande dame hotel was designed by the same architects who designed The Breakers in Palm Beach, which it closely resembles. It opened on December 30, 1930, in the midst of the Great Depression. In 1933, army officers loyal to Machado holed up here following Batista's coup; a gun battle ensued. More famously, in December 1946 Lucky Luciano called a mobster summit to discuss carving up Havana.

The Spanish Renaissance-style hotel was greatly in need of refurbishment when, in 1955, mobster Meyer Lansky persuaded General Batista to let him build a grand casino. Luminaries from Winston Churchill and the Prince of Wales to Marlon Brando have laid their heads here, as attested by the photos in the bar. It is still the preferred hotel for visiting bigwigs.

Beyond the Palladian porch, the vestibule is lavishly adorned with Mudejar patterned tiles. The sweeping palm-shaded lawns to the rear slope toward the Malecón, above which sits a battery of cannons from the independence wars. The cliff is riddled with defensive tunnels built since the 1970s.

The modernist **Hotel Capri** (Calles 21 y N), one block west of the Hotel Nacional, was built in 1958 by the American gangster Santo Trafficante. It was a setting in the movies *The Godfather* and *Soy Cuba*.

MONUMENTO A LAS VÍCTIMAS DEL MAINE

The **Monumento a las Víctimas del Maine** (Maine Monument, Malecón y Calle 17) was dedicated by the republican Cuban government to the memory of the 260 sailors who died when the USS *Maine* exploded in Havana harbor in 1898, creating a prelude for U.S. intervention in the War of Independence. Two

Hotel Nacional, Vedado

Central Vedado

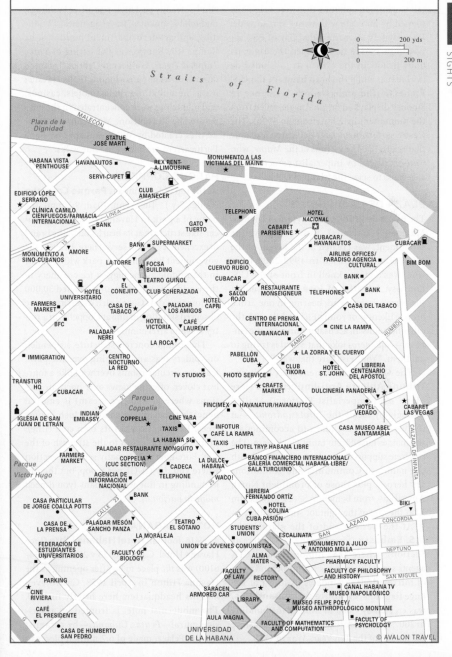

Straits of Florida

Plaza de la Dignidad

MALECÓN

STATUE JOSÉ MARTÍ ★

MONUMENTO A LAS VICTIMAS DEL MAINE ★

HABANA VISTA PENTHOUSE

HAVANAUTOS ■

REX RENT-A-LIMOUSINE

SERVI-CUPET ⛽

CLUB AMANECER

EDIFICIO LÓPEZ SERRANO ★

CLÍNICA CAMILO CIENFUEGOS/FARMÁCIA INTERNACIONAL

LINEA

BANK ■

TELEPHONE ■

GATO TUERTO ▼

CABARET PARISIENNE ★

HOTEL NACIONAL ★

CUBACAR/ HAVANAUTOS ■

CUBACAR ■

MONUMENTO A SINO-CUBANOS ■

AMORE ■

BANK ■ SUPERMARKET ■

AIRLINE OFFICES/ PARADISO AGENCIA CULTURAL ■

BIM BOM

LA TORRE ★

FOCSA BUILDING

EDIFICIO CUERVO RUBIO ★

BANK ■

BANK ■

EL CONEJITO ★

TEATRO GUIÑOL ★

CLUB SCHERAZADA ★

CUBACAR ■

RESTAURANTE MONSEIGNEUR ▼

TELEPHONES ■

CASA DEL TABACO ■

HOTEL UNIVERSITARIO ■

SALÓN ROJO ★

HOTEL CAPRI ■

FARMERS MARKET ■

CASA DE TABACO ★

PALADAR LOS AMIGOS ▼

CENTRO DE PRENSA INTERNACIONAL ■

CINE LA RAMPA ■

BFC ■

HOTEL VICTORIA ■

CAFÉ LAURENT ▼

CUBANACÁN ■

PALADAR NEREI ▼

LA ROCA ▼

RAMPA

IMMIGRATION ■

CENTRO NOCTURNO LA RED ★

PABELLÓN CUBA ★

LA ZORRA Y EL CUERVO ★

TRANSTUR HQ ■

TV STUDIOS ■

PHOTO SERVICE ■

CLUB TIKORA ★

HOTEL ST. JOHN ■

LIBRERIA CENTENARIO DEL APÓSTOL ■

CUBACAR ■

★ CRAFTS MARKET

DULCINERÍA PANADERÍA ■

HOTEL VEDADO ■

CABARET LAS VEGAS ★

IGLÉSIA DE SAN JUAN DE LETRÁN ★

INDIAN EMBASSY ★

Parque Coppelia

COPPELIA ★

FINCIMEX ■

HAVANATUR/HAVANAUTOS ■

Parque Victor Hugo

CINE YARA ★

TAXIS ■

CASA MUSEO ABEL SANTAMARIA ■

FARMERS MARKET ■

INFOTUR ■

CAFÉ LA RAMPA ▼

LA HABANA SÍ ■

PALADAR RESTAURANTE MONGUITO ▼

TAXIS ■

HOTEL TRYP HABANA LIBRE ■

COPPELIA ★ (CUC SECTION)

CADECA ■

LA DULCE HABANA ▼

BANCO FINANCIERO INTERNACIONAL/ GALERIA COMERCIAL HABANA LIBRE/ SALA TURQUINO ■

CALZADA DE INFANTA

AGENCIA DE INFORMACIÓN NACIONAL ■

TELEPHONE ■

WACO! ■

BANK ■

CALLE 23

LIBRERIA FERNANDO ORTÍZ ■

HOTEL COLINA ■

BIKI

CASA PARTICULAR DE JORGE COALLA POTTS ■

CUBA PASIÓN ★

LAZARO

CONCORDIA

CASA DE LA PRENSA ★

PALADAR MESÓN SANCHO PANZA ▼

LA MORALEJA ▼

TEATRO EL SÓTANO ★

STUDENTS' UNION ■

ESCALINATA ★

SAN

MONUMENTO A JULIO ANTONIO MELLA ★

NEPTUNO

FEDERACIÓN DE ESTUDIANTES UNIVERSITARIAS ■

FACULTY OF BIOLOGY ■

UNION DE JÓVENES COMUNISTAS ■

ALMA MATER ★

PHARMACY FACULTY ■

SAN MIGUEL

PARKING ■

FACULTY OF LAW ■

RECTORY ★

FACULTY OF PHILOSOPHY AND HISTORY ■

CANAL HABANA TV MUSEO NAPOLEÓNICO ■

CINE RIVIERA ★

SARACEN ARMORED CAR ■

LIBRARY ■

MUSEO FELIPE POEY/ MUSEO ANTHROPOLÓGICO MONTANE ★

CAFÉ EL PRESIDENTE ▼

AULA MAGNA ■

FACULTY OF MATHEMATICS AND COMPUTATION ■

FACULTY OF PSYCHOLOGY ■

CASA DE HUMBERTO SAN PEDRO ■

UNIVERSIDAD DE LA HABANA

© AVALON TRAVEL

0   200 yds
0   200 m

rusting cannons tethered by chains from the ship's anchor are laid out beneath 12-meter-tall Corinthian columns that were originally topped by an eagle with wings spread wide. Immediately after the failed Bay of Pigs invasion in 1961, a mob toppled the eagle; its body is now in the Museo de la Ciudad de la Habana, while the head hangs in the U.S. Embassy (the ambassador's residence in Siboney displays an original eagle, felled from the monument by a hurricane in 1925). The Castro government later dedicated a plaque that reads, "To the victims of the *Maine*, who were sacrificed by imperialist voracity in its eagerness to seize the island of Cuba."

PLAZA DE LA DIGNIDAD

The **Plaza de la Dignidad** (Plaza of Dignity, Malecón y Calzada), west of the Maine Monument, was created at the height of the Elián González fiasco in 1999-2000 from what was a grassy knoll in front of the U.S. Embassy. A **statue of José Martí** stands at the plaza's eastern end, bearing in one arm a bronze likeness of young Elián while with the other he points an accusatory finger at the embassy—*habaneros* joke that Martí is trying to tell them, "Your visas are that way!"

The Cuban government also built the **Tribuna Abierta Anti-Imperialista** (José Martí Anti-Imperialist Platform)—called jokingly by locals the *"protestadromo"*—at the west end of the plaza to accommodate the masses bused in to taunt Uncle Sam. The concrete supports bear plaques inscribed with the names of Communist and revolutionary heroes, plus those of prominent North Americans, from Benjamin Spock to Malcolm X, at the fore of the fight for social justice.

At the western end of the plaza is the **U.S. Embassy** (formerly the U.S. Interests Section), where U.S. diplomats and CIA agents serve Uncle Sam's whims behind a veil of mirrored-glass windows. A forest of 138 huge flagstaffs, **El Monte de los Banderas,** was erected by Cuba in front of the building in 2007. Each black flag represents a year since the launch of the Ten Years War in 1868.

La Rampa (Calle 23)

Calle 23 rises from the Malecón to Calle L and climbs steadily past high-rise office buildings, nightclubs, cinemas, travel agencies, TV studios, and art deco apartment buildings. La Rampa (the Ramp) was the setting of *Three Trapped Tigers,* Guillermo Cabrera Infante's famous novel about swinging 1950s Havana; it was here that the ritziest hotels, casinos, and nightclubs were concentrated in the days before the Revolution. Multicolored granite tiles created by Wilfredo Lam and René Portocarrero are laid in the sidewalks.

PARQUE COPPELIA

At the top of La Rampa is **Parque Coppelia** (Calle 23 y L, Tues.-Sun. 10am-9:30pm), the name of a park in Havana, of the flying saucer-like structure at its heart, and of the brand of excellent ice cream served here. In 1966, the government built this lush park with a parlor in the middle as the biggest ice creamery in the world, serving up to an estimated 30,000 customers a day. Cuba's rich diversity can be observed standing in line at Coppelia on a sultry Havana afternoon.

The strange concrete structure, suspended on spidery legs and looming over the park, features circular rooms overhead like a four-leaf clover, offering views over open-air sections where *helado* (ice cream) is enjoyed beneath the dappled shade of lush jagüey trees. Each section has its own *cola* (line), proportional in length to the strength of the sun. Foreigners are usually sent to a section where you pay CUC1 per scoop, but the fun is standing in line with Cubans (you'll need *moneda nacional*).

HOTEL HABANA LIBRE

The 416-foot-tall **Hotel Habana Libre** (Free Havana Hotel, Calle L, e/ 23 y 25, tel. 07/834-6100) was *the* place to be after opening as the Havana Hilton in April 1958. Castro even had his headquarters here briefly in 1959. The modernist hotel is fronted by a massive mural—*Frutas Cubanas*—by ceramist Amelia Peláez, made of 6.7 million pieces in the style of Picasso. The mezzanine contains a mosaic mural, *Carro de la Revolución* (the Revolutionary Car) by Alfredo Sosabravo.

CASA MUSEO ABEL SANTAMARÍA

Of interest to students of Cuba's revolutionary history, this **museum** (Calle 25 #164, e/ Infanta y O, tel. 07/835-0891, Mon.-Sat. 9am-4pm, free) occupies a simple two-room, sixth-floor apartment (#603) where Fidel Castro's revolutionary movement, the M-26-7, had its secret headquarters in the former home of the eponymous martyr, brutally tortured and murdered following the attack on the Moncada barracks in 1953. Original furnishings include Fidel's work desk.

Universidad de la Habana and Vicinity

The **Universidad de la Habana** (University of Havana, Calle L y San Lázaro, tel. 07/878-3231, www.uh.cu, Mon.-Fri. 8am-6pm) was founded by Dominican friars in 1728 and was originally situated on Calle Obispo in Habana Vieja. The current edifices were built 1905-1911, when the school was inaugurated in its current location. During the 20th century the university was an autonomous "sacred hill" that neither the police nor the army could enter. The campus is off-limits on weekends and is closed July-August.

From Calle L, the university is entered via an immense, 50-meter-wide stone staircase: the 88-step **Escalinata** (staircase). A patinated bronze **statue of the Alma Mater** cast by Czech sculptor Mario Korbel in 1919 sits atop the staircase. The twice-life-size statue portrays a woman seated in a bronze chair with six classical bas-reliefs representing disciplines taught at the university. She is dressed in a tunic and extends her bare arms, beckoning all who desire knowledge.

The staircase is topped by a columned portico, beyond which lies the peaceful **Plaza Ignacio Agramonte,** surrounded by classical buildings. A **Saracen armored car** in the quadrant was captured in 1958 by students in the fight against Batista. The **Aula Magna** (Great Hall) features magnificent murals by Armando Menocal, plus the marble tomb of independence leader Félix Varela (1788-1853).

The **Monumento a Julio Antonio Mella,** across Calle L at the base of the Escalinata, contains the ashes of Mella, founder of the University Students' Federation and, later, of the Cuban Communist Party.

The **Escuela de Ciencias** (School of Sciences), on the south side of the quadrant,

Universidad de la Habana, Vedado

contains the **Museo de Ciencias Naturales Felipe Poey** (Felipe Poey Museum of Natural Sciences, tel. 07/877-4221, Mon.-Fri. 9am-noon and 1pm-4pm, free), displaying endemic species from alligators to sharks, stuffed or pickled for posterity. The museum dates from 1842 and is named for its French-Cuban founder. Poey (1799-1891) was versed in every field of the sciences and founded the Academy of Medical Sciences, the Anthropological Society of Cuba, and a half-dozen other societies. The **Museo Anthropológico Montane** (Montane Anthropology Museum, tel. 07/879-3488, http://fbio.uh.cu/mmontane.php, Mon.-Fri. 9am-noon and 1pm-4pm, free), on the second floor, displays pre-Columbian artifacts.

MUSEO NAPOLEÓNICO

Who would imagine that so much of Napoleon Bonaparte's personal memorabilia would end up in Cuba? But it has, housed in the **Museo Napoleónico** (Napoleonic Museum, San Miguel #1159, e/ Ronda y Masón, tel. 07/879-1412, mnapoleonico@patrimonio.ohc.cu, Tues.-Sat. 9:30am-5pm, Sun. 9:30am-12:30pm, entrance CUC3, cameras CUC5, guide CUC2) in a three-story Florentine Renaissance mansion on the south side of the university. The collection (7,000 pieces) was the private work of Orestes Ferrara, one-time Cuban ambassador to France. Ferrara brought back from Europe such precious items as the French emperor's death mask, his watch, toothbrush, and the pistols Napoleon used at the Battle of Borodino. Other items were seized from Julio Lobo, the former National Bank president, when he left Cuba for exile. The museum, housed in Ferrara's former home (Ferrara was also forced out by the Revolution), is replete with busts and portraits of the military genius, plus armaments and uniforms.

CALLE 17

This street stretches west from the Monumento a las Víctimas del Maine and is lined with remarkable buildings, beginning with the landmark 35-story **Focsa** (Calle 17

e/ M y N), a V-shaped apartment block built 1954-1956 as one of the largest reinforced concrete structures in the world. The **Instituto Cubano de Amistad con los Pueblos** (Cuban Institute for People's Friendship, Calle 17 #301, e/ H y I) occupies a palatial beaux-arts villa. One block west, the equally magnificent Casa de Juan Gelats is another spectacular exemplar of beaux-arts style; built in 1920 it houses the **Unión Nacional de Escritores y Artistas de Cuba** (National Union of Cuban Writers and Artists, UNEAC, Calle 17 #351, esq. H, tel. 07/832-4551, www.uneac.org.cu).

West of Avenida de los Presidentes, the **Centro Hebreo Sefaradi** (Calle 17 #462, esq. E, tel. 07/832-6623) hosts a small Holocaust museum that is limited to visual displays. The **Museo de Artes Decorativas** (Museum of Decorative Arts, Calle 17 #502, e/ D y E, tel. 07/861-0241 or 07/832-0924, Tues.-Sat. 9:30am-5pm and Sun. 10am-2pm, CUC5 with guide, cameras CUC5, videos CUC10), housed in the former mansion of a Cuban countess, brims with lavish furniture, paintings, textiles, and chinoiserie from the 18th and 19th centuries.

Beyond Paseo, on the west side, to the left, is the **Casa de la Amistad** (Paseo #406, e/ 17 y 19, tel. 07/830-3114), an Italian Renaissance mansion built in 1926 with a surfeit of Carrara marble, silver-laminated banisters, decorative Lalique glass, and Baccarat crystal.

Two blocks west, Calle 17 opens onto **Parque Lennon** (Calle 6), where in 2000, on the 20th anniversary of John Lennon's death, a life-size bronze statue was unveiled in the presence of Fidel (who had previously banned Beatles music). Lennon sits on a cast-iron bench, with plenty of room for anyone who wants to join him. The sculpture is by Cuban artist José Villa, who inscribed the words "People say I'm a dreamer, but I'm not the only one," at Lennon's feet. A *custodio* is there 24/7; he takes care of Lennon's spectacles.

Stroll two blocks north and one block west to reach Calle 11 (bet. 10 and 12), where revolutionary heroine Celia Sánchez once lived. Fidel had an apartment here until his death, and the area was off-limits until 2017. MININT security still patrol the street, where the **Oficinas de Asuntos Históricos del Consejo del Estado** (Línea e/ 10 y 12, c/o tel. 07/832-9149) is located. It houses the official archives of the Cuban Revolution and boasts an astonishing art collection, but is closed to public view.

AVENIDA DE LOS PRESIDENTES

Avenida de los Presidentes (Calle G) runs perpendicular to Calle 23 and climbs from the Malecón toward Plaza de la Revolución. The avenue is named for the statues of Cuban and Latin American presidents that grace its length.

The **Monumento Calixto García** studs the Malecón. One block south, on your right, the **Casa de las Américas** (Presidentes, esq. 3ra, tel. 07/832-2706, www.casa.cult.cu, Mon.-Fri. 8am-4:45pm), formed in 1959 to study and promote the cultures of Latin America and the Caribbean, is housed in a cathedral-like art deco building. Fifty meters south is the Casa's **Galería Haydee Santamaría** (e/ 5ta and G).

The **Museo de la Danza** (Calle Línea #365, esq. Presidentes, tel. 07/831-2198, mus-danza@cubarte.cult.cu, Tues.-Sat. 10am-5pm,

CUC2, guide CUC1) occupies a restored mansion and has salons dedicated to Russian ballet, modern dance, and the Ballet Nacional de Cuba. Divert one block west along Línea to visit **Galería Habana** (Línea 460 e/ E y F, tel. 07/832-7101, www.galerihabana.com, Mon.-Fri. 10am-4pm, Sat. 10am-1pm, free), a superb art gallery showing works by leading contemporary and yesteryear maestros.

Ascending the avenue, you'll pass statues to Ecuadorian president Eloy Alfaro (e/ 15 y 17; note the wall mural called *Wrinkles,* for self-evident reasons, on the southwest corner), Mexican president Benito Juárez (e/ 17 y 19), Venezuelan Simón Bolívar (e/ 19 y 21), Panamanian strongman president Omar Torrijos (e/ 19 y 21), and Chilean president Salvador Allende (e/ 21 y 23).

The tree-shaded boulevard climbs two blocks to the **Monumento a José Miguel Gómez** (Calle 29), designed by Italian sculptor Giovanni Nicolini and erected in 1936 in classical style to honor the vainglorious republican president (1909-1913). Beyond, the road drops through a canyon to the junction with Avenida Salvador Allende.

To the west, on the north side of the road, the once-graceful **Quinta de los Molinos** (e/ Infanta y Luaces, tel. 07/879-8850) was closed

Beaux Arts Museo de Artes Decorativas, Vedado

for restoration at last visit. Built between 1837 and 1840, it was a summer palace for the captains-general. In 1899, it was granted as the private residence of General Máximo Gómez, the Dominican-born commander in chief of the liberation army. The *molino* (mill) refers to a tobacco mill that operated 1800-1835, powered by the waters of the Zanja Real. The *quinta*'s 4.8-hectare grounds form the **Jardín Botánico** (Botanical Gardens, Tues.-Sun. 7am-7pm, free), featuring a *mariposario* (butterfly garden). Guided walks are offered.

★ Necrópolis Cristóbal Colón

The **Necrópolis Cristóbal Colón** (Columbus Cemetery, Zapata, esq. 12, tel. 07/830-4517, daily 8am-5pm, entrance CUC5 includes guide and right to photograph) covers 56 hectares and contains more than 500 major mausoleums, chapels, vaults, tombs, and galleries (in addition to countless gravestones) embellished with angels, griffins, cherubs, and other flamboyant ornamentation. You'll even find Greco-Roman temples in miniature, an Egyptian pyramid, and medieval castles, plus baroque, Romantic, Renaissance, art deco, and art nouveau monuments. The triple-arched entrance gate has marble reliefs depicting the crucifixion and Lazarus rising from the grave and is topped by a marble coronation stone representing the theological virtues of faith, hope, and charity.

Today a national monument, the cemetery was laid out between 1871 and 1886 in 16 rectangular blocks, like a Roman military camp, divided by social status. Nobles competed to build the most elaborate tombs, with social standing dictating the size and location of plots.

Famous *criollo* patricians, colonial aristocrats, and war heroes such as Máximo Gómez are buried here alongside noted intellectuals and politicians. The list goes on and on: José Raúl Capablanca, the world chess champion 1921-1927 (his tomb is guarded by a marble queen chess piece); Alejo Carpentier, Cuba's most revered contemporary novelist; Celia Sánchez, Haydee Santamaría, and a plethora

of other revolutionaries killed for the cause; and even some of the Revolution's enemies. The **Galería Tobias** is one of several massive underground ossuaries.

The major tombs line Avenida Cristóbal Colón, the main avenue, which leads south from the gate to an ocher-colored, octagonal neo-Byzantine church, the **Capilla Central,** containing a fresco of the Last Judgment.

The most visited grave is the flower-bedecked tomb of Amelia Goyri de Hoz, revered as **La Milagrosa** (The Miraculous One, Calles 3 y F) and to whom the superstitious ascribe miraculous healings. According to legend, she died during childbirth in 1901 and was buried with her stillborn child at her feet. When her sarcophagus was later opened, the baby was supposedly cradled in her arms. Ever since, believers have paid homage by knocking three times on the tombstone with one of its brass rings, before touching the tomb and requesting a favor (one must not turn one's back on the tomb when departing). Many childless women pray here in hopes of a pregnancy.

The Chinese built their own cemetery immediately southwest of Cementerio Colón, on the west side of Avenida 26 (e/ 28 y 33, tel. 07/831-1645, daily 8am-4pm, free). Beyond the circular gateway, traditional lions stand guard over burial chapels with upward-curving roofs.

GALERÍA 23 Y 12

The northwest corner of Calles 23 and 12, one block north of Cementerio Colón, marks the spot where, on April 16, 1961 (the eve of the Bay of Pigs invasion), Castro announced that Cuba was henceforth socialist. The anniversary of the declaration of socialism is marked each April 16. A **bronze bas-relief** shows Fidel surrounded by soldiers, rifles held aloft. It honors citizens killed in the U.S.-sponsored strike on the airfield at Marianao that was a prelude to the invasion, repeating his words: "This is the socialist and democratic revolution of the humble, with the humble, for the humble." At last visit, the building (and memorial) were boarded up as unsafe.

Necrópolis Cristóbal Colón

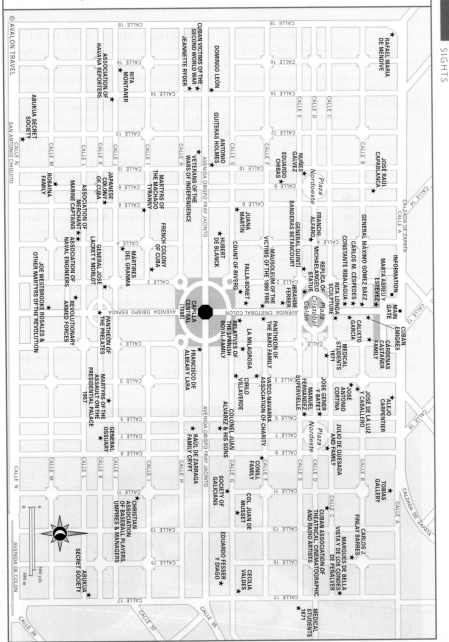

© AVALON TRAVEL

Plaza de la Revolución

Havana's largest plaza, Plaza de la Revolución (Revolution Plaza), which occupies the Loma de los Catalanes (Hill of the Catalans), is an ugly tarred square. The trapezoidal complex spanning 11 acres was laid out during the Batista era, when it was known as the Plaza Cívica. It forms the administrative center for Cuba. All the major edifices date to the 1950s. Huge rallies are held here on May 1.

Among the important buildings are the monumentalist **Biblioteca Nacional** (National Library, tel. 07/855-5542, Mon. 8:15am-1pm, Tues.-Fri. 8:15am-6:30pm, Sat. 8am-4:30pm, guided tours offered), Cuba's largest library, built 1955-1957; the 21-story **Ministerio de Defensa,** originally built as the municipal seat of government on the plaza's southeast side; and the **Teatro Nacional** (National Theater, Paseo y Av. Carlos M. de Céspedes, tel. 07/878-5590, www.teatrona-cional.cu), one block to the northwest of the plaza, built 1954-1960 with a convex glazed facade. Paseo climbs northwest from the plaza to Zapata, where in the middle of the road rises the **Memorial a Ethel y Julius Rosenberg,** bearing cement doves and an inset sculpture of the U.S. couple executed in 1953 for passing nuclear secrets to the Soviet Union. An inscription reads, "Assassinated June 19, 1953." The Cuban government holds a memorial service here each June 19.

MEMORIAL Y MUSEO JOSÉ MARTÍ

The massive **Memorial José Martí** on the south side of the square sits atop a 30-meter-tall base that is shaped as a five-pointed star. It is made entirely of gray granite and marble and was designed by Enrique Luis Varela and completed in 1958. To each side, arching stairways lead to an 18-meter-tall (59-foot) gray-white marble statue of Martí sitting in a contemplative pose, like Rodin's *The Thinker*.

Behind looms a 109-meter-tall marble edifice stepped like a soaring ziggurat from a sci-fi movie. It's the highest point in Havana. The edifice houses the **Museo José Martí** (tel. 07/859-2347, Mon.-Sat. 9am-4:30pm, entrance CUC3, cameras CUC5, videos CUC10), dedicated to Martí's life, with maps, texts, paintings, and a multiscreen broadcast on independence and the Revolution. An elevator whisks you to the top of the tower for a 360-degree view over Havana (CUC2).

PALACIO DE LA REVOLUCIÓN

The center of government is the **Palacio de la Revolución** (Palace of the Revolution),

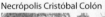

Necrópolis Cristóbal Colón

immediately south of the José Martí monument. This imposing structure was inspired by the architecture then popular in Fascist Europe and was built 1954-1957 as the Palace of Justice. Today, it is where Raúl Castro and the Council of Ministers work out the policies of state. The labyrinthine, ocher-colored palace with gleaming black stone walls and checkered floors adjoins the buildings of the Central Committee of the Communist Party. Before the Revolution, the buildings served as the Cuban Supreme Court and national police headquarters. No visitors are allowed.

MINISTERIO DEL INTERIOR

Commanding the northwest side of the plaza is the seven-story Ministerio del Interior (Ministry of the Interior, MININT, in charge of national security), built in 1953 to be the Office of the Comptroller. On its east side is a windowless horizontal block that bears a soaring **"mural" of Che Guevara** and the words *Hasta la victoria siempre* ("Always toward victory"), erected in 1995 from steel railings donated by the French government. See it by day *and* by night, when it is illuminated.

MINISTERIO DE COMUNICACIONES

In October 2009, a visage of Comandante Camilo Cienfuegos (identical in style to that of Che) was erected on the facade of the **Ministerio de Comunicaciones** (Ministry of Communications), on the plaza's northeast corner. The 100-ton steel mural was raised for the 50th anniversary of Cienfuegos's death and is accompanied by the words *Vas bien, Fidel* ("You're doing fine, Fidel"). Cienfuegos's famous response was in reply to Fidel's question "Am I doing all right, Camilo?" at a rally on January 8, 1959. The ground-floor **Museo Postal Cubano** (Cuban Post Museum, Av. Rancho Boyeros, esq. 19 de Mayo, tel. 07/882-8255, Mon.-Fri. 8am-4pm, entrance CUC1) has a well-catalogued philatelic collection, including a complete range of Cuban postage stamps dating from 1855, plus stamps from almost 100 other countries.

Nuevo Vedado

Nuevo Vedado, which stretches southwest of Plaza de la Revolución, is a sprawling complex of mid-20th-century housing, including postrevolutionary high-rise apartment blocks. The most magnificent and prominent building is undoutedbly the **Coliseo de la Ciudad Deportiva** (Sports Coliseum, colloquially called "El Coliseo"), a giant Olympic stadium with a massive concrete dome. It was built in 1957 at Avenida 26, Avenida de la Independencia (Rancho Boyeros), and Vía Blanca.

Note: Those with children in tow might be tempted to visit the poorly managed **Jardín Zoológico de la Habana** (Havana Zoological Garden, Av. 26 y Zoológico, tel. 07/881-8915, zoohabana@ch.gov.cu, Wed.-Sun. 9:30am-5pm, CUC2), but this depressing zoo is best avoided.

CENTRO DE ESTUDIOS CHE GUEVARA

Opened in 2014, the **Center for Che Guevara Studies** (Calle 47 #772 e/ Conill y Tulipán, tel. 07/814-1013, www.centroche.co.cu) is housed in a handsome contemporary building opposite Che's gorgeous former modernist home (Calle 47 #770), where he lived 1962-1964 and which now houses offices for the center. It has separate *salas* dedicated to Che, Camilo Cienfuegos, and Haydee Santamaría, plus a library, auditorium, and expositions on Che's life.

BOSQUE DE LA HABANA AND PARQUE METROPOLITANO DE LA HABANA

Follow Avenida Zoológica west to the bridge over the Río Almendares to enter the **Bosque de la Habana** (Havana Forest). This ribbon of wild, vine-draped woodland stretches alongside the river. There is no path—you must walk along Calle 49C, which parallels the river. Going alone is not advised; robberies have occurred.

North of Bosque de la Habana, and accessed from Avenida 47, the motley riverside

Nueva Vedado and Cerro

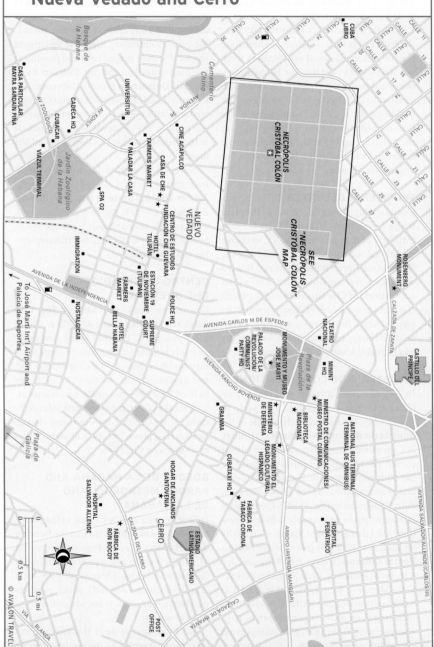

CALLE 11
CALLE 13
CALLE 15
CALLE 17
CALLE 19
CALLE 21
CALLE 23
CALLE 25
CALLE 27
CALLE 28
CALLE 30
CALLE 24
CALLE 22
CALLE 18
CALLE 14
CALLE 12
CALLE 10
CALLE 8
CALLE 6
CALLE 4
CALLE

CUBA LIBRO

Bosque de la Habana

Cementerio Chino

AVENIDA 26

NECRÓPOLIS CRISTÓBAL COLÓN

SEE "NECRÓPOLIS CRISTÓBAL COLÓN" MAP

ROSENBERG MONUMENT

CALZADA DE ZAPATA

CASTILLO DEL PRÍNCIPE

CASA PARTICULAR MAYRA SARDAIN PINA

CADECA HQ

CUBACAR

VIAZUL TERMINAL

AV ZOOLÓGICO

UNIVERSITUR

FARMERS MARKET

PALADAR LA CASA

Jardin Zoológico de la Habana

SPA O2

CINE ACAPULCO

CASA DE CHE

CENTRO DE ESTUDIOS FUNDACIÓN CHE GUEVARA

NUEVO VEDADO

IMMIGRATION

AVENIDA DE LA INDEPENDENCIA

NOSTALGICAR

HOTEL TULIPÁN

ESTACIÓN 19 DE NOVIEMBRE (TULIPÁN)

FARMERS MARKET

HOTEL BELLA HABANA

SUPREME COURT

POLICE HQ

AVENIDA CARLOS M DE ESPEDES

TEATRO NACIONAL

MININT HQ

PALACIO DE LA REVOLUCIÓN/ COMMUNIST PARTY HQ

MONUMENTO Y MUSEO JOSÉ MARTÍ

Plaza de la Revolución

AVENIDA RANCHO BOYEROS

MINISTERIO DE DEFENSA

MINISTRO DE COMUNICACIONES/ MUSEO POSTAL CUBANO

BIBLIOTECA NACIONAL

NATIONAL BUS TERMINAL (TERMINAL DE OMNIBUS)

GRAMMA

MONUMENTO EL LEGADO CULTURAL HISPÁNICO

HOSPITAL PEDIÁTRICO

To José Martí Int'l Airport and Palacio de Deportes

Plaza de Galicia

HOSPITAL SALVADOR ALLENDE

HOGAR DE ANCIANOS SANTOVENIA

CUBATAXI HQ

CALZADA DEL CERRO

CERRO

FÁBRICA DE RON BOCOY

ESTADIO LATINOAMERICANO

FÁBRICA DE TABACO CORONA

AVENIDA SALVADOR ALLENDE (CARLOS III)

ARROYO (AVENIDA MANGLAR)

CALZADA DE INFANTA

POST OFFICE

VÍA BLANCA

© AVALON TRAVEL

0   0.5 km
0   0.5 mi

Parque Metropolitano de la Habana has pony rides, rowboats, mini-golf, and a children's playground. To the south, the woods extend to **Los Jardines de la Tropical** (Calle Rizo, Tues.-Sun. 9am-6pm), a landscaped park built 1904-1910 on the grounds of a former brewery. The park found its inspiration in Antoni Gaudí's Parque Güell in Barcelona. Today it is near-derelict and looks like an abandoned set from *Lord of the Rings*.

PLAYA (MIRAMAR AND BEYOND)

West of Vedado and the Río Almendares, the *municipio* of Playa extends to the western boundary of Havana as far as the Río Quibu. Most areas were renamed following the Revolution. Gone are Country Club and Biltmore, replaced with politically acceptable names such as Atabey, Cubanacán, and Siboney, in honor of Cuba's indigenous past.

Miramar

Miramar is Havana's upscale residential district, laid out in an expansive grid of treeshaded streets lined by fine mansions. Most of their original owners fled Cuba after the Revolution. Nonetheless, Miramar is at the forefront of Cuba's quasi-capitalist remake. The best-stocked stores are here, as are the foreign embassies and many of the city's top *paladares* and private nightclubs.

Primera Avenida (1st Avenue, 1ra Av.) runs along the shore. Time-worn *balnearios* (bathing areas) are found along Miramar's waterfront, cut into the shore. Of limited appeal to tourists, they draw Cubans on hot summer days. Inland, running parallel at intervals of about 200 meters, are 3ra Avenida, 5ta Avenida (the main thoroughfare), and 7ma Avenida.

Tunnels under the Río Almendares connect Miramar to Vedado. The Malecón connects with 5ta Avenida; Línea (Calle 9) connects with 7ma Avenida and Avenida 31, which leads to the Marianao district; Calle 11 connects with 7ma Avenida; and Calle 23

becomes Avenida 47, linking Vedado with Kohly and Marianao.

QUINTA AVENIDA

The wide, fig-tree-lined, eight-kilometer-long boulevard called 5th Avenue, or "Quinta," runs ruler-straight through the heart of Miramar. It is flanked by mansions, many now occupied by foreign embassies; Quinta Avenida (5ta Av.) is known as "Embassy Row."

At its eastern end, the **Casa de la Tejas Verdes** (House of Green Tiles, Calle 2 #318, Miramar, tel. 07/212-5282, tejasverde@patrimonio.ohc.cu, visits by appointment), or Edificio Fraxas, is a restored beaux-arts mansion on the north side of Quinta at Calle 2, immediately west of the tunnel. Built in 1926, after the Revolution it fell into utter decay. It has a sumptuous postmodern interior.

The junction at Calle 10 is pinned by **Reloj de Quinta Avenida,** a large clock erected in 1924 in the central median. At Calle 12, the **Memorial de la Denuncia** (Museum of Denouncement, 5ta Av., esq. 14, tel. 07/206-8802, ext. 108, www.cubadenuncia.cu) opened in 2016 and is dedicated to U.S.-Cuba relations. Six *salas* (rooms) are themed, including one dedicated to the CIA's efforts to dethrone Fidel and another to *el bloqueo* (the embargo). It's run by the Ministry of the Interior.

Parque de los Ahorcados (Park of the Hanged), aka Parque de la Quinta, spans Quinta between Calles 24 and 26. The park is shaded by massive jagüey trees and features a Greek-style rotunda, a bust of Gandhi (north side), and a statue of Emilio Zapata (south side). The park is best avoided on Sunday mornings, when the "Ladies in White" dissident group gathers to march, with no shortage of secret police present. Rising over the west side is **Iglesia de Santa Rita de Casia** (5ta, esq. Calle 26, tel. 07/204-2001). This exemplar of modernist church architecture dates from 1942; its main feature is a statue of Santa Rita by Rita Longa. Music lovers might head two blocks north to **Casa Museo Compay Segundo** (Calle 22 #103, e/ 1ra y 3ra, tel. 07/206-8629 or 202-5922, Mon.-Fri.

Playa

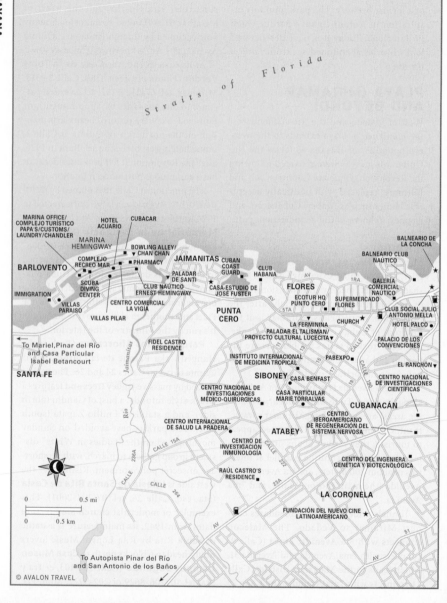

Straits of Florida

MARINA OFFICE/
COMPLEJO TURÍSTICO
PAPA'S/CUSTOMS/
LAUNDRY/CHANDLER

MARINA
HEMINGWAY

HOTEL
ACUARIO

CUBACAR

COMPLEJO
RECREO MAR

BOWLING ALLEY/
CHAN CHAN

BARLOVENTO

PHARMACY

JAIMANITAS

CUBAN
COAST
GUARD

CLUB
HABANA

BALNEARIO DE
LA CONCHA

BALNEARIO CLUB
NÁUTICO

SCUBA
DIVING
CENTER

PALADAR
DE SANTI

FLORES

1RA

GALERÍA
COMERCIAL
NÁUTICO

IMMIGRATION

CLUB NÁUTICO
ERNEST HEMINGWAY

CASA-ESTUDIO DE
JOSÉ FUSTER

ECOTUR HQ
PUNTO CERO

SUPERMERCADO
FLORES

AV

5TA

CLUB SOCIAL JULIO
ANTONIO MELLA

VILLAS
PARAISO

CENTRO COMERCIAL
LA VIGÍA

PUNTA
CERO

HOTEL PALCO

VILLAS PILAR

LA FERMININA

CHURCH

17A

PALACIO DE LOS
CONVENCIONES

PALADAR EL TALISMAN/
PROYECTO CULTURAL LUCECITA

CALLE

To Mariel, Pinar del Río
and Casa Particular
Isabel Betancourt

FIDEL CASTRO
RESIDENCE

13

SANTA FE

INSTITUTO INTERNACIONAL
DE MEDICINA TROPICAL

PABEXPO

15

EL RANCHÓN

Jaimanitas

17

CENTRO NACIONAL
DE INVESTIGACIONES
CIENTÍFICAS

SIBONEY

CASA BENFAST

19

CALLE 190

CENTRO NACIONAL DE
INVESTIGACIONES
MÉDICO-QUIRÚRGICAS

CASA PARTICULAR
MARIE TORRALVAS

Río

CUBANACÁN

CENTRO INTERNACIONAL
DE SALUD LA PRADERA

ATABEY

CENTRO
IBEROAMERICANO
DE REGENERACIÓN DEL
SISTEMA NERVOSA

CALLE 15A

CENTRO DE
INVESTIGACIÓN
INMUNOLOGÍA

CALLE 222

CENTRO DEL INGENIERA
GENÉTICA Y BIOTECNOLÓGICA

236A

CALLE

RAÚL CASTRO'S
RESIDENCE

23A

LA CORONELA

CALLE

CALLE 264

FUNDACIÓN DEL NUEVO CINE
LATINOAMERICANO

0   0.5 mi

0   0.5 km

AV

51

To Autopista Pinar del Río
and San Antonio de los Baños

AV

© AVALON TRAVEL

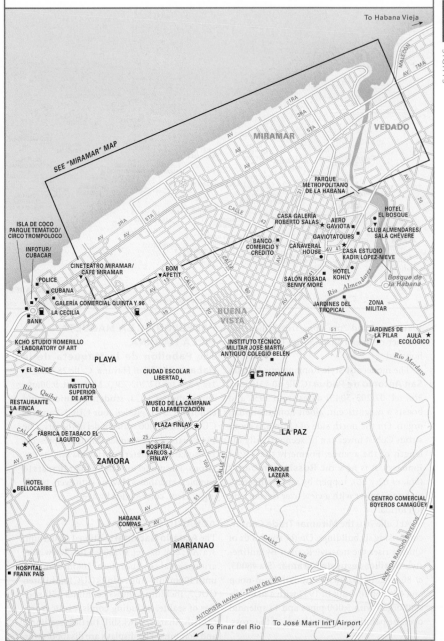

To Habana Vieja

VEDADO

MIRAMAR

SEE "MIRAMAR" MAP

PARQUE METROPOLITANO DE LA HABANA

HOTEL EL BOSQUE

CASA GALERÍA ROBERTO SALAS ★
AERO GAVIOTA ★

CLUB ALMENDARES/ SALA CHÉVERE

ISLA DE COCO PARQUE TEMÁTICO/ CIRCO TROMPOLOCO

INFOTUR/ CUBACAR

BANCO COMERCIO Y CRÉDITO ■
GAVIOTATOURS ★

CAÑAVERAL HOUSE ●

CASA ESTUDIO KADIR LÓPEZ-NIEVE ★

CINETEATRO MIRAMAR/ CAFÉ MIRAMAR

BOM APETIT ▼

SALÓN ROSADA BENNY MORÉ ●

HOTEL KOHLY

POLICE ■

Bosque de la Habana

CUBANA ▼
GALERÍA COMERCIAL QUINTA Y 96
LA CECILÍA ▲

JARDINES DEL TROPICAL ●

ZONA MILITAR ■

BANK

BUENA VISTA

JARDINES DE LA PILAR ■
AULA ECOLÓGICO ★

KCHO STUDIO ROMERILLO LABORATORY OF ART ★

Río Mordazo

PLAYA

INSTITUTO TÉCNICO MILITAR JOSÉ MARTÍ/ ANTIGUO COLEGIO BELÉN ■

EL SAUCE ▼

CIUDAD ESCOLAR LIBERTAD ★

INSTITUTO SUPERIOR DE ARTE ■

Río Quibú

TROPICANA

RESTAURANTE LA FINCA ★

MUSEO DE LA CAMPANA DE ALFABETIZACIÓN ★

FÁBRICA DE TABACO EL LAGUITO ★

PLAZA FINLAY ★

LA PAZ

ZAMORA

HOSPITAL CARLOS J FINLAY ■

PARQUE LAZEAR ★

HOTEL BELLOCARIBE ●

CENTRO COMERCIAL BOYEROS CAMAGÜEY ■

HABANA COMPAS ●

MARIANAO

HOSPITAL FRANK PAÍS ■

AUTOPISTA HAVANA - PINAR DEL RIO

To Pinar del Río

To José Martí Int'l Airport

Miramar

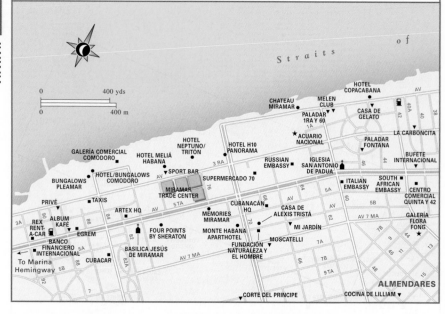

10am-noon and 2pm-4pm, free), where the crooner of *Buena Vista Social Club* fame is honored.

The modernist-style Romanesque **Iglesia San Antonio de Padua** (Calle 60 #316, esq. 5ta, tel. 07/203-5045) dates from 1951 and boasts a magnificent, albeit nonfunctional, organ. On the north side of Quinta, a monstrous Cubist tower can be seen virtually the length of the avenue. Formerly the Soviet Embassy, it is now the **Russian Embassy** (5ta, e/ 62 y 66), topped by an intelligence-gathering tower with a view over the horizon to Florida.

At Calle 70 is the **Miramar Trade Center,** comprising six buildings. On the south side of Quinta rises the massive Roman-Byzantine-style **Basílica Jesús de Miramar** (5ta #8003, e/ 80 y 82, tel. 07/203-5301, daily 9am-noon and 4pm-6pm), built in 1953 with a magnificent organ with 5,000 pipes and 14 splendid oversize paintings of the stations of the cross.

PABELLÓN DE LA MAQUETA DE LA HABANA

The **Pabellón de la Maqueta de la Habana** (Model of Havana, Calle 28 #113, e/ 1ra y 3ra, tel. 07/202-7303, Mon.-Sat. 9:30am-5pm, adults CUC3, students, seniors, and children CUC1, guided tour CUC1, cameras CUC2) is a 1:1,000 scale model of the city. The 144-square-meter *maqueta* (model) represents 144 square kilometers of Havana and its environs. The model took more than 10 years to complete and shows Havana with every building present, color-coded by age.

ACUARIO NACIONAL

The **Acuario Nacional** (National Aquarium, 3ra Av., esq. 62, tel. 07/203-6401, www.acuarionacional.cu, Tues.-Sun. 10am-6pm and until 10pm July-Aug., adults CUC10, children CUC7, including shows) exhibits 450 species of sealife, including corals, exotic tropical fish, sharks, hawksbill turtles, sea lions, and dolphins. The displays are disappointing

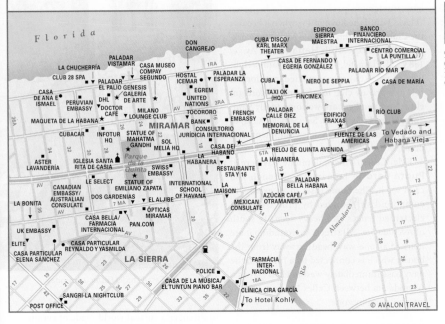

by international standards. Sea lion shows (Tues.-Sun. 11am and 4pm, Sat.-Sun. 11am, 2pm, and 4pm) and dolphin shows (daily noon, 3pm, and 5pm) are offered.

FUNDACIÓN NATURALEZA Y EL HOMBRE

The **Fundación Naturaleza y El Hombre** (Foundation of Man and Nature, Av. 5B #6611, e/ 66 y 70, tel. 07/204-2985, www.fanj. cult.cu, Mon.-Fri. 9am-4pm, CUC2) honors Cuban naturalist and explorer Antonio Nuñez Jiménez. Many of the eclectic exhibits in its **Museo de la Canoa** are dedicated to the 10,889-mile journey by a team of Cubans (led by Nuñez in 1996) that paddled from the source of the Amazon to the Bahamas in dugout canoes. There is a replica of the canoe along with indigenous artifacts, including pre-Columbian erotic ceramics.

Náutico and Jaimanitas

Beyond Miramar, 5ta Avenida curls around the half-moon Playa Marianao and passes through the Náutico district, a setting for Havana's elite prerevolutionary social clubs and *balnearios*. Following the Revolution, the area reopened to the hoi polloi and was rechristened. The beaches—collectively known as Playas del Oeste—are popular with Cubans on weekends. There was even an eponymous mini-version of New York's famous Coney Island theme park, re-created in 2008 as **Isla de Coco Parque Temático** (tel. 07/208-0330, Wed.-Fri. 4pm-10pm, Sat.-Sun. 10am-10pm).

Commanding the scene are the palatial Mudejar-style former **Balneario de la Concha** (5ta e/ 112 and 146) and, immediately west, the **Balneario Club Náutico** with its sweeping modernist entrance. Beyond the Río Quibu, 5ta Avenida passes into the Flores district. The Havana-Biltmore Yacht and Country Club was here, dating from 1928 and fronting Havana's most beautiful expanse of white sand. The "Yacht" was founded in 1886 and became the snootiest place in Havana (it was here that President Fulgencio Batista, mulatto, was famously refused entry for being too "black") until the Revolution, when it became the Club Social Julio Antonio Mella, for workers. Today, as the **Club Habana** (5ta Av., e/ 188 y 214, Playa, tel. 07/204-5700, yanis@club-habana.palco.cu), it has reverted to its former role as a private club for the (mostly foreign) elite. Nonmembers are welcome (daily 9am-7pm, Mon.-Fri. CUC20, Sat.-Sun. CUC30) to use the beach, water sports equipment, and pool.

Fidel Castro's main domicile was here at **Punta Cero** in Jaimanitas, although you can't see it. The home is set in an expansive compound surrounded by pine trees and electrified fences and heavy security south of Avenida 5ta. All streets surrounding it are marked as one-way, heading away from the house, which is connected by a tunnel to the navy base immediately west of Club Havana. Avenida 5ta between Calles 188 and 230 is a no-photography zone.

José Fuster at Casa-Estudio Fuster, Jaimanitas

KCHO ESTUDIO ROMERILLO

In 2014, world-renowned artist Alexis Leiva Machado, better known as "Kcho," opened this contemporary **art complex** (7ma, esq. 120, Playa, tel. 07/208-4750 or 5279-1844, www.kchoestudio.com, by appointment) with a library, theater, experimental graphic workshop, and galleries showing revolving exhibitions of leading artists worldwide. It also has a foundry and carpentry and pottery workshops. Enhancing the complex are the local parks that comprise **Museo Orgánico Romerillo,** which spans 20 blocks. Kcho finances the project himself.

CASA-ESTUDIO DE JOSÉ FUSTER

Artist José R. Fuster, a world-renowned painter and ceramist nicknamed the "Picasso of the Caribbean," has an open-air workshop-gallery at **his home** (Calle 226, esq. Av. 3ra, Jaimanitas, tel. 07/271-2932 or 5281-5421, www.josefuster.com, daily 9am-5pm; call ahead). You step through a giant doorway to discover a surreal world made of ceramics. Many of the naïve, childlike works are inspired by farmyard scenes and icons of *cubanidad,* such as *El Torre del Gallo* (Rooster's Tower), a four-meter-tall statement on male chauvinism. Fuster's creativity now graces the entryways, benches, roofs, and facades of houses throughout his local community.

Cubanacán and Siboney

Cubanacán is—or was—Havana's Beverly Hills, an exclusive area inland of Náutico and Flores. It was developed in the 1920s with winding tree-lined streets on which the most grandiose of Havana's mansions arose. The golf course at the Havana Country Club lent the name "Country Club Park" to what is now called Cubanacán, still the swankiest address in town. Following the Revolution, most of the area's homeowners fled Cuba. Many mansions were dispensed to Communist officials, who live in a manner that the majority of Cubans can only dream of and, of course, never see. The area is replete with military camps and security personnel. Other homes serve either as "protocol" houses—villas where foreign dignitaries and VIPs are housed during visits—or as foreign embassies and ambassadors' homes.

One of the swankiest mansions was built in 1910 for the Marqués de Pinar del Río; it was later adorned with 1930s art deco glass and chrome, a spiral staircase, and abstract floral designs. Today it is the **Fábrica El Laguito** (Av. 146 #2302, e/ 21 y 21A, tel. 07/208-0738, by appointment only), the nation's premier cigar factory, making Montecristos and the majority of Cohibas—*the* premium Havana cigar.

Havana's impressive convention center, the **Palacio de las Convenciones** (Convention Palace, Calle 146, e/ 11 y 13, tel. 07/202-6011, www.eventospalco.com), was built in 1979 for the Non-Aligned Conference. The main hall hosts twice-yearly meetings of the Cuban National Assembly. Two blocks west, **Pabexpo** (Av. 17 e/ 180 y 182, tel. 07/271-3670) has four exhibition halls for trade shows and is Cuba's main expo space.

Cuba's biotechnology industry is also centered here and extends westward into the districts of Atabey and Siboney (a residential area for MININT and military elite), earning the area the moniker "Scientific City." The **Centro de Ingeniería Genética y Biotecnología** (Center for Genetic Engineering and Biotechnology, Av. 31, e/ 158 y 190, Havana, tel. 07/271-8008, http://cigb.edu.cu) is Cuba's main research facility and perhaps the most sophisticated research facility in any developing nation.

INSTITUTO SUPERIOR DE ARTE

Following the Revolution, Fidel Castro and Che Guevara famously played a few rounds of golf at the exclusive Havana Country Club before tearing it up and converting the grounds to house Cuba's leading art academy, the **Instituto Superior de Arte** (Higher Art Institute, Calle 120 #1110, esq. 9na, tel. 07/208-9771, www.isa.cult.cu, appointment only through a tour agency; closed in summer),

featuring the Escuela de Música (School of Music), Escuela de Ballet (Ballet School), Escuela de Baile Moderno (School of Modern Dance), and Escuela de Bellas Artes (School of Fine Arts). The school was designed by three young "rebel" architects: Italians Roberto Gottardi and Vittorio Garatti, and Cuban Ricardo Porro. As the five redbrick main buildings emerged, they were thought too avant-garde. The project was halted, though the school did open. Many buildings were never completed and fell into ruin. Calles 15 and 134 have the best views.

Marianao and La Coronela

This dilapidated *municipio,* on the heights south of Miramar, evolved since the mid-19th century along newly laid streets. During the 1920s, Marianao boasted the Marianao Country Club, the Oriental Park racetrack, and Grand Nacional Casino; it was given a boost on New Year's Eve 1939 when the Tropicana opened as Havana's ritziest nightclub. After the Revolution, the casinos, racetrack, and even Tropicana (briefly) were shut down.

Following the U.S. occupation of Cuba in 1898, the U.S. military governor, General Fitzhugh Lee, established his headquarters in Marianao and called it Camp Columbia. Campamento Columbia later became headquarters for Batista's army, and it was from here that the sergeant effected his *golpes* in 1933 and 1952. Camp Columbia was bombed on April 15, 1960, during the prelude to the CIA-run Bay of Pigs invasion.

Following the Revolution, Castro turned the barracks into **Ciudad Escolar Libertad,** a school complex that became the headquarters for Castro's national literacy campaign. The **Museo de la Campaña de Alfabetización** (Museum of the Literacy Campaign, Av. 29E, esq. 76, tel. 07/260-8054, Mon.-Fri. 8am-5pm, Sat. 8am-noon, free) is dedicated to the campaign initiated on January 1, 1960, when 120,632 uniformed *brigadistas,* mostly students, spread out across the country to teach illiterate peasantry to read and write. The blue building 100 meters west was Fulgencio Batista's former manse.

A tower in the center of the traffic circle—**Plaza Finlay**—outside the main entrance, at Avenida 31 and Avenida 100, was erected in 1944 as a beacon for the military airfield. In 1948 a needle was added so that today it is shaped like a syringe in honor of Carlos Finlay, the Cuban who in 1881 discovered the cause of yellow fever.

The Autopista a San Antonio links Havana with San Antonio de los Baños. Midway between the two cities, you'll pass the **Universidad de las Ciencias Informáticas** (Carretera de San Antonio de los Baños, Km 2, Torrens, tel. 07/837-2548, www.uci.cu), Cuba's university dedicated to making the country a world power in software technology. Immediately north is the gray marble **Memorial al Soldado Internacionalista Soviético,** with an eternal flame dedicated to Soviet military personnel who died in combat.

TROPICANA

The **Tropicana** (Calle 72 e/ 41 y 45, tel. 07/207-0110, www.cabaret-tropicana.com) is an astonishing exemplar of modernist architecture. Most of the structures date from 1951, when the nightclub was restored with a new showroom—the Salon Arcos de Cristal (Crystal Bows)—designed by Max Borges Recio with a roof of five arcing concrete vaults and curving bands of glass to fill the intervening space. Built in decreasing order of height, they produce a telescopic effect that channels the perspective toward the orchestra platform. Borges also added the famous geometric sculpture that still forms the backdrop to the main stage, in the outdoor Salón Bajo las Estrellas.

A ballet dancer pirouettes on the tips of her toes amid the lush foliage in front of the entrance. The statue, by the renowned Cuban sculptor Rita Longa, is surrounded by bacchantes performing a wild ritual dance to honor Dionysius.

ACROSS THE HARBOR

The harbor channel and Bahía de la Habana (Havana Bay) separate Habana Vieja from the communities of Casablanca, Regla, and Guanabacoa. The communities can be reached through a tunnel under the channel (access is eastbound off Avenida del Puerto and the Prado) or along Vía Blanca, skirting the harbor. Little ferries bob their way across the water, connecting Casablanca and Regla with each other and with Habana Vieja.

★ Parque Histórico Militar Morro-Cabaña

Looming over Habana Vieja, on the north side of the harbor channel, the rugged cliff face is dominated by two great fortresses that constitute **Parque Histórico Militar Morro-Cabaña** (Morro-La Cabaña Historical Military Park, Carretera de la Cabaña, Habana del Este, tel. 07/862-4095). Together, the castles comprise the largest and most powerful defensive complex built by the Spanish in the Americas.

Visitors arriving by car reach the complex via the harbor tunnel (no pedestrians or motorcycles without sidecars are allowed) that descends beneath the Monumento al General Máximo Gómez off Avenida de Céspedes. Buses from Parque de la Fraternidad pass through the tunnel and stop by the fortress access road.

CASTILLO DE LOS TRES REYES DEL MORRO

The **Castillo de Los Tres Reyes del Morro** (Castle of the Three Kings of the Headland, tel. 07/863-7941, daily 8am-7pm, entrance CUC6, children under 12 free, guide CUC1) is built into the rocky palisades of Punta Barlovento at the entrance to Havana's narrow harbor channel. The fort—designed by Italian engineer Bautista Antonelli and initiated in 1589—forms an irregular polygon that follows the contours of the headland, with a sharp-angled bastion at the apex, stone walls 10 feet thick, and a series of batteries stepping down to the shore. Slaves toiled under the lash of whip and sun to cut the stone in situ, extracted from the void that forms the moats. El Morro took 40 years to complete and served its job well, repelling countless pirate attacks and withstanding for 44 days a siege by British cannons in 1762.

Enter via a drawbridge across a deep moat, leading through the **Túnel Aspillerado** (Tunnel of Loopholes) to vast wooden gates that open to the **Camino de Rondas,** a small parade ground (Plaza de Armas) containing a two-story building atop water cisterns that supplied the garrison of 1,000 men. To the right of the plaza, a narrow entrance leads to the **Baluarte de Austria** (Austrian Bastion), with cannon embrasures for firing down on the moat.

To the left of the Plaza de Armas, the **Sala de Historia del Faro y Castillo** profiles the various lighthouses and castles in Cuba. Beyond is the **Surtida de los Tinajones,** where giant earthenware vases are inset in stone. They once contained rapeseed oil as lantern fuel for the 25-meter-tall **Faro del Morro** (daily 10am-noon and 2pm-7pm, CUC2 extra), a lighthouse constructed in 1844. Today an electric lantern still flashes twice every 15 seconds. You can climb to the top for a bird's-eye view.

All maritime traffic in and out of Havana harbor is controlled from the **Estación Semafórica,** the semaphore station atop the castle, accessed via the Baluarte de Tejeda. Below the castle, facing the city on the landward side and reached by a cobbled ramp, is the **Batería de los Doce Apóstoles** (Battery of the Twelve Apostles). It boasts massive cannons and El Polvorín (The Powderhouse) bar.

FORTALEZA DE SAN CARLOS DE LA CABAÑA

The massive **Fortaleza de San Carlos de la Cabaña** (Saint Charles of the Flock Fortress, Carretera de la Cabaña, tel. 07/862-4095, daily 10am-10pm, entrance CUC6 adults, children under 12 free, CUC8 for the *cañonazo* ceremony, guide CUC1), half a kilometer east of the Morro, enjoys a fantastic strategic

position overlooking the city and harbor. It is the largest fort in the Americas, covering 10 hectares and stretching 700 meters in length. It was built 1763-1774 following the English invasion, and cost the staggering sum of 14 million pesos—when told the cost, the king after whom it is named reached for a telescope; surely, he said, it must be large enough to see from Madrid. The castle counted some 120 bronze cannons and mortars, plus a permanent garrison of 1,300 men. While never actually used in battle, it has been claimed that its dissuasive presence won all potential battles—a tribute to the French designer and engineer entrusted with its conception and construction.

From the north, you pass through two defensive structures before reaching the monumental baroque portal flanked by great columns with a pediment etched with the escutcheon of Kings Charles III, followed by a massive drawbridge over a 12-meter-deep moat, one of several moats carved from solid rock and separating individual fortress components.

Beyond the entrance gate a paved alley leads to the **Plaza de Armas,** centered on a grassy, tree-shaded park fronted by a 400-meter-long curtain wall: **La Cortina** runs the length of the castle on its south side and formed the main gun position overlooking Havana. It is lined with cannons. The *Ceremonía del Cañonazo* (cannon-firing ceremony, CUC6) is held nightly at 8:30pm, when troops dressed in 18th-century military garb and led by fife and drum light the fuse of a cannon to announce the closing of the city gates, maintaining a tradition going back centuries. The soldiers prepare the cannon with ramrod and live charge. When the soldier puts the torch to the cannon at 9pm, you have about three seconds before the thunderous boom. It's all over in a millisecond, and the troops march away. Opening to the plaza is a small **chapel** with a baroque facade and charming vaulted interior. The building opposite served as the headquarters for Che Guevara following the Triunfo del Revolución, when he oversaw the

Parque Histórico Militar Morro-Cabaña

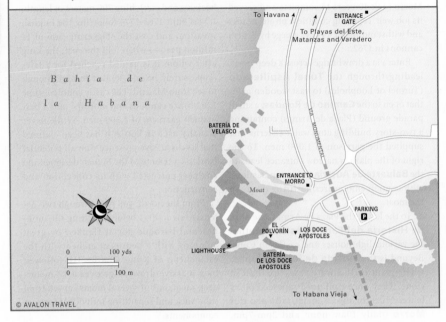

Bahía de la Habana

BATERÍA DE VELASCO

To Havana

ENTRANCE GATE

To Playas del Este, Matanzas and Varadero

VÍA MONUMENTAL

ENTRANCE TO MORRO

Moat

PARKING

EL POLVORÍN

LOS DOCE APÓSTOLES

LIGHTHOUSE

BATERÍA DE LOS DOCE APÓSTOLES

0   100 yds
0   100 m

To Habana Vieja

© AVALON TRAVEL

tribunals for "crimes against the security of the state."

Facing the plaza on its north side is the **Museo de Fortificaciones y Armas.** The museum (set in thick-walled, vaulted storage rooms, or *bovedas*) traces the castle's development and features uniforms and weaponry from the colonial epoch, including a representation of a former prison cell, plus suits of armor and weaponry that span the ancient Arab and Asian worlds and stretch back through medieval times to the Roman era.

A portal here leads into a garden—**Patio de los Jagüeyes**—that once served as a *cortadura,* a defensive element packed with explosives that could be ignited to foil the enemy's attempts to gain entry. The *bovedas* open to the north to cobbled **Calle de la Marina,** where converted barracks, armaments stores, and prisoners' cells now contain restaurants and the **Casa del Tabaco y Ron,** displaying the world's longest cigar (11 meters long).

Midway down Marina, a gate leads down to **El Foso de los Laureles,** a massive moat containing the execution wall where nationalist sympathizers were shot during the wars of independence. Following the Revolution, scores of Batista supporters and "counterrevolutionaries" met a similar fate.

ÁREA DEPÓSITO CRISIS DE OCTUBRE

Displayed atop the **San Julián Revellín** moat, on the north side of Fortaleza de San Carlos, are missiles and armaments from the Cuban Missile Crisis (called the October 1962 Crisis by Cubans). These include an SS-4 nuclear missile; English-language panels explain that it had a range of 2,100 kilometers and a one-megaton load. It was one of 36 such missiles installed at the time. Also here are a MiG fighter jet, various antiaircraft guns, and the remains of the U-2 piloted by Major Rudolf Anderson shot down over Cuba on October 27, 1962. You can view them from the road but it costs CUC1 to get up close and personal.

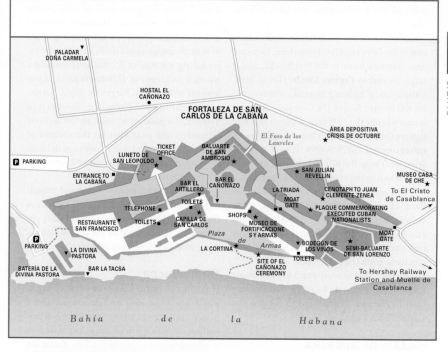

ESTATUA CRISTO DE LA HABANA

The **Estatua Cristo de la Habana** (Havana Christ Statue, Carretera del Asilo, daily 9am-8pm, entrance CUC1, children under 12 free) looms over Casablanca, dominating the cliff face immediately east of the *fortaleza*. The 15-meter-tall statue, unveiled on December 25, 1958, was hewn from Italian Carrara marble by Cuban sculptor Jilma Madera. From the *mirador* surrounding the statue, you have a bird's-eye view of the harbor. It is possible, with the sun gilding the waters, to imagine great galleons slipping in and out of the harbor laden with treasure en route to Spain.

The adjoining **Casa-Museo del Che** (tel. 07/866-4747, daily 9am-7pm, entrance CUC6, guide CUC1) is where Che Guevara lived immediately following the fall of Batista. Today it displays his M-1 rifle, submachine gun, radio, and rucksack, among other exhibits.

A ferry (10 centavos) runs to Casablanca every 20 minutes or so from the Emboque de Luz (Av. del Puerto y Calle Luz) in Habana Vieja. You can walk uphill from Casablanca.

Regla

Regla, a working-class barrio on the eastern shore of Havana harbor, evolved in the 16th century as a fishing village and eventually became Havana's foremost warehousing and slaving center. It developed into a smugglers' port in colonial days. Havana's main electricity-generating plant and petrochemical works are here, pouring bilious plumes over town.

Regla is a center of Santería; note the tiny shrines outside many houses. Calle Calixto García has many fine examples. Many *babalawos* (Santería priests) live here and will happily dispense advice for a fee.

The **Museo Municipal de Regla** (Martí #158, e/ Facciolo y La Piedra, tel. 07/797-6989, Tues.-Sat. 9am-8:45pm, Sun. 1pm-8:45pm, entrance CUC2, guide CUC1), two blocks east of the harborfront, tells the tale of the town's Santería associations. Other displays include colonial-era swords, slave shackles, and the like.

Calle Martí, the main street, leads southeast to the city cemetery; from there, turn east onto Avenida Rosario for two blocks, where steps ascend to **Colina Lenin** (Lenin Hill, Calle Vieja, e/ Enlase y Rosaria). A three-meter-tall bronze face of the Communist leader is carved into the cliff face; a dozen life-size figures (in cement) cheer him from below. A **museum** (tel. 07/797-6899, Tues.-Sat. 9am-5pm, free) atop the hill is dedicated to Lenin and various martyrs of the Cuban Revolution.

The Colina is more directly reached from Parque Guaycanamar (Calle Martí, six blocks east of the harborfront) via Calle Albuquerque and 24 de Febrero; you'll reach a metal staircase that leads to the park. Bus #29 will take you there from the Regla dock.

Ferries (10 centavos) run between Regla and the Emboque de Luz (Av. San Pedro y Luz) in Habana Vieja. Bus P15 departs the Capitolio for Regla.

IGLESIA DE NUESTRA SEÑORA DE REGLA

The **Iglesia de Nuestra Señora de Regla** (Church of Our Lady of Regla, Sanctuario #11, e/ Máximo Gómez y Litoral, tel. 07/797-6228,

daily 7:30am-5:30pm), built in 1810 on the harborfront, is one of Havana's loveliest churches, highlighted by a gilt altar. Figurines of miscellaneous saints dwell in wall alcoves, including a statue of St. Anthony leading a wooden suckling pig. *Habaneros* flock to pay homage to the black Virgen de Regla, patron saint of sailors and Catholic counterpart to Yemayá, the goddess of water in the Santería religion. Time your visit for the seventh of each month, when large masses are held, or for a pilgrimage each September 7, when the Virgin is paraded through town.

Outside, 20 meters to the east and presiding over her own private chapel, is a statue of the Virgen de la Caridad del Cobre, Cuba's patron saint. Syncretized as the *orisha* Ochún, she also draws adherents of Santería.

Guanabacoa

Guanabacoa, three kilometers east of Regla, was founded in 1607 and developed as the major trading center for slaves. An Afro-Cuban culture evolved here, expressed in a strong musical heritage. The **Casa de la Trova** (Martí #111, e/ San Antonio y Versalles, tel. 07/797-7687, hours vary, entrance one peso) hosts performances of Afro-Cuban music and dance, as does **Centro**

Castillo de los Tres Reyes del Morro

Regla and Guanabacoa

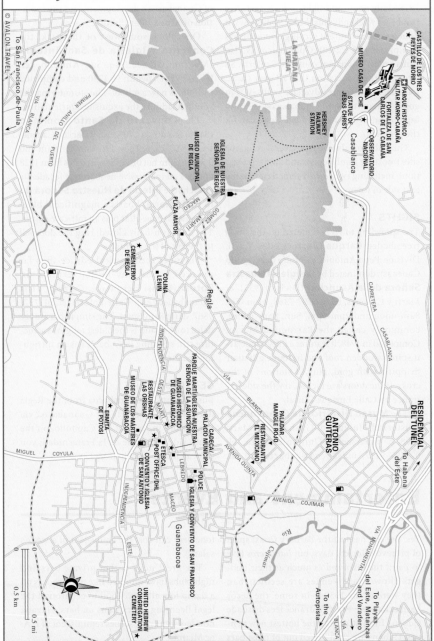

© AVALON TRAVEL

To San Francisco de Paula

PRIMER ANILLO
VIA BLANCA
DEL PUERTO

LA HABANA VIEJA

CASTILLO DE LOS TRES REYES DEL MORRO
PARQUE HISTÓRICO MILITAR MORRO-CABAÑA
FORTALEZA DE SAN CARLOS DE LA CABAÑA
MUSEO CASA DEL CHE
STATUE OF JESÚS CHRIST
OBSERVATORIO NACIONAL

Casablanca

HERSHEY RAILWAY STATION

MUSEO MUNICIPAL DE REGLA
IGLESIA DE NUESTRA SEÑORA DE REGLA
PLAZA MAYOR

MACEO
MARTÍ
GÓMEZ

CARRETERA CASABLANCA

Regla

CEMENTERIO DE REGLA
COLINA LENIN

RESIDENCIAL DEL TÚNEL

To Habana del Este

INDEPENDENCIA
OESTE
MARTÍ

VÍA BLANCA

PARQUE MARTÍ/IGLESIA SEÑORA DE LA ASUNCIÓN
MUSEO HISTÓRICO DE GUANABACOA
CADECA/PALACIO MUNICIPAL
RESTAURANTE LAS ORISHAS
MUSEO DE LOS ORISHAS
MUSEO DE LOS MÁRTIRES DE GUANABACOA
ERMITA DE POTOSÍ

PALADAR MANGLE ROJO
RESTAURANTE EL MEXICANO

ANTONIO GUITERAS

AVENIDA QUINTA

ETESCA
POST OFFICE/DHL
CONVENTO Y IGLESIA DE SAN ANTONIO

LEBREDO
POLICE
IGLESIA Y CONVENTO DE SAN FRANCISCO

MIGUEL COYULA

INDEPENDENCIA
ESTE
MACEO

AVENIDA COJÍMAR

Río Cojímar

Guanabacoa

UNITED HEBREW CONGREGATION CEMETERY

VÍA MONUMENTAL

To Playas del Este, Matanzas and Varadero

To the Autopista

VÍA BLANCA

0   0.5 km
0   0.5 mi

Cultural Recreativo Los Orishas (Calle Martí, e/ Lamas y Cruz Verde, tel. 07/794-7878, daily noon-midnight), which hosts live rumba on weekends plus Friday 9pm shows; it doubles as a restaurant serving *criolla* dishes and pizzas (CUC2-10). Guanabacoa is also Cuba's most important center of Santería. So strong is the association that all over Cuba, folks facing extreme adversity will say "I'm going to have to go to Guanabacoa," implying that only the power of a *babalawo* can fix the problem.

Guanabacoa also boasts several religious sites (most are tumbledown and await restoration), including two Jewish cemeteries on the east side of town.

SIGHTS

The sprawling town is centered on the small tree-shaded **Parque Martí** (Calles Martí, División Pepe Antonio, y Adolfo del Castillo Cadenas), dominated by the **Iglesia Nuestra Señora de la Asunción** (División #331, e/ Martí y Cadenas, tel. 07/797-7368, Mon.-Fri. 8am-noon and 2pm-5pm, Sun. 8am-11am), commonly called the Parroquial Mayor. Completed in 1748, it features a lofty Mudejar-inspired wooden roof and baroque gilt altar dripping with gold, plus 14 stations of the cross. If the doors are locked, try the side entrance on Calle Enrique Güiral.

The **Museo Histórico de Guanabacoa** (Historical Museum of Guanabacoa, Martí #108, e/ Valenzuela y Quintín Bandera, tel. 07/797-9117, musgbcoa@cubarte.cult.cu, Tues.-Sat. 9:30am-5:30pm, entrance CUC2, guide CUC1), one block west of the plaza, tells of Guanabacoa's development and the evolution of Afro-Cuban culture.

One block southwest of the park, the **Convento y Iglesia de San Antonio** (Máximo Gómez, esq. San Antonio, tel. 07/797-7241), begun in 1720 and completed in 1806, is now a school. The *custodio* may let you in to admire the exquisite *alfarje* ceiling.

The **Convento de Santo Domingo** (Santo Domingo #407, esq. Rafael de Cadena, tel. 07/797-7376, Tues.-Fri. 9am-11:30am and 3:30pm-5pm but often closed) dates from 1728 and has an impressive neobaroque facade. Its church, the **Iglesia de Nuestra Señora de la Candelaria,** boasts a magnificent blue-and-gilt baroque altar plus an intricate *alfarje*. The door is usually closed; ring the doorbell to the left of the entrance.

The only ecclesiastical edifice thus far restored is the tiny hilltop **Ermita de Potosí** (Potosí Hermitage, Calzada Vieja Guanabacoa, esq. Calle Potosí, tel. 07/797-9867, daily 8am-5pm). The simple hermitage dates to 1644 and is the oldest religious structure still standing in Cuba. It has an intriguing cemetery.

GETTING THERE

Bus #29 runs to Guanabacoa from the Regla dock. Bus P15 departs for Guanabacoa via Regla from in front of the Capitolio, on the south side of Parque de la Fraternidad; you can catch it in Vedado from G y 23.

Entertainment and Events

Yes, the city has lost the Barbary Coast spirit of prerevolutionary days, but *habaneros* love to paint the town red as much as their budgets allow. Many venues are seedier than they were in the 1950s—in some, the decor hasn't changed. Pricey entrance fees dissuade Cubans from attending the hottest new venues. Cubans are even priced out of most bars (one beer can cost the equivalent of a week's salary).

The great news is that private bars and nightclubs have sprouted like mushrooms on a damp log; all serve food to get around the legal licensing restrictions on bars. Havana now has some chic scenes reminiscent of L.A. or Miami.

For theater, classical concerts, and other live performances it's difficult to make a reservation by telephone. Instead, go to the venue and buy a ticket in advance or just before the performance. Call ahead to double-check dates, times, and venue.

Cartelera, a cultural magazine for tourists published monthly by Artex, has information on exhibitions, galleries, performances, and more. A fantastic Internet source is **La Habana** (www.lahabana.com), which publishes a monthly update of live concerts and other cultural events nationwide. **Havana Club** (www.havana-cultura.com) maintains a pretty cool website with hip profiles on cultural events. And both **Suena Cubano** (www.suenacubano.com) and **Vistar** (www.vistarmagazine.com), two Cuban start-ups, also have up-to-date listings of events.

Radio Taíno (1290 AM and 93.3 FM, daily 5pm-7pm) serves tourists with information on cultural happenings via nightly broadcasts.

Since so many young Cubans lack money for bars and clubs, thousands hang out on the Malecón (principally between Calle 23 and Calle 0) and along Avenida de los Presidentes (Calle G) on weekend nights. The latter chiefly draws *frikis* (Goths and punks), *roqueros,* and what Julia Cooke calls "a genealogical map of youth culture," who mill around sharing beer or rum and listening to music played on cell phones.

NIGHTLIFE
Bars and Lounges
HABANA VIEJA

Every tourist in town wants to sip a *mojito* at **La Bodeguita del Medio** (Empedrado #207, e/ Cuba y Tacón, tel. 07/867-1374, daily 10am-midnight). Go for the ambience, aided by troubadours, rather than the drinks: The *mojitos* are weak, perhaps explaining why Hemingway didn't sup here, contrary to legend. Instead, Hemingway preferred to tipple his mojitos at the **Dos Hermanos** (Av. San Pedro #304, esq. Sol, tel. 07/861-3514, 11am-11pm), a refurbished wharf-front saloon where he bent elbows with sailors and

prostitutes at the long wooden bar. Tourists and a sprinkling of locals are today's clientele, but the mojitos are consistently good (CUC4). There's often live music.

Hemingway enjoyed his sugarless *papa doble* daiquiri (double shot of rum) at **El Floridita** (Obispo, esq. Monserrate, tel. 07/867-1301, bar open daily 11:30am-midnight). It may not quite live up to its 1950s aura, when *Esquire* magazine named it one of the great bars of the world, but to visit Havana without sipping a daiquiri here would be like visiting France without tasting wine. It gets packed; the only Cubans are the musicians and waitstaff.

Now that the de rigueur tourist bars have been addressed, find the real fun at the bi-level **O'Reilly 304** (Calle O'Reilly #304, e/ Habana y Aguiar, tel. 5264-4725, oreilly304@gmail.com, daily noon-midnight), one of the hippest and trendiest spots in town. Most folks come to dine, but you can hang at the bar and sample the mango daiquiri and killer watermelon mojitos while grooving to hip music played by a live band on the stairwell. Get there early for a seat.

Privately run, **Lamparilla Tapas y Cerveza** (Calle Lamparilla #361 e/ Aguacate y Villegas, tel. 5289-5324, daily 11:30am-11:30pm) is a chill place to hang, listen to cool sounds, and savor beer and tapas such as fish *croquetas* and *adobo* pork chops with zucchini tempura. Bare brick walls are festooned with hip art, and the eclectic furnishings add a note of the bohemian.

For chic, try **Sloppy Joe's** (Animas, esq. Zulueta, tel. 07/866-7157, daily noon-2am). This once-legendary bar—founded in 1918 by José Abel, who turned a dilapidated and messy grocery store into "Sloppy Joe's"—reopened in 2013 after decades in ruins. It's been remade as it was, with glossy wood paneling and a long mahogany bar with tall barstools and flat-screen TVs. The Sloppy Joe house drink is made of brandy, Cointreau, port, and pineapple juice (CUC5).

Just around the corner is the trendy **Bar Asturias** (Prado #309 esq. Virtudes, tel.

07/864-1447, 10pm-2am), a cool and colorful club to the rear of the ground floor of the Sociedad Cultural Asturiana. Go for the late-night jazz, jam sessions, and boleros.

Beer lovers should head to Plaza Vieja, where the Viennese-style brewpub **Factoría Plaza Vieja** (San Ignacio #364, tel. 07/866-4453, daily 11am-1am) produces delicious Pilsen (light) and Munich (dark) beer. You can order half liters (CUC2), liters, or a whopping three-liter *dispensa,* a tall glass cylinder fitted with a tap and with beer kept chilled by a thin center tube filled with ice.

The penny-pinching *farandula* (in-crowd) heads to **Bar La Chanchullero** (Brasil, e/ Berraza y Cristo, tel. 07/861-0915, www.el-chanchullero.com, daily 1pm-midnight), a cool and down-to-earth hole-in-the-wall on Plaza del Cristo.

CENTRO HABANA

The suave, state-run **Adagio Barconcert** (Paseo de Martí esq. Neptuno, tel. 07/861-6575, daily 2pm-2am, no cover) combines chic styling with awesome classical music (think Andrea Boccelli), bolero, and jazz, including live performances.

Bohemian, eclectic, and offbeat sum up **Sia Kara** (Calle Industria #502 esq. Barcelona, tel. 07/867-4084, daily 1pm-2am), one of Havana's coolest bars. The brainchild of Cuban ballet dancer José Manuel Carreño and his partner, French-born artist Mateo Royar, it's a true artsy hangout, popular with locals (including Havana's cultural elite) who settle in on well-stuffed sofas and canoodle in the loft-style lounge. Tucked away behind the Capitolio, it's off the tourist radar, but not for long. It serves simple dishes (CUC5) and a full range of cocktails (CUC2.50), but the wine list is feeble. The mojitos are superb, as is the caipiroska—a caipirinha made of vodka.

To find out what happened to the Soviet influence, head to **Nazdarovie** (Malecón #24, e/ Prado y Carcel, tel. 07/860-2947, daily noon-midnight), located upstairs in a townhouse manse overlooking the Atlantic. You'll be greeted by a comrade in Soviet military cap. It's mainly a restaurant serving Slavic-inspired fare, but the bar adds a Russian twist to their cocktails.

For rumba, trova, and even jazz, join the locals at cubbyhole **El Jelengue de Areito** (Calle San Miguel #410, e/ Campanario y Lealtad, no tel). Friday nights are best.

VEDADO AND PLAZA DE LA REVOLUCIÓN

The Hotel Nacional's patio **Bar La Terraza** is a great place to laze in a rattan sofa chair with a cigar and cocktail while musicians entertain with live music. For superb sweeping views of the city, try the **Salón Turquino** (25th floor inside Hotel Habana Libre Tryp, Calle L, e/ 23 y 25, tel. 07/834-6100), or **La Torre** (Calle 17 #55, e/ M y N, tel. 07/838-3088), atop the Focsa building.

At **Esencia Habana** (Calle B #153, e/ Calzada y Línea, tel. 07/836-3031, www.esenciahabana.com, 1pm-3am), owner Juan (a Spaniard) and his Cuban partner have conjured a colonial-style mansion into a classic Cuban bar with quasi-European pretension. It's hugely popular with expats, perhaps because it feels slightly like an English pub. Go for happy hour Friday 5pm-8pm, and for tapas such as carpaccio (CUC6.50) and garlic shrimp (CUC5), best enjoyed on the patio terrace. Three blocks north, the **Corner Café** (Av. 1ra, esq. B, tel. 07/837-1220, daily 10am-close) has a hipper vibe thanks to DJs and live music.

La farandula (the in-crowd) hangs out atop **El Cocinero** (Calle 26, e/ 11 y 13, tel. 07/832-2355, www.elcocinerohabana.com), a former electricity station and fish warehouse turned open-air lounge club with a chic New York City vibe. Adjoining, the **Fábrica de Arte** (Calle 13 #61, esq. 26, tel. 07/838-2260, www.fac.cu, Thurs.-Sun. 8pm-3am, CUC2) is undisputably Havana's chicest bohemian nightspot—a complete cultural venue with theater, film, dance, fashion shows, art exhibitions, concerts, and DJ Iván Lejardi's experimental electronic raves. Alas, it's been taken over by the tourist crowd and is a party stop for

Havana's Gay Scene

Gay life in Havana has loosened considerably from the traditional "scene" around hangout street locales and spontaneous private parties, usually featuring a drag show. Today, there are parties, known as *divino* parties or *fiestas de diez pesos,* at private venues that change nightly and are spread by word of mouth (entrance costs 10 pesos or CUC1-2). To find out where tonight's party is, head to the **Malecón,** opposite Fiat Café near the foot of La Rampa.

Discoteca Escaleras al Cielo (Zulueta #658 e/ Gloria y Apodaca, Habana Vieja, tel. 07/861-9198, Fri.-Sat. 10pm-4am) serves the LGBT crowd, with pole-dancing boys (and sometimes one or two token girls) in hot pants.

Havana's first dedicated, openly gay bar is **Humboldt 52** (Calle Humboldt #52 e/ Infanta y Hospitál, Centro Habana, tel. 5330-2898, www.facebook.com/Humboldt52), which features drag shows, karaoke, and disco. It's an odd mix of wrought-iron furnishings with gingham tablecloths beneath a revolving disco ball.

In Vedado, **Cabaret Las Vegas** (Infanta esq. 25, tel. 07/863-7939, daily 10pm-3am, CUC2-3) is popular for its nightly transvestite cabarets.

Aside from clubs, gay-friendly **Casa de Carlos** (Calle 2 #505 altos e/ 21 y 23, Vedado, tel. 07/833-1329 or 5295-4893, www.carlosincuba.com, CUC35-45 low season, CUC45-55 high season) offers accommodations in a beautifully decorated mansion.

visiting VIPs and tour groups. On last visit I had to ask "where are the Cubans?" It's housed in a former olive oil factory and fish warehouse and has multiple bars on two tiers. Drinks are on credit; you pay on check-out.

A great spot to mingle with Cuba's artsy bohemians, **Café Madrigal** (Calle 17 #809, e/ 2 y 4, tel. 07/831-2433, rafa@audiovisuales. icaic.cu, Tues.-Sun. 6pm-2am) is upstairs in the home of filmmaker Rafael Rosales. This is a spot for tapas and a brain-freezingly chilled daiquiri. Movie memorabilia festoons the red-brick walls, alongside art pieces by Rafael's pal Javier Garver. Relax over cocktails (from daiquiris to whiskey sours; CUC3) to laid-back tunes from Maxwell and Marvin Gaye.

For casual music and romantic ambience check out **Bar Bohemio** (Calle 21 #1065, e/ 12 y 14, tel. 07/833-6918, Tues.-Sun. 6pm-midnight, Fri.-Sat. 6pm-4am), housed in a spacious 1940s manse. Former ballet dancers run this private loungelike bar with an L-shaped terrace. Try the Moscow by Tang (a mojito made of vodka, with basil), best enjoyed on the planter-studded patio.

I love the bohemian ambience at **La Casa de la Bombilla Verde** (Calle 11 #905 e/ 6 y 8, tel. 5848-1331, daily noon-midnight), a chic, unpretentious art-filled lounge billed as a "café cultural."

PLAYA (MIRAMAR AND BEYOND)

This district is ground zero for the hip private lounge club craze sweeping Havana. Many clubs are frequented by high-class *jineteras.*

Risqué artwork is a head-twisting constant at **Espacios** (Calle 10 #513, e/ 5ta y 7ta, tel. 07/202-2921, daily 1pm-2am), catering to bohemian types and Havana's young monied crowd with several indoor lounges and an outdoor party space where live *trova* is played. It serves tapas.

Expats consider the Miami-style alfresco lounge bar at **La Fontana** (3ra Av. #305, esq. 46, tel. 07/202-8337, daily noon-2am) a second home for its cool blue-lit chic and great cocktails.

You're forgiven if you think you've landed in South Beach at **Melem** (Av. 1ra e/ 58 y 60, tel. 07/203-0433, 8pm-3am), a chic and classy contemporary take on a cocktail club; it gets in the groove after midnight. It permits smoking.

Drawing monied young Cubans, the Hotel Meliá Habana's chic alfresco **Sport Bar** (3ra Av., e/ 76 y 80, tel. 07/204-8500, Mon.-Fri.

noon-3am and Sat.-Sun. 9am-3am) has a hip vibe, with omnipresent TVs tuned to sports, a DJ, and occasional live music.

Cabarets Espectáculos

CENTRO HABANA AND CERRO

Cabaret Nacional (San Rafael, esq. Prado, tel. 07/863-2361, CUC5), in the dingy basement of the Gran Teatro, has a modest *espectáculo* nightly at 10pm. The campy show is followed by a disco, drawing Cubans on weekends for steamy dancing; ostensibly only couples are admitted.

VEDADO AND PLAZA DE LA REVOLUCIÓN

The most lavish show is the **Cabaret Parisien** (Calle O, esq. 21, tel. 07/836-3564, CUC30), in the Hotel Nacional. The Cubano Cubano show is offered Sunday-Friday at 10pm and is followed by a Latin dance school. The dinner special (CUC50-70) is best avoided. The place is cramped and fills with smoke, and while the show is nowhere near the scale of the Tropicana, it has plenty of color and titillation and allows patrons to avoid the long trek out to the Tropicana.

The **Cabaret Copa Room** (Paseo y Malecón, tel. 07/836-4051, CUC20), in the Hotel Habana Riviera, hosts a cabaret (Wed.-Mon. 10:30pm). The dated venue features the top names in live Cuban music, such as Los Van Van, and is one of Havana's top spots for serious salsa fans.

Catering to a tourist crowd, **Habana Café** (Paseo, e/ 1ra y 3ra, tel. 07/833-3636, ext. 147, nightly 8pm-3am), adjoining the Hotel Meliá Cohiba, offers cabaret at 8:30pm. A vintage Harley-Davidson, two 1950s classic cars, and an airplane suspended from the ceiling add dramatic chic. Entrance is CUC10, but a *consumo mínimo* applies (CUC30 for top bands such as Los Van Van and Charanga Habanera).

PLAYA (MIRAMAR AND BEYOND)

The small yet popular open-air cabaret at **La Cecilia** (5ta Av. #11010, e/ 110 y 112, tel. 07/204-1562, Fri.-Sat. 10pm-3am, Fri. CUC5, Sat. CUC10) has been running for decades. It still draws monied expats and Cuba's youthful hipsters for the disco that follows. Top bands often perform (CUC20-25).

Cuba's catwalk divas strut at **La Maison** (Calle 16 #701, esq. 7ma, Miramar, tel. 07/204-1543, Thurs.-Sun. 10pm, CUC5), renowned for its *desfiles de modas* (fashion shows) and *cabaret espectáculo* in the terrace garden of an elegant old mansion. A piano bar adjoins, and it has weekend matinees.

★ TROPICANA

Cuba's premier Las Vegas-style nightclub is the **Tropicana** (Calle 72 #4504 y Línea del Ferrocarril, Marianao, tel. 07/267-1717, www.cabaret-tropicana.com, nightly 10pm, entrance CUC75/85/95, cameras CUC5, videos CUC15), which has been in continuous operation since New Year's Eve 1939, when it was the most flamboyant nightclub in the world. In its early days, celebrities such as Nat "King" Cole, Josephine Baker, and Carmen Miranda headlined the show, which was so popular that a 50-passenger "Tropicana Special" flew nightly from Miami for an evening of entertainment. Today patrons watch mesmerized as a troupe of showgirls parades down the aisles wearing glowing chandeliers atop their heads, while searchlights sweep over more gaudily feathered showgirls promenade among the floodlit palm trees. The glitzy, high-octane show boasts more than 200 performers, a fabulous orchestra, and astonishing acrobatic feats. The two-hour cabaret takes place in the open-air Salón Bajo Las Estrellas; on rainy nights, it's held in the Salon Arcos de Cristal.

The entrance fee is outrageous, but includes a bottle of rum with cola, a glass of cheap champagne, and a cheap cigar. It's best to book in advance through your hotel tour desk, as the show often sells out. Beware rip-offs by the waiters, who often wait until the end of the show to bill you for any incidentals, then disappear without bringing your change.

Discos and Nightclubs
CENTRO HABANA AND CERRO

One of the city's most popular venues is **Casa de la Música** (Galiano #253, e/ Concordia y Neptuno, tel. 07/860-8296, Tues.-Sun. 10pm-4am, CUC10-20). A modern theater known as "Dos" (for Casa de la Música 2, or *dos*), it fills with a mostly Cuban crowd for some of the hottest salsa bands and dancing in town. It has a live salsa matinee Saturdays at 5pm.

VEDADO AND PLAZA DE LA REVOLUCIÓN

Salón Turquino (Calle L, e/ 23 y 25, tel. 07/834-6100, Fri.-Sat. 10:30pm-3am, CUC10 cover), atop the Hotel Habana Libre, offers a medley of entertainment that varies nightly, followed by salsa dancing. This expensive and chic hot spot has amazing views. The retractable roof opens at midnight for dancing beneath the stars. Top bands often perform.

The **Salón Rojo** (Calle 21, e/ N y O, tel. 07/833-3747, nightly 10pm-4am, CUC10-25), beside the Hotel Capri, hosts Havana's hottest acts, such as Los Van Van and Bandolero. It's perhaps *the* venue for searing salsa.

Check with locals as to when **Casa Fiesta Jardines del 1830** (Malecón y Calle 20, tel. 07/838-3092, Tues.-Sun. 10pm-2am, CUC3 cover) is happening, as this venue comes and goes in popularity. It's located in the gardens of a mansion overlooking the mouth of the Río Almendares and is known for its Friday night "House Party" with *rueda* (wheel), where circles of couples dance in concert then on cue switch partners.

Despite its lackluster setting, Cubans flock to the **Café Cantante** (Paseo, esq. 39, tel. 07/878-4273, Tues.-Sat. 8pm-3am, CUC10) in the basement of the Teatro Nacional. No hats, T-shirts, or shorts are permitted for men. The plusher **Piano Bar Delirio Habanero** (tel. 07/878-4275), on the third floor, has Saturday afternoon *peñas* (4pm) and live music (Thurs.-Fri. 10pm, CUC5). The mood is similar at the **Café Teatro Bertolt Brecht** (Calle 13, esq. I, tel. 07/832-9359), a sleek low-ceilinged, non-smoking venue that draws a young crowd.

Getting better all the time, **Submarino Amarillo** (Yellow Submarine, Calle 17 esq. Calle 6, tel. 07/830-6808, Mon. 9am-2am, Tues.-Sat. 1pm-7:30pm and 9pm-2am, CUC2 cover), on the corner of Parque Lennon, thrills Beatles fans. The decor plays up the Beatles theme, while live bands perform Fab Four tunes amid Cuban rock. It has weekend matinees at 2pm.

Sarao's Bar (Calle 17, esq. E, tel.

Tropicana

Learn to Salsa

For one-on-one salsa lessons I recommend **Mairym Cuesta** (Calle Estrella #364, e/ Escobar y Lealtad, tel. 07/862-5720, mirianvc@infomed.sld.cu); **Asmara Nuñez** (tel. 5293-0862)—who used to perform as a Tropicana dancer—and her partner, **Yoel Letan Peña**; or **La Casa del Són** (Edpredado #411, e/ Aguacate y Villegas, Habana Vieja), which also teaches *rueda de casino* and rumba. **Club Salseando Chévere** (Calle 49 y Av. 28, Kohly, tel. 07/204-4990, www.salseandochevere.com) offers intensive classes.

07/832-0433 or 5263-8037, daily noon-3am) epitomizes the emerging hip new Cuba, drawing the likes of Usher and Katy Perry to high-octane parties with a South Beach state of mind. This slickly designed venue is the brainchild of several techno DJs and hip-hop artists. With its modern motif and gorgeous staff, this neon-lit nightclub is *the* hot spot for the monied young.

KingBar (Calle 23 #667, e/ D y E, tel. 07/833-0556, daily 5pm-3am) is a homier version of Sarao's, with a pumped-up party scene and occasional live music (from hip hop to electronica). Smooth retro soul and R&B tunes are staples in the garden space decorated with erotic art. The club is hidden away to the rear of a large white mansion and doubles as an open-air restaurant with a charcoal grill.

PLAYA (MIRAMAR AND BEYOND)

Long considered a top salsa venue by monied locals, **Casa de la Música** (Av. 25, esq. 20, tel. 07/204-0447, Wed.-Sun. 5pm-9pm and 10pm-3am, CUC10-20) has sizzling-hot afternoon salsa sessions as well as nightly (Tues.-Sun.) salsa and reggaeton performances by such legends as Alexander Abreu, Bamboleo, and NG La Banda. The headliner normally doesn't come on until 1am. Above the Casa is **Disco Tun Tún Piano Bar** (Tues.-Sun. 11pm-6am, CUC10), which keeps in the groove until dawn.

While I don't get its appeal, **Don Cangrejo** (1ra Av., e/ 16 y 18, tel. 07/204-4169, daily noon-midnight, entrance CUC5-20) is the unlikely Friday and Saturday night hot spot for the Havana elite. The restaurant's open-air

oceanfront pool complex hosts live music by some of Cuba's top performers (such as Buena Fe and Kelvis Ochoa).

The privately owned, neon-lit **Sangri-La** (Calle 42, esq. 21, Playa, tel. 5264-8343, daily noon-3am) is a chic lounge club with kick-ass cocktails, white leather banquettes, and flat-screen TVs showing music videos. A small dance floor is tucked in one corner, but after midnight everyone dances wherever. Get there early on weekends to get in.

Cubans find their fun at **Teatro Karl Marx** (1ra Av., e/ 8 y 10, tel. 07/203-0801, Fri.-Sun. 9pm-2am, CUC10-20), Cuba's largest theater. Buena Fe, Isaac Delgado, and other big names play here. The vast theater also plays host to many of the city's gala events.

Farther out, **Salón Rosado Benny Moré** (Av. 41, esq. 48, tel. 07/203-5322, Fri.-Mon. 7pm-2am for live groups, Tues.-Wed. for cabaret, CUC5-10) is a basic open-air concert arena better known as El Tropical. It's immensely popular on weekends when top-billed Cuban salsa bands perform. Drawing a relatively impecunious crowd, it features killer music and salacious dancing. Rum-induced fights do break out; it's best to go with a Cuban friend.

Traditional Music

HABANA VIEJA

The **Asociación Cultural Yoruba de Cuba** (Prado #615, e/ Dragones y Monte, tel. 07/863-5953) hosts the Peña de Obini Bata with traditional Afro-Cuban music and dance (Fri. 6pm-8pm), plus cultural activities (Sat. 6pm-8pm, Sun. 9am-1pm, CUC5).

Watch for **Gigantería Teatro Callejero,** a group of performing street artists who dress as outlandish living statues. The principal group strolls the streets and plazas on stilts; their coming is announced by wailing of cornets and beating of drums, like an ancient *cabildo.*

The Afro-Cuban All Stars pack in the tourist crowds at **Sociedad Cultural Rosalia de Castro** (Egido #504 e/ Monte y Dragones, tel. 5270-5271, daily 9:30am-11:30pm) for "Gran Concierto Buena Vista Social Club" nightly shows by old Cuban legends from the Buena Vista Social Club era (CUC30 including dinner). And Buena Vista Social Club-era crooners entertain the tour groups at **Café Taberna** (Mercaderes #531, esq. Brasil, tel. 07/861-1637, daily 9:30am-11pm, CUC25), on the northeast side of Plaza Vieja.

CENTRO HABANA AND CERRO

The place to be on Sunday is **Rumba del "Salvador's Alley"** (Callejón de Hamel, e/ Aramburo y Hospital, tel. 07/878-1661, eliasasef@yahoo.es), with Afro-Cuban music and dance (Sun. noon-3pm) and traditional music (9pm last Friday of each month).

VEDADO AND PLAZA DE LA REVOLUCIÓN

Decades old and still going strong, the cramped and moody 1950s-style **Café Concierto Gato Tuerto** (Calle O #14, e/ 17 y 19, tel. 07/838-2696, 10pm-4am, CUC5 cover) nightclub hosts *música filin, trova,* and *bolero* nightly. It gets packed with patrons jammed cheek-to-jowl against the postage stamp-size stage tucked into a corner. I've been hanging out here for two decades and it hasn't lost its edge.

The **Salón 1930** (in the Hotel Nacional, Calle O y 21, tel. 07/836-3663) hosts traditional Buena Vista Social Club-style shows (Tues. and Sun. 9:30pm, CUC25 cover). **El Hurón Azul** (UNEAC, Calle 17 #351, esq. H, tel. 07/832-4551, www.uneac.org.cu, daily 5pm-2am) hosts themed *peñas* (social gatherings) on Wednesday at 5pm (CUC5); the

music varies weekly. This is ground zero for intellectual life in Havana.

The acclaimed **Conjunto Folklórico Nacional** (National Folklore Dance Group, Calle 4 #103, e/ Calzada y 5ta, tel. 07/833-4560, www.folkcuba.cult.cu, CUC5) performs *sábado de rumba* (Saturday rumba) alfresco each Saturday at 3pm. This is Afro-Cuban music and dance at its best.

Who'd have thought a spa would host *trova?* If you dig Cuban ballads, or jazz, visit **O2 Spa & Jardín** (Calle 26 #5 esq. 26B, Nuevo Vedado, tel. 07/883-1663, www.o2habana.com), where top artistes such as Frank Delgado, Abdón Alcarez, and Luna Manzanares perform. Check out the calendar; reservations are essential.

Jazz
HABANA VIEJA

A key jazz venue, **Bar Chico O'Farrill** (Cuba #102, esq. Chacón, tel. 07/860-5080), in the Hotel Palacio O'Farrill, hosts Cuba's top performers Friday-Sunday evenings.

VEDADO AND PLAZA DE LA REVOLUCIÓN

The **Jazz Café** (1ra at the base of Paseo, tel. 07/838-3302, daily 10pm-2am, CUC10 *consumo mínimo*), on the third floor of the Galería del Paseo, is a classy supper club with some of the best live jazz in town, including resident maestro Chucho Valdés. Get there early to snag a seat. In 2015, Cuban jazz musician Lazarito Valdés (leader of the popular band Bamboleo) opened the nonsmoking **Valdés Jazz Club** (Calle E #105, e/ 5ta y Calzada, tel. 07/830-5898, valdesjazz@gmail.com), which features a bar, restaurant, and patio. The all-white decor is a bit cold, but the vibe is hot. Local maestros Bobby Carcassés and Maraca are regulars.

An incongruous red London phone booth serves as the entrance to **La Zorra y el Cuervo** (Calle 23, e/ N y O, tel. 07/833-2402, 10pm-2am, CUC10 including two drinks), a dreary, cramped basement setting (supposedly nonsmoking, but don't count on it) where

Cuban greats such as Roberto Fonseca, Alexis Bosch, and saxophonist Michel Herrera perform. It has blues music on Thursdays, plus a Saturday matinee at 2pm.

Richard Egües—grandson of the eponymous Charanga maestro and lead flautist of Orquesta Aragón—keeps his granddad's legacy alive at **La Flauta Mágica** (Calzada #101 e/ L y M, tel. 07/832-3195, noon-4am). The small and intimate restaurant/bar occupies the penthouse suite of a 1950s high-rise overlooking the U.S. Embassy and Malecón. The live jazz can be sensational, and you can lounge on sofas by the rooftop pool.

PLAYA (MIRAMAR AND BEYOND)

A jazz ensemble performs at the **Tocororo** (Calle 18 y 3ra Av., tel. 07/202-2209, Mon.-Sat. noon-midnight) restaurant, where the lively bar is favored by local expats. The über-chic private club **Privé** (Calle 88A #306, e/ 3ra y 3raA, Miramar, tel. 07/209-2719, Tues.-Sun. 5pm-6am) hosts jazz and *nueva trova* greats such as Frank Delgado and has an open bar (CUC10).

The state entity Artex did a great job refurbishing **Café Miramar** (Calle 5ta, esq. 94, tel. 07/204-6244, Tues.-Sun. noon-2am, CUC2-4) as a snazzy jazz venue where you can catch Pacheco, Aldito López Gavilán, and other hot artists. Music kicks in at 10:30pm, plus it has Sunday afternoon jams. The audience can be quite loud.

THE ARTS
Tango and Flamenco
HABANA VIEJA

The Irene Rodríguez Compañía performs amazing flamenco at **Centro Andaluz en Cuba** (Prado #104, e/ Genios y Refugio, tel. 07/5246-8426, www.irenerodriguezcompania.com, free) each Wednesday, Friday, and Saturday at 9pm. Lessons are offered (Tues.-Thurs. 9am-11am, CUC15 per hour).

El Mesón de la Flota (Mercaderes #257, e/ Amargura y Brasil, tel. 07/863-3838, free) hosts high-energy flamenco shows daily 1pm-3pm and 8pm-11pm; you can even watch

through the bars from the street. **Patio Sevillano** at the Hotel Sevilla (Trocadero, esq. Prado, tel. 07/860-9046) has flamenco on Saturday at 9pm. And the renowned **Ballet Lizt Alfonso** (Compostela e/ Luz y Acosta, tel. 07/866-3688, www.liztalfonso.com) offers flamenco classes and courses.

CENTRO HABANA AND CERRO

Caserón del Tango (Neptuno #309, e/ Águila y Italia, tel. 07/863-0097) hosts tango *peñas* on Monday 5pm-7pm, drawing local aficionados in Argentinian-style garb. **Unión Arabe de Cuba** (Prado e/ Animas y Trocadero, tel. 07/861-0582, www.unionarabecuba.org) hosts occasional tango.

MIRAMAR AND PLAYA

Watch for performances by the incomparable **Habana Compas Dance** (Av. 51 #12202 e/ 122 y 124, Marianao, tel. 07/262-8949, habanacompas@cubarte.cult.cu), a troupe that combines Spanish flamenco with Afro-Cuban drumming.

Theater, Classical Music, and Ballet
HABANA VIEJA

The most important theater in Havana is the renovated **Gran Teatro de la Habana Alicia Alonso** (Paseo de Martí #458, e/ San Rafael y San Martín, Habana Vieja, tel. 07/861-3079, CUC25 for best orchestra seats), on the west side of Parque Central. It's the main stage for the acclaimed Ballet Nacional de Cuba and the national opera company. Performances are Thursday-Saturday at 8:30pm and Sunday at 5pm. A dress code applies.

The **Basílica de San Francisco de Asís** (Calle Oficios, e/ Amargura y Brasil, tel. 07/862-9683) hosts classical concerts at 6pm (CUC2-10) most Saturdays and some Thursdays.

Classical and ecclesiastical concerts are also featured in the **Iglesia de San Francisco de Paula** (Av. del Puerto, esq. Leonor Pérez, tel. 07/860-4210, free or CUC5) on Friday at 7pm, and in the **Oratorio San Felipe Neri** (Calle

Aguiar, esq. Obrapía, tel. 07/862-3243) on Thursday at 7pm and Saturday at 4pm.

Check out the program at the **Museo Nacional de Bellas Artes** (tel. 07/863-9484, www.bellasartes.cult.cu), which hosts classical artists on Thursday and Saturday at 7pm (Cuban section, Trocadero e/ Zulueta y Monserrate) and on Saturday at 4pm (international section, San Rafael e/ Zulueta y Monserrate).

For more avant-garde fare, peruse the schedule at Danza-Teatro Retazos, a contemporary troupe that performs at the **Teatro Retazos** (Calle Amargura #61 e/ San Ignacio y Mercaderes, tel. 07/860-4341).

CENTRO HABANA

The **Palacio de Matrimonio** (Prado #306, esq. Ánimas, tel. 07/866-0661, Tues.-Fri. 8am-6pm) hosts live chamber and classical music.

VEDADO AND PLAZA DE LA REVOLUCIÓN

Performances of the Orquesta Sinfónica Nacional de Cuba (National Symphony) and Danza Contemporánea de Cuba are hosted at the **Teatro Nacional** (Av. Carlos M. de Céspedes, esq. Paseo, Vedado, tel. 07/878-5590, www.teatronacional.cu) every Friday-Saturday at 8:30pm and Sunday at 5pm (CUC1.80-8.90).

The **Teatro Mella** (Línea #657, e/ A y B, Vedado, tel. 07/833-8696, box office Tues.-Sun. 2pm-6pm) is noted for contemporary dance, theater, and ballet (CUC5-10), and hosts the Conjunto Folklórico Nacional.

The last Thursday of each month, **UNEAC** (Calle 17 #351, e/ G y H, Vedado, tel. 07/832-4551, www.uneac.org.cu) hosts an open *peña* for chamber musicians at 6pm.

The **Teatro Amadeo Roldán** (Calzada y D, Vedado, tel. 07/832-1168, CUC5-10) hosts the Simfonía Nacional de Cuba and has two *salas*; it features classical concerts year-round. Nearby is the **Teatro Hubert de Blanck** (Calzada #657, e/ A y B, tel. 07/830-1011, CUC5), known for both modern and classical plays. Shows (in Spanish) are usually Friday-Saturday at 8:30pm and Sunday at 5pm.

The 150-seat **Teatro Buendía** (Calle Loma y 38, Nuevo Vedado, tel. 07/881-6689, five pesos), in a converted Greek Orthodox church, hosts performances by the eponymous theater company, considered to be Cuba's most innovative and accomplished. It performs here Friday-Sunday at 8:30pm.

classical concert in Basílica de San Francisco de Asís, Habana Vieja

The Little Beehive

Unforgettable. Endearing. A tear-jerker. That's a performance by **La Colmenita** (tel. 07/860-7699, colmena@cubarte.cult.cu), an amazing children's musical theater group that has charmed audiences worldwide with high-octane repertoires that mix fairy tales and rock and roll with messages of justice and peace.

La Colmenita—the name means "Little Beehive"—was founded as a small community theater in 1994 by TV producer Carlos Alberto Cremata. His dad was the pilot of the Cubana flight 455 passenger airliner downed by a Cuban American terrorist bomb after it took off from Barbados on October 6, 1976. La Colmenita was begun as homage to Alberto's father (a lover of music and theater) to convey a message of love, humanity, and forgiveness. It has since grown into a worldwide cultural phenomenon, spawning more than two dozen similar "beehives" throughout Cuba and the Americas.

UNICEF has adopted La Colmenita as an official goodwill ambassador, working to help protect and promote the rights of, and improve the lives of, children and women worldwide. The productions, such as "Cinderella by the Beatles" and "The Little Roach Called Martina," are their own. Costumes are prepared by the kids' parents. And any child is welcome to join, even those with physical and mental impairments. The ensemble frequently tours the country to share a positive message with disadvantaged communities and children.

It principally performs at the Teatro de la Orden Tres (Obispo esq. Churrusco), in Habana Vieja.

Circuses

Named for a famed, late Cuban clown, Havana's **Circo Trompoloco** (Calle 112, esq. 5ta Av., Miramar, tel. 07/206-5609 or 07/206-5641, www.circonacionaldecuba.cu, Thurs.-Fri. 4pm, Sat.-Sun. 4pm and 7pm, CUC10) is the headquarters of the Circo Nacional de Cuba, which performs beneath a red-and-white-striped "big top."

FESTIVALS AND EVENTS

For a list of forthcoming festivals, conferences, and events, visit www.lahabana.com.

January

The **Cabildos** festival is held on January 6, when Habana Vieja resounds with festivities recalling the days when Afro-Cuban *comparsas* danced through the streets. Contact Agencia de Viajes San Cristóbal (Oficios #110, e/ Lamparilla y Amargura, tel. 07/861-9171).

February

The **Habanos Festival** (tel. 07/204-0510, www.habanos.com) celebrates Cuban cigars.

It opens at the Tropicana with an elegant dinner and auction for big spenders.

The **Feria Internacional del Libro de la Habana** (Havana Book Fair, Calle 15 #602 e/ B y C, Vedado, tel. 07/832-9526, www.filcuba.cult.cu) is held in Fortaleza San Carlos de la Cabaña.

The **Festival Internacional de Tambor** (International Drum Festival, tel. 07/836-5381, www.fiestadeltambor.cult.cu) is held at various venues.

April

The prestigious **Bienal de la Habana** (Havana Biennial, tel. 07/209-6569, www.bienalhabana.cult.cu) features artists from more than 50 countries. It is hosted in even-numbered years by the Centro Wilfredo Lam (Calle San Ignacio #22, tel. 07/861-2096, www.cnap.cult.cu).

May

On May 1, head to the Plaza de la Revolución for the **Primero de Mayo** (May Day Parade) to honor workers. Intended to appear as a spontaneous demonstration of revolutionary loyalty, in reality it is carefully

Cinemas

Most of Havana's cinemas are mid-20th-century gems that have been allowed to deteriorate to the point of near-dilapidation. Movie houses on La Rampa, in Vedado, tend to be less run-down than those in Habana Vieja and Centro Habana. *Granma* and *Cartelera* (a cultural magazine available at many tourist hotels) list what's currently showing.

The **Sala Glauber Rocha** (Av. 212, esq. 31, La Coronela, tel. 07/271-8967, www.cinelatinoamericano.org), in the Fundación del Nuevo Cine Latinoamericano, shows mostly Latin American movies.

The most important cinemas are:

· **Cine Acapulco** (Av. 26, e/ 35 y 37, Vedado, tel. 07/833-9573).

· **Cine Charles Chaplin** (Calle 23 #1155, e/ 10 y 12, Vedado, tel. 07/831-1101).

· **Cine La Rampa** (Calle 23 #111, e/ O y P, Vedado, tel. 07/878-6146) mostly shows Cuban and Latin American films, plus the occasional obscure foreign movie.

· **Cine Payret** (Prado #503, esq. San José, Habana Vieja, tel. 07/863-3163) is Havana's largest cinema and has as many as six showings daily.

· **Cine Riviera** (Calles 23, e/ H y G, Vedado, tel. 07/832-9564).

· **Cine-Teatro Astral** (Calzada de Infanta #501, esq. San Martín, Centro Habana, tel. 07/878-1001) is the comfiest *cine* in Havana. It functions mostly as a theater for political features.

· **Cine Yara** (Calle 23 y Calle L, Vedado, tel. 07/832-9430) is Havana's "main" theater.

· **Multi-Cine Infanta** (Infanta, e/ Neptuno y San Miguel, tel. 07/878-9323) has four up-to-date auditoriums.

choreographed. Stooges use loudspeakers to work up the crowd of 500,000 people with chants of "*¡Viva Fidel!*" and "*¡Viva Raúl!*" Raúl has toned down the anti-United States flavor since taking over.

The **Festival Internacional de Guitarra** (International Guitar Festival and Contest) is held at the Teatro Roldán in even-numbered years.

June

The **Festival Internacional Boleros de Oro** (International Boleros Festival, UNEAC, Calle 17 #354, e/ G y H, Vedado, tel. 07/832-4571, www.uneac.org.cu) features traditional Latin American folk music.

July

The **Coloquio Internacional Hemingway** (International Hemingway Colloquium, tel. 07/691-0809, mushem@cubarte.cult.cu) takes place in early July every odd-numbered year.

August

The amateurish **Carnaval de la Habana** (Carnival in Havana, tel. 07/832-3742) is held the first or second week of August on the Malecón.

September

The 10-day biennial **Festival Habanarte**, sponsored by the Consejo Nacional de Las Artes (National Council of Arts, Calle 4 #257, Miramar, tel. 07/832-4126, www.habanarte.com), is held in odd-numbered years.

October

The **Festival Internacional de Ballet** (International Ballet Festival) features ballet corps from around the world, plus the acclaimed Ballet Nacional de Cuba (BNC, Calzada #510, e/ D y E, Vedado, Ciudad Habana, tel. 07/832-4625, www.balletcuba.cult.cu).

The annual **Festival de la Habana de Música Contemporánea** (Havana Festival of Contemporary Music, c/o UNEAC, Calle 17 #351, e/ G y H, Vedado, tel. 07/832-0194, www.musicacontemporanea.cult.cu) spans a week in early October, with performances ranging from choral to electro-acoustic.

November

Expo Canina (tel. 07/267-3156, cdc@enet.cu) is Havana's answer to the Crufts and Westminster dog shows.

December

The **Festival del Nuevo Cine Latinoamericano** (Festival of New Latin American Cinema, c/o the Instituto de Cinematografía, Calle 23 #1155, Vedado, tel. 07/838-2354, www.habanafilmfestival.com) is one of Cuba's most glittering events, attended by Cuban actors and directors and their Hollywood counterparts. Movies are shown at cinemas across the city, and the festival culminates with Cuba's own version of the Oscars, the Coral prizes. Buy your tickets well before the programming is announced; you can buy a pass (CUC25) good for the duration of the festival.

The star-studded **Festival Internacional de Jazz** (International Havana Jazz Festival, Calle 15, esq. F, Vedado, tel. 07/862-4938) is highlighted by the greats of Cuban jazz, such as Chucho Valdés and Irakere, and Juan Formell and Los Van Van. Concerts are held at various venues.

Shopping

The Cuban government bans the sale and export of antiques. Hence, there are no stores selling antiques to tourists.

ARTS AND CRAFTS
Habana Vieja

The city's largest market is the **Centro Cultural Almacenes de San José** (Av. Desamparados at San Ignacio, tel. 07/864-7793, daily 10am-6pm), on the waterfront side of the Alameda. Also known as the Feria de la Artesanía, it sells everything from little ceramic figurines, miniature bongo drums, and papier-mâché 1950s autos to banana-leaf hats, crocheted bikinis, straw hats, and paintings.

Habana Vieja contains dozens of *expo-ventas* (commercial galleries representing freelance artists) selling original art. They are concentrated along Calle Obispo. Try **Estudio-Taller Ribogerto Mena** (Calle San Ignacio #154 e/ Obispo y Obrapía, tel. 07/867-5884) or **Taller La 6ta Puerta** (Calle Oficios #6 esq. Obispo, tel. 07/860-6866, www.am-ramirez.com), the gallery of Angel Ramírez.

The **Asociación Cubana de Artesana Artistas** (Obispo #411, tel. 07/860-8577, www.acaa.cult.cu, Mon.-Sat. 10am-8pm, Sun. 10am-6pm) represents various artists.

One of the best galleries is **Galería Victor Manuel** (San Ignacio #46, e/ Callejón del Chorro y Empedrado, tel. 07/861-2955, daily 10am-9pm), on the west side of Plaza de la Catedral. Around the corner is the **Taller Experimental de la Gráfica** (Callejón del Chorro, tel. 07/867-7622, tgrafica@cubarte.cult.cu, Mon.-Fri. 9am-4pm), a cooperative that makes and sells exclusive lithographic prints. It's one of the more fascinating places to buy exceptional art.

You can buy handmade Spanish fans (*abanicos*) at the **Casa del Abanicos** (Obrapía #107, e/ Mercaderes y Oficios, tel. 07/863-4452, Mon.-Sat. 10am-7pm and Sun. 10am-1pm).

The **Tienda El Soldadito de Plomo** (Muralla #164, tel. 07/866-0232, Mon.-Fri. 9am-5pm, Sat. 9am-1:30pm) sells miniature lead (!) soldiers, including a 22-piece War of Independence collection, for CUC5.45 apiece.

A large glass window lets you watch artists painting the pieces.

Centro Habana

This area doesn't abound with galleries. Two exceptions are **Galería Galiano** (Galiano #256 e/ Concordia y Neptuno, tel. 07/860-0224, Mon.-Fri. 10am-6pm, Sat. 10am-noon) and **Collage Habana** (San Rafael e/ Consulado y Industria, tel. 07/833-3826, Mon.-Fri. 10am-6pm, Sat. 10am-noon), both with works by top artists and pertaining to the Fondo be Bienes Culturales (www.fcbc.cu).

Vedado and Plaza de la Revolución

Vedado has an **artisans' market** on La Rampa (e/ M y N, daily 8am-6pm). The **Casa de las Américas** (Av. de los Presidentes, esq. 3ra, tel. 07/55-2706, www.casa.cult.cu, Mon.-Fri. 8am-4:45pm) hosts exhibitions with works for sale.

Servando Galería de Arte (Calle 23, esq. 10, tel. 07/830-6150, www.galeriaservando.com) represents some of the top artists in Cuba. The ever-fascinating **El Espacio Aglutinador** (Calle 6 #602 e/ 25 y 27, tel. 07/832-3531) offers avante-garde works.

Playa (Miramar and Beyond)

Two of my favorite art galleries are **Estudio-Galería Flora Fong** (Calle 11 #4212 e/ 42 y 44, Playa, tel. 07/204-9543) and **Lighthouse Studio** (Av. 47 #3430 e/ 34 y 41, Kohly, tel. 07/206-5772, www.kadirlopez.com), displaying the works of Kadir López-Nieves.

For one-of-a-kind prints signed by world-renowned photographer Roberto Salas, head to his **Galería Roberto Salas** (Calle 30 #3709 e/ 37 y 39, tel. 07/206-5213), where he sells iconic images of Cuba during the past 50 years.

A visit to **Casa-Estudio de José Fuster** (Calle 226, esq. Av. 3ra, tel. 07/271-2932 or 5281-5421, www.josefuster.com, daily 9am-5pm) is a *must* while in Havana, regardless of whether you buy or not. The "Picasso of the Caribbean" sells ceramics priced CUC25 and

up, and main art pieces sell from CUC150 into the thousands.

BOOKS

Habana Vieja

The **Instituto Cubano del Libro** (Cuban Book Institute, Obispo, esq. Aguiar, tel. 07/862-8091, Mon.-Fri. 8am-4:30pm) has a bookshop; most books are in Spanish. To the southeast of Plaza de Armas, tucked off Calle Baratillo, is the setting Feria de Publicaciones y Curiosidades.

Librería La Internacional (Obispo #528, Habana Vieja, tel. 07/861-3258, daily 10am-5:30pm) stocks a limited selection of texts in English, plus a small selection of English-language novels. **La Moderna Poesía** (Obispo #527, esq. Bernaza, tel. 07/861-6983, Mon.-Sat. 10am-8pm) is Cuba's largest bookstore, although virtually the entire stock is in Spanish.

La Papelería (O'Reilly #102, esq. Tacón, Habana Vieja, tel. 07/863-4263, Mon.-Sat. 9am-6:30pm), catercorner to the Plaza de Armas, sells pens and other office supplies.

Vedado and Plaza de la Revolución

Librería Fernando Ortíz (Calle L, esq. 27, tel. 07/832-9653, Mon.-Sat. 10am-5:30pm) is your best bet for English-language books. Its meager collection spans a wide range. **Librería Centenario del Apóstol** (Calle 25 #164, e/ Infanta y O, tel. 07/835-0805, daily 9am-9pm) has used texts.

CIGARS AND RUM

Havana has about two dozen official La Casa del Habano cigar stores (daily 9am-5pm). Buy here; if you buy off the street, you're almost certainly going to be sold fakes, even if they look real.

Habana Vieja

The best cigar store is **La Casa del Habano** (Industria #520, e/ Barcelona y Dragones, tel. 07/866-8086, Mon.-Fri. 9am-7pm, Sat. 9am-5pm, Sun. 10am-4pm) in Fábrica de Tabaco

Partagás. It has a massive walk-in humidor, plus a hidden lounge with a narrow humidified walk-in cigar showcase for serious smokers.

My other favorites are **La Casa del Habano** (Mercaderes #202, esq. Lamparilla, tel. 07/862-9682, daily 10:30am-7pm) in the **Hostal Conde de Villanueva** and **Salón Cuba** (Neptuno, e/ Prado y Zulueta, tel. 07/862-9293, daily 8:30am-9:15pm) in the Hotel Iberostar Parque Central. And the **Casa del Ron y Tabaco** (Obispo, e/ Monserrate y Bernaza, tel. 07/866-0911, daily 9am-5pm), above El Floridita, has knowledgeable staff. This store also lets you sample the rums before buying.

Taberna del Galeón (Baratillo, esq. Obispo, tel. 07/866-8476, Mon.-Sat. 9am-6pm, Sun. 9am-5pm), off the southeast corner of Plaza de Armas, is well stocked with rums.

Vedado and Plaza de la Revolución

The **Casa del Habano** stores in the **Hotel Nacional** (Calle O y 21, tel. 07/873-3564), **Hotel Habana Libre Tryp** (Calle L, e/ 23 y 25, tel. 07/834-6100), **Hotel Meliá Cohiba** (Paseo, e/ 1ra y 3ra, tel. 07/833-3636), and **Hotel Habana Riviera** (Malecón y Paseo, tel. 07/836-4051) are well stocked.

Playa (Miramar and Beyond)

Miramar has the best cigar store in town: **La Casa del Habano** (5ta Av., esq. 16, tel. 07/204-7974, Mon.-Sat. 10am-6pm), run by Carlos Robaina, son of the legendary tobacco farmer Alejandro Robaina. It boasts a vast humidor, executive rooms, private lockers, bar and lounge, and good service. Club Habana's **La Casa del Habano** (5ta Av. e/ 188 y 192, tel. 07/275-0366, daily 9am-5pm) is also excellent.

CLOTHING AND SHOES
Habana Vieja

Men seeking a classic *guayabera* shirt should head to the state's **El Quitrín** (Obispo #163, e/ San Ignacio y Mercaderes, tel. 07/862-0810,

daily 9am-5pm) or **Guayabera Habana** (Calle Tacó #20, e/ O'Reilly y Empedrado, Mon.-Sat. 10am-7pm). El Quitrín also sells embroideries and lace for ladies, plus chic blouses and skirts. Most items are Cuban made and of merely average quality. For quality designer *guayaberas,* head to **PiscoLabis** (Calle San Ignacio #75, e/ Callejón del Chorro y O'Reilly, tel. 5843-3219, www.piscolabishabana.com, daily 9:30am-7:30pm). This private cooperative also sells one-of-a-kind sandals, purses, and adornments.

Nearby, **Sombreros Jipi Japa** (Obispo, esq. Compostela, tel. 07/861-5292, Mon.-Fri. 9am-5pm) is the place to go for hats of every shade. **La Habana** (Obispo, e/ Habana y Compostela, tel. 07/861-5292, and Obispo, esq. Aguacate, Mon.-Fri. 9am-5pm) offers a reasonable stock of shoes and leather goods. Designer shoes and handbags are the expensive name of the game at **Zapatería Obrapía** (Obrapía esq. Oficios). Catercorner, **Carpisa Italia** sells high-end Italian imports.

Jacqueline Fumero Café Boutique (Compostela #1, esq. Cuarteles, tel. 07/862-6562, www.jacquelinefumero.com, daily 10am-10pm) sells exquisite women's fashionwear by the internationally acclaimed designer.

Vedado and Plaza de la Revolución

Adidas and Nike have well-stocked branches selling sportswear in the **Galería Habana Libre** (Calle 25, e/ L y M, daily 8am-7pm).

Playa (Miramar and Beyond)

The **Complejo Comercial Comodoro** (3ra Av., esq. 84, tel. 07/204-5551, daily 8am-7pm), adjoining the Hotel Comodoro, and **Miramar Trade Center** (Av. 3ra, e/ 76 y 80) have outlets for various name-brand European designers.

The boutiques at **La Maison** (Calle 16 #701, esq. 7ma, tel. 07/204-1543, Mon.-Sat. 10am-6:45pm) sell upscale imported clothing, shoes, and duty-free items. Likewise, **Le Select** (5ta Av., esq. 30, tel. 07/204-7410,

Mon.-Sat. 10am-8pm, Sun. 10am-2pm), with its ritzy chandeliers and marble statues, is as close as you'll come to Bond Street or Rodeo Drive.

MUSIC AND FILM
Habana Vieja
Longina Música (Obispo #360, tel. 07/862-8371, Mon.-Sat. 10am-7pm, Sun. 10am-1pm) sells musical instruments and has a large CD collection.

Graphic artist Idania del Rio sells cool contemporary posters and cards at **Clandestina** (Villegas #403 e/ Brasil y Muralla, tel. 5381-4802, www.clandestinacuba.com).

Vedado and Plaza de la Revolución
The **Centro Cultural Cinematográfico** (Calle 23 #1155, e/ 10 y 12, tel. 07/833-6430, Mon.-Sat. 9am-5pm) sells posters and videos of Cuban films; it's on the fourth floor of the Cuban Film Institute (ICAIC). **La Habana Si** (Calle L, esq. 23, tel. 07/832-3162, Mon.-Sat. 10am-9pm) has a large CD selection.

Playa (Miramar and Beyond)
For the widest CD selection in town, head to the **Casa de la Música** (Calle 10 #309, tel. 07/202-6900), the salesroom of Egrem, the state recording agency.

PERFUMES, TOILETRIES, AND JEWELRY
Habana Vieja
Havana 1791 (Mercaderes #156, esq. Obrapía, tel. 07/861-3525, Mon.-Sat. 10am-7pm, Sun. 10am-1pm) sells locally made scents (CUC6-18) in exquisitely engraved bottles with not entirely trustworthy cork tops, in an embossed linen bag. **Farmacia Taquechel** (Obispo #155, e/ Mercaderes y San Ignacio, tel. 07/862-9286, daily 9am-5pm) sells face creams, lotions, and other natural products made in Cuba.

Tienda Museo el Reloj (Oficios, esq. Muralla, tel. 07/864-9515, www.cuervoysobrinos.com, Mon.-Sat. 10am-7pm and Sun. 10am-1pm) will cause a double-take. At this deluxe store, gold-plated fountain pens (each in an elegant cedar humidor with five cigars) sell for CUC1,000 and the cheapest watch costs US$2,000. These are limited editions made in Switzerland and sold under the old Cuevos y Sobrinos label.

Vedado
You'll "ooh!" and "ahh!" over the fine hand-crafted jewelry at **Rox 950** (Calle Linea #256 e/ I y J, tel. 07/209-1479 or 5281-7118, www.rox950.com), where silversmith artist Rosana Varga sells her stunning contemporary silver creations in a fittingly beautiful manse.

Playa (Miramar and Beyond)
Most upscale hotels have quality jewelry stores, as do **La Maison** (Calle 16 #701, esq. 7ma, Miramar, tel. 07/204-1543, daily 9am-5pm), **Le Select** (5ta Av., esq. 30, Miramar, tel. 07/204-7410, daily 9am-5pm), **Joyería La Habanera** (Calle 12 #505, e/ 5ta y 7ma, tel. 07/204-2546, Mon.-Sat. 10am-6pm), and the Club Habana's **Joyería Bella Cantando** (5ta Av. y 188, tel. 07/204-5700, daily 9am-5pm).

DEPARTMENT STORES AND SHOPPING CENTERS
Habana Vieja
Harris Brothers (Monserrate #305, e/ O'Reilly y Progreso, Habana Vieja, tel. 07/861-1644, daily 9am-7pm) has four stories of separate stores that sell everything from fashion and children's items to toiletries. The only photography store in town is in the **Gran Hotel Kempinski Manzana** (Agramonte esq. Neptuno). Opened in June 2017, it sells Canons, Leicas and Nikons at vastly inflated prices.

Centro Habana and Cerro
East of Avenida de Italia (Galiano) is Calle San Rafael—a pedestrian-only shopping zone, known colloquially as "El Bulevar." Havana's main shopping street retains many

department stores from prerevolutionary days. **La Época** (Av. de Italia, esq. Neptuno, Centro Habana, tel. 07/866-9423, Mon.-Sat. 9:30am-7pm, Sun. 9:30am-2pm) is a good place for clothing, including kiddie items and designer fashions. The former Woolworth's, today called **Variedades Galiano** (Av. de Italia, esq. San Rafael, tel. 07/862-7717, Mon.-Sat. 9am-5pm), still has its original lunch counter.

Vedado and Plaza de la Revolución

Galerías de Paseo (1ra Calle, e/ Paseo y A, tel. 07/833-9888, Mon.-Sat. 9am-6pm, Sun. 9am-1pm), at the foot of Paseo, has more than two dozen stores of varying kinds.

Playa (Miramar and Beyond)

La Puntilla Centro Comercial (1ra Av., esq. 0, tel. 07/204-7240, daily 8am-8pm) has four floors of stores covering electronics, furniture, clothing, and more. Similarly, there's **Quinta y 42** (5ta Av. y 42, Miramar, tel. 07/204-7070, Mon.-Sat. 10am-6pm, Sun. 9am-1pm) and **Complejo Comercial Comodoro** (3ra Av., esq. 84, Miramar, tel. 07/204-5551, daily 8am-7pm).

The largest supermarket is **Supermercado 70** (3ra Av., e/ 62 y 70, Mon.-Sat. 9am-6pm and Sun. 9am-1pm), with all manner of imported foodstuffs. The best-stocked store for food items is **Palco** in the Miramar Trade Center (Av. 3ra e/ 76 y 80, Mon.-Sat. 10am-6pm and Sun. 10am-1pm).

Sports and Recreation

Havana has many *centros deportivos* (sports centers). The largest are the **Complejo Panamericano** (Vía Monumental, Km 1.5, Ciudad Panamericano, Habana del Este, tel. 07/795-4140), with an Olympic stadium, tennis courts, swimming pool, and even a velodrome for cycling; and **Ciudad Deportiva** (Vía Blanca, esq. Av. Rancho Boyeros, tel. 07/854-5022), or Sports City, colloquially called "El Coliseo," in Nuevo Vedado.

GOLF

The **Club Habana** (5ta Av., e/ 188 y 192, Rpto. Flores, tel. 07/204-5700) has a practice range. Nonmembers are welcome (entrance CUC20 Mon.-Fri.). **Club de Golf Habana** (Carretera de Vento, Km 8, Boyeros, tel. 07/649-8918, 8:30am-sunset) is about 20 kilometers south of Havana. The nine-hole "golfito" (as the locals know it) has 18 tees positioned for play on both sides of the fairway. It has a minimally stocked pro shop, five tennis courts, a swimming pool, and two restaurants. Membership costs CUC70 plus CUC45 monthly. Nine holes costs nonmembers CUC20 (CUC30 for 18 holes).

Clubs can be rented for CUC15; caddies cost CUC6.

GYMS AND SPAS

Upscale hotels have tiny gyms and/or spas, though most are a letdown. The best are at the **Hotel Nacional** (Calle O y 21, tel. 07/873-3564, nonguests CUC15), **Hotel Meliá Cohiba** (Paseo, esq. 1ra, tel. 07/833-3636), and **Hotel Meliá Habana** (3ra Av., e/ 76 y 80, tel. 07/204-8500).

Gimnasio Biomerica (Calle E, esq. 17, Vedado, tel. 07/832-9087, Mon.-Fri. 8am-8pm), below the Centro Hebreo Sefaradi, charges CUC8 monthly. One of the best facilities is at **Club Habana** (5ta Av., e/ 188 y 192, Rpto. Flores, tel. 07/204-5700, Mon.-Fri. 7:30am-7pm, nonmembers CUC20).

Private spas have blossomed in Cuba. One top-notch option is **Spa O2** (Calle 26, esq. 26B, Nuevo Vedado, tel. 07/883-1663, www.o2habana.com, daily 9am-11:45pm), with a small gym, beauty treatments, and a café. In Habana Vieja, **Spasio** (San Ignacio #364, tel. 07/768-2602, carlos.fente@nauta.cu), on Plaza Vieja, is recommended. And in Miramar, **Vida Spa** (Calle 34 #308 e/ 3ra y 5ta, tel. 07/209-2022 or 5483-3005) offers treatments from massage to skin peels.

SAILING AND SPORTFISHING

Club Habana (5ta Av., e/ 188 y 192, Playa, tel. 07/204-5700) has aqua-bikes and kayaks for rent. Full-size yachts and motor vessels can be rented at **Marina Hemingway** (5ta Av., esq. 248, Santa Fe, tel. 07/273-1867), which also offers sportfishing (from CUC275 for four hours; from CUC375 for eight hours, including skipper and tackle).

SCUBA DIVING

There's excellent diving offshore of Havana. The Gulf Stream and Atlantic Ocean currents meet west of the city, where many ships have been sunk through the centuries. The so-called "Blue Circuit," a series of dive sites, extends east from Bacuranao, about 10 kilometers east of Havana, to the Playas del Este.

Centro de Buceo La Aguja (Marina Hemingway, 5ta Av. y 248, Santa Fe, tel. 07/204-5088 or 07/271-5277, daily 8:30am-4:30pm) rents equipment and charges CUC30 for one dive, CUC50 for two dives, CUC60 for a "resort course," and CUC360 for an open-water certification. The **Centro Internacional Buceo Residencial Club Habana** (5ta Av., e/ 188 y 192, Rpto. Flores, tel. 07/204-5700, Mon.-Fri. 7:30am-7pm, nonmembers entrance CUC20) offers scuba certification.

SWIMMING

Most large tourist hotels have pools and permit use by nonguests. In Habana Vieja, head to **Piscina Hotel Mercure Sevilla** (Prado, esq. Ánimas, tel. 07/860-8560, daily 10am-6pm, entrance CUC20).

The **Hotel Nacional** (Calle O y 21, tel. 07/873-3564, CUC18) and **Hotel Habana Libre Tryp** (Calle L, e/ 23 y 25, tel. 07/834-6100, CUC15), in the Vedado and Plaza de la Revolución, have excellent pools.

In Playa, the best pools are at the **Memories Miramar** (5ta Av., e/ 72 y 76, tel. 07/204-8140) and **Hotel Meliá Habana** (3ra Av., e/ 76 y 80, tel. 07/204-8500). **Club Habana** (5ta Av., e/ 188 y 192, Playa, tel. 07/204-5700, Mon.-Fri. 9am-7pm, entrance CUC20) has a swimming pool. The pool at **Club Almendares** (Av. 49C, esq. 28A, Rpto. Kohly, tel. 07/204-4990, daily 10am-6pm, CUC5) gets mobbed by Cubans on weekends. Farther west, the pool at Papa's Complejo Turistico in **Marina Hemingway** (5ta Av., esq. 248, Santa Fe, tel. 07/209-7920) can get crowded with locals.

SPECTATOR SPORTS

Baseball

Havana's Industriales (colloquially called "Los Leones," or "The Lions") play at the 60,000-seat **Estadio Latinoamericano** (Consejero Aranjo y Pedro Pérez, Cerro, tel. 07/870-6526), the main baseball stadium. Games are played November-May, Tuesday-Thursday and Saturday at 8pm, and Sunday at 2pm (CUC3). Contact the **Federación Cubana de Béisbol** (tel. 07/879-7980, www.beisbolcubano.cu).

Basketball

Havana's Capitalinos play September-November at the **Coliseo de Deportes** (Ciudad Deportiva, Vía Blanca, esq. Av. Rancho Boyeros, Nuevo Vedado, tel. 07/854-5022) and at the **Sala Polivalente Ramón Fonst** (Av. de la Independencia, esq. Bruzón, Plaza de la Revolución, tel. 07/881-1011). Contact the **Federación Cubana de Baloncesto** (tel. 07/648-7156).

Boxing

Championship matches are hosted at the **Coliseo de Deportes** (Vía Blanca, esq. Av. Rancho Boyeros, tel. 07/854-5022), base for the **Federación Cubana de Boxeo** (tel. 07/857-7047). You can watch boxing at the **Gimnasio de Boxeo Rafael Trejo** (Calle Cuba #815, Habana Vieja, tel. 07/862-0266, Mon.-Fri. 8am-5pm) and at **Sala Polivalente**

Kid Chocolate (Prado, e/ San Martín y Brasil, Habana Vieja, tel. 07/862-8634).

Soccer

Cuba's soccer program is not well developed, although there *is* a national league. Havana's *fútbol* team is Ciudad Havana (nicknamed "Los Rojos"—"The Reds"). Games are played at the **Estadio Pedro Marrero** (Av. 41 #4409, e/ 44 y 50, Rpto. Kohly, tel. 07/203-4698).

Food

Havana is in the midst of a gastronomic revolution. Privately owned restaurants (*paladares*) have exploded in number, offering heapings of style and good food. It's hard to stay abreast of new openings. Few state restaurants can compete on ambience and flavorful fare, although many are improving as they convert into workers' cooperatives. Many state restaurants still attain true Soviet-class awfulness, especially the hotel buffets. The best *paladares* have been entirely taken over by U.S. tour groups; if you want to dine with locals opt for budget locales. When the U.S. cruise ships are in town, avoid lunch at popular venues.

HABANA VIEJA
Breakfast and Cafés

Most hotel restaurants are open to nonguests for breakfast. The buffet at the **Mediterráneo** (Neptuno, e/ Prado y Zulueta, tel. 07/866-6627, daily 7am-10am, CUC15) in the Hotel Iberostar Parque Central is the best in town.

If all you want is a croissant and coffee, head to **Pastelería Francesca** (Prado #410, e/ Neptuno y San Rafael, tel. 07/862-0739, daily 8am-noon), on the west side of Parque Central. The ★ **Café El Escorial** (Mercaderes #317, tel. 07/868-3545, daily 9am-10pm), on Plaza Vieja, is the closest in Havana you'll come to a European-style coffee shop. This atmospheric venue with a Tuscan mood sells croissants, truffle cream cakes, ice cream, and gourmet coffees and coffee liqueurs.

Bianchini Croissantería-Dulcería (Sol #12 e/ Av. del Puerto y Oficios, no tel., www. dulceria-bianchini.com, daily 9am-9pm) is a delightfully bohemian, pocket-sized hole-in-the-wall that is the brainchild of Katia, the Italian-Swiss owner who has created a piece of Europe transplanted. She serves quiches, croissants, buns, and tarts, plus coffees and teas. The place is usually packed. Katia has a second outlet—equally small and cozy—in Callejón del Chorro (tel. 07/862-8477), off Plaza de la Catedral.

Paladares

Hugely popular, the cozy ★ **Doña Eutimia** (Callejón del Chorro #60C, tel. 07/861-1332, daily noon-midnight), tucked off Plaza de la Catedral, transports you back two centuries with its antique clocks and quirky oddities. Delightful owner Leticia delivers delicious down-home creole cooking that includes a superb *ropa vieja* (braised lamb prepared with garlic, tomatoes, and spices, CUC7) with heaps of cumin-spiced black beans. Leave room for the chocolate torta (CUC2.50). Reservations are imperative.

Beyoncé and Jay-Z have lunched at **La Moneda Cubana** (Empedrado #152, esq. Mercaderes, tel. 07/861-5304, daily noon-midnight), a colonial military-themed restaurant off Plaza de la Catedral. The creative Cuban cuisine includes lamb in garlic and coffee. Start with ceviche and end with rice pudding with shredded coconut. Tour groups take up much of the space. The rooftop terrace has castle views, good for witnessing the *cañonazo* ceremony at 9pm.

Fidel's former private chef Tomás Erasmo Hernández prepares delicious Cuban dishes at ★ **Mama Inés** (Calle de la Obrapía #60, e/ Oficios y Baratillo, tel. 07/862-2669, Mon.-Sat. noon-10:30pm). The menu features filet mignon (CUC12), veal scallopini (CUC8), and a flavorful and piquant stewed lamb (CUC10), but the succulent *ropa vieja* (CUC12) gets my vote as the best in Havana. The octopus with garlic and pepper is to die for. Erasmo often makes the rounds to chat with guests.

Paladar Los Mercaderes (Mercaderes #207, e/ Lamparillos y Amargura, tel. 07/861-2437, daily noon-midnight) greets you with fresh rose petals on the marble staircase. Upstairs, this lovely colonial space has huge French doors open to the street below. Food is top-notch. I salivated over my octopus with pesto and onion sauce (CUC12), risotto with veggies and dried fruit (CUC8.50), and *ropa vieja* (CUC14).

Restaurante Chef Iván Justo (Calle Aguacate #9, esq. Chacón, tel. 07/863-9697, ivanchefsjusto.restaurant@yahoo.com, daily noon-midnight) rates highly, not least for the charming ambience in a restored and rambling two-story home dating from 1776. The kitchen dishes up such divine treats as cream of squash soup (CUC5), crab claw enchilada (CUC10), veggie and mushroom risotto (CUC12), and even roast pheasant (CUC18), although the *lechón* (suckling pig) and the seafood paella are the signature dishes. Warning: The upstairs restaurant is reached by a steep, narrow staircase. The same owner runs the adjoining **Al Carbón** (same details) downstairs. It specializes in Cuban dishes cooked over charcoal, but the paella is also available.

For something light, check out **Jacqueline Fumero Café Boutique** (Compostela #1, esq. Cuarteles, tel. 07/862-6562, www.jacquelinefumero.com, daily 10am-10pm). The eponymous Cuban fashion designer has conjured a sensational South Beach-style setting—walls of glass, electric-blue lighting, slate-gray tile floors, see-through plastic chairs—in one of Habana Vieja's quintessential colonial *plazuelas*. It's ideal for refueling on coffee, cappuccino, chocolate tarts, smoothies, or delicious sandwiches.

Consider Cinco Esquinas ground zero in the gentrification of Habana Vieja, with several great options. **Café de los Artistas** (Calle Aguilar #22 bajos, e/ Av. de los Misiones y Peña Pobre, tel. 07/866-2418, daily 10am-1am) offers excellent quality and value for a classic Cuban menu, including mouthwatering *tostones* and *ropa vieja*. Owner Luis Carlos is the stage manager for the Ballet Nacional de Cuba and photos of Cuba's elite dancers festoon the walls.

Motorcyclists will love the decor at **Chacón 162** (Chacón #162, esq. Callejón de Espada, tel. 07/860-1386, daily 11am-midnight), owned by Harley-Davidson enthusiasts and a hangout for local *harlistas* since opening in 2016. A motorcycle hangs over the bar, and the cocktails are cued to the theme: Street Bob, Bloody Mary V-Twin, and so forth. The fusion menu is well executed, too. I enjoyed a deliciously spicy *pulpo peruana*—octopus with veggies in tomato salsa (CUC9).

Intimate is an understatement for **Habana 61** (Calle Habana #6, e/ Cuarteles y Peña Pobre, tel. 07/861-9433, www.habana61.com, daily noon-midnight), a cubbyhole restaurant tucked off Cinco Esquinas. It dishes out some of the most creative cuisine in the city, served amid contemporary surrounds in a converted colonial townhouse.

Count your blessings to get a seat at ★ **O'Reilly 304** (Calle O'Reilly #304, e/ Habana y Aguiar, tel. 5264-4725, daily noon-midnight, CUC8-18). Cuba's monied *farandula* (in-crowd) and tourists in the know cram into what has become one of Habana Vieja's trendiest joints. The edgy art and high-energy buzz act like a gravitational force to passersby. Tiny it may be, but the *paladar* serves an imaginative menu of delicious dishes, from to-die-for ceviche to crab tacos.

I wish I could keep **Azúcar** (Mercaderes #315, tel. 07/801-1563, daily 11am-midnight) a secret—this is my favorite lunch spot in town. Owners Allison and Liset serve awesome tapas, tuna sandwiches, and even lobster in *criollo* sauce out of a contemporary colonial townhome that opens to the plaza. At night, the all-female Octava Nota performs.

Penny-pinching *farandulas* head to **Bar La Chanchullero** (Brasil e/ Berraza y Cristo, tel. 5276-0938, daily 1pm-midnight), a down-to-earth hole-in-the-wall on Plaza del Cristo. It serves tapas, plus garlic shrimp (CUC4), pork with parsley (CUC4), and chicken fricassee (CUC4).

Criolla

La Bodeguita del Medio (Empedrado #207, e/ San Ignacio y Cuba, tel. 07/862-1374, restaurant daily noon-midnight, bar 10:30am-midnight, CUC10-20), one block west of Plaza de la Catedral, specializes in traditional Cuban dishes—most famously its roast pork, steeped black beans, fried bananas, garlicky yucca, and sweet guava pudding. Troubadours entertain.

To dine with Cubans, you can't beat ★ **Los Nardos** (Paseo de Martí #563, e/ Teniente Rey y Dragones, tel. 07/863-2985, daily noon-midnight), in a run-down building opposite the Capitolio. The long lines at night hint how good this place is. It has restaurants on three levels; be sure to dine in the atmospheric Los Nardos, not the more ascetic El Trofeo or El Asturianito, on the upper levels. The huge meals include garlic shrimp, lobster in Catalan sauce, paella, and Cuban staples. House sangria is served in a pitcher. The place is run by Cuba's Spanish Asturian association.

The Sociedad Cultural Asturiana runs **La Terraza** (Prado #309, esq. Virtudes, tel. 07/862-3625, daily noon-midnight), a covered open-air rooftop space overlooking the Prado; get there early to snag a seat with a view. Master chef Jorge Falco Ochoa specializes in grilled meats and seafood. Try the grilled octopus with pesto and grilled potatoes, and perhaps a succulent leg of lamb, or grilled sausage in spicy mustard sauce. The food makes up for the ho-hum decor.

European

The modern **Restaurante Prado y Neptuno** (Prado, esq. Neptuno, tel. 07/860-9636, daily noon-midnight) is popular with expats for reasonable Italian fare and pizzas. The *bodega*-style **La Paella** (Oficios #53, esq. Obrapía, tel. 07/867-1037, daily noon-11pm), in the Hostal Valencia, serves paella for two

people only (although one person could ostensibly eat a double serving) for CUC7-15. The *caldo* (soup) and bread is a meal in itself (CUC3). The kitchen also serves the **Bodegón Ouda** (Obrapía, esq. Baratillo, tel. 07/867-1037, Mon.-Sat. noon-7pm), a quaint tapas bar around the corner in the Hotel El Comendador.

Surf and Turf

The ritzy **Café del Oriente** (Oficios, esq. Amargura, tel. 07/860-6686, daily noon-midnight), on Plaza de San Francisco, is considered a showcase state restaurant and draws U.S. tour groups. It has tux-clad waiters and a jazz pianist downstairs in the Bar Café—heck, you could be in New York or San Francisco. The mostly steak and seafood dishes (CUC12-30), include calf's brains with mustard and brandy cream sauce and a divine filet mignon, but it can't hold a candle to the best *paladares*.

A merely adequate state-run restaurant is **Restaurante El Templete** (Av. del Puerto, esq. Narciso López, tel. 07/866-8807, daily noon-midnight), along with adjoining sibling **Restaurante La Barca.** Housed in a restored colonial mansion, this dual restaurant has a diverse menu ranging from delicious fried calamari (CUC5) to overpriced lobster (CUC28) and a chocolate brownie dessert. It's a great place to catch the firing of the cannon across the harbor at 9pm.

Self-Catering

The *agromercado* on Avenida de Bélgica (Egido, e/ Apodada y Corrales) is a great place to stock up on fresh produce. Imported meats are sold at **La Monserrate** (Monserrate, e/ Brasil y Muralles), an air-conditioned butcher shop, and at **Harris Brothers** (Monserrate #305, e/ O'Reilly y Progreso, Habana Vieja, tel. 07/861-1644, daily 9am-6pm), a department store with various foodstuff sections.

CENTRO HABANA
Paladares

Centro Habana boasts the most acclaimed *paladar* in town: ★ **La Guarida** (Concordia

#418, e/ Gervasio y Escobartel, tel. 07/866-9047, www.laguarida.com, daily noon-midnight), on the third floor of a dilapidated 19th-century townhouse turned crowded *ciudadela* (tenement). Don't let the near-derelict staircase put you off the world-class Parisian-style restaurant. The walls are festooned with period Cuban pieces and giant prints of famous personages who've dined here (from Jack Nicholson to Beyoncé, Rhianna, and Madonna) and fashion shoots on the crumbling stairways. (You may recognize it as the setting for the Oscar-nominated 1995 movie *Fresa y Chocolate*.) Owners Enrique Nuñez and Odeysis Baullosa serve such treats as gazpacho (CUC4) and *tartar de atún* (tuna tartare, CUC6) for starters and an out-of-this-world roast chicken in orange sauce and honey (CUC13), plus desserts such as lemon pie (CUC5). Despite the large wine list, only house wine is available by the glass (CUC4). There's also a chic rooftop tapas bar and cigar lounge. Reservations are essential.

Giving La Guarida a run for its money is ★ **San Cristóbal** (Calle San Rafael #469, e/ Campanario y Lealtad, tel. 07/860-1705, rashemarquez@yahoo.com, Mon.-Sat. noon-midnight), with an eclectic museum's worth of antiques, objets d'art, religious and musical icons, and armoires stuffed with old books. Ebullient owner-chef Carlos Cristóbal Márquez and his kitchen team deliver superbly flavorful traditional Cuban dishes, such as grilled lobster, succulent roast pork, and Cuban-style mezze plates. Beyoncé dined here and this was the *only* private restaurant where President Obama dined during his 2016 visit. Good luck booking a table! This is not a place for walking the streets alone late at night; take a taxi.

The homespun **Paladar Doña Blanquita** (Prado #158, e/ Colón y Refugio, tel. 07/867-4958, Tues.-Sun. noon-midnight) offers dining on a balcony overlooking the Prado. The *criolla* menu delivers large portions for CUC5-10. The place overflows with whimsical Woolworth's art, such as cheap *muñequitas* (dolls), plastic flowers, animals, and cuckoo clocks.

For a view over the Malecón, head to **Castropol** (Malecón #107, e/ Genios y Crespo, tel. 07/861-4864, daily 11am-midnight), run by the Sociedad Asturiano. The chef conjures up fusion dishes such as pork tenderloin medallions with honey and Dijon mustard, but I prefer the ceviche (CUC4.50) or delicious octopus Galician style with sweet-and-sour pepper and potatoes (CUC3.65). The downstairs restaurant serves Cuban dishes from the grill; call ahead to book an upstairs terrace table.

The inspiration of Swedish film director and owner Michel Miglis, ★ **Casa Miglis** (Calle Lealtad #120, e/ Animas y Lagunas, tel. 07/863-1486, www.casamiglis.com, daily noon-1am) offers the only Scandinavian cuisine in town, although I'd more accurately call it Cuban-meets-the-world. The menu includes couscous, Mexican chili, and Greek souvlaki. My pork with herb-fried potatoes in bean sauce, chopped shrimp, and balsamic cream induced a sigh of delight. As did a divine vanilla ice cream with raisins and *añejo* rum topped with cacao. Your setting is a centenary townhouse with classically elegant all-white furnishings and place settings from Sweden. The bar is a work of art: Aged seats hang suspended as if floating in air. Miglis hosts live theme nights Friday-Sunday.

Nearby, **Restaurant La California** (Calle Crespo #55 e/ San Lázaro y Refugio, tel. 07/869-7510, californiarestasurant@gmail.com, daily noon-midnight) is justifiably popular with tour groups. I like the four distinct and antique-filled *salas* (salons), including a redbrick terrace, and its clever use of former sewing machine pedestals for tables. The house speciality is oven-grilled pizza. I love the mushroom risotto with squid-ink rice (CUC12), and the chicken supreme in lemon caper sauce (CUC8) is sure to satisfy. Sated? Then climb the spiral staircase to the wine and cigar lounge.

Ice-Cream Parlors

patrons at Coppelia ice cream parlor, Vedado

Street stalls sell ice-cream cones for about 2.50 pesos. However, hygiene is always questionable.

Habana Vieja: For penny-pinchers, the **Cremería el Naranjal** (Obispo, esq. Cuba) sells ice-cream sundaes, including a banana split (CUC1.50-3). Gourmands won't believe they're in Havana at **Helad'oro** (Calle Aguiar #206 e/ Empedrado y Tejadillo, tel. 5305-9131; daily 11am-10pm, CUC1), serving artesanal gelatos. Flavors include mojito, of course.

Vedado: An institution, **Coppelia** (Calle 23, esq. Calle L, tel. 07/832-6149, Tues.-Sun. 10am-9:30pm) serves ice cream of excellent quality. Tourists are often steered toward a special section that, though offering immediate service, charges CUC2.60 for an *ensalada* (three scoops), while the half-dozen communal peso sections (choose from indoor or outdoor dining) offer larger *ensaladas* (five scoops) for only five pesos, a *jimagua* (two scoops) for two pesos, and a *marquesita* (two scoops plus a sponge cake) for 2.50 pesos, all served in simple aluminum bowls. The fun is in waiting in line and dining communally with Cubans; you'll need *moneda nacional*. A kiosk on the west side (Calle K) sells cones. Be prepared for a *long* wait in summer.

Dulce Habana (Calle 25, tel. 07/836-6100, daily 10am-9pm), on the south side of the Hotel Habana Libre Tryp, is run along the lines of Baskin-Robbins and charges accordingly.

My fave spot is **Amore** (Calle 15 #111, esq. L, tel. 5536-5152, daily 10am-midnight), an Italian-owned newcomer in a restored beaux arts mansion serving about 16 flavors of gelatos ranging from mamey to peanut.

Playa (Miramar and Beyond): Yanetzi Anahares dishes up gelato in 16 flavors at her **Casa de Gelato** (1ra Av. esq. 44, tel. 07/202-7938, www.alpescatorehabana.com, daily noon-midnight, CUC1.50-5), in front of the Hotel Copacabana.

Asian

Barrio Chino boasts a score of Chinese restaurants, concentrated along Calle Cuchillo. However, this isn't Hong Kong or San Francisco, so temper your expectations. ★ **Restaurante Tien-Tan** (Cuchillo #17, tel. 07/863-2081, daily 9am-midnight) is the best of a dozen options on Cuchillo. Chef Tao Qi hails from Shanghai. The extensive menu includes such tantalizing offerings as sweet-and-sour fried fish balls with vinegar and soy, and pot-stewed liver with seasoning. The budget-minded will find many options for around CUC2, but dishes run to CUC18. A 20 percent service fee is charged.

One of the best bargains in town is ★ **Flor de Loto** (Salud #313, e/ Gervasio y Escobar, tel. 07/860-8501, daily noon-midnight). Though the staff dress in Chinese robes, about the only Asian item on the menu is *maripositas* (fried wontons). However, the *criolla* fare, such as spicy shrimp (CUC6.50) and grilled lobster (CUC7.50), is tasty and filling.

Self-Catering

For groceries, try the basement supermarket in **La Época** (Galiano, esq. Neptuno, Mon.-Sat. 9:30am-9:30pm, Sun. 9am-1pm). Milk is the hardest item to find in Cuba. Try **La Castillo del Lacteo** (Av. Simón Bolívar, esq. Galiano, daily 9am-8pm), selling ice cream, yogurt, and, hopefully, milk.

VEDADO AND PLAZA DE LA REVOLUCIÓN
Breakfast and Cafés

★ **Café La Rampa** (Calle 23, esq. L, tel. 07/834-6125, 24 hours), at the Hotel Habana Libre Tryp, serves American-style breakfasts, including a breakfast special of toast, eggs, bacon, coffee, and juice for CUC7. The burgers here are surprisingly good (CUC5), as are the tuna and fried egg sandwiches (CUC5) and hot chocolate brownies (CUC3.50).

Paladares

Vedado abounds with great *paladares,* and every month at least one quality private restaurant opens to take advantage of the new legal space. Here's my pick of the ever-expanding litter.

I regularly dine at ★ **Le Chansonnier** (Calle J #259, e/ 15 y Línea, tel. 07/832-1576, daily 1pm-11pm), a gorgeous restaurant in a vast, venerable mansion with soaring ceilings, beige leather banquettes, and sensational art—a testament to owner Héctor Higüera Martínez's Parisian sensibility. Creative fare is highlighted by delicious sauces. The marinated octopus in garlic appetizer is to die for. Other winning dishes include spicy crab appetizer, duck with *salsa guayabana,* pork loin with eggplant, and roasted rabbit in mustard

sauce. The menu is ever-changing. Most dishes cost less than CUC15.

Héctor's influence is also all over ★ **Atelier** (Calle 5 #511, e/ Paseo y 2, tel. 07/836-2025, www.atelier-cuba.com, daily noon-midnight), another chic conversion of a 19th-century Spanish Renaissance mansion—formerly owned by the president of the Senate—adorned with fine Cuban art and, coincidentally, run by Héctor's brother (Herdys Higueras Martínez) and sister (Niuris Higueras Martínez). Daily menus might include candied duck and red snapper ceviche or a superb squash soup (CUC5) and chicken with shrimp *a la crema* (CUC12). Try to snag a table on the rooftop terrace; tour groups fill up the place. Reservations are essential.

The chilled-out **Café Laurent** (Calle M #257, e/ 19 y 21, tel. 07/832-6890, www.cafe-laurent.ueuo.com, daily noon-midnight) is in a fifth-floor penthouse of a 1950s modernist apartment block with veranda dining and white ostrich-leather seats. The three owners have imbued the place with fantastic retro decor and nouvelle Cuban dishes that wow diners. Try the carpaccio ahi tuna, tuna-stuffed peppers (CUC5), or oven-baked chateaubriand with wild mushrooms served in a clay casserole (CUC11.50). And leave room for the delicious chocolate brownie with vanilla ice cream.

What's not to rave about at ★ **El Cocinero** (Calle 26, e/ 11 y 13, tel. 07/832-2355, www.elcocinerohabana.cu, daily noon-midnight)? Visionary entrepreneurs Alexander "Sasha" Ramos and Rafael Muñoz have turned an old redbrick factory that once made cooking oil into a superb *paladar* and lounge club adjoining (and part of) Fábrica de Arte Cubano (FAC). You ascend a spiral staircase augering up the old chimney to a classy second-floor restaurant (grilled lobster with basmati rice, CUC18; chicken with *criolla* sauce, CUC5; pork ribs, CUC5) and, above, an open-air rooftop lounge club favored by *la farandula* (the in-crowd); the latter serves tapas such as whole octopus, gazpacho Andaluz (CUC3), and baguette with goat cheese (CUC5). Leave room for the artisanal ice cream. The lounge also hosts live jazz.

Inside FAC, restaurater siblings Niurys and Hector Higüera Mártinez run the sublime **Tierra** (Calle 26 esq. 11, tel. 5565-2621, Thurs.-Sun. 8pm-1:30am, by reservation only, CUC7-10), using old shipping containers with glass-paneled sides that open to a faux-garden patio. The menu roams the globe from tuna lasagna and lamb moussaka (unimpressive) to a divine fish-and-chips served in newspaper. Start with a mixto Arabe platter (CUC10). You pay the CUC2 entrance to FAC but don't have to wait in line.

Tucked at the end of a brick walkway to the rear of a 1930s mansion and festooned with a decorative arbor, **La Moraleja** (Calle 25 #454, e/ I y J, tel. 07/832-0963, www.lamoraleja-cuba.com, noon-midnight) combines a romantic ambience—choose air-conditioned or patio dining—with superb nouvelle Cuban dishes, prepared in an outdoor brasserie. Try the house octopus salad, roast rabbit with port flambée (CUC10), or divine grilled shrimp with anise and garlic served in an earthenware bowl. The space also hosts live jazz.

Serving some of the best Italian fare in town, **Mediterráneo Havana** (Calle 13 #406, e/ F y G, tel. 07/832-4894, www.

medhavana.com, daily noon-midnight) truly evokes the Mediterranean with its white and, well, Mediterranean blues in this converted 1920s mansion. Sardinian chef Luigi Fiori achieves sublime heights with his superb homemade sausages and ravioli (CUC6.50), lasagna (CUC5.50), and lobster spaghetti (CUC9), plus pizzas (from CUC4.75). The braised goat with herbs and olive oil is delicious (CUC6.50). It has been discovered by American tour groups who frequently take over the place. Two blocks east is **El Idilio** (Cale G #351 esq. 15, tel. 07/831-8182, daily noon-midnight), an unpretentious open-air Italian restaurant with gingham tablecloths. The open kitchen specializes in barbecued meats.

On Saturday night, you'll likely find me at ★ **La Chuchería Café Sport Bar** (1ra esq. C, tel. 07/830-7908, daily 9am-midnight), a hip, straight-from-Miami demonstration of private know-how with its Philippe Starck translucent plastic chairs. There's usually a line to savor delicious thin-crust pizza in the air-conditioned retro-themed diner or on a patio facing the Malecón. It's also a great place to start the day with crêpes or a classic American breakfast (CUC3.50). Plus, it has reasonable burgers, great sandwiches, and

El Cocinero, Vedado

creative salads. It even has pizza and shakes to go.

Guests at the Meliá Cohiba can step across the street to enjoy superb fusion fare at ★ **HM 7** (Paseo #7 e/ 1ra y 3ra, tel. 07/830-2287, www.habanamia7.com, daily noon-11pm), with an open kitchen upstairs. Chic, 21st-century decor includes sleek contemporary styling that extends to the menu. I like the mushroom risotto in squid ink or the spaghetti Bolognese; ceviche (CUC5.25), octopus carpaccio (CUC6.95), and grilled dishes also feature. Downstairs, the bar serves tapas until the wee hours.

On the Malecón seafront (hence the name) is **El Litoral** (Malecón e/ K y L, tel. 07/830-2201, www.ellitoralhabana.com, daily noon-midnight). This maritime-themed restaurant in a graciously restored neo-colonial manse is one of few *paladares* that draws a Cuban elite for the all-you-can-eat antipasto bar—a brilliant and unique idea by owner Alejandro Marcel and chef-partner Alain Rivas. A wide range of seafood dishes include salmon pasta with vodka sauce (CUC18), as well as creative meat dishes such as lamb sausage with sweet potato patties. There's a chic lounge bar with music videos, or hang out on the raised seafront terrace and watch the old cars go by. Next door, **Dolce Vita** (Malecón #159, tel. 07/836-0100 or 5291-1444, daily noon-midnight) raises the bar with its chic styling, glass-enclosed seafront terrace, and excellent Italian fare. Try the spinach ravioli with cream and peanut sauce (CUC12) or gnocchi with Italian sausage and tomato and basil sauce (CUC12), followed by profiteroles (CUC4).

For someplace unpretentious, try **Paladar Los Amigos** (Calle M #253, e/ 19 y 21, tel. 07/830-0880, daily noon-midnight), a cramped and popular little spot adorned with posters and photographs of famous Cuban musicians who've dined here. It serves huge plates of traditional Cuban dishes for about CUC10.

The tiny and cramped **Paladar Restaurante Monguito** (Calle L #408, e/ 23 y 25, tel. 07/831-2615, Fri.-Wed. noon-11pm), directly opposite the Hotel Habana Libre Tryp, is a bargain for simple but filling Cuban dishes such as *pollo asado*, grilled fish, and pork dishes (CUC3-6). Budget hounds are equally well served at **Paladar Mesón Sancho Panza** (Calle J #508, e/ 23 y 25, tel. 07/831-2862, daily noon-3am), on the south side of Parque Don Quijote. It has simple decor and fills with Cubans who come for its vast menu of tapas (such as fried garbanzos), shrimp cocktail (CUC3.30), stuffed eggs (CUC3.50), paellas (from CUC10), and *ropa vieja* (CUC6) at bargain prices.

Chef Osmany Cisnero's **StarBien** (Calle 29 #205, e/ B y C, tel. 07/830-0711 or 5386-2222, starbien.restaurante@gmail.com, Mon.-Sat. noon-midnight, Sun. 7pm-midnight), a fine-dining *paladar* in a restored 1938 building, has garnered a loyal expat clientele. It has a patio, plus an air-conditioned interior with a lofty ceiling and contemporary furnishings. Recommended dishes include the superb ceviche and ravioli with spinach and blue cheese. After dinner, head up to the chic and popular bar to smoke a cigar.

VIP Havana (Calle 9na #454, e/ E y F, tel. 07/832-0178, www.viphavana454.com, daily noon-midnight, CUC25-50) is a soaring and stylishly avant-garde space rehashed from a centenary mansion. Chaplin movies show on a giant screen and a pianist tickles the ivories as you dine on Spanish tapas, pizzas, pastas, paellas, meat, and seafood. The veranda is preferred for lunch on clement days.

Spanish owner Massimo has done a superb conversion of a huge, late-19th-century mansion into ★ **Versus 1900** (Linea #504 altos, e/ D y E, tel. 07/835-1852, versus1900lahabana@gmail.com, daily noon-3am). The ambience stresses antiques and colonial tile floors and floor-to-ceiling shuttered windows that open onto a dining terrace. My favorite dish: charcoal-baked pork in mojo *criollo* sauce with dried fruits (CUC16). The rooftop serves as a stylish neon-lit lounge space, good for postprandial cigars and rum cocktails.

In Nuevo Vedado, ★ **La Casa** (Calle 30

#865, e/ 26 y 41, tel. 07/881-7000, www.restaurantelacasacuba.com, daily noon-midnight) is worth the drive. This 1950s modernist house retains its original decor and is lush with tropical plantings. La Casa serves such delicious dishes as octopus with vinaigrette, tomatoes, and onions (CUC7), ham and spinach cannelloni (CUC75), pasta chicken curry (CUC10), and rabbit with mushroom sauce (CUC12). Actor Matt Dillon and soccer misfit Diego Maradona are among the famous clientele. Savvy owner Alejandro Robaina is usually on hand to fuss over guests. He has an elegant bar upstairs with hookahs and music videos, and hosts Thursday sushi nights.

One of only two dedicated sushi restaurants in town is **PP's Teppanyaki** (Calle 12 #104, e/ L y M, tel. 07/836-2530, ppsteppanyakihavana@yahoo.com, Mon.-Thurs. 6pm-11pm), upstairs in an apartment block. The owner, Pepe, spent eight years as a naval engineer in Japan and has done a good job of replicating Japanese decor, including a teppanyaki bar. He serves professionally presented dishes, such as an excellent octopus vinaigrette and a selection of maki (CUC9), including delicious Danish rolls.

Criolla

Popular with Cubans, the dark, chilly **La Roca** (Calle 21, esq. M, tel. 07/836-3219, daily noon-midnight) has bargain-priced garlic shrimp (CUC9), plus set meals from CUC5, including beer.

ArteChef (Calle 3ra, esq. A, tel. 07/831-1089, www.arteculinario.cu, daily noon-midnight) is operated by the Federación de Asociaciones Culinarias de la República de Cuba, a chefs association that offers professional cooking shows and classes. The space impresses with its classical elegance and wraparound walls of glass. The menu includes traditional dishes such as malanga fritters, plus paella (CUC5), rabbit in wine (CUC6), and lobster thermidor (CUC14).

Continental

La Torre (Calle 17 #155, e/ M y N, tel. 07/838-3088, daily noon-midnight), atop the Focsa building, offers amazing all-around views of the city. Its French-inspired nouvelle cuisine is of higher than usual standard: I recommend the prawns and mushrooms in olive oil and garlic starter (CUC10). I also enjoyed a fish fillet poached in white wine, butter, and cream, and roasted with cheese, served with mashed potatoes and crisp vegetables (CUC15). Order the mountainous and delicious profiteroles (CUC5) for dessert.

The Hotel Meliá Cohiba's baseball-themed **La Piazza Ristorante** (tel. 07/833-3636, daily 1pm-midnight) offers 17 types of pizza (CUC7-20) but also has minestrone (CUC7.50), gnocchi (CUC10), seafood (from CUC11), and an excellent risotto with mushrooms (tinned). Smoking is tolerated and fouls the place.

Self-Catering

There are *agromercados* at Calle 15 (esq. 10), Calle 17 (e/ K y L), Calle 19 (e/ F y Av. de los Presidentes), Calle 21 (esq. J), Calle 16 (e/ 11 y 13), and Pozos Dulces (e/ Av. Salvador Allende and Bruzón).

PLAYA (MIRAMAR AND BEYOND)

This is ground zero for the boom in quality *paladares*. The scene is evolving so quickly that it's truly dizzying.

Breakfast and Cafés

All the tourist hotels have buffet breakfasts. For freshly baked croissants and good coffee, I like **Pain de Paris** (Calle 26, e/ 5ta y 7ma, daily 8am-10pm). **Pan.Com** (Calle 26, esq. 7ma, Mon.-Fri. 8am-2am, Sat.-Sun. 10am-2am), pronounced "pahn POOHN-to com," makes every kind of sandwich. It also has omelets, burgers, and tortillas, all for less than CUC5, plus yogurts, fruit juices, *batidos,* and cappuccinos.

In the Miramar Trade Center, the small, modern, clean, and air-conditioned **Café Amelia** (no tel., daily 8am-10pm) sells simple sandwiches, empanadas, and pastries, all below CUC3.

Paladares

At the homey ★ **Corte de Principe** (Calle 9na, esq. 74, tel. 5255-9091, daily noon-3pm and 7pm-11pm), Italian owner-chef Sergio serves probably the finest Italian fare in town on a simple alfresco patio with a quasi-Italian motif. Go with Sergio's nightly recommendations (there's no written menu), such as a divine beef carpaccio with mozzarella and olive oil, eggplant parmesan, or garlic shrimp. Leave room for real Häagen-Dazs ice cream. Sergio over-chills the red wines, so call ahead to have him open a bottle ahead of time. And if only he wouldn't smoke in his own restaurant! Around the corner, and more elegant and avant-garde, is **Bom Apetíte** (Calle 11 #7210, e/ 72 y 74, Playa, tel. 07/203-3634, open daily 24 hours), an air-conditioned Italian restaurant serving divine pizza, ravioli, and gnocchi.

Gourmet Italian fare is the name of the game at **Nero di Seppia** (Cale 6 #122 e/ 1ra y 3ra, tel. 5478-7871, walterginevri@nauta.cu, Tues.-Sun noon-midnight). Wood-oven pizza, fettuccine with porcini and salsiccia—it's all here, and all beyond good. You'll dine on generous portions in a renovated mansion with various dining rooms and a terrace.

Moscatelli (Av. 7ma #6609 e/ 66 y 70, tel. 07/203-4507, Tues.-Sun. noon-4pm and 5pm-1am) is overseen by Marco, a dietician from Italy's Lazio region. He amazes with his ability to import ingredients from his home. This is classic Italian fare, such as eggplant parmigiana, and seafood fettucine (CUC14). Given its location, it's popular with local business folk and diplomats.

Boasting a one-of-a-kind riverside setting, ★ **Río Mar** (3ra y Final #11, La Puntilla, tel. 07/720-4838, riomarbargrill@gmail.com, daily noon-midnight) has a sensational locale and a ritzy modern aesthetic, thanks to a year-long renovation of a 1950s modernist manse. Choose the alfresco waterfront deck over the snazzy air-conditioned interior, but bring a sweater in winter when a chill wind can kick in. The fusion *criolla* menu includes artfully presented ceviche (CUC5), beef carpaccio (CUC8), lamb with red wine and rosemary (CUC12), and chicken in blue cheese sauce with malanga purée (CUC15). Chef Alberto Álvarez is best known for his house dish: red snapper on a bed of potatoes.

Reservations are vital at the venerable **Cocina de Lilliam** (Calle 48 #1311, e/ 13 y 15, Miramar, tel. 07/209-6514, Sun.-Fri. noon-3pm and 7pm-10pm, CUC15-25), in the lush grounds of a 1930s-era mansion romantically lit at night. The brick-lined patio is shaded by trees and set with colonial lanterns and wrought-iron tables and chairs. Lilliam Domínguez conjures up tasty nouvelle Cuban. Her appetizers include tartlets of tuna and onion, and a savory dish of garbanzo beans and ham with onion and red and green peppers. Entrées include such Cuban classics as simmered lamb with onions and peppers; chicken breast with pineapple; and fresh fish dishes and oven-roasted meats served with creamy mashed potatoes.

By the shore, the suave, South Beach-style ★ **Paladar Vistamar** (1ra Av. #2206, e/ 22 y 24, tel. 07/203-8328, www.restaurantevistamar.com, daily noon-midnight) appeals for its ocean view with the Atlantic breakers crashing in front of an infinity pool. Owner Joel Arcu Otaño's modernist villa is popular for its high-quality seafood. It also serves continental fare as well as Cuban staples. Starters include mussels in white wine sauce (CUC8), while main dishes include swordfish fillet with parmesan sauce (CUC15) and Mediterranean-style seafood pasta (CUC13). I never fail to order the serrano stuffed with honey and fig paste; the lobster presentation is a work of art. Leave room for a thick slab of lemon pie topped with meringue.

Fresh from a makeover, **Paladar Ristorante El Palio** (1ra Av. #2402, esq. 24, tel. 5289-2410 or 5358-6690, daily noon-midnight) has lured Ernesto Cárdenas, former head chef at the Hotel Parque Central. The menu has expanded, but still focuses on

Italian-*criolla* cuisine, such as garlic octopus (CUC4) and shrimp cocktail (CUC6), plus a shrimp and lobster casserole (CUC8). Dine in a shaded garden or in a chic air-conditioned room with white-and-bottle-green settings.

La Fontana (3ra Av. #305, esq. 46, tel. 07/202-8337, www.lafontanahavana.info, daily noon-midnight, CUC2-15) specializes in barbecued meats from an outdoor grill serving T-bone steak. Starters include salads, *escabeche* (ceviche), and onion soup; main dishes include flavorful chicken with rice, pepper, and onions served in an earthenware bowl. Rice and extras cost additional. Choose cellar or garden seating in a traditional country *bohío* setting.

Cuban-Spanish couple Amy Torralbas (an artist) and Álvaro Díez (a sommelier) combine their respective skills at ★ **Otra Manera** (Calle 35 #1810, e/ 20 y 41, tel. 07/203-8315, www.otramaneralahabana.com, Tues.-Sat. noon-3pm and 7pm-11pm). Their *paladar* recreates Amy's grandma's restaurant. Its gorgeous 21st-century minimalist sophistication draws expats to savor the sublime Cuban-Spanish fusion fare such as Andalusian gazpacho, baked snapper with ginger and coconut vinaigrette, or a chicken casserole with candied potatoes. Otra Manera defines Cuba's *nueva cocina* fare.

The unpretentious **Mi Jardín** (Calle 66 #517, esq. 5ta Av. B, tel. 07/203-4627, daily noon-midnight, CUC15-20), in a beautiful 1950s home full of antiques, is run by an affable and conscientious Mexican and his Italian wife. They serve quasi-Mexican fare. The chicken *molé mexicano* and house special fish Veracruz are recommended. You'll also find enchiladas and *totopos* (nachos), plus Italian and *criolla* dishes. You can dine inside or on a patio beneath an arbor.

Doctor Café (Calle 28 #111, e/ 1ra y 3ra, tel. 07/203-4718, www.doctorcafehavana.com, Mon.-Fri. 11am-11pm, Sat. 12:30pm-10pm) has some of the most creative gourmet dishes in town, courtesy of chef Juan Carlos. Every dish I've eaten here has been sublime. Try the crab ceviche or shredded crab enchilada

appetizers, lasagna bolognesa (CUC13), or maybe a "deluxe burger" (CUC16). Choose patio dining or the atmospheric air-conditioned interior. Reservations are required.

Savor the best pizza in town at **La Chuchería** (Av. 1ra esq. 28, tel. 07/212-5013, daily 8am-1am), an oceanfront edition of Vedado's eponymous pizzeria. This converted Spanish Renaissance manse has great ambience, and the bargain-priced pizzas are the best in town. Wash it all down with a milk shake.

Restaurante Habanera (Calle 16 #506, e/ 5ta y 7ma., tel. 07/202-9941 or 5511-8723, habnera506@gmail.com, daily noon-midnight) offers casual elegance in a converted 1930s mansion with faux-washed walls and a checkered floor. Curried shrimp in coconut cream, lobster with mango, and lamb with red wine sauce are highlights of the fusion cuisine menu. In clement weather, opt for the lovely garden terrace.

Out in Jaimanitas, ★ **Santy Pescador** (Calle 240A #3C23, e/ 3raC y Río, tel. 07/272-4998 or 5286-7039, santy_ch2004@hayoo.es, daily noon-midnight, by reservation) is a homey riverfront shack with no menu, but the best sashimi and nigiri you'll ever eat (CUC10-20). Each morning Carlos and Felix, the fishermen-hosts (Santy was their dad), bring in their own catch; they kill and gut the fish to serve minutes before you eat it, prepared with some olive oil, coriander, and soy. There are two private air-conditioned rooms and bi-level riverside dining overlooking the funky fishing boats tethered to even funkier wharves.

Criolla

I return time and again to ★ **El Aljibe** (7ma Av., e/ 24 y 26, tel. 07/204-1583, daily noon-midnight), my favorite state-run restaurant in Havana. It's popular with tour groups. You dine beneath a soaring thatch roof. The sole reason to be here is for the delicious house dish: *pollo asado el aljibe*, roast chicken glazed with a sweet orange sauce, then baked and served with fried plantain chips, rice, french fries, and black beans served until you can eat no more. It's a tremendous bargain at CUC12; desserts and beverages cost extra. Other *criolla* dishes are served (CUC10-20). You can even take away what you don't eat. A 10 percent service charge is also billed. The wine cellar is the city's largest.

Seafood

State-run **Don Cangrejo** (1ra Av., e/ 16 y 18, tel. 07/204-3837, daily noon-midnight) offers some of the finest seafood in town, served in a converted colonial mansion offering views out to sea. It's popular with the monied Cuban elite. The menu features crab cocktail (CUC6), crab claws (CUC18), and seafood mix (CUC25). The wine list runs to more than 150 labels.

Continental

Long a favorite of the Cuban elite, the overpriced **Tocororo** (Calle 18 #302, esq. 3ra, tel. 07/204-2209, Mon.-Sat. noon-midnight, CUC25-35), housed in a neoclassical mansion, has an antique-filled lobby extending into a garden patio with rattan furniture, Tiffany lamps, potted plants, and wooden parrots hanging from gilt perches, plus real parrots in cages. A pianist (by day) and jazz ensemble (by night) entertain. The merely average food is typical Cuban fare, although crocodile and ostrich occasionally feature. Even the bread will be charged, and a 10 percent service charge is automatic.

Self-Catering

Supermercado 70 (3ra Av., e/ 62 y 70, Miramar, tel. 07/204-2890, Mon.-Sat. 9am-6pm, Sun. 9am-1pm) is Cuba's largest supermarket selling imported foodstuffs. However, the best selection is at **Palco** (Mon.-Sat. 10am-6pm, Sun. 9am-1pm), in the Miramar Trade Center; aficionados know that if you can't find it here, it ain't to be found in Cuba. **Zona+** (Av. 7ma 3/ 66 y 68) is the nation's first wholesale store for private businesses, a kind of mini Cuban Costco.

ACROSS THE HARBOR

La Divina Pastora (tel. 07/860-8341, daily noon-midnight), below the Fortaleza de San Carlos de la Cabaña, offers average *criolla* fare in a harborfront setting; go for the setting. Its adjoining **La Tasca** bar-restaurant (tel. 07/860-8341, daily noon-11pm) offers an escape from the tour groups that descend on the main restaurant.

Paladar Doña Carmela (Calle B #10, tel. 07/867-7472, beatrizbarletta@yahoo.com, daily 7pm-11pm) serves delicious *criolla* fare such as a sublime octopus in garlic in an outdoor setting. Competing with Doña Carmela, **El Cañonazo** (Casa #27, tel. 07/867-7476 or 5361-7503), opposite the entrance to Fortaleza de San Carlos, is almost identical. This re-creation of a farmstead with poultry running around underfoot packs in the tourists, brought for commissions by every other taxi driver in town. As such, you pay inflated prices for roast chicken (CUC14), lobster (CUC17), and other dishes.

In Guanabacoa, the best option is the casual **Mangle Rojo** (Av. 1ra #2, e/ 11 y 12, Rpto. Chibas, tel. 07/797-8613, manglerojo.havana@yahoo.es, daily noon-11pm), serving fresh salads, superb pizzas, and tasty *criolla* dishes, all less than CUC10. Opt for either air-conditioned dining or the patio. It's worth the detour to **El Mexicano** (Av. 3ra #6 e/ 2da y 3ra, Rpto. Chibás, Guanabacoa, tel. 5263-5413, daily noon-11pm) for its superb sandwiches and grilled meat dishes. Owner Jorge Luis Pérez has been running his café-counter restaurant with aplomb for two decades.

Accommodations

All hotels have air-conditioned rooms with satellite TVs, telephones, and safes; most have Wi-Fi. With the U.S. tourism tsunami in full flood, tour groups take over the high-end hotels and push up prices astronomically. There is no longer a low season! You'll be wise to make reservations far in advance.

Casas particulares (private room rentals) have air-conditioning and private bathrooms, unless noted. New *casas* open weekly; Havana now has several thousand. The huge demand drives up standards (and prices). Since 2015, several deluxe privately owned "boutique" hotels have opened within the *casa particular* category.

With room availability at such a premium, keep your eyes on new hotels expected to open in the next two years: the 212-room **Sofitel So La Habana** (Prado esq. Malecón), Accor's 112-room **MGallery,** the 202-room **Ibis,** and the 82-room **Pancea Havana Cuba** (Dragones esq. Industriales). Habaguanex plans to open six hotels in 2017-2019: **Catedral** (Mercaderes esq. Empedrado; 24 rooms), **Cueto** (Plaza Vieja; 57 rooms), the **Marque de Cárdenas de Monte Hermoso** (21 rooms), and **Real Aduana** (in the current Customs building; 55 rooms) on Plaza San Francisco. Havana will get its first airport hotel when Canada's Wilton Properties builds the 363-room **Hotel Arte,** near José Martí Aeropuerto Internacional. And China's Suntime International has partnered with Cubanacán to build the 600-room **Hemingway Hotel** at the Hemingway Marina.

Which District?

Location is important in choosing your hotel.

Habana Vieja puts you in the heart of the old city, within walking distance of Havana's main tourist sights. Two dozen colonial-era mansions previously administered by Habaguanex (the commercial branch of the Office of the City Historian) offer yesteryear ambience and modern bathrooms; at press time, these hotels were being transferred to the military's Gaviota tourism branch. There's also a full range of state-run hotels and a wide choice of private room rentals. In this neighborhood the term *hostal* merely refers to small size.

Centro Habana, although offering few sites of interest, has three budget-oriented hotels; Cuba's state tour agencies push the Hotel Deauville, used by many budget package-tour companies, but this gloomy cement tower is terrible and everyone who stays there has a complaint. This run-down residential district also has many *casas particulares,* but safety is a concern.

Vedado and Plaza de la Revolución offer mid-20th-century accommodations well situated for sightseeing, including several first-class modernist hotels with modest decor. Vedado also has dozens of superb *casas particulares.*

Playa (Miramar and Beyond) has moderate hotels popular with tour groups, modern deluxe hotels aimed at business travelers, and deluxe private villas. All are far from the main tourist sights; you'll need wheels or taxis to get around.

HABANA VIEJA
Casas Particulares

Hands-down the most sensational offering is ★ **Casa Vitrales** (Calle Habana #106, tel. 07/866-2607 or 5264-7673, www.cvitrales.com, CUC100 including breakfast). Owner Osmani Hernández bills his nine-bedroom guesthouse as a "boutique hotel" and has exquisitely restored and furnished his *casa particular* with a mix of antiques, '50s modernist pieces, and vibrant contemporary art. The only drawback is the narrow staircase, which winds up four flights to the rooftop breakfast terrace. Situated in the epicenter of Habana

Vieja's gentrification, reservations here are essential.

The pricey ★ **Casa Pedro y María** (Calle Chacón #209, e/ Aguacate y Compostela, tel. 07/861-4641, www.boutiquehotelsincuba. com, CUC100 including breakfast) is in a gorgeously restored 18th-century townhouse. Behind the huge nail-studded door, colonial decor fuses with 21st-century touches; you'll love the rough stone walls. Three bedrooms and one junior suite open to a quiet patio where breakfast is served. (My room had a tiny but delightful en suite shower-bathroom in a space hidden by a curtain.)

Emblematic of the new boutique-type offerings is ★ **Loft Habana** (Calle Oficios #402 e/ Luz y Acosta, tel. 07/864-4685 or 5284-2256, www.lofthabana.com, CUC120-350), with seven unique loft-like units inside a knocked-about building facing the harbor. These stylish air-conditioned units range from standard to deluxe; all have bare stone walls, mezzanine bedrooms, and en suite shower bathrooms. The rooms are kitted out to 21st-century standards and exhibit the good taste of Cuban designer José Antonio Choy. There is a two-night minimum stay.

Hundreds of budget *casas* offer humbler yet adequate lodging. For example, **Hostal del Ángel** (Cuarteles #118 e/ Monserrate y Habana, tel. 07/860-0771 or 5264-7686, www.pradocolonial.com, CUC30-35) offers a better bargain, although it doesn't have the chic of Casa Vitrales or Casa Pedro-María. Restored by German owner Kenia, this centenary town home is stuffed with gorgeous antique furnishings. A spiral staircase leads to a mezzanine library, and balconies hang over the plaza. Its two bedrooms have en suite bathrooms.

Casa de Raquel y Ricardo (Calle Cristo #12, e/ Brasil y Muralla, tel. 07/867-5026, kasarakel@gmail.com, CUC25-30) is a gracious upstairs home; the spacious, airy lounge has rockers and *mediopuntos*. There are two rooms with lofty ceilings; one is air-conditioned and has its own bathroom.

Gay-friendly **Casa de Eugenio Barral**

García (San Ignacio #656, e/ Jesús María y Merced, tel. 07/862-9877, CUC30), in southern Habana Vieja, has seven air-conditioned bedrooms with fans and refrigerators; five have private modern bathrooms. The old home is graciously and eclectically appointed with antiques.

Casa de Pepe y Rafaela (San Ignacio #454, e/ Sol y Santa Clara, tel. 07/867-5551, CUC30-35), on the second floor of a colonial home, has a spacious lounge full of antiques and songbirds. The owners rent three rooms with tall ceilings, fridges, fans, antique beds and furniture, glass chandeliers, and heaps of light pouring in from the balcony windows. Modern bathrooms have large showers.

Hotels
CUC100-200

At press time, the historic **Hotel Inglaterra** (Prado #416, esq. San Rafael, tel. 07/860-8594, www.gran-caribe.cu, from CUC90 s, CUC142 d low season, CUC120 s, CUC175 d high season), on the west side of Parque Central, was in the midst of a much-needed redo and relaunch by U.S. hotel company Starwood. It will reopen as a luxury hotel. No doubt it will retain its extravagant lobby bar and restaurant that whisk you metaphorically to Morocco. Expect its 83 rooms to offer great comfort and furnishings.

I like the **Hotel del Tejadillo** (Tejadillo, esq. San Ignacio, tel. 07/863-7283, from CUC95 s, CUC150 d low season, from CUC120 s, CUC195 d high season), another converted colonial mansion. Beyond the huge doors is an airy marble-clad lobby with a quaint dining area. It offers 32 rooms around two courtyards with fountains. The cool, high-ceilinged rooms are graced by *mediopuntos* (stained glass half-moon windows) and modern furniture.

Playing on a monastic theme, the **Hostal Los Frailes** (Brasil, e/ Oficios y Mercaderes, tel. 07/862-9383, from CUC95 s, CUC145 d low season, from CUC120 s, CUC195 d high season) has staff dressed in monks' habits. It has 22 rooms around a patio with a fountain.

The rooms have medieval-style heavy timbers and wrought iron, religious prints, period telephones, and spacious bathrooms. It has a bar, but no restaurant.

Just one block from Plaza Vieja, **Hotel Beltrán de Santa Cruz** (San Ignacio #411, e/ Muralla y Sol, tel. 07/860-8330, from CUC95 s, CUC150 d low season, from CUC120 s, CUC195 d high season) is a handsome conversion of a three-story 18th-century mansion with exquisite *mediopuntos*. Its 11 rooms and one junior suite have gracious antique reproductions.

The latest of Habaguanex's boutique properties is the delightful **Habana 1612 Hotel** (Calle Habana #612, e/ Brasil y Muralla, tel. 07/866-5035, from CUC95 s, CUC140 d low season, from CUC120 s, CUC195 d high season). The 17th-century townhouse mansion has undergone a gorgeous refurbishing, melding modern decor throughout. With only 12 rooms, it exudes intimacy; seven rooms face the courtyard. The immediate neighborhood awaits restoration, so you're in the heart of earthy Habana Vieja.

If you're struggling to find rooms, there are other properties to try. **El Mesón de la Flota** (Mercaderes #257, e/ Amargura y Brasil, tel. 07/863-3838, CUC80 s, CUC130 d low season, CUC100 s, CUC170 d high season, including breakfast) is a classic Spanish *bodega* bar-restaurant with five intimate rooms. **Hotel Park View** (Colón, esq. Morro, tel. 07/861-3293, CUC62 s, CUC100 d low season, CUC67 s, CUC110 d high season, including breakfast) has 55 lofty and nicely furnished rooms, but minimal facilities. The drab **Hotel Plaza** (Zulueta #267, esq. Neptuno, tel. 07/860-8583, www.gran-caribe.cu, from CUC84 s, CUC120 d low-season) was built in 1909 on the northeast corner of Parque Central. It has 188 rooms (some gloomy; others noisy) that feature antique reproductions.

OVER CUC200

The Moorish-inspired **Hotel Mercure Sevilla Havane** (Trocadero #55, e/ Prado y Zulueta, tel. 07/860-8560, www.accorhotels.com, from CUC132 s, CUC164 d low season, CUC255 s, CUC274 d high season) was built in 1924, with an exterior and lobby straight out of *1,001 Arabian Nights*. Its 178 refurbished rooms feature antique reproductions. There's a sumptuous top-floor restaurant, plus a swimming pool and assorted shops.

Hotel Santa Isabel (Baratillo #9, e/ Obispo y Narciso López, tel. 07/860-8201, from CUC175 s, CUC260 d low season, from CUC210 s, CUC295 d high season), a small and intimate hostelry in the former 18th-century palace of the Count of Santovenia, enjoys a fabulous setting overlooking Plaza de Armas. The hotel has 27 rooms furnished with four-poster beds, reproduction antique furniture, and leather recliners on wide balconies; suites have whirlpool tubs. At press time, it was taken over by U.S. hotel giant Starwood, with plans to upgrade and rebrand as a mega-luxury option.

Overpriced **Hostal Valencia** (Oficios #53, e/ Obrapía y Lamparilla, tel. 07/867-1037, from CUC115 s, CUC165 d low season, from CUC140 s, CUC230 d high season) might induce a flashback to the romantic *posadas* of Spain. The 18th-century mansion-turned-hotel exudes charm with its lobby of hefty oak beams, Spanish tiles, and wrought-iron chandeliers. The 12 spacious rooms and junior suites have cool marble floors. The La Paella restaurant is a bonus. Attached is the **Hotel El Comendador** (Oficios #53, e/ Obrapía y Lamparilla, tel. 07/857-1037, from CUC115 s, CUC165 d low season, from CUC140 s, CUC230 d high season), another endearingly restored colonial home with 14 exquisite rooms.

The **Hotel Ambos Mundos** (Obispo #153, e/ San Ignacio y Mercaderes, tel. 07/860-9530, from CUC115 s, CUC175 d low season, from CUC140 s, CUC230 d high season), one block west of Plaza de Armas, lets you rest your head where Ernest Hemingway found inspiration in the 1930s. The hotel offers 59 overpriced rooms and three junior suites arranged atrium style. Most are small, dark, and undistinguished. Those facing the interior courtyard are quieter. Avoid the fifth floor—a thoroughfare for sightseers.

On the harborfront, **Hotel Armadores de Santander** (Luz #4, esq. San Pedro, tel. 07/862-8000, from CUC115 s, CUC175 d low season, from CUC140 s, CUC230 d high season, CUC300 s/d suite year-round) has 39 spacious rooms with colonial tile floors and handsome furnishings. A contemporary suite boasts a whirlpool tub in the center of a mezzanine bedroom with a four-poster bed.

A fine colonial conversion, the romantic **Hotel Palacio O'Farrill** (Cuba #102, esq. Chacón, tel. 07/860-5080, from CUC115 s, CUC175 d low season, from CUC140 s, CUC230 d high season) is centered on a three-story atrium courtyard lit by a skylight. It has 38 graciously furnished rooms on three floors, with decor reflecting the 18th (mezzanine), 19th (3rd floor), and 20th (4th floor) centuries. Facilities include a cybercafé, an elegant restaurant, and a jazz café.

Dating to 1905, ★ **Hotel Raquel** (San Ignacio, esq. Amargura, tel. 07/860-8280, from CUC115 s, CUC175 d low season, from CUC145 s, CUC230 d high season, including breakfast) is a dramatic exemplar of art nouveau style. The lobby gleams with marble columns and period detailing such as Tiffany lamps and a mahogany bar. It has an elegant restaurant and a rooftop solarium and gym. Located on the edge of the old Jewish quarter, the Hotel Raquel is Jewish themed and the restaurant serves kosher food.

City slickers will love the urbane sophistication of the stylish, 27-room **Hotel Palacio del Marqués de San Felipe y Santiago de Bejucal** (Calle Oficios #152, esq. Mercaderes, tel. 07/864-9194, from CUC145 s, CUC230 d low season, from CUC170 s, CUC280 d high season), on Plaza de San Francisco. The converted 1771 mansion of Don Sebastián de Peñalver blends a chic 21st-century interior—including dark mahogany in a sleek reception area—with a baroque exterior. Rooms (including three suites) have Wi-Fi, DVDs, and flat-screen TVs, plus Jacuzzis.

Entered via giant brass-studded carriage doors, ★ **Hotel Conde de Villanueva** (Mercaderes #202, esq. Lamparilla, tel. 07/862-9293, from CUC115 s, CUC175 d low season, from CUC140 s, CUC230 d high season) is an exquisite conversion of the mansion of the Conde de Villanueva. Doors open to an intimate courtyard with caged birds and tropical foliage. It has nine large and simply appointed rooms and one suite (with whirlpool tub) with 1920s reproduction furnishings. There's an excellent restaurant and bar. The hotel courts cigar smokers with a cigar store and smokers' lounge.

★ **Hotel Florida** (Obispo #252, esq. Cuba, tel. 07/862-4127, from CUC115 s, CUC175 d low season, from CUC140 s, CUC230 d high season) is built around an atrium courtyard with rattan lounge chairs, a stained glass skylight, and black-and-white checkered marble floors. Sumptuously furnished, its 25 rooms feature tasteful colonial decor. Immediately behind the hotel, and part of the same building, is the similarly priced **Hotel Marqués de Prado Ameno** (Obispo #252, esq. Cuba, tel. 07/862-4127). The restored 18th-century mansion has 16 stylishly furnished rooms. A *bodega* (colonial-style bar/restaurant) will whisk you back 200 years.

On Parque Central, **Hotel Telégrafo** (Paseo de Martí #408, esq. Neptuno, tel. 07/861-1010, from CUC115 s, CUC175 d low season, from CUC140 s, CUC230 d high season) melds its classical elements into an exciting contemporary vogue. It has 63 rooms with beautiful furnishings and trendy color schemes. The hip lobby bar is skylit within an atrium framed by colonial ruins.

Perhaps the best hotel in Havana for its combination of location, service, and sophistication, the ★ **Hotel Iberostar Parque Central** (Neptuno, e/ Prado y Zulueta, tel. 07/860-6627, www.iberostar.com, from CUC235 s, CUC295 d year-round) occupies the north side of Parque Central and fuses colonial and contemporary styles in its 281 spacious and tastefully furnished rooms. Ask for a room with a wooden floor, as some rooms with carpets smell mildewed. It has two restaurants, a cigar lounge-bar, a business center, a rooftop swimming pool, and a fitness room. A modern 150-room annex, the similarly priced **Iberostar Parque Central Torre,** offers far hipper decor and postmodern design. It also has a rooftop restaurant and pool.

The finest rooms in Havana are at the ★ **Hotel Saratoga** (Paseo de Martí #603, esq. Dragones, tel. 07/868-1000, www.hotelsaratoga.com, CUC284 s/d low season, from CUC506 s/d high season). European architects and designers have turned this colonial edifice into a visual stunner. Guest room decor varies from colonially inspired to thoroughly contemporary. Most rooms have king-size four-poster beds; all have halogen-lit bathrooms and 21st-century amenities. A rooftop pool, spa, and gym offer fabulous views. The bar and restaurant are New York-chic.

The ultra-deluxe ★ **Gran Hotel Kempinski Manzana** (Agramonte esq. Neptuno, www.kempinski.com, from CUC370 s/d low seasn, CUC499 s/d high season) is *the* place to bed down in town. Located in the reconstructed Edificio Manzana de Gómez (dating from 1918) on Parque Central, the 24-room hotel is managed by Swiss hotel group Kempinski and features a rooftop terrace with a swimming pool, plus three restaurants, a spa, and a business center.

The formerly grandiose building at the corner of Prado and Capdevila lay in ruins for two decades, its facade supported by scaffolding. In 2016, Cuba's Gaviota group began building a new hotel there integrated into the century-old facade. At press time, it was nearing completion as the 300-room deluxe **Hotel Packard** (www.gaviota-grupo.com).

CENTRO HABANA
Casas Particulares

In a townhouse overlooking the Malecón, **Casa de Martha y Leona** (Malecón #115, e/ Crespo y Genios, tel. 07/864-1582, leorangisbert@yahoo.es, CUC25) has a loft room that overlooks the family lounge with floor-to-ceiling windows with ocean views. Although simply furnished, the air-conditioned room has a modern bathroom, fridge, and fan.

For boutique chic, check into the appropriately named ★ **Casa Blanca** (Malecón #413 e/ Manrique y Perseverancia, tel. 07/862-3137, www.casablancacuba.net, CUC35-50), which has all-white decor and European furnishings. It has three rooms, each with a balcony overlooking the Atlantic.

Casa 1932 Habana (Campanario #63, e/ Lagunas y San Lázaro, tel. 07/863-6203, www.casahabana.net, CUC30-35) is an art deco wonder with an antique-filled lounge. There are three bedrooms, all with private bathrooms and hot water. Enjoy coffee or cocktails on the exquisite patio.

Party animals stumbling out of Casa de las Américas in the wee hours will appreciate bedding down at **Casa Elaine González López** (Galiano #257 Apt. 81, e/ Neptuno y Concordia, tel. 07/866-0910 or 5273-9295), on the 8th floor of Edificio América. Choose either a large single bedroom (CUC25-30) with modern bathroom or the entire floor as a two-bedroom apartment (CU50); the lounge has heaps of light and great views toward Vedado.

Perfect for families and small groups, the luxurious and self-contained ★ **Casa Concordia** (Concordia #151, Apt. B, esq. San Nicolás, tel. 5254-5240 or 5360-5300, www.casaconcordia.net, from CUC240 nightly) is furnished to boutique hotel standards. This gorgeous fifth-floor, three-bedroom apartment is adorned with fine-art ceramics and photography, a 32-inch flat-screen TV and other modern accoutrements, plus plush linens, including in the en suite bathrooms. The rate includes maid service, and breakfast and car transfers are offered. The same owners offer a homier one-room unit at the nearby **Tropicana Penthouse** (Galiano #60 Apt 101, e/ San Lázaro y Trocadero, www.tropicanapenthouse.com, CUC50), with modern furnishings, flat-screen TV, breakfast service, and a terrace atop a 10-story apartment block.

Bringing chic to a whole new level is the boutique ★ **Malecón 633** (Malecón #633 e/ Escobar y Lealtad, tel. 5840-5403, www.

malecon663.com, CUC50). Its four rooms are individually themed: the Eclectic Room evokes sumptuous centenary art nouveau; fans of art deco get the bi-level Art Deco Room with mezzanine bedroom; the Modern Room is furnished in 1950s style; and the Contemporary Suite offers a 21st-century take. You even get a Jacuzzi in the rooftop solarium. If midnight hunger pangs strike, downstairs is the eponymous tapas bar-restaurant. (Hopefully the music won't disturb your sweet dreams.) Owners Orlandito (Cuban) and Sandra (French) also offer vintage car tours. A stone's throw away, the three-bedroom ★ Malecón 215 (Malecón #215 esq. Escobar, tel. 5319-7569, CUC295) inspires oohs and aahs with its sumptuous remake. It has terrazo floors, gorgeous furnishings, and a to-die-for ocean view. It rents in entirety.

Hotels
CUC100-200
A stylish boutique option, the ultra-contemporary 14-room **Hotel Terral** (Malecón, esq. Lealtad, tel. 07/860-2100, comercial@hotelterral.co.cu, from CUC850 s, CUC130 d low season, CUC110 s, CUC175 d high season) opens onto the Malecón and features glass walls and heaps of travertine and stainless steel. Flat-screen TVs, minibars, and safes are standard, as are spa tubs. Some rooms have terraces. It has a bar, plus room service, but no restaurant.

VEDADO AND PLAZA DE LA REVOLUCIÓN
Casas Particulares
★ **Casa de Jorge Coalla Potts** (Calle I #456, Apto. 11, e/ 21 y 23, Vedado, tel. 07/832-9032 or 07/5283-1237, www.havanaroomrental.com, CUC30-35) is my favorite *casa particular* in Havana. This delightful home is run by Jorge and his wife, Marisel, who offer two large, well-lit, and well-furnished bedrooms to the rear of their spotless ground-floor apartment, only two blocks from the Hotel Habana Libre Tryp. Each room has a telephone, refrigerator, double bed with firm mattress, ceiling fan, and spacious bathroom

with plentiful hot water. There's a TV lounge with rockers, plus secure parking nearby. The couple and their daughter Jessica (fluent in English) go out of their way to make you feel at home.

I've enjoyed stays with Jorge Praga and Amparo Sánchez at **Casa Fraga** (Calle 11 #452 alto, e/ E y F, tel. 07/832-7184, amparosanchezg@hotmail.com, CUC35), where you are treated like family. They rent four rooms (two share a bathroom). One has lovely antique furnishings. Plus you can use their computer with Internet. A sparsely furnished lounge looks onto the street.

The filling breakfasts—including crêpes with honey—are reason enough to choose **Casa de Eddy Gutiérrez** (Calle 21 #408, e/ F y G, tel. 07/832-5207 or 5281-0041, carmeddy2@yahoo.es, CUC35). Four independent apartments are to the rear of the owner's colonial mansion, including a lovely little cross-ventilated rooftop unit. All have fans and refrigerators. One apartment has its own small kitchen. There's secure parking.

A true standout, ★ **Casa Marta** (Av. de los Presidentes #301, e/ 17 y 19, tel. 07/832-6475, www.casamartainhavana.com, CUC40) is a sensational four-room apartment that takes up the entire 14th floor and boasts wraparound glass windows. The beautifully maintained and spacious rooms feature antique beds and modern bathrooms, and all have spectacular views. Martha is an engaging conversationalist who speaks fluent English. She also offers an impeccably maintained 10th-floor self-contained two-bedroom apartment nearby (Calle 9 #453 e/ F y G, CUC60-70).

One block away from Hotel Presidente, ★ **Casa Nieves** (Calle 9na #485 altos e/ F y F, tel. 07/832-2974, CUC175 s/d) offers boutique hotel ambience. Graced with a delightful hostess, this spacious and airy four-bedroom upstairs manse opens to a lovely courtyard where delicious meals are served. It has been thoroughly renovated with modern bathrooms and consistent hot water.

A delightful hostess adds to your stay at **Casa Elaine Colonial Guesthouse** (Av.

de los Presidentes esq. 13, tel. 07/832-4108 or 5275-1876, travelcuba73@yahoo.com, CUC35), a huge centenary home with lofty ceilings and twin lounges with eclectic furnishings. Elaine rents five large rooms, each different in style.

Casa Blanca (Calle 13 #917, e/ 6 y 8, tel. 07/833-5697, cb1917@hotmail.com, CUC30), in the heart of western Vedado, is a gracious colonial home with a front garden riotous with bougainvillea. Your host, Jorge, rents two antique-filled rooms with clean, modern bathrooms. It has parking.

"Palatial" sums up the 1915 ★ **Palacete de Vedado** (Calle D #154 e/ Linea y Calzada, www.palacetedelvedado.com, CUC400), a fully restored, two-story, four-bedroom manse tastefully furnished in white with cutting-edge art and boutique-hotel-standard bathrooms. There's even a pool table! The owners offer airport pickup in an old Chevy. It rents in entirety. A stone's throw away, ★ **Hostal Boutique Maraby** (Calle 11 #513, tel. 07/833-6276, www.mariby.com, from CUC230 suites, CUC500 entire house) taps the high-end market with uniformed staff and stunning and vibrant period decor. This romantic time warp is run to professional standards as a five-bedroom boutique B&B. There's a reason haute couture designer Jean Paul Gaultier stayed here.

For a room with a view, you can't beat the sensational (albeit pricey) ★ **Habana Vista Penthouse** (Calle 13 #51 es. N, tel. 5388-7866, www.habanavista.com, CUC115-135). It occupies two floors atop a 16-story 1950s high-rise and is accessed by elevator. Three bedrooms have views, retro-themed furnishings fit for a fashion shoot, and modern marble-clad bathrooms and tubs. It even boasts a private rooftop swimming pool and dining terrace for meals prepared by the kitchen staff. Two-night minimum.

Setting an even higher bar is ★ **Artedel Luxury Penthouse** (Calle 17 #260 e/ I y J, tel. 5295-5700, www.cubaguesthouse.com, CUC120), a three-room high-rise owned by

Ydalgo Martínez. The eclectic furnishings are its real charm and include original 1950s lamps and Murano glass items. The suite with a blood-red wall is simply gorgeous. A rooftop wraparound terrace with 360 views will have you blessing your fortune.

Could *this* be the nicest place in Vedado? ★ **Solinos y Yo** (Calle 16 #2, e/ Calzada y Linea, tel. 07/329-9933, www.solinosyyo.com, CUC90), overlooking the Malecón at the far west end of Veado, combines jaw-dropping white-and-salmon decor with superb ocean vistas. With six air-conditioned and sparse yet lovingly furnished bedrooms, it's perfect for families or small groups. The highlight is the huge lounge with an all-glass wall opening onto a seafront balcony. It's staffed and operates like a B&B.

Want to know what $1,000 a night buys you in Havana's new deluxe private property stakes? Then rent the rooftop apartment in the sleek 10-story high-rise at **Atlantic Penthouse** (Calle D, e/ 1ra y 2ra, tel. 5281-7751, renta.atlantic@gmail.com, from CUC200 s/d), with its chic and luxurious all-white interiors and wall-of-glass vistas over the city and Atlantic. You even get your own rooftop swimming pool with butler service.

Hotels
CUC50-100

Hotel Complejo Vedado St. John's (Calle O #206, e/ 23 y 25, tel. 07/833-3740, www.gran-caribe.cu, CUC48 s, CUC70 d low season, CUC56 s, CUC82 d high season) is a dour and gloomy 14-story property with 87 rooms, plus 203 rooms in the adjoining Hotel Vedado. Facilities include a nightclub, rooftop swimming pool, and the Steak House Toro.

A better option for budget hounds is Islazul's **Hotel Paseo Habana** (Calle 17 #618, esq. A, tel. 07/836-0810, CUC34 s, CUC45 d low season; CUC42 s, CUC55 d high season), in a restored former private mansion in a peaceful section of Vedado. It has delightfully decorated rooms with modern bathrooms at bargain prices.

CUC100-200

The art deco high-rise **Hotel Roc Presidente** (Calzada #110, esq. Av. de los Presidentes, tel. 07/855-1801, www.roc-hotels.com, from UC80 s, CUC130 d low season, CUC98 s, CUC150 d high season) was inaugurated in 1927 and retains its maroon and pink interior, with sumptuous Louis XIV-style furnishings. Now Spanish run, it has 160 spacious rooms with tasteful contemporary furnishings, including marble bathrooms. Amenities include an elegant restaurant, swimming pool, gym, and sauna.

Mobster Meyer Lansky's 23-story **Hotel Habana Riviera** (Malecón y Paseo, tel. 07/836-4051, www.gran-caribe.cu, from CUC80 s, CU125 d low season, from CUC95 s, CUC158 d high season) long ago lost its 1950s luxe but still retains its original lobby decor, with acres of marble and glass and original furnishings. The 352 spacious rooms are one by one being upgraded to modern standards; ensure you get a renovated room. It has two restaurants, a 24-hour snack bar, a swimming pool, gym, cigar store, and the Copa Room nightclub. It was being renovated at press time and will be managed by Spain's Iberostar hotel group.

The **Hotel Capri** (Calle 21, esq. M, tel. 07/839-7200 or 07/839-7257, from CUC120 s, CUC150 d low season; CUC135 s, CUC180 d high season) reopened in February 2014 after a 10-year closure. This 1950s classic has been stylishly refurbished with a retro look in classy brown and pistachio tones. Closer inspection reveals many faults, including shoddy workmanship and pathetic lighting in guest rooms.

Almost boutique in style, the well-positioned **Hotel Victoria** (Calle 19 #101, esq. M, tel. 07/833-3510, www.gran-caribe.cu, CUC62 s, CUC85 d low season; CUC90 s, CUC133 d high season) offers 31 small rooms with antique reproduction furnishings and Internet modems. It has a small swimming pool, an intimate lobby bar, and an elegant restaurant.

OVER CUC200

Hotel Tryp Habana Libre (Calle L, e/ 23 y 25, tel. 07/834-6100, www.meliacuba.com, from CUC222 s, CUC280 d low season; from CUC288 s, CUC372 d high season), managed by Spain's Meliá, is Havana's landmark high-rise hotel. It was built in the 1950s by the Hilton chain and became a favorite of mobsters. The modernist atrium lobby with glass dome exudes a 1950s retro feel. The 533 rooms are decorated in a handsome contemporary

Hotel Habana Riviera, Vedado

vogue. The hotel is loaded with facilities, including a 24-hour café, four restaurants, an open-air swimming pool, a business center, underground parking, and one of Havana's best nightclubs.

The deluxe 22-story ★ **Hotel Meliá Cohiba** (Paseo, esq. 1ra, tel. 07/833-3636, www.meliacuba.com, from CUC221 s, CUC230 d low season; from CUC235 s, CUC280 d high season) has 462 spacious and elegant rooms featuring contemporary furnishings. It boasts first-rate executive services, and the magnificent swimming pool, gym, squash court, solarium, boutiques, five top-ranked restaurants, four bars, and the Habana Café nightclub combine to make this one of the city's finest hotels.

The overpriced, state-run **Hotel Nacional** (Calle O y 21, tel. 07/836-3564, www.hotelnacionaldecuba.com, from CUC338 s, CUC468 d year-round) is Havana's flagship hotel and where celebrities flock. A restoration revived much of the majesty of this eclectic 1930s gem, perched overlooking the Malecón. However, furnishings in the 475 large rooms remain dowdy; even the Executive Floor, with 63 specially appointed rooms and suites, has threadbare carpets and other faults. Dining is a letdown except at La Barranca, the open-air garden restaurant serving *criolla* fare. The Cabaret Parisien, the top-floor cocktail lounge, and the open-air terrace bar—perfect for enjoying a cigar and rum—are high points. Features include two swimming pools, upscale boutiques, a beauty salon, spa, tennis courts, a bank, and a business center.

PLAYA (MIRAMAR AND BEYOND)
Casas Particulares

Casa de Fernando y Egeria González (1ra #205, e/ 2 y 4, Miramar, tel. 07/203-3866, martell@alba.co.cu, CUC50) is a superb property. This gracious family home offers two spacious and airy rooms with huge and exquisite tiled bathrooms. Secure parking is available and there's a patio to the rear.

Many homes in Miramar rent out in entirety, including ★ **Casa de Elena Sánchez** (Calle 34 #714, e/ 7ma y 17, tel. 07/202-8969, gerardo@enet.cu, CUC100), one of the nicest 1950s-style rentals in town. It has two rooms, each with TV, fridge, private hot-water bathroom, and a mix of antiques, 1950s modernist pieces, and contemporary furniture. A large TV lounge opens to a shaded garden patio with rockers. There's secure parking.

For a complete apartment, I like ★ **Casa de Reynaldo y Yasmina** (Calle 17 #3401 e/ 34 y 36, tel. 07/209-2958 or 5241-6794, CUC120), whose ground floor apartment in a lovely 1950s home has three bedrooms, two bathrooms, and a full modern kitchen. Meals can be prepared and served on a shaded rooftop terrace. Reynaldo is a fixer and even rents his chauffeured Audi A4.

The three-bedroom ★ **Cañaveral House** (Calle 39A #4402 e/ 44 y 46, tel. 07/206-5338 or 5295-5700, www.cubaguesthouse.com, CUC120) astounds with its tasteful furnishings. Designer Ydalgo Martínez brought artistic sensibility to this gorgeous Spanish-style hacienda villa, furnished with effusive art, antiques, and contemporary pieces, including the state-of-the-art bathrooms. Rented in entirety, you get what you pay for in spades.

If you want to know how Cuba's elite lives, check out **Casa María Torralbas** (Calle 17 #20606, e/ 206 y 214, Siboney, tel. 07/217-2248 or 5258-5025, mariatorralbas@yahoo.es, CUC55), a gorgeous 1950s modernist bungalow in an area occupied by privileged MININT families. Two beautifully furnished rooms include use of a swimming pool in a lush garden.

Exemplary of the deluxe new breed of villas on the market, ★ **Villa Miller Benfast** (Calle 13 #2017 esq. 204, Siboney, tel. 07/2721-5314 or 5280-7636, CUC850 nightly) is a refurbished 1950s modernist gem with six bedrooms in two wings spanning a huge lounge and state-of-the-art kitchen. A lap pool graces the garden. You even get a well-equipped gym and a poolside lounge bar. It comes fully staffed.

A stunner worthy of *Vogue*, ★ VIP **Le Blanc** (Calle 92 #508 e/ 5ta y 5taA, Miramar, tel. 07/212-5436, www.espacios-de-lujo.com, CUC175 s/d) serves travelers with a taste for high living. Run as a deluxe boutique hotel, this six-bedroom villa is fully staffed with a concierge. Rooms include updated, en-suite baths and Wi-Fi. There's a pool with lounge chairs and a staffed bar plus an on-site chef. Children under age 12 are not permitted.

Out in Santa Fe, **Casa Isabel Betancourt** (Calle 1ra #29628 e/ 296 y 298, tel. 07/208-5070 or 5270-4042, CUC20-40) offers a beachfront location in a beautiful coral stone house with a TV lounge and two lovely rooms. For something more upscale, **Villa Yanin** (Av. 3ra A, www.airbnb.com/rooms/11453585, CUC500), in Cayito de Jaimanitas, offers an oceanfront swimming pool with *ranchón* bar, Jacuzzi, and sundeck. The four-bedroom villa is owned by an Italian-Cuban couple (Marco and Yanin) and has been upgraded with gorgeous terrazzo tile bathrooms. It's steps from Fusterlandia and Marina Hemingway and rents in entirety.

Though out of the way in southern La Vibora, the hilltop ★ **La Rosa de Ortega** (Patrocino #252 esq. Juan Bruno Zayas, tel. 07/641-4329 or 5246-4574, www.larosadeortega.com, CUC60-150) is irresistible for its magical ambience. Exposed brick abounds in this rambling Tuscan-like villa with romantic furnishings, city views, a swimming pool, and a Ford Model A in the driveway. One of the three sumptuously appointed rooms is a suite.

Hotels
CUC50-100
Hotel Kohly (Av. 49 y 36A, Rpto. Kohly, Playa, tel. 07/204-0240, www.gaviota-grupo.com, CUC48 s, CUC66 d low season, CUC58 s, CUC86 d) is a 1970s-style property used by budget tour groups, despite its out-of-the-way location. The 136 rooms have tasteful albeit simple furniture. Facilities include a 10-pin bowling alley.

The lonesome **Hotel Chateau Miramar** (1ra Av., e/ 60 y 62, tel. 07/204-1952, www.hotelescubanacan.com, from CUC72 s, CUC94 d year-round), on the shorefront, aims at business clientele. The handsome five-story hotel has 50 nicely furnished rooms (suites have whirlpool tubs), a pool, an elegant restaurant, and a business center. It's a 20-minute walk to several fine *paladares*.

CUC100-200
The Spanish-managed **Memories Miramar** (5ta Av., e/ 72 y 76, tel. 07/204-3584, www.memoriesresorts.com, from CUC120 s, CUC150 d low season, from CUC170 s, CUC200 d high season) lives up to its deluxe billing. This vast modern property features a mix of neoclassical wrought-iron furniture and hip contemporary pieces in the marble-clad lobby. Its 427 cavernous rooms include five wheelchair-accessible rooms. It has a beauty salon, squash court, health center, tennis courts, a business center, three restaurants, and a huge swimming pool.

Used principally by package-tour groups, the mid-priced oceanfront **Hotel Copacabana** (1ra Av., e/ 34 y 36, tel. 07/204-1037, www.hotelescubanacan.com, CUC90 s, CU110 d low season, CUC128 s, CUC150 d high season) has 168 rooms with a quasi-colonial and slightly dated look; however, its modern bathrooms gleam. Its strong suit is its swimming pool (popular with locals on weekends; day pass CUC15) and a disco.

The 1950s-era beachfront **Hotel Comodoro** (1ra Av. y Calle 84, tel. 07/204-5551, www.hotelescubanacan.com, from CUC60 s, CUC92 d low season, from CUC80 s, CUC130 d high season) has 134 spacious rooms, including 15 suites, with modern furnishings. Some rooms have a balcony. The contemporary lobby lounge opens to four restaurants, several bars, and a meager bathing area. A shuttle runs to Habana Vieja five times daily. The Comodoro's **Bungalows Pleamar** are the closest thing to a beach resort in the city. The 320 two-story villas (one-, two-, and three-bedroom) are built around two sinuous swimming pools.

OVER CUC200

Facing the Miramar Trade Center, **Hotel Meliá Habana** (3ra Av., e/ 76 y 80, tel. 07/204-8500, www.meliacuba.com, from CUC344 s, CUC361 d low season, from CUC475 s, CUC513 d high season), with its huge atrium lobby, is a superb hotel that aims at a business clientele. The 397 marble-clad rooms and four suites are suitably deluxe; the executive floor offers more personalized service plus data ports. Facilities include five restaurants, a cigar lounge, a swimming pool, tennis courts, a gym, and a business center.

With a blue-tinted glass exterior, the contemporary **H10 Panorama** (Calle 70, esq. 3ra, tel. 07/204-0100, www.10hotels.com, from CUC148 s, CUC211 d low season, from CUC204 s, CUC208 d high season) high-rise boasts an impressive black-and-gray marble and slate atrium lobby. I like the sophisticated decor in its 317 rooms, all with Internet modems. The executive rooms and suites get their own top-floor restaurant, and floors 7-11 have Wi-Fi. Other facilities include a piano bar, a squash court, an Internet room, Italian- and German-themed restaurants, a swimming pool, and a top-floor piano bar with live jazz.

U.S. hospitality company Starwood took over management of the former Hotel Quinta Avenida in 2016, rebranding it the **Four Points by Sheraton** (5ta Av. e/ 76 y 78, tel. 07/214-1470, from CUC196 s, CUC246 d low season, from CUC333 s, CUC384 high season). It's a pleasant enough place and offers plenty of facilities plus 186 rooms, including six suites, but is hugely overpriced.

ACROSS THE HARBOR

★ **Casa Blanca** (Casa #29, tel. 5294-5397, www.havanacasablanca.com, CUC250) is a great *casa particular* near the El Morro Cabaña complex. This restored, two-bedroom 19th-century villa rents in entirety. It has a pool, shady terraces opening to lovely gardens, and maid service, including for meals.

Information and Services

MONEY

Banks and Exchange Agencies

The **Banco Financiero Internacional** (Mon.-Fri. 8am-3pm, 8am-noon only on the last working day of each month) is the main bank, with eight branches throughout Havana, including one in Edificio Jerusalem in the **Miramar Trade Center** (3ra Av., e/ 70 y 82, Miramar). Its main outlet, in the **Hotel Tryp Habana Libre** (Calle L, e/ 23 y 25, tel. 07/838-4429), has a desk handling credit card advances for foreigners. The Banco de Crédito y Comercio (Bandec), Banco Internacional de Comercio, Banco Popular, and Banco Metropolitano also serve foreigners.

The foreign exchange agency **Cadeca** (Obispo, e/ Cuba y Aguiar, Habana Vieja, tel. 07/866-4152, daily 8am-10pm) has outlets throughout the city, including most hotels.

ATMs

ATMs allowing cash advances of Cuban convertible pesos from Visa cards (but not MasterCard or U.S.-issued Visa cards) are located at **Cadeca** (Obispo, e/ Cuba y Aguiar, Habana Vieja, tel. 07/866-4152, daily 8am-10pm) and major banks.

COMMUNICATIONS

Post Offices and Mail Service

Most major tourist hotels have small post offices and will accept your mail for delivery. In Habana Vieja, there are post offices on the east side of Plaza de la Catedral; at Obispo #102, on the west side of Plaza de San Francisco (Mon.-Fri. 8am-6pm); at Obispo #518; and next to the Gran Teatro on Parque Central.

In Vedado, there's a 24-hour post office in the lobby of the **Hotel Tryp Habana Libre** (Calle L, e/ 23 y 25). Havana's main post office is **Correos de Cuba** (tel. 07/879-6824, 24 hours) on Avenida Rancho Boyeros, one block north of the Plaza de la Revolución.

Servi-Postal (Havana Trade Center, 3ra Av., e/ 76 y 80, Miramar, tel. 07/204-5122, Mon.-Sat. 10am-6pm) has a copy center and Western Union agency.

DHL (1ra Av. y Calle 26, Miramar, tel. 07/204-1578, commercial@dhl.cutisa.cu, Mon.-Fri. 8am-8pm, Sat. 8:30am-4pm) is headquartered at Edificio Habana in the Miramar Trade Center (3ra Av., e/ 76 y 80, Miramar).

Telephone and Fax Service

Etecsa is headquartered on the east side of Edificio Barcelona at **Miramar Trade Center** (3ra Av., e/ 76 y 80, Miramar). The main international telephone exchange is in the lobby of the **Hotel Habana Libre Tryp** (Calle L, e/ 23 y 25, tel. 07/834-6100, 24 hours).

You can rent or buy cellular phones from **Cubacel** (Calle 28 #510, e/ 5 y 7, Miramar, tel. 05/264-2266 or 07/880-2222, www.cubacel.com, Mon.-Fri. 8:30am-7:30pm, Sat. 8am-noon); they can also activate your own cell phone for CUC40. The main Havana office is in Edificio Santa Clara in the Miramar Trade Center (3ra Av., e/ 70 y 82).

Internet Access

Internet access has expanded markedly since 2015. Wi-Fi is installed in most tourist hotels and public Wi-Fi zones are along Paseo de Martí and Parque Central (Habana Vieja); Parque Trillo (Centro Habana); La Rampa, Linea y L, and Parque John Lennon (Vedado); and Av. 1ra y 42 and Parque 13 y 76 (Miramar). In 2016, the government announced that it will create the world's largest Wi-Fi zone the length of the Malecón. In 2017, another 47 public Wi-Fi zones were added. Users must buy a prepaid "Nauta" card (CUC2.50 or CUC6-10 for one hour at some deluxe hotels).

The main **Etecsa** outlets are in Habana Vieja (Obispo, esq. Habana, tel. 07/866-0089, daily 8:30am-9pm); at Calle 17 (e/ B y C) and Edificio Focsa (Calle M, e/ 17 y 19), in Vedado;

and on the west side of Edificio Barcelona, at the Miramar Trade Center.

The **Hotel Nacional** (Calle O y 21, tel. 07/836-3564, daily 8am-8pm) and **Hotel Habana Libre Tryp** (Calle L, e/ 23 y 25, tel. 07/834-6100, daily 7am-11pm) charge CUC10 for Wi-Fi access.

Students at the Universidad de la Habana have free Internet service in the **Biblioteca Central** (San Lázaro, esq. Ronda, tel. 07/878-5573), at the faculty of Artes y Letras (you need to sign up the day before), and at the faculty of Filosofía y Historia, with long lines for use.

GOVERNMENT OFFICES
Immigration and Customs

Requests for visa extensions (*prórrogas*) and other immigration issues relating to foreigners are handled by **Inmigración** (Calle 17 e/ J y K, Vedado, tel. 07/836-7832 or 07/861-3462, Mon.-Wed. and Fri. 8:30am-4pm, Thurs. and Sat. 8:30am-11am); you need CUC25 of stamps purchased at any bank, plus proof of medical insurance and airline reservation to exit. Journalists and others requiring special treatment are handled by the **Ministerio de Relaciones Exteriores** (Ministry of Foreign Relations, Calzada #360, e/ G y H, Vedado, tel. 07/830-9775, www.cubaminrex.cu).

The main customs office is on Avenida del Puerto, opposite Plaza de San Francisco.

Consulates and Embassies

The following nations have embassies/consulates in Havana. Those of other countries can be found in the local telephone directory under *Embajadas.*

- **Australia:** c/o Canadian Embassy

- **Canada:** Calle 30 #518, esq. 7ma, Miramar, tel. 07/204-2516

- **United Kingdom:** Calle 34 #702, e/ 7ma y 17-A, Miramar, tel. 07/204-1771

- **United States:** Calzada, e/ L y M, Vedado, tel. 07/833-3551 or 07/833-3559, emergency/after hours tel. 07/833-3026, http://havana.usembassy.gov

MAPS AND TOURIST INFORMATION
Information Bureaus

Infotur (tel. 07/204-0624, www.infotur.cu), the government tourist information bureau, has nine outlets in Havana, including in the arrivals lounges at José Martí International Airport (Terminal Three, tel. 07/266-4094, 24 hours) and at the Terminal de Cruceros (Cruise Terminal), plus the following outlets in Havana (daily 8:30am-8:30pm):

• Calle Obispo, e/ Bernazas y Villegas, Habana Vieja, tel. 07/866-3333

• Calle Obispo, esq. San Ignacio, Habana Vieja, tel. 07/863-6884

• Calle 23 e/ L y M, Vedado, tel. 07/832-9288

• 5ta Avenida, esq. Calle 112, Miramar, tel. 07/204-3977

MEDICAL SERVICES

Most large tourist hotels have nurses on duty. Other hotels will be able to request a doctor for in-house diagnosis.

Hospitals

Tourists needing medical assistance are steered to the **Clínica Internacional Cira García** (Calle 20 #4101, esq. Av. 41, Miramar, tel. 07/204-2811, www.cirag.cu, 24 hours), a full-service hospital dedicated to serving foreigners. It's the finest facility in Cuba.

The **Centro Internacional Oftalmológica Camilo Cienfuegos** (Calle L, e/ Línea y 13, Vedado, tel. 07/832-5554) specializes in eye disorders but also offers a range of medical services.

Pharmacies

Local pharmacies serving Cubans are meagerly stocked. For homeopathic remedies try **Farmacia Ciren** (Calle 216, esq. 11B, Playa, tel. 07/271-5044).

Your best bets are the *farmacias internacionales,* stocked with imported medicines. They're located at the **Hotel Sevilla** (Prado esq Zulueta, tel. 07/861-5703, daily 8:30am-7:30pm), **Hospital Camilo Cienfuegos**

(Calle L, e/ Línea y 13, Vedado, tel. 07/832-5554, cirpcc@infomed.sid.cu, daily 8am-8pm), the **Galería Comercial Habana Libre** (Calle 25 y L, Vedado, Mon.-Sat. 10am-7:30pm), the **Clínica Internacional Cira García** (Calle 20 #4101, esq. Av. 41, Miramar, tel. 07/204-2880, 24 hours), the **Farmacia Internacional** (Av. 41, esq. 20, Miramar, tel. 07/204-2051, daily 8:30am-8:30pm), and in the Edificio Habana at the **Miramar Trade Center** (3ra Av., e/ 76 y 80, Miramar, tel. 07/204-4515, Mon.-Fri. 8am-6pm).

Opticians

Ópticas Miramar (Neptuno #411, e/ San Nicolás y Manrique, Centro Habana, tel. 07/863-2161, and 7ma Av., e/ Calle 24 y 26, Miramar, tel. 07/204-2990) provides services.

SAFETY

Havana is amazingly safe, and tourist zones are patrolled by police officers 24/7. Still, Havana is not entirely safe. Most crime is opportunistic, and thieves seek easy targets. Centro Habana is a center for street crime against tourists.

Avoid *all* dark back streets at night, especially those in southern Habana Vieja and Centro Habana, and anywhere in the Cerro district and other slum districts or wherever police are not present (these areas can be unsafe by day). I was mugged on a main street in Centro in broad daylight.

Beyond Habana Vieja, most parks should be avoided at night. Be cautious and circumspect of all *jineteros.*

PRACTICALITIES
Haircuts

For a clean cut, head to **ArteCorte** (Calle Aguiar #10, e/ Peña Pobre y Avenida de los Misiones, Habana Vieja, tel. 07/861-0202), on "Hairdressers' Alley." The fun, offbeat setting full of amazingly eclectic art and barber-related miscellany is unique. Or try **Salón Correo Barbería** (Brasil, e/ Oficios y Mercaderes, Habana Vieja, Mon.-Sat.

8am-6pm), an old-style barbershop. I use **Olimpo Salón** (tel. 07/860-6627, ext. 1960, or 5273-1371), in the basement of the Hotel Parque Central Torre.

Laundry

In Miramar, **Aster Lavandería** (Calle 34 #314, e/ 3ra y 5ta, Miramar, tel. 07/204-1622, Mon.-Fri. 8am-5pm, Sat. 8am-noon) has a wash-and-dry service (CUC3 per load) and dry cleaning (CUC2 for pants, CUC1.50 for shirts for three-day service; more for same-day service). There's also a laundry in the **Complejo Comercial Comodoro** (3ra Av., esq. 84, tel. 07/204-5551).

Legal Services

Consultoría Jurídica Internacional (CJI, International Judicial Consultative Bureau, Calle 16 #314, e/ 3ra y 5ta, Miramar, tel. 07/204-2490) provides legal services, as does the **Bufete Internacional** (5ta Av. esq. 40, Miramar, tel. 07/204-436, bufete@bufeteinternacional.cu).

Libraries

The **Biblioteca Nacional** (National Library, Av. de la Independencia, esq. 20 de Mayo, tel. 07/881-5442, www.bnjm.cu, Mon.-Fri. 8:15am-6pm, Sat. 8:15am-4pm), on the east side of Plaza de la Revolución, has about 500,000 texts. Getting access, however, is another matter. Five categories of individuals are permitted to use the library, including students and professionals, but not lay citizens. Foreigners can obtain a library card valid for one year (CUC3) if they have a letter from a sponsoring Cuban government agency and/or ID establishing academic credentials, plus two photographs and a passport, which you need to hand over whenever you wish to consult books. The antiquated, dilapidated file system makes research a Kafkaesque experience. There is no open access to books. Instead, individuals must request a specific work, which is then brought to you; your passport or (for Cubans) personal ID is recorded along with the purpose of your request.

The Universidad de la Habana, in Vedado, has several libraries, including the **Biblioteca Central** (San Lázaro, esq. Ronda, tel. 07/878-5573 or 07/878-3951).

The **Biblioteca Provincial de la Habana** (Obispo, Plaza de Armas, tel. 07/862-9035, Mon.-Fri. 8:15am-7pm, Sat. 8:15am-4:30pm) is a meagerly stocked affair. It's closed the first Monday of each month.

Cuba Libro (Calle 24, esq. 19, Vedado, tel. 07/830-5205, Mon.-Sat. 10am-8pm), a small English-language bookstore, café, and literary salon, has a shaded patio to enjoy the company of expat literati.

Toilets

The only modern public toilet to Western standards is on the ground floor of the Lonja del Comercio, **Plaza de Armas.** Most hotels and restaurants will let you use their facilities. An attendant usually sits outside the door dispensing a few sheets of toilet paper for pocket change (also note the bowl with a few coins, which is meant to invite a tip).

Transportation

GETTING THERE AND AWAY

Air

José Martí International Airport (switchboard tel. 07/266-4644) is 25 kilometers southwest of downtown Havana, in the Wajay district. It has five terminals spaced well apart and accessed by different roads (nor are they linked by a connecting bus service).

Terminal One: This terminal (tel. 07/275-1200) serves domestic flights.

Terminal Two: Charter flights and other select flights from the Caribbean, South America, and Europe arrive at Terminal Two. Occasionally other flights pull in here, although outbound flights will invariably depart Terminal Three.

Terminal Three: All international flights, including United States-Havana flights, arrive at Terminal Three (tel. 07/642-6225 or 07/266-4133 for arrivals and departures) on the north side of the airport. Immigration proceedings are slow. Beware porters who grab your bags outside; they'll expect a tip for hauling your bag the few meters to a taxi. A 24-hour Infotur (tel. 07/266-4094) tourist information office is outside the customs lounge. Check in here if you have prepaid vouchers for transfers into town. A foreign exchange counter is also outside the customs lounge.

Terminal Four: This terminal is for cargo.

Terminal Five: Aero Caribbean flights arrive here, as do private planes. It has taxi service and car rental offices.

In 2016, the Cuban government granted a French company the right to upgrade, expand, and ultimately manage the airport. A military airfield at San Antonio de los Baños is to be converted into a new terminal to handle private planes and possibly all U.S. flights (or cargo). It's one hour from downtown Havana.

DEPARTING CUBA

Since 2015 a CUC25 departure tax is included in your airline ticket price. Make sure you arrive at the correct terminal for your departure. Terminals Two and Three have **VIP lounges** (tel. 07/642-0247 or 07/642-6225, salonvip@hav.ecasa.avianet.cu, CUC25 including drinks and snacks).

Bus

There's no bus service from either of the international terminals. A public bus marked *Aeropuerto* departs from Terminal One (domestic flights) for Vedado and the east side of Parque Central in Habana Vieja. The bus is intended for Cubans, and foreigners may be refused. It runs about once every two hours. When heading to the airport, the *cola* (line) begins near the José Martí statue at Parque Central. There are two lines: one for people wishing to be seated (*sentados*) and one for those willing to stand (*de pie*). The journey costs one peso, takes about one hour, and is very unreliable.

Alternatively, you can catch **Metrobus P12** (originating in Santiago de las Vegas) or Ómnibus #480 from the east side of Avenida de la Independencia, about a 10-minute walk east of the terminal—no fun with baggage. The bus goes to Parque de la Fraternidad on the edge of Habana Vieja (20 pesos). The journey takes about one hour, but the wait can be just as long. When heading to the airport, you can catch Ómnibus #480 or Metrobus P12 from the west side of Parque de la Fraternidad (you can also get on the P12 near the Universidad de la Habana on Avenida Salvador Allende). Both go to Santiago de las Vegas via the domestic terminal (Terminal One), but they will let you off about 400 meters east of Terminal Two. Do not use this bus for the international terminal.

International Airline Offices in Havana

Avianca (tel. 07/833-3114, www.avianca.com) has an office in the Hotel Habana Libre Tryp (Calle L, e/ 23 y 25, Vedado). **Cayman Airways** (tel. 07/649-7644, www.caymanairways.com) is based at Terminal Two, at José Martí International Airport.

The following airlines have offices at Calle 23 #64 (e/ P y Infanta, Vedado):

- **Aerocaribbean** (tel. 07/879-7525, www.fly-aerocaribbean.com)

- **Air Canada** (tel. 07/836-3226, www.aircanada.com)

- **Air Jamaica** (tel. 07/833-2447, www.airjamaica.com)

- **Blue Panorama** (tel. 07/833-2248, www.blue-panorama.com)

- **Condor** (tel. 07/833-3859, www.condor.com)

- **Cubana** (tel. 07/834-4446/7/8/9 or 07/834-4449, www.cubana.cu)

- **Havanatur** (tel. 07/201-9800, for U.S. flights only)

- **LanChile** (tel. 07/831-6186 or 266-4990, www.lanchile.com)

- **LTU** (tel. 07/833-3524, www.ltu.com)

- **Mexicana** (tel. 07/830-9528, www.mexicana.com)

The following have offices at the Miramar Trade Center (5ta Av. y 76, Miramar):

- **Aero Caribe** (Edificio Barcelona, tel. 07/873-3621)

- **Aeroflot** (tel. 07/204-3200, www.aeroflot.com)

- **Air Europa** (Edificio Santiago, tel. 07/204-6904, www.aireuropa.com)

- **Air France** (Edificio Santiago, tel. 07/206-4444, www.airfrance.com/cu)

- **American Airlines** (www.aa.com)

- **COPA** (Edificio Barcelona, tel. 07/204-1111, www.copa.com)

- **Delta** (www.delta.com)

- **Iberia** (Edificio Santiago, tel. 07/204-3460, www.iberia.com)

- **JetBlue** (www.jetblue.com)

- **KLM** (Edificio Santiago, tel. 07/206-4444, www.klm.com)

- **Virgin Atlantic** (Edificio Santa Clara, tel. 07/204-0747, www.virgin-atlantic.com)

Taxi

Cubataxi taxis wait outside the arrivals lounges. Official rates are CUC20-25 to downtown hotels, but most drivers will not use their meter. Avoid private (illegal) taxis, as several foreigners have been robbed.

Car Rental

These companies have booths at Terminal Three: **Cubacar** (tel. 07/649-9800), **Havanautos** (tel. 07/649-5197), and **Rex** (tel. 07/266-6074). These have booths at Terminal Two: **Cubacar** (tel. 07/649-5546), **Havanautos** (tel. 07/649-5215), and **Rex** (tel. 07/649-0306).

Cruise Ship

Havana's **Terminal Sierra Maestra** (Av. del

Metrobus Routes

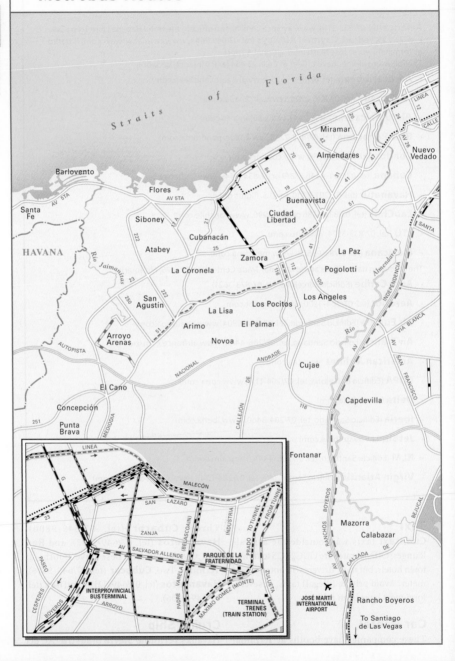

Florida

Straits of

Barlovento

Santa Fe

AV 5TA

Flores

AV 5TA

Siboney

HAVANA

Río Jaimanitas

Atabey

Cubanacán

La Coronela

San Agustín

La Lisa

Arimo

Arroyo Arenas

AUTOPISTA

El Cano

Concepción

Punta Brava

251

MEDIODIA

NACIONAL

CALLEJÓN DE

Miramar

Almendares

Nuevo Vedado

Buenavista

Ciudad Libertad

Zamora

La Paz

Pogolotti

Los Angeles

Los Pocitos

El Palmar

Novoa

ANDRADE

Cujae

Capdevila

Fontanar

Mazorra

Calabazar

Rancho Boyeros

To Santiago de Las Vegas

INTERPROVINCIAL BUS TERMINAL

LINEA

MALECÓN

SAN LAZARO

ZANJA

AV SALVADOR ALLENDE

PASEO

CESPEDES

BOYROS

ARROYO

PADRE VARELA (BELASCOAIN)

INDUSTRIA

PRADO TO TUNNEL

FROM TUNNEL

ZULUETA

PARQUE DE LA FRATERNIDAD

MAXIMO GOMEZ (MONTE)

TERMINAL TRENES (TRAIN STATION)

JOSÉ MARTÍ INTERNATIONAL AIRPORT

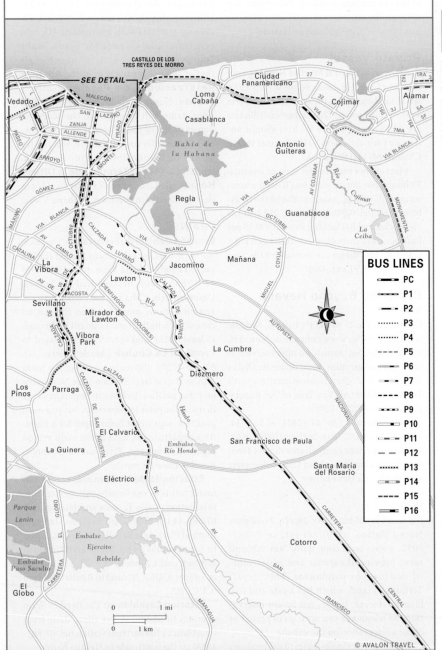

BUS LINES

- PC
- P1
- P2
- P3
- P4
- P5
- P6
- P7
- P8
- P9
- P10
- P11
- P12
- P13
- P14
- P15
- P16

© AVALON TRAVEL

Puerto, tel. 07/862-1925) is a natty conversion of the old customs building. Passengers step through the doorways directly onto Plaza de San Francisco, in the heart of Havana.

Private Vessel

Private yachts berth at **Marina Hemingway** (Av. 5ta y Calle 248, Santa Fe, tel. 07/273-7972, www.nauticamarlin.tur.cu), 15 kilometers west of downtown. The harbor coordinates are 23° 5'N and 82° 29'W. You should announce your arrival on VHF Channel 16, HF Channel 68, and SSB 2790.

Visas are not required for stays of less than 72 hours. For longer stays you'll need a tourist card (CUC25), issued at the harbormaster's office (tel. 07/204-1150, ext. 2884) at the end of channel B. Docking fees (CUC0.35 per foot per day) include water and electricity. Gasoline and diesel are available 8am-7pm (tel. 07/204-1150, ext. 450).

Exploring Beyond Havana

AIR

Cubana (Calle 23 #64, e/ P y Infanta, Vedado, tel. 07/870-9430, www.cubana.cu, Mon.-Fri. 8:30am-4pm, Sat. 8am-1pm) offers service to all major Cuban cities. Most domestic flights leave from José Martí International Airport's **Terminal One** (Av. Van Troi, off Av. Rancho Boyeros, tel. 07/275-1200).

AeroGaviota (Av. 47 #2814, e/ 28 y 34, Rpto. Kohly, tel. 07/204-2621 or 07/203-0668, www.aerogaviota.com) flights depart from Aeropuerto Baracao, about three kilometers west of Marina Hemingway.

BUS

Modern **Víazul** buses (Av. 26, esq. Zoológico, Nuevo Vedado, tel. 07/881-1413 or 07/883-6092, www.viazul.com, daily 7am-9:30pm) serve provincial capitals and major tourist destinations nationwide. They depart Terminal Víazul, which has a café and free luggage storage. It does not accept reservations by telephone; you must go in person or make a reservation on the website.

Ómnibus Nacionales buses to destinations throughout the country leave from the Terminal de Ómnibuses Nacionales. However, they do not accept foreigners, except for students with appropriate ID, who can travel like Cubans for pesos. Make your reservation as early as possible, either at the bus terminal or at the **Agencia Reservaciones de Pasaje** (Factor y Tulipán, Nuevo Vedado, tel. 07/870-9401). Your name will be added to the scores of names ahead of you. If you don't have a reservation or miss your departure, you can try getting on the standby list (*lista de espera,* tel. 07/862-4341) at **Terminal de la Última Hora** (Calle Gancedo e/ Villanueva y Linea de Ferrocarril), in southwest Habana Vieja.

TRAIN

Estación Central de Ferrocarril: The main station is the Central Railway Station (Egido, esq. Arsenal, Habana Vieja, tel. 07/861-2959 or 07/862-1920), or Terminal de Trenes. Unfortunately, Cuba's already dysfunctional system became more so when the station closed for lengthy repairs in 2015 (through at least 2018), and services were moved to **Terminal La Coubre** (Av. del Puerto, tel. 07/860-0700), 400 meters south of the main railway station (and Estación 19 de Noviembre for Pinar del Río). Tickets can be purchased up to one hour prior to departure, but you must purchase your ticket before 8pm for a nighttime departure. As soon as the main station repair is completed, Terminal La Coubre is slated to close for repair.

Estación 19 de Noviembre: Local commuter trains (*ferro-ómnibuses*) operate from this station (Calle Tulipán and Hidalgo, tel. 07/881-4431), also called Estación Tulipán, south of Plaza de la Revolución. Trains depart to San Antonio de los Baños and Rincón at 10:05am and 4:25pm (CUC1.70); to Artemisa at 5:45pm (CUC2.20); and to Batabanó at 5pm (CUC1.80).

Estación Casablanca: The Hershey Train operates to Matanzas five times daily from Casablanca's harborfront station (tel. 07/862-4888) on the north side of Havana harbor.

GETTING AROUND
Bus
TOURIST BUS

Havana has a double-decker tourist bus service, the **HabanaBusTour** (tel. 07/261-9017, daily 9am-9pm), which is perfect for first-time visitors who want to get their bearings and catch the main sights. For just CUC5 a day, you can hop on and off as many times as you wish at any of the 44 stops served by a fleet of buses covering 95 miles of route.

The T1 route (double-decker) begins on the west side of Parque Central and does a figure eight around the perimeter of Habana Vieja, and then heads through Vedado and Miramar. The T3 minibus is a great way to get out to the Playas del Este.

PUBLIC BUS

Havana is served by often crowded public buses, or *guaguas* (pronounced WAH-wahs). No buses operate within Habana Vieja except along the major peripheral thoroughfares.

Most buses run at least hourly during the day but on reduced schedules 11pm-5am. The standard fare for any journey throughout the city is 20 centavos, or 40 centavos on smaller buses called *ómnibuses ruteros,* which have the benefit of being uncrowded. *Taxibuses*—buses

that ply a fixed, nonstop route to the airport and bus and train stations—charge one peso.

Many buses follow a loop route, traveling to and from destinations along different streets. Few routes are in a circle. (If you find yourself going in the wrong direction, don't assume that you'll eventually come around to where you want to be.) Most buses display the bus number and destination above the front window. Many buses arrive and depart from Parque Central and Parque de la Fraternidad in Habana Vieja and La Rampa (Calle 23) in Vedado, especially at Calle L and at Calzada de Infanta.

Taxi

Modern taxis serve the tourist trade while locals make do with wheezing jalopies. Hundreds of *cuentaspropistas* now offer private taxi service, and on almost any street you'll be solicited.

CUC TAXIS

The scene has been flipped on its head since 2013, when Transtur operated all *turistaxis* as **Cubataxi** (tel. 07/855-5555). Cubataxi still exists, but the taxi drivers are now self-employed and lease the vehicles, which can be hailed outside hotels or by calling for radio

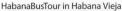
HabanaBusTour in Habana Vieja

dispatch. Taxis range from modern Mercedes to beat-up Ladas. Only the most modern vehicles have functioning seat belts.

Some taxis are metered (CUC1 at flag drop, then CUC0.50 a kilometer); few drivers will use the meter, but will instead ask how much you want to pay. Alas, the U.S. tourist tsunami has inflated taxi rates. Expect to pay CUC10 between Habana Vieja and the Hotel Habana Libre Tryp, and minimum CUC12 to Miramar. Bargain the price before setting off! A light above the cab signifies if the taxi is *libre* (free).

Need a minivan? Gerardo Rojas (tel. 5273-3398) has served me well in a 13-seat Hyundai.

CLASSIC CARS

Fancy tooling around in a 1950 Studebaker or a 1959 Buick Invicta convertible? Private cars can be rented outside most major tourist hotels (CUC40-60 per hour, depending on car). **Nostalgicar** (tel 07/641-4053 or 5295-3842, www.nostalgicarcuba.com) can supply a fleet of hard-top Chevys to meet you at the airport and drive you around. **Vintage Tours** (tel. 5840-5403, www.vintagetour-cuba.com) offers tours (from CUC70 for two hours), as does **OldCarTours** (tel. 07/289-9155, www.oldcartours.com).

The state agency **Gran Car** (Calle Marino, esq. Santa María, Nuevo Vedado, tel. 07/855-5567, grancardp@transnet.cu) rents classic-car taxis for CUC30 per hour (20-km limit the first hour, with shorter limits per extra hour).

PESO TAXIS

Privately owned 1950s-era *colectivos* or *máquinas* run along fixed routes, much like buses, and charge 50 pesos for a ride anywhere along the route. Parque de las Agrimensores, on the north side of the railway station, is the official starting point for most routes. It's fun, so hop in—but don't slam the door!

BICI-TAXIS

Hundreds of homespun tricycle taxis with shade canopies ply the streets of Habana Vieja and Centro. The minimum fare is usually CUC2. You can go the full length of the Malecón, from Habana Vieja to Vedado, for CUC5. Always agree to a fare before setting off. These jalopies are barred from certain streets and areas, so you might end up taking a zigzag route to your destination.

COCO-TAXIS

These cutesy three-wheeled eggshells on wheels whiz around the touristed areas

colectivo taxi

of Havana and charge the same as taxis. However, they are inherently unsafe.

COCHES

Horse-drawn coaches are a popular way of exploring the Malecón and Old Havana, although the buggies are barred from entering the pedestrian-only quarter. They're operated by **San Cristóbal Agencia de Viajes** (tel. 07/861-9171). Their official starting point is the junction of Empedrado and Tacón, but you can hail them wherever you see them. Others can be hailed on Parque Central, and at Plaza de la Revolución. They charge CUC10 per person for one hour.

Car

The narrow one-way streets in Habana Vieja are purgatory for vehicles. The main plazas and streets between them are barred to traffic.

A treacherously potholed four-lane freeway—the Autopista Circular (route Calle 100 or *circunvalación*)—encircles southern and eastern Havana, linking the arterial highways and separating the core from suburban Havana. The intersections are dangerous.

PARKING

A capital city without parking meters? Imagine. Parking meters were detested during the Batista era, mostly because they were a source of *botellas* (skimming) for corrupt officials. After the triumph of the Revolution, *habaneros* smashed the meters. However, the state employs *custodios* in red vests to collect fees around many parks and major streets.

Avoid No Parking zones like the plague, especially if it's an officials-only zone. Havana has an efficient towing system.

Never leave your car parked unguarded. In central Vedado, the Hotel Habana Libre Tryp has an underground car park (CUC0.60 for one hour, CUC6 max. for 24 hours).

CAR RENTAL

All hotels have car rental booths, and there are scores of outlets citywide.

Transtur (Calle L #456, e/ 25 y 27, Vedado, tel. 07/835-0000) operates the two main car rental agencies: **Cubacar** (Calle 21, e/ N y O, Vedado, Havana, tel. 07/836-4038) and **Havanautos** (tel. 07/285-0703).

Rex (tel. 07/273-9166 or 07/835-6830, www.rex.cu) employs Hyundais, VWs, and Audis and has offices at the airport; in Vedado (Malecón y Línea, tel. 07/835-7788); in Miramar at Hotel Neptuno-Triton (tel. 07/204-2213) and 5ta Av. y 92 (tel. 07/209-2207); the cruise terminal (tel. 07/862-6343); and in the Hotel Parque Central Torre (Zulueta esq. Virtudes, tel. 07/860-0096).

Bicycle

Bicycling offers a chance to explore the city alongside Cubans, although very few *habaneros* cycle and the city has no bicycle culture.

Specially converted buses—the *ciclobuses*—ferry cyclists and their *bicis* through the tunnel beneath Havana harbor (10 centavos). Buses depart from Parque de la Fraternidad and Calle Tacón at the corner of Aguiar (Habana Vieja).

Tito, of **Bike Rentals & Tours** (Av. de los Presidentes #359 Apto. 11A e/ 15 y 17, tel. 5841-4839 or 5463-7103, www.bikerentalhavana.com), rents cruiser-type bikes (CUC15 daily) and offers three-hour guided tours (CUC25). He also has bikes equipped for longer journeys beyond Havana (CUC17 per day). **Roma Rent Bike & City Tour** (Compostela #255 e/ Obispo y O'Reilly, tel. 5436-4243 and 5501-3562) charges similar rates for its 18-speed rental bikes.

Ferry

Tiny ferries (standing room only) bob across the harbor between the Havana waterfront and Regla (on the east side of the bay) and Casablanca (on the north side of the bay). The ferries, which operate 24 hours, leave irregularly from Emboque de Luz wharf on Avenida San Pedro at the foot of Calle Luz in Habana Vieja (tel. 07/797-7473 in Regla); the ride costs 10 centavos and takes five minutes.

Organized Excursions

Havanatur (Calle 23, esq. M, Vedado, tel. 07/830-3107 or 07/201-9800, www.havanatur.cu, daily 8am-8pm) offers a city tour, including walking tour, plus excursions to key sights in the suburbs and farther afield.

Agencia de Viajes San Cristóbal (Oficios #110, e/ Lamparilla y Amargura, tel. 07/861-9171, daily 8:30am-5pm) offers city excursions—from a walking tour of Habana Vieja (daily 10am) to modern Havana for architecture buffs. However, at press time it had been taken over the the military economic division, GAESA, and its status was in flux.

Paradiso (Calle 82 #8202 esq. 5ta, Miramar, tel. 07/204-0601, contacto@paradiso.artex.cu, and Calle 23 y P, tel. 07/836-5381) offers cultural programs.

PRIVATE GUIDES

Curated Cuba Tours (www.curatedcubatours.com) arranges personalized multiday itineraries for groups of four people or more, with private guides. **Tours by Locals** (www.toursbylocals.com) offers guiding services with Havana-born guides.

Jineteros (street hustlers) will offer to be your guide. They're usually useless as sightseeing guides, and most will pull a scam.

Havana Suburbs

SANTIAGO DE LAS VEGAS

This rural colonial-era town is 20 kilometers south of Havana. It is accessed via Avenida de la Independencia.

Mausoleo de General Antonio Maceo Grajales

Avenida de los Mártires rises south of Santiago de las Vegas and deposits you at **El Cacahual.** Here, Antonio Maceo Grajales (1845-1896), general and hero of the independence movement, slumbers in a mausoleum engraved in the style of Mexican artist Diego Rivera. The mausoleum also contains the tomb of Capitán Ayudante (Captain-Adjutant) Francisco Gómez Toro (1876-1896), General Máximo Gómez's son, who gave his life alongside Maceo at the Battle of San Pedro on December 7, 1896.

Santuario de San Lázaro

Cuba's most important pilgrimage site is the **Sanctuary of San Lázaro** (Carretera de San Antonio de los Baños, tel. 047/683-2396, daily 7am-7pm, free), on the west side of Rincón, a hamlet about four kilometers southwest of Santiago de las Vegas. The church, **Iglesia de San Lázaro,** is busy with mendicants who have come to have their children baptized. Behind the church is the **Parque de la Fuente de Agua,** where believers bathe their hands and feet in a fountain to give thanks to Babalu Ayé, while others fill bottles with what they consider holy water. The Los Cocos sanatorium, behind the garden, houses leprosy and AIDS patients.

San Lázaro is the patron saint of the sick (in Santería, his avatar is Babalú Ayé). His symbol is the crutch, his stooped figure is covered in sores, and in effigy he goes about attended by his two dogs. Limbless beggars and other unfortunates crowd at the gates and plead for a charitable donation.

A procession to the sanctuary takes place the 17th of each month. The annual **Procesión de los Milagros** (Procession of the Miracles) takes place December 17, drawing thousands of pilgrims to beseech or give thanks to the saint for miracles they imagine he has the power to grant. The villagers of Rincón do a thriving business selling votive candles and flowers. Penitents crawl on their hands and knees as others sweep the road ahead with palm fronds.

Getting There and Away

Buses P12 (from Parque de la Fraternidad) and P16 (from outside Hospital Hermanos Ameijeiras, in Centro Habana) link Havana to Santiago de las Vegas. Ómnibus #480 also serves Santiago de las Vegas from Havana's main bus terminal (Av. Independencia #101, Plaza de la Revolución, tel. 07/870-9401). The **Terminal de Ómnibus** (Calle al Rincón #43, tel. 07/683-3159) is on the southwest side of town, on the road to Rincón.

A three-car train departs Havana's Estación 19 de Noviembre (Tulipán) at 10:05am and 4:25pm, stopping at Rincón (CUC1). Trains run continuously on December 17. If driving, follow Carretera al Rincón, which begins at the bus station on the southwest edge of Santiago de las Vegas; bus #476 also runs from here.

ARROYO NARANJO

This *municipio* lies east of Boyeros and due south of Havana.

Parque Zoológico Nacional

On Avenida Zoo-Lenin, Cuba's **national zoo** (Av. 8, esq. Av. Soto, tel. 07/644-7618 or 643-8063, comercial@pzn.cubazoo.cu, Wed.-Sun. 9:30am-3:15pm, adults CUC3, children CUC2), southeast of the village of Arroyo Naranjo, about 16 kilometers south of central Havana, contains about 1,000 animals, but the cages are small and bare, and many of the animals look woefully neglected.

Tour buses (CUC2) depart the parking lot about every 30 minutes and run through a wildlife park (*pradera africana*) resembling the African savanna, including a *foso de leones* (lion pit).

To get to the main entrance, take Avenida de la Independencia to Avenida San Francisco (the *parque* is signed at the junction), which merges with the *circunvalación*. Take the first exit to the right and follow Calzada de Bejucal south. Turn right onto Avenida Zoo-Lenin (signed).

Metrobus P12 operates from Parque de la Fraternidad, in Habana Vieja.

Parque Lenin

Lenin Park (Calle 100 y Carretera de la Presa, tel. 07/647-1533, Tues.-Sun. 9am-5pm), east of the zoo, was created from a former hacienda and landscaped mostly by volunteer labor. The vast complex features wide rolling pastures and small lakes surrounded by forests. What Lenin Park lacks in grandeur and stateliness (it is badly deteriorated), it makes up for in scale.

The park is bounded by the *circunvalación* to the north and Calzada de Bejucal to the west; there is an entrance off Calzada de Bejucal. A second road—Calle Cortina de la Presa—enters from the *circunvalación,* runs down the center of the park, and is linked to Calzada de Bejucal by a loop road; an **information bureau** (tel. 07/647-1165) is midway down Calle Cortina de la Presa.

The **Galería del Arte Amelia Peláez,** at the south end of Cortina, displays works by the eponymous Cuban ceramist. A short distance to the west is the **Monumento Lenin,** a huge granite visage of the Communist leader and thinker in Soviet-realist style, carved by Soviet sculptor I. E. Kerbel. Farther west, you'll pass an **aquarium** (entrance CUC1) displaying freshwater fish, turtles, and Cuban crocodiles. About 400 meters west of the aquarium is the **Monumento a Celia Sánchez.** Here, a trail follows a wide apse to a small museum fronting a bronze figure of the revolutionary heroine.

On the north side, the **Palacio de Pioneros Che Guevara** displays stainless steel sculptures of Che, plus a full-scale replica of the *Granma* (the vessel that brought Castro and his revolutionaries from Mexico).

An equestrian center, **Centro Ecuestre** (tel. 07/647-2436, daily 9am-5pm), also called Club Hípico, immediately east of the entrance off Calzada de Bejucal, offers one-hour trips (CUC15) plus free riding lessons for children, and has show-jumping exhibitions on Saturday morning, plus an annual show-jumping event (Subasta Elite de Caballos de Salto) in January. Horseback riding is also offered on weekends at **El Rodeo,** the national

Arroyo Naranjo

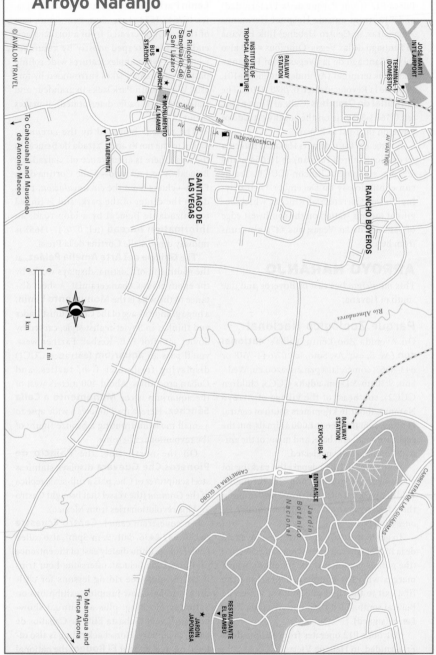

© AVALON TRAVEL

To Rincón and
Sanctuario de
San Lázaro

BUS
STATION

CHURCH

MONUMENTO
AL MAMBI

To Cacahuahal and Mausoleo
de Antonio Maceo

LA TABERNITA

INSTITUTE OF
TROPICAL AGRICULTURE

RAILWAY
STATION

JOSÉ MARTÍ
INTL AIRPORT

TERMINAL 1
(DOMESTIC)

CALLE 188

AV DE LA INDEPENDENCIA

SANTIAGO DE LAS VEGAS

RANCHO BOYEROS

AV VAN TROI

Río Almendares

0   1 km
0   1 mi

RAILWAY
STATION

EXPOCUBA

ENTRANCE

Jardín Botánico Nacional

CARRETERA EL GLOBO

CARRETERA DE LAS GUASIMAS

RESTAURANTE
EL BAMBÚ

JARDÍN
JAPONESA

To Managua and
Finca Alcona

To Havana
HAVANA GOLF CLUB
To Pinar del Río

To Terminal 3 (International)
Terminal 2 (Charters)
REX LIMOUSINES

RÍO VERDE

CALZADA DE BEJUCAL 289

CALABAZAR

ENTRANCE

Parque Zoológico Nacional

FOSO DE LEONES

PRADERA AFRICANO (AFRICAN WILDLIFE PARK)

ENTRANCE

AVENIDA ZOO LENIN

ARROYO NARANJO

AVENIDA VARONA

AVENIDA SOTO

SAN FRANCISCO 100

To Havana 1 A2

EL GALÁPAGO DE ORO RAILWAY STATION

SWIMMING POOLS

BAR/RESTAURANTE CASA DE LA AMISTAD

Presa Paso Sequito

TALLER DE CERÁMICA

MONUMENTO A CELIA SÁNCHEZ

EL GLOBO

CAFÉ RANCHÓN LAS MAJAGUAS

MONUMENTO LENIN

Río Pancho Simón

AQUARIUM

GALERÍA DEL ARTE AMELIA PELÁEZ

ANFITEATRO

EL TRENCITO

MOTEL LA HERADURA/ RESTAURANTE LA RUEDA

CENTRO EQUESTRO (CLUB HÍPICO)

CHE GUEVARA PIONEER PALACE

PARQUE DIVERSIONES

TERMINAL INGLESA RAILWAY STATION

Parque Lenin

Embalse Ejercito Rebelde

TOURIST INFORMATION

EL RODEO

HORSE STABLES

TRAIN STOP/PARRILLADA DE LAS RUINAS

LAS RUINAS

CARRETERA EL GLOBO

MONUMENTO AL VAPORI/ BURÓ DE INFORMACIÓN

ADMINISTRATION

AVENIDA SAN FRANCISCO 100

CIRCUNVALACIÓN

LA GÜINERA

CALZADA DE SAN AGUSTÍN

ELÉCTRICO

To Museo Ernest Hemingway and the Autopista Nacional

AVENIDA DE LA INDEPENDENCIA

243

rodeo arena, in the southeast corner of the park. El Rodeo has rodeo every Sunday, with *rodeo pionero* (for youth) at noon and competitive adult rodeo at 3pm. The Feria de Rodeo (the national championship) is held each August 25.

A narrow-gauge railway circles the park, stopping at four stages. The old steam train (Sat.-Sun. 10am-4pm, four pesos), dating from 1870, departs from the information bureau in winter only and takes 25 minutes to circle the park. Another old steam train—**El Trencito**—is preserved in front of the disused Terminal Inglesa.

A *parque de diversiones* (theme park) in the northwest quarter includes carousels, a Ferris wheel, and pony rides.

Bus P13 operates between La Víbora and the park. Buses #88 and #113 leave from the north side of Havana's main railway station and continue to ExpoCuba.

ExpoCuba

ExpoCuba, on the Carretera del Globo (official address Carretera del Rocío, Km 3.5, Arroyo Naranjo, tel. 07/697-9111, Wed.-Sun. 10am-5pm, closed Sept.-Dec., CUC1), three kilometers south of Parque Lenin, houses a permanent exhibition of Cuban industry, technology, sports, and culture touting the achievements of socialism. The facility covers 588,000 square meters and is a museum, trade expo, world's fair, and entertainment hall rolled into one. It has 34 pavilions, including booths that display the crafts, products, music, and dance of each of Cuba's provinces. Pabellones Central and 14 have Wi-Fi.

Jardín Botánico Nacional

This 600-hectare **botanical garden** (tel. 07/697-9364, daily 8am-4pm, CUC1, or CUC4 including guide), directly opposite ExpoCuba, doesn't have the fine-trimmed herbaceous borders of Kew or Butchart but nonetheless is worth the drive for enthusiasts. Thirty-five kilometers of roads lead through the park, which was laid out between 1969 and 1984.

You can drive your own vehicle with a guide, or take a guided tour aboard a tractor-trailer.

The garden consists mostly of wide pastures planted with copses divided by Cuban ecosystems and by regions of the tropical world (from coastal thicket to Oriental humid forest). There is even a permanent bonsai exhibit, and an "archaic forest" contains species such as *Microcyca calocom,* Cuba's cork palm. The highlight is the **Jardín Japonés** (Japanese Garden), landscaped with tiered cascades, fountains, and a jade-green lake full of koi. The **Invernáculo Rincón Eckman** is a massive greenhouse named after Erik Leonard Eckman (1883-1931), who documented Cuban flora between 1914 and 1924. It is laid out as a triptych with greenhouses for cactus, epiphytes, ferns, insectivorous plants, and tropical mountain plants.

Club Gallístico Finca Alcona

Fascinated by cockfighting or aviculture? The state-run **Club Gallístico Finca Alcona** (Calzada de Managua, Km 17.5, tel. 07/644-9398 or 07/643-1217, Tues.-Sun. 9am-7pm, tours 10am-3pm, CUC10 including lunch), two kilometers northeast of Managua, on the east side of the botanical garden, raises *gallo fino* gamecocks for export. It displays the cocks in a ring (8am-11am Sat.-Sun. Dec.-June, Sat. only July-Nov.) and has brief cockfighting exhibitions, but not to the death. It has two thatched restaurants.

Food

One of Havana's most sensational *paladares,* ★ **Il Divino** (Calle Raquel #50 e/ Esperanza y Lindero, Rpto. Castillo de Averhoff, Mantilla, tel. 07/643-7743 or 5812-7164, www.cubarestaurantedivino.com, daily 11am-midnight), four kilometers northeast of Parque Lenin, feels like a piece of Tuscany transplanted, complete with Italianate furnishings. That's because the owners are Italian businessman Marco DeLuca and his Cuban wife, Yoandra. Try the pumpkin soup (CUC3), stuffed peppers (CUC4), fish fillet in strawberry sauce (CUC8), or lamb in red wine sauce (C7).

Pizzas and pastas are also served. It has a superb basement wine cellar with bar. It can get packed with tour groups; reservations are essential. On Sundays, Cuban families descend to enjoy cultural activities in the organic garden, known as Finca Yoandra.

Las Ruinas (Calle 100 y Cortina, tel. 07/643-8527, Tues.-Sun. noon-5pm), in Parque Lenin, looks like something Frank Lloyd Wright might have conceived. The restaurant was designed in concrete and encases the ruins of an old sugar mill. It serves continental and *criolla* cuisine (lobster Bellevue is a specialty, CUC20).

Parque Lenin has several basic restaurants serving simple *criolla* dishes for pesos.

The **Restaurante El Bambú** (tel. 07/697-9159, Tues.-Sun. noon-5pm), overlooking the Japanese Garden in the Jardín Botánico Nacional, bills itself as an *eco-restorán* and serves vegetables—beetroot, cassava, pumpkin, spinach, taro, and more—grown right there in the garden. It offers an all-you-can eat buffet (CUC1).

SAN MIGUEL DEL PADRÓN

The *municipio* of San Miguel del Padrón, southeast of Habana Vieja, is mostly residential, with factory areas by the harbor and timeworn colonial housing on the hills south of town. The region is accessed from the Vía Blanca or (parallel to it) Calzada de Luyano via the Carretera Central (Calzada de Güines), which ascends to the village of San Francisco de Paula, 12.5 kilometers south of Habana Vieja.

★ Museo Ernest Hemingway

In 1939, Hemingway's third wife, Martha Gellhorn, saw and was struck by **Finca Vigía** (Vigía y Steinhart, tel. 07/691-0809, mushem@cubart.cult.cu, Mon.-Sat. 10am-5pm, entrance CUC5, guided tours CUC5), a one-story Spanish-colonial house built in 1887 and boasting a wonderful view of Havana. They rented Lookout Farm for US$100 a month. When Hemingway's first royalty check from

For Whom the Bell Tolls arrived in 1940, he bought the house for US$18,500. In August 1961, his widow, Mary Welsh, was forced to sign papers handing over the home to the Castro government, along with its contents. On July 21, 1994, on the 95th anniversary of Papa's birth, Finca Vigía reopened its doors as a museum, just the way the great writer left it.

Bougainvilleas frame the gateway to the eight-hectare hilltop estate—today the most visited museum in Cuba. Mango trees and jacarandas line the driveway leading up to the house. No one is allowed inside—reasonably so, since every room can be viewed through the wide-open windows, and the temptation to pilfer priceless trinkets is thus reduced. Through the large windows, you can see trophies, firearms, bottles of spirits, old issues of *The Field, Spectator,* and *Sports Afield* strewn about, and more than 9,000 books, arranged in his fashion, with no concern for authors or subjects.

It is eerie being followed by countless eyes—those of the guides (one to each room) and of the beasts that found themselves in the crosshairs of Hemingway's hunting scope. "Don't know how a writer could write surrounded by so many dead animals," Graham Greene commented when he visited. There are bulls, too, including paintings by Paul Klee; photographs and posters of bullfighting scenes; and a chalk plate of a bull's head, a gift from Picasso.

Here Hemingway wrote *Islands in the Stream, Across the River and into the Trees, A Moveable Feast,* and *The Old Man and the Sea.* The four-story tower next to the house was built at his fourth wife's prompting so that he could write undisturbed. Hemingway disliked the tower and continued writing amid the comings and goings of the house, surrounded by papers, shirtless, in Bermuda shorts. Today, the tower contains exhibitions with floors dedicated to Hemingway's sportfishing and films.

The former garage is to be restored to display Hemingway's last car—a 1955 Chrysler New Yorker convertible, which was recovered

Ernest Hemingway and Cuba

Ernest Hemingway first set out from Key West to wrestle marlin in the wide streaming currents off the Cuban coast in April 1932. The blue waters of the Gulf Stream, chock-full of billfish, brought him closer and closer until eventually he settled on this island of sensual charm. Hemingway loved Cuba and lived for 20 years at Finca Vigía, his home in the suburb of San Francisco de Paula, 12.5 kilometers southeast of Havana.

THE CULT OF HEMINGWAY

Havana's marina is named for the prize-winning novelist. Hemingway's room in the Hotel Ambos Mundos and his home (Finca Vigía) are preserved as museums. And his likeness adorns T-shirts and billboards. The Cuban understanding of Hemingway's "Cuban novels" is that they support a core tenet of Communist ideology—that humans are only fulfilled acting in a "socialist" context for a moral purpose, not individualistically. "All the works of Hemingway are a defense of human rights," said Castro, who claimed that *For Whom the Bell Tolls*, Hemingway's fictional account of the Spanish Civil War, inspired his guerrilla tactics. The two headstrong fellows met only once, during the 10th Annual Ernest Hemingway Billfish Tournament in May 1960. Hemingway invited Cuba's youthful new leader as his guest of honor. Castro was to present the winner's trophy; instead, he hooked the biggest marlin and won the prize for himself.

With the Cold War and the United States' break with Cuba, Hemingway had to choose. Not being able to return to Cuba contributed to Hemingway's depression, said his son Patrick.

PAPA AND THE REVOLUTION

There has been a great deal of speculation about Hemingway's attitude toward the Cuban Revolution. Cuba attempts to portray him as sympathetic, not least because Hemingway's Cuban novels are full of images of prerevolutionary terror and destitution. "There is an absolutely murderous tyranny that extends over every little village in the country," he wrote in *Islands in the Stream*.

Hemingway's widow, Mary Welsh, told the journalist Luis Báez that "Hemingway was always in favor of the Revolution." Another writer, Lisandro Otero, records Hemingway as saying, "Had I been a few years younger, I would have climbed the Sierra Maestra with Fidel Castro."

Hemingway's enigmatic farewell comment as he departed the island in 1960 is illuminating: "*Vamos a ganar. Nosotros los cubanos vamos a ganar.* [We are going to win. We Cubans are going to win.] I'm not a Yankee, you know." Prophetically, in *Islands in the Stream*, a character says: "The Cubans...double-cross each other. They sell each other out. They got what they deserve. The hell with their revolutions."

FINCA VIGÍA'S FATE

After Hemingway's death, Finca Vigía was seized by the Castro government (along with all other U.S.-owned property), though the writer had willed the property to his fourth wife, Mary Welsh. The Cuban government allowed her to remove 200 pounds of papers but insisted that most of their home's contents remain untouched.

In his will, the author left his sportfishing vessel, the *Pilar*, to Gregorio Fuentes (the former skipper couldn't afford its upkeep, and it, too, became the property of the government). Hemingway's sleek red-and-white 1955 Chrysler New Yorker was left to his doctor but soon disappeared. In 2011, it was found in derelict condition and at press time was being restored, thanks to the efforts of actor/director David Soul (most famously Hutch from the 1970s cult detective series *Starsky & Hutch*), with whom I am partnered in a cinematic production about the car and its restoration: www.christopherpbaker.com/cuba-soul-documentary.

in 2011 in destitute shape and at press time was being restored.

Hemingway's legendary cabin cruiser, the *Pilar*, is poised beneath a wooden pavilion on the former tennis court, shaded by bamboo and royal palms. Nearby are the swimming pool (where guests such as Ava Gardner swam naked) and the graves of four of Hemingway's dogs.

Several bus lines service the museum. The P7 Metrobus departs from Industria, between Dragones and Avenida Simón Bolívar, Parque de la Fraternidad, in Habana Vieja. P1 runs from La Rampa; the P2 runs from Paseo, in Vedado.

SANTA MARÍA DEL ROSARIO

The charming colonial village of Santa María del Rosario, 20 kilometers south of Parque Central, is in the *municipio* of Cotorro, about five kilometers southeast of San Francisco de Paula. The village was founded in 1732 by José Bayona y Chacón, the Conde (Count) de Casa Bayona, and was an important spa in colonial days.

Venerable 18th- and 19th-century buildings surround **Plaza Mayor,** the main square. **Casa del Conde Bayona** (Calle 33 #2404, esq. 24, tel. 07/682-3510, daily noon-10pm), the count's former home, includes a coach house. The **Casa de la Cultura** (Calle 33 #202, esq. 24, tel. 07/682-4259), on the west side, features a patio mural by world-renowned Cuban artist Manuel Mendive.

The main reason to visit is to view the baroque **Iglesia de Santa María del Rosario** (Calle 24, e/ 31 y 33, tel. 07/682-2183, Tues.-Sat. 8am-noon, Sun. 3:30pm-6pm), dominating the plaza. One of the nation's finest churches, this national monument features a spectacular baroque altar of cedar dripping with gold leaf, a resplendent carved ceiling, plus four priceless art pieces by José Nicolás de Escalera.

Getting There

From Havana, take the P1 from La Rampa, P2 from Paseo in Vedado, or the P7 from Parque

de la Fraternidad to Cotorro, then catch the #97.

CIUDAD PANAMERICANO AND COJÍMAR

Beyond the tunnel under Havana harbor, you travel the six-lane Vía Monumental freeway to modern **Ciudad Panamericano,** three kilometers east of Havana. It dates from the 1991 Pan-American Games, when a high-rise village was built in hurried, jerry-rigged style. Sports stadiums rise to each side of the Vía Monumental, most significantly the now-disused **Estadio Panamericano** (Vía Monumental, Km 4, Ciudad Panamericano). The desultory town has fallen to ruin.

Ciudad Panamericano is contiguous with **Cojímar,** a forlorn fishing village with a waterfront lined with weather-beaten cottages. Whitecaps are often whipped up in the bay, making the Cuban flag flutter above **Fuerte de Cojímar** (locally called El Torreón), a pocket-size fortress guarding the cove. It was here in 1762 that the English put ashore and marched on Havana to capture Cuba for King George III. It is slated to be restored as a museum.

Ernest Hemingway berthed his sportfishing boat, the *Pilar*, in Cojímar. When he died, every angler in the village donated a brass fitting from his boat. The collection was melted down to create a bust—**Monumento Ernest Hemingway**—that stares out to sea from within a columned rotunda at the base of El Torreón. A plaque reads: "Parque Ernest Hemingway. In grateful memory from the population of Cojímar to the immortal author of *Old Man and the Sea,* inaugurated July 21, 1962, on the 63rd anniversary of his birth."

Cojímar was most famous as the residence of Gregorio Fuentes, Hemingway's former skipper and friend, and the model for "Antonio" in *Islands in the Stream.* Fuentes died in 2002 at the grand old age of 104. The old man (who lived at Calle 98 #209, esq. 3D) could often be found regaling travelers in **La Terraza** (Calle 152 #161, esq. Candelaria, tel. 07/766-5151), where you can toast to his

Habana del Este

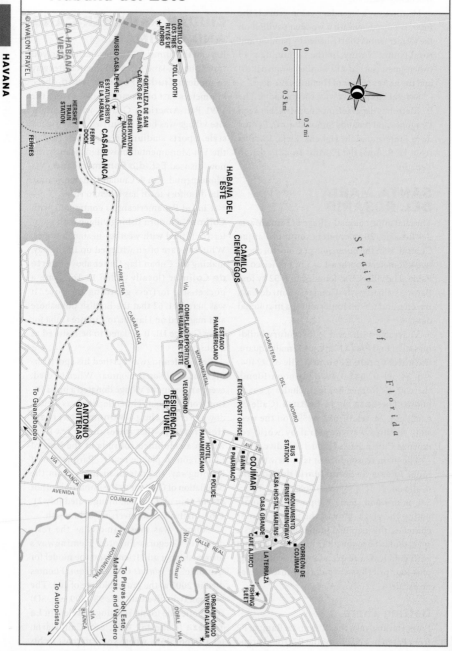

© AVALON TRAVEL

LA HABANA VIEJA

CASTILLO DE LOS TRES REYES DE MORRO

TOLL BOOTH

MUSEO CASA DE CHE

ESTATUA CRISTO DE LA HABANA

FORTALEZA DE SAN CARLOS DE LA CABAÑA

OBSERVATORIO NACIONAL

HERSHEY TRAIN STATION

FERRY DOCK

CASABLANCA

FERRIES

HABANA DEL ESTE

CAMILO CIENFUEGOS

CARRETERA

CASABLANCA

COMPLEJO DEPORTIVO DEL HABANA DEL ESTE

ESTADIO PANAMERICANO

MONUMENTAL

VELODROMO

RESIDENCIAL DEL TUNEL

To Guanabacoa

ANTONIO GUITERAS

VIA BLANCA

AVENIDA

COJÍMAR

VIA MONUMENTAL

VIA BLANCA

To Playas del Este, Matanzas, and Varadero

To Autopista

ETECSA/POST OFFICE

AV. 78

HOTEL PANAMERICANO

BANK

PHARMACY

POLICE

CARRETERA DEL MORRO

BUS STATION

COJÍMAR

CASA HOSTAL MARLINS

CASA GRANDE

CAFÉ AJIACO

LA TERRAZA

MONUMENTO ERNEST HEMINGWAY

TORREÓN DE COJÍMAR

Río Cojímar

CALLE REAL

DOBLE VIA

FISHING FLEET

ORGANIPÓNICO VIVERO ALAMAR

S t r a i t s   o f   F l o r i d a

0
0

0.5 mi

0.5 km

Alamar

Organipónico Vivero Alamar

Immediately east of Cojímar, you'll pass a dormitory city long prized by Fidel Castro as an example of the achievements of socialism. In April 1959, Alamar (pop. 100,000) emerged on the drawing board as the first housing scheme in postrevolutionary Cuba, featuring 4- to 11-story prefabricated concrete apartment blocks. The sea of concrete complexes was built with shoddy materials by microbrigades of untrained "volunteer" workers borrowed from their normal jobs.

Despite its overwhelming deficiencies (the plumbing came from the Soviet Union, the wiring from China, the stoves from North Korea), Alamar was vastly expanded beginning in 1976 and now covers 10 square kilometers. Today it is a virtual slum. Refuse litters the potholed roads, and the roadside parks are untended. There are no jobs here, either, and few stores, no proper transportation, and no logic to the maze of streets or to the addresses of buildings, so that finding your way around is maddening.

Much of Alamar's trash, from rusty old bottles to cash registers, has been recycled as street art at the surreal open-air **Jardin de los Afectos** (Edificio 11-C, Micro-X, tel. 07/765-6270), by local artist Héctor Gallo Portieles.

Well worth a visit is **Organipónico Vivero Alamar** (tel. 5253-6175, ubpc-alamar@minag. cu), an organic produce farm cooperative covering 11 hectares on land leased from the state.

One of the top nightspots in Havana is the **EnGuayabera** (Calle 7ma y 171, Zona 10, Alamar, tel. 07/763-3569, 9pm-3am, free but CUP50-250 for concerts), located in an old textile factory. It replicates the now-touristy Fábrica de Arte, in Vedado, as a multidimensional art and entertainment complex (but without the tourists). It even has a disco, 3-D theater, Wi-Fi, and an ice-cream store.

memory with a turquoise cocktail—Coctel Fuentes. You sense that Papa could stroll in at any moment. His favorite corner table is still there. He is there, too, patinated in bronze atop a pedestal, and adorning the walls in black and white, sharing a laugh with Fidel.

The funky fishing fleet shelters among the mangroves on the southeast bayshore. You might talk your way past the guard, but a footbridge gives you a birds-eye view of fishers bringing in and harvesting sharks (alas) and other fish.

Food and Accommodations

Islazul's **Hotel Panamericano** (Calle A y Av. Central, tel. 07/766-1000), in Ciudad Panermicano, is popular with budget-tour operators. Despite a swimming pool, it offers nothing but regret for tourists.

In Cojímar, the shorefront **Casa Hostal Marlins** (Calle Real #128A, e/ Santo Domingo y Chacón, tel. 07/766-6154, CUC30-35) has a nice air-conditioned apartment upstairs with kitchenette, TV, an enclosed dining patio, and modern bathroom, plus parking.

After exploring, appease your hunger with soup and paella at Hemingway's favorite restaurant, **La Terraza** (Calle 152 #161, esq. Candelaria, tel. 07/766-5151, daily 10:30am-10:30pm), with a gleaming mahogany bar at the front. The wide-ranging menu includes paella (CUC6-12), pickled shrimp (CUC6), oyster cocktail (CUC2), and sautéed calamari (CUC8).

★ **Café Ajiaco** (Calle 92 #267 e/ 3ra y 5ta, tel. 07/765-0514, cafeajiaco@gmail.com, daily noon-midnight) serves delicious Cuban dishes alfresco under thatch. It packs in the tour groups; call ahead.

A steep, winding staircase delivers you to the second floor, open-air and breeze-swept **Casa Grande** (Calle Puezuela #86 esq. Foxa, tel. 07/766-6784, daily noon-midnight), where owner-chef Jorge Falcón cooks up a mean seafood grill (lobster, octopus, shrimp, and whitefish, CUC5-10), served with the usual trimmings. His pork ribs, the house special, earn raves. Reserve ahead.

Getting There and Around

Heading east from Havana on the Vía Monumental, take the first exit marked Cojímar and cross over the freeway to reach Ciudad Panamericano. For Cojímar, take the *second* exit. Metrobus P11 departs Paseo de Martí, opposite the Capitolio Nacional, in Habana Vieja, and runs along the Vía Monumental to Ciudad Panamericano. You can also catch it at the corner of Avenida de los Presidentes y 27 in Vedado.

PLAYAS DEL ESTE

On hot summer weekends all of Havana seems to come to Playas del Este to tan their bodies and flirt. The beaches stretch unbroken for six kilometers east-west, divided by name. A nearly constant breeze is usually strong enough to conjure surf from the warm turquoise seas—a perfect scenario for lazing, with occasional breaks for grilled fish from thatch-roofed *ranchitas* where you can eat practically with your feet in the water. Playas del Este is pushed as a hot destination for foreigners, bringing tourists and Cubans together for rendezvous under *palapas* and palms. It's a nonstarter other than for a day visit.

When driving from Havana via the Vía Monumental, it's easy to miss the turnoff, one kilometer east of the second (easternmost) turnoff for Cojímar, where the Vía Monumental splits awkwardly. Take the narrow Vía Blanca exit to the left to reach Playas del Este; the main Vía Monumental swings south (you'll end up circling Havana on the *circunvalación*).

Tarará

Beyond the Río Tarará you pass **Residencial Tarará** (reception tel. 07/798-2937), a tourist resort at the far western end of Playas del Este, at Vía Blanca (Km 19). Before 1990 it was the Campamento de Pioneros José Martí, used by Cuban schoolchildren who combined study with beachside pleasures. Here, too, victims of the 1986 Chernobyl nuclear disaster in Ukraine were treated free of charge. It was here also that Castro operated his secret government that usurped that of President Manuel Urrutia Lleó after Batista was ousted. Che Guevara was convalescing here after his debilitating years of guerrilla warfare in the Sierra Maestra; **Museo de Che** (Calle 14, esq. 17) recalls his stay.

To the west is a delightful pocket beach that forms a spit at the river mouth; it has a volleyball court and shady *palapas,* plus a restaurant and marina with water sports. Bring snorkel gear: The river mouth channel has corals. The main beach, **Playa Mégano,** to the east, has a sand volleyball court and is served by the **Casa Club** complex (tel. 07/798-3242), with a swimming pool with grill and restaurant.

Entry costs CUC15 including CUC10 *consumo mínimo;* you must show your passport.

Santa María del Mar

Playa Mégano extends east from Tarará and merges into **Playa Santa María del Mar,** the broadest and most beautiful swathe, with golden sand shelving into turquoise waters. The beaches are palm-shaded and studded with umbrellas. Most of Playas del Este's tourist facilities are here, including bars and water sports.

Playa Santa María runs east for about three kilometers to the mouth of the Río Itabo—a popular bathing spot for Cuban families. A large mangrove swamp centered on **Laguna Itabo** extends inland from the mouth of the river, where waterfowl can be admired.

Boca Ciega and Guanabo

Playa Boca Ciega begins east of the Río Itabo estuary and is popular with Cuban families. Moving eastward, Playa Boca Ciega merges into **Playa Guanabo,** the least-attractive beach, running for several kilometers along the shorefront of Guanabo, a Cuban village with plantation-style wooden homes and a vibrant touristic scene. (In 2015, a Chinese company signed a deal to build a $462 million hotel-golf course-condo project here.)

For grand views up and down the beaches, head inland of Guanabo to **Mirador de Bellomonte** (Vía Blanca, Km 24.5, tel. 07/796-3431, daily noon-10pm), a restaurant above the highway; it's signed.

Recreation

Outlets on the beach rent watercraft (CUC15 for 15 minutes), Hobie Cats (CUC20 per hour), and beach chairs (CUC2 per day). **Restaurante Mi Cayito** (Av. las Terrazas, tel. 07/797-1339) rents kayaks and water bikes

on the lagoon. **Havana Kiteboarding Club** (Calle Cobre e/ 12 y 14, tel. 5804-9656, www. havanakite.com) offers kiteboarding and stand-up paddleboarding at Tarará. **Yuniel Valderrama** (tel. 5284-4830, yunielvm80@ nauta.cu) offers surfing and kitesurfing lessons at the west end of Playa Mégano.

Food

Almost a dozen beach grills line the shore and serve *criolla* fare and seafood, including grilled fish and lobster, as does **Restaurante Mi Cayito** (Av. las Terrazas, tel. 07/797-1339, daily 10am-6pm), overhanging the mangroves of Laguna Itabo.

In Guanabo, the best place is ★ **Paladar Italiano Piccolo** (5ta Av., e/ 502 y 504, tel. 07/796-4300, noon-midnight daily), a spacious private restaurant with river-stone walls adorned with Greek murals. Run by Greek owners, it offers surprisingly tasty Mediterranean fare, including wood-fired pizzas, served with hearty salads at low prices (CUC5-10). The private **Restaurant Don Peppo** (Calle 482 #503 e/ 5 y 7, noon-midnight) serves Italian dishes on a shaded terrace with suitably Italian ambience. Try the Hawaiian pizza (CUC5.80), fresh garlic octopus (CUC6), or mixed seafood plate (CUC9).

Air-conditioned **Bim-Bom** (5ta Av., esq. 464, tel. 07/796-6205) serves 32 flavors of ice cream along the lines of Baskin-Robbins.

Accommodations

One of the best *casas particulares* options is ★ **Casa de Julio y Mileydis** (Calle 468 #512, e/ 5ta y 7ma, Guanabo, tel. 07/796-0100, CUC30-35). Set in a beautiful garden, the apartment is equipped for people with disabilities and has a security box, large lounge with a kitchen, a simply furnished bedroom, and a small pool for children. It also has a bungalow. The owners are a pleasure.

If you want a more upscale beachfront villa, check out the stunning two-bedroom ★ **Mayada Beach Villa** (Calle 1ra e/ 490 y 492, Guanabo, www.villamayada.com,

Playas del Este

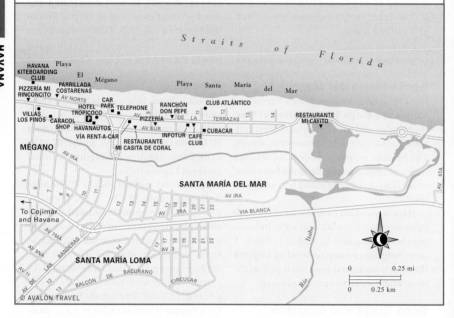

CUC267), adorned to boutique hotel standards in all whites. It has a sundeck, swimming pool, and a garden with outdoor shower and an opening to the beach.

Villas Armonia Tarará (Calle 9na, esq. 14, Villa Tarará, tel. 07/796-0242, www.cubanacan.cu, from CUC27 low season, CUC30 high season for a two-bedroom villa) offers 94 two- to five-bedroom villas—*casas confort*—many with swimming pools. All have a kitchen and private parking. A grocery, laundry, restaurants, and pharmacy are on-site.

The best of several desultory state-run beach hotels is Cubanacán's five-story **Hotel Horizontes Tropicoco** (Av. de las Terrazas, e/ 5 y 7, tel. 07/797-1371, CUC58 s, CUC87 d low season, CUC66 s, CUC95 d high season), with 188 air-conditioned rooms with bamboo furniture plus modern bathrooms.

Gran Caribe's **Villas los Pinos** (Av. 4ta, tel. 07/797-1361, CUC120-220 low season, CUC160-250 high season) is the most elegant option, with 27 two-, three-, and four-bedroom villas; some have private pools. Cuban visitors are prohibited. **Islazul** (www.islazul.cu/es/houses) also rents former private homes.

Services

Infotur (Av. Las Terrazas, e/ 10 y 11, Santa María, tel. 07/796-1261; Av. 5ta esq. 468, Guanabo, tel. 07/796-6868; Mon.-Fri. 8:15am-4:45pm, Sat. 8:15am-12:15pm) provides tourist information.

There are two **post offices** (Edificio Los Corales at Av. de las Terrazas, e/ 10 y 11; in Guanabo, at 5ta-C Av. y 492). The **bank** (tel. 07/796-3320) is at 5ta Avenida (e/ 468 y 470).

Transportation

Tarará (Vía Blanca Km 17), 27 kilometers east of Havana, is signed off the Vía Blanca, as is Playas del Este, with three exits farther east. A taxi will cost about CUC35. Beware the *punto de control* (police control) near Bacuranao; keep to the posted speed limit!

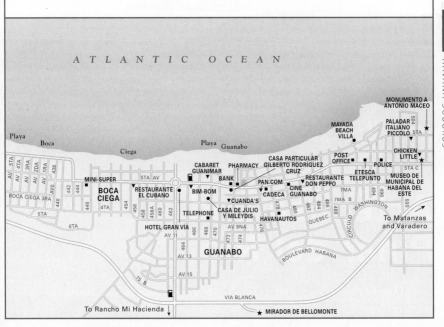

The T3 **HabanaBusTour** (tel. 07/261-0917, daily 9am-9pm) charges CUC5 from Parque Central to Playas del Este.

Cubacar has car rental outlets at Tarará (tel. 07/796-4161) and in the parking lot of Hotel Horizontes Tropicoco (tel. 07/797-1535). There's also **Vía Rent-a-Car** (5ta Av., esq. 11, tel. 07/797-1494). A scooter is the perfect vehicle—rent one from Vía (CUC25 daily).

Cubataxi (tel. 07/796-6666) has taxis at the Hotel Horizontes Tropicoco.

Artemisa and
Pinar del Río

I n Cuba's westernmost province, ox-drawn plows transport you back in time amid quintessentially Cuban land-scapes that attain their most dramatic beauty in Viñales Valley, known for its incredible limestone formations called *mogotes*.

Pinar del Río is dominated by the Cordillera de Guaniguanico, a low mountain chain that forms an east-west spine through the province. The chain is divided by the Río San Diego into two mountain ranges—the Sierra del Rosario in the east and the Sierra de los Órganos in the west. The pine-forested mountains reach 692 meters atop Pan de Guajaibón. Opportunities for ecotourism are available at Soroa, known for its orchid garden, and at Las Terrazas, which has artists' studios, nature trails, cascades, thermal pools, and the remains of 18th-century *cafetales* (coffee plantations). Here, and in the neighboring region of Vuelta Abajo, the world's finest tobacco is grown.

A slender pencil of uninhabited land, the Península de Guanahacabibes, forms the western tip of Cuba, jutting 50 kilometers into the Gulf of Mexico. Smothered in dense brush and cactus, the peninsula is a nature reserve. Playa María la Gorda, in Bahía de

Corrientes, is a center for scuba diving. This area was inhabited at least 4,000 years ago by the Guanahatabey, the island's aboriginal settlers; later the region became a last refuge for the Ciboney, who retreated before the advance of the Taíno.

Between Pinar del Río and Havana lies Artemisa Province, created in 2010 when Havana Province was split into two new provinces. Artemisa incorporates three municipalities formerly in Pinar del Río Province. Sprinkled throughout the province are colonial towns that seem trapped in time. The gently undulating southern plain is the breadbasket of the city and the wealthiest region in Cuba. In counterpoint, the southern shore is a soggy no-man's-land of swamps and mangroves, where lowly fishing villages are among the most deprived and down at the heels in Cuba. Though buses run to most towns, few of the stand-alone sites are served by public transport. You'll need wheels, but be warned:

Previous: Sierra de los Órganos; Valle de Viñales at dusk. **Above:** musician in Viñales.

Look for ★ to find recommended sights, activities, dining, and lodging.

Highlights

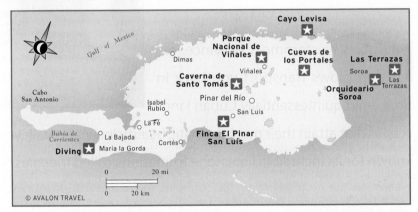

★ **Cayo Levisa:** Serene white-sand beaches and turquoise shallows surround Cayo Levisa, offering fantastic diving (page 175).

★ **Orquideario Soroa:** Hundreds of orchid species, as well as other botanicals, fill this exquisite hillside garden (page 177).

★ **Las Terrazas:** This unique mountain community is home to artists' studios, hiking trails, and a zip line (page 178).

★ **Cuevas de los Portales:** Che Guevara used this huge cave, adorned with dripstone formations, as his headquarters during the Cuban Missile Crisis (page 181).

★ **Parque Nacional de Viñales:** Among Cuba's most famous and fascinating landscapes, skyscraper-scale *mogotes* provide a magnificent backdrop for tobacco fields; there's also great climbing, caving, and a zip line (page 187).

★ **Caverna de Santo Tomás:** Cuba's largest cave system is a fascinating underworld of dripstone formations (page 193).

★ **Finca El Pinar San Luis:** At this world-renowned tobacco farm, visitors gain a complete knowledge of tobacco production (page 195).

★ **Diving at María la Gorda:** Whale sharks, manta rays, and fantastic coral formations are among the highlights (page 196).

The roads that fan out south from Havana are crisscrossed by minor roads that form an unfathomable labyrinth.

PLANNING YOUR TIME

Most visitors to this region justifiably set their sights on **Viñales,** a rustic village fully deserving of two days or more. There's plenty to see and do in the national park that bears its name, and you may wish to budget longer to savor Viñales's fabulous scenery and yesteryear way of life. That said, it has been inundated by travelers, and even "low season" can feel overcrowded with tourists.

To get there, most tourists follow the six-lane Autopista, the concrete highway linking Havana with the provincial capital of **Pinar del Río,** which can be skipped without regret. Take Avenida 25 west from Ciudad Libertad in Marianao; it becomes Avenida 23 and leads to the Autopista. There's relatively little traffic, and the route is pleasingly scenic. There are two refreshment stops along the highway. The only gas station is at the turnoff for **Soroa,** with its lovely orchid garden.

A more interesting route is the Carretera Central through sleepy provincial towns such as **Candelaria, Santa Cruz de los Pinos,** and **Consolación del Sur**—towns memorable for their old churches, faded pastel houses, and covered walkways with neoclassical pillars. The two-lane highway parallels the Autopista along the southern edge of the mountains and grants easy access to Soroa and **Parque Nacional La Güira,** worth visiting for the enormous cavern that once formed a military headquarters for Che Guevara.

For scenery, I prefer the Circuito Norte along the north coast (west of Puerto Esperanza, the road is very badly deteriorated). Offshore, a necklace of cays—the Archipiélago de los Colorados—are protected by a coral reef. There are beaches, though few of great appeal. The star attraction is **Cayo Levisa,** offering excellent diving and accommodations. Scuba enthusiasts should head west to **María la Gorda;** nature lovers might enjoy exploring **Parque Nacional Península de Guanahacabibes.**

The northwest coast and southern plains can be skipped. Historical attractions are few, although modernity overlays a way of life that has changed little since the end of the 19th century. This is especially so in the tobacco fields that are the province's main claim to fame, and never more so than on the outskirts of San Juan y Martínez at **Finca El Pinar San Luis,** renowned to cigar aficionados worldwide.

Central Artemisa Province

The old Carretera Central (Route 2-N1) was the main thoroughfare to Pinar del Río before the Autopista was built. To get there, take Avenida 51 from Marianao to La Lisa and follow the signs. Atmospheric colonial towns line the route. South of Guanajay, midway to Artemisa, is a restored remnant of the **Trocha Mariel-Majana,** a 19th-century fortification built by the Spanish to forestall the Army of Liberation during the wars of independence.

ARTEMISA AND VICINITY

Pedestrian-only **El Bulevar** (Martí e/ 27 y 33) is a public Wi-Fi zone, extending east from **Parque Libertad** and studded by the **Iglesia San Marcos de Artemisa.**

Antiguo Cafetal Angerona

Antiguo Cafetal Angerona lies two kilometers west of Rancho Azucarero and midway to Cayajabos. The site was founded as a coffee (and, later, sugar) plantation in 1813 by

Pinar del Río Province

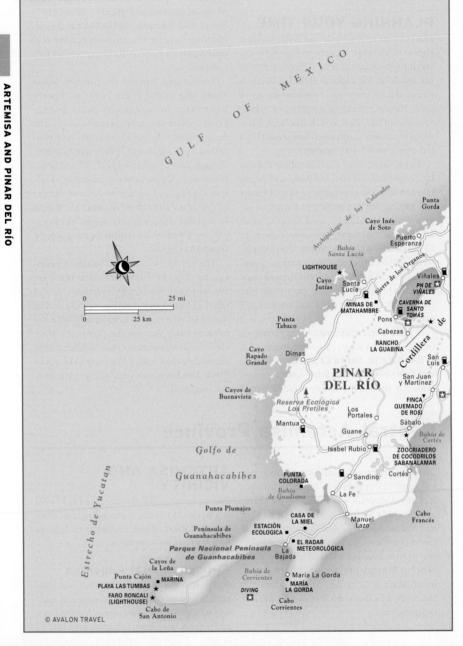

GULF OF MEXICO

Archipiélago de los Colorados

Punta Gorda

Cayo Inés de Soto

Puerto Esperanza

Bahía Santa Lucía

LIGHTHOUSE ★

Cayo Jutías

Santa Lucía

Sierra de los Organos

Viñales

PN DE VIÑALES

MINAS DE MATAHAMBRE ■

CAVERNA DE SANTO TOMÁS

Punta Tabaco

Pons

Cabezas

Cordillera de

RANCHO LA GUABINA

Cayo Rapado Grande

Dimas

San Luis

PINAR DEL RÍO

San Juan y Martínez

Cayos de Buenavista

Reserva Ecológica Los Pretiles

FINCA QUEMADO DE ROSÍ ▼

Los Portales

Mantua

Sábalo

Guane

Bahía de Cortés

Golfo de

Isabel Rubio

ZOOCRIADERO DE COCODRILOS SABANALAMAR ■

Guanahacabibes

PUNTA COLORADA ■

Sandino

Cortés

Bahía de Guadiana

La Fe

Punta Plumajes

Cabo Francés

CASA DE LA MIEL ■

Manuel Lazo

Península de Guanahacabibes

ESTACIÓN ECOLÓGICA ■

EL RADAR METEOROLÓGICA ■

Parque Nacional Península de Guanahacabibes

La Bajada

Estrecho de Yucatán

Cayos de la Leña

Bahía de Corrientes

Punta Cajón

MARINA ■

María La Gorda

PLAYA LAS TUMBAS ★

MARÍA LA GORDA

FARO RONCALI (LIGHTHOUSE) ★

DIVING

Cabo de San Antonio

Cabo Corrientes

0 ___ 25 mi
0 ___ 25 km

© AVALON TRAVEL

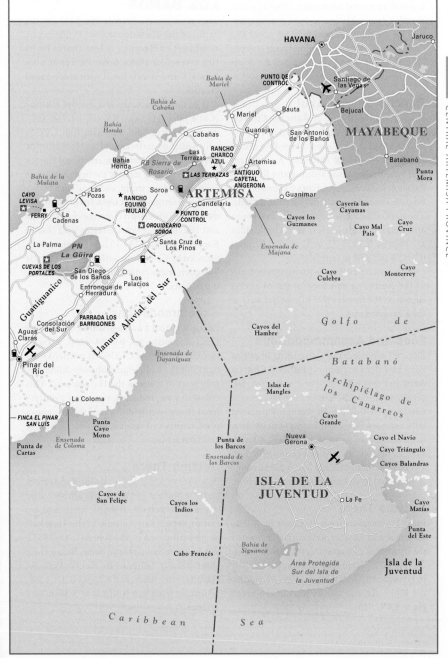

HAVANA
Jaruco

Bahía de Mariel
PUNTO DE CONTROL
Santiago de las Vegas

Mariel
Bauta
Bejucal

Bahía de Cabaña
Cabañas
Guanajay
San Antonio de los Baños
MAYABEQUE

Bahía Honda
RANCHO CHARCO AZUL
Batabanó

Bahía Honda
Las Terrazas
LAS TERRAZAS
Artemisa
ANTIGUO CAFETAL ANGERONA
Punta Mora

RB Sierra de Rosario
Bahía de la Mulata
Las Pozas
Soroa
ARTEMISA
Guanimar
Cayería las Cayamas

CAYO LEVISA
RANCHO EQUINO MULAR
Candelaria
Cayos los Guzmanes
Cayo Mal Pais
Cayo Cruz

FERRY
La Cadenas
ORQUIDEARIO SOROA
PUNTO DE CONTROL

La Palma
Santa Cruz de Los Pinos
Ensenada de Majana
Cayo Culebra
Cayo Monterrey

PN La Güira
CUEVAS DE LOS PORTALES
San Diego de los Baños
Los Palacios

Entronque de Herradura

Guaniguanico
PARRADA LOS BARRIGONES
Llanura Aluvial del Sur
Cayos del Hambre
Golfo   de

Aguas Claras
Consolación del Sur
B a t a b a n ó

Pinar del Río
Ensenada de Dayaniguas
Islas de Mangles
Archipiélago de los Canarreos

La Coloma
Cayo Grande
Cayo el Navio

FINCA EL PINAR SAN LUÍS
Punta Cayo Mono
Punta de los Barcos
Nueva Gerona
Cayo Triángulo
Cayos Balandras

Punta de Cartas
Ensenada de Coloma
Ensenada de los Barcos
ISLA DE LA JUVENTUD
Cayo Matías

Cayos de San Felipe
Cayos los Indios
La Fe
Punta del Este

Cabo Francés
Bahía de Siguanea
Isla de la Juventud

Área Protegida Sur del Isla de la Juventud

C a r i b b e a n   S e a

Cornelio Sauchay, who kept almost 500 slaves. It is now a national monument, albeit in ruins. Novelist James Michener used it as the setting for the sugar plantation in his novel *The Caribbean*. The watchtower and huge cisterns are still intact. There's no entrance fee or official hours; tip any guide.

Rancho Charco Azul

Horses are the theme at **Rancho Charco Azul** (tel. 047/649-1055, or c/o EcoTur, tel. 07/273-1542) at Cayajabos, a breeding center 14 kilometers west of Artemisa. An old farm that once belonged to cattle breeder Rosando Palacios, today Empresa Flora y Fauna breeds English Thoroughbreds and Gertrudis cattle. The stars of the show, however, are Percheron and Belgian draft horses. Horseback rides are offered (CUC5-7), as is guided birding (CUC6) and a farm tour (CUC6).

Rancho Charco Azul is immediately north of the Autopista exit for Cayajabos and is signed on the freeway two kilometers west of the Cayajabos exit.

Food and Accommodations

Flora y Fauna operates a charming boutique hotel in a stone mansion at **Rancho Charco Azul** (tel. 047/649-1055, or c/o EcoTur, tel. 07/273-1542, CUC32 s, CUC58 d low season, CUC33 s, CUC64 d high season). Furnished with antiques, it has four rooms with modern bathrooms, plus six modern cabins. A lovely swimming pool, an outside bar and grill, and an elegant restaurant (daily 7am-9:30am, noon-2:30pm, and 7pm-9pm) round out the picture.

Getting There

Bus #215 operates from Havana's main bus terminal and runs to Artemisa's **Terminal de Ómnibus** (Carretera Central, Km 58, tel. 047/36-3527). Trains depart Estación Tulipán in Havana at 5:45pm for Artemisa (Av. Héroes del Moncada, five blocks west of the main plaza, CUC2.20).

SAN ANTONIO DE LOS BAÑOS

This small town, founded in 1775 on the banks of the Río Ariguanabo (30 kilometers southwest of Havana), is lent charm by its tiny triangular plaza, ocher church (Calles 66 y 41), and streets lined with colonnaded arcades.

The town boasts the **Museo del Humor** (Calle 60 #4116, esq. 45, tel. 047/38-2817, Tues.-Sat. 10am-6pm, Sun. 9am-1pm, CUC2), which displays cartoons and hosts the **Humor Bienal Internacional** (International Humor Festival), drawing some of the best cartoonists from around the world, each odd year.

The prestigious **Escuela Internacional de Cine y Televisión** (International Cinema and Television School, Carretera Villa Nueva, Km 4.5, tel. 047/38-3152, www.eictv.org), founded by Colombian author Gabriel García Márquez, trains cinema artists from developing nations.

Accommodations

Islazul's **Hotel Las Yagrumas** (Calle 40 y Final Autopista, tel. 047/38-4460, www.islazul.cu, CUC56 s, CUC67 d) overlooks the banks of the Río Ariguanabo one kilometer northeast of town on the Havana road. This colonial-style, red-tiled, two-story property has 120 pleasantly decorated rooms, plus a pool, tennis and racquetball courts, bicycle and boat rentals, and boat excursions.

Getting There

Buses serve San Antonio de los Baños from Calle Apodaca between Agramonte and Avenida de Bélgica, Habana Vieja, and arrive or depart San Antonio at the Terminal de Ómnibus (Av. 55, tel. 047/38-2737). Trains serve San Antonio de los Baños from the Estación Tulipán, in Nuevo Vedado, Havana, at 10:05am and 4:25pm (CUC1.50), returning from San Antonio at 5:35am and 1:55pm.

The North Coast

HAVANA TO MARIEL

Departing Havana westward, 5ta Avenida becomes the coast road (Route 2-1-3) via Artemisa province to Pinar del Río. The shore is unremarkable, except for **Playa Baracoa,** 16 kilometers west of Havana and popular with Cubans on hot weekends. Some 5 kilometers farther west, the rather dull **Playa Salado** is the setting for a go-kart racetrack.

About 45 kilometers beyond the marina, you arrive at **Mariel.** Set deep inside a flask-shaped bay, this sleepy yet important port city, founded in 1792, is best known as the site of the April 1980 "boatlift," when 120,000 Cubans departed the island for Florida. Mariel is ringed by docks and factories, including a cement factory that casts a pall of dust over town.

Since 2009 Mariel has been designated as a "special development zone." Brazil is financing a US$1 billion construction project, centered on a huge new deepwater port and container terminal that will handle megaships passaging through the expanded Panama Canal. The facility will replace Havana's harbor as Cuba's main port. Factories producing for export are being built.

Buses depart and drop off at Calle 71.

BAHÍA HONDA TO CAYO LEVISA

Beyond Mariel, Route 2-1-3 continues west to **Cabañas,** beyond which you pass into Pinar del Río Province. It's a stunning drive: a gentle roller-coaster ride as the road runs a few miles inland of the coast.

Beyond the town of **Bahía Honda,** 20 kilometers west of Mariel, the road twists and loops and grows ever more scenic. Soon you are edging along beneath *mogotes,* with lower slopes covered with coffee bushes. The rounded **Pan de Guajaibón** (692 meters, 2,294 feet) looms ahead like the Sugarloaf

of Rio de Janeiro. The dramatic peak lies within the 18,160-hectare **Área Protegida Mil Cumbres,** part of the Sierra del Rosario Biosphere Reserve. One kilometer east of Las Pozas, you can turn south to follow a road into the Sierra del Rosario; it fizzles out at the hamlet of **Rancho Canelo,** from where a rough track continues to the base of Pan de Guajaibón. You can camp at the **Centro de Visitantes El Cuabal** or rent the three simple rooms at the **Casa de Montaña Mil Cumbres** (tel. 048/73-2890, ecoturpr@enet. cu, CUC15) in the community of San Juan de Sagua.

West of Las Pozas you'll see the first cays of the Archipiélago de los Colorados offshore. Ernest Hemingway had a fondness for beach-fringed **Cayo Paraíso** (Cayo Mégano de Casiguas), reachable only by boat. The coral is superb, and there's a sunken vessel to explore eight meters down. Hemingway's presence is venerated by a small monument beside the small wooden dock.

★ Cayo Levisa

About 10 kilometers west of Cayo Paraíso is Cayo Levisa, two kilometers offshore and fringed by a stunning white-sand beach and turquoise waters on its north shore. You need your passport to visit.

Cayo Levisa is popular with divers (the resort has a dive shop; dives cost CUC45). Snorkel gear can be rented for the day. A boat leaves for Cayo Levisa at 10am and 5pm (CUC15 hotel guests, CUC25 others, including lunch and cocktail; CUC35 pp private hire after 10am) from a dock adjacent to the coast guard station at Palma Rubia (the turnoff from the Circuito Norte is 5 kilometers west of the village of Las Cadenas, 10 kilometers west of Las Pozas). The return boats depart the cay at 9am and 5pm. Excursions to Cayo Levisa are offered from tour agencies in Pinar del Río and Viñales.

Accommodations

Missed the ferry to Cayo Levisa? No sweat. Set amid banana fields, **Casa Mario y Antonia** (tel. 048/5335-6310, antonia.felipe@nauta.cu, CUC20), 500 meters before the dock, offers one cross-ventilated room with double and single beds and a cold-water bathroom in a simple farmstead. The charming owners make delicious meals.

★ **Cubanacán Cayo Levisa** (tel. 048/75-6501, reservas@cayolevisa.co.cu, from CUC93 s, CUC133 d low season, from CUC113 s, CUC166 d high season, including meals) has 55 handsome air-conditioned log cabins in three types, including junior suites; all are furnished with satellite TVs, safes, and fridges, plus pine pieces, including four-poster beds with mosquito nets. The food is bland, but the resort offers Hobie Cats, pedal boats, and kayaks for rent.

WEST OF CAYO LEVISA

La Palma is the only town of consequence in the area, with a tiny museum and shops. A road leads south from here over the mountains to Parque Nacional La Güira and San Diego de los Baños. The scenery continues to inspire.

Ten kilometers west of La Palma is the junction for Viñales and the town of Pinar del Río. Continue straight and you reach **San Cayetano,** beyond which the land takes on a new look, with pine forests and, farther west where the land flattens out, citrus orchards. A turnoff leads north from here to the sleepy fishing village of **Puerto Esperanza.**

From San Cayetano it is 22 kilometers to the small port of **Santa Lucía** (the road is deteriorated; far better is to head inland via Viñales and Matahambre). Nearby **Cayo Jutía** (tel. 048/64-8317, daily 9am-5:30pm) offers superb beaches and swimming, plus diving (CUC25) and kayaks (CUC5). The cay is connected to the shore by a *pedraplén* (causeway) accessed by a turnoff, 4 kilometers west of Santa Lucía; it's 17 kilometers to the beach, pinned by a metal lighthouse. Tour companies offer excursions from Viñales. You can camp for free if you bring your own tent.

West of Baja, there's not a soul for miles until you arrive at the pretty hamlet of **Dimas.** Beyond Dimas you pass around the western edge of the Sierra de los Órganos as the badly deteriorated road veers south to **Mantua,** a pleasant little town that in 1896 was the site of a major battle during the War of Independence. This is a lonesome drive through parched scrub-covered land.

Sierra del Rosario

The Sierra del Rosario dominates eastern Pinar del Río Province. The 25,000-hectare (61,775-acre) **Reserva de la Biosfera Sierra del Rosario** protects the easternmost slopes, named a biosphere reserve by UNESCO in 1985 following a decade of reforestation efforts by the Cuban government. The reserve is covered by montane forest of pine and spruce. At any time, the air smells piney fresh.

The 98 bird species (including 11 of Cuba's 24 endemic species) include the national bird, the *tocororo.* The mountains are home to the smallest frog in the world (*Sminthilus*

limbatus). It can get cool at night—bring a sweater.

SOROA

Soroa is an "eco-retreat" set in a valley at about 250 meters elevation. It is called the "Rainbow of Cuba" for its natural beauty, although you need to get above the valley to fully appreciate the setting. The resort is named for Jean-Paul Soroa, a Frenchman who owned a coffee estate here two centuries ago. In the 1930s, it became fashionable as a spa.

Attractions include **Cascadas El Salto** (CUC3), a small waterfall reached from the El

Soroa and Complejo Turístico Las Terrazas

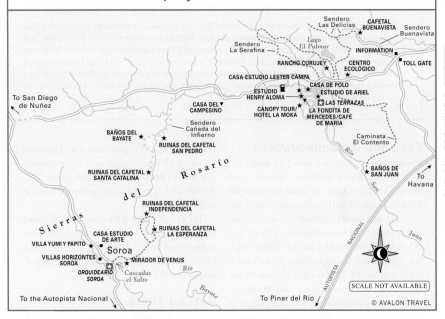

Salto parking lot by deteriorated stairs that descend 400 meters through fragrant woodlands to the bottom of the falls, which tumble 35 meters into pools good for bathing. A bar and restaurant overlook the river. A track leads from the parking lot to **Mirador de Venus,** a hilltop lookout with stupendous views. It's a stiff one-kilometer climb (or you can ride a horse, CUC3). Another trail leads to the ruins of **Cafetal Independencia,** a French coffee plantation (six hours round-trip).

Proyecto Cultural Estudio de Arte, one kilometer north of the Orquideario Soroa, represents six local artists at **Casa Estudio de Arte** (tel. 048/59-8116, infosoroa@hvs. co.cu, daily 8am-pm), where guests can participate in painting and ceramic workshops. Donations of brushes and other art supplies are needed. Jesús Gastell Soto, director, and a graduate of the Instituto Superior de Arte, is known for his large photographic artworks in hallucinogenic detail.

★ Orquideario Soroa

Soroa's prize attraction is this **orchid garden** (Carretera Soroa, Km 8, tel. 048/52-3871, daily 8:30am-4:30pm, CUC3 with obligatory guide, CUC1 camera, CUC2 video), which covers three hectares. It was created in 1943 by Spaniard Tomás Felipe Camacho. The craggy hillside garden offers views down the palm-tufted valley. The garden, nourished by the humid climate and maintained by the University of Pinar del Río, contains more than 20,000 plants representing over 700 species—250 of them indigenous to Cuba. Ask for guide Ana Lidia.

Recreation

The **Hotel and Villa Horizontes Soroa** (Carretera de Soroa, Km 8, Candelaria, tel. 048/52-3534) offers hiking, horseback riding (CUC3 per hour), and guided bird-watching (CUC10).

The Cork Palm

This endemic "palm," found only in Pinar del Río, is a souvenir of the Carboniferous era. The gravely endangered living fossil—*palma corcho*, or *Microcycas calocoma*—isn't a true palm, but rather a member of a primitive cycad family abundant 270 million years ago. It grows to six meters and sheds leaves every other year, leaving a ring around its fuzzy trunk that marks its age. It differs by sex: The masculine and feminine reproductive cells are emitted at different times, thus limiting the plant's propagation. Although some living species are 300 years old, there are few young ones known.

Food and Accommodations

About a dozen families who live along the road linking Soroa with the Autopista rent rooms. My favorite is ★ **Casa Estudio de Arte** (tel. 048/59-8116, infosoroa@hvs.co.cu, CUC25), 400 meters north of the Orquideario Soroa. Delightful hosts Alyshka and Jesús run this large home amid a garden ablaze with frangipani and bougainvillea. They have a cross-ventilated TV lounge. The rustic yet delightful thatched cottage has mosquito nets over two double beds on platforms, plus a modern bathroom with a hot-water shower, and a porch overlooks the rear garden. The home doubles as an art studio and gallery, and Alyshka offers basic Spanish classes with room packages.

Ana Lidia Rodríguez, a charming guide at the orchid garden, rents three independent rooms, all with private bathrooms, at **Casa Los Sauces** (Carretera Soroa, Km 3, tel. 5228-9372, bocourt@af.upr.edu.cu, CUC25), a modern two-story home about five kilometers below the orchid garden and one kilometer from the Autopista. Her garden full of orchids is a treasure.

Cubanacán's **Hotel and Villa Horizontes Soroa** (Carretera de Soroa, Km 8, Candelaria, tel. 048/52-3556, reserva@hvs.co.cu, from CUC45 s, CUC65 d low season, CUC70 s, CUC85 d high season) is a delightful resort complex. Stone pathways lead through landscaped grounds to an Olympic-size swimming pool surrounded by 49 small and pleasantly furnished *cabinas* with cable TV and modern bathrooms, on slopes backed by forest. The

resort also has 20 three- and four-bedroom houses with kitchenettes and private pools. The hotel's **Restaurant Centro** (daily 7am-9:45am and 7pm-9:45pm) serves continental and *criolla* dishes.

The thatched **Bar y Restaurante El Salto** (daily 9am-4pm), by the entrance to the cascade, serves *criolla* fare (CUC4-7) and has a Friday-night *cabaret espectáculo*. Two *paladares* line the road.

Getting There

Soroa is 7 kilometers north of the Autopista. The turnoff is about 80 kilometers west of Havana. The Havana-Pinar Víazul bus will drop you at the Cupet gas station at the Candelaria junction on the Autopista.

★ LAS TERRAZAS

This one-of-a-kind model village of 250 inhabitants, 20 kilometers northeast of Soroa and 4 kilometers northwest of the Autopista, is touted as one of Cuba's prime ecotourism sites. **Complejo Turístico Las Terrazas** (tel. 048/57-8700, www.lasterrazas.cu, CUC2 day visits) was founded in 1971 and is situated in a narrow valley above the shores of Lago San Juan with mountains to all sides. It lies at the heart of a comprehensive rural development project.

French settlers who fled Haiti in 1792 planted coffee in these hills. After the plantations failed, the local campesinos continued to fell the trees for export and eke out a living as charcoal burners. Hillside by hillside, much of the region was deforested. In

1967 the government initiated a 5,000-hectare reforestation project, employing the impoverished campesinos and providing them with housing in a model village. Las Terrazas is named for the terraces of trees (teak, cedar, mahogany, pine) that were planted. The houses of whitewashed concrete are aligned in terraces that cascade down the hillside to the lake, where **Casa de Polo** (daily 8am-5pm) is a museum in the former home of the late singer Polo Montañez. The village **community center,** facing a tiny *plazuela* with a fountain, houses a small **museum** that recounts Las Terrazas's development.

Rancho Curujey (tel. 048/57-8700), the administrative center about 400 meters east of the village, offers a thatched restaurant and bar over its own lake. The **Centro Ecológico** (tel. 048/57-8726, Mon.-Fri. 7am-5pm), a basic ecological center, welcomes visitors.

Sights

The **Cafetal Buenavista** (daily 8am-5pm, closed Sept.-Oct.), about two kilometers east of Hotel Moka, preserves the ruins of a French coffee plantation constructed in 1801. The main building is now a restaurant. Beyond are stone terraces where coffee beans were laid out to dry, the remains of the old slave quarters, and an ox-powered coffee grinder where coffee beans were ground to remove the husks.

Eight kilometers west of Las Terrazas, the **Sendero Cañada del Infierno** follows the Río Bayate south two kilometers to the overgrown ruins of San Pedro French coffee plantation and the sulfur baths of **Santa Catalina** (CUC2 Mon.-Thurs., free Fri.-Sun.). It's easy to miss the turnoff; look for the bridge over the Río Bayate.

Entertainment and Events

The two community bars in the Las Terrazas complex, **El Almacigo** and **Casa de Bota,** usually have someone playing guitar, and **Casa de Polo** hosts live music every second Tuesday (9pm-2am, free). **Discotemba** kicks it up a notch every Wednesday and Saturday night.

Recreation

One of Cuba's two zip line **canopy tours** (CUC25) features a two-cable run spanning the lake. Book at Hotel Moka (tel. 048/57-8600), where the run begins.

A paved road leads south from Las Terrazas three kilometers to the **Baños del Río San Juan** (daily 8am-7pm), with deep pools (good for swimming) and sunning platforms above cascades. A thatched bar and grill serves snacks, and the Restaurante El Bambú (daily 9am-6pm) sits above the falls.

Several poorly marked trails lead into the mountains. **Sendero Las Delicias** climbs Lomas Las Delicias, from where you have a fine view down the valley; the trip ends at the Buena Vista coffee plantation, also reached via the **Sendero Buenavista** (2 km). **Sendero La Serafina** (4 km) is good for birding; the Cuban trogon, the Cuban solitaire, woodpeckers, and the Cuban tody are common. Guided hikes and birding trips (CUC5-19) can be booked at Hotel Moka (tel. 048/57-8600) and Rancho Curujey (tel. 048/57-8700).

Hotel Moka also arranges horse rides (CUC5 per hour) and mountain bikes (CUC2). Rowboats and kayaks can be rented at **Casa de Botes** (tel. 082/75-8519, CUC2 per hour).

Shopping

Whether you intend to invest or not, call at **Casa-Estudio Lester Campa** (tel. 5272-0477, lester@cubarte.cult.cu, 9am-4pm daily), on the lakeshore. Lester Campa's fabulous works begin at around CUC300; his larger paintings fetch thousands of dollars on the international market.

For primitive sculptures, wooden spoons, and wind chimes, head to **Estudio Danny** (Casa 32A, tel. 048/57-8628), and to **Estudio Henry Aloma** (Casa 34B, tel. 082/57-8692, henryaloma79@gmail.com) for exquisite and surreal ecologically inspired drawings and paintings. This tiny hamlet also has a pottery workshop and **Taller de Serigrafo** (daily 8am-5pm), a serigraphy workshop.

Food

At ★ **La Fonda de Mercedes** (c/o Hotel Moka, Unit 9, tel. 048/57-8676, daily 9am-9pm), delightful host Mercedes Dache cooks fabulous *criolla* meals enjoyed on a terrace. A full meal will cost CUC12, including drink and dessert.

The menu (CUC5-10) at the upscale **La Moka** restaurant (Hotel Moka, daily 7:30am-10am, noon-3pm, and 7pm-10pm) includes beef stew, roast chicken, and butterfly lobster.

At **Cafetal Buenavista** (Hotel Moka, daily 9am-5pm) you can have lunch on a tree-shaded terrace. A set lunch costs CUC13, including coffee, dessert, and a fabulous main dish of baked garlic chicken.

Casa del Campesino (tel. 048/77-8555, daily 9am-5pm), two kilometers west of Las Terrazas, re-creates a typical peasant's farm on the ruins of the old Hacienda Unión coffee plantation. Gustavo Golnega and his family raise fowl and serve traditional meals (CUC15) prepared in the open kitchen with wood-fired oven. The place is often packed with tour groups and the kitchen often runs out.

Vegetarians should head to the **Eco-Restaurante El Romero** (tel. 48/77-8555, daily 9am-9pm), which gets rave reviews for its creative organic dishes, such as ceviche made of lotus roots, tempura vegetables, and tempeh steak with eggplant.

Don't miss ★ **Café de María** (no tel., daily 9am-11pm), a quaint open-air coffee shop and a great place to sip a cappuccino or any of 10 other coffee drinks while enjoying the view over the village.

Accommodations

You can rent rustic thatched cabins on stilts (CUC15 s, CUC25 d) or pitch a tent (CUC5 pp own tent, CUC12 tent rental) at **Camping Baños de San Juan** through Rancho Curujey (tel. 048/57-8700).

Sitting atop the village, ★ **Hotel Moka** (tel. 048/57-8602, CUC50 s, CUC80 d low season, CUC80 s, CUC110 d high season) is a contemporary interpretation of Spanish colonial architecture and features an atrium lobby surrounding a lime tree disappearing through the skylight. The two-story accommodations block has magnificent red-barked trees growing up through the balconies and ceiling. Each of the 42 rooms has floor-to-ceiling glass windows and a French door leading

artist Henry Aloma in his studio at Las Terrazas

onto a spacious balcony with tables, reclining chairs, and views through the trees to the lake. Take an upper-story room with high, sloping wooden ceilings. Facilities include a tennis court and swimming pool.

Getting There

Las Terrazas, 75 kilometers west of Havana, is 4 kilometers north of the Autopista at kilometer 51 (there's a sign); a road there runs into the mountains. You can also reach Las Terrazas by traveling north from Soroa, and from the Circuito Norte via an unmarked turnoff.

Tour agencies in Havana offer excursions. The Cupet gas station (daily 8am-5pm) is signed off the main road into Las Terrazas. There's an **information bureau** (daily 8am-5pm) at the toll gate.

SAN DIEGO DE LOS BAÑOS

The once important spa town of San Diego de los Baños is on the banks of the Río San Diego, 120 kilometers west of Havana, 60 kilometers east of Pinar del Río, and 10 kilometers north of the Autopista. It's centered on a tree-shaded plaza with a Greek Orthodox-style church (and public Wi-Fi). The spa waters of the Templado springs were discovered in the 17th century. The resort was later promoted in the United States as the "Saratoga of the Tropics" (the deteriorated Hotel Saratoga, one block west of the park, recalls the era).

The mineral waters (a near-constant 37-40°C) are a salve for rheumatism, skin disorders, and other ailments. A modern facility with subterranean whirlpool baths was built after the Revolution; the deteriorated Balneario San Diego was closed at last visit.

Food and Accommodations

Villa Julio y Cari (Calle 29 #4009, e/ 40 y 42, tel. 048/54-8037, CUC20), 50 meters west of Hotel Saratoga, has two simple air-conditioned rooms with private hot-water bathrooms. Meals are served on a shady terrace fronting the pleasant garden with parking.

Catching the breezes, the bargain-priced hillside **Hotel Mirador** (Calle 23 final, tel. 048/77-8338, carpeta@mirador.sandiego. co.cu, CUC30 s, CUC42 d low season, CUC40 s, CUC65 high season including breakfast) is set above landscaped grounds with a swimming pool. Contemporary flourishes highlight the 30 attractive air-conditioned rooms with simple furnishings, satellite TVs, direct-dial telephones, and modern bathrooms. The classy *criolla* restaurant is lit by Tiffany lamps. It offers guided birding (CUC5 pp) and hiking.

PARQUE NACIONAL LA GÜIRA

Parque Nacional La Güira protects 54,000 acres of wilderness on the higher slopes of the Sierra de los Órganos. Much of the park occupies the former estate of Manuel Cortina, a wealthy landowner who traded in precious woods. Following the Revolution, the land was expropriated and made a preserve, although it sees few visitors.

From the south, you enter the park through a mock fortress gate with turrets (4 km west of San Diego de los Baños), beyond which the road rises to Cortina's former mansion—now in ruins—and a series of modest and deteriorated gardens.

★ Cuevas de los Portales

This dramatic **cave** (daily 8am-5pm, entrance CUC1, guide CUC1, cameras CUC1), on the northwestern edge of the park, has a stunning setting beside the Río Caiguanabo. The river flows beneath a fantastically sculpted natural arch that the water has carved through a great *mogote*. The cave, reaching 30 meters high, lies inside one wall of the arch. The vaulted ceilings are stippled with giant dripstones.

The caves' remoteness and superb natural position made them a perfect spot for Che Guevara to establish his staff headquarters during the 1962 Cuban Missile Crisis, when he commanded the Western Army. The cave opens out to the rear, where stands Che's breeze-block office and dormitory, still containing Che's original table and chairs and narrow, iron bed.

A jeep is essential to negotiate the horribly denuded road that leads north through the park to the caves. Far better is to take the scenic mountain road (Carr. 371) that connects La Palma (on the north coast) with Entronque de Herradura (on the Autopista), 20 kilometers west of San Diego de los Baños. The caves (signed) are one kilometer east of this road.

(Nine kilometers south of La Palma, you can turn left via San Andrés to Viñales.)

Food and Accommodations

Campismo Cuevas Portales (tel. 048/63-6749, www.campismopopular.cu, 40 pesos) has spartan concrete *cabinas* and accepts foreigners, who also pay in *moneda nacional*. It rents tents. Warning: The music here is cranked up!

Pinar del Río and Vicinity

PINAR DEL RÍO

Pinar del Río (pop. 125,000), 178 kilometers west of Havana, is named for the native pine trees that once flourished along the banks of the Río Guamá. It was founded in 1669. Tobacco farmers established themselves nearby, and the city prospered on the trade—Cuba's first tobacco factory was founded nearby in 1761. The town is graced by neoclassical buildings with decorative art nouveau frontages. Tourist sights are few, but it makes a good base for exploring the province.

Orientation

The town is laid out in a grid, although many streets are aligned or curve at odd angles. The Autopista slides into town from the east to become Calle Martí, the main boulevard dividing the town north and south. Most places of interest are along Martí or along Calle Máximo Gómez (one block south). The main cross street is Isabel Rubio, which leads north and south, respectively, to Viñales and Vuelto Abajo. The city rises westward: At the "top" of Martí is Plaza de la Independencia.

Street numbers begin at Calle Martí (east-west) and Calle Gerardo Medina (north-south). Addresses suffixed by "Este" lie east of Gerardo Medina, and addresses suffixed by "Oeste" are west of Gerardo Medina. Similarly, any streets suffixed by "Norte" lie north of Martí and those suffixed by "Sur" lie south of Martí.

Museo de Ciencias Naturales

The small and mediocre **Museum of Natural Sciences** (Calle Martí Este #202, esq. Av. Comandante Pinares, tel. 048/77-9483, Mon.-Sat. 9am-5pm, Sun. 9am-1pm, CUC1) displays the natural history of the province. Concrete dinosaurs stand transfixed in the courtyard, including a T. rex and a *Megalocnus rodens* (an extinct oversized rodent once found in Cuba). The museum is housed in an ornately stuccoed building, the Palacio Gausch, built in 1914 by a Spanish doctor to reflect elements from his world travels. Thus, the entrance is supported by Athenian columns bearing Egyptian motifs, while Gothic griffins and gargoyles adorn the facade.

Entertainment

Cabaret Rumayor (Carretera Viñales, tel. 048/76-3051, Thurs.-Sun. at 10pm, CUC3 including one drink), one kilometer north of town, offers a modest two-hour-long *cabaret espectáculo*. The show is followed by a disco. You need ID to enter. Fans of flesh and feathers might get a kick, too, at **Cabaret El Criollo** (tel. 048/76-3050, Wed., Fri., and Sat., CUC5) on the Carretera Central northeast of town. It's the happening spot for a more impecunious crowd, as is the **Sala Fiesta** (tel. 048/75-5070, weekends) in the Hotel Pinar del Río. **Café Pinar** (Gerardo Medina Norte #34, tel. 048/77-8199, daily 7pm-2am, CUC3 including one drink) draws

Pinar del Río

To Viñales

VIÑALES

RESTAURANTE Y
CABARET RUMAYOR

To San Diego
de los Baños

HOSPITAL
(OLD)

RAFAEL MORALES

CARRETERA DE GUAMA

Río

Guamá

CABARET
EL CRIOLLO

AV. AEROPUERTO

ELISEO CAMAÑO

POLICE

ESTADIO
CAPITÁN SAN LUIS

CAPITÁN SAN LUIS

To Airport

CARRETERA CENTRAL

EUSEBIO GONZÁLEZ

F. REMEDIOS

TEPE PORTILLA

24 DE FEBRERO

JOSÉ LABRADO

CASA
DE DELICIAS

JULIAN ALEMÁN

GUSTAVO LARES

CASA DE
RENÉ GONZÁLEZ

ACUEDUCTO

CASA DE
ELENA RABELO

ANTONIO RUBIO

CORO

SOLANO RAMOS

CMDTE GONZÁLEZ

ERMITA
DE LA CARIDAD
DEL COBRE

ADELA AZCUY

ADELA AZCUY

JUAN GUILBERTO GÓMEZ

MARINA AZCUY

MARIANA GRAJALES

LUIS PÉREZ

COLÓN

To Rancho
La Guabina

VILLA LAS PALMITAS

FARMERS'
MARKET

PEDRO TÉLLEZ

ISIDRO DE ARMAS

20 DE MAYO

IMMIGRATION

EMILIO NÚÑEZ

VIVÓ

ETECSA

ETECSA

MEDINA

COMANDANTE PINARES

HOLDAN

RAFAEL MORALES

ORMANI ARENADO

GERARDO

MARTÍ

ISABEL RUBIO

CELESTINO PACHECO

IGNACIO AGRAMONTE

UNIVERSITY

TARAFA

MÁXIMO GÓMEZ

BUS STATION/
CUBATAXI

PALADAR CAFÉ
ORTUZAR

CARLOS M. DE CÉSPEDES

MONUMENTO Á
LOS HERMANOS SAÍZ

ANTONIO MACEO

CASA DE
JEDREZ

EL MESÓN

PALADAR EL
GALLARDO

HOTEL
PINAR DEL RÍO

CAR
RENTALS

SEE "CENTRAL
PINAR DEL RÍO" MAP

PALADAR LA MIL
Y UNA NOCHES

MUSEO
DE CIENCIAS
NATURALES

CAFETERÍA
LA CHOZA

27 DE NOVIEMBRE

GONZÁLEZ ALCORTA

ANTONIO

CATHEDRAL

CEREFINO FERNÁNDEZ

RAFAEL FERRO

To
Havana

FRANK PAÍS

REMIGIO
RODRÍGUEZ

COLÓN

BANK

To San Juan y Mártinez
and María La Gorda

FÁBRICA DE
BEBIDAS GUAYABITA

2DA

L. SOBRADO

FLORA PALMA

FERROCARRIL

RAILWAY STATION

CASA PARTICULAR
VILLA ANA

26 DE NOVIEMBRE

MAICA

FRANK PAÍS

6TA

ISABEL RUBIO

B

A

NUEVA

0   200 yds

0   200 m

© AVALON TRAVEL

Walking Tour of Pinar del Río

Museo de Ciencias Naturales, Pinar del Río

After perusing the **Museo de Ciencias Naturales** at the foot of Martí, follow Martí west two blocks to the **Teatro José Jacinto Milanés** (Martí, esq. Calle Colón, tel. 048/75-3871, Mon.-Fri. 9am-5pm, CUC1) to admire its ornate fin-de-siècle interior. It dates to 1898. Immediately west, the **Museo Provincial de Historia** (Martí Este #58, e/ Isabel Rubio y Colón, tel. 048/75-4300, Mon. noon-4pm, Tues.-Sat. 8am-10pm, Sun. 9am-1pm, CUC1) traces local history.

Turn left onto Isabel Rubio and walk four blocks to the **Fábrica de Bebidas Guayabita** (Isabel Rubio Sur #189, e/ Cerefino Fernández y Frank País, tel. 048/75-2966, Mon.-Sat. 8am-4:30pm, CUC1 tours), which since 1892 has made *guayabita,* a spicy, brandy-like alcoholic drink made from rum and the fruit of a wild bush—*Psidium guayabita*—that grows only in Pinar del Río.

Retrace your steps two blocks to Antonio Maceo. Turn left and walk west to the **Catedral de San Rosendo** (Maceo Este #2, esq. Gerardo Medina), which dates from 1833 and has a barrel vaulted wooden ceiling and fine gilt altar.

Continuing west, uphill, call in at the **Fábrica de Tabacos Francisco Donatién** (Antonio Maceo Oeste #157, esq. Ajete, tel. 048/77-3069, Mon.-Fri. 9am-noon and 1pm-4pm, CUC5 guided tour), a cigar factory housed in the former jail. No photos.

the young crowd for live music from *bolero* to rap; bring ID.

For traditional music, try the **Casa de Cultura** (Máximo Gómez #108, tel. 048/75-2324, free), with live music nightly at 9pm, and the **Casa de la Música** (Gerardo Medina Norte #21 y Antonio Rubio, tel. 048/75-3605, CUC1).

Pinar hosts a four-day **Carnaval** in early July, when *carrozas* (floats) and *comparsas* (costumed troupes) wind through the streets.

The local **baseball team,** the Vegueros,

plays at the Estadio Capitán San Luis (Calle Capitán San Luis), three blocks west of the Carretera Central for Viñales (Oct.-Mar.).

Food

The *paladar* **El Mesón** (Calle Martí Este #205, tel. 082/75-2867, Mon.-Sat. 11:30am-11pm), opposite the Museo de Ciencias Naturales, serves the usual *criolla* fare for CUC4-6. Next door, **Restaurant El Gallardo** (Martí #20, tel. 048/77-8492, daily 7am-11pm) serves grilled shrimp (CUC5), lobster

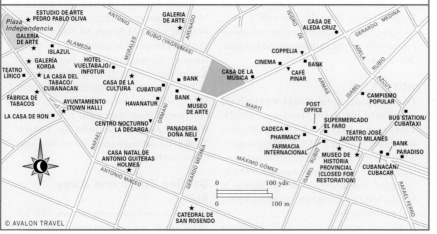

Central Pinar del Río

Plaza Independencia

ESTUDIO DE ARTE ★ PEDRO PABLO OLIVA

GALERIA DE ARTE ★

CASA DE ALEDA CRUZ ★

GALERIA DE ARTE ★

ANTONIO

RUBIO (YAGRUMAS)

ARENIDO

ISIDRO RV

GERARDO MEDINA

ISLAZUL ■

ALAMEDA

MORALES

COPPELIA ▼

ADELA

RUBIO

★ GALERÍA KORDA

HOTEL VUELTABAJO/ INFOTUR

CINEMA ■

BANK ■

CAFÉ PINAR ■

AZCUY

TEATRO LÍRICO ★

★ LA CASA DEL TABACO/ CUBANACAN

CASA DE LA CULTURA ★

CASA DE LA MÚSICA ■

ARMAS

ISABEL

★ CAMPISMO POPULAR ■

FÁBRICA DE TABACOS ■

AYUNTAMIENTO (TOWN HALL) ■

CUBATUR ■

BANK ■

HAVANATUR ■

MARTÍ

POST OFFICE ■

CASA POPULAR ■

BUS STATION/ CUBATAXI ■

LA CASA DE RON ■

CENTRO NOCTURNO LA DECARGA ■

MUSEO DE ARTE ■

ORMANI

SUPERMERCADO EL FARO ■

TEATRO JOSÉ JACINTO MILANÉS ■

BANK ■

PANADERÍA DOÑA NELI ▼

CADECA ■

PHARMACY ■

PARADISO ■

CASA NATAL DE ANTONIO GUITERAS HOLMES ★

FARMACIA INTERNACIONAL ■

MÁXIMO GÓMEZ

ISABEL RUBIO

GERARDO MEDINA

MUSEO DE HISTORIA PROVINCIAL (CLOSED FOR RESTORATION) ■

CUBANACÁN/ CUBACAR ■

RAFAEL FERRO

ANTONIO MACEO

RAFAEL

CATEDRAL DE SAN ROSENDO ★

0   100 yds

0   100 m

© AVALON TRAVEL

enchiladas (CUC7), and *ropa vieja* in a farm-style *ranchón*.

The pleasant **Las Mil y Una Noche** (Martí #132, tel. 048/75-6549, daily noon-11pm) serves a set grilled lunch (CUC7) and, by night, garlic shrimp (CUC4), chicken cordon bleu (CUC8), and *ropa vieja*. Across the street sits **Café Ortuzár** (Martí #127, tel. 5331-2176, daily noon-midnight), adorned with abstract paintings of local *guajiros*. It offers a delightful, clean ambience for coffee or cappuccino, a burger with fries, or even a set three-course meal (CUC15).

For ambience, try the **Restaurante y Cabaret Rumayor** (tel. 048/76-3051, daily noon-midnight), one kilometer north of town on Carretera Viñales. The thatch-and-log dining room is decorated with African drums, shields, and religious icons. *Criolla* dishes include the house special, *pollo ahumado* (smoked chicken, CUC5) and *chirna frita* (fish sautéed with garlic, CUC7).

Coppelia (Gerardo Medina Norte #33, Tues.-Fri. 11am-10pm, Sat. noon-11pm, Sun. 10am-9pm), one block east of Martí, has ice cream for 60 centavos per scoop.

For baked goods, head to **Panadería Doña Neli** (Gerado Medina Sur y Máximo Gómez, daily 7am-10pm). You can buy produce at the ***mercado agropecuario*** (Rafael Ferro y Ferrocarril), four blocks south of Martí.

Accommodations
CASAS PARTICULARES

Secure parking (CUC1) and a fathoms-deep spa-tub in the tree-shaded stone patio are pluses at **Casa de Elena Rabelo** (Antonio Rubio #284, e/ Méndez Capote y Coronel Pozo, tel. 048/75-4295, ghernandez@fcm. pri.sld.cu, CUC20). It has two pleasantly furnished air-conditioned rooms with private bathrooms.

Casa de Aleda Cruz (Gerardo Medina 67, tel. 048/75-3173, CUC20 with fans, CUC25 with air-conditioning) is a venerable colonial home with a choice of two basically furnished rooms with private hot-water bathrooms. A patio has an exquisite garden and a spacious independent apartment with kitchen, plus a plunge pool and secure parking.

Casa de René González (Calle Unión #13, e/ Capitán San Luis y Carmen, Rpto. Villamil, tel. 048/75-7515, CUC20) has two clean air-conditioned rooms upstairs. There's secure parking, and the family runs a *paladar* next door.

On the south side of town, **Casa Villa Ana** (Colón #269, e/ País y 2da, tel. 048/75-3696, CUC15-20) is a good bet for its two comfy rooms with private bathrooms and independent access.

HOTELS

Charm exudes from **Hotel Vueltabajo** (Martí #103, esq. Rafael Morales, tel. 048/75-9381, www.islazul.cu, CUC40 s, CUC60 d low season, CUC45 s, CUC75 d high season), a historic hotel featuring beautiful antiques, stained glass, and a marble staircase; 39 high-ceilinged rooms have simple furnishings. It has the best restaurant in town, plus Internet and an Infotur desk.

Bargain rates are a draw at **Hotel Pinar del Río** (Martí y Final Autopista, tel. 048/75-5070, www.islazul.cu, from CUC26 s, CUC42 d low season, from CUC40 s, CUC54 d high season), on the eastern fringe of town. This post-Stalinist structure has 136 air-conditioned rooms and 13 junior suites with satellite TVs, telephones, and safes. It has car rental, a nightclub, a restaurant, and a swimming pool that draws locals on weekends.

Villa Aguas Claras (Carretera de Viñales, Km 7.5, tel. 048/77-8427, aguasclaras@enet.cu, CUC25 s, CUC40 d including breakfast), eight kilometers north of town on the road to Viñales, bills itself as an eco-resort. It has 50 thatched and modestly furnished air-conditioned *cabinas* amid landscaped grounds. Folkloric shows are performed beside the swimming pool, and it has guided hikes.

Information and Services

Infotur (tel. 048/72-8616, infotur@pinar.infotu.cu, Mon.-Fri. 9:15am-5:15pm) has a tour desk in the Hotel Vueltabajo.

The **post office** and DHL station is at Calle Martí Este #49 (esq. Isabel Rubio, tel. 048/75-5916). **Etecsa**'s *telepunto* (Gerardo Medina, esq. Juan Gualberto Gómez, daily 8:30am-7:30pm) has international phone and Internet service. Parque Independencia and Parque Colón have public Wi-Fi.

Banks include **Banco Financiero Internacional** (Gerardo Medina Norte #44, esq. Isidro de Armas, tel. 048/77-8213). You can change foreign currency at **Cadeca** (Gerardo Medina Norte #35, esq. Isidro de Armas, and Martí, e/ Medina y Isabel Rubio).

The **Farmacia Internacional** (tel. 048/757-7784, Mon.-Sat. 8am-4pm) is at the junction of Martí with Calle Isabel Rubio. **Hospital Abel Santamaría** (tel. 048/76-7379) is on the Carretera Central, one kilometer northeast of town.

Getting There and Away

BUS

Víazul (Juan Gualberto Gómez #14, tel. 048/75-0887, www.viazul.com) buses connect Pinar with Havana and Viñales, with thrice-daily service. Buses arrive and depart the **Terminal de Ómnibus** (Adela Azcuy, e/ Colón y Comandante Pinares, tel. 048/75-2571).

TRAIN

The **railway station** (Comandante Pinares y Ferrocarril, tel. 048/75-2272) is three blocks south of Calle Martí. Train #71 departs Havana's Estación 19 de Noviembre (Tulipán) every second day at 6:10pm (six hours, CUC7). Train #72 departs Pinar del Río for Havana at 1:25pm. (The service will leave/arrive Havana's Estación Central de Ferrocarriles once it reopens.)

TOUR AGENCIES

Tour agencies include **Cubatur** (Martí #51, esq. Rosario, tel. 048/77-8405), **Cubanacán** (Martí #109, esq. Colón, tel. 048/75-0178, and in the Casa del Tabaco, tel. 048/77-2244), and **Havanatur** (Calle Ormany Arenado #2 e/ Martí y Máximo Gómez, tel. 082/77-8494). **Paradiso** (Martí #28, e/ Recreo y Colón, tel. 048/71-7127, www.paradiso.cu) offers cultural tours, and **EcoTur** (Carretera a Ciñales, Km 25, tel. 048/79-6120, ecoturpr@enet.cu) offers ecotourism excursions.

Getting Around

Cubataxi (tel. 048/79-3195) is at the bus station.

Car rental agencies include **Cubacar** (tel. 048/77-8278), **Havanautos** (tel. 048/77-8015), **Rex** (tel. 048/77-1454), and **Vía** (tel. 048/75-7663), all at Hotel Pinar del Río (Martí y Final Autopista). **Cubacar** (tel. 048/72-9381) also has an outlet at Hotel Vueltabajo.

There's a gas station at the bottom of Rafael Morales on the south side of town and two more stations northeast of town, on the Carretera Central.

RANCHO LA GUABINA

Equestrians will delight at **Rancho La Guabina** (Carretera de Luis Lazo, Km 9.5, tel. 048/75-7616, ecoturpr@enet.cu), a horse-breeding and recreational center in the rolling, lake-studded hills northwest of Pinar del Río. The sublime setting is icing on the cake of a relaxing day or two. The focus is the breeding of Pinto Cubano and Appaloosa horses, which are trotted out for display (Mon., Wed., and Fri. at 10am and 4pm.). Explore the farm on a horse-drawn coach (CUC10), then opt for a horseback ride (CUC7 per hour) or rent rowboats (CUC5).

Food and Accommodations

★ **Rancho La Guabina** (CUC42 pp, including breakfast and lunch) has some of the nicest rural digs in all Cuba. The two-story mansion has metamorphosed into lovely air-conditioned accommodations, with five cross-ventilated rooms with huge windows, ceiling fans, and two double beds. Two rooms share a bathroom. It also has three cabins. The elegant restaurant has lake views.

Sierra de los Órganos

Northwest Pinar del Río Province is dominated by the Sierra de los Órganos, boasting the most spectacular scenery in Cuba. The dramatic karst scenery is most fantastic within the Valle de Viñales. The valley (about 11 kilometers long and 5 kilometers wide) is studded with precipitous *mogotes* that tower over *hoyos,* small depressions filled with deep deposits of rich red soil. Thanks to a very special microclimate, tobacco grows well here, dominating the valley economy.

★ PARQUE NACIONAL DE VIÑALES

The Valle de Viñales is enshrined within **Viñales National Park.** Dominating the valley are the dramatic *mogotes,* in whose shadows *guajiros* (farmers) lovingly tend their plots of tobacco and maize. Mists settle above the valley in the early morning.

Viñales

In the heart of the valley is the eponymous village (pop. 10,000), whose sleepy yesteryear charm is a thing of the past. It is well into a tourism boom, thronged with backpacking travelers year-round. The bombast of reggaeton now blares from streetside restaurants, but the spectacular setting remains—and the bucolic Cuba lifestyle continues beyond the village.

Viñales, 26 kilometers north of Pinar del Río, was founded in 1875. Calle Salvador Cisneros, Viñales's wide main street, is lined with red-tile-roofed 19th-century cottages shaded by rows of stately pine trees. The handsome main square is shaded by palms and has a bust of José Martí. To one side is a pretty 19th-century church. On the north side, a beautiful arcaded colonial building houses the **Casa de Cultura** (tel. 048/77-8128), which hosts cultural events and adjoins the tiny **Galería de Arte** (Wed.-Mon. 9am-noon and 1pm-11pm).

Museo Municipal Adela Azcuy (Salvador Cisneros #115, tel. 048/79-3195,

Parque Nacional de Viñales

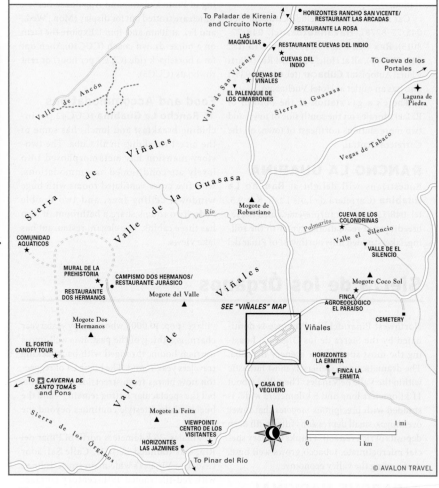

To Paladar de Kirenia
and Circuito Norte

• HORIZONTES RANCHO SAN VICENTE/
RESTAURANT LAS ARCADAS

RESTAURANTE LA ROSA

LAS
MAGNOLIAS

● RESTAURANTE CUEVAS DEL INDIO

CUEVAS DEL
INDIO

To Cueva de los
Portales

CUEVAS DE
VIÑALES

EL PALENQUE DE
LOS CIMARRONES

Laguna de
Piedra

Valle de San Vicente

Sierra la Guasasa

Vegas de Tabaco

Viñales

de

Sierra

Valle

de

la

Guasasa

Río

Mogote de
Robustiano ▲

Palmarito

CUEVA DE LOS
COLONDRINAS
★

Valle el Silencio

VALLE DE EL
SILENCIO
★

COMUNIDAD
AQUÁTICOS
★

MURAL DE LA
PREHISTORIA
★

CAMPISMO DOS HERMANOS/
RESTAURANTE JURÁSICO

Mogote Coco Sol ▲

RESTAURANTE
DOS HERMANOS

Mogote del Valle ▲

FINCA
AGROECOLOGICO
EL PARAÍSO

CEMETERY
■

Mogote Dos
Hermanos ▲

SEE "VIÑALES" MAP

Viñales

EL FORTÍN
CANOPY TOUR
★

HORIZONTES
LA ERMITA
●

FINCA LA
ERMITA ▼

To ✚ CAVERNA DE
SANTO TOMÁS
and Pons

Valle

de

Viñales

CASA DE
VEQUERO ▼

Sierra

de

los

Órganos

Mogote la Feita ▲

VIEWPOINT/
CENTRO DE LOS
VISITANTES
★

0   1 mi

0   1 km

HORIZONTES
LAS JAZMINES
●

To Pinar del Río

© AVALON TRAVEL

Tues.-Sun. 8am-5pm, CUC1) has motley displays telling the history of the region. Outside stands a bronze bust of Adela Azcuy Labrador (1861-1914), a local heroine in the War of Independence.

María Lezcano offers guided tours of **Jardín Botánico de Viñales** (Salvador Cisneros #5, tel. 048/79-6274, daily 8am-7pm, entry by donation), a 0.8-hectare garden full of fruit trees, medicinal plants, and orchids totaling 189 species. The garden is festooned with plastic teddy bears, decapitated dolls' heads, and desiccated fruits, giving it an air of shamanic intrigue. For a more authentic "garden" experience, head east 0.5 kilometer from the village to **Finca Agroecologico El Paraíso** (Carr. al Cementerio Km 1.5, tel. 5818-8581), a private organic farm whose owner, Wilfredo García Correa, offers educational tours.

The **Centro de Visitantes** (Visitors Center, tel. 048/79-6144, daily 8am-8pm)

Mogotes

Dramatic mountain formations called *mogotes* ("haystacks") stud the landscape of Cuba. The isolated, sheer-sloped, round-topped mounds are the remnants of a great limestone plateau that rose from the sea during the Jurassic era, about 160 million years ago. Over the ensuing eons, rain and rivers dissolved and eroded the porous limestone mass, leaving hummocks as high as 1,000 feet.

Rainwater interacts with limestone to produce a mild carbonic acid, which assists the erosive action of underground streams, carving a system of caverns that become so huge that eventually their roofs collapse, forming sheer-sided valleys.

Many species of flora and fauna are found only atop the mesas. Certain species of snails are found only on one or a few *mogotes*. Although the surface soil is thin and water scarce (it percolates rapidly into the rock), the formations are luxuriantly festooned with epiphytes, ferns, and the rare and ancient cork palm (*Mycrocycas calocoma*), a botanical relic that grows only here.

atop a *mogote* to the southwest of the village on the road from Pinar del Río has educational displays on local geology, history, and the ecosystem.

Cuevas del Indio

The **Cuevas del Indio** (tel. 048/79-6280, daily 9am-5pm, guided tour CUC5), five kilometers north of Viñales, were named for the Indian remains found inside. The large grotto is entered via a slit at the foot of a *mogote*. The cave is four kilometers long. A flight of steps leads to a well-lit path (slippery in parts) through the catacomb, which soars 135 meters. Eventually you reach an underground pier where a motorboat departs every 15 minutes for a trip up the subterranean river that runs deep beneath the mountain and is a habitat for opaque fish and blind crustaceans.

Cueva de Viñales (CUC1 with a guide), one kilometer south of Cuevas del Indio, is mostly a curiosity. The cave entrance has been converted into a bar-restaurant and, by night, a discotheque. At the rear, a natural tunnel emerges into another cave entrance with a touristy restaurant that plays up the slave theme.

For an intriguing side trip, turn east along the narrow road two kilometers south of Cuevas del Indio to reach **Laguna de las Rocas**, a scenic lake eight kilometers from

the junction. Nearby is **Valle de El Silencio** (c/o tel. 5310-3342), where owner Raynier serves lunch at a thatched hillside restaurant overlooking a lake and the **Cueva de Colondrinas** (Cave of Swallows). You can explore, hike there, or take an ATV or horseback ride (tel. 5346-7492, www.atcubanstyle.com, CUC5 per hour) along the muddy trail from the village.

Mural de la Prehistoria

The much-touted **Mural de la Prehistoria** (tel. 08/79-6260, daily 8:30am-6pm, CUC3), five kilometers west of Viñales, is painted onto the exposed cliff face of Mogote Dos Hermanos. The mural, which measures 200 feet high and 300 feet long, illustrates evolution in the Sierra de los Órganos, from mollusk and dinosaur to club-wielding Guanajays, the first human inhabitants of the region. It was commissioned by Castro and painted by 25 campesinos in 1961 while the artist, Leovigilda González, directed from below with a megaphone. The cliff face has since been repainted in gaudy colors—a red brontosaurus, a yellow tyrannosaurus, and a blood-red *homo sapiens*—as a testament to bad taste splotched on the wall of what is otherwise a beautiful valley. Horseback (CUC5 per hour) and oxcart (CUC1) rides are offered.

Museo de la Prehistoria (daily 9am-6pm, CUC1) in the Campismo Dos Hermanos

Viñales

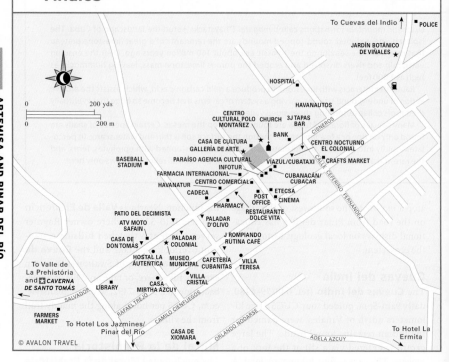

To Cuevas del Indio · POLICE

JARDÍN BOTÁNICO
DE VIÑALES

To Cuevas del Indio · POLICE

HOSPITAL

CENTRO
CULTURAL POLO   CHURCH   3J TAPAS
MONTAÑEZ   BAR

HAVANAUTOS

CISNEROS

BANK

CASA DE CULTURA   CENTRO NOCTURNO
GALLERÍA DE ARTE   EL COLONIAL

PARAÍSO AGENCIA CULTURAL   VIAZUL/CUBATAXI   CRAFTS MARKET
INFOTUR

BASEBALL
STADIUM

FARMACIA INTERNACIONAL   CUBANACÁN/
HAVANATUR   CENTRO COMERCIAL   CUBACAR

CADECA

POST
OFFICE   ETECSA
PHARMACY   CINEMA

RESTAURANTE
DOLCE VITA

PATIO DEL DECIMISTA
ATV MOTO   PALADAR
SAFAIN   D'OLIVO

CASA DE   PALADAR
DON TOMÁS   COLONIAL   J ROMPIANDO
                             RUTINA CAFE

HOSTAL LA   MUSEO   CAFETERÍA   VILLA
AUTENTICA   MUNICIPAL CUBANITAS   TERESA

To Valle de
La Prehistória   VILLA
and CAVERNA   CRISTAL
DE SANTO TOMÁS   LIBRARY   CASA
                           MIRTHA AZCUY

FARMERS
MARKET   To Hotel Los Jazmines/
         Pinar del Río   CASA DE
                              XIOMARA

To Hotel La
Ermita

© AVALON TRAVEL

(opposite the entrance to the mural) displays pre-Columbian artifacts and nature specimens.

Entertainment

The most sophisticated place in town is the French-owned **3J Tapas Bar** (Cisnero #45, tel. 048/79-3334 or 5531-1658), one block east of the plaza. This neon-lit bar tempts patrons with hip sounds and great ambience.

Artex's **Palacio del Decimista** (Salvador Cisneros #102, tel. 048/79-6014, CUC1) has live music nightly. The **Centro Cultural Polo Montañez** (tel. 048/77-6164), on the patio of the Casa de la Cultura on the main plaza, draws crowds for cabaret and live music.

Cueva de Viñales (tel. 048/79-6290) hosts a *cabaret espectáculo*—Cabaret El Palenque—and disco each Saturday at 10pm (CUC1-3), four kilometers north of Viñales.

Recreation

The area is a mecca for caving and climbing. Scores of climbing routes have been mapped up the *mogotes*. The unofficial base is the home of local guide **Oscar Jaime Rodríguez** (Adela Azcuy #43, tel. 048/69-5516, oscar.jaime59@gmail.com). *Cuba Climbing,* by Anibal Fernández and Armando Menocal, is an indispensable guide that includes photos and diagrams of scores of routes (www.quick-drawpublications.com).

Local tour agencies offer five specialist hiking excursions (CUC5-8), biking tours (CUC5 or CUC20 including lunch), and a visit to the **El Fortín Canopy Tour** (CUC8), which has a single 1,000-meter-long cable slung on a *mogote* about two kilometers west of the village. The **Viñales Bus Tour** (CUC5) passes by the roadside canopy station.

ATV excursions are offered at **ATV Moto**

Safain (Cisnero #141, tel. 048/79-6210 or 79-6061), next to Restaurante Don Tomás. You must have a guide (CUC35 for 3 hours or CUC250 full day). It's great fun splashing along muddy trails through the heart of the countryside. **Horseback excursions** (tel. 048/79-3142) get you into the thick of the countryside; my favorite route leads to Valle de El Silencio.

You can buy a day pass to use the pool and facilities at Hotel Villa Rancho San Vicente (CUC7, including CUC6 food and drink).

Food

Most owners of *casas particulares* will prepare filling breakfasts and dinners. Every fourth home along the main drag seems to have a restaurant; most offer variations on the *criolla* theme. The standout is ★ **3J Tapas Bar** (Cisnero #45, tel. 048/79-3334 or 5531-1658, daily 8am-2am), one block east of the plaza. The tapas menu includes stuffed olives (CUC3), Spanish sausage (CUC5.50), squid (CUC7.50), and mains such as ravioli with spinach (CUC6) and *ropa vieja* (CUC12). It also serves breakfast.

At **Restaurante El Olivo** (Cisneros #89, tel. 048/69-6654 or 5283-8045, daily noon-10pm), owner Osnel Carrales Valdes and his Spanish partner have conjured a sophisticated space for enjoying *criolla* fare and Mediterranean tapas (Galician-style octopus, CUC4.25; sautéed battered shrimp, CUC3.90), plus lasagna with mozzarella (CUC6.50). It's hugely popular and reservations are essential.

Next door is **La Cuenca** (Cisneros #97, tel. 048/69-6968, lacuenca@nauta.cu, daily noon-midnight), with an identical menu. Its stark, checkered white-and-black decor feels like dining inside a chess game, but tall windows open to front and side, lending it a pleasant airiness. Start with gazpacho (CUC3) followed by shrimp with olives, mushrooms, peppers, onions, and wine (CU8.50).

For traditional ambience, try **Casa de Don Tomás** (Salvador Cisneros #141, tel. 048/79-6300, daily 10am-10pm), a historic wooden structure festooned with climbing plants. The menu includes *delicias de Don Tomás* (a rice dish with pork, sausage, and lobster, CUC10), and *criolla* staples such as *ropa vieja* (CUC5) and lobster enchiladas (CUC10.95). Troubadours serenade while you eat on the airy rear patio.

Dine with a spectacular view at **Paladar Buena Vista** (tel. 5336-4434), a rustic thatched-roof restaurant on stilts on the hillside next to Hotel Los Jasmines. You're served

tobacco fields, Parque Nacional de Viñales

criolla staples with all the trimmings (CUC5-10). Even better is ★ **Finca Agroecologico El Paraíso** (Carr. al Cementerio Km 1.5, tel. 5818-8581, 11am-10pm), a private hillside farm-restaurant where most of the organic produce served in its delicious *criolla* dishes (slow-roasted pork, shrimp enchiladas) is raised or grown on-site. Your meal begins with a yummy "Anti-Stress" cocktail—coconut milk and pineapple juice blended with honey and herbs (rum optional). Again, what views!

Start the day with a good cup o' joe at **J Rompiando Rutina Cafetería** (Azcuy esq. Rafael Trejo, 7am-10pm).

Accommodations

The accommodations shortage in town is acute, given the surge in tourists. The state has three small hotels, but at last visit only a tiny boutique hotel opposite the plaza was in the works. French company Pansea Hotels has plans for a hilltop resort.

CASAS PARTICULARES

There are more than 900 private house rentals. Most charge CUC20-25 in the low season and CUC25-30 in the high season, and are air-conditioned and offer meals.

The standout ★ **Hostal La Auténtica** (Cisneros #125, tel. 048/69-5838 or 5834-2801, doctoralexis@nauta.cu, CUC30 year-round) is larger and more spacious than other homes. It has four large rooms, all with a signature black-and-white theme; two are in a modern building in the rear garden with wall-of-glass doors, flat-screen TVs, and fans.

I enjoyed a stay at **Villa Corales** (Salvador Cisneros #89, tel. 048/69-6654), where I dined alfresco in the rear patio. The two rooms are small but clean and have fans and hot-water bathrooms. With gracious hosts, **Villa Teresa** (Cienfuegos #10, e/ Azcuy y Fernández, tel. 048/79-3159) has heaps of light in two spacious rooms with modern bathrooms, plus a lush garden terrace. **Casa de Xiomara Duarte** (Calle Orlando Nodarse #50, tel. 048/69-6903 or 5371-5646, aliercubano92@

gmail.com) has three pleasantly furnished rooms with modern bathrooms.

If you don't mind staying outside of town, you can't beat ★ **Buena Vista** (next to Hotel Los Jasmines, tel. 5336-4434, CUC20), which is attached to the thatched restaurant of the same name. Simply furnished rooms offer cozy comfort, modern en suite bathrooms, rockers on a veranda, and sensational views. Hotel facilities are included.

HOTELS

The **Campismo Dos Hermanos** (tel. 048/79-3223, CUC12 s, CUC19 d), a pleasing camp resort opposite the entrance to the Mural de la Prehistoria, has 54 simple air-conditioned cabins with cold water only.

Cubanacán's **Hotel Horizontes Rancho San Vicente** (tel. 048/79-6201, reserva@vinalesrancho.tur.cu, from CUC44 s, CUC66 d low season, CUC55 s, CUC80 d high season, including breakfast), 200 meters north of Cuevas del Indio, has a delightful woodsy ambience. There are 53 modestly furnished *cabinas* spread among forested lawns surrounding a pool. A hotel section contains 20 air-conditioned rooms. Hot mud treatments are offered, and there's a delightful restaurant.

Cubanacán's **Horizontes La Ermita** (Carretera de la Ermita, Km 2, Viñales, tel. 048/79-6071, carpeta@ermita.tur.cu, from CUC51 s, CUC80 d low season, CUC55 s, CUC86 d high season), one kilometer south of town, is perched atop the valley, with great views. The slightly worn property wraps around a sundeck and swimming pool with poolside bar. The 62 air-conditioned rooms are nicely decorated and have balconies (not all have views, however).

Unrivaled in setting, Cubanacán's ridgecrest ★ **Horizontes Las Jazmines** (Carretera de Viñales, Km 25, tel. 048/79-6205, reserva@vinales.tur.cu, from CUC40 s, CUC50 d low season, CUC57 s, CUC71 d high season) is an aging hotel with fabulous vistas. The 16 air-conditioned *cabinas* stairstep the hillside, while 62 rooms are split between those in the original hotel and newer rooms in a separate block. An Olympic-size swimming pool hovers over the valley, and the colonial-style second-floor restaurant-bar offers classical elegance.

Services

Infotur (tel. 048/79-6263, remy2377@gmail.com, Mon.-Sat. 8am-5pm) is opposite the plaza.

The hospital is two blocks east of the plaza. **Etecsa** (Calle Ceferino Fernández, Mon.-Sat. 8:30am-4pm), one block south of the plaza, has telephone and Internet service; the wait is usually long. Use the Wi-Fi zone at **Café Cubanita** (Calles Adela Azcuy and Rafael Trejo) or the main plaza. The post office is opposite Etecsa. The police station is 100 meters north of the gas station, on the road to Cuevas del Indio.

Getting There and Around

The **Víazul** buses link Havana (CUC12) and Viñales twice daily with once-daily service linking Viñales to Cienfuegos (CUC31) and Trinidad (CUC36). Buses depart Viñales from outside the ticket office (Cisneros #63A, tel. 048/79-3195, www.viazul.com, 7am-6pm) opposite the plaza. The less organized **Cubanacán Conectando** service operated by Cubanacán (tel. 048/79-6393, www.viajescubanacan.cu) competes using Transtur tour buses. All buses go via Pinar del Río.

You can rent cars from **Havanautos** (tel. 048/79-6330), opposite the Cupet gas station, and **Cubacar** (tel. 048/79-6060), opposite the plaza. You can rent scooters at Transtur's **ATV Moto Safain** (Cisnero #141, tel. 048/79-6210 or 048/79-6061, CUC13 two hours, CUC25 per day), next to Restaurante Don Tomás.

The **ViñalesBusTour** (tel. 82/77-8078, daily 9am-6pm, CUC5) operates a mini-bus tour making an hour-long circuit of the major sights. You can hop on and off any of the buses.

Tour agencies offer excursions to Viñales

from Havana. In Viñales, **Cubanacán** (tel. 048/79-6393) and **Havanatur** (tel. 048/79-6262) offer local and regional excursions, including bicycle tours (CUC10) and trips to Cayo Jutía (CUC15).

Cubataxi (tel. 048/79-3195) offers service from the plaza. A three-hour tour of the valley costs CUC28.

WEST OF VIÑALES

West of Viñales the Sierra de los Órganos provides for a fulfilling day's excursion. It's a beautiful drive, with serrated *mogotes* to the north. Farther west, tobacco gives way to coffee as you rise to El Moncada and the saddle separating the Valle de Viñales and Valle de Santo Tomás, a scrub-covered, uncultivated valley. At Pons, about 20 kilometers west of Viñales, the road to the right leads via **Matahabre** to **Santa Lucía**, on the north coast.

South from Pons, the deteriorated road leads through the Valle de Quemado and beyond Cabezas to **Valle San Carlos,** offering scenery to rival Viñales. Traveling southwest via sleepy **Sumidero,** you'll arrive on the southwest plains at the town of **Guane.** You can turn southeast from Cabezas to reach Pinar del Río.

★ Caverna de Santo Tomás

At El Moncada (a postrevolutionary village with brick cottages adorned with murals), 15 kilometers west of Viñales, a turnoff leads through coffee fields to the orderly community of **Santo Tomás,** on the cusp of *mogotes*. This is the setting for Cuba's largest cave system, the **Caverna de Santo Tomás** (tel. 048/68-1214, daily 9am-4pm), which has more than 45 kilometers of galleries on eight levels, making it one of the largest underground systems in the New World. Guided 90-minute tours (CUC10) involve some tricky scrambling up and down ladders. Helmets with lamps are provided.

South and Southwestern Pinar del Río

West of the town of Pinar del Río, the climate becomes increasingly dry and the vegetation correspondingly stunted. María la Gorda, in the Bahía de Corrientes, offers great diving, and the Península de Guanahacabibes, Cuba's slender westernmost point, is being developed for ecotourism.

VUELTA ABAJO

The Vuelto Abajo area, centered on the town of San Juan y Martínez, 23 kilometers southwest of Pinar del Río city, has none of the dramatic beauty of Viñales, but due to a unique combination of climate and soil, the tobacco grown here is considered the finest in the world. The choicest leaves of all are grown in about 6,500 hectares around San Juan y Martínez and San Luis, where the premier *vegas* (fields) are given over exclusively to production of wrapper leaves.

San Juan y Martínez has a pretty main avenue lined with colorful columned streets. Just west of town and well worth a visit is **Finca Quemado de Rubi** (tel. 52/64-9191, daily 9am-5pm, CUC5). The tobacco farm of Hector Luis Prieto is well set for visits. Osvaldo, the guide, explains the production process. Linger for lunch in the thatched open-air restaurant (CUC10), or ask to enjoy a cigar and rum pairing. You can stay here in

Tobacco

It is generally acknowledged that the world's best tobacco comes from the 41,000-hectare Vuelta Abajo area of Pinar del Río Province, where the climate and rich reddish-brown sandy loam are ideal.

Most tobacco is grown on small holdings—many privately owned but selling tobacco to the government at a fixed rate. *Vegueros* (tobacco growers) can own up to 67 hectares, although most cultivate less than 4 hectares.

Tobacco growing is labor intensive. The seeds are planted around the end of October in greenhouses. After one month the seedlings are transplanted to the *vegas* (fields). About 120 days after planting, they are ready for harvesting in March and April.

There is a range of leaf choices, from *libra de pie,* at the base, to the *corona,* at the top. The art of making a good cigar is to blend these in such proportions as to give the eventual cigar a mild, medium, or full flavor. The binder leaf that holds the cigar together is taken from the coarse, sun-grown upper leaves, chosen for their tensile strength. Dark and oily, they have a very strong flavor. Wrapper leaves must be soft and pliable and free of protruding veins, and are grown under fine muslin sheets (*tapados*) to prevent them from becoming too oily in a protective response to sunlight.

At harvest, leaves are bundled in a *plancha,* or hand, of five leaves and taken to a barn where they are hung like kippers and cured on poles or *cujes.* Gradually the green chlorophyll in the leaves turns to brown carotene. After 45-60 days, they are taken down and stacked into bundles, then taken in wooden cases to the *escogida*—sorting house—where they are dampened and aired before being flattened and tied in bunches of 50. These are then fermented in large piles for anywhere up to three months.

The leaves are then graded for different use according to color, size, and quality. They are flattened, then sprayed with water to add moisture. Finally they are covered with burlap, fermented again, reclassified, and sent to the factories in *tercios*—square bales wrapped in palm bark to help keep the tobacco at a constant humidity. After maturing for up to two years, they are ready to be rolled into cigars.

a thatched cabin on stilts overhanging a creek; it has four beds, including two in a mezzanine.

★ Finca El Pinar San Luis

If you want an immersion in Tobacco 101 from the master, visit **Finca El Pinar San Luis** (tel. 048/79-7470, ivanterrible@hauta.cu, daily 9am-5pm), the 16-hectare private farm of the late Alejandro Robaina, the unofficial ambassador for Cuba's cigar industry. For six generations, the Robaina family has been renowned for the excellence of their tobacco (the family has farmed their *vegas* since 1845). The Cuban government named a brand of cigar after Alejandro, and there's even a postage stamp with his visage. Alejandro passed away in 2010; Hiroshi now runs the farm in his grandfather's tradition.

Forty-minute **tours** (CUC2) are given. December and January are the best times to visit, as is August 5, when local *guajiros* (farmers) make a pilgrimage to a shrine of Nuestra Señora de los Nieves (patron saint of tobacco), beneath a ceiba tree in Robaina's garden. VIP guests may be invited to a museum room full of mementoes (humidors, photos, paintings), many of Robaina with heads of state and celebs. The *finca* offers lunch by reservation.

To reach the farm, turn south 12 kilometers west of Pinar del Río; San Luis is 3.3 kilometers south of the highway—turn left onto a dirt road. There are several turns along the unsigned country lanes.

ISABEL RUBIO AND VICINITY

The landscape grows increasingly spartan west of the Vuelta Abajo region, with the road arcing close to the coast.

About 15 kilometers southwest of San Juan y Martínez, a turnoff leads south 3 kilometers to **Playa Boca de Galafre.** Five kilometers farther west, near Sábalo, another turnoff leads south eight kilometers to **Playa Bailén.** Both beaches are popular with Cubans, but they're unappealing. Midway to Playa Bailén you pass **Zoocriadero de Cocodrilos Sabanalamar** (daily 8am-6pm, CUC2 entrance, CUC3 camera, CUC5 video), a crocodile farm with some 2,000 American crocs.

Twelve kilometers west of Sábalo you pass through **Isabel Rubio,** a small agricultural town that thrives on the citrus harvest. Beyond is the town of **Sandino.** The area is studded with lagoons stocked with tilapia and bass, including **Laguna Grande,** 18 kilometers northwest of Sandino and reached via a turnoff from the main highway about 5

tobacco leaves hang at Finca El Pinar San Luis

kilometers east of town. The lagoon lies inland of **Punta Colorada,** with a sensational beach.

Two trains run daily between Pinar del Río and Isabel Rubio. *Camiones* connect Sandino and other towns. If continuing to María la Gorda, fill up on gas at Isabel Rubio or Sandino; there are no gas stations farther west.

PARQUE NACIONAL PENÍNSULA DE GUANAHACABIBES

The willowy Península de Guanahacabibes (90 kilometers long and 30 kilometers wide) juts out into the Strait of Yucatán and narrows down to the tip at Cabo San Antonio. The geologically young peninsula is composed of limestone topped by scrubby woodland. The entire peninsula lies within the 121,572-hectare Guanahacabibes Peninsula Biosphere Reserve, created by UNESCO in 1987 to protect the semideciduous woodland, mangroves, and wildlife that live here. The reserve is split into the El Veral and Cabo de Corrientes nature reserves. At least 14 of the more than 600 woody species are found only on the peninsula. More than 170 bird species have been identified. *Jutías* are abundant, as are wild pigs, deer, iguanas, and land crabs that head to the ocean in springtime.

The region became the final refuge for Cuba's aboriginal population as they were driven west by the more advanced Taíno. Several archaeological sites have been uncovered. The few people who live here today eke out a meager living from fishing, farming, and burning charcoal.

The peninsula shelters the Bahía de Corrientes, with waters famed for diving. *Diving and birding are the only reason to visit!*

The access road reaches the shore at **La Bajada,** where you need to present your passport at a military barrier to reach Cabo San Antonio (to the right), the western tip of Cuba. The road to the left swings around the bay and leads 14 kilometers to **María la Gorda,** with a dive center and hotel on a narrow white-sand beach.

The road to Cabo San Antonio is stunningly scenic. After 40 kilometers or so, beyond Punta Holandés, the road opens onto a cactus-studded coral platform (the sharp limestone formations are called *diente de perro*—dog's tooth). After 61 kilometers you reach Cabo San Antonio, dominated by a military post and the **Faro Roncali** lighthouse, built in 1859. Nearby is **Cueva La Sorda,** a labyrinthine cave system that can be explored. The cape hooks around to **Playa Las Tumbas** (a mediocre beach with an "eco-hotel") and dead-ends three kilometers beyond at a small pier at Punta Cajón, where the tarpon fishing is good right off the dock. Scuba divers can explore a wreck off the cape.

Stay clear of the beaches at dusk; tiny no-see-ums (*jejenes*) emerge to feast on humans.

The **Casa de Miel** (House of Honey), eight kilometers east of La Bajada, has displays on beekeeping. Honey from this region is acclaimed.

Recreation

Estación Ecológico (tel. 048/75-0366, daily 9:30am-sunset), at La Bajada, has hiking and birding trips (CUC5-10) and a "Seafari" to Cabo San Antonio (CUC10) that in summer includes viewing turtle nests (July-Aug. is best).

The 1.5-kilometer-long **Sendero Bosque al Mar** (CUC6 including guide) leads from the ecological station to the ocean, where a cave with a *cenote* is good for swimming; much of the "trail" is along the road. The **Sendero Cuevas Las Perlas** (three hours round-trip, CUC8) leads 1.5 kilometers to its namesake cave system, where about 400 meters is accessible. The **Sendero El Tesoro de María** (four hours round-trip, CUC10) leads from María la Gorda.

★ DIVING

Divers rave about the region's waters, with sites ranging from vertical walls to coral canyons, tunnels, and caves just 200 meters from Playa María la Gorda. There are even hulks of Spanish galleons. El Valle de Coral Negro

(Black Coral Valley) has 100-meter-long coral walls. Whale sharks are commonly seen.

Centro Internacional de Buceo María la Gorda (tel. 048/77-8131) has dives at 8:30am, 11am, and 3:30pm (CUC35, CUC40 at night) plus a four-day certification course (CUC365). Use of equipment costs CUC7 extra. Snorkeling costs CUC5.

Diving and fishing are also offered at **Marina Cabo de San Antonio** (tel. 033/75-0118).

Food and Accommodations

Reserve in advance—you're a long way from the nearest alternative accommodation if the resort is full. If the two Gaviota-run hotels are booked, there's one *casa particular* in Manuel Lazo, the nearest town (33 kilometers east of La Bajada). Locals at the humble hamlet of La Bajada will rent rooms and cook you a lobster meal; bring insect repellent and expect very basic facilities.

The better option (which isn't saying much) is **Hotel María la Gorda** (tel. 048/77-8131, comercial@mlagorda.co.cu, from CUC40 s, CUC54 d low season, CUC43 s, CUC65 d high season), which doubles as a dive resort. The air-conditioned rooms come in four types: older and simple cabins with basic bathrooms; newer yet mediocre rooms in two-story units; 20 spacious wooden cabins set back from the beach; and hotel rooms set back from the beach and lacking ocean views. It has a small bar, and the restaurant serves à la carte buffet lunches and dinners (CUC15). Credit cards are accepted, but processing is often not possible.

Villa Cabo San Antonio (tel. 048/77-7656, comercial@mlagorda.co.cu, CUC55 s, CUC72 d low season, CUC62 s, CUC86 d high season), at Playa Las Tumbas, is at the tip of the peninsula. Billed as an "eco-resort," it has 16 huge and nicely equipped duplex cabins on stilts. Each has a telephone, satellite TV, fridge, and safe; some have king beds. French doors open to balconies, but none has a sea view because the cabins are in the woods. It has a dive center and arranges sportfishing. The lackluster restaurant serves motley meals.

Getting There and Away

A taxi from Pinar del Río costs about CUC85 one-way. **Vía** has transfers to/from Havana (CUC215 s or d), Pinar del Río (CUC94 s or d), and Viñales (CUC124 s or d). A Jeep-taxi from María la Gorda to Cabo San Antonio costs CUC90 round-trip (up to four people); call Alexy Suárez (tel. 5271-4950). **Vía** rents scooters and cars at Hotel María la Gorda.

beach at María la Gorda

Isla de la Juventud

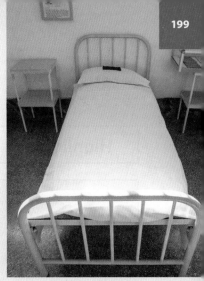

Slung below the underbelly of Artemisa Province in the shallow Golfo de Batabanó is Isla de la Juventud, the largest of Cuba's offshore islands and one with an intriguing history.

Scattered across the ocean to the east are 350 or so isles and cays that make up the Archipiélago de los Canarreos. Together they compose the special municipality of Isla de la Juventud.

Isla de la Juventud (Isle of Youth, so named for the erstwhile socialist experiment of International Youth Brigades), about 100 kilometers south of the mainland, receives relatively few visitors and is sparsely populated. The island was once smothered with native pine and was previously called the Isle of Pines. The island's appeal lies in some of the finest diving in the Caribbean, several historical sites of importance, and untapped nature reserves. The entire southern half of Isla de la Juventud comprises brush and marsh that harbor wild boar, deer, *jutías*, and *Crocodilus rhombifer*, the endemic Cuban crocodile.

Most of the islands of the 160-kilometer-long Archipiélago de los Canarreos necklace contain beaches of the purest white and are haloed by barrier reefs guarding bathtub-warm waters. For now, tourism development is limited to Cayo Largo, the easternmost island and the only one accessible from the mainland.

The cays are a scuba diver's delight. In addition to astounding coral formations, some 200 shipwrecks have been reported in the Canarreos. The Nueva España treasure fleet, for example, foundered in 1563 on the reefs between Cayo Rosario and Cayo Largo. One of the best sites is Cabeza Sambo, 70 kilometers west of Cayo Largo. Over 800 species of fish gambol among the exquisite coral.

The cays shelter tens of thousands of seabirds, along with hawks, orioles, cormorants, and pelicans. Marine turtles are always in the water, particularly during the nesting seasons, when females lay their eggs above the high-water mark.

Previous: Presidio Modelo, Isla de la Juventud; the *sucu sucu* dance, Nueva Gerona. **Above:** Fidel Castro's bed at Presidio Modelo.

Look for ★ to find recommended sights, activities, dining, and lodging.

Highlights

★ **Presidio Modelo:** Fidel Castro and other revolutionaries who survived the attack on the Moncada barracks were confined in this prison-turned-museum (page 206).

★ **Refugio Ecológico Los Indios:** This swampy and scrubby wilderness area offers fabulous bird-watching and is home to the Cuban sandhill crane (page 210).

★ **Criadero de Cocodrilos:** Get up close and personal with Cuba's endemic crocodile at this breeding farm (page 211).

★ **Parque Nacional Punta Francés:** Gorgeous beaches and turquoise waters await at the southwest tip of the island. Just off the coast scuba divers will find fantastic coral formations, sponges, and Spanish galleons and Soviet military vessels to explore (page 211).

★ **Cayo Largo:** Secluded from the mainland, the gorgeous beaches and turquoise waters of Cayo Largo provide the perfect spot to get that all-over tan (page 212).

PLANNING YOUR TIME

Unless you're keen on bird-watching or div-ing, or are an aficionado of revolutionary his-tory, you can safely skip Isla de la Juventud. Two days is sufficient, although scuba divers will want to pack in a few more days for ex-ploring the waters off **Punta Francés,** where the diving rivals anywhere in the Caribbean.

Nueva Gerona, the capital city, can be explored in mere hours. Outside of town, be sure to visit the **Presidio Modelo,** for-merly Cuba's main prison, where Fidel Castro and other participants of the attack on the Moncada barracks were held, and **El Abra,** a farmstead where national hero José Martí once labored under sentence for sedition.

An entire day is needed for a visit to the **Área Protegida Sur de la Isla de la**

Juventud, a swampy wilderness area offering fabulous bird-watching and wildlife-viewing. Guided excursions are compulsory, includ-ing to the white-sand beach of **Playa Punta del Este,** where the Cueva del Punta del Este is adorned with pre-Columbian paintings; to the **Criadero de Cocodrilos,** where you can learn the ecology of the Cuban crocodile; and to the **Refugio Ecológico Los Indios,** where Cuba's endemic crane and parrots can be seen.

Cayo Largo is popular with package tour vacationers, including European nudists. Its beaches shelving into warm turquoise waters are superb. It can be visited on daylong and overnight excursions from Havana.

Traveling between Isla de la Juventud and Cayo Largo is impossible. You need to back-track to Havana.

Isla de la Juventud

Isla de la Juventud (pop. 70,000), or "La Isla," as it is known throughout Cuba, is shaped like a giant comma. Most of the island is flat. Marmoreal hills—the **Sierra de Caballo** and **Sierra del Casas**—flank the city of Nueva Gerona and are the source of most of the gray marble found in buildings throughout Cuba.

The north is predominantly flat or roll-ing lowland, perfect for raising cattle in the east and citrus (especially grapefruit) in the west, where the fertile flatlands are irrigated by streams dammed to create reservoirs. The sweet smell of jasmine floats over the island January-March, when the citrus trees bloom. To the south, the marshy **Ciénaga Lanier** extends the width of the island and is a habi-tat for crocodiles, wild pigs, and waterfowl. Beautiful white-sand beaches rim the south shore. The entire southern half of the island is a protected area and accessed by a single dirt road; an official guide is compulsory for visitors.

The local drink—a mix of grapefruit juice, white rum, and ice—is named a *pinerito.* Local lore says it's an aphrodisiac.

History

The island was inhabited in pre-Colum-bian days by the Ciboney, whose legacy can be seen in cave paintings at Punta del Este on the south coast. The early Indians knew the island as Siguanea. Columbus named it La Evangelista. Pirates, who used the isle as a base, named it the Isle of Parrots for the many endemic *cotorras.* The southwestern shore is known as the Pirate Coast. Welsh pi-rate Henry Morgan even gave his name to one of the island's small towns.

Although the Spanish established a fort to protect the passing treasure fleets, the is-land remained a neglected backwater and the first colony wasn't established until 1826. Throughout the century, the Spanish used the island they had renamed Isla de los Pinos (Isle of Pines) as a prison, while the Spanish military sent soldiers with tropical diseases to the mineral springs in Santa Fe. After the Santa Rita hotel was built in 1860, tourists from North America began to ar-rive. Settlers of English and Scottish descent from the Cayman Islands also arrived in the

Isla de la Juventud

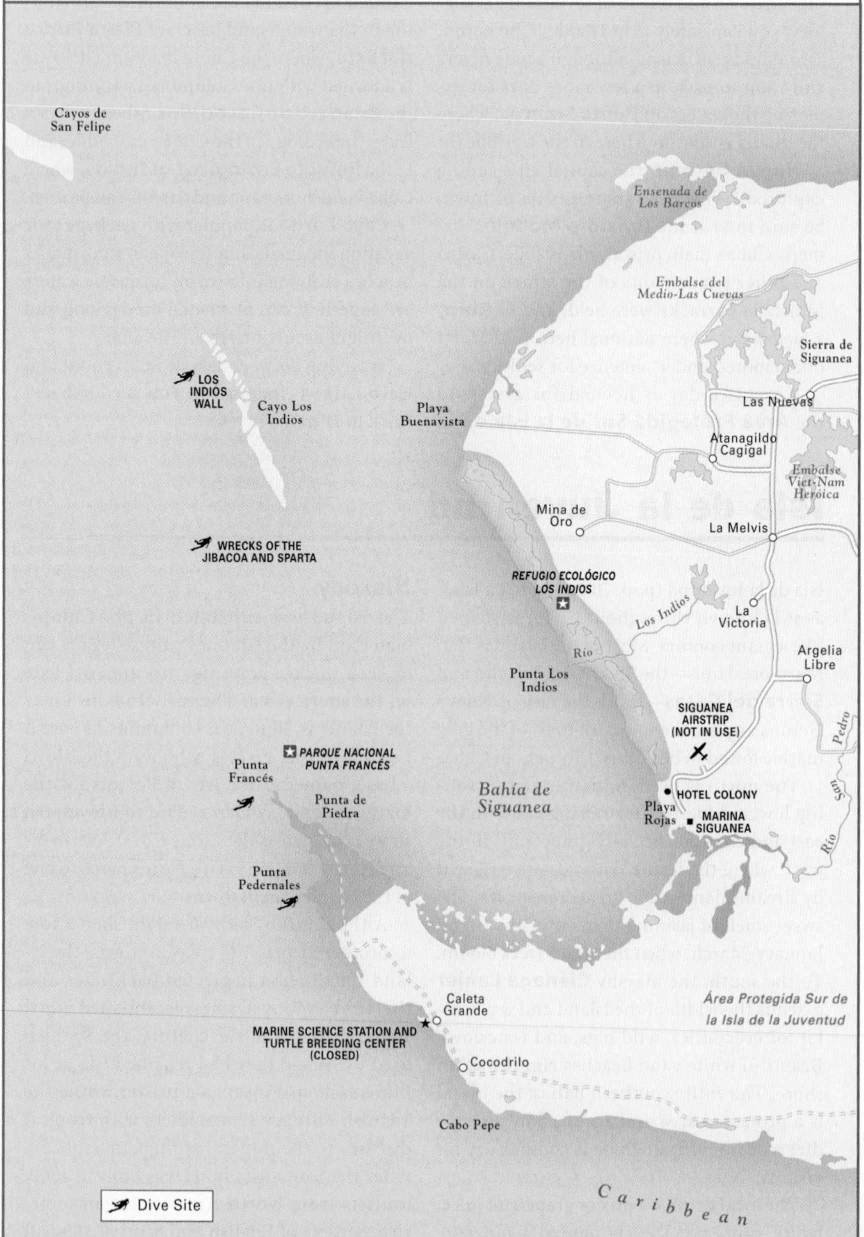

Cayos de
San Felipe

Ensenada de
Los Barcos

Embalse del
Medio-Las Cuevas

Sierra de
Siguanea

LOS
INDIOS
WALL

Cayo Los
Indios

Playa
Buenavista

Las Nuevas

Atanagildo
Cagigal

Embalse
Viet-Nam
Heroica

WRECKS OF THE
JIBACOA AND SPARTA

Mina de
Oro

La Melvis

REFUGIO ECOLÓGICO
LOS INDIOS

Los Indios

La
Victoria

Argelia
Libre

Rio

Punta Los
Indios

SIGUANEA
AIRSTRIP
(NOT IN USE)

Punta
Francés

PARQUE NACIONAL
PUNTA FRANCÉS

Punta de
Piedra

Bahía de
Siguanea

HOTEL COLONY

Playa
Rojas

MARINA
SIGUANEA

Rio San Pedro

Punta
Pedernales

Área Protegida Sur de
la Isla de la Juventud

Caleta
Grande

MARINE SCIENCE STATION AND
TURTLE BREEDING CENTER
(CLOSED)

Cocodrilo

Cabo Pepe

C a r i b b e a n

Dive Site

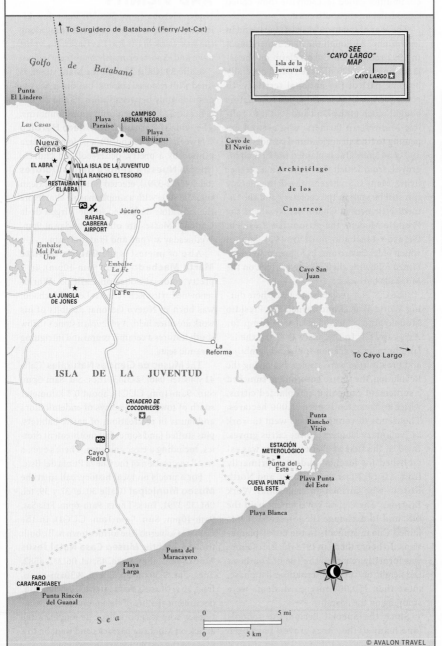

To Surgidero de Batabanó (Ferry/Jet-Cat)

Golfo de Batabanó

Punta El Lindero

Las Casas

Playa Paraíso

CAMPISO ARENAS NEGRAS

Playa Bibijagua

Nueva Gerona

★ **PRESIDIO MODELO**

★ **EL ABRA**   ■ **VILLA ISLA DE LA JUVENTUD**
■ **VILLA RANCHO EL TESORO**

▲ **RESTAURANTE EL ABRA**

PC ✕

RAFAEL CABRERA AIRPORT

Júcaro

Cayo de El Navío

Archipiélago de los Canarreos

SEE "CAYO LARGO" MAP

Isla de la Juventud

CAYO LARGO ✚

Embalse Mal País Uno

Embalse La Fe

★ **LA JUNGLA DE JONES**

La Fe

Cayo San Juan

La Reforma

To Cayo Largo →

ISLA DE LA JUVENTUD

✚ **CRIADERO DE COCODRILOS**

Punta Rancho Viejo

MC

Cayo Piedra

ESTACIÓN METEROLÓGICO
■ Punta del Este

★ **CUEVA PUNTA DEL ESTE**

Playa Punta del Este

Playa Blanca

Punta del Maracayero

Playa Larga

■ **FARO CARAPACHIABEY**
■ Punta Rincón del Guanal

S e a

0   5 mi

0   5 km

© AVALON TRAVEL

19th century and founded a turtle-hunting community called Jacksonville (now called Cocodrilo) on the south coast.

The War of Independence left the island in legal limbo. Although the Platt Amendment in 1902 recognized Cuba's claim on the island, only in 1925 did the island officially become part of the national territory. In consequence, Yankee real estate speculators bought much of the land and sold it to gullible Midwestern farmers, who arrived expecting to find an agricultural paradise. The 300 or so immigrants planted the first citrus groves, from which they eked out a meager living. Many U.S. citizens stayed; their legacy can still be seen in the cemetery and the ruined settlement at Columbia. Nearby is the Presidio Modelo, the prison that President Gerardo Machado built in 1931 and in which Fidel Castro and 25 followers were detained following their abortive attack on the Moncada barracks.

The U.S. Navy established a base here during World War II and turned the Presidio Modelo into a prisoner-of-war camp for Axis captives. In the postwar years, the island became a vacation spot, and gambling and prostitution were staples. Following the Revolution, the Castro government launched a settlement campaign and planted citrus, which today extends over 25,000 hectares. Thousands of young Cubans went to work as "voluntary laborers" in the citrus groves. In 1971, the first of over 60 schools was established for foreign students—primarily from Africa, Nicaragua, Yemen, and North Korea—who formed International Work Brigades. The Cuban government paid the bill, and in exchange the foreign students joined Cuban students in the citrus plantations. To honor them, in 1978 the Isle of Pines was formally renamed the Isle of Youth. At the height of Cuba's internationalist phase, more than 150,000 foreign students were studying on the island.

Since the Special Period the schools (and many of the citrus groves) have been abandoned.

NUEVA GERONA AND VICINITY

Nueva Gerona (pop. 36,000) lies a few kilometers inland from the north coast along the west bank of the Río Las Casas. It's a port town and exports primarily marble and citrus.

Calle 39 (Calle Martí), the main street, is lined with restored colonial buildings; it's pedestrian-only between Calles 20 and 30 and is beautified with sculptures and fountains. The node is **Parque Guerrillero Heróico** (between Calles 28 and 30), a wide-open plaza pinned by a pretty, ocher-colored church, **Iglesia Nuestra Señora de los Dolores** (tel. 046/32-3791), erected in 1929 in Mexican colonial style with a simple marble altar. Note the side altar dedicated to the Virgen de la Caridad. Masses are offered Sunday at 9am, Wednesday at 7pm, and Friday at 9am.

Also of interest is the **Galería de Arte Marta Machado** (daily 9am-10pm), in a pretty colonial house on Calle 39. World-renowned artist Kcho (Alexis Leyva Machado) was born in Nuevo Gerona; exhibits of his work are often held. A *plazuela* a stone's throw south features a ceramic mural and intriguing ceramic seats.

The **Museo de Ciencias Naturales** (Calle 41 y 46, tel. 046/32-3143, Tues.-Sat. 8am-5pm, Sun. 9am-1pm, CUC1), about 0.8 kilometer south of town, has displays of endemic flora and fauna in re-creations of native habitats, plus stuffed (and somewhat moth-eaten) exotics, including a tiger and apes. There's even a small re-creation of the Cueva Punta del Este.

For a précis on local history, call in at the **Museo Municipal** (Calle 30, e/ 37 y 39, tel. 061/32-3791, Tues.-Thurs. 9am-6pm, Fri.-Sat. 9am-10pm, Sun. 9am-1pm, CUC1), in the Casa de Gobierno (the former town hall), built in 1853. And the **Museo Casa Natal Jesús Montané** (Calle 24, esq. 45, tel. 061/32-4582, Tues.-Sat. 9:30am-5pm, Sun. 8:30am-noon, free), alias **Museo de la Lucha Clandestina,** documents the life of the eponymous revolutionary who was born here; he fought in the attack on Moncada barracks and went on to a place in the revolutionary government.

Nueva Gerona

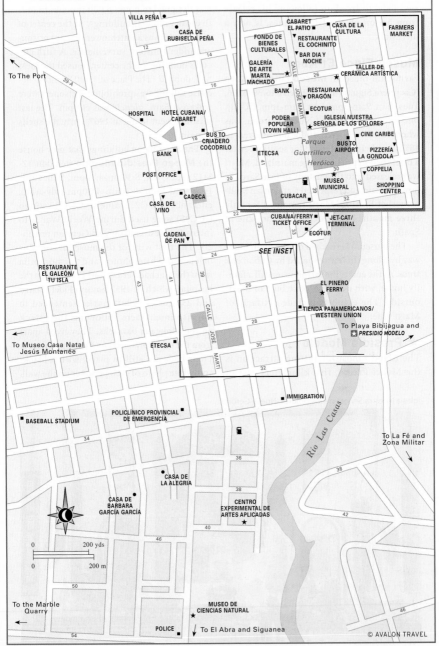

VILLA PEÑA

CASA DE RUBISELDA PEÑA

To The Port

39-A

HOSPITAL

HOTEL CUBANA/ CABARET

BUS TO CRIADERO COCODRILO

BANK

POST OFFICE

CADECA

CASA DEL VINO

CADENA DE PAN

RESTAURANTE EL GALEÓN/ TU ISLA

ÉTECSA

To Museo Casa Natal Jesús Montanéé

BASEBALL STADIUM

POLICLÍNICO PROVINCIAL DE EMERGENCIA

CASA DE LA ALEGRIA

CASA DE BARBARA GARCÍA GARCÍA

CENTRO EXPERIMENTAL DE ARTES APLICADAS

To the Marble Quarry

MUSEO DE CIENCIAS NATURAL

POLICE

To El Abra and Siguanea

Inset:

CABARET EL PATIO

CASA DE LA CULTURA

FARMERS MARKET

FONDO DE BIENES CULTURALES

RESTAURANTE EL COCHINITO

BAR DIA Y NOCHE

GALERÍA DE ARTE MARTA MACHADO

TALLER DE CERÁMICA ARTÍSTICA

CALLE JOSÉ MARTI

BANK

RESTAURANT DRAGÓN

ECOTUR

PODER POPULAR (TOWN HALL)

IGLESIA NUESTRA SEÑORA DE LOS DOLORES

CINE CARIBE

ETECSA

Parque Guerrillero Heróico

BUS TO AIRPORT

PIZZERÍA LA GONDOLA

COPPELIA

MUSEO MUNICIPAL

SHOPPING CENTER

CUBACAR

CUBANA/FERRY TICKET OFFICE

JET-CAT/ TERMINAL

ECOTUR

SEE INSET

EL PINERO FERRY

TIENDA PANAMERICANOS/ WESTERN UNION

To Playa Bibijagua and PRESIDIO MODELO

CALLE JOSE MARTI

IMMIGRATION

Río Las Casas

To La Fé and Zona Militar

0   200 yds

0   200 m

© AVALON TRAVEL

Once the town's major draw, *El Pinero* (Calle 33, e/ 26 y 28), the large ferry that carried Fidel to freedom following his release from prison on the Isle of Pines, is now a mere hulk.

Museo Finca El Abra

Farm-cum-museum **Museo Finca El Abra** (Carretera Siguanea, Km 2, tel. 046/39-6206, Tues.-Sun. 9am-5pm, Sun. 9am-1pm, CUC1), one kilometer south of Nueva Gerona, was where José Martí lived under house arrest in 1870 after being sentenced for sedition. After a brief spell in prison on the mainland, Martí was released into the custody of José Sardá (a family friend and respected Catalonian landowner) at El Abra. Martí remained for only three months before departing for exile in Spain.

The museum is reached off the main highway by a long driveway shaded by Cuban oak trees. At the end is the farmhouse, still a family home, with a large bronze bust of Martí outside. The exhibits include artifacts of Martí's life.

★ Presidio Modelo

The island's most interesting attraction is the Model Prison, five kilometers east of Nueva Gerona. It was built 1926-1931 during President Machado's repressive regime and was designed to house 6,000 inmates in four five-story circular buildings. At the center of each rondel was a watchtower that put prisoners under constant surveillance. A fifth circular building, in the center, housed the mess hall, dubbed "The Place of 3,000 Silences" because talking was prohibited. Prisoners were woken at 5am, *silencio* was at 9pm. The last prisoner went home in 1967. Only the shells remain.

The two oblong buildings that now house the **Museo Presidio Modelo** (tel. 046/32-5112, Tues.-Sat. 8:30am-4:30pm, Sun. 9am-1pm, and Mon. 8:30am-4:30pm July-Aug., entrance CUC2, camera CUC3, video CUC25) were used during World War II to intern Japanese Cubans and German prisoners. The first wing of the museum contains black-and-white photos and memorabilia from the Machado era. Another wing was the hospital, which in 1953 housed Fidel Castro and 25 other revolutionaries sentenced to imprisonment here following the attack on the Moncada barracks. They lived apart from the other prisoners and were privileged. Their beds are still in place, with a black-and-white photo of each prisoner on the wall.

Iglesia Nuestra Señora de los Dolores, Nueva Gerona

Fidel's bed is next to last, to the left, facing the door. Batista foolishly allowed Castro to set up a school (Academia Ideológica Abel Santamaría), where the group studied revolutionary theory and guerrilla tactics. On May 15, 1955, the revolutionaries were released to much fanfare. Immediately to the left of the museum entrance is the room where Fidel—prisoner RN3859—was later kept in solitary confinement. It's surprisingly large, with a spacious bathroom with shower of gleaming white tiles. A glass case contains some of his favorite books.

A taxi from town to the prison will cost about CUC6 round-trip. Buses depart Nueva Gerona for Presidio Modelo and Bibijagua at 7am, 4:10pm, and 5:30pm.

Entertainment and Events

Carnaval is held in March. Watch for performances by **Mongo Rivera y su Tumbita Criolla,** masters of the compelling dance rhythm *sucu suco*, born here early in the 19th century. (The word comes from the onomatopoeic sound of feet moving to its infectious rhythm.) They perform at the **Casa de la Cultura** (Calle 24, esq. 37, tel. 046/32-3591), which has a rumba on Saturday at 3pm.

The happening scene is open-air **Plaza El Pinero** (Calle 33, e/ 26 y 28), where reggaeton gets cranked up and live bands pack in the young crowd. **Cabaret El Patio** (Calle 24, e/ Martí y 37, tel. 046/32-2346, nightly 9pm-2am, CUC5) offers a campy cabaret on Saturday and Sunday evenings, plus discotemba on Thursday.

Baseball games are played October-April at **Estadio Cristóbal Labra** (Calle 32, e/ 49 y 51, tel. 046/32-1044).

Recreation

The Sierra del Casas, immediately southwest of town, is good for hiking. By following Calle 22 westward you can ascend via a dirt track to the summit of **Loma de Cañada** (310 meters), which offers views over the island. At the base, the **Cueva del Agua** has a slippery staircase leading down to a natural lagoon surrounded by dripstone formations. By following Calle 54 west you'll loop around to where gray *mármol* (marble) is quarried.

Food

Nuevo Gerona still awaits a *paladar* revolution. The best of the few private restaurants is the pirate-themed **Paladar El Galeón/Tu Isla** (Calle 24 #4510, e/ 45 y 47, tel. 046/50-9128 or 5350-9128, marco.cecchi.80@gmail.

Fidel's cell at Presidio Modelo

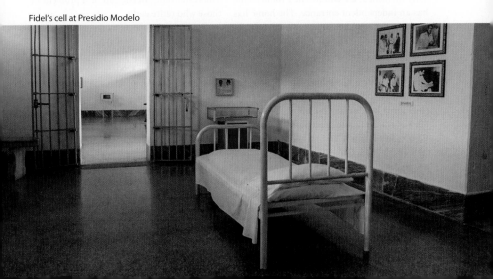

com daily 8am-10:30pm, noon-2:30pm, and 7pm-10pm), serving a steadfast *criolla* menu, including fresh-caught seafood and roast suckling pig prepared on an open rooftop grill. A screen shows music videos and live bands occasionally strike up at night on the rooftop bar.

Restaurante El Cochinito (Calle 39, esq. 24, tel. 046/32-2809, daily noon-10pm) specializes in pork dishes, especially roast suckling pig. Meals are served at set hours. **Restaurante El Abra** (tel. 046/32-4927, Wed.-Sun. noon-5:40pm), about four kilometers south of town, offers a delightful lakeside setting with simple yet tasty local fare.

Coppelia (Calle 32, esq. 37, tel. 046/32-2225, Thurs.-Tues. 11am-9:45pm) sells ice cream for pesos. You can buy fresh produce from the *mercado agropecuario* at Calles 24 and 35, and on Calle 41 at the south end of town. Go to **Cadena de Pan** (Martí, e/ 22 y 24, daily 8am-noon and 1pm-4pm) for fresh bread.

grilled snapper at Tu Isla, Nueva Gerona

Accommodations
CASAS PARTICULARES

One of the best private rentals is **Casa de la Alegría** (Calle 43 #3602, e/ 36 y 38, tel. 046/32-3664, CUC20), which offers two modestly furnished, air-conditioned rooms. One has an independent entrance. The home has parking plus a patio where meals are served.

Villa Peña (Calle 10 #3710, e/ 37 y 39, tel. 046/32-2345, CUC15-20 year-round) is a pleasant home with a two-room air-conditioned unit with telephone, double and single bed, plus private hot-water bath. Meals (including vegetarian) are offered. It has secure parking. In the same family, **Casa de Rubiselda Peña** (Calle 10 #3707, e/ 37 y 39, tel. 046/32-2345, CUC10) is run by a gracious hostess who rents two well-lit air-conditioned rooms upstairs with fans and a small shared hot-water bathroom. There's a TV lounge with rockers, private bathrooms, and a rooftop terrace.

Well placed close to the town center, **Tu Isla** (Calle 24 #4510, e/ 45 y 47, tel. 046/50-9128 or

5350-9128, CUC25) has a rooftop restaurant (Paladar El Galeón) and a patio Jacuzzi. Its eight pleasantly furnished, air-conditioned rooms are on two levels; five have private modern bathrooms and three have balconies. The restaurant's music can be a problem for those who retire early.

HOTELS

The state-run **Villa Isla** (Carretera La Fe, Km 1.5, tel. 046/32-3290, recepcionvilla@iju-campismopopular.cu, CUC8 s, CUC12 d) is a basic hotel property. A better bet is the nearby **Hotel Rancho El Tesoro** (Carretera La Fe, Km 2.5, tel. 046/32-3035, direccionrancho@ijucampismopopular.cu, CUC18 s, CUC24 d), although it too is tired.

Information and Services

You can change money at **Cadeca** (Calle 39 y 20, tel. 046/32-3462, Mon.-Sat. 8:30am-12:30pm and 1pm-3pm), which has an ATM. Services include a **post office** (Calle 39, esq. Calle 18, tel. 046/32-2600, Mon.-Sat.

8:30am-10pm) and **Etecsa** (Calles 41 y 28, daily 8:30am-7:30pm), which has Internet. The *bulevar* is a public Wi-Fi zone.

The **Hospital Héroes de Baire** (Calles 18 y 41, tel. 046/32-3012) has a recompression chamber. Foreigners are also treated at the **Policlínico Provincial de Emergencia** (Calle 41, e/ 32 y 34, tel. 046/32-2236). The **pharmacy** (Calle 39, esq. 24, tel. 046/32-6084, Mon.-Sat. 8am-11pm) is meagerly stocked.

The **police station** (Calle 41, esq. 54) is one kilometer south of town.

Getting There and Away

A passport is compulsory for travel to Isla de la Juventud.

AIR

The **Aeropuerto Rafael Cabrera** (tel. 046/32-2690 or 046/32-2300) is 15 kilometers south of Nueva Gerona. **Cubana** (tel. 046/32-4259, Mon.-Fri. 8:30am-noon and 1:30pm-4:30pm), in the ferry terminal, operates twice-daily flights from Havana (CUC88 round-trip). **AeroCaribbean** also flies twice daily.

A bus marked *Servicio Aereo* connects flights with downtown Nueva Gerona (one peso). The bus to the airport departs from Calle 53 and passes by Cine Caribe (Calle 37, e/ 28 y 30). A taxi costs CUC5.

FERRY

High-speed catamarans serve Nueva Gerona from **Surgidero de Batabanó,** 70 kilometers south of Havana (CUC50, plus CUC5 bus from Havana, two hours). Departures from Surgidero are daily at 1pm, and at 5pm Friday and Sunday; actual departure times depend on the number of passengers. The 350-passenger catamaran has 20 seats reserved for foreigners; the 240-passenger one has 10 seats for foreigners. The journey takes two hours (CUC50).

You'll need your passport when buying a ticket and when boarding. In Surgidero, you can ostensibly buy your ticket at the wharf-side **Viajero** ticket office (tel. 047/58-8240), but this rarely is so. Far safer is to buy your ticket 24 hours in advance from **Naviera Cubana Caribeña** (tel. 07/878-1841, 7am-noon) in the main bus terminal in Havana (Av. Boyeros, Plaza de la Revolución), then check in at 7am for the bus to Surgidero (CUC5); the bus departs around 9:30am, but the security line takes forever. Buy return (*regreso*) tickets when you purchase your outbound (*ida*) tickets. There's a 20-kilogram baggage limit. No bicycles are permitted. On board, you're served a sandwich and drink. Bring something warm to wear and earplugs for the incessant TV.

In Nueva Gerona vessels berth at the **Naviera Cubana Caribeña** ferry terminal (Calles 31 y 24, tel. 046/32-4977 or 046/32-4415). Catamarans depart Nueva Gerona for Surgidero at 8am and at 1pm Friday and Sunday; they are timed to connect with a bus to Havana (buy your bus tickets at the ferry terminal when you buy your catamaran passage). Get here two hours ahead of departure time.

TAKING A VEHICLE

You can ship your car or motorbike (CUC75 each way) aboard a *transitaria* (flatbed barge) towed by a tug. You, however, will have to take a catamaran and meet the barge in Nueva Gerona. The barge departs Surgidero Wednesday, Friday, and Sunday at 8pm. The dock is next to the ferry terminal in Surgidero (tel. 047/58-8945; ask for Jorge); you must register your vehicle at least two hours in advance. The barge arrives in Nueva Gerona the following day, docking two kilometers north of the ferry terminal. The return barge departs Tuesday, Thursday, and Saturday; make your reservations in advance at the ***transitaria* office** (Calle 24 e/ 31 y 33, tel. 046/32-7224, Mon.-Fri. 8am-11pm).

Getting Around

TAXI

Taxis congregate at the corner of Calles 32 and 39.

CAR

Cubacar (Calles 39 y 32, tel. 046/32-4432, daily 7am-7pm) rents cars. You have to pay cash for a full tank of gas (supposedly you get your money back for any gas left above 10 liters).

BUS

Buses for around the isle depart from Calles 39A and 45 (ticket office tel. 046/32-2413, 8am-noon and 1pm-5pm).

EXCURSIONS

EcoTur (Calle Martí e/ 26 y 28, tel. 046/32-7101, Mon.-Fri. 8am-5pm, Sat. 8am-noon) offers ecotourism excursions (CUC8-12, including guide; you'll need a rental car).

SOUTHWEST OF NUEVA GERONA

Carretera Siguanea leads southwest from Nueva Gerona through a rolling landscape studded with reservoirs and stands of pines amid citrus groves. Side roads lead west to the Bahía de Siguanea, lined with mangroves. Supposedly, Columbus landed here on June 13, 1494.

The region is served by the motley Hotel Colony, 30 kilometers southwest of Nueva Gerona. It backs a mediocre beach whose shallows have seagrasses and urchins; day passes can be purchased for CUC1 (you'll need your passport). The **Marina El Colony** (tel. 046/39-8181) offers fishing for bonefish and tarpon, and the **Centro Internacional del Buceo** (International Scuba Diving Center, tel. 046/39-8181) is also here. An Italian company, **Avalon Fishing Center** (http://cuban-fishingcenters.com), offers live-aboard fishing packages.

A monument at Marina El Colony is dedicated to six Cubans killed during a CIA attack on December 23, 1963, when scuba divers attached mines to a Cuban Navy torpedo boat.

★ Refugio Ecológico Los Indios

Much of the bay shore is a 4,000-hectare reserve protecting a fragile environment that includes mangroves, savanna, and endemic pines and palms. There are at least 60 native floral species, 15 of them limited to this spot (14 are endangered, including a species of carnivorous plant). The 153 species of birds include the endemic and endangered Cuban sandhill crane (called *la grulla*) and the *cotorra*, the equally threatened Cuban parrot.

Trails lead into the reserve from Siguanea. A guide is compulsory and can be arranged through the hotel or EcoTur (CUC8).

Accommodations

The **Hotel Colony** (tel. 046/39-8181, reservas@colony.co.cu, CUC25 s, CUC35 d low season, CUC35 s, CUC55 d high season) is a deteriorated 1950s hotel that began life as a Hilton. The 24 modestly decorated, air-conditioned bungalows and 56 standard rooms have been spruced up with new fabrics and furnishings.

Getting There and Away

Bus #441 departs Nueva Gerona for Siguanea at least thrice daily. A taxi from Nueva Gerona will cost about CUC30. **Marina El Colony** (tel. 046/39-8181) has 15 berths with electricity, water, gas, and diesel.

SOUTH OF NUEVA GERONA

A four-lane freeway runs south from Nueva Gerona to **La Fe,** an agricultural town that was founded by U.S. citizens and was originally called Santa Fe. Some of their plantation-style houses still stand around the main square.

Serious botanists might get a thrill at **La Jungla de Jones** (no tel.), about three kilometers west of La Fe. This 30-hectare botanical reserve was founded in 1902 by a U.S. couple, Harry and Helen Jones, who introduced exotic tree species for study in cooperation with the U.S. Department of Agriculture. Today the rather overgrown reserve displays some 72 species, including 10 bamboo species. The highlight is the "Bamboo Cathedral," a

100-meter-long vaulted glade. It's closed to the public except for guided excursions offered by **EcoTur** in Nueva Gerona (Calle Martí, e/ 26 y 28, tel. 046/32-7101, CUC8).

★ Criadero de Cocodrilos

This **crocodile breeding farm** (daily 7am-5pm, CUC3, or CUC9 EcoTur excursion), 30 kilometers south of Nueva Gerona, has over 500 crocodiles separated by age (older crocs are cannibalistic). A trail leads to natural lagoons where mature beasts swim freely. The juveniles feast upon the remains of sardines and lobster, while the full-grown monsters are fed hacked-up cattle. Feeding time is usually between 9am and 10am.

ÁREA PROTEGIDA SUR DEL ISLA DE LA JUVENTUD

The entire isle south of Cayo Piedra along its east-west parallel lies within the Área Protegida Sur del Isla de la Juventud, a wilderness of bush and swamp populated by wild pigs, deer, and crocodiles. The coast is lined with beaches whose sugar-white sands slope down to calm turquoise waters protected by reefs.

This is a military zone, guarded by a checkpoint just south of Cayo Piedra. A day pass and official guide are compulsory, arranged through EcoTur in Nueva Gerona (CUC15).

From Cayo Piedra, a dirt road leads east 20 kilometers through the Ciénaga de Lanier to Punta del Este. There's a beautiful beach here—**Playa Punta del Este**—but the main attraction is **Cuevas Punta del Este,** a group of caves containing 238 aboriginal pictographs that date from about AD 800 and are among the most important aboriginal petroglyphs in the Antilles. The petroglyphs seem to form a celestial plan thought to represent the passage of days and nights. On March 22, when spring begins, the sun appears in the very center of the cave entrance, revealing a red phallus penetrating a group of concentric circles on the back wall, an apparent allusion to procreation.

The road south from Cayo Piedra leads to **Playa Larga,** a stunning beach. Rising over the shore to its west, the **Faro Carapiachibey** lighthouse stands 63 meters tall.

★ Parque Nacional Punta Francés

Covering 6,079 hectares, of which 4,313 are ocean terrain, this national park is at the southwesterly tip of the island, some 120 kilometers from Nueva Gerona. It is distinguished by its semideciduous forest. Blind shrimp inhabit *cenotes* (water-filled sinkholes) that stud the shore. Offshore, gorgonias, corals, and marine turtles abound.

The main draw is the gorgeous beach at **Playa El Francés,** where Spanish galleons and coral formations await scuba divers a short distance from shore. Amenities include a pleasant restaurant, lounge chairs, and water sports. Cruise ships berth offshore and tender passengers ashore for day visits, so the place can be crowded.

The badly deteriorated coast road begins eight kilometers south of Cayo Piedra and runs inland of the shore the whole way from Playa Larga; there is no view of the beautiful shoreline until you reach the tiny seaside community of **Cocodrilo,** originally settled by turtle hunters from the Cayman Islands. It's a full-day drive from Nueva Gerona and back. **EcoTur** (Calle Martí, e/ 26 y 28, Nueva Gerona, tel. 046/32-7101, CUC8) offers excursions.

SCUBA DIVING

The bay offers spectacular diving. There are 56 dive sites concentrated along **La Costa de los Piratas** (the Pirate Coast), whose tranquil waters are protected from the Gulf Stream currents. The sites extend along a 15-kilometer-long axis between Punta Pedernales and Punta Francés. Off Punta Francés, the basin's wall begins at 20 meters and plummets into the depths of the Gulf of Mexico. The wall is laced with canyons, caves, and grottoes. Site 39 is renowned for the **Caribbean Cathedral,** said to be the tallest coral column in the world. Two other sites of interest are **Black Coral Wall** and **Stingray Paradise.**

A naval battle between Thomas Baskerville's pirate ships and a Spanish fleet resulted in many ships being sunk near Siguanea. Northeast of Punta Francés are three well-preserved Spanish galleons. Several freighters were scuttled several decades ago to provide bombing and naval gunnery targets for the Cuban armed forces.

Punta Francés extends northwest as a submarine limestone ridge, with a wall along its west side. **Cayo Los Indios** and the beach-fringed **Cayos de San Felipe,** hanging under the belly of Pinar del Río Province

(and famous for masses of iguanas), offer additional dive sites. German dive specialist **Cuba Diving** (tel. 49/9131-9706-771, www.cuba-diving.de) has an eight-day "Ruta de los Indios" package.

The **Centro Internacional del Buceo** (International Scuba Diving Center, tel. 046/39-8181), 1.5 kilometers south of the Hotel Colony, offers dives (CUC35). It takes well over one hour to reach the dive spots—a tedious journey in basic launches. Drop-in visitors hoping for a day's diving are often taken to the nearest sites, rather than the most interesting. Diving with a guide is compulsory.

Archipiélago de los Canarreos

Uninhabited cays extend for miles east of Isla de la Juventud. Sprinkled like diamonds across a sapphire sea, they are a yachting and diving paradise. The Archipiélago de los Canarreos boasts some of the best wildlife-viewing in Cuba, from a small population of monkeys on **Cayo Cantiles** (the only monkeys in Cuba) to the flamingos inhabiting the lagoons of **Cayo Pasaje. Cayo Iguana,**

a nature reserve immediately north of Cayo Largo, is noted for its large population of endemic iguanas.

Cayo Largo has the only facilities.

★ CAYO LARGO

Cayo Largo, 177 kilometers south of Havana and 120 kilometers east of Isla de la Juventud, is a 3-kilometer-wide, 25-kilometer-long,

dolphins at the Delfinario, Cayo Largo

Cayo Largo

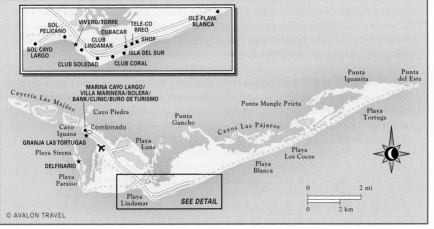

© AVALON TRAVEL

boomerang-shaped sliver of land fringed by an unbroken 20-kilometer stretch of beaches with sand as blindingly white as Cuban sugar. The beaches merge gently into waters that run from lightest green through turquoise and jade. There are water sports and a top-class hotel (plus several less impressive options). Cayo Largo is favored by Canadians and Europeans in budget package groups. Uniquely, the Cuban government tolerates nude sunbathing here, and many people on the beach are in the buff (there's a section of Playa Blanca marked for "Families" where nudity is discouraged). You won't learn a thing about Cuban life, however, as everything here is a tourist contrivance and all the Cubans are workers on 20-day stints.

A single road links the airport, at the northwest end of Cayo Largo, with the resort (3 kilometers south) and continues east, unpaved as far as Playa Los Cocos (14 kilometers). The sole community, **Combinado** (but known to everyone as "El Pueblo"), north of the airport, has a turtle farm—**Granja de las Tortugas** (daily 7am-6pm, CUC1 payable in the adjacent Buro de Turismo)—where you can see turtles in pools. If lucky, you'll witness hatchlings emerging from their nests (Cayo Largo is Cuba's main turtle nesting site). To date, some 12,000 baby green and leatherback turtles have been released to the sea (you can join in the release for CUC3). Free guided tours are offered.

Hidden away in the undergrowth east of Sol Pelicano, the **Vivero Torre** (no tel.) is a tiny garden where crocodiles, freshwater turtles, and tarpon lurk amid the reeds of an inky black lagoon.

The **Delfinario** (no tel.) at Playa Sirena offers dolphin shows thrice daily (CUC90 adult, CUC65 children) and you can swim with these magnificent mammals. Excursions are offered by hotel tour desks. However, the conditions are below international standards: the waters are too shallow and the area is too small for the dolphins.

Entertainment and Events

The waterfront **El Pirata Taberna** (tel. 045/24-8213) is a good spot to imbibe before moseying over to the marina's Disco Bar El Torreón or adjacent Bolera bowling alley.

Recreation

CATAMARANS

Catamaran excursions to Cayo Rico (CUC45), including a sunset "seafari," are offered from the **marina** (tel. 045/24-8133). Cayo Rico is colloquially called Cayo Iguana for its many iguanas, which hang out by the thatched bar.

BEACHES AND WATER SPORTS

Cayo Largo has 27 kilometers of serene beaches, which run the length of the seaward side (the leeward side is composed of mangroves and salty lagoons). The loveliest beach is 2.3-kilometer-long **Playa Sirena,** at the western end of the island, where there's a restaurant and bar. Sailboards and catamarans can be rented. The beach is reached by dirt road; you can also hike a shoreline trail (7 km). The *trencito* shuttle operates to **Playa Paraíso,** immediately west of Playa Sirena, at 9am, 10:30am, and 11:30am (CUC2); it departs Paraíso at 1pm, 3pm, and 5pm. Hotels offer excursions and water sports.

FISHING

Bonefish (*macabí*) and tarpon (*sábalo*) abound inshore. Bookings are handled by **Avalon Fishing Club** (www.avalonfishing-center.com), which offers fly-fishing packages and day trips from the marina.

SNORKELING AND SCUBA DIVING

Several galleons and corsairs lie on the seabed amid coral reefs teeming with fish. Dives are available from **Marina Marlin** (tel. 045/24-8214, buceo.marina@repgc.cls.tur.cu, CUC40 one dive, plus CUC10 equipment rental).

Food and Accommodations

Most guests arrive on an all-inclusive basis. There are few eateries outside the resort hotels. Nonguests can buy day passes to the Sol properties (CUC60) and can also dine at their restaurants.

Olé Villa Marinera (tel. 045/24-8384), at El Pueblo, has 16 nicely furnished air-conditioned log cabins overlooking the mangrove-lined shallows. French doors open to balconies with lounge chairs. Rooms adjoin to form family units, and walls are thin. There's no beach, but it has a pool, and a boat is available to run guests to Playa Sirena. An elegant clubhouse with Internet and pool table wards off boredom by night.

All other hotels are operated on an all-inclusive basis by Cuba's Gran Caribe chain. Rooms have air-conditioning, satellite TV, refrigerators, and safes. The properties have water sports and entertainment on-site.

Hotel Club Cayo Largo (tel. 045/24-8111) comprises four adjacent and mediocre properties. Its **Club Isla del Sur** and neighboring **Club Lindamar** are used exclusively by Italian tour companies. The adjacent and overpriced **Club Coral** and neighboring **Club Soledad** are dismal.

The state-run **Hotel Pelícano** (tel. 045/24-8333, from CUC85 s, CUC120 d low season, CUC140 s, CUC230 d high season) is a mediocre and overpriced low-rise hotel haphazardly built in vaguely Spanish colonial style around a freeform pool amid unkempt grounds. It has 307 rooms and *cabinas,* all with modestly appealing decor.

Far better is the more upscale ★ **Sol Cayo Largo** (tel. 045/24-8260, www.solmeliacuba.com, from CUC152 s, CUC173 d low season, from CUC197 s, CUC281 d high season), a deluxe all-inclusive with 296 spacious rooms in fourplex units graced by sponge-washed walls, ice-cream colors, and pleasingly understated furnishings. A splendid beach restaurant serves an impressive buffet luncheon. There's a 24-hour snack bar, a game room, several bars, and Wi-Fi.

The **Olé Playa Blanca** (tel. 045/24-8088, www.olehotels.com, CUC85 s, CUC150 d low season, CUC140 s, CUC250 d high season, suites cost CUC30 additional) has 306 rooms in two-story bungalows and the three-story main building. Its contemporary design won't suit all tastes, the grounds are poorly laid out, and construction standards are questionable, but it has plenty of amenities and the rooms are pleasant enough.

Information and Services

The **Buro de Turismo** (tel. 045/24-8214, daily 7am-7pm) adjoins the marina in El Pueblo. The **Clínica Internacional** (tel. 045/24-8238, 24 hours) is across the street. The **bank** (tel. 045/24-8225, 9am-noon) is also here; bring your passport. The **post office** (Mon.-Fri. 8am-noon and 4pm-6:30pm) opposite the Isla del Sur Hotel has telephone, DHL, and fax service. **Inmigración** (tel. 045/24-8250) and **customs** (tel. 045/24-8244) are at the airport.

Getting There and Away

International travelers can arrive without a visa if they don't intend to visit the mainland. You can obtain a visa upon arrival in Cayo Largo.

Charter flights operate from Canada, Europe, Mexico, and Grand Cayman to **Vilo Acuña International Airport** (tel. 045/24-8141). **Cubana** (www.cubana.cu) serves Cayo Largo from Havana and Varadero. **AeroGaviota** (tel. 045/24-8364) flies from the Baracoa airstrip, 15 kilometers west of Havana. In 2016, **Silver Airways** (tel. 801/401-9100, www.silverairways.com) initiated scheduled flights from Fort Lauderdale on Saturdays for licensed U.S. travelers.

The cheapest option is a package excursion through a Cuban tour agency (one-day package from CUC199 including tax and catamaran cruise, two-day from CUC230 including overnight). You need to book at least 48 hours in advance.

Private yachters can berth at **Cayo Largo del Sur Marina** (tel. 045/24-8133, VHF channel 16).

Getting Around

You can rent bicycles and scooters (CUC10 hours, CUC18 per day) as well as jeeps (CUC33 three hours, CUC52 per day) at the hotels.

Mayabeque and Matanzas

Created only in 2011, the province of Mayabeque lies between Havana and Matanzas. Its northeast is scalloped as the Valle de Yumurí, a huge basin lush with sugarcane enfolded by a crescent of low mountains famed for mineral springs.

Matanzas Province, to the east, is a triptych of diverse appeal. Its north shore boasts some of the island's finest beaches. The lodestone is Varadero, Cuba's biggest beach resort, occupying the slender 20-kilometer-long Península de Hicacos; it's a mini-Cancún with almost three-quarters of all hotel rooms on the island. Between Havana and Varadero is the namesake city of Matanzas, a once-wealthy sugar- and slave-trading port. Today, it is a center for Afro-Cuban culture.

Hills separate the coastal strip from a vast central plain where red soils support sugarcane fields and citrus orchards that extend east into Villa Clara Province.

The southern part of Matanzas Province is taken up by the low-lying Península de Zapata, the Caribbean's largest marshland system, harboring fantastic birdlife and a large population of Cuban crocodiles. In April 1961 the Zapata region was the setting for the Bay of Pigs invasion by Cuban exiles. Today the region is enshrined within Parque Nacional Ciénaga de Zapata, luring travelers keen on bird-watching and fishing. There are pleasant beaches at Playa Larga and Playa Girón, both major landing sites for the CIA-inspired invasion.

The entire coastline from the Bay of Pigs (21° 45') to Cienfuegos harbor (21° 50') is strictly off-limits to boaters.

PLANNING YOUR TIME

The Vía Blanca, or Circuito Norte, runs along the coast between Havana and Matanzas (102 kilometers), and thence to Varadero, 34 kilometers farther east. Many visitors make **Varadero** their main center for a vacation in Cuba. It has improved immensely of late—perfect if sun and sand are your main interests. Two or even three days relaxing on the beach here should suffice. Scuba diving is excellent, boat trips are fun, and organized

Previous: Playa Girón; bee hummingbird at Casa del Zunzuncito in Palpite. **Above:** José Martí monument in Matanzas.

Highlights

★ **Castillito de San Severino:** This restored fortress houses the Museo de la Ruta del Esclavo, an intriguing museum on slavery and Afro-Cuban religions (page 227).

★ **Cuevas de Bellamar:** Visitors will find dripstones galore in this cool underground cavern system (page 228).

★ **Las Américas/Mansión Xanadú:** An exorbitant mansion built by industrial magnate Irénée Du Pont overhangs the crashing Atlantic in Varadero (page 233).

★ **Scuba Diving and Snorkeling off Varadero:** Wreck diving highlights include a Russian frigate, patrol boat, and airplane (page 235).

★ **Parque Echevarría:** This quiet colonial plaza in Cárdenas has three museums, including the superb Museo Oscar María de Roja and even one to Elián González (page 248).

★ **Parque Nacional Ciénaga de Zapata:** The Caribbean's preeminent wetland area is chock-full of birdlife, crocodiles, and game fish (page 254).

★ **Museo Playa Girón:** Featuring warplanes and U.S. and Soviet military hardware, this excellent museum recalls the failed CIA-sponsored Bay of Pigs invasion (page 257).

Matanzas Province

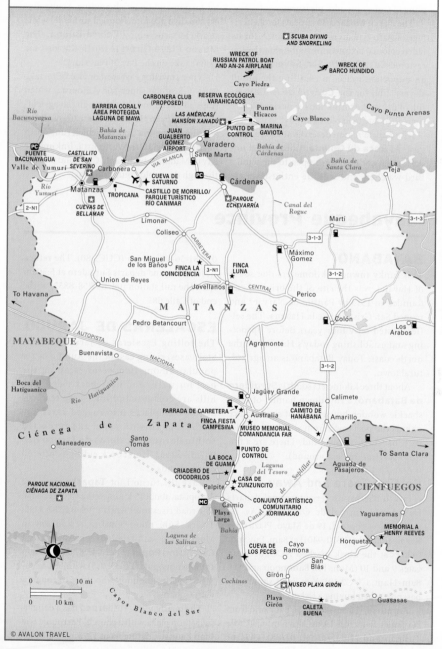

SCUBA DIVING
AND SNORKELING

WRECK OF
RUSSIAN PATROL BOAT
AND AN-24 AIRPLANE

WRECK OF
BARCO HUNDIDO

Cayo Piedra

Cayo Punta Arenas

Río
Bacunayagua

Bahía de
Matanzas

CARBONERA CLUB
(PROPOSED)

BARRERA CORAL Y
ÁREA PROTEGIDA
LAGUNA DE MAYA

RESERVA ECOLÓGICA
VARAHICACOS

LAS AMÉRICAS/
MANSIÓN XANADÚ

Punta
Hicacos

Cayo Blanco

PUENTE
BACUNAYAGUA

CASTILLITO
DE SAN
SEVERINO

JUAN
GUALBERTO
GÓMEZ AIRPORT

PUNTO DE
CONTROL

MARINA
GAVIOTA

Valle de Yumurí

Carbonera

VIA BLANCA

Varadero

Bahía de
Cárdenas

Bahía de
Santa Clara

La
Teja

Río
Yumurí

Matanzas

CUEVA DE
SATURNO

Santa Marta

2-N1

TROPICANA

Cárdenas

CUEVAS DE
BELLAMAR

CASTILLO DE MORRILLO/
PARQUE TURÍSTICO
RÍO CANIMAR

PARQUE
ECHEVARRÍA

Canal del
Rogue

Martí

3-1-3

Limonar

Coliseo

CARRETERA

3-1-3

Máximo
Gomez

San Miguel
de los Baños

FINCA LA
COINCIDENCIA

3-N1

FINCA
LUNA

To Havana

Union de Reyes

Jovellanos

CENTRAL

Perico

M A T A N Z A S

Colón

Los
Arabos

Pedro Betancourt

Agramonte

AUTOPISTA

NACIONAL

3-1-2

MAYABEQUE

Buenavista

Boca del
Hatiguanico

Río Hatiguanico

Jagüey Grande

Calimete

MEMORIAL
CAIMITO DE
HANÁBANA

PARRADA DE CARRETERA

Australia

Amarillo

FINCA FIESTA
CAMPESINA

MUSEO MEMORIAL
COMANDANCIA FAR

To Santa Clara

C i é n e g a   d e   Z a p a t a

Maneadero

Santo
Tomás

PUNTO DE
CONTROL

Aguada de
Pasajeros

CIENFUEGOS

LA BOCA
DE GUAMÁ

Laguna
del Tesoro

PARQUE NACIONAL
CIÉNAGA DE ZAPATA

CRIADERO DE
COCODRILOS

Palpite

CASA DE
ZUNZUNCITO

CONJUNTO ARTÍSTICO
COMUNITARIO
KORIMAKAO

de Soplillar

Yaguaramas

MEMORIAL A
HENRY REEVES

MC

Caimito

Playa
Larga

Bahía

Canal

CUEVA DE
LOS PECES

Cayo
Ramona

San
Blás

Horquetas

Laguna de
las Salinas

de

Girón

Guasasas

0   10 mi

0   10 km

Cochinos

MUSEO PLAYA GIRÓN

Playa
Girón

CALETA
BUENA

Cayos   Blanco   del   Sur

© AVALON TRAVEL

excursions to the timeworn historic city of Cárdenas and farther afield provide a sampling of Cuba's broader pleasures.

The city of **Matanzas** appeals for its heritage of Afro-Cuban music and dance; for its faded colonial architecture highlighted by the restored **Castillito de San Severino,** with an important museum recalling the era of slavery; and for the **Cuevas de Bellamar,** full of dripstone formations. One day is more than adequate to explore the city.

The Zapata region deserves at least a day's visit. At **Boca de Guamá,** Cuba's most important crocodile farm is open to the public. Bird-watchers and wildlife enthusiasts are in their element. **Laguna del Tesoro** and **Laguna de las Salinas** set a world standard for tarpon and bonefish angling. Scuba divers can dive a *cenote* (flooded sinkhole) while snorkelers can enjoy **Caleta Buena.** The **Museo Playa Girón** is worth the visit for Cuba's take on the Bay of Pigs story.

When traveling east-west or vice versa, take your pick of the super-fast Autopista, which skips all towns and runs through flat agricultural lands from Havana to Santa Clara, or the winding Carretera Central, which runs north of and parallel to the Autopista, linking the city of Matanzas with Santa Clara and passing through dusty old country towns.

Mayabeque Province

BATABANÓ

This funky town, 51 kilometers due south of Havana, was the site of the original city founded in 1515 by Pánfilo de Narváez and named San Cristóbal de la Habana. The settlers lasted only four years before uprooting and establishing today's Havana on the north coast. Today Batabanó is an agricultural town.

About three kilometers south is **Surgidero de Batabanó,** a run-down hamlet of ramshackle wooden houses and of significance only as the port town from which ferries depart for Isla de la Juventud. There are a few *casas particulares* (ask around).

Getting There and Away

A bus to Batabanó's ferry terminal departs Havana's Terminal de Ómnibus (Av. de Rancho Boyeros, esq. 19 de Mayo, Plaza de la Revolución, tel. 07/870-9401) at 8am. Buy your tickets at the kiosk marked NCC, between gates 9 and 10 (Mon.-Fri. 8am-noon and Sat. 8am-11am, CUC2.10). You must show your passport when buying a ticket.

A train serves Surgidero de Batabanó from Havana's Estación 19 de Noviembre (Calle Tulipán and Hidalgo, tel. 07/881-4431 or 07/881-3642) at 5pm (CUC1.80). The return train to Havana departs Surgidero at 5:30am from the rail station (tel. 047/58-8855) at the end of Calle 68.

ESCALERAS DE JARUCO

The rolling Escaleras de Jaruco (Jaruco Staircases) rising east of the Autopista are popular among *habaneros* escaping the heat for walks and horseback rides. The hills are composed of limestone terraces denuded in places into rugged karst formations laced with caves and protected within **Parque Escaleras de Jaruco** (tel. 047/87-3266). Horseback riding is offered on weekends.

Take the turnoff for **Tapaste** from the Autopista, about 15 kilometers east of Havana. The road rises to **El Arabe** (tel. 047/87-3292, Thurs.-Sun. noon-5pm), a restaurant in Mogul style with fabulous views. There's a **Campismo Popular** (tel. 047/87-2666, www.campismopopular.cu, CUC5) with basic cabins for budget hounds who want to rough it with Cubans.

The quaint village of **Jaruco** has a delightful hilltop plaza with a church, Parroquia San Juan Bautista, dating from 1778.

Mayabeque Province

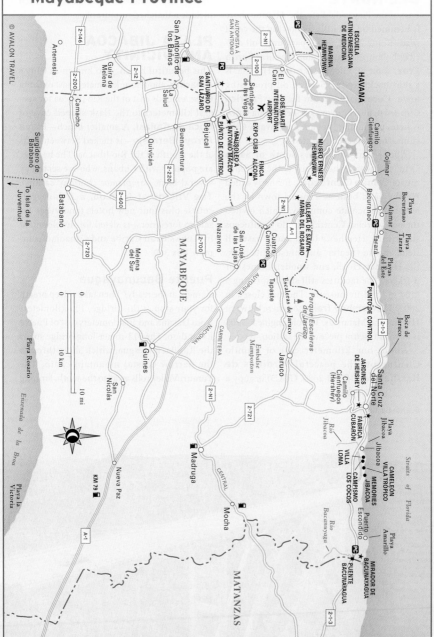

© AVALON TRAVEL

HAVANA

MAYABEQUE

MATANZAS

Straits of Florida

Ensenada de la Broa

To Isla de la Juventud

SANTA CRUZ DEL NORTE

East of the Playas del Este, the Atlantic shore is hemmed by low hills. Following the coast road (Route 2-1-3), you'll pass small oil derricks bobbing languidly atop the cliffs. **Santa Cruz,** some 30 kilometers east of Havana, is a ramshackle industrial and oil-processing town. Cuba's largest rum factory, **Fábrica Cubarón,** also known as Ronera Santa Cruz, is here, producing the famous Havana Club rums. No visits are permitted.

About four kilometers south of Santa Cruz and worth the detour is the community of **Camilo Cienfuegos,** formerly called Hershey and built as a model town by the Hershey chocolate company, which owned the now-derelict Central Camilo Cienfuegos sugar mill. Hershey's town had a baseball field, movie theater, an amusement park, the Hershey Hotel, and wooden homes for workers. The facilities still stand, forming a kind of lived-in museum. The mill closed in 2002. The **Hershey Train** stops here between Havana and Matanzas. The old engine #21203 is now a museum piece at the station.

About one kilometer east of Camilo Cienfuegos, the peaceful **Jardines de Hershey** (tel. 047/20-2685, CUC3) occupy a valley and hillside. Paths (and a river) wind through the somewhat wild gardens, which include a thatched restaurant.

PLAYA JIBACOA AND VICINITY

This beautiful beach, also known as **Playa Amarillo,** about four kilometers east of Santa Cruz, extends east of the Río Jibacoa for several kilometers to the flask-shaped cove of **Boca de Canasí.** A smaller beach—**Playa Arroyo Bermejo**—is tucked between cliffs at the mouth of the Río Jibacoa. The beaches are popular with Cubans, who are served by several basic *campismos* (holiday camps). **The Village at Jibacoa,** a 27-hole golf course plus four new hotels (and villas for sale to foreigners) is slated for development by Cuba's Gran Caribe and Canadian company Vox 360.

Puente Bacunayagua

Camera at the ready? Then take a deep breath for your stop at this bridge, 106 kilometers from Havana and 10 kilometers east of Puerto Escondido. The 313-meter-long bridge spans the Río Bacunayagua, which slices through the narrow coastal mountain chain. The Yumurí Valley rolls away to the south, fanning

Puente Bacunayagua

out spectacularly as if contrived for a travel magazine's double-page spread.

The *mirador* (lookout) has a restaurant.

Food and Accommodations

Budget-focused foreigners can stay at **Campismo Los Cocos** (Playa Jibacoa, tel. 047/29-5231, www.campismopopular.cu, CUC8 low season, CUC9 high season, including breakfast), which has simply furnished concrete *cabinas* (nine of higher standard for tourists) amid well-kept lawns; they have kitchenettes and modern bathrooms. There's a swimming pool, game room, and basic restaurant. You'll be among Cubans here, so expect loud music all night long.

At the east end of the beach, Gran Caribe's all-inclusive **Cameleón Hotel Villa Trópico** (Vía Blanca, Km 60, tel. 47/29-5205, reserva@clubtropico.gca.tur.cu, CUC29 s, CUC46 d low season, CUC70 s, CUC100 d high season) offers nicely furnished bungalows with modern bathrooms, plus water sports and other activities.

A more upscale option, the all-inclusive **Memories Jibacoa** (Vía Blanca, Km 60, tel. 047/29-5122, from CUC150 pp), run by Mexico's Blue Diamond Resorts, is a pleasing four-star resort. Its 250 spacious and tastefully decorated rooms and 10 suites are centered on a vast swimming pool. It has heaps of facilities. Reservations are required.

A couple of simple *casas particulares* (room rentals) and *paladares* (private restaurants) are a few minutes' walk inland of Breezes Jibacoa. A 10-minute drive east, **MonteECOcorales** (Vía Blanca Km 65, tel. 07/205-9015 or 5385-6682, www.montecorales.com, CUC25) rents two independent apartment rooms in a simple redbrick casita (with hammocks on a veranda) set amid fruit gardens just steps from the fishing village at Boca de Canasí. Owner Natacha Fábregas will prepare fresh seafood meals.

Matanzas and Vicinity

MATANZAS

The city of Matanzas (pop. 142,000) borders the deep, 11-kilometer-long, 5-kilometer-wide Bahía de Matanzas (more than 20 Spanish galleons lie at the bottom of Matanzas Bay, sunk by Dutch admiral Piet Heyn in 1628). The city was founded at the end of the 17th century on the site of an Indian village, Yacayo, and was populated by settlers from the Canary Islands. In 1694 a castle, Castillito de San Severino, was initiated to guard the bay.

During the 18th century, Matanzas grew as a port city. During the mid-19th century, the region accounted for more than 50 percent of national sugar production. The city was a center for the importation of slaves and established itself as Cuba's most important center of cult religions (Matanzas remains a potent center for African-derived religions and Afro-Cuban music and dance). Many white citizens grew wealthy on the sugar and slave trades, and a fashionable café society evolved. In 1828 the citizens began Cuba's first newspaper. A philharmonic society and a library were formed, followed by theaters, and the city acquired its "Athens of Cuba" moniker.

Matanzas was a battleground during the wars of independence and was shelled by the USS *New York*. Today the bay is filled with oil tankers and freighters waiting to be loaded with sugar. Tall chimney stacks belong to a geothermal plant, a chemical factory, and a paper mill that uses *bagazo* (crushed cane fiber). Nonetheless, the town's setting is pleasing, in the cusp of gentle hills.

Orientation

Matanzas lies on the western and southern bayshore and is divided by the Ríos Yumurí and San Juan into distinct sections. To the north is **Reparto Versalles,** a late colonial addition climbing the gentle slopes. The

Matanzas

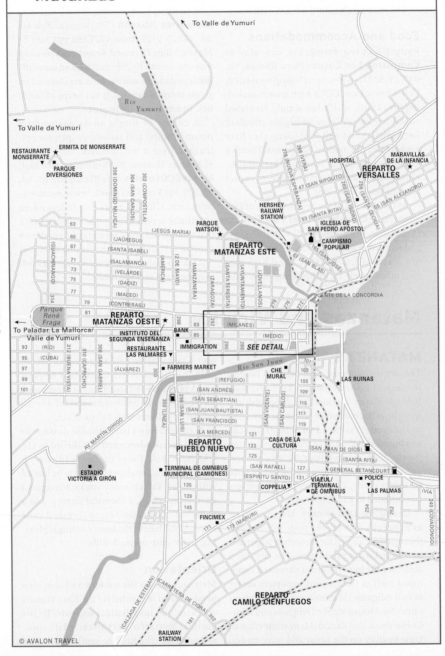

To Valle de Yumurí

Río Yumurí

To Valle de Yumurí

RESTAURANTE MONSERRATE ▼
ERMITA DE MONSERRATE ★
PARQUE DIVERSIONES

To Valle de Yumurí

306 (DOMINGO MUJICA)
304 (SAN CARLOS)
302 (COMPOSTELA)

63
65
67 (JAÚREGUI)
71 (SANTA ISABEL)
73 (SALAMANCA)
75 (VELARDE)
77 (DAOIZ)
79 (MACEO)
81 (CONTRERAS)

(JESÚS MARÍA)
PARQUE WATSON ★
REPARTO MATANZAS ESTE

314
(GUACHINANGO)

Parque René Fraga
REPARTO MATANZAS OESTE ★

To Paladar La Mallorca/
Valle de Yumurí

93 (RÍO)
95 (CUBA)
97
99
101

312 (BUENA VISTA)
310 (SAN GABRIEL)
308
300

INSTITUTO DEL SEGUNDA ENSEÑANZA ■
RESTAURANTE LAS PALMARES ▼
(ÁLVAREZ)
FARMERS MARKET ■

2 DE MAYO
AMÉRICA
MANZANERA
(ZARAGOZA)
(SANTA TERESTA)
(AYUNTAMIENTO)
JOVELLANOS

298
83
85

BANK ■
IMMIGRATION ■

292
(MILANES)
290
288 (MEDIO)
SEE DETAIL

AV. MARTÍN DIHIGO
300 (LÍNEA)
298 (SAN LUIS)

REPARTO PUEBLO NUEVO

ESTADIO VICTORIA A GIRÓN

(REFUGIO)
(SAN ANDRÉS)
(SAN SEBASTIÁN)
(SAN JUAN BAUTISTA)
(SAN FRANCISCO)
(LA MERCED)
121
123
125
127 (SAN RAFAEL)
131 (ESPÍRITU SANTO)
135
139
145

SAN VICENTE
SAN CARLOS

Río San Juan
101
CHE MURAL ★
103
105
109
115
117
119

CASA DE LA CULTURA ■
SAN JUAN DE DIÓS
(SANTA RITA)
GENERAL BETANCOURT

VÍAZUL/ TERMINAL DE ÓMNIBUS
POLICE ■
LAS PALMAS

TERMINAL DE ÓMNIBUS MUNICIPAL (CAMIONES) ■
COPPELIA ▼

FINCIMEX ■
171
173 (MARURÍ)

254
252
240 (COVADONGA)
(VÍA)

LAS RUINAS ★

266 (VERA)
218 (NUEVA ESPERANZA)
47 (SAN HIPÓLITO)
260 (SAN ISIDRO)
256 (SANTA CECILIA)
55 (SAN ALEJANDRO)
53 (SANTA RITA)
45 (SANTA CECILIA)

HOSPITAL
MARAVILLAS DE LA INFANCIA ★
REPARTO VERSALLES

HERSHEY RAILWAY STATION

IGLESIA DE SAN PEDRO APÓSTOL ■
CAMPISMO POPULAR
166 (SAN JOSÉ)
67 (SAN BLAS)

282
278
272

PUENTE DE LA CONCORDIA

REPARTO CAMILO CIENFUEGOS

(CALZADA DE ESTEBAN)
(CARRETERA DE CIORA)
181
302

RAILWAY STATION ■

© AVALON TRAVEL

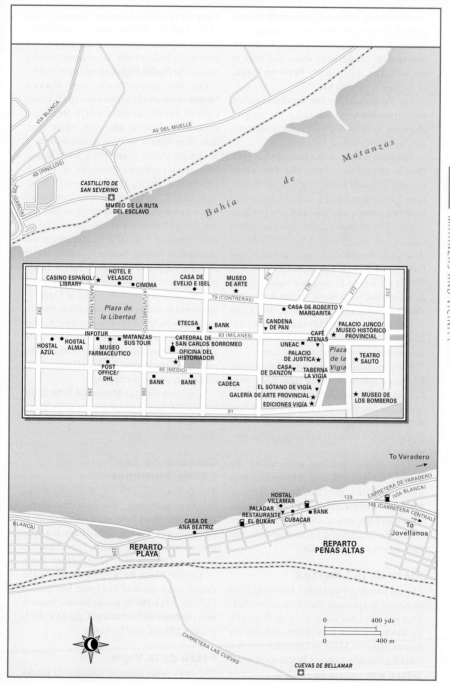

VÍA BLANCA

AV DEL MUELLE

Matanzas

de

49 (PINILLOS)

229 (GARCIA)

CASTILLITO DE
SAN SEVERINO

MUSEO DE LA RUTA
DEL ESCLAVO

Bahía

CASINO ESPAÑOL/
LIBRARY

HOTEL E
VELASCO

CINEMA

CASA DE
EVELIO E ISEL

MUSEO
DE ARTE

278

SANTA TERESITA

Plaza
de la Libertad

AYUNTAMIENTO

79 (CONTRERAS)

CASA DE ROBERTO Y
MARGARITA

276

272

270

292

ETECSA

BANK

280

CANDENA
DE PAN

PALACIO JUNCO/
MUSEO HISTÓRICO
PROVINCIAL

INFOTUR

MATANZAS
BUS TOUR

83 (MILANES)

CAFÉ
ATENAS

HOSTAL
AZÚL

HOSTAL
ALMA

MUSEO
FARMACÉUTICO

CATEDRAL DE
SAN CARLOS BORROMEO

OFICINA DEL
HISTORIADOR

UNEAC

PALACIO
DE JUSTICA

Plaza
de la
Vigía

TEATRO
SAUTO

POST
OFFICE/
DHL

85 (MEDIO)

CASA
DE DANZÓN

TABERNA
LA VIGIA

290

288

BANK

BANK

CADECA

EL SÓTANO DE VIGÍA

MUSEO DE
LOS BOMBEROS

GALERÍA DE ARTE PROVINCIAL

EDICIONES VIGÍA

91

To Varadero

CARRETERA DE VARADERO

(VÍA BLANCA)

HOSTAL
VILLAMAR

129

145 (CARRETERA CENTRAL)

BLANCA)

226

PALADAR
RESTAURANTE
EL BUKÁN

CASA DE
ANA BEATRIZ

CUBACAR

BANK

To
Jovellanos

REPARTO
PLAYA

REPARTO
PEÑAS ALTAS

CARRETERA LAS CUEVAS

0   400 yds

0   400 m

CUEVAS DE BELLAMAR

predominantly 19th-century **Pueblo Nuevo** extends south of the Río San Juan along flatlands. The historic city center, **Reparto Matanzas,** lies between them and rises to the west. The 20th-century **Reparto Playa,** to the east, fronts the bay.

The Vía Blanca from Havana descends into town from the north and skirts the Reparto Playa bay shore as Calle General Betancourt (Calle 129) en route to Varadero.

The town is laid out in a near-perfect grid. Odd-numbered streets run east-west, even-numbered streets north-south. Many streets have both a name *and* a number; most also have *two* names, one pre- and one postrevolution. For example, Calle 79 is also called Calle Contreras, though locals still refer to it as Calle Bonifacio Byrne. Contreras and Calle 83 (Milanés) run west from the Vía Blanca six blocks to the main square, Plaza de la Libertad. Calle Santa Teresita (Calle 290) runs perpendicular to the west, and Calle Ayuntamiento (Calle 288) runs perpendicular to the east. The first three digits of a house number refer to the nearest cross street.

For a fabulous view over town, follow Calle Contreras uphill westward from Plaza de la Libertad to **Parque René Fraga.** En route, turn right (north) onto Calle 306 and follow it to **Ermita de Monserrate** (Monserrate Hermitage), a *mirador* offering spectacular views.

The eight-kilometer-wide **Valle de Yumurí** is held in the cusp of 150-meter-high limestone cliffs—the Cuchillas de Habana-Matanzas—immediately west of Matanzas, from which it is separated by a high ridge. Two rivers, the Yumurí and Bacunayagua, thread their silvered way to the sea.

Plaza de la Libertad

The old parade ground (once known as Plaza de Armas) is a pleasant place to sit under shade trees and watch the world go by. At its heart is the **Monumento a José Martí,** with life-size bronze figures of Martí and an Indian maiden breaking free of her chains. Buildings of architectural note include the much-deteriorated **Casa de la Cultura,** in the former Lyceum Club, and the **Biblioteca** in the former Casino España, both on the north side. The former city hall on Calle Ayuntamiento today houses the **Poder Popular,** on the east side.

On the south side, the **Museo Farmacéutico** (Pharmaceutical Museum, Calle 83 #49501, tel. 045/24-3179, farmaceutico@atenas.cult.cu, Mon.-Sat. 10am-5pm, Sun. 9am-2pm, CUC3) is a wood-paneled pharmacy dating from 1882, when it was opened as La Botica Francesa by French pharmacist Ernesto Triolet Lefevre. It functioned until 1964, when it metamorphosed into a museum preserving the store just as it was the day it closed, with pharmaceutical instruments and original porcelain jars neatly arranged on the shelves. Out back a laboratory contains copper distilleries. Note the bright red and orange *vitrales.* Originally they were red, white, and blue—the colors of France—but Spanish authorities insisted that they be replaced with Spain's national colors. Ascend the Carrera marble staircase to the **Sala Celia Triolet,** displaying and selling stained glass pieces, and the **Museo de Arte Decorative,** displaying period furnishings.

One block east, the **Museo de Arte** (Calle 9 #28007, e/ 280 y 282, tel. 045/29-0735, Tues.-Sat. 9am-5pm, Sun. 9am-noon, CUC1) displays art and antiques.

Catedral de San Carlos Borromeo

This **cathedral** (Calle 282, e/ 83 y 85, Mon.-Fri. 8am-noon and 3pm-5pm, Sun. 9am-noon), one block southeast of Plaza de la Libertad, was built in 1878. Today the opulently frescoed ceiling gleams. The curator has an office at the side of the church (Tues.-Sun.).

The tiny **Plaza de la Iglesia** fronting the church has a statue of local poet José Jacinto Milanés (1814-1863), whose former home is now the **Archivo Histórico** (Calle 83 #28013, e/ 280 y 282, tel. 045/24-4212).

Plaza de la Vigía

The city's other plaza of note is four blocks

east of Plaza de la Libertad, at the junction of Milanés and Calle 270, immediately north of the **Puente Calixto García** over the Río San Juan. At its heart is a marble statue of an unnamed freedom fighter of the independence wars. The neoclassical **Teatro Sauto** (tel. 045/24-2721, Tues.-Sat. 9am-5pm, Sun. 2pm-4pm, CUC2 guided) was built in 1863 at the height of the city's prosperity. In its heyday, it attracted the likes of Sarah Bernhardt, Enrico Caruso, and Anna Pavlova. A lengthy restoration of the three-tiered auditorium, with its circular balconies supported by thin bronze columns, was almost complete at last visit.

On the plaza's north side is the Palacio de Junco, an 1840 mansion housing the **Museo Histórico Provincial** (Calles 83 y 91, tel. 045/24-3195, Tues.-Sat. 10am-6pm, Sun. 9am-noon, CUC2), tracing the city's development. The antique furnishings, clocks, and weaponry are impressive.

South of the theater, the neoclassical fire station houses the **Museo de los Bomberos** (tel. 045/24-2363, Mon.-Fri. 10am-4pm, Sat. 9am-noon, free), displaying antique fire engines; the oldest, from London, dates from 1864.

Facing the fire station is the **Galería de Arte Provincial** (Calle 272, Calles 85 y 91, Mon.-Fri. 9am-5pm, Sat. 10am-2pm, Sun. 9am-1pm, free). The **Ediciones Vigía** (Plaza de la Vigia, e/ 85 y 91, tel. 045/24-4845, Mon.-Fri. 8am-4pm, CUC1) produces handmade books in limited editions.

★ Castilito de San Severino

This restored fortress (Carretera del Puerto), completed in 1745 on the west side of the bay, is the most intriguing site in town. Slaves were landed here and held in dungeons, awaiting sale to sugar plantations. During the 19th century Cuban nationalists were imprisoned here; 61 patriots were executed, and you can see the bullet holes in the moat on the south side of the castle.

The fortress houses the excellent **Museo de la Ruta del Esclavo** (Carretera del Puerto, tel. 045/28-3259, Tues.-Sat. 10am-4pm, Sun. 9am-noon, entrance CUC2, camera CUC2). One room regales visitors with local pre-Columbian and colonial history. The Sala de Orishas is dedicated to Afro-Cuban religions and displays life-size figures of the *orishas*. A third exhibit is dedicated to slavery. It also has a gallery dedicated to Cuban artists Wilfredo Lam and Nelson Domínguez, whose works are infused with Santería mythology.

The castle stands at the east end of Reparto

Castillo de San Severino, Matanzas

A Sugar of a Journey

Rail journeys hold a particular magic, none more so in Cuba than the Hershey Train, which runs lazily between Casablanca and Matanzas year-round, three times a day. Before the Revolution, the Hershey estates belonging to the Pennsylvania-based chocolate company occupied 179 square kilometers of lush cane fields around a modern factory town (now called Camilo Cienfuegos), with a baseball field, movie theater, amusements, and a hotel.

At its peak, the estate had 19 steam locomotives. Their sparks, however, constituted a serious fire hazard, so they were replaced in 1921 with seven 60-ton General Electric locomotives built especially for the Hershey-Cuban Railroad. Milton Hershey also introduced a three-car passenger train service between Havana and Matanzas every hour, stopping at Hershey. The diminutive vermilion MU electric locomotive was replaced in 1998 with two antique Spanish cars from 1944.

The train winds in and out of palm-studded hills, speeds along the coast within sight of the Atlantic, and slips past swathes of sugarcane in the Yumurí Valley. Two hours into the journey, you'll arrive at a station still bearing the Hershey sign. You're now in the heart of the old Hershey sugar factory. After a mesmerizing 3.5-hour journey (with 47 stops!), you finally arrive at the Matanzas station.

The train (CUC1.40 to Hershey, CUC2.80 round-trip) departs the Estación de Casablanca (Carretera de los Cocos, tel. 07/793-8888), on the north side of Havana harbor, at 4:45am, 12:21pm, and 4:35pm, arriving at Matanzas 3.5 hours later. Return trains depart **Terminal Hershey** (Calles 55 y 67, tel. 045/24-4805) in Reparto Versalles, three blocks northeast of the Río Yumurí bridge, at 4:39am, 12:09pm, and 4:25pm. Tickets go on sale one hour before departure.

Versalles, accessed from downtown via the **Puente de la Concordia,** built in 1878 over the Río Yumurí with decorative Babylonian-style columns at each end. The region was settled last century by French-Haitian refugees and is pinned by the twin-towered **Iglesia de San Pedro Apóstol** (Calles 57 and 270). Nearby, the **Maravillas de la Infancia** (Calle Colón #23615, e/ 236 y 244, tel. 045/28-2989, mariae.romero@nauta.cu) sociocultural project works to uplift disadvantaged children through music, dance, and cultural and ecological projects. A visit to their center is well rewarded.

★ Cuevas de Bellamar

These **caves** (Carretera a las Cuevas, tel. 045/25-3538 or 045/25-3190, Tues.-Sun. 9am-5pm, CUC5 for one-hour guided tour, cameras and videos CUC5), in the hills about three kilometers southeast of downtown, form one of Cuba's largest cave systems. A 159-step staircase leads to more than 3,000 meters of galleries full of stalactites and stalagmites, including the 80-meter-long, 26-meter-high

Gothic Temple, with shimmering flower-like crystal formations known as dahlias. A small museum describes the geological formations. Tours (45 minutes) depart at 9:30am, 10:30am, 11:30am, 1:15pm, 2:15pm, 3:15pm, and 4:15pm. Avoid weekends.

Bus #16 departs Calle 300 (esq. 83) and will drop you at Calle 226, from where it's a 30-minute uphill hike along the road to the caves (cars will need to take Calle 254).

Entertainment and Events

In mid-October, the city hosts the **Festival del Bailador Rumbero,** with performances by Cuba's finest Afro-Cuban rumba bands, including the homegrown Los Muñequitos. The **Festival Cuba-Danzón** (tel. 045/24-3512) is a biennial held in November, with workshops and competitions of *danzón* and folk dance. For further information, contact **Puesto de Mando Cultura** (tel. 045/24-2210 or 045/26-0323, www.atenas.cult.cu).

The **Casa de Danzón** (Calle Medio #27405, e/ 280 y 282, tel. 045/28-7061) has programs Saturday at 8pm and Sunday at 2pm.

Musicians also play the **Casa de la Cultura Bonifacio Byrne** (Calle 272 #11916, e/ 119 y 121, tel. 045/29-2709) most evenings.

Resembling an Irish bar, the historic **Taberna La Vigía** (Calle 85, esq. Plaza de la Vigía, tel. 045/25-3076, 11am-11pm) is the best place to enjoy a chilled beer. Below, the basement **El Sotano de Vigía** nightclub (Mon.-Fri. 9:30pm-2am, Sat.-Sun. 6:30pm-2am) has a varied program spanning classical to contemporary music. It's a popular gay hangout and has drag shows.

The hot dance spot on weekends is Artex's open-air **Las Palmas** (tel. 045/25-3252, Mon.-Wed. noon-midnight, Fri.-Sun. noon-2am), aka "El Palacio" because it's next to the Palacio de Los Matrimonios. It has live music nightly. For Las Vegas-style cabaret, head to the open-air **Tropicana Matanzas** (Autopista Varadero, Km 4.5, tel. 045/26-55380, Tues.-Sat. 10pm, CUC49, including a half bottle of rum). A separate karaoke bar with dance floor is the hottest ticket in town for hip locals (10pm-3am, CUC.2.50); the dancing here seems straight out of a hip-hop video. Book in advance with a tour agency.

Matanzas's baseball team, Los Cocodrilos, play at **Estadio Victoria a Girón** (Av. Martín Dihigo), one kilometer west of town, October-May.

Kids might get a minor kick at **Parque Watkin** (Calle 290, esq. 63, Tues.-Fri. 1pm-5pm and Sat.-Sun. 10am-6pm, CUC1), a small and desultory park displaying flamingos and other endemic Cuban species.

Food

Matanzas's best private restaurant is ★ **Paladar La Mallorca** (Calle 334 #7705 e/ 77 y 79, tel. 045/28-3282, paladarmallorca. matanzas@yahoo.es, Wed.-Sun. 12:30pm-9:30pm), hidden away atop the hill west of Parque René Fraga; turn right at the gas station 200 meters beyond the park. An upstairs conversion of the owner's home hosts a modern lounge with large-screen TV and an air-conditioned restaurant where musicians often play live (for better or worse). The large menu

ranges from *criolla* such as shrimp cocktail in tomato cream (CUC2.50) to international dishes such as shrimp chop suey and fish fillet in white wine sauce with spinach (CUC5). Try the house specialty: three breaded meats stuffed with shrimp and cheese (CUC5).

Paladar El Bukán (Calle 210, esq. 127, tel. 045/28-9999, www.elbukan.com, Wed.-Sun. 11:30am-10:30pm) is on the bayfront in Reparto Altas. Air-conditioned, it offers grilled seafood and meat dishes, including wood-fired pizza, plus lasagna and pasta. It has live music.

Downtown, **Taberna La Vigía** (Calle 85, esq. Plaza de la Vigía, tel. 045/25-3076, ext. 106, daily 8:30am-1am) serves burgers (CUC1-3) and beer.

Accommodations

One block from Plaza Independencia, **Hostal Alma** (Calle 83 #29008 altos, e/ 290 y 292, tel. 045/24-2449, hostalalma@gmail.com, CUC25-30) makes you feel welcome. Three rooms have high ceilings, fans, fridges, and modern private bathrooms. The vast upstairs lounge has a balcony. Next door, and owned by the same family, is **Hostal Azul** (Calle 83 #29012, e/ 290 y 292, tel. 045/24-2449, hostalazul.cu@gmail.com, CUC25-30), a huge and delightful colonial home with four simply furnished rooms with small modern bathrooms.

Huge (and tasty) breakfasts and dinners are reason enough to stay at **Casa de Roberto y Margarita** (Calle 79 #27608, e/ 276 y 280, tel. 045/24-2577, CUC20), a colonial home with one spacious room with floor-to-ceiling windows opening to a courtyard. Roberto and Margarita are a delight.

It's upstairs, but **Casa de Evelio e Isel** (Calle 79 #28201, e/ 282 y 288, tel. 045/24-3090 or 5281-4966, evelioisel@yahoo.es, CUC25) gets my thumbs-up. This condo home has two rooms furnished with good mattresses and modern accoutrements, including refrigerator, fan, TV, safe, and private hot-water bathrooms. Each has a balcony.

In the Reparto Playa district, **Casa de Ana Beatriz** (Calle General Betancourt 129

#21603, e/ 216 y 218, tel. 045/26-1576, CUC25-30) is a bayfront 1940s home with two spacious rooms with modern bathrooms. A rear garden gets the breezes. Nearby, ★ **Hostal Villa Mar** (Calle 27 #20809, e/ 208 y 210, tel. 045/28-8132 or 5296-9894, lictik87@gmail.com, CUC25-35) is a superb bargain. This gorgeous villa rents a small, air-conditioned, two-bedroom independent apartment in the rear garden where you dine overlooking the water. A spiral staircase leads to a cove. It has secure parking.

Hotel E Velasco (Calle Contreras, e/ Santa Teresa y Ayuntamiento, tel. 045/25-3880, CUC50 s, CUC08 d low season, CUC65 s, CUC114 d high season), on Plaza de la Libertad, originally opened as a hotel in 1902. It has been beautifully restored and has an elegant marble lobby and 17 graciously furnished guest rooms. Standard rooms lack windows; four suites have balconies overlooking the plaza. Live music is offered in the atrium restaurant and bar. It has a cybercafé plus Wi-Fi.

Information and Services

The **post office** (Calles 85 and 290, tel. 045/24-3231, Mon.-Sat. 7am-8pm) has DHL service. **Etecsa** (Calle 83, esq. 282, daily 8:30am-7pm) has Internet and international telephones. Plaza de la Libertad, Parque René Fraga, and Cafetería Plaza La Vigia have public Wi-Fi zones. **Bandec** (Calle 85, e/ 282 y 288, tel. 045/24-2781) and **Banco Financiero Internacional** (Calles 85 y 298, tel. 045/25-3400, Mon.-Fri. 8am-3pm) have branches, as does **Cadeca** (Calle 286, e/ 83 y 85, Mon.-Sat. 8am-6pm, Sun. 8am-noon). **Hospital Faustino Pérez** (tel. 045/25-3426) is on the Carretera Central about two kilometers southwest of town.

Getting There and Away

AIR

International flights serve the **Juan Gualberto Gómez International Airport** (tel. 045/24-7015), 20 kilometers east of Matanzas.

BUS

Buses operate to and from the **Terminal de Ómnibus Nacional** (Calles 131 and 272, tel. 045/29-1473) on the south side of town. **Víazul** buses (tel. 045/29-2943 or 045/29-1473, www.viazul.com) link Matanzas with Havana and Varadero four times daily in each direction. The **Terminal de Ómnibus Municipal** (Calles 298 y 127, tel. 045/29-2701) serves destinations throughout Matanzas Province.

A taxi will cost about CUC120 one-way between Matanzas and Havana and about CUC60 between Matanzas and Varadero.

TRAIN

The rail station (Calle 181, tel. 045/29-9590) is on the south side of town. All trains between Havana and Santiago de Cuba stop here, calling at provincial capitals en route: Camagüey (CUC22), Santa Clara (CUC6.50), Sancti Spíritus (CUC11), Ciego de Ávila (CUC14), Las Tunas (CUC20), and Holguín (CUC24). In 2016, service was reduced to train #7 every second day; trains #13 and #15 are every fourth day (Havana, CUC4).

Getting Around

The **Matanzas Bus Tour** (CUC10, daily 11:15am, 12:45pm, 3:45pm, and 5:15pm) leaves from Plaza de la Libertad and makes a simple circuit along Contreras to Parque Reve Fraga and down Calle José, then on to Varadero. Buses depart Varadero for Matanzas at 9:30am, 11am, 2pm, and 3:30pm. You can also use the Varadero Bus Tour at no extra cost. Bus #16 runs to the Terminal de Ómnibus Municipal from Calle 79, one block west of the main square. There are gas stations on the Vía Blanca, east of downtown. **Cubacar** (Calle 129, esq. 208, tel. 045/25-3294) rents cars.

RÍO CANIMAR AND PLAYA CORAL

Four kilometers east of Matanzas, immediately beyond the bridge over the Río Canimar, a road to the left loops downhill into **Parque Turístico Río Canimar** (tel. 045/26-1516, daily 9am-4:30pm), with a tiny beach and restaurant. It has a three-hour boat trip upriver (daily 12:30pm, CUC10, or CUC25 with snorkeling, plus horseback riding and lunch), including a visit to **Cueva La Eloísa** (a flooded cave where you may swim) and **Arboleda,** a *finca* with crocodiles, buffalo, and hiking trails. Book through **Cubamar** (tel. 045/66-8855), which also has a full-day tour combining the river excursion with a Matanzas city tour.

A small fort, **Castillo El Morrillo** (Tues.-Sun. 10am-5pm, CUC1), stands over the west bank of the river mouth. Built in 1720, it is now a museum dedicated to revolutionary leaders Antonio Guiteras Holmes (1906-1935), founder of the radical student group Joven Cuba (Young Cuba), and Venezuelan revolutionary Carlos Aponte Hernández (1901-1935), executed nearby by General Machado's henchmen. They are buried in the fort. Prehistoric artifacts and native remains are displayed.

Immediately east of the river mouth, a broad peninsula bulges into the Atlantic. A coast road that parallels the Circuito Norte loops around the peninsula, passing **Playa Coral,** a tiny beach popular with excursion groups from Varadero. It's part of the **Reserva Barrera Coralina y Laguna de Mayo,** which protects an offshore barrier reef and an onshore lagoon. It has lounge chairs, beach volleyball, and a simple thatched restaurant. You can snorkel (CUC5) at Playa Coral, which has a dive center (tel. 045/66-8063, daily 8am-5pm). The dive center also has trips to **Cueva de Saturno** (tel. 045/25-3272, daily 8am-6pm, CUC3 entrance, CUC5 extra for snorkeling), one kilometer south of the Vía Blanca on the road to Varadero airport about 10 kilometers east of Matanzas. The 17-kilometer-long cave system has dripstones. A small museum explains the geology. The Matanzas Bus Tour passes by here.

About 15 kilometers east of Matanzas, you pass **Carbonera** and the turnoff to the south for Varadero airport. U.K. development company London + Regional has inked a deal to build a golf resort with a 150-room boutique hotel and 1,000 residences for sale to foreigners.

Accommodations

Islazul's **Hotel Canimao** (tel. 045/26-1014, comercial@canimao.co.cu, CUC43 s, CUC54 d year-round), off the Vía Blanca about eight kilometers east of Matanzas, is a pleasant, no-frills bargain. The 158 air-conditioned rooms are modestly furnished, with satellite TV, safes, and modern bathrooms. The hotel, adjacent to the Tropicana nightclub, has a swimming pool.

Varadero

"In all the beaches in Cuba the sand was made of grated silver," says a character in Robert Fernández's *Raining Backwards,* "though in Varadero it was also mixed with diamond dust." Varadero, 34 kilometers east of Matanzas and 140 kilometers east of Havana, is Cuba's tourist mecca. It is frequented by budget-minded Canadian and European charter groups and, of late, by Cuban vacationers, who've added vitality and a touch of normality. There are more than 60 hotels, and the gaps are being filled in. All-inclusive resorts dominate the scene.

Strictly speaking, Varadero is the name of the *beach* area. It lies on the ocean-facing side of the 20-kilometer-long Península de Hicacos, which encloses Bahía de Cárdenas and is separated from the mainland by the Laguna de Paso Malo. The peninsula is only 1.2 kilometers at its widest; it slants to the northeast, where Punta Hicacos is the northernmost point in Cuba. The scrub-covered eastern half is broken by a series of flat-topped mesas and raised coral platforms pitted with sinkholes and caves.

The main beach, Playa Mayor, is a virtually unbroken 11.5-kilometer-long swath that widens eastward and has most of the deluxe hotels. The beaches shelve gently into waters the color of a Maxfield Parrish painting. A coral reef lies offshore, good for diving. Facilities include a mega-marina that is one of the largest in the Caribbean, with more than 1,000 yacht berths.

HISTORY

The Spanish settled the region around 1587, when charcoal and salt-pork enterprises supplied Spanish fleets. A small community of fisherfolk later sprouted on the south shore, in the village today known as Las Moralas. In the 1870s, families from Cárdenas built wooden summer homes and developed the beach with boardinghouses for summer vacationers. Rowing regattas evolved, and the first hotel opened in 1915.

In 1926, U.S. industrialist Irénée Du Pont bought much of the peninsula and built himself a large estate, complete with golf course. Other wealthy *norteamericanos* followed. (Du Pont, who had paid four centavos a square meter, sold them the land for 120 pesos a square meter.) Al Capone bought a house here. So did the dictator Fulgencio Batista. By the 1950s, Varadero had a casino and was a favored hangout of Hollywood stars and Havana's middle class. The Castro government likes to claim that Cubans were banned from the beach, but in reality this was only on privately owned sectors, and everyone had access to the long swath in front of the village and hotels (ironically, during the 1990s only Cubans who lived in the village were permitted access to Varadero).

ORIENTATION

There is only one way onto Varadero: the bridge over Laguna de Paso Malo, at the extreme west end of the Hicacos Peninsula and from where two roads run east along the peninsula. The fast Autopista Sur runs along the bayfront all the way to the end of the peninsula. Avenida Primera (1ra), the main street, runs along the oceanfront from Calle 8 in the west to Calle 64 in the east. West of Calle 8, Avenida Primera becomes Avenida Kawama, which runs through the Kawama district to the westernmost tip.

Cross streets begin at Calle 1, in the Kawama suburb, and run eastward consecutively to Calle 64, in the La Torre area. Farther east, they are lettered, from Calle A to L. The luxury hotel zone begins east of Calle 64, where Avenida 1ra becomes Avenida las Américas. The old village occupies the central section of town, roughly between Calles 23 and 54.

SIGHTS

A castellated water tower next to the Mesón del Quijote restaurant, atop a rise on Avenida las Américas, was built in the 1930s and has been given a quaint touch by a modernist **sculpture of Don Quixote** on his trusty steed. The small **Museo de Varadero** (Calle 57 y 1ra, tel. 045/61-3189, daily 10am-7pm, CUC1), in the 1920s-era summer home of Leopoldo Abreu, has sections dedicated to local flora and fauna, aboriginal culture, Irénée Du Pont, and Varadero's historic regattas.

Varadero's well-kept **Parque Retiro Josone** (Av. 1ra, e/ 54 y 59, tel. 045/66-7228, daily 9am-midnight, activities 9am-5pm, free) is centered on an old mansion furnished with colonial-era antiques. Businessman José Fermín Iturrioz and his wife, Onelia, lived here in the 1950s. After departing Cuba following the Revolution, Señor Fermín had to relinquish his property to the Castro regime in exchange for safe passage from the country. Facilities include a lake with geese, a swimming pool (CUC3 entrance), four restaurants, and pedal boats (CUC5 one hour).

Dolphins are the star performers at the **Delfinario** (Autopista, Km 11, tel. 045/66-8031, daily 9am-5pm), a coral-rimmed lagoon 400 meters east of Marina Chapelín. Shows are offered at 11am and 3:30pm (CUC15 adults, CUC5 children). You can even swim with the dolphins at 9:30am, 11:30am, 2:30pm, and 4pm (CUC93 adults, CUC73 children).

★ Las Américas/ Mansión Xanadú

Varadero's most interesting attraction is **Las Américas** (Carretera Las Morlas, tel. 045/66-8482 or 045/66-7388), munitions magnate Irénée Du Pont's Spanish-style mansion at the far eastern end of Avenida las Américas. The tile-roofed mansion, which Du Pont named Xanadu, was built in 1926 as a sumptuous winter hideaway complete with a nine-hole golf course. He fitted his house with a Carrara marble floor, great dark wooden eaves and precious timbers, original hardwood antiques, an organ, and a massive wine cellar. On the top floor is a bar (once a ballroom) decorated in Italian rococo. A tapestry in the dining room transcribes the lines of Samuel Coleridge's poem: *In Xanadu did Kubla Khan, A stately pleasure dome decree.*

The six bedrooms can be rented and the on-site restaurant is among Varadero's finest.

Reserva Ecológica Varahicacos

This 450-hectare reserve (tel. 045/61-3594, varahicacos@csam.cu, daily 9am-4:30pm, CUC3) of scrub and woodland at the eastern tip of the peninsula is riddled with limestone caves. The most important is **Cueva Ambrosia,** accessed by trail from the park entry. It displays pre-Columbian petroglyphs. A second trail leads to **Cueva de los Musulmanes** (Cave of Muslims), once used as an indigenous tomb (replete with a replica of a cadaver). A separate 17-hectare section surrounds **Cueva del Pirata** (closed by day, it hosts a cabaret by night).

ENTERTAINMENT AND EVENTS

The all-inclusive hotels feature their own bars, cabarets, and entertainment.

Nightlife

BARS

You'll find several unremarkable open-air bars along Avenida 1ra. Keeping it simple, the small **Café Bar** (esq. Calle 55, tel. 045/61-3506, daily 9pm-2am) is a great place to enjoy cocktails or cappuccinos on the street-front patio. **Café Bar Benny** (Camino del Mar, e/ 12 y 13, 24 hours) is lent ambience by silky jazz riffs on the sound system and occasional live music. The genteel **Bar Mirador Casablanca** (Carretera Las Morlas, daily 10am-11:45pm), in Mansión Xanadú, has live jazz each afternoon at 4pm.

Calle 62 Snack Bar (Av. 1ra, esq. 62, tel. 045/66-8167, daily 8am-2am) hosts free live music nightly 9:30pm-midnight, when the plaza fills shoulder to shoulder with tourists. **The Beatles Bar** (Av. 1ra & Calle 59, tel. 045/66-7415, daily 1pm-1am) hosts live bands performing Fab Four music and other rock faves alfresco. The music begins at 9:30pm; get there early to snag a seat.

To sample rums, head to **Bar Tienda Maqueta** (Av. 1ra, esq. 63, tel. 045/66-8393, daily 9am-9pm), in La Casa del Ron. It serves 75 types of rum and offers sample shots, and there's a scale model reproduction of the Distilería Santa Elena rum factory (1906-1938) with a working railway.

CABARETS ESPECTÁCULOS

Hotel tour desks sell excursions to the Tropicana Varadero in Matanzas, a far more satisfying emporium of exotica than the all-inclusive hotel cabarets. The local options include **Cueva del Pirata** (Autopista Sur, Km 11, tel. 045/66-7751, Mon. 10pm, CUC10 including all drinks), a tiny swashbuckling cabaret—think eye patches and cutlasses with G-strings and high heels—that takes place in a natural cave. It's followed by a disco.

La Comparsita (Calle 60, esq. 3ra, tel. 045/66-7415, Wed.-Mon. 11pm-2am, CUC7 including drinks) also packs 'em in. The open-air venue downstairs hosts a *cabaret espectáculo* and/or live music, with disco to follow. It has karaoke upstairs.

Varadero Area

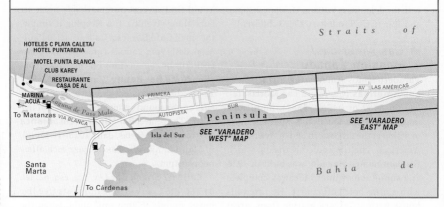

HOTELES C PLAYA CALETA/
HOTEL PUNTARENA
MOTEL PUNTA BLANCA
CLUB KAREY
RESTAURANTE
CASA DE AL
MARINA
ACUA
To Matanzas VIA BLANCA
Laguna de Paso Malo
AUTOPISTA SUR
AV. PRIMERA
Isla del Sur
Peninsula
Straits of
AV. LAS AMÉRICAS
SEE "VARADERO
WEST" MAP
SEE "VARADERO
EAST" MAP
Santa
Marta
To Cárdenas
Bahía de

DISCOS AND NIGHTCLUBS

Several all-inclusive hotels have their own discos. The **Casa de la Música** (Av. de la Playa y Calle 42, tel. 045/66-8918, Wed.-Sun. 5pm-9pm and 10:30pm-3am, CUC10-15), a classy venue hosting live bands, sizzles to salsa. It has a dress code, and ID is needed for entry. It's *the* hot spot in town. To learn the moves, head to **ABC Academia de Baile** (Av. 1ra, e/ 34 y 35, tel. 045/61-2623, www.varaderobaila.com, daily 9:30am-7pm), offering two-hour salsa dance classes (CUC15) at 9am, 11:30am, 2pm, and 5:30pm.

Cubans from out of town flock on weekends to the **Palacio de la Rumba** (Carretera Las Américas, Km 3.5, tel. 045/66-8210, daily 10pm-3am, CUC10 including all drinks), a Western-style disco with a dress code; **Club Nocturno Havana Club** (Calle 62 final, tel. 045/66-5178, daily 10:30pm-3am, CUC5), in Centro Comercial Copey; **Mambo Club** (Carretera Las Morlas, Km 14, tel. 045/66-8564, Mon.-Fri. 10pm-2am, Sat.-Sun. 10pm-3am, CUC10 including drinks), outside the Club Amigo Varadero at the east end of the peninsula; and **Disco La Bamba** (Av. Las Américas, Km 2, tel. 045/66-7560, daily 10:30pm-3am, CUC10) in the Hotel Tuxpan.

Festivals and Events

Varadero's **World Music Festival,** held each June, attracts artists from throughout Latin America. Cuba's *harlistas* (owners of Harley-Davidson motorcycles) roar into town in February for the annual five-day **Harlistas Cubanas** (tel. 07/866-2559, www.harlistascubanosrally.com). Varadero has a full-blown **Centro de Convenciones** (Autopista Sur, Km 11, tel. 045/66-8181) at Plaza América.

SPORTS AND RECREATION

Most resort hotels have tennis courts (non-guests pay a fee) and include water sports in their room rates. Beach outlets offer snorkeling (CUC3 per hour), sea kayaks and aqua bikes (CUC5 per hour), sailboards (CUC10), and banana-boat rides (CUC5 for 10 minutes). **Barracuda Scuba Cuba** (Av. 1ra, esq. 2, tel. 045/61-3481, comerical@barracuda.mtc.tur.cu) and the **Marlin Náutica** (Av. 1ra, e/ 58 y 59, tel. 045/5244-0961) rent sailboards and kiteboards and offer *parapente* (kitesurfing) instruction. They're based at the Hotel Cuatro Palmas, where you can rent boards and get instruction (CUC60 one hour, CUC670 one week).

Todo En Uno (Autopista Sur y Calle 54, Tues.-Thurs. 6pm-11pm, Fri.-Sun. 11am-11pm, CUC1 per ride) has a 24-hour *bolera* (bowling alley), plus *carros locos* (bumper cars) and a small roller coaster that doesn't

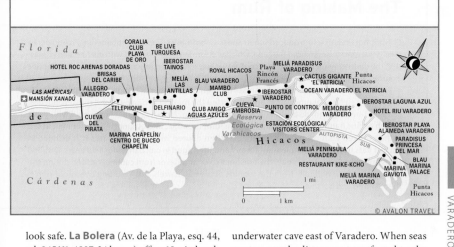

look safe. **La Bolera** (Av. de la Playa, esq. 44, tel. 045/61-4887, 24 hours) offers 10-pin bowling and pool tables.

★ Scuba Diving and Snorkeling

There are more than 30 dive sites off Varadero. Most sites are in **Parque Marino Cayo Piedras del Norte,** a one-hour boat ride. It features an AN-24 aircraft and a 102-meter frigate with missiles. Another good site is the Blue Hole—**Ojo de Mégano**—an underwater cave east of Varadero. When seas are too rough, divers are transferred to the Playa Girón (Bay of Pigs, a three-hour ride; CUC70).

Marlin Náutica (www.nauticamarlin. tur.cu) operates three dive outlets (resort course CUC70, two-tank dive CUC50, night dive CUC65, certification course CUC365). **Barracuda Scuba Cuba** (Av. 1ra, esq. 2, tel. 045/61-3481 or 045/66-7072, comercial@barracuda.mtc.tur.cu, daily 8am-7pm) is the main outlet. **Diving Center Marina Chapelín**

Mansión Xanadú, Varadero

The Making of Rum

Christopher Columbus introduced sugarcane to Cuba in 1493. *Trapiches* (rudimentary ox-powered mills) squeezed *guarapo* from the cane, which was fermented and mixed with *miel de caña* (molasses), the dark brown residue left after crystallized sugar has been processed from cane, to produce a crude type of "molasses wine."

The introduction of steam power (and of distilleries in the manufacturing process) in the early 1800s increased sugar production and permitted the making of more-refined rum. Production involves fermentation, distillation, aging, and blending. Molasses is first fermented with yeast (which occurs naturally in sugarcane) to transform the sugar into ethanol. The fermented liquid is then heated with compressed vapor and then diluted with distilled water. It is distilled in copper vats to eliminate unpleasant flavors and then aged in oak barrels for 1-15 years. Distilled rums are clear. Darker rums gain their distinct color and flavor from caramels added during the aging process, or naturally from the tannins of the oak barrels. The resulting overproof rum is then diluted and bottled.

(tel. 045/66-8871, daily 9am-4pm), at Marina Chapelín, is solely for certified divers.

Marlin offers a snorkeling package to Playa Coral and Cueva de Saturno (daily 9am-2pm, CUC36), including transfers and lunch. Many all-inclusive hotels have dive facilities and rent snorkeling gear (CUC5).

Sportfishing

Sportfishing trips are offered at the three marinas: **Marina Dársena** (tel. 045/66-8060), on the Vía Blanca, one kilometer west of Varadero; **Marina Chapelín** (tel. 045/66-8727), toward the east end of the Autopista Sur; and **Marina Gaviota** (tel. 045/66-4115, reserva@marinagav.co.cu), at the far east end of the Autopista. Typical prices are CUC350 for four people, offered daily 9am-4pm.

Boat Excursions

Marlin runs all water-based activities. You can hop aboard a catamaran at **Marina Gaviota** (tel. 045/66-4115, reserva@marinagav.co.cu) for a "seafari" to Cayo Blanco (CUC75 adults, CUC38 children, including lunch) or a snorkeling cruise (CUC30 adults, CUC15 children). Rent your own Jet Ski at **Marlin Náutica y Marinas** (Autopista Sur y Calle 35, tel. 045/66-8063) for rides on the inner bay.

Golf

You can practice your swing at **Varadero Golf Club** (Carretera Las Morlas, tel. 045/66-8482, www.varaderogolfclub.com, daily 7am-7pm, CUC130 includes club rental and golf cart). The 18-hole, par-72 course has a well-stocked pro shop, plus a restaurant and snack bar. Golf classes are offered (tel. 045/66-7788). An all-inclusive special costs CUC95. Fans of mini-golf can putt around a crude "crazy golf" course at **El Golfito** (Av. 1ra, e/ 41 y 42, daily 9am-10pm, CUC0.50).

SHOPPING

Crafts markets line Avenida Primera. For world-class ceramics head to **Taller de Cerámica Artística** (Av. 1ra y 59, tel. 045/66-7554, daily 9am-7pm). Look for dining sets and individual plates by renowned artists such as Osmany Betancourt, Lázaro Zulueta, and Beatríz Santacana. Next door is Varadero's **Galería de Arte** (tel. 045/66-8260, daily 10am-6pm), with wooden statues, paintings, and artwork.

The **Plaza de Artesanía** (Av. 1ra, e/ 15 y 16) is the largest open-air crafts market in Varadero. It has cafés and public toilets. **Centro Comercial de Caimán** (Av. 1ra, e/ 61 y 62) has boutiques and cosmetic stores. **Adidas** and **Reebok** have sportswear stores on Calle 63. **Plaza América** has designer boutiques and a duty-free jewelry store. **Joyería Coral Negro** (Calle 64 y 3ra, tel. 045/61-4870) sells duty-free name-brand watches plus perfumes and quality Cuban jewelry. And **El Quitrín** (Av. 1ra, e/ 55 y 56, tel. 045/61-2580) sells hand-made *guayaberas,* lace skirts, and blouses.

The outlets of **La Casa del Habano** (Av. 1ra y 39, tel. 045/61-4719; Calle 63, e/ 1ra y 3ra, tel. 045/66-7843; and Plaza América, tel. 045/66-8181, ext. 251) are the best-stocked cigar shops in town. Each has a bar and smokers' lounge and sells Cuba's export-grade coffees. **La Casa del Ron** (Av. 1ra, esq. 63, tel. 045/66-8393, daily 9am-9pm) stocks about 75 rum types.

FOOD

Buffet meals in most all-inclusive hotels are mediocre, while menus in street-side restaurants vary little; deluxe hotels managed by international hotel groups usually offer fare approaching international quality.

Paladares

The two best restaurants in Varadero are both privately run. Operated by two Cuban brothers, ★ **Varadero 60** (Calle 60, esq. 3ra, tel. 045/61-3986, daily noon-midnight) offers super-attentive service and great fare. Choose a shaded outdoor patio or two air-conditioned rooms in this converted mansion, which plays up the 1950s with old ads and posters. All dishes are wood-fired. Start with fried garbanzo (CUC4.50) or cream of seafood soup (CUC5.50), followed by shrimp with brandy (CUC11) or steak Roquefort (CUC16), then crêpes with fruit sauce (CUC5.50).

★ **Salsa Suárez** (Calle 31 #103, tel. 045/61-2009, Wed.-Mon. noon-midnight) is one of the finest *paladares* outside Havana. It has shaded patio dining and an elegant air-conditioned option. Yoel Suárez has put years of experience as a hotel food and beverage manager to good effect. Gourmands will appreciate the divine dishes on the weekly menu, such as beef carpaccio with capers and olive oil (CUC5.50), seafood cannelloni

(CUC8), spiced octopus and mussels (CUC10), and a house special of pork and chicken with onions, pepper, and Roquefort (CUC10). *Do* leave room for the divine rice pudding with blue cheese and blue curaçao liqueur. Staff in sharp black uniforms are friendly and efficient.

The other standout *paladar* is the whimsically named **Waco's Club** (Calle 59 #212, esq 3ra, tel. 045/61-3728 or 5297-1408, noon-11pm), serving elegantly presented surf and turf and local seafood staples. The house dish is lobster tail prepared with coconut milk cream, mushrooms, and gratin cheese (CUC15). Patio dining is available.

The down-home **Paladar Don Alex** (Calle 31 #106, e/ 1ra y 2da, no tel., Tues.-Sun. 12:30pm-11pm), opposite Salsa Suárez, is hugely popular. It serves no-frills Italian and *criolla* fare on a shaded patio of a simple bungalow.

Criolla

Shrimp in rum is on the menu at **Restaurante La Vega** (Av. 1ra y 31, tel. 045/61-1431, daily 10am-11pm), where you can dine alfresco with ocean views. And lobster in pepper sauce (CUC6) and beef fillet stuffed with bacon (CUC7) feature at **Restaurante El Criollo** (Av. 1ra y 18, tel. 045/61-4794, daily noon-midnight), a rustic colonial home-turned-restaurant whose menu also includes bean soup (CUC1.50).

Restaurante La Vicaria (Av. 1ra y 38, tel. 045/67-4721, daily noon-10:45pm) offers pleasant alfresco dining under thatch, with the usual roast chicken and fish dishes (CUC5-8). Live music, a 1914 Ford, and a 1955 Oldsmobile add ambience to the **Restaurante Esquina Cuba** (Av. 1ra y 38, tel. 045/61-4019, daily noon-11pm), an open-air restaurant offering *ropa vieja* (CUC8).

Continental

★ **Restaurante La Fondue** (Av. 1ra, esq. 62, tel. 045/66-7747, daily noon-10:30pm) lists a large range of fondues using Cuban cheeses (CUC7-18). Special cheeses such as Gruyère,

Varadero West

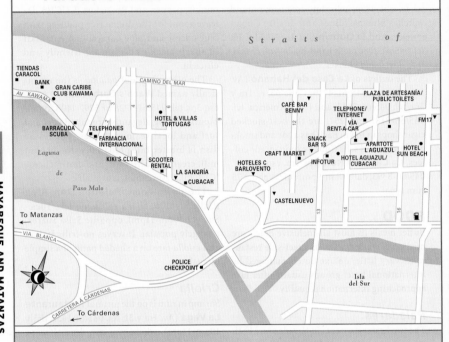

Straits of

TIENDAS CARACOL
BANK
GRAN CARIBE CLUB KAWAMA
AV KAWAMA
CAMINO DEL MAR
HOTEL & VILLAS TORTUGAS
BARRACUDA SCUBA
TELEPHONES
FARMACIA INTERNACIONAL
Laguna
KIKI'S CLUB
SCOOTER RENTAL
de
LA SANGRÍA
CUBACAR
Paso Malo
HOTELES C BARLOVENTO
CAFÉ BAR BENNY
PLAZA DE ARTESANÍA/ PUBLIC TOILETS
TELEPHONE/ INTERNET
VÍA RENT-A-CAR
FM17
SNACK BAR 13
CRAFT MARKET
APARTOTEL AGUAZUL
HOTEL SUN BEACH
INFOTUR
HOTEL AGUAZUL/ CUBACAR
CASTELNUEVO
To Matanzas
VIA BLANCA
Isla del Sur
POLICE CHECKPOINT
CARRETERA A CÁRDENAS
To Cárdenas

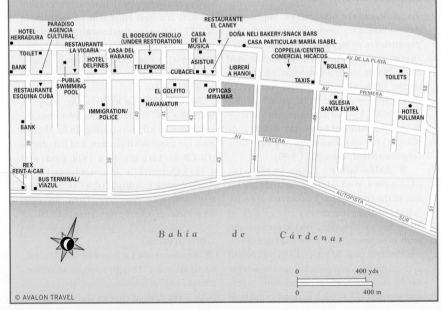

RESTAURANTE EL CANEY
HOTEL HERRADURA
PARADISO AGENCIA CULTURAL
EL BODEGÓN CRIOLLO (UNDER RESTORATION)
CASA DE LA MÚSICA
DOÑA NELI BAKERY/SNACK BARS
CASA PARTICULAR MARÍA ISABEL
TOILET
RESTAURANTE LA VICARIA
CASA DEL HABANO
COPPELIA/CENTRO COMERCIAL HICACOS
AV DE LA PLAYA
BANK
HOTEL DELFINES
TELEPHONE
ASISTUR
CUBACEL
LIBRERÍA HANOI
BOLERA
TOILETS
PUBLIC SWIMMING POOL
TAXIS
PRIMERA
RESTAURANTE ESQUINA CUBA
EL GOLFITO
OPTICAS MIRAMAR
AV
IMMIGRATION/ POLICE
HAVANATUR
IGLESIA SANTA ELVIRA
HOTEL PULLMAN
BANK
AV
TERCERA
REX RENT-A-CAR
BUS TERMINAL/ VIAZUL
AUTOPISTA
SUR
Bahía   de   Cárdenas

0   400 yds
0   400 m

© AVALON TRAVEL

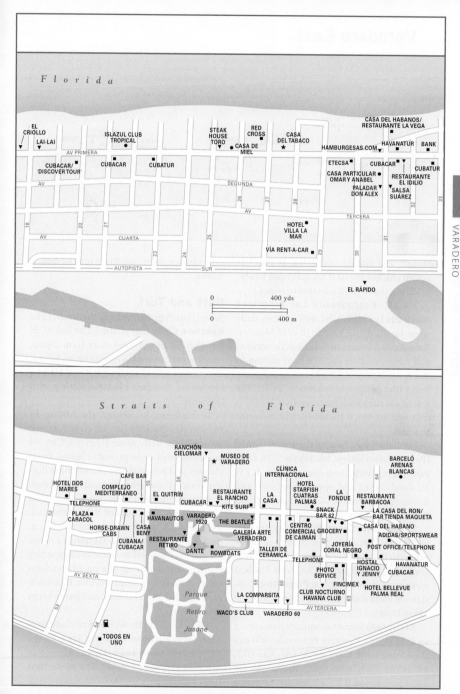

Florida

EL CRIOLLO
LAI-LAI
AV PRIMERA
ISLAZUL CLUB TROPICAL
STEAK HOUSE TORO
CASA DE MIEL
RED CROSS
CASA DEL TABACO
CASA DEL HABANOS/ RESTAURANTE LA VEGA
HAMBURGESAS.COM
HAVANATUR
BANK
CUBACAR/ 'DISCOVER TOUR'
CUBACAR
CUBATUR
ETECSA
CASA PARTICULAR OMAR Y ANABEL
CUBACAR
CUBATUR
AV
SEGUNDA
PALADAR DON ALEX
RESTAURANTE EL IDILIO
SALSA SUÁREZ
18 20 21 26 27 28 AV 25 TERCERA 32 33
AV CUARTA 23 24
HOTEL VILLA LA MAR
31
AUTOPISTA SUR 29 30
VÍA RENT-A-CAR

0   400 yds
0   400 m

EL RÁPIDO

Straits   of   Florida

RANCHÓN CIELOMAR
MUSEO DE VARADERO
BARCELÓ ARENAS BLANCAS
CAFÉ BAR
COMPLEJO MEDITERRÁNEO
55 56 57
CLÍNICA INTERNACIONAL
64
HOTEL DOS MARES
EL QUITRÍN
RESTAURANTE EL RANCHO
HOTEL STARFISH CUATRAS PALMAS
LA FONDUE
RESTAURANTE BARBACOA
TELEPHONE
CUBACAR
KITE SURF
LA CASA
SNACK BAR 62
LA CASA DEL RON/ BAR TIENDA MAQUETA
52
PLAZA CARACOL
HAVANAUTOS
VARADERO 1920
THE BEATLES
CENTRO COMERCIAL DE CAIMÁN
GROCERY
CASA DEL HABANO
HORSE-DRAWN CABS
CASA BENY
GALERÍA ARTE VERADERO
ADIDAS/SPORTSWEAR
CUBANA/ CUBACAR
RESTAURANTE RETIRO
DANTE
ROWBOATS
JOYERÍA CORAL NEGRO
62
POST OFFICE/TELEPHONE
TALLER DE CERÁMICA
TELEPHONE
HOSTAL IGNACIO Y JENNY
HAVANATUR CUBACAR
AV SEXTA
58 59 60
PHOTO SERVICE
FINCIMEX
HOTEL BELLEVUE PALMA REAL
53
Parque Retiro Josone
LA COMPARSITA
CLUB NOCTURNO HAVANA CLUB
63
54
WACO'S CLUB
VARADERO 60
AV TERCERA
TODOS EN UNO

Varadero East

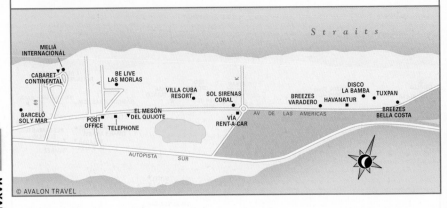

MELIÁ INTERNACIONAL

CABARET CONTINENTAL

BE LIVE LAS MORLAS

VILLA CUBA RESORT

SOL SIRENAS CORAL

DISCO LA BAMBA

TUXPAN

BREEZES VARADERO

HAVANATUR

BARCELÓ SOL Y MAR

EL MESÓN DEL QUIJOTE

POST OFFICE

TELEPHONE

VÍA RENT-A-CAR

AV DE LAS AMERICAS

BREEZES BELLA COSTA

AUTOPISTA SUR

Straits

© AVALON TRAVEL

Sbrinz, and Gouda cost extra. It also has grilled chicken breast (CUC4.50) and lobster (CUC16), plus a good selection of wines.

The ★ **Restaurante Las Américas** (Carretera Las Morlas, tel. 045/66-7388, daily noon-10pm), on the ground floor of Mansión Xanadú, specializes in French-style seafood and meats, such as appetizers of shrimp in sherry vinaigrette (CUC10), and seared goose liver with cabbage and balsamic (CUC11). The seared ahi tuna with green sauce (CUC20) is first-rate; so, too, is the artistically presented tiramisu.

For Italian fare, head to the stylish **Dante** (Parque Retiro Josone, tel. 045/66-7738, daily 9am-10pm), with views over the lake. It has air-conditioned and open-air options, and features pastas (from CUC6) and pizzas (from CUC4.50) plus a large wine list.

Restaurante Castel Nuevo (Av. 1ra y 11, tel. 045/66-7786, daily 2pm-10pm) has an appropriately Italianate motif and serves spaghetti, pastas, and pizzas (CUC2-10). The best pizza around, however, is at **Pizza Nova** (upstairs in Plaza América, tel. 045/66-8181, daily 11am-10pm).

Al Capone's former oceanfront home (built in 1934 on the Kawama Peninsula) is today the atmospheric **Casa de Al** (Av. Kawama, tel. 045/66-8018, 10am-10pm). Paella (CUC15) and filet mignon (CUC15) feature. Choose a

tiny terrace for romantic over-the-beach dining.

Surf and Turf

Several beach grills overhang the sands. I like **Ranchón Cielo Mar** (Calle 57, 24 hours). **El Rancho** (tel. 045/61-4760, daily 11am-10pm), opposite the entrance to Parque Retiro Josone, also serves grilled seafood (CUC6-14) in a handsome thatched roadside setting with live music.

Specializing in lobster, the hilltop **El Mesón del Quijote** (Av. las Américas, tel. 045/66-7796, daily noon-11pm, CUC10-30) boasts beamed ceilings, metal lamps, brass plaques, and potted plants on a solarium dining terrace. It also prepares good steak dishes.

Perhaps the most exclusive restaurant in Varadero, ★ **Restaurant Kike-Kcho** (tel. 045/66-4115, reserva@marina.gov.co.cu, daily noon-11pm, CUC20-35) fulfills a desire for gourmet seafood in a chic contemporary setting, with the bonus of a superb perch on stilts overlooking Marina Gaviota. It's known for its grilled lobster dishes, and paella earns rave reviews.

Bulls' heads on the wall and rawhide seats adorn **Steak House Toro** (Av. 1ra y 25, tel. 045/66-7145, daily noon-11pm), where you can dine alfresco or inside. The menu runs from veal chops (CUC14) to smoked salmon

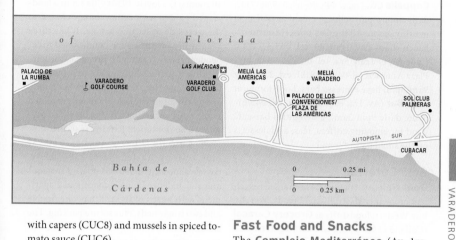

with capers (CUC8) and mussels in spiced tomato sauce (CUC6).

Asian

Taking a stab at Asian ambience and fare, **Lai-Lai** (Av. 1ra, e/ 18 y 19, tel. 045/66-7793, daily 1pm-9:30pm) features spring rolls, fried rice with shrimp or lobster, and lobster chop suey (CUC5-15). It ain't Hong Kong, but the dishes here are passable.

Fast Food and Snacks

The **Complejo Mediterráneo** (Av. 1ra, e/ 54 y 55) has two eateries in one: **Café Aladdin** offers sandwiches 24 hours, and **D'Prisa Mediterráneo** is a 24-hour open-air grill serving *criolla* fare and pizzas. Good sandwiches are served at **Pan.Com** (Centro Comercial Hicacos, Av. 1ra, e/ 44 y 46, tel. 045/61-4613, daily 9am-9pm). Clean and modern, it would fit well in L.A. or London.

Restaurante Las Américas, Mansion Xanadu, Varadero

Cafés and Desserts

Coppelia (Av. 1ra, e/ 44 y 46, tel. 045/66-7147, daily noon-8pm) sells ice cream at CUC0.50 per tiny scoop. All the **Casa del Habano** tobacco shops (Av. 1ra y 39, tel. 045/61-4719; Calle 63, e/ 1ra y 3ra, tel. 045/66-7843; and Plaza América, tel. 045/66-8181, ext. 251, daily 9am-9pm) have espresso bars. Look for me at **Café Bar** (Av. 1ra, esq. Calle 55, tel. 045/61-3506, daily 9pm-2am), a delightful bar-café good for enjoying coffees, teas, and desserts on the small patio.

Self-Catering

Doña Neli (Av. 1ra y 43, 24 hours) sells excellent croissants, pastries, and breads. You can buy Western foodstuffs at **Grocery Caracol** (Calle 15 e/ 1ra y 3ra), **Grocery La Trovatta** (Av. 1ra y A), and in **Plaza América,** which has a fully stocked supermarket (daily 8:30am-8pm).

ACCOMMODATIONS

There are scores of hotels to choose from, but low-price options are few; for that, seek out a *casa particular.* Air-hotel packages from abroad offer discounts. Most hotels are all-inclusive: meals, alcoholic beverages, entertainment, and water sports are included in the room rate. Few live up to the standards of all-inclusives elsewhere in the Caribbean, and standards are generally higher in foreign-managed hotels than in Cuban-managed properties. Hotels become more upscale eastward, though these are far from the action, which concentrates between Calles 11 and 64. Constantly to-ing and fro-ing can rack up a hefty taxi bill, although the Varadero Bus Tour serves most hotels.

Prices have skyrocketed in recent years, and the few so-called budget hotels that remain no longer represent a bargain. Hotels are listed here west to east. There are far more hotels than are listed here.

Casas Particulares

A true standout, ★ **Casa Beny** (Calle 55 #124, e/ 1ra y 2da, tel. 045/61-1700, www.

benyhouse.com, CUC110 house or CUC35-40 rooms) is a lovely 1950s villa set in a landscaped garden with rattan lounge chairs, to the west side of Parque Josone. It has three beautifully furnished air-conditioned independent rooms, each with private bathroom, making it perfect for couples and families. Owner Beny Nordarse Cruz and his family are totally professional. Meals are included in the rates, including a filling breakfast plus sandwiches for lunch. Parking is secure.

★ **Casa de Omar y Anabel** (Calle 31 #104, e/ 1ra y 3ra, tel. 045/61-2587, sherly-dayi@yahoo.es, CUC30-35) offers a spacious and airy independent air-conditioned apartment with heaps of light. It has one double and two single beds, plus secure parking. The small modern bathroom has hot water, and the apartment has its own kitchen and patio.

For a waterfront option, check out **Casa de María Isabel** (Av. de la Playa #4303, e/ 43 y 45, tel. 045/61-2363, varaderotorres@gmail.com, CUC30), with two rooms in a small cottage with secure parking.

Superbly situated near the thick of the action, **Hostal Ignacio y Jenni** (Calle 63 #6203, esq. Av. 2da, no tel., CUC35) gets rave reviews for the hospitable hosts and cozy comforts, plus modern accoutrements such as the flat-screen TV in the single clean, modestly furnished bedroom. Jenni's parents prepare breakfasts (CUC5).

Under CUC50

Popular with budget travelers, down-to-earth **Hotel Pullman** (Av. 1ra y Calle 49, tel. 045/66-2702, www.islazul.cu, CUC24 s, CUC38 d low season, CUC76 s, CUC88 d high season, including a meager breakfast) occupies a colonial mansion. The 15 rooms have colonial furniture and modern bathrooms; however, not all inspire. It has a small, airy restaurant and a patio bar. Operated jointly with the Pullman, the neighboring **Hotel Dos Mares** (Av. 1ra and Calle 53, same rates) has a certain bed-and-breakfast charm. It has 34 large, modestly furnished, no-frills rooms and a meager restaurant.

Others in this price bracket include: **Villa La Mar** (3ra Av., e/ 28 y 30, tel. 045/61-3910, vlamar@enet.cu); **Hotel Herradura** (Av. de la Playa, e/ 35 y 36, tel. 045/61-3703, carpeta@herradura.co.cu); and **Varadero Naviti Resort Hotel** (Vía Blanca, Km 130, tel. 045/66-7380).

CUC100-150

Islazul targets Italians at its all-inclusive **Hotel Los Delfines** (Av. 1ra, e/ 38 y 39, tel. 045/66-7720, www.islazul.cu, CUC120 per person low season, CUC138 per person high season), but the property is open to all comers. The 89 rooms have a lively contemporary decor. There are four suites and nine junior suites, and the price is a bargain.

Though overpriced, **Motel Punta Blanca** (Av. Kawama y Final, tel. 045/66-2410, www.islazul.cu, CUC90 s, CUC103 d year-round) is recommended for its refreshingly not-a-hotel status. Comprising three converted 1950s modernist villas, this extension of Club Kare has 21 spacious rooms with quasi-functional furnishings, plus a restaurant and bar. You're at the peninsula's western tip, away from the crowds. I like the contemporary motif at Gran Caribe's **Hotel & Villas Tortuga** (Calle 7, e/ Camino del Mar y Bulevar, tel. 045/61-4747, www.gran-caribe.cu, from CUC84 s, CUC112 d low season, from CUC114 s, CUC150 d high season), a modern, 280-room, two-story complex centered on a pool. The rooms have heaps of light but no TVs or telephones. You can also rent villas.

Islazul's **Hotel Club Tropical** (Av. 1ra, e/ 21 y 22, tel. 045/61-3915, www.islazul.cu, CUC120 s, CUC144 d low season, CUC115 s, CUC142 d high season) is an all-inclusive property with 143 rooms and apartments with lively fabrics. Its pleasant lobby bar and elegant restaurant appeal. Otherwise don't expect much here.

CUC150-250

Gran Caribe's all-inclusive **Gran Hotel Club Kawama** (Av. 1ra, esq. 1, Rpto. Kawama, tel. 045/66-4416, www.gran-caribe.cu, from CUC84 s, CUC130 d low season, CUC120 s, CUC160 d high season) dominates the Kawama peninsula on seven hectares and has 235 nicely furnished villas. The resort has several bars and restaurants, plus water sports, bike, scooter, and car rentals.

Gran Caribe's lively, albeit worn, 282-room, all-inclusive **Starfish Cuatro Palmas** (Av. 1ra, e/ 61 y 62, tel. 045/66-7040, www.starfishresorts.com, CUC115 s, CUC170 d low season, CUC140 s, CUs220 d high season) has a great location at the heart of the action. This popular hotel, run by the Barbadian Blue Diamond chain, is built on the grounds of Fulgencio Batista's summer house and is centered on an attractive swimming pool. It has apartment units across the street.

Managed as an all-inclusive by the Spanish Roc Hotels group, the **Hotel Roc Arenas Doradas** (tel. 045/66-8150, www.en.roc-hotels.com, from CUC136 s, CUC210 d) has 316 rooms set amid 20 acres of landscaped grounds surrounding a freeform pool with sunken pool bar and open-air whirlpool tub. Interior decor is attractive, though this is no Ritz. It has water sports and entertainment.

Hoteles Roc Barlovento (Av. 1ra, e/ 10 y 12, tel. 045/66-7140, www.en.roc-hotels.com, CUC88 s, CUC140 d low season, CUC133 s, CUC190 d high season) is a handsome, modern all-inclusive hotel done up in a contemporary interpretation of Spanish colonial style, with 269 attractively appointed rooms and three suites. The complex surrounds a large pool and offers water sports and entertainment.

I like the contemporary aesthetic of the all-inclusive **Hotel Bellevue Palma Real** (Av. 2da y 64, tel. 045/61-4555, jrecep.palmreal@hotetur.com, CUC100 s, CUC130 d low season, CUC104 s, CUC210 d high season), although this hotel faces the bay, not the sea. It has 466 rooms with lively decor, two restaurants and three bars, and entertainment. The two-tiered pool is a highlight.

Gran Caribe's venerable 1950s-era Hotel Varadero Internacional was demolished in 2015 and is scheduled to be replaced by the all-inclusive 934-room **Meliá Internacional** (Carretera las Américas), which was under construction at press time. Expect it to be one of Varadero's finest hotels when completed.

Farther east, Cubanacán's all-inclusive, six-story postmodernist **Hotel Tuxpan** (Av. Las Américas, Km 2, tel. 045/66-7560, www.hotelescubanacan.com, from CUC152 s, CUC200 d high season) boasts a large swimming pool and plenty of recreational facilities, including tennis, beach volleyball, and Hobie Cats, plus the La Bamba disco. Its 232 small, refurbished bedrooms have pleasant travertine-clad bathrooms.

The best bargain resort in Varadero is also one of my faves: Gaviota's ★ **Blau Marina Palace Resort** (Punta Hicacos Final, tel. 045/66-9966, www.blauhotels.com, from CUC94 s, CUC149 d low season, from CUC145 s, CUC233 d high season), at the very tip of the peninsula. Sprawling along the shore between the road and sand dunes, it boasts pleasing architecture and a contemporary quasi-maritime vogue to its 296 junior suites and four suites. All the required facilities are here, including a waterslide dropping into a huge pool.

Over CUC250

Gran Caribe's all-inclusive ★ **Barceló Solymar Arenas Blancas** (Carretera Las Américas y Calle 69, tel. 045/61-4499, www.barcelo.com, from CUC115 s, CUC170 d low season, CUC138 s, CUC228 d high season) is a modern resort with a contemporary design. Its 525 rooms and 193 bungalows all have exquisite marble-top bathrooms. The resort has a vast pool complex.

For a uniquely romantic experience, check into ★ **Mansión Xanadú** (Carretera Las Morlas, tel. 045/66-7388, www.varaderogolfclub.com, CUC145 s, CUC216 d low season, CUC198 s, CUC264 d high season, including breakfast and greens fees) at the Varadero Golf Club. This mansion's six gracious rooms feature marble floors, wrought-iron beds, throw rugs, and all-marble bathrooms with

vast walk-in showers. There's a splendid restaurant.

The **Meliá Las Américas Suites & Golf Resort** (Playa de las Americas, tel. 045/66-7600, www.solmeliacuba.com, from CUC184 s, CUC263 d low season, from CUC246 s, CUC354 d high season) boasts a stunning lobby. Arched terraces support a beautiful pool and sundeck overlooking its own private beach. The 340 rooms and suites feature kitchenettes and small lounges below mezzanine bedrooms with pleasing bamboo and wicker furniture.

The all-inclusive **Meliá Varadero** (Carretera Las Morlas, tel. 045/66-7013, www.solmeliacuba.com, from CUC165 s, CUC236 d low season, from CUC182 s, CUC274 d high season), adjoining Plaza América, makes a dramatic first impression with 490 rooms and suites in six arms that fan out from a soaring circular atrium with a curtain of vines cascading down from the balconies. Better still is the sibling ★ **Paradisus Varadero** (Carretera Las Morlas, tel. 045/66-8700, www.solmeliacuba.com, from CUC284 s, CUC315 d low season, from CUC300 s, CUC472 d high season), a beautiful all-inclusive centered on a huge freeform pool. It has 420 exquisitely appointed junior suites and suites, and a garden villa (with butler service) with sponge-washed walls, canopy beds, and wrought-iron and rattan furniture. Facilities include water polo, archery, volleyball, and tennis courts.

The outstanding ★ **Blau Varadero Hotel** (Carretera Las Morlas, Km 15, tel. 045/66-7545, www.blauhotels.com, from CUC151 s, CUC188 d low season, from CUC280 s, CUC350 d season) is a dramatic take on a Mayan pyramid. The lobby opens to a dramatic soaring atrium with skylight. A contemporary vibe infuses the guest rooms, with marble-clad bathrooms and spacious balconies. A hip buffet restaurant, an alfresco poolside restaurant, a beach grill, a bi-level pool, a large kids' club, and state-of-the-art theater and gym are among the amenities. The similarly priced **Iberostar Varadero** (Carretera Las Morlas, Km 17.5, tel. 045/66-999, www.iberostar.com) gets two thumbs up for its calming mood and creative design subtly infused with Mughal influences. At its heart is a vast freeform pool.

The **Royalton Hicacos Resort & Spa** (Carretera Las Morlas, Km 14, tel. 045/66-8844, www.royaltonresorts.com, from CUC215 s, CUC350 d low season, from CUC250 s, CUC420 d high season) is visually impressive: The entrance plays on a Polynesian theme, with thatched walkways over landscaped water courses. Lively Caribbean colors meld with rich ocher. It has 404 junior suites with a lovely contemporary feel, but the food leaves much to be desired.

Families might consider **Breezes Varadero** (Carretera Las Américas, Km 3, tel. 045/66-7030, www.superclubscuba.com, North America tel. 800/467-8737, U.K. tel. 01/749-677200), a 270-suite all-inclusive property managed by Jamaica's SuperClubs chain. It has heaps of facilities and its elegantly furnished guest rooms are spacious.

The nautically themed, 423-room all-inclusive ★ **Meliá Marina Varadero** (Autopista del Sur y Final, tel. 045/66-7330, www.melia-marinavaradero.com, from CUC228 s, CUC326 d low-season, from CUC265 s, CUC377 d high season) sets the standard for sophistication in Varadero. Enfolding the Marina Gaviota, this luxury four-phase hotel offers all the services of a beach resort. The largest touristic project in Cuba also features 220 luxury apartments for long-term stays, plus a tourist village, full-service spa, Casa de la Música, a bowling alley, dive center, and more. The white-and-turquoise rooms all have king beds and Wi-Fi (although only at the luxury level is it free). Its 10 restaurants and 9 bars include a tapas bar plus the clubby, Hemingway-themed Don Ernesto for Cuban-fusion fare. Casa Burguete serves French-inspired dishes.

At the far east end of the peninsula are several virtually identical options: the 1,035-room **Memories Varadero** (www.memoriesresorts.com); the 998-room **Hotel Riu Varadero** (tel. 045/66-7966, www.

riuvaradero.ca); the adjoining and equally sprawling 814-room **Iberostar Laguna Azul** (tel. 045/66-7900, www.iberostar.com); the Meliá-managed **Meliá Las Antilles** (tel. 045/66-8470, www.solmeliacuba.com); and **Paradisus Princesa del Mar** (tel. 045/66-7200, www.solmeliacuba.com). All are owned by Cuba's Grupo Gaviota, but under foreign management.

With the beachfront developed, hotels are popping up on the offshore cays. In 2017, Singapore's Banyan Tree Resorts (www.banyantree.com) was slated to break ground on the ultra-deluxe **Banyan Tree Cayo Buba** and **Angsana Cayo Buba** hotels.

INFORMATION AND SERVICES

Infotur (Calle 13 y 1ra, tel. 045/66-2966, infovar@enet.cu, daily 8am-5pm) provides tourist information. Alternatively, try **Havanatur** (1ra y 64, tel. 045/66-7279, daily 8am-5pm) or any of the other tour bureaus.

Money

Euros are accepted as direct payment in Varadero. Banks include **Banco Financiero Internacional** (Av. Kawama; Av. Playa y 32; and in Plaza América, Mon.-Fri. 8am-12:30pm and 1:30pm-7pm); **Bandec** (Av. 1ra y 36, Mon.-Fri. 8am-3pm); and **Banco Popular** (Av. 1ra y 36, Mon.-Fri. 8am-noon and 1:30pm-4:30pm). The **Cadeca** foreign exchange bureau is at 1ra and 59; the clerk there tried to scam me, as often happens in Cadeca bureaus. *Always ask for a receipt!*

Fincimex (Av. 2da y 63, tel. 045/61-4413, Mon.-Sat. 8:30am-noon and 1pm-4pm) represents foreign credit card companies.

Communications

Varadero has post offices at Avenida 1ra and Calle 36 (Mon.-Sat. 8am-7pm, Sun. 8am-5:30pm); in the gatehouse at Avenida las Américas and Calle A (tel. 045/61-4551, 8am-8pm); and at Avenida 1ra and Calle 64 (tel. 045/61-2882, daily 8am-8pm), which also represents DHL.

Etecsa (daily 8:30am-7pm) has international phone and Internet service at Avenida 1ra (esq. 30), which gets crowded; upstairs in Plaza América; and in Centro Comercial Hicacos (Av. 1ra, e/ 44 y 46), where **Cubacel** (Mon.-Sat. 8am-4pm) has an office for mobile phone service. The Complejo Todo por Uno mall has public Wi-Fi.

Medical Services

Clínica Internacional (Av. 1ra y 61, tel. 045/66-7710 or 045/66-8611, clinica@clinica. var.cyt.cu, 24 hours, CUC25 per consultation, CUC30 after 4pm, CUC60 for hotel visits) has an ambulance and pharmacy. There are also international pharmacies at Plaza América (tel. 045/66-4610), Avenida Kawama (e/ 3 y 4, tel. 045/61-4470), and Centro Comercial Hicacos (Av. 1ra e/ 44 y 46, tel. 045/61-4610, ext. 145, daily 8am-7pm).

Ópticas Miramar (Av. 1ra, esq. 43, tel. 045/66-7525, daily 8am-7pm) has optician services.

Legal Aid and Safety

The **police** station is at Avenida 1ra and Calle 39. The **Canadian Consulate** (Calle 13 #422, e/ 1ra y Camino del Mar, tel. 045/61-2078, varadero@international.gc.ca) also represents Australia. **Asistur** (Edificio Marbella, Apto. 6, Av. 1ra esq. Calle 42, tel./fax 045/66-7277, www.asistur.cu, Mon.-Fri. 9am-noon and 1:30pm-4:30pm, Sat. 9am-noon) provides assistance in an emergency.

Red flags are flown when swimming is dangerous.

GETTING THERE AND AWAY
Air

The **Aeropuerto Juan Gualberto Gómez** (tel. 045/61-2133 or 045/61-3036) is 16 kilometers west of Varadero. Air Berlin, Condor, and Thomas Cook Airways are among the charters that fly here from Europe. From the United States, **American Airlines** (tel. 800/433-7300, www.aa.com) launched twice-daily service from Miami in 2016; **Silver Airways** (tel. 801/401-9100, www.silverairways.com) initiated four flights weekly from Fort Lauderdale.

A taxi from the airport to the Varadero hotels will cost about CUC25. **Víazul** (tel. 045/61-4886, www.viazul.com) buses link the airport and Varadero (CUC6).

Sea

You can berth at **Marina Marlin Dársena** (Vía Blanca, Km 31, tel. 045/66-8060, HF-2790 or VHF-1668) and the full-service **Marina Gaviota Varadero** (Carretera Las Morlas, Km 21, tel. 045/66-4115, reserva@marinagav. co.cu). The latter has been expanded to 1,200 slips, making it one of the Caribbean's largest marinas.

Bus

Víazul buses (tel. 045/61-4886, www. viazul.com, daily 7am-6pm) arrive and depart the **Terminal de Ómnibus Interprovinciales** (Calle 36 y Autopista Sur, tel. 045/61-2626), connecting Varadero to Havana, Trinidad, and Santiago de Cuba and cities in between.

Bus #236 departs hourly for Cárdenas from the **Terminal Ómnibus de Cárdenas,** next to the main bus station, and from Avenida 1ra y Calle 13 (CUC1).

Car and Taxi

Most hotels have car rental outlets. Main offices include **Havanautos** (Av. 1ra y Calle 31, tel. 045/61-8196; Av. 1ra y 64, tel. 045/66-7094), **Cubacar** (Av. 1ra y 21, tel. 045/66-0332; Av. 1ra, e/ 54 y 55, tel. 045/61-1875; and Av. las Américas y A, tel. 045/61-7326, www. transturvaradero.com), and **Vía Rent-a-Car** (Calle 29, e/ Autopistas y 3ra, tel. 045/61-4391; and opposite Sol Club Coral). **Rex** (Calle 36 y Autopista, tel. 045/66-2112) has outlets at the **Hotel Iberostar Varadero** (tel. 045/66-7739) and the **airport** (tel. 045/66-7539).

Foreign drivers pay a CUC2 toll on the Vía Blanca, two kilometers west of Varadero. There are **gas stations** at Autopista Sur (esq.

17 and esq. 54) and next to Marina Aqua on the Vía Blanca west of town.

A taxi from Havana costs about CUC100 one-way.

Organized Excursions

You can book excursions farther afield in the major tourist hotels. Tour agencies include **Cubanacán** (Calle 24 y Playa, tel. 045/33-7061), **Cubatur** (Av. 1ra y 33, tel. 045/66-7217), **Havanatur** (Av. 3ra, e/ 33 y 34, tel. 045/66-7027), and **Paradiso** (1ra, esq. 36, tel. 045/61-2643). **Cubacar** (Av. 1ra, esq. 21, tel. 045/61-1808) has a "Discover Tour" by self-drive Suzuki jeep.

GETTING AROUND
Bus

The **Varadero Beach Tour** (tel. 045/66-8212, comercial.var@transtur.cu, daily 9am-8pm, CUC5) double-decker bus runs up and down Avenida 1ra and the length of the peninsula hourly. A full circuit takes two hours. It stops at all the major hotels and you can hop on or off at any of 45 stops. You can buy tickets at

hotels; a ticket is valid all day and can be used on the Matanzas Bus Tour.

With pesos you can also hop aboard buses #47 and #48 (20 centavos), which run along Avenida 1ra between Calle 64 and the Santa Marta district, west of the access bridge, and bus #220, on the Autopista Sur.

Car and Taxi

Cubataxi taxis (tel. 045/61-4444) wait outside tourist hotels. No journey between Calle 1 and Calle 64 should cost more than CUC8. **Grancar** (tel. 045/66-2454, CUC30 per hour) rents chauffeured prerevolutionary cars.

Coco-taxis, hollow egg-shaped three-wheel vehicles known locally as *huevitos* ("little eggs"), cost CUC3 minimum and rent for CUC20 hourly. Horse-drawn *coches* ply Avenida 1ra (CUC10 pp, 90 minutes).

Bicycle and Scooter

Scooters can be rented at most hotels and at **Cubacar** (tel. 045/61-4555, CUC15 for two hours, CUC25 per day).

Central Matanzas

From Havana, the Autopista runs east-west through south-central Matanzas Province. There are no diversions to distract you until you reach kilometer 142 and the turnoff for Jagüey Grande, Australia, and the Península de Zapata. Farther east, at the junction for Amarillo (one kilometer north of the Autopista), stands the **Memorial Caimito de Hanábana** (daily 8am-5pm, free), a small museum commemorating the site where, in 1862, nine-year-old José Martí wrote a letter to his mother recording the horrors of slavery. The structure is designed using astronomical computations so that each day the sunlight strikes a different date on a calendar noting important dates in Martí's life.

Alternatively, you can follow the Carretera Central (Route 3-N-1) through a string of dusty old towns; or the Circuito Norte coast

road, an unremarkable route whose only town of interest is Cárdenas.

CÁRDENAS

The Península de Hicacos forms a natural breakwater protecting Bahía de Cárdenas and the town of Cárdenas (pop. 82,000), a world away from the commercialism of Varadero, 10 kilometers to the northwest.

The city, founded in 1828, developed rapidly as a port serving the prosperous sugar-producing hinterland. Otherwise, Cárdenas has a lackluster history, punctuated by a singular event in 1850, when the Cuban flag was first flown here. That year, a Venezuelan adventurer called Narciso López came ashore with a mercenary army to free the locals from Spanish rule and annex Cuba himself. Although López's ragtag army captured the town, his meager force failed to rally local support and the invaders beat a hasty retreat. Cárdenas has forever since been called the Flag City.

Most of the town is dilapidated, despite being spruced up for news photographers after hometown boy Elián González was rescued in November 1999 after his mother and 10 others drowned at sea in a bid to flee Cuba for the United States. However, Cárdenas boasts a colonial cathedral and one of the nation's most impressive museums.

Orientation

Potholed streets running northeast-southwest are called *avenidas,* and streets running northwest-southeast are *calles.* Those *avenidas* northwest of Avenida Céspedes, the main boulevard, are suffixed with *oeste* (west); those to the southeast are *este* (east). *Calles* run consecutively from the bay. From Varadero, you enter town along Calle 13 (Calzada) but exit eastward along Calle 14.

★ Parque Echevarría

This charming tree-shaded plaza, one block east of Avenida Céspedes, is the cultural heart of town. On its east side stands a life-size bronze bust of José Antonio Echevarría, the leader of the anti-Batista Directorio Revolucionario Estudantil (Students Revolutionary Directorate). Echevarría led the students' assault on Batista's palace in March 1957; from a captured radio station he announced that Batista had been killed and called for a general strike, but the plug had been pulled and his words never made the air. He was killed later that day in a shootout with police.

Museo Casa Natal de José Antonio Echevarría (Av. 4 Este #560, esq. 12, tel. 045/52-4145, Tues.-Sat. 10am-6pm, Sun. 9am-1am, entrance CUC1, cameras CUC5, guided tours CUC5), on the park's west side, is a two-story house built in 1873. The namesake hero was born in this house in 1932. Downstairs features memorabilia relating to the wars of independence and fight against Batista;

upstairs is accessed by a beautiful hand-carved spiral staircase and has displays that honor Echevarría.

On the park's south side is the not-to-be-missed **Museo Oscar María de Roja** (Av. 4 Este, e/ Echevarría y Martí, tel. 045/52-2417, Tues.-Sat. 10am-6pm, Sun. 9am-1am, entrance CUC1, cameras CUC5, guided tours CUC5). Housed in the former home of the lieutenant governor (1861-1878), then the town hall (1878-1966), it's one of Cuba's oldest (founded in 1900), finest, and most expansive museums. Fourteen rooms are arrayed by theme, ranging from pre-Columbian culture to armaments, coins, independence, José Martí, and so on. The pièce de résistance is an ornate baroque 19th-century horse-drawn hearse.

On the park's northeast corner, the **Museo a la Batalla de Ideas** (Av. 6, e/ 11 y 12, tel. 045/52-7599, www.museobatalladeideas.cult.cu, Tues.-Sat. 10am-6pm, Sun. 9am-noon, entrance CUC2, cameras CUC5) is housed in the old firehouse (dating from 1872). It is dedicated to Elián González's father's fight with Miami's Cuban American community for custody of his son. Mementos include photographs of the boy, and even the T-shirt worn by Donato Dalrymple, the angler who plucked Elián from the sea. A copy of the statue of José Martí holding Elián that stands in front of the U.S. Embassy in Havana stands in the lobby.

Avenida Céspedes

Tiny **Parque Colón** (Céspedes, e/ 8 y 9), or Columbus Park, is dominated by the **Catedral de la Concepción Inmaculada,** a neoclassical cathedral consecrated in 1848 (but looking much older); it is fronted by an impressive statue of Columbus with a globe at his feet. The church has notable stained glass windows. Kitty-corner, the former mayor's mansion, now the near-derelict **Hotel Dominica,** is a national monument—it was here that Narciso López first raised the Cuban flag. Avenida Céspedes continues north to a bay-front **flagpole** and monument commemorating the events of 1850.

At the southwest end of Céspedes, a small **fortress** stands in the central median. Elián González's home faces the fortress on the east side of the street; he lives with his father, Juan Miguel, at Av. Céspedes #275. There's a similar fortress at the west end of town on Avenida 13 (Calzada).

Plaza Molokoff

Occupying an entire city block (Av. 3 Oeste, e/ 12 y 13), this two-story plaza is taken up by a farmers market. The historic market building was built of iron in 1856 in the shape of a cross, with a metal domed roof in Moorish style. Its wrought-iron balustrades are held aloft by colonnades. Molokoff refers to the dome-like crinoline skirts fashionable in the mid-19th century.

Food and Accommodations

Casa Hostal Angelo (Espriu #656, e/ Velásquez y Cristina, tel. 045/52-2451, CUC30) has one clean, simply furnished room. The delightful hosts make filling meals, enjoyed on a courtyard with a plunge pool. Perhaps the best place to bed in town is **Casa Grande** (Calle 18B #712, e/ Campiña y Portilla, tel. 5270-1135, CUC35), with two bedrooms in a delightful and spacious home. Filling meals are served and there is secure parking.

The best of few dining options, **Don QKQ** (Céspedes #1001, e/ 21 y 22, tel. 5268-5882, Wed.-Sun. 7pm-11pm) has tables arrayed alfresco around a kidney-shaped pool. Don Kuko caters mostly to a local crowd, hence the de rigueur live music and cabaret. He serves *criolla* staples, from shrimp cocktail to fish fillet *uruguayano* (stuffed with ham and cheese).

Paladar Las Delicias (Av. Céspedes #1314, tel. 045/52-7061, daily 11am-11pm) is a delightful private restaurant with uniformed waitresses, live musicians, and home-cooked *criolla* fare served on a shaded garden patio.

Services

There's a **post office** (Céspedes y Calle 8, Mon.-Sat. 8am-6pm); an **Etecsa** *telepunto* (Céspedes y Calle 13, daily 7am-11pm);

Bandec (Céspedes #252, esq. 11); and a **Cadeca** (Av. 3 Oeste, e/ 12 y 13, daily 8am-5pm) where you change dollars for pesos. Parque José Antonio Echevarría is a public Wi-Fi zone.

Hospital José M. Aristegui (Calle 13, tel. 045/52-4011, 24 hours daily) is one kilometer west of town.

Getting There and Away

Buses depart the **Terminal de Ómnibus Provincial** (Céspedes, e/ 21 y 22, tel. 045/52-1214). Bus #376 runs between Varadero and Cárdenas (30 minutes, CUC1), arriving and departing from Calle 14 and Avenida 8. Also serving Varadero, bus #236 arrives and departs Calle 13 and Avenida 13 Oeste.

A taxi from Varadero costs about CUC20.

Getting Around

For a taxi call **Cubataxi** (tel. 045/52-3160). There's a Cupet gas station at the west end of Calle 13, on the road to Varadero.

ALONG THE CARRETERA CENTRAL

The Carretera Central runs east from Matanzas city through a string of dusty agricultural towns. First up is **Coliseo,** at the junction for Cárdenas. Six kilometers east of Coliseo, at Guasimal del Toro, I highly recommend relaxing at **Finca La Coincidencia** (tel. 045/81-3923, daily 10am-5pm). The organic garden and pottery workshop of agronomist Hector Correa Almeida. This erudite farmer has studded his lovely garden with surreal sculptures; other treats include the *melapona* stingless bee hives, and the orchards of bananas, mangos, and tamarind, plus gardens where Hector lovingly tends his legumes. His wife Odalysa welcomes visitors with turmeric tea. Pottery workshops are offered.

The Carretera continues east past fields of sugarcane via the small agricultural town of **Jovellanos,** where **Finca Luna** (Av. 10 final, tel. 045/81-3956 or 5806-5520, www.fincaluna.com) is an upscale carbon copy of Finca La Coincidencia, for good reason: It's run by

Hector Correa's brother Luis and his wife, Nancy. Also potters, they have a micro-zoo of local fauna on their organic farm with lovely landscaped gardens with peacocks. There's a Cupet gas station at the east end of town.

Colón, 33 kilometers east of Jovellanos, is worth a quick browse. Its colonnaded streets are lined with tumbledown neoclassical structures centered on Parque de Libertad, two blocks south of the main street, Máximo Gómez (aka El Bulevar; it has public Wi-Fi). At its heart is a life-size, patinated bronze statue of the town's namesake, Christopher Columbus (Cristóbal Colón). There's a Cupet gas station on Máximo Gómez and another on Route 3-1-2, which leads south to the Autopista.

San Antonio de los Baños

Worth the detour off the Carretera Central is **San Miguel de los Baños,** a little spa town hidden deep amid rolling hills. It's reached via a turnoff from the Carretera Central at Coliseo, 37 kilometers east of Matanzas, at the junction with Route 3-1-1 to Cárdenas. The town's lofty setting, combined with the healing properties of its mineral waters, fosters growth as a popular health spa. The gentry built villas here in neoclassical and French provincial style with gingerbread woodwork. Most are in tumbledown condition. Most significant is the former **Gran Hotel y Balneario,** a once-grandiose spa modeled on the Grand Casino in Monte Carlo.

For a view over town ascend the 448 concrete steps—lined with faded murals of the stations of the cross—that lead to the top of **Loma de Jacán.**

Food and Accommodations

Hector Correa and his wife, Odalysa, welcome you at **Finca La Coincidencia** (tel. 045/81-3923, CUC20). The memorable and delicious meals are reason enough to stay here; try *moringa* soup with a veritable banquet of pumpkin, okra, chicken, pork, or sweet potato.

★ **Finca Luna** (Av. 10 final, tel. 045/81-3956 or 5806-5520, www.fincaluna.com,

CUC35), in Jovellanos, has three lovely thatched air-conditioned cabins on an organic farm with convivial hosts. The "Family Room" sleeps six people (CUC45). A swimming pool anchors the landscaped garden. Meals are served noon-3pm and 6pm-9pm.

JAGÜEY GRANDE AND VICINITY

Jagüey Grande, one kilometer north of the Autopista at kilometer 142, is an agricultural town encircled by citrus and sugarcane fields. Kilometer 142 is a major hub at the junction (south) for the Península de Zapata and Playa Girón (Bay of Pigs).

Finca Fiesta Campesina (tel. 045/91-2045, daily 9am-5pm, free, parking CUC1), 200 yards south of the junction, is a contrived "peasant farm" and restaurant popular with tour groups. It has a small zoo with deer, agoutis, snakes, crocodiles, and birds. There are gas stations 100 meters west of Parador de Carretera and at the junction of Calles 13 and 70 (at the south end of Jagüey Grande), which has public Wi-Fi in the main plaza.

Australia

The derelict Central Australia sugar factory looms over the sugarcane fields two kilometers south of Jagüey Grande and one kilometer south of the kilometer 142 junction, on the road to Playa Girón. Fidel Castro set up his military headquarters here on the afternoon of April 15, 1961, during the Bay of Pigs invasion, as he knew that the sugar factory had the only telephone for miles around.

Today, the mill's former headquarters houses the small **Museo Memorial Comandancia FAR** (Armed Forces Command Center Memorial Museum, tel. 045/91-2504), which remained closed at press time. Remains of aircraft shot in the fighting lie outside. (If it reopens, expect to see photographs, maps, and the desk and telephone used by Fidel, plus an antiaircraft gun and uniforms.)

To the west side are four antique steam trains. One train, dating from 1913, offers

90-minute rides one kilometer into the countryside for groups (tel. 045/91-3224, CUC10 pp).

Food and Accommodations

Cubanacán's **Villa Horizontes Don Pedro** (tel. 045/91-2825, www.hotelescubanacan.com, CUC25 s, CUC35 d low season, CUC30 s, CUC40 d high season), adjoining Finca Fiesta Campesina about 200 yards south of the junction at kilometer 142, has two modern air-conditioned cabins plus 10 roomy thatched log cottages with satellite TVs, ceiling fans, large bathrooms, and small kitchenettes. Some have loft bedrooms for four people. *Criolla* meals are served. You feel like you're on a farm.

Pío Cua (tel. 045/91-2525, CUC24 s/d, CUC30 including breakfast), south of Jagüey Grande about two kilometers south of the Central Australia factory, has three simply furnished, air-conditioned cabins: one for two people, two each for four people. Rooms have local TV and modern bathrooms. It has an atmospheric restaurant (daily 11:30am-4pm) and bar popular with tour groups.

Parador de Carretera (tel. 045/91-3224, sistema@cienaga.var.cyt.cu), at the kilometer 142 junction, is a café-restaurant (daily 11:30am-10pm) colloquially known as "El Barco." It doubles as a tourist information center (daily 8am-8pm) that arranges excursions and handles bookings for local hotels.

Península de Zapata and Vicinity

South of the hamlet of Australia, the sugarcane fields end and the sawgrass begins. This swampland (the Ciénega de Zapata) sweeps south to the Caribbean Sea, smothering the Península de Zapata, a great shoe-shaped extension jutting west into the Golfo de Batabanó. Most of the 4,230-square-kilometer limestone landmass is in Parque Nacional Ciénega de Zapata, within the larger Reserva de la Biosfera Ciénega de Zapata.

Zapata extends west of a deep, finger-like bay, the 20-kilometer-long Bahía de Cochinos—Bay of Pigs, named for the local *cochinos cimarrones,* wild pigs, which were a dietary staple for local Indians. The bay is renowned as the site for the 1961 invasion, when 1,300 heavily armed, CIA-trained Cuban exiles came ashore to topple the Castro regime.

Route 3-1-18 runs like a plumb line from Australia to Playa Larga, a small fishing village tucked into the head of the bay. Concrete monuments rise along the coast road, each one representing a Cuban soldier (161 in all) who fell during the three-day battle in April 1961.

About 8,000 people inhabited the area on the eve of the Revolution, when there were no roads, schools, or electricity. Charcoal-making was the major occupation of the impoverished population. The *cenague-ros* were among the first beneficiaries of the Revolution. The youthful Castro government built highways into the swamps, established a small hospital and schools, and sent more than 200 teachers from the national literacy campaign.

RESERVA DE LA BIOSFERA CIÉNAGA DE ZAPATA

This 628,171-hectare UNESCO Biosphere Reserve enshrines the entire Península de Zapata and surrounding wilderness. The park entrance (no fee) is midway along Route 3-1-18. The entrance to the actual wildlife reserve is at Buena Ventura, two kilometers west of Playa Larga, 32 kilometers south of Australia; a fee applies and a guide is obligatory.

For a perspective on the reserve and its flora and fauna, call in at the **Centro Ecológico** (tel. 045/91-5539, Mon.-Fri. 8am-4pm, CUC2 including an interpretive trail

Peninsula de Zapata and Vicinity

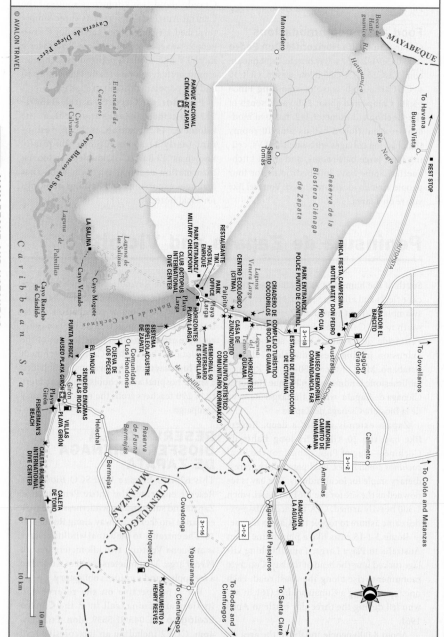

Crabs!

Mid-March through April, legions of giant land crabs (*cangrejos*) emerge from the vegetation and swarm to meeting grounds where they gather for breeding and egg-laying. They move in such numbers that the coast road between Playa Larga and Playa Girón, and those along much of the southern and eastern coasts of Cuba, become a veritable carpet of crushed crabs. For travelers it can be a daunting challenge to avoid a puncture.

In *Mi Moto Fidel: Motorcycling Through Castro's Cuba,* I write: "The air stank of fetid crabmeat. Vultures hopped about, drawn greedily to the prodigal banquet. I passed my first live crab. Bright orange. A newborn. Then a large black crab with terrifying red pincers ran across my path, the forerunner of a lethal invasion heading the other way. Suddenly I was surrounded by a battalion of armored, surly crustaceans that turned to snap at my tires. I slalomed between them as they rose in the road with menacing claws held high. Then I hit one square on. POOF! It sounded like bubble wrap exploding."

The surreal crabfest is usually over by May. Until then, there's no way around them. If you choose to drive, be sure to have a spare tire.

walk), a visitors center five kilometers south of La Boca de Guamá. It features an exhibition on the region. A separate exhibit details the indigenous heritage.

Mosquitoes are ferocious here; bring repellent!

Complejo Turístico La Boca de Guamá

Complejo Turístico La Boca de Guamá (tel. 045/91-5662), 19 kilometers south of Jagüey Grande, is an important roadside stop at the edge of Laguna del Tesoro. It has restaurants, a souvenir shop, and a gas station. No credit cards are accepted.

Criadero de Cocodrilos (tel. 045/91-5666, daily 7am-7pm, CUC5 adults, CUC3 children) is Cuba's most important crocodile farm, with more than 4,000 crocodiles. Visitors can learn about the breeding cycle and ecology. When they're seven years old, some are released to the wild; others are killed for meat and leather.

The 16-square-kilometer **Laguna del Tesoro** (Treasure Lagoon) is stocked with bass, tarpon, and meter-long *manjuarí*. The lake, reached via a five-kilometer-long canal from La Boca, is named for the Taíno religious objects that have been raised from the water and are now exhibited at **Villa Guamá,** on

an island in the middle of the lake; this hotel features a mock Taíno village and 32 life-size sculptures depicting Taíno engaged in daily activities. A tour boat leaves La Boca for Villa Guamá on a regular basis (CUC12).

Rowboats (CUC2) can be hired. Fishing trips are offered (tel. 045/91-3224).

Four kilometers south of Boca de Guamá, and midway to Playa Larga, is the hamlet of **Palpite,** where a roadside billboard indicates that the "mercenaries" (invading force in 1961) reached here, just four kilometers inland. The community is famous for its **Conjunto Artístico Comunitario Korimakao** (tel. 045/59-5651), a renowned art, dance, and theater project that tours nationwide. Up a dusty street 100 meters to the north, the **Casa del Zunzuncito** (tel. 5422-0701, bernabe.hernandez@nauta.cu, CUC5) has hummingbird feeders that draw the world's smallest bird, the bee hummingbird.

Playa Larga and Bahía de los Cochinos (Bay of Pigs)

Playa Larga, at the head of the Bahía de los Cochinos, was one of the two main landing sites during the Bay of Pigs invasion. The formerly sleepy fishing village of **Caletón,** at the east end of the two-kilometer-long white-sand beach, is in the throes of a tourism and construction boom, with several dozen *casas particulares* and restaurants. There's a water sports outlet (c/o Rigo, tel. 5227-9637) at Villas Playa Larga (pedal boats CUC4 per hour, kayaks CUC2, Hobie Cats CUC10).

A road leads west from Caletón two kilometers to the entrance to the Parque Nacional Ciénaga de Zapata.

East of Playa Larga, white beaches extend around the bay. At **Caleta del Rosario,** about three kilometers from Playa Larga, is a splendid little cove with good swimming. The route is lined with *cenotes,* limestone sinkholes filled with freshwater. **Cueva de los Peces** (Cave of Fishes, tel. 5253-9004, daily 9am-5pm), 15 kilometers from Playa Larga, is one of the largest *cenotes:* 70 meters deep, it's a superb spot for swimming, although it can get packed with tour groups. The beach in front of the *cenote* offers good snorkeling and diving in jade-colored waters.

Between Playa Larga and Cueva de los Peces, a sign points to **Memorial de Sopillar.** The deteriorated road leads five kilometers to a rustic *bohío* commemorating where Fidel celebrated Christmas Eve dinner in 1959.

A little east of Cueva de los Peces is **Bar/Restaurante Punta Perdiz** (daily 9am-4pm), a small recreation area with a bird-watching trail. Nearby, the **Sistema Espeleolacustre de Zapata** investigates marine caverns. It has two one-kilometer-long trails through endemic woodlands. You can swim in *cenotes.* Guided hikes are offered four times daily.

The **Club Octopus International Dive Center** (Playa Larga, tel. 045/98-7294) offers dives daily 9am-5pm (CUC25 one dive, CUC40 cave dive and Nitrox dives, CUC365 certification) and rents snorkeling gear (CUC3). Marlin also has a dive outlet at El Tanque, about 10 kilometers south of Playa Larga. It also has guided snorkeling trips to the barrier reef (CUC10).

★ Parque Nacional Ciénaga de Zapata

The 490,417-hectare **Ciénaga de Zapata National Park** protects Cuba's most important wetland area. The ecosystems include marsh grass, mangrove thickets, and swamp forest. It is a biological mirror of the Everglades of Florida. Vegetation includes the button tree, so small that it looks like a bonsai. Zapata harbors more than 900 species of flora, 171 species of birds, 31 of reptiles, and 12 of mammals, including the pygmy *jutía* native to the Zapata swamp, and manatees. The alligator gar (*manjuarí*), the most primitive of Cuban fish, is found in lagoons, as are crocodiles and caimans.

A unique way to explore the park is by kayak. **ROW Adventures** (tel. 800/451-6034, www.rowadventures.com) includes three days kayaking and snorkeling in Zapata in its eight-day Cuba program.

BIRD-WATCHING

Of Cuba's 25 endemic bird species, 18 inhabit the marshes. Zapata protects the bee hummingbird (the world's smallest bird) as well as an endemic tanager, the Zapata sparrow, Zapata rail, Zapata wren, the Cuban trogon or *tocororó,* and Cuban parrots. Zapata is also a favorite stop for tens of thousands of migratory birds. The best time is October to April, when migrants flock in, among them sandhill cranes and wood ibis.

The best spots for bird-watching are **Laguna de las Salinas,** a 36,400-hectare expanse of flats, watercourses, and islets on the southern shores of Zapata and where flamingos flock in the thousands; and also around **Santo Tomás,** about 30 kilometers west of Playa Larga (CUC10 pp by jeep, including guide). **Refugio de Fauna Bermejas,** accessed from north of Playa Girón, is a separate section of the park (the entrance fee is payable in the Hotel Playa Larga) with a bird-watching trail. Local birding guides include **Armando Herrera** (tel. 045/98-7249).

FISHING

Zapata has been isolated from fishing pressure since 1959, making this huge reserve as close to a virgin fishery as one can find in today's world. There are said to be places where you can catch the fish with your bare hands, the way the indigenous people did. There are two distinct areas for fishing—the Río Hatiguanico (for tarpon) and Laguna de las Salinas (for bonefish). Several well-traveled anglers consider Las Salinas the standard by which all other locations should be judged worldwide. Bonefishing is most productive late fall through June; tarpon fishing peaks late February/early March through June. Underpowered skiffs mean long periods getting to the best lagoons.

PERMITS AND GUIDES

Access is by permit only (CUC12 pp, including an obligatory guide), obtained from the **Oficina Parque Nacional** (tel. 045/98-7249, sistema@cienaga.var.cyt.cu, daily 8am-4:30pm), beside the highway in Playa Larga. You can also hire a guide and arrange hikes, bird-watching, fishing (CUC170 fullday), and crocodile tours through Parador de Carretera, at kilometer 142. You'll need your own vehicle (4WD recommended), with a spare seat for the guide.

Food

At La Boca, the modestly elegant **Colibrí Restaurant** (daily 9:30am-5pm, CUC5-12) serves *criolla* fare, including crocodile (CUC10) and lobster (CUC11), but the wait can be long when tour groups are in. The open-air **Bar y Restaurante La Rionda** (daily 9:30am-8pm, CUC5-12), adjacent, is nicer on cooler days.

Cueva de los Peces (daily 8am-5pm, CUC5-12), overhanging the *cenote,* has a thatched restaurant serving *criolla* fare. Tour groups often take over the place. Several *paladares* line the beachfront in Caletón. My favorite is **Tiki** (tel. 45/98-7285 or 5471-5922, tikibarbahia@gmail.com, daily 10am-midnight), where you dine on delicious seafood on a thatched open-air deck.

Accommodations
LA BOCA DE GUAMÁ

Laguna Tesoro was one of Castro's favorite fishing spots. The Cuban leader spent many weekends in a *cabina* that became known as "Fidel's Key." One day he supposedly announced, "We're going to build a Tahitian village here!" And they did. The result is a replica Taíno village, now **Horizontes Villas Guamá** (tel. 045/91-5551, CUC34 s, CUC40 d), with 13 tiny islands connected by hanging bridges. The 44 thatched, air-conditioned wooden bungalows on stilts are simply furnished, but pleasant. They have TVs and there's a swimming pool. Bring bug spray!

PLAYA LARGA

The boom is on in Playa Larga, where several dozen homes rent rooms. The most sophisticated is the ever-expanding ★ **Hostal Enrique** (tel. 045/98-7425 or 5268-6785, enriqueplayalarga@gmail.com, CUC25-30), which has 10 air-conditioned rooms: six in the original ground-floor section and four atop the roof terrace. Rooms have modern en suite bathrooms. Filling seafood dishes are served on the terrace. The only potential drawback: it's extremely popular with tour groups who come to lunch.

Hostal Mayito (tel. 043/98-7428 or 5368-9739, hostalcasamayito@gmail.com, CUC30-35 including bike use), with stone walls and modern furnishings, has three upstairs air-conditioned rooms, each with a fridge and fans; one good for families has a double bed and a Murphy bed. The English-speaking owner rents snorkel gear.

Villa Juana (Batey Caletón, Playa Larga, tel. 045/98-7308, caribesolpz@yahoo.es, CUC20-25) is a pleasant blue-painted and decorated home with modern amenities. The single air-conditioned room with its own refrigerator, fan, and modern bathroom opens to a charming garden patio where meals are served. The family is a delight.

The Bay of Pigs

The Bay of Pigs invasion—Cubans call it *la victoria* (the victory)—was the brainchild of Richard Bissell, deputy director of the CIA. The "Program of Covert Action Against the Castro Regime" called for creation of a Cuban government in exile, covert action in Cuba, and "a paramilitary force outside of Cuba for future guerrilla action." In August 1959, President Eisenhower approved a US$13 million budget with the proviso that "no U.S. military personnel were to be used in a combat status."

The CIA recruited Cuban exiles for the invasion force and used an abandoned naval base at Opa-Locka, outside Miami, to train the brigade. They were later moved to U.S. military locations in Guatemala and Puerto Rico (in violation of U.S. law). Meanwhile, a "government in exile" was chosen from within a feud-riven group of political exiles, many of them corrupt right-wing politicians nostalgic for the Batista days.

The plan called for the invasion force to link up with counterrevolutionary guerrillas operating out of the Sierra Escambray, more than 100 kilometers east of the Bay of Pigs, where the brigade would land at three beaches 25 kilometers apart and surrounded by swamps. In photos taken by U-2 spy planes, the CIA identified what it claimed was seaweed offshore. Cuban brigade members identified the formations as coral heads, but the CIA wouldn't listen.

The invasion plan relied on eliminating the Cuban air force. On April 15, 1961, two days before the invasion, B-26 bombers painted in Cuban air force colors struck Cuba's military air bases. Thus Castro was fully forewarned. Worse, only five aircraft were destroyed. Cuba still had three T-33 jet fighters and four British-made Sea Fury light-attack bombers.

THE INVASION

The U.S. Navy aircraft carrier *Essex* and five destroyers escorted six freighters carrying the Cuban fighters and their supplies. The landings began about 1:15am on April 17. Landing craft came roaring in. About 140 meters offshore, they hit the coral reefs the CIA had dismissed as seaweed. The brigade had to wade ashore. Meanwhile, the Cubans had installed searchlights on the beach. "It looked like Coney Island," recalls Gray Lynch, the CIA point man who ended up directing the invasion. The brigade had also been told that "no communications existed within 20 miles of the beach." In fact, there was a radio station only 100 meters inland. By the time the brigade stormed it, Castro had been alerted.

President Kennedy had approved taking the Cubans to the beaches; beyond that, they were on their own. Worried about repercussions at the United Nations, Kennedy ordered cancellation of a U.S. air strike designed to give the invasion force cover.

Castro set up headquarters in the Central Australia sugar mill and from there directed the Cuban defense. As the exiles landed, Cuba's aircraft swooped down. Two supply ships containing ammunition and communications equipment were sunk. The brigade did, however, manage to unload World War II-era Sherman tanks. They fought against Cuba's equally outdated T-34 and Stalin tanks.

Despite the CIA's predictions, the local people defended their homeland until the first Cuban battalion arrived in buses (many were killed when the convoy was strafed by the brigade's B-26s). Reinforcements poured in and encircled the invasion forces, and the fight became a simple matter of whittling away at the exiles.

Although a U.S. jet-fighter squadron flew reconnaissance and was forbidden to engage in combat, six U.S. pilots flew combat missions under CIA orders without President Kennedy's knowledge. Four were shot down and killed. The Cubans recovered the body of one pilot, Thomas Ray; his corpse remained in a Havana morgue, unclaimed by the U.S. government, until Ray's daughter brought his body home for burial in 1979.

On the third day, U.S. destroyers advanced on the shore to pick up those *brigadistas* who had made it back to sea. The brigade had lost 114 men (the Cubans lost 161); a further 1,189 were captured. Eventually, 1,091 prisoners were returned to the United States in exchange for US$53 million in food and medical supplies.

The overpriced beachfront **Horizontes Playa Larga** (Batey Caletón, Playa Larga, tel. 045/98-7241, CUC55 s, CUC74 d low season, CUC66 s, CUC93 d high season, including breakfast) has 68 spacious, modestly furnished, air-conditioned *cabinas* with basic kitchenettes. The restaurant serves ho-hum meals and the swimming pool can get overly lively when rowdy Cuban families pour in for the day. It has water sports.

Getting There and Around

The 7am Havana-Trinidad **Víazul** and 4pm Trinidad-Havana buses travel via Playa Larga and Girón (CUC13). Transtur operates the hop-on/hop-off **Guamá Bus Tour** (tel. 045/98-7212, commercial@peninsula. cyt.cu, CUC3) twice daily between Guamá (departs at 10:30am and 3:30pm) and Caleta Buena via Playa Larga and Playa Girón (departs 9am and 2pm), stopping at key sites en route. Tour agencies in Havana and Varadero offer excursions.

PLAYA GIRÓN

You finally arrive at the spot where socialism and capitalism slugged it out, and what do you find? Vacationers from cool climates, lathered with suntan oil, splashing in the shallows where 50-odd years before blood and bullets mingled with the sand on the surf.

Playa Girón is a small, single-road *pueblo* of a few hundred people. It was named in honor of Gilbert Girón, a French pirate captured here. The community lies inland of the hotel and beautiful white-sand beach, which is enclosed within a concrete barrier (*rompeola*) that protects against any future wave of CIA-backed anti-Castroites foolish enough to come ashore. Nonetheless, it's a carbuncle on the coast and made worse by the military watchtower to its east end. (The hotel takes up much of the beach, but go around it to the east for the public beach.)

A decade ago, there were no *casas particulares*, no *paladares*. The village has since seen

an explosion in independent tourism and is prospering.

The paved coastal highway (Route 3-1-16) turns inland at Girón and runs 39 kilometers through scrubland via Bermejas, where the road bifurcates. Forsake the road north to Covavango; it's terribly deteriorated. East from Bermejas the road runs through the communities of Babiney and Horquitas (amid rich agricultural country) to Yaguaramas, beyond which it connects with Route 3-1-2, which runs north to the Autopista and east to Cienfuegos.

Immediately east of Babiney is a billboard stating *"Hasta aquí llegaron los mercenarios"* ("The Mercenaries reached here"), referring to the parachute drop of Cuban-American invaders during the 1961 Bay of Pigs invasion. Exactly midway between Horquitas and Yaguaramas, the **Monumento a Henry Earl Reeves** marks the site where the eponymous U.S. mercenary, who rose to be a general in the Cuban army (he is known to Cubans as "El Inglesito"), was killed in 1876 during the Ten Years War.

★ Museo Playa Girón

This excellent **museum** (tel. 045/98-4122, daily 9am-5pm, entrance CUC2, guide CUC1, cameras CUC1), 100 meters inland of the beach at Playa Girón, gives an accurate portrayal of the Bay of Pigs invasion. Black-and-white photographs confirm the poverty of the local peasantry before the Revolution. Others profile the events culminating in the act to which the museum is dedicated—the invasion of April 15, 1961, by 1,297 CIA-trained Cubans.

Maps trace the evolution of the 72-hour battle. There are photographs, including gory pictures of civilians caught in the midst of explosions, and of all the martyrs—the "Heroes de Girón"—killed in the fighting (the youngest, Nelson Fernández Estévez, was only 16 years old; the oldest, Juan Ruíz Serna, was 60). Displays include weapons and a Sea Fury fighter-aircraft, which sits on the forecourt alongside Soviet T-34 and SAU-100 tanks.

A 15-minute black-and-white documentary is shown in the cinema to the rear of the museum (CUC1).

Caleta Buena

This exquisite **cove** (tel. 045/91-5589, daily 10am-5pm, CUC15), eight kilometers east of Playa Girón, contains a natural pool good for swimming. There are pocket beaches atop the coral platform, with red-tiled *ranchitas* for shade and lounge chairs for sunning. The seabed is a multicolored garden of coral and sponges, ideal for snorkeling (CUC3 one hour, CUC5 per day) and diving (CUC25). Lunch is served 12:30pm-3pm (the bar is open until 5pm).

Accommodations

There are several dozen *casas particulares,* most being similar in style and price (CUC20-25). A standout is ★ **Hostal Luis** (tel. 045/98-4258, hostaluis@yahoo.es, CUC25-30), run by a gracious couple, Luis García Padrón and his wife Marleyn, with four well-lit, air-conditioned rooms in two buildings; all have modern bathrooms, and one unit is a two-room apartment. It has parking and a laundry.

I also like **Casa de Ivette y Ronel** (tel. 045/98-4129, www.playagironcasa.com, CUC20), with two rooms—the Blue Room and the Red Room (each air-conditioned and with flat-screen TVs)—set in a garden and with secure parking. Ronel is a certified dive instructor.

Cubanacán's lackluster, beachfront, and overpriced all-inclusive **Villas Playa Girón** (tel. 045/98-7206, www.hotelescubanacan. com, from CUC110 s, CUC164 d high season) has 127 rooms in villas scattered amid lawns. Some have shared bathrooms; all have satellite TV, telephone, and fridge, but furnishings are basic. The restaurant's buffet is pathetic. It's popular with budget package tourists, including Cubans.

Services

There's a pharmacy, a post office, a café, and shops opposite the museum.

Getting There and Around

Víazul (www.viazul.com) buses depart for Girón from Havana at 7am, arriving at 11:30am and continuing to Cienfuegos and

British Sea Fury at Museo Playa Girón

Trinidad at 10:45am; from Trinidad at 4pm, arriving at 7:10pm en route to Havana.

A truck *(camion)* departs Girón daily at 5am for Cienfuegos. A bus *(guagua)* departs Jagüey Grande at 8am for Girón; it returns at 6am. A bus runs from Matanzas Monday-Friday at 1pm, departing Girón for Matanzas at 4:20am.

Cubacar (tel. 045/98-4126) has a rental agency (scooters CUC13 two hours or CUC25 full day; cars from CUC60 with insurance). There's a gas station adjacent.

Cienfuegos and Villa Clara

Villa Clara and Cienfuegos Provinces lie due east of Matanzas Province, with Villa Clara north of Cienfuegos. Together they share some of the prettiest scenery in Cuba.

The southern and eastern portions of Villa Clara Province are dominated by rolling uplands called the Alturas de Santa Clara, which rise gradually to the steep, pine-clad Sierra Escambray. Cool forests tantalize bird-watchers and hikers, with man-made lakes good for fishing, a famous health spa, and an invigorating climate. The mountains extend south and west into Cienfuegos Province.

Industry is centered on the city of Cienfuegos, a major port town that also boasts some splendid colonial architecture and, nearby, a fine botanical garden, while the city of Santa Clara (an important industrial and university city) should be on every traveler's itinerary for the fascinating Museo de Che (Guevara).

Villa Clara is second only to Pinar del Río as a center of tobacco production, centered on the scenic Vuelta Arriba region, east of the provincial capital. Here, the historic town of Remedios is caught in a delightful time warp. Remedios and neighboring villages are renowned for their *parrandas*, unique carnival-style revelries that border on mayhem. Nearby, gorgeous beaches beckon in the Cayos de Villa Clara.

PLANNING YOUR TIME

All the main highways merge into (or radiate from) the city of **Santa Clara,** which boasts the must-see **Complejo Monumental Comandante Ernesto Che Guevara.** A full day is sufficient for this city.

Northwest of Santa Clara, the Circuito Norte linking Villa Clara with Matanzas Province skirts the north coast and offers little visual appeal. You can enjoy a massage and steep in mud at Hotel Elguea & Spa. Northeast of Santa Clara, the route passes through **Vuelta Arriba** and is superbly scenic. Stay overnight in the town of **Remedios** to savor its historical charm. If possible, time your visit for Christmas week, when the entire town explodes in revelry; accommodation is in short supply at year's end. When the dust settles, head out to **Cayos de Villa Clara** for sunning,

Previous: Palacio del Valle at dusk; Complejo Monumental Comandante Ernesto Che Guevara in Santa Clara. **Above:** Casa de la Cultura in Cienfuegos.

Highlights

★ **Parque Martí:** Cienfuegos's expansive plaza is surrounded by impressive neoclassical structures and a cathedral (page 266).

★ **Jardín Botánico Soledad:** This vast arboretum on the outskirts of Cienfuegos has a huge collection of tropical trees and shrubs (page 274).

★ **El Nicho:** The placid Sierra Escambray features beautiful waterfalls and hiking at this recreational site (page 277).

★ **Complejo Monumental Comandante**

Ernesto Che Guevara: A splendid museum sits beneath the imposing Che Guevara monument in Santa Clara. A mausoleum contains the revolutionary hero's remains (page 280).

★ **Remedios:** Time your visit to this beautiful colonial town for year's end to catch the *parranda*—a fireworks battle like no other (page 287).

★ **Cayos de Villa Clara:** A 50-kilometer-long land bridge provides access to stunning white-sand beaches and jade waters on remote cays with fishing, scuba diving, and resorts (page 291).

Cienfuegos and Villa Clara Provinces

© AVALON TRAVEL

Caribbean Sea

MATANZAS

VILLA CLARA

CIENFUEGOS

SANCTI SPIRITUS

Alturas de Santa Clara

To Havana

Los Arabos

Aguada de Pasajeros

Yaguaramas

Rodas

Cartagena

Santa Isabel de las Lajas

Cruces

Palmira

Pepito Teyo

Rancho Luna

La Sierrita

Cumanayagua

Manicaragua

Hanabanilla

Mataguá

La Ya Ya

Ranchuelo

Esperanza

Jicotea

San Diego del Valle

Cifuentes

Encrucijada

Manacas

Cascajal

Rancho Veloz

Carahatas

Quemado de Güines

Sagua la Grande

El Santo

Emilio Cordova

Camajuaní

San Antonio de las Vueltas

Placetas

Zulueta

Buena Vista

Fomento

Ciudad Nuclear

Pascaballo

Rancho Luna

Punta Gavilán

San Juan

Pico (1,140m)

Topes de Collantes

Ciego Montero Spring

Central Maltiempo

Central Nacional

JARAGUA NUCLEAR REACTOR
FORTALEZA DE NUESTRA SEÑORA DE JAGUA
FARO LUNA (LIGHTHOUSE)
DELFINARIO
Playa Rancho Luna
EL NARANJO AND LA PUNTA ARRIBA (DIVE SITES)

OIL REFINERY

PALACIO DEL VALLE
PARQUE MARTÍ

Bahía de Cienfuegos

AEROPUERTO JAIME GONZÁLEZ
NECROPOLIS TOMÁS ALEA
JARDÍN BOTÁNICO SOLEDAD

Sierra del Escambray

EL NICHO

Presa del Hanabanilla

Valle de Yaguanabo
CAMARONERA DE YAGUANABO

RESTAURANTE EL QUEDARAS

EL RAPIDO 259

SANTA CLARA

COMPLEJO MONUMENTAL COMANDANTE ERNESTO CHE GUEVARA

AEROPUERTO ABEL SANTAMARÍA

RESTAURANTE LA LEGUA

Presa Minerva

Presa Alacranes

Presa del Valle

Río Sagua la Chica

REMEDOS
MUSEO DEL AZÚCAR
FORTÍN DE LA TROCHA

FINCA RESTAURANTE EL CURUJEY

San Antonio de las Vueltas

Caibarién

TOLL BOOTH

To Picuas-Cayo del Cristo
To Refugio Nacional
Las Picuas-Cayo del Cristo

4-011
4-13
4-241
4-N1
4-13
4-321
4-21
4-112
4-206
4-474
4-474
4-432
4-N1
4-401
4-461
4-321
4-221

To Morón
To Ciego de Ávila

SANCTI SPIRITUS

REFUGIO GUANAROCA

Cayo Fragoso
Cayo Francés
Cayo Las Brujas
Cayo Santa María
Cayo Conuco

To CAYOS DE VILLA CLARA,
Cayo Las Bruja, and
Cayo Santa María
(see detail)

CAYOS DE VILLA CLARA

To Casilda
To Trinidad

25 km
25 mi

CARRETERA CENTRAL

AUTOPISTA NACIONAL

swimming, and to reel in some game fish from the placid jade waters.

The Carretera Central through central Villa Clara will take you through aged provincial towns, although there are no sights of significance. The Autopista (freeway) runs through northern Cienfuegos and southern Villa Clara Province. East of Santa Clara city, the scenery takes a dramatic turn as the Autopista cuts through the beautiful hills of the Alturas de Santa Clara and passes into Sancti Spíritus Province. The main turnoff for the city of Cienfuegos is at Aguada de los Pasajeros.

The city of **Cienfuegos** is a popular destination with an intriguing historic city core.

Nearby, the ho-hum beach at **Playa Rancho Luna** has a *delfinario* with dolphin shows, and anyone with a love of flora will find fascination in the **Jardín Botánico Soledad.** By following the scenic southern coast road, you can use Cienfuegos as a gateway for exploring the Sierra Escambray.

You'll need at least a week to see all the highlights, with two days for Cienfuegos, a day in the Sierra Escambray, one night in Santa Clara, at least one night in Remedios, and one or two days in the Cayos de Villa Clara.

Santa Clara and Cienfuegos are served by Víazul buses, and Santa Clara is a stop for Havana-Santiago de Cuba trains.

Cienfuegos and Vicinity

CIENFUEGOS

Cienfuegos (pop. 105,000), 340 kilometers east of Havana and 69 kilometers southwest of Santa Clara, lies on the east side of the Bahía de Cienfuegos, a deep, 88-square-kilometer bay with an umbilical entrance. It's Cuba's third-largest port.

Cienfuegos means "100 fires" but citizens call their town La Perla del Sur (The Pearl of the South). The city's appeal lies partly in the French flavor of its colonial hub, with a wide Parisian-style boulevard and elegant colonnades and an ambience that inspired Benny Moré, the celebrated Cuban *sonoro,* to sing, "Cienfuegos is the city I like best." Not least, it has a swinging nightlife and tremendous *casas particulares.*

Orientation

Approaching from the Autopista, the highway enters the city from the north and becomes a broad boulevard, the Paseo del Prado (Calle 37), the city's main thoroughfare leading to the historic core, called Pueblo Nuevo. Parque Martí, the main plaza, is four blocks west of the Prado and reached via Avenidas 54 and 56. Avenida 54 (El Bulevar), the principal shopping street, is pedestrian-only.

At Avenida 46, the Prado becomes the Malecón, a wide seafront boulevard stretching south one kilometer along a narrow peninsula ending at Punta Gorda, a once-exclusive residential district that recalls 1950s North American suburbia, with Detroit classics still parked in the driveways of mid-20th-century homes.

The city is laid out in a grid: Even-numbered *calles* run north-south, crossing odd-numbered *avenidas* running east-west. A six-lane highway, the *circunvalación,* bypasses the city.

History

Columbus supposedly discovered the bay in 1494. Shortly after the Spanish settled Cuba and established their trade restrictions, the bay developed a thriving smuggling trade. Sir Francis Drake and Henry Morgan were among the privateers who visited for plunder. Construction of a fortress, **Castillo de Jagua,** was begun in 1738 to protect the bay and to police smuggling. It wasn't until 1817 that Louis D'Clouet, a French émigré from Louisiana, devised a settlement scheme that he presented to Don José Cienfuegos, the

Cienfuegos

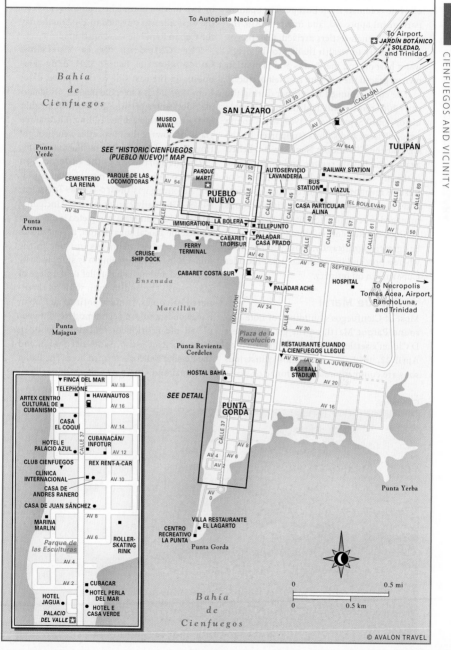

To Autopista Nacional

To Airport,
JARDÍN BOTÁNICO SOLEDAD,
and Trinidad

Bahía de Cienfuegos

MUSEO NAVAL

SAN LÁZARO

AV 70
(CALZADA)
64
AV
AV 64A
TULIPÁN

SEE "HISTORIC CIENFUEGOS (PUEBLO NUEVO)" MAP

Punta Verde

CEMENTERIO LA REINA

PARQUE DE LAS LOCOMOTORAS

PARQUE MARTÍ
AV 58
AV 54
CALLE 37
AUTOSERVICIO LAVANDERÍA
RAILWAY STATION
PUEBLO NUEVO
CALLE 41
CALLE 45
BUS STATION
VIAZUL
(EL BOULEVAR)
CALLE 65
CALLE 69

CALLE 21
AV 48
Punta Arenas

IMMIGRATION
LA BOLERA
TELEPUNTO
CASA PARTICULAR ALINA
CALLE 49
CALLE 53
CALLE 57
CALLE 61
AV 50

FERRY TERMINAL
CABARET TROPISUR
PALADAR CASA PRADO
CALLE 37
AV 46

CRUISE SHIP DOCK
CABARET COSTA SUR
AV 42
AV 38
AV 5 DE SEPTIEMBRE

Ensenada
PALADAR ACHÉ
HOSPITAL
To Necropolis Tomás Acea, Airport, RanchoLuna, and Trinidad

Marcillán
(MALECÓN)
32
AV 34
CALLE 45
AV 30

Punta Majagua

Punta Revienta Cordeles

Plaza de la Revolución
RESTAURANTE CUANDO A CIENFUEGOS LLEGUÉ
AV 26 (AV. DE LA JUVENTUD)
BASEBALL STADIUM
AV 20

HOSTAL BAHÍA

SEE DETAIL

PUNTA GORDA
CALLE 37
AV 16
AV 8
AV 4 AV 6
AV 2

Punta Yerba

AV 0

VILLA RESTAURANTE EL LAGARTO
CENTRO RECREATIVO LA PUNTA
Punta Gorda

Bahía de Cienfuegos

0   0.5 mi
0   0.5 km

Detail inset

FINCA DEL MAR
AV 18
TELEPHONE
ARTEX CENTRO CULTURAL DE CUBANISMO
HAVANAUTOS
AV 16
CASA EL COQUI
AV 14
HOTEL E PALACIO AZUL
CUBANACÁN/ INFOTUR
AV 12
CLUB CIENFUEGOS
REX RENT-A-CAR
CLÍNICA INTERNACIONAL
AV 10
CASA DE ANDRES RANERO
CASA DE JUAN SÁNCHEZ
AV 8
MARINA MARLIN
AV 6
ROLLER-SKATING RINK
CALLE 37
Parque de las Esculturas
AV 4
AV 2
CUBACAR
HOTEL JAGUA
HOTEL PERLA DEL MAR
PALACIO DEL VALLE
HOTEL E CASA VERDE

© AVALON TRAVEL

Spanish captain-general: The Spanish government would pay for the transportation of white colonists from Europe. The Spanish parliament approved, and in April 1819, the first 137 French settlers arrived. Cienfuegos grew rapidly to wealth thanks to the deep-water harbor, and merchants and plantation owners graced the city with a surfeit of stucco.

The city continued to prosper during the early 20th century and had an unremarkable history until September 5, 1957, when young naval officers and sailors (supported by the CIA) at the Cienfuegos Naval Base rebelled against the Batista regime and took control of the city's military installations. Members of Castro's revolutionary 26th of July Movement and students joined them. Batista's troops managed to recapture the city by nightfall.

Since the Revolution, the city's hinterland has grown significantly, mostly to the west, where a port and industrial complex includes Cuba's main oil refinery.

★ Parque Martí

Most of Cienfuegos's buildings of note surround Parque Martí, on the ground where D'Clouet's settlers proclaimed the town on April 22, 1819. The city's most illustrious sons are commemorated in bronze or stone.

Pinning the park is a statue of José Martí, while the east entrance of the park is guarded by two marble lions. The triumphal arch on the west side was unveiled in 1902 on the day the Cuban Republic was constituted.

The **Catedral de la Purísima Concepción** (tel. 043/52-5297, daily 7am-noon), on the east side of the square, dates from 1870. It has a splendid interior, with marble floors and a pristine gilt Corinthian altar beneath a Gothic vaulted ceiling. The stained glass windows of the 12 apostles were brought from France following the revolution of 1789.

On the north side is the **Colegio San Lorenzo,** a handsome neoclassical building. Adjoining it is **Teatro Tomás Terry** (tel. 043/51-3361, daily 9am-6pm, CUC2 including guide, CUC5 cameras), completed in 1895 and named for a local sugar baron, a Venezuelan who had arrived penniless in Cuba in the mid-1800s. The proscenium is sumptuously decorated and has a bas-relief centerpiece of Dionysius. The auditorium, with its three-tiered balconies, is made entirely of Cuban hardwoods and can accommodate 900 people in old-fashioned, fold-down wooden seats. Enrico Caruso, Sarah Bernhardt, and the Bolshoi Ballet performed here. The Ballet Nacional and Ópera de Cuba still perform,

Cienfuegos

bringing the bats from their hiding places to swoop over the heads of the audience.

On the west side, the **Casa de la Cultura** (Calle 25 #5403, tel. 043/51-6584, daily 8:30am-midnight, free) occupies the dilapidated Palacio Ferrer, an eclectically styled former mansion of sugar baron José Ferrer Sirés.

The former Spanish Club (the initials CE, inset in the pavement, stand for Club Español), on the south side, dates from 1898 and now houses the **Museo Histórico Provincial** (Av. 54 #2702, esq. Calle 27, tel. 043/51-9722, Tues.-Sat. 10am-5pm, Sun. 9am-1pm, CUC2). It displays a modest assortment of antiques, plus an archaeological room honoring the indigenous people of the Americas. Fifty meters east is the **Primer Palacio,** now the Poder Popular, the local government headquarters.

Kitty-corner to the Poder Popular is the **Casa del Fundador** (Av. 54, esq. 29, tel. 043/55-2144, Mon.-Sat. 9am-5:30pm, Sun. 9am-12:30pm, CUC1), the former home of city founder Louis D'Clouet.

Paseo del Prado and Malecón

Calle 37—the Prado—is lined with a central median with plaques and busts honoring illustrious citizens, including a life-size bronze figure of Benny Moré (esq. Av. 54). Note the

Casa de los Leones (e/ 58 y 60), an old mansion guarded by two life-size bronze lions.

The **Club Cienfuegos** (Calle 37, e/ Av. 8 y 12, tel. 043/52-6510, free), a baroque building erected in 1920, served for decades as the yacht club. The lobby exhibits antique silver trophies and other yachting memorabilia. One block south, at the tip of the peninsula, a cultural park exhibits avant-garde sculptures.

Cienfuegos's architectural pride and joy is **Palacio del Valle** (Calle 37, esq. Av. 2, tel. 043/51-1003, ext. 812, daily 10am-11pm) at the tip of Punta Gorda. This architectural stunner—now a restaurant of the Hotel Jagua—originated as a modest home for a trader, Celestino Caceres. It passed out of his hands and was given as a wedding present to a member of the local Valle family, who added to it in Mogul style, with carved floral motifs, cupped arches, bulbous cupolas, and delicate arabesques in alabaster. Note the mural of the Magi on the Carrara marble staircase. Two other rooms are in gauche English Gothic and Louis XIV style. A spiral staircase deposits you at a rooftop *mirador* (CUC2, free after 5pm).

Necrópolis Tomás Acea

This cemetery (Av. 5 de Septiembre, tel.

Parque Martí, Cienfuegos

043/52-5257, daily 9am-5pm, free, CUC1 guide), two kilometers east of town on the road to Rancho Luna, has impressive neo-classical structures and tombs. The main structure is inspired by Athens's Parthenon. It is entered via a gate supported by 64 Doric columns.

Cementerio La Reina

Anyone with a morbid fascination for graveyards, or a love of baroque architecture, might find this evocative and derelict Carrara marble **cemetery** (Av. 50 y Calle 7, daily 7am-7pm, free) appealing. The walls contain tombs of soldiers from the War of Independence. Most tombs are caved in, with the skeletons open to view. Take Avenida 48 west, then turn right.

Four antique steam trains are preserved at the **Parque de los Locomotoras** on Calle 19 (esq. Av. 54).

Museo Histórico Naval

The excellent **Museo Histórico Naval** (Calle 21, e/ 60 y 62, tel. 043/51-6617, Tues.-Sat. 10am-6pm, Sat.-Sun. 9am-1pm, CUC1 including guide, CUC1 cameras), in the former navy headquarters, is worth a visit for its model ships, colonial armory, and nautical miscellany. It was here in 1957 that naval officers rebelled against the Batista regime.

Entertainment and Events

The **Festival Internacional de Música Benny Moré** (tel. 043/51-8783, www.festivalbennymore.azurina.cult.cu) is held every other year (no set month). A local band plays a free show on Thursday (3pm) in Parque Martí and on Sunday (3pm) on the Prado.

The **Teatro Tomás Terry** (tel. 043/51-1772, box office 9am-6pm and 90 minutes prior to performances, CUC1-10), on Parque Martí, hosts performances ranging from classical symphony to live salsa music. The **Cantores de Cienfuegos** (tel. 5343-6214, www.cantoresdecienfuegos.com) choral group is not to be missed, if they're performing here or at other venues. So, too, the **Orquesta Cámara Concierto Sur** (tel. 5270-3533, enmeerl@yahoo.es), and the astounding **Orquesta de Guitarra,** which frequently performs at the Hotel Jagua. Check with the Paradiso Cultural Agency (Av. 54 #3301, tel. 5287-5336, paradise@sccfg.artex.cu) for a schedule. And be sure to attend any performance of the children's theatrical group **La Colmenita** (Calle 41 #1803, e/ 18 y 20, Punta Gorda, tel. 043/52-6984).

Palacio del Valle, Cienfuegos

Historic Cienfuegos

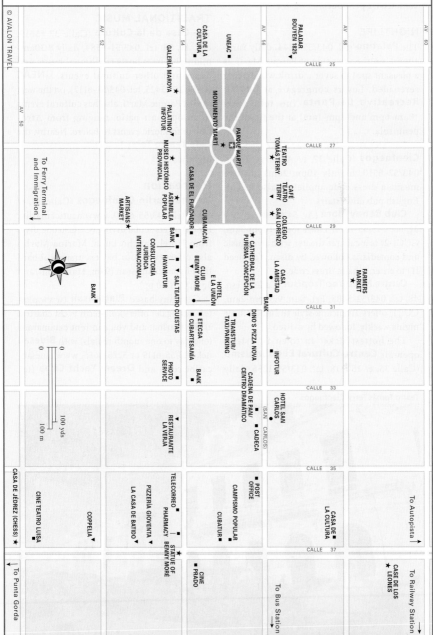

© AVALON TRAVEL

To Ferry Terminal and Immigration

AV 60
AV 58
AV 56
AV 54
AV 52
AV 50

PALADAR BOUYEN 1825 ▼

CASA DE LA CULTURA ■

UNEAC ■

GALERIA MAROYA ★

PALATINO/INFOTUR ▼

MUSEO HISTÓRICO PROVINCIAL ★

ARTISANS MARKET ★

ASEMBLEA POPULAR ■

CONSULTORIA JURÍDICA INTERNACIONAL ■

HAVANATUR ■

SAL TEATRO CUESTAS ■

BANK ■

BANK ■

MONUMENTO MARTÍ

PARQUE MARTÍ

CASA DE EL FUNDADOR ■

CUBANACAN ■

CLUB BENNY MORÉ ▼

CATHEDRAL DE LA PURÍSIMA CONCEPCIÓN ★

HOTEL E LA UNIÓN ●

TEATRO TOMÁS TERRY ■

CAFÉ TEATRO TERRY ▼

COLEGIO SAN LORENZO ★

CASA LA AMISTAD ■

BANK ■

DINO'S PIZZA NOVA ▼

CADENA DE PAN/CENTRO DRAMÁTICO ■

TRANSTUR/TAXI/PARKING ■

ETECSA ■

CUBARTESANIA ■

BANK ■

INFOTUR ■

FARMERS MARKET ★

HOTEL SAN CARLOS ■

CADECA ■

PHOTO SERVICE ■

RESTAURANTE LA VERJA ▼

POST OFFICE ■

CAMPISMO POPULAR ■

CUBATUR ■

CASA DE JEDREZ (CHESS) ★

CINE TEATRO LUISA ▼

COPPELIA ▼

TELECORREO ■

PHARMACY ■

PIZZERIA GIOVENTA ▼

LA CASA DE BATIDO ▼

STATUE OF BENNY MORÉ ▼

CINE PRADO ■

CASA DE LA CULTURA ■

CASE DE LOS LEONES ★

CALLE 25
CALLE 27
CALLE 29
CALLE 31
CALLE 33
CALLE 35
(SAN CARLOS)
CALLE 37

0   100 yds
0   100 m

To Punta Gorda
To Autopista
To Railway Station
To Bus Station

For bowling or billiards, head to **La Bolera** (Calle 37, esq. 48, tel. 043/55-1379, daily 11am-2am, CUC2 per hour).

NIGHTLIFE

The **Palatino** (tel. 043/55-1244, daily 9am-10pm), on the west side of Parque Martí, is a pleasant spot to savor a drink while being serenaded. Lovers congregate at **Centro Recreativo La Punta** (no tel., daily 10am-6pm and 8pm-1am) at the tip of the peninsula.

For elegance, the terrace bar of **Club Cienfuegos** (Calle 37, e/ Av. 8 y 12, tel. 043/52-6510, nightly 10pm-2am) has live music; a dress code applies. It also has an English pub downstairs.

Club Benny Moré (Av. 54 #2904, e/ 29 y 31, tel. 043/55-1674, Thurs.-Sun. 10pm-3am, CUC1-2) is a cabaret theater with live music and comedians, followed by disco. You need ID to enter; it has a dress code.

Centro Nocturno Tropisur (Calle 37, esq. 48, tel. 043/52-5488, Fri.-Sun. 9:30pm-2am, CUC1) offers Tropicana-style titillation three nights weekly, followed by a disco.

The hottest ticket in town is Artex's open-air **Centro Cultural El Cubanismo** (Calle 35, e/ 16 y 18, tel. 043/55-1255, daily 9pm-2am), with a live music medley that draws locals.

TRADITIONAL MUSIC

The **Casa de la Cultura** (Calle 37 #5615, esq. Av. 58, tel. 043/51-6584, daily 8:30am-midnight, free) hosts traditional music and dance and other cultural events. **UNEAC** (Calle 25 #5425, tel. 043/51-6117), on the west side of Parque Martí, also has cultural events in an open-air patio, ranging from Afro-Cuban folkloric events to *bolero*. Nearby, the **Café Teatro Terry** hosts live entertainment nightly.

Recreation

Marina Marlin Cienfuegos (Calle 35, e/ 6 y 8, tel. 043/55-6120, www.nauticamarlin.tur.cu) offers scuba diving (CUC30 one dive) from Hotel Rancho Luna. Marina Marlin also offers two-hour bay excursions aboard the *Flipper* catamaran (9am, 11am, 2pm, and 5pm, CUC10 pp).

Germany-based **Plattensail** (www.platten-sailing.de) offers long-term yacht charters at the marina, and you can rent catamarans (one-day to one-month rentals) with **Bluesail** (tel. 043/55-6119 or 5285-8685, www.bluesail-caribe.com) and **Dream Yacht Cuba** (tel.

Teatro Tomás Terry, Cienfuegos

5391-4274, www.dreamyachtcharter.com) at **Club Cienfuegos** (Calle 37, e/ Av. 8 y 12, tel. 043/52-6510, daily 10pm-2am). However, you must book the excursions *prior* to arriving in Cuba. The club grounds also have a beautiful public swimming pool (daily 11am-6pm, CUC3, or CUC10 with drinks), plus crazy cars (*carros locos*, CUC0.50), go-karts (CUC1), and tennis.

The gym at the **Hotel La Unión** (Av. 54 y Calle 31, tel. 043/55-1020) is open to the public. **Estadio 5 de Septiembre** (Av. 20, e/ 45 y 55, tel. 043/51-3644) hosts baseball games October-May.

Shopping

Galería Maroya (Av. 54 #2506, tel. 043/55-1208, Mon.-Sat. 9am-6pm, Sun. 9am-1pm), on the west side of Parque Martí, has a splendid collection of arts and crafts. Several galleries have opened along the Prado.

Food

Paladares abound. For outdoor ambience, head to ★ **El Lagarto** (Calle 35 #4B, e/ Av. 0 y Litoral, tel. 043/51-9966), at the tip of Punta Gorda. The fixed-price dinner (CUC18) includes bruschetta with garlic tomato, followed by salad and soup, fruit plate, and a choice of lobster, shrimp, chicken, or pork.

★ **Finca del Mar** (Calle 35 e/ 18 y 20, tel. 043/52-6598), on the bay shore drive, is one of the top *paladares* outside Havana. I love its stylish open-air setup with shade umbrellas. Groups typically sit in an air-conditioned salon. Service is excellent and the diverse menu boasts some international flavors. I enjoyed fried garbanzo (CUC6), seafood carpaccio with olive oil and basil (CUC6), and lamb with herbs and olive oil (CUC14.50). The icing on the cake is the large-screen TV playing subdued live-music DVDs of Stevie Wonder, the Stones, or Elton John. Reservations are a must!

Despite its windowless, somewhat claustrophobic space, **Casa Prado** (Calle 37 #4626 e/ 46 y 48, tel. 5262-3858, www.casapradorestaurant.com, daily 11:30am-10:30pm) is hugely popular with locals, budget travelers, and tour groups alike. It serves well-executed *criolla* staples, plus paellas and pizza. Immediately south of the Hotel Jagua is **Pelicano** (Av. 0 #3506-B altos, e/ 35 y 37, tel. 5377-1351, pelicano@nauta.cu, Wed.-Mon. noon-3pm and 6pm-11pm), with open-air upstairs terrace dining and the usual *criolla* favori]tes.

Hotel Jagua's **Palacio de Valle** (Calle 37, e/ 0 y 2, tel. 043/55-1003, ext. 812, daily 10am-10pm) is a must if only for the remarkable

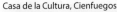

Casa de la Cultura, Cienfuegos

ambience. It has a large seafood menu, including lobster (CUC15), though dishes disappoint. Far better, however, is the restaurant's **Los Laureles,** where a superb suckling pig roast buffet is offered in the garden beneath a giant fig tree.

Coppelia (Calle 37, esq. 52, Tues.-Sun. 11am-11pm) is good for ice cream (pesos only). For an espresso or cappuccino head to the **Café Teatro Terry** (daily 9am-10pm) on Parque Martí. Delicious fresh fruit *batidos* (shakes) will help you beat the heat at **La Casa del Batido** (Av. 37, e/ 52 y 54, daily 9am-10pm).

Accommodations
CASAS PARTICULARES
Cienfuegos has scores of excellent room rentals. Many are in Punta Gorda, where noise from El Cubanismo disco (Thurs.-Sun.) can cause insomnia.

A wonderful downtown option, **Casa La Amistad** (Av. 56 #2927, e/ 29 y 31, tel. 043/51-6143, casamistad@correodecuba.com, CUC20-25), one block east of Parque Martí, is upstairs in a creaky colonial home. The two simple rooms share a bathroom. It's not luxe, but you're here to share with the welcoming hosts who gets rave reviews.

Book early to snag a room at Omar and Diana's remarkable ★ **Hostal Bahía** (Av. 20 #3502 altos, esq. 35, tel. 043/52-6598, hostalbahia@yahoo.es, CUC35-40) in Punta Gorda. It has a shaded bay-view balcony and a 40-inch plasma TV in the cross-ventilated lounge. Modern art adorns the walls. The owners run the superb Finca del Mar *paladar,* adjacent.

Of the many 1950s modernist homes, my favorite is ★ **Casa de Juan Sánchez** (Av. 8 #3703, e/ 37 y 39, tel. 043/51-7986, CUC30 including breakfast), with original furnishings and heaps of stained glass. The lounge connects to a garden with shade trees. Its single spacious room is well lit and cross-ventilated, with a large handsome bathroom.

I've always enjoyed staying with Alina at **Hostal D'Carmen Alina** (Av. 54 #4923,

e/ 49 y 51, tel. 043/51-9056 or 5337-8499, alieli1996@hayoo.es, CUC25). She has three rooms with private bathrooms and private entrance; one has a kitchen. Filling meals can be enjoyed.

HOTELS
A shortage of hotel space means rates are exorbitant relative to standards. Gran Caribe's **Hostal E Palacio Azul** (Calle 37 #1201, e/ 12 y 14, tel. 043/55-5829, reserva@union.cfg.tur.cu, CUC71 s, CUC106 low season, CUC81 s, CUC135 d high season, including breakfast) offers seven huge rooms with high ceilings and colonial tile floors in a restored mansion on the Malecón. It has a charming little bar and restaurant and the staff is friendly.

★ **Hotel La Unión** (Av. 54 y Calle 31, tel. 043/55-1020, reserva@union.cfg.tur.cu, CUC74 s, CUC118 d low season, CUC98 s, CUC157 d high season), one block east of Parque Martí, is a beautifully restored neoclassical re-creation of a 19th-century hotel. It has 49 rooms (11 are junior suites, 2 are suites, 1 is a signature suite) arrayed around a courtyard. The open-air pool has a Romanesque setting, and you get a sauna, whirlpool tub, gym, business center, and commendable restaurant.

Popular with tour groups, Gran Caribe's high-rise 1950s modernist-era **Hotel Jagua** (Calle 37, e/ 0 y 2, tel. 043/55-1003, reservas@jagua.gca.tur.cu, CUC78 s, CUC126 d low season, CUC98 s, CUC160 d high season) boasts 149 large rooms plus 13 poolside *cabinas.* You get more facilities than at the other hotels, including a swimming pool. At press time, it was due to be managed by Meliá.

The green 1930s-era mansion opposite the Hotel Jagua is today the eight-room **Hotel E Casa Verde** (c/o Hotel Jagua, CUC75 s, CUC92 d). It's up to European standards with its gracious furnishings, plasma TVs, and mobile phones. Two rooms have king beds. It has a pool with snack bar, and buffet lunch and dinner.

The ★ **Hotel Perla del Mar** (c/o Hotel Jagua, CUC86 s, CUC128 d low season,

CUC102 s, CUC170 d high season) is a modernist 1950s waterfront mansion that has been restored with finesse as a nine-room boutique hotel. It is furnished with chic contemporary style in an olive-and-cream color scheme, and it has silent air-conditioning and flat-screen TVs.

A last resort is the overpriced **Hotel Islazul Punta La Cueva** (Carretera a Rancho Luna, Km 3.5 y Circunlavación, tel. 043/57-3952, www.islazul.cu, CUC33 s, CUC50 d low season, CUC63 s, CUC71 d high season), east of town. None of its 67 rooms even have windows.

The lodging scene should improve with the opening of the **Hotel San Carlos** (Av. 56 e/ 33 y 35), a six-story eclectic-style former hotel dating from 1925 that was being brought back to life at press time. Gran Caribe will manage the 48-room property. The roof garden—the tallest point in the city—promises fantastic views.

Several other boutique hotels—the 22-room **Hotel E Ciervo de Oro,** 24-room **Hotel E Bristol,** 28-room **Hotel E Palacio de Ferrer,** and 12-room **Hotel E Fernandina**—are planned, as is a 100-room hotel (**Villa Náutica Residencial**) at the to-be-expanded marina.

Information and Services

Infotur (Av. 56, e/ 31 y 33, and Calle 37, esq. 18, tel. 043/51-4653, daily 8am-5pm) has tour bureaus at the Casa del Fundador, on the east side of Parque Martí. The following companies sell guided excursions, including a city tour (CUC10): **Cubanacán** (Av. 54, e/ 29 y 31, tel. 043/55-1680), **Cubatur** (Calle 37, e/ 54 y 56, tel. 043/55-1242), and **Havanatur** (Av. 54 #2906, e/ 29 y 31, tel. 043/51-1639).

The **post office** is at Avenida 54 and Calle 35, but the *telecorreo* (Av. 54 #3514, tel. 043/55-6102) has DHL service. **Etecsa** (Av. 54, e/ 35 y 37, daily 8am-7:30pm) has international phone and Internet service. Public Wi-Fi zones include Parque Martí, Parque Villuendas, and El Rápido complex (Malecón y 26).

Banks include **Banco Financiero Internacional** (Av. 54 y Calle 29, Mon.-Fri. 8am-3pm), on the southeast corner of Parque Martí, and **Bandec** (Av. 56 y Calle 31). **Cadeca** (Av. 56, e/ 33 y 35) also converts foreign currency for pesos.

The **Clínica Internacional** (Av. 10, e/ 37 y 39, tel. 043/55-1622) has a pharmacy, as does the Hotel 242. The **Consultoría Jurídica Internacional** (Av. 54 #2904, e/ 29 y 31, tel. 043/55-1572) provides legal services.

Getting There and Away

AIR

Aeropuerto Internacional Jaime González (tel. 043/55-2047) is three kilometers east of downtown. A taxi into town will cost about CUC10. In 2016, **American Airlines** (tel. 800/433-7300, www.aa.com) launched daily scheduled service from Miami; **Silver Airways** (tel. 801/401-9100, www.silverairways.com) initiated five weekly flights from Fort Lauderdale.

BUS

The bus terminal (Calle 49, e/ Av. 56 y 58) is six blocks east of the Prado. **Víazul** (tel. 043/51-5720, www.viazul.com) buses link Cienfuegos to Havana, Trinidad, Varadero (via Bay of Pigs), and Santa Clara. The slightly dysfunctional **Cubanacán Conectando** service offered by Cubanacán (Av. 54, e/ 29 y 31, tel. 043/55-1680, www.viajescubanacan.cu) competes with Víazul using Transtur tour buses.

TRAIN

The **train station** (Calle 49, e/ Av. 58 y 60, tel. 043/52-5495) is one block north of the bus station. At last visit, trains departed Cienfuegos for Havana at 7am (CUC11), for Santa Clara at 4am (CUC2.10, second class only), and for Sancti Spíritus at 2pm. You can also catch an *especial* from Havana to Santa Clara and then connect to Cienfuegos, which lies at the end of a branch line off the main Havana-Santiago railroad. At press time, train #73 departed Havana's Estación 19 de Noviembre for Cienfuegos at 7:15am, from Santa Clara at 5:40pm, and from Sancti Spíritus at 3:53pm.

SEA

Marina Marlin Cienfuegos (Calle 35, e/ 6 y 8, tel. 043/55-1699, www.nauticamarlin.tur. cu) has moorings for 30 yachts.

Getting Around

Bus #9 runs the length of Calle 37 (10 centavos), as do horse-crawn *coches* and *bici-taxis* (CUC2-5). **Cubataxi** (Av. 50 #3508, esq. 37, tel. 043/51-9145) charges CUC3 between the Hotel Jagua and downtown. Rent cars from **Cubacar,** which has three locations (Hotel La Unión, tel. 043/55-1700; Calle 37 y Av. 18, tel. 043/55-1211; and Hotel Jagua, tel. 043/55-2166). There are gas stations at Calle 37 (e/ Av. 18), about 10 kilometers east of town on the road to Rancho Luna, and at the north end of Calle 37, at the entrance to town.

★ JARDÍN BOTÁNICO SOLEDAD AND PEPITO TEY

This splendid **arboretum** (tel. 043/54-5115, Mon.-Thurs. 8am-5pm, Fri.-Sun. 8am-4:30pm, CUC5, guide CUC10) is about 10 kilometers east of Cienfuegos, on the road to Trinidad. It was begun in 1899 by a New Englander, Edward Atkins, who owned sugar estates in the area and brought in Harvard botanists to develop more productive sugarcane strains. Later, Harvard University assumed control under a 99-year lease, and a general collection making up one of the tropical world's finest botanical gardens was amassed. Since the Revolution, the arboretum has been maintained by the Cuban Academy of Science's Institute of Botany.

Pathways lead through the 94-hectare garden, reached along an avenue of royal palms. It harbors some 1,490 species, 70 percent of which are exotics. A bamboo collection has 23 species. Of rubber trees, there are 89 species; of cactus, 400. The prize collection is the 245 varieties of palms. The facility has a café and

restaurant, and well-versed bilingual guides give informative tours.

The avenue of royal palms extends south to the former sugar-processing community of **Pepito Tey.** A stroll around this village, which is an educational center, is a fascinating study in how the Communist state has attempted to employ former sugarcane workers.

The bus from Cienfuegos to Cumanayagua passes the garden. A taxi from Cienfuegos will cost about CUC40 round-trip. Tour agencies in Cienfuegos offer tours (CUC10).

PLAYA RANCHO LUNA AND VICINITY

About 15 kilometers southeast of Cienfuegos, the pleasant beach of Playa Rancho Luna hosts some small resort hotels used by package tour groups. The coast road swings west past the **Faro Luna** lighthouse and follows the rocky coast eight kilometers to **Pasacaballo,** facing the Castillo de Jagua across the 400-meter-wide mouth of Cienfuegos Bay, 22 kilometers from Cienfuegos.

See it now, as the area is slated to be developed in a $580 million deal with a Spanish company, with twin golf courses, several hotels, and up to 3,000 villa-condos for sale to foreigners.

Recreation

There are better beaches in Cuba than Playa Rancho Luna. The main draw is the **Delfinario** (tel. 043/54-8120, Thurs.-Tues. 8:30am-4pm, CUC10 adults, CUC6 children), an enclosed lagoon offering dolphin shows at 10am and 2pm. You can kiss the dolphins (CUC10) and swim with them (CUC50 adults, CUC33 children).

Scuba diving is offered at the **Club Amigo Rancho Luna** (Km 18, tel. 043/54-8087). At least eight ships lie amid the coral reefs. You can rent catamarans and pedal boats through **Villa Rancho Luna** (tel. 045/54-8189), a simple beachfront restaurant (daily 9am-9pm).

Refugio Guanaroca Punta Gavilán (Carretera Cienfuegos-Rancho Luna, Km 12, tel. 043/54-8019 or 043/54-8117), 12 kilometers from Cienfuegos, protects a flock of about 50 young flamingos that migrate from Zapata and the Río Máximo zone off the north coast of Camagüey province. The refuge offers birding tours (CUC10) at 8am and 11:30am by boat on Laguna Guanaroca, reached by hiking a 1.5-kilometer trail. It has a café.

Food and Accommodations

There are several private rentals at Rancho Luna, including **Casa Isidro Vera León** (tel. 5275-7090, isidrovera@nauta.cu, CUC20-25), a lovely two-story home with four simply appointed rooms with modern bathrooms.

Farther west, and doubling as a *paladar*, the **Hostal El Farito** (Carretera de Pasacaballo, Km 18, Playa Rancho Luna, tel. 043/54-8044, CUC35-40) enjoys a breeze-swept position on the cliffs 100 meters east of the lighthouse. English-speaking owner José Piñeiro prepares Cuban cuisine served beneath an arbor. The home abounds in antiques and modern furnishings. Five modestly furnished, cross-ventilated rooms include a two-bedroom apartment; some rooms have metal-frame antique beds.

Gran Caribe's all-inclusive **Hola Club Rancho Luna** (Carretera de Rancho Luna, Km 18, tel. 043/54-8012, www.gran-caribe.cu, CUC75 s, CUC105 d low season, CUC100 s, CUC145 d high season) is a staple of Canadian and European tour groups. Boasting lively tropical pastels and rattan furnishings, it's a noisy, unsophisticated beach resort with canned entertainment and dismal food. It has 222 nicely furnished rooms and water sports.

The more intimate 46-room **Hotel Faro Luna** (tel. 043/54-8030, reservas@ranluna.cfg.tur.cu, CUC62 s, CUC86 d), run by Gran Caribe, offers spacious modern rooms with cable TV.

The overpriced Soviet-style **Hotel Pasacaballo** (Carretera de Rancho Luna, Km 22, tel. 043/59-2100, www.islazul.cu, CUC42 s, CUC60 d low season, CUC79 s, CUC90 d high season, including meals) is out on a limb atop cliffs on the east side of the bay. I like its stylish modernist interior, despite its ugly exterior and mishmash furnishings; some rooms have king beds. Check out the tiny museum honoring Benny Moré—**Salón Alma Mía**—on the ground floor. Beware of the dangerous step on the lobby staircase.

The road past Hotel Pasacaballo ends at La Milpa, a hamlet where local fishers make seafood meals. Also nearby is **Paladar Playa Las Dunas** (tel. 5220-3264, daily noon-10pm), serving seafood meals for CUC8 on a bayfront patio.

Getting There

A taxi from Cienfuegos costs about CUC12. Ferries leave Cienfuegos for Pasacaballo on a regular basis from the terminal at Avenida 46 and Calle 25 (CUC1).

FORTALEZA DE NUESTRA SEÑORA DE JAGUA

Across the bay from Pasacaballo, a restored 17th-century Spanish fort, the **Fortaleza de Nuestra Señora de Jagua** (tel. 043/96-5402, Tues.-Sat. 9am-5pm, Sun. 9am-1pm, entrance CUC1, cameras CUC1) guards the entrance to the Bahía de Cienfuegos. The original fortress was expanded in the 18th century to defend against the English Royal Navy. Two Ordoñez cannons guard the entrance of the fort, which overlooks a fishing village from its perch above the water. At midnight, a ghost—the Blue Lady—is said to haunt the building.

Up on the hill behind Jagua is **Ciudad Nuclear** (Nuclear City), a modern city built in the 1980s to house workers constructing Cuba's first nuclear power station nearby at Juragua. The half-completed reactor, about two kilometers west of town, stands idle. Construction began in 1983, when Soviet aid flowed freely. The facility was mothballed in 1992.

Getting There

Passenger ferries depart Cienfuegos (Av. 46 and Calle 25) at 8am, 1pm, and 5pm (30 minutes, CUC1). Ferries also link Jagua and Pasacaballo six times daily.

SANTA ISABEL DE LAS LAJAS AND VICINITY

Famed musician Benny Moré (1919-1963) was born in the village of Santa Isabel de las Lasas, eight kilometers north of the town of Cruces (30 kilometers northeast of Cienfuegos), and he is buried in the town cemetery. The **Museo Municipal** (Calle Dr. Machín #99, e/ Martí y Calixto García, lajaz@azurina.cult.cu, Tues.-Sat. 10am-6pm, Sun. 9am-1pm) pays homage to the crooner considered Cuba's most influential musician of his era. The **Festival Internacional de Música Benny Moré** is held here every other December.

Palmira, midway between Cienfuegos and Cruce, has deep Afro-Cuban roots and is a center for Santería, as told in its **Museo Municipal** (Villuendas #41, e/ Cisneros y Agramonte, tel. 043/54-4533, Tues.-Sat. 10am-6pm, Sun. 9am-1pm, CUC1), on the main plaza.

THE CIRCUITO SUR

The Circuito Sur coast road dips and rises east of Cienfuegos, with the Sierra Escambray to the north. Beaches lie hidden at the mouths of rivers that wash down from the hills. **Hacienda La Vega** (Km 52, tel. 043/55-1126, daily 9am-6pm), about three kilometers west of Playa Inglés, is a cattle farm (*vaquería*) where horseback riding is offered (CUC5 per hour) and demonstrations of traditional farm life are given. A roadside restaurant serves snacks and *criolla* fare. Lather up with insect repellent!

Crossing the **Río Yaguanabo,** 53 kilometers from Cienfuegos, you pass into Sancti Spíritus Province. Immediately beyond the river, a giant shrimp stands over the road, marking the **Camaronera Yaguanabo** shrimp farm. At Kilometer 56 you can follow a rugged dirt track seven kilometers inland to **Finca Protegida Yaguanabo-Arriba,** also with horseback riding and guided birding in the foothills of the Sierra Escambray. The highlight is the **Monumento Nacional Cueva Martín Infierno,** a stupendous cavern that boasts the world's largest stalagmite (68 meters tall) as well as gypsum flowers (*flores de yeso*).

Food and Accommodations

★ **Villa Guajimico** (Carretera Cienfuegos-Trinidad, Km 42, tel. 042/54-0646, guajimico@enet.cu, CUC25 s, CUC43 d low season, CUC32 s, CUC49 d high season) sits over the mouth of the Río La Jutía. Some of the 51 air-conditioned brick cabins line a tiny white-sand beach in the river estuary. Others stairstep a hill where a swimming pool and restaurant offer spectacular views. It has scuba diving daily at 9am and 1:30pm, plus Hobie Cats.

Pleasing, but overpriced, the **Villa Yaguanabo** (Carretera a Trinidad, Km 55, tel. 042/54-1905, www.islazul.cu, CUC42 s, CUC60 d low season, CUC80 s, CUC93 d high season) has 34 rooms in cabins at the river mouth, with a pleasant restaurant and bar. For eats, you can't beat **Restaurante La Covacha,** a thatched *paladar* overlooking the Río Yaguanabo.

SIERRA ESCAMBRAY

The Sierra Escambray (officially the Sierra de Guamuhaya), Cuba's second-highest mountain range, lies mostly within Cienfuegos Province, descending gradually into Villa Clara Province to the north, edging into Sancti Spíritus Province to the east, and dropping steeply to the southern coast. The forested peaks are protected in Gran Parque Natural Topes de Collantes, in the southeast (in Sancti Spíritus), where most of the attractions are found.

In the late 1950s, these mountains were the site of a revolutionary front against Fulgencio Batista, led by Che Guevara. After the revolutionaries triumphed in 1959, the Escambray hid counterrevolutionaries who opposed Castro. The CIA helped finance and arm these resistance fighters, whom the Castro regime tagged "bandits." Castro formed counterinsurgency units called Battalions of Struggle Against Bandits, and forcibly evacuated campesinos to deny the anti-Castroites local support. The *bandidos* weren't eradicated until 1966.

Access from Cienfuegos is via the Circuito Sur and the community of **La Sierrita,** about 30 kilometers east of Cienfuegos; the road, badly deteriorated in places, continues to Topes de Collantes in Sancti Spíritus province. It's a stupendously scenic route that rises past sheer-walled, cave-riddled limestone *mogotes,* at their most impressive near the village of **San Blas,** eight kilometers east of La Sierrita. San Blas sits in the lee of great cliffs where huge stalactites and stalagmites are exposed in an open cave high atop the mountains.

★ El Nicho

El Nicho (tel. 043/43-3351, daily 8am-6pm, CUC10), a recreational site in the northern foothills of the Sierra Escambray, is popular for its spectacular waterfalls set amid ferns and forest. The **Sendero El Reino de las Aguas** trail leads from the entrance along the banks of the Río Hanabanillo for 1.5 kilometers to the 20-meter-tall cascade, from which waters then tumble down into a series of turquoise-colored pools good for swimming.

Simple meals are served at thatched **Restaurante El Helechón.** Alternatively, head to **Paladar El Orquidea** (tel. 5247-2289, mathalbe@yahoo.es), about 100 meters beyond the entrance to El Nicho.

El Nicho is reached via **Camanayagua,** 30 kilometers east of Cienfuegos; the turnoff is 3 kilometers farther east at El Mamey (on the Cumanayagua-Manicaragua road). You can reach the falls (14 km south from El Mamey) by ordinary sedan. You'll pass through the community of **El Jovero,** known for its Grupo Teatro de los Elementos theatrical group, as you snake towards the mountains. The place can get crowded with groups arriving by Soviet trucks from Topes de Collantes and Trinidad; if you're driving this route a 4WD vehicle is required.

You can take a bus to Cumanayagua or Manicuragua from either Cienfuegos or Santa Clara; a *colectivo* runs to El Nicho from Cumanayagua at 5am and 5pm. Excursions are offered from Cienfuegos, Santa Clara, and Trinidad.

Santa Clara and Vicinity

SANTA CLARA

Santa Clara (pop. 175,000), 300 kilometers east of Havana, is the provincial capital of Villa Clara. Straddling the Carretera Central and within five minutes of the Autopista, it is strategically located at the center of Cuba. The city was established within the confluence of the Ríos Bélico and Cubanicay in 1689, when residents of Remedios grew tired of constant pirate raids and moved inland. Later it functioned as a plum in Cuba's wars of independence. On December 28, 1958, Che Guevara's rebel army attacked the town and derailed a troop train carrying reinforcements and U.S. armaments bound for Oriente. Two days later, the rebel army captured the city, which became known as *el último reducto de la tiranía batistiana* (the last fortress of Batista's tyranny). Within 24 hours, the dictator fled the island.

Today Santa Clara is an industrial town and home to the **Universidad Central de las Villas** (www.uclv.edu.cu/en), where a small botanical garden is of modest interest.

Orientation

Santa Clara is laid out roughly in a rectilinear grid of one-way streets and encircled by a ring road (*circunvalación*). The Carretera Central enters from the west and arcs south around

Santa Clara

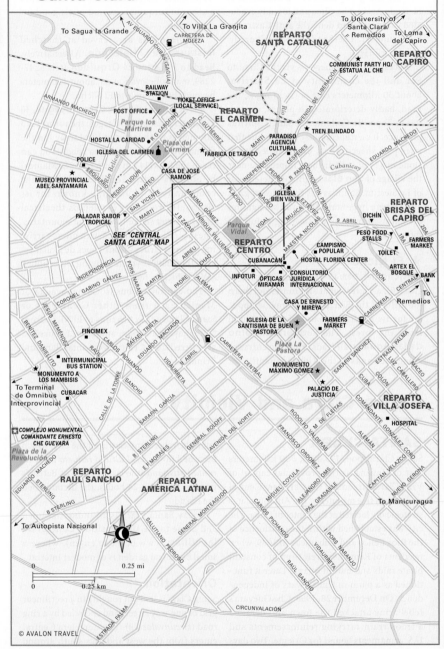

To Sagua la Grande

AV EDUARDO CHIBAS (SIGUA)

To Villa La Granjita
CARRETERA DE MOLEZA

To University of
Santa Clara/
Remedios

To Loma
del Capiro

REPARTO
SANTA CATALINA

REPARTO
CAPIRO

COMMUNIST PARTY HQ/
ESTATUA AL CHE

ARMANDO MACHEDO

RAILWAY
STATION

TICKET OFFICE
(LOCAL SERVICE)

POST OFFICE

R G GARÓFINO

CANYEDA

C. GUTIERREZ

REPARTO
EL CARMEN

Rio

AVENIDA DE LIBERACIÓN

EDUARDO MACHEDO

TREN BLINDADO

Parque los
Mártires

MARTI

CESPEDES

PARADISO
AGENCIA
CULTURAL

Cubanicay

HOSTAL LA CARIDAD

Plaza del
Carmen

INDEPENDENCIA

PEDRO

R. PARDO

CHIQUITIN PEDROZA

ESQUERDO

Rio Belico

IGLESIA DEL CARMEN

FÁBRICA DE TABACO

POLICE

PEDRO TUDURI

CASA DE JOSÉ
RAMÓN

SAN MATEO

R. PARDO ESTEVEZ

IGLESIA
BIEN VIAJE

REPARTO
BRISAS DEL
CAPIRO

MUSEO PROVINCIAL
ABEL SANTAMARÍA

SAN VICENTE

MÁXIMO GÓMEZ

ENRIQUE VILLUENDAS

PLÁCIDO

MACEO

MUJICA

MAESTRA NICOLAS

DICHÍN

9 ABRIL

PALADAR SABOR
TROPICAL

MARTI

J B ZAYAS

VIDAL

Parque
Vidal

PESO FOOD
STALLS

1RA

2DA

FARMERS
MARKET

SEE "CENTRAL
SANTA CLARA" MAP

ABREU

CHAO

REPARTO
CENTRO

CAMPISMO
POPULAR

TOILET

INDEPENDENCIA

PORS NARANJO

MARTA

PADRE

ALEMAN

CUBANACÁN

HOSTAL FLORIDA CENTER

ARTEX EL
BOSQUE

BANK

CORONEL GABINO GALVEZ

INFOTUR

ÓPTICAS
MIRAMAR

CONSULTORIO
JURÍDICA
INTERNACIONAL

UNIÓN

CENTRAL

To
Remedios

JESÚS MENÉNDEZ

CASA DE ERNESTO
Y MIREYA

CARRETERA

FINCIMEX

RAFAEL TRISTA

EDUARDO MACHADO

VIDAURRETA

4 ABRIL

IGLESIA DE LA
SANTISIMA DE BUEN
PASTORA

FARMERS
MARKET

SARAFÍN SÁNCHEZ

ESTRADA PALMA

LUZ CABALLERO

MACEO

BENITEZ DANIELITO

RAÚL

CARLOS PICHANDO

SANCHO

Plaza La
Pastora

COLÓN

INTERMUNICIPAL
BUS STATION

CARRETERA CENTRAL

MONUMENTO
MÁXIMO GÓMEZ

CUBA

REPARTO
VILLA JOSEFA

MONUMENTO A
LOS MAMBISIS

CALLE DE LA TORRE

SANCHO

PALACIO
DE JUSTICIA

COMANDANTE GONZÁLEZ CORO

HOSPITAL

To Terminal
de Ómnibus
Interprovincial

CUBACAR

SARAFÍN GARCÍA

RODOLFO

M DE FLEITAS

ALEMAN

CAPITÁN VELAZCO

NUEVO GERONA

COMPLEJO MONUMENTAL
COMANDANTE ERNESTO
CHE GUEVARA

GENERAL ROLOFF

FRANCISCO ORDOÑEZ

VALDERAS

To Manicuragua

Plaza de la
Revolución

B. STERLING

E. F MORALES

AVENIDA DEL NORTE

MIGUEL COYULA

ALEJANDRO OMS

PAZ GRADAILLE

EDUARDO MACHADO

STERLING

REPARTO
RAUL SANCHO

REPARTO
AMÉRICA LATINA

CARLOS PICHANDO

PORS NARANJO

B STERLING

SALUTIANO PEDROSO

GENERAL MONTEAGUDO

VIDAURRETA

To Autopista Nacional

RAÚL SANCHO

CIRCUNVALACIÓN

ESTRADA PALMA

0   0.25 mi

0   0.25 km

© AVALON TRAVEL

Central Santa Clara

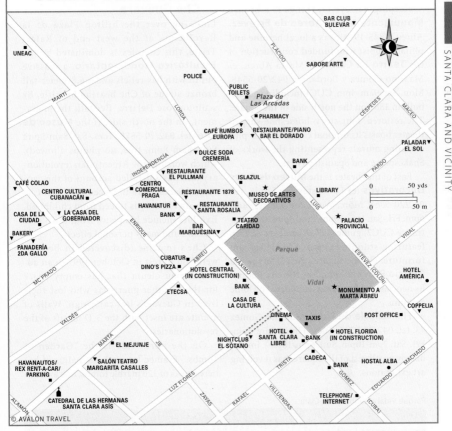

UNEAC

POLICE

PUBLIC TOILETS

Plaza de Las Arcadas

PHARMACY

BAR CLUB BULEVÁR

SABORE ARTE

CAFÉ RUMBOS EUROPA

RESTAURANTE/PIANO BAR EL DORADO

PALADAR EL SOL

DULCE SODA CREMERÍA

BANK

RESTAURANTE EL PULLMAN

ISLAZUL

CAFÉ COLAO

CENTRO CULTURAL CUBANACÁN

CENTRO COMERCIAL PRAGA

RESTAURANTE 1878

MUSEO DE ARTES DECORATIVOS

LIBRARY

HAVANATUR

RESTAURANTE SANTA ROSALIA

CASA DE LA CIUDAD

LA CASA DEL GOBERNADOR

BANK

PALACIO PROVINCIAL

BAKERY

TEATRO CARIDAD

BAR MARQUESINA

PANADERÍA 2DA GALLO

Parque

CUBATUR

Vidal

HOTEL AMÉRICA

DINO'S PIZZA

HOTEL CENTRAL (IN CONSTRUCTION)

MONUMENTO A MARTA ABREU

ETECSA

BANK

COPPELIA

CASA DE LA CULTURA

CINEMA

TAXIS

POST OFFICE

NIGHTCLUB EL SÓTANO

HOTEL SANTA CLARA LIBRE

BANK

HOTEL FLORIDA (IN CONSTRUCTION)

HAVANAUTOS/ REX RENT-A-CAR/ PARKING

EL MEJUNJE

SALÓN TEATRO MARGARITA CASALLES

CADECA

BANK

HOSTAL ALBA

CATEDRAL DE LAS HERMANAS SANTA CLARA ASÍS

TELEPHONE/ INTERNET

50 yds

50 m

© AVALON TRAVEL

the town center, accessed from the west by Rafael Tristá and from the south by Calle Colón, which runs to Parque Vidal, the main square. Calle Marta Abreu runs west from the square and connects with the Carretera Central, which continues east to Placetas.

Independencia, one block north of Parque Vidal, runs parallel to Marta Abreu, crosses the Río Cubanicay (eastward), and (as Avenida de Liberación) leads to Remedios. Independencia between Zayas and Maceo is a pedestrian precinct known as El Bulevar (The Boulevard).

Máximo Gómez (Cuba) and Luis Estévez (Colón) run perpendicular to Abreu, on the west and east side of the park, respectively. Maceo (one block east of Estévez) runs north seven blocks to the railway station and becomes Avenida Sagua, which leads to Sagua la Grande and the north coast. Enrique Villanueva (one block west of Máximo Gómez) runs south to Manicaragua.

Parque Vidal

This large paved square is named for revolutionary hero Leoncio Vidal. A curiosity of the square is its double-wide sidewalk. In colonial days, this was divided by an iron fence: whites perambulated on the inner half while blacks kept to the outside. The bandstand hosts concerts on weekends.

Keeping her eye on things is a bronze **Monumento Marta Abreu de Estévez.** Abreu (1845-1904) was a local heroine and philanthropist who funded construction of the **Teatro La Caridad** (Marta Abreu, e/ Máximo Gómez y Lorda, tel. 042/20-5548, Mon.-Sat. 9am-4pm, CUC1 including guide), built in 1885 on the north side of the square. The restored, four-story, horseshoe-shaped theater boasts its original cast-iron seats plus stunning murals representing the works of Shakespeare and Spanish writers.

East of the theater is the **Museo de Artes Decorativos** (e/ Luis Estévez y Lorda, tel. 042/20-5368, Mon., Wed., and Thurs. 9am-6pm, Fri.-Sat. 1pm-10pm, Sun. 6pm-10pm, entrance CUC2, guide CUC1, cameras CUC5), featuring stunning colonial antiques and furniture. On the square's east side, the old **Palacio Provincial** houses the city library; its neoclassical frontage is supported by Ionic columns.

The **Galería de Arte** (Máximo Gómez #3, tel. 042/20-7715, Tues.-Thurs. 9am-5pm, Fri.-Sat. 2pm-10pm, Sun. 6pm-10pm), immediately northwest of the square, has revolving art exhibitions.

★ Complejo Monumental Comandante Ernesto Che Guevara

Looming over the hilltop Plaza de la Revolución, at the west end of Rafael Tristá, this complex is dominated by the **Escultórico Monumentario,** a massive plinth with bas-reliefs and a 6.8-meter-tall bronze statue of Che bearing his rifle, by sculptor José Delarra. Beneath the monument, on the north side, is the **Museo de Che** (tel. 042/20-5878, Tues.-Sat. 8am-9pm, Sun. 8am-8pm, free, no photos allowed), which worships the Argentinian revolutionary and has a detailed account of the capture of Santa Clara in December 1958. Che Guevara's history is traced from childhood. Exhibits include his pistol from the Sierra Maestra and many personal effects.

Che's remains (discovered in Bolivia) were laid to rest in October 1997 in an adjacent mausoleum that has empty space for the 37 other guerrillas who lost their lives in Guevara's last campaign. Walls of granite are inset with the 3-D motifs of the revolutionaries.

On the north side is the "Garden of Tombs." Framed by symbolic palms, it has tiered rows of 220 marble tombs, one for each

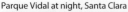

Parque Vidal at night, Santa Clara

of Che's *combatientes* (soldiers), arcing around an eternal flame.

Museo Provincial Abel Santamaría

Housed in the Escuela Abel Santamaría, the **Museo Provincial Abel Santamaría** (Calle Esquerra, tel. 042/20-3041, Tues.-Sat. 9am-5pm, entrance CUC1, cameras CUC1), at the north end of Calle Esquerra in the Reparto Osvaldo Herrera neighborhood, is full of colonial furniture but is dedicated to the province's role in the independence wars and the fight against Batista. It features weaponry plus natural history exhibits. The school was formerly a military barracks, fulfilling Castro's dictum to turn all Batista's barracks into centers of learning.

From here, walk west 300 meters to **NaturArte** (Abel Santamaría, esq. Calle Sub Planta, tel. 042/20-8354, daily 8:30am-11:30pm, donation requested), founded by Ermes Ramírez Criado and Idania Moreno to turn a garbage-strewn site into a multidimensional art and ecological project. Gardens studded with eclectic sculptures host events. The complex also breeds and displays exotic birds and offers environmental education, plus work projects for community members at risk.

Plaza del Carmen

This exquisite little plaza, at the north end of Máximo Gómez, five blocks north of Parque Vidal, is dominated by the **Iglesia Nuestra Señora del Carmen,** a national monument dating to 1748. It is fronted by a granite monument where the first mass was held to celebrate the founding of Santa Clara on July 15, 1689. The church is riddled with bullet holes fired from the former police station—now named El Vaquerito—across the street during the battle of December 29, 1958. On the north side of the church is a life-size figure of revolutionary hero Roberto Rodríquez Fernández—*el vaquerito*—of whose death Che Guevara said, "We have lost one hundred men."

Two blocks east, the **Fábrica de Tabaco Constantino Pérez Carrodegua** (Maceo #181, e/ Julyo Jover and Berenguer, tel. 042/20-2211) has 30-minute guided tours of the tobacco factory (9am-11am and 1pm-3pm, CUC4), making Hoyo de Monterey, Montecristo, Pártagas, Robaina, and Romeo y Julieta cigars for export. You need to buy your ticket in advance from Cubatur, Cubanacán, or Havanatur. No photos or children are permitted. You can stock up on cigars across the street at **La Casa del Tabaco**

Complejo Monumental Comandante Ernesto Che Guevara, Santa Clara

La Veguita (Maceo #176A, tel. 042/20-8952, Mon.-Sat. 9am-5pm), where Marilín Morales Bauta, the cigar sommelier, will give a lighting demo.

Plaza la Pastora and Vicinity

This small plaza, on Calle Cuba, five blocks south of Parque Vidal, has at its heart the Iglesia de la Santísima de Buen Pastora (tel. 042/20-6554, daily 10am-4pm). It features a beautiful stained glass window. On its northeast corner is Monumento a Miguel Gerónimo Gutiérrez, honoring a local patriot. Two blocks south, the Monumento General Máximo Gómez stands in front of the neoclassical Palacio de Justicia, the courthouse.

Monumento a la Toma del Tren Blindado

At the east end of Independencia beyond the railway crossing, the Monumento a la Toma del Tren Blindado (tel. 042/20-2758, Mon.-Sat. 9am-5pm, entrance CUC1, guide CUC1, cameras CUC1) was where, on December 29, 1958, 18 rebel troops led by Che Guevara derailed one of Batista's troop trains. They used a bulldozer and Molotov cocktails, setting in rapid motion the chain of events that toppled Batista. Four rust-colored carriages are preserved higgledy-piggledy as they came to rest after the train was run off the rails. There is an exhibit inside carriage #4; the bulldozer rests atop a plinth.

Continue east 300 meters to the Communist Party headquarters (Av. Liberación esq. Calle F); in the forecourt stands the bronze statue El Che de los Niños by Casto Solano showing Che holding a boy in his arms, with a ram on his shoulders. A close-up view reveals scenes from his life engraved into the sculpture.

Still on the revolutionary trail, continue east three blocks to the Cupet gas station and turn right. After two blocks turn left. After another two blocks, turn right again. In 400 meters, you'll arrive at Loma del Capiro, where steps lead to an avant-garde

stainless steel monument marking the hilltop site where the battle of December 1958 commenced.

Entertainment and Events

Troubadours play most evenings and weekend afternoons at the Casa de la Cultura (tel. 042/20-7181), on the west side of Parque Vidal. Don't miss Piquete Melodías Antillana if the group is performing. They play late-18th-century danzón while old-timers of the Club Alegría de Vivir dance. Contact Paradiso Cultural Agency (Independencia #314, e/ La Cruz y San Isidro, tel. 042/20-1374, paradisovc@artex.cu) for the calendar.

The no-frills, overly air-conditioned Piano Bar (Luis Estévez #13, e/ Independencia y Parque Vidal, tel. 042/21-5215, daily 9pm-1am) hosts boleros, instrumental music, and trova. Classical and other performances are hosted at Teatro la Caridad (Tues., Wed., Sat., and Sun. at 9pm, 5 pesos).

Everything from comedy to live music is featured at Bar Club Bulevar (Independencia #225, e/ Unión y Maceo, tel. 042/21-6236, daily 10pm-2am, CUC2), a hip space where performances are followed by disco. Get the ball rolling with a shot of rum or cold beer at Bar Marquesina (tel. 043/22-4848, daily 9am-midnight), on the northwest corner of Plaza Vidal; it has live music at 9pm.

The in-spot in town is El Mejunje (Marta Abreu #107, e/ Zayas y Alemán, tel. 042/28-2572, Tues.-Fri. 4pm-1am, Sat.-Sun. 10am-1pm), an open-air space amid brick ruins that hosts an eclectic program, from rap to traditional trova (some of the best in Cuba). It's famous nationwide for its LGBTQ Saturday night parties with diva drag show (10pm). Saturday morning it hosts Afro-Cuban music and dance (10am), then bolero and jazz at 5pm. It's the main venue for the Concurso Miss Transvesti beauty pageant, held each March.

A small cabaret is hosted at La Casa del Gobernador (Independencia, esq. Zayas, tel. 042/20-2273, Tues.-Sat. 11am-5pm and

Che Guevara

Ernesto "Che" Guevara was born into a leftist middle-class family in Rosario, Argentina, in 1928. He received a medical degree in 1953, then set out on an eight-month motorcycle odyssey through South America (as portrayed in Brazilian director Walter Salle's 2004 movie, *The Motorcycle Diaries*).

In 1954, he was working as a volunteer doctor in Guatemala when the Arbénz government was overthrown by a CIA-engineered coup that left Che intensely hostile to the United States. He fled to Mexico where, in November 1955, he met Fidel Castro and joined the revolutionary cause.

The two had much in common. They were both brilliant intellectuals. Each had a relentless work ethic, total devotion, and an incorruptible character. Although the handsome, pipe-smoking rebel was a severe asthmatic, Che also turned out to be Castro's best field commander, eventually writing two books on guerrilla warfare. He commanded a revolutionary front in the Sierra Escambray and led the attack that on December 28, 1958, captured Santa Clara and finally toppled the Batista regime. Che took command of Havana's main military posts on New Year's Day 1959.

SHAPING THE REVOLUTION

The revolutionary regime granted Guevara Cuban citizenship. Che (an affectionate Argentinian appellation meaning "pal" or "buddy") became head of the National Bank of Cuba and Minister of Finance and, in 1961, Minister of Industry. He also led the tribunals that dispensed with scores of Batista supporters and was instrumental in stamping out "counterrevolutionaries."

Guevara supervised radical reforms and negotiated trade deals with the Soviet Union as a bulwark for the break with the United States. Though born into a bourgeois family, he developed an obsessive hatred of bourgeois democracy, the profit motive, and U.S. interests. He believed that the individualistic motivations that determine behavior in a capitalist system would become obsolete when collective social welfare became the stated goal. Che believed that liberty eroded moral values: Individualism was selfish and divisive.

Guevara's ambition was to export peasant revolution around the world. The forces he helped set in motion in Latin America created a dark period of revolutionary violence and vicious counter-repression throughout the continent.

However, Guevara was greatly at odds with Castro on fundamental issues. Where Castro was pragmatic, Guevara was ideological. And Guevara was fair-minded toward Cubans critical of the Castro regime, unlike Castro. Guevara gradually lost his usefulness to Fidel's revolution. His frankness eventually disqualified him, forcing him into exile. (Che's popularity with the public also probably played against him. *Time* magazine named him one of the "One Hundred Most Important People of the Century." Fidel, a supreme egoist, did not make the list.)

Guevara left Cuba in early 1965. He renounced all his positions in the Cuban government, as well as his citizenship.

DEATH AND ETERNAL GLORY

Che fought briefly in the Congo with the Kinshasa rebels before returning in secret to Cuba. He reemerged in 1966 in Bolivia, where he unsuccessfully attempted to rouse the Bolivian peasantry and "to create another Vietnam in the Americas" as a prelude to what he hoped would be a definitive world war in which socialism would be triumphant. Che was betrayed to the Bolivian army by the peasants he had hoped to set free. He died on October 9, 1967, ambushed and executed along with several loyal Cuban followers—the "men of Che."

After Guevara's death, Castro built an entire cult of worship around Che, exploited as a "symbol of the purest revolutionary virtue." The motto *Seremos como Che* ("We will be like Che") is the official slogan of the Young Pioneers, the nation's youth organization.

In 1997 Che's remains were delivered to Cuba and interred in Santa Clara.

7pm-midnight, CUC5). **Artex El Bosque** (Carretera Central, tel. 042/20-4444, Wed.-Sun. 9pm-2am, CUC6), overhanging the Río Cubanicay, also has an open-air cabaret at 10:30pm. And outside of town, **Cubanacán Villa La Granjita** (Carretera Malezas, Km 2.5, tel. 042/22-8190) has a nightly "Fiesta Campesina" show poolside at 9:30pm.

The local team, Los Naranjas (the Oranges) play baseball October-April at **Estadio Sandino** (Av. 9 de Abril), about one mile east of Parque Vidal.

Food

For a bargain, head to **Restaurant El Sol** (Maceo #52, e/ Prado y Vidal, tel. 042/27-1463 or 5312-4139, daily noon-10pm), a no-frills place that packs in Cubans for filling *criolla* dishes—such as superb ropa vieja, and garlic lobster—charged in *moneda nacional*. It's on three levels; try the third-floor rooftop terrace.

Owner Ángel and chef Wilfredo at ★ **Restaurante Florida Center** (Maestra Nicolasa #56, e/ Colón y Maceo, tel. 042/20-8161, daily 6pm-8:30pm) serve a divine *ropa vieja,* a house dish of sublime lobster with prawns in a zesty tomato sauce, and huge seafood platters on the candlelit patio of this *casa particular.* Reservations are essential.

Although lacking Florida Center's amazing decor, **Sabore Arte** (Maceo #7, e/ Céspedes y Independencia, tel. 042/22-3969, CUC10) competes with excellent *criolla* fare, plus international staples (such as spaghetti Bolognese), enjoyed on a spacious patio. It has friendly and efficient service.

The state's elegant **Restaurante Santa Rosalia** (Máximo Gómez, e/ Independencia y Abreu, tel. 042/20-1439, daily 11am-11pm), in a colonial mansion, serves chickpea soup (CUC3.40), roasted veal with olives (CUC5), and a house dish of beef with onion (CUC6.40). It hosts fashion shows Wednesday and Thursday nights, and has a cabaret on Fridays and Saturdays.

El Bulevar has several snack bars facing Plaza de las Arcadas, including **Café Europa** (tel. 042/21-6350, daily 9am-1:30am). It's a hangout for tourists, not least for its draft Cristal beer. *Peso* food stalls surround the *mercado agropecuario* (1ra, e/ Morales y General Roloff, Mon.-Sat. 8am-5pm, Sun. 8am-noon), which sells fresh produce.

Panadería Doña Neli (Maceo Sur, esq. Av. 9 de Abril, 6:30am-6pm) sells bread, croissants, and pastries. **Café Colao** (Callejón de la Palma #6, e/ Zayas y Esquerra, tel. 042/5825-9655, daily 7am-11:45pm) is a private coffee shop serving cappuccino, iced coffees, mochas, and scrumptious café cuisine. Owners Salvador de la Torre and Yuniel Leyva play alternative music.

Coppelia (Calle Colón, esq. Mujica, tel. 042/20-6426, Wed.-Fri. noon-10pm, Sat. 10am-4:30pm, Sun. 10am-4:30pm and 5pm-11:30pm), one block south of the main square, sells ice cream for pesos. **Dulce Crema Sodería** (Independencia, esq. Luis Estéves, daily 11am-11pm) charges in CUC.

Accommodations
CASAS PARTICULARES

I always enjoy staying at **Hostal La Caridad** (Calle San Pablo #19, e/ Carolina y Máximo Gómez, tel. 042/22-7704, lacaridad8@gmail.com, CUC25-30), on the north side of Plaza del Carmen. The delightful hosts, Lidia and Santiago, have a spacious lounge with color TV, nicely decorated in 1950s style. The air-conditioned ground-floor bedroom has a private bathroom and five beds, and an upstairs room has a balcony overlooking the plaza. Filling meals can be enjoyed in a shady garden patio. The couple also runs **Hostal Oshún** (Calle Bonifacio Martínez #58, e/ Sindico y Caridad, tel. 042/22-7704, hostaloshun@gmail.com), with two rooms, a shared bathroom, kitchen, and a lovely patio garden.

Near Plaza del Carmen, **Casa de José Ramón** (Máximo Gómez #208 altos, e/ Berenguer y Yanes, tel. 042/20-7239, josetur2009@gmail.com, CUC15-20) has an independent upstairs apartment with full kitchen and stairs to a rooftop terrace.

English-speaking owner Ángel Rodríguez

runs a remarkable rental at ★ **Hostal Florida Center** (Maestra Nicolasa #56, e/ Colón y Maceo, tel. 042/20-8161, www.hostalfloridacenter.com, CUC30). Teeming with antiques, including Baccarat chandeliers, this colonial home opens to a lush patio with an aviary. One bedroom is colonial-themed and has bronze and wrought-iron beds; the other features art deco. Angel's partner, Wilfredo, has a rental with similarly impressive furnishings nearby at **Hostal Alba** (Machado #7, e/ Cuba y Colón, tel. 042/29-4108, albahostal@ yahoo.com, CUC20 s, CUC25 d).

The bargain-priced **Casa de Ernesto y Mireya** (Calle Cuba #227 altos, e/ Sindico y Pastora, tel. 042/27-3501, www.rentasantaclara.com, CUC20) is recommended for its independent upstairs apartment with handsome lounge overlooking Plaza la Pastora. The spacious, simply appointed air-conditioned bedroom has an attractive bathroom. There's parking. Ernesto and Mireya also have a lovely mid-century home—you'll love the '50s features—with three rooms around the corner. Together, the units are perfect for a family or group.

HOTELS

Islazul's lackluster and overpriced high-rise **Hotel Santa Clara Libre** (Parque Vidal #6, e/ Trista y Padre Chao, tel. 042/20-7548, CUC32 s, CUC40 d low season, CUC64 s, CUC72 d high season), overlooking Parque Vidal, is a last resort.

Far superior is Cubanacán's contemporary **Hotel América** (Mujica, e/ Maceo y Colón, tel. 042/20-1585, www.hotelescubanacan.com, from CUC55 s, CUC84 d), with 27 delightful rooms in a pistachio color scheme and with modern mahogany furnishings. Facilities include a cyber café, swimming pool, and restaurant.

Justifiably popular with tour groups, **Cubanacán Los Caneyes** (Av. de los Eucaliptos y Circunvalación de Santa Clara, tel. 042/21-8140, www.hotelescubanacan. com, CUC47 s, CUC72 d low season, CUC58 s, CUC86 d high season), two kilometers west

of town, has 96 appealing air-conditioned rooms in thatched, wooden octagonal *cabinas* amid landscaped grounds. Facilities include an excellent restaurant and a swimming pool. East of town, its similarly priced sibling **Cubanacán Villa La Granjita** (Carretera Malezas, Km 2.5, Santa Clara, tel. 042/22-8190, www.hotelescubanacan.com) has 71 thatched cabins around a handsome pool and sundeck. It has a tennis court, restaurant, and shop.

Information and Services

Infotur (Cuba #66, e/ Machado y Maestro Nicolás, tel. 042/20-1352, director@infotur. vcl.tur.cu) offers tourist information and assistance. Infotur has an office at the airport (tel. 042/21-0386). The **post office** (tel. 042/20-3862, Mon.-Fri. 9am-6pm, Sat. 8:30am-noon) is at Colón #10 (e/ Parque Vidal y Machado). **DHL** (Cuba #7, e/ Tristá y San Cristóbal, tel. 042/21-4069) is one block west.

Etecsa (Marta Abreu, esq. Villuendas, daily 8am-7:30pm) has international telephone and Internet service. You can tap into public Wi-Fi around Parque Vidal, Parque de los Mártires, and Plaza de la Revolución. **Bandec** (Marta Abreu y Luis Estéves, and Máximo Gómez y Rafael Tristá) and **Banco Financiero Internacional** (Cuba #6, e/ Triste y Machado) have branches on Parque Vidal. You can change foreign currency at **Cadeca** (Máximo Gómez, esq. Rafael Tristá, Mon.-Sat. 8:30am-8pm, Sun. 9am-6pm).

The **Consultoría Jurídica Internacional** (Colón #119, e/ San Miguel y Candelaria, tel. 042/20-8458) offers legal assistance.

Getting There and Away
AIR

Flights arrive at **Aeropuerto Internacional Abel Santamaría** (tel. 042/21-4402), 10 kilometers northeast of the city. In 2016, **American Airlines** (tel. 800/433-7300, www. aa.com) launched twice-daily scheduled service from Miami; **JetBlue** (tel. 800/538-2583, www.jetblue.com) initiated thrice-weekly flights from Fort Lauderdale; and **Silver**

Airways (tel. 801/401-9100, www.silverairways.com) initiated five weekly flights from Fort Lauderdale.

BUS

The **Terminal de Ómnibus Interprovincial** (Av. Cincuentenario, Independencia y Oquendo, tel. 042/29-2214) is on the Carretera Central, 2.5 kilometers west of the city center. **Víazul** (tel. 042/22-2524, www.viazul.com) buses between Havana and Santiago stop in Santa Clara, as do once-daily Trinidad-Cayo Santa María and Trinidad-Varadero services. The **Cubanacán Conectando** (Colón, e/ Candelaria y San Cristóbal, tel. 042/20-5189, www.viajescubanacan.cu) competes with more limited service using Transtur tour buses.

TRAIN

Ten departures weekly serve Santa Clara from Terminal La Coubre (through 2018). The **Estación de Ferrocarriles** (tel. 042/20-0893) is at the northern end of Luis Estévez, seven blocks from Parque Vidal. Seats on the *regular* are sold up to 24 hours in advance; seats on the *especial* can be bought only one hour in advance of departure. The local train ticket office is 50 meters south of the national train office. Local trains run to Cienfuegos Sunday-Friday at 5:30pm and to Morón every second day at 5:30am.

Getting Around
BUS AND TAXI

Local buses depart the **Terminal de Ómnibus Intermunicipal** (Marta Abreu, tel. 042/20-3470), 10 blocks west of Parque Vidal. Bus #11 runs between Parque Vidal and Hotel Los Caneyes.

    Cubataxi (tel. 042/22-2691) taxis can be hailed from hotels.

CAR AND SCOOTER

You can rent cars from **Cubacar** (tel. 042/20-9118) and **Rex** (tel. 042/22-2244). **Palmares** (tel. 042/22-7595) rents scooters for CUC24 one day, CUC126 weekly. All three offices are at Marta Abreu #130. There are gas stations on the Carretera Central at the corner of General Roloff and two blocks north at Carretera Central and the corner of Avenida 9 de Abril.

ORGANIZED EXCURSIONS

Tour agencies include **Cubanacán** (Colón, e/ Candelaria y San Cristóbal, tel. 042/20-5189), **Cubatur** (Marta Abreu #10, e/ Máximo Gómez y Villuendas, tel. 042/20-8980), and **Havanatur** (Máximo Gómez #13, e/ Independencia y Barreras, tel. 042/20-4001).

ALTURAS DE SANTA CLARA

The Alturas de Santa Clara rise south and east of the city and merge into the Sierra Escambray. The valleys are pocked with timeworn villages and quilted by tobacco fields. The Autopista and Carretera Central pass through the region. One of the most scenic drives in Cuba is Route 4-474 south from Santa Clara to Manicaragua and Topes de Collantes.

    The 32-square-kilometer **Embalse Hanabanilla** is an artificial lake that beautifies the northern foothills of the Sierra Escambray, below a serrated backdrop of pine-studded mountains. It is stocked with trout and largemouth bass. It's a popular vacation spot for Cubans and a great option for nature lovers who make their base at the **Hotel Hanabanilla** (tel. 042/20-8461).

    Activities offered at the hotel (and by independent guides touting their services locally) include fishing trips (CUC25 pp), plus guided hikes such as the 13-kilometer trek to **El Nicho** (CUC12) and a five-kilometer hike to the **Casa del Campesino** (CUC3), a small working farm where you can get a taste for the campesino life. Boat excursions take you to El Nicho (CUC35) and Casa de Campesino (CUC10), and to a trailhead for a short hike to the **Cascada Arroyo Trinitario** waterfall (CUC10).

    Islazul's dour-looking Soviet-style **Hotel Hanabanilla** (tel. 042/20-8461, www.islazul. cu, CUC26 s, CUC40 d low season including breakfast, CUC74 s, CUC84 d all-inclusive), perched on the lake's western shore, offers great views, but can be noisy with Cuban families on weekends. The 125 air-conditioned rooms are pleasantly furnished and have modern bathrooms.

The turnoff for Embalse Hanabanilla is midway between Cumanayagua and Manicuragua, on Route 4-206, at La Macagua, just west of Ciro Redondo. You can catch buses to Cumanayagua and Manicuragua from Cienfuegos and Santa Clara.

Eastern Villa Clara

VUELTA ARRIBA

East of Santa Clara, the Carretera Central and Route 4-321 run through the Vuelta Arriba region, one of Cuba's premier tobacco-growing districts. The scenery is marvelous as you pass fields tilled by ox-drawn plows and stir up the dust in small agricultural towns lent a Wild West feel by horses tethered to sagging arcades.

The district is unique for *parrandas,* festivals in which rockets whiz through the streets and handheld fireworks and "mortars" explode as the townsfolk of each community divide into two camps and vie to see who can produce the best parade float and the loudest din. In all, 14 local communities hold *parrandas,* most notably Camajuani (March), Placetas, Remedios (late December), Zulueta, and San Antonio de las Vueltas (January or February).

★ REMEDIOS

This lost-in-time town (pop. 18,000), 45 kilometers northeast of Santa Clara, is full of colonial charm. The entire city is a national monument. The historic core has been restored with funding and expertise from the World Monument Fund (www.wmf.org). A *circunvalación* (ring road) wraps around the city to the east.

Remedios was founded in 1514 when a land grant was given to conquistador Vasco Porcallo de Figueroa. It was originally situated closer to the shore. In 1544, it was moved a short distance inland to escape pirates. The town continued to come under constant attack, and in 1578, the townsfolk uprooted

again and founded a new settlement. In 1682, a group of citizens left to found Santa Clara, which in time grew to become the provincial capital. Apparently, in 1691 the clique returned to Remedios, determined to raze it to the ground. They were rebuffed in a pitched battle.

Plaza Martí

The town's main square is shaded by tall royal palms, beneath which you can sit on marble and wrought-iron benches. Dominating the square is the venerable **Parroquia de San Juan Batista** (Camilo Cienfuegos #20, Mon.-Sat. 9am-11am), dating from 1692. Its pious exterior belies the splendor within, not least a carved cedar altar that glimmers with 24-carat gold leaf, and its Moorish-style ceiling of carved mahogany is gabled and fluted. The church was badly damaged by an earthquake in 1939 and was restored over the ensuing 15 years at the behest of a local benefactor, who also donated European paintings.

Museo Casa Alejandro García Caturla (Camilo Cienfuegos #5, tel. 042/39-6851, Tues.-Sat. 9am-noon and 1pm-6pm, Sun. 9am-1pm, entrance CUC1, cameras CUC5), on the north side, honors one of Cuba's foremost avant-garde composers. The house features period furniture and Caturla's original manuscripts. The musical prodigy began writing music in 1920, when he was only 14. The iconoclastic composer was an incorruptible lawyer who became a municipal judge. He was assassinated in 1940.

On the park's northwest corner stands the **Iglesia Buen Viaje** (Alejandro del

Remedios

CUBACAR

↑ To Caibarién

JOSÉ PENA

DEL RÍO

ANDRÉS

TELEPUNTO

TEATERO GUIÑOL ★

CREMERÍA AMÉRICA

MUSEO DE LA MÚSICA ALEJANDRO GARCÍA CATURLA

JESÚS CRESPO IGLESIA BIEN VIAJE

MERCADO AGROPECUARIO

HOTEL E REAL

PARROQUIA DE SAN JUAN BATISTA

HOSTAL LA ESTANCIA

Plaza Martí

ENRIQUE MALARET

CASONA CUETO ●

CADECA ■

★ DRIVER'S BAR

■ TEATRO RUBEN MARTÍNEZ

MUSEO DE LAS ★ PARRANDAS

MÁXIMO GÓMEZ

HOTEL CAMINO DEL PRINCIPE

HOTEL MASCOTTE

LAS LEYENDAS

CASA DE LA CULTURA

EL LOUVRE ■ BANK

● HOTEL BARCELONA

ANTONIO MACEO

★ CASA DE JÉDREZ

JOSÉ MARTÍ

MARGALIS

ANDRÉS DEL RÍO

INFOTUR ●

HOSTAL EL CHALET ●

BRIGADIER GONZÁLEZ

■ PHARMACY

INDEPENDENCIA

A ROMERO

HERMANOS GARCÍA

RUIZ QUINTANA

To Santa Clara ↓

© AVALON TRAVEL

0   200 yds

0   200 m

Río #66), a prim little church with a three-tiered bell tower with a life-size figure of the Virgin Mary and Jesus in the "dove-hole." It is fronted by a marble statue of Cuba's indigenous maiden of liberty.

One block west of the plaza, the **Museo de las Parrandas Remedianas** (Calle Máximo Gómez #71, tel. 042/39-5400, Tues.-Sat. 9am-noon and 1pm-6pm, Sun. 9am-1pm, entrance CUC1, cameras CUC1) celebrates the festivals unique to the region. Given the ostentation

of the actual *parrandas,* the museum is anticlimactic.

Entertainment and Events

If possible, time your visit for Christmas week for the annual *parranda,* which in Remedios culminates on December 24. The wild and racket-filled event is a dangerous business, as rockets whiz into the crowd and every year several people are injured. Don't wear flammable nylon clothing. Be sure to check out the midnight mass in the cathedral. The next day the streets are littered with spent drunks and fireworks. On December 26 those citizens who have recovered celebrate the city's "liberation" by Che Guevara's rebel army. Pickpockets abound, so leave your valuables behind.

There's a good reason that **El Louvre** (tel. 042/39-5639, daily 8am-2am), on the plaza's south side, gets packed: It serves draft Cristal beer. Next door, **Las Leyendas** (tel. 042/39-6131, daily 8am-2am) hosts a *cabaret espectáculo* (Fri.-Sun. at 10pm, CUC1). Traditional music and dance is performed at the **Casa de la Cultura** (Gómez, esq. José de Pena, tel. 042/39-5581, Tues.-Sun. 9am-11pm), one block east of the main square.

The **Teatro Rubén Martínez** (Cienfuegos #30, tel. 042/39-5364, Mon.-Fri. 8am-noon and 1pm-5pm, Sat. 8am-noon), built in the late 19th century with a triple-tiered horseshoe-shaped auditorium, hosts classical and other performances.

Food

El Louvre (tel. 042/39-5639, daily 7:30am-midnight), on the south side of the plaza, claims to be the oldest bar in Cuba. It serves omelets, sandwiches, and burgers. The **Restaurante La Arcada** (daily noon-3pm and 7pm-10pm), in the Hotel E Mascotte (Calle Máximo Gómez, tel. 042/39-5341), has spiced up its menu with beef carpaccio (CUC7) and such entrées as pork mignon with creole sauce (CUC8) and grilled fish with parsley, lemon, and butter sauce (CUC8.50).

Fireworks Fever

The villages and towns due east of Santa Clara are renowned islandwide for *parrandas,* noisy revels that date back more than a century. The festival apparently began in Remedios on Christmas Eve in 1822, when a zealous priest went through the streets making frightening noises meant to rouse the townspeople and scare them into attending midnight mass. The villagers took the fiesta-like idea to heart and gradually evolved a classic Mardi Gras-type carnival celebrated during the days around Christmas and New Year's.

Eventually the *parrandas* spread to the neighboring villages (14 communities now have *parrandas*). Fireworks were introduced and the revels developed into competitions—really, massive fireworks battles—to see who could make the loudest noise. Each of the villages divides into two rival camps represented by mascots: the Carmelitos of Remedios, for example, are represented by a *gavilán* (hawk), and the Sansacrices (from San Salvador) by a *gallo* (rooster).

The villagers invest much emotional value in their wars and spend months preparing in secret. Warehouses are stocked full of explosives and sawhorses studded with fireworks, and the final touches are put on the floats (*trabajos de plaza*) that will be pulled by field tractors around 3am. Spies infiltrate the enemy camp. Even sabotage is not unknown.

The rivals take turns parading all through the night. Rum flows. Conga lines weave through town. Huge banners are waved, to be met by cheers or shouts of derision. *¡Viva la Loma! ¡Viva Guanijibes!* The excitement builds as each neighborhood stages fireworks displays. The opposing sides alternately present their pyrotechnics. The streets are filled with deafening explosions from stovepipe mortars, rockets, and whirling explosives whizzing overhead and sometimes into the panicked crowd, and the smoke is so thick that you can barely see your way through the streets. Finally, the wildest fireworks are unleashed and the fiesta culminates in an orgy of insane firepower. Pretty fireworks don't earn points; the most relentless, voluminous bombast determines who wins.

For quality, the state can't compete with private restaurants such as ★ **Restaurante La Estancia** (Cienfuegos #34, e/ General Carillo y José Peña, tel. 042/39-5582, www.laestanciahostal.com), which offers huge buffets poolside with live music. An unusually diverse à la carte menu includes pumpkin soup, curried chicken (CUC12), *ropa vieja* (CUC14), and pot-roast pork (CUC12), all wonderfully seasoned.

A delightfully rustic alternative is **Restaurante El Curujey** (Carr. a Caibarien, tel. 042/39-5764, daily 10am-5pm), one kilometer east of town. Dishes include a fried banana with beef hash appetizer (CUC2) and rabbit in red wine sauce (CUC19). This amateurish re-creation of a peasant farmstead has horseback rides, a mini-zoo, and a cow-milking demo. Beat the heat with ice cream at **Cremería América** (Jesús Crespo, esq. Andres del Río, no tel., daily 9am-9:45pm), to the northwest side of the plaza.

Accommodations

Dozens of homes are licensed as *casas particulares.* For colonial ambience, check into ★ **Casona Cueto** (Alejandro del Río #72, e/ Enrique Malaret, tel. 042/39-5350, luisenrique@capiro.vcl.sld.cu, CUC25), a delightful 18th-century home full of antiques. The owners rent five air-conditioned rooms with fans and modern bathrooms. One is a loft bedroom reached via a spiral church pulpit staircase. Two more are in a cottage in the courtyard with caged birds and a landscaped rooftop terrace.

An almost identical alternative next to Teatro Rubén Martínez is ★ **Hostal La Estancia** (Cienfuegos #34, e/ General Carillo y José Peña, tel. 042/39-5582, www.laestanciahostal.com, CUC30), an antique-filled centenary home with three spacious rooms; it even boasts a grand piano, swimming pool, and lounge with home theater. Delightful owners Amarelys and Manuel also operate the B&B

as a *paladar* known for its scrumptious buffet meals; B&B guests have their own dining room.

Owners Gisela and Jorge fuss over guests in their well-furnished 1950s modernist ★ **Hostal El Chalet** (Brigadier González #29, tel. 042/39-6538 or 5809-7315, toeva@capiro.ucl.sld.cu, CUC25), two blocks south of the plaza. They rent two rooms. One has an independent entrance reached via spiral stairs and has its own sunny lounge and patio, fridge, spacious cross-lit bedroom, and modern bathroom. The second (entered via the house) has fans. There's a rooftop patio for sunbathing. Parking is secure.

Remedios also has two boutique hotels. Cubanacán's comfy **Hotel E Mascotte** (Máximo Gómez, tel. 042/39-5341, www.cubanacan.cu, CUC40 s, CUC60 d low season, CUC60 s, CUC80 d high season) has 14 air-conditioned rooms with satellite TV and modern marble-clad bathrooms. Some interior rooms lack windows.

The similarly priced ★ **Hotel E Barcelona** (José Peña #67, e/ La Pastora y Antonio Maceo, tel. 042/39-5144, www.cubanacan.cu), on the southeast corner of Plaza Martí, offers a lovely ambience behind an original colonial facade. Exposed brick walls add to the charm of its lounge, which has leather sofas and board games. The hotel has 24 rooms, including five junior suites, surrounding a three-story atrium with creeping ivy. Most rooms are interiors with one tiny window, but they have gracious furnishings and bathrooms.

In 2016, Cubanacán added a boutique option on the main plaza: the **Hotel E Camino del Príncipe** (Cienfuegos #9 e/ Montalvan y Alejandro del Río, tel. 042/39-5144, www.cubanacan.cu), with 26 spacious modern rooms and an elegant restaurant. Try to secure a room with a plaza view. The **Hotel E Real** (Cienfuegos #6 /e Andres del Río y Alejandro del Río, tel. 042/39-5144, www.cubanacan.cu) opened in 2016 with eight delightful rooms. Breakfast is served on a rooftop terrace overlooking Iglesia Buen Viaje.

Information and Services

There's an **Infotur** office (tel. 042/39-7227, Mon.-Fri. 8:30am-noon and 1pm-5pm) at the corner of Calle Margalis and Brigadier González. The plaza is a public Wi-Fi zone.

Getting There and Away

The bus station (tel. 042/39-5185) is on the road to Santa Clara. **Cubacar** (tel. 042/39-5555) has a car rental office at the Oro Negro gas station on the north side of town.

CAIBARIÉN

This sprawling, down-at-the-heels coastal town (pop. 39,000), eight kilometers east of Remedios, has some intriguing, albeit much-deteriorated, colonial structures. There's a 19th-century *trocha* (fort) at the southern entrance to town, where a huge stone crab raises its claws defiantly in the road divide.

The main street, Máximo Gómez, leads to **Parque de la Libertad,** surrounded by period edifices and with a bandstand at its heart (free performances are held Thursday at 3pm and Sunday at 10:30am). On its east side, the **Museo María Escobar Laredo** (tel. 042/36-4731, Tues.-Fri. 10am-6pm, Sat. 2pm-10pm, Sun. 9am-1pm, CUC1), upstairs next to the Havanatur office, has simple exhibits relating to local geology and history. It's named for a heroine of the independence wars. Most impressive is the old Linotype print shop—**La Imprenta Villagraf**—on the park's northeast corner.

Avenida 5, one block west of Máximo Gómez, is a broad boulevard pinned by the **Monumento José Martí.** It makes for a pleasant stroll, as does (on the east side of town) the palm-lined shorefront **Malecón,** which leads east to a funky fishing fleet. Interested in community projects? Check out the bayside **Proyecto de Arte por la Costa** (Calle 39, esq. Malecón, tel. 042/35-3599), where crude and garish artworks are made from recycled garbage. Inland one block, you can buy intriguing art at the **Estudio Galería Noa,** in the quaint clapboard home of artist and project leader Madelin Pérez Noa.

Caibarién explodes into life for its year-end *parranda*.

Museo de Agroindustria Azucarera

The defunct Central Marcelo Salado sugar-processing factory, at La Reforma, three kilometers west of town, is today the excellent **Museo de Agroindustria Azucarera** (tel. 042/36-3586, www.tecnoazucar.azcuba.cu, Mon.-Sat. 9am-4pm, CUC3). First up is an informative video (an English version is offered) on the history of slavery and sugar production in Cuba. Then you tour the old mills *(molinos)*, with fascinating exhibits. Twenty-one antique steam locomotives are on display (the oldest dates from 1904). You can hop aboard a steam train for an excursion from the museum to Remedios (CUC10).

Food and Accommodations

Three blocks from the bayfront, **Pensión Villa Virginia** (Agramonte #73, Ciudad Pesquera, tel. 042/36-3303, virginiaspension@aol.com, CUC25-30) is a tremendous *casa particular* in a prefab home in a quiet residential area on the east side of town. Take your pick of three nicely furnished rooms. Virginia offers free Internet and serves delicious meals in a shaded garden patio.

Three blocks from the plaza is the delightful **Hostal Calle 12** (Calle 12 #1116, e/ 11 y 13, tel. 042/36-4274, caibarienhostalcalle12@gmail.com, CUC25), with three spacious, air-conditioned bedrooms with en suite bathrooms; it also doubles as a *paladar.* Juan and Clara serve delicious and filling *criolla* meals (noon-10pm, CUC8-15) in a lovely colonial-era space.

Islazul runs the 17-room **Hotel Brisas del Mar** (Rept. Mar Azul, tel. 042/35-4699, recepcion@brisas.co.cu, CUC20 s, CUC25 d year-round), at the tip of a breeze-swept peninsula at the east side of town. The rates are a bargain for this simple yet charming modern option with a swimming pool.

Information and Services

Banks include **Banco Financiero**

Internacional (Av. 7, esq. Calle 6, Mon.-Fri. 8am-3:30pm, Sat. 8am-1pm). **Etecsa** (Av. 11, esq. Calle 10, tel. 042/36-3131, 8:30am-7:30pm), one block east of the plaza, has Internet and international phone service. There is public Wi-Fi on the main plaza.

★ CAYOS DE VILLA CLARA

About five kilometers east of Caibarién, a 50-kilometer-long causeway departs the coast road—you need your passport for a toll booth checkpoint (CUC2 each way)—and leaps from cay to cay, ending at **Cayo Las Brujas, Cayo Ensenachos,** and **Cayo Santa María,** 45 kilometers from the mainland. Miles of beaches run along their north shore, shelving into turquoise waters with a coral reef beyond. The cays are in the last phase of development that calls for 10,000 hotel rooms; 17 hotels were open at press time. Day visitors can buy passes at some (from CUC20).

The southeast quarter of Cayo Santa María is protected as **Reserva Cayo Santa María,** a nature reserve with a trail. Flamingos can be seen in the shallows on the south side of Cayo Santa María and at **Las Salinas** (salt pans) on Cayo Las Brujas; turn left immediately east of the airport to get there. **Playa Cañon,** between Hotel Sol Cayo Santa María and Hotel Buenavista, is clothing optional.

Recreation

The impressive **Acuario-Delfinario** (tel. 042/35-0013, CUC5 adults, CUC3 kids), with six large dolphin pools, offers twice-daily shows (10:30am and 3pm) plus a swim "interaction" with dolphins (10am and 3pm, CUC75 adults, CUC40 children 7-12). It includes an aquarium, sea lions, and a lobster farm (to feed all the hungry hotel guests). It has a bar and restaurant specializing in lobster.

Marina Gaviota (tel. 042/35-2246, www.nauticamarlin.tur.cu, daily 9am-5pm), adjoining Villa Las Brujas, offers a one-hour visit to dolphin training tanks, including snorkeling (CUC35); excursions by catamaran (CUC42 half day, CUC72 full day, CUC57 sunset cruise with dinner); and fishing for tarpon (CUC260/350 half/full day). Fishing here is top-notch, and scuba diving is spectacular (CUC45 one dive).

You can book excursions, including a speedboat trip (CUC32 including snorkeling) through **Gaviotatours** (tel. 042/35-0085, comercial@gaviotatoursvc.co.cu), which has tour desks in all the hotels. The guided **MotoNatura** scooter tour takes you to the nature reserve (CUC52 s, CUC76 d).

Food and Entertainment

Pueblo La Estrella (tel. 042/35-0400), between the Husa Cayo Santa María and the Memories Paraíso Beach Resort, has more than one dozen restaurants (including Italian and Japanese), a jazz bar and piano bar, a disco (11pm-3am, CUC5 including one drink), and a small gym.

Pueblo Las Dunas (tel. 042/35-0205), between Meliá Cayo Santa María and Meliá Las Dunas, has restaurants, a bowling alley, and a nightclub. **Pueblo Las Terrenas** (at the eastern end of Cayo Santa María) also has a bowling alley. The **Pueblo Flor de Sal** (on Cayo Las Brujas) restaurant, shopping, and entertainment complexes were being completed at press time.

Restaurante El Bergantin (tel. 042/35-0013, daily 10am-7pm), at Acuario-Delfinario, serves fresh lobster dishes (CUC15-20) from its own nursery, but you can choose other seafood staples too. Fresh seafood and simpler fare can be enjoyed from an over-the-beach perch at **Restaurante Farallón** (tel. 042/35-0025, daily 7am-10am, noon-3pm, and 7pm-10pm), open to the public at Villa Las Brujas.

Accommodations

The 17 hotels open at press time are operated by Cuba's Gaviota chain (www.gaviota-grupo.com); all but Villa Las Brujas are all-inclusive resorts and most are under foreign management. Here's the pick of the litter.

CUC50-100

Villa Las Brujas (tel. 042/35-0025, reserva@villa.lasbrujas.co.cu, from CUC68 s, CUC89 d low season, CUC73 s, CUC95 d high season, including breakfast) has 24 spacious *cabinas* atop Punta Periquillo, on Cayo Las Brujas. Nicely appointed, each has two double beds, satellite TV, and modern bathrooms. The resort has sailboats. The Restaurante El Farallón overlooks the beach but the food wins no prizes.

yachts in the marina at Cayo Santa María

OVER CUC250

Spain's Meliá (www.meliacuba.com) manages four deluxe, all-inclusive, self-contained resort hotels. **Sol Cayo Santa María** (tel. 042/35-1500, CUC128 s, CUC183 d low season, CUC175 s, CUC207 d high season) offers 300 *cabinas*, done up in Meliá's lively trademark pastels and built on piles separated by small bridges. The hotel has a VIP extension, the two-bedroom **Villa Zaida del Río,** with its own swimming pool and gardens.

The similarly priced ★ **Meliá Cayo Santa María** (tel. 042/35-0500) has 358 beautifully decorated rooms and a classy elegance to the public areas, which include three swimming pools. It offers all the water sports you could wish for.

For top-of-the-line luxe, check into the gorgeous **Iberostar Ensenachos** (Cayo Ensenachos, tel. 042/350-301, www.iberostar.com), an all-inclusive with three separate sections in English colonial style, with marble floors throughout. It has 400 rooms, including 10 bungalows, 50 honeymoon rooms, and 10 suites, most a considerable distance from the beach. Every room comes with concierge service. The "Royal Suites" are three kilometers away—a resort within a resort. Kids will love this hotel for its water park.

The hip and adults-only **Royalton Santa María** (tel. 042/35-0900, www.royaltonresorts.com, CUC215 s, CUC290 d low season, CUC261 s, CUC382 d high season) has 122 suites and offers butler service.

The French-run 800-room **Warwick Cayo Santa María** (tel. 042/35-0630, warwickhotelscuba.com) opened in 2016 and stands out for its chic 21st-century room styling and gorgeous freeform pool complex.

Cuba will take a step into the future if plans come through for the **Angsana Cayo Santa María,** run by Singapore's Banyan Tree Resorts. Meanwhile, the **Dhawa Cayo Santa María** (tel. 42/35-0893, www.dhawa-cuba.com) raised the bar when it opened in January 2017 with 512 rooms (in five categories), all infused with a super-chic Modernism-meets-vaguely-Zen aesthetic.

Information and Services

The **police station** and **immigration office** and a **Clínica Internacional** (tel. 042/35-0310, director@clinicacsm.co.cu, daily 24 hours) are on the south side of the highway, opposite the Hotel Playa Cayo Santa María.

Getting There and Around

AeroGaviota has two flights daily from

dolphins in training at Acuario-Delfinario, Cayo Santa María

Havana to Cayo Las Brujas airport (tel. 042/35-0009) on Cayo Las Brujas. Most international visitors fly into Santa Clara's Aeropuerto Abel Santamaría, 116 kilometers away. **Víazul** (www.viazul.com) has once-daily bus service between Trinidad and Cayo Santa María (CUC20) via Cienfuegos, Santa Clara, Remedios, and Caibarien.

Gaviota operates a **Panoramic Bus Tour** (daily 8am-5pm, CUC1) aboard an open-top double-decker bus. It runs the length of the cays, with stops at all the hotels, the aquarium, Puebla Las Dunas, and Pueblo La Estrella.

Taxis are available 24/7 (CUC3-5 between any points on the cays; about CUC35 to Caibarién, CUC40 to Remedios, and CUC60 to Santa Clara each way). There's a gas station adjacent to the airport, where **Vía Rent-a-Car** (tel. 042/39-5398) has an office. Scooters can be rented at most hotels.

Sancti Spíritus

Look for ★ to find recommended
sights, activities, dining, and lodging.

Highlights

★ **Complejo Histórico Comandante Camilo Cienfuegos:** A moving tribute to one of the Revolution's most popular figures, this off-the-beaten-track museum is a must-see on the revolutionary trail (page 305).

★ **Trinidad's Plaza Mayor:** This is the most complete colonial town center outside Havana, with a fabulous yesteryear ambience and lively Afro-Cuban traditions (page 310).

★ **La Boca and Península de Ancón:** Close to Trinidad, Playa Ancón offers scintillating sands and excellent diving (page 320).

★ **Valle de los Ingenios:** Planted in sugarcane, this valley is noted for its ruined colonial sugar mills. Stop at Torre de Manaca-Iznaga, a former sugar estate with a 43.5-meter-tall tower that can be climbed (page 321).

★ **Gran Parque Natural Topes de Collantes:** This national park hosts magnificent mountain hiking and bird-watching. It has horseback-riding excursions and waterfalls (page 323).

No trip is complete without a visit to Trinidad, the country's best-pre-served colonial city. Its unique combi-nation of 18th-century architecture, a breeze-swept hillside setting, and time-honored way of life is irresistibly charming.

This UNESCO World Heritage Site lies in the lee of the Sierra Escambray within a 15-minute drive of Playa Ancón—the most beautiful beach along Cuba's south shore. Although the Sierra Escambray lies mainly within the provinces of Cienfuegos and Santa Clara, most of the trails and accessible sites of interest are within Sancti Spíritus's Gran Parque Natural Topes de Collantes, easily accessed from Trinidad. Trinidad grew to colonial wealth from sugar, and the nearby and scenic Valle de los Ingenios (Valley of the Sugar Mills) recalls that era.

The eponymous provincial capital struggles to compete but has its own colonial charms. To the north, rolling hills flow down towards the coastal plains, farmed in sugarcane and without noteworthy beaches. The southern coastal plains are mostly inhospitable marshland, with few villages or roads, although bird-watchers are served by wetland reserves.

PLANNING YOUR TIME

A week will barely suffice to enjoy this region, with the bulk of your time centered on **Trinidad.** The town itself needs two full days for exploring the sights. However, the Trinidad experience is more about slowing down and immersing oneself in the local life, so a full week here should not be considered too much. Budget one day for an excursion to **Gran Parque Natural Topes de Collantes** to hike mountain trails and go birding. You'll want beach time, too, so plan one day for sunning, snorkeling, and perhaps even scuba diving at **Playa Ancón.** If you prefer the company of Cubans, head to **La Boca,** where locals flock on weekends. A sojourn from Trinidad to the **Valle de los Ingenios** is also de rigueur.

The city of **Sancti Spíritus** deserves at least half a day's exploration; you'll be hard pressed to find more than a full day's worth of things to see and do. Outdoors enthusiasts

Sancti Spíritus Province

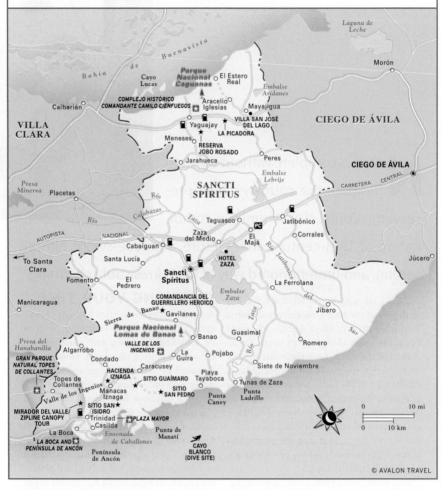

might visit nearby **Embalse Zaza,** a vast wetland full of birdlife and where the fishing for bass and tarpon is world-class.

The Autopista runs 15 kilometers north of the city and continues east for 20 kilometers before ending abruptly in the middle of nowhere, near the city of **Jatibónico.** The Circuito Norte cuts across the northern province inland of the coast, which has no beaches of appeal. Nature lovers, however, might get a thrill at **Parque Nacional Caguanes,** although there are no facilities and getting there is difficult. Interested in revolutionary history? The **Complejo Histórico Comandante Camilo Cienfuegos,** nearby at Yaguajay, is one of the better provincial museums.

Sancti Spíritus and Vicinity

SANCTI SPÍRITUS

Sancti Spíritus (pop. 100,000), the provincial capital 390 kilometers east of Havana, is laid out around a colonial core on a rise above the Río Yayabo. It straddles the Carretera Central, midway between Havana and Santiago.

The settlement of Espíritu Santo was founded in 1514 by Diego Velázquez and Fernández de Cordoba, who conquered the Yucatán. The city began life about six kilometers from its current position but was moved eight years later. The city prospered from cattle ranching and sugar.

In 1895, Winston Churchill arrived in Sancti Spíritus. He thought the city "a very second-rate place, and a most unhealthy place" (an epidemic of yellow fever and smallpox was raging). It has improved vastly since Churchill passed through. Quaint cobbled streets and venerable houses with iron filigree and wide doors for carriages attest to the city's antiquity, aided by a restoration of much of the central core. Still, it receives relatively few visitors. The city plays second string to nearby Trinidad—now overwhelmed with tourists—and is all the more peaceful for it.

Orientation

The Carretera Central enters town from the north as Bartolomé Masó (connecting the city to the Autopista) and passes down the town's eastern side before arcing east for Ciego de Ávila.

Streets are laid out in a grid, running northwest-southeast and northeast-southwest. The most important east-west thoroughfare, Avenida de los Mártires, runs west from Bartolomé Masó to Plaza Serafín Sánchez (also called Plaza Central), the main square. Avenida Jesús Menéndez runs south from the plaza, crosses the river, and continues to Trinidad. The main street, Independencia, runs south from the square and divides the city into *este* (east) and *oeste* (west). Avenida

de los Mártires divides the city into *norte* (north) and *sur* (south).

Plaza Serafín Sánchez

The town's modest Parque Central was laid out in 1522 and named for Serafín Sánchez, a homegrown general in the War of Independence. It has none of the charm or grandeur of main plazas elsewhere in Cuba, although it is surrounded by neoclassical buildings, including the impressive *biblioteca* (library) on the west side and the **Teatro Principal** on the south side. The **Museo Provincial General** (tel. 041/32-7435, Mon.-Wed. 10am-6pm, Thurs. and Sat. 2pm-10pm, Sun. 8:30am-12:30pm, CUC1), next to the library, is full of antiques and has exhibits on local history, sports, music, and more. The **Museo de Historia Natural** (Máximo Gómez Sur #2, tel. 041/32-6365, Mon.-Thurs. and Sat. 9am-5pm, Sun. 8am-noon, CUC1), half a block south, has a motley collection of stuffed beasts, plus insects, seashells, and more.

To the northeast, the plaza extends one block along Independencia and opens into a tiny square with a statue of local journalist-politician Judas Martínez Moles (1861-1915).

Plaza Honorato del Castillo and Vicinity

This diminutive plaza, at the junction of Calle Jesús Menéndez and Honorato, honors a local general in the War of Independence but is pinned by a statue of Rudesindo Antonio García Rojo, an eminent doctor. The **Farmacia de Medicinas Verdes** (Máximo Gómez #38, tel. 041/32-4101, Mon.-Fri. 8am-noon and 2pm-6pm, Sat. 8am-noon), on the west side of the plaza, is full of old apothecary jars.

On the plaza's south side, the **Parroquial Mayor del Espíritu Santo** (Agramonte Oeste #58, tel. 041/32-4855, Tues.-Sun.

Sancti Spíritus

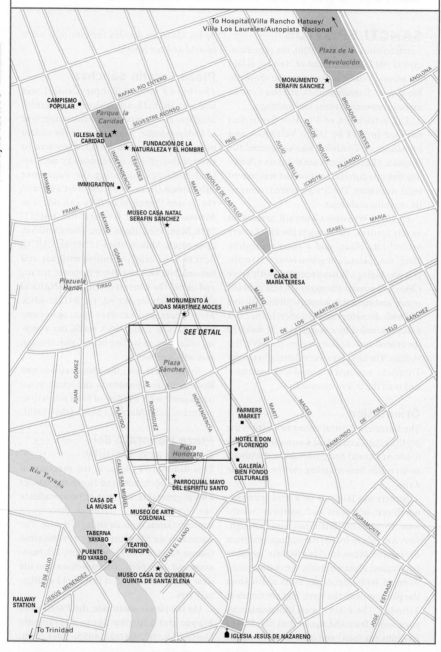

To Hospital/Villa Rancho Hatuey/
Villa Los Laureles/Autopista Nacional

Plaza de la
Revolución

ANGLONA

MONUMENTO
SERAFÍN SÁNCHEZ ★

RAFAEL RÍO ENTERO

BRIGADIER REEVES

CAMPISMO
POPULAR ■

Parque la
Caridad

SILVESTRE ALONSO

CARLOS ROLOFF
(FAJARDO)

IGLESIA DE LA ★
CARIDAD

CÉSPEDES

FUNDACIÓN DE LA
NATURALEZA Y EL HOMBRE

PAÍS

JULIO
MELLA
(CMDTE

BAYAMO

INDEPENDENCIA

MARTÍ

ADOLFO DE CASTILLO

IMMIGRATION ■

FRANK

MÁXIMO

MARÍA

ISABEL

GÓMEZ

MUSEO CASA NATAL
SERAFÍN SÁNCHEZ
★

Plazuela
Honor

TIRSO

CASA DE
MARÍA TERESA ●

LABORÍ

MONUMENTO Á
JUDAS MARTÍNEZ MOCES
★

GÓMEZ

AV. DE LOS MÁRTIRES

TELO
SÁNCHEZ

SEE DETAIL

MACEO

JUAN

AV.

Plaza
Sánchez

PLÁCIDO

RODRÍGUEZ

INDEPENDENCIA

MARTÍ

MACEO

DE PISA

RAIMUNDO

FARMERS
MARKET ■

HOTEL E DON
FLORENCIO ●

Río Yayabo

Plaza
Honorato

GALERÍA/
BIEN FONDO
CULTURALES ■

CALLE SAN MIGUEL

PARROQUIAL MAYO
DEL ESPÍRITU SANTO ★

LAGRAMONTE

CASA DE
LA MÚSICA ▼

MUSEO DE ARTE
COLONIAL ★

CALLE EL LLANO

TABERNA
YAYABO ▼

PUENTE
RÍO YAYABO

TEATRO
PRÍNCIPE ■

26 DE JULIO

JESÚS MENÉNDEZ

MUSEO CASA DE GUYABERA/
QUINTA DE SANTA ELENA

ESTRADA

RAILWAY
STATION ■

JOSÉ

To Trinidad

IGLESIA JESÚS DE NAZARENO

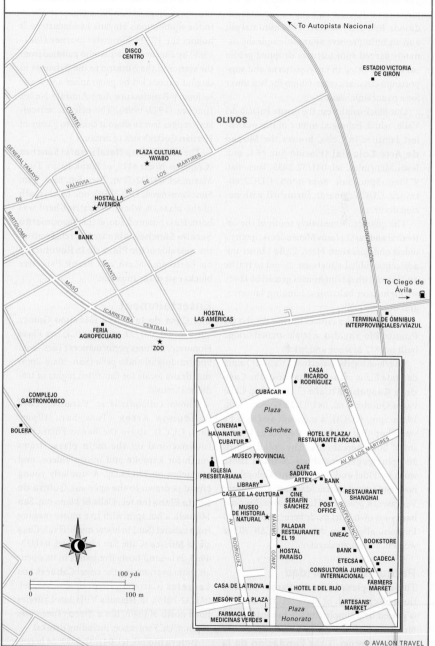

To Autopista Nacional

DISCO CENTRO

ESTADIO VICTORIA DE GIRÓN

OLIVOS

CUARTEL

GENERAL TAMAYO

VALDIVIA

AV. DE LOS MÁRTIRES

PLAZA CULTURAL YAYABO

DE

BARTOLOMÉ

HOSTAL LA AVENIDA

LEPANTO

BANK

MASÓ

CIRCUNVALACIÓN

To Ciego de Ávila

(CARRETERA CENTRAL)

HOSTAL LAS AMÉRICAS

FERIA AGROPECUARIO

ZOO

TERMINAL DE ÓMNIBUS INTERPROVINCIALES/VÍAZUL

COMPLEJO GASTRONÓMICO

BOLERA

0   100 yds
0   100 m

CASA RICARDO RODRÍGUEZ

CUBÁCAR

Plaza Sánchez

CINEMA
HAVANATUR
CUBATUR

HOTEL E PLAZA/ RESTAURANTE ARCADA

CÉSPEDES

AV. DE LOS MÁRTIRES

MUSEO PROVINCIAL

IGLESIA PRESBITARIANA

CAFÉ SADUNGA
ARTEX
BANK

RESTAURANTE SHANGHAI

LIBRARY

CASA DE LA CULTURA

CINE SERAFÍN SÁNCHEZ

POST OFFICE

INDEPENDENCIA

MUSEO DE HISTORIA NATURAL

PALADAR RESTAURANTE EL 19

UNEAC

BOOKSTORE

AV RODRÍGUEZ

MÁXIMO GOMEZ

HOSTAL PARAÍSO

BANK
ETECSA

CADECA

CONSULTORÍA JURÍDICA INTERNACIONAL

FARMERS MARKET

CASA DE LA TROVA

MESÓN DE LA PLAZA

HOTEL E DEL RIJO

ARTESANS' MARKET

FARMACIA DE MEDICINAS VERDES

Plaza Honorato

9am-11am and 2pm-5pm) is well preserved. The church dates from 1680, though the triple-tiered bell tower and cupola are later additions. Relatively austere, it has minimal gilt and an unimpressive altar, although the ornately carved roof features dropped gables carved and fitted in cross patterns and supporting a circular center. Climb the bell tower for a panoramic view.

One block southwest, the ornate Palacio del Valle, which belonged to one of the wealthiest families in Cuba, houses the **Museo de Arte Colonial** (Plácido Sur #64, esq. Jesús Menéndez, tel. 041/32-5455, Tues.-Sat. 9:30am-5pm, Sun. 8am-noon, CUC2 entrance, CUC1 camera), furnished with period decor.

The quarter immediately south of the cathedral and east of Jesús Menéndez is the city's oldest and quaintest. Here, **Calle Llano** and adjacent cobbled streets are closed to traffic and lined with quaint houses graced by fancy wrought-iron balconies, hanging lanterns, and wooden grills.

Jesús Menéndez crosses the Río Yayabo via **Puente Río Yayabo,** a triple-arched bridge built in 1817 of stone and brick.

Overlooking the waterfront, the old Quinta de Santa Elena mansion today hosts the **Casa de la Guayabera** (Calle El Llano, esq. Calle Padre Quintero, tel. 041/32-2205, Tues.-Sun. 10am-5pm, CUC1), a museum and tailor's workshop that celebrates the classic Cuban shirt, born hereabouts. The collection of 200-plus *guayabera* shirts includes those worn by Fidel and Raúl Castro, Colombian novelist Gabriel García Márquez, and former Venezuelan president Hugo Chávez. You can have your own shirt made here (up to CUC40 for men, allow two days; up to CUC70 for women, allow four days).

Parque de la Caridad

This small plaza (officially Parque Maceo), three blocks north of Plaza Serafín Sánchez, is graced by a simple church, the **Iglesia de Nuestra Señora de la Caridad.** On the southeast corner is the **Fundación de la**

Naturaleza y el Hombre (Calle Cruz Pérez #1, tel. 041/32-8342, www.fanj.cult.cu, Mon.-Fri. 10am-4pm, CUC0.50), a regional cousin to the foundation's Havana headquarters. It honors the 17,524-kilometer journey (1987-1988) by a team of Cubans who paddled from the source of the Amazon to the Bahamas in dugout canoes led by geographer and revolutionary Renaissance man Antonio Nuñez Jiménez (1923-1998). The eclectic miscellany ranges from a dugout canoe to a copy of Hernán Cortés's suit of armor.

The **Museo Casa Natal Serafín Sánchez** (Céspedes Norte #112, e/ Frank País y Tirso Marín, tel. 041/32-7791, Tues.-Sat. 8am-5pm, Sun. 8am-noon, CUC0.50), one block south of the plaza, is where the patriot-hero was born. He is honored, too, at the **Monumento Serafín Sánchez,** a bronze bas-relief wall on the west side of the **Plaza de la Revolución** on Bartolomé Masó and Frank País, five blocks east of the museum.

Entertainment

The **Casa de la Trova** (Máximo Gómez Sur #26, tel. 041/32-8048, CUC1), on Plaza Honorato, features performances (Tues.-Sun. 9pm-midnight) and a *peña* (Sun. 10am-2pm) that draws locals for fun-filled nights of traditional music.

Known colloquially as "Karaoke," **Café Sandunga Artex** (Tues.-Sun. 10pm-2am, CUC1), above the Banco Financiero Internacional on the main plaza, draws youth for karaoke and music videos, and reggaeton on Thursday. A similarly young crowd is drawn to the open-air **Quinta de Santa Elena** (no tel., Calle El Llano esq. San Miguel), a hot spot with live music ranging from cabaret (Sat.) to house music (Fri.). **Casa de la Música** (Calle San Miguel, tel. 041/32-4963, Fri.-Sun.) hosts live bands in its open-air patio overlooking the river. **Cabaret Los Laureles** (Carretera Central, Km 383, tel. 041/32-7016), in Islazul's Villa Los Laureles hotel north of town, has a **disco** (Tues.-Sun. 10pm, CUC5 entrance, including drinks).

Bolera (Roloff, tel. 041/32-2339, 24 hours,

CUC1 for 20 "bowls"), three blocks south of Avenida de los Mártires, has bowling and pool tables. The **Feria Agropecuario** (Carretera Central esq. Raimundo de Pisa) is one of Cuba's major rodeo venues and a setting for regular musical shows.

The local baseball team, Los Gallos (the Roosters) plays October-May at **Estadio Victoria del Girón,** in Reparto Olivos.

Food

The cream of the private restaurant crop is the elegant ★ **Restaurante El 19** (Máximo Gómez, tel. 041/33-1919, www.restaurantel19cuba.esy.es, daily 11am-10pm), with efficient uniformed waitstaff, an airy colonial setting, and a creative menu that includes shellfish cream soup (CUC3), paella (CUC7.50), and pork loin with caramelized onions (CUC8).

Don your finest to dine at Hotel E Plaza's **Restaurante Arcada** (tel. 041/32-7102, daily 7:30pm-9:30pm), on the east side of Parque Central. Enjoy a candlelight dinner of chicken in beer with rice (CUC5), or pork mignon with creole onion sauce and sour orange (CUC8).

For romance under the stars, choose the patio of the **Hostal E del Rijo** (Calle Honorato del Castillo #12, tel. 041/32-8588, daily 7:30am-10am, 11am-3pm, and 6pm-10:30pm). The food's pretty good too, although the menu is limited. Try tuna with olive salad (CUC4), pork mignon with creole sauce (CUC9), and caramel pudding (CUC3).

Perfect for penny-pinchers, **Mesón de la Plaza** (Máximo Gómez #34, tel. 041/32-8546, daily 9am-10:45pm), opposite Hostal E del Rijo, is styled as a Spanish *bodega,* with rough-hewn tables and cowhide chairs. Try the *garbanzo mesonero* (garbanzos with bacon, pork, and sausage, CUC2) or *ensalada de garbanzo* (baked chickpeas, green peas, onions, and peppers, CUC1.50), plus *ropa vieja* (CUC5), washed down with sangria.

For alfresco views, head to ★ **Taberna Yayabo** (Jesús Menéndez #106, tel. 041/83-7552 or 5447-8665, daily 9am-10:30pm, CUC8-15), a huge Spanish tapas bar with a balcony overhanging the river. It specializes in *criolla* staples such as roast pork. A resident sommelier presides over an exceptional wine list. You can buy produce at the *mercado agropecuario* (Independencia, esq. Honorato, Mon.-Sat. 7am-5:30pm, Sun. 7am-noon).

Accommodations
CASAS PARTICULARES

The ★ **Hostal Las Américas** (Carretera Central #157 Sur, tel. 041/32-2984, hostallasamericas@yahoo.es, CUC25-30) is the best rental in town and is close to the bus station. This well-kept 1950s modernist home has a large TV lounge plus dining room, with three new rooms opening to a garden patio. Two spacious, cross-ventilated bedrooms in the house are delightful. Meals include a superb lamb special.

Among the colonial-era options downtown, I like the **Hostal Paraíso** (Máximo Gómez #11 Sur, e/ Cervantes y Honorato, tel. 041/33-4658, www.paraiso.trinidadhostales.com, CUC25-30), with four spacious, nicely furnished, air-conditioned rooms around a fern-filled patio with rockers. The two upstairs rooms are modern additions with their own terrace.

A heart-of-affairs option, **Casa de Ricardo Rodríguez** (Independencia #28 altos, tel. 041/32-3029, CUC25) is upstairs in a centenarian house on the northeast corner of the main plaza. It has a large lounge with a balcony. Two spacious upstairs rooms are simply furnished and have private bathrooms.

HOTELS

Islazul's **Hotel E Plaza** (tel. 041/32-7102, www.islazul.cu, CUC38 s, CUC60 d low season, CUC47 s, CUC75 d high season), on the east side of Parque Central, is one of Cuba's better boutique hotels, with 27 handsomely furnished rooms with modern bathrooms and balcony views. The small lobby bar is a nice spot to tipple, and the romantic restaurant is above par.

★ **Hotel E del Rijo** (Calle Honorato del

Castillo #12, tel. 041/32-8588, www.islazul. cu, CUC38 s, CUC60 d low season, CUC47 s, CUC75 d high season) exudes colonial charm. The 1818 neoclassical structure is entered through soaring carriage doors. The 16 large rooms (including a suite) surround a patio and boast beamed ceilings, wrought-iron lamps, period art, and modern marble bathrooms.

Islazul's latest boutique entry is the 12-room **Hotel Don Florencio** (Independencia Sur #62, tel. 041/32-8588, www.islazul.cu, CUC44 s, CUC68 d low season, CUC55 s, CUC90 d high season), an exquisitely refurbished colonial property that mirrors the Hotel E del Rijo. It even has twin Jacuzzis.

Islazul's lackluster alternative is the **Villa Los Laureles** (Carretera Central, Km 383, tel. 041/36-1016, CUC24 s, CUC38 d low season, CUC28 s, CUC44 d high season), four kilometers north of town, offering 78 modest *cabinas* in meagerly landscaped grounds that include a swimming pool. The slightly more upscale **Villa Rancho Hatuey** (Carretera Central, Km 382, tel. 041/32-8315, www.islazul.cu, CUC30 s, CUC48 d low season, CUC38 s, CUC60 d high season) has 74 rooms in two-story *cabinas* in a contemporary Mediterranean style.

Information and Services

The **post office** (Independencia Sur #8, Mon.-Fri. 8am-4pm) is one block south of the main plaza; another branch (Bartolomé Masó #167, tel. 041/32-3420) has DHL service. **Etecsa** (Independencia, daily 8:30am-7pm), 50 meters south of Plaza Sánchez, has international telephone plus Internet service. For public Wi-Fi, join the Cubans in Parque Serafin Sánchez, Plaza Cultural Yayabo, and Complejo Gastronómico Mar y Cielo, on the west side of the Feria Agropecuaria.

Banco Financiero Internacional (Independencia Sur #2) is on the southeast corner of Plaza Sánchez; **Banco Popular** is one block south. You can also change foreign currency at **Cadeca** (Independencia Sur #31). Most banks are open Monday-Friday 8am-3:30pm and Saturday 8am-1pm.

Hospital Provincial Camilo Cienfuegos (tel. 041/33-8000) is on Bartolomé Masó, opposite the Plaza de la Revolución. There's a **Farmacia** (Independencia #123, tel. 041/32-4660, 24 hours) on Parque la Caridad, and **Farmacia de Plantas Medicinales** (Máximo Gómez Sur #40, tel. 041/32-4101, Mon.-Fri. 8am-noon and 2pm-6pm, Sat. 8am-noon) on Plaza Honorato.

The **Consultoría Jurídica Internacional** (Independencia #39 Altos Sur, e/ Ernesto Valdés Muñoz y Cervantes, tel. 041/32-8448, Mon.-Fri. 8am-12:30pm and 1:30pm-5:30pm) provides legal assistance.

Getting There and Away

The **Terminal Provincial de Ómnibus** (tel. 041/32-4142) is at the junction of Bartolomé Masó and the *circunvalación*, east of town. **Víazul** buses (tel. 041/33-4983, www.viazul.com) traveling Havana, Varadero, and Trinidad to/from Santiago de Cuba stop in Sancti Spíritus.

Local buses and *camiones* serve nearby towns from the **Terminal Municipal** (Calle Sánchez and Carlos Roloff, tel. 041/22162), one block south of Avenida de los Mártires.

The **train station** (Av. Jesús Menéndez, esq. 26 de Julio, tel. 041/32-9228 or 041/32-7914 for express trains) is 400 meters southwest of Puente Yayabo (ticket office open daily 8am-4pm, until 9pm when there are departures). At press time, train #7 departed Havana every second day for Sancti Spíritus via Matanzas and Santa Clara at 9:21pm; train #8 departed Sancti Spíritus at 8:45pm every second day (CUC14).

The *tren especial* between Havana and Santiago de Cuba previously stopped at Guayos, 15 kilometers north of Sancti Spíritus, but at press time this appeared not to be the case. If it is running, you should be in the front carriage of the train to alight at Guayos; taxis are available to Sancti Spíritus. If departing Sancti Spíritus to catch the *especial* you should buy your ticket at the rail station before departing for Guayos.

Getting Around

Cubatur (tel. 041/32-8518, cubaturss@enet.cu), on the west side of Plaza Serafín Sánchez, offers excursions.

You can rent cars from **Havanautos,** in Hotel Los Laureles; **Vía** (tel. 041/33-6697), on Plaza Honorato; and **Cubacar** (tel. 041/32-8181), on Plaza Serafín Sánchez. There's a Cupet gas station on the Carretera Central, about four kilometers north of downtown.

EMBALSE ZAZA

Six kilometers east of the city, Embalse Zaza is a huge lake studded with flooded forest. It is stocked with trout and bass, and marsh birds flock from far and wide, making Zaza a favorite spot for bird-watchers and anglers.

Expect no frills at Islazul's **Hotel Zaza** (tel. 041/32-7015, recepcion.hzaza@islazulssp.tur.cu, CUC20 s, CUC33 d year-round including breakfast), a faceless and dowdy two-story Soviet-inspired hotel with 124 air-conditioned rooms, most with lake views. At least it has a swimming pool (often empty); birding and boating are offered. European anglers and hunters are the main clientele.

EcoTur (tel. 041/54-7419), in Sancti Spíritus, offers fishing (Nov.-Mar., CUC80 pp, eight hours).

NORTH OF SANCTI SPÍRITUS

The Circuito Norte coast road parallels the shore some miles inland, connecting Remedios (in Villa Clara Province) and Morón (in Ciego de Ávila Province).

★ Complejo Histórico Comandante Camilo Cienfuegos

The main sight of interest is in the town of **Yaguajay,** 40 kilometers east of Caibarién, where a five-meter-tall bronze statue of Camilo Cienfuegos stands one kilometer north of town. Within its base is an excellent **museum** (Calle Eladio Carlata, tel. 041/55-2689, Mon.-Sat. 8am-4pm, Sun. 9am-1pm, CUC1) dedicated to the revolutionary

commander and the battle he led here against Batista's troops in the closing days of December 1958. Its displays include Camilo's stuffed horse enshrined in a glass case.

To the rear, the **Mausoleo Frente Norte de las Villas** has an eternal flame and marble tombs for Camilo's troops. They're surrounded by 24 palms symbolizing the date of liberation of Yaguajay. Schoolchildren are bused in each October 28 to toss "a flower for Camilo" into a moat on the anniversary of his death in a mysterious plane crash in 1959.

The hospital opposite the monument was formerly the army barracks, and the focus of the battle in 1958. A replica of a small tank (converted from a tractor) used in the assault stands outside.

Reserva la Biosfera Buenavista

Northeast of Yaguajay the sugarcane fields meld into the swampy coastal flats, now protected within **Parque Nacional Cuguanas.** The park harbors almost 200 species of fauna, including Cuba's largest colony of Cuban cranes. Caves have subterranean galleries and pre-Columbian petroglyphs. Iguanas are found on Cayo Piedra. Access is via **Mayijagua,** about 15 kilometers east of Yaguajay. Getting there is another matter: The dirt road is fit for four-wheel drive only.

The park is part of the 313,503-hectare **Reserva de la Biosfera Buenavista,** enshrining 11 separate protected areas that include **Reserva Jobo Rosado,** a "managed resource" area southeast of Yaguajay that protects 41 square kilometers of forested limestone hills (the Sierra de Meneses-Cueto) studded with *mogotes* and riddled with caves. A monument marks where Camilo Cienfuegos established his headquarters for the attack on Yaguajay. Two kilometers east of Yaguajay, **Rancho Querete** (Tues.-Sun. 9am-4pm) is a visitors center and restaurant with a mini-zoo and a blue hole; it gets packed with Cubans on weekends. Interpretive trails lead to the Cueva de Valdés and La Solapa de Genaro cascades.

EcoTur (Calle Pedro Díaz #54, Yaguajay, tel. 041/55-4930, ffauna@yag.co.cu or ecoturss@enet.cu) offers excursions.

La Picadora

This **agritourism project** (tel. 5230-1043, la.picadora.cuba@gmail.com), at the community of La Picadora, two kilometers west of Mayijagua, lets you savor the campesino lifestyle while getting some dirt beneath your fingernails. The Manuel Montaña cooperative of 53 farmers and their families welcome visitors to pick fruit and produce, milk cows, or make fruit preserves. You can stay with farmers in three rustic thatched cabins with compost toilets; the farmers' wives prepare meals. Guided hikes and horseback rides to archeological and geological sites are offered.

Accommodations

Just east of Mayijagua, Islazul's **Villa San José del Lago** (tel. 041/54-6108, reserve. loslagos@islazulssp.tur.co.cu, CUC26 s, CUC35 d low season, CUC64 s, CUC75 d high season) is a spa resort centered on a lagoon with pedal boats and rowboats, plus three swimming pools (one with thermal water). Thirty small, simple air-conditioned *cabinas* have satellite TV and modern bathrooms.

Massages and mud treatments are offered. It's popular with Cubans and gets lively on weekends.

SANCTI SPÍRITUS TO TRINIDAD
Parque Nacional Alturas de Banao

The road that leads southwest from Sancti Spíritus to Trinidad is a stupendous scenic drive that rises and dips along the foothills of the Alturas de Banao.

From the village of **Banao,** 20 kilometers west of Sancti Spíritus, you can follow the valley of the Río Banao seven kilometers into the foothills, where a pristine 3,050-hectare swath is protected in the **Parque Nacional Alturas de Banao** (Banao Heights Ecological Reserve, tel. 041/39-9205, CUC4 entrance). The ecosystems include semideciduous forest, tropical moist forest, and cloud forest topping out with Las Tetas de Juana (842 m). The region is rich in flora, with more than 700 flowering plants (more than 100 are endemic), including over 60 orchid species. Banao is a paradise for bird-watchers.

During the war to oust Batista, Che Guevara established his headquarters near the community of Gavilanes. The **Comandancia**

Parque Nacional Alturas de Banao

del Guerrillero Heróico, in the heart of the mountains, is reached by a dirt trail; the turnoff is at the hamlet of Las Brisas, five kilometers east of Banao. It's a stiff hike (about 10 kilometers) from the trailhead, near Campismo Planta Cantú. There's an obelisk at the *comandancia*.

The **visitors center** at Jarico, four kilometers north of Banao, offers horseback riding (CUC5) and hikes (from CUC3) to caves and the Cascada Bella waterfall. It also has eight basic cabins (CUC25) with cold-water showers, plus a lovely thatched restaurant (daily 8am-3:30pm). You can overnight at the more remote Sabina cabin (CUC56 including meals), reached by a six-kilometer trail.

EcoTur (tel. 041/54-7419 or 07/641-0306, ecoturss@enet.cu) offers tours. Drop-in visitors pay CUC5 entry (CUC10 with lunch).

Trinidad and Vicinity

TRINIDAD

Trinidad (pop. 45,000), the crown jewel of Cuba's colonial cities, is 67 kilometers southwest of Sancti Spíritus and 80 kilometers east of Cienfuegos. It was the fourth of the seven cities founded by Diego de Velázquez in 1514. No other city in Cuba is so well preserved or so charming. The entire city is a national monument lent appeal by its setting astride a hill, where it catches the breezes and gazes out over the Caribbean against a backdrop of verdurous Sierra Escambray.

Its narrow, unmarked cobbled streets are paved with river stones. The maze of streets is lined with terra-cotta tile-roofed houses in soft pastel colors. Much of the architecture is neoclassical and baroque, with a Moorish flavor. The exquisite buildings are fronted by mahogany balustrades and massive wooden doors with *postigos* that open to let the breezes flow through cool, tile-floored rooms connected by double-swing half-doors (*mamparas*) topped by *vitrales.*

Mule-drawn carts and cowboys on horseback clip-clop through the cobbled streets. Old folks rock gently beneath shady verandas, serenaded by twittering songbirds in bamboo cages—a Trinidad tradition. At night, cool air flows downhill, and it's a special joy to stroll the traffic-free streets that make the town feel even more adrift from the 21st century.

However, since 2015 the city has witnessed a massive tourist boom. The main plaza throngs with visitors and the city's infrastructure (water, sewage) is under stress. As the number of room rentals continues to grow—there are more than 3,000—authorities are contemplating banning additional *casas particulares* to stem the unsustainable growth.

Trinidad is steeped in Santería and Catholicism. Easter and Christmas are good times to visit.

History

The initial settlement, named Villa de la Santísima Trinidad, was founded in 1514 by Diego de Velázquez on a site settled by the Taíno, who panned for gold in nearby rivers. The Spanish established a lucrative (but short-lived) gold mine that lent vigor to the young township and the wharves of nearby Casilda. Hernán Cortés set up base in 1518 to provision his expedition to conquer the Aztec empire. Soon fleets bearing the spoils of Mexico gathered, eclipsing Trinidad's meager mines.

Trinidad was far enough from the reach of Spanish authorities in Havana to develop a bustling smuggling trade. Its position on Cuba's underbelly was also perfect for trade with Jamaica, the epicenter of the Caribbean slave trade. Trinidad also grew prosperous importing slaves, many of whom were put to work locally, stimulating the sugar industry. Money poured in from the proceeds of sugar grown in the Valle de los Ingenios. When the English occupied Cuba in 1762-1763, Trinidad

Trinidad and Vicinity

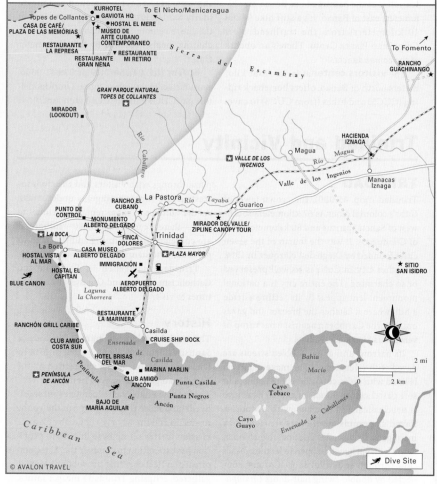

KURHOTEL
GAVIOTA HQ
Topes de Collantes
To El Nicho/Manicaragua
HOSTAL EL MERE
CASA DE CAFÉ/
PLAZA DE LAS MEMÓRIAS
MUSEO DE
ARTE CUBANO
CONTEMPORANEO
RESTAURANTE
LA REPRESA
RESTAURANTE
MI RETIRO
RESTAURANTE
GRAN NENA
To Fomento
RANCHO
GUACHINANGO
Sierra   del   Escambray
GRAN PARQUE NATURAL
TOPES DE COLLANTES
HACIENDA
IZNAGA
MIRADOR
(LOOKOUT)
Río Caballero
Magua
Río Magua
VALLE DE LOS
INGENIOS
Valle de los Ingenios
Manacas
Iznaga
RANCHO EL
CUBANO
La Pastora
Río Tayaba
Guarico
PUNTO DE
CONTROL
MONUMENTO
ALBERTO DELGADO
MIRADOR DEL VALLE/
ZIPLINE CANOPY TOUR
LA BOCA
FINCA
DOLORES
Trinidad
La Boca
CASA MUSEO
ALBERTO DELGADO
PLAZA MAYOR
HOSTAL VISTA
AL MAR
IMMIGRACIÓN
SITIO
SAN ISIDRO
HOSTAL EL
CAPITÁN
BLUE CANON
AEROPUERTO
ALBERTO DELGADO
Laguna
la Chorrera
RESTAURANTE
LA MARINERA
RANCHÓN GRILL CARIBE
Casilda
CLUB AMIGO
COSTA SUR
Ensenada
de
Casilda
CRUISE SHIP DOCK
HOTEL BRISAS
DEL MAR
MARINA MARLIN
Bahía
Macío
PENÍNSULA
DE ANCÓN
CLUB AMIGO
ANCÓN
Punta Casilda
Península
de
Ancón
Punta Negros
Cayo
Tobaco
BAJO DE
MARÍA AGUILAR
Cayo
Guayo
Ensenada de Caballones
Caribbean
Sea
0   2 mi
0   2 km

Dive Site

© AVALON TRAVEL

became a free port and prospered even further, entering its golden age.

Wealthy citizens built their sumptuous homes around the main square—Plaza Mayor—and along the adjoining streets. Ships unloaded pianos from Berlin; sumptuous furniture from France; and linens, lattices, and silverware from Colombia.

By the early 19th century, Cienfuegos, with its vastly superior harbor, began to surpass Casilda, which had begun silting up. Trinidad

began a steady decline, hastened by tumult in the slave trade and new competition from more advanced sugar estates elsewhere in Cuba. Isolated from the Cuban mainstream, by the turn of the 20th century Trinidad had foundered.

In the 1950s, Trinidad was declared a "jewel of colonial architecture." A preservation law was passed. Development was prohibited and the city continued to stagnate in its own beauty. The town was named a national

Trinidad

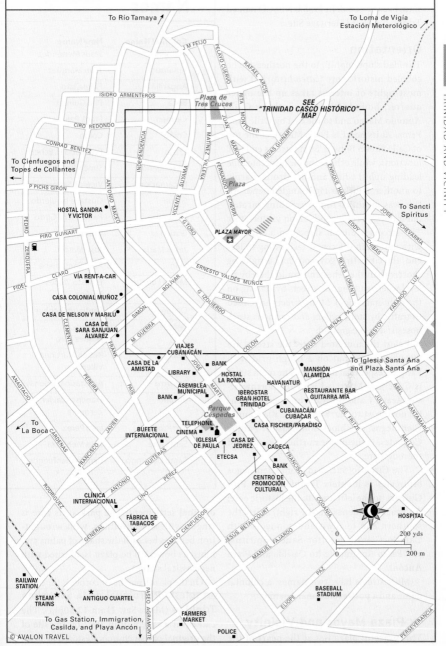

To Río Tamaya

To Loma de Vigía
Estación Meterológico

J M FEIJO

PELAYO CUERVO

RAFAEL ARCIS

ISIDRO ARMENTEROS

Plaza de
Tres Cruces

SEE
"TRINIDAD CASCO HISTÓRICO"
MAP

CIRO REDONDO

RITA

JUAN

R. MARTÍNEZ VILLENA

MONTELIER

RIVAS GUINART

CONRAD BENÍTEZ

To Cienfuegos and
Topes de Collantes

P. PICHS GIRÓN

INDEPENDENCIA

ANTONIO MACEO

SUYAMA

FERNANDO H. ECHERRI

Plaza

ENRIQUE HART

To Sancti
Spíritus

PEDRO

PIRO GUINART

HOSTAL SANDRA
Y VICTOR

VICENTE

F. G. TORO

PLAZA MAYOR

JOSÉ
ECHEVARRÍA

ZERQUERA

FIDEL

CLARO

VÍA RENT-A-CAR

CASA COLONIAL MUÑOZ

ERNESTO VALDÉS MUÑOZ

EDDY
CHIBAS

REYES LORENTI

CASA DE NELSON Y MARILÚ

SIMÓN

BOLÍVAR

G. IZQUIERDO

SOLANO

RESTOY

FARAJDÓ

LUZ

CASA DE
SARA SANJUAN
ÁLVAREZ

M. GUERRA

CLEMENTE

FRANK

VIAJES
CUBANACÁN

COLÓN

AGUSTÍN

BENAZ PAZ

To Iglesia Santa Ana
and Plaza Santa Ana

CASA DE LA
AMISTAD

JOSÉ MARTÍ

BANK

MANSIÓN
ALAMEDA

ABEL

JULIIO

SANTAMARÍA

ANASTACIO

PEREIRA

PAÍS

LIBRARY

ASEMBLEA
MUNICIPAL

HOSTAL
LA RONDA

HAVANATUR

RESTAURANTE BAR
GUITARRA MÍA

JOSÉ FRITZE

A. MELLA

To
La Boca

CÁRDENAS

JAVIER

BANK

IBEROSTAR
GRAN HOTEL
TRINIDAD

CUBANACÁN/
CUBACAR

A

FRANCISCO

BUFETE
INTERNACIONAL

Parque
Céspedes

TELEPHONE

CINEMA

CASA FISCHER/PARADISO

RODRIGUEZ

ANTONIO

GUITERAS

IGLESIA
DE PAULA

CASA DE
JEDREZ

CADECA

FRANCISCO

LINO

PÉREZ

ETECSA

BANK

CODAINA

CLÍNICA
INTERNACIONAL

CENTRO DE
PROMOCIÓN
CULTURAL

HOSPITAL

GENERAL

FÁBRICA DE
TABACOS

CAMILO CIENFUEGOS

JESÚS BETANCOURT

MANUEL FAJARDO

0   200 yds

0   200 m

RAILWAY
STATION

STEAM
TRAINS

ANTIGUO CUARTEL

PASEO AGRAMONTE

FARMERS
MARKET

PAZ

ELIOPE

BASEBALL
STADIUM

PERSEVERANCIA

To Gas Station, Immigration,
Casilda, and Playa Ancón

POLICE

© AVALON TRAVEL

monument in 1965. A restoration committee was established, and the historic core has since been restored. In 1988 UNESCO named Trinidad a World Heritage Site.

Orientation

Trinidad slopes uphill, to the northeast. The cobbled historic core (*casco histórico*) with most sights of interest takes up the upper quarter, bounded to the south by Calle Antonio Maceo and to the east by Calle Lino Pérez. At its heart is Plaza Mayor, at the top of Calle Simón Bolívar. Some streets end at T junctions, while others curl or bifurcate, one leading uphill while another drops sharply to another Y fork or right-angled bend. All this was meant to fool marauding pirates, but it does a pretty good job on visitors, too. The streets are each sloped in a slight V, with gutters in the center (according to legend, the city's first governor had a right leg shorter than the other and could thereby be level when walking the streets by staying on the right-hand side). Many streets are closed to traffic by stone pillars and cannons stuck nose-first in the ground.

Below the touristed core, the streets are paved and laid out on a rough grid with Parque Céspedes at its center. The main street is Calle José Martí, which runs northwest-southeast. Calle Bolívar runs perpendicular northeast to Plaza Mayor. Calle Camilo Cienfuegos, one block southeast of Parque Céspedes, is the major northeast-southwest thoroughfare.

The Circuito Sur road from Cienfuegos bifurcates as it enters Trinidad: Calle Piro Guinart (to the left) leads to the historic core; Anastacio Cárdenas (to the right) skirts the southern end of town and connects with Camilo Cienfuegos (for Sancti Spíritus) and Paseo Agramonte (to Casilda and Playa Ancón).

Most streets have two names: a colonial name and a postrevolutionary name.

★ Plaza Mayor and Vicinity

This graceful plaza lies at the heart of the

Trinidad Street Names

Colonial Name	New Name
Alameda	Jesús Menéndez
Amargura	Juan Márquez
Angarilla	Fidel Claro
Boca	Piro Guinart
Carmén	Frank País
Colón	Colón
Cristo	Fernando H. Echerrí
Desengaño	Simón Bolívar
Encarnación	Vicente Suyama
Gloria	Gustavo Izquierdo
Guaurabo	Pablo Pichs Girón
Gutiérrez	Antonio Maceo
Jesús María	José Martí
Lirio	Abel Santamaría
Media Luna	Ernesto Valdés Muñoz
Olvido	Santiago Escobar
Peña	Francisco Gómez Toro
Real	Rubén Martínez Villena
Reforma	Anastasio Cárdenas
Rosario	Francisco Javier Zerquera
San Procopio	Lino Pérez
Santa Ana	Jose Mendoza
Santo Domingo	Camilo Cienfuegos

original settlement. The park at its core is ringed with silver trellises, with wrought-iron benches beneath the shade of palms and hibiscus bowers. The plaza is adorned with neoclassical statues.

On the plaza's northeast corner is the modest **Iglesia Parroquial de la Santísima Trinidad** (Mon.-Sat. 11am-12:30pm). The cathedral was rebuilt in 1892 on the site of the original parish church. Restored in 1996,

Trinidad Casco Histórico

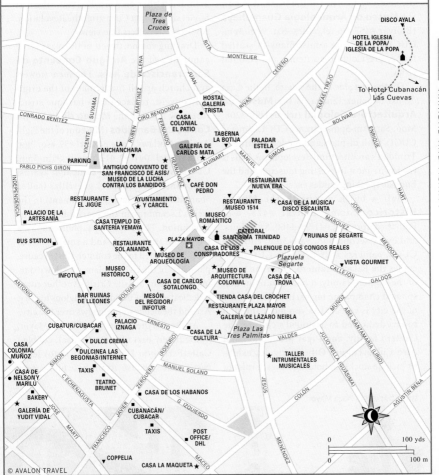

it is more English than Spanish inside, with a Victorian-Gothic vaulted ceiling and altar carved from mahogany; there's no baroque extravagance, although the carved statuary is intriguing, as is the 18th-century Cristo de la Vera Cruz (Christ of the True Cross).

On the northwest corner is Palacio Brunet, a beautifully preserved, two-story mansion dating from 1741 and housing the **Museo Romántico** (Calle Echerrí #52, esq. Calle Bolívar, tel. 041/99-4363, Tues.-Sun.

9am-5pm, entrance CUC2, cameras CUC2). The dozen rooms are filled with intriguing artwork and fabulous antiques. Note the solid carved-cedar ceiling, dating from 1770, and the *mediopunto* arches. Upstairs, step out onto the balcony to admire the view over the square. The stunning wrought-iron bed is the only heirloom of the Brunet family original to the house. The museum is frequently closed for lengthy periods of rehabilitation.

During his investigative sojourn in Cuba

in 1801, German explorer Alexander von Humboldt stayed at the Casa Padrón, on the southwest corner of the plaza. It is now the **Museo de Arqueología Guamuhaya** (Bolívar #457, no tel., Tues.-Sat. 9am-5pm, CUC1), exhibiting a miscellany of stuffed fauna, pre-Columbian items, and colonial relics.

On the east side of the square, in the Casa de los Sánchez Iznaga, is the **Museo de Arquitectura Colonial** (tel. 041/99-3208, Mon.-Sat. 9am-5pm, entrance CUC1, cameras CUC1), with displays and models relating to Trinidad's architectural development. This is the town's most interesting museum, and the English-speaking guides excel.

Half a block downhill, the **Museo Histórico** (Simón Bolívar #423, esq. Francisco Toro, tel. 041/99-4460, Sat.-Thurs. and every second Sun. 9am-5pm, entrance CUC2, cameras CUC1, videos CUC5) occupies the Palacio Cantero. Once the home of the Cantero family, it had a fountain that spouted champagne for parties. The history of the city is revealed as you move through rooms dedicated to Trinidad's culture, the Cantero family, and sugar production and Afro-Cuban culture. Other intriguing exhibits include stocks for holding slaves, a *volanta*

(single-axle horse-drawn carriage), and a scale model of the *Andrei Vishinsky,* which entered Trinidad harbor on April 17, 1960—the first Soviet ship to visit Cuba after the Revolution. A watchtower offers fine views.

Drawing you northwest of the plaza is the campanile of the **Antiguo Convento de San Francisco de Asís.** The *torre* (tower) and church are all that remain of the original convent, replaced by a baroque structure now housing the **Museo de la Lucha Contra Los Bandidos** (Museum of the Fight Against Outlaws, Calle Echerrí #59, esq. Pino Guinart, tel. 041/99-4121, daily 9am-5pm, CUC1), which traces the campaign against the counterrevolutionary guerrillas (called "bandits" by the Castro government) in the Sierra Escambray in the years following the Revolution. There are maps, photographs, a CIA radio transmitter, and a small gunboat the CIA donated to the counter-Castro cause, plus parts of the U-2 spy plane shot down during the Cuban Missile Crisis. Another room is dedicated to the building's religious history. Ascend the bell tower for views over the city.

At the northeast corner of Plaza Mayor, immediately east of the cathedral, cobbled Calle Fernando Hernández (Cristo) leads past a wide staircase. At the base of the steps

street buskers in Plaza Mayor

is a handsome ocher-colored house—the **Mansión de los Conspiradores**—with an ornately woodworked balcony. The house is so named because La Rosa Blanca (the secret organization against Spanish colonial rule) met here.

One block east on Cristo brings you to the triangular **Plazuela de Segarta** and Calle Jesús Menéndez, containing some of the oldest homes in the city, among them the **Casa de la Trova,** dating to 1777. Off the northeast corner of the *plazuela* is Calle Juan Manuel Márquez, featuring a trio of houses with wonderfully photogenic elevated galleries.

Plazuela Real del Jigüe

This charming triangular plaza (Piro Guinart y Villena), one block northwest of Plaza Mayor, has a calabash tree in the center. The tree, planted in December 2009, is the youngest in a succession of trees kept alive since 1514, the year the Spanish celebrated their first mass here. Kitty-corner to El Jigüe is the **Ayuntamiento y Cárcel** (Piro Guinart #302), the old town hall and jail, with a portion of the original stone-and-lime masonry exposed for view.

Immediately east, the **Casa Templo de Santería Yemayá** (Villena #59) features a Santería altar to Yemayá, *orisha* of water and maternity. Host *santero* Israel gives well-rehearsed explanations about the religion and may even offer to cleanse you with "holy" water and a horsehair brush.

Plaza de Tres Cruces

Four blocks northwest of Plaza Mayor along Villena is **Plaza de Tres Cruces,** a bare-earth area pinned by three wooden crosses that for several centuries have formed the terminus of Trinidad's annual Easter procession. Note the houses with metal crosses on their exterior walls: these are way-stops on the procession and extend along Calle Juan Manuel Márquez.

This zone is the heart of untouristed Trinidad. It's especially worth visiting in early morning when the cobbled streets resound to the clip-clopping of passing cowboys and men on burros.

Parque Céspedes and Vicinity

Trinidad's main square today is six blocks southeast of Plaza Mayor, on Calle Martí and Lino Pérez, and thronged with locals using public Wi-Fi. On the southwest side is the tiny **Iglesia de Paula,** with the town hall kitty-corner.

One block northwest of the plaza, at the

Museo Histórico

restored Casa Frias, **La Maqueta** (Colón esq. Gutiérrez, Mon.-Sat. 9am-5pm, CUC1) displays a model of the city with every building shown to scale and in detail.

Follow Lino Pérez south five blocks to the **Antigua Cuartel de Dragones** (Prolongación de Camilo Cienfuegos), a former dragoons' barracks built in 1844. At press time it was awaiting conversion into a conference center. Three retired antique **steam trains** to the rear are for ogling only.

Entertainment and Events

Chess fans should check out the **Casa de Jedrez** (Lino Pérez #292) on the east side of Parque Céspedes.

Trinidad is known for its local beverage, the *canchánchara,* made from *aguardiente* (raw rum), mineral water, honey, and lime. Try it at the atmospheric **Taberna La Canchánchara** (Rubén Martínez, esq. Girón, tel. 041/99-6231, daily 24 hours), where a cigar roller gives demonstrations and live bands kick up for tourist groups. For a more authentic experience, head to **Taberna La Botija** (Márquez, esq. Piro Guinart, tel. 041/28-3047, www.labotija.trinidadhostales.com, 24 hours), re-created as a bodega of yore serving chilled beer in ceramic mugs.

State entity Palmares has re-created both of Havana's Hemingway dives in Trinidad. **La Floridita** (General Lino Pérez #313, esq. Francisco Codania, 24 hours) is replete with a life-size replica of the author propping up the bar. **Bodeguito del Medio** (Villena #29, esq. Girón, noon-midnight) is festooned with graffiti signatures.

Local youth showcase their salsa moves during concerts in the courtyard at **Casa de la Música** (Juan Manuel Marquéz, e/ Bolívar y Menéndez, tel. 041/90-3414, CUC2). The steps that lead to it from Plaza Mayor get thronged with locals and tourists alike as live salsa bands hit the high notes.

Around midnight, the Casa de la Música crowd heads uphill for a memorable dancing experience at **Disco Ayala** (nightly 10pm-3am, CUC10 including open bar), in a giant cavern above and behind Hotel Pansea La Popa. Flashing lights and reggaeton amid the stalagmites and stalactites? Awesome! *Jineteros* and *jineteras* are as thick as the mosquitoes.

For rumba, don't miss the **Palenque de los Congos Reales** (Echerri #146, esq. Jesús Menéndez, daily 1:30pm-midnight, CUC1), half a block northeast of Plaza Mayor, which has a lively *espectáculo afrocubano* at 10pm. A stone's throw east, musicians drift in to jam and locals whisk tourists onto the dance floor at **Casa de la Trova** (Echerri #29, tel. 041/99-6445, daily 10am-2am, CUC1), where *son* is the name of the game. The **Casa de la Cultura** (Zerquera, esq. Ernest Valdes, tel. 041/99-4308, daily 8am-10pm, free) also hosts traditional music, as does **Casa Fischer** (Lino Pérez #312, e/ Cadahia y Martí, tel. 041/99-6486), which also hosts daily dance and drumming lessons (CUC5).

The roofless ruins of Teatro Brunet house **La Casa de Cerveza** (Maceo #461, e/ Bolívar y Zerquera, daily 10am-midnight, CUC2), a beer hall serving Cristal and Bucanero. It also hosts live music and an *espectáculo campesino* (peasant show) on Wednesday.

Trinidad has a tradition for *madrugadas,* early-morning performances of regional songs sung in the streets. Though rarely heard today, *madrugadas* highlight the town's weeklong **Semana de la Cultura** in early January.

Every Easter during **El Recorrido del Vía Crucis** (The Way of the Cross), devout Catholics follow a route through the old city, stopping at 14 sites marked with crosses. The weeklong **Festival de Semana Santa** (Holy Week celebration) features street processions.

For nine days during Christmas, Trinitarios observe **Fiestas Navideñas,** a street re-creation of Mary and Joseph's journey by donkey. Each night the procession ends at a different house, with a fiesta for children.

Recreation

"Horse whisperer" Julio Muñoz offers guided horseback rides at **Centro Ecuestre Diana** (tel. 041/99-3673, www.trinidadphoto.com/

The Cuban Horse Whisperer

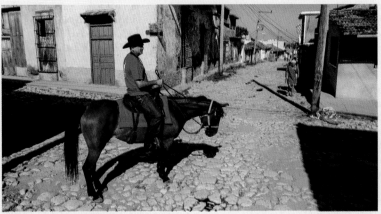

"Horse-whisperer" Julio Muñoz

Local "horse whisperer" Julio Muñoz founded **Proyecto Diana** (Calle Martí #401, esq. Santiago Escobar, tel. 041/99-3673, www.diana.trinidadphoto.com) to make the world, or at least Cuba, a better place for horses. Despite rural Cuba still being an equine culture, care of horses leaves much to be desired. For example, when horses sicken they are often treated with home remedies that sometimes aggravate the horse's condition, or they're left to die because the owner lacks the means to treat the condition. And the traditional method of breaking in a horse causes pain and damage.

Julio started the project after his horse Diana died of colic, and he has since studied the methods of "horse whisperer" Monty Roberts. He wants to change things by educating local farmers, farriers, and horse owners. Donations of books, farriers' tools and equipment, and equine medicines are requested.

riding.html, CUC25 pp), a farm about three kilometers north of town in the hamlet of La Pastora. Julio also offers riding lessons. A highlight is to watch him pacify and mount an untrained horse using "horse whisperer" techniques. Reservations are required. You can lunch here on traditional campesino fare at the farm-style **Restaurante El Paraíso** (tel. 5819-1697 or 5380-6720, daily 9am-7pm).

Horseback riding is offered at **Parque Nacional El Cubano** (tel. 041/99-6611, daily 8am-4pm, CUC9 entrance including a drink), a fish farm one kilometer west of Trinidad. Trails lead to the Cascada Javira. Tour agencies in Trinidad handle bookings for

horseback riding (CUC15) at **Finca Dolores** (tel. 041/99-6481), a rustic farm-turned-tourist attraction on the banks of the Río Guaurabo, two kilometers west of Trinidad. This representation of a traditional farm features an aviary, cockfights, milking, and other farm activities during folkloric shows.

Shopping

All manner of arts and crafts are sold at the **artisans markets** held in Plazuelita Las Tres Palmitas and elsewhere around Plaza Mayor.

Galería-Estudio Lázaro Niebla (Real del Jigüe #452, tel. 5294-0210, www.lazaronie-bla.com), next to the Restaurant Plaza Mayor, features one-of-a-kind works of art: bas-relief carvings of old Trinitarios carved into antique door panels. Lázaro also sells exquisite conceptual pieces (from CUC150). His wife, Leanys, is part of a 36-member lace-making cooperative whose wares are sold around the corner at **La Casa El Crochet** (Zerquera, esq. Real del Jigüe).

A favorite place for quality art is the **Galería de Carlos Mata** (Piro Guinart #367, e/ Juan M. Márquez y Fernando H. Echerrí, tel. 041/99-4380), selling international-quality collector's pieces, including Carlos's night scenes of Trinidad. The internationally acclaimed works of Yudit Vidal are sold at **Galería Yudit Vidal** (Desengaño #295 e/ Jesús María y Carmen, tel. 5290-3681, www.yuditvidal.com).

Galería Orbeín Licor Zayas (Zerquera #407 e/ Rubén Villena y Ernesto Valdés Muñoz, tel. 5248-9761, orbein.licor@nauta.cu) sells beautiful handcrafted silverwork.

For cigars and rum, head to **Casa del Habano** (Maceo, esq. Zerquera, tel. 041/99-6256, daily 9am-7pm).

The **Casa de la Música** (Juan Manuel Márquez, e/ Bolívar y Menéndez, tel. 041/99-3414) has a wide selection of CDs. Musical instruments can be bought at the **Taller de Instrumentales Musicales** (Menéndez #127-A, e/ Ernesto Valdés y Colón, tel. 041/99-3617), where bongos, *timbales,* and other instruments are made.

Much of the ceramic work sold locally is made at **El Alfarero Casa Chichí** (Andres Berro Macias #51, e/ Pepito Tey y Abel Santamaría, tel. 041/99-3146, daily 8am-8pm), where the Santander family carries on a tradition of pottery making.

Food

Most *casas particulares* provide meals. The following *paladares* are the tip of the iceberg.

The best meal in town is served at ★ **Vista Gourmet** (Callejón de Galdós, e/ Ernesto Valdéz y Callejón de Gallegos, tel. 041/99-6700 or 5277-0905, tahiri_bolo@yahoo.es, daily noon-midnight), where owner and

sommelier "Bolo" oversees an incredible rooftop alfresco buffet (CUC17, or CUC10 vegetarian) that includes hot plates and desserts. On the à la carte menu, try the lamb in Pernod or seafood mix with white wine. You get fantastic views while musicians entertain.

For cozy ambience try **Guitarra Mía** (Jesús Menéndez #19, e/ Cienfuegos y Pérez, tel. 041/99-3452 or 5270-3174, restaurantequitarramia@yahoo.es, daily noon-midnight), owned by Pepito, son of famous guitarist Pepe López. Redbrick walls are decorated with guitars painted with Trinitario scenes and troubadours usually play. I enjoyed a superb *tostones rellenos* (stuffed plantain cups) with tuna served with squash shaped like a guitar.

The stunning ★ **Restaurante Sol Ananda** (Calle Real #45, esq. Simón Bolívar, tel. 041/99-8281, daily noon-midnight, CUC8-15) faces north onto Plaza Mayor and combines delicious local cuisine and antique elegance—the silverware and the antique bed in one room are something to behold. The *ropa vieja* is delicious, but my favorite is the truly sublime shrimp in coconut curry sauce.

Of state-run restaurants, **Restaurante Plaza Mayor** (Zerquera, esq. Villena, tel. 041/99-6470, daily noon-10pm, CUC10) offers a superb all-you-can-eat buffet, but at peak hours it's usually packed with tour groups.

Feeling flush? Then dress up to dine at the **Restaurant Gourmet,** in the Iberostar Gran Hotel Trinidad. The creative fare includes smoked salmon appetizer and such entrées as sautéed shrimp over spinach in white wine sauce, and candied tenderloin steak in red wine with mashed potatoes. You can purchase a buffet breakfast (7am-10am, CUC15), lunch (12:30pm-3pm), or dinner (7pm-10pm, CUC20 for appetizer and dessert, or CUC35 for three courses).

For ice cream, head to **Dulce Crema** (Antonio Maceo, e/ Bolívar y Zerquera, daily 10am-10pm) or **Coppelia** (Martí e/ Zerquera y Colón, tel. 041/99-6468, daily 8am-8:40pm). State-run **Dulcinea La Begonia** (tel. 041/99-4287, daily 7:30am-10pm), opposite Dulce Crema, is the best café around, with espressos, cappuccinos, and yummy cakes and pastries. This is the liveliest corner in town and Dulcinea the place to watch the world go by.

Competing for most relaxing café is the private **Café Don Pepe** (Piro Guinart, esq. Villena, tel. 041/99-3573, 8am-midnight), with a tree-shaded patio where you can savor a huge menu of coffee drinks—iced coffee with cola, simple espresso, or cappuccino—served in ceramic mugs with a square of Cuban chocolate.

The best-stocked supermarket is **Galería Comercial Universo** (Martí, e/ Zerquera y Colón). You can buy produce at the *mercado agropecuario* (Pedro Zerquera, esq. Manuel Fajardo, Mon.-Sat. 8am-6pm, Sun. 8am-noon) and baked goods at the bakery at Simón Bolívar and Martí (7am-7pm).

Accommodations

A good resource for additional listings is **TrinidadRent** (tel. 41/99-3673 or 5290-0810, www.trinidadrent.com).

CASAS PARTICULARES

Trinidad has thousands of *casas particulares*. More are being added and city planners talk of banning new units. Finding a room in high season can be a challenge. Owners will call around to help you find a place if you don't have a reservation.

I stay at ★ **Casa Colonial Muñoz** (Calle Martí #401, esq. Santiago Escobar, tel./fax 041/99-3673, www.casa.trinidadphoto.com, CUC35), a venerable home built in 1800 and featured in *National Geographic*. The timeworn house has period furnishings, including swords, old clocks, and centenary prints. Its three lofty-ceilinged bedrooms and bi-level duplex (the upper room has a king four-poster) each have two double beds and fans, and modern, private bathrooms. Julio Muñoz, the English-speaking owner and a professional photographer, offers horseback rides and photo tuition. You can reserve by credit card. Beware: Some other *casa particular* owners pretend to be Julio Muñoz to steal his business, and *jineteros*

are known to steer you to such houses for a commission.

I've enjoyed several stays with Julio's neighbor at **Casa de Nelson y Marilú** (Santiago Escobar #172, e/ Frank País y Martí, tel. 041/99-2899, hostalmarilu@yahoo.es, CUC25), with three rooms, including a pleasant cross-ventilated rooftop chamber with a modern bathroom. Meals are served under an arbor on the rooftop terrace with rockers, hammock, and a plunge pool.

Casa de Carlos Sotolongo (Calle Rubén Martínez Villena #33, tel. 041/99-4169, galinkapuig@gmail.com, CUC30), on the southeast corner of Plaza Mayor, is another atmospheric winner. Vast front doors open to a cavernous lounge with antiques, modern art, and a colonial tile floor. Local art critic Carlos Sotalongo rents two rooms with terra-cotta floors, metal-frame beds, and private hot-water bathrooms.

The antiquities are even more impressive at **Casa Sara Sanjuan Álvarez** (Simón Bolívar #266, e/ Frank País y Martí, tel. 041/99-3997, CUC30), a well-kept, beautifully furnished colonial home that opens to an exquisite rose garden with rockers. Four rooms (two up, two down) have fans, refrigerators, and modern bathrooms. There's secure parking.

Hostal Sandra y Victor (Antonio Maceo #613, e/ Piro Guinart y Pablo Pichs, tel. 041/99-6444, www.hostalsandra.com, CUC25 low season, CUC30 high season), just 100 meters from the bus station, has three upstairs rooms with private bathrooms and hot water. A spacious lounge has rockers, and a delightful rooftop terrace features artistic ceramic walls and a bar.

An amazing colonial option, ★ **Casa Colonial El Patio** (Ciro Redondo #274, e/ Juan M. Márquez y Fernando H. Echerrí, tel. 5359-2371, ssofiapg@yahoo.es, CUC30) was recently restored with aid from the historian's office. It retains its original *alfarje* roof, exposed wall murals, and colonial tile floor. The rear garden patio is an exquisite space, and the two rented rooms are furnished with period pieces.

In 2017, the sublime 10-bedroom ★ **Mansión Alameda** (Calle Jesus Mendez #69, e/ Lino Perez y Bernaz Paz, tel. 041/99-8313 or 5485-1229, www.mansionalameda.com, CUC125-240 s, CUC135-250 d low season, CUC140-290 s, CUC150-300 d high season) opened as a restored 18th-century mansion offering boutique hotel standards and staggering European rates. It operates like a hotel, with 24/7 room service. There's a minimum two-night stay.

HOTELS

Lovely and intimate define Cubanacán's **Hotel E La Ronda** (Calle Martí #239, e/ Lino Pérez y Colón, tel. 041/99-8538, www.hotelescubanacan.com, CUC107 s, CUC143 d low season, CUC128 s, CUC170 d high season), on the northwest corner of Parque Céspedes. This restored 1868 building offers 14 delightfully furnished air-conditioned rooms with a turn-of-the-20th-century retro feel. Alas, it's vastly overpriced.

Despite its breeze-swept hillside setting with views, the 114 rooms at **Hotel Cubanacán Las Cuevas** (Calle General Lino Pérez final, tel. 041/99-6133, reservas@cuevas.co.cu, CUC77 s, CUC118 d, including breakfast) are overpriced. A thatched restaurant

and bar serve mediocre food, but a swimming pool, car rental, game room, and nightly cabaret are pluses. It's a stiff uphill hike from town on a hot day.

Cubanacán's delightful and peaceful (if overpriced) riverside **Horizontes Finca Ma Dolores** (tel. 041/99-6481, comercial@dolores.co.cu, CUC45 s, CUC70 d low season, CUC57 s, CUC82 d high season, including breakfast), two kilometers west of Trinidad, enjoys an appealing rustic setting and offers 19 modern rooms, plus 26 cabins. *Criolla* meals are served in a lovely thatched restaurant. It has a swimming pool and horseback rides.

The gorgeous ★ **Iberostar Gran Hotel Trinidad** (Martí 262, esq. Lino Pérez, tel. 041/99-6070, comercial@iberostar.trinidad.co.cu, from CUC165 s, CUC220 d low season, CUC245 s, CUC380 d high season), on Parque Céspedes, is perhaps the finest urban hotel outside Havana. It mixes colonial elegance with sumptuous contemporary refinements. Highlights include a clubby cigar lounge, game room with pool table, and a chic bar and restaurant.

At press time, the derelict La Popa church was being integrated as the entrance to the deluxe, hacienda-themed **Hotel Pansea La**

antique furnishings at Casa Sara Sanjuan Álvarez

Popa (www.pansea.com), under construction atop the hill on the north side of town. The 52-suite hotel will be managed by a French company. Restoration has been stop-and-go for several years, but hopes are that it will open soon.

Information and Services

Infotur (Izquierda e/ Bolívar y Guinart, tel. 041/99-8257, Mon.-Fri. 8:30am-6pm, Sat.-Sun. 8:30am-5pm) has a tourist information bureau opposite the bus terminal.

Banks include **Bandec** (Martí #264, e/ Colón y Zerquera), **Banco Popular** (Colón y Miguel Calzada), and **Banco Financiero Internacional** (Cienfuegos, esq. Martí). You can exchange currency at **Cadeca** (Martí #164, e/ Lino Pérez y Céspedes, Mon.-Fri. 8am-3pm).

The **post office** (Maceo #418, e/ Zerquera y Colón, tel. 041/99-2443) has DHL service. The usually crowded **Etecsa** (Lino Pérez y Francisco Pettersen, tel. 041/99-6020, daily 8:30am-7:30pm) has international phone and Internet service. Parque Céspedes and the steps below Casa de la Música are public Wi-Fi zones. **Dulcinea Las Begonias** (Maceo #473, esq. Bolívar, daily 9am-9pm) has Internet service, but charges CUC3 per 20 minutes.

The **Clínica Internacional** (Lino Pérez #103, esq. Cárdenas, tel. 041/99-6492, 24 hours) has a pharmacy; it charges CUC25 per consultation and CUC50 for house calls. **Hospital General** (Maceo #55, esq. Elipe Paz, tel. 041/99-4012) is a kilometer southeast of the colonial core.

The **police station** (Julio Cuevas Díaz #20, e/ Pedro Zerquera and Cárdenas, tel. 041/99-6900) is one block east of Paseo Agramonte, on the south side of town.

Bufete Internacional (Frank País, esq. Colón, tel. 041/99-6489, notario@bufete.tdad. cyt.cu, Mon.-Fri. 8am-5pm) can assist with legal matters.

Getting There and Away
BUS

Buses arrive and depart the **Terminal de Ómnibus** (Izquierda, esq. Piro Guinart, tel. 041/99-6676), including **Víazul** buses (tel. 041/99-2214, www.viazul.com, ticket office daily 8am-5pm) that link Trinidad with Havana (CUC25, via Matanzas, Varadero, and Cienfuegos twice daily, and via Cienfuegos and Playa Girón once daily); plus once-daily service to/from Viñales (CUC37, via Cienfuegos and Pinar del Río); Varadero (CUC20, via Cienfuegos and

Iberostar Gran Hotel Trinidad

Santa Clara); Cayo Santa María (CUC20, via Cienfuegos, Santa Clara, and Remedios); and Santiago de Cuba (CUC33, via all cities in between).

Transtur operates bus transfers between Trinidad and Cienfuegos, Havana, Varadero, and Santiago de Cuba, offered (for the same price as Víazul) as the ill-organized **Cubanacán Conectando** service by Cubanacán (Martí, e/ Lino Pérez y Cadahia, tel. 041/99-4753, www.viajescubanacan.cu).

TRAIN

The train station (tel. 041/99-3348, ticket booth open daily 4:30am-5pm) is at the bottom of Lino Pérez. The only service at last visit was a daily diesel commuter train to Casilda and to Meyer, in the Valle de los Ingenios. A diesel-hauled, two-car tourist train heads into the valley at 9:30am, stopping at Hacienda Iznaga, and returning about 2pm; buy your ticket (CUC10) from tour agencies.

Getting Around

Cubataxi (tel. 041/99-2340) provides taxi service. **Coco-taxis** (tel. 041/99-2214) cruise the streets (CUC1 minimum).

The **Trinidad Bus Tour** (CUC2) hop-on/hop-off minibus departs Cubatur (Maceo y Zerquera) at 9am, 11am, 2pm, 4pm, and 6pm and runs to Playa Ancón, La Boca, and Finca Ma Dolores.

CAR

For car rental, try **Cubacar** (Lino Pérez, e/ Martí y Francisco Cadalia, tel. 041/99-6633; and Bolívar, esq. Maceo, tel. 041/99-6257); **Gaviota** (tel. 041/99-6235), which offers house-to-house taxi service between Havana and Trinidad (about CUC110); or **Vía** (Frank País, e/ Fidel Claro and Bolívar, tel. 041/99-6388).

The Oro Negro gas station is northeast of town on Fausto Pelayo. A Cupet gas station is south of town on Paseo Agramonte (the road to Casilda).

EXCURSIONS

Cubatur (Maceo y Zerquera, tel. 041/99-6314), **Cubanacán** (Martí, e/ Lino Pérez y Cadahia, tel. 041/99-4753), and **Havanatur** (Calle Lino Pérez e/ Morón y Cadahia, tel. 041/99-6317) offer excursions. **Paradiso** (Lino Pérez, e/ Cadahia y Martí, tel. 041/99-6486, paradiso@sctd.artex.cu), in Casa Fischer, specializes in cultural tours, including a guided city tour (CUC10).

★ LA BOCA AND PENÍNSULA DE ANCÓN

La Boca, five kilometers west of Trinidad, is a quaint fishing village with traditional tile-roofed *bohíos* and a single coastal road. It appeals for its pocket beaches amid coral coves favored by Trinitarios on weekends. **Casa Museo Alberto Delgado** (tel. 5219-9801, Tues.-Sat. 9am-5pm, Sun. 9am-12:30pm, free), two kilometers east of La Boca, honors a Castroite killed during the counterrevolutionary war. It has his pistol, uniform, and some personal effects.

The coast extends south of La Boca to a small point beyond which the long, narrow Península de Ancón curls east to **Playa Ancón,** enfolding a mangrove-lined lagoon—the Ensenada de Casilda. The four-kilometer-long beach has sugary white sand and turquoise waters, plus two all-inclusive hotels. During certain times of year a microscopic sea lice (*agua mala* or *caribe*) can cause infections.

The peaceful charm of this region is about to change. The peninsula is slated to be developed with two 18-hole golf courses, the 400-room **Meliá Trinidad** hotel, an aquatic park, and 2,850 villa-condos for sale to foreigners.

Recreation

Ancón's offshore reefs have more than 30 dive spots, including sunken vessels. **Cayo Blanco,** nine kilometers southeast of Ancón, is famous for its kaleidoscopic corals and sponges.

Scuba diving and snorkeling (CUC10) are offered at **Club Amigo Ancón** (tel.

041/99-6120, CUC35 per dive, CUC320 open-water course) and at **Cayo Blanco International Dive Center**, at the marina. **Marina Marlin** (tel. 041/99-6205) offers a sunset cruise (CUC20) and "seafari" excursion to Cayo Blanco (9am, CUC50), including snorkeling, plus fly-fishing (CUC280 up to six people), and deep-sea fishing (CUC300 up to four people).

Food and Accommodations

Of the two dozen *casas particulares* in La Boca, I like **Hostal Vista al Mar** (Calle Real #47, tel. 041/99-3716, CUC25), a simply furnished yet meticulously maintained home overlooking the beach and river mouth. Manolo and Sylvia, the owners, are gracious and fun hosts. Choose from three rooms, two with private bathrooms; you can also rent the whole house. It has parking.

★ **Hostal El Capitán** (Playa La Boca #82, tel. 041/99-3055, captaincasanovatrinidad@ yahoo.es, CUC25-30), 400 meters south of the village, has a nice location above the coral shore. The two rooms are cross-ventilated and well-lit with louvered windows and king beds. Delicious homemade meals are served on a patio—perfect for sunset. It has parking.

Cubanacán operates three all-inclusive hotels at Playa Ancón. The lackluster Soviet-style **Club Amigo Ancón** (tel. 041/99-6123, reserva@ancon.co.cu, from CUC84 s, CUC108 d low season, CU89 s, CUC124 d high season) is a favorite of Canadian and European charter groups. It has 279 air-conditioned rooms, plus a huge swimming pool and scuba diving.

Tucked on its own little beach west of Playa Ancón, Cubanacán's intimate **Club Amigo Costasur** (tel. 041/99-6174, reservas@costasur.co.cu, from CUC59 s, CUC92 d low season, CUC63 s, CUC96 d high season) is popular with German tour groups and has 112 pleasantly furnished rooms and 20 bungalows with contemporary wrought-iron furnishings. Still, this is no prizewinner, with mediocre food and entertainment.

The fanciest Cubanacán option is **Brisas Trinidad del Mar** (tel. 041/99-6500,

reservas@brisastdad.co.cu, from CUC92 s, CUC146 d low season, from CUC125 s, CUC156 d high season), a neocolonial low-rise haphazardly arrayed around a large freeform pool. The 241 rooms are spacious and have appealing bathrooms, and the buffet meals are passable.

The thatched **Rancho Grill Caribe** (no tel., daily 9am-10pm), above the coral shore between La Boca and Ancón, is a seafood grill. The best dining is at **Restaurante La Marinera** (Jovellanos #179 e/ Perla y Iglesia, tel. 041/99-5454 or 5248-9684, www.facebook. com/PaladarLaMarinera, daily noon-10pm), on a back street in Casilda. Fans blow up a storm in the shaded open-air patio to the rear, done up in maritime décor. The restaurant grows its own veggies to accompany the likes of lobster tails in salsa (CUC15), grilled fish (CUC13), and paella (CUC16.50). It provides transport for groups.

Getting There and Around

The **Trinidad Bus Tour** (CUC2) shuttle bus departs Cubatur (Maceo y Zerquera) at 9am, 11am, 2pm, 4pm, and 6pm and runs to Playa Ancón. A taxi to/from Trinidad costs about CUC10 one-way.

Marina Marlin (tel. 041/99-6205, www. nauticamarlin.tur.cu) has moorings, but it is *not* an international entry port. Bare-boat and skippered yachts and catamarans can be chartered here for inclusive multiday tours to the Jardines de la Reina and Archipiélago de ls Canarreos (from CUC300 per day up to eight people); reservations must be made prior to arrival in Cuba.

★ VALLE DE LOS INGENIOS

East of Trinidad, the Carretera de Sancti Spíritus drops into the Valle de los Ingenios, known more correctly as the Valle de San Luis. This UNESCO Cultural Heritage Site is named for the many sugar mills, or *ingenios* (43 at its peak), that sprang up over the centuries. The valley was Cuba's most important sugar-producing region into the 19th century.

Many of the mills and estate houses remain, mostly in ruin.

Sitio Histórico San Isidro de los Destiladeros (CUC1, daily 9am-5pm), signed from the highway about 10 kilometers east of Trinidad, features a three-story campanile. Partially restored, it is slated to become a museum on the sugar industry and slavery.

Most notable is **Sitio Histórico Guaímaro** (daily 7am-7pm), about 20 kilometers east of Trinidad, which boasts spectacular wall murals. The former estate of *marques* and sugar baron José Mariano Borrell has a chapel and a thatched bar. Guaímaro is about 600 meters off the highway via a dirt road that continues 11 kilometers (to be attempted in dry season only) to **Sitio Histórico San Pedro,** a rural village of tumbledown wattle-and-daub huts with a couple of restored colonial homes.

For a spectacular view over the valley, stop at **Mirador del Valle de los Ingenios** (no tel., daily 8am-5pm), a café-restaurant about five kilometers east of Trinidad, immediately before you drop into the valley.

Manaca-Iznaga

The quaint village of **Iznaga** is a picture-perfect gem with a prim little railway station.

The village, 14 kilometers east of Trinidad, is most famous for **Hacienda Iznaga** (tel. 041/99-7241, daily 9am-5pm), founded in 1750 by Manuel José de Tellería. In 1795 it was purchased by Pedro Iznaga, who rose to become one of the wealthiest slave traders and sugar planters in Cuba. The hacienda features a 43.5-meter-tall bell tower with seven levels, each smaller than the one beneath. It was built 1835-1845 by Alejo María del Carmen e Iznaga. You can ascend the 186 steps (CUC1) for a sensational view.

The hacienda is now a restaurant with a traditional *trapiche* (sugar press) out back. Lacework, a local specialty, is made and sold here.

Recreation

You can ride horses at **Casa Guachinango** (no tel., daily 9am-5pm), three kilometers north of Iznaga; a one-hour ride leads to mineral springs good for bathing. This 200-year-old hacienda-turned-restaurant boasts a beautiful setting above the Río Ay. It can be reached by walking along the train track (45 minutes) east from Iznaga.

In 2016, Cuba's third **zip line canopy tour** (tel. 5548-4912 or 5408-2620, daily 8am-5pm, CUC10) opened at the Mirador

Sitio Histórico Guaímaro

del Valle de los Ingenios, five kilometers east of Trinidad. It's a 15-minute run with four short cables.

Food and Accommodations
The **Hacienda Iznaga** (tel. 041/99-7241, daily 9am-5pm) serves *criolla* meals, as does **Casa Guachinango** (no tel., daily 9am-5pm), which is popular with tour groups on the excursion train. Savor fresh-squeezed *guarapo* (sugarcane juice) as the traditional band kicks up.

Getting There
A local diesel commuter train departs Trinidad for Meyer via the Valle de los Ingenios at 5am and 5:20pm (CUC5). It stops at Iznaga and Guachinango. Trains depart Meyer for Trinidad at 6am and 6:10pm.

A diesel train hauls two open-air carriages from Trinidad to Guachinango daily at 9:35am, with a lunch stop at Iznaga or Guachinango (CUC10; pay for lunch separately). It departs Guachinango at 2:30pm. Tour agencies make reservations.

The paved road from Iznaga to the Guachinango turnoff snakes through stupendously scenic mountains and connects with Fomento in Villa Clara.

★ GRAN PARQUE NATURAL TOPES DE COLLANTES
Five kilometers west of Trinidad, a turnoff from the coast road leads into the Sierra Escambray. Cuba's second-largest mountain range has slopes swathed in pines and ancient tree ferns, bamboo, and eucalyptus that are tremendous for hiking and birding. Although the bulk of the Sierra Escambray lies within Cienfuegos and Villa Clara provinces, most tourist attractions and hiking trails are accessed from Topes. Gran Parque Natural Topes de Collantes, officially a "Paisaje Natural Protejido" (Protected Natural Landscape), comprises four smaller parks administered by Gaviota, the Cuban military-run tourist entity.

At a refreshingly cool 790 meters is **Complejo Turístico Topes de Collantes** (tel. 042/54-0330 or 042/54-0117, www.gaviota-grupo.com, daily 8am-7pm), the administrative and interpretative center at **Parque Altiplano,** 21 kilometers from Trinidad. Topes is dominated by a massive concrete structure—the grotesque Kurhotel—built in 1936, when it served as a sanatorium for tuberculosis patients. Following the Revolution, the disease was eradicated in Cuba. The complex was developed as a resort area in the late 1970s and now focuses on nature and health tourism.

Check out the giant sundial outside the **Centro de Visitantes**, which has maps and interpretive exhibits and handles bookings.

One hundred meters below the visitors center is the incongruous **Museo de Arte Cubano Contemporáneo** (tel. 043/54-0347, daily 8am-8pm, CUC2), in the former home of a Cuban senator; it later housed Communist Party VIPs during visits. Its four rooms of stunning art include some 70 works by Flora Fong, Esteban Leyva, and other big names in Cuban art.

The **Casa Museo del Café** (7am-7pm), 400 meters south of the Kurhotel, is a delightfully rustic coffee shop selling drinks made from locally grown coffee. It has historical photos plus simple tools of the trade, and offers demonstrations of coffee production, plus two dozen coffee varieties growing in the **Jardín de Variedades del Café** up the hill. It sells its own Cristal Mountain brand. A stone's throw away, nip into the **Plaza de las Memorias** museum (Mon.-Sat. 8am-5pm) to learn about local history. Downhill 100 meters, **La Casa de Elida** and **Casa del Artesano** are re-creations of typical country homes.

Hiking Trails
A guide is not compulsory, but some trailheads are remote and are best reached on an organized excursion. You'll need sturdy footwear, as many trails are slippery.

Still Puffing Away

Until a few years ago, Cuba maintained about 200 operating steam trains, projecting yet another surreal image of an island lost in time. Most are of U.S. progeny and date from the 1920s (the first Cuban railway was built by the British in 1837). A few are still capable of thundering down the slim tracks with a full load of sugarcane. The trains are kept going because the sugar mills operate only four to five months a year, providing plenty of time to overhaul the engines and keep them in good repair so as to extract a few more thousand miles of hard labor.

However, the drastic closures of sugar mills initiated in 2002 delivered many clunky old engines to the grave. Others have been spruced up for passenger and tourist endeavors. Tourist steam trains currently operate from Australia, Morón, and Rafael Freyre.

PARQUE ALTIPLANO

The popular **Sendero Caburní** trail (CUC9, six kilometers round-trip) begins beside Villa Caburní, east of the Kurhotel, and zig-zags steeply downhill to **Salto de Caburní**, a spectacular 62-meter-high waterfall (in dry season the falls can dry up). You can also reach Caburní via the **Sendero Vegas Grandes**, which begins at the Soviet-style apartment blocks (known as Reparto El Chorrito) one kilometer below the Centro de Visitantes. It leads to the Cascada Vegas Grande, then continues to Caburní along unmarked trails; hire a guide.

The less demanding, 500-meter **Sendero Jardín de Gigantes** trail (CUC4) leads from the Plaza de las Memorias and sidles downhill through natural gardens of ferns to Parque La Represa, with a riverside restaurant. Towering trees top out with the *gigante*—supposedly the tallest mahogany in Cuba.

PARQUE CODINA

From the Casa Museo del Café, **Sendero La Batata** (CUC4, five kilometers round-trip) leads west to a cave system with an underground river and pools good for swimming. From La Batata, **Sendero de Alfombra Mágico** (CUC6) continues to **Hacienda Codina**, an erstwhile coffee estate that serves as a post for bird-watchers and hikers. Luncheons are laid on for tour groups, with roast suckling pig. Codina has an orchid garden with trails that lead to waterfalls and caves. It can also be reached by 4WD from the Topes-Manicuragua road via a dirt road that begins 1.5 kilometers north of the Kurhotel.

PARQUE GUANAYARA

About 15 kilometers northwest of Topes, **Parque Guanayara** is reached via a trail opposite the turnoff for Hacienda Codina on the Topes-Manicuragua. It descends to the **Casa La Gallega,** a farm-style riverside restaurant at the center of Parque Guanayara (it specializes in roast chicken). Most visitors arrive on excursions by Soviet trucks and begin hiking here by following the riverside **Sendero Centinelas del Río Melodioso** (CUC9) trail to the **Poza del Venado** blue hole or to the **Salto El Rocío** waterfall.

Food and Accommodations

Camping (CUC6) is allowed at Vegas Grandes and at Casa de Gallega.

The only *casa particular* at Topes is **Hostal Restaurante El Mere** (CUC20), a simple, rustic house. It has one no-frills, cross-ventilated rooftop room with a hot-water bathroom.

The area's top choice is the remarkable ★ **Ecoalojamiento El Manantial** (tel. 042/54-1325, manantial@nauta.cu, CUC25), six kilometers below Topes. This sensational two-story home of red brick and natural timbers has homemade beds in two simply furnished rooms. A balcony has hammocks for enjoying views over the fruit orchard and natural pool. Owners Aray and Oscar prove wonderful hosts and prepare meals, including roast suckling pig, on an open woodstove.

Masochists may enjoy the brutal Stalinist aesthetic of the massive **Kurhotel Escambray** (tel. 042/54-0180, from CUC35 s, CUC40 d low season, from CUC50 s, CUC48 d high season), reached via a stone staircase on a Siberian scale. The 210 air-conditioned rooms and 16 suites boast the essentials, including modern bathrooms. It has a modest restaurant, gyms, a beauty salon, movie theater, and a thermal swimming pool where massage and therapeutic treatments are offered. But the overriding feel is eerily clinical. The hotel's **Villa Caburní** (CUC23 s, CUC33 d low season, CUC27 s, CUC40 d high season) has apartment *cabinas* for up to four people.

Hotel Los Helechos (tel. 042/54-0330, from CUC29 s, CUC37 d low season, from CUC32 s, CUC45 d high season) hides in a cool valley below the Kurhotel. The shocking pink-and-green exterior befits this boxy oddity, with bamboo decor in spacious yet dowdy air-conditioned rooms with satellite TVs and modern bathrooms. Take a room in the front; the rest are poorly lit. It has a swimming pool and bowling alley, but the restaurant induces groans.

The only *paladar* is **Restaurante Gran Nena** (tel. 042/54-0338, daily 24 hours), a lovely place adjoining the museum. Occupying a historic *casona*, it has alfresco patio dining and serves Cuban dishes and seafood, plus pasta, using fresh produce from its own garden.

The riverside **Restaurante La Represa,** below Casa de Elida, would be a lovely spot to dine alfresco, but the peace is shattered by speakers blasting reggaeton.

Getting There

A public *camión* runs between Topes and Trinidad. The road rises in a steep, potholed, badly eroded switchback that eventually drops to Manicaragua, on the northern slopes. Drive with utmost caution! Stop at **Mirador de Hanabanilla,** eight kilometers north of Topes, for the spectacular views over Embalse Hanabanilla; the roadside café (daily 7am-7pm) even has beers and cappuccinos. All other routes through the mountains are suitable for four-wheel drive only.

Tour operators sell excursions by truck to Topes from Trinidad (CUC55). A taxi will cost CUC20 each way.

Ciego de Ávila and Camagüey

These contiguous and geographically similar provinces are dominated by rolling savannas and by the Cayería del Norte, low-lying, coral islands where Cuba's spectacular beaches dissolve into peacock-blue waters.

Officially called the Archipiélago de Sabana-Camagüey, but known to all Cubans as the Jardines del Rey (King's Gardens), this wilderness extends for some 470 kilometers in a great line parallel to the coast, between 10 and 18 kilometers from shore. Tourism development is concentrated on Cayo Coco and Cayo Guillermo.

The islands are mostly covered with low scrub—a perfect habitat for wild pigs and iguanas and birds. The briny lagoons are favored by pelicans, ibis, and flamingos. Running along the northern edge of the cays is coral reef.

Ernest Hemingway pursued German submarines here in the 1940s, immortalizing his adventures in his novel *Islands in the Stream*. It is possible to follow the route of the novel's protagonists as they hunted the U-boats east-west along the cays, passing Confites, Paredón Grande, Coco, Guillermo, and Santa María.

Much of the coastal plain is covered with scrubland and swampy marshland, perfect for bird-watching, and by lagoons, perfect for fishing. Inland, the undulating seas of green sugarcane merge with cattle country dominated by ranches—*ganaderías*—worked by *vaqueros* (cowboys) with lassoes.

Pancake-flat Ciego de Ávila (average elevation is less than 50 meters above sea level) is Cuba's least-populous province, and though it's the nation's leading pineapple producer, almost three-fourths of the province is devoted to cattle. The wedge-shaped province (6,910 square kilometers) forms Cuba's waist, stretching only 50 kilometers from coast to coast. There are few rivers and no distinguishing features, and few sights of historical interest, even in Ciego de Ávila and Morón, the only two towns of importance. By contrast, the city of Camagüey, capital of the nation's largest province, offers plenty of colonial charm. The surrounding honey-colored rolling plains are reminiscent of Montana,

---

Previous: Cayo Guillermo; Cayo Coco. **Above:** Playa Los Cocos.

Look for ★ to find recommended
sights, activities, dining, and lodging.

Highlights

★ **Parque Nacional Jardines de la Reina:** World-class sportfishing and diving await at way-off-the-beaten-track offshore cays studding crystal-clear shallows (page 336).

★ **Cayo Coco and Cayo Guillermo:** Beaches don't get any more gorgeous than at these sibling isles, with turquoise waters, flamingos, and top-class all-inclusive resort hotels (pages 341 and 345).

★ **Plaza San Juan de Dios:** This square is the most impressive of several atmospheric colonial plazas in the large provincial capital of Camagüey (page 351).

★ **Finca La Belén:** There's good hiking and bird-watching at this farm with exotic wildlife (page 356).

★ **Refugio de Fauna Silvestre Río Máximo:** The Caribbean's largest breeding ground for flamingos will wow you (page 358).

★ **Cayo Sabinal:** Coral fringes this lonesome cay with gorgeous white sand and peacock-blue waters (page 359).

★ **Scuba Diving at Playa Santa Lucía:** Though the Playa Santa Lucía beach resort is otherwise a dud, the diving is superb (page 360).

parched in summer by a scouring wind that bows down the long flaxen grasses. These upland plains are bounded to the north by a line of low mountains, the Sierra de Cubitas.

The sparsely populated southern plains are covered almost entirely by marshland and swamps. A slender archipelago—the Jardines de la Reina—lies off the southern coast, sprinkled east-west across the Golfo de Ana María. This necklace boasts fabulous beaches and birdlife, coral formations perfect for scuba diving, and shallow waters that offer angling delights. The region is gradually being opened to tourism.

PLANNING YOUR TIME

Running through the center of the provinces, the Carretera Central connects Ciego de Ávila and Camagüey cities with Havana and Santiago de Cuba. The cities are also major stops on the main east-west railway. The paved and less-trafficked Circuito Norte highway parallels the north coast at an average distance of five kilometers inland. Feeder roads connect it with the Carretera Central.

The 400 or so cays of the **Jardines del Rey** are separated from one another by narrow channels and from the coast by shallow lagoons. *Pedraplenes* (causeways) link Cayo Coco, Cayo Romano, and Cayo Sabinal to the mainland. Two days is barely sufficient for relaxing on **Cayo Coco** and neighboring **Cayo Guillermo** (connected by another *pedraplén*), the most developed of the keys, with more than a dozen all-inclusive resort hotels. If all you want is to relax with a rum cocktail on fine white sand, with breaks for water sports,

then this could be for you. You can rent a car for forays farther afield.

Gateway to these two cays is **Morón,** a small-scale town that boasts the excellent **Museo Caonabo** and the **Museo de Azúcar,** where a steam train ride is offered. Anglers can cast for game fish in nearby **Lago La Redonda.** Morón is served by trains, with direct connection to both Havana and Ciego de Ávila, the provincial capital.

More interesting by far is **Camagüey.** You could easily justify three days in this colonial city, which boasts several historic plazas. Camagüey is a gateway to **Playa Santa Lucía.** This beach resort appeals mostly to budget-minded Canadians and Europeans, with second-rate hotels and a desultory nightlife. Sure, the diving is exceptional, but that's about it. The hinterland is physically unappealing, although a worthwhile excursion is to **Cayo Sabinal,** with spectacular beaches and waters touted for future development. At **Rancho King,** you can watch a rodeo and even play cowboy for half a day.

Opportunities abound for bird-watchers, not least at **Finca La Belén,** a wilderness area southeast of Camagüey city. Set amid scenic terrain, it provides a rare opportunity for hiking and is served by a delightful hotel.

Divers, anglers, and yachters should set their sights on **Parque Nacional Jardines de la Reina.** This necklace of cays off the southern coast is accessed solely from the funky fishing village of Júcaro, south of Ciego de Ávila. Since 2016, visitation is no longer exclusively through a single agency; specialist cruise vessels are beginning to enter.

Ciego de Ávila and Camagüey Provinces

© AVALON TRAVEL

SANCTI SPIRITUS

Caribbean Sea

Archipiélago de los Jardines de La Reina

Golfo de Ana María

Caribbean Sea

PARQUE NACIONAL JARDINES DE LA REINA

WRECK OF THE FAISY

TORTUGA LODGE

Sanguily
Venezuela
Júcaro
AVALON DIVE CENTER
Baragua
Gaspar
SUR DE CIEGO DE AVILA GAME RESERVE

Cayos
Cayo Caoba
Ana María
Cayo Algodón Grande
Cayo Chocolate
Playa de Florida
Cayo Caguamas
Cayo Cabeza
Cayo Pilón
Cayo Media Luna

Laguna Lamar
Vertientes
Florida
Piedrecitas
Presa Caonao

CAMAGÜEY
Sierra de Cubitas

PLAZA SAN JUAN DE DIOS
CAMAGÜEY
AEROPUERTO IGNACIO AGRAMONTE

Cubitas
Sola
Caidijo
RESERVA ECOLÓGICA LIMONES TUABAQUEY
SILVESTRE RÍO MÁXIMO
RESERVA DE FAUNA
FARO COLON
CAYO SABINAL

Concordia
Jimaguayú
Contramaestre
Santa Cruz del Sur

CENTRAL
Najasa
Siboney
Sibanicú

FINCA LA BELÉN

Sierra del Chorillo

Guáimaro

LAS TUNAS

GRANMA

Dive Site

LAS TUNAS

LOS CANGILONES DEL RÍO MÁXIMO
Gurugú
Minas
CRIADERO DE COCODRILOS
SENADO
FABRICA DE INSTRUMENTOS MUSICALES
Crucero de Lugareño
INGENIO SANTA ISABEL
INGENIO DE SAN MIGUEL de Bagá
RANCHO KING
Camalote
Nuevitas
Bahía de Nuevitas

Presa Amistad Cubano-Búlgara
Presa La Mañana de Santa Ana
Cascorro
Palo Seco

MININT CHECKPOINT
Playa los Pinos
WRECK OF THE MORTERO
Playa Los Cocos
La Boca
Santa Lucía
Playa Bonita
Santa Cruz

(BADLY DETERIORATED)
SCUBA DIVING

CARRETERA
Río
Presa
Río

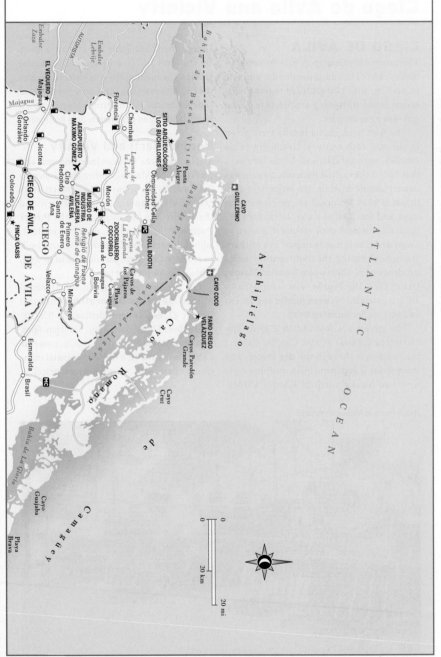

Ciego de Ávila and Vicinity

CIEGO DE ÁVILA

This provincial capital (pop. 85,000), 460 kilometers east of Havana, is worth a day's browse in passing, with two excellent regional museums, some intriguing architecture, and a pleasant pleasure park.

The first land grants locally were given in the mid-16th century. Gradually cattle ranches were established. Local lore says that one of the earliest hacienda owners was named Jacomé de Ávila. His property, established in 1538, occupied a large clearing, or *ciego*, and was used as a way station for travelers. A settlement grew around it, known as Ciego de Ávila. It rose to import as a military stronghold during the 19th-century independence wars. Cuba's own fortified Mason-Dixon Line, the Trocha, was completed in 1872; it extended between Morón and Júcaro and was connected by railroad.

The streets are laid out in a grid. The Carretera Central (Calle Chicho Valdés) runs east-west through the city center. The main street is Independencia, running east-west two blocks north of Chicho Valdés.

Independencia divides the city into *norte* (north) and *sur* (south) sections; Marcial Gómez, the main north-south street, divides the city into *este* (east) and *oeste* (west). Calle Independencia west of Parque Martí is now a lovely landscaped pedestrian-only boulevard.

Parque Martí and Vicinity

The central plaza, between Independencia and Libertad, and Marcial Gómez and Honorato del Castillo, has a bust of José Martí at its center. Victorian-era lampposts surround the square. On the south side, the **Poder Popular,** the town hall, dating from 1911, adjoins **Iglesia San Eugenio,** a church built in 1951; part art deco, part modernist in style, it boasts an impressive facade.

On the southeast corner, the splendid **Museo de Artes Decorativos** (Marcial Gómez #2, esq. Independencia, tel. 033/20-1661, Mon.-Thurs. 9am-5pm, Sat. 1pm-6pm, Sun. 8am-noon, entrance CUC1, cameras CUC1) is housed in a restored colonial mansion replete with all manner of priceless

steam trains at Museo de Azúcar

Ciego de Ávila

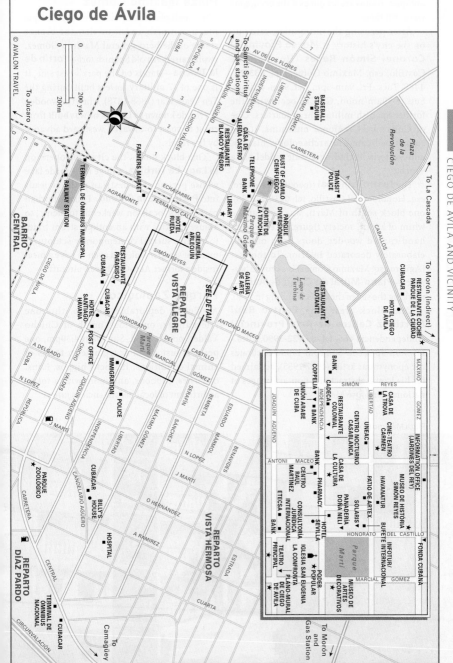

© AVALON TRAVEL

antiques; rooms are set out as if the occupants were still there.

After perusing the antiquities, catch up on the city's history at **Museo Provincial Coronel Simón Reyes** (Honorato de Castillo, esq. Máximo Gómez, tel. 033/20-4488, Tues.-Fri. 9am-5pm, Sat. 9am-4:30pm, Sun. 8:30am-noon, CUC1), occupying the former Spanish military headquarters. One of Cuba's best regional museums, it has rooms dedicated to archaeology, history, and Santería, including a scale model of La Trocha.

The **Teatro Principal** (Joaquín de Agüero, esq. Honorato del Castillo, tel. 033/22-2086), one block south of Martí, was built at the whim of a local society figure. Its enormous hand-carved wooden doors open onto an elaborately decorated interior. To the east (Agüero esq. Máximo Gómez) is a bronze bas-relief—**Plano-Mural de Ciego de Ávila**—marking the site of the city's founding in 1840.

One block west, the **Centro Raúl Mártinez Centro de Arte Provincial** (Independencia #65, tel. 033/22-3990, Tues.-Fri. 9am-9pm, Sat.-Sun 2pm-10pm) celebrates the eponymous artist (1927-1955), acclaimed for his iconic abstract and pop-art images of national hero José Martí.

Plaza Máximo Gómez

This small plaza, four blocks west of Parque Martí, is worth a visit to view the bronze statue of the hero-general Máximo Gómez, sword raised. An old Spanish fort—**Fortín de la Trocha**—stands on the park's east side. It is one of 17 military towers built during the Ten Years War (1868-1878), when the wooden barricade known as La Trocha was built from coast to coast to thwart a westward advance by the rebels.

One block north, the cityscape opens on to **Lago La Turbina,** a huge man-made lake whose perimeter pedestrian pathway leads into **Parque de la Ciudad.** This vast urban park draws locals on weekends to picnic, to amuse the kids with an antique steam train, to admire surreal contemporary sculptures made of scrap metal, and even to have a meal inside a former AeroCaribbean aircraft.

Parque Zoológico

As Cuba's deplorable zoos go, this one (Hernández, one block north of Chicho Valdés, no tel., Wed.-Sun. 9am-4:30pm, one peso) is just about acceptable in terms of animal conditions. It stocks hippos, lions, ostriches, baboons, and more with a token assortment of local beasts, such as *jutías*.

Plaza Máximo Gómez

Entertainment and Events

Patio de Artex (Libertad #162, tel. 033/26-6680) hosts an eclectic bag of live performances on its patio (Tues.-Sun. 8pm-2am), drawing the Generation Y crowd. The **Casa de la Trova** (Libertad #130, CUC3 including one drink) hosts traditional music for an older crowd, as does the **Casa de la Cultura** (Independencia #76, tel. 033/72-3974), which has *danzón* every Wednesday afternoon. The **Museo de Artes Decorativas** (Marcial Gómez #2, esq. Independencia, tel. 033/20-1661) has various cultural events, including classical and chorale.

Gotta get your kicks? The showgirls (and guys) at **Cabaret La Piñas** (Wed.-Sun., 10pm-2am, CUC2) perform Tropicana-style routines alfresco at Circulo Social Esteban López, beside the Carretera Central one kilometer west of the Circunvalación. After the show, patrons flood the stage to dance. The most popular disco is the Hotel Ciego de Ávila's **Discoteca Batanga** (Carretera Caballos, tel. 033/22-8013, 10pm-2am, CUC5).

Once the joke of Cuba's baseball leagues, Ciego's Tigres won the championship in 2012, 2015, and 2016. They play October-April at **Estadio José R. Cepero** (Máximo Gómez y Calle 5).

As expected for "The City of Pineapples," the highlight of the annual calendar is the **Festival de Música Fusión Piña Colada,** held at venues throughout town in April and ranging from jazz to trova and popular dance.

Food

Paladares are surprisingly few, but outstanding is **Restaurante Blanco y Negro** (Independencia #388 e/ 2 y 3, tel. 033/20-7744, daily noon-11pm, CUC8-15), a clean, nonsmoking option with a retro 1950s feel. Chef Alfredo Carbonnell delivers tasty and filling *criolla* staples. The house special is *trio de carnes* (chicken, fish, and pork, each with its own sauce).

La Casona (Calle 3 #16, e/ Independencia y Joaquín de Agüero, tel. 033/22-8355, www.privavila.com/lacasona, Tues.-Sun.

noon-3pm and 7pm-midnight) goes one better than Blanco y Negro. Its house special is La Picadera, with four types of fish and meat. A buffet guarantees to fill all comers.

State-run **La Confronta** (Marcial Gómez, esq. Joaquín de Agüero, tel. 033/20-0931, daily noon-3:45pm and 7pm-11:45pm), in a restored centenary mansion, whisks you back in time with its colonial decor and Benny Moré memorabilia. Pork dishes are the name of the game here. Even foreigners pay in pesos—even for cocktails!

The **Restaurante El Colonial** (Independencia Oeste #110, tel. 033/22-3595, daily 6pm-midnight) replicates a Spanish *bodega*, complete with statues of flamenco dancers, a bull's head over the bar, and cowhide chairs. The menu offers the usual *criolla* staples. Across the street, the **Unión Arabe de Cuba** (tel. 033/22-4865, Mon.-Fri. 8am-4pm and Sat.-Sun. 8am-10pm) spices its *criolla* menu with hummus and Levantine pastries.

For ice cream, join the line at **Coppelia** (Independencia Oeste, esq. Simón Reyes, Tues.-Sun. 9am-2pm and 4pm-10pm) or, one block west, **Cremería Arlequin** (esq. Agramonte, Mon. and Wed.-Fri. 10am-5pm and 7pm-10pm, and Sat.-Sun. until 11pm).

You can buy produce at the *mercado agropecuario* (Mon.-Sat. 6am-6pm), beneath the overpass at Chicho Valdés and Fernando Calleja, and baked goods at **Panadería Doña Neli** (daily 9am-9pm), on the northwest corner of Parque Martí.

Accommodations

CASAS PARTICULARES

Under new ownership, but still tops, is ★ **La Casona** (Calle 3 #16, e/ Independencia y Joaquín de Agüero, tel. 033/22-8355, www. privavila.com/lacasona, CUC25-30), a well-preserved 1959 middle-class home that whisks you back with its retro furnishings. It has three air-conditioned rooms; the spacious, wood-paneled upstairs room opens to a vast rooftop terrace. La Casona doubles as a *paladar*. There is secure parking.

Close to the center, **Billy's House** (Agüero

#206 e/ Onelio Hernández y Arnaldo, tel. 033/22-4869, CUC25-30) is a delightful home with two air-conditioned rooms featuring comfy mattresses. Owner Milena's clean, modern bathrooms would make anyone proud. Parking is free.

HOTELS

Typical of the Soviet-inspired staples throughout Cuba, Islazul's **Hotel Ciego de Ávila** (Carretera Caballos, tel. 033/22-8013, carpeta@hca.co.cu, CUC20 s, CUC32 d low season, CUC26 s, CUC42 d high season, including breakfast), in the heart of Parque de la Ciudad two kilometers northwest of downtown, has 143 pleasantly furnished air-conditioned rooms. Meals are ho-hum and the swimming pool is noisy on weekends.

Information and Services

Infotur (Honorato del Castillo, e/ Libertad y Independencia, tel. 033/20-9109, Mon.-Fri. 8:30am-4:30pm, alternate Saturdays 8:30am-4:30pm) provides tourist information with a smile.

The **post office** (Marcial Gómez, esq. Chico Valdés, tel. 033/22-2096), two blocks south of Parque Martí, has DHL service. **Etecsa** (Joaquín de Agüera, e/ Honorato y Maceo, daily 8:30am-7:30pm) has international phone and Internet service. Parque Martí and Parque Máximo Gómez have public Wi-Fi.

Bandec (Independencia Oeste, esq. Simón Reyes, and Independencia Oeste, esq. Antonio Maceo) and **Banco Popular** (Independencia, e/ Simón Reyes y Maceo) have branches. You can also change foreign currency at **Cadeca** (Independencia Oeste #118, e/ Maceo y Simón Reyes).

The **Hospital General** (Máximo Gómez #257, tel. 033/22-4015) is at the east end of town.

The **Consultoría Jurídica Internacional** (Independencia, e/ Honorato y Maceo, tel. 033/26-6238, Mon.-Fri. 8:30am-5pm) offers legal aid; the **police station** (Delgado, e/ Libertad and Independencia) is one block east of the main square. **Inmigración** (Mon. noon-7pm, Tues., Wed., and Fri. 8am-5pm, Thurs. and Sat. 8am-noon) is on Independencia, 50 meters east of the square.

Getting There and Around

AIR

The **Aeropuerto Máximo Gómez** (tel. 033/22-5717) is 22 kilometers north of town. **Cubana** (Chicho Valdés #83, e/ Maceo y Honorato, tel. 033/22-1117) offers flights from Havana.

BUS

The **Terminal de Ómnibus Nacional** (tel. 033/22-5114) is on the Carretera Central, 1.5 kilometers east of town. **Víazul** buses (tel. 033/20-3086, www.viazul.com) stop here between Havana and Santiago de Cuba.

The **Terminal de Ómnibus Municipal** (tel. 033/22-3076), next to the railway station, serves towns within the province.

TRAIN

The **Estación Ferrocarril** (Agramonte, tel. 033/22-3313) is on the south side of Parque Maceo. Trains #13 and #15 (Havana-Santiago de Cuba eastbound) and trains #12 and #16 (westbound) each stop here every fourth day.

CAR AND TAXI

You can rent cars at **Cubacar** (tel. 033/20-7133), on Candelario Agüero and at the bus station (tel. 033/20-5114). There are gas stations at the junction of the *circunvalación* and Carretera Morón (northeast of town); on Chicho Valdés and Martí; and two blocks east at Chicho Valdés and Independencia. For a taxi, call **Cubataxi** (tel. 033/22-7636).

★ PARQUE NACIONAL JARDINES DE LA REINA

The Garden of the Queens archipelago comprises around 660 deserted coral cays in a long chain that extends east-west for some 350 kilometers off the southern coast of Ciego de Ávila and Camagüey Provinces. The ecosystem is protected within Cuba's first marine park—the largest no-take marine reserve in the Caribbean. Flamingos wade in the briny shallows of the Golfo de Ana María. An extensive coral reef runs along the chain's southern shore, which is lined by white-sand beaches. The reef is one of the best-preserved such ecosystems in the world. Sharks are particularly numerous and divers often encounter curious (but apparently friendly) crocodiles.

The cays are nirvana for sportfishing and diving. Visitation is strictly controlled, with only 1,000 visitors a year permitted. Italian company **Avalon** (tel. 033/49-8104, www.cubandivingcenters.com and www.cubanfishingcenters.com) once held a monopoly on services, though its control has loosened since 2015.

Recreation

Avalon offers six-day/seven-night diving and fishing packages mid-October through August using six live-aboard vessels. Other specialist companies use Avalon's vessels, including Montana-based **Yellowdog Flyfishing Adventures** (tel. 406/585-8667, www.yellowdogflyfishing.com).

In 2016, **Lindblad Expeditions** (tel. 212/261-9000 or 800/397-3348, www.expeditions.com) was granted permission to visit Jardines de la Reina during its 11-day adventure cruises. **Aggressor Fleet** (tel. 706/993-2531 or 800/348-2628, www.aggressor.com) spends a week in the Jardines de la Reina during its 10-day "people-to-people" diving cruises. U.S. citizens can visit on a licensed travel program offered by **Ocean Doctor** (tel. 202/695-2550, http://oceandoctor.org/gardens).

Diving is permitted only with a guide, even if you arrive on your own yacht (contact Avalon). Professional scuba instructors even stage shark riding!

Getting There

You can hire catamarans and yachts from the European charter companies based in Cienfuegos and Marina Trinidad, but reservations must be made before arrival in Cuba. Private vessels must report to **Marina Júcaro** (www.nauticamarlin.tur.cu). Yachts can moor at the cays only with prior permission.

MORÓN AND VICINITY

The crossroads city of Morón (pop. 50,000), 37 kilometers due north of Ciego de Ávila, is the main gateway to Cayo Coco and Cayo Guillermo. It is perfectly positioned for day excursions to the cays and several intriguing sites outside town. It is known as the City of the Rooster, a name bequeathed in the 18th century by settlers from Morón de la Frontera, in Andalusia, Spain. Morón featured prominently during the independence wars. The Spanish colonial army built the 50-kilometer-long wooden barricade (La Trocha) from Morón to Júcaro. The town was captured by rebel troops in 1876.

Sights

The most worthwhile sight in town is the modestly impressive **Museo Municipal Caonabo** (Martí #115, tel. 033/550-4501, Tues.-Sat. 9am-5pm, Sun. 8am-noon, CUC1), occupying a three-story neoclassical former bank. Downstairs is dedicated to pre-Columbian culture. Upstairs the historical artifacts range from Spanish swords and mantillas to revolutionary icons, all thoughtfully displayed and labeled.

The city boasts the impressive **Terminal de Ferrocarriles** (Varhorne esq. Martí), a seemingly Teutonic-inspired railway station completed in 1924. To the rear is Cuba's largest locomotive works, occupying the former Baldwin Locomotive Works.

In the 1950s, Morón's city fathers erected a rooster, **El Gallo de Morón,** at the entrance to town. Fulgencio Batista was present for the unveiling. After the Revolution, an officer in the rebel army ordered the monument's destruction. In 1981, the city government decided to erect another cockerel in bronze at the foot of a clock tower outside the entrance to the Hotel Morón. It's fitted with

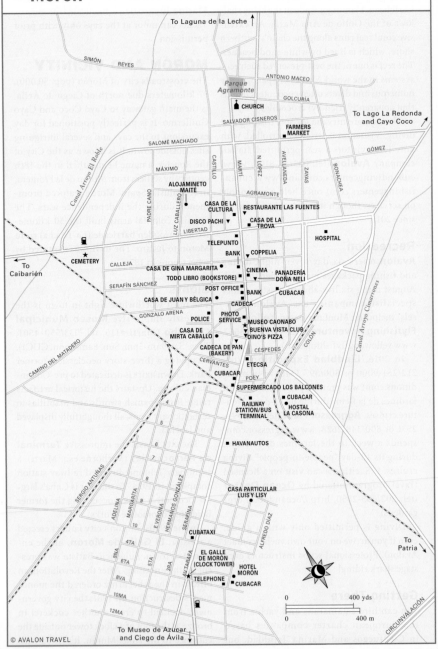

Morón

To Laguna de la Leche

SIMÓN REYES

ANTONIO MACEO

Parque Agramonte

GOLCURÍA

To Lago La Redonda and Cayo Coco

CHURCH

SALVADOR CISNEROS

FARMERS MARKET

SALOMÉ MACHADO

GÓMEZ

MÁXIMO

CASTILLO

MARTÍ

N LÓPEZ

AVELLANEDA

ZAYAS

BONACHEA

Canal Arroyo El Roble

PADRE CANO

LUZ CABALLERO

ALOJAMINETO MAITÉ

AGRAMONTE

CASA DE LA CULTURA

RESTAURANTE LAS FUENTES

DISCO PACHI

LIBERTAD

CASA DE LA TROVA

HOSPITAL

TELEPUNTO

BANK

COPPELIA

To Caibarién

CEMETERY

CALLEJA

CASA DE GINA MARGARITA

CINEMA

PANADERÍA DOÑA NELI

SERAFÍN SÁNCHEZ

TODO LIBRO (BOOKSTORE)

POST OFFICE

BANK

CUBACAR

CASA DE JUAN Y BÉLGICA

CADECA

GONZALO ARENA

POLICE

PHOTO SERVICE

MUSEO CAONABO

BUENVA VISTA CLUB

CASA DE MIRTA CABALLO

DINO'S PIZZA

CÉSPEDES

COLÓN

CADECA DE PAN (BAKERY)

CERVANTES

CAMINO DEL MATADERO

ETECSA

POEY

CUBACAR

SUPERMERCADO LOS BALCONES

CUBACAR

RAILWAY STATION/BUS TERMINAL

HOSTAL LA CASONA

4

5

6

HAVANAUTOS

7

SERGIO ANTUÑAS

8

ADELINA

MARGARITA

E VERONA

HERMANOS GONZÁLEZ

SERAFINA

9

CASA PARTICULAR LUIS Y LISY

10

ALFREDO DÍAZ

To Patria

CUBATAXI

9NA

6TA

5TA

3RA

AV TARAFA

4TA

EL GALLE DE MORÓN (CLOCK TOWER)

HOTEL MORÓN

8VA

TELEPHONE

CUBACAR

10MA

12MA

0 400 yds

0 400 m

CIRCUNVALACIÓN

To Museo de Azucar and Ciego de Ávila

© AVALON TRAVEL

an amplifier so that citizens could hear the rooster crow daily at 6am.

Entertainment

The **Casa de la Trova** (Libertad #74, e/ Martí y Narciso López) hosts traditional music, as does the **Casa de la Cultura** (Martí #224, tel. 033/50-4309), which has dance lessons Wednesday and Friday at 5pm.

La Casona de Morón (Cristóbal Colón #41) hosts an outdoor disco (Tues.-Sun.) to wake the dead. **Disco La Cueva,** three kilometers north of town on the road to Laguna de la Leche, warms up with a *cabaret espectáculo* (CUC1).

The **Buena Vista Club** (Martí #111, tel. 033/50-2045) has live music (Wed.-Mon. 2pm-2am) and Arctic air-conditioning.

Food

Pickings are slim, but no worries, as Morón boasts one of the best *paladares* in Cuba. ★ **Restaurante Maité La Qaba** (Luz Caballero #40b e/ Libertad y Agramonte, tel. 033/50-4181, 24 hours, CU8-15) is where Maité conjures delicious homemade pastas, paellas, and *criolla* dishes—including garlic lobster—with love and flair. Reservations are essential.

For ice cream, head to **Coppelia** (Martí esq. Calleja, Tues.-Sun. noon-10pm). You can buy bread at **Panadería Doña Neli** (Serafín Sánchez #86, e/ Narciso López y Martí, daily 7am-noon and 1pm-8pm), produce at the *mercado agropecuario* (Machado, esq. Avellaneda), and groceries at **Supermercado Los Balcones** (Av. Tarafa y Calle 3).

Accommodations

Casa de Gina Margarita (Callejas #89, e/ Martí y Castillo, tel. 33/50-4340 or 5295-6585, CUC20-25), an attractive 1950s home full of antiques and kitsch, earns raves from past guests, including me. It has two modestly furnished, cross-ventilated air-conditioned rooms with small private bathrooms and independent entrance. There's parking and a delightful patio.

I've twice slept comfortably at **Casa de Juan y Bélgica** (Castillo #189, e/ San José y Serafín Sánchez, tel. 033/50-3823, juanclen@ enet.cu, CUC20), a well-kept home with the usual mix of antiques and kitsch. Two air-conditioned rooms have fans and modern bathrooms. Meals are served on a patio with planters.

Ever-expanding ★ **Alojamiento Maité** (Luz Caballero #40b e/ Libertad y Agramonte, tel. 033/50-4181, CUC25-30) features a swimming pool and seven graciously appointed, impeccably clean rooms, all with en suite bathrooms. There is secure parking. Maité, the delightful owner, runs the best *paladar* in town here; guests get breakfast on the rooftop terrace.

Islazul's modest two-story **Hotel Morón** (Av. Tarafa, tel. 033/50-2230, www.islazul. cu, CUC24 s, CUC35 d low season, CUC36 s, CUC62 d high season including breakfast) offers 144 no-frills rooms. Facilities include a massage salon, barber shop, swimming pool, and a disco that can leave guests sleep-deprived.

Hostal La Casona (Cristóbal Colón #41, tel. 033/22-8013, www.islazul.cu, CUC32 s, CUC48 d low season, CUC44 s, CUC53 d high season), a refurbished colonial mansion, has seven lovely rooms with flat-screen cable TVs and a wraparound veranda. It has a swimming pool and car rental; bring earplugs for the boom-boom of the patio disco.

Services

Etecsa (Céspedes, esq. Martí, tel. 033/50-2399, daily 8:30am-7pm) offers phone and Internet service. Parque Martí, Parque Morón, Parque de los Madres, and Parque Máximo Gómez are Wi-Fi zones. **Bandec** (Martí e/ Serafín Sánchez and Gonzalo Arena) has a branch; you can change foreign currency at **Cadeca** (Martí, esq. Gonzalo Arena, Mon.-Sat. 9am-4:30pm and Sun. 9am-noon), immediately south. The **Hospital General** (tel. 033/50-5011) is at the east end of Libertad.

Getting There and Around

The **bus station** (tel. 033/50-3398) and **railway station** (tel. 033/50-5398) are next to each other on Avenida Tarafa. Eight buses daily connect Morón with Ciego de Ávila. Víazul buses no longer serve Morón; at press time, train service had been reduced to thrice-daily service to Ciego de Ávila (CUC1). The colloquially known "La Morón" service to Camagüey has ceased.

Cubacar (tel. 033/50-2152) has four outlets, including at Hotel Morón; the Cupet gas station is one block south.

Laguna de la Leche

Morón is enclosed to the north and east by a vast quagmire of sedges, reeds, and water. **Laguna de la Leche** (Milk Lake), five kilometers due north of the city, is named for its milky complexion, which derives from deposits of gypsum. Birdlife includes flamingos, and fish from tilapia to tarpon abound. Fishing trips and boat tours are offered (daily 10am-5:30pm, CUC20) from La Cueva, on the west shore; check in at the Flora y Fauna (tel. 033/50-5632) office.

Nautically themed ★ **Restaurante La Atarralla** (tel. 033/50-5351, Tues.-Sun. 2:30pm-5pm) overhangs the lagoon and serves paella (CUC5), oyster cocktails (CUC2.50), and grilled lobster (CUC7). Each September, the **Carnival Acuático** (Water Carnival) takes place in a canal leading to Laguna de la Leche. Musicians serenade the crowd while the city's prettiest young maidens row boats decorated with garlands of flowers.

Laguna La Redonda

Northeast of Morón, **Lago La Redonda** claims the largest concentration of bass in Cuba. **Centro Turístico La Redonda** (tel. 033/30-2489, daily 8am-7pm), 14 kilometers north of Morón, has a bar-restaurant and offers fishing (CUC75 for four hours, four person minimum) and boat trips (CUC7) amid the mangrove-lined shores. There are crocodiles in the water, so don't dip your hand in.

COMUNIDAD CELIA SÁNCHEZ

Much has been made of this community at Turiguanó, 28 kilometers north of Morón, known locally as the Pueblo Holandés because it was modeled on a "Dutch village" (coincidentally, Cuba's first wind-turbine scheme was built here; two giant turbines loom to the east of the village). Turiguanó was a U.S.-owned private cattle estate before the Revolution. In 1960-1961, the land was expropriated and the Dutch-style houses were built for the 30 or so families who live here. The 59 gable-roofed houses supported by timber-beam facades transport you lyrically back to Holland, except they are in a sad state of disrepair.

The cattle estate is now the Ganado Santa Gertrudis, breeding cattle of that name. Its **Agroturístico Rodeo** has rodeos that are part of tour excursions from the cays, but you might chance on local cowboys chasing and lassoing bulls.

Museo de la Industria Azúcarera Avileña

The defunct Central Patria o Muerte sugar mill at Patria, three kilometers southeast of town, has been turned into the excellent **Museo de la Industria Azúcarera Avileña** (tel. 033/50-5511, www.tecnoazucar.azcuba. cu, Mon.-Fri. 8am-5pm, Sat. 8am-11am, CUC3), with exhibits describing sugarcane cultivation and refining. Much of the original machinery is in place and functioning within the restored building. To the rear are 18 steam trains; rides are offered on a 1917 Baldwin (Mon. 10am and 3pm, CUC12), ending at the Rancho La Palma farmstead.

Refugio de Fauna Loma de Cunagua and Cayos de los Pájaros

Floating over the surrounding flatlands 18 kilometers east of Morón, the great hummock of **Loma Cunagua** (no tel., www.snap.cu, daily 7am-7pm, CUC1) rises to 364 meters. Bird-filled forests smother the slopes, giving way on the north side to wetlands and mangroves that extend to the coast. All of this is protected within the flora and fauna reserve. There are hiking trails and a mountaintop restaurant; horses can be rented to take you to caves displaying aboriginal pictographs. Excursions are offered through **EcoTur** (tel. 033/30-8163, comercial@cat.ecotur.tur.cu) or hotel tour desks on Cayo Coco.

Although crocodiles inhabit the wetlands, you'll have a better chance of seeing them at the **Zoocriadero Cocodrilo** (no tel., daily 9am-7pm, CUC3 including drink and guide), midway between Morón and the entrance to the reserve.

The reserve extends east to a vast swathe of sugar-white sands and cays. The **Cayos de los Pájaros** (Bird Cays) culminate at a curling spit and the fishing hamlet of **Cunagua,** with tumbledown shacks on stilts over the jade waters. The cays are a major breeding site for gulls and terns. You can wade to many of the cays across the thimble-deep shallows to count the seabirds. Cunagua is 12 kilometers north of the town of Bolivia, eight kilometers east of the reserve.

Sitio Arqueológico Los Buchillones

This national monument at Punta Alegre (about 30 km northwest of Morón) is one of Cuba's most important archaeological digs. The National Geographic Society is helping with the excavation of a Taíno village preserved in coastal mud; it was discovered in the 1940s, but not excavated until 1980. The remains of canoes and pile-supported wooden houses have been remarkably well preserved. Many figurines, tools, and other items discovered in the mud are displayed in a tiny museum. Visits can be arranged to **La Cueva de los Murciélagos** (Bat Cave).

The site is 35 kilometers north of **Chambas,** where the **Museo Municipal** (Calle Agramonte #80, e/ Calixto García y Martí) also hosts exhibits from Los Buchillones.

Cayo Coco and Cayo Guillermo

These contiguous islands, separated from the mainland by the Bahía de Perros (Bay of Dogs) and joined to it by a *pedraplén* (causeway), are the third-largest tourist destination in Cuba, after Havana and Varadero. It's no wonder why: They boast the finest beaches in Cuba and some of the country's most beautiful jade-colored waters. Mangroves line the southern shores. Although two small facilities cater to budget travelers, this is the domain of ever-more numerous and increasingly high-end all-inclusive resort hotels. Long-term plans call for 22,000 rooms for the twin islands, with heaven knows what ecological consequences. *Bring insect repellent!*

The narrow, elevated, 27-kilometer *pedraplén* connecting Cayo Coco to the mainland was originally made of solid landfill. It cut the Bahía de Perros in two and prevented the flow of currents, resulting in damage to the mangrove systems (sluices have since been added). There's a toll booth (CUC2 each way, passport required) and security checkpoint at the entrance to the *pedraplén*. Drive carefully—there are no barriers! At the traffic circle, the road straight ahead leads to the hotel complex and main beaches of Cayo Coco. That to the left leads to Cayo Guillermo.

Cubans must buy a prepaid package (CUC8) from **Cubatur** (tel. 033/52-0106) beside the toll booth.

★ CAYO COCO

This 364-square-kilometer cay is a stunner on account of its 21 kilometers of superlative beaches. It's second only to Varadero in number of hotel rooms—6,000 and counting. Most hotels front the sands of Playa Larga, Playa Palma Real, and Playa Flamenco. Huge sand dunes—Las Dunas de los Puertos—rise

Cayo Coco and Cayo Guillermo

© AVALON TRAVEL

IBEROSTAR PILAR
RANCHÓN PILAR
Playa Pilar
HORSE-RIDING STABLE
CAYO GUILLERMO
DELFINARIO
BOAT ADVENTURES
MARINA MARLIN/
DIVE CENTER

SOL CAYO GUILLERMO
MELIÁ CAYO GUILLERMO
BOLERA
IBEROSTAR
DAIQUIRI
ALLEGRO CLUB CAYO GUILLERMO

AGUACHALES DE FALLA
GAME RESERVE ★
RESTAURANTE LA ATALAYA ▼
LA CUEVA ▼

Punta Jiguani

Cayo
Botella

Punta del
Perro

Bahía
de

CARRETERA A CAYO GUILLERMO

Parque
Ecológico
Sima

Laguna de
la Leche

COMUNIDAD
CELIA SÁNCHEZ ★

CENTRO
TURÍSTICO
LA REDONDA ■

WIND
TURBINES ○
La Loma ○

AGROTURÍSTICO
RODEO ★

PG TOLL BOOTH

Playa Uva Caleta
CAMPISMO ●

Playa
Uva Caleta

Parque
Nacional
El Bagá

SITIO LA
GUIRA
VILLA
AZUL
POLICE ■
BANK/
HAVANAUTOS ■

Manati

THE PEDRAPLEN

Laguna
de
Playa la Tinaja

PARADOR
LA SILLA ●

Laguna de los
Flamencos

Laguna la Redonda

Perros

CAYO COCO ✠

Playa Larga

SEE DETAIL

✈ NEW HOTEL UNDER CONSTRUCTION
Punta Almacigo

0   5 km
0   5 mi

Cayo
Judas

Cayo
Romano

MG BRIDGE

Cayo Paredón
Grande

FARO
DIEGO VELÁZQUEZ ★

Playa del Norte

WATERSPORTS/
FISHING CLUB ■

Playa Los Pinos

RANCHÓN
PLAYA FLAMINGO
PESTANA CAYO COCO
BEACH RESORT
MEMORIES
FLAMENCO
MEMORIES
CARIBE

HOTEL
PLAYA COCO

CLÍNICA INTERNACIONAL/
SPA TALASO TERAPIA

HOTELS
FLAMINGO 3&4

Playa
Flamingo

Sendero
Playa
Rocarena

CUEVA
DE JABALÍ ★

HOTEL TRYP CAYO COCO
CENTRO DE INVESTIGACIONES
DE LAS ECOSISTEMAS COSTEROS

BLAU COLONIAL
CAYO COCO

VILLA
GAVIOTA
ECOTUR

HOTEL NH
KRYSTAL LAGUNA
SOL
CAYO COCO

ROCARENA
CLIMBING
CENTER

MELIÁ CAYO
COCO
PULLMAN
CAYO COCO

RANCHÓN
LAS DUNAS
IBEROSTAR
MOJITO

RANCHO
PULLMAN

MARINA AGUA
TRANQUILA
CAYO COCO

Ernest Hemingway, Nazi Hunter

In May 1942, Ernest Hemingway showed up at the U.S. Embassy in Havana with a proposal to fit the *Pilar* out as a Q-boat, with 0.50-caliber machine guns and a trained crew with himself at the helm. The boat would navigate the cays off the north coast of Cuba, ostensibly collecting specimens on behalf of the American Museum of Natural History, but in fact on the lookout for Nazi U-boats, which Hemingway intended to engage and disable.

Hemingway's friend Col. John W. Thomason Jr. was Chief of Naval Intelligence for Central America and pulled strings to get the plan approved. The vessel was "camouflaged" and duly set out for the cays. Gregorio Fuentes—who from 1938 until the writer's death was in charge of the *Pilar*—went along and served as the model for Antonio in *Islands in the Stream,* Hemingway's novel based on his real-life adventures.

They patrolled for two years. Several times they located and reported the presence of Nazi submarines that the U.S. Navy or Air Force was later able to sink. Only once, off Cayo Mégano, did Hemingway come close to his dream: A U-boat suddenly surfaced while the *Pilar* was at anchor. Unfortunately, it dipped back below the surface before Hemingway's boat could get close.

over the west end of Playa Flamenco, offering fabulous views along the coast and an inland lagoon.

Cayo Coco has a flamingo colony, sadly few in number since the airport opened (some years see greatly diminished flocks). Every day, they fly over the north end of the *pedraplén* shortly after sunrise and again at dusk. Scrub-covered Cayo Coco, which is named for the roseate ibis, or *coco,* was immortalized by Ernest Hemingway in *Islands in the Stream.*

The 158 bird species here also include migratory waterfowl. The most prominent animals are *jabalís*—wild pigs—and endemic iguanas. There are even deer. The 769-hectare **Parque Nacional El Bagá** (tel. 033/30-1063, daily 9:30am-5:30pm) protects the brush-covered west end of Cayo Coco (named for the three-meter-tall *bagá* tree that grows in wetland), though speedboat tours through the mangroves harass the bird and fish colonies, and dynamiting for hotel development does the same. Guided trail tours are available through **EcoTur** (tel. 033/30-8163, comercial@cav.ecotur.tur.cu), next to the **Centro de Investigaciones de las Ecosistemas Costeros** (tel. 033/30-1161, www.ciec.cu), immediately east of the Hotel Tryp Cayo Coco.

Cayo Paredón Grande

From the traffic circle, you can follow a road east past the service area (with a workers complex and warehouses) to a channel separating Cayo Coco from Cayo Romano. Cross the bridge and ask the military personnel in tatterdemalion uniforms to lift the rope that serves as a barrier. The lonesome road swings north to **Cayo Paredón,** where the cay's northern tip is studded by a lighthouse—**Faro Diego Velázquez**—built in 1859. A side road fit for jeeps only leads to **Playa Los Pinos,** popular for day excursions by catamaran from Cayo Coco.

Entertainment

All the hotels offer theme parties, cabarets, and discos. The only other option is a *cabaret espectáculo* at the **Cueva del Jabalí** (1.6 km west of Villa Gaviota, tel. 033/30-1206, Tues.-Thurs. 10:30pm-2am, CUC15). Bring repellent.

Recreation

All the hotels have water sports. Nonguests can pay for banana-boat rides, snorkeling, and Hobie Cat rentals at outlets on the beaches.

Diving (CUC40 one dive, CUC365 open-water certificate) is available at most all-inclusive resorts and through **Centro**

Internacional de Buceo Coco Diving (tel. 033/30-1020, cocodiving.cav@tur.cu), at the Hotel Tryp Cayo Coco.

Horseback riding (CUC10 per hour) is offered at **Sitio La Güira** (tel. 033/30-1208), a rather hokey facility six kilometers west of the Servi-Cupet roundabout. It displays farm animals and hosts a **Fiesta Campesino** (folkloric country show) each Tuesday at noon.

Cuba's only climbing facility is the German-built **Rocarena Climbing Center** (tel. 5315-6628, CUC26 adults, CUC12 9-16 years, CUC5 4-9 years). This triple-tier, 90-meter-tall structure opened in 2015 with climbing poles, a kids climbing wall, and a rope circuit. Those who make it to the top of the tower can opt for a zip line descent, and auto-belay, or a freefall.

Sportfishing (CUC270 half day, CUC410 full day, up to six people) and fly-fishing (CUC129 half day, CUC179 full-day) at Cayo Paredón is offered from **Marina Marlin Aguas Tranquilas** (tel. 033/30-1328, www.nauticamarlin.tur.cu). **EcoTur** (tel. 033/30-8163, comercial@cav.ecotur.cu) offers fishing trips, an eight-hour jeep safari, and birding.

Catamaran cruises include snorkeling (CUC20 adult, CUC10 child), sunset trips (CUC30 adult, CUC15 child), and a full-day safari (tel. 033/30-1323, CUC75 adult, CUC38 child) with snorkeling and a lobster lunch.

Food

Nonguests can purchase a day or night pass to most all-inclusive hotels. To escape the resorts, four identical thatched beach grill restaurants serve up seafood dishes: **Ranchón Las Dunas** (daily 8am-8pm), **Ranchón Playa Flamenco** (daily noon-3:30pm), **Ranchón Playa Prohibida** (daily 8am-8pm), and **Ranchón Playa Los Colorados** (daily 8am-5pm).

Parador La Silla (tel. 033/30-2137), a simple thatched café on one of the cays that precede Cayo Coco, offers sandwiches and has a lookout for spotting flamingos.

Accommodations

There are a couple of choices for budget travelers. Islazul's soulless and overpriced 142-room **Villa Azul** (tel. 033/30-8121, jrecepcion@villazul.tur.cu, CUC42 s/d low season, CUC64 s/d high season) was built to house workers in three-story blocks two kilometers from the beach. All units are simply furnished suites. Price aside, I don't see any upside to staying here. The yin to Villa Azul's yang is rustic, farm-style **Sitio La Güira** (tel. 033/30-1208, CUC25 s/d including breakfast), six kilometers west of the Servi-Cupet roundabout. It has four thatched air-conditioned cabins, plus a thatched restaurant. Bring your bug spray!

All other lodging options are all-inclusives: 13 at last count. All have water sports and entertainment. Here's the pick of the litter.

At Playa Flamenco, the 508-room **Pestana Cayo Coco Beach Resort** (tel. 033/30-4200, www.pestana.com, from CUC92 s, CUC146 d low season, CUC119 s, CUC190 d high season) offers contemporary chic that makes competing hotels look dowdy. Rooms in three-story blocks have minimalist decor in tropical colors. The price is a relative bargain.

An elevated contemporary lobby with bar and shopping arcade overlooking a serpentine swimming pool makes a great first impression at the venerable **Hotel Tryp Cayo Coco** (tel. 033/30-1300, www.solmeliacuba.com, from CUC125 s, CUC178 d low season, from CUC144 s, CUC207 d high season). The food at this sprawling Sol Meliá property is OK at best, but the 508 rooms are nicely furnished and have cavernous bathrooms. Families like it for the kids facilities.

Sol Meliá's gracious, adults-only **Meliá Cayo Coco** (tel. 033/30-1180, www.solmeliacuba.com, from CUC200 s, CUC287 d low season, from CUC226 s, CUC328 d high season) boasts 250 spacious rooms done in a subdued contemporary take on traditional Spain. A specialty seafood restaurant is suspended over the lagoon, as are two-story villas.

The first hotel in Cuba with Wi-Fi in every room opened in 2016. That's the chic, French-run 522-room ★ **Pullman Cayo**

Coco (tel. 07/860-5212, www.pullmanhotels. com, from CUC161 s, CUC233 low season, CUC267 s, CUC372 d high season), on Playa Las Colorados at the extreme east end of Cayo Coco. An adults-only section has sumptuous suites with hip, all-white decor. Eight restaurants include Japanese and French cuisine.

Information and Services

Infotur (tel. 033/30-9109, Mon.-Sat. 8am-5pm) has a bureau in the airport. DHL (tel. 033/30-1300, Mon.-Fri. 8am-5pm, Sat. 8am-1pm) has an office in the Hotel Tryp Cayo Coco. There's a Banco Financiero Internacional (Mon.-Fri. 8am-noon and 1pm-3pm) outside the Cupet gas station.

Clínica Internacional (tel. 033/30-2158, 24 hours), one kilometer west of the Hotel Tryp, has a dental clinic, clinical lab, high-pressure oxygen chamber, plus massage and hydrotherapy at the adjoining Spa Talasoterapia. The police station is one kilometer west of the Servi-Cupet roundabout.

Getting There and Away

Flights from Canada and Europe serve Cayo Coco International Airport (tel. 033/30-9165). AeroGaviota has service from Havana. Other flights arrive at Máximo Gómez International Airport in Ciego de Ávila, from where travelers are bused to Cayo Coco.

There is no public bus service to Cayo Coco. A taxi from Morón costs about CUC45.

Skippers can berth at Marina Marlin Aguas Tranquilas (tel. 033/30-1328, www. nauticamarlin.tur.cu).

Getting Around

Getting around is a breeze thanks to Transtur's hop-on/hop-off Jardines del Rey BusTour (tel. 033/30-1175, daily 8am-4pm, CUC5); double-decker buses run five times daily between the Pullman Cayo Coco and Playa Pilar (Cayo Guillermo).

Cubataxi (tel. 033/50-3290) charges CUC25-30 for an island tour in a classic car. A 45-minute tour by horse-drawn coche costs CUC5 per person. And tren shuttles (open-sided faux trains) run between the hotels (CUC2).

You can hire bicycles, scooters, and cars at most hotels. Rent cars from Havanautos (tel. 033/30-1371), at the airport and at the Cupet gas station, and from Rex (tel. 033/30-2244), at Sol Cayo Coco.

★ CAYO GUILLERMO

This 18-square-kilometer cay lies west of Cayo Coco, to which it is joined by a short pedraplén. Hotels are laid out along chalky, five-kilometer-long postcard-perfect Playa El Paso. Westward is Playa Pilar, where dunes pile 15 meters high and white-as-snow sands dissolve into shallow ocean waters of astonishing blues and greens. Cayo Media Luna, a former haunt of Fulgencio Batista, hovers on the horizon 1.5 kilometers offshore. Excursions (CUC25) can be booked at the hotel tour desks.

Ernest Hemingway immortalized Cayo Guillermo in Islands in the Stream, recounting his WWII adventures hunting U-boats in these cays aboard his beloved Pilar. He's now immortalized by life-size bronze statues along the pedraplén showing him in fishing.

Recreation

The Delfinario (tel. 033/30-1529), at the east end of the cay, has dolphin shows daily at 9:30am, 11:30am, 1:30pm, and 3:30pm. Viewing from the oceanside platform costs CUC25 adult (CUC15 child), or you can interact (CUC55 adult, CUC25 child) or even swim with the dolphins (CUC110 adult, CUC60 child). Boardwalks lead through mangroves to the disconcertingly small pens.

Marina Marlin (tel. 033/30-1718, commercial@marlin.cco.tur.co), across the road from the Delfinario, offers sportfishing. Scuba diving, paragliding, and kitesurfing are available at the Green Moray Dive Center (tel. 033/30-1680, greenmoray@marlin.cco.tur. cu), at Meliá Cayo Guillermo. The Sol Cayo Guillermo has kitesurfing (CUC50 per session; or CUC250 for a full course), as does

Havana Kiteboarding Club (tel. 5804-9656, www.havanakite.com), beside the Iberostar Daiquirí.

On rainy days, head to **Bolera** (tel. 033/30-1697, daily 10am-11pm), just west of Iberostar Daiquiri, for 10-pin bowling.

Food and Accommodations

Seven all-inclusive resorts were operating at press time; all have water sports and entertainment. Two more were nearing completion and four others were due to break ground for completion by 2020.

The 312-room **Iberostar Daiquirí** (tel. 033/30-1560, www.ibersostar.com, from CUC140 s, CUC180 d low season, from CUC160 s, CUC240 d high season), with its contemporary Spanish colonial-inspired design, lush landscaping, and excellent children's facilities, is a favorite. In 2016, Iberostar upped the ante with its sleek 482-room ★ **Iberostar Playa Pilar** (tel. 033/30-6300, www.ibersostar.com from CUC190 s, CUC280 d low season, from CUC240 s, CUC320 d high season). It has a fresh 21st-century feel, five vast pools with lounge beds, and a water park for the kids.

Sol Meliá manages the 264-room **Sol Cayo Guillermo** (tel. 033/30-1760), a second-tier option to the neighboring and superior **Meliá Cayo Guillermo** (tel. 033/30-1680, www.sol-meliacuba.com, from CUC166 s, CUC240 d low season, from CUC189 s, CUC269 d high season), with 301 rooms furnished in the company's trademark turquoise and Caribbean pastels.

Overlooking the gorgeous sands and turquoise waters at Playa Pilar, thatched restaurant **Ranchón Pilar** (noon-3pm) serves seafood and *criolla* dishes. It has lounge chairs beneath shade umbrellas, perfect for postprandial lazing.

Getting Around

The hop-on, hop-off **BusTour** (tel. 033/30-1175, daily 9am-5pm, CUC5) runs five times daily between the Meliá Cayo Coco and Ranchón Pilar, with stops at all the hotels. Horse-drawn *coches* await outside the hotels.

Camagüey and Vicinity

CAMAGÜEY

Camagüey (pop. 270,000), 570 kilometers east of Havana and 110 kilometers east of Ciego de Ávila, sits in the center of the namesake province on a bluff above the vast plains. Cuba's third-largest city (and perhaps its most loyally Catholic) is full of beautifully restored colonial plazas that lend the city one of its nicknames, "City of Squares." The historic core is laid out in a haphazard fashion to confuse pirates (so it is claimed) and is a national monument. In 2008 it was named a UNESCO World Heritage Site. It received a substantial facelift for the city's 2014 quincentennial, including four lovely new boutique hotels

It's a pleasure to walk the colonial streets, especially in late afternoon, when the sun gilds the facades like burnished copper, and at night, too, when moonlight silvers the Spanish grills of the poorly lit streets, full of intrigue. In the dark, full of shadows, it is easy to imagine yourself cast back 200 years.

Warning: Camagüey has more *jineteros* (hustlers), and more aggressive ones, than most cities. *Jineteros* on bicycles (and scooters) accost tourists arriving in the city and will pursue you to guide you to *casas particulares,* in which case you'll have to pay a commission. Pay no attention to young Cuban males who approach unsolicited to offer assistance.

History

Camagüey was one of the original seven settlements founded by Diego Velázquez, though the first buildings were erected in 1515 miles to the north, on the shores of

Camagüey

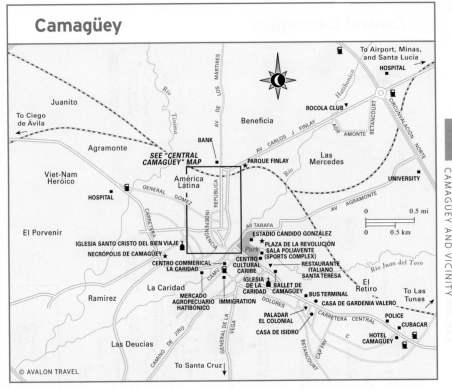

Bahía de Nuevitas. The site lacked fresh water and came under constant attack from local Indians. It was finally moved to its present location, where it was built on the site of a native settlement.

The early settlers were beset with water shortages. The town's Catalonian potters therefore made giant earthenware amphorae called *tinajones* to collect rainfall. Soon the jars (up to 2.5 meters tall and 1.5 meters wide) were a standard item outside every home, partly buried in the earth to keep them cool, but always under the gutters that channeled the rain from the eaves. Citizens began to compete with each other to boast the most *tinajones* and demonstrate their wealth. According to local legend, an outsider offered water from a *tinajón* will fall in love and never leave.

The city prospered from cattle raising and, later, sugar, which fostered a local slave-plantation economy. Descendants of the first Spanish settlers evolved into a modestly wealthy bourgeoisie that played a vital role in the national culture. The wealth attracted pirates. The unfortunate city was sacked and almost destroyed twice during the 17th century—in 1688 and 1679. Many Camagüeyans were themselves notorious smugglers who went against the grain of Spanish authority. The city also birthed Ignacio Agramonte (1841-1873), a cattle rancher who went on to become a hero of the Ten Years War (1868-1878) for independence. As head of the Camagüeyan rebel forces, in July 1869 he led a destructive assault on the Spanish-held city. (Agramonte is the hometown hero par excellence, and locals are often referred to as *agramontinos*.)

"This town has always been looked upon

Central Camagüey

© AVALON TRAVEL

Plaza del Cristo

Plaza del Carmen

CONVENTO DE NUESTRA SEÑORA DEL CARMEN

ESTUDIO GALERIA MARTA JIMENEZ

EL OVEJITO

RAMOS

BEMBETA

LA

AURELIA

CRISTO

CASTILLA

DE

RAUL

BAYAMESA

FEBRERO

HOSPITAL

RED CROSS

LAMAR

MATIAS

LUGAREÑO

24

MARTI

10

DE

DE

OCTUBRE

SAN RAMON

CASA NATAL DE NICOLAS GUILLEN

200 yds

200 m

CASA NATAL DE CARLOS FINLAY

CASA DE LA DIVERSIDAD

CASA DE LA TROVA

LIBRARY

UNEAC/ GALERIA JUAN MORALES

CASA ALFREDO Y MILAGRO

CATEDRAL DE SANTA IGLESIA

ESTUDIO GALERIA JOVER

RESTAURANTE 1800

PLAZA SAN JUAN DE DIOS

COMPAÑA DE TOLEDO

OSINEROS

PARADOR DE LOS TRES REYES

IGLESIA SAN JUAN DE DIOS/ MUSEO DE ARQUITECTURA COLONIAL

INDEPENDENCIA

VARONA

MATADERO

BANCO FINANCIERO INTERNACIONAL

HOTEL E EL MARQUES

CAFÉ CIUDAD

Parque Agramonte

MAQUETA DE LA CIUDAD

EL CAMBIO

BAKERY

GALERIA DE ARTE ALEJO CARPENTIER

HOTEL E LA SEVILLANA

CAFÉ LAS RUINAS

FARMACIA INTERNACIONAL LA ELEGANTE

FINCIMEX

CADECA

PIANO BAR

PHOTO SERVICE

COPPELIA

MACEO

GENERAL

Plaza de los Trabajadores

CINE ENCANTO

CASABLANCA

GRAN HOTEL

DOÑA NELI DULCERIA

ASISTUR/ CUBATUR

HOTEL E CAMINO DEL HIERRO

HOTEL E LA AVELLENADA

Plaza de la Solidaridad

LUCES

REPUBLICA

GOMEZ

MUSEO JESUS SUAREZ GAYOZ

POLICLINICO

IGLESIA SAGRADO CORAZON DE JESUS

CASA COLONIAL LOS VITRALES

Parque Martí

OTALLA

LA CARIDAD

PUENTE

TELEPHONE

CUBACAR

CASA DE MATRIMONIO

LIBERTADORES

AV. DE LOS

CARRETERA

PUENTE LA HATIBONICO

Río Hatibónico

CENTRAL

INSTITUTO DE SEGUNDA ENSEÑANZA

R

PINTO

ENRIQUE

VILLUENDAS

ZOO

CASINO CAMPESTRE

CAMAGÜEY AND VICINITY

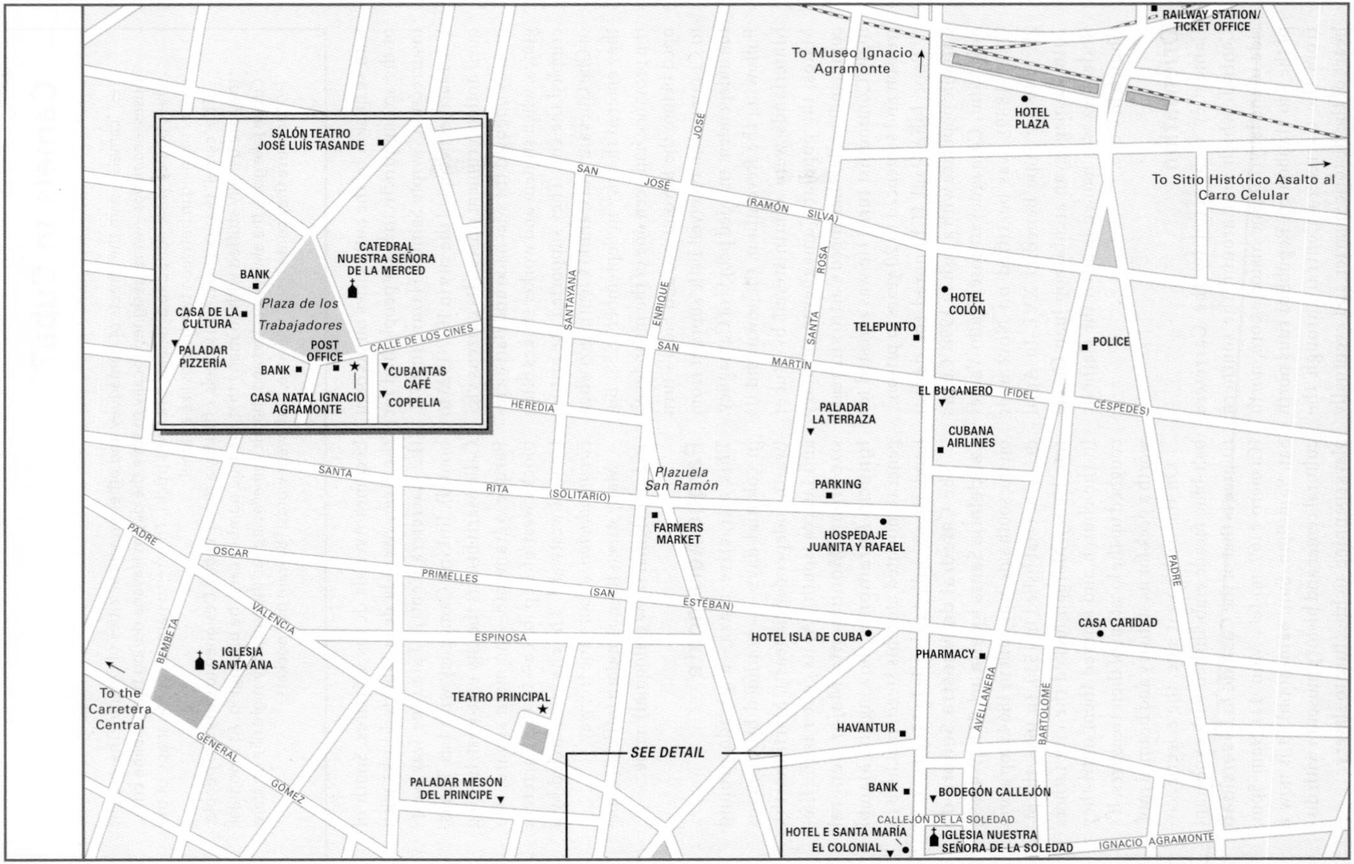

Camels in Cuba?

Yes, "camels" roam the streets of Camagüey and other provincial cities of Oriente. These giant buses—*camellos*—were designed locally to save the day in Havana during the gasoline crisis, when bodies were added to articulated flatbed trucks. They're so named for the shape of the coach: sagging in between two humps like a camel.

The "camel" is a warehouse on wheels, officially a *supertrenbus*. Designed to carry 220 people, they are usually stuffed with so many that the true number can't be untangled. As a popular Cuban joke goes, the always-packed and chaotic *camellos* are like the Saturday-night film on state TV, "because they contain sex, violence, and swear words!" Beware pickpockets.

with suspicion by the authorities on account of the strong proclivities its people had for insurrection," wrote Samuel Hazard in 1871. U.S. Marines occupied the city in 1917-1923 to quell antigovernment unrest. Its citizens vigorously opposed the Machado and Batista regimes, when student and worker strikes often crippled the city. They supported the armies of Che Guevara and Camilo Cienfuegos when they entered the city in September 1958. But the province had been one of the most developed before the Revolution, and Fidel's turn to Communism received little support from the independent-minded people of Camagüey. Following the Revolution, the town and its hinterlands were administered by Huber Matos, the popular Camagüeyan military commander, who challenged Castro's increasingly Communist turn. He was arrested for treason and sentenced to 20 years in prison.

Pope John Paul II honored the devout Catholic populace with a visit in 1998. Cuba's only saint, Camagüeyan José Olallo Valdés (1820-1889), was beatified on November 29, 2008 by Pope Benedict XVI. In April 2016, Camagüeyan archbishop Juan García Rodríguez was named head of the Catholic Church in Cuba.

Orientation

Camagüey is bisected by the Carretera Central, which arcs around the southern side of the labyrinthine historic core, north of the Río Hatibónico. República runs north from the Carretera Central through the heart of the historic quarter and eventually

becomes Avenida de los Mártires. South of the river, Avenida de la Libertad links with the Carretera Central Este (one-way westbound), linking Camagüey with Las Tunas. Calle Martí bisects the city east-west, linking Parque Agramonte—the main square, two blocks west of República—to the Carretera Central westward. The city is encircled by a *circunvalación,* a four-lane freeway.

Many streets have a modern (official) name and an original (now colloquial) name.

Parque Agramonte

This attractive plaza—a parade ground in colonial days—is bounded by Cisneros (west), Independencia (east), Martí (north), and Luaces (south). At its center is the life-size bronze **Monumento Major General Ignacio Agramonte** showing the Mambí general mounted atop his steed, machete in hand. He was killed in battle in May 1873.

The **Catedral de Nuestra Señora de Candelaria Santa Iglesia** (tel. 032/29-4965), on the south side, was built in 1864 atop a predecessor established in 1530. In 1688, the pirate Henry Morgan locked the city fathers in the church and starved them until they coughed up the location of their treasures. It's worth a peek for its statuary and beamed roof.

On the park's west side, the eclectic, cobalt-blue facade embellished with exuberant filigree is that of the **Casa de la Diversidad** (Cisnero #169, no tel., Mon.-Fri. 9am-5pm, Sat. 9am-9pm, Sun. 8am-noon). It is now a cultural center and history museum with displays spanning architecture to slavery.

Afro-Cuban poet Nicolás Guillén (1902-1989) was born in **Casa Natal de Nicolás Guillén** (Hermano Agüiro #57, e/ Cisneros y Principe, tel. 032/29-3706, Mon.-Fri. 8am-4:30pm, free), one block north of the plaza. A loyal nationalist and revolutionary, Guillén served as chairman of the National Union of Cuban Writers and Artists (UNEAC), which he helped found. The house contains some of his personal possessions. It now doubles as a music study center of the Instituto Superior de Arte.

Casa Natal de Carlos Finlay (Cristo #5, tel. 032/29-6745, Mon.-Fri. 9am-5pm, Sat. 8am-noon, CUC1), 50 meters west of the plaza, is the birthplace of the scientist who discovered that the *aedes aegypti* mosquito is the vector for yellow fever. It has apothecary jars.

Pinned by a small statue of José Martí, **Parque Martí,** four blocks east of Parque Agramonte, is worth the visit to admire the neo-Gothic **Iglesia Sagrado Corazón de Jesús.** Dating from 1920, it features beautiful trompe l'oeil.

Plaza del Carmen

This intimate, pedestrian-only cobbled square (Martí and 10 de Octubre), six blocks west of Parque Agramonte, features life-size ceramic figures: an old man pushing a cart, three women sipping *tazas* of coffee, two elderly lovers sharing gossip, and my favorite—Norberto Subirat Betancourt reading a newspaper (he often hangs out to re-create the pose next to his likeness for a tip). The tiny plaza is surrounded by venerable houses in bright pastels. On the west side, the former **Convento de Nuestra Señora del Carmen** (tel. 032/23-7577), built in 1825, today houses the **Galería de Arte Fidelio Ponce de León** (tel. 032/25-7577, Tues.-Sat. 8am-5pm, Sun. 8am-noon, CUC1).

Four blocks south of Plaza del Carmen is the **Iglesia de San Cristo del Buen Viaje** and **Plaza del Cristo.** Initiated in 1794 and updated in 1840, it was splashed with yellow paint for the quincentennial. It's attached

to the far more interesting **Necropolis de Camagüey,** the city cemetery that contains the remains of Ignacio Agramonte, one of many notable *agramonsistas* who lie beneath bleached marble tombs. Guided tours are offered (CUC1).

On the north side, **Estudio-Taller Martha Jiménez** (tel. 032/29-1696, www.martha-jimenez.es) displays superb paintings and sculptures by the artist. She's always happy to break her work to welcome visitors. The life-size statues in the plaza are hers.

★ Plaza San Juan de Dios

Hidden away two blocks south of Parque Agramonte, one block west of Cisneros, this plaza is a national monument boasting 18th-century buildings with huge doorways and beautifully turned window bars, plus two of the city's top restaurants. To the southwest corner, **Estudio-Galería Jover** (Paco Recio, tel. 032/29-2305) displays the work of Joel Jover, one of Camagüey's world-renowned artists.

On the east side, the Moorish **Antiguo Hospital de San Juan de Dios** is a former military hospital dating from 1728. Its arcaded cloisters were presided over by José Olallo Valdés, the nurse-friar who attended to the wounded Spanish and rebel troops during the Ten Years War (1868-1878). In 2008, he was beatified as Cuba's only saint. Today it houses the **Museo de Arquitectura Colonial** (tel. 032/29-1388, Tues.-Sat. 9am-5pm, Sun. 8am-noon, entrance CUC1, cameras CUC2), chronicling the city's history. Adjoining it is the **Iglesia de San Juan de Dios** (open Mon.), featuring a splendid mahogany ceiling and a bell tower, which can be climbed for the view.

Several blocks west is **Casino Campestre,** a leafy park on the south side of the river that is accessed from the historic center via the stone-and-metal **Puente Hatibónico** bridge dating from 1773. It has prerevolutionary statues plus a small and dispiriting **zoo** (daily 7:30am-6pm, 0.50 peso), with African animals. To its west, across the

Carretera Central, rises the imposing neoclassical **Instituto de Segunda Enseñanza** (Institute of Secondary Education). To the east of the park, the **Plaza de la Revolución** features an impressive marble and granite **Monumento Ignacio Agramonte** inscribed with 3-D sculptures of Fidel, Che, and other revolutionaries.

Plaza de los Trabajadores

The triangular Workers' Plaza, three blocks north of Parque Agramonte and two blocks west of República, has a venerable ceiba tree at its heart and is surrounded by striking buildings.

On the east side rises **Catedral Nuestra Señora de la Merced** (tel. 032/29-2740, daily 8:30am-11:30am and 4pm-6pm), dating to 1748 and boasting an elaborate gilt altar beneath a barrel-vaulted ceiling with faded murals. The devout gather to request favors at a silver coffin, the Santa Sepulcro, made of thousands of old coins and topped by a prostrate figure of Christ. Check out the catacombs, with skeletons in situ.

Ignacio Agramonte was born on September 23, 1841, at **Casa Natal Ignacio Agramonte** (Agramonte #459, esq. Candelaria, tel. 032/29-7116, Tues.-Sat. 9am-4:45pm, Sun.

9am-2:30pm, entrance CUC2, cameras CUC1), on the south side of the square. Beautifully restored, it is now a museum containing an important art collection, colonial furniture, and mementos such as Agramonte's pistol.

One block east of the plaza, the baroque, redbrick **Iglesia Nuestra Señora de la Soledad** (República, esq. Agramonte) dates from 1755. It has impressive interior frescos, an elaborate gilt altar, and a beamed ceiling, and it dominates the recently created **Plaza de la Solidaridad.** Connecting it to Plaza de los Trabajadores is **La Calle de los Cines** (Cinemas Street, but formally Calle Agramonte), so named because the Cine Casablanca and Cine Encanto opened here in the 1940s and '50s. In 2015, the street was remodeled for the 500-year celebrations. The cinemas have since reopened and the street is dedicated to the movie theme.

My favorite spot is **La Maqueta de la Ciudad** (Martí #160, Mon.-Sat. 9am-9pm, Sun. 9am-1pm, CUC1), which opened in 2014 in the restored and air-conditioned Edificio Collado, on the north side of the square. The 1:500 scale model of the city features buildings in accurate, exquisite detail. A wraparound mezzanine gallery offers a bird's-eye view.

Santa Sepulcro in Catedral Nuestra Señora de la Merced

Entertainment and Events

In early February, the **Jornadas de la Cultura Camagüeyana** festival celebrates the city's founding. The **Festival del Teatro de Camagüey** is a biennial celebration held in September. A religious festival, the **Nuestra Señora de la Caridad,** is held on September 8 to honor the city's patron saint.

On Saturday nights, República is closed to traffic for the raucous rum-soaked fiesta **Noche Camagüeyana.**

One of Cuba's best traditional music venues is the **Casa de la Trova** (Cisneros #171, tel. 032/29-1357, Mon.-Fri. noon-6pm and 9pm-midnight, Sat. 11am-6pm and 9pm-2am, and Sun. 11am-3pm, CUC3), on the west side of Parque Agramonte. It draws young couples and oldsters alike for music from *chachachá* to *trova.*

You half expect the Rat Pack to show up at the Gran Hotel's moody **Jazz Club** (Calle Maceo #67, tel. 032/29-2314, daily 4pm-2am); the hotel also hosts aquatic ballet shows in its swimming pool at 9pm. The **Piano Bar** (tel. 032/23-8935, Sun.-Fri. noon-11pm and Sat. noon-2am), 50 meters to the south, is popular with a thirtysomething crowd, despite being darker than an underground cave.

Most dive bar action takes place on Parque Agramonte, where **El Cambio** (daily 10am-2am), on the northeast corner, attracts an offbeat crowd. It serves Bucanero draft beer, including in tall three-liter dispensers (CUC8). Alas, it has *jineteros* and *jineteras* on the scrounge, as does **Café Las Ruinas,** a tiny yet hugely popular open-air bar with live music, at Plaza Maceo.

Camagüeyans get their cabaret kicks at **Centro Cultural Caribe** (Narciso Montreal esq. Freyre, tel. 032/29-8112, 9pm-2am, CUC5), on the east side of Club Campestre and where the flashing of flesh and feathers is followed by disco. For highbrow culture, the acclaimed **Ballet de Camagüey** performs at the **Teatro Principal** (Padre Valencia #64, tel. 32/29-3048, Fri.-Sat. 8:30pm, Sun. 5pm, CUC5-10), dating to 1850 and where notables such as Enrico Caruso once sang.

The local Alfareros (Ceramists) baseball team plays at the **Estadio Cándido González** October-April.

Food

The lovely ★ **Café Ciudad** (tel. 032/25-8412, daily 9am-11pm), on the northwest corner of Plaza Agramonte, occupies a marvelous colonial building adorned with massive sepia lithographs. It's a tremendous venue for cappuccino (CUC1.20), hot chocolate, coffee, and tea, and maybe a *jamón serrano* sandwich.

For a splurge, the ★ **Restaurante de Hierro** (Plaza de la Solidaridad #76, e/ Maceo y República, tel. 032/28-4264, daily noon-midnight), in the Hotel Camino de Hierro, offers colonial elegance—think eye-pleasing gold, mahogany, and white color scheme, and real silverware—in a beamed dining room cross-ventilated by soaring windows. Bargain-priced meals range from a tuna sandwich (CUC4.50) to shrimp enchiladas (CUC9) and grilled pork steak with garlic (CUC4).

A superb colonial ambience and an unbeatable setting on Plaza San Juan de Dios are big draws to the private ★ **Restaurant 1800** (tel. 032/28-3619, www.restaurante1800.com, daily noon-midnight), one of the best *paladares* in Cuba. A creative menu includes marinated lobster and Moorish kebab starters, and entrées of lamb stew and grilled pork chops (CUC5-15). In the rear patio awaits a superb buffet (CUC12). It even has a large wine cellar and sommelier.

The owners of **Ristorante Italiano Santa Teresa** (Av. de la Victoria #12 e/ Padre Carmelo y Freyre, tel. 032/29-7108, daily noon-midnight), one block east of Casino Campestre, serve genuine Italian fare, with yummy pizza and homemade ravioli and cannelloni served on a pleasant patio (CUC5-12). With the completion of the Calle de los Cines renovation, the state-run **Restaurante La Isabella** (Agramonte esq. Independencia, tel. 032/22-1540, daily noon-10pm) offers fun seating in canvas directors' chairs. Admire the movie-themed posters and photos while enjoying pretty good pizzas and pasta (CUC5-12).

For Spanish cuisine, head to **Bodegón Callejón** (República, esq. Callejón de la Soledad, tel. 032/29-1961, daily 11am-11pm), where Spanish flags, thick *taberna* benches and tables, and tapas (below CUC2) and paella (CUC6.50) whisk you to Iberia.

Coppelia (Independencia, e/ Agramonte y Gómez, tel. 032/29-4851, Sun.-Fri. 10am-10pm, Sat. 10am-11pm) serves ice cream for pesos.

You can buy baked goods for dollars at **Panadería Doña Neli** (Maceo, daily 8am-9pm), opposite the Gran Hotel, and fresh produce from the **Mercado Agropecuario Hatibónico** (Carr. Central e/ Desengaño y 24 de Febrero, daily 7am-6pm).

Accommodations
CASAS PARTICULARES

I enjoyed a stay at **Casa Particular Alfredo y Milagro** (Cisneros #124, e/ Raúl Lamar y Padre Olallo, tel. 032/29-7436, allan.carnot@gmail.com, CUC20-25), a huge, nicely furnished 1950s house with a pleasant host. Two spacious rooms open to a patio. A lush patio garden is also a highlight at ★ **Casa Caridad** (Calle Oscar Primelles #310A, e/ Bartolomé Masó y Padre Olallo, tel. 032/29-1554, abreucmg@enet.cu, CUC20), where three identical bedrooms with private bathrooms open to an atrium corridor. Meals are served beneath an arbor. Caridad proved a delightful host. Her son Eduardo runs a *casa particular*.

Hosts fuss over you at **Hospedaje Juanita y Rafael** (Santa Rita #13, e/ República y Santa Rosa, tel. 032/28-1995, CUC15-20), a beautifully kept colonial home with a sunlit, breezy lounge filled with contemporary art. The owners rent two spacious, modestly furnished rooms with modern bathrooms.

For immersion in colonial ambience try **Casa Colonial Los Vitrales** (Avellanada #3 e/ General Gómez y Martí, tel. 032/29-5866 or 5294-2522, requejobarreto@gmail.com, CUC25-30). Owners Emma and Rafael

have lovingly restored a former convent steps from the historic core. The *vitrales*, *tinajones*, aged murals, and heaps of potted plants create a wonderful atmosphere. Four rooms surround the courtyard, where filling breakfasts are served. Reservations are essential.

Handily close to the bus station, **Casa de Gardenia Valero** (Carretera Central #515, e/ Argentina y 2da, tel. 032/27-1203, CUC20) is a splendid middle-class home with two air-conditioned rooms with fans and private hot-water bathrooms; one bathroom is a stunner. It has secure parking.

Northeast of town, the sensational ★ **Rocola Club** (Av. Carlos J. Finlary #462, no tel., CUC30) has Italian Cuban owners. This spacious 1950s home is hung with tasteful art and has a vine-draped patio, plus four thoughtfully furnished rooms. You're a good distance from the center, but it has secure parking and doubles as a *paladar*.

HOTELS

Cubanacán (www.cubanacan.cu) has been restoring historic properties and turning them into boutique hotels, so you can say *adios* to the dour Soviet-style Hotel Camagüey and lackluster Hotel Plaza and Isla de Cuba.

You'll be delighted upon entering the ★ **Hotel Camino de Hierro** (Plaza de la Solidaridad #76, e/ Maceo y República, tel. 032/28-4264, www.cubanacan.cu, CUC96 s, CUC138 d year-round), with a rambling layout in a restored colonial building. Lovely antique reproduction furnishings fill the spacious guest rooms. Its restaurant is one of the best in town. The gorgeous ★ **Hotel E Santa María** (República esq. Agramonte, tel. 032/28-3990, CUC104 s, CUC150 d year-round) evokes a deluxe hotel with its airy lobby, gracious Republican furnishings, and uplifting color scheme.

With Cubanacán's new offerings, Islazul's 48-room **Hotel Colón** (República #472, e/ San José y San Martín, tel. 032/25-4878, www.islazul.cu, CUC40 s, CUC54 d low season, CUC108 s, CUC132 d high season including breakfast) now looks dowdy and overpriced.

Still, you can't fault the atmospheric lobby bar and fine restaurant.

Popular with tour groups, the venerable **Gran Hotel** (Calle Maceo #64, e/ Gómez y Agramonte, tel. 032/29-2314, reserva@granhotel.cmg.tur.cu, CUC44 s, CUC66 d low season, CUC108 s, CUC152 d high season, including breakfast) has 72 rooms, but the highlights are its top-floor bar-restaurant, swimming pool, and jazz bar.

Information and Services

Infotur (tel. 032/26-5805, infocmg@enet.cu) has an impressive tour bureau at the airport and another at Agramonte #461 (tel. 032/25-6794, daily 9am-5pm).

The **post office** (Agramonte #461, esq. Cisneros, tel. 032/29-3958, 8am-5pm Mon.-Fri.), on the south side of Plaza de los Trabajadores, has DHL service. **Etecsa** (Avellada, e/ San Martín y Primelles, daily 8:30am-7:30pm) has international telephone and Internet service. Public Wi-Fi zones include Casino Campestre, Parque Agramonte, Plaza de los Trabajadores, and Parque Céspedes.

You can change foreign currency at **Bandec** (Plaza de los Trabajadores; and on República, one block north of Ignacio Agramonte); **Banco Financiero Internacional** (Independencia, on Parque Maceo); and **Cadeca** (República #353, e/ Primelles y Solitario, Mon.-Sat. 8:30am-6pm, Sun. 8:30am-1pm).

Hospital Provincial (Carretera Central, Km 4.5, tel. 032/28-2012) is on the west side of town. The **Policlínico José Martí** (tel. 032/29-5706, 24 hours) on Parque Martí will treat foreigners for free in an emergency. **Farmacia Internacional** (Agramonte, 20 meters east of Plaza de los Trabajadores; and Maceo #88, e/ Gómez y Parque Maceo, tel. 032/28-0896, Mon.-Fri. 9am-5pm, Sat. 9am-1pm) stocks imported medicines.

Consultoría Jurídica Internacional (Joaquín de Agüero #165, e/ Tomás Betancourt y Julio Sanguily, Rpto. La Vigía, tel. 032/28-3159, cjicamaguey@enet.cu) offers legal assistance. **Asistur** (Agramonte #449, e/ López Recio e Independencia, tel. 032/28-6317, asisturcmg@enet.cu, Mon.-Fri. 8am-5pm, Sat. 8am-1pm) assists travelers in distress.

Getting There and Away

AIR

Ignacio Agramonte Airport (tel. 032/26-1000 and 032/26-7154) is nine kilometers northeast of the city. A taxi costs about CUC10. **Cubana** (República #400, esq. Correa, tel. 032/29-2156, www.cubana.cu) flies daily from Havana. Bus #22 runs past the airport from Parque Finlay, by the train station.

From the United States, **American Airlines** (tel. 800/433-7300, www.aa.com) has daily service from Miami.

BUS

The **Terminal de Ómnibuses Intermunicipales** (Carretera Central Oeste, esq. Perú, tel. 032/27-2480) is two kilometers southeast of town. **Víazul** buses (tel. 032/27-0396, www.viazul.com) between Havana and Santiago de Cuba (thrice daily) stop here, as do once-daily buses between Varadero-Santiago de Cuba and Trinidad-Santiago de Cuba, and twice-daily buses between Havana and Holguín.

Buses and *camiones* to provincial destinations depart from the **Terminal de Municipales** (tel. 032/28-1525), adjoining the train station.

TRAIN

The railway station is at the north end of Avellaneda; the ticket office (tel. 032/25-3132) is on the north side of the station. All trains on the Havana-Santiago de Cuba route stop in Camagüey; train #11 (6:13pm) via Santa Clara and #13 (7:25pm) and #15 (6:53pm) via Matanzas, Santa Clara, and Ciego de Ávila all depart every fourth day (as of November 2016; CUC23). Train #11 continues direct to Santiago de Cuba without stops; #13 continues to Bayamo and Manzanillo; #15 continues to Cacocúm

(Holguín) and Guantánamo. Train #9 operates from Santa Clara to Camagüey every second day, continuing to Santiago de Cuba (train #8 does the reverse).

The **Terminal de Ferro-Ómnibus** (tel. 032/28-7525), adjacent to the main station, serves local destinations. Trains depart for Santa Cruz del Sur (CUC3) at 5:45am (return trains depart Santa Cruz at 3:15pm).

Getting Around

For a taxi, call **Cubataxi** (tel. 032/28-1245).

You can rent cars from **Havanautos** (Independencia, esq. Martí, tel. 032/27-2239, and at the airport, tel. 032/28-7067), **Cubacar** (tel. 032/28-5327, in the Café Buro de Turismo on the southeast side of Plaza de los Trabajadores), and both **Rex** (tel. 032/26-2444) and **Vía** (tel. 032/24-2498) at the airport.

There are gas stations on the Carretera Central, just west of Puente La Caridad; outside town, on the road to Nuevitas; and on the Carretera Central, at the corner of General Gómez.

Cubatur (Agramonte #421, e/ Independencia y República, tel. 032/25-4785) and **Havanatur** (tel. 032/28-8604) offer excursions. **EcoTur** (San Estebán #453, e/ Lopes Rocio y Popular, tel. 032/24-3693, comercial@cmg.ecotur.tur.cu) offers ecotourism excursions.

ÁREA PROTEGIDA DE RECURSOS MANEJADOS SIERRA DEL CHORRILLO

Southeast of Camagüey is an upland area—the Sierra Chorrillo—studded by *mogotes*. The limestone formations lie within the 4,115-hectare Área Protegida de Recursos Manejados Sierra del Chorrillo (CUC4 entrance), about 13 kilometers south of the community of **Najasa,** 43 kilometers southeast of Camagüey. The reserve has distinct regions of semideciduous woodland and tropical montane forest, and protects 110 species of vascular plants, a rare endemic cactus, *jutías,* and at least 80 bird species, including parrots and *tocororos*.

★ Finca La Belén

From the entrance, on the south side of the community of El Pilar, a dirt track winds two kilometers uphill to this working farm, where zebu and other exotic cattle species are raised. There are even zebras and various species of antelope (previously raised for the hunting pleasure of Communist bigwigs).

Finca La Belén

The **Sendero Santa Gertrudis** hiking trail (4.5 km) leads to mineral springs with pools and a cave; **Sendero de los Aves** (1.8 km) is best for birders (guided, CUC17). Other excursions include horseback riding (two hours CUC5), show jumping (CUC7), birding (CUC7), and hiking (CUC7) to "Casa Perico" (a peasant home with animals), where lunch is served.

Continue past the entrance to the reserve and the dirt road delivers you at a trailhead for Cuba's only fossil forest, **Bosque Fósiles de Najasa,** featuring fallen trees of 3 million-year-old petrified wood.

The farm has a surprisingly modern hotel, ★ **Motel La Belén** (tel. 5219-5744, CUC28 s, CUC34 d low season, CUC40 s, CUC56 d high season, including breakfast), with a swimming pool, TV lounge, and 10 spacious air-conditioned rooms with modern bathrooms. Its rustic restaurant specializes in meals of antelope. It was renovated in 2017.

Tours and reservations are handled through **EcoTur** (San Estebán #453, e/ Lopes Rocio y Popular, tel. 032/24-3693 or 032/24-4957, comercial@cmg.ecotur.tur.cu), in Camagüey.

GUÁIMARO

This small town, straddling the Carretera Central 65 kilometers east of Camagüey, has an intriguing granite obelisk in the town square, **Parque Constitución.** The monument—with bronze bas-reliefs of various heroes of the wars of independence—commemorates the opening in April 1869 of the Constitutional Assembly, where the first Cuban constitution was drafted, Carlos Manuel de Céspedes was elected president of the Free Republic of Cuba, and the abolition of slavery was decreed. The building where the 1869 Assembly was held today houses the **Museo Histórico de Guáimaro** (Constitución #85 e/ Libertad y Máximo Gómez, Mon.-Fri. 9am-5pm, CUC1).

Between Camagüey and Guáimaro, **Sitio Histórico Ingenio Oriente,** an old sugar mill where General Ignacio Agramonte launched his first attack of the Ten Years War in 1868, is promoted along the Carretera Central. Beginning 2 kilometers east of Sibanicú and 8 kilometers west of Guáimaro, it's a 14-kilometer drive along a dirt track to the community of Oriente Rebelde, but the site is of interest only to serious historians.

North Coast of Camagüey

The Circuito Norte coast road runs west-east about 10 kilometers inland of the coast. Floating offshore are the heretofore inaccessible cays of the Archipiélago de Camagüey.

CAYO ROMANO AND CAYO CRUZ

Cayo Romano, immediately east of Cayo Coco, is the largest of Camagüey's cays. It and dozens of other cays sprinkled offshore were off-limits to visitors until 2014. The government's tourism master plan contemplates 4,700 hotel rooms for Cayo Romano and, beyond, **Cayo Cruz.** The 550-room Hotel Quebrada was expected to open on **Cayo Cruz** in late 2017, the first of five hotels slated to be built by 2020.

Cayo Romano is accessed via the sugar-processing town of **Brasil,** from where a road leads north 5 kilometers to a 12-kilometer-long *pedraplén* that leapfrogs to Cayo Romano and Cayo Cruz. There's a military checkpoint; you'll need your passport.

Besides the beaches, the big draw is year-round fly-fishing for barracuda, bonefish, permit, snapper, and tarpon (April-June) in the jade-colored flats and lagoons off Cayo Romano's north shore. **EcoTur** (tel. 032/27-4995 or 07/641-0306, www.ecoturcuba.co.cu) offers guided fishing trips to Cayo Cruz, as does Italian company **Avalon Fishing** (www.

cubanfishingcenters.com), which has 3-, 5-, and 7-day packages.

Brasil is fascinating for its classic U.S. colonial architecture, when the sugar mill and *batey* (community) were laid out in 1919-1921 in an orderly tree-lined grid by the American Sugar Refining Company. By the 1950s it was Cuba's largest sugar mill; after being nationalized in 1961, it was renamed Central Brasil. In 2008, the community was named a national heritage site, **Monumento Nacional Central Jaronú.**

Accommodations

Dating from 1919, when it was the home of the sugar mill owner, the stately **Hotel Casona de Romano** (Calle 6 e/ B y C, from CUC50), in Brasil, was restored in 2013 to cater to anglers. Its nine air-conditioned rooms overlook a courtyard (with church).

RESERVA ECOLÓGICA LIMONES TUABAQUEY

Created in 2010, the 19,600 hectare **Reserva Ecológica Limones Tuabaquey,** in the Sierra de Cubitas 32 kilometers north of Camagüey, draws hikers and nature lovers. Rising to 365 meters atop **Cerro de Tuabaquey** are karstic formations pitted with caves. Caverns such as **Cueva María Teresa** and **Cueva La Pichardo** preserve some of the best pre-Columbian pictographs in Cuba. Other draws include the **Paso de los Paredones,** a natural gorge with sheer walls; and **Hoyo de Bonet,** a 90-meter-deep sinkhole with a re-creation of a Taíno *bohío* community.

Birding towers offer a chance to spot tocororó, Cuban woodpeckers, and Cuban parrots (the reserve has 17 of Cuba's endemic bird species), while with luck you might chance upon a Cuban boa underfoot.

The visitors center (CUC6 entrance) is 5 kilometers east of **Pese de Lesca,** on Carretera Sierra Cubitas 20 kilometers north of Camagüey's Ignacio Agramonte International Airport (the turnoff is opposite the airport entrance). A guide is compulsory for hiking. You can cool off by jumping in the Río Máximo.

MINAS AND AROUND

The small town of Minas, 61 kilometers southeast of Brasil and 37 kilometers northeast of Camagüey, is known for its **Fábrica de Instrumentos Musicales** (tel. 032/69-6232, Mon.-Fri. 7am-2pm, Sat. 7am-11am, free), at the south end of town. Workers turn native hardwoods into elegantly curved violins, violas, cellos, and guitars. It was founded by revolutionary *comandante* Juan Almeida Bosque, who rose to become Cuba's Vice President of the Council of State.

Ingenio de Santa Isabel, roadside about 15 kilometers east of Minas on the way to Santa Lucía, is the ruins of a historic sugar mill; it has a pleasant café under shade trees.

A **Zoocriadero de Cocodrilos** (daily 7am-4pm, CUC2), or crocodile farm, outside Senado, about 10 kilometers northwest of Minas on the road to Sola, raises American crocodiles for leather. A guided tour is fascinating. Divert in Senado to the derelict sugar factory, where a 19th-century steam train stands outside.

Nature lovers might call at **Los Cangilones del Río Máximo** (no tel., 7am-5pm), between Minas and Solas, a restored natural site with swimming pools, weirdly sculpted marble rocks, and a *campismo* with thatched restaurant. You can hike to a cave good for spelunkers. It's eight kilometers west of Caidije, via dirt road.

★ REFUGIO DE FAUNA SILVESTRE RÍO MÁXIMO

The Río Máximo trickles into the Bahía de la Gloria southeast of Cayo Romano. The wetlands and shallows between the mouths of the Máximo and Cagüey Rivers are protected within the **Río Máximo Wildlife Refuge.** Covering 35,562 hectares of saline flats, this area claims to have the largest breeding population of flamingos in the Caribbean (as many as 60,000 nests in good years). It also hosts the largest population of American crocodiles on Cuba's north coast, plus manatees and at least 217 other bird species, including migratory waterfowl. Access is by rough dirt track via the community of Mola (the turnoff from the Circuito Norte is 2 kilometers west of Gurugú and about 16 kilometers east of Sola). **EcoTur** (tel. 032/24-3693, comercial@cmg.ecotur.tur.cu) offers excursions.

RANCHO KING

This **cattle ranch** (tel. 5219-4139, daily 8am-4:30pm), on the Circuito Norte about seven kilometers west of the junction for Santa Lucía, was once held by the owners of the famous King Ranch in Texas. The Castro regime expropriated the property. Though still a working ranch, it today serves tourists with a rodeo show (CUC50) featuring bull riding and steer wrestling. You can saddle (CUC3) to join *vaqueros* on the trails or take a wagon. A ranch tour includes a visit to a rural elementary school (this exists merely for the excursion), plus lunch in a thatched restaurant with chickens underfoot.

The ranch rents three air-conditioned **rooms** (CUC16 s, CUC25 d low season, CUC19 s, CUC30 d high season, including breakfast). Tour desks in Playa Santa Lucía offer excursions (CUC29 including lunch).

★ Cayo Sabinal

Stunningly beautiful Cayo Sabinal is the easternmost cay in the archipelago and one of my favorites. It is attached to the north coast of Camagüey by a hair's-breadth isthmus and encloses the flask-shaped Bahía de Nuevitas. This virginal isle has 33 kilometers of beaches protected by coral reefs, within one kilometer of shore; the turquoise shallows can be waded.

For now, there is nowhere to stay. In 2016 plans were announced for two hotels with 1,405 rooms to be built by 2020; the Cuban government reckons Sabinal has a potential capacity for 12,000 hotel rooms. Until they are built, all you'll pass is a couple of military posts and a half-dozen humble *bohíos* belonging to impoverished charcoal burners and fisherfolk. There are plenty of birds and iguanas, and wild pigs called *jabalí*. Flamingos wade in the inland shallows of **Laguna de los Flamencos.** Bring insect repellent!

The best place to spend your time is the fantastically lonesome **Playa Los Pinos** (it has a thatched restaurant towards its eastern end). Occasionally a small tour group arrives for a day visit from Santa Lucía, but it's more likely you will have the place to yourself.

Near the eastern end of Cayo Sabinal is a lighthouse—**Faro Colón**—built in 1850 and,

Fábrica de Instrumentos Musicales

beyond, a circular fortress—**Fuerte San Hilario**—built in 1831 to protect the entrance to Bahía de Nuevitas.

GETTING THERE

Most visitors to Cayo Sabinal arrive on boat excursions from Playa Santa Lucía. If driving, Cayo Sabinal is reached via a bridge over the Ensenada de Sabinal, where there's a military checkpoint (you'll need your passport). The gate is usually locked; honk your horn to summon the guard, or retreat 200 yards and drive down to the guard post visible on the flat. Your car will be thoroughly searched coming and going. A CUC5 entrance charge is collected about 600 meters beyond the gate. After 10 kilometers, you reach the shore, where Playa Los Pinos unfurls to the east. To reach Faro Colón, turn right at the traffic circle two kilometers inland of the shore; turn left after 14 kilometers and it's 3.5 kilometers from here. The track extends another 6 kilometers to Fuerte San Hilario. In places, the narrow tracks are smothered in sand. The going can be challenging after heavy rains, when four-wheel drive is essential.

If traveling east along the Circuito Norte, the turnoff is at an unsigned junction for Lugareno, about 11 kilometers west of the junction for Nuevitas (and about 700 meters west of a railroad crossing). The dirt road snakes north eight kilometers to the guard post. If coming from the east, the best route is through the port town of Nuevitas, 12 kilometers north of the Circuito Norte and 65 kilometers northeast of Camagüey. When approaching town, turn left for Centro Termoeléctrica 10 de Octubre, then turn left immediately after crossing the railroad (two kilometers). The road becomes hard-packed dirt that runs along the Bahía de Nuevitas and leads to Cayo Sabinal.

Trains depart Camagüey for Nuevitas.

PLAYA SANTA LUCÍA AND VICINITY

Popular with budget-oriented German, Italian, and Canadian charter groups, Playa Santa Lucía, 110 kilometers east of Camagüey, 85 kilometers north of Las Tunas, and 20 kilometers north of the Circuito Norte (the turnoff is just north and west of Camalote, about 30 kilometers east of Nuevitas), is touted as a major resort destination. Forget the hype! Santa Lucía is an ugly duckling with minimal infrastructure and zero pizzazz. The meager facilities spread out over several kilometers, with stretches of nothingness between them. What Santa Lucía *does* have is an astounding 20 kilometers of beach protected by an offshore coral reef.

The shorefront road extends west of Santa Lucía to a funky fishing hamlet—**La Boca**—with its own beach, **Playa Los Cocos,** with atmospheric restaurants and showers. The dirt road to La Boca is full of deep pools and mud. Mangrove-lined **Laguna Daniel** and **Laguna El Real** form a swampy morass inland of the shore. Flamingos occasionally flock to wallow by day, then take off in a flash of bright pink at dusk.

Marlin Náutico (tel. 032/33-6404, www.nauticamarlin.tur.cu), at the west end of Playa Santa Lucía, offers fishing (three hours, CUC204 for four people) and catamaran excursions, and hotel tour desks offer flamingo-viewing tours (CUC59) and trips to Cayo Sabinal (CUC69) and Rancho King (CUC50).

★ Scuba Diving

Scuba diving at Playa Santa Lucia is superb. The warm waters support dozens of coral and fish species. And the mouth of the Bahía de Nuevitas is a graveyard of ships, including the steamship *Mortera,* which sank in 1898, its prow resting at a depth of 20 feet. Diving (including resort, certification, and specialized courses) is offered from **Centro Internacional de Buceo Shark's Friend** (tel. 032/36-5182, shark_friend@nautica.stl.tur.cu), on the beach between Brisas and Hotel Gran Club Santa Lucía, with dive trips daily at 9am and 1pm (CUC40, CUC40 night dive). It has a "shark show," in which you can witness bull sharks being hand fed (CUC65), plus snorkeling trips (CUC20).

Food

There are few options beyond the dismal hotel restaurants. The Italian-themed beachfront **Restaurante Luna Mar,** in the Centro Comercial Villa Vientos, serves spaghetti and pizza (CUC4-9) plus seafood. At Playa Los Cocos, **Bar y Restaurante Bucanero** (tel. 032/36-5226, daily 9am-6pm) serves seafood and *criolla* fare, including lobster (CUC18), and rents lounge chairs.

Accommodations

Locals are permitted to rent rooms as *casas particulares*. **Casa Martha Santana** (Residencial #32, tel. 032/33-6135, CUC25) is an independent two-room apartment near Hotel Tararaco and just steps from the beach. One room is small and has a basic bathroom; the second is larger. Martha prepares filling breakfasts and other meals by request. At Playa Los Cocos, try **Hostal Coco Beach** (tel. 5248-9359, CUC25), a beachfront bungalow with two simply furnished air-conditioned rooms with modern bathrooms literally atop the sands.

Apartamentos Santa Lucía (tel. 032/33-6373, www.islazul.cu, CUC28-36) offers simply furnished two- and three-bedroom units in a spruced-up Soviet-style former apartment block. Functional furnishings belie the homey touch.

A good option is Islazul's ★ **Hotel Costa Blanca** (Rpto. Residencial district, tel. 032/33-6373), two kilometers east of the main hotel zone. It has 12 rooms (CUC27 s, CUC33 d) and 16 one- to four-room villas (CUC28-53), all with modern bathrooms and accoutrements, plus a pleasant restaurant.

Cubanacán runs the four all-inclusive resort hotels (and badly at that); all have some water sports plus entertainment.

The classiest option, albeit no prizewinner, is the **Oasis Brisas Santa Lucía** (tel. 032/33-6317, CUC70 s, CUC90 d low season, CUC96 s, CUC120 d high season), a modern, 214-room all-inclusive low-rise combining a contemporary design with traditional thatch. At its heart is a pleasant swimming pool.

Information and Services

Etecsa (tel. 032/33-6126, daily 8:30am-7:30pm), next to the gas station at the east end of Santa Lucía, has international telephone and Internet service. The resort hotels have Wi-Fi.

Bandec (Mon.-Fri. 8am-3:30pm, Sat. 8am-1pm) has a branch on the coast road, 1.5 kilometers east of the tourist center. A **Clínica Internacional** (tel. 032/33-6370, 24 hours) is 200 meters farther east; the Gran Club and Brisas hotels have pharmacies. The **police station** is 400 meters west of the bank.

Getting There and Around

International charter flights arrive at Camagüey and Las Tunas airports. A taxi from Camagüey will cost about CUC75 one-way. You can rent cars at the hotels and from **Cubacar** (tel. 032/36368), 50 meters west of Gran Club Santa Lucía. **Cubatur** (tel. 032/33-5383) and **Cubanacán** (tel. 032/33-6404) offer excursions. *Coches* ply the shorefront strip (CUC2 between points, or CUC5 one hour). You can rent bicycles and scooters at the hotels.

Las Tunas and Holguín

Rich in history and physically diverse, this region is as interesting as any in the nation. Holguín, rather than Las Tunas, steals the show.

Las Tunas Province forms a flat, narrow band across the island, broadening to the northeast. The capital city occupies a low-lying ridge on the eastern edge of the great plains that dominate central Cuba. It is dull, unvarying terrain, mostly farmed for cattle. The scenery begins to grow more lush and interesting eastward. The province has few beaches, but Playa Herradura is a stunner popular with Cubans and virtually undiscovered by foreign visitors. There are few sights of interest other than in the eponymous provincial capital.

Holguín, by contrast, is chock-full of things to see and do. The capital city itself boasts several colonial plazas and an active nightlife, and the hinterlands have several unique sites, foremost among them Fidel Castro's birthplace. Holguín's north-central shore is in the throes of touristic development, centered on Playas Guardalavaca and Pesquero. Inland, the dramatic formations of the Grupo de Maniabon will have you reaching for your camera, and there are

pre-Columbian museums and archaeological sites to explore.

East of Holguín city, the coastal plain narrows to a panhandle extending along the shore at the base of the Sierra de Nipe, Sierra del Cristal, Cuchillas del Toa, and Alturas de Moa. These mountains are nirvana to bird-watchers and hikers. The color of heated chrome, the mountains are also rich in cobalt, manganese, and nickel. The ores are processed at the coastal town of Moa, in the far east of Holguín Province; the immediate area is blighted by the mineral extraction industry.

PLANNING YOUR TIME

The city of **Las Tunas** is worth a quick browse in passing. All routes through the province pass through the capital. Out-on-a-limb **Playa Covarrubias** rewards the trek with superb diving and a fascinating agritourism project, **La Y de Calzadilla**.

The larger city of **Holguín** offers considerably more to see, including three plazas. Holguín also has a well-developed cultural

---

Previous: Playa Esmeralda in Guardalavaca; Museo Conjunto Histórico Birán in Holguín. **Above:** flamingo at Refugio de Fauna Silvestre Monte Caganiguán-Ojo de Agua.

Look for ★ to find recommended
sights, activities, dining, and lodging.

Highlights

★ **Playas La Herradura and La Boca:**
These beaches, popular with Cubans, offer stunning white sands and turquoise waters and have virtually no foreign visitors for miles (page 372).

★ **Plaza Calixto García:** The largest of Holguín's three plazas, this one is home to two museums of note (page 376).

★ **Gibara:** This laid-back fishing town with fine colonial architecture makes a cool place to steep in Cuban culture (page 381).

★ **Guardalavaca:** The scorching beaches, magnificent teal-blue waters, and fabulous

diving offshore could keep you plenty happy, but be sure to make time for Museo Aborigen Chorro de Maíta, an excellent small museum and archaeological site recording pre-Columbian culture (page 384).

★ **Museo Conjunto Histórico Birán:**
Fidel's birthplace and childhood home provides fascinating insight into the early years of Cuba's enigmatic leader (page 390).

★ **Pinares de Mayarí:** Crisp mountain air, pine forests, and gorgeous waterfalls tempt birders and hikers to this alpine retreat formerly reserved for the Communist elite (page 391).

scene, with everything from an excellent Casa de la Cultura to a bargain-priced cabaret. I recommend a two-day stay.

The slightly down-at-heels seafront town of **Gibara** appeals for its marvelous setting, laid-back lifestyle, and bracing ocean airs. It has an excellent natural history museum. To its west, I love **Playa Herradura**—probably the nicest beach in Cuba for an almost 100 percent Cuban experience.

The beach resort of **Guardalavaca** and nearby **Playa Pesquero** are imbued with all-inclusive resorts plus plenty of options for day-trippers from Holguín, including scuba diving, a dolphin show, bird-watching, horseback riding, and kayaking. You can even take a ride into the Grupo de Maniabon in a 1920 Baldwin steam train. Nearby is the eminently rewarding **Museo Aborigen Chorro de Maíta,** a pre-Columbian archaeological site, and the similarly focused **Museo Indocubano,** in Banes. And how about **Museo Conjunto Histórico Birán,**

Fidel Castro's not-to-be-missed birthplace and childhood home?

Birders and hikers should head for **Pinares de Mayarí,** a cool alpine retreat in the Sierra de Nipe, where the **Salto El Guayabo** waterfall is a must-see, or to **Cayo Saetía,** where the wildlife-viewing is surreal (think camels and zebras).

The Carretera Central cuts through the center of the provinces. At Holguín, it turns southwest for Bayamo, in Granma Province. If heading from Camagüey direct to Granma Province and Santiago, you can bypass Holguín via a paved road that leads southeast from Las Tunas to Bayamo and cuts across the Río Cauto plains via the town of Jobabo.

The Circuito Norte (north coast road) is disjointed and diverts you inland through the cities of Las Tunas and Holguín. Roads radiate to Puerto Padre, Gibara, Guardalavaca, and Banes. West of Manatí and east of Moa, much of the Circuito Norte is badly deteriorated.

Las Tunas and Vicinity

LAS TUNAS

Las Tunas (pop. 80,000) is a small-time capital of a small-time province. The town is officially known as La Victoria de las Tunas, a name bequeathed by the Spanish governor in 1869 to celebrate a victory in the Ten Years War. Patriots under General Vicente García recaptured the town in 1895. Two years later, it was put to the torch by rebels as Spanish forces attempted to retake it. Thus the town today lacks edifices of architectural note.

Las Tunas (nicknamed "City of Sculptures") is famed for its terra-cotta ceramics, expressed in contemporary art scattered all over the city. Look for works by some of Cuba's leading artists, such as *Liberation of the People* by Manuel Chong, opposite the Asamblea Provincial. It's a pleasant enough place to overnight and spend a half day browsing before moving on.

Orientation

The town sits astride the Carretera Central, which enters from the west along Avenida 1ro de Enero, becomes Avenida Vicente García, and slopes up to the central square, Parque Vicente García, where it turns 90 degrees and runs southeast for Holguín as Calle Francisco Verona. A *circunvalación* bypasses the town.

The historic core is laid out in a grid centered on Parque García, at the top of Vicente García, between Calles Francisco Varona and Francisco Vega. Frank País runs northeast to the railway station, where it forks for the airport and Puerto Padre, on the north coast.

Museo de Mártires de Barbados

The **Museo de Mártires de Barbados** (Luca Ortíz #344, tel. 031/34-7213, Tues.-Sat. 10am-6pm, Sun. 8am-noon, free), at the

Las Tunas and Holguín Provinces

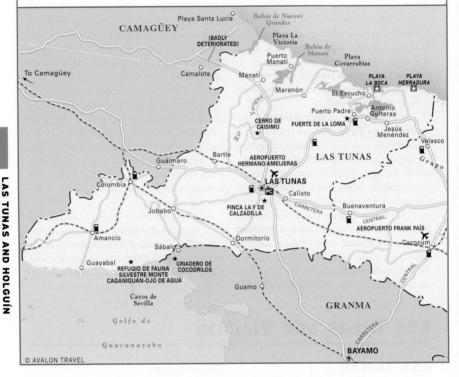

base of Vicente García, occupies a structure where lived Carlos Leyva González, Cuba's champion *florete* (fencer). Leyva died, along with his brother and the entire Cuban fencing team, when Cubana flight CU-455 was destroyed by a bomb after taking off from Barbados on October 6, 1976. All 73 people aboard died, including 57 Cubans, 5 Koreans, and 11 Guyanese. Cuban-American exiles Otto Bosch and Luis Posada Carilles were convicted. Bosch was pardoned by President George H. W. Bush, and Posada, who escaped prison in Venezuela and lives a free man in Miami, is hailed as a hero by extremist Cuban Americans.

Note the dramatic sculpture of an arm and clenched fist (like a fencer's clutching a foil) made from wreckage of the doomed aircraft.

The museum faces onto **La Fuente de las Antilles,** a sprawling and somewhat grotesque fountain (usually devoid of water) by celebrated sculptor Rita Lonja. Sculptural figures represent the emergence of aboriginal peoples from the Caribbean Sea.

Parque Vicente García

The town's main square, at the top of Avenida Vicente García, features a marble statue of the local hero, Major General Vicente García González, who burned the city rather than let it fall into Spanish hands. On the southwest corner is a small limestone church, the **Iglesia de San Jeronimo.** On the park's northeast corner, separated by Calle Colón, is the petite **Plaza Martiana,** with a contemporary sculpture of José Martí and a massive sundial, also by Rita Lonja.

The **Centro Histórico** (Francisco Verona,

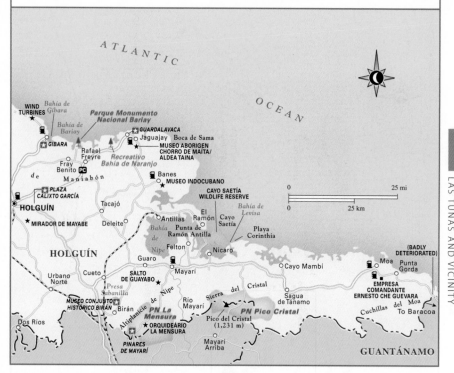

esq. Vicente García, tel. 031/34-8201), on the northwest corner, features meager exhibits on local history. Note the ceramic bas-relief map of the city on its wall. Kitty-corner, the **Museo Provincial** (Francisco Varona and Vicente García, tel. 031/34-8201, Tues.-Thurs. 9am-5pm, Fri.-Sat. 1pm-9pm, Sun. 8am-noon, CUC1) has eclectic exhibits on local history and culture, including 10-syllable rhyming songs called *décimas.* Another room is dedicated to *internacionalismo*—Cuba's support for revolutionary causes throughout the world. Upstairs the natural history room has a whale skeleton.

One block south of the park, **Casa Memorial Mayor General Vicente García González** (Vicente García #5, tel. 031/34-5164, Tues.-Sat. 9am-6pm, Sun. 8am-noon, CUC1) is where, on September 26, 1876,

General Vicente García purportedly began the fire that burned the city. The building, which was rebuilt in 1919, is now a museum commemorating the wars of independence.

Plaza de la Revolución

The ungainly Revolution Plaza, on the northeast side of town, is dominated by the huge **Monumento a Mayor General Vicente García González,** hewn in pink concrete with bas-reliefs showing the local hero of the wars of independence with his sword held high. The **Salón de los Generales** features bronze busts of other generals in the wars.

Entertainment and Events

The **Feria Interprovincial** agricultural fair in mid-February features rodeos in Parque 26 de Julio, at the base of Vicente García. Las

Las Tunas

© AVALON TRAVEL

To Camagüey

CARRETERA CENTRAL

AV. 1RA DE ENERO

ROBERTO REYES

REPARTO
AGUILERA

Río Hormiguero

CABARET TAINO

TELEPHONES

Parque
26 de Julio

VICENTE

COLÓN

MUSEO DE
MÁRTIRES DE
BARBADOS

LA FUENTE DE
LAS ANTILLAS

CREMERÍA
LAS ANTILLAS

CAFÉ PIROPO
EL MESÓN

LUCAS ORTIZ

LICO CRUZ

MARTÍ

24 DE FEBRERO

13 DE OCTUBRE

REPARTO
SANTO
DOMINGO

RAMÓN

ANGEL

GUERRA

SATURNO

CENTRO DE ARTES
PLÁSTICOS

CUBANA

GARCÍA

ORTUÑO

JULIÁN
SANTANA

VEGA

FRANCISCO
FRANCISCO VERONA

Parque
Vicente García

Parque
Maceo

ANTONIO MACEO

GONZALO DE QUESADA

LORA

NICOLÁS HEREDIA

PANADERÍA DOÑA NELI

JOAQUÍN AGÜERA

CREMERÍA LAS COLUMNAS

HOSPEDAJE
DOÑA NELY

SEE "CENTRAL LAS
TUNAS CITY" MAP

TONY ALOMA

BUS STATION

REPARTO
LA LOMA

REPARTO
AURORA

CUBACAR/
HAVANAUTOS

FARMERS
MARKET

POLICE

BANK

AV. 2 DE DICIEMBRE

PALADAR
LA BAMBA

FRANK
PAÍS

RAILWAY
STATION

TERMINAL
INTERMUNICIPALES

REPARTO CASA PIEDRO

FERRO-OMNIBUS STATION/
CAMIONES

To Airport and
Santa Lucía

To Holguín

AV. 30 DE NOVIEMBRE

STADIUM

Plaza de la
Revolución

HOTEL
LAS TUNAS

MONUMENTO A
MAYOR GENERAL
VICENTE GARCÍA
GONZÁLEZ

BASEBALL STADIUM

REPARTO
VELÁSQUEZ

CANO CIENFUEGOS
FARMERS
MARKET

0   800 yds
0   800m

Central Las Tunas

© AVALON TRAVEL

To Cupet Gas Station
and Camagüey

BANK

CONSULTORIA
JURIDICA
INTERNACIONAL

EN FAMILIA

PUBLIC
TOILETS

CENTRO CULTURAL HUELLAS

ETECSA

CASA DE
MARIELY
JORGE

RISTORANTE
LA ROMANA

BANK

CASA MEMORIAL DE
MAYOR GENERAL VICENTE
GARCÍA GONZÁLEZ

CASA
IBEROAMERICANA
DE LA DÉCIMA

PIANO BAR

DULCERÍA LAS
DELICIAS

IGLESIA DE
SAN JERÓNIMO

CREMERÍA
LA COPA

CENTRO HISTÓRICO

POST OFFICE/
DHL

HAVANATUR/
VÍA RENT-A-CAR

CABILDO SAN
PEDRO LUCUMÍ

MONUMENTO A
VICENTE GARCÍA

CASA DE LA
JOVEN CREADOR

CADECA

CASA DE
JEDREZ

CADECA

SUNDIAL

HOTEL CADILLAC/
CLUB CADILLAC

CACHE

GALERÍA
DEL ARTE

MUSEO
PROVINCIAL

INFOTUR

TELEPHONE

FONDO CUBANO DE
BIENES CULTURALES

CINE SALA TUNAS

PARKING/
CUBATAXI

Parque
Vicente García

Plaza
Martí

Parque
Diversiones

Parque
Maceo

SALÓN ROJO

FÁBRICA DE TABACOS
ENRIQUE CASAL

CASA PARTICULAR
MARÍA DEL PILAR

CABALLO BLANCO

To Railway Station

RED CROSS

CINE
LUANDA

To Hotel Las Tunas
and Holguín

0   0
100m 100 yds

Tunas hosts a carnival in September, but the highlight is the **Jornada Cucalambeana** (Cucalambé Folkloric Festival, tel. 031/34-7770), when songsters from all parts of Cuba compete with *décimas* (impromptu poems). It takes place at Motel El Cornito (tel. 031/34-5015), 10 kilometers west of town, each June or July.

At all times of year, the **Casa Iberoamericana de la Décima** (Calle Colón #161, e/ Francisco Vega y Julian Santana, tel. 031/34-7380, cdecima@tunet.cult.cu) has daily poetry recitals and *peñas*.

Culture vultures can also get a fix of poetry and live music at **Centro Cultural Huellas** (Calle Francisco Vegas e/ Luca Ortíz y Vicente García, Mon.-Fri. 9am-5pm, Sat. 9am-noon). The **Cabildo San Pedro Lucumí** (Francisco Verona, e/ Angel Guardia y Lucas Ortíz, tel. 031/34-6461, free) celebrates Afro-Cuban drumming and dance on Sunday at 9pm.

Titillating feathers and flesh are at **Cabaret Taíno** (tel. 031/34-3823), at the base of Vicente García, with a *cabaret espectáculo* Saturday at 9pm (35 pesos). The local millennials come for the disco after, although the hottest salsa scene is **Cine Disco Luanda** (Carretera Central, esq. Saturno Lora, tel. 031/34-8671, Mon.-Sat. 11pm-3am, Sun. 3pm-8pm, CUC3-5, including drinks), a Western-style disco featuring laser lights. It also has a cinema.

From October to April you can catch Los Magos (the Wizards) baseball team at **Estadio Julio Antonio Mella,** at the north end of Avenida 2 de Diciembre.

Food

The best *paladar* is **El Caballo Blanco** (Calle Frank País #85, esq. Gonzalo de Quesada, tel. 031/34-2586, daily 10am-11pm), an excellent dining spot set in a travertine-clad patio with open-air bar. The menu includes chicken with wine (CUC2.50), garlic shrimp (CUC2.75), and a superb *ropa vieja* (CUC2).

A violinist serenades at antique-filled **Ristorante La Romana** (Francisco Varona #331, tel. 031/34-7755, daily noon-11pm),

where Italian owner Franco whips up home-made bruschetta and pasta, drawing any Italian tourist for miles.

Appropriately named **Caché** (Francisco Varona, e/ Nicolás Heredia y Joaquin Agüera, tel. 031/99-5557, daily noon-2am, CUC3-8) has exposed redbrick walls, blood-red leather seating, and neon lighting. The cozy and fully stocked lounge bar-restaurant stirs up a killer piña colada, though the food (sandwiches, burgers, garlic shrimp, and fried chicken) seems an afterthought.

Join the Cubans in line for ice cream sundaes (for pesos) at **Cremería La Copa** (daily 9am-3:30pm and 4:30pm-10pm), on the west side of Parque Vicente García, and **Cremería Las Antillas** (Vicente García, esq. Ángel Guerra, Mon.-Fri. 10am-11pm, Sat.-Sun. 10am-midnight).

For baked goods, head to **Panadería Doña Neli** (Carretera Central, daily 7am-10pm), next to the Oro Negro gas station. The *mercado agropecuario* on Camilo Cienfuegos, 200 meters north of the railway station, sells produce.

Accommodations
CASAS PARTICULARES
Near the center, the standout is ★ **El Caballo Blanco** (Calle Frank País #85, esq. Gonzalo de Quesada, tel. 031/37-3658 or 5281-8264, CUC20 low season, CUC25 high season), where Dr. José "Pepe" Luis Viguero Pavón offers two nicely furnished upstairs rooms with modern bathrooms and a lounge. The best *paladar* in town is here, too. **Casa de María de Pilar** (Frank País #82A, e/ Gonzalo de Quesada y Iran Durañeno, tel. 031/34-0467 or 5294-7078, mariadelpilar412@yahoo.es, CUC25) is a lovely modern home with two pleasant rooms and parking.

I've twice enjoyed stays at **Hospedaje Doña Nelly** (Lucas Ortíz #111, e/ Gonzalo de Quesada y Coronel Fonseca, tel. 031/34-2526, cl8rbt@frcuba.co.cu, CUC20-25), a large colonial home with a piano in the lounge, plus an air-conditioned room with a private bathroom. Laundry service is offered.

HOTELS

If nondescript neo-Stalinist prefab hotels are your thing, check into Islazul's **Hotel Las Tunas** (tel. 031/34-5014, www.islazul. cu, CUC36 s, CUC59 d low season, CUC64 s, CUC75 d high season), one kilometer east of town on Avenida de 2 Diciembre. It has 142 no-frills air-conditioned rooms.

More appealing is the art deco **Hotel E Cadillac** (Joaquín Agüero, esq. Francisco Verona, tel. 031/37-2791, www.islazul.cu, CUC25 s, CUC35 d low season, CUC40 s, CUC50 d high season), built in 1945 in the shape of a slanting, rounded prow with porthole windows. Its eight rooms and two suites have plasma TVs, modern bathrooms, and cheap modern furniture (looking a bit knocked-about at last visit).

Information and Services

Infotur (Francisco Varona #298, esq. Ángel de la Guardia, tel. 031/37-2717, Mon.-Fri. 8am-4:30pm) provides tourist information with a smile.

Change your currency at **Cadeca** (Colón #41), **Bandec** (Av. 30 de Noviembre and Vicente García #69), **Banco Financiero Internacional** (Vicente García, esq. 24 de Octubre), or **Banco Popular** (Vicente García, esq. Francisco Vega).

The **post office** (Vicente García #6, tel. 031/34-3863), on the west side of Parque García, has DHL service. **Etecsa** (Francisco Varona, e/ Lucas Ortí and Vicente García, daily 8am-7pm) has international telephone and Internet service. The city's public Wi-Fi zones include Parque Martiana, Parque Antonio Maceo, and Complejo Las Antillas.

Hospital Che Guevara (Av. Carlos J. Finlay, esq. Av. 2 de Diciembre, tel. 031/34-5012) is 400 meters east of Plaza de la Revolución.

The **Consultoría Jurídica Internacional** (Vicente García, e/ 24 de Febrero y Ramón Ortuño, tel. 031/34-6845, Mon.-Fri. 8:30am-noon and 1:30pm-5:30pm) offers legal assistance.

Getting There and Around

AIR

The **Aeropuerto Hermanos Ameijeras** (tel. 031/34-2484) is three kilometers north of town. **Cubana** (Lucas Ortíz, esq. 24 de Febrero, tel. 031/34-6872) serves Las Tunas from Havana.

BUS

The **Terminal de Ómnibus** (tel. 031/34-3060 interprovincial buses, tel. 031/34-2117 municipal buses) is on the Carretera Central, one kilometer east of Parque Vicente García. The following **Víazul** (tel. 031/37-4295, www.viazul.com) buses stop in Las Tunas: Havana-Holguín (twice daily), Havana-Santiago de Cuba (thrice daily), Varadero-Santiago de Cuba (once daily), and Trinidad-Santiago de Cuba.

TRAIN

The **train station** (Terry Alomá e/ Lucas Ortíz y Ángel de la Guardia, tel. 031/34-8146) is northeast of downtown near the baseball stadium. At press time, only trains #11 and #15 eastbound (#12 and #16) between Havana and Santiago de Cuba stop in Las Tunas (CUC23 to/from Havana, CUC7 to/from Santiago) two days out of four. A two-car commuter train—*ferro-ómnibus*—runs to towns throughout the province.

CAR AND TAXI

You can rent cars from **Havanautos** (tel. 031/34-6228), in the Hotel Las Tunas, and **Cubacar** (Francisco Verona, esq. Av. 30 de Noviembre, tel. 031/37-1505). There are gas stations on the Carretera Central: one about 400 meters west of Parque Lenin and one four blocks east of Parque Vicente García. For taxis, call **Cubataxi** (tel. 031/34-2036).

REFUGIO DE FAUNA SILVESTRE MONTE CAGANIGUÁN-OJO DE AGUA

The 14,500-hectare **Monte Caganiguán-Ojo de Agua Wildlife Refuge** (Calle

Hermanos Acosta #10-A, e/ Frank País y Chibás, Jobabo), bordering the Golfo de Guacanayabo (and within the much larger Refugio de Fauna Silvestre Delta del Cauto, in Granma Province), is a premier breeding site for American crocodiles, which inhabit the pristine mangroves and swamp-lined delta complex of the Río Cauto. Flamingos also breed here alongside kestrels, Cuban parrots, roseate spoonbills, and dozens of species of waterfowl. Supposedly the 300 or so breeding female crocs represent the largest concentration of the species from Cuba to Venezuela; the nesting sites are concentrated along the beaches and a two-hectare patch of raised land in the swamps. A breeding center at **Zabalo** (Sábalo) can be visited; it's 20 kilometers south of the gateway community of **Jobabo,** 26 kilometers southwest of Las Tunas.

EcoTur (tel. 031/37-2073, www.ecoturcuba.tur.cu) offers nature excursions via Jobabo. The U.K.'s **Earthwatch Institute** (www.earthwatch.org) occasionally offers volunteer opportunities.

PUERTO PADRE AND VICINITY

This pleasant port town, about 30 kilometers northeast of Las Tunas, is one of Cuba's oldest. The settlement first appeared as Portus Patris on early 16th-century maps of the New World. During the 19th century, Puerto Padre grew to become Cuba's most important port for sugar export. Today it's a gateway to a couple of emerging beach resorts where you can laze alongside Cubans with your feet in turquoise waters and savor lobster meals under thatch for a pittance.

The town featured prominently in the independence wars. In 1875 the Spanish built a medieval-style fortress, **Fuerte de la Loma** (Tues.-Sat. 9:30am-4:30pm, Sun. 8:30am-11:30am, CUC1), to protect the southern entrance to town. Well preserved, it still stands atop the hill at the end of Puerto Padre's Las Ramblas-like sloping boulevard (Avenida Libertad), pinned by the **Monumento Máximo Gómez.** The boulevard descends downhill to a lovely park with a bandstand and a statue of the liberty maiden.

Playa Covarrubias

Las Tunas's north coast is lined with beautiful beaches, although the only one with a resort hotel is Playa Covarrubias, a four-kilometer-long strip of white sands with turquoise waters protected by a coral reef with superb diving (CUC45). The beach is 22 kilometers north of the rural community of Marañon, 15 kilometers west of Puerto Padre; it's virtually all scrub and briny pools to each side the whole way. You can buy a day pass (CUC25) to utilize the hotel facilities at Brisas Covarrubias. The road west from Marañon is pitted with hollows that can swallow a car!

Accommodations
CASAS PARTICULARES
Puerto Padre has several private room rentals. My favorite is **Casa de Elvis and Migdalia** (Calle Paco Cabrera esq. Céspedes, tel. 031/51-3124 or 5834-6419, CUC20-25), on the breeze-swept Malecón. Two simply furnished upstairs rooms open to terraces with rockers facing the sea, and they have clean bathrooms.

Catering almost exclusively to package tourists, **Brisas Covarrubias** (Playa Covarrubias, tel. 031/51-5530, www.hoteles-cubanacan.com, from CUC78 s, CUC96 d low season, from CUC95 s, CUC140 d high season) is a tranquil property with 180 spacious, if dated rooms. The huge freeform pool has a thatched bar and theater, plus there's a playground, disco, gym, water sports, and diving.

Services
Etecsa (Av. Libertad #144, e/ Masó y Flor Crombet, tel. 031/51-5316, daily 8am-7pm) has international telephone and Internet service. The **Cupet gas station** is one block south.

★ PLAYAS LA HERRADURA AND LA BOCA

The singular not-to-miss spot in Las Tunas Province, this string of gorgeous white beaches is easily reached from the north coast road with not a tourist in sight. About 10 kilometers east of Puerto Padre, you pass through Jesús Menéndez and Loma, where a road leads north eight kilometers via **Playa Corelia** to **Playa La Herradura** and, eight kilometers farther west, **Playa La Boca.** The seas are of stunning hues, made more dramatic by the inland lagoons with flamingos and salt flats. *Bring mosquito repellent* and avoid the beaches at dawn and dusk.

The beaches are popular with locals on weekends; Playa Herradura is probably the nicest beach on the island for sharing a purely Cuban experience. A boat for La Boca (one peso) leaves from the wharf at El Secucho, 16 kilometers north of Puerto Padre.

Food and Accommodations

There's no shortage of room rentals and budget seafood eateries. Options at Playa La Boca include **Casa de Jorge and Ana** (tel. 031/54-7357 or 5828-3732, CUC25), with a pleasing air-conditioned room with TV and DVD player. There's a *paladar* next door.

At Playa La Herradura, the beachfront **Villa Carolina** (Calle de la Playa, tel. 5238-7272, giuseperradura@gmail.com, CUC25-30) is run by Gioseppe and Yanet, who offer two spacious, gaily colored rooms with fan, fridge, and TV.

Holguín and Vicinity

HOLGUÍN

Holguín (pop. 320,000), 775 kilometers east of Havana and 200 kilometers northwest of Santiago de Cuba, was one of Cuba's original seven cities and is today the country's fourth largest. Although known as an industrial city (especially for brewing), the colonial core boasts many fine plazas and houses of Spanish origin. Holguín is renowned for one of the most vibrant cultural scenes in Cuba, lending the city a laid-back appeal.

When Columbus landed nearby in 1492, believing he had arrived in Asia, he sent an expedition inland to carry salutations to the Japanese emperor's court. The explorers came across a large native village called Cubanacán.

Playa Herradura, Holguín

Holguín

LAS TUNAS AND HOLGUÍN
HOLGUÍN AND VICINITY

ZAYAS

LIBERTAD

EL LLANO

LENIN

VISTA ALEGRE

PIEDRA BLANCA

JOSÉ DÍAZ

PUEBLO NUEVO

JULIO G. PERALTA

LA QUINTA

PLAZA DE LA REVOLUCIÓN

LA ADUANA

CEMETARY

SEE CENTRAL HOLGUÍN MAP

RESTAURANTE LOMA DE LA CRUZ
LOMA DE LA CRUZ
SNACK BAR
PALADAR LOS ALMENDROS
VILLA LIBA
HOSPEDAJE LA PALMA
RED CROSS
CASA DE ROSA
LA BOLERA
Parque Diversiones
HOSPITAL LENIN
Parque Quijote
MONUMENTO A LOS PATRIOTAS FUSILADOS
PALADAR DELICIAS CUBANAS
RESTAURANTE LOS ALMENDROS
PALADAR EL CRUELO
FINCIMEX
FINCIMEX FREKES
PALADAR YELLY BOOM
RESTAURANTE EL MILANO
MUSEO DE HISTORIA
POST OFFICE
PLAZA CALIXTO GARCÍA
IGLESIA DE SAN JOSÉ
GALERIA HOLGUÍN
BANK
Cemetery
RESTAURANTE LA TERNIDA
RESTAURANTE BAR 1910
CINE TEATRO MARTI
PANADERIA DOÑA NELI
PHARMACY
CADECA
MONUMENTO A BENITO JUÁREZ
Plaza Julio Graves de Peralta (LIBERTAD)
CABLES
CASA DE DON SANTIAGO
IMMIGRATION
MONUMENTO A SIMÓN BOLÍVAR
RAILWAY STATION / CAMIONES
CASA DE OLGA MERINA
CUBATAXI
HOSPITAL
ESTADIO CALIXTO GARCÍA
BIM-BOM
TERMINAL DE OMNIBUS MUNICIPAL
MONUMENTO A MÁXIMO GÓMEZ
CUBACAR
COMMUNIST PARTY HEADQUARTERS
HOTEL PERNIK
TABERNA PANCHO
Plaza de la Revolución
MONUMENTO A CALIXTO GARCÍA
MONUMENTO A LUCÍA IÑIGUEZ LANDÍN
VILLA EL BOSQUE
TELECORREO
BANK
UNIVERSIDAD DE HOLGUÍN
MONUMENTO A ANTONIO MACEO
MONUMENTO A CHE GUEVARA

TERMINAL DE INTERPROVINCIALES / VIZUL
TERMINAL LA MOLIENDA (CAMIONES)

To Gas Station, Centro Nocturno, and Las Tunas
To Villa El Cocal, Airport, and Bayamo
To Mirador de Mayabe
To Fábrica de Órganos / Gibara
COLECTIVO TAXIS
To Guardalavaca
To Cuerto and Pinares de Mayari

0   0.5 km
0   0.5 mi

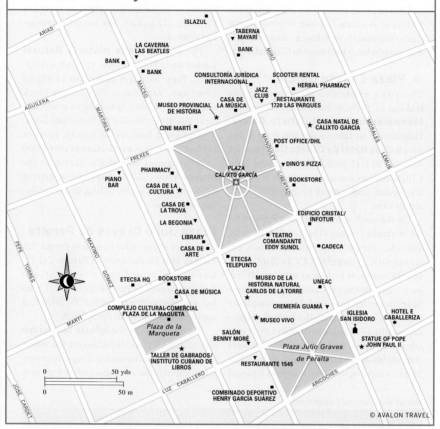

Central Holguín

Within the map:

ISLAZUL
ARIAS
TABERNA MAYARÍ
BANK
LA CAVERNA LAS BEATLES
BANK
BANK
MIRÓ
MACEO
CONSULTORÍA JURÍDICA INTERNACIONAL
SCOOTER RENTAL
HERBAL PHARMACY
JAZZ CLUB
RESTAURANTE 1720 LAS PARQUES
AGUILERA
MÁRTIRES
MUSEO PROVINCIAL DE HISTÓRIA
CASA DE LA MÚSICA
MANDULEY
MORALES
LEMUS
CASA NATAL DE CALIXTO GARCÍA
CINE MARTÍ
POST OFFICE/DHL
FREXES
DINO'S PIZZA
LIBERTAD
PHARMACY
PLAZA CALIXTO GARCÍA
BOOKSTORE
PIANO BAR
CASA DE LA CULTURA
CASA DE LA TROVA
EDIFICIO CRISTAL/INFOTUR
LA BEGONIA
PEPE TORRES
MÁXIMO GÓMEZ
LIBRARY
CASA DE ARTE
TEATRO COMANDANTE EDDY SUNOL
CADECA
ETECSA TELEPUNTO
ETECSA HQ
BOOKSTORE
MUSEO DE LA HISTÓRIA NATURAL CARLOS DE LA TORRE
UNEAC
CASA DE MÚSICA
COMPLEJO CULTURAL-COMERCIAL PLAZA DE LA MAQUETA
CREMERÍA GUAMÁ
IGLESIA SAN ISIDORO
HOTEL E CABALLERIZA
MARTÍ
Plaza de la Marqueta
SALÓN BENNY MORÉ
MUSEO VIVO
STATUE OF POPE JOHN PAUL II
Plaza Julio Graves de Peralta
TALLER DE GRABADOS/INSTITUTO CUBANO DE LIBROS
RESTAURANTE 1545
ARICOCHES
JOSÉ CARDEI
LUZ CABALLERO
COMBINADO DEPORTIVO HENRY GARCÍA SUÁREZ

0   50 yds
0   50 m

© AVALON TRAVEL

Three decades later, a land grant was made to Capitán García Holguín, who built a settlement named for himself. Granted the title of city in 1752, San Isidro de Holguín later became a prize in the Ten Years War (1868-1878), when it was captured from the Spanish by General Calixto García, Holguín's native-born hero.

Orientation

The Carretera Central enters from the west and swings south for Granma Province, skirting the city center. Aguilera (eastbound) and Frexes (westbound) link the Carretera Central to the city center. At its heart is Parque Calixto García, bounded by Calles Frexes (north), Martí (south), Libertad (also known as Manduley; east), and Maceo (west).

Martí runs east from the square and merges to the east with Avenida de los Libertadores, which leads through the modern Plaza de la Revolución district and continues to Moa and Baracoa. The city is bypassed to the south by a *circunvalación* linking the Carretera Central with the road to Moa. Avenida de los Libertadores is lined with monuments to South American "liberators" and revolutionary heroes: Benito Juárez (esq. Aricoches), Simón Bolívar (esq. Cables), Máximo Gómez (esq. San Carlos), Antonio Maceo (400 meters west of Av. de los Internacionalistas), and Che Guevara (esq. Av. de los Internacionalistas).

Libertad runs north from Parque Calixto García to Avenida Capitán Urbino, which leads northeast to Gibara. Avenida XX Aniversario leads northeast to Guardalavaca.

★ Plaza Calixto García

The city's expansive main square was laid out in 1719. At its heart is the marble **Monumento General Calixto García.** Holguín's most famous son was born in the simple **Casa Natal de Calixto García** (Miró #147, tel. 024/42-5610, Tues.-Sat. 9am-5pm, CUC1), one block east of the square. His deeds are regaled, and some of his personal effects are on view.

On the north side, the **Museo Provincial de Historia** (Frexes #198, tel. 024/46-3395, Tues.-Sat. 8am-4:30pm, Sun. 8am-noon, entrance CUC1, cameras CUC1) displays an eclectic range of historical artifacts. It was built 1860-1868 as the Casino Español, where Spanish gentry caroused. It is colloquially known as La Periquera—the Parrot's Cage— supposedly after Spanish troops in their garish yellow, blue, and green uniforms were trapped inside the building, with its cage-like barred windows, when the town was besieged in 1868 by García's troops. The museum's pride and joy is a 35-centimeter-long pre-Columbian axe (the *hacha de Holguín*) carved in the shape of a human. The axe is the provincial symbol.

The **Museo de la Historia Natural Carlos de la Torre** (Maceo #129, tel. 024/42-3935, Tues.-Sat. 9am-noon and 12:30pm-5pm, Sun. 9am-noon, CUC1), one block south of the square, is housed in a neoclassical building guarded by two stone lions. The museum features an eclectic array of stuffed fauna, plus a collection of over 4,000 colorful painted snail shells. Next door, the **Museo Vivo** (CUC1) displays live marine denizens in tanks, including the antediluvian *manjuarí*.

Plaza Julio Graves de Peralta

This small square (also known as Parque Las Flores), four blocks south of Parque Calixto García, is anchored by a marble statue of General Graves de Peralta (1834-1872), who led a rebel assault on October 30, 1868, that captured Holguín from the Spanish.

On the east side, the **Iglesia San Isidro** dates from 1720 and is named for the town's patron saint. The wooden ceiling is noteworthy, although the most gawked-at feature is

Monumento General Calixto García

the larger-than-life statue of Pope John Paul II outside.

The dramatic bas-relief of famous local citizens, called *Origenes,* on the park's west side, traces the city's evolution since pre-Columbian times.

Other Plazas

Tiny **Plaza de la Marqueta,** between Máximo Gómez, Mártires, Martí, and Luz Caballero, occupies the site of a former market and candle factory (*marqueta* refers to the molds). In April 2016, a long-anticipated restoration of the derelict structure was completed. The new **Complejo Cultural-Comercial Plaza de la Marqueta** serves as an artisans' market. Life-size figures of local personalities dot the square. The **Instituto Cubano de Libros** print shop (Callejón de Mercado #2, tel. 024/42-4051), on the south side, still makes books using Linotype.

Plaza José Martí, seven blocks south of Plaza Calixto García, features a bust of the eponymous national hero in front of a bas-relief wall mural of Che Guevara, Simón Bolívar, and other Latin American revolutionary heroes, including former Chilean socialist president Salvador Allende.

The antique cobbled **Plaza San José** (aka Parque Céspedes), two blocks north of Parque Calixto García, is surrounded by colonial buildings and has a statue to local patriots executed during the wars of independence. On its east side, the beautiful **Iglesia de San José** is topped by a domed neoclassical clock tower. The church dates from 1820 and features baroque innards. The **Museo de Historia** (tel. 024/46-2121, Mon.-Fri. 8am-noon and 1pm-4:30pm, free), on the north side, has a motley display relating to the city's past.

The huge **Plaza de la Revolución,** on Avenida XX Aniversario, is dominated by a huge frieze depicting important events in Cuba's history; Fidel is most prominent, of course. Calixto García's mausoleum is here; his mother (also a patriot) is buried east of the plaza beneath a copse.

Loma de la Cruz

Looming over Holguín to the north is the **Loma de la Cruz** (Hill of the Cross), named for the cross that has stood here since 1790. From here you can look out over the city and across the plains towards the mountain formations of the Grupo de Maniabon. To get there, climb the 450 or so steps that begin at the north end of Calle Maceo, 10 blocks north of Plaza San José, or drive via Avenida Capitán Urbino. Security guards are present 24/7.

Entertainment and Events

You can schmooze with intellectuals at **UNEAC** (National Union of Cuban Writers and Artists, Libertad #148, tel. 024/46-4066, daily 8am-midnight), which hosts cultural events. **Teatro Comandante Eddy Suñol** (Martí #111, tel. 024/46-3161), on Parque Calixto García, hosts ballet, classical, and theatrical performances.

For 10-pin bowling, head to **La Bolera** (Habana, esq. Libertad, tel. 024/46-8812, daily 10am-1am, CUC1). You can watch the local baseball team, Los Perros (the Dogs) playing October-April at **Estadio Calixto García** (Av. XX Aniversario, tel. 024/46-2606).

NIGHTLIFE

It's only appropriate that Cuba's main brewing city pours draft Mayabe beer, served in ceramic mugs, at the German-style **Taberna Pancho** (Av. Dimitrov, tel. 024/48-1868, daily noon-11pm), next to Hotel Pernik, and downtown at **Taberna Mayabe** (Libertad, esq. Aguilera, tel. 024/46-1543, Tues.-Sun. noon-6pm and 8pm-midnight).

Islazul's open-air **Cabaret Nocturno** (tel. 024/42-5185, Wed.-Mon. 10pm-midnight, CUC8 including one drink), a mini-Tropicana on the Carretera Central two kilometers west of town, is followed by the city's top disco.

Timeworn crooners perform *danzón* and *son* staples at the **Casa de la Trova "El Guayabero"** (Maceo #174, tel. 024/45-3104, Tues.-Sun. 11am-6pm and 8pm-1am, CUC1), on the west side of Parque Calixto García.

For contemporary sounds, hot spots include **Salón Benny Moré** (Maceo, esq. Luz Caballero, CUC2), with a nightly open-air show at 10:30pm. Midweek, try the insanely packed **Disco Cristal** (Edificio Cristal, Manduley esq. Martí, Tues.-Thurs. 9pm-2am). On weekends it's the Hotel Pernik's hot-hot-hot **Disco Havana Club** (Fri.-Sun. 10pm-2am, CUC2).

The **Casa de la Música** (Libertad, esq. Frexes) has a medley of venues. Upstairs, musicians tickle the ivories of the **Piano Bar Las Musas** (daily 4pm-2am, CUC3); live bands perform downstairs in the air-conditioned **Salon Santa Palabra** (nightly 9pm-2am, CUC1-5); and rooftop **Terraza Bucanero** serves draft beer. Nearby **Bar Terraza** atop Salon 1720 (Frexes #190, e/ Manduley y Miró, tel. 024/42-1078) hosts live music each Friday and Saturday at 9pm.

There's live jazz at the **Jazz Club** (Libertad, esq. Frexes, tel. 024/47-4312, nightly 3pm-2am, CUC5); piped music cranks up after midnight. **La Caverna The Beatles** (tel. 024/45-3440, nightly 4pm-2am, 25 pesos) attempts to re-create Liverpool's the Cavern, replete with life-size figures of the Fab Four.

FESTIVALS AND EVENTS

Mid-January bursts with cultural events during **Semana de Cultura Holguinera.** Every May 3, Holguín comes alive with **Las Romerías de Mayo,** when theater, music, and dance events are held around the city, and pilgrims ascend to the top of Loma de la Cruz for a special mass. The **Festival Internacional de Ballet** is held in November every even-numbered year, and the **Fiesta Iberoamericana de la Cultura** in October celebrates the Spanish heritage in music, dance, and theater.

Food

Holguín has seen an explosion of *paladares*, including **Restaurant El Milano** (Maceo #88, e/ Agramonte y Garajalde, tel. 024/42-5052, daily 11am-11pm), an Italian-run joint with red-and-green decor and a menu featuring pizza, risotto, and lasagna (CUC5-8).

The city's top *paladar*, **Restaurante 1910** (Calle Mártires #143, e/ Aricochea y Cables, tel. 024/42-3994 or 5326-7098, Wed.-Mon. noon-midnight) specializes in roasts and seafood with a broad-ranging international and *criolla* menu that varies from onion soup to filet mignon. Owner Ignacio graces his

bowling at La Bolera

restaurant with pleasant decor and his staff delivers top-notch service.

It doesn't get more Cuban than at **Restaurante Los Almendros** (Calle José A. Cardet #68, tel. 024/42-9652, daily noon-11pm, CUC10-15), which replicates a thatched rural farmstead, including *tabu-rete* (cowhide) seats and authentic country fare from the open kitchen. Lobster and shrimp dishes are offered. Meals come with heapings of rice, delicious black beans, and plantains.

State-run **Restaurante Salón 1720** (Frexes #190, e/ Manduley y Miró, tel. 024/45-8150, daily noon-10:30am) offers classical elegance in a restored colonial mansion. The menu is unusually creative for a state venue and includes onion soup, smoked salmon (CUC6), creole shrimp in brandy (CUC13), and paella (CUC5). Reservations are recommended. Penny-pinchers can look out on Plaza Julio Graves at the atmospheric **Restaurant 1545** (Maceo, esq. Luz Caballero, no tel., daily noon-4pm and 6pm-midnight), serving *criolla* fare for pesos. A dress code applies at both restaurants.

Taberna Pancho (Av. Dimitrov, tel. 024/48-1868, noon-10pm), near Hotel Pernik, serves set *criolla* meals, including decent shrimp and pork dishes (CUC2.50-5, including two beers).

For views over town, ascend the Loma de la Cruz to the open-air **Restaurante Loma de la Cruz** (tel. 024/46-8037, daily noon-9:30pm). The simple menu is limited to *criolla* staples.

The patio snack bar at **La Begonia** (daily 8am-2am), on the west side of Parque Calixto García, is *the* unofficial meeting spot for foreign travelers seeking ham-and-cheese sandwiches, chilled beer, and boy-meets-girl company.

The wait is worthwhile for ice cream at **Cremería Guamá** (daily 10am-10pm), on Plaza Julio Graves; 2.40 pesos buys you a full glass.

For baked goods head to **Panadería Doña Neli** (Manduley #285, daily 8am-8pm), two blocks south of Plaza Julio Graves.

You can buy fresh produce at the *mercado agropecuario* at the east end of Coliseo.

Accommodations

CASAS PARTICULARES

My favorite abode is ★ **Villa Liba** (Maceo #46, esq. 18, Rpto. El Llano, tel. 024/42-3823, marielayoga@cristal.hlg.sld.cu, CUC25), a 1950s bungalow replete with period furnishings. Two cross-ventilated rooms have private bathrooms. Gracious owners Jorge and Mariela make wholesome meals served on a patio with a vine arbor and dipping pool. There's secure parking.

★ **Hospedaje La Palma** (Maceo #52, tel. 024/42-4683, CUC25-30) is a marvelous 1950s home done in Southern California style. One of the two large rooms has a soaring beamed ceiling and a bathroom with piping-hot water. The second room has more classical furniture. The place is festooned with art, including a dramatic terra-cotta bust of Che Guevara, plus there's a huge garden. Owner Enrique is a great host.

You won't regret staying at **Casa de Don Santiago** (Narciso López #25, Apto. 3, e/ Coliseo y 2da, tel. 024/42-6146, CUC20-25), on the second floor of a Soviet prefab apartment complex. The single bedroom has a TV, DVD player, and ceiling fan, but the main reason to stay here is your friendly host, Santiago Andraca, an educated conversationalist.

HOTELS

The '70s Soviet-style **Hotel Pernik** (Av. Dimitrov, tel. 024/48-1011, www.islazul.cu, CUC32 s, CUC48 d low season, CUC45 s, CUC64 d high season), near the Plaza de la Revolución, has 202 pleasantly refurbished rooms (some have modems), plus a swimming pool and a disco to wake the dead. Part of the same complex, the more intimate and similarly priced **Villa El Bosque** (tel. 024/48-1012, www.islazul.cu) has 69 rooms in cabins with modern solar-heated bathrooms and uninspired, sprawling grounds.

By far the best choice is the boutique **Hotel E La Caballeriza** (Miró #203, e/ Luz

Caballero y Aricochea, tel. 024/42-9191, www. cubanacan.cu, CUC110 s, CUC150 d high season), a lovingly restored 1810 mansion that once served as a military stable. This cozy gem has 21 rooms furnished to international standards, plus the city's most elegant restaurant.

Information and Services

Infotur (tel. 024/42-5013, holgdir@enet.cu, Mon.-Fri. 8am-5pm, Sat. 8am-1pm) has tourist information bureaus upstairs in Edificio Cristal and at the airport (tel. 024/47-4774, when flights arrive).

The **post office** (Máximo Gómez, e/ Aguilera y Arias) is on the east side of Parque Calixto García. **DHL** (Manduley, esq. Frexes, tel. 024/46-8254, Mon.-Fri. 9am-6pm, Sat. 8:30am-noon) has an office in the Edificio Cristal. **Etecsa** (Martí, e/ Mártires y Máximo Gómez, daily 8am-7pm) has international telephone and Internet service. Parque Calixto Gracía, Parque Julio Grave de Peralta, and Loma de la Cruz are public Wi-Fi zones.

Banks include **Bandec** (on the south side of Plaza San José as well as on Maceo, esq. Aguilera), **Banco Financiero Internacional** (Aguilera, esq. Maceo), and **Banco Popular** (Maceo, e/ Aguilera y Arias, as well as one block south of the Villa El Bosque). You can change currency at **Cadeca** (Libertad e/ Martí y Luz Caballero, Mon.-Sat. 8am-5pm).

Consultoría Jurídica Internacional (Libertad #171, e/ Frexes y Aguilera, tel. 024/42-1066, Mon.-Fri. 8am-5pm, Sat. 8am-1pm) provides legal services.

Seeking a soothing massage after walking the streets? Mariela Gógora is renowned for yoga and massage classes and services. Contact her at **Villa Liba** (Maceo #46, esq. 18, Rpto. El Llano, tel. 024/42-3823).

Getting There and Around

AIR

Aeropuerto Frank País (tel. 024/46-2512) is 10 kilometers south of town, on the Carretera Central. The domestic terminal is served by a bus from Calle Rodríguez, near the train station six blocks south of Parque Calixto García.

Cubana (Edificio Cristal, tel. 024/46-8148 or 46-8114, Mon.-Fri. 8am-4pm) flies between Havana and Holguín daily.

From the United States, **American Airlines** (tel. 800/433-7300, www.aa.com) has daily scheduled service from Miami and Fort Lauderdale.

BUS

The **Terminal de Ómnibus Interprovinciales** (Carretera Central #19, e/ 20 de Mayo e Independencia, tel. 024/42-2111) is on the west side of town. Most (but not all) **Víazul** buses (tel. 024/42-6822, www. viazul.com) stop in Holguín traveling between Havana (CUC44), Varadero (CUC38), and Trinidad (CUC26) to Santiago de Cuba (CUC11).

Buses to and from Guardalavaca and towns east of Holguín arrive and depart the **Terminal de Ómnibus Municipales** (Av. de los Libertadores, tel. 024/48-1170), opposite the baseball stadium. West and southbound trucks leave from **Terminal La Molienda** (Carretera Central y Comandante Fajardo, tel. 024/42-2322), on the west side of town. Bus #16 connects the Hotel Pernik with downtown.

TRAIN

Cuba's main railway line serves **Cacocum** train station (tel. 024/32-7194), 15 kilometers south of town; an hourly bus connects Holguín's **Estación de Ferrocarriles** (Calle Pita, tel. 024/42-2331), eight blocks south of Plaza Calixto García, with Cacocum. Service is highly irregular and subject to change; check current schedules at the stations.

At press time, train #15 from Havana (every third day at 6:53pm) stopped at Cacocum (10:17am, CUC26) and continued to Guantánamo. Train #11 from Havana (6:13pm) also stops at Cacocum every fourth day, continuing to Santiago de Cuba (CUC24.50). Westbound, train #12 from Santiago de Cuba (11:45pm) calls at Cacocum, continuing to Havana via Camagüey, Ciego de Ávila, Santa Clara and Matanzas; and train

#16 from Guantánamo (8:50am) makes similar stops.

CAR AND TAXI

You can rent cars through **Cubacar** (tel. 24/42-8196 at Hotel Pernik, tel. 024/46-8414 at the airport, com.renta.hlg@transtur.cu), **Havanautos** (tel. 024/46-8412, domestic terminal), **Rex** (tel. 024/46-4644, international terminal at Aeropuerto Frank País), and **Vía** (Cine Martí, tel. 024/42-1602). There are gas stations on Carretera a Gibara, on Avenida de los Libertadores, on Avenida de los Internacionalistas, and at the junction of the Carretera Central and *circunvalación*. **Cubataxi** (tel. 024/42-3290) offers taxi service.

Excursions are offered by **Cubatur** (Edificio Cristal, tel. 024/42-1679).

MIRADOR DE MAYABE

The **Mirador de Mayabe** (CUC2 entrance), high above the Mayabe Valley eight kilometers southeast of town, offers magnificent views. The ridgetop facility includes a thatched restaurant and bar (daily 7am-9pm) and draws locals on weekends. Islazul's **Villa Mirador de Mayabe** (tel. 024/42-2160, www.islazul.cu, CUC35 s, CUC47 d low season, CUC50 s, CUC73 d high season) has 24 nicely furnished hilltop *cabinas* and a swimming pool. There's also Casa de Pancho, a fully staffed four-bedroom house.

Adjoining, **Finca Mayabe** is an ersatz farmstead with turkeys, geese, and other farm animals, as well as a *galleria* (a cock pit) where you can watch cockfights.

North of Holguín

★ GIBARA

Delightful for its sleepy ambience, Gibara (pop. 20,000), 28 kilometers north of Holguín, is a browbeaten, salt-encrusted fishing port that overlooks the Bahía de Gibara. Founded in 1817, it was a major sugar-trading port in colonial days, when it was known as Villa Blanca and colloquially as La Perla del Oriente (the Pearl of the Orient). It has no shortage of intriguing colonial structures, though only remnants of the original 18th-century city walls still stand.

The town was devastated by Hurricane Ike in November 2008 (more than 70 percent of homes in the area were damaged). It has since been given a fresh coat of paint and government investment has gone a long way toward restoration. Funky fishing boats sit at anchor in a bay with sensational views southeast toward the flat-topped mountain **Silla de Gibara** (Saddle of Gibara), considered to be the hill described by Christopher Columbus when he landed on October 28, 1492.

The streets rise steeply south and west of the main plaza. Follow Independencia west, uphill past charming little **Plaza Colón,** and turn right at Calle Cabada to reach the paltry ruins of **Fuerte Eel Cuartelón** (a 30-minute hike), a remnant of the old city wall that once surrounded the town. The view is worth the effort.

From the Eddy Suñol Ricardo primary school (at the west end of Independencia), the Sendero Antonio Nuñez Jiménez trail leads to **Caverna de los Panaderos,** a cave system with fantastical dripstone formations and an underground river and lake (plus bats). The system is part of the much larger labyrinthine Polja del Cementerio system. Contact naturalist guide Alexis Silva García (tel. 024/84-4458) at the Museo de Historia Natural.

Gibara's seafront promenade, the **Malecón,** boasts a **statue of Camilo Cienfuegos** on the north side of town.

You can hire a boat to **Playa Blanca,** a glorious white-sand beach on the east side of the bay (CUC5 round-trip); take a rickety twice-daily ferry to **Playa Los Bajos** (CUC1) from the pier on Ronda de la Marina (esq. Peralta); or drive the 15 kilometers northwest to **Playa**

Caletones via a wind farm with six turbines. The latter is popular with locals on weekends and the pleasant **Restaurante La Esperanza** here serves fresh seafood.

Parque Calixto García

The pretty main plaza is framed by African oaks and is pinned by a **Monumento a Los Libertadores de la Patria,** commemorating those who fought in the wars of independence. The restored **Iglesia de San Fulgencio** church (Tues.-Sun. 8am-noon and 2pm-5pm), with Byzantine-style cupolas, dates from 1850.

The excellent **Museo de Historia Natural** (Luz Caballero #23, tel. 024/84-4458, Mon. 1pm-5pm, Tues.-Sat. 9am-noon and 1pm-5pm, Sun. 9am-noon, entrance CUC1, cameras CUC1, guide CUC5) displays stuffed animals and other natural history exhibits.

The **Museo de Arte Decorativo** (Independencia #19, tel. 024/84-4687, Tues.-Sat. 9am-noon and 1pm-5pm, Sun. 8am-noon, entrance CUC2, cameras CUC1), in a restored neoclassical mansion 50 meters southwest of the square, boasts period furniture and paintings upstairs.

Batería Fernando 7mo, one block east of the square, preserves an old fortress.

Entertainment and Events

The open-air **Centro Cultural El Colonial** (Peralta, esq. Sartorio, CUC2), on the northwest corner of the main square, has live music Tuesday-Sunday nights. Alternatively, head to **Siglo XX,** a similar cultural venue on the park's east side for live and canned music.

Gibara is famed nationwide for its love of cinema. The **Cine Jiba** (Luz Caballero #17), on the main plaza, hosts Cuba's annual **Festival Internacional de Cine Pobre** (International Low-Budget Film Festival, tel. 07/836-9493, www.festivalcinepobre.cult.cu), drawing rising movie stars and producers to this unlikely venue each April. The festival is a big deal, and the town goes wild with carnival-like celebrations.

Food

The best of few eateries is the **Restaurant Las Terrazas** (corner Céspedes and Calixto García)—aka "Michael's Place." It exudes rustic ambience, not least thanks to its old fishing bar on the open-air rooftop terrace. It serves *criolla* fare and seafood, as does the thatched farmhouse-style **Restaurant La Cueva** (Calle 2da #131, tel. 024/84-5333, daily noon-midnight, CUC8-12), one kilometer north of town. English-speaking owner Pedro Rodríguez and his efficient staff serve superb crab, lobster, shrimp, and fish dishes accompanied by homegrown organic salads and veggies.

Six pesos (25 cents) will buy you a garlic shrimp dish at the no-frills hilltop **Restaurante El Mirador** (tel. 024/84-5259, daily noon-8pm), with views over town.

Accommodations

The standout among several excellent *casas particulares* is the antiques-filled ★ **La Casa de los Amigos** (Céspedes #15, e/ Luz Caballeros y Peralta, tel. 024/84-4115, lacasadelosamigos@yahoo.fr, CUC25), where the walls are covered in fabulous murals (some erotic). The two gorgeous air-conditioned bedrooms open to a patio with a thatched bar and dining space, and have fans, batik spreads and linens, and exquisite bathrooms. Lilian is your delightful host.

You'll fall in love with **Hostal los Hermanos** (Céspedes #13, e/ Peralta y Luz Caballero, tel. 024/84-4542, www.hostaloshermanos.com, CUC20), where owner Odalis rents four antiques-filled rooms. ★ **Villa Caney** (Céspedes #36, e/ Peralta y Luz Caballero, tel. 024/84-4552, CUC20-25) is another colonial gem full of period pieces. It opens to a delightful garden terrace with hammocks, palms, and a thatched restaurant. The owners rent two air-conditioned rooms with fans and private bathrooms with hot water.

★ **Hotel E Ordoño** (Calle J. Peralta e/ Donato Mármol e Independencia, tel. 024/84-4448, www.cubanacan.cu, CUC44 s, CUC56 d low season, CUC65 s, CUC82 d high season) shines after a complete restoration of a derelict family mansion. Beyond its columned lobby is an impressive restaurant. Upstairs are 21 beautifully furnished rooms on two levels (there's no elevator). The master suite features an extravagant bathroom mural.

Cubanacán upped the ante in 2015 when it opened the two-story **Hotel E Arsenito** (Sartorio #22 e/ Martí y Luz Caballero, tel. 024/84-4400, www.cubanacan.cu, CUC97 s, CUC141 d high season), a remodeled centenary manse kitted out with modern accoutrements. Two of its 12 bedrooms boast king beds.

Information and Services

Plaza de la Cultura (Independencia y Agüero) has public Wi-Fi. The **post office** is at Independencia #15 (Mon.-Sat. 8am-8pm). You can change money at **Bandec** (Independencia y J. Peralta).

Getting There and Around

The **bus station** (tel. 024/84-4215) is at the entrance to town. Buses depart Holguín for Gibara twice daily. A taxi will cost about CUC25. **Cubacar** (Calle Independencia Final, tel. 024/84-4222) has a rental agency at Restaurante El Faro in Hostal Buena Vista. There's a gas station at the entrance to town.

RAFAEL FREYRE AND VICINITY

This small town, 35 kilometers northeast of Holguín (mid-way to Guardalavaca), is dominated by the defunct Rafael Freyre sugar mill. The *central* is the setting for what is touted as the **Museo de Locomotora de Vapor** (Steam Train Museum, tel. 024/85-0493, Mon.-Fri. 9:30am-11:30pm). There are six engines (the oldest dates from 1882) in derelict sheds.

The town (also known as Santa Lucía) lies a few kilometers inland of Bahía de Bariay. If you zigzag through Rafael Freyre and go past the *central,* the road north will take you to the bay and **Playa Blanca,** a gorgeous beach with a commemorative plaque to Columbus that declares this the "site of the first landing of Christopher Columbus in Cuba."

Parque Monumento Nacional Bariay

Created in 2002 to honor Columbus's landing, this 206-hectare **park** (tel. 024/43-3311, daily 9am-5pm, CUC8 entrance including cocktail) is within the broader Parque Cristóbal

Hotel E Ordoño

Colón. This meager facility features a re-created village—**Aldea Aborigen**—where reenactments of Taíno life take place, with Cubans in indigenous garb. There's also an archaeological site with a small museum, and the Hellenistic **Monumento al Medio Milenio,** commemorating Columbus's landing. Horseback rides are offered (CUC4).

To get there, take the road west from Rafael Freyre for Frey Benito; the park is signed four kilometers west of town. The Rafael Freyre-Frey Benito road continues to Gibara, passing the **Silla de Gibara,** a saddle-shaped lime-stone massif that Columbus recorded during his visit: CUC2 buys you entry to trails at Campismo Silla, four kilometers west of Frey Benito. It also has horseback riding, plus some two dozen climbing routes (contact naturalist guide Alexis Silva García, tel. 024/84-4458, in Gibara).

Accommodations

Campismo Silla de Gibara (tel. 024/42-1586, CUC5 pp), enjoying a fabulous location at the base of a *mogote,* is a simple holiday camp with 42 basic cabins (some air-conditioned) with cold-water showers. It has a swimming pool, café, and horseback riding.

Hosts José and Daylin Portelles welcome you to **Hostal Cayo Bariay** (Calle 2 #18, tel. 024/85-0758 or 5338-8993, cayobariayhostal@gmail.com, CUC20-25), a *casa particular* in a hamlet that is steps from the entrance to Parque Monumental Nacional Bariay. The couple rents three simply furnished rooms (two air-conditioned). Meals are served on a lovely, leafy patio.

The all-inclusive **Hotel Don Lino** (tel. 024/43-0308, www.islazul.cu, CUC45 s, CUC66 d low season, CUC80 s, CUC198 d high season), in its own beach-lined cove near Playa Blanca, has 36 pleasantly furnished air-conditioned rooms in bungalows (18 have ocean views). Expect canned entertainment and mediocre food. The hotel was scheduled for a major upgrade and expansion at press time.

★ GUARDALAVACA

Guardalavaca (the name means "Guard the Cow") is a resort about 55 kilometers northeast of Holguín, stitching together a string of gorgeous beaches. Scuba diving and snorkeling are excellent. Most hotels are all-inclusive and cater almost exclusively to package charter groups. It's a small fry compared to Varadero or Cayo Coco, and a stay here may come as a disappointment to

native reenactment at Parque Monumento Nacional Bariay

sun-sea-and-sand-loving tourists who are expecting the scope of Cancún.

The original (and main) resort, comprising Guardalavaca proper, is at the twin-beach strip of **Playa Mayor** and, to its east, **Playa Las Brisas;** farther east is the lovely, as-yet-undeveloped beach of **Playa El Cayuelo.** High-end development has focused farther west at **Playa Esmeralda, Playa Pesquero,** and **Playa Yuraguanal,** midway between Guardalavaca and Rafael Freyre. Additional hotels are being built here, but there are no other services.

Museo Aborigen Chorro de Maíta

This **museum** (tel. 024/43-0201, Mon.-Sat. 9am-5pm, Sun 9am-1pm, entrance CUC2, cameras CUC5), on a hilltop seven kilometers east of Guardalavaca and two kilometers south from the highway, is on a large aboriginal burial site where almost 200 skeletons have been unearthed. A gallery surrounds the burial ground within a building where 62 skeletons lie in peaceful repose. Pre-Columbian artifacts are displayed. A life-size model indigenous village, **Aldea Taína,** has been re-created across the road (CUC5 additional) with an ensemble of locals dressed like Taíno who perform at noon Monday-Saturday.

Bahía de Naranjo

This huge flask-shaped bay, about four kilometers west of Guardalavaca, is fringed by mangroves and dry forest protected in **Parque Natural Bahía de Naranjo.** The eastern headland is accessible via **Las Guanas Sendero Eco-Arqueológico** (daily 8:30am-5:30pm, CUC3), where self-guided trails lead to archaeological sites and Cueva Ciboney, a funerary cave with petroglyphs. Lookout towers provide a bird's-eye view. An interpretive center offers introductions to the flora and fauna.

Acuario Cayo Naranjo (tel. 024/43-0132, daily 9am-9pm, cameras CUC2, videos CUC5) occupies a natural lagoon on the tiny island in the middle of the bay. Sea lions and dolphins perform acrobatics at noon. The hotels offer excursions.

Recreation

Horseback riding (CUC16 per hour) is offered at **Centro Hípico Rancho Naranjo** (Playa Esmeralda) and **Bioparque Rocazul** (daily 9am-5pm, entrance CUC8, cameras CUC1, videos CUC2), a 1,487-hectare recreational

human skeletons at Museo Aborigen Chorro de Maíta

Guardalavaca and Vicinity

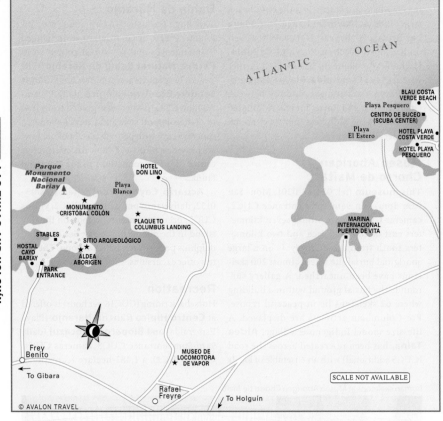

© AVALON TRAVEL

facility on the west side of the bay. Hiking trails (guide compulsory, CUC8 one hour) lead through the scrub and mangroves, and to **Finca Monte Bello** (CUC16), a display farm hosting rodeos (Mon., Wed., and Fri. 10:30am, CUC9 adults, CUC5 children).

Marlin Club Las Brisas (tel. 024/43-0774), at the east end of Playa Las Brisas, offers banana-boat rides, waterskiing, kayak and Hobie Cat rental, sportfishing, and catamaran excursions. **Marlin Eagle Ray Dive Center** (tel. 024/43-0316), at the west end of Playa Mayor, offers scuba diving (CUC45 one dive) at 9am, 11am, and 2pm. There's also a dive

center at the Blau Costa Verde Beach hotel, at Playa Pesquero.

Hotel tour desks sell snorkeling and sunset cruises plus sportfishing from **Marina Gaviota Puerto de Vita** (tel. 024/43-0132, reservas@mvita.co.cu), near Playa Pesquero, and at the marina in the fishing village of **Boca de Samá,** nine kilometers east of Guardalavaca.

Havana Kiteboarding Club (tel. 5804-9656, www.havanakite.com) has an outlet at Hotel Brisas Guardalavaca. *Cuentapropista* (private entrepreneur) Luis Riveron (tel. 5378-4857, luiskitesurf@nauta.cu) offers lessons

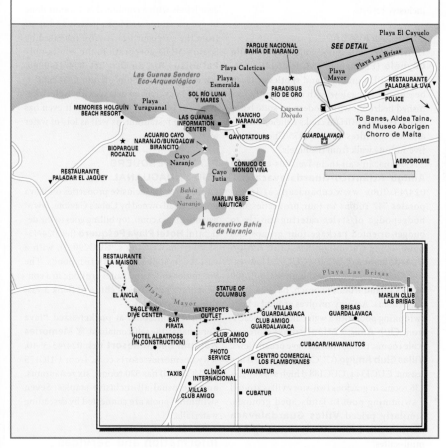

(CUC25 per hour) and board rental (CUC8 per hour) by Bar Pirata on Playa Mayor.

Food

Tops by far is ★ **Restaurant La Maison** (100 meters west of Playa Mayor, tel. 024/48-0839, daily noon-11pm), a *paladar* with an enviable hilltop position overlooking Playa Mayor with great ocean views. The excellent food includes paella (CUC5) and lobster (from CUC12.50). It has a lovely setting in a coral-stone home with patio dining under an arbor.

Forsake the hotel buffets for authentic Cuban fare at **Restaurante Doña Bárbara**

(tel. 5278-7505, www.actiweb.es/donabarbara, daily 11:30am-11pm, CUC10-15), at Yaguajay two kilometers south of Guardalavaca. Filling meals—from perfectly cooked pork dishes to garlic lobster—are served on a rear patio. State-run **El Ancla** (tel. 024/43-0381, daily 10am-10pm, from CUC8), atop a coral outcrop at the west end of Playa Mayor, serves fish dishes (lobster costs a ludicrous CUC31).

Most hotels sell day and evening passes (CUC35-50), which include all-inclusive use of their restaurants and other facilities.

Accommodations

Private room rentals are perfect for budget

hounds and those who prefer to avoid the all-inclusive resorts.

GUARDALAVACA

Hotel-goers will envy your stay at **Villa Cayuelo** (El Cayuelo #38, tel. 5246-9446, CUC35-40), a gracious and spotlessly clean beachfront bungalow with a pleasantly furnished bedroom with modern en suite bathroom. Hostess Miriam cooks delicious meals and her son hires out his 1955 Chevy. It's a five-minute walk from the hotels.

Cubanacán's all-inclusive, '70s-era **Club Amigo Atlántico-Guardalavaca** (tel. 024/43-0180, www.cubanacan.cu) incorporates 747 rooms in four properties in a hodgepodge of styles catering mostly to budget-oriented package tour groups and noise-loving Cuban families. **Club Amigo Guardalavaca** (CUC60 s, CUC90 d low season, CUC105 s, CUC152 d high season), 100 meters inland from the beach, has 234 standard rooms. Activity revolves around a huge swimming pool with a waterslide. The beachfront **Club Amigo Atlántico** has more upscale rooms, though not all have ocean views. **Villas Club Amigo** (CUC80 s, CUC110 d low season, CUC134 s, CUC188 d high season) has 136 rooms in gracious two-story villas around a swimming pool in landscaped grounds. Similarly priced **Villas Guardalavaca** has 144 beachside *cabinas* including four mini-suites.

Somewhat more elegant and upmarket, **Brisas Guardalavaca** (tel. 024/43-0218, www.cubanacan.cu, from CUC95 s, CUC126 d low season, from CUC118 s, CUC150 d high season), on Playa Las Brisas, is less boisterous. It has 357 pleasantly furnished rooms, 80 mini-suites, and 4 junior suites divided into villa and hotel complexes with two large pools.

PLAYA ESMERALDA

A step up from the Guardalavaca options, the **Sol Río de Luna y Mares** (tel. 024/43-0030, www.meliacuba.com, from CUC150 s, CUC200 d low season, from CUC163 s, CUC220 d high season) comprises two adjacent hotels with a combined 564 rooms done in eye-pleasing Caribbean pastels and steps from the gorgeous beach. Also managed by Spain's Meliá corporation, the adults-only **Paradisus Río de Oro** (tel. 024/43-0090, www.meliacuba.com, from CUC333 s, CUC477 d) verges on deluxe, with lively tropical decor in its 254 junior suites. It even has a Japanese restaurant, as well as lots of water toys.

PLAYAS PESQUERO AND YURAGUANAL

Of the three all-inclusive properties on Playa Pesquero (all owned by Cuba's Gaviota, www.gaviota-grupo.com), top billing goes to the delightful **Hotel Playa Pesquero** (tel. 024/43-3530, from CUC185 s, CUC290 d), with a vast Asian-style lobby with fish ponds. The 968 junior suites and suites are done in a contemporary neoclassical chic and flank a vast three-pool complex.

On its lonesome at pocket-sized Playa Yuraguanal, the self-contained ★ **Memories Holguín Beach Resort** (tel. 024/43-3540, www.memoriesresorts.com, from CUC175 s, CUC240 d) has 520 rooms, six restaurants, and the usual all-inclusive staples. Seven swimming pools are connected by cascading waterfalls.

Information and Services

The post office and DHL service are in the Brisas Guardalavaca resort. International calls from hotels are expensive; use the *minipuntos* (telephone kiosks) roadside at Playa Mayor and Playa Esmeralda. All hotels have Wi-Fi.

There's a **Banco Financiero Internacional** (Mon.-Fri. 9am-3pm) in Centro Comercial los Flamboyanes.

Getting There and Away

Guardalavaca has no airport. Vacationers on package tours land at Holguín.

Transtur has a tourist shuttle that leaves Holguín's Parque Calixto García daily at 1pm for Guardalavaca via Playas Pesquero and Esmeralda (CUC15 round-trip). The return shuttle departs Brisas Guardalavaca at 8:45am, Playa Esmeralda at 9am, and Playa Pesquero at 9:30am.

There is a taxi stand west of Club Amigo, or call **Cubataxi** (tel. 024/43-0330). A taxi between Guardalavaca and Holguín will cost about CUC40 one-way; a *colectivo* costs about CUC5.

You can rent cars from **Cubacar** (tel. 024/43-0389), adjacent to Club Amigo Atlántico-Guardalavaca; or **Rex** (tel. 024/42-0476), at Brisas Guardalavaca. The gas station is between Playa Esmeralda and Guardalavaca.

Excursions can be purchased at hotel tour desks or direct with **Cubatur** (tel. 024/43-0170), 50 meters south of Centro Comercial Los Framboyantes; **Havanatur** (tel. 024/43-0406, noryuan@havanatur.cu), at the west end of Guardalavaca; or **Gaviota** (tel. 024/43-0903, travel.hog@gaviotatours.co.cu).

Marina Gaviota Puerto de Vita (tel. 024/43-0132445, reservas@mvita.co.cu), one kilometer west of Playa Pesquero, has 38 slips and handles international yacht arrivals.

Getting Around

Horse-drawn *coches* charge CUC3 for a tour around Guardalavaca (CUC15 to the *acuario*).

You can hop on and off Transtur's **Guardalavaca Beach Tour** (CUC5) double-decker shuttle bus, which travels between Guardalavaca, Acuario Cayo Naranjo, and other beaches, and east to Aldea Taíno.

Bicycles and scooters (CUC13 one hour, CUC25 per day) can be rented at Vía Rent-a-Car.

BANES

Banes (pop. 84,000), about 34 kilometers southeast of Guardalavaca—the rolling, palm-fringed route is superbly scenic—and 70 kilometers northeast of Holguín, is a large provincial sugar-processing town. This is the real Cuba, with all the sundry life that Guardalavaca lacks. For much of the past century, the town was run by the United Fruit Company, which owned virtually all the land hereabouts and had a now-defunct sugar mill called Boston (since renamed Nicaragua) five kilometers south of town.

Former dictator-president Fulgencio Batista was born here in 1901. His future archenemies, Fidel and Raúl Castro, were born nearby at Birán. On October 12, 1948, Fidel married Mirta Diaz-Balart, daughter of the mayor of Banes (and a close friend of Batista, who gave the couple $1,000 as a wedding gift), in the art deco **Iglesia de Nuestra Señora de la Caridad,** on the main square, **Parque Martí,** at the northeast side of town.

The **Museo Indocubano** (General Marrero #305, tel. 024/80-2487, Tues.-Sat. 9am-5pm, Sun. 8am-noon, CUC1, cameras CUC5) exhibits a collection of more than 20,000 pre-Columbian artifacts, most importantly a small gold fertility idol wearing a feather headdress. English-speaking curator Luis Quiñones García (tel. 024/90-2691, votico@gmail.com) offers tours around town and can explain replica aboriginal cave paintings displayed in **Plaza Aborigen,** adjoining the museum. The plaza also hosts "El Panchito," a tiny steam locomotive made in 1888 by the H. K. Porter Locomotive Works of Pittsburgh and used in the Boston sugar-processing mill.

For now, visitors can glory in the pearly beauty of **Playa de Morales**, 10 kilometers east of Banes via rough unpaved road. To the north is **Playa Puerto Rico,** where prim bungalows and rustic fishers' shacks overhang pristine sands. The beaches and those of **Peninsula de Ramón Antilla** southeast are to be developed as a major tourist resort.

Food and Accommodations

Casas particulares include the lovely **Casa Evelyn Feria Dieguez** (Bruno Merino #3401-A, e/ Delfín Pepo y Heredia, tel. 024/80-3150, CUC20), with two upstairs rooms opening to a terrace. Each has modern private bathroom. The hostess is a delight. There's secure parking. If she's full, Evelyn will call around for alternatives, such as **Hostal Paraíso** (Capitán Capdevilla #505, e/ Céspedes y Maceo, tel. 024/80-4096 or 5878-3956, CUC25), a charming wooden colonial home one block from Parque Martí. Gracious owners Dania and Julio rent three rooms. Banes's top *paladar* is **Restaurante Don Carlos** (Veguitas #1702, esq. H, tel. 024/80-2176, daily noon-10pm), a no-frills option serving filling *criolla* and seafood dishes.

Getting There and Away

Buses operate between Holguín and Banes; the terminal is at Calle Los Angeles and Tráfico. Taxis between the towns will cost about CUC25.

Holguín to Guantánamo Province

★ MUSEO CONJUNTO HISTÓRICO BIRÁN

Fidel Castro was born on August 13, 1926, at Finca Las Manacas in **Birán**, a rural hamlet below the western foothills of the Altiplanici de Nipe, 60 kilometers southeast of Holguín and 65 kilometers south of Banes via Cueto. Castro's father, Ángel, began leasing land from the United Fruit Company in 1910, farmed sugarcane to sell to the mills, and grew wealthy on the proceeds of his 26,000-acre domain. Eventually, he acquired a sawmill and a nickel mine, and was the powerful patriarch of the region. Fidel, however, worked to downplay his social privilege and preferred to exaggerate the simplicity of his background. "The house was made of wood. No mortar, cement, or bricks," he told Brazilian theologian Frey Beto in *Fidel: My Early Years*. In truth, it's a substantial house—clearly the home of a well-to-do man. The two-story house on wooden pilings with a cattle barn (and a 1918 Ford pickup that once belonged to Ángel) underneath is a replica—the original burned to the ground in 1954. The property also contained a slaughterhouse, repair shop, store, bakery, and other facilities.

In 2002 the **Finca Las Manacas** (tel. 024/28-6114, Tues.-Sat. 8am-4pm, Sun. 8am-noon, entrance CUC10, cameras CUC10, videos CUC10), which is guarded by MININT soldiers, opened to the public as a national

Fidel's sniper rifle, Museo Conjunto Histórico Birán

Big Fruit

After the wars for independence, the vast sugarcane fields of Holguín gradually fell into the hands of U.S. corporations, especially the United Fruit Company (UFC), which bought the land for a pittance and came to dominate economic and political life in the region. While the UFC was also a philanthropic agent locally—paying, for example, for a sewer system for the town of Banes—Tad Szulc explains that it was "emblematic of almost everything that was wrong in Cuba's relationship with the United States: the powerlessness, the degree to which the mill constituted a world unto itself in which Cubans had no rights except those conceded by the company." One of the few Cubans who benefited economically from the UFC arrangement was Fidel Castro's father, Ángel Castro, who leased lands from UFC and grew to be both prosperous and powerful. The pitiful existence of many among the Cuban peasantry was not lost on the young Fidel, who, it is claimed, first agitated on workers' behalf as a boy—and on his father's estate.

Telex from Cuba: A Novel, by Rachel Kushner (New York: Scribner, 2008), tells the tale.

historic site. A guide will accompany you as you're shown the graves of Castro's parents, Ángel and Lina; the simple schoolhouse that Fidel attended (his desk is front row, center, of course); and the local post office and telegraph office. The huge main house has many original furnishings, plus Fidel's personal effects (including his baseball glove and basketball) and the bed in which it is claimed he was born. (In *After Fidel,* author and former CIA analyst Brian Latell cites convincing evidence that Fidel, who was born illegitimate and not legally acknowledged by his father until he was 17, lived his first few years with his mother, the family housemaid, and apart from his father and his formal wife.)

From Holguín, take the Cueto road (Route 6-123). Turn south five kilometers west of Cueto to Loynaz Echevarría. Turn east (left) just beyond the *central.* The community of Birán is seven kilometers farther, and Finca Las Manacas is two kilometers to the north. You can also reach Birán from Palma Soriano, to the south, by a badly potholed road via Mella, a sugar town with an artists' cooperative.

★ PINARES DE MAYARÍ

From the small town of Mayarí Abajo, 80 kilometers east of Holguín, a partially paved and muddy road (badly deteriorated at last visit) climbs sharply to a broad *altiplano* (plateau)

high in the Sierra Cristal, where mists drift languidly through the pine forest. It's a great place to beat the heat and for bird-watching (65 species) and hiking; activities are centered on Villa Pinares de Mayarí, an eco-focused hotel at the mountain peak of Loma de Mensura (995 meters elevation), 20 kilometers south of Mayarí. The distinctly alpine region is enshrined in Parque Nacional La Mensura.

At Loma de Mensura, the Cuban Academy of Sciences' Estación de Investigación Integral de la Montaña includes Orquideario La Mensura (daily 8am-5pm, no tel., CUC2 payable in the hotel), an orchid garden; and the 2.4-kilometer-long Sendero La Sabina (CUC6) self-guided nature trail, which is named for a local juniper species.

Two kilometers north of the Orquideario is La Plancha, another lovely garden set amid eucalyptus; it was ravaged by Hurricane Sandy in 2012 and remained under restoration at last visit, as was Finca Los Exóticos (8 km west of the Pinares road), where elk, nilgai, and deer are bred (originally for the hunting pleasure of the Communist elite).

Salto El Guayabo

The high point of the altiplano is the not-to-be-missed Salto El Guayabo (daily 8:30am-5pm, c/o EcoTur, tel. 5408-8452, aliomar@hlg.sld.cu, CUC5), 17 kilometers north of Villa

Pinares de Mayarí. The *salto* is a twin waterfall (120 and 140 meters, respectively), Cuba's highest. A *mirador* offers sensational views of the cascade and forested river canyon, and far out to the Atlantic. It has a delightful restaurant in a garden of ferns and poincianas. You can hike two trails: One descends to the base of the falls, and the second leads to the top, with natural pools atop the plunge.

Cueto and Mayarí towns form part of the **Ruta de Chan Chan,** colloquially named for the opening chorus line to "Chan Chan," Compay Segundo's canonical theme song from the blockbuster *Buena Vista Social Club* album. U.S. tour operator **Cuba Unbound** (tel. 208/770-3359, www.cubaunbound.com) features the route as part of a 12-day walking tour that includes Mayarí.

Food and Accommodations

You will be wowed upon arrival at **Villa Yoya** (Calle 4ta #3, tel. 5542-7619, www.villayoya1901.com, CUC25 including breakfast), a superb two-story middle-class home in Chaveleta Norte, one kilometer east of Mayarí. Its two bedrooms are luxuriously decked out and lavish meals are served in a rooftop *rancho*. There's secure parking.

A middle-class gem, Marina and Raulito's

Casa Juan Vicente (Loma #50, tel. 024/50-1316 or 5245-4040, www.juanvicente.webs.com, CUC25 including breakfast) enjoys a country setting at Juan Vicente, four kilometers west of downtown Mayarí (a 10-minute drive from Playa Juan Vicente). Two rooms—one upstairs, the other in a wooden cottage—have modern furnishings and en suite bathrooms with hot-water showers. Filling country meals are served beneath thatch in the backyard.

Pack some cold-weather clothes for a stay at **Villa Pinares de Mayarí** (tel. 024/50-3308, comercial@vpinares.co.cu, CUC32 s, CUC40 d low season, CUC36 s, CUC48 d high season), a rustic eco-resort at 680 meters elevation. It has 29 spacious yet rustic wooden one-, two-, and three-bedroom cottages with private bathrooms. There's a swimming pool and restaurant.

CAYO SAETÍA

This 42-square-kilometer cay (CUC10 entrance), 18 kilometers north of the coast highway, is separated from the mainland by a hair's-breadth waterway. Its ecosystems range from mangrove swamps to evergreen forests harboring endangered species, including *jabalí* (wild boar), plus exotic animals—ostrich,

cabin at Villas Pinares de Mayarí

zebra, giraffes, camels, and so forth—originally imported for the hunting pleasure of top Communist officials, for whom Cayo Saetía was once a private vacation spot.

One-hour jeep safaris (CUC9) and horseback riding (CUC6 per hour) are available; spotting the wildlife all but requires a safari with guide. There are superb white-sand beaches beneath cliffs.

If driving, note that many maps show a nonexistent road direct from the Carretera Costa Norte to Cayo Saetía. The real road leads to Felton, a T junction with an unmarked turnoff to the right for Cayo Saetía.

Food and Accommodations

Villa Cayo Saetía (tel. 024/51-6900, comercial@cayosaetia.co.cu, from CUC55 s, CUC80 d low season, CUC74 s, CUC100 d high season) has 12 rustic *cabinas* and more handsome suites with satellite TVs. The eyes of animals that wandered between crosshairs glower eerily as you dine in the restaurant.

Ranchón El Cristo (daily 9am-4pm), four kilometers east of the hotel, sits on stilts atop a gorgeous scoop of vanilla beach; lunch is included with your visit. Snorkeling (CUC15) and kayaking (CUC6) are offered.

MOA

East of Mayarí, the Circuito Norte coast road leads past a series of port towns that rely on the mineral ore industries. Tall chimneys belching out smoke announce your arrival at the coastal town of Moa, which is smothered with red dust from the nearby processing plants. It has been claimed (probably in jest) that Cuban engineers would rather sacrifice their careers than work here. Nonetheless, Moa has the only accommodations (and about the only food) in the many lonesome miles between Mayarí and Baracoa.

Two kilometers east of Moa you'll pass **Empresa Comandante Ernesto Che Guevara,** a huge smelting plant guarded by a statue of Che towering over the gates. The environment here has been hammered and sickled into a grotesque gangue pitted with pestilential lagoons. Gnarled, splintered trees add to the dramatic effect, like the aftermath of a World War I bombardment. Photography is prohibited.

Accommodations

Islazul's Soviet-era **Hotel Miraflores** (Av. Amistad, tel. 024/66-6103, jcarpeta@miraflores.co.cu, CUC24 s, CUC29 d year-round) has 148 modestly furnished rooms, plus a swimming pool, restaurant, disco, and car rental.

Getting There and Away

Cubana (tel. 024/66-7916) flies from Havana on Monday to Moa's **Orestes Acosta Airport** (tel. 024/66-7012), three kilometers east of town. A bus departs Holguín daily for Moa, from where *camiones* and jeep *colectivo* taxis operate to Baracoa (70 kilometers farther east). There's a gas station one kilometer west of town.

Granma

Cuba's southwestern most province abounds with sites of historical import. Throughout Cuba's history, the region has been a hotbed of insurrection.

In 1512, Hatuey, the local Indian chieftain, rebelled against Spain. The citizens of Bayamo were at the forefront of the drive for independence, and the city, which became the capital of the provisional republic, is filled with sites associated with the days when Cuba's *criollo* population fought to oust Spain. Nearby, at La Demajagua, Carlos Céspedes freed his slaves and proclaimed Cuba's independence. And Dos Ríos, in the northeast of the province, is the site where José Martí chose martyrdom in battle in 1895.

The region also became the first battleground in the revolutionary efforts to topple the Batista regime, initiated on July 26, 1953, when Castro's rebels attacked the Bayamo garrison in concert with an attack on the Moncada barracks in Santiago. In 1956, Castro, Che Guevara, and 80 fellow revolutionaries came ashore at Las Colorados to set up their rebel army. The province is named for the vessel—the *Granma*—in which the revolutionaries traveled from Mexico.

Several sites recall those revolutionary days, not least La Comandancia de la Plata (Fidel Castro's guerrilla headquarters), deep in the Sierra Maestra. An enormous swath of Granma Province is protected within Gran Parque Nacional Sierra Maestra, fabulous for bird-watching and hiking. You can even ascend the trail to Pico Turquino, Cuba's highest mountain.

For physical drama, Granma Province is hard to beat. The province is neatly divided into plains (to the north) and mountains (to the south). The Río Cauto—Cuba's longest river—runs north from these mountains and feeds the rich farmland of the northern plains. The river delta is a vast mangrove and grassy swampland (birding is spectacular, not least for flamingoes and roseate spoonbills). Whereas the north side of the Sierra Maestra has a moist microclimate and is lushly foliated, the south side lies in a rain shadow. Greenery yields to cacti-studded semidesert.

Previous: Monumento Celia Sánchez in Manzanillo; bell at Museo Histórico La Demajagua. **Above:** lighthouse at Cabo Cruz.

Look for ★ to find recommended
sights, activities, dining, and lodging.

Highlights

© AVALON TRAVEL

★ **Parque Céspedes:** The setting for important events in Cuban history, Bayamo's main plaza has two fine museums. It adjoins Plaza del Himno, an intimate cobbled square with one of the nation's finest and most important churches (page 400).

★ **La Comandancia de la Plata:** Castro's former (and well-preserved) guerrilla headquarters is reached via a splendid hike along a ridgetop trail (page 408).

★ **Hiking to Pico Turquino:** For the ultimate high, this overnight guided hike to the summit of Cuba's highest peak is strenuous but richly rewarding (page 408).

★ **Parque Nacional Desembarco del Granma:** Trails through tropical dry forest provide ample opportunities for spotting rare birds. Caves with dripstone formations are a bonus, and you can hike a revolutionary trail that follows the course of Fidel's rebels after they landed their crippled vessel, the *Granma*, here in 1956 (page 415).

★ **Marea del Portillo to Santiago de Cuba:** The country's ultimate scenic drive is also a challenging adventure. Break out the camera (page 417)!

Granma

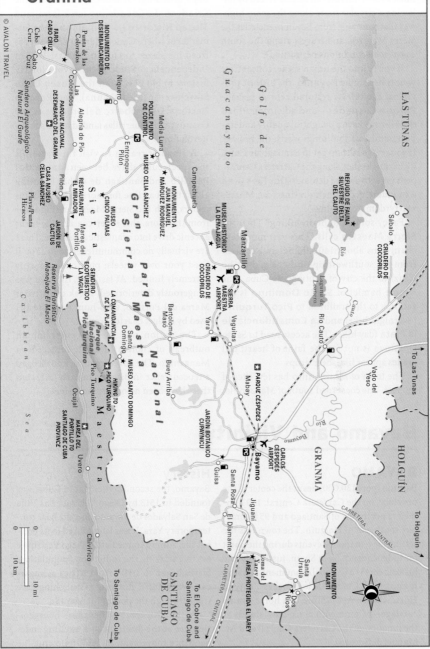

© AVALON TRAVEL

FARO
CABO CRUZ
Cabo
Cruz

Cabo
Cruz

Sendero Arqueológico
Natural El Guafe

MONUMENTO DE
DESEMBARCARDERO

Punta de las
Colorados

Las
Colorados

Niquero

Parque Nacional
Desembarco del Granma

Alegría de Pío

Pilón

Media Luna

Entronque
Pilón

POLICE PUNTO
DE CONTROL
MUSEO CELIA SÁNCHEZ

Campechuela

Golfo de
Guacanayabo

LAS TUNAS

MONUMENTO A
JUAN MANUEL
MÁRQUEZ RODRÍGUEZ

REFUGIO DE FAUNA
SILVESTRE DELTA
DEL CAUTO

Sábalo

CRIADERO DE
COCODRILOS

CASA-MUSEO
CELIA SÁNCHEZ

RESTAURANTE
EL MIRADOR

Playa/Punta
Hicacos

JARDÍN DE
CACTUS

Marea del
Portillo

Reserva Florística
Manelajad El Macío

Caribbean

MUSEO
CINCO PALMAS

Sierra

Gran Sierra

Parque Nacional

SENDERO
ECOTURÍSTICO
LA YAGUA

Parque
Nacional
Pico Turquino

Ocujal

Chivirico

To Santiago de Cuba

MUSEO HISTÓRICO
LA DEMAJAGUA

Manzanillo

Río

Cauto

Laguna de
Leoneros

Bartolomé
Maso

Yara

Veguitas

SIERRA
MAESTRA
AIRPORT

CRIADERO DE
COCODRILOS

LA COMANDANCIA
DE LA PLATA

Santo
Domingo

Buey Arriba

MUSEO SANTO
DOMINGO

Pico Turquino

HIKING TO
PICO TURQUINO

MAREA DEL
PORTILLO TO
SANTIAGO DE CUBA
PROVINCE

Uvero

Sea

Maestra

Mabay

Río Cauto

To Las Tunas

Vado del
Yeso

PARQUE CÉSPEDES

JARDÍN BOTÁNICO
CUPAYNICU

Río

Bayamo

GRANMA

CARLOS
CÉSPEDES
AIRPORT

Bayamo

Guisa

Santa Rosa

El Diamante

Jiguaní

Santa
Úrsula

Loma del
Yarey

AREA PROTEGIDA EL YAREY

MONUMENTO
MARTÍ

Dos
Ríos

HOLGUÍN

To Holguín

CARRETERA   CENTRAL

CARRETERA   CENTRAL

To El Cobre and
Santiago de Cuba

SANTIAGO
DE CUBA

0   10 mi

0   10 km

N

PLANNING YOUR TIME

Most sites of interest can be discovered by following a circular route along the main highway that runs west from Bayamo, encircles the Sierra Maestra, and travels along the south coast (road conditions permitting).

If you're into the urban scene, concentrate your time around **Bayamo,** the historic provincial capital. Its restored central plaza—**Parque Céspedes**—and adjoining **Plaza del Himno** have a delightful quality and important historic buildings worth the browse. If you're in a rush to get to Santiago de Cuba, it's a straight shot along the Carretera Central, perhaps with a short detour to **Dos Ríos** (with a monument commemorating José Martí's martyrdom here in 1895).

Fancy some mountain hiking? Then the **Sierra Maestra** calls. This vast mountain chain runs about 140 kilometers west-east from the southwest tip of the island (Cabo Cruz) to the city of Santiago de Cuba. The remote hamlet of **Santo Domingo** is the gateway to the trailhead to **Pico Turquino** (overnight hike) and **La Comandancia de la Plata** (day hike). The access road to Santo Domingo is not for the faint of heart; hill grades appear like sheer drops.

The town of **Manzanillo** has few sites of interest. The coast road south of Manzanillo, however, has attractions sufficient for a day's browsing. Of modest interest are the **Criadero de Cocodrilos** (croc farm) and **Museo Histórico La Demajagua,** the former farm where Carlos Manuel de Céspedes freed his slaves to launch the first War of Independence. Students of revolutionary history might check out the **Museo Celia Sánchez** (in Media Luna), and **Parque Nacional Desembarco del Granma,** where Castro and his guerrillas landed to pursue the Revolution.

A singular reason to visit this region is the spectacular drive between **Marea del Portillo** and Santiago de Cuba. Running along the coastline for more than 100 kilometers, with the Sierra Maestra rising sheer from the shore, this roller-coaster ride turns a scenic drive into a fantastic adventure. There are virtually no communities en route. You'll need your own wheels; public transport is extremely limited. At last visit, the road was dangerously deteriorated. Break the drive at Marea del Portillo, a ho-hum beach resort used by budget charter groups.

The region was the epicenter for an outbreak of cholera in 2012, centered on Manzanillo. The government acknowledged a reoccurrence in Bayamo in early 2013, but there have been no occurrences since.

Bayamo and Vicinity

BAYAMO

Bayamo (pop. 130,000) lies at the center of the province, on the Carretera Central, 130 kilometers northwest of Santiago and 95 kilometers southwest of Holguín. The town was the setting for remarkable events during the quest for independence from Spain. Justifiably, the historic core is a national monument. Bayamo is known as "Ciudad de los Coches" (City of Horse-Carts). A sculpture of a horse-drawn carriage—Monumento al Coche—stands at the junction of the Carretera Central and Av. Manuel de Socorro.

History

Bayamo, the second settlement in Cuba, was founded in 1513 by Diego Velázquez as Villa de San Salvador de Bayamo on a site near contemporary Yara. It was later moved to its present site. Almost immediately Diego Velázquez set to enslaving the indigenous population. Slaves began to arrive from Africa as sugarcane was planted, fostering a flourishing slave trade through the port of Manzanillo.

By the 19th century, Bayamo's bourgeoisie were at the forefront of a swelling independence movement. In 1867, following the

Bayamo

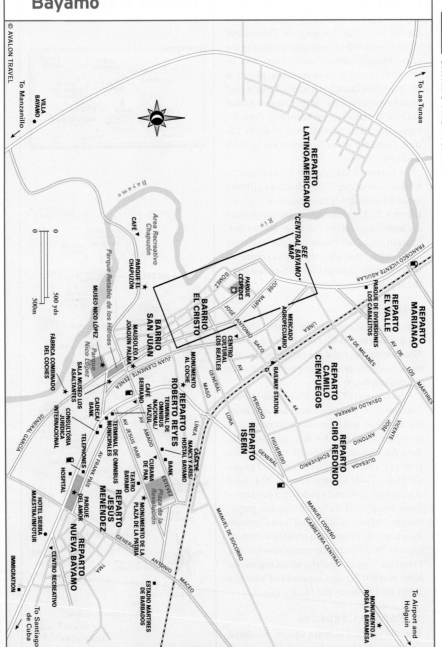

coup that toppled Spain's Queen Isabella, Carlos Manuel de Céspedes and the elite of Bayamo rose in revolt. The action sparked the Ten Years War that swept the Oriente and central Cuba. Other nationalists rallied to the cause, formed a revolutionary junta, and, in open defiance of Spanish authority, played in the parochial church the martial hymn that would eventually become the Cuban national anthem (composed by homeboy Perucho Figueredo). With a small force of about 150 men, Céspedes seized Bayamo from Spanish forces on October 20.

In January 1869, Spanish troops were at Bayamo's doorstep. The rebellious citizens razed Bayamo rather than cede it to Spanish. Internal dissent arose among the revolutionary leadership and the Ten Years War fizzled. Spanish troops left Bayamo for the final time on April 28, 1898, when the city was captured by rebel leader General Calixto García during the War of Independence.

Orientation

Bayamo is laid out atop the eastern bluff of the Río Bayamo, which flows in a deep ravine. The historic core sits above the gorge, with the more modern city spreading north, east, and south like a fan.

The Carretera Central (Carretera Manuel Cedeño) from Holguín enters Bayamo from the northeast and skirts the historic core as it sweeps southeast for Santiago. Avenida Perucho Figueredo leads off the Carretera Central and runs due west to Parque Céspedes. Calle General García—the main commercial street and a pedestrian precinct—leads south from Parque Céspedes, paralleled by Calles José Martí and Juan Clemente Zenea, which merge south with the Carretera Central. To the north they merge into Avenida Francisco Vicente Aguilera, which begins one block north of Parque Céspedes and leads to a Y fork for Las Tunas and Manzanillo.

★ Parque Céspedes

The city's beautiful main square, bordered by Libertad, Maceo, General García, and

Cacique Guamá streets, is surrounded by important buildings. At its center is a granite column topped by a larger-than-life bronze statue of Carlos Manuel de Céspedes. There's also a bust of local patriot Perucho Figueredo (1819-1870), inscribed with the words (in Spanish) he wrote for the *himno nacional,* "La Bayamesa":

> To the battle, run, Bayamesas
> Let the fatherland proudly observe you
> Do not fear a glorious death
> To die for the fatherland is to live.

Céspedes was born on April 18, 1819, in a handsome two-story dwelling on the north side of the square. The house, **Casa Natal de Carlos Manuel de Céspedes** (Maceo #57, tel. 023/42-3864, Tues.-Fri. 9am-5pm, Sat. 9am-2pm and 8pm-10pm, Sun. 10am-1pm, entrance CUC1, cameras CUC5, guide CUC1) was one of only a fistful of houses to survive the fire of January 1869. Downstairs are letters, photographs, and maps, plus Céspedes's gleaming ceremonial sword. The ornately decorated upstairs bedrooms are full of his mahogany furniture. His law books are there, as is the printing press on which Céspedes published his *Cubana Libre,* the first independent newspaper in Cuba.

Next door, the **Museo Provincial** (Maceo #58, tel. 023/42-4125, Wed.-Mon. 9am-5pm, Sat.-Sun. 9am-1pm, entrance CUC1, cameras CUC5), in the house where Manuel Muñoz Cedeño, composer of the *himno nacional,* was born, contains further historical miscellany.

On the east side of Parque Céspedes is the house, now the **Poder Popular** (town hall), where Céspedes, as president of the newly formed republic, announced the abolition of slavery.

Parque Céspedes opens to the northwest onto the charming **Plaza del Himno,** dominated by the beautifully restored **Iglesia Parroquial del Santísima Salvador** (tel. 023/42-2514, Sun.-Fri. 9am-1pm and 3pm-5pm, Sat. 9am-1pm), a national monument that amazingly survived the fire. The revolutionary national anthem was sung for the first time in the cathedral (by a choir of 12 women—the Bayamesas) during Corpus Christi celebrations on June 11, 1868, with the dumbfounded colonial governor in attendance. The church's most admirable feature is the beautiful mural of Céspedes and the Bayamesas above the altar. The building occupies the site of the original church, built in 1516, rebuilt in 1733, and rebuilt again following the fire of 1869. It has a Mudejar ceiling and a baroque gilt altarpiece. On the north

souvenir sellers at Parque Céspedes

side of the cathedral is a small chapel, **Capilla de la Dolorosa,** that dates to 1630.

The quaint **Casa de la Nacionalidad Cubana** (tel. 023/42-4833, Mon.-Fri. 8am-noon and 1pm-5pm, alternate Saturdays 8am-noon, free), on the west side, houses the town historian's office and displays period furniture.

El Bulevar

This pedestrian-only main street (Calle General García) runs south from Parque Céspedes for six blocks. It's graced by ceramic tiles and sculptures, including lampposts turned into faux trees and bottles.

At Masó, four blocks south of the square, are four key sites. The **Gabinete de Arqueología** (tel. 023/42-1591, Tues.-Fri. 8am-5pm, Sat.-Sun. 9am-noon, CUC1) displays pre-Columbian stoneware and other artifacts. Next door, the **Acuario** (no tel., Tues.-Sat. 9am-5pm and Sun. 9am-1pm, free) displays tanks with tropical fish.

The **Museo de Cera** (Calixto García #254, tel. 023/42-5421, Tues.-Fri. 9am-5pm, Sat. 10am-1pm and 7pm-10pm, Sun. 9am-noon, entrance CUC1, cameras CUC5) is Cuba's only wax museum. It displays 13 life-size waxworks, from world-renowned Cuban musician

Compay Segundo to Ernest Hemingway and Colombian Nobel Prize-winning novelist Gabriel García Márquez.

Across the street, La Maqueta (tel. 023/42-3633, Mon.-Fri. 8am-noon and 1pm-5pm, one peso) displays fascinating scale models of the city.

Parque Ñico López

This small plaza (Calle General García, esq. Amado Estévez) eight blocks south of Parque Céspedes is named for a revolutionary hero who, along with 24 other members of Fidel Castro's rebels, attacked Batista's army barracks on July 26, 1953. López survived, fled to Mexico, and was with Fidel aboard the *Granma.* He was killed shortly after landing in Cuba in 1956.

López is honored on the **Retablo de los Héroes** (Calles Martí and Amado Estévez), a bas-relief in the center of the square; in the **Museo Parque Ñico López** (Abihail González, tel. 023/42-3742, Tues.-Fri. 9am-5pm, Sat. noon-8pm, Sun. 8am-noon, CUC1), in the former medieval-style barracks, 100 meters west of the square; at the tiny **Sala Museo Los Asaltantes** (Agusto Marquéz, tel. 023/42-3181, Tues.-Sat. 9am-5pm, Sun. 8am-noon, CUC1), 50 meters southeast of

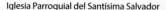

Iglesia Parroquial del Santísima Salvador

the square; and on the **Plaza de la Patria** (Amado Estévez and Av. Jesús Rabi, one kilometer east of Parque **Ñico López**), where the **Monumento de la Plaza de la Patria** features a bas-relief of heroes of the *Granma* landing.

Fábrica de los Coches

The city's ubiquitous horse-drawn carriages are produced in Cuba's only coach-making factory, the state-run **Combinado de Coches** (Prolongación General García #530, tel. 023/41-1902, Mon.-Fri. 8am-3pm), 300 meters south of Parque Ñico López. The coaches are handcrafted using centuries-old tradition. Blacksmiths, carpenters, saddlers, and upholsters are employed to shape the 143 pieces into a finished product—exact replicas of the Milord and Duquesa (Duchess) coaches. Each takes about three months' labor. Workers also make tiny souvenir replicas for sale.

Entertainment and Events
NIGHTLIFE
The lively **Casa de la Trova** (Martí, esq. Maceo, tel. 023/42-5673, Tues.-Sat. 10am-1am, free by day, CUC1 at night) is acclaimed for its traditional music honoring singer/songwriter

Pablo Milanes. *Bolero* is performed in the Casa de Tomás Estrada Palma at **UNEAC** (Céspedes #158, tel. 023/42-3670, Sat. 4pm, free); the building is the birthplace of Tomás Estrada Palma, the first president of Cuba following independence.

The **Sala Teatro José Joaquín Palma** (Céspedes, tel. 023/42-4423) hosts drama, children's theater, and folkloric performances. The **Casa de la Cultura** (Parque Céspedes, tel. 023/42-5917, daily 8am-8pm) hosts cultural programs. Teatro Bayamo (Av. Jesús Rabí, tel. 023/42-5106, Wed.-Sun.), on the southeast corner of Plaza de la Patria, is one of Cuba's most impressive regional theaters. You can occasionally catch an English-language Hollywood hit at Cine Céspedes on Parque Céspedes.

La Bodega (Plaza del Himno, tel. 023/42-1011, Fri.-Sun. 10pm-1am), a Spanish-style *bodega* with seats made of barrels and cart wheels, offers heaps of charm. It has music in a patio overhanging the river canyon.

Beatles tribute groups hail the Fab Four on weekends at the open-air **Centro Cultural Los Beatles** (Zenea, e/ Saco y Figueredo, tel. 023/42-1799, Tues.-Sun. 7am-midnight, 5-10 pesos), where life-size figures of the group greet you. Busty wooden figures hold aloft

Casa de la Trova

the bar at **Bar La Esquina** (Marmól, esq. Maceo, tel. 023/42-1731, daily noon-1am), a clean modern bar playing music videos.

You can get your titillating cabaret kicks at **Centro Recreativo Cultural El Bayam** (tel. 023/48-1698, Sat.-Sun. 4pm and 10pm, CUC1), opposite the Hotel Sierra Maestra. The *cabaret espectáculo* is followed by a disco.

Parque Diversiones Los Caballitos (Av. Aguilera) is one of the most complete children's fun parks in the country, with all the fun of the fair. Join the local families enjoying picnics in Parque El Chapuzón (Av. Amado Estévez), a leafy natural park on the west side of town; it has a small theme park.

FESTIVALS AND EVENTS

Fireworks and candles are lit each January 12 on Parque Céspedes to commemorate El Incendio de Bayamo, the burning of the town in 1869, and a procession of horses symbolizes its abandonment. In mid-May, the city hosts the **Festival de las Flores**—a flower festival. Time your arrival for August 6 to catch the annual **carnival,** when neighborhoods let loose.

The bayameses honor the struggle with the Fiesta de la Cubanía (Oct. 17-20), a mounted parade of Mambisi (independence fighters) and horse carts, plus cultural events, parties, and concerts.

Each Saturday night, locals set up lechoneras (suckling pig barbecues), dust off pipe organs, and crank up the reggaeton for a weekly dance. You can drink and be merry near the Hotel Sierra Mastra.

Granma's baseball team, Los Alazanes, plays at Estadio Mártires de Barbados (General Antonio Maceo, esq. 13ra, Oct.-Apr.).

Food

Bayamo is a bit of a culinary wasteland still craving a great *paladar*; it's best to avoid street-cart fare. Dine instead at your *casa particular*.

On the *bulevar,* Spanish-themed **La Sevillana** (Calixto García #171, e/ Perucho Figueredo y General Lora, tel. 023/42-1472,

daily noon-2pm and 6pm-10pm) serves simple *criolla* dishes, plus garbanzos and paella for pesos. It has dinner sittings at 6pm-8pm and 8pm-10pm; men must wear long pants. One block south, **Paladar La Estrella** (General García #209, e/ Lora y Masó, tel. 023/42-3950, daily 10:30am-10:30pm) is a pleasant, simple option for *criolla* staples, such as shrimp enchiladas (CUC3).

The best private restaurant is upstairs at the charming **Restaurante San Salvador de Bayamo** (Maceo #107, e/ Marmól y Martí, tel. 023/42-6942, daily 11am-midnight). The menu is predictably criolla, including garlic shrimp and delicious flan.

Tropi Crema (Mon.-Fri. 10am-10pm, Sat.-Sun. noon-midnight), on Parque Céspedes, serves ice cream for pesos. The well-run **Café Serrano** (Carretera Central, esq. Estévez) is a great place to savor freshly brewed coffee. For bohemian ambience, you can't beat Café Literario Ventana Sur (Figueredo #62, daily 10am-midnight), on Parque Céspedes, where the city's *farándula* (in-crowd) gathers for music and debate.

Accommodations

CASAS PARTICULARES

Among the better town-center options is **Casa de Ana Martí Vázquez** (Céspedes #4, e/ Maceo y Canducha, tel. 023/42-5323, marti@enet.cu, CUC20-25), a gracious home beautifully furnished with antiques and chandeliers. The lounge opens to a shady stone patio. Ana hosts two rooms: One, in a loft, is like a honeymoon suite.

I enjoyed several stays with the wonderful hosts at **Casa de Manuel y Lydia** (Donato Mármol #323, e/ Figueredo y Lora, tel. 023/42-3175, nene19432001@yahoo.es, CUC20-25). The house has a simply furnished, air-conditioned room with fan and shared hot-water bathroom. It opens to a spacious patio with a hammock and rockers.

The enjoyable **Casa de Nancy y Aris** (Amado Estévez #67, e/ 8 y 9, Rpto. Jesús Menéndez, tel. 023/42-4726, CUC20-25), close to Plaza de la Patria and overseen by delightful owners, has three air-conditioned rooms with fans and private bathrooms. It has secure parking and a rooftop plunge pool. Their upstairs neighbors also have pleasing rooms at **Hostal Bayamo** (tel. 023/42-9127, www. hostalbayamo.com, CUC25).

HOTELS

A splendid boutique hotel, the **Hotel E Royalton** (Maceo #53, tel. 023/42-2290, CUC31 s, CUC50 d low season, CUC40 s, CUC70 d high season), on the north side of Parque Céspedes, has a marble staircase leading to 33 small rooms with modern bathrooms, flat-screen TVs, and a restaurant and terrace bar overlooking the plaza.

Cubanacán's Bauhaus-style **Hotel Sierra Maestra** (Carretera Central, Km 7.5, tel. 023/42-7970, www.islazul.cu, CUC30 s, CUC48 d low season, CUC36 s, CUC58 d high season), three kilometers southeast of the city center, is adequate for a night or two. Modern bathrooms are the high point of its 114 simply furnished rooms. It has a swimming pool and disco.

Information and Services

Infotur (tel. 023/42-3468, infogran@enet.cu), on Plaza del Himno, supplies tourist information. **Paradiso** (Antonio Maceo #112, e/ 2da y Frank País, tel. 023/48-1956, paradisogr@ scgtr.artex.cu) can provide information on cultural events.

The **post office** (tel. 023/42-3305, Mon.-Sat. 9am-6pm), on the west side of Parque Céspedes, has DHL service. **Etecsa** (Marmól e/ Saco y Figueredo, tel. 023/42-8353, daily 8am-7pm) has international telephone and Internet service (upstairs). El Bulevar, Parque del Amor, Parque los Coches, and Plaza de la Patria have public Wi-Fi.

Banks include **Bandec** (General García, esq. Saco, and García, esq. Figueredo) and **Banco Popular** (General García, esq. Saco). You can also change foreign currency at **Cadeca** (Saco #101), on the Carretera Central, next to the bus station.

Hospital Carlos Manuel de Céspedes

(Carretera Central, Km 1.5, tel. 023/42-5012) is west of the Hotel Sierra Maestra, which has a **Farmacia Internacional** (Mon.-Fri. 8:30am-noon and 1pm-5pm, Sat. 8:30am-noon).

The **Consultoría Jurídica Internacional** (Carretera Central, e/ Av. Figueredo y Calle Segunda, tel. 023/42-7379, Mon.-Fri. 8:30am-noon and 1:30pm-5:30pm) provides legal services.

Getting There and Away

The **Aeropuerto Carlos Céspedes** (tel. 023/42-7514) is four kilometers northeast of town; a bus operates between the airport and the Terminal de Ómnibus. **Cubana** (Martí, esq. Parada, tel. 023/42-7511, airport tel. 023/42-3695) flies between Havana and Bayamo twice weekly.

Interprovincial buses arrive and depart the **Terminal de Ómnibus** (Carretera Central, esq. Augusta Márquez, tel. 023/42-4036). **Víazul's** Santiago de Cuba-bound buses (tel. 023/42-1438, www.viazul.com) stop in Bayamo between Havana (thrice daily), Varadero (once daily), and Trinidad (once daily). Immediately south is the **Terminal de Ómnibus Intermunicipal** (tel. 023/6892), serving local buses to nearby communities.

Camiones (passenger trucks) to towns throughout Granma depart from opposite the **railway station** (Saco, esq. Línea, tel. 023/42-4955). In 2016, rail service was reduced to train #13 between Havana and Manzanillo (every fourth day). Check for updates at the station. Local trains connect with Manzanillo daily. You can rent cars from **Havanautos** (tel. 023/42-7375), in Hotel Sierra Maestra. There are gas stations on the Carretera Central (by Parque del Amor; at Av. Amado Estévez; and at Av. Perucho Figueredo) and on Av. Vicente Aguilar.

Havanatur (General García #237, e/ Lora y Masó, tel. 023/42-7662), on the west side of Parque Céspedes, offers excursions, as does eco-focused **EcoTur** (tel. 023/48-7006, agencia@grm.ecotur.tur.cu), in Hotel Sierra Maestra.

Getting Around

Horse-drawn *coches* are the staple of local transport; they congregate outside the railway station. The main route runs along the Carretera Central via the bus station and Hotel Sierra Maestra. For a taxi, call **Cubataxi** (tel. 023/42-4313).

SOUTHEAST OF BAYAMO

The Carretera Central runs east from Bayamo across the Río Cauto floodplain. At Santa Rita, about 15 kilometers east of Bayamo, head south 1 kilometer to reach the hamlet of **El Diamante**, where several families make a living carving marble into souvenirs. Check out the family cooperative of **Yoelvis Labrada** (tel. 5398-3017) and his homemade lathe made of a Lada gearbox, bicycle chain, shaft drives, and other parts from various vehicles.

Dos Ríos

At Jiguaní, a nondescript town 26 kilometers east of Bayamo, a road leads north to Dos Ríos (Two Rivers), the holy site where José Martí gave his life for the cause of independence.

On April 11, 1895, Martí had returned to Cuba from exile in the United States. On May 19, General Máximo Gómez's troops exchanged shots with a small Spanish column. Martí, as nationalist leader, was a civilian among soldiers. Gómez halted and ordered Martí and his bodyguard to place themselves to the rear. Martí, however, took off down the riverbank towards the Spanish column. His bodyguard took off after him—but too late. Martí was hit in the neck by a bullet and fell from his horse without ever having drawn his gun. Revolutionary literature describes Martí as a hero who died fighting on the battlefield. In fact, he committed suicide for the sake of martyrdom.

Monumento Martí is a simple 10-meter-tall obelisk of whitewashed concrete in a trim garden of lawns and royal palms. White roses surround the obelisk, an allusion to his famous poem *Cultivo una Rosa Blanca*. A stone wall bears a 3-D bronze visage of Martí and the words, "When my fall comes, all the sorrow of life will seem like sun and honey." A plaque on the monument says simply, "He died in this place on May 19, 1895." A tribute is held each May 19.

Jardín Botánico Cupaynicu

A turnoff from the Carretera Central about two kilometers east of Bayamo leads south to **Guisa**, a charming town in the foothills

Monumento Martí

of the Sierra Maestra. About one kilometer north of Guisa you'll pass a Saracen armored car roadside: It's now the **Monumento Nacional Loma de Piedra,** recalling the battle for the town that took place on November 20, 1958.

Two kilometers before reaching Guisa, a sign at La Nieñita points the way to the **Jardín Botánico Cupaynicu** (tel. 023/39-1330, Tues.-Sun. 8am-4:30pm, CUC2), at Los Mameyes. It's named for a local palm, one of 2,100 species of flora found here. Two-hour guided trips are offered of the 104-hectare garden, divided into 14 zones, including palms (72 species, of which 16 are Cuban), cacti (268 species), rock plants, and tropical flowers, accessed via a 1.8-kilometer loop trail. It also has a greenhouse of ornamentals, plus an herbarium. Local tour companies offer excursions, as does **Anley Rosales Benítez** (Carretera Central #478, tel. 5292-2209, www.bayamotravelagent.com), in Bayamo.

The Sierra Maestra

The Sierra Maestra hangs against the sky along the entire southern coast of Oriente, from the western foothills near Cabo Cruz eastward 130 kilometers to Santiago de Cuba. The towering massif gathers in serried ranges that precede one another in an immense chain rising to Pico Turquino. It is forbidding terrain creased with steep ravines and boulder-strewn valleys. These mountains were the setting for the most ferocious battles in the fight to topple Batista.

The hardy mountain folk continue to eke out a subsistence living, supplemented by a meager income from coffee.

PARQUE NACIONAL PICO TURQUINO

This 17,450-hectare national park is named for **Pico Turquino,** Cuba's highest mountain (1,974 meters). These mountains are also important for their diversity of flora and fauna. At least 100 species of plants are found nowhere else, and 26 are peculiar to tiny enclaves within the park. Orchids cover the trunks of semideciduous montane forest and centenarian conifers. Higher up is cloud forest, festooned with old man's beard, bromeliads, ferns, and vines, fed by mists that swirl through the forest primeval. Pico Turquino is even tipped by marshy grassland above 1,900 meters, with wind-sculpted, dwarf species on exposed ridges. The calls of birds ring through the green silence of the jungle. Wild pigs and *jutías* exist alongside three species of frog found only on Pico Turquino.

Pico Turquino looms over the tiny gateway community of **Santo Domingo,** on the east bank of the Río Yara, 20 kilometers south of the sugarcane processing town of **Bartolomé Masó** (60 kilometers southwest of Bayamo). The road requires first-gear ascents and descents.

Santo Domingo was the setting for fierce fighting in 1958. The small **Museo Santo Domingo** (open by request, CUC1) features a 3-D model of the Sierra Maestra with a plan of the battles. Small arms and mortars are displayed.

Entrance to the park is permitted daily 7:30am-2:30pm (10am is the latest you are allowed to set off for Pico Turquino). A guide is compulsory, arranged through EcoTur's **Centro de Visitantes** (daily 7am-10am) at Santo Domingo. You can book in advance through **EcoTur** (tel. 023/56-5635 at Villa Santo Domingo, tel. 023/48-7006 at Bayamo).

From Santo Domingo the corrugated cement road is inclined 40 degrees in places—a breathtakingly steep climb with hairpin bends. After five kilometers the road ends at Alto del Naranjo (950 meters elevation), the trailhead to Pico Turquino and La Comandancia de la Plata. The drive is not for the fainthearted, and not all rental cars can make it! Hire a jeep taxi (CUC5). To hike from Santo Domingo to Alto del Naranjo is a relentless four-hour ascent.

★ La Comandancia de la Plata

Fidel named his **rebel army headquarters** (CUC33 or CUC27 pp for more than four people, including transport, lunch, and entrance, plus CUC5 cameras, CUC5 videos) in the Sierra Maestra after the river whose headwaters were near his camp on a western spur ridge of Pico Turquino. The 16 buildings were dispersed over one square kilometer on a forested ridge crest, reached by a tortuous track from Alto de Naranjo that's a two-hour scramble over rocks and mud. The wooden structures were hidden at the edge of the clearing and covered with hibiscus arbors to conceal them from air attacks. Castro's house was built against the ravine, with a hidden entrance and an escape route into the creek. Amazingly, the compound is preserved pretty much exactly as it was in 1958.

You'll also see the small **hospital** (run by Che Guevara, who was the group's doctor) and a guesthouse that is now a **museum** with a 3-D model of the area, plus rifles, machine guns, and other memorabilia. Plata was linked by radio to the rest of Cuba (a transmitter for Radio Rebelde loomed above the clearing); it's a steep and slippery ascent to the radio hut.

★ Hiking to Pico Turquino

From Alto de Naranjo it's 13 kilometers to the summit. Even here you can't escape the Revolution. In 1952 soon-to-be revolutionary heroine Celia Sánchez and her liberal-minded father, Manuel Sánchez Silveira, hiked up Turquino carrying a bronze bust of José Martí, which they installed at the summit. In 1957 Sánchez made the same trek with a CBS news crew for an interview with Fidel beside the bust.

The **Sendero Pico Turquino** begins at Alto de Naranjo (a 7am departure from Santo Domingo is recommended). En route you'll pass through the remote communities of Palma Mocha, Lima, and Aguada de Joaquín. Hikers normally ascend the summit the same day, then descend to overnight in a dorm at Aguada de Joaquín.

From the summit, you can continue down the south side of the mountain to Las Cuevas by prearrangement; a second guide will meet you at the summit.

Hikers need to take their own food and plenty of water. You can buy packaged meals

La Comandancia de la Plata

(CUC10) at Villa Santo Domingo. There are no stores hereabouts. Warm clothing and waterproof gear are essential (the mountain weather is fickle and can change from sunshine to downpours in minutes), as are a flashlight and bedroll.

EcoTur (tel. 023/56-5635 at Villa Santo Domingo, tel. 023/48-7006 at Bayamo, reservas@grm.ecotur.tur.cu) handles all visits and offers three guided hikes to the summit: **Pico Turquino 1** (one night/two days, CUC68), with overnight at Aguada; **Pico Turquino 2** (two nights/three days, CUC90); and **Pico Turquino 3** (two nights/three days, CUC104), including La Comandancia de la Plata. Prices include transport, entrance, food, and water. Tip your guide!

Food and Accommodations

Serving Cubans and backpackers, the riverside **Campismo La Sierrita** (tel. 023/56-5584, www.campismopopular.cu/campismo/525, CUC6-8 pp), six kilometers south of Bartolomé Masó, has 27 simple two- and four-person cabins, plus a basic restaurant. You can make reservations c/o **Campismo Popular** (General García #112, tel. 023/42-4425) in Bayamo.

To sample local life, spend a night at **Casa de Ernesto y Arcadia** (CUC25 including breakfast), a humble home on the hillside opposite Villa Santo Domingo. I enjoyed a wonderful evening with the gracious hosts. The sole room has a comfy double bed, fan, and a shared bathroom with modern toilet and cold-water shower in the garden. Bring mosquito repellent.

Across the river in Santo Domingo is ★ **Casa Sierra Maestra** (tel. 023/56-4491, www.casasierramaestra1.com, CUC20-30 low season, CUC25-40 high season), whose owner Ulises rents two spacious rooms in a modern bungalow; two smaller wooden cabins have outside bathrooms. Filling campesino meals are served alfresco in a riverside ranchón, where suckling pig is prepared for groups.

A pleasing but overpriced state option, Islazul's **Villa Santo Domingo** (tel. 023/56-5568, www.islazul.cu, rooms CUC60 s, CUC74 d low season, CUC82 s, CUC88 d high season, bungalows CUC70 s, CUC84 d low season, CUC110 s, CUC116 d high season, including breakfast), on the banks of the river in Santo Domingo, has 20 simple air-conditioned cabins, each with TV and modern bathrooms, plus 20 more luxurious quadplex two-story wooden "bungalows." An open-air riverside restaurant serves *criolla* staples.

Getting There

A *camión* departs Masó for Santo Domingo on Thursday at 5:45am and 4pm and departs Santo Domingo for Masó at 8am and 6pm.

A jeep-taxi from Bayamo costs about CUC45 each way, CUC15 from Masó. In Bayamo, **Anley Rosales Benítez** (tel. 5292-2209, www.bayamotravelagent.com) offers taxi service, plus guided excursions that include La Comandancia (CUC115 two people) and Pico Turquino.

Manzanillo to Cabo Cruz

MANZANILLO

Off-the-beaten-track Manzanillo (pop. 105,000) extends along three kilometers of shorefront on the Gulf of Guacanayabo. In colonial days, it was a smuggling port and center of slave trading. The city became the main underground base for Castro's rebel army in the late 1950s (Celia Sánchez coordinated the secret supply routes, under the noses of Batista's spies, from here). Today the weatherworn town functions as a fishing port. Many structures have been influenced by Moorish design, but once-glorious buildings are crumbling to ruin. In Barrio de Oro, the cobbled streets are lined with rickety wooden houses with cacti growing between the faded roof tiles.

The **Malecón** seafront boulevard features a life-size bronze statue of Cuban crooner Benny Moré plus various naked mermaids and maidens. Offshore, the easternmost cays of the Jardines de la Reina archipelago float on the horizon.

This 66,374-hectare Refugio de Fauna Silvestre Delta del Cauto extends along the gulf shoreline north of town, protecting the swamp-lined delta complex of the Río Cauto. American crocodiles, manatees, and flamingos breed here. EcoTur (tel. 023/48-7006, agencia@grm.ecotur.tur.cu, in Bayamo) offers nature excursions, including fishing in jade-colored Laguna de Leonero (mid-Dec.-Mar.).

Orientation

The road from Bayamo enters Manzanillo from the east as Avenida Rosales, which runs west to the shore, fronted by Avenida 1 de Mayo and the Malecón and paralleled five blocks inland by Avenida Martí. These roads run west to Avenida Jesús Menéndez. The old city lies within this quadrangle.

To the east of the city Avenida Camilo Cienfuegos (the *circunvalación*) runs south from Avenida Rosales, intersects Avenida Jesús Menéndez, and drops to the Malecón.

Parque Céspedes

City life revolves around this handsome square bounded by Martí, Maceo, Merchan, and Masó. The square has little stone sphinxes at each corner and is ringed by royal palms and Victorian-era lampposts. The most notable feature is a Moorish-style *glorieta* (bandstand), inlaid with cloisonné and inspired by the Patio de los Leones in Alhambra, Spain.

Dating from 1834, the neoclassical **Iglesia Parroquia Purísima Concepción,** on the north side, has a beautiful barrel-vaulted ceiling and elaborate gilt altar.

The **Casa de la Cultura** (Masó #82, tel. 023/57-4210, daily 8am-6pm, free), on the south side, is an impressive colonial building with mosaics of Columbus's landing and Don Quixote tilting at windmills.

On the east side, the **Museo Histórico** (Martí #226, tel. 023/57-2053, Tues.-Fri. 9am-5pm, Sat. noon-8pm, Sun. 8am-noon, free) displays cannons and antiques.

The lovely, restored **Teatro Manzanillo** (Villuendas, esq. Maceo, tel. 023/57-2973), one block northwest of the square, dates to 1856.

Monumento Celia Sánchez

Manzanillo's main attraction takes up two entire blocks along Caridad (e/ Martí y Luz Caballero), where a terra-cotta tile staircase is graced on each side by ceramic murals. At the top is the monument to Celia Manduley Sánchez and a tiny room with portraits and personal effects (Mon.-Fri. 8am-noon and 2pm-6pm, Sat. 8am-noon, free) dedicated to the memory of *"La más hermosa y autóctona flor de la Revolución"* (the most beautiful native flower of the Revolution). The **Plaza de la Revolución** (Av. Camilo Cienfuegos) has a bas-relief mural of Celia Sánchez and other revolutionary heroes.

Entertainment and Events

The **Casa de la Cultura** (tel. 023/57-4210)

and **Casa de la Trova** (Merchan #213, esq. Masó, tel. 023/57-5423), both on the main square, host traditional music performances and cultural events.

Piano Bar Mi Manzanillo (J. M. Gómez, esq. Calixto García, tel. 023/57-5312, Tues.-Sun. noon-midnight, free) applies a dress code. A quartet plays jazz, *música filin*, and even salsa. Music videos and live music draw young adults to **Artex Centro Cultural** (Wed.-Mon. noon-midnight), on the north side of the plaza.

The endearing open-air *cabaret espectáculo* at **Costa Azul** (Av. 1ra de Mayo, esq. Narciso López, tel. 023/57-3158, Fri.-Sun. 10pm, CUC1) is followed by a disco. The bar is in a ship hauled ashore.

Teatro Manzanillo (Villuendas, esq. Maceo, tel. 023/57-2973, 5 pesos) hosts cultural programs.

Baseball games are played October-April at **Estadio Wilfredo Pages,** off Avenida Céspedes. The town hosts a carnival in August.

Food

The town has few *paladares*. The best is **Paladar Rancho Luna** (Calle José Miguel Gómez #169, e/ Narciso López y Aguilera, tel. 023/57-3858), a huge and airy restaurant with lofty ceiling, wrought-iron furnishings, and natural stone walls. It specializes in *criolla* seafood. Service can be excruciatingly slow. I enjoyed a delicious garlic seafood plate (CUC7) at **Paladar La Roca** (Mártires de Vietnam #68, e/ Benítex and Caridad, c/o Adrian tel. 023/57-3028, daily 24 hours).

The most elegant state option is **Restaurant La Catalana** (Martí, esq. Narciso López, no tel., daily noon-2pm and 6pm-10pm), serving shrimp cocktail, garbanzo, paella, and *criolla* dishes for pesos.

It's a pleasure to slurp ice cream beneath shade canopies at **Unidad La Fuente** (no tel., 24 hours), on the plaza's northeast corner. **Cremería El Nectar** (Martí, esq. Maceo, daily 10am-10pm), on the southeast corner, sells four scoops for a mere 2.80 pesos.

You can buy fresh produce at the *mercado agropecuario* (Martí, e/ Batería y Concepción, daily 6am-5pm).

Accommodations

The standout *casa particular* is ★ **Casa de Adrián y Tonia** (Mártires de Vietnam #49, esq. Caridad, tel. 023/57-3028, CUC20-25), a delightful house with a TV lounge with rockers and a balcony overlooking the stairs to the Monumento Celia Sánchez. The owners rent a splendid cross-ventilated, air-conditioned independent apartment upstairs with modern bathroom plus roof terrace with super views.

You get a spacious, nicely furnished, air-conditioned upstairs room at **Casa de Eldris y Yosdanis** (Miguel Gómez #347, esq. León, tel. 023/57-2392, nayabo1@yahoo.com, CUC15-25). The hostess is a delight. There should be no regrets at **Hostal Reliance** (Sariol #245 altos, e/ Saco y Codina, tel. 023/55-9154 or 5452-2153, hostalreliance@gmail.com, CUC20-25), a lovely middle-class home full of Cuban kitsch; it's located above a car rental agency. The vast bedroom has a modern bathroom.

Islazul's hilltop **Hotel Guacanayabo** (Av. Camilo Cienfuegos, tel. 023/57-4012, CUC24 s, CUC33 d low season, CUC25 s, CUC40 d high season, including breakfast) has 108 uninspired rooms, and hot water is only available 6am-9am and 6pm-10pm. At least you get satellite TV, modern bathrooms, a swimming pool, and services. Noise from the disco reverberates on weekends.

Information and Services

The **post office** is on Martí (e/ Saco y Codina). **Etecsa** (Codina e/ Gómez y Martí, tel. 023/57-8890) has Internet and international phone service. Pedestrian-only El Bulevar (Martí e/ Masó y Aguilera) is a public Wi-Fi zone.

You can change foreign currency at **Bandec** (Merchan, esq. Codina), **Banco Popular** (Merchan, esq. Codina, and Merchan, esq. Calixto), and **Cadeca** (Martí #184, e/ Figueredo y Narciso López).

Manzanillo

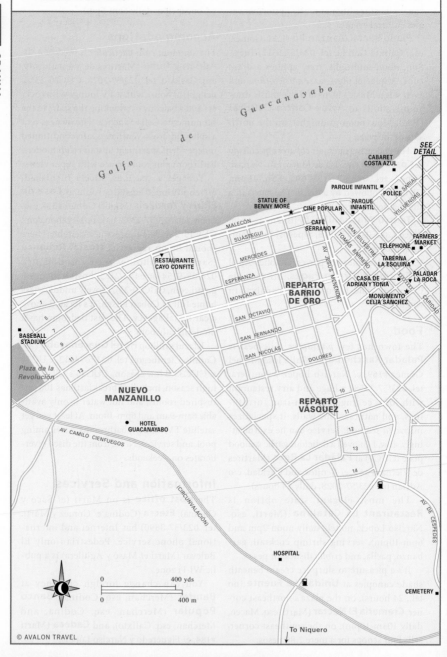

Golfo de Guacanayabo

SEE DETAIL

CABARET COSTA AZUL

PARQUE INFANTIL

POLICE

SARIAL

VILLUENDAS

STATUE OF BENNY MORÉ

CINE POPULAR

PARQUE INFANTIL

MALECÓN

CAFÉ SERRANO ▼

SUÁSTEGUI

SAN SILVESTRE

FARMERS MARKET

TELÉPHONE

RESTAURANTE CAYO CONFITE ▼

MERCEDES

TOMÁS BARRERO

TABERNA LA ESQUINA ▼

PALADAR LA ROCA ▼

ESPERANZA

AV JESÚS MENÉNDEZ

REPARTO BARRIO DE ORO

CASA DE ADRIÁN Y TONIA ●

CARIDAD

MONCADA

MONUMENTO CELIA SÁNCHEZ ★

SAN OCTAVIO

SAN FERNANDO

SAN NICOLÁS

DOLORES

BASEBALL STADIUM

Plaza de la Revolución

1

5

7

9

11

13

NUEVO MANZANILLO

10

11

REPARTO VÁSQUEZ

12

13

14

HOTEL GUACANAYABO ●

AV CAMILO CIENFUEGOS

(CIRCUNVALACIÓN)

AV DE CÉSPEDES

HOSPITAL

CEMETERY

0   400 yds

0   400 m

To Niquero

© AVALON TRAVEL

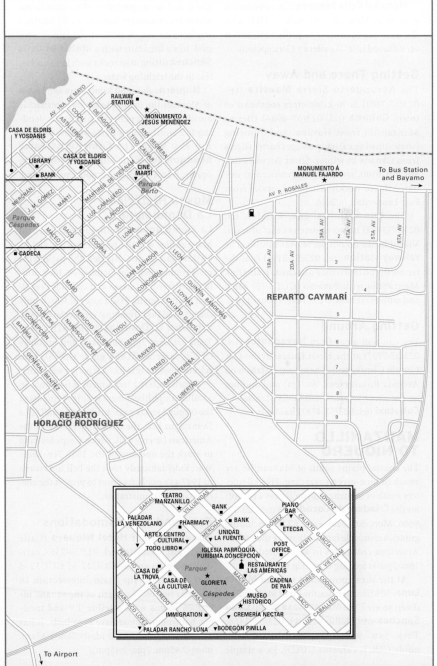

Hospital Celia Sánchez (Circunvalación y Av. Jesús Menéndez, tel. 023/57-4011) is on the west side of town. The **police station** is on Villuendas (e/ Aguilera y Concepción).

Getting There and Away

The **Aeropuerto Sierra Maestra** (tel. 023/57-7401) is 10 kilometers southeast of town. **Cubana** (tel. 023/57-4984) flies to Manzanillo from Havana, and Sunwing (www.sunwing.ca) has package charter flights from Canada in winter. Silver Airways (tel. 801/401-9100, www.silverairways.com) initiated thrice-weekly scheduled service from Fort Lauderdale in 2016.

The **bus terminal** (Av. Rosales, tel. 023/57-3404) is two kilometers east of town. Víazul buses do not serve Manzanillo. The **railway station** (tel. 023/57-2195) is at the far north end of Avenida Merchan. Trains link Manzanillo with Bayamo (CUC1.70) daily, and with Havana (CUC28) every fourth day.

Getting Around

You can rent a car from **Havanautos** (tel. 023/57-7737) at the Hotel Guacanayabo (Av. Camilo Cienfuegos). There's a gas station on Avenida Rosales (esq. Av. 1ra) and another on the *circunvalación* (esq. Jesús Menéndez). **Cubataxi** (tel. 023/57-4782) has taxis.

MANZANILLO TO NIQUERO

The coastal plains south of Manzanillo are awash in lime-green sugarcane. Five kilometers south of Manzanillo you'll pass a turnoff for the **Criadero de Cocodrilos** (tel. 023/57-8606, Mon.-Sat. 7am-4pm, CUC5 including guide), a crocodile farm with more than 8,000 American crocodiles in algae-filled ponds; 1pm-2pm is feeding time. Tip the guide.

At the sugar-processing town of **Media Luna,** 50 kilometers southwest of Manzanillo, divert to view the **Museo Casa Natal Celia Sánchez** (Av. Podio #11, tel. 023/59-3466, Tues.-Sun. 9am-5pm, entrance CUC5, guide CUC5, cameras CUC5), in a simple green-and-white gingerbread wooden house where revolutionary heroine Celia Sánchez was born on May 9, 1920. Media Luna's town park has a fountain with a **statue of Celia Sánchez** sitting atop rocks with her shoeless feet in the trickling water.

Niquero, about 60 kilometers southwest of Manzanillo, is unique for its ramshackle buildings in French colonial style, lending it a similarity to parts of New Orleans and Key West. The **Communist Party headquarters,** one block from the main square, is in a fabulous art nouveau building.

Museo Histórico La Demajagua

La Demajagua, 13 kilometers south of Manzanillo, was the sugar estate owned by Carlos Manuel de Céspedes, the nationalist revolutionary who on October 10, 1868, unilaterally freed his slaves and called for rebellion against Spain. His house (of which only the original floor remains) is now the **Museo Histórico La Demajagua** (tel. 5219-4080, Tues.-Sat. 8am-5pm, Sun. 8am-1pm, entrance CUC1, cameras CUC5, guide CUC5), with eclectic displays that include period weaponry.

A path leads to a monument of fieldstone in a walled amphitheater encircling remnants of the original sugar mill. Inset in the wall is La Demajagua bell, the Cuban equivalent of the American Liberty Bell, which Céspedes rang to mark the opening of the 1868 Ten Years War. Fidel famously took the bell to Havana in 1947 as a publicity stunt to protest the corrupt Grau administration.

Food and Accommodations

Islazul's pleasant **Hotel Niquero** (Calle Martí, esq. Céspedes, tel. 023/59-2367, caridad@hotelnq.co.cu, CUC22 s, CUC32 d year-round), at the main intersection in Niquero two blocks north of the square, offers 26 rooms with satellite TV and modern bathrooms; some have king beds. It has an appealing restaurant (daily 7am-9:45am, noon-2:45pm, 7pm-9:45pm).

For Whom the Bell Tolls

Since independence, La Demajagua bell had been entrusted to Manzanillo to maintain as a national shrine. In November 1947, a politically ambitious law student named Fidel Castro arranged for the venerable 300-pound bell to be brought to Havana to be pealed in an anti-government demonstration. Castro accompanied the bell from Manzanillo to Havana, to great popular fanfare. The bell was placed in the Gallery of Martyrs in the university, but disappeared overnight, presumably at the hands of President Grau's police. Castro, who likely set up the theft himself, took to the airwaves denouncing the corrupt Grau government.

Several days later, the bell was delivered "anonymously" to President Grau and was immediately sent back to Manzanillo. The incident helped young Castro achieve fame as a rising political star.

★ PARQUE NACIONAL DESEMBARCO DEL GRANMA

This UNESCO World Heritage Site, 100 meters south of the hamlet of **Las Colorados,** about 20 kilometers south of Niquero, protects the southwesternmost tip of Cuba, from Cabo Cruz to Punta Hicacos. The land stairsteps toward the Sierra Maestra in a series of marine terraces left high and dry over the eons. More than 80 percent of the park is covered by virgin woodland. Flora and fauna species are distinct. Drier areas preserve cacti more than 400 years old. Two endemic species of note are the blue-headed quail dove and the Cuban Amazon butterfly. Even endangered manatees inhabit the coastal lagoons.

The entrance station (tel. 5219-0004) has a visitors center with exhibits; pay your park entrance (CUC5) here. The **Sendero Arqueológico Natural El Guafe,** about eight kilometers south of the entrance, leads through mangroves and scrub to caverns containing dripstone formations. One, the Idolo del Agua, is thought to have been shaped by pre-Columbian Taínos. You can hire guides (CUC5) or hike solo. **EcoTur** (tel. 023/48-7006 in Bayamo, www.ecoturcuba.tur.cu) offers guided hikes.

The two-kilometer-long **Sendero Morlotte-Fustete** leads to caverns and a sinkhole; it is accessed by a shake-your-teeth-till-they-fall-out road from Alegría del Pío, 28

kilometers southeast of Niquero. EcoTur (tel. 023/48-7006, agencia@grm.ecotur.tur.cu) offers a 4x4 Jeep Safari that includes the trail hike.

The park is named for the spot where Fidel and his band of revolutionaries came ashore at Playa las Coloradas on December 2, 1956. The exact spot where the *Granma* ran aground is one kilometer south of Las Colorados. Here, the **Monumento de Desembarcadero** consists of a replica of the *Granma* and a tiny museum (entrance is overpriced at CUC5) with a few photos, rifles, and a map showing the route of the *desembarcaderos* into the Sierra Maestra.

A concrete pathway leads 1.8 kilometers through the mangroves to the exact spot where the *Granma* bogged down.

Cabo Cruz

The potholed road south from Las Colorados dips and rises through dense scrubland, twists around Laguna Guafes, and ends at the fishing hamlet of Cabo Cruz, the southwesterly tip of Cuba. The **Faro Cabo Cruz** lighthouse (off-limits; it's a military zone), built in 1871, rises 33 meters above a shrimp farm. A plaque atop the cliff states that Christopher Columbus arrived here in May 1494.

Restaurante El Cabo (tel. 023/90-1317, daily noon-2:30pm, 3pm-5:30pm, and 6pm-9:40pm) offers seafood beside the lighthouse in Cabo Cruz.

Route of the *Desembarcados*

After landing their stricken leisure yacht amid mangroves just south of Los Colorados (Che Guevara called it "a shipwreck") and wading ashore, the tale of the 82 revolutionaries' fate reads like a movie script. The rebels made it inland 18 kilometers, as far as Alegría de Pío, where on day five they were ambushed by Batista's troops and air force. The survivors dispersed. At one point Fidel found himself hiding in a sugarcane field with only two others—doctor Faustino Pérez (weaponless) and Universo Sánchez (shoeless), Fidel's bodyguard—as Batista's warplanes strafed the field. After four days the exhausted and starving trio crawled away and successfully dodged army patrols as they crept to safety. On December 13 they met up with campesino Guillermo García, who guided them to the prearranged meeting point at **Cinco Palmas.**

On December 18, Raúl Castro arrived with four others. Then, on December 21, Che Guevara, Camilo Cienfuegos, and five others staggered in. On Christmas Day the 15 survivors then headed into the Sierra Maestra, along with some new peasant recruits, in their march to safety and destiny.

Sites: Cinco Palmas, 27 kilometers southeast of Media Luna via a denuded road, has a **monument** and **museum** (in a *bohío* replicating the simple home of peasant farmer Ramón "Mongo" Pérez) marking the site where the survivors linked up. Alegría de Pío also has a **monument,** and guides will lead you to the **Cueva del Che,** where Che & Co. hid out following the attack.

Recreation: You can arrange at the park entrance or with Ecotur (tel. 023/48-7006, agencia@grm.ecotur.tur.cu) for a guided, rugged 18-kilometer hike between Los Colorados and Alegría de Pío that follows the route of the revolutionaries.

The South Coast

From Entronque Pilón, five kilometers north of Niquero, a scenic road cuts east through the foothills of the Sierra Maestra and drops down through a narrow pass to emerge on the coastal plains near Pilón, where a gas station is the last before Santiago de Cuba, 200 kilometers to the east.

PILÓN AND MAREA DEL PORTILLO

The scruffy fishing (and former sugar-processing) town of **Pilón** is ringed on three sides by mountains and on the fourth by the Caribbean Sea. The land west of Pilón is smothered in sugarcane. East of Pilón, the land lies in the rain shadow of the Sierra Maestra and is semidesert. Cacti appear, and goats graze amid stony pastures. The town's sole attraction is **Casa Museo Celia Sánchez** (Conrado Benitez #20, tel. 023/59-4107, Tues.-Fri. 8am-noon and 1:30pm-5:30pm, Sat 8am-noon, free), a beautiful red-and-yellow clapboard house once used by Celia Sánchez as a base for her underground supply network for Castro's rebel army. The museum is dedicated to the revolutionary underground and Castro's literacy campaign.

Fifteen kilometers east of Pilón the mountains shelve gently to a wide bay at **Marea del Portillo,** rimmed by a beach of pebbly gray-brown sand. Marea del Portillo is favored by budget-minded Canadian and European charter groups plus Cuban families, but facilities are limited.

Recreation

Water sports, sportfishing (CUC45), and scuba diving (CUC30 per dive) are offered at **Marlin Albacora Dive Center** (tel. 023/59-7139), at Club Amigo Marea del Portillo. Dive sites include the wreck of the *Cristóbal Colón,* a Spanish warship sunk in the war of 1898 (CUC70 for two dives).

Excursions offered by the hotel tour desks

include horseback rides (from CUC5); a "seafari" with snorkeling at Cayo Blanco; jeep tours; and hiking to La Comandancia de la Plata.

Food and Accommodations

In Pilón, friendly hosts Milka and Mayumi welcome guests to their pleasant **Casa La Palma** (Calle Segunda #41, tel. 023/59-4162 or 5857-4093, milkac.reyes@nauta.cu, CUC20-25), which is both a three-bedroom B&B and a *paladar* (daily 10am-10pm) that serves paella and lasagna in the shaded garden patio.

Cubanacán (www.hotelescubanacan.com) operates three hotels at Marea del Portillo. The somewhat lifeless **Villa Punta Piedra** (tel. 023/59-7062, CUC34 s, CUC60 low season, CUC48 s, CUC70 d high season, including breakfast), five kilometers west of Marea, has 13 spacious, simply furnished air-conditioned villas, plus a restaurant and bar-disco.

The all-inclusive, no-frills beachfront **Club Amigo Marea del Portillo** (tel. 023/59-7102, reservas@marea.co.cu, from CUC62 s, CUC90 d) is divided into a beachfront property and a much nicer hilltop Farallón del Caribe section (from CUC98 s, CUC128 d), with superb views but open November-April only. Together they have 283 rooms and suites, including 56 *cabinas*. Each section has a restaurant, bar, and swimming pool. A simple cabaret is offered, and Farallón del Caribe has a disco, but the constant need to walk between the hotels grows old.

To escape the dreary hotel food, head to the elegant **Restaurant El Mirador** (tel. 5269-0599, daily noon-9pm), on a hillside two kilometers west of Villa Punta Piedra. It serves tasty *criolla* fare and seafood.

Getting There and Around

A *camión* runs between Pilón and Santiago de Cuba on alternate days. You can rent cars and scooters at the Club Amigo properties through **Cubacar** (tel. 023/59-7185). Horse-drawn *coches* charge CUC3 for a tour of the nearby fishing village. A rugged mountain road links Bartolomé Masó and Marea del Portillo; a jeep is required.

★ MAREA DEL PORTILLO TO SANTIAGO DE CUBA

The rugged coast that links Marea del Portillo and Santiago de Cuba is an exhilarating and daunting drive. The paved but dangerously deteriorated road hugs the coast the whole way, climbing over steep headlands and dropping through river valleys. The teal-blue sea is your constant companion, with the Sierra Maestra pushing up close on the other side. There are no villages or habitations for miles, and no services whatsoever. Landslides occasionally block the road, much of which has been washed away; near La Cueva you have to run along the shingle beach. It may be impassable at high tide and in storms. A jeep is essential.

In springtime, giant land crabs march across the road in fulfillment of the mating urge. Amazingly, the battalions even scale vertical cliffs. The dangerously derelict bridge over the Río Macio, 15 kilometers from Marea, marks the border with Santiago de Cuba Province. Ford the river instead.

Santiago de Cuba

Santiago de Cuba Province is one of the most historically important regions in the country and claims to be the Cradle of the Revolution.

The first charge of machete-wielding Mambí was at Baire in 1868. And in 1953 Fidel Castro's attack on Batista's barracks took place at Moncada, in the city of Santiago, initiating the Revolution that six years later brought Castro to power.

The province's namesake capital city, second only to Havana in size, is distinctive in mood and teems with sites of historical and cultural interest, from a castle and the 16th-century house where Diego Velázquez governed Cuba to a notable cathedral and the Moncada barracks. Nearby there are beaches, the holy shrine of El Cobre, Reserva Baconao, and Parque Nacional Gran Piedra, reached by a serpentine road that leads through cool pine forest to a splendid garden perched atop a peak at over 1,200 meters.

The Santiagüeros carry themselves with a certain lassitude and speak in a lilting tongue with a musical tone. French and African words appear, a legacy of the many French and Haitian families that settled here in the late 18th century. Santiago has the highest percentage of African blood in Cuba; though the traditional architecture is mostly Spanish, the faces are mostly black. Such musical forms as *son* were birthed here, and the city remains Cuba's most vital center of Afro-Cuban culture, a legacy not only of slavery but of the many Jamaicans and Haitians imported as laborers during the late 19th century, for which reason Santiago is known as the "most Caribbean" city in Cuba.

Most of the province is mountainous. The Sierra Maestra rises west of Santiago. East of the city, an elevated plateau extends for miles, slanting gradually to the sea, with the serrated Cordillera de la Gran Piedra behind. Behind these rise the Sierra de Baracoa and Sierra Cristal, extending into Holguín and Guantánamo Provinces.

The region was dealt a devastating blow on October 25, 2012, when Hurricane Sandy blasted ashore, causing significant damage in and around the city of Santiago de Cuba (171,380 houses were damaged, and 15,889 collapsed) and killing 11 people.

Previous: El Morro castle at dusk; changing of the guard at Cementerio de Santa Ifigenia. **Above:** José Martí tomb at Cementerio de Santa Ifigenia.

Look for ★ to find recommended sights, activities, dining, and lodging.

Highlights

Complejo Histórico de
Museos del Segundo Frente ★

Mangos de
Baragua

Mayarí
Arriba

Bayamo

Casa de Don Diego
Velázquez

Palma
Soriano

Museo Municipal
Emilio Bacardí Moreau

0   25 mi

Cuartel
Moncada

Cementerio de
Santa Ifigenia

0   25 km

Filé

El Cobre

Santiago
de Cuba

Basílica de
Nuestra Señora
del Cobre ★

★

★ Siboney

Ocujal

Parque
Histórico
El Morro

Museo de la Guerra
Hispano-Cubano-
Americano

Caribbean   Sea

© AVALON TRAVEL

★ **Casa de Don Diego Velázquez:** The building from where Diego Velázquez ruled Cuba is the island's oldest house. In superb condition, it houses a fine museum (page 428).

★ **Museo Municipal Emilio Bacardí Moreau:** The museum begun by a member of the famous rum-making family holds an eclectic and fascinating collection inside a beautiful neoclassical edifice (page 430).

★ **Cuartel Moncada:** This is where it all began: The scene of the attack by Castro and company that launched the Revolution is now a school and museum (page 432).

★ **Parque Histórico El Morro:** An enormous restored 17th-century castle with a dramatic clifftop setting holds a nightly cannon-firing ceremony (page 435).

★ **Cementerio de Santa Ifigenia:** Important figures in Cuban history, not least José Martí and Fidel Castro, are buried here (page 436).

★ **Basílica de Nuestra Señora del Cobre:** Make a pilgrimage here to see the Cubans praying and making offerings to the Virgen de la Caridad (page 447).

★ **Complejo Histórico de Museos del Segundo Frente:** A superb museum and mausoleum honoring the efforts of Raúl Castro and Vilma Espin and the martyrs of the Second Front (page 450).

★ **Museo de la Guerra Hispano-Cubano-Americano:** This small yet excellent museum displays maps, artillery pieces, and other articles relating to the Spanish-American War (page 452).

Santiago de Cuba

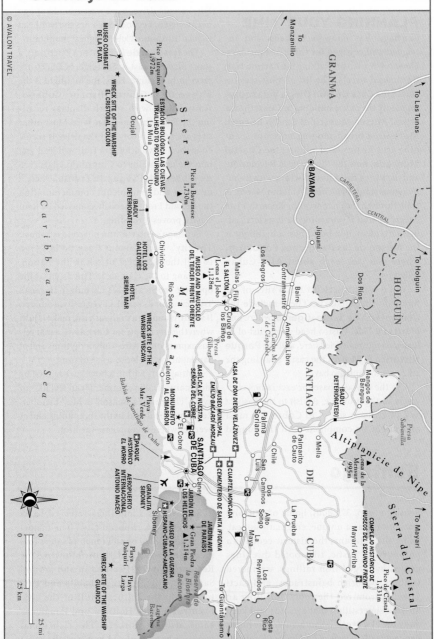

© AVALON TRAVEL

The government has done a splendid job of restoration.

PLANNING YOUR TIME

Santiago has enough to keep you intrigued and engaged for three or four days. Downtown, plan on walking the narrow, traffic-clogged streets. The list of must-sees includes the **Casa de Don Diego Velázquez,** reputedly the oldest building in Cuba; the excellent **Museo Municipal Emilio Bacardí Moreau,** a broad-ranging museum spanning arts, history, and culture; the **Cuartel Moncada,** now the Museo de la Revolución; and the **Plaza de la Revolución,** with its humongous statue of General Antonio Maceo. A walk through the once-wealthy Reparto Vista Alegre district is rewarding for its eclectic albeit tatterdemalion buildings; a highlight is the **Museo de las Religiones Populares,** where you can learn about Afro-Cuban religions.

You'll want wheels to reach sites of interest on the outskirts. These include the **Cementerio de Santa Ifigenia,** where José Martí and Fidel Castro head a long list of illustrious figures buried here, and the **Parque Histórico El Morro,** the castle guarding the entrance to Santiago bay.

Use the city as a base for excursions elsewhere in the province. A visit to the basilica and pilgrimage site of **El Cobre** is a must and might be combined with the rugged drive to **El Saltón,** a mountain resort that is a good base for bird-watching and hiking. For a scenic drive, head west from Santiago to **Chivírico,** beyond which lies the trailhead to Pico Turquino, Cuba's highest mountain.

The **Reserva de la Biosfera Baconao,** a short distance east of Santiago, is an eco-reserve only in name. Here, the highlight is the **Museo de la Guerra Hispano-Cubano-Americano,** with superb displays recalling the Spanish-American War. Most other sites are rather hokey, but the drive is scenic enough. A Revolution-era trail will lead you into the mountains to **Complejo Histórico de Museos del Segundo Frente,** where a museum and mausoleum commemorating the Second Front established and led by Raúl Castro proves rewarding.

Santiago's entertainment scene is robust. The city's world-famous **Casa de la Trova** is still the heartbeat of *son* in the nation. The yang to the Casa de la Trova's yin is the open-air **Tropicana,** second only to Havana's Tropicana for its sexy Las Vegas-style cabaret. If you're planning a midyear visit, make it July, when the city erupts for **Carnaval,** a marvelous expression of Afro-Cuban rhythms and of Santiagüeros' let-loose sense of fun.

Santiago sits within a bowl surrounded by mountains, and in summer it can feel like an oven. The rainiest season is May-October. Relief may be found in the mountains and at beaches where breezes ease the heat.

Santiago

Santiago (pop. 375,000), home of rum and revolution, has a unique, enigmatic appeal. Older than Havana, the historic center is a potpourri of rustic, tile-roofed dwellings graced by forged-iron railings, weathered timbers, Moorish balustrades, and cacti growing from red-tile roofs, fulfilling an Oriente superstition that a cactus will keep away the evil eye. If a Santiagüero lets his or her cactus die, a year of bad luck will follow.

Santiago is sometimes referred to as "Cuba's most Caribbean city." The majority of the 30,000 or so French planters and merchants who fled Haiti following the Revolution in 1791 settled in and around Santiago, stitching their habits and customs onto the cultural quilt of the city. Eventually black Haitians and Jamaicans came also, as workers. The rich racial mixture has produced some of the most exciting music, art, and architecture in the Caribbean.

Proud Santiagüeros tout their city as the "Hero City," or the *capital moral de la Revolución*, birthed here on July 26, 1953, when Fidel and his band of revolutionaries attacked the Moncada barracks.

A world away from Havana, Santiago arouses mixed feelings in visitors. Often appearing brash, manic, and perpetually hilly and hot, it has more than its fair share of aggressive *jiniteros* (hustlers), swarms of take-no-prisoners motorcycle-taxis, pollution, and a frenetic and cacophonous energy level. Relax, and you'll love it.

HISTORY

Diego Velázquez founded the city in 1515 and named it for the king of Spain's patron saint, St. James. The city, built on hills on the east side of the Bahía de Santiago, was named the Cuban capital and grew rapidly thanks to its splendid harbor and wealth from nearby copper mines at El Cobre. Its first *capitán-general* was none other than Hernán Cortés, soon to be conqueror of Mexico. Other famous conquistadores resided here, too, including Francisco Pizarro (conqueror of Peru), Don Pedro de Alvarado (founder of Guatemala), and Juan Ponce de León (colonizer of Puerto Rico). Many of the original buildings still stand, including Velázquez's own sturdy home.

Santiago remained capital of Cuba only until February 1553, when the governor transferred his residence to Havana. Santiago had lost its advantage and the El Cobre mines closed shortly thereafter. It was subsequently damaged by earthquakes and razed by pirates, including the French buccaneer Jacques de Sores and Welsh pirate Henry Morgan.

Spanish settlers from Jamaica boosted Santiago's numbers when that island was seized by the English in 1655. At the close of the century, when Santiago's population approached 10,000, a massive influx of French émigrés from Haiti doubled the city population and added new vitality. Another boost in fortunes came in 1793, when Spanish authorities granted Santiago an *asamiento* (unlimited license) to import slaves. Countless West African slaves gained their first look at the New World as they stepped shackled and confused into the harsh light on Santiago's wharves.

Santiago's reputation as a liberal city dates to 1836, when city fathers proclaimed local elections in defiance of the governor in Havana. Governor Tacón won the battle, but Santiago had asserted an autonomy that propelled it to the forefront in the quest for independence. During the wars for independence, the city became a concentration camp held by Spanish troops and enclosed by barbed wire. On July 1, 1898, after the United States entered the fray, U.S. troops reached the outskirts of Santiago and the defenses atop San Juan Hill that protected the city. Throughout the morning, the U.S. artillery softened up the Spanish defenders before 3,000 U.S. Rough Riders stormed the hill under cover of punishing fire. Though Teddy Roosevelt's part in the assault has been vastly overblown by U.S. history texts, the victory sealed the war. The Spanish navy, meanwhile, had sheltered in Santiago harbor. On July 3, it attempted to escape. A battle ensued and the Spanish fleet was destroyed.

The Spanish surrender was signed on San Juan Hill on July 17. The Spanish flag came down and up went the Stars and Stripes.

The city became a hotbed of revolutionary activity during the decades before 1950. The opening shots in Castro's revolution were fired here on July 26, 1953, when the 26-year-old lawyer and his followers attacked the Moncada barracks at dawn in an attempt to inspire a general uprising.

Assassinations by Batista's thugs were common. The terror and turmoil reached a crescendo on November 30, 1956, when a 22-year-old Santiago teacher named Frank País led a group of Castro's 26th of July Movement (M-26-7) rebels in a daring attack on the police headquarters in Santiago, timed to coincide with the landing of the *Granma*

Santiago

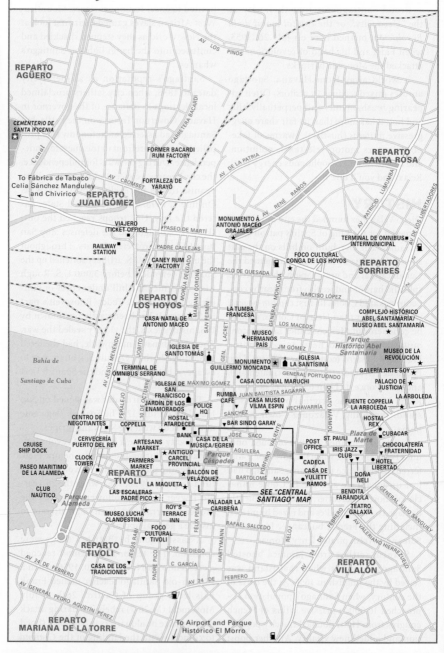

REPARTO AGÜERO

AV LOS PINOS

CARRETERA BACARDI

CEMENTERIO DE
SANTA IFIGENIA

Canal

FORMER BACARDI
RUM FACTORY ★

AV DE LA PATRIA

REPARTO
SANTA ROSA

AV CROMBET

To Fábrica de Tabaco
Celia Sánchez Manduley
and Chivirico

FORTALEZA DE
YARAYÓ ★

REPARTO
JUAN GÓMEZ

AV RENÉ RAMOS

AV PATRICIO LUMUMBA

AV DE LOS LIBERTADORES

VIAJERO
(TICKET OFFICE) ■

PASEO DE MARTÍ

MONUMENTO A
ANTONIO MACEO
GRAJALES ★

TERMINAL DE OMNIBUS
INTERMUNICIPAL ■

RAILWAY
STATION ■

PADRE CALLEJAS

CANEY RUM
FACTORY ★

GONZALO DE QUESADA

FOCO CULTURAL
CONGA DE LOS HOYOS ★

REPARTO
SORRIBES

NARCISO LÓPEZ

REPARTO
LOS HOYOS

LA TUMBA
FRANCESA ★

LOS MACEOS

COMPLEJO HISTÓRICO
ABEL SANTAMARÍA/
MUSEO ABEL SANTAMARÍA ★

CASA NATAL DE
ANTONIO MACEO ■

MUSEO
HERMANOS
PAÍS ★

JM GÓMEZ

Parque
Histórico Abel
Santamaría

MUSEO DE LA
REVOLUCIÓN ★

Bahía de

Santiago de Cuba

TERMINAL DE
OMNIBUS SERRANO ■

IGLESIA DE
SANTO TOMÁS ✝

MONUMENTO
GUILLERMO MONCADA ★

IGLESIA
LA SANTÍSIMA ✝

GENERAL PORTUONDO

GALERÍA ARTE SOY ★

PALACIO DE
JUSTICIA ★

IGLESIA DE
SAN
FRANCISCO ✝

CASA COLONIAL MARUCHI ■

CENTRO DE
NEGOTIANTES ■

JARDÍN DE LOS
ENAMORADOS ★

POLICE
HQ ■

RUMBA
CAFÉ ★

CASA MUSEO
VILMA ESPIN ★

LA ARBOLEDA
★

FUENTE COPPELIA
LA ARBOLEDA ★

CRUISE
SHIP DOCK

CERVECERÍA
PUERTO DEL REY ■

COPPELIA
★

HOSTAL
ATARDECER ■

BANK ■

BAR SINDO GARAY ★

JOSÉ SACO

POST
OFFICE ■

HOSTAL
REX ■

ST. PAULI ★

Plaza de
Marte

CUBACAR ●

PASEO MARITIMO
DE LA ALAMEDA ★

CLOCK
TOWER ★

ARTESANS
MARKET ■

FARMERS
MARKET ■

ANTIGUO
CARCEL
PROVINCIAL ■

CASA DE LA
MUSICA/EGREM ■

Parque
Céspedes

AGUILERA

IRIS JAZZ
CLUB ●

CADECA ■

CHOCOLATERÍA
FRATERNIDAD ●

HOTEL
LIBERTAD ●

CLUB
NÁUTICO ★

Parque
Alameda

REPARTO
TIVOLI

BALCÓN DE
VELÁZQUEZ ★

HEREDIA

MASÓ

CASA DE
YULIETT
RAMOS ●

DOÑA
NELI ●

LA MAQUETA ★

BARTOLOMÉ

SEE "CENTRAL
SANTIAGO" MAP

BENDITA
FARANDULA ●

LAS ESCALERAS
PADRE PICO ★

PALADAR LA
CARIBEÑA ●

TEATRO
GALAXIA ■

MUSEO LUCHA
CLANDESTINA ■

ROY'S
TERRACE
INN ●

FÉLIX PEÑA

RAFAEL SALCEDO

REPARTO
TIVOLI

FOCO
CULTURAL
TIVOLI ■

JOSÉ DE DIEGO

REPARTO
VILLALÓN

AV 24 DE FEBRERO

CASA DE LOS
TRADICIONES ■

C GARCÍA

AV 24 DE FEBRERO

AV GENERAL PEDRO AGUSTÍN PÉREZ

REPARTO
MARIANA DE LA TORRE

To Airport and Parque
Histórico El Morro

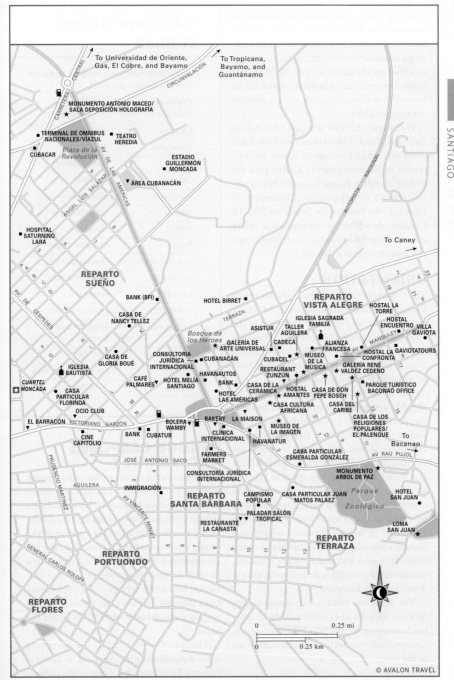

To Universidad de Oriente,
Gas, El Cobre, and Bayamo

To Tropicana,
Bayamo, and
Guantánamo

CARRETERA CENTRAL

CIRCUNVALACIÓN

MONUMENTO ANTONIO MACEO/
SALA DEPOSICIÓN HOLOGRAFÍA

TERMINAL DE OMNIBUS
NACIONALES/VIAZUL

TEATRO
HEREDIA

CUBACAR

Plaza de la
Revolución

ESTADIO
GUILLERMÓN
MONCADA

ÁREA CUBANACÁN

ÁNGEL LUIS SALAZAR

AV. DE LAS AMÉRICAS

AUTOPISTA NACIONAL

HOSPITAL
SATURNINO
LARA

To Caney

REPARTO
SUEÑO

AV. DE CÉSPEDES

BANK (BFI)

HOTEL BIRRET

REPARTO
VISTA ALEGRE

HOSTAL LA
TORRE

HOSTAL
ENCUENTRO

CASA DE
NANCY TELLEZ

TERRAZA

ASISTUR

IGLESIA SAGRADA
FAMILIA

VILLA
GAVIOTA

Bosque de
los Héroes

GALERÍA DE
ARTE UNIVERSAL

TALLER
AGUILERA

CADECA

MANDULEY

ALIANZA
FRANCESA

HOSTAL LA
CONFRONTA

GAVIOTATOURS

CASA DE
GLORIA BOUÉ

CONSULTORIA
JURÍDICA
INTERNACIONAL

CUBANACÁN

CUBACEL

MUSEO
DE LA
MÚSICA

GALERÍA RENÉ
VALDEZ CEDEÑO

IGLESIA
BAUTISTA

CAFÉ
PALMARES

HOTEL MELIÁ
SANTIAGO

HAVANAUTOS

RESTAURANT
ZUNZUN

CUARTEL
MONCADA

CASA
PARTICULAR
FLORINDA

BANK

CASA DE LA
CERÁMICA

HOSTAL
AMANTES

CASA DE DON
PEPE BOSCH

PARQUE TURÍSTICO
BACONAO OFFICE

HOTEL
LAS AMÉRICAS

CASA CULTURA
AFRICANA

CASA DEL
CARIBE

OCIO CLUB

EL BARRACÓN

VICTORIANO GARZÓN

BOLERA
WAMBY

BAKERY

LA MAISON

CASA DE LOS
RELIGIONES
POPULARES/
EL PALENQUE

To
Bacanao

CINE
CAPITOLIO

BANK

CUBATUR

CLÍNICA
INTERNACIONAL

MUSEO DE
LA IMAGEN

HAVANATUR

AV. RAÚL PUJOL

PRUDENCIO MARTÍNEZ

JOSÉ ANTONIO SACO

FARMERS
MARKET

CASA PARTICULAR
ESMERALDA GONZÁLEZ

AGUILERA

CONSULTORIA JURÍDICA
INTERNACIONAL

MONUMENTO
ARBOL DE PAZ

INMIGRACIÓN

AV. VICENTE MINIET

REPARTO
SANTA BÁRBARA

CAMPISMO
POPULAR

CASA PARTICULAR JUAN
MATOS PALAEZ

Parque
Zoológico

HOTEL
SAN JUAN

GENERAL CARLOS ROLOFF

PALADAR SALÓN
TROPICAL

RESTAURANTE
LA CANASTA

REPARTO
TERRAZA

LOMA
SAN JUAN

REPARTO
PORTUONDO

REPARTO
FLORES

0   0.25 mi

0   0.25 km

© AVALON TRAVEL

bringing Castro and other revolutionaries from exile in Mexico. País's attack was ill-fated, and Batista's henchmen initiated a campaign of indiscriminate murders. Frank País was shot on the street on July 30, 1958. His funeral erupted into a massive protest led by Santiago's mothers, inspiring similar protests throughout Cuba.

On January 2, 1959, two days after Batista fled the island, Fidel Castro and his rebel army arrived in Santiago to accept the surrender of Batista's general. Castro gave his victory speech in Parque Céspedes before setting off on a victory parade—Caravana de la Libertad—for Havana. (In December 2016, La Caravana de la Libertad was reversed as Fidel's remains traveled to Santiago to be laid to rest in Cementerio Santa Ifigenia.)

ORIENTATION

The Carretera Central from Bayamo enters Santiago from the north, descends to Plaza de la Revolución, and runs into the heart of the city as Avenida de los Libertadores. The coast road from Marea del Portillo enters the city from the west as Paseo de Martí, which rises to Avenida de los Libertadores.

The historic core (*casco histórico*) is roughly arranged in a grid. At its heart is Parque Céspedes, bounded by Félix Pena and Lacret (north-south) and Aguilera and Heredia (east-west). Most sights of interest are within a few blocks of the park. Aguilera leads east from Parque Céspedes uphill to Plaza de Marte, a major hub on the eastern edge of the historic quarter. From here, Avenida 24 de Febrero leads south to the airport and Parque Histórico El Morro. Avenida Victoriano Garzón leads east from Plaza de Marte to the Reparto Sueño and Vista Alegre districts, also accessed from Plaza de la Revolución via Avenida de las Américas.

The Autopista Nacional (freeway) begins in Vista Alegre and extends only 45 kilometers before petering out near Palma Soriano. A *circunvalación* circles the east and south sides of the city.

Santiago Street Names

Most streets have both modern and older names; locals use the latter.

Old Name	New Name
Alameda	Jesús Menéndez
Calvario	Porfirio Valiente
Carnicería	Pío Rosado
Clarín	Padre Quiroga
Corona	Mariano
Enramada	José Antonio Saco
Jagüey	Cornelio Robert
Marina	Aguilera
Reloj	Mayía Rodríguez
San Agustín	Donato Marmól
San Basilio	Bartolomé Masó
San Félix	Hartmann
San Pedro	General Lacret
Santa Lucía	Joaquín Castillo Duany
Santo Tomás	Félix Pena
Trinidad	General Portuondo
Trocha	24 de Febrero

PARQUE CÉSPEDES AND VICINITY

This square at the heart of the city is ringed with gas lamps, shade trees, and marvelous buildings spanning the centuries (including a jarring 1950s glass-fronted bank on the southwest corner). At its center is a statue of the square's namesake hero, Carlos M. Céspedes, who sparked the independence movement in 1858. To best appreciate the colorful ambience, take to the terrace of the 1905 **Hotel Casa Grande** (Heredia esq. General Lacret) and sip a chilled beer while overlooking the plaza.

The beautiful building on the north side is the **Ayuntamiento** (Aguilera, e/ General Lacret y Félix Pena; not open to the public),

Central Santiago de Cuba

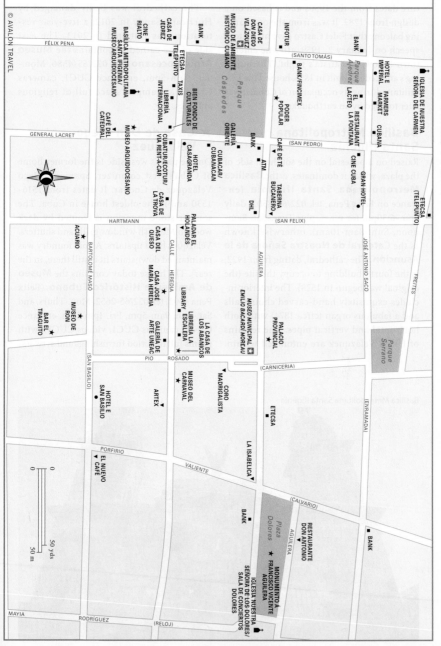

© AVALON TRAVEL

FÉLIX PENA

GENERAL LACRET

HARTMANN

BARTOLOMÉ MASO

PORFIRIO

MAYIA

RODRÍGUEZ

(RELOJ)

CASA DE JEDREZ
CINE RIALTO
BASÍLICA METROPOLITANA STA. IFIGENIA
MUSEO ARQUIDIOCESANO

BANK

CASA DE DON DIEGO VELÁZQUEZ
MUSEO DE AMBIENTE HISTÓRICO CUBANO

INFOTUR

BANK

(SANTO TOMÁS)

HOTEL E IMPERIAL
FARMERS MARKET

IGLESIA DE NUESTRA SEÑORA DEL CARMEN

ETECSA (TELEPUNTO)

ETECSA
TELEPUNTO
TAXIS

LIBRERÍA INTERNACIONAL

Parque Céspedes

Parque Ajedrez

BANK/FINCIMEX

EL RESTAURANT LÁCTEO LA FONTANA

CUBANA

CAFÉ DEL CATEDRAL

MUSEO ARQUIDIOCESANO

CUBATUR/ECOTUR/ VÍA RENT-A-CAR

BIEN FONDO DE CULTURALES

GALERÍA ORIENTE

CUBACAR/ CUBANACAN

PODER POPULAR

CAFÉ DE TÉ

(SAN PEDRO)

BANK

ATM

CINE CUBA

GRAN HOTEL

CASA DE LA TROVA

HOTEL CASAGRANDA

TABERNA BUCANERA

DHL

(SAN FELIX)

PALADAR EL HOLANDÉS

CALLE

AGUILERA

JOSÉ ANTONIO SACO

FRETES

ACUARIO

MUSEO DE RON

BAR EL TRAGUITO

CASA DEL QUESO

HEREDIA

CASA JOSÉ MARÍA HEREDIA

GALERÍA DE ARTE UNEAC

LIBRERÍA ESCALERA

LIBRERÍA LA ESCALERA

LA CASA DE LOS ABANICOS

MUSEO MUNICIPAL EMILIO BACARDÍ MOREAU

PALACIO PROVINCIAL

Parque Serrano

(ENRAMADA)

PIO   ROSADO

(CARNICERIA)

(SAN BASILIO)

ARTEX

HOTEL E SAN BASILIO

MUSEO DEL CARNAVAL

CORO MADRIGALISTA

ETECSA

LA ISABELICA

EL NUEVO CAFÉ

VALIENTE

(CALVARIO)

BANK

Plaza Dolores

AGUILERA

RESTAURANTE DON ANTONIO

BANK

MONUMENTO A FRANCISCO VICENTE AGUILERA

IGLESIA NUESTRA SEÑORA DE LOS DOLORES/ SALA DE CONCIERTOS SALA DOLORES

0   50 yds
0   50 m

or town hall. The original building was first occupied by Hernán Cortés; the current structure dates from the 1950s and is based on a design from 1783. It was from the overhanging balcony that Fidel Castro gave his victory speech on January 2, 1959, after he entered town following Batista's flight. The building's antecedent, built in 1855, housed the U.S. military during its occupation of Cuba; it was later toppled by an earthquake.

Basílica Metropolitana Santa Ifigenia

Raised on a pedestal on the southern side of the plaza, which it dominates, is the **Basílica Metropolitana Santa Ifigenia** (entrance on Félix Pena, tel. 022/62-8502, daily 5pm-6:30pm for mass, plus Tues.-Sat. 8am-noon, Sun. 8am-10am), otherwise known as the **Catedral de Nuestra Señora de la Asunción.** The cathedral, dating from 1922, is the fourth building to occupy the site (the original was begun in 1528). The interior includes exquisitely hand-carved choir stalls and a fabulous organ (circa 1874) with both horizontal and vertical pipes. The remains of Diego Velázquez are entombed within.

Between the church's twin towers is a statue of an angel holding a trumpet.

The cathedral was badly damaged by Hurricane Sandy in 2012; a five-year restoration was initiated in 2013. The east side of the cathedral contains the **Museo Arquidiocesano** (tel. 022/65-4586, Mon.-Sat. 9am-5pm, entrance CUC1, cameras CUC1), a cramped space full of religious antiques.

★ Casa de Don Diego Velázquez

On the park's west side is the former home of Cuba's first colonizer, Spaniard Diego Velázquez de Cuellar. It dates from 1516-1530 and is the oldest house in Cuba. The somber stone mansion is fronted by dark wooden Moorish window grills and shutters. Velázquez lived upstairs. A gold foundry was maintained downstairs (it is still there, in the rear). The house today contains the **Museo de Ambiente Histórico Cubano** (Félix Pena #602, tel. 022/65-2652, Mon.-Thurs. and Sat.-Sun. 9am-5pm, Fri. 1pm-5pm, entrance CUC2, cameras CUC1, videos CUC5), with rooms full of period furnishings and artwork.

Basílica Metropolitana Santa Ifigenia

PLAZA CÉSPEDES TO PLAZA DE MARTE

Calles Heredia (full of musical atmosphere and intriguing sites) and, to the north, Saco (the city's main commercial thoroughfare, now thankfully pedestrianized) slope east from Parque Céspedes uphill to **Plaza de Marte,** a small plaza built in 1860 as the Spanish parade ground and execution spot for Cuban patriots. Busts of Cuban patriots speckle the square, pinned by an odd-looking column topped by a red French revolutionary cap representing liberty.

Your first stop on Heredia should be the **Casa de la Trova** (Heredia #208, tel. 022/65-2689, daily noon-1am). Formerly the home of revered composer Rafael Salcedo (1844-1917), it is Cuba's oldest such *casa,* having opened in 1968. Most afternoons and evenings, the haunting melodies and plaintive *boleros* of the *trova* reverberate down the street.

Casa Natal José María Heredia (Heredia #260, tel. 022/62-5350, Tues.-Sat. 9am-7pm, Sun. 9am-1pm, CUC1) is the birthplace of the 19th-century nationalist poet José María Heredia (1803-1839). The house is furnished in colonial fashion. It hosts cultural events.

Break out your camera at **La Librería La Escalera** (Heredia #265), a tiny bookstore festooned with intriguing bric-a-brac. Across the street, the **Galería de Arte UNEAC** (Heredia, e/ Hartmann y Pio Rosada, tel. 022/65-3465, ext. 106) is worth a peek for its superb art. Next, take the stairs to the **Museo del Carnaval** (Heredia #304, tel. 022/62-6955, Mon. 2pm-5pm, Tues.-Sat. 9am-5:15pm, Sun. 9am-1pm, entrance CUC1, cameras CUC5), which tells the history of Santiago's colorful carnival. Some of the outlandish costumes are on display. Folkloric shows are held at 4pm.

At the junction of Heredia and Valiente, turn north and walk one block into **Plaza Dolores,** a delightful little plaza with wrought-iron seats surrounding a larger-than-life bronze statue of Francisco Vicente Aguilera (1821-1877), a revolutionary leader in the Ten Years War. The **Iglesia Nuestra Señora de los Dolores,** on the east side, is now a concert hall and adjoins the **Colegio Jesuita Dolores,** where Fidel Castro was educated as a youth.

One block south on Calle Heredia, at the junction of Bartolomé Masó and Pío Rosado, is the small **Museo del Ron** (tel. 022/62-08884, Mon.-Sat. 9am-5pm, CUC1), with basic displays on rum-making plus a huge collection of bottled rums; you can tipple in the basement bar.

antique armor in Casa de Don Diego Velázquez

★ Museo Municipal Emilio Bacardí Moreau

This **museum** (Pío Rosado, e/ Aguilera and Heredia, tel. 022/62-8402, Mon. 1pm-4:30pm, Tues.-Sat. 9am-4:30pm, Sun. 9am-noon, entrance CUC2, cameras CUC5), one block east of Parque Céspedes, was founded in 1899 by Emilio Bacardí Moreau (1844-1922) and contains his astounding collection. A member of the Bacardí rum family (after the Revolution, the family had to flee Cuba), Emilio, the mayor of Santiago, was imprisoned in the Castillo del Morro for revolutionary activities.

The museum is housed in a huge neoclassical edifice with Corinthian columns. The first floor contains colonial artifacts, from slave shackles and stocks to antique weapons. A small but impressive display of pre-Columbian artifacts from throughout the Americas includes a shrunken head (*cabeza reducida*) and Peruvian mummies. The second-floor art gallery includes 19th-century and contemporary works.

On the museum's north side rises the 1920s neoclassical **Palacio Provincial,** the seat of local government.

REPARTO TIVOLI

The hilly 17th-century Tivoli district southwest of Parque Céspedes was first settled by French colonists from Saint Domingue and is full of sites associated with figures in the revolutionary pantheon.

Beginning at the park's southwest corner, follow Félix Pena south one block to Masó. Turn left. One block along, at the corner of Calle Corona, you'll pass the **Balcón de Velázquez** (daily 9am-9pm, free, cameras CUC1), a small plaza atop an old Spanish fort with views toward the harbor. On the next block south, **La Maqueta de la Ciudad** (Mariano Corona, e/ Masó y Duany, tel. 022/65-2095, Tues.-Sun. 9am-9pm, CUC1 including guide) displays a huge 3-D scale model of the city showing every building in detail and covering the entire bay from the Castillo del Morro. Various maps edify on the city's evolution, geography, and future development.

Continue west 100 meters to Calle Padre Pico. Turn left. The broad and much-photographed steps (popular for fashion and *quinceañera* shoots) are known as **La Escalanita.** Here, three members of the 26th of July Movement were killed on November 30, 1956, while attacking a nearby police

Museo Lucha Clandestina

station. To learn more, ascend the steps to the former station, now the **Museo Lucha Clandestina** (Jesús Rabi #1, tel. 022/62-4689, Tues.-Sun. 9am-5pm, CUC1, cameras CUC5), which tells the tale of Castro's 26th of July Movement (M-26-7). Fidel Castro lived across the street (Jesús Rabi #6) as a youth and, following the attack on Moncada, was imprisoned in the **Antiguo Carcel Provincial** (Aguilera #131), two blocks north.

Three blocks south of the museum is **La Casa de los Tradiciones** (Rabí #154, e/ Princesa y San Fernando, tel. 022/65-3892, daily 9am-midnight), an old wooden home and traditional music forum festooned with photos of famous musicians.

REPARTO LOS HOYOS

The neighborhood of Los Hoyos, north of Parque Céspedes, is known for its 18th-century churches: **Iglesia de Nuestra Señora del Carmen** (Félix Pena #505, esq. Tamayo Freites), noted for its statuary; **Iglesia de San Francisco** (Sagarra #121, esq. Mariana Corona), with its triple nave; austere **Iglesia de Santo Tomás** (Félix Pena #308, esq. General Portuondo); and **Iglesia de la Santísima Trinidad** (General Portuondo, esq. General Moncada), overlooking a tiny plaza dedicated to Guillermo Moncada (1840-1895), a Liberation Army general who was born nearby.

Avenida Sánchez Hechavarría, three blocks north of Parque Céspedes (between Hartmann and Valiente), is lined with houses used by revolutionaries during the effort to topple Batista; they're marked by bronze plaques. Here is the former home (1939-1959) of Vilma Espin, an M-26-7 member in the urban underground who later became a guerrilla fighter, married Raúl Castro, and led the Women's Federation of Cuba. Today it is **Museo Memorial Vilma Espín** (Hechavarría #473, e/ Porfirio Valiente y Pio Rosada, tel. 022/62-2295, Mon.-Sat. 9am-5pm, free), with six rooms dedicated to the life of this revolutionary heroine.

The **Museo Hermanos País** (Banderas #266, e/ General Portuondo y Habana, tel. 022/65-2710, Mon.-Sat. 9am-4:45pm, CUC1, cameras CUC5) is the birthplace of brothers Frank and José País, who headed the Santiago M-26-7 organization and were killed by Batista's police. The **Museo Casa Natal de Antonio Maceo** (Maceo #207, e/ Corona y Rastro, tel. 022/62-3750, Mon.-Sat. 9am-5pm, closed during rains, CUC1, cameras CUC5) occupies the birthplace of Antonio Maceo Grajales, the *mulato* general who rose to second in command of the Liberation Army during the War of Independence and, in the Protest of Baraguá, refused to accept the 1878 armistice.

THE WATERFRONT

Six blocks west, downhill from Parque Céspedes, is Avenida Jesús Menéndez, running along 1.5 kilometers of harbor waterfront. The boulevard is the main venue for the carnival parade in July. At its north end is **Fábrica de Ron Caney** (Av. Peralejo, e/ Gonzalo de Quesada y Padre Callejas). The oldest rum factory in Cuba, it was built in 1868 by the Bacardí family and nationalized in 1959, after which the Cuban government has continued to make rum (as Ron Santiago, Ron Caney, Ron Varadero, and Isla Tesoro) while Bacardí operates in Puerto Rico. It is not open to view, but you can sample the goods in the tasting room (Av. Peralejo #103, tel. 022/62-5575, Mon.-Sat. 9am-5pm, Sun. 9am-noon). The main rum factory of the Bacardí corporation is four blocks north, on Carretera Bacardí at the corner of Crombet.

To the south, the avenue divides around **Parque Alameda,** studded at its north end by a French Renaissance-style **clock tower** outside the cruise ship dock, and paralleling a lovely landscaped waterfront park, **Paseo Marítimo de la Alameda.**

REPARTO SUEÑO

This 19th-century district lies northeast of the old city and **Plaza de Marte**. The district is framed by Avenida Victoriano Garzón, Avenida de las Américas, and Avenida de los

The Attack on Moncada

At 5am on Sunday, July 26, 1953, Fidel Castro and 122 young followers sang the national anthem. Then, dressed in brown Cuban Army uniforms, they set out from Granjita Siboney crammed inside 16 cars, with Castro in the fifth car—a brand-new 1953 Buick sedan. The third car, containing Raúl (leading a second unit), took a wrong turn and arrived at its target—the Palace of Justice—after the fighting had begun. Another car had a flat tire and yet another car took a wrong turn, which reduced the fighting force to 105 men, who attacked Moncada with a few Winchester rifles, hunting shotguns, a single M-1 rifle, a single Browning submachine gun, and assorted sporting rifles.

Castro had concluded that the fort could be rushed through the southeastern gate. The commandos would then fan out through the barracks with newly seized weapons. At first, the attack went according to plan. The sentinels were taken by surprise and disarmed. As the commandos rushed into the barracks, an army patrol appeared. Gunfire erupted. The alarm bells were sounded. Then a volley of machine-gun fire sprayed the rebels, who were forced to retreat. The battle lasted less than 30 minutes. Only 8 rebels were killed in combat, but more than 60 others were caught and summarily tortured to death.

Batista's army, which lost 19 soldiers, claimed that Moncada was attacked by "between 400 and 500 men, equipped with the most modern instruments of war," and that Castro's men had been gunned down at Moncada. A photographer, however, managed to get photos of the tortured *fidelistas* (the film was smuggled out in journalist Marta Rojas's bra). The gruesome photos were printed, exposing Batista's lie and unleashing a wave of disgust.

Libertadores, a broad boulevard lined with bronze busts of revolutionary heroes.

In 2016, city fathers unveiled the **Fuente Coppelia La Arboleda** (Garzón, esq. Avenida de los Libertadores), a huge fountain with ponds and a pedestrian tunnel beneath an arcade of water jets. It faces the headquarters of the **Partido Comunista de Cuba,** adorned with visages of the Castro brothers.

Complejo Histórico Abel Santamaría

The **Complejo Histórico Abel Santamaría** (General Portuondo, esq. Av. de los Libertadores) features a huge granite cube carved with the faces of Abel Santamaría and José Martí. A fountain seems to hold the cube aloft. To its north, the **Museo Abel Santamaría** (tel. 022/62-4119, Mon.-Thurs. and Sun. 9am-5pm, Fri. 1pm-5pm, CUC1, cameras CUC5) occupies the former hospital where Abel Santamaría and 22 fellow rebels fired at the Moncada barracks on July 26, 1953, and where they were later captured, tortured, and killed. Here, too, Fidel Castro gave his famous "History Will Absolve Me"

speech while being judged by an emergency tribunal. Nine rooms house exhibits relating to the event and to the life of Abel Santamaría.

Immediately south is the 1940s **Palacio de Justicia,** still functioning as a courthouse. It was attacked by Raúl Castro's contingent during the assault on Moncada.

★ Cuartel Moncada

This former **military barracks** (General Portuondo, e/ Av. de los Libertadores y Carlos Aponte), with castellated walls and turrets, is renowned for the fateful day on July 26, 1953, when Fidel Castro and his poorly armed cohorts stormed the barracks. After the Revolution, Moncada was turned into a school, the Ciudad Escolar 26 de Julio. A portion of the building near the entrance gate is riddled with bullet holes. They're not the originals; Batista's troops filled those in. Castro had the holes redone using photographs. This section houses the **Museo Histórico 26 de Julio** (tel. 022/66-1157, Tues.-Sat. 9am-4:30pm, Sun. 9am-12:30pm, entrance CUC2, cameras CUC5), which tells the tale of the attack and subsequent revolutionary history. Weaponry displayed includes Castro's rifle.

Plaza de la Revolución

This vast plaza at the junction of Avenida de las Américas and Avenida de los Libertadores is dominated by the massive **Monumento Antonio Maceo,** dedicated to the homegrown son of a local merchant who rose to become the hero-general of the War of Independence as second-in-command of the rebel forces. Maceo was nicknamed the "Bronze Titan"—a sobriquet referring to both his bravery and skin color. Appropriately, the mammoth statue of the general on a rearing horse is cast in bronze. On the north side, an eternal flame flickers in a marble-lined bowl cut into the base by the entrance to the **Sala Deposición Holografía** (tel. 022/64-3053, Mon.-Sat. 8am-4pm, free), with holograms telling of Maceo's life and of the War of Independence.

The **Teatro Heredia** on the plaza's east side is fronted by a giant steel mural of revolutionary *comandante* Juan Almeida Bosque (1927-2009).

REPARTO VISTA ALEGRE

This leafy, formerly upscale residential district is bounded on the west by Avenida de las Américas and on the south by Avenida Pujol (Carretera Siboney). Avenida Manduley runs east-west through the center of Vista Alegre and is lined with the once sumptuous villas of Santiago's long-departed upper class.

The **Museo de la Imagen** (Calle 8 #106, esq. 5, tel. 022/64-2234, Mon.-Fri. 9am-5pm, Sat.-Sun. 2pm-5pm, CUC1) was established by cameraman Bernabé Muñiz, who filmed Fulgencio Batista's coup d'état in 1952, the surrender of the Moncada barracks to the revolutionaries in 1959, and Fidel's victory parade from Santiago to Havana. The museum features almost 500 photographic, film, and TV cameras—from CIA espionage cameras to a stereoscopic viewfinder from 1872—plus a library of feature films and documentaries dating back to 1926.

Parque Histórico Loma de San Juan

Teddy Roosevelt and his Rough Riders defeated the Spanish at **San Juan Hill** (although there was no cavalry charge, as popularly believed), which rises on the south side of Avenida Pujol (esq. Calle 13) to a palm-shaded

Cuartel Moncada

A Walk Through Vista Alegre

making pottery at Casa de la Cerámica

Begin at the Hotel Meliá Santiago, on Avenida de las Américas. Kitty-corner, on the east side of the boulevard, the **Bosque de los Mártires de Bolivia** (esq. Calle 2) features bas-relief tableaux of Che Guevara and the band of revolutionaries who died in Bolivia. The **Galería de Arte Universal** (Calle 1, esq. M, tel. 022/64-1198, Mon.-Sat. 9am-5pm), on the east side of the park, is worth a peek before continuing south along Calle 1 three blocks to Avenida Manduley, where facing you is **La Maison** (Manduley #52, esq. Calle 1), a mansion that hosts a nightly fashion show.

Eastward, on the next block, you'll pass the **Casa Cultura Africana Fernando Ortíz** (Manduley, esq. Calle 5, tel. 022/66-7129, Tues.-Sun. 8am-5pm, free), displaying artifacts from Africa. On the next block, stop in at **Casa de la Cerámica** (Manduley #102, e/ 3 y 5, tel. 022/66-7211) to watch beautiful pots, vases, and plates being handcrafted for sale. Three blocks farther along Manduley brings you to **Casa de José "Pepín" Bosch** (esq. Calle 11), a grand neobaroque mansion (circa 1910) and the former home of the head of the Bacardi rum empire. It's now the **Palacio Provincial de Pioneros** (Young Pioneers' School), with a Soviet MiG fighter jet in the playground. Cross Manduley and walk uphill one block to **Iglesia Sagrado Familia** (Calle 11, e/ 4 y 6, open for mass only, Mon. and Fri. at 5pm and Sun. at 10:30am), a Gothic-style Catholic church built in 1898 with fine stained glass.

Continue along Manduley to Calle 11 and **Galería René Váldes Cedeño** (Av. Manduley #304 e/ 11 y 13, tel. 022/66-8238, www.caguayo.co.cu, Tues., Fri., and Sun. 10am-5pm, Sat. 10am-noon), a stunning contemporary art venue with a café.

Now turn right onto Calle 11. One block away, at the corner of Calle 8, is the **Casa del Caribe** (Calle 13 #154, tel. 022/64-3609, Mon.-Sat. 8am-5pm), with exhibits honoring Caribbean cultures. One block south, the **Museo de las Religiones Populares** (Calle 13 #206, e/ 8 y 10, tel. 022/64-2285, ext. 114, daily 9am-5:30pm, CUC1 entrance, CUC1 guide) is dedicated to the Santería religion and related Afro-Cuban sects; it hosts musical *peñas* in the patio.

park containing a replica fort, plus monuments and cannons, including a Tomb of the Unknown Mambí, Cuba's independence fighters. One memorial is dedicated to "the generous American soldiers who sealed a covenant of liberty and fraternity between the two nations." The Cuban liberationists who helped storm the hill weren't even invited to the surrender ceremony on July 16, 1898, beneath a huge ceiba tree. The **Monumento Arbol de Paz,** in its own little park off Avenida Pujol 100 meters west of San Juan Hill, occupies the site of the original "peace tree." Cannons and howitzers surround giant bronze plaques (shaped as open books) inscribed with the names of all the U.S. and Cuban soldiers killed in the war.

SUBURBS
Jardín de los Helechos

For an escape from the frenetic bustle, head to the **Jardín de los Helechos** (Carretera de la Caney #129, tel. 022/64-8335, manolito@ bioeco.siess.info.cu, Mon.-Sat. 9am-5pm, Sun. 9am-noon, CUC1), a fern garden in the colonial village of Caney, three kilometers northeast of Reparto Vista Alegre. What began as a private collection in the mansion of Manuel "Manolito" Caloff now boasts more than 360 fern species plus orchids and about 1,000 other plant species divided into zones and specialties, such as miniatures and medicinal plants. It's best visited in winter, when the orchid blooms are profuse. Take bus #5 from Plaza de Marte.

★ Parque Histórico El Morro

A UNESCO World Heritage Site, the **Castillo de San Pedro del Morro** (tel. 022/69-1569, daily 8:30am-7:30pm, entrance CUC4, cameras CUC5) is an enormous piece of military architecture poised atop the cliffs at the entrance to Santiago Bay, about 14 kilometers south of the city. Begun in 1638, the castle was rebuilt in 1664 after Henry Morgan's pirates reduced it to rubble. Cannons are everywhere, and the views from the battlements are spectacular. Exhibits in the **Museo de Piratería**

include old muskets, cutlasses, and more. A *cañonazo* ceremony is usually held at 6pm (CUC4), when soldiers in period costume put a torch to a cannon in a time-honored tradition that once announced the nightly sealing of the harbor.

The cliff is pinned by the **Faro del Morro,** a lighthouse built in 1920 and still using the original hand-wound Fresnel lens. Part of the adjoining military complex, it's off-limits to visitors.

Do call in at the clifftop **Restaurante El Morro** (tel. 022/69-1576, daily noon-10pm), where the excellent *criolla* dishes are accented by fabulous views. Hopefully there'll be space between the tour groups.

Bus #212 runs from downtown to Embarcadero Cayo Granma, from where you can hike up to the castle (20 minutes). If driving, follow Avenida 12 de Agosto south from Plaza de Marte; this leads to Carretera del Morro. Alternatively, you can drive the Carretera Turística, which begins at the southern end of Avenida Jesús Menéndez, following the bay shore to emerge atop the cliffs by the castle. En route, you'll pass **Punta Gorda,** a slender peninsula once fashionable with Santiago's upper class. A large statue of revolutionary hero Frank País looms over the point overlooking Marina Marlin.

Cayo Granma

This small island sits in the bay offshore of Punta Gorda. Its down-at-heels fishing colony looks and feels as if it has been magically transferred from the Mediterranean, with its rowboats berthed beneath the eaves of waterfront houses. A trail circles the isle, and narrow streets lead up to a hilltop church, **Iglesia de San Rafael.** The state-run **Restaurante El Cayo** (tel. 022/69-7109, daily noon-5pm), on the east side of the cay, serves seafood and *criolla* dishes, as does *paladar* **Restaurante Nuevo Paraíso** (tel. 022/69-7104, daily 9am-9pm), on the west side.

A passenger ferry (20 centavos) serves the cay four times daily from Embarcadero Cayo Granma and continues to **Playa Socapa,** a

Santiago de Cuba Outskirts

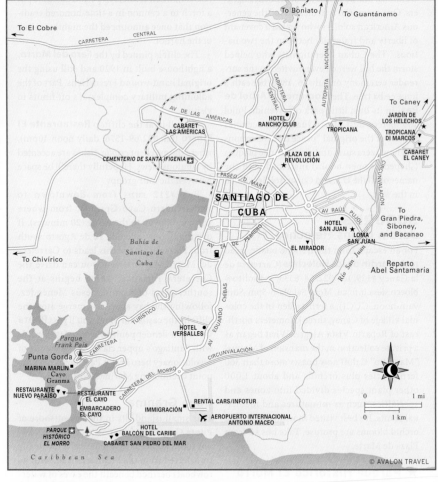

beach with a cannon battery on the headland facing El Morro. An excursion boat runs from Marina Marlin (daily 8:30am-4:30pm, CUC3).

★ Cementerio de Santa Ifigenia

This grandiose **cemetery** (Calzada Crombet, tel. 022/63-3522, 6am-5pm, entrance CUC1, cameras CUC1, videos CUC5) is the final resting place of key figures in Cuban history, among them Carlos Manuel Céspedes, rum

magnate, mayor, and revolutionary Emilio Bacardí, Cuba's first president Tomás Estrada Palma, and homegrown M-26-7 leader Frank País. Also interred are heroes of the attack on the Moncada barracks (look for the red and black flags on their graves), 11 of the 31 generals of the War of Independence (who are entombed in a tiny castle), and singer Compay Segundo (of Buena Vista Social Club fame). The grand gateway is dedicated to Cuban soldiers who died fighting in Angola.

The main draw is the **Mausoleo de Martí,** the tomb of national hero José Martí, beneath a crenellated hexagonal tower (each side represents one of the six original provinces of Cuba). Marble steps lead down to a circular mausoleum, designed so that the sun would always shine on Martí's coffin, draped with the Cuban flag. Military guards stand duty 24/7 and change shifts with a goose-stepping march every 30 minutes. Don't miss it.

On the north side of Martí's mausoleum, and directly in front of the pink marble Panteón de los Mártires del 26 de Julio (aka Retablo de los Héroes, or Heroes Altarpiece), is the **memorial of Fidel Castro.** On December 4, 2016, the ashes of Fidel Castro were interred within a boulder bearing a simple bronze plaque that reads *Fidel.* The rear tableau, the Panteón de los Caidos de la Insurgencia (Pantheon of the Fallen of the Insurgency), contains 180 niches inset in limestone. Each has a plaque naming an insurgent, some of whom are still living.

The three-kilometer **Avenida de la Patria** links the graveyard to Plaza de la Revolución. To get here, you'll pass **Fuerte de Yarayó** (Carretera Bacardí, esq. Paseo de Martí), a small fort built in the late 19th century.

ENTERTAINMENT AND EVENTS

The **Sala Juegos,** at Hotel San Juan (Av. Siboney y Calle 13), has two miniature bowling lanes plus pool tables.

Nightlife

BARS

The **Hotel Casa Granda** (Heredia #201, esq. General Lacret) is ground zero for a chilled beer; the rooftop terrace bar competes with sensational views.

Serving sophisticates, the **Pico Real** lobby bar in the Hotel Meliá Santiago (Av. de las Américas, esq. M, daily 6pm-2am) is a relaxing spot to enjoy cocktails while a pianist tickles the ivories or a live jazz or traditional music *conjunto* performs. For city views, take the elevator to the hotel's top-floor **Bello Bar** (daily 6pm-2am, CUC5 including one drink; hotel guests free), which hosts live music at times.

A shot of quality rum costs a mere CUC1 at the **Bar El Traguito** (Pío Rosado, e/ San Basilio y Santa Lucía, tel. 022/64-1705, Tues.-Fri. noon-midnight, Sat.-Sun. 2pm-2am), a simple *bodega*-style bar beneath the Museo del Ron. Cuba's own *peso*-conscious sudsters sup at **Taberna Bucanero** (Hartmann, esq.

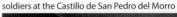

soldiers at the Castillo de San Pedro del Morro

Aguilera, daily 10am-11:45pm), serving draft Bucanero by the glass (CUC0.75) or 10-glass ice-core dispenser (CUC7.50).

In 2015 the government converted a former tobacco factory into the **Cervecería Puerto del Rey** (Av. Jesús Menéndez esq. Aduana), a stylish microbrewery perfect for chilling over a delicious artisanal beer (CUC2). It also serves *criolla* fare, while *troubadors* add to the merriment.

TRADITIONAL MUSIC AND DANCE

Don't miss Santiago's **Casa de la Trova** (Heredia #208, tel. 022/65-2689, noon-1am, CUC1 by day, CUC5 at night), the island's original and most famous "house of *trova*." The *trova* tradition of romantic ballads was born here, and famous Cuban musicians perform. Nearby, **Patio de Artex** (Heredia #304, tel. 022/65-4814, daily 11am-1pm, 4pm-7pm, and 9:30pm-2am, CUC2) packs in a younger crowd for traditional music performed live. Even livelier, earthy **La Casa de los Tradiciones** (Rabí #154, e/ Princesa y San Fernando, tel. 022/65-3892, Mon.-Fri. 6pm-midnight, Sat.-Sun. 4pm-midnight) is an old wooden home where even the beer bottles get up and dance. **Bar Sindo Garay** (Tamayo Fleites, esq. General Lacret, daily 11am-11pm),

named for serenader Antonio Gumesindo Garay (1867-1968), serves live *trova* and a house cocktail of *aguardiente* (cheap rum) with lime and coffee liqueur. The **Museo de Ambiente Histórico Cubano** (Félix Pena #602, tel. 022/65-2652) hosts traditional music and other cultural activities.

The following Afro-Cuban *comparsas* (folkloric associations) host workshops and rehearsals that keep alive African-derived music and dance traditions: **Tumba Francesa "La Caridad del Oriente"** (Pío Rosado #268, e/ Los Maseo y Sao del Indio, no tel., Tues. and Fri. at 9pm), which maintains French-Haitian traditions; **Foco Cultural El Tivoli** (Desiderio Mesnier #208, tel. 022/62-0142, Mon., Wed., and Fri. at 8:30pm, Sun. at 2pm); and **Ballet Folklórico Cutumba** (Teatro Galaxia, Av. 24 de Febrero, esq. Av. Valeriano Hierrezuelo, tel. 022/62-5173, Tues.-Fri. 9am-1pm).

Cuba's diverse ethnic heritages are synthesized in performances by **Compañia Danzaría Foklórica Kokoyé** (Calle 13 #154, tel. 022/64-3609, Sat. afternoon, Sun. evening) at Casa del Caribe, and by the more contemporary **Ballet Folklórico de Oriente** (tel. 022/64-4049), in the Teatro Heredia.

Hotel Casa Granda

CABARETS AND NIGHTCLUBS

Second only to Havana's own emporium of glitz, the open-air **Tropicana** (Autopista Nacional, Km 1.5, tel. 022/68-7020, Mon.-Sat. 10pm high season, Sat. only low season, CUC20), four kilometers northeast of town, hosts a colorful show tracing Caribbean history and culture. This is saucy Las Vegas-style *cabaret espectáculo* at its best.

If you don't mind the eight-kilometer trek south of town, the gay-friendly **Cabaret San Pedro del Mar** (Carretera del Morro Km 7.5, tel. 022/69-2373, Sat.-Wed. 10pm-2am, CUC5), near El Morro castle, features a small *espectáculo* that precedes a disco. The colonial-themed **Santiago Café** (Sat. 10pm-2am low season, nightly high season, CUC5), in the Hotel Meliá Santiago (Av. de las Américas, esq. M), features a small cabaret followed by disco. **La Maison** (Manduley #52, tel. 022/64-0108, daily at 10:30pm, CUC5 including one drink) offers an alfresco fashion show followed by a cabaret.

Jazz fans are served by the suave **Iris Jazz Club** (Paraíso e/ Saco y Aguilera, off Plaza de Marte, tel. 022/62-7312, Tues.-Sun. 9pm-2am, CUC3), which hits all the right notes with performances by top musicians.

Salsa fans fire up the dance floor at **Casa de la Música** (Corona #564 e/ Aguilera y Heredia, tel. 022/65-2227, 10pm-3am, CUC3-5).

The Arts

The modern **Teatro Heredia** (Av. de las Américas, esq. Av. de los Desfiles, tel. 022/64-3190, box office 9am-4pm), by the Plaza de la Revolución, hosts performances from classical to rock and theater. The **Plaza Cultural Aguilera** (Saco, esq. Reloj, tel. 022/62-6130) hosts programs from *trova* to orchestral music and children's performances (Fri.-Sun. 8:30pm).

Festivals and Events

Every Saturday night, beer and food stalls set up along Calle Saco for **Noche Santiaguera,** when a cacophony of music draws **the city's youth**. On Friday and Saturday night, local youth gather at **Área Cubanacán** (Avenida de las Américas) to hear live bands and watch big-screen music videos. The spiritual heartland of Cuba's music traditions, Santiago abounds with festivals, kicked off in June with the quasi-religious **Festival de San Juan**, which *santiagueros* turn into an excuse for mini-carnivals of conga and general partying.

Making its debut in 2016 was **Manana**

Tumba Francesa

Carnaval!

Carnaval has been held in Santiago de Cuba since the 19th century, when it was an Easter celebration. Originally it was called the Fiesta de las Mamarrachos (Festival of the Nincompoops), when slaves were given time to release their pent-up energies and frustrations in a celebration full of sexual content. The celebration was bound irrevocably to the secret societies of ancient Africa, transformed in Cuba into neighborhood societies called *carabalí* that vied with one another to produce the most elaborate processions (*comparsas*).

Today the hourglass drums of the ancestors pound out their *tun q'tu q'tu q'tun* rhythm. The wail of Chinese cornets adds to the racket. And young and old alike rush to join the conga lines full of clowns and celebrants in colonial period dress. The conga lines are followed by floats graced by girls (*luceros*—morning stars) in riotous feathers and sequined bikinis or outrageous dresses. Huge papier-mâché heads supported by dancing Cubans bash into each other. There are representations of the *orishas* in the *comparsas*, and characters representing the various gods lead the way. Every year there's a different theme, and contestants are judged on originality and popularity.

For further information, contact **Casa del Caribe** (tel. 022/64-3609, www.casadelcaribe. cult.cu).

(www.mananacuba.com), a three-day festival of electronica fused with hip-hop and Afro-Cuban rhythms.

The big enchilada is the weeklong, slightly licentious **Carnaval** (Fiesta del Caribe) in late July, when everyone in town gets caught up in the street rumbas and conga lines. The main parade takes place along Avenida Jesús Menéndez, but impromptu parties happen around town. The **Fiesta del Caribe** (aka Fiesta del Fuego, www.casadelcaribe.cult.cu) warms things up in early July with nine days of *comparsas*, parades, and eclectic cultural events.

Every odd November/December, lovers of choral music head to town for the **Festival Internacional de Coros.** Santiago de Cuba has three professional choirs.

The local baseball team, **Las Avispas** (the Wasps), plays at **Estadio Guillermo Moncada** (Av. de las Américas y Calle E, tel. 022/64-2640, CUC1) October-April.

SHOPPING

For fine art head to **Galería de Arte UNEAC** (Heredia, e/ Hartmann y Pio Rosada, tel. 022/65-3465, ext. 106); **Taller Aguilera** (Calle 6 #211, esq. 9, Vista Alegre, tel. 022/64-1817 or 5368-7678), where sibling artists Carlos and Josefina Aguilera and their father José display sensational works; or **Galería René Váldes Cedeño** (Av. Manduley #304 e/ 11 y 13, tel. 022/66-8238, www.caguayo.co.cu, Tues., Fri., and Sun. 10am-5pm, Sat. 10am-noon), representing works by several top artists from Oriente.

The tasting room adjoining **Fábrica de Ron Caney** (Av. Peralejo #103, tel. 022/62-5575, daily 9am-5pm) sells a wide range of national rums, including rare 25-year-old Ron Paticruzado. It is also well stocked with cigars, as are the **Casa del Habano** (Aguilera, esq. Jesús Menéndez, tel. 022/65-4207, Mon.-Sat. 9am-5pm, Sun. 9pm-noon) and **Casa del Tabaco** (daily 8am-8pm) in the Hotel Meliá Santiago (Av. de las Américas, esq. M).

For a genuine hand-embroidered blouse or *guayabera,* head to **El Quitrín** (Hechavarría #477, e/ Porfirio Valiente y Pío Rosada, tel. 022/62-2528, Mon.-Fri. 8:30am-4pm). **La Casa de los Abanicos** (Heredia, esq. Pio Rosada, Mon.-Sat. 9:20am-5:20pm) sells handmade fans from CUC5. For music CDs, check out **Discoteca Egrem** (Saco #309, e/ Lacret y Hartmann, tel. 022/62-7611, Mon.-Sat. 10am-6pm), specializing in recordings by local maestros.

FOOD
Paladares

Santiago's private restaurant scene has been slow to take off; pickings remained slim at last visit. The standout newcomer is ★ **St. Pauli** (Saco #605, e/ Barnada y Paraíso, tel. 022/65-2292, daily noon-midnight), tucked up a narrow, mural-lined corridor a stone's throw west of Plaza Marte. The menu holds few surprises, but the preparation and seasoning are spot on. You can't go wrong with *ropa vieja,* lobster thermidor (CUC18), and a divine garlic octopus (CUC12). The decor includes a glass roof.

Although gloomily lacking light, **Bendita Farándula** (Bernada #513, e/ Aguilera y Heredia, tel. 022/65-3739, daily noon-11pm) makes up with flavorful *criolla* staples (shrimp in garlic tomato sauce), including the occasional twist (fish in coconut milk), and delicious homemade lemonade. Its brick walls are scrawled with customers' doodles.

The vine-draped rooftop terrace at ★ **Roy's Terrace Inn** (Diego Palacios #177, e/ Padre Pico y Mariana Corona, tel. 022/62-0522, www.facebook.com/pg/roysterraceinn, CUC25) is a romantic venue for delicious down-home Cuban fare. Reserve early; there are just five tables.

One of the city's original *paladares,*

Paladar Salón Tropical (Fernández Marcané #310, e/ 9 y 10, tel. 022/64-1161, daily noon-midnight) is located up a steep, narrow metal staircase. It offers rooftop dining beneath an arbor or a romantic cross-ventilated room with stained glass windows. The menu ranges from pizza (CUC4) to fricasseed lamb (CUC8). Next door, ★ **Paladar La Canasta** (Fernández Marcané #51, e/ 9 y 10, tel. 022/64-2964, daily noon-midnight) is run by former Cuban basketball star and coach Alejandro Castañeira Rivero, who has themed the garden restaurant accordingly. You even get to shoot a hoop as you enter! It offers excellent *criolla* fare.

In the *casco histórico,* you're served filling plates of tasty *criolla* fare at **El Holandes** (Heredia #251, esq. Hartman, tel. 022/62-4878, Raquel.halley2012@yahoo.es, daily noon-midnight).

In Reparto Hoyo, **Rumba Café** (San Félix #455A, e/ San Francisco y San Gerónimo, tel. 5802-2153, Mon.-Thurs. 9:30am-9pm, Fri.-Sat. 9:30am-10pm) is a café-lounge run by a Cuban-Italian couple, Vilma and Fabio, and offering European sophistication (think world music on the sound system). The kitchen conjures up salads, tapas, fruit tarts, and various

Paladar La Canasta

coffees, enjoyed in the lounge or under an arbor in the patio with poured-concrete sofas.

Opened in late 2016, **Setos Cuba** (Av. Manduley #154, e/ 5 y 7, tel. 022/66-7256 or 5355-2204, daily 11:30am-11:30pm) appeals for its fantastic setting: a restored high-ceilinged centenary mansion with patio dining. The menu features experimental dishes by Santiago standards, including ceviche and octopus risotto.

State Restaurants

El Barracón (Av. Garzón, esq. Prudencio Martínez, tel. 022/66-1877, daily noon-11pm) plays up the runaway slave theme with life-size models, medieval-style tables and chairs, wrought-iron lanterns, and a pork-focused menu (CUC5-10).

Despite its ritzy elegance and exceptional cuisine at reasonable prices, not many folks dine at **Restaurant La Isabelica** (tel. 022/68-7070, daily 7pm-11pm), in the Hotel Meliá Santiago (Av. de las Américas, esq. M). I savored a pumpkin curried soup (CUC3) and jumbo shrimp flambéed with rum (CUC16), plus profiteroles (CUC3). The Hotel Meliá Santiago's open-air ★ **Restaurant La Fontana** (daily noon-11pm) is a hit for its Italian dishes, including tasty pizza, plus continental dishes such as fish fillet with capers in white wine sauce (CUC12).

Restaurant Zunzún (Av. Manduley #159, tel. 022/64-1528, daily noon-10pm), in a mansion in Vista Alegre, has a varied menu ranging from *tapas* (CUC2) to lobster enchiladas (CUC25).

Cafés and Desserts

After exploring the frenetic streets, revive at **Café de Té** (Calle Aguilera, esq. General Lacret, tel. 022/65-8067, daily 9:15am-8:45pm), which sells herbal and flavored teas, plus coffee drinks. It hosts *boleros* and traditional music on Saturday at 6pm.

Freshly baked goodies are sold at **Doña Neli** (no tel., Mon.-Sat. 7am-7pm and Sun. 7am-2pm), on the southwest corner of Plaza de Marte. And *do* treat yourself to artisanal chocolates made on-site at **Chocolatería Fraternidad** (Mon.-Fri. 9:15am-9:15pm, Sat.-Sun. 10am-10pm), on Parque de Marte's southeast corner.

For ice cream, head to ★ **Coppelía La Arboleda** (Av. de los Libertadores, esq. Av. Garzón, tel. 022/62-0435, Tues.-Sun. 9am-11pm), a temple of delight with numerous sales points and outdoor patios to speed along the lines. This workers' cooperative competes with **Jardín de las Enramadas** (Calle Jagüey, e/ Peralejo y 10 de Octubre, Tue.-Fri. 9am-10:45pm, Sat.-Sun. 9am-11:45pm), where you slurp ice cream amid a garden full of ornamental plants.

Self-Catering

You can buy fresh produce and meats at the *mercado agropecuario* (Aguilera and Padre Pico, Mon.-Sat. 6am-5pm) and the squeaky-clean **El Avileño** market (Saco e/ Félix Pena y General Lacret, Tues.-Sat. 8am-noon and 4pm-7pm, Sun. 8am-noon).

ACCOMMODATIONS
Casas Particulares
DOWNTOWN

Stuffed with antiques and Santería icons, and justifiably popular, ★ **Casa Colonial Maruchi** (San Félix #357, e/ Trinidad y San Germán, tel. 022/62-0767 or 5261-3791, maruchib@yahoo.es, CUC25-30) is named for owner Maruchi Berbes, an expert on Afro-Cuban culture. Downstairs, her beautiful colonial house has two rooms (one with a brass bed) with en suite hot-water bathrooms; upstairs, an apartment has its own terrace. Maruchi serves delicious meals on a lush patio, and hosts dance and drumming classes.

Exuding charm, **Casa de Yuliett Ramos** (San Basilio #513, e/ Clarin y Reloj, tel. 022/62-0546, CUC15-25) is endearingly decorated with stone walls and wood paneling. One of the three rooms opens to a patio balcony; another has a quaint sundeck. Yuliett, her spouse, and three kids are super friendly. Canadian tour operator Kate Daley and her Cuban husband, Abel, run ★ **Hostal**

Atardecer (Jagüey #164, e/ Padre Pico y Corona, tel. 022/65-9320, www.realcubaonline.com, CUC25), on a steep street one block from the main square. It's a neocolonial home with massive doors, wide verandas with railings, a high ceiling, period furniture, and a patio plus roof terrace with fabulous view. The house has two large air-conditioned bedrooms with private bathrooms. Kate's gourmet meals are reason enough to stay here and include vegetarian and nonobservant kosher. Kate offers discounts for long-term stays and volunteers, plus special-interest tours of the region.

Steps from Parque Céspedes, ★ Roy's Terrace Inn (Diego Palacios #177, e/ Padre Pico y Mariana Corona, tel. 022/62-0522, www.facebook.com/pg/roysterraceinn, CUC25) is named for its vine-draped rooftop terrace—which doubles as a *paladar*—with views over Tivoli. Multilingual owner Roy Pérez once worked on cruise ships (as do many Cubans) and has brought his service-oriented savvy to bear. Choose from three themed rooms (sea, Santería, and mythology), each lovingly furnished and with modern bathroom.

REPARTO SUEÑO

I feel like adopted family at Casa de Florinda Chaviano Martínez (Calle I #58, e/ 2da y 3ra, tel. 022/66-3660, CUC25), a home away from home. Liberal and attentive hosts Florinda and Jorge rent a single, well-lit room with modern hot-water bathroom. A handsome patio with grapevine arbor proves perfect for enjoying breakfast. Florinda can call around to several dozen neighbors, who also rent rooms.

REPARTOS VISTA ALEGRE AND TERRAZA

These leafy residential suburbs offer some of the nicest middle-class houses in town. One of my favorites is *Casa Particular Esmeralda González* (Av. Pujol #107, esq. 5ta, tel. 022/64-6341, rachelbarreiro@yahoo.es, CUC20-25), where Esmeralda rents a spacious, well-lit, cross-ventilated room with

fans, kitchenette, TV, independent entrance, marvelous period bathroom, and parking. Another is ★ *Casa Particular Juan Matos Palaez* (Calle Bitirí #102, esq. Taíno, tel. 022/64-1427, cmatos@eccs.ciges.inf.cu, CUC25-30), a beautiful 1950s-style home with two nicely furnished rooms with exquisite tiled hot-water bathrooms, plus huge patios to the front and rear.

Hotels

UNDER CUC50

The Oficina del Conservador de la Ciudad (City Conservationist's Office, Av. Rafael Manduley #203 e/ 7 y 9, Vista Alegre, tel. 022/64-9690) has opened four small *hostals* in refurbished villas in Vista Alegre. All cost CUC18 s, CUC22 d, or CUC20 s, CUC25 d with breakfast. A three-night minimum is required.

CUC50-100

Islazul's Hotel Libertad (Aguilera #658, tel. 022/62-1589, www.islazul.cu, CUC30 s, CUC42 d low season, CUC48 s, CUC66 d high season, including breakfast), on the south side of Plaza de Marte, has a classical motif and exquisite tilework and hardwoods throughout. It offers 42 smallish but amply furnished rooms with small modern bathrooms. It has a lobby bar and an elegant restaurant and a thumping disco.

In a residential district away from the city clamor, Villa Gaviota (Manduley #502, e/ 19 y 21, tel. 022/64-1370, jefe.recepcion@gaviota.co.cu, from CUC25 s, CUC35 d low season, from CUC29 s, CUC40 d high season), in Vista Alegre, features 46 modestly furnished bargain-priced villas and offers good value. It has a swimming pool and disco.

A stone's throw from Parque Céspedes, Cubanacán's almost boutique Hotel E San Basilio (San Basilio #403, e/ Calvario y Carnicería, tel. 022/65-1702, www.cubanacan.cu, CUC65 s, CUC95 d year-round) has conjured a former colonial mansion into a delightful eight-room hotel. Rooms are regally decorated and have beautiful modern bathrooms. It has a small restaurant and 24-hour lobby bar.

South of the city, Cubanacán's 72-room hillside **Hotel Versalles** (Alturas de Versalles, Km 1.6, Carretera del Morro, tel. 022/69-1016, www.cubanacan.cu, from CUC50 s, CUC72 d low season, CU58 s, CUC80 d high season) is striking for its stylish contemporary furnishings, lovely bathrooms, and large balconies with city views. Its pool deck is a great place to lounge, but can be crowded on weekends.

Popular with tour groups, **Hotel San Juan** (Av. Siboney y Calle 13, tel. 022/68-7200, www.islazul.cu, CUC40 s, CUC72 d low season, CUC55 s, CUC90 d high season, including breakfast), on San Juan Hill, has 110 modestly furnished rooms in villa-style blocks—take an upstairs room with a lofty ceiling to help dissipate the heat. Facilities include a swimming pool and nightclub, but you're a long way from the center and the restaurant disappoints. Islazul's similarly priced Soviet-style, 70-room **Hotel Las Américas** (Av. de las Américas y General Cebreco, tel. 022/64-2011), is uninspired, but is closer to the center.

Used in 1953 as a base for the assault on the Moncada barracks, the ★ **Hotel Rex** (Av. Garzón #10, tel. 022/68-7092, www.islazul.cu, CUC45 s, CUC60 d year-round, including breakfast), just off traffic-thronged Plaza de Marte, has been resurrected as a 24-room hotel with unusually contemporary styling. A highlight is its snazzy restaurant and bar.

In 2016 the once majestic **Hotel E Imperial** (Saco #251, e/ General Lacret y Félix Peña, tel. 022/65-3021, www.cubanacan.cu, CUC50 s, CUC70 s low season, CUC68 s, CUC98 d high season) regained its stature after years of abandonment. Beautifully restored, it combines yesteryear elegance with 39 chic 21st-century guest rooms. Don't miss the views from the rooftop terrace bar.

CUC100-150

Santiago's grand dame, the **Hotel Casa Granda** (Heredia #201, esq. General Lacret, tel. 022/65-3021, www.cubanacan.cu, CUC60 s, CUC95 d low season, CUC85 s, CUC120 d high season) retains much of the airs that novelist Graham Greene described when he stayed here and penned *Our Man in Havana*. There's nothing exceptional here, although Edwardian furnishings appeal, and you can't beat the location and the rooftop restaurant-bar for the views.

Setting the gold standard is Cubanacán's ★ **Hotel Meliá Santiago** (Av. de las Américas, esq. M, tel. 022/68-7070, www.meliacuba.com, from CUC198 s, CUC215 d year-round), a 15-story modernist structure with 270 rooms, 30 junior suites, and 3 suites (with free wireless Internet), all with contemporary furniture. It has heaps of facilities, including restaurants, a sauna, gym, swimming pool, business center, and nightclub.

INFORMATION AND SERVICES

There's an **Infotur** booth in the airport car park (tel. 022/69-2099) and another on the northwest corner of **Parque Céspedes** (Aguilera, esq. Felix Peña, tel. 022/669401, daily 8am-5pm low season, daily 8am-7pm high season). Alternatively, try **Cubatur** (Heredia, esq. General Lacret, tel. 022/68-6033, and Garzón e/ 3ra y 4t).

Inmigración (Aguilera, esq. 5ta, Rpto. Santa Barbara, tel. 022/68-7135) handles visa issues. No shorts are allowed.

You can exchange foreign currency at **Cadeca** (Aguilera #456, e/ Reloj y Calvario; in Hotel Meliá Santiago, Av. de las Américas y M, tel. 022/68-7182, daily 7:30am-7:30pm; and Hotel Las Américas, Av. de las Américas y Garazón) and **Banco Financiero Internacional** (on Félix Pena one block north of Parque Céspedes; on Saco, at the corner of Porfirio Valiente; and on Avenida de las Américas, esq. J).

The **post office** (Aguilera #310, esq. Padre Quiroga) adjoins **DHL** (tel. 022/68-6323 or 022/65-4750). **Etecsa** (Freites, esq. Hartmann, tel. 022/65-7524, and Heredia, e/ Félix Pena y General Lacret, tel. 022/65-7524, daily 8:30am-7:30pm), on the south side of Parque Céspedes, and the **Centro de Negocios** (Alameda e/ Jagüey y Saco, tel. 022/68-7135) have international telephone and Internet service. Public Wi-Fi zones include Parque Céspedes, Plaza de Marte, Parque Maritimo la Alameda, and, in Vista Alegre, Galería René Váldes Cedeño (Av. Manduley #304 e/ 11 y 13).

The **Clínica Internacional** (Av. Raúl Pujol, esq. Calle 8, tel. 022/64-2589, 24 hours) charges CUC25 per consultation, or CUC30 between 4pm and 7am and for hotel visits. The clinic has a modestly stocked pharmacy, as does that in Hotel Meliá Santiago (Av. de las Américas, esq. M, tel. 22/6807070, daily 8am-6pm).

Asistur (Calle 4, esq. 7, Rpto. Vista Alegre, tel. 022/68-7259, asisturstago@enet.cu, Mon.-Sat. 9am-5pm) provides emergency assistance for medical and insurance issues. The **Consultoría Jurídica Internacional** (Calle 8 #54, e/ 1 y 3, Rpto. Vista Alegre, tel. 022/64-4546) provides legal services.

GETTING THERE AND AWAY
Air
Aeropuerto Internacional Antonio Maceo (tel. 022/69-8612 or 022/69-1053), off Carretera del Morro, is eight kilometers south of Santiago. Buses #212 and #213 (via Punta Gorda) operate between the airport and Avenida de los Libertadores, downtown. A taxi costs about CUC12 one-way. The departure lounge has Wi-Fi.

Cubana (Saco, esq. San Pedro, tel. 022/65-1577, airport tel. 022/69-1214) serves Santiago from Europe, plus daily from Varadero, Camagüey, and Baracoa, and thrice daily from Havana. From the United States, **Silver Airways** (tel. 801/401-9100, www.silverairways.com) has daily scheduled service from Fort Lauderdale.

Bus
Víazul buses (tel. 022/62-8484, www.viazul.com) for Santiago arrive and depart the **Terminal de Ómnibus Nacional** (Av. de los Libertadores, esq. Av. Juan Gualberto Gómez, tel. 022/62-3050). Buses depart Santiago three times daily for Havana (CUC51), and once daily for Baracoa (8am, CUC15), Trinidad (7:30pm, CUC33), and Varadero (8pm, CUC49).

Local buses and *camiones* operate to outlying destinations from the **Terminal de Ómnibus Municipales** (Av. de los Libertadores y Calle 4, tel. 022/62-4329), including twice daily to El Cobre. *Camiones* for Bayamo and Guantánamo leave from the **Terminal de Ómnibus Intermunicipales Serrano** (Av. Jesús Menéndez, e/ Máximo Gómez y Juan Bautista Sagarra, tel. 022/62-4325).

Train
Trains arrive and depart the **railway station** (Av. Jesús Menéndez y Martí, tel. 022/62-2836). The schedule is ever in flux (check ahead). At press time, trains #1, 2, 3, and 4 had been canceled until further notice. The only service was train #9 departing Havana's Terminal Le Coubre every fourth day at 6:13pm and arriving in Santiago de Cuba at 10:05am, with stops in Santa Clara and Camagüey. The return train (#12) departs Santiago de Cuba at 11:45pm and arrives in Havana at 2:33am. Train #9 originates in Santa Clara, departing at 2:25pm and arriving in Santiago de Cuba at 6:05am, every second day, with stops in Ciego de Ávila, Camagüey, and Cacocum (Holguín). Train #10 departs Santiago for Santa Clara at 7:10am.

Buy your tickets at the **Viajero** ticket office (tel. 022/65-1381, daily 9am-6pm) on the station's north side; you must go 24 hours beforehand for the regular train.

Sea
Ships berth at the **cruise terminal** (Av. Jesús Menéndez, tel. 022/65-1763). Santiago de Cuba is on the itineraries of U.S.-based **Fathom** (tel. 855/932-8466, www.fathom.org) and U.K.-based **Noble Caledonia** (tel. 020/7752-0000, www.noble-caledonia.co.uk).

Marina Marlin (tel. 022/69-1446), at Punta Gorda, has moorings for arriving yachts and offers water sports, sportfishing, and watercraft rental.

GETTING AROUND
Bus

Bus #1 runs between Parque Céspedes and both the interprovincial and municipal bus terminals. Most people get around on *camiones*, penned in shoulder to shoulder like cattle.

Car

All tourist hotels have rental agencies, but often there are no cars available. **Havanautos** (Hotel Las Américas, tel. 022/68-7160), **Cubacar** (Hotel Meliá, tel. 022/62-7177; Hotel San Juan, tel. 022/68-7206; Av. de los Libertadores, esq. Av. Juan Gualberto Gómez, tel. 022/62-3884; Plaza de Marte, tel. 022/62-9194; beneath the Hotel Casa Granda, tel. 022/68-6107), **Vía** (on the southeast corner of Parque Céspedes, tel. 022/62-4646), and **Rex** (tel. 022/68-6445 downtown, airport tel. 022/68-6444) all have offices at the airport.

There are **gas stations** at Pase de Martí at the corner of Moncada; Avenida de los Libertadores at the corner of Céspedes; Avenida de las Américas at the Carretera Central; and Avenida Garzón at the corner of Calle 4.

Taxi and Scooter

Taxis hang out on the south side of Parque Céspedes and outside the tourist hotels. **Cubataxi** (tel. 226/65-1038) has taxis on call. However, small motorcycles are the taxis of choice for locals; thousands buzz through the streets—just wave one down and hang on for the ride of your life. **Grantaxi** (tel. 022/66-9100) offers rides in classic Yankee autos.

You can rent scooters at the **Hotel San Juan** (Av. Siboney y Calle 13) and **Hotel Las Américas** (Av. de las Américas y Garzón).

Organized Excursions

City tours are offered by **Cubatur** (Heredia #701, esq. General Lacret, tel. 022/68-6033, and Garzón, e/ 3ra y 4ta), **Cubanacán** (Av. de las Américas y M, tel. 022/64-2202), **Gaviotatour** (Av. Manduley #456, tel. 022/68-7135), and **Paradiso** (Heredia #305, tel. 022/62-7037), which specializes in cultural tours. **EcoTur** (Heredia #701, esq. General Lacret, tel. 022/68-7279) specializes in ecotours.

Spanish speakers can join guided tours of the *casco histórico* offered by the **Oficina del Conservador de la Ciudad** (Av. Rafael Manduley #203, e/ 7 y 9, Vista Alegre, tel. 022/64-9690, 8 pesos). They begin at Parque Céspedes (Tues., Thurs., and Sat. 9:30am) and at the Museo Emilio Bacardí Moreau (Wed., Fri., and Sun. 9:30am).

Marina Marlin (tel. 022/69-1446) offers an hour-long bay excursion (CUC15 including cocktail) with a 10-passenger minimum.

Canadian Kate Daley and her husband, Abel (Jagüey #164, e/ Padre Pico y Corona, tel. 022/65-9320, www.realcubaonline.com), offer **history tours** of the city; excursions and tours farther afield focused on art, gardens, ecosystems, and geography; Spanish classes; and music and dance instruction.

North and West of Santiago

EL COBRE

The village of El Cobre, on the Carretera Central, 20 kilometers northwest of Santiago, takes its name from the copper (*cobre*) mine that the Spanish established in the mid-1500s. In 1630, it was abandoned, and the African slave-miners were unilaterally freed. A century later it was reopened by Colonel Don Pedro Jiménez, governor of Santiago, who put the slaves' descendants back to work. The slaves were officially declared free in 1782, a century before their brethren in the cane fields. Although the mine closed in 2000, the pit (filled with a turquoise lagoon) can be seen from the **Monumento al Cimarrón,** beyond the village. This monument, reached by steep stairs, is dedicated to the slaves who rebelled.

★ Basílica de Nuestra Señora del Cobre

Dominating the village is the ocher-colored, triple-towered hilltop **Basílica de Nuestra Señora del Cobre** (tel. 022/34-6118, daily 6am-6pm). Cuba's only basilica was erected in 1927 (a hermitage has occupied the site since 1608, however) and is a national shrine dedicated to the Virgin of Charity, the patron saint of Cuba to whom miraculous powers are ascribed.

The front entrance is reached via a steep staircase. More usual is to enter at the rear, from the parking lot, where the **Sala de Milagros** (Salon of Miracles) contains a small chapel with a silver altar crowded with votive candles and flowers. To the left and right are tables with miscellaneous objects placed in offering. On the walls hang scores of silver *milagros;* the two centuries of ex-votos include a small gold figure left by Castro's mother, Lina Ruz, to protect her two sons, Fidel and Raúl, during the war in the Sierra Maestra.

Steps lead up to a separate altar where the **Virgen de la Caridad del Cobre** resides in effigy in an air-conditioned glass case. Clad in a yellow cloak and crown (Ochún's color is yellow), the 40-centimeter-tall statue is surrounded by a sea of flowers and the entire shrine is suffused with narcotic scents. Once a year thousands of devotees make their way along the winding road, many crawling painfully uphill to fulfill a promise made to the saint at some difficult moment in their lives. The unlucky angler in Ernest Hemingway's *The Old Man and the Sea* promises to "make a pilgrimage to the Virgin de Cobre" if he wins his battle with the massive marlin. In 1952, Hemingway dedicated his Nobel Prize for Literature to the Virgin, placing it in her shrine (it's not on view, having been briefly stolen in 1980).

Touts will rush forward to sell you flower wreaths, miniature *cachitas* (images of the Virgin), and iron pyrite—fool's gold—culled from the residue of the nearby mine. *"Es real!"* they say, attempting to put a small piece in your hand. A firm "No gracias!" should suffice.

Food and Accommodations

The **Hospedaje El Cobre** (tel. 022/34-6246), behind the church, serves pilgrims and has 16 basic rooms where foreigners are welcome when space allows; each room has three single beds and a private bathroom (20 pesos pp). Couples must be married and show ID with the same address. A refectory serves basic fare at 7am, noon, and 6pm. For reservations, write Hermana Elsa Aranda, Hospedaje El Cobre, El Cobre, Santiago.

Getting There

Bus #2 operates four times daily to El Cobre from Santiago's Terminal de Ómnibus Intermunicipales. *Camiones* run from Avenida de las Américas at the corner of Calle M and from Avenida de los Libertadores and Calle 4. A taxi will cost about CUC30 round-trip. Tour operators offer excursions.

The Legend of the Virgen de la Caridad

All Cubans know the legend of the Virgen de la Caridad (colloquially known as the Virgen del Cobre, or Cachita), the most revered religious figure in Cuba. According to folklore, in 1608, two mulatto brothers, Rodrigo and Juan de Hoyos, and a young black boy, Juan Moreno, were fishing in the Bahía de Nipe, off the north coast of Cuba, when they were caught in a storm. As their boat was about to capsize, a small raft appeared bearing a statue of a black Virgin Mary holding a black baby Jesus and a cross. The statue was inscribed with the words *Yo soy la Virgen de la Caridad* (I am the Virgin of Charity). At that moment the seas calmed.

The story gained popularity and miracles were ascribed to the Virgen de la Caridad. In time a shrine was built near the copper mine at El Cobre. Pope Benedict XV declared her the patron saint of Cuba on May 10, 1916.

Today, the Virgen de la Caridad is associated with Ochún, the Santería goddess of love and water. She is depicted in a yellow gown, standing atop the waves with the three fishermen in their little boat at her feet.

EL SALTÓN AND VICINITY

The easternmost spurs of the Sierra Maestra rise west of Santiago. Nestled in a valley, El Saltón is touted as a mountain health resort, with picture-perfect cascades. It's excellent for bird-watching and hiking. The lodge offers massage, guided hikes (CUC2), and birding (CUC2).

El Saltón is at the end of the road about 15 kilometers west of **Cruce de los Baños,** a regional center overlooking the Río Contramaestre. The **Mausoleo del Tercer Frente Oriental** (Av. de los Mártires, Tues.-Sat. 9am-4pm, Sun. 9am-noon) contains the remains of Comandante Juan Almeida Bosque (1927-2009), who led the "third eastern front" during the Revolution; he is buried alongside 216 other guerrilla fighters. In the town center, the **Museo Tercer Frente Guerrillero** (Av. de los Mártires, Tues.-Sat. 9am-4pm, Sun. 9am-noon) tells their tale.

Food and Accommodations

Cubanacán's **Villa El Saltón** (Carretera Puerto Rico a Filé, III Frente, tel. 022/56-6326, CUC39 s, CUC48 d) is an eco-lodge built in the 1970s as an anti-stress center for the Cuban elite. The setting, plus the lodge's sauna and massage services, make up for ho-hum accommodations in 25 modestly appointed double rooms with modern bathrooms. An open-sided, thatched restaurant overlooks the river.

Getting There

El Saltón is reached from Contramaestre, on the Carretera Central about 70 kilometers northwest of Santiago, then 27 kilometers south to the village of Cruce de los Baños, where the paved road gives out. El Saltón is eight kilometers west of Cruce via the community of Filé. El Saltón can also be reached by jeep and a steep clamber from Río Seco, on the coast near Chivírico.

SANTIAGO TO CHIVÍRICO

The bone-rattling drive west along the coast from Santiago to Marea del Portillo, in Granma Province, is magnificent, with the Sierra Maestra plummeting to a crashing sea. The road becomes gradually more lonesome as you pass rustic fishing villages and pocket beaches. The section between Palma Mocha and La Plata is frequently washed out by storms (it was impassable at last visit, although repair crews were at work); don't be surprised to find the road impassable, or to find heavy-duty trucks ferrying passengers across washed-out sections.

The only settlement is **Chivírico,** a fishing village about 80 kilometers west of Santiago.

Here you'll find two foreign-operated hotels with knockout views. Nearby **Las Cuevas de Murciélagos** is full of bats, while about 22 kilometers farther west of Chivírico, at **Uvero** and reached via a glade of palms, is a monument marking the site where Castro's rebel army won its first major victory against Batista's troops on May 28, 1957.

About 12 kilometers west of Ocujal (48 kilometers west of Chivírico), you cross the mouth of the Río La Plata. It was here, on January 17, 1957, that Castro's rebel army first came down from the Sierra Maestra to attack a small garrison of Batista's Rural Guard. The **Museo Combate de la Plata** (CUC1) is 400 meters off the road, beside the river, on the west side of the bridge. Three thatched huts exhibit uniforms, maps, small arms, and more. The watchman, who lives adjacent, will open up on demand.

Hiking to Pico Turquino

Pico Turquino (1,974 meters) lures the intrepid who seek the satisfaction of reaching the summit of Cuba's highest peak, heart of the 17,450-hectare Parque Nacional Pico Turquino. Most hikers set off from Santo Domingo, in Granma Province, on the north side of the mountain. On the south side, a dauntingly steep 13-kilometer trail begins at **Estación Biológica Las Cuevas del Turquino,** at **Las Cuevas,** 55 kilometers west of Chivírico. A guide is compulsory (CUC20 pp, plus CUC5 for cameras, plus mandatory tip).

You'll need to set off around 4am to summit before clouds set in (no departures are permitted after 7am). You normally ascend and return in one day, a 10-hour feat, although you can shelter at 1,650 meters on Pico Cuba (with a rudimentary kitchen with stove) and at La Esmajagua, midway between Pico Cuba and Las Cuevas (CUC30 for a two-day hike). If you want to cross the sierra, you can hike all the way to Alto del Naranjo, on the north side of the mountain, a two-night/three-day journey (CUC48). You'll need two sets of guides—one for each side of the mountain—arranged in advance.

You must be self-sufficient (bring all the food and water you need). The weather is unpredictable; dress accordingly. Cold winds often kick up near the summit; the humidity and wind-chill factor can drop temperatures to near freezing. Rain is always a possibility, downpours are common, and fog is almost a daily occurrence at higher elevations by midmorning.

Book through **EcoTur** (Santo Domingo tel. 023/56-5635; Bayamo tel. 023/48-7006; Santiago tel. 022/62-5438 or 5289-3558; Havana tel. 07/641-0306). You need to carry your own gear. No sleeping bags or blankets are available.

Scuba Diving

Brisas Sierra Mar (Carretera de Chivírico, Km 60, tel. 022/32-9110) offers scuba diving (CUC30, or CUC60 for a wreck dive, CUC365 for a certification course). The most popular dive site is the wreck of the Spanish cruiser *Colón*, sunk on July 3, 1898, by the U.S. Navy. It rests just 20 meters below the surface, 35 meters from shore just east of Ocujal. Offshore from kilometer 24.7 is the wreck of the warship *Juan González*, and off Asseredero, at kilometer 32, lies the wreck of the cruiser *Viscaya*.

Food and Accommodations

Planning to hike Pico Turquino? You can camp (you'll need to be self-sufficient) at **Estación Las Cuevas,** which has a basic dormitory with three beds (CUC5 pp). Alternatively, **Campismo La Mula** (tel. 022/32-6262, or c/o Campismo Popular, Jagüey #163, e/ Mariano Corona y Padre Pico, Santiago, tel. 022/62-9000, CUC5 pp), at the mouth of the Río La Mula, 12 kilometers east of Las Cuevas, has basic cabins with cold showers, plus a simple restaurant.

Campismo Caletón Blanco (c/o Campismo Popular), 30 kilometers west of Santiago, also has simple cabins and accepts foreigners.

Canadian **Kate Daley** and her Cuban hubby, **Abel** (Jagüey #164 e/ Padre Pico y Corona, Santiago de Cuba, tel. 022/65-9320, www.realcubaonline.com, CUC50 including housekeeper), rent a three-room hilltop bungalow at Caletón Blanco, with a three-day minimum rental. It has heaps of light. Single rooms with traditional furniture cost CUC15-20. A *paladar* 400 meters east of Campismo Caletón Blanco serves meals.

Cubanacán's clifftop **Brisas Sierra Mar** (Carretera de Chivírico, Km 60, tel. 022/32-9110, www.cubanacan.cu, from CUC58 s, CUC76 d low season, from CUC106 s, CUC148 d high season) is a beautiful all-inclusive 10 kilometers east of Chivírico. The 200 nicely furnished rooms have modern accoutrements. Its heaps of facilities include water sports, tennis, scuba diving, and a swimming pool with views. It shares facilities with the more intimate yet similarly priced 34-room **Brisas Los Galeones** (Carretera de Chivírico, Km 60, tel. 022/32-6163), perched atop a headland about 10 kilometers east of Brisas Sierra Mar; a shuttle connects the two. The spacious rooms have king-size beds and balconies. A charming restaurant overlooks a pool, and there is a game room, tiny gym, and sauna. A 296-step staircase leads to a beach.

Nonguests can buy day passes to the Brisas hotels (CUC27 pp 9am-6pm, CUC39 9pm-11pm including all meals and drinks, or CUC9 dinner only).

★ COMPLEJO HISTÓRICO DE MUSEOS DEL SEGUNDO FRENTE

The small town of **Mayarí Arriba** squats at the end of the road in the rugged Sierra del Cristal northeast of Santiago. Carlos Manuel de Céspedes established his revolutionary government here in the 1860s, and Raúl Castro established his military headquarters here when he opened the second front in 1958. Access is via the crossroads village of Alto Songo, 23 kilometers northeast of Santiago.

The superb **Complejo Histórico de Museos del Segundo Frente** (Av. de los Mártires, tel. 022/42-5749, Mon.-Sat. 9am-5pm, free), on the north side of Mayarí Arriba, includes the main museum displaying photos, maps, and military hardware, including a helicopter and even full-scale models of a P-51 Mustang (delivered secretly from the U.S. to the rebel army in November 1958) and other U.S. warplanes. The museum focuses on the work of Raúl Castro, Frank País, and Vilma Espin (Frank's chauffeur, later Raúl's wife, and later still head of the Women's Federation) in liberating the region from Batista's troops and setting up a public service administration in the region in 1958—"a grand experiment for the near future."

Uphill, a palm-lined boulevard leads to the **Mausoleo del Segundo Frente** (daily 9am-4pm, free), a dramatic marble mausoleum set in an arc of royal palms, surrounded by red *califo rojo* plants (they represent the blood of revolutionary martyrs). A ceremony is held here each March 11. The ashes of Vilma Espín are buried beneath a huge rock in the garden, where Raúl has prepared his own grave. The rock bears a plaque with the Cuban emblem with Raúl and Vilma's names to each side.

Reserva de la Biosfera Baconao

The 32,400-hectare **Baconao Biosphere Reserve** extends 40 kilometers from the eastern suburbs of Santiago to the border with Guantánamo Province. The park was named a biosphere reserve by UNESCO for its bio-diversity, including many species endemic to the region. It is reached from Santiago via the Carretera Siboney, lined with 26 monuments to the heroes of the Moncada attack.

The region has beaches popular with locals on weekends. Few are inspiring (except Playa Daiquirí, which is exclusively for the use of Cuban military personnel and their families).

Getting There and Away

Bus #214 departs Santiago's **Terminal de Ómnibus Municipales** (Av. de los Libertadores, esq. Calle 4) to Playa Siboney and Baconao, which are also served by *camiones*. A **taxi** from Santiago will cost about CUC35 round-trip to Siboney (about CUC50 to Baconao; arrange a return pickup). The only **gas station** (24 hours) is 26 kilometers east of Santiago.

PARQUE NACIONAL GRAN PIEDRA

This park encompasses the Cordillera de la Gran Piedra, a lush mountain environment for bird-watching and hiking. Access is from a T junction at Las Guasimas, 13 kilometers from Santiago, where the **Prado de las Esculturas** (daily 8am-4pm, CUC1) is a sculpture garden with about 20 uninspired contemporary works lining a trail.

The deteriorated road—subject to land-slides—winds up through ravines, growing ever steeper and more serpentine until it deposits you at **Pico Gran Piedra** (1,234 meters), a distance of 14 kilometers, on a ridge with a view down the mountains. It's cooler up here and clouds swirl through the pines and bamboo.

The Villa Gran Piedra restaurant and hotel sits at 1,150 meters elevation, where a 454-step stairway leads up to the **Gran Piedra** (Great Rock, CUC2); you can climb a steel ladder onto the massive boulder for a spectacular view. On a clear day you can see the Blue Mountains in Jamaica.

A bus from Santiago runs weekly.

Jardín Ave de Paraíso

This 45-hectare **garden** (daily 7am-4pm, CUC1), 800 meters west of Villa Gran Piedra, was created in 1960 on a former coffee planta-tion. The garden is a riot of color and scents, difficult to dampen in even the wettest of weather. Guides will show you around a series of juxtaposed gardens, surrounded by topi-ary hedges. Amaryllises grow with carnations, *salvia roja* spring up beside daisies, blood-red dahlias thrive beside the garden's namesake birds of paradise. There are potting sheds, too, full of begonias and anthuriums, and a prim courtyard with a café. Visits are permit-ted only with a voucher (CUC5) sold by tour agencies in Santiago.

Cafetal La Isabelica

Two kilometers east of Gran Piedra via a rut-ted dirt road are the remains of a coffee plan-tation built by Victor Constantin Couson, a French immigrant who fled Haiti in 1792. Now a **museum** (daily 8:30am-4:30pm, CUC1), the ruins of the two-story *finca* ex-hibit farming implements and furniture. The coffee-crushing wheel can still be seen. Trails lead through the estate and forests. It has guided tours in Spanish.

Food and Accommodations

Islazul's **Villa Gran Piedra** (Carretera de la Gran Piedra, Km 14, tel. 022/68-6147, CUC35 s, CUC50 d) has 22 rustic, modestly furnished redbrick cottages atop the ridge crest—a spec-tacular setting at a crisp 1,225 meters. An at-mospheric restaurant/bar offers views. It has

Reserva de la Biosfera Baconao

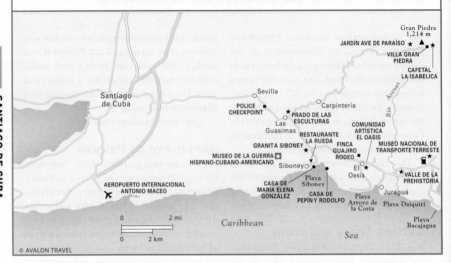

© AVALON TRAVEL

struggled to get back on sound footing since Hurricane Sandy, and consistently has issues with electricity and water supply.

SIBONEY

The little village of Siboney, replete with wooden French-style Caribbean homes, lies in a sheltered bay with a mediocre beach, **Playa Siboney.** Being the closest beach to Santiago, it's popular with Cubans who flock on weekends. A war memorial recalls the landing of U.S. troops on June 24, 1898. Renowned composer-guitarist Compay Segundo was born here: he composed "Chan Chan," the hit theme song of the Buena Vista Social Club album and movie that launched Compay to worldwide fame at the age of 90.

Granjita Siboney

This red-tile-roofed farmhouse, one kilometer inland of Siboney, is the site at which Fidel Castro and his loyal cohorts gathered for their attack on the Moncada barracks: They sang the national anthem in whispers, and at five o'clock on the morning of Sunday, July 26, 1953, the rebels set out in a convoy; the 1950 Oldsmobile used by Abel Santamaría is

here. The farmhouse is now a **museum** (tel. 022/39-9168, Mon. 9am-1pm, Tues.-Sun. 9am-5pm, entrance CUC1, cameras CUC1, videos CUC5) displaying weapons and bloodstained uniforms. Newspaper clippings tell of horrific torture. Six of the rebels died in the attack; more than 60 others died in captivity. Batista's henchmen then took the already-dead revolutionaries to Granjita Siboney, where they were blasted with gunfire to give the impression that they had been caught plotting and were shot in a battle.

★ Museo de la Guerra Hispano-Cubano-Americano

This excellent little **museum** (tel. 022/39-9119, Mon.-Sat. 9am-5pm, CUC1), 100 meters east of Granjita Siboney, is dedicated to the Spanish-Cuban-American War of 1898. Its thoughtful and detailed presentations include huge historical photos, superb maps, scale models of warships and the battles, and original cannons and other weaponry, including two Spanish torpedoes.

Food and Accommodations

The standout property is **Casa de Pepín &**

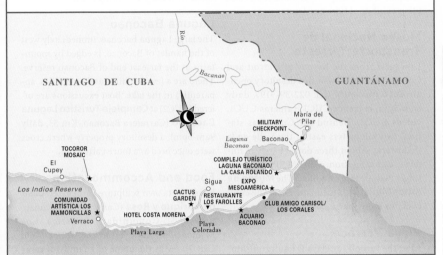

Rodolfo (Calle La Marina #21, tel. 022/39-9245 or 5293-6992, seoane90@hotmail.com, CUC30 room, CUC40-50 bungalow), on the clifftop east of the footbridge at the east end of the beach. This gorgeous 1950s villa has access to its own tiny beach good for snorkeling. The couple rents a two-room bungalow with a simple kitchen and shared bathroom. A dining room opens to a broad terrace and lawns.

I also like **Casa de María Elena González** (Obelisco #10, tel. 022/39-9200, marielana. sgto2013@yahoo.es, CUC20-25), a clean, cross-ventilated modern three-story house with a swimming pool in the stone patio. One of its two rooms opens to a breeze-swept terrace with fabulous views; the second, atop the roof, has floor-to-ceiling louvered glass windows.

About the only eatery here is **Restaurante La Rueda** (tel. 022/39-9325, Sun.-Fri. noon-5pm, Sat. noon-10pm), which serves superb *criolla* fare (less than CUC5) and has ocean views.

SIBONEY TO LAGUNA BACONAO

From a T junction at Granjita Siboney, a spur road leads east through Reserva de la Biosfera Baconao. First up is **Comunidad Artística El Oasis,** a hamlet of fieldstone cottages about three kilometers from the T junction. The entire community, comprising 10 families, works as artists and has open studios: check out the Santería-inspired works of Evelio Ramos Pérez. His neighbor Clemento Ríos, a *santero,* can offer a genuine Santería experience in his home with an astonishing shrine.

Beyond Verraco, a massive limestone plateau shoulders up against the coast, with the road running at its base. The Carretera Baconao ends just beyond the hamlet of Baconao, where there's a military barrier.

Valle de la Prehistoria

It's a shock to find a *Tyrannosaurus rex* prowling the **Valle de la Prehistoria** (Carretera de Baconao, daily 8am-5pm, entrance CUC1, cameras CUC1, videos CUC5), about six kilometers east of Comunidad Artística El Oasis. The beast is one of dozens of life-size dinosaurs that lurk in a natural setting. An *Apatosaurus* wallows in a pool. There are even woolly mammoths, and a pterodactyl perches atop a hillock. Real-life goats nibble amid the make-believe beasts made of concrete. A

Museo de Ciencias Naturales (daily 8am-4:45pm, CUC1) displays painted snails and other exhibits of flora and fauna.

Museo Nacional de Transporte Terreste

Dowagers from the heyday of Detroit and Coventry are on view at this desultory open-air auto museum (tel. 022/39-9197, daily 8am-5pm, entrance CUC1, cameras CUC1, videos CUC2), behind the Cupet gas station, two kilometers east of the Valle de la Prehistoria. About three dozen barely maintained cars range from a 1912 Model-T Ford to singer Benny Moré's Cadillac. The Museo de Autos Miniaturas (Miniature Car Museum) contains more than 2,500 tiny toy cars.

Playa Verraco

After the turnoff for Playa Daiquirí (off-limits), you'll come to a bend in the road with a huge mosaic of a *tocororo,* the national bird of Cuba, inlaid in the hillside. A few kilometers beyond is Comunidad Artística Los Mamoncillas, at Playa Verraco. Here, the entire community is engaged in arts. You can browse open studios.

Farther east the land grows more arid. Inland of Playa Sigua you'll pass the Jardín de Cactos (daily 8am-3pm, CUC2), displaying about 200 species from around the world. Expo Mesoamérica is a cactus garden containing Mesoamerican sculptures at the base of cliffs opposite the Club Amigo Los Corales.

Acuario Baconao

This aquatic park (tel. 022/35-6176, Tues.-Sun. 9am-4pm, CUC7), about 50 kilometers east of Santiago, has a small yet impressive museum on nautical miscellany and marine life. The real-life exhibits, which include moray eels, marine turtles, and a shark tank with walk-through glass tunnel, are dismal. The highlights are the daily dolphin shows at 10:30am and 3pm; you can even get in the water with these endearing beasts.

Laguna Baconao

The large Laguna Baconao, immediately west of the hamlet of Baconao, is edged by mountains at the far east end of Baconao reserve. There are a few dolphins (and crocodiles, apparently) in the lake. Boat excursions are offered (CUC2) at Complejo Turístico Laguna Baconao (Carretera Baconao, Km 53, daily 9am-5pm), a desultory property where crocs were once bred as a tourist attraction.

Food and Accommodations

Boasting its own sculpture garden, ★ Casa de Enrique y Rosa (Carretera de Baconao, Km 17.5, Comunidad Artística Los Mamoncillas, Playa Verraco, tel. 022/62-5766, CUC20-25) is the home of a family of ceramists who rent one spacious air-conditioned room with fan, refrigerator, and a delightful tiled bathroom. It has secure parking.

Islazul's 115-room, stone-lined Hotel Costa Morena (Playa Larga, Carretera de Baconao, Km 38.5, tel. 022/35-6126, www.islazul.cu, CUC36 s, CUC65 d low season, CUC58 s, CUC820 d high season, all-inclusive) sits in ungainly grounds that overlook a narrow pebble beach. The high point is its atmospheric Restaurant Las Orquideas.

Cubanacán's Club Amigo Carisol-Los Corales (tel. 022/35-6155, www.cubanacan.cu, from CUC75 s, CUC100 d all-inclusive) is divided into two adjoining properties: Carisol is for adults only, Caracol caters to families. There's nothing scintillating here, but the large pool area appeals and you get your cocktails, water sports, and buffets included. You can rent scooters for exploring.

The thatched La Casa Rolando (tel. 022/35-6196, daily 9am-4pm), at Complejo Turístico Laguna Baconao, serves *criolla* dishes.

Guantánamo

Look for ★ to find recommended sights, activities, dining, and lodging.

Highlights

★ **Zoológico de Piedra:** This mountainside zoo featuring life-size critters hewn from boulders is one of a kind (page 465).

★ **La Farola:** A steep mountain road snaking into the pine-clad Sierra Cristal offers fabulous vistas, but watch those bends (page 466)!

★ **Museo Arqueológico Cueva del Paraíso:** This fascinating albeit simple museum of Taíno culture is set in hillside funerary caverns with pre-Columbian skeletons still in situ (page 470).

★ **Parque Natural Duaba and El Yunque:** Rugged mountain terrain provides a challenging but rewarding hike to the top of the famous rock formation El Yunque, with incredible views as an added bonus (page 474).

★ **Parque Nacional Alejandro de Humboldt:** Wilderness supreme! This park provides great opportunities for bird-watching and hiking into the mountains, and manatees can be spotted along the shore (page 474).

Guantánamo is both a city and province, the latter of which tapers eastward to Punta Maisí, the easternmost point of the island.

It may be best known as the site of a U.S. naval base… or as the setting for the popular song "Guantanamera."

The province is almost wholly mountainous. Except for a great scalloped bowl surrounding the town of Guantánamo, the uplands push up against a barren coastal plain. The wild eastern shore and secluded mountains offer fantastic opportunities for hiking. Traces of indigenous culture linger around Baracoa, Cuba's oldest city, near where a ball court similar to those of the Mayan culture has been discovered. Baracoans claim that Columbus first set foot in Cuba here and left a wooden cross (now on view in the town's cathedral) as a memento. Whatever the truth, it's undisputed that the Spanish conquistadores who came on Columbus's heels established the first town in Cuba at Baracoa. The town retains an aged colonial feel in a to-die-for setting, despite being hammered by hurricanes Sandy (2013) and Matthew (2016).

Today the mountain region is protected within a system of reserves slowly being developed for ecotourism. These mountains harbor rare plant and bird species and the *Polymita pictas* (snails that haul fabulously colored shells on their backs). The northeast coast and north-facing mountains form the rainiest region in Cuba. By contrast, valleys along the southern coast are pockets of aridity, and cacti grow in the lee of Cuba's wettest slopes.

The already deteriorated coast road linking Baracoa to Holguín was badly damaged by Hurricane Matthew in October 2016 when a bridge collapsed. A replacement bridge (pedestrians only) was completed in December of that year. At press time, the road remained closed to traffic.

PLANNING YOUR TIME

A single badly deteriorated road hugs the north coast, linking Holguín and Baracoa (public transport along this route is infrequent). For scenery, you should definitely plan on traveling the Guantánamo city-to-Baracoa route via **La Farola,** a wheezing

---

Previous: Baracoa's regional cuisine; Plaza Martí. **Above:** Cruz de la Parra in Baracoa.

Guantánamo Province

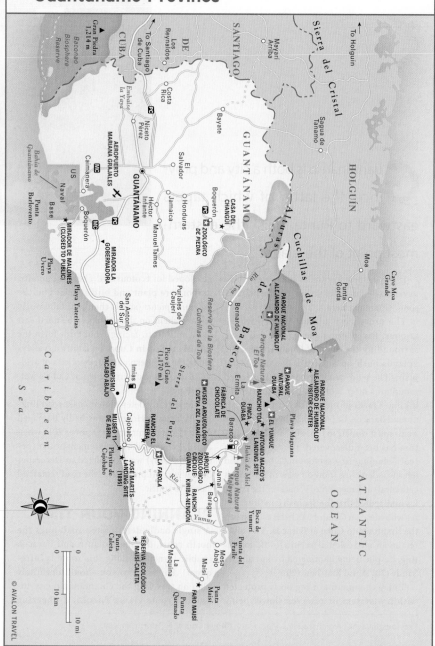

© AVALON TRAVEL

mountain switchback that has some nerve-wracking bends and slingshots you over the Sierra Cristal. The other option is the remote, arid, and dramatically scenic eastern shore route via **La Maquina.** Trains connect Guantánamo city to Santiago de Cuba and Havana. Víazul also offers daily bus service from Santiago de Cuba to Guantánamo and Baracoa.

The town of **Guantánamo** is more a place to overnight in passing. However, it has a lovely colonial plaza, and the cultural and music scene is striking, with more traditional Afro-Cuban cultural centers than you can shake a stick at.

The hinterlands of Guantánamo township boast two sites of unique appeal. First, the U.S. naval base holds a fascination that many travelers can't resist. While the chances of visiting the base are less than you winning the lottery, you *can* get a look at it from **Mirador La Gobernadora.** Not to be missed is the

Zoológico de Piedra. Within a one-hour drive of the city, this "stone zoo" features more than 200 life-size animals hewn from rock.

History buffs on the trail of José Martí should make a pilgrimage to **Cajobabo,** with its **Museo Municipal 11 de Abril** honoring Martí's landing at nearby Playitas, where a clamber over beach boulders reveals a marble monument at the exact spot where the nationalist hero stepped ashore. You can take in both the stone zoo and Cajobabo in a drive between Guantánamo and Baracoa.

Baracoa deserves two days minimum. One day is more than sufficient for sightseeing, with the highlights being the **Catedral Nuestra Señora de la Asunción** and the not-to-be-missed **Museo Arqueológico Cueva del Paraíso.** The second day you'll want to hike to the top of **El Yunque,** perhaps combined with horseback riding nearby or kayaking in search of manatees in **Parque Nacional Alejandro de Humboldt.**

Guantánamo and Vicinity

GUANTÁNAMO

Guantánamo, 82 kilometers east of Santiago de Cuba, is a large city (pop. 180,000) at the head of a deep bay of the same name and some 25 kilometers inland of the U.S. naval base, which lies at the mouth of the bay. The attractive colonial heart of the otherwise ungainly city has been spruced up; it's an architecturally fascinating place, with many fine examples of art nouveau and art deco. Much of the population is descended from Haitian and English-speaking Caribbean immigrants who arrived in the 1920s to work in the sugar fields. The cultural connections are strong, and the city is epicenter of *tumba francesa* and *changüí* musical genres.

Given the proximity of the U.S. naval base, there's a strong Cuban military presence. U.S. Marines first arrived here in June 1898 during the Spanish-Cuban-American War, following which the town developed a near-total

economic dependency on the base, which employed hundreds of Cuban workers.

Orientation

Guantánamo is laid out in a grid and approached from Santiago de Cuba by a four-lane highway that enters town from the northwest. The historic district is accessed by Paseo (Avenida Estudiantes), and further south by Avenida Camilo Cienfuegos, a wide boulevard that runs along the southern edge of downtown. North of Paseo is Reparto Caribe, where the Hotel Guantánamo overlooks Plaza de la Revolución. The center of town is Parque Martí, six blocks north of Camilo Cienfuegos and four blocks south of Paseo. Flor Crombet (El Bulevar), to the park's south, and Aguilera, on the north side, are pedestrian precincts.

Calle 5 de Prado (one block north of Parque Martí) leads east across the Río Bano for

Guantánamo

PARQUE DIVERSIONES

MERCADO AGROPECUARIO

IMMIGRATION

RESTAURANTE LOS GIRASOLES

CASA DE DOÑA MIMI

To Santiago, Villa Turística La Lupe, and Cupet Gas Station

HOTEL GUANTÁNAMO

BANK

CUBACAR

HOSPITAL

Plaza de la Revolución

COMMUNIST PARTY HQ

MONUMENTO A LOS HÉROES

ETECSA (PHONES)

BANK

Río Bano

To Cabaret Hanoi

(13 DE JUNIO)

AHOGADO

MÁXIMO GÓMEZ

JOSÉ MARTÍ

PEDRO PÉREZ

Río Guaso

CASA DE NORLAND PÉREZ

To ZOOLÓGICO DE PIEDRA

CARRETERA SANTA MARÍA

PASEO (AV ESTUDIANTES)

POST OFFICE

RAILWAY STATION

Plaza Pedro Agustín Pérez

NARCISO LÓPEZ

CINEMA

JESÚS DEL SOL

SEE "CENTRAL GUANTÁNAMO" MAP

5 DEL PRADO

FLOR CROMBET

CEMETERY

BARTOLOMÉ MASÓ

BERNACE VERONA

AV CAMILO CIENFUEGOS

CENTRAL

CASA DE LA TROVA

PEDRO PÉREZ

Parque Martí

ANTONIO MACEO

BRITISH WEST INDIAN WELFARE CENTER

TUMBA FRANCESA

CASA DE CHANGÜÍ/ CASA DE SON

CARRETERA

To Bus Station and Niceto Pérez

CALLE PINTO

To Caimanera

ESTADIO VAN TROI (BASEBALL STADIUM)

0   0.5 mi

0   0.5 km

© AVALON TRAVEL

Baracoa. A *circunvalación* (ring road) runs north of the city.

Parque Martí and Vicinity

What little there is to see downtown surrounds this attractive square with a beautifully restored church, **Iglesia Parroquial de Santa Catalina,** on the north side; note its impressive *alfarje* ceiling. A **monument to José Martí** is on the west side of the church.

Built in Parisian fashion and topped by a cupola—La Fama—bearing a herald with trumpet, the exquisite **Palacio Salcido** one block northwest of the square houses the **Museo de Artes Decorativos** (Pedro Pérez #804, esq. Prado, tel. 021/32-4407), displaying period furniture, vases, and more.

One block west, the small but impressive **Museo Provincial** (Martí #804, tel.

021/32-5872, Mon.-Fri. 8pm-4:30pm, Sat. 8am-noon, CUC1) dates from 1862 and was once a prison. It has exhibits on pre-Columbian culture and natural history; cigar bands; coins; plus a bas-relief map of the U.S. naval base and Cuban defense system. A 1940s-era Harley-Davidson in the lobby belonged to revolutionary messenger Capitán Asdrúbal.

The neoclassical **Plaza del Mercado** (Antonio Maceo, esq. Prado), two blocks northeast of the square, still houses an agricultural market.

The **British West Indian Welfare Center** (Serafín Sánchez #663, e/ Paseo y Narciso López, tel. 021/32-5297 or 5425-8183, derrick@infosol.gtm.sld.cu), an association for English-speaking citizens (locally called *ingleses*—Englishmen), works to keep alive the language and traditions of their descendants.

Central Guantánamo City

CUBACAR ■

CASA DE
OSMAIDA BLANCA ●

PASEO

NARCISO   LÓPEZ

CASA PARTICULAR   FLORA Y FAUNA
SEÑOR CAMPOS ●   (ECOTUR) ●

JESÚS   DEL   SOL

CASA DE
ELYSE CASTILLO OSORIA ●

MUSEO
PROVINCIAL ■   BANK ■ 5   DEL PRADO

PALACIO SALCIDO/ ★   DIRECCIÓN   ■ CADECA
★ MUSEO DE ARTES   PROVINCIAL DE
DECORATIVOS   CULTURA ▼

CASA DE LA   HOTEL
SUPERACIÓN ■   CAFÉ LA MARTÍ ●   HAVANATUR
AGUILERA   PRIMADA ▼   CUBATUR |

POST
OFFICE ■
CASA DE LA   IGLESIA   PIZZERÍA
CULTURA ■   PARROQUIAL DE   LA VENECIANA
SANTA CATALINA ▼
CAMPISMO
POPULAR ▼   Parque Martí   CINEMA/
FLOR CROMBET   ■ VIDEO BAR

RESTAURANT CASA DE CASA LA ▼   FARMACIA ■
E LA CRIOLLA LA TROVA INDIANA ▼   INTERNACIONAL
RESTAURANTE   HOTEL BRASIL
1870   (IN CONSTRUCTION) ●
EMILIO GIRO   CASA DE LA MÚSICA▼ ■ INFOTUR
LA RUINA ■   BAKERY ▲

PABELLÓN
GUANTÁNAMO▼   BANK ■
■ CUBANA   PHOTO
SERVICE
■ CADECA   ▲ BAKERY
■ PHARMACY   BANK ■
BARTOLOME MASÓ

PESCARÍA ■
(FISHMONGERS)   ★
PARQUE
CLUB NEVADA▼   ANTONIO
MACEO

DONATO MARMÓL

COPPELIA
▼
BERNACE VERONA

POLICE
■
Parque
Zoológico
RAMÓN PINTO

0   0.1 mi

☾   SABOR MELIÁN▼   0   0.1 km

AV ━ CAMILO ━ CIENFUEGOS

© AVALON TRAVEL

JOSÉ MARTÍ
PEDRO PÉREZ
CALIXTO GARCÍA

Some of the members were young men working on the U.S. military base when the Revolution succeeded; many continued to do so, commuting daily, until the last retired in January 2013.

Plaza de la Revolución Mariana Grajales Coello

This huge, barren square is enlivened by the **Monumento a los Héroes,** a huge concrete structure with the faces of heroes from the War of Independence and dedicated to the Brigada Fronteriza—the brigade that mans the Cuban defensive zone around the U.S. base. The bones of Los Mártires de Angola (Cuban military personnel who died fighting in Angola) are interred here.

Entertainment and Events

Every Saturday evening, Pedro Pérez is cordoned off for a street party, **Noches Guantanamera,** when local youth gather at Plaza Pedro Agustín Pérez to hear live bands perform. **Fiesta a la Guantanamera,** in early December, highlights traditional music and dance, as does the **Festival Nacional de Changüí** in mid-December.

The **Casa de la Trova** (Pedro Pérez, esq. Flor Crombet, no tel., Tues.-Sun. 8am-midnight, CUC1 entrance) is a great spot to hear traditional music performed live. Watch for performances by Orquesta Revé, a local (and world-famous) exponent of *changüí* (an antecedent of *son*). A second **Casa de la Trova** (Máximo Gómez #1062, e/ Marmól y Verona, tel. 021/35-5499), colloquially called "El Patio," draws a younger crowd for fusion, hip-hop, and reggaeton. The **British West Indian Welfare Center** (Serafín Sánchez #663, e/ Paseo y Narciso López, tel. 021/32-5297, derrick@infosol.gtm.sld.cu) hosts music and dance sessions featuring *changüí,* as does the **Casa de Changüí** (Serafín Sánchez #715), a stone's throw south. Opposite, **Tumba Francesa** (Serafín Sánchez #715, e/ Jesús del Sol y Narciso López, Tues., Thurs., and Sat. 9:30am-1pm) is a great place to experience Haitian music and dance.

Guantanamera...

Everywhere in Cuba you'll hear "Guantanamera" played by troubadours. It's become a kind of signature tune. The melody was written in 1928 by Joseito Fernández (1908-1979), who at the time was in love with a country girl *(guajira)* from Guantánamo and adopted the term *"guajira guantanamera"* into the original song. When the song was first played on the radio in 1934, it became an overnight hit. In 1962, Cuban classical composer Julian Orbon (1925-1991) added four verses from José Martí's *Versos Sencillos* (simple verses) to Fernández's melody and played it to friends and family, including Hector Angulo, one of his students. In the early 1960s, Angulo taught the song to folk singer Pete Seeger, who transcribed it for guitar and intended it as a peace song in the *We Shall Overcome* album (1963) at the time of the Cuban Missile Crisis. Angulo and Seeger launched it to international fame.

La Ruina (Calixto García, e/ Crombet y Gulo, tel. 021/92-9565, daily 9am-1am, free) is the place to sip suds in a colonial structure run *bodega*-style with wooden benches and big-screen music video; karaoke fans will love it.

The in-spots are **Club Nevada** (Pedro Pérez, esq. Masó, tel. 021/35-5447, Wed.-Sun. 7:30pm-2am, CUC1), an open-air nightclub with big-screen music videos that hosts karaoke (Wed.) and live music (Thurs.), and **Casa de la Música** (Calixto García e/ Flor Crombet y Emilio Giro, tel. 021/32-7266, nightly 9pm-2am, CUC1), for sizzling salsa and jazz.

Cabaret Hanoi (tel. 021/38-2901, CUC1), four kilometers northeast of town, offers a *cabaret espectáculo* followed by a disco (Sat.-Sun. 10pm). The **Hotel Guantánamo** (Calle 13, e/ Ahogado y Oeste, tel. 021/38-1015, CUC5) also has disco nightly (8pm-1am).

Baseball fans can catch the provincial team, Los Indios, at **Estadio Van Troi** (Calle 4 Este, Oct.-Apr.), one kilometer southwest of the Servi-Cupet gas station on the east side of town.

Food

Cuba's gastro-revolution is even reaching Guantánamo. The standout *paladar* is **El Paladar de Edgar,** which has marble floors and flat-screen videos playing music videos. The menu includes standards such as garlic shrimp and *ropa vieja*, but the flavors sing. With a clean and pleasant brick-lined space,

Sabor Melián (Camilo Cienfuegos #407, e/ Pedro Pérez y Martí, tel. 021/32-4422, sabormelian777@yahoo.com, daily noon-midnight) serves local fare such as fried chicken and grilled shrimp.

El Bulevar on the north side of the plaza hosts **Café La Primada** (tel. 021/32-9182, daily 8am-3pm and 4pm-11pm), a fabulous coffee shop and chocolate store selling truffles, cakes, and Cuban chocolates and drinks for pesos. For romance, head to ★ **Restaurante Los Girasoles** (Ahogados #6501, esq. 15 Norte, Rpto. Caribe, tel. 021/38-4178, daily noon-9:30pm), which offers candlelit dinners, including a superb shrimp in *criolla* sauce (CUC6), in an elegant 1950s home.

Five pesos will buy you a slice of what passes for pizza at **Pizzería La Veneciana** (Mon.-Sat. 10am-2:45pm and 5:30pm-10:45pm), on the east side of Parque Martí. **Coppelia** (Pérez, esq. Bernace Verona, Tues.-Sun. 10am-10pm) serves delicious ice cream for pesos. You can buy produce at the *mercado agropecuario* (Antonio Maceo, esq. Prado, Mon.-Sat. 8am-6pm, Sun. 8am-2pm).

Accommodations
CASAS PARTICULARES

One block northeast of Plaza de la Revolución and handy for services at the Hotel Guantánamo, **Casa Doña Mimi** (Ahogados #3106, e/ 14 y 15 Norte, Rpto. Caribe, tel. 021/38-4161, CUC20-25) offers good value.

This modern bungalow has one cool, spacious room with local TV and a large hot-water bathroom, plus secure parking.

Downtown has several dozen options. I enjoyed a stay at **Casa Señor Campos** (Calixto García e/ Narciso López y Jesús del Sol, tel. 021/35-1759 or 5290-0847, mcamposcreme@yahoo.com, CU20-25), with a large room with double and single bed, a TV, refrigerator, and 1950s retro decor. If full, Señor Campos can direct you to alternatives.

HOTELS

The best option is Islazul's **Hotel Martí** (Calixto García, esq. Aguilera, tel. 021/32-9500, www.islazul.cu, CUC45 s, CUC60 d low season, CUC50 s, CUC68 high season), on the northeast corner of Parque Martí. It has 21 pleasantly furnished air-conditioned rooms with cable TVs and clinically clean modern bathrooms. The restaurant is ho-hum and *jineteras* take up the street-terrace seats, but the rooftop terrace bar has Wi-Fi. Islazul's similarly priced and Cubist **Hotel Guantánamo** (Calle 13, e/ Ahogado y Oeste, tel. 021/38-1015), by Plaza Mariana Grajales, has simple, no-frills rooms with modern bathrooms. Services include a swimming pool and disco.

Islazul's **Villa Turística La Lupe** (tel. 021/38-2634, www.islazul.cu, CUC40 s, CUC48 d year-round), four kilometers north of town on the banks of the Río Bano, draws Cubans to the noisy poolside bar on weekends. It has 50 lovely rooms with modern bathrooms in two-story units.

Information and Services

Infotur (Calixto García e/ Crombet y Giro, tel. 021/35-1993, Mon.-Sat. 8:30am-5pm) offers tourist info. **Cubatur** (Aguilera e/ Maceo y Calixto García, tel. 021/32-8342) and the adjacent **Havanatur** (tel. 021/32-6365) can arrange excursions.

The **post office** (Pérez, esq. Aguilera, tel. 021/32-4668) has DHL service. **Etecsa** (Maceo, e/ Aguilera y Prado, tel. 021/32-7878, daily 8am-7pm) has international phone and Internet service. Parque Martí and Parque Máximo Gómez are public Wi-Fi zones.

The **Farmacia Internacional** (Flor Crombet e/ Calixto García y Maceo, tel. 021/35-1129, Mon.-Fri. 9am-5pm, Sat. 9am-4pm) is relatively well stocked. **Hospital Agostinho Neto** (Carretera El Salvador, Km 1, tel. 021/35-5450) is to the west of Plaza Mariana Grajales.

Getting There and Away
Aeropuerto Mariana Grajales (tel. 021/32-3564), 12 kilometers east of town, is not served by international flights. **Cubana** (Calixto García #817, e/ Prado y Aguilera, tel. 21/32-5453, www.cubana.cu) flies between Havana and Guantánamo.

The **bus terminal** (tel. 021/32-5588) is two kilometers south of town. **Víazul** (tel. 021/32-3713, www.viazul.com) buses for Guantánamo depart Santiago de Cuba at 8am (CUC6) and Baracoa at 2pm (CUC10). Buses depart Guantánamo for Santiago de Cuba at 5:40pm and for Baracoa at 9:30am.

The **train station** (tel. 021/32-5518) is on Pedro Pérez, one block east of Paseo. Train #15 departs Havana for Guantánamo every third day at 6:53pm (CUC32). Train #16 departs Guantánamo for Havana at 8:50am, with stops at most provincial capitals.

Getting Around
Bus #9 runs past the Hotel Guantánamo from Paseo. **Cubataxi** (tel. 021/32-3636) offers taxi service. **Cubacar** (tel. 021/35-5515) has car rental in the Hotel Guantánamo (Calle 13, e/ Ahogado y Oeste) and on Paseo (esq. Calixto García, tel. 021/35-5129). You can rent scooters from **Palmares Motoclub** (Calixto García e/ Crombet y Giro, tel. 021/32-9565).

GUANTÁNAMO BAY
The U.S. naval base occupies both sides of the entrance to Guantánamo Bay, which is inhabited by endangered manatees and marine turtles (iguanas, the unofficial Gitmo mascot, roam on land).

The bay is ringed by Cuban military bases,

Guantánamo U.S. Naval Base

The **Naval Station Guantanamo Bay** (tel. 011/5399-4520, https://cnic.navy.mil/regions/cnrse/installations/ns_guantanamo_bay.html), which is colloquially referred to as Gitmo (for the official airport code, GTMO), is the only U.S. military base in a Communist country. Since 1903 the United States has held an indefinite lease on the 117-square-kilometer property, which it claimed as a prize at the end of the Spanish-American War.

The Platt Amendment, which "granted" use of the base as a "fueling station" to Uncle Sam, was dropped in 1934, and a new treaty was signed. Although it confirmed Cuba's "ultimate sovereignty," the treaty stipulated that the lease would be indefinite; it also upped the original lease fee from US$2,000 in gold per year to US$4,085, payable by U.S. Treasury check. Since 1959, Cuba has refused to cash the checks and has called the base "a dagger plunged in the heart of Cuban soil."

The base's gates were closed on January 1, 1959, and have not been reopened except to a small number of Cubans who were permitted to continue commuting through the base's Northeast Gate following the Revolution. The last of these workers retired in 2013.

In 1964 the Cuban government cut off the base's water supply. A seawater desalinization plant today provides 3,000,000 gallons of fresh water daily, and electrical power is generated from wind turbines.

The facility was ringed by the largest U.S. minefield in the world, laid down during the Cuban Missile Crisis of 1962 but dug up in 1999. The Cuban mines remain.

Since 2002, the base has housed suspected Taliban and Al Qaeda terrorists at "Camp Delta."

LIFE ON THE BASE

The Naval Air Station (NAS), on the western side of the bay, is separated by four kilometers of water from the naval station, on the east side. The bay is crisscrossed by helicopters, boats, and an hourly ferry, while Cuban vessels also pass to and fro (the treaty guarantees free access to the waters to Cuban vessels and those of its trading partners).

By 2001 the base was virtually inactive, with reduced staffing. Since then it has ramped up because of the importance of Camp Delta, which at press time held 56 prisoners.

Today, 9,500 U.S. service personnel and their families live here amid all the comforts of a small Midwestern town. There are five swimming pools, four outdoor movie houses, 400 miles of paved road, and a golf course. McDonald's, KFC, Pizza Hut, Taco Bell, and even Starbucks have concessions—the only ones in Cuba. Another 7,000 civilians work here.

GETTING THERE

Prior permission to visit Gitmo is required from the U.S. military and isn't granted to your average Joe. Media, family of military personnel, and other categories classify. Flights to Gitmo depart Andrews Air Force Base in Maryland. **IBC Air** (tel. 954/834-1700, www.flyibcair.com) has charters twice weekly from Fort Lauderdale.

two Cuban naval facilities (Glorieta and Boquerón), and Mirador de Malones (U.S. Marines call it "Castro's Bunker"), a command center buried deep beneath the mountain on the east side of the bay. Unbelievably, visits to the bunker have been permitted in past years, but no longer. Check with Infotur in town, or MINTUR agent Orlando Román Cuba (tel. 021/35-5991, comercial@gtm.mintur.tur.cu).

The main gate (closed since 1959) is at **Caimanera,** 22 kilometers south of Guantánamo. This small Cuban town is surrounded by desert and salt flats; its economy is based on salt, fishing, and a Frontera Brigada military complex. Before the Revolution, many *caimaneros* worked on the U.S. naval base, while *caimaneras* worked in the strip joints and brothels that were the town's staple industry.

Caimanera is a restricted military zone, and visits by foreigners are limited to guided excursions offered by **Gaviotatours** and **Havanatur** (daily 9am-5pm, CUC14 pp with cocktail and lunch); 72 hours' notice is required so that MININT can check you out. The situation is fluid and depends on the state of international relations. From the balcony of room 101 at Hotel Caimanera you can look out past Cuban watchtowers to the naval base, which blazes at night like a mini-Las Vegas. Bring binoculars.

Far easier is to bring binoculars to **Mirador La Gobernadora** (tel. 021/57-8908, daily 24 hours), a roadside restaurant at the crest of the breeze-swept ridge on the bay's southeast side, at **Glorieta,** 25 kilometers east of Guantánamo city. It has a spectacular view of the entire bay (including Cuba's Soviet T-62 battle tanks, directly below) from a lookout tower and serves simple *criolla* dishes plus sandwiches. It's signed two kilometers east of the military checkpoint and the turnoff for Mirador de Malones.

Islazul's breeze-swept, hilltop **Hotel Caimanera** (Loma Norte, Caimanera, tel. 021/49-9415, director@hotelcm.co.cu, CUC25 s, CUC40 d) has 17 modest yet perfectly adequate air-conditioned rooms plus a swimming pool and open-air restaurant. Reservations must be requested 72 hours in advance.

NORTH OF GUANTÁNAMO

North of the city, sugarcane fields merge into mountains. You need your passport for a police *punto de control* one kilometer before the Zoológico de Piedra, beyond which a security zone is off-limits.

★ Zoológico de Piedra

Zoológico de Piedra (no tel., daily 8am-5pm, CUC1 entrance, CUC1 camera, CUC5 video), in the mountains 25 kilometers northeast of Guantánamo, features a menagerie of wild animals from around the world—lions, tapirs, hippopotamuses, elephants, and other species—hewn from huge calcareous rocks with hammer and chisel by a coffee farmer, Ángel Iñigo. Iñigo (1935-2004) carved 426 animals that he had seen only in photographs, representing more than 30 years of work. Stone pathways lead through the thick foliage, revealing such scenes as a buffalo being attacked by mountain lions, two monkeys picking fleas from each other, and Stone Age figures killing a wild boar. The zoo is a work in progress.

viewing the U.S. naval base from Mirador La Gobernadora

The thatched **Restaurante Mirador La Piedra** (Tues.-Sun. 11am-midnight), at the zoo, has fantastic views, but don't count on food being available. Alternatively, you can arrange a meal at **Casa del Changüí** (tel. 021/39-5188, by appointment only c/o 021/33-3210), a small and rustic farm about three kilometers north of the stone zoo. Here, the family of Eduardo "Pipi" Goul and his Estrellas Campesinas ensemble perform traditional music and dance.

GUANTÁNAMO TO BARACOA

Beyond Mirador El Gobernador, the road drops to the coast and you emerge at **Playa Yateritas,** a golden beach popular with residents of Guantánamo on weekends. For the next few miles, you'll pass little coves cut into the raised coral shore.

Beyond the hamlet of **Imias,** the terrain turns to semidesert, with valley bottoms filled with palms. **Campismo Yacabo Abajo** (tel. 021/88-5188, CUC10 pp), about five kilometers west of Imias, has modern yet basic beachfront cabins. It has a café and offers horseback rides (CUC3).

Cajobabo

The community of Cajobabo, 45 kilometers east of Guantánamo, is hallowed ground. At **Playitas,** two kilometers farther east, José Martí, Máximo Gómez, and four other patriots put ashore in a rowboat on April 11, 1895, after years in exile. The tiny beachfront **Museo Municipal 11 de Abril** (no tel., daily 8:30am-noon and 1pm-5:30pm, CUC1) honors Martí. A replica of the boat sits outside the museum and is used each April 11, when the landing is reenacted and cultural activities are hosted. Playita can be reached by road or via a challenging three-kilometer coast trail (hire a local to guide you). Beyond the rocks at the far east end of the beach hides a tiny cove with a **marble monument** inset into the cliff face. The monument was laid in 1947 at the exact spot of Martí's landing.

The shorefront road continues east to Punta Maisí at the eastern tip of Cuba. One of the most dramatic drives in all Cuba is rarely taken by travelers but richly rewards with incredible vistas as you ascend cactus-studded limestone plateaus that comprise **Reserva Ecológica Maisí-Caleta.**

★ La Farola

Immediately beyond Cajobabo, the highway turns north and climbs into the Sierra del Purial along **La Farola,** initiated during the Batista era (it was called the Vía Mulata) and completed since the Revolution to link Baracoa with the rest of Cuba. This highway switchbacks uphill through the valley of the Ríos Yumurí and Ojo. The road narrows with the ascent, the bends growing tighter, the views more dramatic and wide-ranging. Soon you are climbing through pine forests.

The summit (Alto de Coltillo) hosts a tiny café, beyond which the road drops through a moist valley until you emerge by the sea at Baracoa. The unlit road is subject to landslides.

Baracoa and Vicinity

BARACOA

Baracoa (pop. 65,000) lies 200 kilometers east of Santiago, 120 kilometers east of Guantánamo, and is miles from anywhere. The somnolent town nestles hard up against the ocean beneath the hulking flat-topped mass of El Yunque. Baracoa curves around the wide Bahía de Miel (Honey Bay), lined with black-sand beaches.

Isolation breeds individuality, and Baracoa is both isolated and individual. The town looks and feels antique, with its little fortresses and streets lined with venerable wooden edifices, rickety and humbled with age. Many did not survive the ravages of Hurricane Matthew in October 2016. At last visit, the town had recovered remarkably.

Baracoans have a good deal of indigenous heritage, identified by their short stature, olive-brown skin, and squared-off faces.

History

On October 27, 1492, approaching Cuban shores for the first time, Christopher Columbus saw "a high, square-shaped mountain, which looked like an island." For centuries, it was widely accepted that the mountain he saw was El Yunque. It is now thought that Columbus was actually describing a similar flat-topped mountain near Gibara, many miles to the west (Baracoans, however, are staunchly partisan on the subject).

In 1511, Don Diego Velázquez de Cuellar arrived fresh from Spain with 300 men and founded La Villa de Nuestra Señora de la Asunción, the first of the original seven cities founded by Velázquez. As such, it is the oldest colonial city in the Americas.

Baracoa's remote geographical circumstance did little to favor the settlement. After five years, Santiago de Cuba, with its vastly superior harbor, was proclaimed the new capital. Baracoa languished in limbo for the next four centuries, without road or rail link to the rest of Cuba until La Farola was completed in the early 1960s.

Orientation

La Farola enters town from the east as Calle

Baracoa at dawn

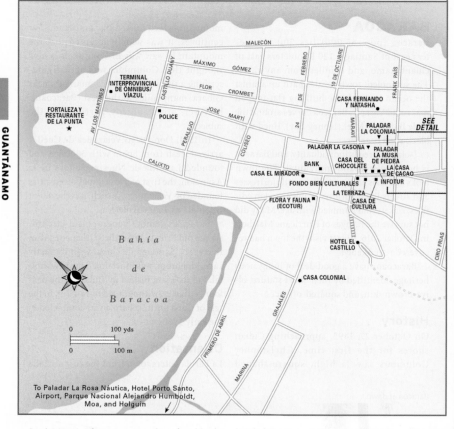

Baracoa

MALECÓN
MÁXIMO GÓMEZ
FLOR CROMBET
JOSÉ MARTÍ
CALIXTO

TERMINAL INTERPROVINCIAL DE OMNIBUS/ VIAZUL
FORTALEZA Y RESTAURANTE DE LA PUNTA ★
POLICE
CASTILLO DUANY
AV LOS MÁRTIRES
PERALEJO
COLISEO

FEBRERO
10 DE OCTUBRE
FRANK PAÍS
DE
24
MARAVÍ

CASA FERNANDO Y NATASHA
PALADAR LA COLONIAL
SEE DETAIL
PALADAR LA CASONA ▼
PALADAR LA MUSA DE PIEDRA
PALADAR LA CASONA
BANK
CASA DEL CHOCOLATE
LA CASA DE CACAO
CASA EL MIRADOR
FONDO BIEN CULTURALES
INFOTUR
LA TERRAZA
FLORA Y FAUNA (ECOTUR)
CASA DE CULTURA

CIRO FRÍAS

B a h í a
d e
B a r a c o a

HOTEL EL CASTILLO
CASA COLONIAL
GRAJALES
PRIMERO DE ABRIL
MARINA

0   100 yds
0   100 m

To Paladar La Rosa Náutica, Hotel Porto Santo, Airport, Parque Nacional Alejandro Humboldt, Moa, and Holguín

José Martí. The town is only a few blocks wide, with narrow roads running parallel to the shore. The Malecón runs along the seafront, two blocks north of Martí. From Holguín, the town is accessed via Avenida Primero de Abril, which curls around the western harbor.

Fortresses

Dominating the town is **El Castillo,** a fortress—**Castillo Seboruco**—atop the rocky marine terrace that looms above Baracoa, offering a bird's-eye view. It was built during the War of Jenkins' Ear (1739-1741) between Spain and Britain, when the two nations' navies

battled it out over the issue of trading rights in the New World. It has metamorphosed as the Hotel El Castillo and is accessed by a steep staircase at the southern end of Frank País.

Tiny **Fuerte Matachín,** at the east end of Martí and the Malecón, dates to 1802 and guards the eastern entrance to town. A bronze bust of General Antonio Maceo stands outside the fortress. The storehouse contains the **Museo Matachín** (tel. 021/64-2122, daily 8am-noon and 2pm-6pm, CUC1 entrance, CUC1 camera), tracing the history of the region since pre-Columbian days. It also displays shells of the painted snail. The round tower—**Torreón de Toa**—immediately

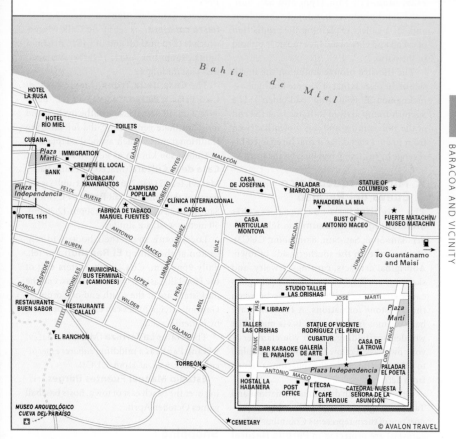

south of the fort served as a Spanish customs checkpoint.

The **Fortaleza de la Punta,** at the west end of Martí, was built in 1803 to guard the harbor entrance.

Plaza Independencia

This triangular plaza (Antonio Maceo, e/ Frank País y Ciro Frias) is the town hub and is pinned by a **bust of Hatuey,** the native chief who led resistance to Spanish rule. It is dominated by the recently restored **Catedral Nuestra Señora de la Asunción** (daily 7am-11am and 4pm-7pm), dating from 1805 on the site of an earlier church destroyed by pirates in 1652. The church is famous for the "Cruz de la Parra," a dark, well-worn, meter-tall cross that is supposedly the oldest European relic in the Americas. Baracoans believe that Columbus left the cross upright amid stones at the harbor entrance in 1492. Carbon-dating analysis confirms that it is indeed about 500 years old, although scientific study by experts determined that the cross was made of *Coccoloba diversifolia,* a native New World hardwood that grows abundantly around Baracoa. Perhaps Columbus whittled the cross himself in Cuba!

Avenida Maceo runs west from the plaza as a lovely pedestrian boulevard studded with sculptures. **Casa de Cacao** (tel. 021/64-2125, Mon.-Fri. 7am-11pm and Sat.-Sun. until 2am) produces handmade chocolates and has a gallery explaining the production of cacao and chocolate. Live music is offered in the patio.

The life-size bronze statue on the north side of the plaza is that of Vicente Rodríguez—nicknamed "El Pelú" (the "bad omen"). The Spanish tramp arrived in Baracoa at the end of the 19th century and was violently driven from town. Legend has it that he enacted his revenge by inflicting bad luck on the town.

★ Museo Arqueológico Cueva del Paraíso

The highlight of Baracoa is this **archaeological museum** (no tel., Mon.-Fri. 8am-5pm, Sat.-Sun. 8am-noon, CUC3), inside a cave on the southern side of town. Aboriginal artifacts, carvings, jewelry, and skeletons are displayed within floodlit glass cases ensconced within crevices between the dripstone formations. A funerary cave has skeletons in situ; access is via makeshift wooden scaffolding, which you clamber at your own risk. Follow Calle Moncada uphill to a tiny traffic circle; the museum is signed from here.

Other caves with dripstone formations and Taíno petroglyphs (local archaeologists purport one of them represents Columbus's three caravels) are protected in **Parque Natural Majayara,** reached by walking along the shore east of town.

Parque Zoológico Cacique Guamá

This small **zoo** (tel. 021/64-3409, Tues.-Sun. 8am-4pm, 20 centavos), seven kilometers east of Baracoa, displays monkeys, a hippo, a lion, birds, crocodiles, rodent-like *jutías,* and a near-extinct relative, the *almique,* endemic to eastern Cuba.

Entertainment and Events

The **Semana de la Cultura,** a weeklong cultural festival, kicks off on April 1 to celebrate

Antonio Maceo's landing at nearby Duaba in 1895.

Every Saturday night, a street party—*fiesta callejera*—is set up on Calle Maceo, which is cordoned off and lit with Christmas lights. Boom-box music reverberates until well past midnight.

The **Casa de la Trova** (Maceo #149, e/ Ciro Frías y Pelayo Cuervo, no tel., daily 9pm-2am, 10 pesos) is one of the liveliest and most intimate venues in Cuba for savoring traditional music, such as local adaptations of Cuban *son* known as *nengón* and *kiriba.* **Casa de la Cultura** (Maceo, e/ Frank País y Maraví, tel. 021/64-2364), where rumba is the name of the game, and **El Patio BFC** (Mon.-Sat. 5pm-12:30am and Sun. 8:30pm-12:30am), 50 meters west, are similar.

Local youth shake their booties to reggaeton at the hilltop **El Ranchón** (no tel., daily 9pm-2am, CUC1), 800 meters east of the Hotel El Castillo (you can also ascend the dark staircase at the south end of Coroneles Gajano); foreign males can expect to be hit on by *jiniteras.*

The rooftop **La Terraza** (Maceo, e/ Maraví y Frank País) has a middling *cabaret espectáculo* (Tues.-Sun. at 11pm, CUC1).

Estadio Manuel Fuentes Borges, rising over the beach east of town, hosts baseball games October-April.

Shopping

Galería Eliseo Osoris (Félix Ruenes #25, Mon.-Fri. 9am-noon and 4pm-9pm, Sat.-Sun. 4pm-10pm), on the north side of Plaza Independencia, sells paintings and sculptures. Also try the **Bien Fondo Culturales** (Maceo #120); the **Taller la Musa** (Calle Maceo #124, e/ Maraví y Frank País), where noted artists Roel Caboverde and Orlando Piedra sell original paintings; and **Estudio Taller Las Orishas** (Martí #131, e/ Frank País y Pelayo Cuervo).

Food

The best *paladar* is ★ **El Poeta** (Maceo #159, e/ Ciro Frias y Céspedes, tel. 021/64-3017, daily 9am-10pm). The kitchen delivers delicious Baracoan specialties, including soup served in a gourd, *tamal* stuffed with crab, and spicy shrimp with coconut-flavored rice.

Restaurante Calalú (Calixto García #151, esq. Céspedes, tel. 5310-4810, restaurantecalalu@gmail.com, daily noon-midnight) is a spacious *paladar* with an alfresco upstairs patio. I relished the sea crab in creole sauce (CUC10) served with *calalú* (spinach) with *tetí* (tiny fish) appetizer and *natilla* (custard) dessert.

La Casona (Martí 114, esq. Maravi, tel. 021/64-1122, daily 11am-11pm) occupies an airy colonial home with heaps of cozy charm and great service. The special is seafood in coconut milk (CUC12), but I enjoyed both a lobster (CUC12) and lamb in wine (CUC8). The bargain prices include soup and salad. **La Colonial** (Martí #123, e/ Maraví y Frank País, tel. 021/64-5391, daily 10am-11pm) serves swordfish, shark, and *dorado* in huge portions (most dishes CUC7).

I enjoy **La Rosa Náutica** (1ra de Abril #85 altos, tel. 021/64-5764 or 5814-4654, daily noon-midnight), with rooftop dining and a simple elegance. The menu features gazpacho (CUC1), chicken soup (CUC1), lobster (CUC10), and the house dish of marinated rabbit (CUC7).

Although it has its off nights, **Restaurante La Punta** (tel. 021/64-1480, daily 10am-10pm), in Fortaleza de la Punta, can't be beat for its setting and colonial ambience. The limited *criolla* menu includes a fish, crab, and shrimp special (CUC9).

Accommodations
CASAS PARTICULARES
There are scores of private rooms for rent. All are air-conditioned and most serve meals. Here are a few of my faves.

For an independent apartment, try **Casa Fernando y Natasha** (Flor Crombet #115, e/ Frank País y Maraví, tel. 021/64-3820, CUC20-25), where the friendly owners were tremendously attentive when I stayed there. They offer two spacious upstairs rooms with modern bathrooms and heaps of light. Meals are served on a rooftop terrace. I also enjoyed my stay at **Casa de Josefina** (Flor Crombet #269, tel. 021/64-1928, CUC15-20), where the pleasant hosts offer two rooms, each with fan, private bathroom, and terrace.

Casa Particular El Mirador (Maceo #86, e/ 24 de Febrero y 10 de Octubre, tel. 021/64-2647, ilianacu09@gmail.com, CUC15-20) is one of the best room rentals. Hostess Iliana Sotorongo Rodríguez's attractive colonial home has two spacious upstairs rooms with fans and lofty ceilings that open to a balcony with rockers and views.

My preferred option is ★ **Casa Colonial** (Mariana Grajales #35, tel. 021/64-2267, CUC15-20), a lovely old home with 1950s retro decor and run by attentive owner Isabel Castro. The home opens directly to a rear garden patio that gets the sun. It has secure parking.

HOTELS
All hotels are operated by Gaviota (reservas@gavbcoa.co.cu) and have air-conditioned rooms with satellite TV. The ★ **Hostal La Habanera** (Maceo #126, esq. Frank País, tel. 021/64-5273, www.gaviota-grupo.com, CUC30 s, CUC35 d low season, CUC35 s, CUC40 d high season) is a splendid restoration of a colonial-era hotel. Its 10 rooms around a central atrium patio have high ceilings, pleasant rattan furniture, and modern bathrooms. There's a small bar and restaurant.

The **Hotel Río Miel** (Calle Ciro Frias, tel. 21/64-1236, CUC53 s, CUC86 d) offers a pleasing boutique elegance in its 12 rooms with mahogany furnishings and snazzy modern bathrooms. It has a hip bar and an air-conditioned shorefront restaurant. The exquisite yet tiny **Hostal 1511** (Ciro Frias e/ Maceo y Ruber López, CUC30 s, CUC35 d low season, CUC35 s, CUC46 d high season) has tasteful modern furnishings and modern bathrooms. There's no restaurant, but you're a stone's throw from several *paladares*.

For a room with a view opt for **Hotel El Castillo** (Calle Calixto García, Loma del Paraíso, tel. 021/64-5106, CUC42 s, CUC56 d low season, CUC44 s, CUC60 d high season), built atop the foundations of El Castillo. It has 62 rooms (those in a newer block are the best) furnished in colonial style, with balconies with El Yunque views. The swimming pool is a major reason to stay here.

A lesser yet identically priced alternative is **Hotel Porto Santo** (Carretera del Aeropuerto, tel. 021/64-5106, CUC42 s, CUC56 d low season, CUC44 s, CUC60 d high season), on the west side of the bay. Its 36 rooms and 24 *cabinas* surround an amoeba-shaped pool, and it has tennis.

A last resort is the 12-room **Hotel La Rusa** (Máximo Gómez #161, tel. 021/64-3011, larusa@enet.cu, CUC20 s, CUC25 d low season, CUC25 s, CUC30 d high season), facing the Malecón.

You can buy a chocolate drink, *natilla* (a kind of chocolate mousse), and chocolate bars for pesos at the **Casa del Chocolate** (Antonio Maceo #121, esq. Maraví, tel. 021/64-1553, daily 7:30am-10:30pm), and at **Casa de Cacao** (tel. 021/64-2125, Mon.-Fri. 7am-11pm and Sat.-Sun. until 2am), where artisanal chocolates are made on-site.

Information and Services

Infotur (Maceo #129-A, e/ Maravi y Frank País, tel. 021/64-1781, Mon.-Sat. 8:30am-5pm) has a tourist information bureau with Internet service (CUC6 per hour). The **post office** (daily 8am-8pm) is on Plaza Independencia. Next door, **Etecsa** (Maceo #134, tel. 021/64-2543, Mon., Wed., and Fri. 8:30am-4pm, Tues. and Thurs. 12:30pm-7pm, and Sat. 8:30am-11:30am) has international telephone and Internet service. Parque Central is a public Wi-Fi zone. **Bandec** has branches at Maceo (esq. Marina Grajales) and on Plaza Martí.

Hospital General Docente (tel. 021/43014, 021/42568 for emergencies) is two kilometers east of town. The **Clínica Internacional** (Martí, esq. Reyes, tel. 021/64-1038, daily 8am-8pm) has a small pharmacy. The **police station** is on Martí (e/ Duany y Coliseo).

Getting There and Away

Aeropuerto Gustavo Rizo (tel. 021/64-2216) is on the west side of the bay. **AeroGaviota** flies between Havana and Baracoa on Wednesday and Saturday. **Cubana** (Martí #181, tel. 021/64-2171) has four flights a week.

Hotel El Castillo

Local Flavors

Baracoa is acclaimed for its original cuisine based on the coconut, which finds its way into such local delicacies as *calalú,* a spinach-like vegetable simmered in coconut milk; *bacán,* a tortilla made of baked plantain paste mixed with coconut milk, wrapped in banana leaves, and filled with spiced pork; *cucurucho,* an ambrosial sweet made of shredded coconut mixed with papaya, orange, nuts, and sugar or honey, served wrapped in folded palm leaves; delicious *turrón de coco,* a baked bar of grated coconut mixed with milk and sugar; and *frangollo,* a dish of green bananas toasted and mashed.

For drinks, try *chorote,* a tasty chocolate drink thickened with cornstarch; *sacoco,* a concoction of rum and coconut milk served in green coconuts; *sambumbia,* made of honey, lemon, and water; and *pru,* made from pine needles and sugar syrup.

Cuban chocolates come from here too. They're made at the **Fábrica de Chocolate Che Guevara** (not open to visits), two kilometers west of Baracoa.

Fishers also net a local oddity, *tetí,* a tiny fish that migrates like salmon up the Río Toa. The fish arrive at the mouth of the river enveloped in a gelatinous cocoon that splits apart on contact with freshwater. *Tetí* is eaten raw with cocktail sauce.

Buses arrive and depart the **Terminal Interprovincial** (Los Mártires, esq. Martí, tel. 021/64-3880). **Víazul** buses (tel. 021/64-1550, www.viazul.com) depart Santiago de Cuba daily at 8am via Guantánamo for Baracoa; and depart Baracoa daily at 2pm for Guantánamo and Santiago de Cuba.

You can rent cars from **Cubacar** (Martí #202, tel. 021/64-2555) and **Vía** (tel. 021/64-5135) at the airport and at Café El Parque on Plaza Independencia.

Getting Around

For a taxi, call **Cubataxi** (tel. 021/64-3737), or hail one of the old Willys Jeep private taxis, which are a staple of local transport. **Cubatur** (Martí #181, tel. 021/64-5306), **Havanatur** (Martí #202, tel. 021/64-5358), and **Gaviotatours** (Calle Calixto García, Loma del Paraíso, tel. 021/64-4115), in the Hotel La Habanera, offer excursions. Gaviotatours also has an office in Cafetería El Parque (tel. 021/64-5164). **EcoTur** (Calixto García, esq. Marina Grajales, tel. 021/64-3665, ecoturbc@enet.cu, Mon.-Sat. 8am-6pm) handles excursions into the nearby national parks.

There are gas stations beside Fuerte Matachín and one kilometer east of town.

RESERVA DE LA BIOSFERA CUCHILLAS DE TOA

West of Baracoa, the 208,305-hectare **Cuchillas de Toa Biosphere Reserve** encompasses most of the Alturas de Sagua-Baracoa, Cuchillas de Toa, and Cuchillas de Moa mountain ranges, and rises from sea level to 1,139 meters in elevation. The reserve has diverse climate types and ecosystems and protects the richest flora and fauna in Cuba, including more endemic species than anywhere else on the island, not least the *Polymita pictas* (a colorful snail species).

Much of the area is forested in Cuban pine, a perfect habitat for the ivory-billed woodpecker and its cousin, the endemic and endangered royal woodpecker. The ivory-billed woodpecker was once common throughout the American South, but it has not been seen in the United States since the 1940s. The bird was considered extinct until the mid-1980s, when it was identified in these mountains. The sightings led the Cuban government to establish a 220-square-kilometer protected area. No sightings have since been made.

The reserve is divided into several national parks. Visits are coordinated through **EcoTur** (Calixto García, esq. Marina Grajales, tel.

021/64-3665, ecoturbc@enet.cu), which has an office at Campismo El Yunque.

★ Parque Natural Duaba and El Yunque

At the mouth of the Río Duaba, five kilometers west of Baracoa, is **Playa Duaba,** a black-sand beach where General Antonio Maceo and 22 compatriots landed in April 1895 to wage the War of Independence. Immediately beyond is the site where he fought his first battle. He is honored by a roadside monument with bust and cannon.

You can turn inland here and follow a dirt road one kilometer to **Finca Duaba** (tel. 021/64-5224, daily 10am-4pm), a fruit farm with a restaurant serving *criolla* meals. Guided tours (CUC1) include a demonstration of cacao processing.

The park enfolds El Yunque ("the anvil"), the spectacular flat-topped mountain (575 meters) that dominates the landscape west of Baracoa. This sheer-sided giant—the remains of a mighty plateau that once extended across the entire area—was hallowed by the Taíno. Mists flow down from the summit in the dawn hours, and it glows like hot coals at dusk. Waterfalls pour from its summit.

You can hike to the summit daily 8am-3pm (four hours round-trip, CUC13 from Campismo El Yunque, CUC15-18 from Baracoa; a guide, water, and lunch are compulsory). From the coast highway, take the signed turnoff for Finca Duaba, then keep left at the Y fork (the *campismo* is to the left; Finca Duaba is to the right). **Sendero El Jutiero** from the *campismo* leads to cascades and pools good for swimming (CUC8, 40 minutes).

Parque Natural El Toa

This park, immediately west of Parque Natural Duaba, extends into the interior mountains. The seven-kilometer-long **Sendero Juncal Rencontra** trail transcends the mountains, leading from the Río Duaba to the Río Toa; **guided hikes** (CUC22 from Baracoa) end with a boat or jeep return.

★ Parque Nacional Alejandro de Humboldt

This 70,835-hectare park extends into Holguín Province. A guide is compulsory. There's a two-meter-tall statue of the namesake German explorer roadside near the **visitors center** (daily 8am-7pm). The center, on the east side of Recreo, five kilometers west of the Río Nibujón, has a 3-D map of the park.

El Yunque viewed from the national park headquarters

The **Sendero Balcón de Iberia** leads inland to waterfalls and natural swimming pools (five hours, last departure at 11am, CUC10, or CUC22 with transport from Baracoa). The shorter **Sendero El Recreo** (CUC10) hugs the shore of **Parque Natural Bahía de Taco,** incorporated within Parque Nacional Alejandro de Humboldt and protecting 2,263 hectares of marine ecosystems, including mangroves, an offshore cay, and white-sand beaches shelving to a coral reef. Manatees are often seen. The **Sendero Bahía de Taco** includes a boat excursion (CUC5).

Intrepid hikers can follow an arduous and muddy trail to **Salto Fino,** said to be the Caribbean's tallest waterfall at 305 meters. The main fall—Arroyo El Infierno (Hell's Stream)—plummets over the precipice of a rainforest-shrouded mesa and plunges 258 meters into the Devil's Inferno, a swirling pool that feeds the Río Toa. The river needs to be waded several times to reach the falls.

Food and Accommodations

Campismo El Yunque (tel. 021/64-5262, www.campismopopular.cu), midway between Finca Duaba and the summit of El Yunque, has 16 basic huts, each sleeping up to six people. Even more rustic, **Finca La Esperanza** (CUC20 pp, including meals and boat tour), at the mouth of the Río Toa, has four basic rooms, each with four beds and fans.

Gaviota's ★ **Villa Maguana** (Carretera de Moa, Km 20, tel. 021/64-5106, CUC75 s, CUC90 d low season, CUC85 s, CUC105 d high season, including meals), 28 kilometers west of Baracoa, nestles in its own cove with a white-sand beach and turquoise waters. It has 16 lovely rooms with modern bathrooms in two-story fourplex wooden structures.

A preferred alternative at Maguana is **Casa de Hidiolvis** (tel. 5310-4875, hidiolvis@nauta.cu, CUC20-25), where the namesake host and her family rent out two rooms in their simple yet cozy home set back from the beach.

BARACOA TO PUNTA MAISÍ

The coast road east from Baracoa follows a winding course inland via the hamlet of Jamal, touching the coast again 20 kilometers east of Baracoa at **Playa Baragua**—a ruler-straight silver-sand beach with a fabulous view towards El Yunque.

About 15 kilometers east of Baracoa, divert off the main road to the hamlet of **El Güirito,** where descendants of Taíno people keep alive

Parque Nacional Alejandro de Humboldt

Painted Snails

Polymita pictas is a species of tiny snail unique to the Baracoa region. It is commonly called the painted snail or Cuban land snail. This diminutive critter is much sought by collectors for its coat of many colors, which are as unique to each individual snail as fingerprints are to humans. However, the species is endangered and it is illegal to catch, buy, or export it.

According to an Indian legend, the snails' shells were originally colorless. One snail, while slowly roaming the region, was taken by the area's lush beauty and asked the mountains for some of their green. Then he admired the sky and asked for some blue. When he saw the golden sands, he asked for a splash of yellow, and for jade and turquoise from the sea.

the *kiriba* and *nengón* music and dance traditions. The **Kiriba-Nengón** cultural group dresses in traditional country attire (long flowery skirts and frilled lace blouses) and performs for visitors.

Beyond Baragua, the road eventually passes through a cleft in the vertical cliffs spanned by a natural arch called Túnel de los Alemanes (Germans' Tunnel). Beyond, you emerge at **Boca de Yumurí,** where the Río Yumurí cuts through a deep canyon to meet the Atlantic breakers. You can rent pedal boats at **Café Yumurí** (daily 10am-6pm), and locals will accost you as you step from your car to row you upriver (CUC2 round-trip).

Punta Maisí

Immediately east of the Río Yumurí, the road begins a daunting first-gear switchback ascent and winds its way into the mountains and the town of **La Máquina,** the center of a coffee-growing region on the cooler eastern slope of the Meseta de Maisí, 22 kilometers beyond the river mouth.

La Máquina looks down over a vast plain studded with cacti. Far below, a *faro* built in 1862 at Punta Maisí pins the easternmost tip of Cuba, where day breaks 40 minutes before it occurs in Havana. A paved road track descends from La Máquina past **Laguna de Limones** (a lake accessed by trails) to the lighthouse, 14 kilometers away. You have reached land's end, 1,280 kilometers from Havana.

At press time, a new road was being constructed along the coast from Yumurí to Maisí as an alternative to the dangerous switchback.

Background

The Landscape

Cuba lies at the western end of the Greater Antilles group of Caribbean islands, which began to heave from the sea about 150 million years ago.

Cuba is by far the largest of the Caribbean islands at 110,860 square kilometers. It is only slightly smaller than the state of Louisiana and half the size of the United Kingdom. It sits just south of the Tropic of Cancer at the eastern perimeter of the Gulf of Mexico, 150 kilometers south of Key West, Florida, 140 kilometers north of Jamaica, and 210 kilometers east of Mexico's Yucatán Peninsula. It is separated from Hispaniola to the east by the 77-kilometer-wide Windward Passage.

Cuba is an archipelago with some 4,000-plus islands and cays dominated by the main island (104,945 square kilometers), which is 1,250 kilometers long—from Cabo de San Antonio in the west to Punta Maisí in the east—and between 31 and 193 kilometers wide. Plains cover almost two-thirds of the island.

Slung beneath the mainland's underbelly is Isla de la Juventud (2,200 square kilometers), the westernmost of a chain of smaller islands—the Archipiélago de los Canarreos—that extends eastward for 110 kilometers across the Golfo de Batabanó. Farther east, beneath east-central Cuba, is a shoal of tiny coral cays—the Archipiélago de los Jardines de la Reina—poking up a mere four or five meters from the sapphire sea. The central north coast is rimmed by a necklace of coral jewels—the Jardines del Rey—lined by Cuba's most beautiful beaches. Most beaches along the south coast can't compare; exceptions include Playa Ancón and Cayo Largo.

TOPOGRAPHY

Cuba is the *least* mountainous of the Greater Antilles, with a median elevation of less than 100 meters above sea level. The flatlands are disjoined by three mountain zones, where the air is cool and inviting. The westernmost mountains are the slender, low-slung Sierra del Rosario and Sierra de los Órganos, which together constitute the Cordillera de Guaniguanico, forming a backbone along the length of northern Pinar del Río Province. In their midst is the striking Valle de Viñales, a classic karst landscape of limestone formations called *mogotes*.

The Sierra Escambray rises steeply over west-central Cuba, dominating eastern Cienfuegos and southern Villa Clara Provinces.

A third mountain zone, incorporating several adjacent ranges, overshadows the provinces of Granma, Santiago de Cuba, and Guantánamo and spills into Holguín Province. To the west, the precipitous Sierra Maestra rises steeply from the sea, culminating atop Pico Turquino (1,974 meters), Cuba's highest mountain. To the east are the Cuchillas de Toa, Sierra de Puriscal, and Sierra de Cristal.

The north coast is indented by huge, flask-shaped bays, not least of which is Bahía de Habana, on whose western shores grew Havana.

Cuba has more than 500 rivers, most of them short, shallow, and unnavigable. The principal river, the 370-kilometer-long Río Cauto, which originates in the Sierra Maestra and flows northwest, is navigable by boat for about 80 kilometers.

Cuba's Vital Statistics

Area: 110,860 square kilometers (42,804 square miles)
Population: 11,179,995 (2016)
Annual Population Growth: -0.3 percent
Urbanization: 77.1 percent
Capital: Havana, pop. 2,137,000
Literacy: 99.8 percent
Life Expectancy: 78.7 years
Annual Birth Rate: 10.8 per 1,000
Infant Mortality Rate: 4.5 per 1,000

CLIMATE

Cuba lies within the tropics, though its climate—generally hot and moist—is more properly semi- or subtropical. There are only two seasons: wet (May to November) and dry (December to April), with regional variations.

The island is influenced by the warm Gulf Stream currents and by the North Atlantic high-pressure zone that lies northeast of Cuba and gives rise to the near-constant *brisa,* the local name for the trade winds that caress Cuba year-round. Despite its more southerly latitude, Havana, wrote Ernest Hemingway, "is cooler than most northern cities in [July and August], because the northern trades get up about ten o'clock in the morning and blow until about five o'clock the next morning." Summer months, however, can be insufferably hot and humid.

Temperatures

Cuba's mean annual temperature is 25.2°C, with an average of eight hours of sunshine per day throughout the year. There is little seasonal variation, with an average temperature in January of 22°C, rising (along with humidity) to an average of 27.2°C in July. Nonetheless, in summer the temperature can rise to 32°C or more, and far higher in the Oriente, especially the lowlands of Guantánamo Province (the hottest part of the country). The southern coast is generally hotter than the north coast, which receives the trades. Winds sometimes rip across the central plains in summer.

Midwinter temperatures can fall below 10°C when severe cold fronts sweep down from Canada. Atop the higher mountains temperatures may plunge at night to 5°C.

Rainfall

Rain falls on Cuba an average of 85-100 days a year, totaling an annual average of 132 centimeters. Almost two-thirds falls during the May-October wet season, which can be astoundingly humid. Summer rain is most often a series of intermittent showers, but afternoon downpours and torrential storms are common. Years of relative drought are common.

Central and western regions experience a three- to five-month dry period known as La Seca. February through April and December are the driest months. Nonetheless, heavy winter downpours are associated with cold fronts sweeping south from North America.

The Atlantic coast tends to be slightly rainier than the southern coast. The mountains receive the highest rainfall, especially the uplands of eastern Oriente (up to 400 centimeters fall in the Cuchillas de Toa). The mountains produce regional microclimates, forming rain shadows along the southeast coast, so that pockets of cacti and parched scrub grow in the lee of thick-forested slopes.

Hurricanes

Cuba lies within the hurricane belt. August through October is hurricane season, but freak tropical storms can hit Cuba in other months, too. Most hurricanes that strike Cuba originate in the western Caribbean during October and move north over the island. Cuba has been struck by several hurricanes in recent years. In fact, 2008 was one of the worst years in history, with three direct hits in two months. In October 2012, Hurricane Sandy struck Santiago de Cuba, killing 11 people—the worst hurricane in decades—and Hurricane Matthew devastated Baracoa in 2016.

Rainfall

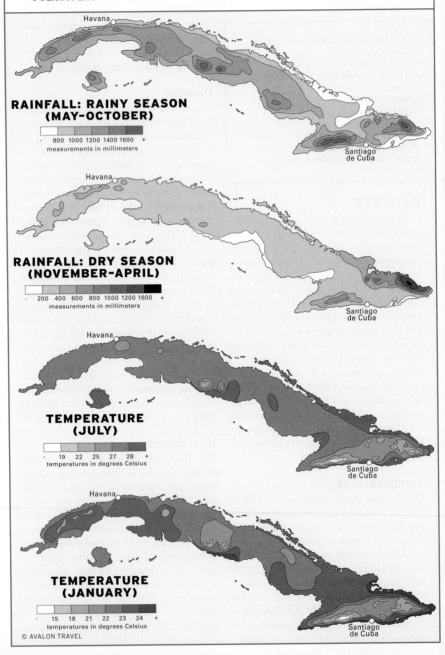

Havana

**RAINFALL: RAINY SEASON
(MAY–OCTOBER)**

- 800 1000 1200 1400 1600 +
measurements in millimeters

Santiago
de Cuba

Havana

**RAINFALL: DRY SEASON
(NOVEMBER–APRIL)**

- 200 400 600 800 1000 1200 1600 +
measurements in millimeters

Santiago
de Cuba

Havana

**TEMPERATURE
(JULY)**

- 19 22 25 27 28 +
temperatures in degrees Celsius

Santiago
de Cuba

Havana

**TEMPERATURE
(JANUARY)**

- 15 18 21 22 23 24 +
temperatures in degrees Celsius

© AVALON TRAVEL

Santiago
de Cuba

Cuba's Climate

Jan.	Feb.	Mar.	Apr.	May	June	July	Aug.	Sept.	Oct.	Nov.	Dec.
National Average (degrees Celsius)											
26	26	27	29	30	31	32	32	31	29	27	26
Havana Average (degrees Celsius)											
22	22.5	23	25	26	27	28	28	27.5	26	24	22.5
Days with Rainfall (Havana)											
6	4	4	4	7	10	9	10	11	11	7	6

The country has a highly developed disaster preparedness and exemplary civil defense network for evacuations.

ENVIRONMENTAL ISSUES

Cuba is likened by socialists to the setting of Ernest Callenbach's novel *Ecotopia,* about an environmental utopia where everything is recycled and nothing is wasted; where there are few cars and lots of bicycles; where electricity is generated from methane from dung; and where city dwellers tend agricultural plots designed to make the island self-sufficient in food and break its traditional dependence on cash crops for export.

Though simplistic, there's truth in this vision. The Cubans are ahead of the times in coping with problems the entire world may eventually face. Cuba's advances are recent, necessitated by the collapse of the Soviet bloc. The fuel shortage caused Cubans to relinquish their cars in favor of bicycles. Everything from solar power to windmills is now being vaunted as alternative energy. Five wind farms were in operation nationwide in 2016; solar panels are also being installed, including a five-hectare farm outside Cienfuegos. Meanwhile, most of Cuba's sugar mills are now powered by *bagazo* (waste from cane processing).

However, there is a lack of public education about ecological issues and few qualified personnel to handle them. And despite much-touted environmental laws, Cuba suffers from horrific waste and pollution. Industrial chimneys cast deathly palls over parts of Havana and other cities. The cement works at Mariel smother the town in a thick coat of dust. Then there are the decades-old Yankee automobiles and the Hungarian-made buses that, in Castro's words, "fill the city with exhaust smoke, poisoning everybody; we could draw up statistics on how many people the Hungarian buses kill" (conveniently, he forgot to mention who ordered them). In townships nationwide, rivers and streams are polluted like pestilential sewers, which, in many cities, are broken. Rotting garbage litters streets and goes uncollected.

Recent engineering projects to promote tourism in the northern cays have been ecological disasters. Construction of the *pedraplén* (causeway) linking Cayo Coco to mainland Ciego de Ávila Province cut off the flow of tidal waters, to the severe detriment of local ecology. And dynamiting for hotel construction has scared away flocks of flamingos, while previously protected areas are gerrymandered to make way for massive new all-inclusive hotels.

Cuba's coral reefs are in fine shape, thanks to sound management. But even while Cuba has had notable success in bringing the Cuban crocodile back from the dead, the government campaigns to get sales of hawksbill turtles legalized again internationally. Endangered black coral is a staple of Cuba's jewel industry. Lobsters are becoming endangered in Cuban waters because of overharvesting. And zoos nationwide are a disgrace for their filthy conditions and tiny cages, with animals openly taunted by Cuban patrons displaying insensitivity.

Reforestation

When Christopher Columbus arrived in Cuba, more than 90 percent of the island was covered in forest. On the eve of the Revolution, only 14 percent of the land was forested. The revolutionary government undertook a reforestation program in the mid-1960s. Following the collapse of the Soviet bloc, the government announced a second reforestation plan. Virtually the entire reforestation program, however, is in firs, not diverse species. There is little effort to regenerate primary forest.

National Parks

Cuba officially claims 13 national parks, 23 ecological reserves, 5 nature reserves, 11 fauna refuges, 9 flora reserves, and dozens of other protected areas, under the Sistema Nacional de Áreas Protegidas (SINAC, or National System of Protected Areas), covering one-fifth of the national territory. The **Ministerio de Ciencia, Tecnología y Medio Ambiente** (Ministry of Sciences, Technology, and Environment, or CITMA, www.medioambiente.cu) has responsibility for the environment. The **Empresa Nacional para la Protección de Flora y Fauna** (Calle 18A #4114, e/ 43 y 47, Playa, Havana, tel. 07/202-7970, www.snap.cu) is charged with developing protected areas as touristic sites through its **EcoTur** tour agency (tel. 07/614-0306, www.ecoturcuba.tur.cu).

Plants and Animals

Cuba touts the most impressive species diversity of any Caribbean island. Despite four centuries of devastating deforestation, extensive tracts remain cloaked in a dozen shades of tropical green. Coastal mangroves and wetlands, dry forest, scrubby pine forest, pockets of lowland rainforest and montane cloud forest, and desert-dry terrain supporting cacti are strewn like isles within an isle.

Cuba boasts more than 6,700 vascular plant species, of which some 3,180 are endemic and about 950 are endangered. The countryside flares with color. Begonias, anthuriums, "Indian laburnum," oleander, and poinsettia are common, as are mimosa, hibiscus, bright pink morning glory, and bougainvillea in its rainbow assortment of riotous colors. Cuba's national flower is the brilliant white, heady-scented *mariposa,* a native species of jasmine that became a symbol of rebellion and purity at the time of the wars for independence.

Cuba has several hundred species of orchids. At any time of year dozens of species are in bloom, from sea level to the highest reaches of the Sierra Maestra. The greatest diversity exists in humid mid-elevation environments, where they are abundant as tropical epiphytes.

Most of Cuba's fauna species are invertebrates (mostly insects), with a great many species endemic to specific regions. Unique species and subspecies include the world's smallest frog (*Sminthillus limbatus*) and smallest bird (the bee hummingbird, or *zunzuncito*); an endemic crocodile species; and unique, beautifully colored snails of the genus *Polymita.*

TREES

Indigenous tree species include mahogany, cedar, pine, rosewood, ebony, lignum vitae, cottonwood, *majagua,* and the deciduous, silvery *yagruma*, which shimmers as if frosted and bursts forth with huge lily-like blooms. Many species are in short supply following centuries of logging to supply the furniture makers of Europe and to clear the land for sugar. Mountain ranges still have ecosystems typical of original Antillean vegetation.

Archetypal species include the silver-trunked *kapok*, or silk-cotton, better known in Cuba as the revered ceiba, with broad trunk and wide-spreading boughs. The bully of trees is the *jagüey*, a species of strangler fig. It sprouts from the tops of trees from seeds dropped by birds or bats. It then sends roots to the ground, where they dig into the soil and provide a boost of sustenance. Slowly—it may take a full century—the roots grow and envelop the host tree, choking it until it dies and rots away, leaving the hollow, freestanding fig tree.

There are fruit trees, too, such as mangos and mameys, whose pulpy red fruit is the queen of Cuban fruits. One of Sierra del Rosario's endemic species, *Psidium guayabita*, produces a berry from which sweet *licor de guayabita* and dry *guayabita seca* brandy are made.

With elevation, palms and large-leafed undergrowth such as the "everlasting plant" give way to ferns, bracken, pine trees, feathery-leafed *palo de cotorra* (parrot tree), and parasitic *conde de pino* (count of the pine) vine. Above 2,000 meters, the vegetation changes abruptly to cloud forest. Some wind-battered elfin woods on exposed ridges are dwarfed, whereas more protected areas have majestically tall trees festooned with bromeliads, lichens, mosses, and lianas and creepers.

Many trees host bromeliads—spiky-leafed "air plants" up to 120 centimeters across—and other epiphytes, arboreal nesters ("epiphyte" comes from the Greek, "upon plants") that attach themselves to tree trunks or branches.

Palms

Visually, the predominant species are the palms, of which Cuba has more than 30 types, including the rare cork palm, found in the western part of Cuba. Those palms with swollen lower trunks are *barrigonas,* or belly palms, so named because of their remarkable ability to store water. The coconut palm is severely outnumbered, although it holds its own in northeast Cuba.

The king of palms is the ubiquitous silver-sheathed *Roystonea regia,* the royal palm, which grows singly or in great elegant clumps. Its smooth gray trunk, which can tower 25 meters, resembles a great marble column with a curious bulge near the top. Its fronds (*pencas*) make good thatch, and the thick green base—the *yagua*—of the *penca,* being waterproof, also makes an excellent roof or siding material. The trunk itself makes good timber. Bees favor palm honey. The seeds are used for pig feed. And birds love its black fruit and carry the seeds (*palmiche*) all over the country. As part of the national emblem, it is protected by law, despite its ability to thrive almost anywhere.

Mangroves

Cuba's shorelines are home to five species of mangrove. Mangroves are halophytes, plants that thrive in salty conditions. Although they do not require salt (they grow better in fresh water), they thrive where no other tree can. These pioneer land builders thrive at the interface of land and sea, forming a stabilizing tangle that fights tidal erosion and reclaims land from the water. The irrepressible shrubby mangroves rise from the dark water on interlocking stilt roots. Brackish labyrinthine creeks wind among them like snakes.

Their sustained health is vital to the health of other marine ecosystems. Cuba's rivers carry silt out of the mountains onto the coastal alluvial plains, where it is trapped by mangroves. The nutrient-rich mud fosters algae and other small organisms that form the base of the marine food chain. Mangrove swamps are esteemed as nurseries of marine life and havens for water birds—cormorants, frigate birds, pelicans, herons, and egrets—which feed and nest here, producing guano that makes the mangroves grow faster.

Mangroves build up the soil until they strand themselves high and dry. In the end they die on the land they have created.

BIRDS

Cuba has 374 recorded species of birds, of which 149 species breed on the island and 25 are native to Cuba. Birds that have all but disappeared in other areas still find tenuous safety in protected pockets of Cuba, although some 37 species are listed as threatened due to habitat destruction, pollution, and hunting.

Spoonbills and flamingos are common on the cays and coastal lagoons. White egrets (*coco blanco*) are found around cane fields and mudflats, and their cousins the ibis (*coco negro*) and blue heron (*garza*) can be seen picking at a buffet that extends for miles. Frigate birds, coast dwellers with long scimitar wings and forked tails, hang like sinister kites in the wind. *Gaviotas,* or gulls, also prefer maritime regions, as does the *gincho* (osprey).

Of terrestrial species, the wood stork can be seen in scrub areas. Tanagers and woodpeckers brighten the forests. Listen at night for the hoot of the barn owl and pygmy owls. The *tocororo,* or Cuban trogon, is the national bird, perhaps because its brilliant blue, white, and red plumage copies the colors of the national flag. It wears a scarlet sash across its breast. Listen for its onomatopoeic call.

There were so many parrots and macaws in the New World 500 years ago that the Americas were shown on maps as Terra Psittacorum, land of the free parrot. These are now on the road to extinction (the Cuban macaw became extinct in the 19th century). The best place to spot parrots is the Los Indios forest reserve on Isla de la Juventud, inhabited by 153 species of birds, including the Cuban *grulla* (sandbill crane).

Cuba also has three species of hummingbirds, whose magnificent emerald and purple liveries shimmer iridescent in the sunlight as they sip nectar from the blooms and twirl in midair, their wings a filmy blur. The bee hummingbird or *zunzuncito,* also called the *pájaro mosca*—fly bird—for its diminutive size, is the smallest bird in the world. It weighs less than a penny. Hummers earned a place in the mythology of the Taíno, who called them *colibrí,* meaning "god bird." They worshipped the bird as a *zemi,* a fetish idol.

AMPHIBIANS AND REPTILES

The most common reptiles are any of 46 lizard species, especially the comical curly-tailed lizard, and geckos. The dragonlike iguana, which can grow to two meters in length, can be seen on the cays. Its head is crested with a frightening wig of leathery spines, its heavy body encased in a scaly hide, deeply wrinkled around the sockets of its muscular legs. Despite its menacing "one million years BC" appearance, it is a nonbelligerent vegetarian. Aquatic turtles (terrapins) are also common, particularly in the Península de Zapata.

The amphibians are primarily represented by the frogs and toads, most of which you're more likely to hear than to see.

Cuba is also home to 14 species of neotropical snakes. None of them are venomous. Among the more common species are the wide-ranging boas. The *majá,* or Cuban boa, can grow to four meters in length. Its converse is the 20-centimeter-long pygmy boa, found solely in the caves of the Valle de Viñales.

Crocodiles and Caimans

The endemic freshwater *Crocodylus rhombifer* is found only in the Península de Zapata but is being reintroduced to the Lanier swamps, Río Cuato estuary, and other native areas. The crocodile was hunted to near extinction during colonial days and today has the most restricted geographical range of any crocodile species in the world. *Lagarto criollo* (as the Cuban croc is colloquially known) is more aggressive than its cousin, the American crocodile, which inhabits many of the estuaries and brackish environments around the island. Climate change is causing the sea level to rise, and the first hybrids have been discovered as a result of interbreeding as freshwater and brackish-water species now meet. Cuba has an active breeding program to save the indigenous species. Today the population is abundant and healthy (about 6,000 exist in the wild). In 1995, the Cuban government was authorized by the Convention of International Trade in Endangered Species to market the skins of the American crocodile worldwide to be turned into shoes and handbags, with the money to be plowed back into conservation; only crocs in the captive-breeding program are culled.

The creatures, which can live 80 years or more, spend much of their days basking on mud banks. At night, they sink down into the river for the hunt.

Marine Turtles

Marine turtles, notably the hawksbill and the green, nest on Cuban beaches, mostly on Isla de la Juventud and southern cays. Most of the important nesting sites in Cuba are now protected, and access to some is restricted. Despite legislation outlawing the taking of turtle eggs or disturbance of nesting turtles, adult turtles continue to be captured for meat by Cuban fishers. Hawksbills are also hunted illegally in Cuba (which lobbies to reopen international trade in hawksbill shell products) for the tourist trade.

Of the hundreds of eggs laid by a female in one season, only a handful survive to maturity. Cayo Largo has Cuba's only turtle farm.

FISH AND SHELLFISH

The warm waters off Cuba's coast are populated by more than 900 species of fish and crustaceans—from octopus, crabs, turtles, and lobsters the size of house cats to sharks, tuna, and their cousins the billfish, which approach aerodynamic perfection. The sailfish has been timed swimming over short distances at 110 kilometers per hour—faster than cheetahs can run.

The lucky diver may also spot whale sharks (the largest fish in the world) and manta rays up to seven meters across.

Fish to avoid include the fatally toxic and heavily camouflaged stonefish and the or-ange-and-white-striped lionfish, whose long spines can inflict a killer sting. The bulbous puffer, which can blow itself up to the size of a baseball, is also toxic. And don't go probing around inside coral, where moray eels make their home—their bite can take your fingers off.

Inland, the waters of Zapata harbor the rare *manjuarí,* the Cuban "alligator gar" (*Atractosteus tristoechus*), a living fossil.

Coral Reefs

Coral reefs—the most complex and variable community of organisms in the world—rim much of Cuba at a distance of usually no more than one kilometer offshore. Those of the Jardines de la Reina are considered as pristine as any on earth. On the sea floor sit the massive brain corals and the delicate, branching sea fans and feathers; nearer the surface are elkhorn corals, frond-like gorgonians spreading their fingers upward toward the light, lacy outcrops of tubipora such as delicately woven Spanish mantillas, and soft flowering corals swaying to the rhythms of the ocean currents.

Corals are animals that secrete calcium carbonate. Each individual soft-bodied coral polyp resembles a small sea anemone and is surrounded by an intricately structured calyx of calcium carbonate, an external skeleton that is built upon and multiplied over thousands of generations to form massive reef structures. Though stinging cells protect it against some predators, coral is perennially gnawed away by fish, surviving by its ability to repair itself and provide both habitat and food for other fauna.

MAMMALS

Given the diversity of Cuba's ecosystems, it may come as a surprise that only a few dozen mammal species live here. Wild boar (*jabalí*) are common in many wild regions, including the cays of Jardines de la Rey, the Lanier swamps of Isla de la Juventud, and the Península de Guanahacabibes, all areas where white-tailed deer are also found.

Much of the wildlife is glimpsed only as shadows, such as the *jutía* (*Capromys*), a large forest rodent related to the guinea pig and coypu of South America. It is edible and has been hunted for meat since indigenous times. Today it is endangered though found island-wide. A well-known indigenous animal that you are *not* likely to see is the solenodon, a primitive insectivorous mammal. The solenodon was thought to have become extinct in the 1990s, but in 2012 seven were captured and tagged by scientists. This ratlike mammal (also called the *almiqué*) has large padded feet and claws and a long proboscis good for sucking up ants.

Bats are by far the most numerous mammals: Cuba has 27 species. You may come across them slumbering by day halfway up a tree or roosting in a shed. Most species—like the Cuban flower bat and the giant Jamaican fruit bat, with a wingspan of more than 51 centimeters—are frugivores or insectivores. The smallest bat in the world is Cuba's butterfly bat, also known as the moth bat. Cuba has no vampire bats.

Cuba has few marine mammals, though the endangered West Indian manatee inhabits coastal lagoons. This herbivorous, heavily wrinkled beast looks like a tuskless walrus, with no hind limbs—just a large, flat, spatulate tail. The creature can weigh up to 900 kilograms and reach 4.3 meters in length.

INSECTS

With almost 200 identified species of butterflies and moths (at least 28 endemic), Cuba is a lepidopterist's paradise. You can barely stand still for one minute without checking off a dozen dazzling species: the transparent Cuban clear-wing butterfly, metallic gold monarch, delicate black-winged heliconius splashed with bright red and yellow, the scintillating yellow orange-barred sulphur, and huge swallowtails fluttering and diving in a ballet of stupendous color. At dusk the air trills with the sound of cicadas (*cigarras*), while fireflies flit by all a-twinkle with phosphorescence. Unfriendly bugs also exist: chiggers, wasps and bees, mosquitoes, and the famous "no-see-ums" (*jejenes*).

History

Cuba has a sunny geography shadowed by a dark, brooding history. A sound knowledge of the island's history is integral to understanding Cuba today. It is as fascinating a tale of pathos as that of any nation on earth.

PRE-COLUMBIAN HISTORY

The indigenous people numbered no fewer than 100,000 when Christopher Columbus chanced upon the island in 1492. The Spaniards who claimed the island lent the name Arawaks to the indigenous peoples, but there were several distinct groups that had left the Orinoco basin of South America and island-hopped their way up the Caribbean over centuries.

The earliest to arrive were the Gauanajatabeys, hunter-gatherers who lived in the west, in what is now Pinar del Río Province. They were followed by the Ciboneys, who settled along the south coast, where they established themselves as farmers and fishers. Little is known of these preceramic peoples (3500 BC–AD 1200). The preceramic tribes were displaced by the Taíno, who arrived from Hispaniola around AD 1100 and, in a second wave, in the mid-15th century, when they were driven from Hispaniola by the Caribs.

A Peaceable Culture

The Taíno lived in *bohíos*, thatched circular huts. Villages, which allied with one another, consisted of 15 or so families who shared property and were governed by a *cacique*, or clan leader. Since the land produced everything, the indigenous peoples were able to live well and peaceably. They culled fish from the rivers and birds from the trees, which also produced tropical fruits and nuts in abundance. The Taíno also used advanced farming techniques to maximize yields of yucca (also called manioc) and corn (*mahis,* or maize).

Although they went naked, the Taíno were skilled weavers who slept in tightly woven cotton nets (a precursor to today's hammocks) strung from poles; the Spaniards would later use native labor to weave sailcloth. They were also skilled potters and boat builders who hewed canoes from huge tree trunks. It seems they had evolved at least basic astronomical charts, painted on the walls of caves.

Columbus "Discovers" Cuba

After making landfall in the Bahamas in 1492 during his first voyage to the New World, Columbus threaded the maze of islets that lay to the southwest. On the evening of October 27, 1492, Columbus first set eyes on Cuba. He voyaged along the north coast for four weeks and finally dropped anchor on November 27, 1492, near today's Gibara.

"They are the best people in the world," Columbus recorded of the Indians, "without knowledge of what is evil; nor do they murder or steal.... All the people show the most singular loving behavior...and are gentle and always laughing." The Spaniards would change that forever.

THE SPANISH TAKE OVER

In 1509 King Ferdinand gave Christopher Columbus's son, Diego, the title of Governor of the Indies, with the duty to organize an exploratory expedition led by Diego Velázquez de Cuellar (1465-1524). In 1511 four ships from Spain arrived, carrying 300 settlers under Diego Columbus and his wife, María de Toledo (grandniece of King Ferdinand). Also on board was Velázquez, the new governor of Cuba, and his secretary, young Hernán Cortés

(1485-1547), who later set sail from Havana for Mexico to subdue the Aztecs.

Velázquez founded the first town at Baracoa in 1511, followed within the next few years by six other crude *villas*—Bayamo, Puerto Príncipe (today's Camagüey), San Cristóbal de la Habana, Sancti Spíritus, Santiago de Cuba, and Trinidad.

A Sordid Beginning

The Spaniards were not on a holy mission. Thus the indigenous island cultures—considered by the Spaniards to be a backward, godless race—were subjected to the Spaniards' ruthless and mostly fruitless quest for silver and gold. A priest named Bartolomé de las Casas (1474-1566) accompanied Velázquez and recorded in his *History of the Indies:*

> The Indians came to meete us, and to receive us with victuals, and delicate cheere...the Devill put himselfe into the Spaniards, to put them all to the edge of the sword in my presence, without any cause whatsoever, more than three thousand soules, which were set before us, men, women and children. I saw there so great cruelties, that never any man living either have or shall see the like.

Slavery was forbidden by papal edict, but the Spaniards immediately found a way around the prohibition. Spain parceled its new conquests among the conquistadores. The Indians were turned into *peones*—serfs under the guise of being taught Christianity. Each landowner was allotted from 40 to 200 Indian laborers under a system known as the *encomienda,* from the verb "to entrust." Those Indians not marched off to work in mines were placed on plantations. Since the Indians were supposed to be freed once converted, they were literally worked to death to extract the maximum labor.

The resistance was led by Hatuey, a *cacique* who had fought the Spanish on the island of Hispaniola and fled to Cuba after his people were defeated. The Spaniards captured the heroic chief and burned him at the stake on February 2, 1512. The Spaniards, in their inimically cruel fashion, provided Cuba with its first martyr to independence.

The 16th century witnessed the extinction of a race. Those Taíno not put to the sword or worked to death fell victim to European diseases (measles, smallpox, and tuberculosis) to which they had no natural resistance. Within 100 years of Columbus's landfall, virtually the entire indigenous population had perished.

The Key to the New World

The Spanish found little silver and gold in Cuba. They had greater luck in Mexico and Peru, whose indigenous cultures flaunted vast quantities of precious metals and jewels. Cuba was set to become a vital stopover for Spanish galleons and traders carrying the wealth of the Americas back to Europe.

In 1564 a Spanish expedition reached the Philippines. The next year it discovered the northern Pacific trade winds that for the next 250 years propelled ships laden with Chinese treasure to Acapulco, from where the booty was carried overland to Veracruz, on the Gulf of Mexico, and loaded onto ships bound for Havana and Europe. Oriental perfumes, pearls, silks, and ivories passed through Havana. To these shipments were added silver from Bolivia and alpaca from Peru, plus Cuban tobacco, leather, fruit, and precious woods. To supply the fleets, the forests were felled, making room for cattle ranches and tobacco (and, later, sugar) plantations that would supply European markets.

With the Indian population devastated, the Spanish turned to West Africa for labor. By the 17th century, a slave trade had developed. Landowners, slave traders, and merchants were in their heyday. The Spanish crown heavily taxed exports, which fostered smuggling on a remarkable scale.

The Period of Piracy

As early as 1526, a royal decree declared that ships had to travel in convoy to Spain. En route, they gathered in Havana harbor. The crown had a vested interest in protecting the wealth from pirates: it received one-fifth of the treasure. In 1537, Havana was raided. One year later, French pirate Jacques de Sores sacked the capital.

Soon, pirates were encouraged (and eventually licensed) by the governments of France, Holland, and England to prey upon Spanish shipping. In 1587 King Philip of Spain determined to end the growing sea power of England and amassed a great armada to invade her. Sir Francis Drake, John Hawkins, and Sir Walter Raleigh assembled a fleet and destroyed the armada, breaking the power of Spain in the Old World.

Now, no Spanish-held city was safe. There were hundreds of raids every year. Spain was impotent. In 1662, Henry Morgan and his buccaneers ransacked Havana, pilfered the cathedral bells, and left with a taunt that the Spanish weren't equal to the stone walls that Spain had built: "I could have defended Morro Castle with a dog and a gun."

The Spanish crown treated Cuba as a cash cow to milk dry as it pleased. For example, it had monopolized tobacco trading by 1717. The restriction so affected farmers' incomes that the *vegueros* (tobacco growers) marched on Havana. The rebellion, the first against Spain, was brutally crushed. In 1740, Spain created the Real Compañía, with a monopoly on all trade between Cuba and Spain. It bought Cuban products cheaply and sold necessities from Europe at inflated prices.

England Takes Over

On January 4, 1762, George III of England declared war on Spain. On June 7, a British fleet of 200 warships carrying 11,000 troops put ashore and Havana erupted in panic. The Spanish scuttled three ships in the harbor mouth, ineptly trapping their own warships inside the harbor. That night, when Spanish guards atop the fort began firing at British scouts, the Spanish warships began blasting the ridge, causing their own troops to flee. The British took the ridge and laid siege to Havana. On July 29 sappers blew an enormous hole in the Castillo del Morro, and the flag of St. George was raised over the city.

The English immediately lifted Spain's trade restrictions. Foreign merchants flocked, and Cuba witnessed surging prosperity. Jamaican sugar planters, however, pressured England to cede back to Spain what would otherwise become a formidable rival for the English sugar market. On February 10, 1763, England exchanged Cuba for Florida in the Treaty of Paris. In the interim, Spain had acquired a more enlightened king, Charles III, who continued the free-trade policy, encouraged a decade later when the United States began trading directly with Cuba.

KING SUGAR RULES

North Americans' collective sweet tooth fostered the rapid expansion of sugar plantations in Cuba. Wealthy Cuban and U.S. slave merchants funded planting of new lands by granting loans for capital improvements. Land planted in sugar multiplied more than tenfold by the end of the 18th century and was boosted with the Saint Domingue (Haiti) rebellion in 1791. About 30,000 French planters washed up in Cuba, bringing their superior knowledge of sugar production.

These events sent the slave trade soaring. In 1713, the Treaty of Utrecht, which ended the War of the Spanish Succession, granted the British sole rights to the Spanish-American slave trade. The trade grew throughout the century: As many as 200 slaving ships called into Havana annually during the 1830s. Although in 1817 Spain signed a treaty with England to abolish the trade, Cuban officials were so enriched by bribes that the industry continued unabated. Only in 1886 was slavery in Cuba abolished.

By 1760 Havana was already larger than New York or Boston. The first University of Havana had been established in 1728, the first newspaper in 1763, and the postal service in 1764. Spanish ships unloaded builders and craftsmen, hired to help citizens display their earnings in an outpouring of architectural sophistication. They brought with them a Moorish aesthetic, which they translated into what Juliet Barclay calls a unique "tropical synthesis of column, courtyard, and chiaroscuro." Monuments and parks were erected, along with public libraries and theaters. Streets were paved, and beautiful colonial homes were erected. While the British went out to their colonies to grow rich and return, the Spanish went to grow rich and stay.

THE WARS FOR INDEPENDENCE

Spain's colonial policy, applied throughout its empire, was based on exploitation, with power centralized in Madrid and politics practiced only for the spoils of office and to the benefit of *peninsulares*—native-born Spaniards. "The Spanish officials taxed thrift right out of the island; they took industry by the neck and throttled it," thought Frederic Remington on his visit in 1899. Cuban-born *criollos* resented the corrupt *peninsulares* who denied them self-determination: No Cuban could occupy a public post, set up an industry or business, bring legal action against a Spaniard, or travel without military permission.

Following the Napoleonic wars in Europe, Spain's New World territories were wracked by wars of independence. By 1835 only Cuba and Puerto Rico had not gained independence from Spain. Meanwhile, young Cuban intellectuals and patriots began to make their voices heard. In 1843, Miguel Tacón became governor. He suppressed patriotic sentiment and executed or exiled leading nationalists. Meanwhile, the island, says historian Louis A. Pérez Jr., "had achieved a level of modernity that far surpassed Spain's. Spain could not provide Cuba with what it did not itself possess." Spain clung to its colony with the support of wealthy *criollos* (concentrated in western Cuba), who feared that independence would lead to abolition of slavery in Cuba.

Uncle Sam Stirs

Annexation sentiment in the United States had been spawned by the Louisiana Purchase of 1803. The Mississippi River became the

Slave Society

Black slavery in Cuba began in 1513 and it wasn't abolished until 1886. At the peak of the trade, in the 1840s, slaves formed about 45 percent of Cuba's population.

The majority of slaves who were shipped to Cuba came from highly developed West African tribes such as the Fulani, Hausa, and Yoruba. Distinct ethnic groups were kept together, unlike in North America. As a result, their traditions and languages have been retained and passed down.

After being captured and herded to African ports, slaves were packed onto ships like sardines. Chained together body-to-body in the rancid hold, they wallowed in their own excrement and vomit on the nightmare voyage across the Atlantic. Thousands died. They arrived in Cuba diseased and half-starved. Once ashore, they were sold to plantation owners or to work as domestics in the cities. Parents, children, and siblings were torn asunder forever.

Rebellion was always around the corner. The first slave revolt occurred in 1532 in Oriente. A few years later, Havana was sacked by slaves in the wake of an attack by French pirates. Other slaves fled to the mountains. When a slave was caught, it was standard to cut off one ear as a warning to others.

Nonetheless, slaves had the legal right to buy their own and their relatives' freedom. Slaves could keep a percentage of whatever fee their masters charged for hiring them out as labor and apply it toward buying their manumission. Free blacks formed a significant part of Havana's populace: Once free, they could even own and sell property, and there evolved a significant slave-owning black middle class. An overseer called the *síndico* existed to ensure that slaves' rights were enjoyed: For example, if a slave wished to change his master, the *síndico* could force an owner to grant a slave three days' absence to look for one; he could also ask the owner to value the price, after which that sum could not be increased.

Slave owners bred slaves like cattle for sale. The healthiest women were expected to produce healthy babies every year. It was common for white men to take a black mistress, and their off-spring usually received their freedom.

Plantation slaves lived in primitive barracks *(barracoons)*. By 6am they were marching in file to the fields, where they worked until sunset. Slaves stopped working if they reached 60 years of age. Sunday was rest day. Small private plots were the slaves' salvation. Here, they could grow vegetables and raise livestock for sale.

The most comprehensive account of plantation life is *Autobiography of a Runaway Slave,* by Esteban Montejo, who related his life as a slave and runaway *(cimarron)* in 1963 at the age of 105.

main artery of trade, and Cuba's position at the mouth of the Gulf of Mexico took on added strategic importance. Thus in 1808 Thomas Jefferson attempted to purchase Cuba from Spain. By 1848, 40 percent of Cuba's sugar was sold to the U.S. market; manufactures began flowing the other way. Yankees yearned for expanded trade. President James Polk (1845-1849) offered Spain US$100 million for Cuba. President Franklin Pierce (1853-1857) upped the ante to US$130 million. His successor, James Buchanan, tried twice to purchase Cuba for the same price. But Spain wasn't selling.

The American Civil War changed the equation. With slavery in the United States ended, it became impossible for Spain to keep the lid on Cuba. In 1868 the pot boiled over.

The Ten Years War

On October 10, 1868, a planter named Carlos Manuel de Céspedes freed the slaves on his plantation at La Demajagua, near Manzanillo, in Oriente. Fellow planters rushed to join him. Within a week, 1,500 men had flocked to Céspedes's calling (they called themselves the Mambí, after a freedom fighter in Santo Domingo). For the next 10 years Cuba would be roiled by the first war of independence (the Ten Years War, 1868-1878), in which white and black *criollos* fought side by side against 100,000 Spanish volunteers shipped from Spain with a virtual carte blanche to terrorize the people of Cuba. Led by two brilliant generals—one a white, Máximo Gómez, and the other a mulatto, Antonio Maceo—the rebels liberated much of the island. However, the movement collapsed, and in 1878 the forces signed the Pact of Zanjón. The rebels were given a general amnesty, and slaves who had fought with the rebels were granted their freedom.

The Cuban economy had been devastated. Huge tracts of land lay abandoned. North American investors bought up ravaged sugar plantations and mills at ludicrously low rates. Meanwhile, the Spanish reverted to the same old recipe of tyranny.

The long, bloody war claimed the lives of 250,000 Cubans (almost one-fifth of the population) and 80,000 Spaniards. At least 100,000 Cubans were forced to flee; their lands were expropriated and given to loyalists. Among those arrested was a teenager named José Martí y Pérez. After a brief imprisonment, the gifted orator, intellectual, poet, and political leader was exiled to Spain.

Martí's Martyrdom

Following his exile, José Martí traveled to the United States, where he settled. In 1892 he formed the Cuban Revolutionary Party, and through his writings and indefatigable spirit he became the acknowledged "intellectual author" of the independence movement.

In 1895 Martí joined General Máximo Gómez in the Dominican Republic. Together they sailed to Cuba. On April 11, they landed at Cajobabo at the eastern end of the island. They linked up with General Maceo and together they launched the War of Independence (1895-1898).

Barely one month after returning from exile, Martí martyred himself on May 19, 1895, at the age of 42. His motto was, "To die for the fatherland is to live." Martí's death left Cuba without a spiritual leader. But the Cubans were determined to seize their freedom. Generals Gómez and Maceo led an army of 60,000 the full length of Cuba, smashing

Spanish forces en route. Maceo's brilliant tactics earned worldwide acclaim until he was finally killed in battle in December 1896.

After Maceo's death, the struggle degenerated into a destructive guerrilla war. In a desperate bid to forestall independence, the ruthless Spanish governor, Valeriano Weyler, herded virtually the entire campesino population into concentration camps. The *reconcentración* campaign claimed the lives of 10 percent of Cuba's population. In turn, the rebels torched the sugarcane fields until the conflagration licked at the fringe of Havana.

THE SPANISH-CUBAN-AMERICAN WAR

The ideal of *¡Cuba libre!* (Free Cuba!) had support among the U.S. populace, which saw echoes of its own struggle for independence a century earlier. The public hungered for information about the war. The *New York World* and *New York Journal*, owned by Joseph Pulitzer and William Randolph Hearst, respectively, started a race to see which newspaper could first reach one million subscribers. While Hearst's hacks made up stories from Cuba, the magnate himself worked behind the scenes to orchestrate events. He sent the photographer Frederic Remington to Cuba in anticipation of the United States entering the war. At one point Remington wired Hearst: "There will be no war. I wish to return." Hearst replied: "Please remain. You furnish the pictures and I'll furnish the war."

Remember the *Maine!*

Responding to public pressure, President McKinley sent a warship, the USS *Maine*, to Havana to protect U.S. citizens living there. On February 5, 1898, the ship exploded and sank in Havana Harbor, killing 258 people. Evidence suggests this was an accident, but Hearst had his coup and rushed the news out in great red headlines. He blamed the Spanish, and so did the public. His *New York Journal* coined the phrase "Remember the *Maine,* to hell with Spain." Theodore Roosevelt, then assistant secretary of the navy, also fanned the

Heroes of the Wars for Independence

Carlos Manuel de Céspedes (1819-1874), known in Cuba as the "Father of Our Country," was a sugar planter who published the first independent newspaper in Cuba. On October 10, 1868, he freed his slaves, enrolled them in an army, and in an oration known as the *Grito de Yara* (Shout of Yara) declared an open revolt against Spain, starting the Ten Years War. Céspedes was named head of the government but in 1874 was cut down in a hail of bullets—ambushed by the Spanish while awaiting a ship for a life in exile.

Calixto García Iñiguez (1840-1898) was born in Holguín and rose to become top commander of the rebel army in the Oriente in the Ten Years War (1868-1878), during which he was captured by the Spanish and survived attempted suicide. When he was second-in-command of the rebel Mambí army during the War of Independence (1895-1898), his troops liberated many Spanish-held cities and participated alongside U.S. troops in the assault on Santiago de Cuba that sealed Cuba's independence from Spain. García, who died of pneumonia, was buried with full U.S. military honors in Arlington National Cemetery.

Máximo Gómez y Baez (1836-1905) was born in Santo Domingo, Dominican Republic. He joined the Spanish army in 1856 and commanded Spanish troops in Cuba before switching sides and rising to become commander in chief of the Army of Liberation. Prominent Cuban leaders invited Gómez to run for the presidency of the newly independent republic, but he declined. He died in Havana.

Antonio Maceo Grajales (1845-1896), of African and Spanish descent, hailed from Santiago and rose to become a general in the rebel army in the Ten Years War. A brilliant guerrilla strategist, Maceo was known for his whirlwind strikes against superior forces. He was wounded 24 times, earning the nickname the "Bronze Titan." The fearless leader refused to accept the treaty ending the war in 1878 and fought on for several months until fleeing into exile. He returned on March 30, 1895, to help lead the War of Independence; as a commander of the Army of Liberation he led his forces all the way to Pinar del Río before being killed in battle near Havana on December 7, 1896.

flames, seeing the venture as "good for the navy." On April 25, 1898, Congress declared war against Spain.

The Cuban general, Máximo Gómez, did not want U.S. troops. His guerrilla army—the Mambí—was on the verge of victory and would have undoubtedly won independence before the close of the century. However, Cuba's freedom fighters soon found themselves forced into the backseat. Where the Mambí did fight, heroically, their part was dismissed, as at the pivotal engagement at San Juan Hill in Santiago de Cuba, where, on July 1, 1898, a charge led by Theodore Roosevelt sealed the war. In a decisive naval battle on July 3, the U.S. Navy destroyed the Spanish fleet as it attempted to escape Santiago harbor. On July 17, Spain surrendered. The Spanish flag was lowered and the Stars and Stripes raised, ending one of the most foolishly run

empires in the world. Cuba ended the century as it had begun—under foreign rule.

Uncle Sam Takes Over

The U.S. military occupation formally began on January 1, 1899, when 15 infantry regiments, one of engineers, and four of artillery arrived to "pacify" Cuba. They would remain for four years. Washington dictated the peace terms embodied in the Treaty of Paris, signed on April 11, 1899. Even the Cuban constitution was written by Washington in 1901, ushering in a period known as the Pseudo-Republic. Rubbing salt in the wound of Cuban sensibilities was a clause called the Platt Amendment, named for Senator Orville H. Platt of Connecticut but written in 1903 by Secretary of War Elihu Root. Through it, the United States acquired the Guantánamo naval base and the right to intervene in Cuban affairs whenever the United States deemed it necessary.

Nonetheless, the United States pumped millions of dollars into reconstruction. Under General Leonard Wood, the U.S. authorities set up schools, started a postal system, established a judiciary and civil service, organized finances, paved roads in cities throughout the nation, and eradicated yellow fever.

On May 20, 1902, the U.S. flag was lowered and the lone-star flag of Cuba rose into the sunny sky. "It's not the republic we dreamed of," said Máximo Gómez.

THE PSEUDO-REPUBLIC

Washington "granted" Cuba "independence"—at the end of a short leash. The Pseudo-Republic was an era of Yankee colonization and domestic acquiescence. Economically, North America held sway. Politically, Washington called the shots. As Hugh Thomas suggests: "This continuous U.S. presence, benevolent though it often set out to be, paternalistic though it usually was in practice, fatally delayed the achievement of political stability in Cuba."

The United States installed Cuba's first president, Tomás Estrada Palma, who received his salary and instructions directly from Washington. Palma, though reelected in 1905, was too honest and weak to hold greedy politicians in check. Each Cuban president forged new frauds of his own and handed out sinecures (which the Cubans called *botellas*—milk bottles given to babies) to cronies. The U.S. government was constantly influenced to support this or that Cuban who had given, or would give, opportunities to U.S. investors or had borrowed from North American banks. When U.S. economic interests were threatened, Uncle Sam sent in troops. The United States landed marines in 1906, 1912, and 1917. Dollar diplomacy was blind to the corruption, state violence, and poverty plaguing the country.

A U.S. Colony

Cuba witnessed a great influx of capital as U.S. companies invested in every major industry—tobacco, railroads, utilities, mining, and, above all, sugar. U.S. citizens arrived, bringing their North American style and sensibilities to the island. In short order, every major industry was U.S.-owned. U.S. interests in the sugar industry increased almost overnight from 15 percent to 75 percent. Cuba had become a giant Monopoly board controlled by U.S. interests.

Thanks to billions of dollars of investment, the Cuban economy bounced back with vigor, though the mass of rural families struggled to survive. Although the sugar workers had no other way of earning a living, the sugar companies paid them wages for only half a year. Employment lasted only as long as the dry season. Most workers and their families lived in squalor and suffered miserably for half the year. (Not all estates were of this model. For example, the Hershey company built modern homes for its Cuban employees and provided clinics, schools, and social services.)

Profits from sugar were so great that Cubans sold out their other properties and poured their money into the industry, deriving dividends from sweetening the desserts of the world. The peak of the sugar boom—the "dance of the millions"—lasted from 1915 to 1920, when the price of sugar climbed to US$0.22 a pound. Then came the crash. In 1924, Cuba produced more than 4.5 million tons of sugar. The next year it produced a million tons more—but the sugar sold for less than US$0.01 a pound.

Sugar money paid for massive civic constructions and public utilities and for the plush mansions in beaux-arts and art deco style then blossoming in cities all over Cuba. Cuba of the 1920s was far and away the richest tropical country anywhere, with a per capita income equivalent to that of Ireland, two-thirds that of Britain, and half that of the United States. As Prohibition and a wave of morality swept through the United States, Yankees flocked to Havana, which, wrote Juliet Barclay, was filled with "milkshakes and mafiosi, hot dogs and whores. Yanqui Doodle had come to town and was having martini-drinking competitions in the Sevilla Bar."

This was a period of overt racism. Rarely reported (even the post-Revolution government has kept the story under wraps) was the massacre in 1912 of thousands of black Cubans—an event known as "Negro Rebellion" or the "Little Race War." Many of those murdered were members of the Partido Independiente de Color (Independent Party of Color), Cuba's first black political party founded in 1908 to combat the marginalization of nonwhites following independence in 1902. After being ordered to disband by President José Miguel Gómez, the party leaders initiated an armed rebellion in Oriente. At least 3,000 people were slaughtered, with the assistance of U.S. Marines, mainly in Guantánamo. (In 1937, many Cubans of Haitian descent were also forcibly repatriated to Haiti.)

The Machado Epoch

In 1924, President Alfredo Zayas, having made his millions, declined to run for reelection. General Gerardo Machado y Morales (1871-1939) stepped into the breach. Machado acted on his promises to construct schools, highways, and a health care system, and initiated an ambitious development plan for Cuba. However, he was also a uniquely corrupt man susceptible to la mordida (literally, "the bite"—bribes). In 1928 Machado manipulated a phony election and became a tropical Mussolini, supported by a ruthless police force. His politics were to make himself rich and to protect U.S. investments. His method was to assassinate anyone who opposed his government.

When the Great Depression hit, Cuba's one-crop economy was dealt a death blow, bringing misery throughout the country. The United States raised its import tariffs on sugar, exacerbating Cuba's plight. The Cuban economy collapsed, and the nation disintegrated into violent mayhem. Havana and other cities were swept by random bombings and assassinations. Machado responded to hunger marches, strikes, and antigovernment demonstrations with greater repression. (President Calvin Coolidge thought that "under Machado, Cuba is a sovereign state.... Her people are free, independent, in peace, and enjoying the advantages of democracy.") Finally, in the summer of 1933, a general strike brought the whole country to a halt. On August 11, Machado fled the country carrying a suitcase full of gold. A typhoon of retributory violence took the lives of at least 1,000 Machadistas.

Batista Days

Carlos Manuel de Céspedes (grandson of the hero of the Ten Years War) was named provisional president. Within a month he was overthrown by an amalgam of students and army officers. In short order, a 32-year-old sergeant named Fulgencio Batista y Zaldivar (1901-1973) led a golpe called the Sergeant's Revolt, which ousted the senior officers. They handed power to a five-man civilian commission that named a leftist university professor, Dr. Ramón Grau San Martín, president.

Grau lasted only four months. He was far too reformist for Washington. Batista, self-promoted to colonel and chief of the army, was under no illusions as to the intentions of the United States, which sent 30 warships to Cuba as a warning. On January 14, 1934, Batista ousted Grau and seized the reins of power. Impressed by Batista's fealty to Washington, in 1934 the United States agreed to annul the Platt Amendment—with the exception of the clause regarding the Guantánamo naval base. Following promulgation of a new and progressive constitution in 1940, Batista ran for the presidency himself on a liberal platform. Cuban voters gave him a four-year term (1940-1944) in what was perhaps the nation's first clean election.

Batista at first displayed relative benevolence and good sense. He maintained enlightened attitudes on elections, civil liberties, public welfare, and workers' rights, and he enacted progressive social reforms and a new, liberal constitution. For pragmatic reasons, Batista legalized the Partido Comunista de

Cuba, and two leading Communists became ministers in his 1940-1944 government.

After serving his term, in 1944 Batista retired to Florida a wealthy man, leaving his country in the hands of men who permitted their administrations to again sink into chaos. Assassinations and bombings were daily events. Rival gangster groups ruled the streets. The public suicide on August 5, 1951, of Senator "Eddy" Chibás, incorruptible head of the Ortodoxo party, brought together a broad spectrum of Cubans fed up with corruption and student gangsterism.

In 1952 Batista returned to Cuba and again put himself up as a presidential candidate in the forthcoming elections. It soon became clear that he wouldn't win. On March 10, only three months before the election, he upended the process with a bloodless predawn *golpe*. (One of the reform-minded candidates for congress whose political ambitions were thwarted by Batista's coup was a 25-year-old lawyer named Fidel Castro, who had risen to prominence as the most outspoken critic of corrupt government and was being hailed as a future president.) In November 1954, Batista won the presidential election. Though the elections were rigged, Washington immediately recognized the regime. Batista had forsaken his interest in the Cuban people. He had lingered too long in Miami with mafiosi and had come back to commit grand larceny hand in hand with the mob.

Batista initiated massive civic construction work that conjured a tourist boom, spurring economic growth and fueling prosperity. Gangsters began to take over the hotels and casinos with Batista's blessing—for a cut of the proceeds, of course—creating the mobster-run, Las Vegas-style Havana with which pre-revolutionary Cuba will always be associated. North Americans arrived by plane or aboard the *City of Havana* ferry from Key West to indulge in a few days of sun and sin. They went home happy, unaware that behind the scenes chaos and corruption were rife.

Batista maintained his cynical rule with a brutal police force. Many Cubans were disgusted by the repression and depravity into which Havana had sunk, made more wretched by the poverty and destitution endemic in the slums of the capital and by the illiteracy and malnourishment that were part of the rural condition.

THE GATHERING STORM

Almost immediately following Batista's *golpe*, Fidel Castro began to plot Batista's downfall. Castro possessed a vision of his place in Cuba's future that seemed preordained. He was also ruthlessly focused. His plan: street protests and legal challenges to the Batista regime and a secret conspiracy simmering underneath. He organized an underground movement and ran it with military discipline.

The Attack on Moncada

Castro, then 26 years old, launched his revolution on July 26, 1953, with an attack on the Moncada barracks in Santiago de Cuba. It quickly collapsed in a hail of bullets. Batista declared a state of emergency. His propaganda machine went to work to convince the nation that the rebels had committed all kinds of atrocities. Unknown to Batista, however, the torture and assassination of more than 60 rebels who had been captured had been photographed. When the gruesome photos were published, revulsion swept the land. The Catholic hierarchy stepped in and negotiated a guarantee of the lives of any future captives.

Castro was eventually captured by an army detachment whose commander—a 53-year-old black lieutenant named Pedro Sarría—disobeyed orders to kill Castro on sight (Batista jailed Sarría, who would go on to become a captain in Fidel's Revolutionary Army). Amazingly, Fidel was allowed to broadcast his story over the national radio to demonstrate how subversive he was—a public relations coup that sowed the seeds of future victory. "Imagine the imbecility of these people!" Fidel later said, "At that minute, the second phase of the Revolution began."

History Will Absolve Me

Castro, who acted as his own attorney, was sentenced in a sealed court that opened on September 21, 1953. Castro never attempted to defend against the charges leveled at him and his fellow conspirators. He relied solely on attacking Batista's regime, and proudly defended his own actions, citing history's precedents for taking up arms against tyrants and ending with the words, "Condemn me, it does not matter. History will absolve me!" (The Moncada attack parallels in many ways Hitler's failed Rathaus Putsch in 1924. Indeed, Castro had studied *Mein Kampf,* and his "History Will Absolve Me" speech was closely modeled on the words of Adolf Hitler at the end of his Putsch trial, which ended with the words, "You may pronounce us guilty, [but] history will smile.... For she acquits us!")

Castro was cheered as he and 25 other companions were led away to serve 15 years in jail on the Isle of Pines (now Isla de la Juventud). José Martí had also been imprisoned on the Isle of Pines, adding to Castro's symbolic association with the original revolutionary hero. The media gave wide coverage to Castro, whose stature increased with each day in jail. In May 1955 Batista bowed to mounting public pressure and signed an amnesty bill. Castro and the Moncada prisoners were free. Nonetheless, Castro was forced to move constantly for his own safety. On July 7, 1955, he boarded a flight to Mexico.

Castro's Exile

Castro's goal in exile was to prepare a guerrilla army to invade Cuba. Fidel's enthusiasm and optimism were so great that he managed to talk Alberto Bayo, a hero of the Spanish Civil War, into giving up his business to train his nascent army—now known as M-26-7 (Movimiento Revolucionario 26 Julio)—in guerrilla warfare. (One of the foreigners who signed up was Ernesto "Che" Guevara, an Argentinean doctor and intellectual.)

In a brilliant coup, Fidel sent a powerful message to the congress of the Ortodoxo party, in which he called for the 500 delegates to reject working with Batista through congressional elections and to take the high road of revolution. The delegates jumped to their feet chanting "Revolution!" (The Communists continued to shun him—the "objective conditions" defined by Karl Marx didn't exist. Castro shunned the Communist Party, whose members were excluded from the movement; even Castro's Communist brother, Raúl, was kept out for a time.) Castro also authored the movement's manifesto, laying out the revolutionary program in detail: "The outlawing of the *latifundia,* distribution of the land among peasant families.... The right of the worker to broad participation in profits.... Drastic decrease in all rents.... Construction by the state of decent housing to shelter the 400,000 families crowded into filthy single rooms, huts, shacks, and tenements.... Extension of electricity to the 2,800,000 persons in our rural and suburban sectors who have none.... Confiscation of all the assets of embezzlers."

Castro's plan called for a long-term war in both countryside and urban areas, although he eschewed random violence against the public. To raise money for the endeavor, he toured the United States, speechmaking to thousands of Cuban exiles and Yankees alike. Batista's secret police tortured suspected opposition members and hanged them from trees. "The president's regime was creaking dangerously towards its end," wrote Graham Greene in *Our Man in Havana.*

The *Granma* Landing

Shortly after midnight on November 25, 1956, Castro and his revolutionaries set off from Tuxpán, Mexico, for Cuba aboard a 38-foot-long luxury cruiser. The *Granma* had been designed to carry 25 passengers. Battered by heavy seas and with a burden of 82 heavily armed men and their supplies, the vessel lurched laboriously toward Cuba. One engine failed and the boat fell two days behind schedule. At dawn on December 2, it ran aground two kilometers south of the planned landing site at Playa Las Coloradas. The men had to abandon their heavy armaments and supplies and wade ashore through dense mangroves. Just after dawn, Fidel Castro stood on terra firma alongside 81 men, with minimal equipment, no food, and no contact with the movement ashore. "This wasn't a landing, it was a shipwreck," Che Guevara later recalled.

Within two hours of landing, the *Granma* had been sighted and a bombardment began. On December 5, the exhausted column was ambushed. Only 16 men survived, including Fidel and Raúl Castro and Che Guevara. On December 13, Castro's meager force finally met a peasant member of the 26th of July Movement. Aided by an efficient communications network and support from the mountain peasants, the rebel unit moved deeper into the mountains and to safety.

THE CUBAN REVOLUTION

Soon men began joining the rebel army, mostly idealists keen to help oust a corrupt regime, but many of them, according to Jon Lee Anderson, were "former rustlers, fugitive murderers, juvenile delinquents, and marijuana traffickers."

The initial year in the mountains was difficult. The tiny rebel band won small skirmishes with Batista's troops but gained their major coup on February 16, 1957, when Herbert L. Matthews of the *New York Times* was led into the mountains to meet the next day with Castro. Matthews's report hit the newsstands on February 24. It began, "Fidel Castro, the rebel leader of Cuba's youth, is alive and fighting hard and successfully in the rugged, almost impenetrable vastness of the Sierra Maestra." Batista had lifted censorship the week before, and Matthews's story created a sensation that Castro milked by releasing a manifesto calling for violent uprising against the regime.

The rebel army consolidated its control of the mountains throughout 1957 from its base at La Plata, on the northwest slope of Pico Turquino. The first real battle occurred on May 28, when Castro and a force of 80 men attacked a garrison at El Uvero, on the coast. They lost six men but gained two machine guns and 46 rifles. In early 1958, the rebel army split into four separate units. Castro continued to lead from La Plata, Che Guevara held the northern slopes, Camilo Cienfuegos led a group on the plains near Bayamo, and Raúl Castro opened a new front near Santiago. By spring the rebel army had control of most of the mountain regions of Oriente. The enemy was being denied more and more territory. And a radio station— Radio Rebelde—was set up to broadcast revolutionary messages to the nation.

Batista responded with a ruthless campaign against the local populace, while B-26 bombers and P-47 fighter planes supplied by the United States strafed the Sierra Maestra. Batista managed to alienate the peasantry upon whom Castro's forces relied, while the rebel army cemented the support of the *guajiros* (peasant farmers) by assisting with the coffee harvest. "The story of how Castro was able to recover from a terrible initial defeat, regroup, fight, start winning against Batista units, and form an ultimately victorious rebel army is the story of the extraordinary support he received from Sierra Maestra peasants," writes Tad Szulc in *Fidel: A Critical Portrait.*

War in the Cities and Countryside

While the rebel army nibbled away at its foes in the mountains, a war of attrition spread throughout the countryside and cities. Sugarcane fields were razed; army posts, police stations, and public utilities were destroyed. On March 13, an assault on the presidential palace in Havana by the Students' Revolutionary Directorate failed, and 35 students died in the attack. Castro, far off in the mountains of Oriente, increasingly found himself in a battle for revolutionary leadership with the movement's urban wings and on July 12 committed himself to "free, democratic elections" to assuage the growing leadership crisis. Castro and eight leading opposition groups signed an agreement to create a civic coalition and affirmed the movement's choice

Revolutionary Heroes

Camilo Cienfuegos Gorriarán (1932-1959) joined Castro's guerrilla army in Mexico and participated in the *Granma* landing. He was named chief of staff, established himself as a brilliant commander, and, although not a Communist, was considered in the top triumvirate, alongside Fidel Castro and Che Guevara, in the early Castro regime. In October 1959, Castro sent Cienfuegos to arrest anti-Communist commander Hubert Matos; while returning to Havana on October 28, Cienfuegos's Cessna disappeared under mysterious circumstances.

Julio Antonio Mella (1903-1929) led Communist-inspired demonstrations that included a student takeover of the University of Havana. He founded the University Students Federation and the periodical *Juventud,* and in August 1925 cofounded the Cuban Communist Party. He was expelled from the university and later imprisoned, and in 1926 was exiled to Mexico, where he became embroiled in infighting within the Mexican Communist Party and was assassinated in 1929.

Frank País (1935-1958) was born in Santiago de Cuba, where he founded the anti-Batista Movimiento Nacional Revolucionario, which he merged with Castro's 26th of July Movement (M-26-7). País was named head of Cuban-based revolutionary activities during Castro's absence in Mexico and led the ill-fated attack on the police headquarters in Santiago on November 30, 1956, timed to coincide with the *Granma* landing. País was assassinated by Batista's police in July 1957.

Celia Sánchez Manduley (1920-1980) was born in Media Luna, Oriente, and at an early age became a dedicated anti-Batista revolutionary. Later, as a leader in Castro's 26th of July Movement, she set up and ran the networks that smuggled men and munitions to Castro's rebel army in the mountains; saw combat at the Battle of Uvero; and became Castro's secretary and, some say, his lover. For many years she was the most important person in Fidel Castro's life; she helped balance and minimize Fidel's absolutist side and was one of only a handful of people who could give him news and opinions he didn't want to hear. Her death from cancer in January 1980 profoundly shook Castro.

Brother and sister **Abel** (1925-1953) and **Haydee** (1931-1980) **Santamaría** were early participants in the efforts to oust Batista. Castro's designated successor in the revolutionary movement, Abel Santamaría helped organize the attack on the Moncada barracks and led a contingent that captured the hospital across the street. Batista's troops stormed the hospital (Haydee was also one of the attackers and pretended to be a nurse) and ruthlessly tortured Abel to death. Following the Revolution, Haydee became head of the Casa de las Américas; she committed suicide in 1980.

of a respected liberal judge, Manuel Urrutia Lleó, to head a provisional government after Batista's fall. Urrutia promptly left for exile in the United States, where he was instrumental in Eisenhower's pledge to stop arming Batista. However, Washington kept shipping arms secretly (including napalm, used to bomb peasant villages) and even rearmed Batista's warplanes at Guantánamo naval base.

In May 1958 Batista launched an all-out offensive in the Sierra Maestra with 10,000 men—Operation FF (Fin de Fidel). By June 19, Castro's troops were virtually surrounded atop their mountain retreat. The rebels rained mortars down into the valley, along with a psychological barrage of patriotic songs and exhortations blasted over loudspeakers

to demoralize Batista's tired troops. Then at the battle of Jigüe, which lasted 10 days, Castro's rebels defeated a battalion whose commander, Major José Quevedo, joined the rebels. Batista's army collapsed and retreated in disarray.

Castro then launched his counteroffensive. In August 1958 Castro's troops came down out of the mountains to seize, in swift order, Baire, Jiguaní, Maffo, Contramaestre, and Palma Soriano. In September, Castro led an offensive to take Santiago de Cuba. On December 30, Che Guevara captured Santa Clara. The scent of victory was in the air.

The Revolution Triumphs

Washington persuaded Batista to hand over

power to a civilian-military junta. At midnight on New Year's Eve 1958, Batista and his closest supporters boarded a plane for the Dominican Republic. (Batista settled in Spain, where he lived a princely life until his death in 1973. The poor cane cutter died as one of the world's wealthiest men, having milked Cuba of almost US$300 million.) On January 2, the same day that the rebel armies of Camilo Cienfuegos and Che Guevara entered Havana, Castro's army took over Santiago de Cuba. Castro walked up the stairs of the Moncada barracks to accept the surrender of Batista's army in Oriente at the very site where he had initiated his armed insurrection six years before. That night he delivered a televised victory speech, and the following day the triumphant guerrilla army began a five-day victory march to Havana, with crowds cheering Castro atop a tank, all of it televised to the nation.

Castro was intent from day one on turning the old social order upside down. Fidel moved cautiously but vigorously to solidify his power under the guise of establishing a pluralist democracy, but his aim was clear. Although Manuel Urrutia had been named president and an unusually gifted coalition cabinet had been formed (the U.S. government recognized Urrutia's government on January 4, 1959), Castro—the real power-holder—set up a parallel government behind the scenes. He began secretly negotiating with the Communists to co-opt them and build a Marxist-Leninist edifice (many of his wartime *compadres* who resigned over this issue were jailed for treason).

Castro recognized that the Cuban people were not yet ready for Communism; first he had to prepare public opinion. He also had to avoid antagonizing the United States. Castro manipulated Urrutia by forcing his prime minister, José Miró Cardona, to resign and getting *himself* named prime minister with power to direct government policy. Speaking before large crowds, he molded and radicalized the public mood as a tool to pressure the Urrutia government, which he said must obey "the will of the people." Meanwhile, hundreds of Batista supporters and "enemies of the Revolution" were dispatched following summary trials. The executions, presided over by Che Guevara, were halted after international protests.

Uncle Sam Responds

Castro, determined to assert Cuba's total independence, feared that U.S. Marines would steal his revolution as they had stolen independence at the end of the Spanish-Cuban-American War in 1898. An antagonistic relationship between a Castroite Cuba and the United States was inevitable. The Revolution was born when the East-West struggle for power was at its zenith. There was no way Uncle Sam could tolerate a left-leaning revolution beyond its control only 90 miles from Florida, especially one soon aligned with America's principal enemy.

In March 1959, Castro visited the United States and met with Vice President Nixon. Castro disingenuously promised not to expropriate foreign-owned property and affirmed that elections would *follow* "democracy," which he publicly defined as when all Cubans were employed, well fed, well educated, and healthy. "Real democracy is not possible for hungry people," he said.

Let the Reforms Begin!

On March 6, 1959, all rents in Cuba were reduced by 50 percent. Two months later, Cuba enacted an Agrarian Reform Law acclaimed, at the time, by the U.N. as "an example to follow." Large sugar estates and cattle ranches were seized without compensation by Castro's National Institute of Agrarian Reform (INRA), headed by the rebel army. The agrarian reform increased tensions between Cuba and Washington and established a still-unresolved grievance: nonpayment for illegally seized land (over time, all claims by Spanish, British, French, Canadian, and Dutch owners were settled).

Miami received a flood of unhappy exiles. At first, these were composed of corrupt elements, from pimps to political hacks escaping prosecution. As the reforms extended to affect the upper and middle classes, they, too, began to make the 90-mile journey to Florida. The trickle turned into a flood, including about 14,000 children sent to Miami by their parents in the Operation Peter Pan airlift (1960-1962). About 250,000 Cubans left by 1963, most of them white, urban professionals—doctors, teachers, engineers, technicians, businesspeople, and others with entrepreneurial skills. As Castro's revolution turned blatantly Communist and authoritarian, many of his revolutionary cohorts also began to desert him. Later, intellectuals and homosexuals joined the flood. (Those who were forced to leave Cuba had to leave their possessions behind. Their houses were confiscated ("donated to the Revolution" is the official verbiage) and divvied up to loyal *fidelistas* and to citizens in need of housing, while others became schools, medical facilities, and social centers.

On July 13, 1959, President Urrutia denounced the growing Communist trend. Meanwhile, Castro had arranged for peasants to be brought to Havana from all over Cuba to celebrate the anniversary of the attack on Moncada. Castro appeared on television, denounced Urrutia for refusing to sign his decrees, then resigned as prime minister. The streets of Havana erupted in calls for the president's resignation and pleas for Castro's return. Urrutia was forced to resign. Castro had carried out the world's first coup d'état by TV. Speaking the next day at the Plaza de la Revolución, he declared that there was no need for elections. The will of the people was supreme. "This is real democracy!" he concluded.

Into Soviet Orbit

Castro had decided on a profound new relationship. He knew, wrote Lee Anderson, "if he was ever to govern as he saw fit and achieve a genuine national liberation for Cuba, he was going to have to sever [U.S. relations] completely." To the Kremlin, Cuba seemed like a perfect strategic asset, so Castro and Khrushchev signed a pact. Ever fearful of a U.S. invasion and unsure as yet of the depth of Soviet assistance, Castro initiated a massive militia-training program, while emissaries began to purchase arms overseas. The first shipment arrived from Belgium on March 4, 1960, aboard the French ship *Le Coubre*. One week later, the steamship exploded in Havana Harbor, killing 80 Cubans. During the funeral ceremony for the victims, Castro uttered the rallying cry that would later become the Revolution's supreme motto: ¡*Patria o muerte!* (Patriotism or death!). Recalls Nobel Laureate Gabriel García Márquez: "The level of social saturation was so great that there was not a place or a moment when you did not come across that rallying cry of anger.... And it was repeated endlessly for days and months on radio and television stations until it was incorporated into the very essence of Cuban life."

When Soviet oil began to arrive in May 1960, U.S.-owned refineries refused to refine it. In response, the Cuban government took over the refineries. In July, President Eisenhower refused to honor a purchase agreement for Cuban sugar. Cuba's biggest market for virtually its entire source of income had slammed the door. Washington couldn't have played more perfectly into the hands of Castro and the Soviet Union, which happily announced that it would purchase the entire Cuban sugar stock. Hit with Eisenhower's right cross, Castro replied with a left hook: He nationalized *all* Yankee property. In October the Eisenhower administration banned exports to Cuba. In January 1961 the Kennedy administration broke diplomatic ties with Cuba; on February 3, Kennedy extended the embargo to include Cuban imports, sealing a complete trade embargo. Kennedy pressured Latin American governments to follow suit. Every Latin American country except Mexico fell in line.

The United States had severed Cuba's umbilical cord. The island faced economic collapse. During that period of intense Cold War, there were only two routes for underdeveloped nations. One way led west, the other east.

The Bay of Pigs Fiasco

Meanwhile, internal opposition to Castro was growing as government repression increased. Bands of counterrevolutionary guerrillas had set up a front in the Sierra Escambray. Many former Castro supporters fought against him when they realized that he had turned into a Communist caudillo and that a personality cult was being erected. The Lucha Contra Bandidos (Struggle Against Bandits) lasted until 1966 before finally being eradicated (local farmers were forcibly relocated in order to isolate counterrevolutionaries).

Castro, with his highly efficient intelligence operation, knew that the CIA was plotting an invasion of Cuba by exiles. In mid-1960 he began to suppress the press. He also established the Committees for the Defense of the Revolution (CDRs)—a countrywide information network for "collective vigilance." Cuba's State Security began a nationwide sweep against suspected "counterrevolutionaries" and opponents.

On April 15, 1961, Cuban exiles strafed Cuban airfields as a prelude to a CIA-sponsored invasion. Castro turned the funeral for the seven persons killed into a stirring call for defiance: "What the imperialists cannot forgive us for...is that we have made a socialist revolution under the nose of the United States." It was his first public characterization of the Revolution as socialist. The debacle thus created the conditions by which socialism became acceptable to a nation on the brink of invasion.

President Kennedy was assured that the Cuban people would rise up in arms. They did, and within 72 hours they had defeated the CIA-backed invasion at the Bay of Pigs on April 17, 1961. U.S. ambassador Philip Bonsal declared that the Bay of Pigs "consolidated Castro's regime and was a determining factor in giving it the long life it has enjoyed." As Castro admitted: "Our Marxist-Leninist party was really born at Girón; from that date on,

socialism became cemented forever with the blood of our workers, peasants, and students."

The debacle not only solidified Castro's tenure but also provoked a repressive house-cleaning of anyone thought to be too independent or deviant. By 1965, at least 20,000 political prisoners—including homosexuals, practicing Catholics, and other "social deviants"—languished in jails.

The Cuban Missile Crisis

On December 1, 1961, Castro informed Cuba and the world that Cuba was officially a Marxist-Leninist state. The news was a bombshell to the Kennedy administration, which in March 1962 launched Operation Mongoose, a six-phase program to oust Castro. Four hundred CIA agents were assigned full-time to the operation, which was led by Bobby Kennedy. The CIA's plans read like a James Bond novel—or a comedy of errors. Some plots were straightforward, like the attempt to kill Castro with a bazooka. The CIA's Technical Services Division was more imaginative. It impregnated a box of cigars with botulism—they were tested on monkeys and "did the job expected of them"—and hoped, in vain, to dupe Castro into smoking one. No one knows whether they reached Castro or whether some innocent victim smoked them.

Kennedy's threat to do away with socialist Cuba virtually obliged Fidel to ask the Soviets for rockets to defend Cuba in the event of a U.S. invasion. In August 1962, Soviet personnel and MiG fighter-bombers began to arrive. Kennedy had warned the Soviets that the United States would not tolerate the installation of missiles. Khrushchev promised Kennedy that no "offensive weapons" were being supplied to Cuba. His deceit had near-calamitous consequences. The Soviet Union felt severely threatened by the U.S. deployment of intermediate-range ballistic missiles on Turkey's border with the USSR. To the Soviets, the Bay of Pigs fiasco provided an opportunity to establish bases at equally close range to the United States, which could then be used as bargaining chips for a reduction

The U.S. Embargo

Since the 1960s, Washington has clamped a strict trade embargo on Cuba in the expectation that economic distress would oust Castro or at least moderate his behavior. Since 1996 it has been embodied in law (heretofore it was an executive order enacted on February 3, 1962, by President Kennedy). The 1996 Helms-Burton Law requires that U.S. presidents seek congressional approval if they wish to modify or lift the embargo; stipulates that the embargo can only be lifted when a "transition government" is in place in Cuba that meets U.S. criteria; denies entry into the U.S. territory to anyone who has done business with Cuban nationals or the Cuban government; fines *foreign* banks and corporations from trading U.S. assets (such as dollar bills) with or on behalf of Cuba; and will allow any U.S. citizen whose property was confiscated after the Revolution to sue any foreign corporation that has "benefited" from the property or from its use.

Critics call it a violation of international law that injures and threatens the welfare of Cuban people. The United Nations General Assembly routinely votes to condemn it (the 2016 vote was 192-0, with the United States abstaining).

Although no Cuban goods can be sold to the United States, the United States *does* permit sales of "agricultural" and certain other goods to Cuba under a waiver that runs from daiquiri mix to rolls of newsprint (even the Communist rag, *Granma,* is printed on paper from Alabama), to the tune of almost US$1 billion a year.

The effects of the embargo (which the Cuban government calls *el bloqueo,* or blockade) are much debated. In 2012, Cuba claimed it had suffered losses valued at US$1.6 trillion. However, in 2000, the International Trade Commission (ITC) determined that the embargo has had a minimal impact on the Cuban economy, citing domestic policies as the main cause of Cuba's economic woes (for three decades, the effects of the embargo were offset by massive subsidies from the Soviet Union).

The paradox is that the policy achieves the effect opposite of its stated goals. Says *The Economist:* "The 50-year-old economic embargo...has done more than anything else to keep the Castros in power. The abiding trope of the brothers' propaganda is the need for 'unity' against the aggressor over the water—the official justification for the lack of political freedom and for one-party rule."

Although State Department officials privately admit that the embargo is the fundamental source of the Castros' hold on power, U.S. presidents have traditionally been wed to a policy geared toward short-term electoral gains in Florida in response to fanatically anti-Castroite Cuban-American interests. Contemporary U.S. policy toward Cuba has been largely shaped by this constituency, whose U.S.-Cuba Democracy Political Action Committee has evolved into one of the most powerful lobbying groups in the United States. It works hard to keep Washington from cutting a deal. (The hard-line Cuban-American congressional caucus is also firmly opposed to rapprochement.)

In 2014, President Obama significantly watered down the embargo's bite through executive actions to facilitate more commerce, including relaxing financing terms and permitting more travel. The newly formed (Cuban-American) Cuba Study Group and Engage Cuba business lobby are leaning on Congress to throw in the towel.

What can you do to help end the embargo and travel ban? Contact your senator or representative in Congress (U.S. Congress, Washington, DC 20510, tel. 202/224-3121 or 800/839-5276, www.house.gov and www.senate.gov).

Write or call the president (The President, The White House, Washington, DC 20500, tel. 202/456-1414, president@whitehouse.gov). Also call or fax the **White House Comment Line** (202/456-1111, www.whitehouse.gov) and the **Secretary of State** (202/647-4000, www.state.gov/secretary).

Support the freedom to travel campaign. Contact the **Latin America Working Group** (424 C St. NE, Washington, DC 20002, tel. 202/546-7010, www.lawg.org), which campaigns to lift the travel restrictions and U.S. embargo, monitors legislators, and can advise on how representatives have voted on Cuba-related issues.

of U.S. bases in Turkey. Castro learned of Khrushchev's decision to back down over the radio, along with the rest of the world. He was livid. When United Nations Secretary-General U Thant met Castro immediately after the crisis to arrange for verification that the missiles had been removed, Castro refused.

Castro may have correctly calculated that the threat of nuclear conflict could save him from a nonnuclear attack. The 13-day Cuban Missile Crisis (Cubans call it the October 1962 Crisis) ended with a guarantee from Kennedy that the United States would not invade Cuba (the non-explicit no-invasion pledge was withdrawn after Castro refused to permit verification). Nonetheless, the Kennedys had initiated another invasion plan for 1964—OPLAN 380-63. Before it could be implemented, the president was dead, shot by Lee Harvey Oswald.

Castro was now free to move forward with his socialist revolution.

MAKING THE REVOLUTION

Cuba in 1959 was comparatively advanced in socioeconomic terms. It had a huge middle class. And the island's per capita rankings for automobiles, telephones, televisions, literacy, and infant mortality (32 per 1,000 live births) were among the highest in the Western Hemisphere. But hundreds of thousands of Cubans also lived without light, water, or sewage. Poverty was endemic, and thousands of citizens lived by begging and prostitution.

Castro's government poured its heart and soul into improving the lot of the poor. Castro, for example, dubbed 1961 the Year of Education. "Literacy brigades" were formed of university students and high school seniors, who fanned out over the countryside with the goal of teaching every single Cuban to read and write. Within two years, the regime had added 10,000 classrooms. By the end of its first decade, the number of elementary schools had nearly doubled and the number of teachers had more than tripled. Castro also set up special schools for the indigent, for the

blind, deaf, and mute, and for ex-prostitutes. Electricity, gas, and public transport fees were dramatically lowered, as were rents and other fees. The government poured money into health care. And the Revolution brought unparalleled gains in terms of racism and social relations.

However, Castro's reforms came at the cost of politicizing all private choices and the totalitarian precedence over individual liberties. Havana and other cities were neglected and left to deteriorate. And the middle class was effaced. Cuba's far-reaching social programs also had a price tag that the national economy could not support.

Mismanaging the Economy

The young revolutionaries badly mismanaged the Cuban economy, swinging this way and that as Castro capriciously tacked between Soviet dictate and personal whim. Castro's economic errors were worsened by bureaucratic mismanagement and abrupt reversals in direction. Trained managers were replaced with Communist cadres, while sound economic decisions were sacrificed to revolutionary principles intended to advance the power of the state over private initiative.

Gradually, inventories of imported goods and cash at hand were exhausted. As machinery broke down, no replacements could be ordered from the United States because of the trade ban enacted in 1961. Raw materials could not be bought. Soon the economy was in appalling shape. In 1962 rationing was introduced. The black market began to blossom.

Sugar monoculture was blamed. Castro decided to abandon a sugar-based economy and industrialize. When that attempt failed, Castro switched tack and mobilized the entire workforce to achieve a record sugar harvest: 10 million tons a year by 1970 (the previous record was 6.7 million tons). Tens of thousands of inexperienced "voluntary" workers left their jobs in the cities and headed to the countryside. Holidays were abolished. Every inch of arable land was turned over to sugar. Nonetheless, only 8.5 million tons were harvested, and the severely disrupted economy was left in chaos.

To make matters worse, in 1968 Castro nationalized the entire retail trade still in private hands. More than 58,000 businesses—from corner cafés to auto mechanics—were eliminated in the "Great Revolutionary Offensive." As a result, even the most basic items disappeared from the shelves.

The Soviets saved the day. Castro's zealous experimentations gave way to a period of enforced pragmatism. In 1976, Cuba joined COMECON, the Soviet bloc's economic community. Cuba would henceforth supply sugar to the European socialist nations in exchange for whatever the island needed.

Adventurism Abroad

Castro was committed to exporting his revolution (he had been complicit in armed plots against several neighboring countries, including support for a failed invasion of the Dominican Republic in June 1959). In 1962 Guevara launched a wave of Cuban-backed guerrilla activity throughout Latin America that was endorsed by Castro in his "Second Declaration of Havana"—a tacit declaration of war on Latin American governments. At the Organization of Latin American Solidarity conference in Havana in August 1967, Castro launched his Fifth International, to "create as many Vietnams as possible" in defiance of the Soviet Union's policy of coexistence with the United States. Said Castro: "The duty of every revolutionary is to make the revolution."

Cuban troops had already been sent to countries as far afield as Algeria and Zaire. Soon revolutionary fighters from Angola, Mozambique, and elsewhere were being trained at secret camps on Isla de la Juventud. In Ethiopia and Angola, Cuban troops fought alongside Marxist troops in the civil wars against "racist imperialism," while in Ethiopia they shored up a ruthless regime. In Nicaragua, Cubans trained, armed, and supported the Sandinista guerrillas that toppled the Somoza regime. More than 377,000 Cuban troops were rotated through Angola during the 15-year war (the last troops came home in May 1991), proportionally far greater than the U.S. troop commitment in Vietnam. Tens of thousands of Cuban doctors and technical specialists were also sent to more than two dozen developing nations.

Castro launched his international initiatives at a time when Washington was looking at rapprochement with Cuba, beginning with the Ford administration, which had initiated secret talks in Havana to end the embargo and, as a show of intent, permitted U.S. subsidiary companies abroad to trade with Cuba. Castro didn't want rapprochement, and his adventurism nixed the deal.

The Mariel Boatlift

In 1980, 12 Cubans walked through the gates of the Peruvian embassy in Havana and asked for asylum. The Peruvians agreed. President Jimmy Carter announced that the United States would welcome Cuban political refugees with "open arms." In a fit of pique, Castro removed the embassy guards, and 11,000 Cubans rushed into the Peruvian embassy. Castro decided to allow them to leave, along with dissidents and other disaffected Cubans. Many "antisocial elements" were coerced to leave, while Castro added to the numbers by emptying his prisons and lunatic asylums. Thus Castro disposed of more than 120,000 critics and disaffected.

In the 1980s President Ronald Reagan took a much harder line. In 1983, U.S. Marines stormed the Caribbean island of Grenada to topple Maurice Bishop's Cuban-backed socialist regime. The Reagan administration also spawned the Cuban-American National Foundation to give clout to the right-wing Cuban-American voice. In 1985 it established Radio Martí to broadcast anti-Castro propaganda into Cuba.

THE BUBBLE BURSTS

Meanwhile, Mikhail Gorbachev, the new leader of the Soviet Union, was initiating reforms—just as Castro turned more sharply toward Communist orthodoxy. In 1986, for example, Castro closed free farmers markets, a brief fling that had led to an increase in the food supply. He was alarmed at the success of the free-market experiment and railed against "millionaire garlic growers." *Glasnost* and *perestroika,* Gorbachev's "heresies," would not be tolerated in Cuba.

In 1989 the Berlin Wall collapsed and the Communist dominoes came tumbling down. However, the news in Cuba was dominated by a political show trial that made it clear that reform was not in the cards. General Arnaldo Sánchez Ochoa, a reform-espousing, powerful and charismatic national hero with impeccable credentials going back to the Sierra Maestra, was accused (on false charges) of colluding with the Colombian drug cartel to smuggle drugs to the United States via Cuba. After a closed trial, Ochoa and 13 other high-ranking officers were convicted of treason and corruption. Ochoa and three others were executed. A purge followed, notably of the Ministry of the Interior (MININT), but also of dissidents and private entrepreneurs.

The "Special Period"

With the Eastern bloc lifeline severed, Cuba's economy collapsed. In January 1990, Castro declared that Cuba had entered a Special Period in a Time of Peace. He also announced a draconian, warlike austerity plan. A new slogan appeared throughout Cuba: *¡Socialismo o muerte!* (Socialism or death!). Inevitably, rising political discontent boiled over on April 21, 1991, when clashes erupted against the police—the first act of spontaneous rebellion since 1959. Then on August 18, 1991, on the last day of the highly successful Pan-American Games in Havana (which Cuba won with 140 gold medals), the Soviet Union began its dizzying unraveling. Reformer Boris Yeltsin took power. Subsidies and supplies to Cuba virtually ceased.

After the last Soviet tanker departed in June 1992, the government began imposing electricity blackouts. There were no fans, no air-conditioning, no refrigeration, no lights. Nor fuel for transportation. Buses and taxis

gave way to horse-drawn carts. Factories closed down and state bureaucracies began transferring laid-off workers to jobs in the countryside. Gaiety on the streets was replaced with a forlorn melancholy.

Harvests simply rotted in the fields for want of distribution. People accustomed to a government-subsidized food basket guaranteeing every person at least two high-protein, high-calorie meals a day were stunned to suddenly be confronting shortages of almost every staple. When East German powdered milk ceased to arrive, Cuba eliminated butter; when Czechoslovakian malt no longer arrived, Cuban beer disappeared. Soaps, detergents, deodorants, toilet paper, clothing—everything vanished. Cubans had to resort to making hamburger meat from banana peels and steaks from grapefruit rinds. Many Cubans began rearing *jutías,* ratlike native rodents. The most desperate resorted to rats. Cuba, the only country in Latin America to have eliminated hunger, began to suffer malnutrition and debilitating diseases. Meanwhile, believing that Cuba was on the verge of collapse, the Bush administration tightened the screws by passing the Cuban Democracy Act, which reduced economic assistance to countries trading with Cuba and prohibited U.S. subsidiary companies abroad from trading with Cuba.

The reformist movement found an unexpected ally in Raúl Castro, who argued for deregulating key sectors of the economy. Market-savvy reformers were elevated to positions of power and cobbled together a recovery plan led by tourism. Possession of the dollar was legalized and limited private enterprise was permitted.

The *Balsero* Crisis

On August 5, 1994, crowds gathered along Havana's Malecón in response to a rumor that a major exodus was to be permitted and that a flotilla of boats was en route from Florida. When police attempted to clear the boulevard, a riot (the "Maleconazo") ensued, and two police officers were killed. Castro saw a chance to defuse a dangerous situation and benefit.

He declared that Cuba would no longer police the U.S. borders: If the United States would not honor its agreement to allow people to migrate legally, then Cuba would no longer try to prevent anyone from going illegally.

Leaving Cuba without an exit permit was illegal; Cubans were rarely granted such visas. Meanwhile, the United States' 1966 Cuban Adjustment Act *guaranteed* residency to Cubans who step foot on U.S. soil. The United States had agreed to accept an annual quota of 20,000-plus Cuban immigrants, but most Cubans who petitioned the United States for a visa were rejected. The more difficult the economic circumstances became in Cuba, the fewer legal immigrants were accepted. Thousands of *balseros* (rafters) fled Cuba on makeshift rafts.

Meanwhile, a Miami-based volunteer group called Brothers to the Rescue had been operating rescue missions. When the flood of *balseros* stopped, pilots of the organization began buzzing Havana and dropping "leaflets of a subversive nature." On February 24, 1996, Cuban jet fighters shot two Brothers to the Rescue Cessnas down, killing both pilots. Cuban-American exiles and Republican presidential candidates campaigning for the mid-March Florida primary erupted in fury. The incident scuttled the Clinton administration's carefully calibrated policy on Cuba of promoting democratic change as a prelude to easing the embargo.

Following the Brothers to the Rescue incident, Senator Jesse Helms and Representative Dan Burton Helms rode the wave of anti-Castro sentiment in Miami and Washington and steered the Cuban Liberty and Democratic Solidarity Act through Congress. Clinton signed the bill, which sealed the U.S. embargo (hitherto merely an executive order) into law. The law, which violates international law, earned the wrath of the United States' leading allies (Canada and the U.K. even enacted retaliatory legislation) and united Cubans behind the Castro government as nothing had done in years. Meanwhile, in 1997, Miami-based Cuban-American exiles launched a bombing campaign against the Cuban tourist industry, killing an Italian tourist.

Reasserting State Control

On January 1, 1999, Cubans celebrated the 40th anniversary of the Cuban Revolution. The economy was bouncing back, driven by dollars from tourism, and was given a boost in January when President Clinton eased the trade embargo, permitting U.S. citizens to send up to US$1,200 annually to Cuban individuals and nongovernmental organizations. Castro called the move a "fraud."

Meanwhile, serious crime had returned to the streets of Cuba. Thousands of young Cuban women had turned to quasi-prostitution. And corruption was becoming entrenched. Castro announced draconian legislation—the Law for the Protection of Cuba's National Independence and Economy. Thousands of Special Brigade police were deployed on street corners throughout major cities. The policy was officially "a battle against disorder, crime, disrespect for authority, illegal business, and lack of social control." Outlawed, too, were the "supply, search, or gathering of information" for and "collaboration" with foreign media. The state was also reasserting control throughout the private economy.

INTO THE NEW MILLENNIUM
The Elián González Crisis

Cuba began the new millennium with a new battle with Uncle Sam, this one over a five-year-old boy, Elián González, saved by the U.S. Coast Guard after his mother and 10 other people drowned when their boat sank en route from Cuba to Florida. Miami's anti-Castroite Cubans and right-wing politicians demanded that the boy remain in the United States against his Cuban father's wishes. Castro turned the issue into an anti-American crusade by organizing "Free Elián" rallies. Castro vowed that protests would last "10 years, if necessary," while the case wound through the Florida courts. Elián's custodians refused to hand him over to his father when he arrived in the United States in April 2000 to collect his son. In a dawn raid, the INS grabbed Elián and reunited him with his father. In late June Elián and his father returned to Cuba after the U.S. Supreme Court affirmed the father's right to custody of his son.

To Fidel Castro, the battle for Elián was personal, recalling with astonishing parallels an incident that occurred more than four decades earlier (as reported by journalist Ann Louis Bardach) when he refused to hand over his own son, Fidelito, to his mother, whom the Cuban courts had awarded custody after their divorce. The mother was Mirta Diaz-Balart, whose nephew, Lincoln Diaz-Balart (then a Republican Congressman representing Miami, Florida), an arch anti-Castroite, had championed the crusade to keep Elián González in the United States.

New Battles

In 2001, as the George W. Bush administration initiated an increasingly hard-line approach to Cuba, Castro launched the "Battle of Ideas," an ideological campaign meant to shore up flagging support for socialism.

The following spring, Jimmy Carter made a five-day visit to Havana. Just days before Carter's arrival, a dissident group, Proyecto Varela (Varela Project), delivered to the National Assembly a petition containing 11,020 signatures demanding sweeping reforms in Cuba. Amazingly, Fidel permitted Carter to address the nation live on TV. Carter denounced the U.S. embargo, as Fidel no doubt had wished, but focused primarily on the call for greater freedoms in Cuba and mentioned Proyecto Varela by name—the first time most Cubans learned of the organization.

Three weeks later, with Carter safely off the island, the Varela Project leaders were arrested and given harsh prison sentences. The Castro regime then pulled out of its hat a petition of more than eight million signatures, it claimed, calling for a resolution to make the existing constitution "eternal" and "untouchable." In March 2003, Castro initiated a crackdown on dissidents, independent journalists, and librarians. Meanwhile, two Cuban planes were successfully hijacked to the United States, and an attempt to hijack a ferry failed when it ran out of fuel 30 miles from Havana. The Cuban military towed the vessel back to Havana; following a swift trial, three of the hijackers were executed by firing squad.

The Post-Fidel Decade

The Bush administration implemented new restrictions aimed at stopping all travel to Cuba as part of a broader attempt to cut the flow of dollars to Cuba. Meanwhile, having allied himself ever more closely with Venezuela's Hugo Chávez and increasingly with China (now Cuba's second-largest trading partner), Castro stepped up retrenchment of the socialist system. Many foreign companies were ousted, and the U.S. dollar was banned. Meanwhile, the first of tens of thousands of poor patients from Latin America arrived for free eye operations bankrolled by Venezuela.

On July 31, 2006, Fidel Castro was taken seriously ill and underwent intestinal surgery for diverticulitis on the eve of his 80th birthday. In February 2008, an extremely frail Fidel handed power to his brother Raúl Castro, who was duly elected as head of state by the National Assembly. The transition went smoothly. Raúl stated that he wanted normalized relations with Uncle Sam. The inauguration of President Barack Obama in January 2009 augured possibility of a new thaw between Washington and Havana. In March, President Obama rescinded all restrictions on travel to Cuba for family visits and called for "constructive engagement" with Cuba. In February 2010, U.S. and Cuban officials reinstated the first direct talks between the two nations since Bush scrapped them in 2004. In June, the Organization of American States voted to readmit Cuba (which responded that it had no such interest).

However, the animosity between Cuba and the United States was reinforced when, in March 2011, Cuba sentenced a U.S. citizen,

The Cuban Five

The faces of the "Cuban Five" are ubiquitous throughout Cuba. The five Cubans—Fernando González, René González, Antonio Guerrero, Gerardo Hernández, and Ramón Labañino—were convicted in U.S. federal court on June 8, 2001, and sentenced to 15 years to life in prison.

The five "innocents" or "heroes," as they are called in Cuba, were indeed agents of Cuban intelligence and had infiltrated Cuban-American groups such as Brothers to the Rescue and extremist organizations such as Omega 7 and Alpha 66 that continue to perpetrate terrorist acts against moderate Cuban-Americans espousing dialogue with Cuba; against Cuba-bound travelers and Cuba-travel suppliers; and against Cuba, including, in 1997, a hotel bombing campaign in Havana that killed an Italian tourist.

Such groups have acted with impunity for decades, and the U.S. government has basically turned a blind eye to their terrorist acts. For example, anti-Castroite Orlando Bosch was convicted of conspiring in the bombing of Cubana flight 455 on October 6, 1976, which killed 73 passengers, but he was pardoned by President George H. W. Bush. His coconspirator, Luis Posada Carrilles, was convicted of the bombing in Venezuela but escaped from jail and returned to Miami, where he has never been prosecuted. Because the U.S. government refuses to prosecute Cuban-American terrorists, Cuban agents have infiltrated such groups to monitor them and identify future threats.

What Cubans don't learn is that the five were all also employed at the Key West Naval Air Station (and had attempted to infiltrate the U.S. Southern Command) and were passing information about military installations and movements back to Havana.

René González was freed in October 2011 and in April 2013 was allowed to return to Cuba provided that he renounce his U.S. citizenship. Fernando González returned to Cuba on February 28, 2014, after completing his term. On December 17, 2014, the final three came home in a secret deal that also freed two American spies.

Alan Gross, to 15 years in prison on charges of "crimes against the integrity of the state" while working for a project, backed by the United States Agency for International Development, to spread democracy in Cuba. Still, in January 2011 President Obama reinstated the Clinton-era license for "people-to-people" educational exchange, permitting *any* U.S. citizen to travel to Cuba.

Raúl Castro initiated economic reforms (called an "updating of the economic model") that have begun to stimulate the rebirth of capitalism. More than one million state workers have been laid off and transferred to the private sector in an effort to get the economy rolling. Cubans can even buy and sell houses (as of November 2011), and cars (since 2013). But Raúl also initiated an anti-corruption purge, not least against people in government who have been entrenching themselves financially. In the sixth Communist Party Congress, in April 2011, Raúl even called for a separation between party and government.

In January 2013, Raúl declared that he would step down in 2018. An heir apparent was named: First Vice President Miguel Díaz-Canel (born 1960), former Minister of Higher Education, representing the generation born after the Revolution. When Presidents Obama and Castro shook hands in January 2014 at the funeral ceremonies for Nelson Mandela, few expected that it would lead to a deeper thaw any time soon. In December 17, 2014, the presidents simultaneously announced that the two governments had negotiated to reestablish diplomatic relations. Relations were formally restored the following summer when the two nations reopened their respective "interest sections" as embassies. President Obama sealed the rapprochement on March 20, 2016, by becoming the first U.S. president to visit Cuba since Calvin Coolidge in 1928.

On November 25, 2016, Fidel finally passed away. He was cremated and buried next to José Martí in Santiago de Cuba. The nation mourned while exiles celebrated on the streets of Miami. Castro's demise marked the end of a post-Fidel decade marked by Raúl's reforms and rapprochement with Uncle Sam.

As Miguel Díaz-Canel has said: "[Cuba has made] progress on the issues that are easiest to solve. What is left are the most important choices that will be decisive in the development of the country." That will happen after 2018, when the Castros will no longer be making the choices. Now that will be revolutionary!

Meanwhile, the election of President Donald Trump (and his immediate appointment of pro-embargo advocates) sent a chill down the spine of Cubans hoping for better times. In June 2017, Trump tightened restrictions, including banning independent travel to Cuba.

Government

Cuba is an independent socialist republic. The Cuban constitution, adopted in 1975, defines it as a "socialist state of workers and peasants and all other manual and intellectual workers." General Raúl Castro Ruz is head of both state and government. In February 2008, Raúl succeeded his elder brother Fidel, who had served as top dog 1959-2008. Total power is legally vested in Raúl Castro as President of the Republic, President of the Council of State, President of the Council of Ministers, First Secretary of the Communist Party, and Commander in Chief of the armed forces. Miguel Díaz-Canel is First Vice President of both the Council of State and the Council of Ministers.

There are no legally recognized political organizations independent of the Communist Party, which controls the labyrinthine state apparatus and which the constitution (copied largely from the Soviet constitution of 1936) recognizes as "the highest leading force of the society and of the state."

STATE STRUCTURE
The Central Government
The highest-ranking executive body is the Consejo de Ministros (Council of Ministers), headed by Raúl and comprising several vice presidents and ministers. Its Executive Committee administers Cuba on a day-to-day basis and is ostensibly accountable to the National Assembly of People's Power, which "elects" the members at the initiative of the head of state. The council has jurisdiction over all ministries and central organizations and effectively runs the country under the direction of Raúl, who has replaced Fidel's ministers with loyal military figures dedicated to regime survival in lockstep with Raúl.

The 612-member Asamblea Nacional (National Assembly) is invested with legislative authority but is mostly a rubber-stamp legislature. The assembly is elected for a five-year term (with a two-term limit) and meets only twice annually. Deputies are elected directly by voters, and independent candidates are allowed but must be approved by Provincial Assemblies.

The 31-member Consejo del Estado (Council of State) is modeled on the Presidium of the former Soviet Union and functions as the Executive Committee of the National Assembly when the latter is not in session.

Since 2013, at Raúl's initiative, *politicos* in high political and state positions will be limited to two five-year terms.

The Cuban Communist Party
The sole political party is the Partido Comunista de Cuba (PCC), of which Raúl is head. The PCC, whose goal is "to guide common efforts toward the construction of socialism," occupies the central role in all government bodies and institutions. It is led by the 15-member Buró Político (Politburo; currently half are military figures loyal to Raúl) and steered by the Comité Central (Central

Committee), whose 115 members are selected by Raúl and the Council of Ministers. It meets every six months and is the principal forum through which the party leadership disseminates party policy. Youth organizations are the most common avenue for passage into the PCC. Current membership is about 600,000 (about 5 percent of the population).

Castro has drawn from "the elite of the elite" of the party to maintain his government. Loyalty takes precedence over all other considerations. Although the Council of State and Council of Ministers ostensibly make the decisions, Raúl Castro shapes those decisions, as did his brother before him.

Local Government

The country is divided into 15 provinces plus a Special Municipality (Isla de la Juventud) and 169 municipalities (*municipios*), dominated by the city of Havana, a separate province. Each province and municipality is governed by an Assembly of Delegates of People's Power, representing state bodies at the local level. Members are elected by popular ballot and serve two-and-a-half-year terms.

The organs of *poder popular* (popular power) also serve as forums for citizens' grievances and deal with problems such as garbage collection and housing improvement.

Raúl has proposed a gradual decentralization of central government, giving local governments more power. In 2011, Havana Province was split into two new provinces—Artemisa and Mayabeque—specifically designed as an experiment in streamlining and devolving powers at the local government level.

Committees for the Defense of the Revolution

The linchpins in maintaining the loyalty of the masses and spreading the Revolution at the grassroots level are the neighborhood Comités para la Defensa de la Revolución. There are 15,000 CDRs in Havana and 100,000 throughout the island. Almost every block has one. On one hand, the CDRs perform wonderful work:

They collect blood for hospitals, discourage kids from playing hooky, and so on. But they are also the vanguard in watching and snitching on neighbors (the CDRs are under the direction of MININT, the Ministry of the Interior). Above the voluntary CDR head is the *jefe del sector*, the sector boss in charge of four CDRs, who specifically looks for revolutionary delinquency.

Other Mass Organizations

Citizen participation in building socialism is manifested through mass organizations controlled by the PCC. Prominent among them are the Federation of Cuban Women, the Confederation of Cuban Workers, and the Union of Communist Youth. No independent labor organizations are permitted. Membership in mass organizations is a virtual prerequisite for getting on in Cuban society. Promotions, access to university, and other rewards are based on being a "good revolutionary" through participation in an organization.

The Judiciary

Courts are a fourth branch of government and are not independent. The individual in Cuba enjoys few legal guarantees. The judiciary is charged with "maintaining and strengthening socialist legality." The Council of State can overturn judicial decisions, and Fidel Castro frequently did so in political trials. Interpretation of the constitution is the prerogative of the National Assembly, not the courts. Cuba's legal system requires that defendants prove their innocence, rather than for prosecutors to prove the defendants' guilt. Hence, thousands of Cubans languish in jails for crimes the state finds it convenient to convict them of.

The highest court in the land is the People's Supreme Court in Havana. The president and vice president are appointed by Castro; other judges are elected by the National Assembly. Private practice of law is not permitted. Capital punishment by firing squad remains on the books for 112 offenses (79 for violations of state security), but in 2008 all death sentences were commuted.

Cuba has a policy of criminal rehabilitation for all but political crimes. The penal system guarantees an individual's job upon release from prison.

Military and Security

Cuba once boasted a formidable military under the aegis of the Fuerzas Armadas Revolucionarias (Revolutionary Armed Forces, or FAR). However, the number of men and women on active duty has shrunk from over 180,000 in 1993 to about 55,000 in 2009. In addition, Cuba has about 1.3 million in the territorial militias. (All males between the ages of 16 and 45 are subject to conscription; women between 17 and 35 may volunteer.) The key to defense is the "Guerra de Todo el Pueblo" (War of All the People): In the event of an attack, the *entire* population of Cuba will be called into action.

In 1991 the military was re-engineered and now earns its way by investments in tourism, agriculture, and industry, and today employs 20 percent of all workers in Cuba. High-ranking military figures hold key positions throughout the economy and government. Under Raúl, the military's business wing, GAESA, has taken over larger chunks of the economy. In 2016, it assumed responsibility for both Habaguanex, the business entity of Havana's Office of the City Historian, and the principal bank doing business with foreign entities. CIMEX, a division of GAESA, has long had responsibility for all imports into Cuba.

State security is the responsibility of the Ministry of the Interior, which operates a number of intelligence-related services, plus the National Revolutionary Police (PNR). Other intelligence units—most notoriously, the much-feared Seguridad del Estado or G-2—are operated by the Department of State Security and the General Directorate of Intelligence. There are more security-linked officials than meet the eye.

Cuba has for six decades been a *fidelista* state in which Marxist-Leninism has been loosely grafted onto Cuban nationalism, then tended and shaped by one man. Since 2006 Cuba has transitioned from the domineering role of Fidel to the more pragmatic commanding rule of his younger brother, Raúl. Fidel preferred to leave his development choices open, allowing a flexible interpretation of the correct path to socialism. Ideological dogma was subordinated to tactical considerations. Fidel's decision making involved the minutest aspects of government.

Government officials had to study Castro's speeches intently to stay tuned with his ever-changing views. The fear of repercussions from on high remains so great that the bureaucracy—Cubans call it a "*burro*cracy"—has evolved as a mutually protective society. Bureaucratic incompetence affects nearly every aspect of daily life. Nonetheless, the past decade has seen the rise of a new generation of capable managers with greater decision-making powers in the upper echelons of Cuba's self-supporting state enterprises.

Fidel Castro ran Cuba as much by charisma as through institutional leadership: *personalismo* was central in *fidelismo*. He called Western democracies "complete garbage." He preferred "direct democracy"—his appeals ("popular consultations") to the people, relying on his ability to whip up the crowds at mass rallies with persuasive arguments to keep revolutionary ardor alive. Although a less gifted orator than his elder brother, Raúl has continued the style while elevating pragmatic and economically gifted apparatchiks (mostly army officers with engineering backgrounds) to share his vision for greater liberalization. The *históricos* who fought for the Revolution, and have since run the government, are dying off. A new generation is now at the fore.

FIDEL CASTRO

Born and dispatched into this world with the engine of an athlete, Castro has the

Human Rights

"It is fair to say that under [Fidel] Castro, Cubans have lost even the tenuous civil and political liberties they had under the old regime," claims Professor Wayne Smith, former head of the U.S. Interests Section in Havana. "Woe to anyone who gets on a soapbox in downtown Havana and questions the wisdom of the Castro government." The United Nations' Human Rights Commission places Cuba on its list of worst offenders; Amnesty International named Cuba the worst offender in Latin America; and Human Rights Watch names Cuba as the only country in Latin America that represses virtually all forms of political dissent.

The Cuban penal code states that disrespect for authorities is good for one to seven years in prison. As a result, Cubans are circumspect about publicly criticizing the government for fear of police informers. People face harsh retribution if they cross the line into political activism.

Contemporary Cuba, however, is a far cry from the 1960s, when crushing sentences were imposed en masse. Repression runs hot and cold. Since succeeding his brother, Raúl Castro has released the majority of dissidents. In 2008 his government even signed the U.N. covenants on human rights. He has permitted more legitimate and blunt debate and criticism. And leaders of the Damas en Blanco (Ladies in White) dissident group, plus dissident blogger Yoani Sánchez (http://generacionyen.wordpress.com), were even allowed to travel abroad in 2013 to receive international human rights prizes.

In 2011, the Cuban Council of Human Rights listed only 43 political prisoners in jail. Nonetheless, Raúl Castro's government has increasingly relied on arbitrary short-term detention to harass and intimidate dissidents. It's hard to be sure of true numbers: Cuba does not allow international organizations to inspect its prisons. And forget habeas corpus—Cuba uses a law called "pre-criminal dangerousness" to lock up anyone it so chooses.

Cuba's small, faction-ridden dissident groups are heavily infiltrated by state security. The government refers to dissidents as "mercenaries," as the U.S. Embassy offers financial support, effectively turning dissidents into paid agents of a foreign government.

discipline of a warrior, the intellect of a chess master, the obsessive mania of a paranoiac, and the willfulness of an infant.

Ann Louise Bardach

Whatever you think of his politics, Fidel Castro was unquestionably one of the most remarkable and enigmatic figures of the 20th century, thriving on contradiction and paradox like a romantic character from the fiction of his Colombian novelist friend Gabriel García Márquez.

Fidel Castro Ruz was born on August 13, 1926, at Manacas *finca* near Birán in northern Oriente, the fifth of nine children of Ángel Castro y Argiz. Fidel's father was an émigré to Cuba from Galicia in Spain as a destitute 13-year-old. In Cuba, he became a wealthy landowner who employed 300 workers on a 26,000-acre domain; he owned 1,920 acres and leased the rest from the United Fruit Company, to whom he sold cane. Fidel's

mother was the family housemaid, Lina Ruz González, whom Ángel later married after divorcing his wife. Fidel, who seems to have had a happy childhood, liked to obfuscate the true details of his illegitimacy and early years.

As a boy Fidel was extremely assertive and combative and seems to have developed a pathological need to have enemies to fight. He was a natural athlete. He was no sportsman, however; if his team was losing, he would leave the field and go home. Gabriel García Márquez has said, "I do not think anyone in this world could be a worse loser." It became a matter of principle to win at everything.

Star Rising

In October 1945 Fidel enrolled in Havana University's law school, where he plunged into politics as a student leader. Fidel earned his first front-page newspaper appearance following his first public speech,

How Cubans Feel About the Revolution

A large segment of Cubans saw Fidel Castro as a ruthless dictator who cynically betrayed the democratic ideals that he used to rally millions to his banner. To Miami exiles especially, Fidel was just a common tyrant. Nonetheless, the Revolution retains the admiration of many Cuban people, to whom Fidel remains a hero: Countless families hang framed photographs of him.

Many of the same Cubans who complain about harrowing privation and the ubiquitous and oppressive presence of the state will profess loyalty to the Revolution. Those with a hate-hate relationship are resigned to sullen silence, prison, or exile. Most Cubans, however, have a love-hate relationship with Fidel and Raúl (they are the "Gray Zone," the majority, neither committed to nor directly opposed to the government), a result of the unifying power of national pride, the very real achievements of the Revolution, Fidel's unique charisma, and the way Fidel was able to shape the minds of *cubanos* like a hypnotist.

Cuba has invested 50 years of resources to become one of the few underdeveloped nations that protect virtually all members of society from illiteracy and ill health. This, plus tremendous advances in racial and sexual equality, has produced mammoth goodwill, especially in the countryside, where support for the Revolution is strongest. Many among the party faithful, of course, espouse support because they're the beneficiaries of the system, which nurtures its own privileged elite. For loyalists, defending the system is a knee-jerk reaction.

Despite the gains (and despite Raúl's reforms), the majority of urbanites long ago lost faith in the Castro government. The mood on the streets is one of frustration. Most Cubans are pained by their own poverty and the political posturing to disguise it. Urbanites, especially, are anxious for a return to the market economy and a chance to control and improve their own lives. Most Cubans are tired of the inefficiencies, the endless hardships, the constant sacrifices, and having to live under the stress of being caught for the slightest transgression. Which does not mean they're unhappy—far from it.

There is a tendency to judge Cuba by this single yardstick. Cubans, and the Cuban Revolution, demonstrate the naiveté in that thinking. Most Cubans are immeasurably better off than their Caribbean neighbors thanks to a revolutionary government that takes its obligation seriously to guarantee health care and literacy for all. It wasn't that way before 1959, and that bears remembering.

denouncing President Grau, on November 27, 1946. In 1947, Fidel was invited to help organize Edward Chibás's Ortodoxo party. He stopped attending law school and rose rapidly to prominence, including as head of the revolutionary group Orthodox Radical Action.

The period was exceedingly violent, and Fidel never went anywhere without a gun. Fidel was soon on the police hit list, and several attempts were made on his life. In February 1949, Fidel was accused of assassinating a political rival. After being arrested and subsequently released on "conditional liberty," he went into hiding.

On October 12, 1949, Fidel married a philosophy student named Mirta Díaz-Balart. They honeymooned extravagantly—even staying in the Waldorf-Astoria—for several weeks in the United States. Fidel, the consummate opportunist, may have married for political gain: Mirta's father was mayor of Banes, a Cuban congressman, and a close friend of Fulgencio Batista, who gave the couple US$1,000 for their honeymoon.

In November, Fidel gave a speech in which he named all the gangsters, politicians, and student leaders profiting from the "gangs' pact." In fear for his life, Fidel left Cuba for the United States. He returned four months later to cram for a multiple degree. In September 1950, Fidel graduated with the title of Doctor of Law.

Congressional Candidate

By 1951, Fidel was preparing for national office. His personal magnetism, his brilliant speeches, and his apparent honesty aroused the crowds. Batista, who had returned from retirement in Florida to run for president, even asked to receive Fidel to get the measure of the young man who in January 1952 shook Cuba's political foundation by releasing a detailed indictment of President Prío.

Fidel was certain to be elected to the Chamber of Deputies. It was also clear that Batista was going to be trounced in the presidential contest, so at dawn on March 10, 1952, Batista effected a *golpe*. Says Tad Szulc: "Many Cubans think that without a coup, Fidel would have served as a congressman for four years until 1956, then run for the Senate, and then made his pitch for the presidency in 1960 or 1964. Given the fact that Cuba was wholly bereft of serious political leadership and given Fidel's rising popularity...it would appear that he was fated to govern Cuba—no matter how he arrived at the top job."

A Communist Caudillo

At 30 years old, Fidel was fighting in the Sierra Maestra, a disgruntled lawyer turned revolutionary who craved Batista's job. At 32, he had it. He was determined not to let go. Fidel used the Revolution to carry out a personal *caudillista* coup. "Communist or not, what was being built in Cuba was an old-fashioned personality cult," wrote Jon Lee Anderson.

Fidel outlasted 10 U.S. presidents, each of whom predicted his imminent demise and plotted to hasten it by fair means or foul. He said he would never relinquish power while Washington remained hostile—a condition he thrived on and worked hard to maintain. Fidel—who knew he could never carry out his revolution in an elective system—was consummately Machiavellian. Says Guillermo Cabrera Infante, "Fidel's real genius lies in the arts of deception, and while the world plays bridge by the book, he plays poker, bluffing and holding his cards close to his olive-green chest." Adds historian Hugh Thomas: "Often the first person he deceived was himself."

Nonetheless, Fidel genuinely believed that disease, malnutrition, and illiteracy are criminal shames and that a better social order could be created through the perfection of good values. Despite the turn of events, Fidel clung to the thread of his dream: "If I'm told 98 percent of the people no longer believe in the Revolution, I'll continue to fight. If I'm told I'm the only one who believes in it, I'll continue." But he was far from the saint his ardent admirers portray.

A Hatred of Uncle Sam

Fidel turned to Communism for strategic, not ideological reasons, but his bitterness toward the United States also shaped his decision. He was less committed to Marxism than to anti-imperialism, in which he was unwavering. He cast himself in the role of David versus Goliath, in the tradition of José Martí. Fidel saw himself as Martí's heir, representing the same combination of New World nationalism, Spanish romanticism, and philosophical radicalism.

His boyhood impressions of destitution in Holguín Province under the thumb of the United Fruit Company and, later, the 1954 overthrow of the reformist Arbenz government in Guatemala by a military force organized by the CIA and underwritten by "Big Fruit" had a profound impact on Fidel's thinking. Ever since, Fidel viewed world politics through the prism of anti-Americanism. During the war in the Sierra Maestra, Fidel stated, "When this war is over, it will be the beginning, for me, of a much wider and bigger war; the war I'm going to wage against [the Americans]. I realize that that's going to be my true destiny."

He brilliantly used the Cold War to enlist the Soviet Union to move Cuba out of the U.S. orbit, and was thus able—with Soviet funds—to bolster his stature as a nationalist redeemer by guaranteeing the Cuban masses substantial social and economic gains while exerting constant energy and creativity to keep the United States at a distance.

Many Talents

Fidel had a gargantuan hunger for

information, a huge trove of knowledge, and an equally prodigious memory. He never forgot facts and figures, a remarkable asset he nourished at law school, where he forced himself to depend on his memory by destroying the materials he had learned by heart. He was a micromanager. There was a sense of perfection in everything he did, applied through a superbly methodical mind and laser-clear focus. He had astounding political instincts, notably an uncanny ability to predict the future moves of his adversaries (Fidel was a masterly chess player). Fidel's "rarest virtue," said his intimate friend Gabriel García Márquez, "is the ability to foresee the evolution of an event to its farthest-reaching consequences."

Fidel was also a gambler of unsurpassed self-confidence. He stood at the threshold of death several times and loved to court danger. Above all, Fidel had an insatiable, almost manic, appetite for the limelight, and a narcissistic focus on his theatrical role. The one thing that infuriated Fidel was to be ignored. He never laughed at himself unless he made the joke. And he assiduously avoided singing or dancing—he was perhaps the only male in Cuba who was never seen to dance.

Fidel nurtured his image with exquisite care, feigning modesty to hide his immense ego. He saw himself as a leader of vast international significance, and the "absolute patriarch" of his country, suggests Bardach. He also claimed that his place in history did not bother him. Yet in the same breath he haughtily likened himself to Jesus Christ, cultivating a myth of Fidel the redeemer figure.

Fidel's revolutionary concept was built on communicating with the masses through public speeches, televised in entirety. Fidel was masterfully persuasive, an amazingly gifted speaker who in his better days could hold Cubans spellbound with oratory, using his flattery and enigmatic language to obfuscate and arouse. His speeches lasted for hours. Fidel's loquaciousness is legendary. He was not, however, a man of small talk; he was deadly serious whenever he opened his mouth. His digressive repertoire was immense: "Fidel,

the former lawyer, can argue anything from any side at any time," writes Bardach.

Dilettante Extraordinaire

Cubans' bawdy street wisdom says that Fidel had various domiciles so that he could attend to his lovers. Fidel was an avid consumer of Cuba's anti-cholesterol drug, PPG, renowned for its Viagra-like side effects. He admitted to having at least 12 children but acknowledged there may be others.

Many highly intelligent and beautiful women dedicated themselves to Fidel and his cause. But Fidel saved his most ardent passions for the Revolution, and the women (and children) in his life were badly treated. Delia Soto del Valle, Fidel's second wife, with whom he had five sons, was rarely seen in public, and almost never with her husband. The average Cuban in the street knows virtually nothing of Fidel's private life.

Fidel retains the loyalty of millions of Cubans, but he was only loyal to those who were loyal to him. His capacity for Homeric rage was renowned, and no official in his right mind dared criticize him. Paradoxically, he could be extremely gentle and courteous, especially towards women, in whose company he was slightly abashed. Cubans feared the consequences of saying anything against him, discreetly stroking their chins—an allusion to his beard—rather than uttering his name. In 1996 his biographer Tad Szulc wrote, "He is determined not to tolerate any challenge to his authority, whatever the consequences." Fidel did not forget, or pardon, and never apologized as a matter of policy. Beneath the gold foil lay a heart of cold steel. Thus, he was prepared to eliminate anyone, no matter who, if it served him.

His policies divided countless families, and Fidel's family is no exception. His sister, Juanita, left for Miami in 1964 and is an outspoken critic of her brothers' policies (in her 2009 autobiography, *Fidel and Raúl, My Brothers: The Secret History,* she revealed that she even worked for the CIA against her brother before fleeing Cuba). Fidel's daughter, Alina Fernández Revuelta, fled in disguise in

Raúl Castro

Born at Birán on June 3, 1931, Raúl is the youngest of the three Castro brothers (Cubans refer to him as *el chino* and slant their eyes to denote him—an allusion to the belief that he was fathered by a Chinese man, Batista loyalist Felipe Miraval). Although a mediocre student, he proved a capable commander in Fidel's guerrilla army and has been at the forefront of government since 1959. He enjoys the absolute loyalty of the army, which he led with skill and savvy until taking over the reins of the government.

He is a delegator, not the obsessive micromanager that Fidel was. Nor is he filled with his brother's vast ego. Although an immensely capable manager, Raúl has little of his brother's charisma and has been far less popular than Fidel, from whom he derived his political strength. That is changing, however, as Cubans have been surprised by, and come to appreciate, Raúl's reforms.

Raúl has been a Communist since youth. Although he seems absolutely devoted to preserving the socialist revolution and one-party state, he is far more pragmatic than Fidel and has demonstrated a desire to dramatically step up the pace of reform while keeping a tight lid on political dissent; Fidel would never have permitted Raúl's reforms.

The real test will come with Raúl's passing, when the true power struggle begins.

1993 and vilified her father from her home in Miami.

The indefatigable Cuban leader was taken ill in July 2006 and underwent emergency surgery for diverticulitis. He never fully recovered and became a frail old man rarely seen in public. He lived quietly in a modest home on the western outskirts of Havana with his wife.

Fidel—and now Raúl—denied that a personality cult exists. Yet monuments, posters, and billboards are adorned with their quotations and faces. Since his death on November 25, 2016, Fidel's visage is everywhere, headlined by the new refrain: YO SOY FIDEL! (I am Fidel!).

Economy

One may wait 15 minutes to buy a pound of rice, or 30 minutes for a bus that never shows. Another may wait four days in a provincial terminal for an airplane that's sitting in a hangar in some other province waiting for repairs from a mechanic who happens to be waiting in line at the doctor's office, but the doctor is late, still waiting for a permission slip from a government functionary who's behind schedule because she, too, had to wait in line all morning trying to reschedule her daughter for an eye exam that was delayed because the optometric lens was waiting to be repaired by the technician who was busy waiting at the train station for his relatives to arrive.

Ben Corbett, *This Is Cuba*

THE REVOLUTIONARY ECONOMY

For several decades prior to the Revolution, U.S. corporations virtually owned the island. Most of the cattle ranches, more than 50 percent of the railways, 40 percent of sugar production, 90 percent of mining and oil production, and almost 100 percent of telephone and utility services were owned by U.S. companies. Every year, beginning in 1934, the U.S. Congress established a preferential quota for Cuban sugar. In exchange for a guaranteed price, Cuba had to guarantee tariff concessions on U.S. goods sold to Cuba. The agreement kept Cuba tied to the United States.

Nonetheless, despite immense poverty throughout the country, Cuba's national income in 1957 of US$2.3 billion was topped only by that of the much larger countries of Argentina, Mexico, and Venezuela.

Fidel and Che Guevara, who became the Minister of Industry, might have been great revolutionaries, but they didn't have the skills to run an efficient economy, which they swiftly nationalized. There were few coherent economic plans in the 1960s—just grandiose schemes that almost always ended in near ruin. They replaced monetary work incentives with "moral" incentives, set artificially low prices, and got diminishing supplies in return. Socialism had nationalized wealth, leaving Cuba with a ruined economy.

Soviet Largesse

For almost three decades, the Soviet Union acted as Cuba's benefactor, providing aid estimated at around US$11 million per day—the greatest per capita aid program in world history. Says P. J. O'Rourke, "The Cubans got the luxury of running their economy along the lines of a Berkeley commune, and like California hippies wheedling their parents for cash, someone else paid the tab." The Soviet Union also sustained the Cuban economy by supplying 85 percent of its imports in barter for sugar.

After the collapse of the Soviet bloc, Cuba's economy was cut adrift. Between 1990 and 1994, the economy shrank as much as 70 percent. The work force was left idle. To compound the problem, the world market price of sugar (which in the 1980s accounted for 80 percent of Cuba's export earnings) also plummeted, along with Cuba's sugar harvest.

Farewell to Marxism

In October 1991 the Cuban Communist Party Congress adopted a resolution establishing profit-maximizing state-owned Cuban corporations that operate independently of the central state apparatus. In 1995 Cuba passed a law allowing foreign businesses to enter into joint partner ventures with Cuban state entities. Cuba began sending its best and brightest abroad for crash courses in capitalist business techniques. The Castros have handed over large chunks of the economy to the military, which began sweeping experiments under GAESA, the business arm of the army (its CEO is Alberto Rodríguez López-Callejas, son-in-law to Raúl Castro). Today generals in civilian clothes run at least 60 percent of the Cuban economy.

In 1993, to soak up foreign currency floating freely in the black market as cash remittances *(remesas)* from families in the United States or as tips from foreign tourists, the Cuban government legalized possession of the U.S. dollar (greenbacks are called *fula,* a reference to the green-gray gunpowder used in Santería to invoke the spirits) and opened "foreign exchange recovery stores" (shops) selling imported items, from toothpaste to Japanese TVs. The government also legalized self-employment: By mid-1995, 210,000 Cubans (about 5 percent of Cuba's labor force) had registered as *cuentapropistas,* subject to taxation up to 50 percent.

Back from the Brink

By 2005, with the economy stabilized (and bolstered by growing economic ties to China and Venezuela), the government began rolling back reforms. By the end of that year, only a handful of foreign investors remained. Joint-venture enterprises lost much of their autonomy. In 2016, Cuba's self-employed, who typically earn far more than the average monthly salary of about 700 pesos (equivalent to US$25), found Cuban-style capitalism bruising in the face of regulations meant to restrain success.

TODAY'S ECONOMY

Cuba, with an annual GDP of US$128 billion (2014), is running a massive trade deficit that topped $9.5 billion in 2015. The economy is kept afloat with substantial aid from Venezuela, which supplies Cuba with oil and financial assistance. Brazil, China, and Russia have also substantially increased their investments. In 2016, Cuba renegotiated its debt with Russia (which forgave $29 billion!),

What a Joke!

After the Revolution, Che Guevara was named president of the bank and Minister of Finance. He loved to regale listeners with the joke of how he'd gotten the job, according to author Jon Lee Anderson. Supposedly, at a cabinet meeting to decide on a replacement of bank president Felipe Pazos, Castro asked who among them was a "good *economista*." Che raised his hand and was sworn in as Minister of Finance and head of the National Bank. Castro said: "Che, I didn't know you were an economist." Che replied, "I'm not!" Castro asked, "Then why did you raise your hand when I said I needed an economist?" To which Guevara replied, "Economist! I thought you asked for a Communist."

China, and other nations. The top sources of income are family remittances sent from abroad (perhaps as high as US$5 billion), plus tourism, and exports of nickel, pharmaceuticals, and professional services (doctors and teachers, which earned $8.2 billion in 2014).

The 3,700 or so state companies, managed by government ministries, still control almost 100 percent of manufacturing and most of the farm sector. Raúl Castro has replaced key ministers with military disciplinarians charged with bringing efficiency to the economy. A new salary bonus system that rewards productivity was introduced as a prelude to dramatic reforms. The private sector (limited to service industries) is booming.

Raúl's Reforms

In April 2011, the Communist Party Congress approved 313 "guidelines" *(lineamientos)* that comprise a detailed road map for economic reforms. Despite a rearguard action by sclerotic, self-interested bureaucrats, Raúl Castro has initiated a slow and measured but irreversible dismantling of Communism in an effort to revive the moribund economy and change the state's role from administrating the economy to regulating it. Today, small private businesses (*cuentapropistas,* meaning "on their own account") are being given government support. More than 500,000 *cuentapropistas* now exist in 206 permissible categories of self-employment, from plumbers to "dandies" (posers for tourist cameras), all in service sectors. *Cuentapropistas* can now hire their own employees and have multiple businesses, and even sell their goods and services to state entities. They alone in Cuba pay taxes (top marginal rate is 50 percent).

Meanwhile, unprofitable state enterprises—which have traditionally operated as extensions of government ministries, which issue directives and quotas—will be closed. Managers will be given more autonomy in decision making. The ram to push the reforms forward is Manuel Murillo, former Minister of Economics, named as head of the new Permanent Government Commission for Implementation of Development.

The blueprint calls for creating more *zonas especiales de desarrollo* (ZEDs, or special development zones), intended as powerhouses for economic growth and offering special incentives to foreign investors. However, a desire to increase foreign investment remains stymied by Cuba's fickleness and its highly selective approach to project approval; the Cuban government acknowledges it needs at least $2.5 billion annually (ten times the current level). Foreign investors remain spooked by the Cuban government's capriciousness and history of asset-grabbing. "There's no turning back," Raúl has insisted, while making plain that the economy will be shaped by state planning, not the market.

Also in 2011, the 7th Communist Party Congress—the last presided over by the *históricos* (original revolutionary leaders)—acknowledged that the preceding five years had failed to live up to the hopes of the *"lineamientos"* (guidelines) for economic reform. The death of Venezuela's Hugo Chávez in 2013 fostered Cuba's understanding that it must seek rapprochement with the United States as an economic lifeline in the likely event of a collapse of Venezuelan support. The government reinstituted price controls in the face of inflation.

It's a tricky balancing act. The reforms have exposed the country's enormous potential and extraordinary entrepreneurial spirit. But Cuba's leaders fear the private sector growing so large that it threatens the system. Meanwhile, the military's economic division has become the country's biggest hotelier, importer, and retailer.

AGRICULTURE

Traveling through Cuba, you'll sense the vast potential that caused René Dumont, the outstanding French agronomist, to say that "with proper management, Cuba could adequately feed five times its current population."

Before the Revolution, Cuba certainly couldn't feed itself: The best arable lands were planted in sugarcane for export. Alas, since the Revolution, management of agriculture has been inept. Having seized all large estates and foreign holdings, Fidel organized land in a system of centralized, inefficient state farms dedicated to sugarcane monoculture to satisfy the Soviet sweet tooth. Since the Soviet collapse, Cuba lost its sugar market; fully 50 percent of land now lies idle, much of it overgrown with a tenacious acacia called *marabú*. Declining agricultural production was exacerbated in the early 1990s by a lack of machinery, fertilizers, and alternating droughts and torrential storms. Food distribution is also centralized and highly inefficient.

In September 1993 Cuba established autonomous cooperatives that farm government land but own the crop they harvest (although they must follow state directives and sell their crops to the state at fixed prices). Private owners utilize about 40 percent of Cuba's 6.7 million hectares of cultivable land but account for about 70 percent of all produce (they, too, must sell 80 percent of their produce to the state at fixed prices; the surplus can be sold

on the free market). Meanwhile, several thousand community-operated gardens have eased food shortfalls; alongside private farms, these *agropónicos* account for about half the food grown in Cuba.

Since taking over, Raúl has initiated significant reforms. More than 1.5 million hectares of vacant state land have been leased free of charge in usufruct to farmers; prices paid to farmers have been increased; local councils have been given greater autonomy over food production; and the state has supposedly paid its outstanding debts to farmers and increased the prices it pays for produce. In 2012, the government began to permit private cooperatives to take over. The state has begun to address the dramatic shortage of agricultural inputs and hardware by opening stores, and Brazil is providing loans for Cuban farmers to buy Brazilian mini tractors to be made on the island. In 2015, a U.S. company became the first in half a century to sign a commercial deal to manufacture mini tractors in Cuba.

Despite these changes, production remains insufficient to meet domestic needs.

Cattle, Citrus, and Coffee

Cuba always had a strong cattle industry, particularly in the provinces around Camagüey, which has been famous for beef and dairy production since before the Revolution. There were 6.5 million head of cattle on the eve of the Revolution, when milk production was 9.6 million liters a year. Following the Revolution, ranching was nationalized and the herds were slaughtered to compensate for falling production of other foods; by 1963, there were only 2 million head. That year, Castro took a lively interest and made animal husbandry a national priority, resulting in the breeding of Cuba's home-grown F1 strain. By 1980, Cuba had replenished its herds, which peaked at 7.3 million head; they have since dwindled back to about 3.7 million head, or 1915 levels, while their average weight has dropped 60 percent. Milk production has also fallen by more than 50 percent since the 1980s. Private farmers are again permitted to raise cattle, but killing cattle for private consumption or sale of meat is illegal, and farmers are fined for each head of cattle they lose. Nonetheless, dairy production is inching up as bureaucrats take more of a backseat under Raúl's liberalizing directive.

Cuba produces about one million tons of citrus. Most goes to produce juices and extracts, much of it for export to Europe. Effort has been made in recent years to upgrade with investments from Chile and Israel.

Cuba produces excellent coffee. The finest is grown in the Sierra Escambray, although most coffee is grown in the mountains of eastern Cuba. Cuba enjoyed modest exports on the eve of the Revolution, following which Fidel initiated a massive and disastrous coffee-planting scheme that cordoned lowland Havana with the upland plant. Production has since declined markedly. The 2010 harvest yielded only 5,500 tons (the lowest in two centuries and only 10 percent of production in 1955), while Cuba spent $47.5 million purchasing coffee abroad. The highest quality coffee is exported. Domestic coffee is adulterated with roasted wheat.

Sugar

The whole country reeks of sweet, pungent sugar, Cuba's curse and blessing. The unusual depth and fertility of Cuba's limestone soils are unparalleled in the world for producing sugar. The nation's bittersweet bondsman has been responsible for curses like slavery and the country's almost total dependence on not only the one product, but on single imperial nations: first Spain, then the United States, and most recently the Soviet Union.

Production rose gradually from about 5 million tons a year in the early 1970s to 7.5 million tons on average in the late 1980s. Three-quarters went to feed the Soviet bear; the rest went to capitalist markets to earn hard currency. The collapse of the Soviet bloc rendered a triple whammy to Cuba's obsolete sugar industry. Cuba had to produce more and more sugar to generate the same income while facing growing competition from new producers such as Brazil and India and sugar beet producers.

In 2002, the government announced that more than 3.1 million acres of cane fields were to be converted to food crops. All but 39 of the nation's 156 sugar mills have since been closed and 100,000 sugar workers made redundant. From 7 million tons in 1991, the harvest plummeted to 1.1 million tons in 2010; the 2014-2015 harvest brought in 1.8 million tons.

Tobacco

About 29,000 hectares are given to tobacco, Cuba's second most important agricultural earner of foreign exchange. It is grown predominantly in a 145-kilometer-long, 16-kilometer-wide valley—Vuelta Abajo—in Pinar del Río, on small privately owned properties; the average holding is only 10 hectares. The Vuelta Arriba region of Villa Clara and Sancti Spíritus Provinces produces a strongly scented dark tobacco for cigarettes and strong cigars.

The tobacco industry has been devastated by hurricanes, heavy rains, and drought, causing massive losses within the industry. Cuba's state-run Habanos S. A. has struggled to maintain quality, not least due to overproduction in some years. Production peaked at 54,600 metric tons in 1982; production was 24,300 metric tons in 2015 (state farms account for barely 1 percent of production), when Cuba exported about 150 million cigars, worth US$439 million.

INDUSTRY

Cement, rubber, and tobacco products, processed foods, textiles, clothing, footwear, chemicals, and fertilizers are the staple industries. Many factories date from the antediluvian dawn. An exception is in pharmaceuticals, where the country's investments in biotechnology generate more than US$300 million a year. Cuba has also invested in metal processing, spare-parts industries, and factories turning out domestic appliances, albeit often of shoddy quality. It also has steel mills, bottling plants, paper-producing factories,

The *Zafra*

With the onset of the dry season, Cuba prepares for the *zafra,* the sugar harvest, which runs from November through June. Then *macheteros* (cane-cutters) are in the fields from dawn until dusk, wielding their blunt-nosed machetes after first burning the cane stalks to soften them for the cut. The *macheteros* grab the three-meter-tall stalks, which they slash close to the ground (where the sweetness concentrates). Then they cut off the top and strip the dry leaves from the stalk.

Today, three-quarters of the crop is harvested mechanically. The Cuban-designed combine-harvester can cut a truckload of cane (close to seven metric tons) in 10 minutes, three times more than the most skilled *macheteros* can cut by hand in a day.

The cut cane is delivered to the sugar mills in Cuba, which operate 24 hours a day, pouring black smoke into the air. Here the sugarcane is fed to the huge steel crushers that squeeze out the sugary pulp called *guarapo,* which is boiled, clarified, evaporated, and separated into molasses and sugar crystals. The molasses makes rum, yeast, and cattle feed. *Bagazo,* the fiber left after squeezing, fuels boilers or is shipped off to mills to be turned into paper and wallboard. The sugar is shipped by rail to bulk shipping terminals for transport to refineries abroad.

and animal feed factories. Even Sony TVs, Cuban-designed computers, and vehicles are assembled from foreign parts.

Cuba boasts large resources of chromite, cobalt, iron, copper, manganese, lead, and zinc, all concentrated in the island's northeast. Cuba is also the world's sixth-largest producer of nickel and has about 37 percent of the world's estimated reserves.

In April 1960, the Soviet ship *Chernovci* arrived with 70,000 barrels of oil—the beginning of a 10,000-kilometer petroleum pipeline that was maintained for three decades. Cuba traded nickel, citrus, and sugar to the Soviet Union in return for 10-12 million tons of crude oil and petroleum per year. As much as half of this was re-exported for hard currency to purchase necessities on the world market (by the mid-1980s, oil surpassed sugar as the island's major moneymaker). Today, Cuba meets the bulk of its needs with discounted Venezuelan oil, paid for in part in medical and other services (much of the crude is resold on work markets for hard currency).

Cuba *does* have oil, and crude is pumped from 20 oil fields concentrated near Varadero—enough to cover 50 percent of the island's needs. However, Cuba's crude oil is heavy, with high sulfur content (it's used to generate electricity). Seeking higher-quality oil, the Cuban government has opened a 112,000-square-kilometer zone of the Gulf of Mexico for deepwater exploration by foreign companies. The U.S. embargo, however, prevents Cuba accessing *any* international rigs or technology that contain 10 percent U.S. parts or intellectual property. In 2012, the *Scarabeo 9* moveable drilling platform arrived from China and began exploration. It is being leased to international oil companies but has come up dry.

There's new urgency to the need to strike oil. Venezuela is in crisis and oil supplied dropped from 125,000 barrels daily in 2014 to fewer than 90,000 in 2016.

TOURISM

Before 1959 Cuba was one of the world's hottest tourist destinations. When Batista was ousted, most foreigners stayed home. Apart from a handful of Russians, the beaches belonged to the Cubans throughout the 1960s, '70s, and '80s, when tourism contributed virtually nothing to the nation's coffers. With the demise of the Soviet Union, Cuba set itself an ambitious long-term goal of five million tourists annually by 2010. Tourism has yo-yoed, nowhere near to that mark, but since 2014—when President Obama announced major liberalization for travel to

Cigars

The tobacco leaves, which arrive at the factories after 1-5 years of fermenting and aging, are first moistened and stripped, then graded by color and strength (each type of cigar has a recipe). A blender mixes the recipes and the leaves then go to the production room, where each *torcedor* (roller) receives enough to roll approximately 50-150 cigars for the day, depending on cigar size and shape.

The rollers sit at rows of *galeras* (workbenches). The rollers' sole tool is a *chaveta*, a rounded, all-purpose knife for smoothing and cutting leaves, tamping loose tobacco, and circumcising the tips. While they work, a *lector* (reader) reads aloud from a platform. Morning excerpts are read from the newspaper; in the afternoon, the *lector* reads a book (Alexandre Dumas's *The Count of Monte Cristo* was such a hit in the 19th century that it lent its name to the Montecristo cigar).

The *torcedor* chooses two to four filler leaves, which are rolled into a tube and then enveloped by the binder leaves to make a rough-looking "bunch." This is then placed with others in a mold that is screwed down to press each cigar into a solid cylinder.

THE WRAPPER

Next, the *torcedor* selects a wrapper leaf, which he or she trims to size. The "bunch" is then laid at an angle across the wrapper, which is stretched and rolled around the "bunch," overlapping with each turn. Finally, a piece of wrapper leaf the size and shape of a quarter is cut to form the cap; it is glued (using flavorless tragapanth gum, made from Canadian pine) and twirled into place, and the excess is trimmed.

AND SO TO MARKET

The roller ties cigars of the same size and brand into bundles of 50. These are then fumigated in a vacuum chamber. Quality is determined according to eight criteria, such as length, weight, firmness, and smoothness of wrappers. Professional smokers then blind test the cigars for aroma, draw, and burn.

Once fumigated, cigars are placed in humidors for three weeks to settle fermentation and remove any excess moisture. The cigars are then graded according to color and then shade. A trademark paper band is then put on. Finally, the cigars are laid in pinewood boxes, with the lightest cigar on the right and the darkest on the left. A thin leaf of cedarwood is laid on top to maintain freshness, and the box is sealed with a green-and-white label guaranteeing the cigars are genuine Havanas, or *puros habanos* (today the terms *puro* and *habano* are synonyms for cigar).

Cuba—it has boomed. In 2016, Cuba received more than 4 million visitors, earning Cuba US$3.5 billion.

Canada accounted for roughly 50 percent of arrivals (almost all of it at all-inclusive beach resorts), followed by the United States (614,433 in 2016, including Cuban-Americans), Great Britain, Italy, and Spain. Cuba is currently focusing on the former Soviet bloc market.

In March 2016, Tourism Minister Manuel Marrero Cruz announced that Cuba planned to add 60,000 hotels by 2030 on top of an existing crop of 60,552 that is now insufficient to keep up with demand. In 2016, the first U.S. cruise ships arrived, as did the first U.S. hotel corporation since the Revolution when Starwood took over management of three Cuban hotels.

Cuban Society

DEMOGRAPHY

Cuba's population was 11,164,000 according to the 2012 census, of which 76 percent were classified as urban; 20 percent live in the city of Havana, with a population of about 2.2 million. Santiago de Cuba, the second-largest city, has about 350,000 people. Population growth halted in 2003. Since then, Cuba has been the only nation in the Americas whose population is falling.

The low birth and mortality rates, long life expectancy, and a steady drain of young Cubans to the United States and other countries also mean a rapidly aging population. About 16 percent of the population is 60 years or older (by 2025, at current trends, the number of pensioners will be on a par with that of workers)—an enormous social security burden for the beleaguered government (pensions cost almost 8 percent of Cuba's GDP).

The United Nations Human Development Index ranks Cuba third in the Caribbean (behind the Bahamas and Barbados) and fifth in Latin America (behind Argentina, Chile, Uruguay, and Costa Rica).

Ethnicity and Race Relations

Officially about 37 percent of the population is "white," mainly of Spanish origin. About 11 percent is black, and 52 percent is of mixed white-black ethnicity—in truth, there is some African in every Cuban's blood. Chinese constitute about 0.1 percent.

After emancipation in 1888, the island was spared the brutal segregation of the American South, and a black middle class evolved alongside a black underclass, with its own social clubs, restaurants, and literature. "Cuba's color line is much more flexible than that of the United States," recorded black author Langston Hughes during a visit in 1930. Gradually, U.S. visitors began to import Southern racial prejudice to their winter playground. To court their approval, hotels that were formerly lax in their application of color lines began to discourage even mulatto Cubans. Cuba on the eve of the Revolution had adopted discrimination. When dictator Fulgencio Batista—who was a mixture of white, black, and Chinese—arrived at the exclusive Havana Yacht Club, they turned the lights out to let him know that although he was president, as a mulatto he wasn't welcome.

The Castro government outlawed institutionalized discrimination and vigorously enforced laws to bring about racial equality. The social advantages that opened up after the Revolution have resulted in the abolition of lily-white scenes. Cuban society is as intermixed as any other on earth. Mixed marriages raise no eyebrows in Cuba.

Nonetheless, the most marginal neighborhoods still have a heavy preponderance of blacks. Most Cuban blacks still work at menial jobs and earn, on average, less than whites. And blacks are notoriously absent from academia and the upper echelons of government. (Since 1994, when Havana witnessed what were essentially race riots, the government has been promoting black officials and elevating blacks to more prominent positions in tourism.) Nor has the Revolution totally overcome stereotypical racial thinking and prejudice. Black youths, for example, claim to be disproportionately harassed by police (though, ironically, blacks are well represented among the uniformed police). And you still hear racist comments.

CHARACTER, CONDUCT, AND CUSTOMS

Although a clear Cuban identity has emerged, Cuban society is not easy to fathom. Cubans "adore mystery and continually do their damnedest to render everything more intriguing," thought author Juliet Barclay. The Cubans value context, and the philosophical approach to life differs markedly from North

Spanish Surnames

Spanish surnames are combinations of the first surname of the person's father, which comes first, and the mother's first surname, which comes second. Thus, the son of Ángel Castro Argiz and Lina Ruz González was Fidel Castro Ruz.

After marriage, women do not take their husbands' surnames; they retain their maiden names. A single woman is addressed as *señorita* if less than 40 years old, and *señora* if above 40.

America or northern Europe. Attempts to analyze Cuba through the North American value system are bound to be wide of the mark.

In the decades since the Revolution, most Cubans have learned to live double lives. One side is spirited, inventive, irrepressibly argumentative and critical, inclined to keep private shrines at home to both Christian saints and African gods, and profit however possible from the failings and inefficiencies of the state. The other side commits them to be good revolutionaries and to cling to the state. When loyalists speak of the "revolution," they don't mean the toppling of Batista's regime, or Castro's seizure of power, or even his and the country's conversion to Communism. They mean the ongoing process of building a society where everyone supposedly benefits. Despite a pandemic of disaffection, many Cubans seem happy to accept the sacrifice of individual liberties for the abstract notion of improving equality.

The Cuban people are committed to social justice. The idea that democracy includes every person's right to guaranteed health care and education is deeply ingrained in their consciousness. True, Cubans crave the opportunity to better their lives materially, but few are concerned with the *accumulation* of material wealth, although that is now changing as Raúl's economic reforms (and increased relations with U.S. tourists) are fostering a rapidly growing middle class with disposable income. Most Cubans are more interested in sharing something with you than getting something from you. They are unmoved by talk of your material accomplishments, although a growing "consumerism" is noticeable.

Cubans are also notoriously toilet- and fashion-conscious. Even the poorest Cuban manages to keep fastidiously clean and well dressed.

The struggles of the past decades have fostered a remarkable sense of confidence and maturity. As such, there's no reserve, no emotional distance, no holding back. Cubans are self-assured and engage you in a very intimate way. They're not afraid of physical contact; they touch a lot. They also look you in the eye: They don't blink or flinch but are direct and assured. And free of social pretension. They're alive and full of emotional intensity.

Cubans lack the social caste system that makes so many Europeans walk on eggshells. There is absolutely no deference, no subservience. Cubans accept people at face value and are slow to judge others negatively. They are instantly at ease, and greet each other with hearty handshakes or kisses. Women meeting for the first time will embrace like sisters. A complete stranger is sure to give you a warm *abrazo,* or hug. Cuban loyalists call each other *compañero* or *compañera,* which Martha Gellhorn described as having a "cozy sound of companionship."

Social Divisions

The Revolution destroyed social stratification. As an agrarian-populist movement, *fidelismo* eliminated the middle class, eradicating their hard-earned wealth and tearing families asunder. The "privileged" classes were replaced by a new class of senior Communist

Party members and army officials who enjoy benefits unavailable to other Cubans.

In the past few decades, however, a more stratified society has emerged. The values and ethics are becoming strained. An economic elite of *masetas* (rich Cubans, or *consumistas* flaunting their wealth) has become visible, as has a class of impoverished, mostly blacks. Not least, most families that receive remittances from the United States are white. The new class of wealthy includes successful farmers, artists, musicians, and enterprising owners of private restaurants and even nightclubs. Reports Marc Frank: "A recent study found a 15-to-1 difference in purchasing power between the top tenth of society and the bottom tenth, with access to foreign exchange the most important differentiating factor."

Plus, low-level corruption, long a necessity for getting around Cuba's socialist inefficiencies, has blossomed into more insidious high-level graft and racketeering. Many people are alternately sad and high-spirited.

Many families are torn by divided feelings towards the Revolution. The worst divisions are found among families split between those who departed for Miami and those who stayed. *Se fue* (he/she left) and *se quedó* (he/she stayed) carry profound meaning. Every year tens of thousands plot their escape to Miami, often without telling their relatives, sometimes not even their spouses. Cubans thus tend to evolve speedy relationships and/or grasp at opportunity. "All the Cubans' experience tells them that there is no time to go slow, that pleasures and love must be taken fast when they present themselves because tomorrow...*se fue*," wrote Claudia Lightfoot.

Meanwhile, while the exodus continues and the exciting changes accelerating within Cuba are buoying millennials and many among those who've left. They see greater possibility to achieve their ambition—the very opposite of what inspired them to leave in the first place. Many are returning flush with cash. Those thinking of leaving are now hesitant, seeing the chance to lead a more globalized life in Cuba. An excitement for tomorrow has taken hold.

Cuban Curiosity

You would imagine that a sense of isolation and a high level of cultural development would have filled Cubans with intense curiosity. Many will guess your nationality and quiz you about the most prosaic matters of Western life, yet rarely do they ask about its most profound. Issues of income and cost are areas of deep interest. Otherwise, Cubans are amazingly non-inquisitive.

Cubans watch U.S. programs and Hollywood movies and often converse with a worldly erudition. If you tell them you are a *yanqui*, most Cubans light up. They are genuinely fond of U.S. citizens. However, although Cubans thrive on debate, those who despise the government are hesitant to discuss politics openly except behind closed doors. Only in private, and once you have earned their trust, will you be able to gauge how they really feel about Cuba and Castro. Despite their hardships, Cubans have not lost the ability to laugh. Stand-up comedy is a tradition in Cuban nightclubs. Cubans turn everything into a *chiste* (joke), most of which are aimed at themselves. Their penetrating black humor spares no one—the insufferable bureaucrat, *jineteras*, the Special Period. Not even Fidel and Raúl are spared the barbs, although no one in his right mind would tell such a joke in public.

Cubans also boast a great wit. They lace their conversations with risqué double entendres.

The Nationalist Spirit

Cubans are an intensely passionate and patriotic people united by love of country. The revolutionary government has engaged in consciousness-raising on a national scale, instilling in Cubans that they can have pride as a nation. Schoolchildren not only lisp loyalty to the flag (and Che) daily at school, they recite their willingness to *die* for it.

Cubans had not expected socialism from the Revolution, but those who could accept it did so not simply because so many benefited but because, as Maurice Halperin suggests, "it came with nationalism; that is, an assertion of economic and political independence from the United States, the goal of Cuban patriots for a half century." This provides Cubans with a different perspective and viewpoint on history.

Labor and the Work Ethic

Cubans combine their southern joy of living with a northern work ethic. The entrepreneurial spirit isn't dead, as attested by the success of the self-employed since Raúl initiated his reforms.

The majority of Cubans work for the state, which with few exceptions dictates where an individual will work. However, a huge proportion of the adult population has no productive work, despite official figures. The degree of anomie is great. Many Cubans ask their doctor friends to issue *certificados* (medical excuses) so that they can take a "vacation" from the boredom of employment that offers little financial reward. *Socio* is the buddy network, used to shield you from the demands of the state. *Pinche* and *mayimbe* are your high-level contacts, those who help you get around the bureaucracy. Meanwhile, so many teachers left their profession to work in tourism that tourism companies are forbidden from hiring teachers.

The improvements in the living standards among rural families in the early decades of the Revolution have not been enough to keep the younger generation on the land. There has been a steady migration from the *campos*.

Under Fidel, wages were according to a salary scale of 22 levels, with the top level getting six times that of the lowest. Highly trained professionals share the same struggles as unskilled workers. Life is little different for those who earn 250 pesos (US$10) a month and those who earn 1,000 (US$40). In 2015 average monthly wage for state workers was about 700 pesos, or US$28. Such wages don't go far in contemporary Cuba. In 2008, Raúl lifted caps on state wages and directed state employers to develop a sliding scale to reward productive workers with higher pay. The legalization of self-employment and mass dismissals of many state workers created a freer labor market, and competitiveness is driving a newfound competence. Nonetheless, the Cuban government is not about to let anyone get rich. Foreign corporations have always paid illegal hard currency supplements to Cuban workers; in 2008, these were made legal, but they had to be declared and the income is now taxed, as are the burgeoning self-employed.

Sexual Mores

The traditional Afro-Cuban tropical culture has proved resistant to puritanical revolutionary doctrine. Cubans are sensualists of the first degree. Judging by the ease with which couples neck openly and spontaneously slip into bed, the dictatorship of the proletariat that transformed Eastern Europe into a perpetual Sunday school has made little headway in Cuba. The state may promote the family, but Cubans have a notoriously indulgent attitude towards casual sex.

As journalist Jacobo Timerman wrote, "Eros is amply gratified in Cuba and needs no stimulation." A joyous eroticism pervades Cuban men and women alike. Seduction is a national pastime pursued by both sexes—the free expression of a high-spirited people confined in a politically authoritarian world. After all, Cubans joke, sex is the only thing Castro can't ration.

Both genders are unusually bold. Long glances—*ojitos*—often accompanied by uninhibited comments, betray envisioned improprieties. Even the women murmur *piropos* (catcalls or courtly overtures) and sometimes comic declarations of love.

Homosexuality

Cuban homosexuals must find it ironic that the heart of the homosexual world is Castro Street in San Francisco. It is assuredly not named in Fidel's honor, as gays—called *maricones* (queens), *mariposas* (butterflies), *pájaros* (birds), *patos* (ducks), or *gansos* (geese)

Prostitution or Opportunity?

Before the Revolution, Batista's Babylon offered a tropical buffet of sin. In 1959, the revolutionary government closed down the sex shows and brothels and sent the prostitutes to rehabilitative trade schools, thereby ostensibly eliminating the world's oldest trade.

"It is not legal in our country to practice prostitution, nor are we going to legalize it.... We are not going to repress it either," Castro told *Time* magazine, while boasting that Cuba had the healthiest and best-educated prostitutes in the world.

However, the Cuban government was clearly stung by foreign media reports on the subject. In 1996, Cuban women were barred from tourist hotels, and a mandatory two-year jail term (since increased to four years) was imposed for any female the government considers a "prostitute." Thousands of young women (many of them innocent) were picked up on the streets and jailed. Several provinces temporarily banned sexual relations between Cubans and foreigners entirely.

Foreigners may once again legally bed with Cubans, including in hotels. *Jineteras* (the word comes from *jineta,* horsewoman, or jockey) continue to work the tourist bars, discos, and hotel lobbies. Cuban males, too, tout themselves as gigolos to foreign females.

Like everything in Cuba, the situation is complex and needs some explaining.

Many women who form intimate relationships with tourists are ordinary Cubans who would laugh to be called *jineteras.* A pretty *cubana* attached to a generous suitor can be wined and dined and get her entrance paid into the discos, drinks included, to which she otherwise wouldn't have access. "Few romantic liaisons between locals and foreigners are deemed prostitution," says Julia Cooke in *The Other Side of Paradise.* "Rather, most fall under the banner of relationships with *amigos.* Any non-Cuban is eligible, and what locals want from *amigos* is neither finite nor clear: a mix of money, attention, and the sense of possibility linked to anyone with a non-Cuban passport."

For many women the ultimate hope is that a relationship may develop. Their dream is to find a foreign boyfriend who will marry them and take them away. It happens all the time, especially for good-looking *negras de pelo* (black women with straight hair). "Italian and German men are *locos* for *negras y mulatas de pelo,*" says Lety, in Isadora Tattlin's *Cuban Diaries.* "Ay, being *una negra de pelo* in Cuba is as good as having a visa to Canada or western Europe, guaranteed."

In a society where promiscuity is rampant and sex on a first date is a given, any financial transaction is reduced to a charitable afterthought to a romantic evening out. Thus, educated and morally upright Cuban women smile at tourists passing by on the street or hang out by the disco doorways, seeking affairs and invitations, however briefly, to enjoy a part of the high life.

in the Cuban vernacular (and *tortillas* for lesbians)—were persecuted following the Revolution. Castro (who denies the comment) supposedly told journalist Lee Lockwood that a homosexual could never "embody the conditions and requirements of a true revolutionary." Homosexuals were classified as "undesirable."

Gays and lesbians met with "repression and rejection" in Cuba, just as they did in the United States. In Cuba, however, it was more systematic and brutal. The pogrom began in earnest in 1965; homosexuals were arrested and sent to agricultural work and reeducation camps—UMAP (Units for Military Help to Agricultural Production). Echoing Auschwitz,

over the gate of one such camp in Camagüey was the admonition "Work Makes You Men." Many brilliant intellectuals lost their jobs. Homosexuals were not allowed to teach, become doctors, or occupy positions from which they could "pervert" Cuban youth.

Although UMAP camps closed in 1968 and those who had lost their jobs were reinstated, periodic purges occurred throughout the 1970s and early '80s. Many homosexuals were forced to leave on the Mariel boatlift. However, by the mid-1980s, Cuba began to respond to the gay rights movement that had already gained momentum worldwide. The new position is that homosexuality and bisexuality are no less natural or healthy than heterosexuality. An official atonement was made through the release at the 1993 Havana Film Festival of *Vidas Paralelas* (*Parallel Lives*) and the hit movie *Fresa y Chocolate* (*Strawberry and Chocolate*).

Sexologist Mariela Castro Espín (Raúl's daughter and head of the National Sex Education Center) leads the effort to treat the LGBT community as equals.

LIFE IN CUBA

On the eve of the Revolution, Cuba was a semideveloped country with more millionaires than anywhere south of Texas and an urban labor force that had achieved "the eight-hour day, double pay for overtime, one month's paid vacation, nine days' sick leave, and the right to strike." On the other hand, in 1950, a World Bank study team reported that 40 percent of urban dwellers and 60 percent of rural dwellers were undernourished, while over 40 percent of Cuban people had never gone to school, and only 60 percent had regular full-time employment.

The Revolution has immeasurably improved the condition of millions of Cubans, eliminating the most abject poverty while destroying the middle and wealthy urban classes and imposing a general paucity on millions of others. At least everyone had the essentials and enjoyed two two-week vacations a year at the beach. In better days, the government provided newlyweds with a wedding present and honeymoon, and birthday cakes for kids under 10.

The deal, acceptable to many, was that Cubans would surrender their liberty in exchange for guaranteed security with the state providing their basic needs—a deal that worked well until the Special Period. Today the average Cuban faces absences of everything we take for granted in life.

The Bare Essentials

The *libreta*—the ration book meant to supply every Cuban citizen with the basic essentials—provides, at best, supplies for perhaps 10 days per month (Raúl Castro has stated that

the system may be abandoned, but the subject is so sensitive that his proposal to phase out the *libreta* was dropped from the reform guidelines of the 2011 party congress). A fixed amount is allowed per person per month—six pounds of rice, eleven ounces of beans, five pounds of sugar, four ounces of lard, eight eggs—although the items aren't always available.

The U.S. embargo—*el bloqueo*—is blamed, even though Cuba purchases about 40 percent of its foods from U.S. suppliers, peaking at $710 million in 2008 (agricultural goods are permitted by U.S. law).

The real problem is that Cubans are paid virtual slave-labor wages in pesos, but all things worth buying—including daily necessities such as toilet paper and soap—are sold by Cuban state enterprises for "convertible pesos" (obtainable only in exchange for foreign currency) at an average markup of 240 percent. Fortunately, rent and utilities are so heavily subsidized that they are virtually free, as is health care and education, and no one has to pay rent or a mortgage. Still, the past few years witnessed rapid inflation (28 percent for basic foods in 2014), and in January 2016 the government reinstituted price controls.

The Black Market

The black market, known as the *bolsa* (the exchange), resolves the failings of the state-controlled economy. Most Cubans rely on the underground economy, doing business illegally; on theft or fortuitous employment; or, for the exceedingly fortunate, on a wealthy relative or a lover abroad. Cubans have always survived by *resolviendo*—the Cuban art of barter, the cut corner, or theft. The black market touches all walks of life. Even otherwise loyal revolutionaries are forced to break the law: Almost every Cuban is self-employed by necessity, either legally or illegally, as a means to survive. (In October 2005, after disclosing that half the gasoline in the country was being stolen, Castro fired gas station attendants en masse and replaced them with thousands of graduates serving

National Holidays

January 1:	Liberation Day (Día de la Liberación)
January 2:	Victory Day (Día de la Victoria)
January 28:	José Martí's birthday
February 24:	Anniversary of the War of Independence
March 8:	International Women's Day (Día de la Mujer)
March 13:	Anniversary of the students' attack on the presidential palace
April 19:	Bay of Pigs Victory (Victoria del Playa Girón)
May 1:	Labor Day (Día de los Trabajadores)
July 26:	National Revolution Day (anniversary of the attack on the Moncada barracks)
July 30:	Day of the Martyrs of the Revolution
October 8:	Anniversary of Che Guevara's death
October 10:	Anniversary of the Ten Years War
October 28:	Memorial day to Camilo Cienfuegos
December 2:	Anniversary of the landing of the *Granma*
December 7:	Memorial day to Antonio Maceo

their *trabajo social* [social work]—payback for education.)

Life is organized around a mad scramble for foreign currency and *pesos convertibles*. The lucky ones have access to family cash, known as *fula,* sent from Miami. Cubans joke about getting by on *fé,* which is Spanish for faith, but today it's an acronym for *familia extranjera*—family abroad. Cuban economists reckon that about 60 percent of the population now has some form of access to *pesos convertibles*. The rest must rely on their wits. Every morning people prepare to cobble together some kind of normalcy out of whatever the situation allows. Cubans are masters at making the best of a bad situation. The very elderly with no access to foreign currency, however, fare poorly, and thousands exist in poverty at a level barely above *sobrevivencia* (mere survival).

True, a large percent of the people now own cellular phones and other contemporary accoutrements, and the mostly white nouveau riche living rich on *fula* sent from Miami can now be seen driving around Havana in new Audis and other fancy cars (the only others with big bank balances are Cuba's top artists, in a country where creativity still trumps business acumen and entrepreneurship). For most, everything else is a hand-me-down—mummified American cars, taped-together Russian refrigerators, and 45-pound Chinese bicycles. The staple of transport in cities is the horse-drawn cart. The staple for intercity travel is the open-topped truck, often without any seats.

There's always *la yuma*—the United States (from the 1957 film *3:10 to Yuma* starring Glenn Ford and Van Heflin)—beckoning just 90 miles away. Cubans lucky enough to receive visas to immigrate to the United States were traditionally bilked by the Cuban government (to the tune of almost US$1,000). Until 2013, when Raúl Castro lifted all restrictions on Cubans traveling freely abroad, the families' possessions were seized by the government; a state inspector took an inventory, and if anything was missing on the day of departure the *carta blanca* was revoked and with it any chance of leaving. Now Cubans can come and go as they wish (in response, the U.S. government seems to be issuing visas only to Cubans who express their wish to leave Cuba behind).

Real Estate

After half a century during which Cubans could only swap, not buy or sell houses, the sunshine socialist state is on the block. In November 2011, Raúl Castro lifted a five-decade-old ban on the real estate market.

Cubans (and permanent residents) are now permitted to buy and sell property freely (previously owners could only exchange two properties of roughly equal value, if the creaky and corrupt state bureaucracy approved). They can now own a residence *and* a vacation home.

Thousands of houses are now on the market. Prices range from about CUC10,000 for a small one-bedroom in crowded Centro Habana to $1,000,000 or more for humongous villas and modernist marvels in Miramar or Siboney, Havana's toniest areas.

Ground zero for sales is the Paseo del Prado, where on weekends sellers advertise their houses on crude cardboard or simple flyers while intermediaries tout listings written in longhand in school exercise books. There are even a couple of real estate websites—www.cubanismima.com and www.revolico.com—for those lucky enough to have Internet access. Intermediaries (i.e., real estate agents, called *corredores* or "runners") are illegal. They exist, of course, as do lawyers to process the paperwork (equally illegal), and many have since become wealthy. The real value of properties is hard to assess, as both sellers and buyers must pay a 4 percent tax; hence they disguise the true amount of money that passes hands. Transactions are required to take place through bank accounts to avoid tax evasion.

Prices have been driven up by a flood of money from Miami (and, to a lesser degree, Europe), as Cuban Americans have been buying up properties in the names of their relatives on the island.

Simple Pleasures

Cuba has no fiesta tradition. The Cubans are too busy playing baseball or practicing martial arts while others while away the long, hot afternoons playing dominoes or making love. In rural areas pleasures are simple: cockfights, rodeos, cigars, cheap rum, and sex. Urban life is more urbane, offering movies, discos, theater, cigars, cheap rum, and sex.

Cuban social life revolves around the family and friends and neighbors. Cubans are a gregarious people, and foreigners are often amazed by the degree to which Cubans exist in the public eye, carrying on their everyday lives behind windows open to the streets.

For all its musical gaiety and pockets of passionate pleasure, and an increasing disposable income for many, life for the average urbanite is dreary, even melancholy: see Julia Cooke's *The Other Side of Paradise*.

Living Conditions

Half an hour in Havana is enough to cure you of a taste for that distressed look so popular in Crate & Barrel stores.

P. J. O'Rourke

Until the Revolution, government expenditures were concentrated mostly in and around Havana and the provincial cities. According to the 1953 census, only 15 percent of rural houses had piped water, 54 percent had no toilet whatsoever, and 43 percent had no electricity. Since the Revolution, the government has concentrated its energies on developing the countryside, where tens of thousands of bungalows were built by the state and given to people living in hovels. In the cities, hundreds of concrete apartment block units of a standard Bulgarian design—the ugly Bauhaus vision of uniform, starkly functional workers' housing—went up. Most were built with the unskilled volunteer labor (microbrigades) of future tenants.

The typical country house, or *bohío*, is a low, one-story structure with thick walls to keep out the heat, built of adobe or porous brick covered with stucco and roofed with thatch or red tiles. And thousands of rural dwellers still live in simple shacks. (Urban shantytowns, eliminated following the Revolution, have also reappeared, notably in Havana, such as the overcrowded slums of El Romerillo district of Miramar, populated mostly by migrants from eastern cities.) However, virtually every house has electricity.

Cities ache with penury and pathos. Havana needs a million gallons of paint. Most prerevolutionary housing is deteriorated to a point of dilapidation: Havana municipal authorities have admitted that 7 percent of houses are officially considered unsafe, and 20 percent of the population lives in housing considered to be in "precarious condition." In fact, three buildings a day collapse in Havana on average. Many Cubans cling to family life behind crumbling facades festooned with makeshift wiring and inside tottering buildings that should have faced the bulldozer's maw long ago. The housing shortage is so critical that many Cubans live in a *barbecue,* a room divided in two. Due to lack of space, the high-ceilinged rooms of many old colonial buildings have been turned into two stories by adding new ceilings and staircases. Several generations are often crowded together unwillingly; there is simply nowhere for the offspring to go. Still, there *are* many fine, well-kept houses, and every city has a section that resembles its middle-class American counterpart.

By law, no renter can pay more than 10 percent of his or her salary in rent, and about 95 percent of Cubans own their own homes. Those who fled Cuba had their property seized by the state: Nice houses in good neighborhoods were often taken by the government for the political elite or for government offices. Owners of commercial properties were forced to sell to the state, which then granted ownership of former rental apartments to the tenants (owners were compensated at declared tax value).

Meanwhile, municipal administration is a disaster. When sidewalks collapse, no repairs are made; when pavements buckle, they go unattended. Sewers and electrical boxes aren't maintained, so over time everything is jerry-rigged and/or deteriorates without hope of repair.

Supplies for repairs have been virtually impossible to find. Nails? Paint? Forget it. Everything has had to be foraged. The equivalent of Home Depot doesn't exist. In 2011, the government attempted to stop the rot by allowing private entrepreneurs to sell materials on the open market. The government also opened the first chain of hardware stores and initiated bank loans to ease the burden on repair and even to build rooms from scratch. And private purchase and sale of homes was legalized. A real estate market has developed, fostering urban renewal by savvy owners keep to up their homes' values.

CHILDREN AND YOUTH

One of the simplest pleasures for the foreign traveler is to see smiling children in school uniforms so colorful that they reminded novelist James Michener of "a meadow of flowers. Well nourished, well shod and clothed, they were the permanent face of the land." And well behaved, too!

Children are treated with as much indulgence by the state as by family members. The government has made magnificent strides to improve the lot of poor children. And it teaches youngsters magnificent values.

After high school, all Cuban males must perform two years of military service; girls serve two years as *trabajadores sociales* doing "social" work.

The "I" Generation

More than 65 percent of the Cuban population was born after the Revolution. Where their parents use "we," Cuba's youth use "I"—I want to do so and so. The majority are bored by the constant calls for greater sacrifice. They want to enjoy life like kids the world over, and in much the same way. Many youths realize they can get further on their own and are going into business for themselves as *cuentapropistas* (freelancers), making a buck waiting tables in *paladares.* When you ask young Cubans what are their dreams, most reply "to leave Cuba." Few have dreams bigger than the tiny rooms they've grown up in. Says Julio Cooke: "This generation has detached from its country's fate in some deep and meaningful way.... They are the last generation raised under Fidel, the first generation raised in globalization, the first generation to come into adulthood in a time when it's largely acknowledged that nothing works and they won't have an impact."

Cuba's millennials think the Castros are dinosaurs. They don't give a hoot about politics. They're expressing their individuality—they want to be themselves, which today means showing a marked preference for anything North American. They wouldn't be caught dead in a *guayabera,* the traditional tropical shirt favored by older men (and considered a sure sign of someone who works for the government). Young men and women dress in the latest fashions, as well as their budgets allow. A cell phone is de rigueur for those with the means to afford one. They listen to reggaeton and hip-hop and are fast becoming addicted to Facebook. They're fueling an entirely avant-garde art and cultural scene that's exciting yet worryingly consumerist and challenging to Cuba's marvelous traditional values.

FEMINISM AND MACHISMO

The country has an impressive record in women's rights. A United Nations survey ranks Cuba among the top 20 nations in which women have the highest participation in politics and business. Women make up 50 percent of university students, 60 percent of doctors, and 48 percent of high government.

Women are guaranteed the same salaries as men and receive 18 weeks of paid maternity leave—six before the birth and the remainder after. Working mothers have the right to one day off with pay each month, or the option of staying home and receiving 60 percent of their full salary for the child's first year. And every woman and girl can get free birth control assistance, regardless of marital status.

Despite this, prejudices born of the patriarchal Spanish heritage still exist. Male machismo continues, while the Revolution has not been able to get the Cubanness out of Cuban women who, regardless of age, still adore coquetry.

RELIGION

Cuba was officially atheist from the early 1960s until 1992 (it has since officially been a secular state). Nonetheless, a recent government survey found that the majority of Cubans are *creyentes,* believers of one sort or another.

Christianity

Cubans have always been relatively lukewarm about Christianity. In colonial times, there were few churches in rural districts, where it was usual for a traveling priest to call only once a year to perform baptisms and marriages. Moreover, the conservative Roman Catholic Church sided with the Spanish against the patriots during the colonial era and was seen by *criollos* as representing authoritarianism hand in hand with the Spanish crown. Later, the Catholic Church had a quid pro quo with the corrupt Machado, Grau, and Batista regimes. When the Revolution triumphed, many of the clergy left for Miami along with the rich to whom they had ministered.

When Fidel nationalized the church's lands, the Catholic Church became a focus of opposition. Many priests were expelled. Practicing Catholics were banned from the Communist Party. Practitioners were harassed. Religious education was eliminated from the school curriculum, and a rational scientific understanding of the world replaced superstition.

In 1986 Fidel Castro performed an about-face: Religion was no longer the opiate of the masses. In 1991, the Communist Party opened its doors to believers. It was a timely move, co-opting the shifting mood. The collapse of the Soviet Union and onset of the Special Period left a spiritual vacuum that fed church attendance. Castro attempted to go with the rising tide. In November 1996, he met with Pope John Paul II in Rome. The pontiff's visit to Cuba in January 1998 boosted the

Sweet 15

Decades of socialism have killed off many traditional celebrations—but not **fiestas de quince,** the birthday parties celebrating a girl's 15th birthday and her coming of age. There is nothing like a *quince* party (a direct legacy of a more conservative Spanish era) for a young *cubana*.

Parents will save money from the day the girl is born to do her right with a memorable 15th. A whole arsenal might be involved, from the hairdresser and dressmaker (a special dress resembling a wedding gown or a knock-'em-dead Scarlett O'Hara outfit is a must) to the photographer and the classic American car with chauffeur to take the young woman and her friends to the party.

influence of the Catholic Church and reignited an expression of faith. It also prompted a flood of Protestant missionaries, who seem more fearful of the spread of "papism" than of Communism. Protestants are estimated to number about 300,000.

The Catholic Church has continued to be highly critical of the Castro government, although it has lent its support to Raúl's reform process. Raúl himself even attends mass. Although about 60 percent of Cubans are baptized Catholic, only about 5 percent practice their religion. A huge percentage of Cubans remain atheistic, or at least agnostic.

Santería

Santería, or saint worship, has been deeply entrenched in Cuban culture for 300 years and is far more significant than Catholicism. The cult is a fusion of Catholicism with the Lucumí religion of the African Yoruba tribes of modern-day Nigeria and Benin. Because slave masters had banned African religious practice, the slaves cloaked their gods in Catholic garb and continued to pray to them in disguise. Thus, in Santería, Catholic figures are avatars of the Yoruban *orishas* (divine beings, or guardian spirits, of African animism). Metaphorically *orishas* change their identity—even their gender—at midnight. By day, adherents may pray in front of a figure of Santa Bárbara and at night worship the same figure as Changó. There are about 400 guardian spirits in the pantheon, but only about 20 are honored in daily life.

It is thought that the *orishas* control an

individual's life, performing miracles on a person's behalf. They are thus consulted and besought. A string of bad luck will be blamed on an *orisha*, who must be placated in order to attain harmony—a state of order and balance being the quintessential goal of Santería belief. The *orishas* are too supreme for mere mortals to communicate with directly: *Santeros* or *babalawos* (priests) act as go-betweens to interpret their commands (for a fee). *Babalawos* use divination to interpret the *obi* and *ifá* (oracles) and solve everyday problems using pieces of dried coconut shells and seashells.

Many a home has a statue of an *orisha* to appease the spirits of the dead. Even Fidel Castro, a highly superstitious person, was said to be a believer. He had triumphed on January 1, a holy day for the *orishas*. The red and black flag of the revolutionaries was that of Elegguá, god of destiny. Then, on January 8, 1959, as Fidel delivered his victory speech before the nation, three doves flew over the audience and circled the brightly lit podium; miraculously, one of the doves alighted on Fidel's shoulder, touching off an explosion from the ecstatic onlookers: *"Fee-del! Fee-del! Fee-del!"* In Santería, doves are symbols of Obatalá, god of peace and purity. To Cubans—and perhaps Fidel himself—the event was a supreme symbol that the gods had chosen Fidel to guide Cuba. (In truth, the doves were trained by Luis Conte Agüero, Secretary-General of the Othodox Party, "to put a touch of religiosity to the first speech of the great leader.")

Nonetheless, following the Revolution, the government stigmatized Santería as *brujería* (witchcraft) and tried to convert it into a folkloric movement. In the late 1980s, Santería bounced back. In 1990 the Castro government began to co-opt support for the faith. Reportedly, many *babalawos* have been recruited by MININT, for they above all know people's secrets.

Throughout Cuba, you'll see believers clad all in white, having just gone through their initiation rites as *santeros* or *santeras*. A follower of Santería may choose at any stage in life to undertake an elaborate initiation that will tear the follower away from his or her old life and set their feet on *la regla de ocha*—the way of the *orishas*. During this time, the *iyawó* will be possessed by, and under the care of, a specific *orisha* who will guide the initiate to a deeper, richer life. Initiations are highly secret and involve animal sacrifice (usually pigeons and roosters). The rites are complex. They include having to dress solely in white and stay indoors at night for a year, though exceptions are made for employment. And an *iyawó* may not permit him- or herself to be touched, except by the most intimate family members or, this being Cuba, by lovers.

Santería is a sensuous religion—the *orishas* let adherents have a good time. The gods themselves are fallible and hedonistic philanderers, such as the much feared and respected Changó (or Santa Barbara; yes, he is female in Catholicism), whose many mistresses include Ochún (the Virgen de la Caridad), the sensuous black goddess of love.

Each saint has specific attributes. Changó, for example, dresses in red and white and carries a scepter with a double-headed axe. Followers of Changó wear collars decorated with red and white plastic beads. Ochún wears yellows; her followers wear yellow and white beads. Obatalá, god of peace and creation (but the female Virgen de la Merced in Catholicism), dresses in white. Yemayá (the Virgen de Regla), goddess of the sea and of motherhood, wears blue and white. Each saint also has an "altar" where offerings (fruits, rum-soaked cakes, pastries, and coins) are placed. Devout *santeros* even keep a collection

Santería Terms

- *babalawo:* a high priest of Lucumí

- *batá:* set of three drums of Yoruba origin—*iya, itotele,* and *okonkolo*

- *Changó:* the mighty *orisha* of fire, thunder, and lightning

- *Eleggúa:* messenger of all *orishas;* guardian of the crossroads and god of destiny

- *fundamento:* a strict repertoire of rhythms for each *orisha*

- *iyawó:* Santería initiate; "bride" of the *orishas*

- *Obatalá: orisha* of peace and purity

- *obi* and *ifá:* oracles

- *Ochún:* the sensuous black goddess that many Cuban women identify as the *orisha* of love

- *Ogún: orisha* represented as a warrior

- *orishas:* deities symbolic of human qualities and aspects of nature

- *toque:* specific rhythm attributed to an *orisha*

of vases in their bedrooms in which one's personal *orisha,* plus Obatalá, Yemayá, Ochún, and Changó live, in that hierarchical order.

African Cult Religions

Other spiritualist cults exist in Cuba. The most important is the all-male Abakuá secret mutual protection society that originated in Nigeria, appearing in Cuba in the early 19th century. It still functions among the most marginalized black communities, where it is known as *ñañiguismo*. The first duty of an adherent is to protect a fellow member. Membership is restricted to "brave, virile, dignified, moral men" who contribute to their communities. It involves worship of ancestral devil figures, called *diablitos* or *iremes,* where dancers dress from head to toe in hooded hessian costumes.

Palo Monte (known also as *reglas congas*) also derives from west-central Africa and is a spirit religion that harnesses the power of the deceased to control supernatural forces. Adherents (called *paleros*) use ritual sticks and plants to perform magic.

EDUCATION

Cuba's education system is a source of national pride. One in every 15 people is a college graduate. And even in the most remote Cuban backwater, you'll come across children laden with satchels, making their way to and from school in pin-neat uniforms.

Official statistics are contradictory. The Cuban government claims that on the eve of the Revolution, 43 percent of the population was illiterate and half a million Cuban children went without school; however, the U.N. Statistical Yearbook suggests that as much as 80 percent of the population was literate, behind only Argentina, Chile, and Costa Rica for the time.

Private and religious schools are forbidden.

Accomplishments

In December 1960, the government announced a war on illiteracy. On April 10, 1961, 120,000 literacy workers—*brigadistas*—spread throughout the island to teach reading and writing to one million illiterates. The government established about 10,000 new classrooms in rural areas. Today literacy is 99.9 percent, according to UNESCO, exceeding all other Latin American nations (compared to 97 percent for the United States and 99.4 percent for the United Kingdom). At 16 about 60 percent of secondary students go on to study at technical schools; the rest begin two years at a PRE, for *pre-universitario*. Children with special talents may compete to attend specialist schools that foster skills in art, music, or sports. About 8 percent of school graduates go on to higher education.

A UNESCO study of language and mathematics skills throughout Latin America found that Cuba was well ahead of all other nations (the World Bank's *World Development Indicators* data show Cuba as topping virtually all other poor countries in education statistics). But standards are slipping.

Cuba has five universities.

The Downside

Cuba's hyper-educated population is hard pressed to find books and other educational materials. Few schools have a library or gym or laboratory, and many are unclean and deteriorated. The entire literary panorama is severely proscribed: Only politically acceptable works are allowed. The state often dictates what university students will study. Options for adult education are virtually nonexistent. Thousands of qualified Cuban school graduates are denied university places reserved for Venezuelans and other "solidarity" students.

Cubans also complain about a dramatic decline in teaching quality; many teachers are straight out of high school themselves, in response to a mass exodus of professional teachers to become *cuentapropistas* or work in tourism. Tele-classes also filled teachers' shoes: As much as 60 percent of classroom time is now spent watching TV programming.

HEALTH

According to the Castro government, in pre-revolutionary Cuba only the moneyed class could afford good medical care. Many people (especially in rural areas) lacked medical services. According to the United Nations Statistical Yearbook, however, in 1958 Cuba had an advanced medical system that ranked third in Latin America (behind only Uruguay and Argentina), with 128 physicians and dentists per 100,000 people—the same as the Netherlands, and ahead of the United Kingdom. And Cuba's infant mortality rate of 32 per 1,000 live births in 1957 was the lowest in Latin America and the 13th lowest in the world (today it is the 28th lowest).

From the beginning, health care has assumed a prominent place in revolutionary government policies (about 12 percent of its budget). Today, 20 medical schools churn out thousands of doctors each year.

Cuba's life expectancy of 79.4 years is behind only Costa Rica (79.8) and Chile (79.5) in Latin America and is on a par with that of the United States. In 2013 Cuba's infant mortality rate of 4.76 per 1,000 births also bettered that of the United States (5.2) and was almost as good as the United Kingdom's (4.5).

The Success Story

The Revolution's accomplishment is due to its emphasis on preventative medicine and community-based doctors. A near 100 percent immunization rate has ensured the total eradication of several preventable contagious diseases, such as measles.

According to the World Health Organization, Cuba has a doctor for every 170 residents, ahead of the United States with 1:188. (Dental care lags far behind, however.) Every community has a *casa del médico* (family doctor's home), with a clinic. Every town also has a hospital, plus a maternity home and a day-care center for the elderly, and mobile laboratories travel the country. All medical services are free.

Cuba also commands the kind of technology that most poor countries can only dream about: ultrasound for obstetricians, CAT scans for radiologists, stacks of high-tech monitors in the suites for intensive care. Cuba has performed heart transplants since 1985, heart-lung transplants since 1987, coronary bypasses, pacemaker implantations, microsurgery, and a host of other advanced surgical procedures. Even sex-change operations are provided free of charge. Cuban doctors "have turned mass-production eye operations into a fine art," says the BBC's Michael Voss.

Cuba has also made notable leaps in advancing the field of molecular immunology. It even manufactures interferons for AIDS treatment, a meningitis vaccine, and a cure for the skin disease vitiligo.

The Downside

Resources have also been shifted from primary care toward turning Cuba's medical system into a profit-making enterprise catering to foreigners, notably in the surgical and advanced medicine fields. Dr. Hilda Molina, founder of Havana's International Center for Neurological Restoration, claims that "foreigners are assigned the highest priority, followed by government functionaries and their families, followed by athletes with good records of performance, then dancers, and lastly, ordinary Cuban patients."

Cubans also complain that the plethora of Cuban medical staff serving abroad has sapped local clinics and hospitals. Other medical staff, being low-paid, have simply opted to earn more money as taxi drivers and other *cuentapropistas* (self-employed).

Meanwhile, conditions in hospitals and clinics are often of third-world standard; everywhere, medical equipment is broken and many hospitals are filthy and constitute their own health risk.

In 2000, the U.S. rescinded restrictions preventing medicines and medical equipment manufactured in the United States or under U.S. patent from being exported to Cuba. Cuba began purchasing millions of dollars of U.S. medical products, although it still balks at buying U.S. medicines.

Cuba's Flying Doctors

Since 1963, when Cuba sent 56 doctors to newly independent Algeria, the country has provided medical assistance to developing countries regardless of its own economic straits. In 1985 the *New York Times* dubbed Cuba's international medical aid program "the largest Peace Corps-style program of civilian aid in the world." Cuba regularly deploys medical brigades to regions struck by disasters and has donated entire hospitals to developing countries. In 2014 medical personnel were serving in more than 80 countries around the world, earning hard currency for themselves and the Cuban state. When the Haiti earthquake struck on January 12, 2010, Cuba already had 344 doctors serving there. As many as 37,000 Cuban medical professionals also work in Venezuela (another 10,000 work in Brazil) for hard currency.

Cuba has also offered free medical care in Cuba for patients from abroad, most famously for 20,000 child victims of the Chernobyl nuclear disaster in the Soviet Union. And since it was initiated in 2005, Cuba's Operación Milagro (Operation Miracle) has performed more than 100,000 free eye operations on indigent people from throughout the Americas and Caribbean.

In November 1999, Cuba converted a naval academy into the Latin American School for Medical Sciences, offering free medical education to students from developing countries (including full scholarships for students from disadvantaged communities in the United States).

The Arts

Since the Revolution, the government's sponsorship of the arts has yielded a rich harvest in every field. The Centro Nacional de Escuelas de Arte (National Center of Schools of Art), created in 1960, has 41 schools under its umbrella, including the national Escuela de la Música, a national folkloric school, two ballet schools, two fine-arts schools, and a school of modern dance, plus schools at the provincial level. The graduates are superbly trained, despite great shortages of instruments and other materials.

During the first two years of the Revolution, Fidel enjoyed being the "bohemian intellectual," and artists and writers enjoyed relative freedom. As the romantic phase of the Revolution passed into an era of more dogmatic ideology, the Culture Council took a hard line. In 1961 the government invited intellectuals to a debate on the meaning of cultural liberty at which Fidel offered his "Words to the Intellectuals," which he summed up with a credo: "Within the Revolution, everything. Outside the Revolution, nothing!" The government acquired full control of the mass media. Intellectuals, writers, and artists were intimidated into ideological straitjackets. Raúl has since lightened up considerably.

MUSIC AND DANCE

Music—the pulsing undercurrent of Cuban life—is everywhere. Dance, from the earliest *guaguancó* to the mambo craze, has always been a potent expression of an enshrined national tradition: Cuban sensualism. Girls are whisked onto the dance floor and whirled through a flurry of complicated steps and sensuous undulations just a little closer than cheek to cheek.

Folkloric Music and Dance

In Cuba, folkloric music (*música folklórica*) usually refers to Afro-Cuban music. The earliest influence was Spanish. The colonists brought the melodies, guitars, and violins from which evolved folk music, or *guajira*, influenced through contact with black culture. The fusion gave rise to *punto campesino*

The *Buena Vista Social Club*

In 1996, Cuban music promoter Juan de Marcos rounded up a clique of legendary but largely forgotten veteran musicians to make a comeback album. Guitarist Ry Cooder happened to make a musical pilgrimage to Cuba around the same time; he struck a deal with Marcos, and they gifted to the world the *Buena Vista Social Club,* naming the album for a Havana venue where many of the artists performed in the 1950s. German film director Wim Wenders tagged along with his Beta steadicam to chronicle how Cooder ushered the half-forgotten relics of prerevolutionary Cuba into recording studios, cut an album of sepia-toned tunes, and dispatched them on a world tour that met with runaway success. The documentary (also called *Buena Vista Social Club*) celebrates the elderly musicians' performance on the world stage and offers a portrait of their life back in an impoverished Cuba.

This suave old bunch of codgers wowed the world when the documentary movie was released in 1999, introducing the richness of *son, danzón,* and *bolero* in a style untouched by contemporary trends. The CD won the Grammy for Tropical Music and topped the charts among Latin albums, taking Cuban music international for the first time, selling several million copies worldwide, and creating international nostalgia for the old Havana whose charmingly dilapidated streets are the setting for Wenders's wonderful movie.

Alas, all the main stars except Eliades Ochoa and Omara Portuondo (who in 2009 won a Grammy at the age of 79) have since passed away.

(peasant dances), including the all-important *danzón* (the first dance in Cuba in which couples actually touched each other), the *zapateo,* the slow and sensual *yambú,* and the *colombia* (a solo men's dance performed blindfolded with machetes)—all popular in past centuries among white country people and accompanied by small accordions, kettle drums, gourds, and calabashes.

From Europe, too, came the *trovas,* poetic songs (*canciones*) concerned with great historical events and, above all, with love. *Trovas,* which were descended from the medieval ballad, were sung in Cuba throughout the colonial period. *Trovadores* performed for free, as they still do at *casas de la trova* islandwide. The duty of the *casas* is to nurture the music of the provinces, and their success is one reason why Cuba is today a powerhouse on the international music scene.

Last century saw the evolution of the sultry *bolero* (a fusion of traditional *trovas* with Afro-Cuban rhythms) and more recently *trovas nuevas,* which often include subtle criticism of governmental dogma, as echoed by Pablo Milanés, Silvio Rodríguez, and more recently Buena Fe.

The African Influence

Almost from the beginning, the Spanish guitar (from the tiny *requinto* to the *tres,* a small guitar with three sets of double strings) joined the hourglass-shaped African *bata* and bongo drum, claves (two short hardwood sticks clapped together), and *chequerí* (seed-filled gourds) to give Cuban music its distinctive form. Slaves played at speakeasies in huts in the slaves' quarters. Their jam sessions gave birth to the *guaguancó,* an erotic rumba in which the man tries to make contact with the woman's genitals and the woman dances defensively, with handfuls of skirt in front of her groin. Later, slaves would take the *guaguancó* a few steps farther to create the sensuous *rumba,* a sinuous dance from the hips from which tumbled most other forms of Cuban music, such as the *tumba francesa,* a dance of French-African fusion, and *son.*

Son, which originated in the eastern provinces of Oriente, derived as a campesino-based form combining African call-and-response verse to Spanish folk tunes using *décima* verses (octosyllabic 10-line stanzas). Popularized on radio by 1920s artists such as Rita Montaner, *son* became the national music form.

By the 1930s, *son* was adopted and melded with U.S. jazz influences by large band orchestras (*orquestas típicas*) with percussion and horn sections and tall conga drums called *tumbadores,* epitomized by the roaring success of Benny Moré (born Bartolomé Maximiliano Moré, 1919-1963), the flamboyant *bárbaro del ritmo*—the hot man of rhythm—who became a national idol and had his own big band, the Banda Gigante. The success of big band paved the way for the evolution of salsa. Such contemporary salsa groups as Los Van Van have incorporated the *son,* which has its own variants, such as *son changüí* from Guantánamo Province, typified by the music of Orquesta Revé.

The mambo, like the cha-cha, which evolved from *son,* is a derivative of the *danzón* jazzed up with rhythmic innovations. Mambo is a passé but still revered dance, like the jitterbug in the United States, danced usually only by older people. Created in Cuba by Orestes López in 1938, mambo stormed the United States in the 1950s, when Cuban performers were the hottest ticket in town. Though the craze died, mambo left its mark on everything from American jazz to the old Walt Disney cartoons where the salt and pepper shakers get up and dance.

The mix of Cuban and North American sounds created blends such as *filin* music, a simple, honest derivative of the *bolero,* as sung by Rita Montaner and Nat "King" Cole, who performed regularly in Havana; and *Cu-bop,* which fused bebop with Afro-Cuban rhythms, epitomized by Moré, who was considered the top artist of Cuban popular music.

Modern Sounds

Salsa is the heartbeat of most Cuban nightlife and a musical form so hot it can cook the pork. Los Van Van—one of Cuba's hottest big, brassy salsa-style bands—and Irakere have come up with innovative and explosive mixtures of jazz, classical, rock, and traditional Cuban music that have caused a commotion in music. They regularly tour Europe and

Latin America. And Bamboleo is a leader in *timba* (high-speed new-wave salsa).

For a long time, the playing of jazz in Cuba was discouraged as "representative of Yankee imperialism." The government began to lighten up in the 1980s. Today, Cuba boasts wonderful jazz players. The undisputed king of contemporary jazz is pianist Chucho Valdés, winner of five Grammy awards for his scorching-hot compositions.

More recently, rap has come to Cuba. Although the rhythms, gestures, and posturing take their cues from U.S. urban ghettoes, Cuban hip-hop is gentler, less dependent on guttural, driving aggression and more based on melodic fusion. Rap-based, reggae-influenced reggaeton is now the most universally popular and ubiquitous sound on the island, performed by such groups as Sintesis and Obsesión (in Oriente, a more hard-edged, direct style called *perreo* has spun off). Beginning in 2002, the government responded to increasingly critical hip-hop content with a severe yank on the leash, ironically by lending it official support, permitting the government to usurp and control it. The state decides what music can be played, and when and where, and it is not unknown for officials to literally pull the plug on unofficial concerts. The same holds true for rock, which has been lassoed by the Unión Juventud de Cuba (the Young Communists) to corral disaffected youth. Rock was once officially banned. Cuba's *roqueros* (rockers) and *frikis* (freaks, known for their torn clothes and punkish hair) faced a hard time of things for many years, as the government considered them social deviants.

Classical Music and Ballet

It is astounding how many contemporary Cubans are accomplished classical musicians. Everywhere you go, you will come across violinists, pianists, and cellists serenading you for tips while you eat. Cuba also boasts several classical orchestras, notably the Orquesta Sinfónica Nacional. Watch, too, for performances by Frank Fernández, Cuba's finest classical pianist.

Cubans love ballet, which is associated in Cuba with one name above all: Alicia Alonso, born to an aristocratic family in Havana on December 21, 1921. Alonso was a prima ballerina with the American Ballet Theater since its inception in the 1940s. She returned to Cuba and, sponsored by Batista (who hated ballet but considered her star status a propaganda bonus), founded the Ballet Alicia Alonso, which in 1955 became the Ballet de Cuba. Alonso was outspoken in her criticism of the "Sordid Era," and she went into exile in 1956 when Batista withdrew his patronage. The Revolution later adopted her, and her ballet company was re-formed and renamed the Ballet Nacional de Cuba, renowned worldwide for its original choreography and talent. The Camagüey Ballet—founded by Alicia's husband, Fernando Alonso—is also renowned for its innovative streak, as is the Santiago-based Ballet Folklórico de Oriente, which lends contemporary interpretations to traditional themes.

In 2014, ballet superstar Carlos Acosta formed **Acosta Danza** (Linea #857 e/ 4 y 6, Vedado, Havana, tel. 07/833-5699, www.acostadanza.com), a premier company fusing contemporary and classical dance.

ART

Artists followed classical European prescriptions throughout the early colonial period, and only in the 19th century did a distinctly national school arise, with mulatto artists José Nicolás de la Escalera and Vincente Escobar at the fore. Their *costumbrista* movement presented an idealized vision of *criollo* culture. In 1818, Juan Bautiste Vermay opened the Academia Nacional de Bellas Artes, which perpetuated the French allegorical, neoclassical stylistic form of painting.

The coming of independence opened Cuba to a wave of new influence, led by Armando García Menocal. Europe's avant-garde movement swept in as painters such as Eduardo Abela and Cabrera Moreno adopted international styles to represent emblematic Cuban themes, such as the figure of the *guajiro* (peasant farmer). Victor Manuel García and Marcelo Pogolotti were instrumental in formation of a Cuban post-impressionist school, while Wilfredo Lam, perhaps the greatest painter to emerge from Cuba during the 20th century, adopted Afro-Cuban mysticism to his exploration of the surrealist style inspired by Picasso, marrying Cubism and surrealism with Afro-Cuban and Caribbean motifs. The traditions of Afro-Cuban Santería also influenced the works of René Portacarrero.

The artists who grew up *after* the 1959 revolution have been given artistic encouragement (even entire villages, such as Verraco near Santiago, exist as art communities). In the late 1960s, the government tried to compel Cuban artists to shun then-prevalent decadent abstract art and adopt the realistic style of the party's Mexican sympathizers, such as Diego Rivera and David Alfaro Siqueiros. In 1980 the Cuban government began to loosen up. The artists began shaking off their clichés and conservatism. Contemporary Cuban artists express an intense Afro-Latin Americanism in their passionate, visceral, colorful, socially engaged, and eclectic body of widely interpretive works. Eroticism—often highly graphic—is an integral component of contemporary Cuban art, as exemplified by the works of Chago Armada, Carlos Alpizar, and Aldo Soler. Much of current art subtly criticizes the folly of Cuba's sociopolitical environment, but usually in a politically safe, universal statement about the irony in human existence, expressing the hardships of daily life in a dark, surreal way.

Cuba has 21 art schools, organized regionally with at least one per province. The very best artists graduate to the Instituto Superior de Arte, Cuba's premier art school.

Until recent years, artists were employed by Cuban state institutions and received a small portion of receipts from the sale of their work. In 1991 the government finally recognized that copyright belongs with the artist. It

Cuban Poster Art

Cuba's strongest claim to artistic fame is surely its unique poster art, created in the service of political revolution and acclaimed as "the single most focused, potent body of political graphics ever produced in this hemisphere." The three leading poster-producing agencies have turned out more than 10,000 posters since 1959. Different state bodies create works for different audiences: Artists of the Cuban Film Institute (ICAIC), for example, design posters for movies from Charlie Chaplin comedies to John Wayne westerns; Editora Política (the propaganda arm of the Cuban Communist Party) produces posters covering everything from AIDS awareness, baseball games, and energy conservation to telling children to do their homework.

Cuba's most talented painters and photographers rejected Soviet realism and developed their own unique graphic style influenced by Latin culture and the country's geography. The vibrant colors and lush imagery are consistent with the physical and psychological makeup of the country, such as the poster urging participation in the harvest, dripping with psychedelic images of fruit and reminiscent of a 1960s Grateful Dead poster.

See *¡Revolución! Cuban Poster Art*, by Lincoln Cushing (San Francisco: Chronicle Books, 2003).

has created independent profit-making, self-financing agencies to represent individual artists on a contractual basis whereby the agency retains 15 percent of sales receipts from the sale or licensing of copyrights abroad, making artists a hugely privileged group (Cuba's few true millionaires are all world-renowned, royalty-earning artists and musicians).

Among Cuba's most revered contemporary artists is Alfredo Sosabravo, the most versatile and complete artist among those making up the plastic-arts movement in Cuba today. Look, too, for the works (inspired by nature and Santería) of Manuel Mendive; the naïve works of José Fuster; the existential works by Alicia Leal; and the iconographic works of plastic artist Kcho (Alexis Leiva Machado).

LITERATURE

Cuba's goals and struggles have spawned dozens of literary geniuses whose works are mostly clenched fists that cry out against social injustice. The most talented Cuban writers all produced their best works in exile. Cirilo Villaverde (1812-1894) fought with the rebel army and was imprisoned as a nationalist, and his spellbinding novel *Cecilia Valdés*, written in exile in the 1880s, helped establish Villaverde as Cuba's foremost 19th-century novelist. From exile, too, José Martí,

the 19th-century nationalist leader whose works helped define the school of modern Latin American poetry, produced a long list of brilliant works, including the seminal *Versos Sencillos*.

There evolved in the 1930s and '40s a *poesía negra* (black poetry) that drew heavily on memories of slavery, very socialist in content, as portrayed by the works of mulatto poet Nicolás Guillén (1902-1989). Guillén also spent time in exile during the closing years of the Batista regime, having become a Communist while serving as a journalist covering the Spanish Civil War. Following the Revolution, he helped found the **Unión Nacional de Escritores y Artistas de Cuba** (National Union of Cuban Writers and Artists, or UNEAC, Calle 17 #351, esq. H, Vedado, Havana, tel. 07/832-4551, www.uneac.org.cu).

Similarly, Alejo Carpentier (1904-1980), acclaimed as Cuba's greatest 20th-century writer, was imprisoned by the dictator Machado but escaped and fled Cuba for Paris on a false passport. He returned to Cuba in 1937 but in 1946, during the violent excesses of the Batista era, fled Cuba for Venezuela, where he wrote his best novels. When the Castro revolution triumphed, Carpentier returned and was named head of the state publishing house. He is known for his erudite and verbally explosive works, which were seminal in defining the surreal Latin American magic-realist style. Following the Revolution, Carpentier became a bureaucrat and sycophant and in 1966 was appointed ambassador to Paris, where he died in 1980.

In the first two years of the Revolution, literary magazines such as *Lunes de Revolución* attained an extraordinary dynamism. In 1961, however, Castro dictated that only pro-revolutionary works would be allowed. Ever since, the state has determined who gets published, as well as who speaks on radio or television. Such state control came to a climax in 1970-1976, a period euphemistically called "the gray five years" (*quinquenia gris*). The worst years ended when the Ministry of Culture was founded in 1976, ushering in a period of greater leniency. Most of the boldest and best writers, many of whom had been devoted revolutionaries, left. Among them were Guillermo Cabrera Infante, Carlos Franqui, Huberto Padilla, Reinaldo Arenas, and Virgilio Piñera. Although much of the cream of the crop left Cuba, the country still maintained a productive literary output. Notable examples are Lezama Lima (1912-1976); Nicolás Guillén; and Dulce María Loynaz (1902-1997).

The 1990s saw a thaw. The Cuban government began to salvage those artists and writers who, having produced significant works, were never allowed to publish. In 1996, writers began to feel a sharp tug on the leash. There are no independent publishing houses. Hence, many splendid writers find it difficult to get their books published. Some authors have resorted to sending manuscripts with foreigners, such as Pablo Juan Gutiérrez, whose blistering *Dirty Havana Trilogy* is an indictment on the hardships of life in contemporary Cuba. Others become "official writers," producing pablum that panders to the Castro government's self-congratulatory ego.

Things have eased up under Raúl, but reading matter remains severely proscribed. Bookstores are few and meagerly stocked, so that tattered antique editions do the rounds until they crumble to dust. Nonetheless, Cubans are avid readers, and not just of home-country writers. The works of many renowned international authors, such as Gabriel García Márquez and Isabel Allende, are widely read. Tens of thousands of Cubans subscribe to the underground *paqueta semanal* (weekly package)—a compendium of U.S.-sourced programming, magazines, soap operas, and news sources delivered on flash drives by creative entrepreneurs.

FILM

In 1959 Cuba established a high-quality cinema institute to produce feature films, documentaries, and newsreels. All movies in Cuba are under the control of the **Instituto Cubano de Cinematografía** (ICAIC, Calle 23 #1155, e/ 10 y 12, Vedado, Havana, tel. 07/831-3145, www.cubacine.cult.cu), the Cuban Film Institute.

Undoubtedly the most respected of Cuba's filmmakers was Tomás Gutiérrez Alea (1928-1996), whose works were part of a general questioning of things—part of the New Latin American Cinema. The Film Institute granted a relative laxity to directors such as Gutiérrez, who was instrumental in its formation and whose populist works are of an irreverent picaresque genre. For example, his 1966 *La Muerte de un Burócrata* (*Death of a Bureaucrat*) was a satire on the stifling bureaucracy imposed after the Revolution; and *Memorias del Subdesarrollo* (*Memories of Underdevelopment*), made in 1968, traced the life of a bourgeois intellectual adrift in the new Cuba.

Gutiérrez's finest film is *Fresa y Chocolate* (*Strawberry and Chocolate*), released in 1994. The poignant and provocative movie, set in Havana during the repressive heyday of 1979, explores the nettlesome friendship between a flagrant homosexual and a macho party member, reflecting the producer's abiding questioning of the Revolution to which he was nonetheless always loyal.

Humberto Solas (born 1941) is another

leading director within the New Latin American genre. His *Lucía* (1969), which tells the tale of three women of that name living in different epochs, is considered a classic of feminist sensitivity. His *Miel para Oshun* (*Honey for Oshun,* 2001) addresses the story of exiled Cubans returning to the island. As a tale of loss, longing, and rediscovery the movie is a visceral, moving examination of the emotional scars created by the Revolution.

Another leading Cuban director is Juan Carlos Tabío (born 1944), who follows in the tradition of Alea, with whom he codirected *Guantanamera,* a farcical parody on Communist bureaucracy, told through the tale of a cortege attempting to return a body to Havana for burial. Tabío's *Lista de Espera* (*The Waiting List,* 2000), another magical-realist whimsy, aims its arrow at the dire state of transportation in Cuba, focusing on a group of disparate Cubans waiting in vain for a bus, eventually transforming the bus station into a kind of socialist utopia in which the characters find transformation.

The annual **International Festival of New Latin American Cinema** (www.habanafilmfestival.com) is held each December, and the **Festival Internacional de Cine Pobre** (International Low-Budget Film Festival, www.cubacine.cult.cu/cinepobre) is held in April, in Gibara.

Essentials

U.S. Law and Travel to Cuba

Moon Cuba provides complete travel information for all travelers, regardless of origin. Cuba has no restrictions on international travel. However, the U.S. government does. Most *yanquis* harbor the false impression that it's illegal for U.S. citizens to visit Cuba; it's not. The Supreme Court determined in the 1950s that U.S. citizens have a right to unrestricted travel under the Fifth Amendment. However, for decades, it has been illegal to spend money in Cuba, or to do so in pursuit of travel, without a license. The U.S. government invokes the 1916 Trading with the Enemy Act to prohibit travelers from *trading* with Cuba.

Except as specifically licensed by the Office of Foreign Assets Control (OFAC), payments of any kind in connection with travel to Cuba are prohibited, including prepaid tours to companies in third countries. The regulations change frequently and are open to interpretation by OFAC staff.

The regulations apply to U.S. citizens and permanent residents wherever they are located: all people and organizations physically in the United States (including airline passengers in transit) and all branches and subsidiaries of U.S. companies and organizations throughout the world. Now the good news...

New Regulations

On December 17, 2014, President Obama liberalized travel to Cuba. However, he did *not* end travel restrictions. That's the prerogative of Congress. Tourism (recreational travel) is not among the travel exemptions listed by the White House. These are changes made since December 2014:

- All 12 existing categories of licensed travel are covered by a general license. Previously, most categories (freelance journalists, humanitarians, athletes, etc.) had to request a specific license (i.e., written authorization) from OFAC, which could deny such requests. Now, under a general license all such individuals are *pre-authorized* to travel to Cuba.

- U.S. citizens are represented in Cuba by an embassy in Havana that opened in August 2015.

- U.S. travelers will be able to use their U.S. debit and credit cards in Cuba.

- U.S. travelers will be permitted to import Cuban goods up to $800 per trip, including $100 in cigars and rum.

Since July 2016, *all* U.S. citizens can travel to Cuba with any tour company or other entity licensed to operate "people-to-people educational exchange" group programs. The new regulations also permit any tour company, educational institution, or other entity that wishes to operate such educational exchange programs to do so without written authority. U.S. students wishing to study in Cuba may also now simply travel to Cuba with pre-authorization using the general license, so long as it's for a formal program of study. Plus, all licensed travelers are permitted to travel to Cuba by any means.

Tourism is still banned, which means no beach vacation! The truth is, since 2011, the U.S. government more or less stopped policing the regulations, and the people-to-people license (under which the majority of U.S. citizens now travel) ostensibly permits "disguised tourism" because the regulations are now unenforceable.

However, in June 2017 President Trump rescinded President Obama's provision permitting independent travel by individuals for "self-directed" people-to-people exchange.

At press time, the only permissible way for all U.S. travelers to legally visit Cuba is on organized people-to-people programs.

The regulations are overseen by the Licensing Division, **Office of Foreign Assets Control** (U.S. Department of the Treasury, 1500 Pennsylvania Ave. NW, Washington, DC 20200, tel. 202/622-2480, www.treas.gov).

The U.S. government recommends that its citizens arriving in Cuba register at the U.S. Embassy in Havana.

General Licenses

The following categories of travelers are permitted to spend money for Cuban travel without the need to obtain special permission from OFAC on a case-by-case basis. They are not required to inform OFAC in advance of their visit to Cuba. *However, they must maintain a full-time schedule of activities relating to their license category; be able to document that their travel qualifies under a general license; and keep a written record of their activities in Cuba as relates to the authorized travel transactions for five years.*

Official government travelers, including representatives of international organizations of which the United States is a member, traveling on official business.

Journalists and supporting broadcasting or technical personnel regularly employed in that capacity by a news reporting organization and traveling for journalistic activities. (The Cuban government requires that you be issued a journalist's visa, not a tourist card.) The new regulations now permit freelance journalists with a suitable record of publication who are traveling to do research for a freelance article to do so under a general license.

Full-time professionals whose travel is directly related to "noncommercial, academic research" in their professional field and whose research will comprise a full work schedule in Cuba and has a likelihood of public dissemination; or whose travel is directly related to attendance at professional meetings or conferences that do not promote tourism or other commercial activity involving Cuba or the production of biotechnological products, so long as such meetings are organized by "qualifying international bodies."

Persons visiting Cuban family (or persons visiting "close relatives" who are U.S. government employees assigned to the U.S. Embassy in Havana) may visit them as often as desired and for an unlimited period.

Faculty, staff, and students of accredited U.S. graduate and undergraduate degree-granting academic institutions traveling for educational activities. University students may travel to Cuba for purposes of study toward their graduate or undergraduate degree for any length of time, provided that they have authorization from their university and a letter verifying that credit toward their degree will be granted for their study in Cuba.

Religious activities under the auspices of a religious organization located in the United States.

Humanitarian projects designed to directly benefit the Cuban people.

Activities intended to provide support for the Cuban people including but not limited to (1) activities of recognized human rights organizations; (2) activities of independent organizations designed to promote a rapid, peaceful transition to democracy; and (3) activities of individuals and nongovernmental organizations that promote independent activity intended to strengthen civil society in Cuba.

Professional research, conferences, and meetings so long as such activities do not include touristic activities, and conferences and meetings do not promote tourism in Cuba.

Academic educational activities for accredited U.S. graduate or undergraduate degree-granting academic institutions.

Educational exchanges not involving academic study pursuant to a degree program and that promotes people-to-people contact.

Academic seminars, conferences, and workshops related to Cuba or global issues involving Cuba and sponsored or cosponsored by the traveler's accredited U.S. graduate or undergraduate academic institution.

Athletic competitions by amateur or semiprofessional athletes or teams selected by the relevant U.S. federation.

Participation in a **public performance, clinic, workshop, competition, or exhibition** in Cuba.

Activities by **private foundations or research or educational institutes** that have an established interest in international relations to collect information related to Cuba for noncommercial purposes.

Persons traveling to engage in exportation, importation, or transmission of **informational materials.**

Marketing, sales negotiation, accompanied delivery, or servicing of exports consistent with the **export or re-export licensing policy** of the Department of Commerce.

Marketing, sales negotiation, accompanied delivery, or servicing of **medicine, medical supplies, or certain telecommunications equipment** by a U.S.-owned or -controlled firm in a third country.

Individuals traveling to conduct business in the field of **agricultural and medicinal product sales** (including marketing, negotiation, delivery, or servicing of exports), and in **telecommunications,** including conferences and meetings.

Spending Limits

Authorized travelers are now permitted to spend any amount of money "for transactions directly related to the activities for which they received a license." Money may be spent only for purchases of items directly related to licensed travel, such as hotel accommodations, meals, and goods personally used by the traveler in Cuba.

Also, as of January 2015, U.S. citizens are allowed to use debit and credit cards in Cuba (although only one U.S. bank had a functioning relationship at press time). Plus, the new regulations allow U.S. citizens to return to the United States with up to $800 of Cuban commercial purchases, including cigars and rum, and an unlimited amount of informational material, which includes art, CDs, and films.

U.S. regulations apply even to foreigners in transit through U.S. airports. Since the United States has no transit entry, *all* passengers in transit, say, from Mexico to Europe, must pass through U.S. Immigration and Customs; any Cuban items beyond the $800 limit may be confiscated, whether bought in Cuba or not.

Qualified Travel Service Providers

Any U.S. travel agent can now provide travel services involving travel-related transactions regarding Cuba. Moreover, persons subject to U.S. jurisdiction are now authorized to provide carrier service by aircraft to, from, and within Cuba. The first scheduled service to Cuba since 1961 was initiated on August 31, 2016, by JetBlue. The first U.S. cruise ships began service in 2015. Such entities are required to maintain certificates from each traveler for five years, demonstrating that they are legally authorized to travel to Cuba.

"Illegal" Travel

Individuals who choose to circumvent U.S. law do so at their own risk and the author and publisher accept no responsibility for any consequences that may result from such travel.

Thousands of U.S. citizens have slipped into Cuba through Canada, Mexico, and other third countries. Since 2012, Cuban immigration officials have been stamping all passports of arriving visitors. Persons subject to U.S. jurisdiction who travel to Cuba without a license bear a "presumption of guilt" and may be required to show documentation that all expenses incurred were paid by a third party not subject to U.S. law.

To my knowledge no one has been issued a "pre-penalty notice" since 2011. However, on paper trading with Cuba illegally is grounds for a fine up to US$55,000 under provisions of the Helms-Burton Bill, plus up to US$250,000 under the Trading with the Enemy Act, but most demands for fines have been US$7,500.

Getting There and Away

AIR

About 40 airlines service Cuba. Most flights arrive at Havana's José Martí International Airport or Varadero's Juan Gualberto Gómez International Airport. Cuba has eight additional international airports: Camagüey, Cayo Coco, Cayo Largo del Sur, Ciego de Ávila, Cienfuegos, Holguín, Santa Clara, and Santiago de Cuba.

Cuba's national airline, **Cubana de Aviación** (www.cubana.cu), generally offers lower fares than competing airlines. Cubana has DC-10s and Airbus A-320s that serve Europe and Mexico. The workhorses in the stable remain Soviet-made aircraft, including modern Antonovs.

Fares quoted in this book are based on rates advertised at press time. They are subject to change and should be used only as a guideline.

To get the cheapest fares, make your reservations as early as possible, especially during peak season, as flights often sell out. Low-season and midweek travel is often cheaper, as are stays of more than 30 days.

Most scheduled airlines permit two pieces of checked baggage, although a fee may apply; most charter airlines permit 20 kilos of baggage and charge extra for overweight bags. Cubana (20-40 kilograms, depending on class) charges extortionate rates for each kilo over your limit. Keep any valuable items, such as laptop computers, in your carry-on luggage. Always reconfirm your reservation and return flight within 72 hours of your departure (reservations are frequently canceled if not reconfirmed; Cubana is particularly bad), and arrive at the airport with plenty of time to spare. Always keep a photocopy of your ticket separate from your ticket and other documents as a safeguard in the event of loss or theft.

Online Bookings

Scheduled flights from the United States were authorized in 2016. Licensed travelers can legally book and pay by credit card for flights via U.S. websites such as www.orbitz.com and www.travelocity.com, as well as direct with any airline servicing Cuba. Travelers must sign a form affirming that they are traveling under one of the 12 approved categories of licensable travel. However, since June 2017 independent travel for people-to-people educational exchange is no longer permitted.

From the United States

Scheduled commercial flights between the United States and Cuba were authorized in 2016. At press time, seven airlines—Alaska Airlines, American Airlines, Frontier Airlines, JetBlue, Southwest Airlines, and Sun Country Airlines—had service to Cuba's provincial airports, solely for licensed passengers as permitted by the U.S. Treasury Department. A total of 110 weekly flights have been approved in a joint U.S.-Cuban accord. Havana will receive 20 flights daily: 14 will be from Florida, and the remainder from Atlanta, Charlotte, Houston, Los Angeles, Newark, and New York. (However, early demand was less than expected, and by mid-2017 several airlines had already reduced flights.) The average cost round-trip from Miami is about $150, including tourist visa and mandatory travel insurance.

Additionally, about two dozen companies—called Carrier Service Providers (CSPs)—are authorized to fly direct charters to Cuba from the United States. Charters use aircraft operated by American Airlines (www.aa.com), Eastern Airlines (www.easternairlines.aero), JetBlue (www.jetblue.com), World Airways (www.flywaa.com), and United Airlines (www.united.com). However, none was operating at press time.

From Canada

Most flights from Canada land at Varadero

Private Aircraft

Private pilots must contact the **Instituto de Aeronáutica Civil de Cuba** (Calle 23 #64, e/ Infanta y P, Vedado, tel. 07/834-4949, www.iacc.gob.cu) at least 10 days before arrival in Cuba and at least 48 hours before an overflight.

U.S. owners of private aircraft, including air ambulance services, who intend to land in Cuba must obtain a temporary export permit for the aircraft from the U.S. Department of Commerce before departure.

Air Journey (tel. 561/841-1551, www.airjourney.com) offers group tours for private pilots who fly their own planes to Cuba.

and other beach destinations. You can find cheap airfares—about C$400 round-trip—through **Travel Cuts** (tel. 800/667-2887, www.travelcuts.com).

A. Nash Travel Inc. (5865 McLaughlin Rd., Unit 2B, Mississauga, ON L5R 1B8, tel. 905/755-0647 or 800/818-2005, www.nashtravel.com) is a recommended Cuba specialist.

Air Canada (tel. 800/247-2262, www.air-canada.com) serves various destinations in Cuba from Canada. **Cubana** (675 King St. W. #206, Toronto, tel. 416/967-2822 or 866/428-2262, www.cubana.cu) flies from Montreal to Camagüey, Cayo Largo, Cienfuegos, and Havana; and from Toronto to Camagüey, Cayo Largo, Cienfuegos, Havana, Holguín, Santa Clara, and Santiago de Cuba.

Most charter flights are designed as beach vacation packages, but charter operators also sell "air-only" tickets. Try **Air Canada Vacations** (tel. 866/529-2079, www.vacations.aircanada.com); **Air Transat** (tel. 866/847-1112, www.airtransat.com); **SunWing** (tel. 877/786-9464, www.sunwing.ca); and **Westjet** (tel. 888/937-8538, www.westjet.com).

From Europe

From France: Havana is served by **Air France** (tel. 09-69-39-02, www.airfrance.com), with daily flights from Paris's Charles de Gaulle Airport (from about €605 round-trip). **Cubana** (41 Blvd. du Montparnasse, 75006 Paris, tel. 01/53-63-23-38) flies from Paris Orly airport to Havana via Santiago de

Cuba, and via Santa Clara (from about €950 round-trip). **Air Europa** (tel. 971/080-235 in Spain, www.aireuropa.com) flies between Charles de Gaulle and Havana via Madrid (from about €1,200).

From Germany: Charter company **Condor** (tel. 0180/6-76-77-76, www.condor.com) flies from Frankfurt and Munich to Havana and Holguín. **AirBerlin** (tel. 917/26-13-165, www.airberlin.com) flies from Berlin to Varadero.

From Italy: You can use **Alitalia** (tel. 89-20-10, www.alitalia.it) to connect with Air France, Iberia, or Virgin Atlantic flights. **Blue Panorama** (tel. 06/9895-6666, www.bluepanorama.com) carries the bulk of Italian tourists to Cuba with flights to Cayo Largo, Havana, Holguín, Santa Clara, and Santiago de Cuba.

From the Netherlands: Havana is served by **KLM** (tel. 20/474-7747, www.klm.com) from Amsterdam (from about €1,100 round-trip).

From Russia: Russia's **Aeroflot** (tel. 095/223-5555 or 800/444-5555, www.aeroflot.ru/cms/en) flies from Moscow to Havana. **Cubana** (tel. 095/238-4343, www.cubana.ru) operates once a week from Moscow.

From Spain: Havana is served by **Iberia** (tel. 800/772-4642, www.iberia.com) from Madrid daily, as well as by **Air Europa** (tel. 902/401-501, www.air-europa.com). **Cubana** (tel. 091/758-9750, www.cubana.cu) flies from Madrid to Havana and Santiago de Cuba.

From the United Kingdom: Virgin

Humanitarian Couriers

You can make tax-deductible donations to relief organizations licensed by OFAC to run food, medicine, and other humanitarian aid to Cuba using ordinary U.S. citizens as volunteer couriers. However, since 2011, OFAC has denied most humanitarian organizations a license. Currently, **Global Health Partners** (39 Broadway, Suite 1540, New York, NY 10006, tel. 212/353-9800, www.ghpartners.org) sends medical supplies to Cuba via its people-to-people humanitarian program.

Atlantic (tel. 0344/874-7747, www.virgin-atlantic.com) flies from Gatwick to Havana (from £539 round-trip) twice weekly. Good online resources for discount tickets include www.ebookers.com, www.cheapflights.co.uk, and www.travelsupermarket.com; for charter flights, there's **Charter Flight Centre** (tel. 0845/045-0153, www.charterflights.co.uk).

From the Caribbean
From the Bahamas: Bahamasair (tel. 242/377-5505, http://up.bahamasair.com) has Nassau-Havana flights three times weekly.

From the Cayman Islands: Havana is served daily by **Cayman Airways** (tel. 345/949-2311, www.caymanairways.com) from Grand Cayman.

From the Dominican Republic and Haiti: Cubana (tel. 809/227-2040, www.cubana.cu) serves Havana from Santo Domingo and Fort-de-France, twice weekly.

From Central America
Copa (tel. 507/217-2672 or 800/359-2672 in the U.S., www.copaair.com) flies to Havana from Panama City six times daily. **Avianca** (www.avianca.com) has daily flights from El Salvador and Costa Rica to Havana with connecting flights from the United States.

Cubana (tel. 52-55/52-506355 in Mexico City, tel. 52-9988/87-7210 in Cancún, www.cubana.cu) flies from Mexico City five times weekly and daily from Cancún.

From South America
Latam Airlines (tel. 866/435-9526, www.latam.com), formerly Lan Chile, flies to Havana from Santiago de Chile twice weekly.

Cubana (www.cubana.cu) flies to Havana from Quito, Ecuador; Buenos Aires, Argentina; Sao Paulo, Brazil; Bogota, Colombia; and Caracas, Venezuela.

From Asia
In 2016, **Air China** (tel. +86-10-95583, www.airchina.com) has twice-weekly flights from Beijing to Havana, with a stop in Montreal. You can also fly to Paris, London, Madrid, or Canada and connect with flights to Cuba. Eastbound, flying nonstop to Los Angeles or Miami, is perhaps the easiest route.

From Australia and New Zealand
The best bet is to fly to either Los Angeles or San Francisco and then direct to Havana or via Miami. **Air New Zealand** (Australia tel. 132-476, New Zealand tel. 0800/737-000, www.airnewzealand.com), **Qantas** (Australia tel. 13-13-13, New Zealand tel. 0800/808-767, www.qantas.com.au), and **United Airlines** (Australia tel. 131-777, New Zealand tel. 0800/747-400, www.united.com) offer direct service between Australia, New Zealand, and North America. A route via Santiago de Chile and then to Havana is also possible.

Specialists in discount fares include **STA Travel** (Australia tel. 134-782, www.statravel.com.au; New Zealand tel. 0800/474-400, www.statravel.co.nz). A good online resource for discount airfares is **Flight Centre** (Australia tel. 133-133, www.flightcentre.com.au).

SEA

As yet, no ferry service between Florida and Havana has been approved by Cuba (although as of 2014 President Obama approved such services).

Cruise Ship

Since 1961, the U.S. embargo restricted the cruise industry's access to Cuba (no vessel of any nation could berth in U.S. ports within 180 days of visiting Cuba). In April 2016, President Obama relaxed these regulations and the first U.S. cruise ship—**Fathom**'s (tel. 855/932-8466, www.fathom.org) 700-passenger MV *Adonia*—arrived, initiating a regular schedule of so-called "people-to-people" cruises. In January 2017 **Pearl Sea Cruises**' 100-passenger *Pearl Mist* initiated three-times per-month 10-day cruises (Nov.-Mar., from US$7,810). **Royal Caribbean Lines** (tel. 866/562-7625, www.royalcaribbean.com) and **Norwegian Cruise Line** (tel. 866/234-7350, www.ncl.com) have also initiated cruises from Florida using much larger vessels. Carnival Corporation has requested permission to initiate "people-to-people" cruises for its Holland-America, P&O, Princess, and Seabourn lines. At press time, **Victory Cruise Lines** (tel. 888/907-2636, www.victorycruiselines.com) was awaiting Cuban authorization for its 202-passenger *M/V Victory*.

Lindblad Expeditions (tel. 800/397-3348, www.expeditions.com) offers 11-day "Land-Sea" programs aboard the 46-passenger *Harmony V* (Nov.-Mar.); **Variety Cruises** (tel. 800/833-2111, www.groupist.com) offers small-group sailings aboard the M/Y *Callisto* and *Sea Voyager.*

England's **Noble Caledonia** (tel. 020/7752-0000, www.noble-caledonia.co.uk) includes Cuba on its Caribbean itineraries using the M/S *Serenissima*. **Thomson Holidays** (tel. 0871/231-4691, www.thomson.co.uk) offers Caribbean itineraries featuring Cuba aboard the 1,500-passenger *Thomson Dream.*

Sea Cloud Cruises (www.seacloud.com) offers deluxe cruises aboard its legendary windjammers, *Sea Cloud* and *Sea Cloud II.*

Private Vessel

No advance permission is required to arrive by sea. However, it's wise to give at least 72 hours notice by faxing details of your boat, crew, and passengers to the six official entry ports operated by Cuba's **Marlin Náutica y Marinas** (tel. 07/273-7912, www.nautica-marlin.com). Cuba has 15 marinas, including one of the largest marinas in the Caribbean, at Varadero. Most offer fresh water, 110-volt electrical hookups, plus diesel and gasoline. Expansion and modernization at key marinas is underway.

For cruising, you'll need to register your boat upon arrival and receive a *permiso especial de navegación* (from CUC50, depending on the length of your boat). You'll need an official clearance (a *despacho*) to depart for your next, and every, stop. Authorities will usually ask for a planned itinerary, but insist on flexibility to cruise at random toward your final destination. A *permiso de salida* will be issued listing your final destination and possible stops en route.

As of 2016, all U.S. boaters are pre-authorized to sail to Cuba. All persons subject to U.S. law aboard vessels, including the owner, must be licensed travelers and have a valid reason for travel. (Since June 2017, U.S. citizens are no longer authorized for "people-to-people" travel except with an organized group through a licensed entity).

The United States and Cuba do not have a Coast Guard agreement (however, the U.S. Embassy *has* arranged such assistance to U.S. yachters). There are many reports of Cuban authorities being indifferent to yachters in distress, some of whom have had their vessels impounded; in several cases, foreign yachters have lost their vessels to corrupt officials. In case of emergencies requiring financial transactions, such as repair of vessels, travelers should contact OFAC (tel. 202/622-2480) for authorization.

Haut Insurance (tel. 978/475-0367, www.

johngalden.com) handles insurance coverage for yachters cruising in Cuban waters.

ORGANIZED TOURS

Joining an organized tour offers certain advantages over traveling independently. Cuba isn't easy to fathom, so choosing a tour with an acclaimed Cuba expert is a major advantage. Check the tour inclusions to identify any hidden costs, such as airport taxes, tips, service charges, or extra meals. Most tours are priced according to quality of accommodations.

From the United States
PEOPLE-TO-PEOPLE PROGRAMS

People-to-people (P2P) educational programs are offered by U.S. entities such as National Geographic Expeditions. By law, they must provide a full schedule of "educational exchanges" with Cubans. The rationale is that by meeting with Cubans, participants become ambassadors for democratic values.

These organizations are among the best offering P2P programs:

- **Cross Cultural Journeys** (tel. 800/353-2276, http://crossculturaljourneys.com) offers a wide range of special-interest tours in Cuba.

- **Cuba Motorcycle Tours** (tel. 760/327-9879, www.cubamotorcycletours.com) offers 8-, 12-, and 14-day motorcycle trips using BMWs and Harley-Davidsons.

- **Cuba Unbound** (tel. 208/770-3359, http://www.cubaunbound.com) offers special-interest trips, from biking to kayaking.

- **National Geographic Expeditions** (tel. 888/966-8687, www.nationalgeographicexpeditions.com) offers a fun and highly educational eight-day "Cuba: Discovering Its People & Culture."

- **Plaza Cuba** (tel. 510/848-0911, www.plazacuba.com) specializes in music and dance workshops.

The following can arrange trips for academic and cultural organizations and business groups:

- **Curated Cuba Tours** (tel. 760/285-9827, www.curatedcubatours.com) specializes in customized tours for small groups.

- **Marazul Tours** (tel. 305/559-7114 or 800/993-9667, www.marazulcharters.com).

Tours from Canada

Cuba Education Tours (tel. 888/965-5647, www.cubaeducationaltravel.ca) offers "solidarity" and special-interest tours.

Real Cuba (tel. 306/205-0977, www.realcubaonline.com) offers special themed trips, including bicycling, walking, and bird-watching trips, as well as photography workshops and volunteer programs.

WowCuba (tel. 902/368-2453, www.wowcuba.com) specializes in bicycle tours of Cuba but has other programs, including scuba diving.

Tours from the United Kingdom

Captivating Cuba (tel. 44/01438-310099, www.captivatingcuba.com) offers a wide range of trips.

Cuba Direct (tel. 020/3811-1987, www.cubadirect.co.uk) offers tailor-made itineraries.

Journey Latin America (tel. 020/3811-5828, www.journeylatinamerica.co.uk) offers trips from a "Havana Weekend Break" to self-drive packages.

GETTING AWAY

A CUC25 departure tax is built into the cost of international flights.

Customs

Cuba prohibits the export of valuable antiques and art without a license.

Returning to the United States: U.S. citizens are now allowed to bring back $800 of Cuban purchases, plus an unlimited value of informational materials (art, music, literature). This includes the two bottles of liquor and up to 100 loose cigars or two boxes of cigars. For details, contact the **U.S. Customs Service** (1300 Pennsylvania Ave. NW, Washington DC 20229, tel. 703/526-4200, www.cbp.gov/travel).

Returning to Canada: Canadian citizens are allowed an "exemption" of C$800 for goods purchased abroad, plus 1.14 liters of spirits, 200 cigarettes, and 50 cigars. See www.cbsa-asfc.gc.ca.

Returning to the United Kingdom: U.K. citizens may import goods worth up to £390, plus 200 cigarettes, 50 cigars, and one liter of spirits. See www.hmrc.gov.uk/customs/arriving.

Getting Around

AIR

Most major Cuban cities have an airport. Cuba's state-owned airlines have a monopoly. Their safety records do not inspire confidence, although many old Soviet planes have been replaced by modern aircraft. Flights are often booked up weeks in advance, especially in peak season. Tickets are normally nonrefundable. If you reserve before arriving in Cuba, you'll be given a voucher to exchange for a ticket upon arrival in Cuba. Arrive on time for check-in; otherwise your seat will be given away. Delays, cancellations, and schedule changes are common. You can book at hotel tour desks.

Cubana (Calle 23, e/ 0 y P, Havana, tel. 07/834-4446, www.cubana.cu) serves most airports. Fares are 25 percent cheaper if booked in conjunction with an international Cubana flight. **Aerocaribbean** (Calle 23 #64, Vedado, tel. 07/879-7524) and **Aerogaviota** (Av. 47 #2814, e/ 28 y 34, Rpto. Kohly, Havana, tel. 07/203-0668, www.aerogaviota.com) also operate flights.

Since they're all state-owned, don't be surprised to find yourself flying Aerogaviota even if you booked with Cubana.

BUS
Tourist Buses

Víazul (Av. 26, esq. Zoológico, Nuevo Vedado, Havana, tel. 07/881-1413, www.viazul.com, daily 7am-9pm) operates bus services for foreigners to key places on the tourist circuit using modern air-conditioned buses. Children travel at half price. Bookings can only be made via the website (six days in advance) or at a Víazul ticket office. A 10 percent fee applies for cancellations made more than 24 hours before departure; a 25 percent fee applies if you cancel within 24 hours. A 20-kilo baggage limit applies. Excess baggage is charged 1 percent of your ticket cost per kilo.

Transtur (tel. 07/831-7333, www.transtur.tur.cu) operates tourist bus excursions within Havana and Varadero by open-top double-decker bus, and in Matanzas, Viñales, Playa Girón, Trinidad, Cayo Coco, Holguín, Guardalavaca, and Baracoa by minibus.

Public Buses

There are two classes of buses for long-distance travel: *Especiales* are faster (and often more comfortable) than crowded and slow *regulares,* which in many areas are still old and rickety with butt-numbing seats.

Most towns have *two* bus stations for out-of-town service: a Terminal de Ómnibus Intermunicipales (for local and municipal service) and a Terminal de Ómnibus Interprovinciales (for service between provinces). Often they're far apart.

Caution: Pickpockets plague the buses and often work in pairs; foreigners are their first targets.

INTERPROVINCIAL SERVICES

The state agency **Ómnibus Nacionales** (Av. Independencia #101, Havana, tel. 07/870-9401, ext. 100) operates all interprovincial services linking cities throughout the island. However, it is off-limits to foreigners except for students registered at Cuban institutions.

Víazul Bus Schedule

Route	Departure Times	Duration	One-Way Fare
Havana-Santiago	6am, 3:15pm, and 8pm	13 hours	CUC51
Santiago-Havana	6am, 3:15pm, and 8pm	13 hours	CUC51

Stops are made at Entronque de Jagüey (CUC12), Santa Clara (CUC18), Sancti Spíritus (CUC23), Ciego de Ávila (CUC27), Camagüey (CUC33), Las Tunas (CUC39), Holguín (3:15pm departure only, CUC44), and Bayamo (CUC44).

Route	Departure Times	Duration	One-Way Fare
Havana-Trinidad	7am and 10:45am	5.75 hours	CUC25
Trinidad-Havana	7:45am and 2:30pm	5.75 hours	CUC25

Stops are made at Entronque de Jagüey (CUC12), Playa Larga and Playa Girón (8:15am departure only, CUC13), Aguada de Pasajeros (1pm departure only, CUC13), Yaguarama (CUC14), Rodas (CUC15), and Cienfuegos (CUC20).

Route	Departure Times	Duration	One-Way Fare
Havana-Varadero	8am, 10am, 1pm, and 5pm	3 hours	CUC10
Varadero-Havana	Noon, 2pm, 4pm, and 6pm	3 hours	CUC10

Stops are made at Playas del Este (8am departure only, CUC6), Matanzas (CUC7), and Aeropuerto de Varadero (by request).

Route	Departure Times	Duration	One-Way Fare
Havana-Viñales	9am and 2:30pm	3.25 hours	CUC12
Viñales-Havana	8am and 2pm	3.25 hours	CUC12

Stops are made at Las Terrazas (9am departure only, CUC6) and Entronque de Candelaria (9am departure only, CUC6), and in Pinar del Río (CUC11).

Route	Departure Times	Duration	One-Way Fare
Santiago-Baracoa	8am	5 hours	CUC15
Baracoa-Santiago	2pm	5 hours	CUC15
Trinidad-Santiago	8am	12 hours	CUC33
Santiago-Trinidad	7:30pm	12 hours	CUC33
Varadero-Trinidad	7:25am and 2pm	6 hours	CUC20
Trinidad-Varadero	7am and 1:55pm	6 hours	CUC20
Varadero-Santiago	9pm	15 hours	CUC49
Santiago-Varadero	8pm	15 hours	CUC49

INTERMUNICIPAL SERVICES

You may or may not be denied service; it's a crapshoot. No reservations are available for short-distance services between towns within specific provinces. You'll have to join the queue.

CAMIONES

The staple of travel between towns is a truck, or *camión*. Most travel only to the nearest major town, so you'll need to change *camiones* frequently for long-distance travel. Some are open-sided flatbeds with canvas roofs.

Sometimes it's a truck with a container of makeshift windows cut out of the metal sides and basic wooden seats welded to the floor. They depart from designated transportation hubs (often adjacent to bus or railway stations). You pay in pesos (1-10 pesos), depending on distance. Officially, foreigners are banned, so expect to be turned away by the drivers.

WITHIN TOWNS

Provincial capitals have intracity bus service, which can mean *camiones* or makeshift horse-drawn *coches*. Buses—*guaguas* (pronounced WAH-wahs)—are often secondhand Yankee school buses or uncomfortable Hungarian or Cuban models. They're usually overcrowded and cost 10-50 centavos. Many cities use *camellos,* uncomfortable and crowded homemade articulated bodies hauled by trucks.

Bus stops—*paradas*—are usually well marked. To stop the bus, shout *¡pare!* (stop!), or bash the box above the door in Cuban fashion. You'll need to elbow your way to the door well in advance (don't stand near the door, however, as you may literally be popped out onto your face; exiting has been compared to being birthed). Don't dally, as the bus driver is likely to hit the gas when you're only halfway out.

TRAIN

The nightmarishly dysfunctional **Ünion de Ferrocarriles de Cuba** operates rail service. One main line spans the country connecting major cities, with secondary cities linked by branch lines. Commuter trains called *ferroómnibus* provide suburban rail service in and between many provincial towns.

Published schedules change frequently: Check departure and arrival times and plan accordingly, as many trains arrive (and depart) in the wee hours of the morning. The carriages haven't been cleaned in years (windows are usually so dirty you can barely see out), and most are derelict in all manner of ways. Few trains run on time, departures are frequently canceled, and safety is an issue.

At last visit, an upgrade of tracks, signals, and communications was underway, and a fleet of brand-new Chinese locomotives was operating.

Bicycles are allowed in the baggage compartment (*coche de equipaje*). You usually pay (in pesos) at the end of the journey.

U.K.-based train enthusiast Mark Smith maintains "The Man in Seat 61" website (www.seat61.com/cuba.htm) with the latest info on Cuba train travel.

Reservations

The state agency **FerroCuba** (tel. 07/861-9389 or 07/861-8540, ferrotur@ceniai.cu) handles ticket sales and reservations for all national train service. Foreigners pay in CUC, for which you get a guaranteed first-class seat (when available). In Havana, tickets for foreigners are sold at the dysfunctional Terminal La Coubre (tel. 07/862-1000, Mon.-Fri. 9am-3pm), 100 meters south of the main railway station (Av. de Bélgica, esq. Arsenal, Habana Vieja, tel. 07/862-1920). Elsewhere you can normally walk up to the FerroCuba office at the station, buy your ticket, and take a seat on board within an hour. Buy your ticket as far in advance as possible. You should also buy your ticket for the next leg of your journey upon arrival in each destination. Reservations can sometimes be made through Infotur offices (tel. 07/866-3333, www.infotur.cu) and other regional tour agencies. You'll need your passport.

Reservations for local commuter services can't be made.

Service

Service has been reduced considerably since 2014, when trains #1, #2, #3, and #4 were taken out of service. The fast and generally reliable *especial* (train #11, also known as the Tren Francés [French train]), operates between Havana (departs Terminal Le Coubre at 6:15pm) and Santiago de Cuba (with stops in Matanzas, Santa Clara, and Camagüey) every fourth day and takes 13.5 hours for the 860-kilometer journey, arriving in Santiago

Last in Line

Cuban lines (*colas*), or queues, can be confusing to foreign travelers. Cubans don't line up in order in the English fashion. Lines are always fluid, whether in a shop, bank, or bus station. Follow the Cubans' example and identify the last person ahead of you by asking¿*el último?* ("who's last?"). It's like a game of tag. You're now *el último* until the next person arrives. Thus you don't have to stand in line, but can wander off to find some shade and then simply follow the person ahead of you onto the bus.

de Cuba at 11:40am. The return train (#12) departs Santiago de Cuba at 11:45pm and arrives at Havana at 3:41pm. At press time, the following service also operated from Havana: train #7 to Sancti Spíritus (departs 9:21pm every second day) via Matanzas and Santa Clara; train #13 to Manzanillo (departs 7:25pm every fourth day) with five stops en route; train #15 to Guantánao (departs 6:53pm every fourth day) with five stops en route; train #71 to Pinar del Río (departs 6:10am every second day); and train #73 to Cienfuegos (departs 7:15am).

Expect bone-chilling air-conditioning, TVs showing movies (loudly), a poorly stocked *cafetería* car, and *ferromoza* (rail hostess) meal service. Regardless, take snacks and drinks. Relieve yourself before boarding as toilets are grim (and some have no doors); bring toilet paper!

Fares

At press time, the following fares applied between Havana and: Santiago de Cuba, CUC30; Matanzas, CUC10; Sancti Spíritus, CUC14; Ciego de Ávila, CUC20; Morón, CUC24; Camagüey, CUC24; Cacocum (Holguín), CUC26; Bayamo/Manzanillo, CUC26; Guantánamo, CUC32. Children aged 5-11 are charged half price; children under 5 travel free.

TAXI
Tourist Taxis

Cubataxi operates radio-dispatched *turistaxis,* also found outside tourist hotels nationwide, and at *piqueras* (taxi stands) around the main squares. Since 2011, taxi drivers have leased the vehicles from the state. Few taxi drivers use their meters, and most now negotiate a fare (which have shot up in Havana due to U.S. travelers' willingness to overpay and overtip).

In tourist venues, modern Japanese or European cars are used. Beyond tourist areas, Cubataxi's vehicles are often beat-up Ladas. Few have seatbelts.

Peso Taxis

Havana and most provincial capitals have peso taxis serving locals and charging in pesos. Since 2009, peso-only taxis have been permitted to carry foreigners.

The workhorses are the *colectivos,* shared cabs that pick up anyone who flags them down (they also hang outside railway and bus terminals), often until they're packed to the gills. Sometimes called *máquinas* (machines) or *almendros* (almonds), they run along fixed routes much like buses and charge similar fares. Most are old Yankee jalopies. They usually take as many passengers as they can cram in.

Private Cabs

Private taxis were legalized in 2009; your vehicle could be anything from a clapped-out Lada to a ritzy Audi. Freelance driver-guides hang outside tourist hotels, restaurants, and discos. Your fare is negotiable. Educate yourself about *turistaxi* fares to your destination beforehand, as many drivers attempt to gouge you and you may end up paying more than you would in a tourist taxi. Agree on the fare *before* getting in. Make sure you know whether it is one-way or round-trip.

Coco-Taxis

These bright yellow fiberglass motorized tricycles look like scooped-out Easter eggs on wheels. You'll find them outside major hotels and cruising the tourist zones in large cities. They charge about the same as tourist taxis. However, they have no safety features, and several accidents involving tourists have been reported.

Bici-Taxis

Bici-taxis—the Cuban equivalent of rickshaws—patrol the main streets of most Cuban cities. These tricycles have been cobbled together with welding torches, with car-like seats and shade canopies. They offer a cheap (albeit bumpy) way of sightseeing and getting around if you're in no hurry. Some *ciclotaxis* are only licensed to take Cubans (who pay pesos). Always negotiate a fare before setting off.

Coches

These horse-drawn cabs are a staple of local transport. In Havana, Varadero, and other beach resorts, antique carriages with leather seats are touted for sightseeing. Elsewhere they're a utility vehicle for the hoi polloi and are often decrepit, with basic bench seats. They operate along fixed routes and usually charge one to three pesos, depending on distance.

CAR

Cuba is a great place to drive if you can handle the often perilous conditions. There are no restrictions on where you can go. Cuba has 31,000 kilometers of roads (15,500 kilometers are paved), though even major highways are deteriorated to the point of being dangerous.

The main highway, the Carretera Central (Central Highway), runs along the island's spine for 1,200 kilometers from one end of the country to the other. This two-laner leads through sleepy rural towns. For maximum speed take the A-1, or Autopista Nacional (National Expressway), the country's only freeway—eight (unmarked) lanes wide but much deteriorated in recent years. About 650 kilometers have been completed, from Pinar del Río to a point just east of Sancti Spíritus, and from Santiago de Cuba about 30 kilometers northwestward.

Only a few highways are well signed, although things are improving. You can buy the excellent *Guía de Carreteras* road atlas at tour desks and souvenir outlets. It's extraordinary how little Cubans know of regions outside their own locale. Rather than asking, "Does this road go to so-and-so?" (which will surely earn you the reply, *"¡sí!"*), ask *"¿Dónde va esta ruta?"* ("Where does this route go?").

Traffic Regulations and Safety

To drive in Cuba, you must be 21 years or older and hold either a valid national driver's license or an international driver's license (IDL), obtainable through automobile associations worldwide (www.aaa.com, United States; www.caa.ca, Canada; www.theaa.com, U.K.; www.aaa.asn.au, Australia; or www.aa.co.nz, New Zealand).

Traffic drives on the right. The speed limit is 100 kph (kilometers per hour) on the Autopista, 90 kph on highways, 60 kph on rural roads, 50 kph on urban roads, and 40 kph in children's zones. Speed limits are vigorously enforced. Ubiquitous, overzealous traffic police (*tránsitos* or *tráficos*) patrol the highways. Oncoming cars will flash their lights to indicate the presence of police ahead. Major highways have *puntos de control*—police control points, for which you must slow. If you receive a traffic fine, the policeman will note this on your car rental contract, to be deducted from your deposit. The *tráfico* cannot request a fine on the spot, although Cuban police occasionally attempt to extract a subtle bribe. If so, ask for the policeman's name and where you can fight the ticket (this usually results in you being waved on your way).

Seatbelt use is mandatory in front seats; motorcyclists are required to wear helmets.

Cuba's Vintage American Cars

Automotive sentimentality is reason enough to visit Cuba, the greatest living car museum in the world. American cars flooded into Cuba for 50 years, culminating in the Batista era. Then came the Cuban Revolution and the U.S. trade embargo. In terms of American automobiles, time stopped when Castro took power.

Today, Cuba possesses about 600,000 cars, of which about one-sixth are prerevolutionary American autos. In certain areas, one rarely sees a vehicle that is *not* a venerable, usually decrepit, classic of yesteryear.

Lacking proper tools and replacement parts, Cubans adeptly cajole one more year out of their battered hulks. Their intestinally reconstituted engines are monuments to ingenuity—decades of improvised repairs have melded parts from Detroit and Moscow. One occasionally spots a shining example of museum quality. The majority, though, have long ago been touched up with house paint. That said, more cars today look better than ever thanks to the new accessibility of real car paint and replica car parts from the States.

Owners of prerevolutionary cars can sell them freely to anyone with money to buy, but the chances of owning a more modern car are slim. Virtually all cars imported since 1959—Ladas (a Russian-made Fiat described by Martha Gellhorn as "tough as a Land Rover, with iron-hard upholstery and, judging by sensation, no springs"), Soviet UAZs, jeep-like Romanian AROs, and more recently Mercedes-Benzes, Nissans, Citroëns, and Chinese Geelys—are owned by the state. New such cars were leased out to Communist bigwigs, high-level workers, and state executives. Sports stars and top artists were also gifted or allowed to buy cars. Since 2011, Cubans have been permitted to buy and sell cars freely, regardless of vintage. Cuba's new breed of middle class is finally flaunting its wealth with imported BMWs and Audis, although the state still controls sales of all imported vehicles, charges a fortune, and restricts who can buy (the self-employed, farmers, and foreign company employees, for example, must make do with the higher-priced private used car market).

Cuba Classics: A Celebration of Vintage American Automobiles (http://christopherpbaker.com/cuba-classics-2) is an illustrated coffee-table book that offers a paean to the cars and their owners.

Note that it's illegal to: 1) enter an intersection unless you can exit; 2) make a right turn on a red light unless indicated by a white arrow or traffic signal (*derecha con luz roja*); or 3) overtake on the right. You must stop at *all* railway crossings before crossing. Headlights by day are illegal, except for emergency vehicles, but you should use yours and be seen.

Road conditions often deteriorate without warning, and obstacles are numerous and comprise everything from wayward livestock to mammoth potholes. Driving at night is perilous, not least because few roads are lit. Sticks jutting up in the road usually indicate a dangerous hole. *Keep your speed down!*

Accidents and Breakdowns

Rental car agencies have a clause to protect against damage to the car from unwarranted repairs. Call the rental agency; it will arrange a tow or send a mechanic.

In the event of an accident, *never* move the vehicles until the police arrive. Get the names, license plate numbers, and *cédulas* (legal identification numbers) of any witnesses. Make a sketch of the accident. Then call the **transit police** (tel. 07/882-0116 in Havana; tel. 116 outside Havana) and your rental agency. In case of injury, call for an **ambulance** (tel. 104 nationwide). Do not leave the accident scene; the other party may tamper with your car and the evidence. Don't let honking traffic pressure you into moving the cars. If you suspect the other driver has been drinking, ask the police officer to administer a Breathalyzer test—an *alcolemia*.

Accidents that result in death or injury are treated like crimes, and the onus is on the

Making Sense of Addresses

In most Cuban cities, addresses are given as locations. Thus, the Havanatur office is at Calle 6, e/ 1ra y 3ra, Miramar, Havana, meaning it is on Calle 6 between (e/ for *entre*—between) 1st and 3rd Avenues (Avenidas 1ra y 3ra).

Street numbers are occasionally used. Thus, the Hotel Inglaterra is at Prado #416, esq. San Rafael, Habana Vieja; at the corner (esq. for *esquina*—corner) of Prado and Calle San Rafael, in Old Havana (Habana Vieja).

Reparto (abbreviated to Rpto.) is a district. *Final* refers to the end of a street, or a cul-de-sac.

Piso refers to the floor level (thus, an office on *piso 3ro* is on the third floor). *Altos* refers to "upstairs," and *bajos* refers to "downstairs."

Most cities are laid out on a grid pattern centered on a main square or plaza, with parallel streets (*calles*) running perpendicular to avenues (*avenidas*).

Many streets have at least two names: one predating the Revolution (and usually the most commonly used colloquially) and the other a postrevolutionary name. On maps, the modern name takes precedence, with the old name often shown in parentheses.

driver to prove innocence. Prison sentences can range 1-10 years. If you are involved in an accident in which someone is injured or killed, you will not be allowed to leave Cuba until the trial has taken place, which can take up to a year. Contact your embassy for legal assistance.

Gasoline

Gasoline (*petróleo*) and diesel (*gasolina*) are sold at Cupet and Oro Negro stations (*servicentros*) nationwide. Most are open 24 hours. Gas stations are supposed to sell only *especial* (usually about CUC1.40 per liter—about CUC5.60 a gallon) to tourists in rental cars, and you may be refused cheaper *regular* (CUC1.20 per liter), even if that's all that's available. (Local gas stations, *bombas,* serve *regular* to Cubans only.) Electricity blackouts often shut the pumps down. Few stations accept credit cards.

Insurance

If you have your own vehicle, the state-run organization **ESEN** (Calle 5ta #306, e/ C y D, Vedado, Havana, tel. 07/832-2508, www. esen.cu) insures automobiles and has special packages for foreigners. However, this does not include "liability" insurance similar to the United States or United Kingdom.

Rental

Don't rent a car at the airport; relax for a day or two first.

Demand exceeds supply. During Christmas and New Year's, you'll need reservations, which can only be made within 15 days of your arrival; it's no guarantee that your reservation will be honored (ask for a copy of the reservation to be faxed to you and take this with you). If one office tells you there are no cars, go to another office (even of the same company). In a worst-case scenario, head to the next town (cars are always in short supply in Havana but are often available in Matanzas).

Expect to pay CUC50-185 per day with unlimited mileage, depending on vehicle; a two-day minimum applies for unlimited mileage. Added charges apply for one-way rentals, for drivers under 25 years of age, and for second drivers (CUC15). Discounts apply for rentals over seven days. The companies accept cash or credit cards (except those issued by U.S. banks). You must pay a deposit of CUC200-500; the agency will run off a credit card authorization that you will receive back once you return the car, assuming it has no damage. You must pay in cash for the first tank of gas before you drive away, although your contract states that you must return the tank empty (an outrageous state-run rip-off). Gaviota's Vía is preferred—its gasoline policy is the international norm: You return the car with the same amount as when rented. Check the fuel level *before* setting off; if it doesn't look full to the brim, point this out to the rental agent and demand a refund, or that it be topped off (but good luck getting that). Clarify any late-return penalties, and that the time recorded on your contract is that for your *departure with the car,* not the time you entered into negotiation.

Rental cars are poorly serviced and often not roadworthy, although in 2014 Transtur (www.transtur.tur.cu), the parent company of Cubatur, Havanautos, and Rex, purchased several thousand new Audi, MG, Peugeot, Volkswagen, and other European and Asian sedans. Inspect your car thoroughly before setting off; otherwise, you may be charged for the slightest dent when you return. Don't forget the inside, plus radio antenna, spare tire, the jack, and wrench. Don't assume the car rental agency has taken care of tire pressure or fluids. Note the *Aviso Próximo Mantenimiento* column on the rental contract. This indicates the kilometer reading by which you—*the renter*—are required to take the car to an agency office for scheduled servicing; you're granted only 100 kilometers leeway. If you fail to honor the clause, you'll be charged CUC50. This scam is a disgrace, as you may have to drive miles out of your way to an agency and then wait hours, or even overnight, for the car to be serviced.

Most agencies offer a chauffeur service (CUC50-120 a day). A four-wheel-drive vehicle is recommended only for exploring mountain areas.

RENTAL COMPANIES

Only state-owned car rental agencies operate. **Transtur** (Calle L #456, e/ 25 y 27, Vedado, www.transtur.tur.cu) operates **Cubacar** (tel. 07/835-0000), **Havanautos** (tel. 07/273-2277), and **Rex** (tel. 07/835-6830, www.rex.cu). There are scores of offices nationwide. There's no difference between the companies, although rates vary. For example, Havanautos offers 20 types of vehicles—from the tiny Geely CK (about CUC325 weekly) to an eight-passenger VK Transporter minivan (CUC1,400 weekly) and BMW 5-series and Audi A6 (CUC1,450 weekly). Rex has nine models—from the Seat Ibiza (from CUC65 daily low season, CUC80 high season) to the Mercedes #200 (CUC225 daily). Rates may vary between agencies but typically include 150 kilometers daily (unlimited on rentals of three days or more).

Gaviota's **Vía Rent-a-Car** (tel. 07/206-9935, www.gaviota-grupo.com) mostly rents Peugeots and Chinese-made Geelys, plus the tiny Suzuki Jimny jeep.

INSURANCE

Be sure to purchase insurance offered by the rental agency. You have two choices: CDW (Collision Damage Waiver, CUC15-20 daily, with a deductible of CUC200-500) covers accidents but not theft. Super CDW (CUC20-40) offers fully comprehensive coverage, except for the radio and spare tire. The insurance must be paid in cash. If you decline, you'll be required to put down a huge cash deposit. If your car is broken into or otherwise damaged, you must get a police statement (a *denuncia*), otherwise you will be charged for the damage. You can also name any licensed Cuban driver on your rental policy. However, there is no comprehensive liability coverage in Cuban insurance packages: If you (or anyone else driving your rented vehicle) are deemed at fault in an accident, rental agencies will nullify coverage and seek damages to cover the cost of repairs. You may be prevented from leaving the country until payment is obtained.

SAFETY

Theft, including of car parts, is a huge problem. Always park in *parqueos,* designated parking lots with a *custodio* (guard). Alternatively, tip the hotel security staff or hire someone to guard your car.

Your car rental contract states that picking

Travel Distances in Cuba

DISTANCES IN KILOMETERS

	Havana	Pinar del Río	Matanzas	Santa Clara	Cienfuegos	Sancti Spíritus
Baracoa	1,168	1,331	1,087	890	957	804
Bayamo	819	984	740	543	610	457
Camagüey	546	711	467	270	337	184
Ciego de Ávila	438	603	359	162	229	78
Cienfuegos	243	419	193	74	—	153
Guantánamo	1,026	1,191	825	750	817	664
Guardalavaca	802	967	723	526	593	440
Havana	—	176	102	276	243	362
Holguín	748	913	699	472	539	388
Las Tunas	670	835	591	394	461	308
Matanzas	102	267	—	197	193	283
Pinar del Río	176	—	267	441	419	527
Sancti Spíritus	362	527	283	86	153	—
Santa Clara	276	441	197	—	74	88
Santa Lucía	658	823	579	382	446	296
Santiago de Cuba	944	1,109	865	668	735	582
Soroa	86	89	188	362	329	448
Trinidad	321	497	271	89	78	67
Varadero	144	309	42	196	177	282
Viñales	193	28	295	469	436	555

up hitchhikers is not allowed. Foreign embassies report that many tourists have been robbed, and I do not endorse picking up hitchhikers.

Motorcycles and Scooters

You cannot rent motorcycles in Cuba (except, perhaps, from private individuals). Scooters can be rented in Havana and at resort hotels. California-based **Cuba Motorcycle Tours** (tel. 760/327-9879, www.cubamotorcycletours.com) offers 8-, 12-, and 14-day "people-to-people" programs by motorcycle, but does not rent bikes. It can customize tours for small groups.

BICYCLE

Bike rental is increasingly available in Cuba from private entrepreneurs; feeble beach cruisers can be rented at resort hotels. You'll need to bring your own bike. A sturdy lock is essential.

HITCHHIKING

Roadways are lined with thousands of hitchers, many of them so desperate that they wave peso bills at passing vehicles—be it a tractor, a truck, or a motorcycle. If it moves, in Cuba it's fair game. The state has even set up *botellas* (hitchhiking posts) where officials wearing mustard-colored uniforms (and therefore termed *coges amarillas,* or yellow-jackets) wave down state vehicles, which must stop to pick up hitchers.

It can be excruciatingly slow going, and there are never any guarantees for your safety. Hence, I don't recommend or endorse hitchhiking. If you receive a ride in a private car, politeness dictates that you offer to pay for your ride: *"¿Cuánto le debo?"* after you're safely delivered.

Visas and Officialdom

DOCUMENTS AND REQUIREMENTS
Cuban Tourist Visas

A passport valid for six months from date of entry is required. Every visitor needs a Cuban visa or tourist card (*tarjeta de turista*) valid for a single trip of 30 days (90 days for Canadians); for most visitors, including U.S. citizens, a tourist card will suffice. No tourist card is required for transit passengers continuing their journey to a third country within 72 hours. Tourist cards are issued outside Cuba by tour agencies or the airline providing travel to Cuba. They cost US$85 (£30-40 in the U.K., or £15 if you go in person to the Cuban consulate; flights from Canada include the fee). In some cases, tourist cards can be obtained at the airport upon arrival within Cuba (CUC100 in Miami and other U.S. airports).

Journalists require a journalist visa; students and academics entering to take classes or engage in research need a student or academic visa. U.S. citizens entering under the general license category for professional research need a Cuban visa to that effect, including an invitation from a formal Cuban entity.

Don't list your occupation as journalist, police, military personnel, or government employee, as the Cuban government is highly suspicious of anyone with these occupations.

EXTENSIONS

You can request up to two 30-day tourist visa extensions (*prórroga,* CUC25, payable in stamps—*sellos*—purchased at Cuban banks) in Havana at **Inmigración** (Calle 17, e/ J y K, Vedado, tel. 07/861-3462, Mon.-Wed. and Fri. 8:30am-4pm, Thurs. and Sat. 8:30am-11am), or at immigration offices in major cities. Dress conservatively; short shorts and flip-flops are not allowed. You need CUC25 of stamps purchased at any bank, plus proof of medical insurance and airline reservation to exit; if you're staying in a *casa particular* you also need a receipt for the house.

Visitors who overstay their visas may be held in custody until reports are received on their activities in the country. In such an event, you are billed daily! Do not overextend your stay.

CUBAN ÉMIGRÉS

Cuban-born individuals who permanently left Cuba after December 31, 1970, must have a valid Cuban passport to enter and leave Cuba (you will also need your U.S. passport to depart and enter the United States). Cuban passports can be obtained from the **Cuban Embassy** (2630 16th St. NW, Washington DC 20009, tel. 202/797-8515, www.cubadiplomatica.cu) or any Cuban consulate in other countries. Cuban émigrés holding Cuban passports do not need to apply for a visa to travel to Cuba. Cuba does not recognize dual citizenship for Cuban citizens who are also U.S. citizens; Cuban-born citizens are thereby denied representation through the U.S. Embassy in the event of arrest.

Non-Tourist Visas

If you enter using a tourist visa and then wish to change your visa status, contact the **Ministerio de Relaciones Exteriores** (Ministry of Foreign Affairs; MINREX, Calle

Regional Immigration Offices

The following regional offices have varying hours for handling requests for visa extensions (*prórrogas*) and other immigration issues:

- **Baracoa:** Maceo #48

- **Bayamo:** Carretera Central y 7ma, Rpto. Las Caobas, tel. 023/48-6148

- **Camagüey:** Calle 3ra #156, e/ 8 y 10, Rpto. Vista Hermosa, tel. 032/27-5201

- **Ciego de Ávila:** Independencia Este #14, tel. 033/27-3387

- **Cienfuegos:** Av. 48, e/ 29 y 31, tel. 043/52-1017

- **Guantánamo:** Calle 1 Oeste, e/ 14 y 15 Norte, tel. 024/43-0227, one block north of the Hotel Guantánamo

- **Holguín:** General Vásquez y General Marrero, tel. 024/40-2323

- **Las Tunas:** Av. Camilo Cienfuegos, esq. Jorge Rodríguez Nápoles, Rpto. Buena Vista

- **Manzanillo:** Martí, esq. Masó, tel. 023/57-2584

- **Matanzas:** Calle 85 #29408, e/ 2 de Mayo y Manzaneda

- **Nueva Gerona:** Calle 35 #3216, esq. 34, tel. 046/30-3284

- **Pinar del Río:** Gerardo Medina, esq. Isabel Rubio, tel. 048/77-1404

- **Sancti Spíritus:** Independencia Norte #107, tel. 041/32-4729

- **Santa Clara:** Av. Sandino, esq. 6ta, three blocks east of Estadio Sandino, tel. 042/20-5868

- **Santiago de Cuba:** Centro Negocios, Av. Jesús Menéndez, esq. José Saco, tel. 022/65-7507 (There's also an office outside the airport.)

- **Trinidad:** Concordia #20, off Paseo Agramonte, tel. 041/99-6950

- **Varadero:** Calle 39 y 1ra, tel. 045/61-3494

Calzada #360, e/ G y H, Vedado, tel. 07/835-7421 or 07/832-3279, www.cubaminrex.cu). Journalists must enter on a journalist's D-6 visa. Ostensibly these should be obtained in advance from Cuban embassies, and in the United States from the **Cuban Embassy** (2639 16th St. NW, Washington, DC 20009, tel. 202/797-8518, recepcion@usadc.embacuba.cu). However, processing can take months. If you enter on a tourist visa and intend to exercise your profession, you must register for a D-6 visa at the **Centro de Prensa Internacional** (International Press Center, Calle 23 #152, e/ N y O, Vedado, Havana, tel. 07/832-0526, cpi@cpi.minrex.gov.cu, Mon.-Fri. 8:30am-5pm). Ask for an Acreditación de Prensa Extranjera (Foreign Journalist's Accreditation). You'll need passport photos. Here, a journalist's visa (CUC70) can be got in a day, but you might not get your passport back for a week.

A commercial visa is required for individuals traveling to Cuba for business. These must also be obtained in advance from Cuban embassies.

Other Documentation

Visitors need a return ticket and adequate finances for their stay. The law requires that you carry your passport and tourist card with you at all times. Make photocopies of all your important documents and keep them separate from the originals, which you can keep in your hotel safe.

Cuban Embassies and Consulates

Cuba has Cuban embassies and representation in many nations. For a complete list, visit www.misiones.minrex.gob.cu.

- **Australia:** 1 Gregory Place, O'Malley, ACT 2606, tel. 02/6286-8770, asicuba@cubaus.net.

- **Canada:** 388 Main St., Ottawa, ON K1S 1E3, tel. 613/563-0141, consulcuba@emba-cubacanada.net (embassy and consulate); 4542 Decarie Blvd., Montreal, QC H4A 3P2, tel. 514/843-8897, seconcgc@bellnet. ca (consulate); 5353 Dundas St. W. #401, Toronto, ON M9B 6H8, tel. 416/234-8181, toronto@embacubacanada.net (consulate).

- **United Kingdom:** 167 High Holborn, London WC1V 6PA, tel. 020/7240-7463, consulcuba@uk.embacuba.cu.

- **United States:** 2630 16th St. NW, Washington DC 20009, tel. 202/797-8515, recepcion@usadc.embacuba.cu.

CUSTOMS

Visitors to Cuba are permitted 20 kilos of personal effects plus "other articles and equipment depending on their profession," all of which must be re-exported. An additional 2 kilos of gifts are permitted, if packed separately. Visitors are also allowed 10 kilos of medicines. An additional US$51 of "objects and articles for noncommercial use" can be imported free; thereafter, items up to $501 are subject to a tax

equal to 100 percent of the declared value, and items $501-1,000 to a tax 200 percent of declared value, but this applies mostly to Cubans and returning foreign residents. Both the Obama and Raúl Castro administrations have lifted restrictions on many goods, such as computers, DVD players, and TVs. "Obscene and pornographic" literature is banned—the definition includes politically unacceptable tracts. (If you must leave items with customs authorities, obtain a signed receipt to enable you to reclaim the items upon departure.)

For further information, contact **Aduana** (Customs, Calle 6, esq. 39, Plaza de la Revolución, Havana, tel. 07/883-8282, www. aduana.gob.cu).

EMBASSIES AND CONSULATES

The following nations have embassies and consulates in Havana. Those of other countries can be found at www.embassypages. com/cuba.

- **Australia:** c/o Canadian Embassy.

- **Canada:** Calle 30 #518, esq. 7ma, Miramar, tel. 07/204-2516, www.lahabana.gc.ca.

- **United Kingdom:** Calle 34 #702, e/ 7ma y 17-A, Miramar, tel. 07/214-2200, embrit@ ceniai.inf.cu.

- **United States:** Calzada, e/ L y M, Vedado, Havana, tel. 07/839-4100, https:// cu.usembassy.gov. Readers report that it has been helpful to U.S. citizens in distress, and that staff are not overly concerned about policing infractions of travel restrictions.

Recreation

BICYCLING AND MOTORCYCLING

Bicycle touring offers a chance to explore the island alongside the Cubans themselves. Roads are little trafficked yet full of hazards. Wear a helmet! Most airlines treat bicycles as a piece of luggage and require that bicycles

be boxed; Cubana does not. Bring essential spares, plus locks.

If planning an all-Cuba trip, touring is best done in a westerly direction to take advantage of prevailing winds. A good resource is *Bicycling Cuba,* by Barbara and Wally Smith.

In Cuba, **WowCuba** (Centro de Negocios

Kohly, Calle 34 e/ 49 y 49A, Kohly, Havana, tel. 07/796-7655, www.wowcuba.com) offers bicycle tours, as do U.K.-based **Cubania Travel** (tel. 0208-355-7608, www.cubaniatravel.com) and Canada's **Exodus** (tel. 800/267-3347, www.exodustravels.com).

Motorcycling is big business, and four fleets of imported BMWs, Harley-Davidsons, and Suzukis serve foreigners. **Cross Cultural Journeys** (tel. 800/353-2276, http://www.crossculturaljourneys.com); **Cuba Motorcycle Tours** (tel. 760/327-9879, www.cubamotorcycletours.com); and **RTW Moto Tours** (tel. 480/328-3039, www.rtwmototours.com) serve the U.S. market. **Edelweiss** (tel. +43 5264-5690, www.edelweissbike.com) serves Europeans.

BIRD-WATCHING

The Península de Zapata is one of the best bird-watching areas in the Caribbean (its 203 species include 18 of the nation's 21 endemics), as are Cayo Coco (more than 200 species, including flamingos), Isla de la Juventud (for cranes and endemic parrots), and mountain zones such as the Reserva de la Biosfera Sierra del Rosario, Reserva de la Biosfera Baconao, and Reserva de la Biosfera Cuchillas de Toa.

U.S. company **Naturalist Journeys** (tel. 520/558-1146 or 866/900-1146, www.naturalistjourneys.com) has birding trips in Cuba, as does **Quest Nature Tours** (491 King St., Toronto, ON M5A 1L9, tel. 416/633-5666 or 800/387-1483, www.questnaturetours.com).

ECOTOURISM AND HIKING

Cuba has the potential to be a hiking and ecotourism paradise. Both activities are relatively undeveloped. Notable exceptions are the trails in the Reserva de la Biosfera Sierra del Rosario and Parque Nacional Península de Guanahacabibes, in Pinar del Río; and Parque Nacional Pico Turquino and Cuchillas de Toa, in Oriente.

Guides are compulsory in national parks. Pinares de Mayarí (in Holguín Province), El Saltón (in Santiago Province), and Hotel Moka (in Pinar del Río) are Cuba's three so-called "eco-lodges," although they are really lodges merely set in wilderness areas.

EcoTur, S.A. (tel. 07/649-1055, www.ecoturcuba.tur.cu) offers eco-oriented tours—that include hunting and Jet Skiing!

FISHING
Freshwater and Inshore Fishing

Cuba's freshwater lakes and lagoons boil with tarpon, bonefish, snook, and bass. The star of the show is largemouth bass, which is best at Embalse Hanabanilla in the Sierra Escambray; Embalse Zaza in Sancti Spíritus Province; and Lago La Redonda, near Morón in Ciego de Ávila Province. As for bonefish and tarpon, few (if any) destinations can compare. This feisty shallow-water game fish is abundant off Cayo Largo and the Cayos de Villa Clara; in the Jardines de la Reina archipelago south of Ciego de Ávila Province; and in the coastal lagoons of Península de Zapata. In Cuba, **EcoTur** (tel. 07/649-1055, www.ecoturcuba.tur.cu) also offers fishing trips.

Italian company **Avalon** (http://cubanfishingcenters.com) has a monopoly for fishing in the Jardines de la Reina.

U.S. tour operator **Orvis** (tel. 800/547-4322, www.orvis.com) offers fly-fishing trips in Cuba, as does U.K.-based **CubaWelcome** (in Cuba tel. 5344-8888, U.K. tel. 020/7731-6871, www.cubawelcome.com), which has an office in Havana.

Deep-Sea Fishing

So many game fish travel through the Gulf Stream—Ernest Hemingway's "great blue river"—that hardly a season goes by without some IGFA record being broken. The marlin run begins in May, when the sailfish swim against the current close to the Cuban shore. The Cubans aren't yet into tag-and-release, preferring to let you sauté the trophy (for a cut of the steak).

Fishing expeditions are offered from **Marlin Náutica y Marinas** (www.nautica-marlin.com) nationwide.

GOLF

Before the Revolution, Cuba had several golf courses. After 1959, they were closed and fell into ruin. The only courses currently open are the 9-hole Havana Golf Club and an 18-hole championship course in Varadero. For years, Cuba has been talking about investing in its future as a golfing destination. Ten new golf course projects are on the books. In 2010, Cuba announced it would finally approve financing the resorts through residential real estate sales to foreigners—a prerequisite for foreign investors. In 2015, Cuba created CubaGolf, a division of the state entity Palmares, to manage the planned golf courses.

ROCK CLIMBING AND SPELUNKING

Cuba is riddled with caverns, and caving (spelunking) is growing in popularity, organized through the **Sociedad Espeleológica de Cuba** (Calle 9na #8402, esq. 84, Havana, tel. 07/202-5025, funatss@enet.cu), which also has a climbing division (c/o Anibal Fernández, Calle Águila #367, e/ Neptuno y San Miguel, Centro Habana, tel. 07/862-0401, anibalpiaz@yahoo.com). Many climbing routes have been established in Viñales. Climbing routes are open and no permission is necessary. Cuban American climber Armando Menocal (U.S. tel. 307/734-6034) is a good resource. Fernández and Menocal's superb *Cuba Climbing* (www.quickdrawpublications.com) guidebook is indispensable.

SAILING AND KAYAKING

Most all-inclusive resort hotels have Hobie Cats for hourly rental. Some also have kayaks. Yachts and catamarans can be rented at most marinas; try **Marlin Náutica y Marinas** (tel. 07/273-7912, www.nauticamarlin.com). You can also charter through Germany-based **Plattensail** (www.platten-sailing.de), which offers yacht charters out of Cienfuegos. However, they must be reserved *before* arrival in Cuba.

Cuba Unbound (tel. 208/770-3359, www.cubaunbound.com) and **Cuba Adventure Company** (tel. 902/759-9096, www.cubaadventurecompany.com) offer kayaking trips for U.S. citizens.

SCUBA DIVING

Cuba is a diver's paradise. There are dozens of sunken Spanish galleons and modern vessels and aircraft, and the coral formations astound. Visibility ranges from 15 to 35 meters. Water temperatures average 27-29°C.

Cuba has almost 40 dive centers. Most large resort hotels have scuba outlets. Certification courses are usually for the American and Canadian Underwater Certification (ACUC), not PADI. Cuban dive masters are generally well trained, but equipment is often not up to Western standards, and dive shops are meagerly equipped. Spearfishing is strictly controlled. Spearguns and gigs are *not* allowed through customs.

Cuba has four principal dive areas: the Archipiélago de Las Colorados, off the north coast of Pinar del Río; the Jardines de la Rey archipelago, off the north coast of Ciego de Ávila and Camagüey Provinces; the Jardines de la Reina archipelago off the southern coast of Ciego de Ávila and Camagüey Provinces; and Isla de la Juventud and Cayo Largo. The so-called Blue Circuit east of Havana also has prime sites, as do the waters off the tip of Cabo de Corrientes, at the westernmost point of Cuba (good for whale sharks). Isla de la Juventud, with many of the best wrecks and walls, is primarily for experienced divers. Varadero is of only modest interest for experienced divers, although it has caves and wrecks.

For U.S. Citizens: Yes, you can finally dive in Cuba legally. Dr. David E. Guggenheim leads "people-to-people" trips through **Ocean Doctor** (tel. 202/695-2550, www.oceandoctor.org) to the "Garden of the Queens."

Entertainment and Events

Cuba pulsates with the Afro-Latin spirit, be it energy-charged Las Vegas-style cabarets or someone's home-based celebration (called *cumbanchas,* or rumbas), where drummers beat out thumping rhythms and partners dance overtly sexual *changüí* numbers. And *noches cubanas* take place in most towns on Saturday nights, when bars and discos are set up alfresco and the street is cleared for dancing.

Havana is now throbbing to a new breed of sizzling nightclubs, many privately owned, that rival the best of New York and South Beach. That said, Cuba's nocturnal entertainment scene is a far cry from days of yore, and in many locales you are hard-pressed to find any signs of life.

LaHabana (www.lahabana.com) is the best source for information on artistic and cultural events, festivals, courses, and workshops.

NIGHTLIFE
Bars and Discos

Cuba's bar scene is anemic. Cuban cities are relatively devoid of the kind of lively sidewalk bars that make Rio de Janeiro buzz and South Beach hum, although Havana has gained several sensational new bars in recent years. Tourist-only hotel bars are with few exceptions pretty dead, while those serving locals are run-down to the point of dilapidation (and often serving beer or rum in sawn-off beer bottles).

The dance scene is much livelier. Most towns have at least one disco or *centro nocturno* (nightclub or open-air disco) hosting live music from salsa bands to folkloric trios. Romantic crooners are a staple, wooing local crowds with dead-on deliveries of Benny Moré classics. Foreign males can expect to be solicited outside the entrance to a disco: Cuban women beg to be escorted in because the cover charge is beyond their means and/or because

the venue only permits couples to enter. Drink prices can give you sticker shock: It's cheaper to buy a bottle of rum and a Coca-Cola. Few discos get their groove on before midnight.

Many clubs apply a *consumo mínimo* (minimum charge) policy that covers entry plus a certain value of drinks.

Folkloric Music Venues

Every town has a *casa de la trova* and a *casa de la cultura* where you can hear traditional *música folklórica* (folkloric music), including ballad-style *trova* (love songs rendered with the aid of guitar and drum), often blended with revolutionary themes. UNEAC (National Union of Cuban Writers and Artists, www.uneac.org.cu) also has regional outlets hosting cultural events.

Cabarets

One of the first acts of the revolutionary government was to kick out the Mafia and close down the casinos and brothels. "It was as if the Amish had taken over Las Vegas," wrote Kenneth Tynan in a 1961 edition of *Holiday.* Not quite! Sure, the strip clubs and live sex shows are gone. But sexy Las Vegas-style cabarets (called *espectáculos,* or shows) remain a staple of Cuban entertainment; every town has at least one. They're highlighted by long-legged dancers wearing high heels and G-strings, with lots of feathers and frills. Singers, magicians, acrobats, and comedians are often featured.

Outshining all other venues is the Tropicana, with outlets in Havana, Matanzas, and Santiago de Cuba.

THE ARTS

Theater is the least developed of Cuba's cultural media. Theater was usurped by the Revolution as a medium for mass-consciousness-raising. As such it became heavily politicized. In recent years, however, an avant-garde theater scene has evolved. The run-down theaters are used mostly for operatic, symphonic, and comic theater. However, you'll need to be fluent in Spanish to get many giggles out of the comedy shows, full of burlesque and references to politically sensitive third-rail issues.

CINEMA

Cubans are passionate moviegoers, although most cinemas are extremely run-down. Entrance usually costs a peso, and the menu is surprisingly varied and hip. Movies are often subtitled in Spanish (others are dubbed; you'll need to be fluent in Spanish). No children under 16 are admitted; most towns have special children's screenings. Many cinemas also have *salas de videos*—tiny screening rooms.

FESTIVALS AND EVENTS

The annual calendar is filled with cultural events ranging from "high culture," such as the Festival Internacional de Ballet, to purely local affairs, such as the year-end *parrandas* of Villa Clara Province, where the townsfolk indulge in massive fireworks battles. A highlight is Carnaval, held in Havana (August) and Santiago (July). Religious parades include the Procession of the Miracles (December 17), when pilgrims descend on the Santuario de San Lázaro, at Rincón, on the outskirts of Santiago de las Vegas in suburban Havana. The old Spanish holiday El Día de los Reyes Magos (Three Kings' Day), on January 6, is the most important religious observance.

Consumo Mínimo

You'll come across this term everywhere for entry to nightclubs and many other facilities. The term means "minimum consumption." Basically, it means that patrons have a right to consume up to a specified amount of food and/or beverage with a cover charge. For example, entry to the swimming pool at the Hotel Sevilla costs CUC20 but includes a *consumo mínimo* of up to CUC16 of food and beverage. There are no refunds for unused portions of the fee. The system is rife with *estafas* (swindles).

For a list of events, check out **LaHabana** (www.lahabana.com).

SPECTATOR SPORTS

Cuba is a world superstar in sports and athletics, as it was even before the Revolution, especially in baseball and boxing. Following the Revolution, professional sports were abolished and the state took over all sports under the **Instituto Nacional del Deportivo y Recreo** (National Institute for Sport, Physical Education, and Recreation, INDER, www.inder.cu).

The Cuban calendar is replete with sporting events. **Cubadeportes** (Calle 20 #706, e/ 7 y 9, Miramar, tel. 07/204-0946, www.cubadeportes.cu) specializes in sports tourism and arranges visits to sporting events and training facilities.

Major Festivals

Festival/Event	Month	Location
Habanos Festival (Cigar Festival)	February	Havana
Festival Internacional de Jazz (International Jazz Festival)	February	Havana
Festival de Semana Santa (Easter)	April	Trinidad
Festival Internacional de Percusión (International Percussion Festival)	April	Havana
Festival Internacional de Cine Pobre (International Low-Budget Film Festival)	April	Gibara
Carnaval de la Habana	August	Havana
Fiesta del Caribe (Carnaval)	July	Santiago de Cuba
Festival de la Habana de Música Contemporánea (Havana Festival of Contemporary Music)	October	Havana
Fiesta Iberoamericana de la Cultura (Festival of Latin American Culture)	October	Holguín
Festival Internacional de Ballet (International Ballet Festival)	October	Havana
Festival del Nuevo Cine Latinoamericano (Festival of New Latin American Cinema)	November	Havana
Festival Internacional de Música Benny Moré (Benny Moré International Music Festival)	December	Cienfuegos

Shopping

Department stores and shopping malls can be found in Havana. These, and smaller outlets in every town, sell Western goods from toiletries, Levi's, and Reeboks to Chinese toys and Japanese electronics sold for CUC at vastly inflated prices. If you see something you want, *buy it!* If you dally, it most likely will disappear. Most stores selling to tourists accept foreign credit cards except those issued by U.S. banks, but an 11 percent surcharge applies. Peso stores are meagerly stocked with second-rate local produce.

ARTS AND CRAFTS

For quality arts and crafts, Cuba is unrivaled in the Caribbean. Arts and crafts are sold by artisans at street stalls and in state agency stores such as the Fondo Cubano de Bienes Culturales and Artex. The best stuff is sold in upscale hotels, which inflate prices accordingly. Tourist venues are overflowing with kitschy paintings, busty cigar-chomping ceramic mulattas, erotic carvings, and papier-mâché vintage Yankee cars. There is also plenty of true-quality art, ranging from paintings to hand-worked leather goods. You'll also see *muñequitas* (dolls) representing the goddesses of the Santería religion.

Most open-air markets offer silver-plated jewelry at bargain prices (a favorite form is old cutlery shaped into bracelets), while most upscale hotels have *joyerías* (jewelry stores)

Turning Out Champions

Tiny Cuba is one of the world's sports powers, excelling in baseball, volleyball, boxing, and track and field. Cuba is by far the strongest Olympic power in Latin America.

Cuba's international success is credited to its splendid sports training system. When the Revolution triumphed, sports became a priority alongside land reform, education, and health care. In 1964 the Castro government opened a network of sports schools—Escuelas de Iniciación Deportiva (EIDE)—as part of the primary and secondary education system, with the job of preparing young talent for sports achievement. There are 15 EIDE schools throughout Cuba. The island also has 76 sports academies and an athletic "finishing" school in Havana, the Escuela Superior de Perfeccionamiento Atlético.

Sports training is incorporated into every school curriculum. School Games are held islandwide every year and help identify talent to be selected for specialized coaching. For example, María Colón Rueñes was identified as a potential javelin champion when she was only seven years old; she went on to win the gold medal at the Moscow Olympics. Many of Cuba's sports greats have passed through these schools—track-and-field stars such as world-record-holding high jumper Javier Sotomayor, world-record sprinters Leroy Burrel and Ana Fidelia Quirot, and volleyball legends such as Jel Despaigne and Mireya Luis. The system has been so successful that little Cuba was fifth in medal totals at the 1992 Summer Olympics in Barcelona.

Sports figures are considered workers and "part of the society's productive efforts." As such, sports stars are paid a salary on par with other workers, although most national team members also receive special perks, such as new cars. Not surprisingly, almost every international competition outside Cuba results in at least one defection.

selling international-quality silver jewelry, much of it in a distinctly Cuban contemporary style. *Avoid buying black coral, turtle shell jewelry, and other animal "craft" items.* The Cuban government doesn't seem conscientious in this regard, but European and North American customs officials may seize these illegal items.

A limited amount of bargaining is normal at street markets. However, most prices are very low to begin with. If the quoted price seems fair, pay up and feel blessed that you already have a bargain.

Exporting Arts and Antiques

Antiques may not be exported, including antiquarian books, stamp collections, furniture, and porcelain. An export permit is required for all quality artwork; the regulation doesn't apply to kitschy tourist art. State-run commercial galleries and *expo-ventas* (galleries representing freelance artists) will issue an export permit or arrange authorization for any items you buy.

Export permits for items for which you have not received an official receipt may be obtained from the **Registro Nacional de Bienes Culturales** (National Registry of Cultural Goods, Calle 17 #1009, e/ 10 y 12, Vedado, Havana, tel. 07/831-3362, Mon.-Fri. 9am-noon), in the Centro de Patrimonio Cultural, or at regional offices in provincial capitals. A single work costs CUC10, but CUC30 is good for up to 50 works of art. You must bring the object for inspection, or a photo if the object is too large. Allow up to two days for processing.

CIGARS

Cuba produces the world's best cigars (*habanos, tabacos,* or *puros*) at perhaps one-half the price of similar cigars in London.

Since 1985, handmade Cuban cigars have carried the Cubatabaco stamp plus a factory mark and, since 1989, the legend *"Hecho en Cuba. Totalmente a Mano."* (Made in Cuba. Completely by Hand.). If it reads *"Hecho a Mano,"* the cigars are most likely hand

The *Guayabera*

The traditional *guayabera*, Cuba's all-purpose gift to menswear, was created in central Cuba (or Mexico, no one is certain) more than 200 years ago and is the quintessential symbol of Latin masculinity. In 2010, the Cuban government anointed it Cuba's "official formal dress garment."

Despite the infusion of New York fashion, this four-pocket, straight-bottom shirt remains the essence of sartorial style. The *guayabera*, thought Kimberley Cihlar, "is possessed of all the sex appeal any Latin peacock could want." Nonetheless, younger Cubans shun the shirt as a symbol of someone who works for the government.

The *guayabera*, which comes short sleeved or long, is made of light cotton perfect for weathering the tropical heat. In shape, it resembles a short-sleeved jacket or extended shirt and is worn draped outside the pants, usually as an outer garment with a T-shirt beneath. Thus it fulfills the needs of summertime dressing with the elegance of a jacket and the comfort of, well, a shirt. It is embellished with patterned embroidery running in parallel stripes *(alforzas)* down the front and is usually outfitted with pockets—with buttons—to stow enough *habanos* for a small shop.

finished (i.e., the wrapper was put on by hand) rather than hand *made*. If it states only *"Hecho en Cuba,"* the cigars are assuredly machine made. All boxes feature a holographic seal (any other boxes are subject to seizure by Cuban customs).

There are about 40 brands, each in various sizes and even shapes; sizes are given specific names, such as Corona (142mm) and Julieta (178mm). Fatter cigars—the choice of connoisseurs—are more fully flavored and smoke more smoothly and slowly than those with smaller ring gauges. As a rule, darker cigars are also more full-bodied and sweeter.

All cigar factories produce various brands. Some factories specialize in particular flavors, others in particular sizes. Several factories might be producing any one brand simultaneously, so quality can vary markedly even though the label is the same. Experts consider cigars produced in Havana's El Laguito factory to be the best. As with fine wines, the quality of cigars varies from year to year. The source and year of production are marked in code on the underside of the box. The code tells you a lot about the cigars inside. Even novices can determine the provenance and date of cigars if they know the codes. However, the code system keeps changing to throw buyers off, so that cigars of different ages have

different codes. The first three letters usually refer to the factory where the cigars were made, followed by four letters that give the date of manufacture.

The expertise and care expressed in the factory determine how well a cigar burns and tastes. Cigars, when properly stored, continue to ferment and mature in their boxes—an aging process similar to that of good wines. Rules on when to smoke a cigar don't exist, but many experts claim that the prime cigars are those aged for 6-8 years. Everyone agrees that a cigar should be smoked either within three months of manufacture or not for at least a year; the interim is known as a "period of sickness." Cigars should be slightly soft when gently squeezed; have a fresh, robust smell; be smooth and silky in texture; and free of any protuberances or air pockets. The cigars should be of near identical color and shape.

You may leave Cuba with up to CUC5,000 worth of cigars with purchase receipts (or 90 without receipts). You can buy additional cigars in the airport duty-free lounge after passing through customs controls. Cigars can be bought at virtually every tourist hotel and store, or at dedicated *casas del habano* or *casas del tabaco* nationwide. Most shop clerks know little about cigars. Prices can vary up to 20 percent from store to store. If one store doesn't have what you desire, another surely will. Inspect your cigars before committing to a purchase.

In cities, *jineteros* (street hustlers) will offer you cigars at what seems the deal of the century. Forget it! The vast majority are low-quality or defect cigars sold falsely as top-line cigars to unsuspecting travelers. The hustlers use empty boxes and seals stolen by colleagues who work in the cigar factories, so the unknowing buyer is easily convinced that this is the real McCoy.

LITERATURE

Books are severely restricted by the government, which maintains firm control over what may be read. There are few newsstands or newsagents and no foreign periodicals.

Most tourist outlets sell a limited range of English-language coffee-table books, travel-related books, and political treatises that have been approved by the censors. Otherwise the few bookstores that exist stock mostly Spanish-language texts, mainly socialist texts glorifying the Revolution.

Food and Drink

A standing joke in Cuba is: What are the three biggest failures of the Revolution? Breakfast, lunch, and dinner. The poor quality of food has long been a source of exasperation. Before the Revolution, Cuba boasted many world-class restaurants. After 1959 many of the middle- and upper-class clientele fled Cuba along with the restaurateurs and chefs, taking their knowledge and entrepreneurship with them. In 1967 all remaining restaurants were taken over by the state. It was downhill from there.

The blasé socialist attitude to dining, tough economic times, and general inefficiencies of the system became reflected in boring (usually identical) menus, abysmal standards (tablecloths rarely get washed), and lack of availability. Some of the lousiest service and dishes can be had for the most outrageous prices. And don't assume that a restaurant serving good dishes one day will do so the next. Restaurants have traditionally relied upon the dysfunctional state distribution system to deliver daily supplies.

In the provinces trying to find somewhere with palatable food can *still* be a challenge. Shortages are everywhere. Plan ahead. Stock up on sodas, biscuits, and other packaged snacks at CUC-only stores before setting out each day.

Now the good news! Since 2011, restrictions on private restaurants have been lifted, leading to a boom in quality dining options. Havana is now blessed with dozens of world-class *paladares* (private restaurants). And many state restaurants have vastly improved, as the government has invested in culinary (and management) training and turned most such restaurants over to the workers to run as cooperatives. In general, the best meals are served in *paladares* (which outside Havana mostly serve *criolla*, or Cuban fare) and in the upscale hotels, which tend toward "continental" cuisine. Few places other than hotel restaurants serve breakfast; most offer variations on the same dreary buffets.

Sometimes service is swift and friendly, sometimes protracted and surly. You're likely to be serenaded by musicians, who usually hit up any available tourists for a tip (or to sell a CD or cassette recording). Eating in Cuba doesn't present the health problems associated with many other destinations in Latin America. However, hygiene at streetside stalls is often questionable.

Peso Eateries

Pesos-only restaurants are for Cubans. Food availability tends to be hit or miss and the cuisine undistinguished at best. Many restaurants offer an *oferta especial* (special offer), usually a set meal of the day. Some sell *cajitas,* bargain-priced boxed take-out meals for a few pesos.

Restaurant Scams

The creativity that Cubans apply to wheedle dollars from foreigners has been turned into an art form in restaurants. Here are a few tricks:

Added Items: Bread and butter is often served without asking, but you are charged extra. Mineral water and other items often appear on your bill, even though you didn't ask for them, or they never arrived.

Á la Carte Be Damned: The restaurant has a fixed price for a set menu but your bill charges separately for itemized dishes, which add up to considerably more. Beware menus that don't list prices.

Bait and Switch: You ask for a cola and are brought an imported Coca-Cola (CUC2) instead of Tropicola (CUC0.50), a perfectly adequate Cuban equivalent.

Commissions: The *jinetero* who leads you to a recommended *paladar* gets his commission added to your bill, even if he's merely picked you up outside the *paladar* you've already chosen.

Dollars or Pesos? The dollar sign ($) is used for both dollars and pesos. In a peso restaurant you may be told that the $ prices are in dollars. Sometimes this is true. Even so, change may be given in pesos.

¡No Hay! You're dying for a Hatuey beer but are told *¡no hay!* (there is none). The waiter brings you a Bucanero. Then you notice that Cubans are drinking Hatuey. You're then told that the Hatueys aren't cold, or that Bucanero (which is more expensive) is better.

Overpricing: Compare the prices on your bill against those on the menu. One or two items on your bill may be inflated.

Variable Pricing: Always ask for a printed menu with prices. Some places charge according to how much they think you are worth. If you're dressed in Gucci, expect to pay accordingly.

State-run *merenderos* and private roadside snack stalls—the staple for local dining—display their meager offerings in glass cases. A signboard indicates what's available, with items noted on strips that can be removed as particular items sell out. These stalls are an incredibly cheap way of appeasing your stomach with snacks. The "$" sign at peso eateries refers to Cuban pesos, not U.S. dollars.

The staple of street stalls is basic *pizzeta* (pizza), usually five pesos per slice. Pizzas are dismal by North American standards—usually a bland doughy base covered with a thin layer of tomato paste and a smattering of cheese and ham. Other staples are fatty pork *bocaditos, pan con queso* (basic but tasty cheese sandwich), *fritura de maíz* (corn fritters), and *pay de coco* (coconut flan).

Eating at street stalls poses a serious health risk.

PALADARES

Private restaurants—*paladares*—have been permitted since September 1994. The word means "palate" and comes from the name of the restaurant of the character Raquel, a poor woman who makes her fortune cooking, in the popular Brazilian TV soap opera *Vale Todo.* Here you can fill up for CUC5-35, depending on snazziness of the restaurant—from simple, albeit huge *criolla* meals to creative fusion fare in joints that would do London and New York proud. Some are open 24 hours. Not all owners are honorable, however; lack of a written menu listing prices can be a warning sign: Don't order food without seeing the menu, or the price is likely to be jacked up.

Taxi drivers and *jineteros* may offer recommendations. Their commission will be added to your bill.

FOOD CHAINS

There are as yet no McDonald's or KFCs in Cuba (except at the U.S. military base at Guantánamo). However, the Cuban government has established a chain of tacky equivalents, including KFC-style fried-chicken joints called El Rápido. Food often runs out or is severely limited, and the quality is usually awful. Cuba's answer to McDonald's is Burgui, open 24 hours.

The government has done a better job with seafood. The Dimar chain has roadside restaurants in major cities selling seafood at fair prices. The Baturro chain of Spanish-style *bodegas* has outlets in major cities, with charming ambience and *criolla* fare of acceptable standard.

SELF-CATERING

There are scant groceries and no roadside 7-Eleven equivalents. The state-run groceries, called *puestos,* where fresh produce often of questionable quality is sold, can make Westerners cringe. Cuba's best fruits and vegetables are exported for hard currency or turned into juices. Cheese and milk are precious scarcities. As a result, most Cubans rely on the black market or private produce markets called *mercados agropecuarios* (or *agros* for short). Every town has at least one *agro.* Carrots, cucumbers, chard, and pole beans are about the only vegetables available year-round; tomatoes disappear about May and reappear around November, when beets, eggplants, cabbages, and onions are also in season. Chicken and pork are sold at *agros,* but not beef. The government-run *pescaderías especiales* sell fish and other seafood.

You can buy imported packaged and canned goods (at inflated prices) at CUC-only stores.

CAFÉS AND BAKERIES

Cuba has few sidewalk cafés, and most of the prerevolutionary *cafeterías* (coffee stands) and tea shops (*casas de té* or *casas de infusiones*) have vanished. Still, cafés in the purist Parisian tradition have begun to sprout, notably in Havana.

Most towns have bakeries serving sugary confections and bread (served as buns or twisted rolls). The situation has improved following the arrival of French expertise to run the Pain de Paris bakery chain. Doña Neli bakeries and the Pan.Com snack restaurant chain, in most large cities, offer quality baked goods and sandwiches, respectively. In Havana, several private *dulcerías* offer baked goods of international quality.

WHAT TO EAT
Cuban Dishes

Cuban food is mostly peasant fare, usually lacking in sauces and spices. *Cerdo* (pork) and *pollo* (chicken) are the two main protein staples, usually served with *arroz y frijoles negros* (rice and black beans) and *plátanos* (fried banana or plantain). *Cerdo asado* (succulent roast pork), *moros y cristianos* (Moors and Christians—rice and black beans), and *arroz congrí* (rice with red beans) are the most popular dishes. *Congrí oriental* is rice and red beans cooked together. *Frijoles negros dormidos* are black beans cooked and allowed to stand till the next day. Another national dish is *ajiaco* (hotchpotch), a stew of meats and vegetables.

Cubans like *pollo frito* (fried chicken) and *pollo asado* (grilled chicken), but above all love roast pork, the most ubiquitous dish along with ham. Beef is virtually unknown outside the tourist restaurants, where filet mignon and prime rib are often on the menu, alongside *ropa vieja* (a braised shredded beef dish). Meat is used in snacks such as *empanadas de carne,* pies or flat pancakes enclosing meat morsels; and *picadillo,* a snack of spiced beef, onion, and tomato. Crumbled pork rinds are an ingredient in *fufu,* mixed with cooked plantain, a popular dish in Oriente. And ham and cheese find their way into fish and are stuffed inside steaks as *bistec uruguayo.*

Corvina (sea bass), *filet de emperador* (swordfish), and *pargo* (red snapper) are the most common fish, and lobster and shrimp are widely available.

Vegetables

Few Cubans understand the concept of vegetarianism. Since colonial days meat has been at the very center of Cuban cooking. Cubans disdain greens, preferring a sugar- and starch-heavy diet. Only a few restaurants serve vegetarian dishes, and servers in restaurants may tell you that a particular dish is vegetarian, even though it contains chunks of meat. Most beans are cooked in pork fat, and most *congrí* (rice with red beans) dishes contain meat. *"Protein vegetal"* translates as "soy product."

Ensaladas mixtas (mixed salads) usually consist of a plate of lettuce or *pepinos* (cucumbers) and tomatoes (often served green, yet sweet) with oil and vinaigrette dressing. *Palmito,* the succulent heart of palm, is also common. Often you'll receive canned vegetables. Sometimes you'll receive shredded *col* (cabbage), often alone.

Plátano (plantain), a relative of the banana, is a staple and almost always served fried, including as *tostones,* fried green plantains eaten as a snack. Yucca (manioc) is also popular: It resembles a stringy potato in look, taste, and texture and is prepared and served like a potato in any number of ways. *Boniato* (sweet potato) and *malanga* (taro), a bland root crop rich in starch, are used in many dishes.

Fruits

Until recently you could pass field after field of pineapples, melons, oranges, and grapefruits but not see any for sale along the road. Virtually the entire state fruit harvest goes to produce fruit juice. But these days private farmers can freely sell their produce, resulting in an explosion of roadside stalls and *mercado agropecuarios* selling well-known fruits such as papayas (which should be referred to as *fruta bomba;* in Cuba, "papaya" is a slang term for vagina), plus such lesser-known types as the furry *mamey colorado,* an oval, chocolate-brown fruit with a custardy texture and taste; the cylindrical, orange-colored *marañon,* or cashew-apple; the oval, coarse-skinned *zapote,* a sweet granular fruit most commonly found in Oriente; and the large, irregular-shaped *guanábana,* whose pulp is sweet and "soupy," with a hint of vanilla.

Coconuts are rare, except in sweets and around Baracoa, where coconut forms a base for the nation's only real regional cuisine.

Desserts

Cubans have a sweet tooth, as befits the land of sugar. They're especially fond of sickly sweet sponge cakes (*kek* or *ke*) covered in soft "shaving-foam" icing and sold for a few centavos at *panaderías* (bakeries). *Flan,* a caramel custard, is also popular (a variant is a delicious pudding called *natilla*), as is marmalade and cheese. Also try *tatinoff,* chocolate cake smothered with cream; *chu,* bite-size puff pastries stuffed with an almost-bitter cheesy meringue; and *churrizo,* deep-fried doughnut rings sold at every bakery and streetside stalls, where you can also buy *galletas,* sweet biscuits sold loose.

Coconut-based desserts include *coco quemado* (coconut pudding), *coco rallado y queso* (grated coconut with cheese in syrup), and the *cucurucho,* a regional specialty of Baracoa made of pressed coconut and sugar or honey.

Cubans are lovers of ice cream, sold at *heladerías* (ice-cream stores) and street stalls. Cubans use specific terms for different kinds of scoops. *Helado,* which means "ice cream," also means a single large scoop; two large scoops are called *jimagua;* several small scoops is an *ensalada;* and *sundae* is ice cream served with fruit.

DRINKING
Nonalcoholic Drinks

Water is not always reliable, and many water pipes are contaminated through decay. Stick to bottled mineral water, readily available carbonated (*con gas*) or non-carbonated (*sin gas*). Coca-Cola and Pepsi (or their Cuban-made equivalent, Tropicola), Fanta (or Cuban-made Najita), and other soft drinks are widely available. Malta is a popular nonalcoholic drink that resembles a dark English stout but tastes like root beer.

Far more thirst-quenching and energy-giving, however, are *guarapo,* fresh-squeezed sugarcane juice sold at roadside *guaraperías; prú,* a refreshing soft drink concocted from

Cuba's Cocktails

CUBA LIBRE

Who can resist the killer kick of a rum and Coke? Supposedly, the simple concoction was named more than a century ago after the war cry of the independence army: "Free Cuba!"

The Perfect Cuba Libre: Place ice cubes in a tall glass, then pour in 2 ounces of seven-year-old Havana Club *añejo* rum. Fill with Coca-Cola, topped off with 1 ounce of lemon juice. Decorate the rim with a slice of lemon. Serve with a stirrer.

DAIQUIRI

The daiquiri is named for a Cuban hamlet 16 miles east of Santiago de Cuba, near a copper mine where the mining firm's chief engineer, Jennings S. Cox, created the now world-famous cocktail that Hemingway immortalized in his novels. It is still associated with El Floridita bar and Hemingway's immortal words: *"Mi mojito en La Bodeguita, mi daiquirí en El Floridita."*

Shaved ice, which gave the drink its final touch of enchantment, was added by Constante Ribailagua, El Floridita's bartender, in the 1920s. The "Papa Special," which Constante made for Hemingway, contained a double dose of rum, no sugar, and a half ounce of grapefruit juice.

The Perfect Daiquiri: In an electric blender, pour half a tablespoon of sugar, the juice of half a lemon, and 1.5 ounces of white rum. Serve semi-frozen blended with ice (or on the rocks) in a tall martini glass with a maraschino cherry.

MOJITO

The *mojito* is considered the classic drink of Cuba.

The Perfect Mojito: With a stirrer, mix half a tablespoon of sugar and the juice of half a lime in an eight-inch highball glass. Add a sprig of yerba buena (mint), crushing the stalk to release the juice; two ice cubes; and 1.5 ounces of Havana Club Light Dry Cuban rum. Fill with soda water, add a small splash of angostura, then dress with a mint sprig. ¡Salud!

---

fruit, herbs, roots, and sugar; *batidos,* fruit shakes blended with milk and ice; and *refrescos naturales,* chilled fruit juices (avoid the sickly sweet water-based *refrescos*); and *limonadas* (lemonade).

No home visit is complete without being offered a *cafecito.* Cubans love their coffee espresso-style, thick and strong, served black in tiny cups and heavily sweetened. Much of Cuban domestic coffee has been adulterated—*café mezclado*—with other roasted products. Stick with export brands sold vacuum packed. *Café con leche* (coffee with milk) is served in tourist restaurants, usually at a 1:1 coffee-to-hot milk ratio. Don't confuse this with *café americano,* diluted Cuban coffee.

Alcoholic Drinks

Cuba makes several excellent German-style beers, usually served chilled, although only two are usually available: Bucanero, a heavy-bodied lager that comes light or dark; and lighter Cristal. Imported Heineken and Canadian and Mexican brands are sold in CUC stores and hotel bars. Clara is a rough-brewed beer for domestic consumption (typically one peso) sold at *cervecerías* (beer dispensaries) for the hoi polloi; often these are roadside dispensers on wheels where you can buy beer in paper cups or bottles sawed in half for a few centavos.

About one dozen Cuban rum distilleries produce some 60 brands of rum. They vary widely—the worst can taste like paint thinner. Cuban rums resemble Bacardi rums, not surprisingly, as the company was based in Santiago de Cuba. Each brand generally has three types of rum: clear "white rum," labeled *carta blanca,* which is aged three years (about CUC5 a 0.75-liter bottle); the more assertive "golden rum," labeled *dorado* or *carta oro,* aged five years (about CUC6); and *añejo,* aged seven years or longer (CUC10 or more). The best in all categories are Havana Club's rums, topped only by Matusalem Añejo Superior. A few limited-production rums, such as the 50-year-old Havana Club Máximo (from CUC1,300 per bottle) and Ron Santiago 500 Aniversario (CUC3,000) exceed the harmony and finesse of fine cognacs.

Golden and aged rums are best enjoyed straight. White rum is ideal for cocktails such as a piña colada (rum, pineapple juice, coconut cream, and crushed ice) and, most notably, the daiquiri and the *mojito*—favorites of Ernest Hemingway, who helped launch both drinks to world fame.

Impecunious Cubans drink *tragos* (shots) of *aguardiente*—cheap, overproof white rum.

Cuba's rum manufacturers also make liqueurs, including from coffee, crème de menthe, cocoa, guava, lemon, pineapple, and other fruits. Certain regions are known for unique liqueurs, such as *guayabita*, a drink made from rum and guava exclusive to Pinar del Río.

Imported South American, French, and Californian wines (*vinos*) are widely available. Avoid the local and truly terrible Soroa brand, made of unsophisticated Italian wine blended with local grapes from Soroa, Pinar del Río.

Accommodations

RESERVATIONS

Cuba is in the midst of a tourism boom and accommodations are at a premium. It's wise to prebook rooms for at least your first few nights.

Christmas and New Year's are particularly busy, as are major festivals. And these days, many all-inclusive beach hotels offer deep discounts to Cubans in summer low season. Book well ahead; call direct, send an email, or have a tour operator abroad make your reservation (the latter are sometimes cheaper thanks to wholesalers' discounts). Insist on written confirmation and take copies with you, as Cuban hotels are notorious for not honoring reservations. Pay in advance for all nights you intend to stay; otherwise you might be asked to check out to make room for someone else.

Charter package tours with airfare and hotel included may offer the cheapest rates, although the less notable hotels are often used.

If you are a journalist or in a similar sensitive occupation, expect your assigned hotel room to be bugged. (Don't believe me? Read *The Double Life of Fidel Castro*, by Juan Reinaldo Sánchez.)

Private room rentals, *casas particulares,* offer by far the best bargains and permit you to experience *real* Cuban life alongside the Cubans themselves.

PRICES

The Cuban government has a monopoly on hotels, and it jacks up and reduces prices nationwide according to market trends; since 2015 rates in Havana have doubled to outrageous levels. Rates also vary for low (May-June and Sept.-Nov.) and high season (Dec.-Apr. and July-Aug.). Cuba has no room tax or service charge.

Often it's cheaper to pay as you go rather than prepaying. The same goes for meals. A "modified American plan" (MAP; room rate that includes breakfast and dinner) can be a bargain at beach resorts, where ordering meals individually can be a lot more expensive. In Havana, you're better off with a European plan (EP; room with breakfast only). If you're not intent on exploring beyond your resort, consider an all-inclusive property, where the cost of all meals, drinks, and activities is included in the room rate.

TYPES OF ACCOMMODATION
Camping

Cuba is not geared for camping. Tent sites don't exist and you need permission to camp "wild." While urbanites are savvy about the rules, rural folks may not be; you potentially expose farmers to ruinous fines merely for having you on their land. The system assumes guilt unless the farmer can prove that he or she has not, or was not going to, accept money.

Cuba has dozens of *campismos,* simple holiday camps with basic cabins and facilities operated by **Campismo Popular** (Calle 13 #857, e/ 4 y 6, Vedado, Havana, tel. 07/835-2502, www.campismopopular.cu), which has booking offices islandwide. Often camps are closed Monday-Thursday and in the off-season; in summer they're often full with Cubans.

Hotels

In 2016, Cuba claimed more than 65,000 hotel rooms (with a goal of 130,000 by 2030), of which 60 percent were declared to be four- or five-star. All hotels in Cuba are owned by four state-run entities that ostensibly compete for business, some in cooperative management agreements with foreign (mostly Spanish) hotel groups. However, hotels frequently juggle between the following entities:

- **Cubanacán** (www.cubanacan.cu) has more than 50 hotels. Its Hoteles Brisas and Hoteles Club Amigo are (supposedly) four-star and three-star all-inclusive beach resorts. Its Hoteles Horizontes are urban hotels (usually lackluster two- or three-star ones). Hoteles E are small boutique hotels. It also has modest Hoteles Cubanacán.

- **Gaviota** (www.gaviota-grupo.com), a branch of the military, owns eco-lodges, deluxe city hotels, and all-inclusive beach resorts.

- **Gran Caribe** (www.gran-caribe.cu) once managed deluxe hotels; today it has some three dozen hotels ranging from two to five stars.

- **Islazul** (www.islazul.cu) operates inexpensive hotels catering primarily to Cubans (who pay in pesos). Some of its properties are splendid bargains.

Habaguanex, the commercial division of the Oficina del Historiador de la Habana, has controlled some 20 boutique hotels in Habana Vieja. It was being disbanded at press time and Gaviota is expected to assume responsibility for the properties.

The ratings Cuba gives its hotels are far too generous; most fall one or two categories below their international equivalents. Most towns have one or two historic hotels around the central park and a concrete Soviet-era hotel on the outskirts. Hotels built in recent years are constructed to international standards, although even the best suffer from poor design, shoddy construction, and (often) poor management. The top-line hotels run by foreign management groups are usually up to international par.

Many hotels use both 220-volt and 110-volt outlets (usually marked), often in the same room. Check before plugging in any electrical appliances, or you could blow a fuse. Note that "minibars" in most hotel guest rooms are actually small (and empty) refrigerators.

Upon registering, you'll be issued a *tarjeta de huésped* (guest card) at each hotel, identifying you as a hotel guest. Depending on your hotel, the card may have to be presented when ordering and signing for meals and drinks, changing money, and often when entering the elevator to your room.

Many hotels open their swimming pools to Cuban locals; most all-inclusive hotels sell day passes to nonguests wishing to use the facilities.

ALL-INCLUSIVE RESORTS

Most beach resorts are run as all-inclusives: cash-free, self-contained properties where your room rate theoretically includes all meals and beverages, entertainment, and water sports at no additional fee. Standards vary. Properties managed by international name-brand hotel chains are preferred to the purely Cuban-run affairs.

APARTHOTELS AND *PROTOCOLOS*

Aparthotels offer rooms with kitchens or kitchenettes. Most are characterless. Many are linked to regular hotels, giving you access to broader facilities.

Cubanacán and Gran Caribe handle reservations for *protocolos*—special houses reserved for foreign dignitaries. Most are in mansions in the Cubanacán and Siboney regions of Havana (they include Frank Sinatra's former home), but most other towns have at least one.

NATURE LODGES

About half a dozen quasi-"ecotourism" properties can be found in mountain areas or close to nature reserves. Cuba has no eco-lodges to international standards. The most prominent is Hotel Moka (Pinar del Río), though it's an eco-lodge only in name; others include Villa Pinares de Mayarí (Holguín) and Villa El Saltón (Santiago de Cuba).

SECURITY

All tourist hotel lobbies have security staff, posted following the spate of bombs planted in Havana's hotels in 1997 by Cuban American terrorists. They serve to prevent a repeat performance, but also do double duty to keep out unsavory characters and unregistered Cubans slipping upstairs with foreign guests.

Theft is an issue in hotels. If your hotel has a safe deposit box, use it. Before accepting a room, ensure that the door is secure and that someone can't climb in through the window. *Always* lock your door. Keep your suitcase locked when you're not in your room, as maids frequently make off with clothing and other items.

Casas Particulares

My recommendation is to stay wherever possible in a *casa particular* (private house)—a room in a family home, granting you a chance to gain a perspective on Cuban life. This can be anything from a single room with a live-in family to a self-sufficient apartment. Increasingly, foreign money is being invested to turn larger properties into boutique hotels, such that the term *casa particular* is morphing to mean any privately owned property—from a single room to a 10-bedroom "hotel."

The going room rate in Havana is CUC25-40 (but up to CUC1,000 for entire houses), and CUC15-35 outside Havana, but boutique properties may charge CUC100-300 per room.

Legally licensed houses post a blue Arrendador Divisa sign, like an inverted anchor, on the front door (those with a red sign are licensed to rent only to Cubans, in pesos). Avoid illegal, unlicensed *casas particulares*.

Check to see if hot water is available 24 hours, or only at specific times. Avoid rooms facing streets, although even rooms tucked at the backs of buildings can hold an unpleasant surprise in predawn hours, when all manner of noises can intrude on your slumber.

Reservations are recommended during high season (since 2012, state tourism agencies are allowed to make reservations for *casas particulares*). If you arrive in a town without a reservation, owners of *casas particulares* are happy to call around on your behalf. Touts do a brisk business trying to steer travelers to specific *casas,* and are not above telling independent travelers lies, such as that a particular house you might be seeking has closed. The tout's commission will be added to your rent. Many touts pose as hitchhikers on roads into major cities; others chase you around by bicycle.

Spell out all the prices involved before settling on a place to stay. Remember, most homeowners have cut their rates to the bare bones while facing punitive taxes. Most serve meals: breakfasts usually cost CUC3-5, dinners typically cost CUC5-10. Many homes have shower units with electric heater elements, which you switch on for the duration of your shower. Beware: It's easy to give yourself a shock.

Your host must record your passport details, to be presented to the Ministry of the

Interior within 24 hours (hence, MININT is always abreast of every foreigner's whereabouts). Honor regulations and avoid attracting undue attention to your host's home, as the legal repercussions of even the hint of an infraction can be serious.

Many *casa particular* owners maintain their own websites, but you can also book online via AirBnB (www.airbnb.com) and similar booking agencies.

Unauthorized Accommodations

Tourists must receive written permission from immigration authorities to stay anywhere other than a hotel or licensed *casa particular*. If you wish to stay with Cuban friends, you must go to an immigration office within 24 hours to convert from a tourist visa to an A2 visa (CUC25). You must be accompanied by the person you wish to stay with. If an unregistered foreigner is found staying in a house (or camping), the Cuban host must prove that the foreigner is not a paying guest—an almost impossible situation. Thus, the Cuban is automatically found guilty of

renting illegally. The regulations are strictly enforced, and fines are ruinous.

Cuban Guests

Since 2008, Cubans have been allowed to room in hotels. The new rulings also permit foreigners and Cubans to share a hotel room. Foreigners staying in *casas particulares* are also permitted to share their room with Cubans of either gender; in all cases, your host must record your guest's *cédula* (ID) details for presentation to MININT within 24 hours. MININT runs the Cuban guest's name through a computer database; if the name of a woman appears three times with a different man, she is arrested as a "prostitute" and gets a mandatory jail term; no equivalent exists for Cuban male "prostitutes."

The rules keep changing. A foreigner is permitted to host only one Cuban partner during his or her stay in a hotel or *casa particular*. Woe betide any *casa particular* owner whose guest is discovered with an unrecorded Cuban in his or her room, let alone underage. In such cases, the owner of the *casa particular* can lose his or her license and receive a jail term.

Health and Safety

BEFORE YOU GO

Dental and medical checkups are advisable before departing home. Take along any medications; keep prescription drugs in their original bottles to avoid suspicion at customs. I had my spectacles stolen in Cuba—a reminder to take a spare pair (or at least a prescription for eyewear). If you suffer from a debilitating health problem, wear a medical alert bracelet.

A basic health kit should include alcohol swabs and medicinal alcohol, antiseptic cream, Band-Aids, aspirin, diarrhea medication, sunburn remedy, antifungal foot powder, antihistamine, surgical tape, bandages and gauze, and scissors. Most important? A bottle of hand sanitizer: Use it frequently!

Information on health concerns can

be answered in advance of travel by the **Department of State Citizens Emergency Center** (tel. 888/407-4747 or 202/501-4444 from overseas, http://travel.state.gov), the **Centers for Disease Control and Prevention** (tel. 800/232-4636, www.cdc.gov), and the **International Association for Medical Assistance to Travellers** (tel. 716/754-4883, www.iamat.org), with offices worldwide.

Travel and Health Insurance

Travel insurance is recommended. Travel agencies can sell you travelers' health, baggage, and trip cancellation insurance. Check to see if policies cover expenses in Cuba, which now requires that all arriving travelers demonstrate that they have health insurance. If you can't show proof of insurance, you will be required to purchase an insurance package from **Asistur** (Prado #212, e/ Trocadero y Colón, Habana Vieja, tel. 07/866-4499, 07/866-8527, or 5280-3563 and 5805-6292, www.asistur.cu, Mon.-Fri. 8:30am-5pm), which represents about 160 insurance companies in 40 countries. It has offices at all international airports. Rates vary from CUC3 daily (for CUC7,000 medical and CUC15,000 evacuation coverage) to CUC4.50 daily (CUC25,000 medical and CUC15,000 evacuation).

Vaccinations

No vaccinations are required to enter Cuba unless you are arriving from areas of cholera and yellow fever infection. Epidemic diseases have mostly been eradicated throughout the country. However, viral meningitis and dengue fever occasionally break out. Consult your physician for recommended vaccinations. Consider vaccinations against tetanus and infectious hepatitis.

MEDICAL SERVICES

Sanitary standards in Cuba are a mixed bag. As long as you take appropriate precautions and use common sense, you're not likely to incur a serious illness or disease. Cuba's vaunted public health system faces severe shortages of medicines and equipment; with few exceptions, facilities and standards are not up to those of North America or northern Europe. In many local hospitals, hygiene conditions are appalling, facilities rudimentary, and medical know-how often lacking. Local pharmacies are mostly well stocked. *Turnos regulares* pharmacies are open 8am-5pm; *turnos permanentes* are open 24 hours.

Facilities for Foreigners

Foreigners receive special treatment through **Servios Médicos Cubanos** (tel. 07/204-4811, www.servimedcuba.com), a division of Cubanacán that promotes health tourism,

from "stress breaks" to advanced treatments such as eye, open-heart, and plastic surgery.

Most major cities and resort destinations have 24-hour international clinics (*clínicas internacionales*) staffed by English-speaking doctors and nurses, plus foreigners-only international pharmacies (*farmacias internacionales*) stocked with Western pharmaceuticals. Larger tourist hotels also have nurses on duty and doctors on call, and some have pharmacies. **Óptica Miramar** (7ma Av., e/ 24 y 26, Miramar, tel. 07/204-2269, direccion@opticam.cha.cyt.cu) provides optician services and sells contact lenses and eyeglasses. It has outlets nationwide.

Pay in CUC or by credit card (unless issued by a U.S. bank). Get a receipt with which to make an insurance claim once you return home. You can call your insurance company in advance of medical treatment. If approved, the company can pay direct to Asistur (Prado #208, Havana, tel. 07/866-4499, or 5280-3563 and 5805-6292, www.asistur.cu), which then pays the Cuban clinic. However, U.S. citizens should note that even if visiting Cuba legally, payment for "nonemergency medical services" is prohibited.

Medical Evacuation

Uncle Sam has deemed that even U.S. emergency evacuation services cannot fly to Cuba to evacuate U.S. citizens without a license from the Treasury Department. The rules keep changing, so it's worth checking the latest situation with such companies as **Traveler's Emergency Network** (tel. 800/275-4836, www.tenweb.com), **International SOS Assistance** (tel. 215/942-8226, www.internationalsos.com), and **MedJet Assist** (tel. 800/527-7478, www.medjetassist.com), which provide worldwide ground and air evacuation.

HEALTH PROBLEMS

Cuba is a tropical country and the health hazards are many: filthy public fixtures, garbage rotting in the streets, polluted watercourses, broken sewer pipes, holes in sidewalks, dilapidated buildings, and so on. In addition, molds, fungus, and bacteria thrive. The slightest scratch can fester quickly. Treat promptly with antiseptic and keep any wounds clean.

Intestinal Problems

Cuba's tap water is questionable. Drink bottled water, which is widely available. Don't brush your teeth using suspect water. Milk is pasteurized, and dairy products in Cuba are usually safe.

Diarrhea: The change in diet may briefly cause diarrhea or constipation. Most cases of diarrhea are caused by microbial bowel infections resulting from contaminated food. Don't eat uncooked fish or shellfish, uncooked vegetables, unwashed salads, or unpeeled fruit. Diarrhea is usually temporary, and many doctors recommend letting it run its course. If that's not preferable, medicate with Lomotil or similar antidiarrheal product. Drink lots of liquids. Avoid alcohol and milk. If conditions don't improve after three days, seek medical help.

Dysentery: Diarrhea accompanied by severe abdominal pain, blood in your stool, and fever requires immediate medical diagnosis. Tetracycline or ampicillin is normally used to cure bacillary dysentery. More complex treatment is required for amoebic dysentery.

Cholera: Symptoms of this potential killer include extreme diarrhea resulting in dehydration and drowsiness. Urgent medical care and quarantine are required. Cholera can be caused by infected water, seafood, and vegetables. Follow good hygiene at all times. In 2012 a cholera outbreak (the first since the Revolution) swept eastern Cuba, causing at least three deaths. It was soon eradicated.

Other Infections: Giardiasis, acquired from infected water, causes diarrhea, bloating, persistent indigestion, and weight loss. Intestinal worms can be contracted by walking barefoot on infested beaches, grass, or ground. Hepatitis A can be contracted through unhygienic foods or contaminated water (salads and unpeeled fruits are major culprits). The main symptoms are stomach pains, loss of appetite, yellowing skin and eyes, and extreme tiredness. The much rarer hepatitis B is usually contracted through unclean needles, blood transfusions, or unprotected sex.

Sunburn and Skin Problems

The tropical sun can burn even through light clothing or shade. Use a suncream or sunblock of at least SPF 15. Bring sunscreen; it's not readily available beyond beach resorts in Cuba. Wear a wide-brimmed hat.

Sun glare can cause conjunctivitis; wear sunglasses. Prickly heat is an itchy rash, normally caused by clothing that is too tight or in need of washing; this and athlete's foot (a fungal infection) are best treated by airing the skin and washing your clothes. Ringworm, another fungal infection, shows up as a ring, most commonly on the scalp and groin; it's treated with over-the-counter ointments.

Dehydration and Heat Problems

The tropical humidity and heat can sap your body fluids like blotting paper. Leg cramps, exhaustion, dizziness, and headaches are signs of dehydration. Drink lots of water. Avoid alcohol.

Excessive exposure to too much heat can cause potentially fatal heat stroke. Excessive sweating, extreme headaches, and disorientation leading to possible convulsions and delirium are symptoms. Emergency medical care is essential.

The common cold (*gripe,* pronounced GREE-pay, or *catarro cubano*) is a pandemic among Cubans.

Critters

Snakes (*culebras*) are common in Cuba; they're nonvenomous. Scorpions (*alacranes*) also exist; their venom can cause nausea and fever but is not usually serious. In the wild, watch where you're treading or putting your hands. Crocodiles are a serious threat in swampy coastal areas and estuaries; don't swim in rivers! Most areas inhabited by crocodiles, such as the Zapata swamps, are off-limits to foreigners without guides.

Mosquitoes abound. Repellent sprays and lotions are a must by day for many areas. Citronella candles, electric fans, and mosquito coils (*espirales,* which are rarely sold in Cuba) help keep mosquitoes at bay at night. Bites can easily become infected in the tropics; avoid scratching! Treat with antiseptics or antibiotics. Antihistamines and hydrocortisone can help relieve itching.

Malaria isn't present in Cuba. However, mosquitoes *do* transmit **dengue fever,** which *is* present. Its symptoms are similar to those for malaria, with severe headaches and high fever and, unlike malaria, additional severe pain in the joints, for which it is sometimes called "breaking bones disease." It is not recurring. There is no cure; dengue fever must run its course. The illness can be fatal (death usually results from internal hemorrhaging).

Chiggers (*coloradillas*) inhabit tall grasslands. Their bites itch like hell. Nail polish apparently works (over the bites, not on the nails) by suffocating the beasts.

Tiny, irritating *jejenes* (known worldwide as "no-see-ums"), sand flies about the size of a pinpoint, inhabit beaches and marshy coastal areas. This nuisance is active only around dawn and dusk, when you should avoid the beach. They are not fazed by bug repellent, but Avon's Skin-So-Soft supposedly works.

Jellyfish (*agua mala*) are common along the Atlantic shore, especially in winter and spring. They can give a painful, even dangerous, welt that leaves a permanent scar. Dousing in vinegar can help neutralize the stingers, while calamine and antihistamines should be used to soothe the pain. In Caribbean waters, a microscopic mollusk that locals call *caribe* can induce all manner of illnesses, from diarrhea and severe fever to itching. It, too, is more frequent in winter.

Sea urchins (*erizos*) are common beneath the inshore waterline and around coral reefs. These softball-size creatures are surrounded by long spines that will pierce your skin and break off if you touch or step on them. This is excruciatingly painful. You'll have to extract the spines.

Rabies, though rare in Cuba, can be contracted through the bite of an infected animal. It's always fatal unless treated.

Sexually Transmitted Diseases

Cubans are promiscuous, and sexually transmitted diseases are common, although the risk of contracting AIDS in Cuba is extremely low (the rate of infection is among the world's lowest). Use condoms (*preservativos*), widely available in Cuba.

SAFETY
Crime and Hustling

All the negative media hype sponsored by Washington has left many people with a false impression that Cuba is unsafe. Far from it. In rural areas many residents still say they can hardly remember the last time a crime was committed. Sexual assault is rare. However, the material hardships of Cubans combined with the influx of wealthy tourists *has* fostered crime. Pickpockets (*carteristas*) and purse slashers work the streets and buses. Chambermaids pilfer items from guests' luggage. Theft from luggage occurs at the airport, where bogus tour operators and taxi drivers also prey on tourists (the British embassy also reports attempted robberies from vehicles on the Havana airport road). Muggings have escalated. Car-related crime is on the increase, notably by bogus hitchhikers and staged punctures (if you get a puncture, drive several kilometers, preferably to a town, before stopping).

There have even been several unreported murders of tourists in recent years. Most, but not all, have involved sexual relations between foreigners and Cubans. *Never* go to a *casa clandestina* (an illegal room rental, usually rented by the hour), and *always* check a Cuban partner's *carnet* (ID) and leave a copy with someone you trust if possible.

Most crime is opportunistic snatch-and-grab. Caution is required when walking city

Cuba's War on AIDS

Cuba has one of the world's most aggressive and successful campaigns against AIDS. The World Health Organization (WHO) and the Pan-American Health Organization have praised as exemplary Cuba's AIDS surveillance system and prevention program. The program has stemmed an epidemic that rages only 50 miles away in Haiti and has kept the spread of the disease to a level that no other country in the Americas can equal. According to UNAIDS (www.unaids.org), as of 2015 fewer than 500 people had died of AIDS in Cuba, which has an adult HIV prevalence rate of 0.3 percent, the lowest in the Americas and on a par with Finland and Singapore. Although in Cuba in the early years it was predominantly a heterosexual disease, today 81 percent of HIV sufferers are gay men.

Cuba's unique response to the worldwide epidemic that began in the early 1980s was to initiate mass testing of the population and a "mandatory quarantine" of everyone testing positive. Twelve AIDS sanatoriums were developed throughout the island. By 1994, when the policies of mandatory testing and confinement were ended, about 98 percent of the adult population had been tested. Voluntary testing continues. An outpatient program was implemented so that sufferers could continue to lead a normal life; residents live in small houses or apartments, alone or as couples.

Cuba's biogenetic engineering industry has been at the forefront of research for an AIDS vaccine and cure. Plus, the government distributes more than 100 million free condoms a year.

streets (especially at night) and in crowded places. If you sense yourself being squeezed or jostled, elbow your way out of there immediately.

The **U.S. State Department** (tel. 888/407-4747, from overseas tel. 202/501-4444, www.travel.state.gov) and **British Foreign and Commonwealth Office** (tel. 020/7008-1500, from overseas tel. 020/7008-0210, www.fco.gov.uk) publish travel advisories.

HUSTLING AND SCAMS

Your biggest problem will probably be hustling by *jineteros* (street hustlers), plus scams pulled by restaurants, hotels, and other tourist entities. And the *consumo mínimo* charge in many bars and nightclubs is an invitation to fleece you. Be prepared for charges for things you didn't consume or which didn't materialize, and for higher charges than you were quoted. Insist on an itemized bill at restaurants, add it up diligently, and count your change. *Always* ask for a receipt at Cadeca exchange bureaus; staff regularly scam tourists.

Car rental companies and tour agencies (and their employees) are adept at scams. You pay for a deluxe hotel, say, on a package to Cayo Largo, but are told when you arrive

that the hotel in question doesn't honor such packages. You're then fobbed off to the cheapest hotel. When you return to Havana to request a refund, the documents relating to your trip can't be found. Rarely is there a manager available, and usually they say there's nothing that can be done. If the scam amounts to outright theft, take the staffer's name and threaten to report him or her to the head office and police. Don't pay cash in such conditions. Pay with a credit card and challenge the bill. Or simply refuse to pay. Once it has your money, the Cuban government is not about to give refunds under virtually any condition.

COMMONSENSE PRECAUTIONS

Make photocopies of all important documents. Carry the photocopies with you, and leave the originals along with your other valuables in the hotel safe. Prepare an "emergency kit" to tide you over if your wallet gets stolen.

Never carry more cash than you need for the day. Never carry your wallet in your back pocket; wear a secure money belt. Spread your money around your person. Thread fanny pack straps through the belt loops of your pants, and never wear your purse or camera loosely slung over your shoulder. Wear an

Jineterismo

Jineteros (male hustlers) and *jineteras* (females who trade sex for money) are a persistent presence in tourist zones, where they pester foreigners like flies around fish.

Jineteros try to sell you cigars, tout places to stay or eat, or even suggest a good time with their sisters. In provincial cities, touts on bicycles descend on tourists at traffic lights and will trail you through town, sometimes merely in the hope that you'll give them money to go away. If you're a female tourist, expect to be hustled by Cuban males ingratiating themselves as potential boyfriends.

The best defense is to completely ignore them. Don't say a word. Don't look them in the eye. Don't even acknowledge their presence. Just keep walking.

inexpensive watch. Don't flaunt jewelry. Be wary when cashing money at a bank. Do *not* deal with *jineteros*. Insist that credit card imprints are made in your presence. And make sure any imprints incorrectly completed are torn up; destroy the carbons yourself.

Never leave items unattended. Always keep an eye on your luggage on public transportation. Don't carry more luggage than you can adequately manage. And have a lock for each luggage item. Always keep purses fully zipped and luggage locked, even in your hotel room. Don't leave *anything* within reach of an open window or in your car, which should always be parked in a secure area overnight.

Drugs

Few countries are so drug-free. You may occasionally come across homegrown marijuana, but serious drug use is unknown in Cuba. Nonetheless, drug use has increased in recent years with the blossoming of tourism and as Colombian and Jamaican drug lords take advantage of Cuba's remote, scattered cays to make transshipments en route to the United States. Draconian laws are strictly enforced and foreigners receive no special favors. Sentences in excess of 20 years are the norm.

Traffic and Pedestrians

Be wary when crossing streets. Stand well away from the curb—especially on corners, where buses often mount the sidewalk. *Watch your step!* Sidewalks are full of gaping potholes and tilted curbstones. And drive with

extreme caution. Driving in Cuba presents unique dangers, from treacherous potholes and wayward bicyclists to cattle and ox-drawn carts wandering across four-lane freeways. Use extra caution when passing tractors and trucks, which without warning tend to make sweeping turns across the road.

Racial Discrimination

Despite all the hype about Cuba being a color-blind society, racial discrimination still exists (although it pales in comparison to the U.S.). Nonwhite tourists can expect to be mistaken for Cubans and hassled on the streets by police requesting ID. Likewise, tourists of non-European descent are more likely to be stopped at the entrances to hotel lobbies and other tourist venues. Mixed-race couples can expect to draw unwanted attention from the police.

Officialdom

Cuba has an insufferable bureaucracy, and working with government entities can be a perplexing and frustrating endeavor. Very few people have the power to say "Yes," but everyone can say "No!" Finding the person who can say "Yes" is the key. Logic and ranting get you nowhere. Charm, *piropos* (witty compliments), or a gift of chocolate works better.

The Policía Revolucionario Nacional (National Revolutionary Police, or PNR) is a branch of the Ministry of the Interior (MININT) and its major task is to enforce revolutionary purity. Uniformed police officers also perform the same functions as in

Bite Your Tongue!

Cubans are a paranoid people, never sure who might be a *chivato,* a finger pointer for the CDR or MININT, the much-loathed Ministry of the Interior. In this regard, Cuba doesn't seem to have changed much since the 1930s, when Hemingway told Arnold Samuelson, "Don't trust anybody. That fellow might have been a government spy trying to get you in bad. You can never tell who they are."

Since Raúl took over from Fidel, things have eased. These days, Cubans aren't so frightened to voice their frustrations verbally on the street. Still, no one in his or her right mind would dare to *overly* criticize the government or the Castros in public. Sometimes a diatribe against the government (usually offered in hushed tones) will end in midstream as the speaker taps his two forefingers on his opposite shoulder, signifying the presence of a member of State Security. Hence, Cubans have developed a cryptic, elliptical way of talking where nuance and meaning are hidden from casual tourists.

Even foreigners are not above surreptitious surveillance by the General Directorate for State Security (G2). Foreign journalists may even be assigned specific hotel rooms that may be bugged. The Cuban government looks with suspicion on U.S. travelers entering on religious or humanitarian licenses, and U.S. "people-to-people" programs are handled exclusively by Celimar, a division of Havanatur that is said to report to MININT and is heavily laden with ex-MININT staffers.

Tourists are free to roam wherever they wish without hindrance or a need to look over their shoulders, but nay-saying the Revolution in public can swiftly land you in trouble.

Western countries, although with far less professionalism than you may be used to in the United States or Europe. Cuban police officers are trained to be paranoid about foreigners. Never attempt to photograph police or military without their permission.

If a police officer wants to search you, insist on it being done in front of a neutral witness—*"solamente con testigos."* Do *not* allow an official to confiscate your passport. Tell as little as circumspection dictates—unlike priests, policemen rarely offer absolution for confessions. If a police officer asks for money, get his name and badge number and file a complaint with the Ministry of Foreign Relations.

If Trouble Strikes

In emergencies, call:

- 104 for an ambulance
- 105 for fire
- 106 for police

If things turn dire, contact **Asistur** (Prado #212, e/ Trocadero y Colón, Habana Vieja, tel. 07/866-4499, 07/866-8527, 5280-3563, or 5805-6292, www.asistur.cu, Mon.-Fri.

8:30am-5pm), which assists tourists in trouble. It has a 24-hour "alarm center," plus outlets in Camagüey, Ciego de Ávila, Cienfuegos, Guardalavaca, Santiago de Cuba, and Varadero. You should also contact your embassy or consulate. It can't get you out of jail, but it can help locate a lawyer or arrange for funds (U.S. citizens in Cuba can request help in an emergency).

If you're robbed, immediately file a police report with the **Policía Revolucionaria Nacional** (PNR, in Havana, Calle Picota, e/ Leonor Pérez y San Isidro, tel. 07/867-0496 or 07/862-0116). You'll receive a statement (*denuncia*) for insurance purposes. Proceedings can take hours (readers report Kafkaesque experiences). If you're involved in a car accident, call the *tránsitos* (transit police, tel. 07/862-0116 in Havana, 106 outside Havana).

If you're charged with a crime, request that a representative of your embassy be present, and that any deposition be made in front of an independent witness (*testigo*).

There are reports of Cuban police jailing victims of passport theft while the crime and victim are investigated. Report to your embassy *before* reporting ID theft to the police.

HELP FOR U.S. CITIZENS

Travelers report that the **U.S. Embassy** (Calzada, e/ L y M, Vedado, tel. 07/839-4100, emergency/after-hours tel. 07/839-4100 +1, https://cu.usembassy.gov, Mon.-Fri. 8am-4:30pm) has a good record in helping U.S. citizens in need in Cuba. The U.S. Department of State has a **Hotline for American Travelers** (tel. 202/647-5225), and you can call the **Overseas Citizen Service** (tel. 888/407-4747, from overseas tel. 202/501-4444 for after-hours emergencies, http://travel.state.gov, Mon.-Fri. 8am-8pm) if things go awry. If arrested, U.S. citizens should ask Cuban authorities to notify the U.S. Embassy. A U.S. consular officer will then try to arrange regular visits. Cuba does not recognize dual citizenship for Cuban citizens who are also U.S. citizens; Cuban-born citizens are denied representation through the U.S. Embassy.

LEGAL ASSISTANCE

Consultoría Jurídica Internacional (CJI, International Judicial Consultative Bureau, Calle 16 #314, e/ 3ra y 5ta, Miramar, tel. 07/204-2490, www.cji.co.cu) provides legal advice and services. It can assist travelers, including those who lose their passports or have them stolen.

Travel Tips

WHAT TO PACK

Dress for a tropical climate. Pack a **warm sweater** and a **windbreaker** for winter visits. In summer, the weather is hot and humid; you'll want **light, loose-fitting shirts and shorts.** Ideally, everything should be drip-dry, wash-and-wear. Cubans dress informally, though neatly, for all occasions.

A comfortable, well-fitting pair of **sneakers** will work for most occasions. Pack a pair of **dress shoes** for your evening ensemble. Take all the **toiletries** you think you'll need, including toilet paper and face cloth. Medicines are rarely available except in Havana and other key tourist venues; come prepared with aspirin and other essentials. Hand sanitizer is a must—use it regularly!

International credit cards are accepted throughout Cuba, although the system is dysfunctional and unreliable. At press time, most U.S. citizens need to operate on a **cash-only** basis.

MONEY
Currency

Cuba has two currencies. At press time, the government's announced intention to unify the currencies was far from fruition.

CONVERTIBLE PESOS

All prices in this book are quoted in Cuban convertible pesos (*pesos convertibles*), denominated by "CUC" (pronounced "say-ooh-say" and colloquially called *kooks*) and often, within Cuba, by "$." Foreigners must exchange their foreign currency for convertible pesos (at press time the CUC is at parity with the U.S. dollar), issued in the following denominations: 1-, 3-, 5-, 10-, 20-, 50-, and 100-peso notes, along with 1-, 5-, 10-, 25-, and 50-centavo coins plus CUC1 and CUC5 coins. Euros are acceptable tender in Varadero, Cayo Coco, and Havana.

Always carry a wad of small bills; change for larger bills is often hard to come by.

CUBAN PESOS

The Cuban currency (*moneda nacional*), in which state salaries are paid, is the peso, which is worth about US$0.05 (the exchange rate at press time was 25 pesos to the dollar). It is also designated "$" and should not be confused with the CUC or US$ (to make matters worse, the dollar is sometimes called the peso). The peso is divided into 100 centavos.

There is very little that you will need pesos for. Exceptions are if you want to travel on local buses or buy ice cream at Coppelia.

EXCHANGING CURRENCY

Foreign currency can be changed for CUC at tourist hotels, banks, and official *burós de cambios* (exchange bureaus) operated by **Cadeca** (tel. 07/855-5701), which has outlets throughout Cuba; a 3 percent commission is charged for all exchanges. They can also change CUC or foreign currency for *moneda nacional*. Cadeca charges a 3 percent commission plus an additional 10 percent commission for exchanging U.S. dollars. To avoid the surcharge, U.S. visitors should bring Canadian dollars or euros. Check the current exchange rates at the **Banco Central de Cuba** website (www.bc.gob.cu). Always ask for a receipt before changing your money, as Cadeca clerks often shortchange tourists.

Jineteros may offer to change currency on the streets. Many tourists are ripped off, and muggings have been reported. One scam is for *jineteros* to tell you that the banks are closed and that they can help. *Never* change money on the street. It's also illegal; tourists who have been scammed and have reported it to the police have been fined.

Banks

All banks in Cuba are state entities. No foreign banks are present. The most important of the banks catering to foreigners is the **Banco Financiero Internacional,** which offers a full range of services. Branches nationwide are open Monday-Saturday 8am-3pm (but 8am-noon only on the last working day of each month). **Banco de Crédito y Comercio** (Bandec) is the main commercial bank, with outlets islandwide (most are open weekdays 8:30am-3pm). **Banco Popular** and **Banco Metropolitano** also provide foreign transaction services.

Cuban banks have been known to pass off counterfeit CUC50 and CUC100 bills to *foreigners. When receiving such bills, always check for watermarks.*

Credit Cards and ATMs

Most hotels, larger restaurants, and major shops accept credit cards, as long as they are not issued or processed by U.S. banks (other nationalities should check that their cards can be used; for example, about 20 percent of British-issued cards are outsourced to U.S. companies). Credit card transactions are charged 11 percent commission (comprising an 8 percent levy on currency exchange, plus a 3 percent conversion fee).

Automated teller machines (ATMs) at major banks dispense CUC to Cubans with cash cards. Many ATMs are linked to international systems such as Cirrus (non-U.S. Visa-designated cards work, but not MasterCard). Use them only during bank hours, as they often eat your card. You can use your non-U.S. credit card to obtain a cash advance up to CUC500 (CUC100 minimum).

Although use of U.S. credit cards was legalized in 2016, at press time only cards issued by **Stonegate Bank** (www.stonegatebank.com) functioned in Cuba. The bureaucratic financial system was still treating Cuba as pariah. Plan on needing to travel on a cash-only basis.

Problem with your card? Contact **Fincimex** (Calle 8 #319, e/ 3ra y 5ta, Miramar, Havana, tel. 07/224-3191), which has branches in major cities.

U.S. citizens should avoid checking their bank statements online while in Cuba, which can result in an instant block on your account when the financial infrastructure identifies the Cuban IPC address.

Travelers Checks

Travelers checks (unless issued by U.S. banks) are accepted in some tourist restaurants, hotels, and foreign-goods stores. They can also be cashed at most hotel cashier desks, as well as at banks. You should *not* enter the date or the place when signing your checks—a quirky Cuban requirement.

Studying in Cuba

Thousands of people every year choose to study in Cuba, be it for a monthlong dance course or six years of medical training. Be prepared for basic living conditions if signing up for a long-term residential course. Restrictions for U.S. students apply.

UniversiTUR (Calle 30 #768, e/ Kohly y 41, Nuevo Vedado, tel. 07/261-4939 or 07/855-5978) arranges study at centers of higher learning. For study at the Universidad de la Habana (Calle J #556, e/ 25 y 27, Vedado, www.uh.cu), contact Isabel Milán Licea (tel. 07/832-1692, imilan@rect.uh.cu).

Study Abroad (www.studyabroad.com/in-cuba) is a clearinghouse for institutions offering study opportunities in Cuba.

STUDENT VISAS

You can study in Cuba using a tourist visa only if you travel via UniversiTUR. All others require a student visa (CUC80), which can be requested in advance from the Director of Graduate Degrees of the relevant university 20 days prior to your intended arrival date. Visas are good for 30 days but can be extended upon arrival in Cuba for CUC25.

You can *arrive* in Cuba with a tourist visa, however. You then have 48 hours to register for your university program and request a change of visa status (CUC65). You'll need six passport photos, your passport and tourist card, and a license certificate for the *casa particular* where you'll be staying.

ARTS, MUSIC, AND DANCE

The Cátedra de Danza (Calzada #510, e/ D y E, Vedado, tel. 07/832-4625, www.balletcuba.cult.cu) offers monthlong ballet courses for intermediate- and advanced-level professionals and students.

The Centro Nacional de Conservación, Restauración y Museología (Calle Oficios, e/ Jústiz y Obrapía, Habana Vieja, tel. 07/861-5846) offers courses for urban planners, conservationists, and architects.

The Instituto Superior de Arte (Calle 120 #1110, e/ 9na y 13, Cubanacán, tel. 07/208-8075, www.isa.cult.cu) offers courses in music, dance, theater, and visual arts.

The Taller Experimental de Gráfica (Callejón del Chorro #6, Plaza de la Catedral, Habana Vieja, tel. 07/864-6013, tgrafica@cubarte.cult.cu) offers courses in engraving and lithography.

MEDICAL TRAINING

Cuba offers scholarships for disadvantaged and minority students from the United States and developing nations to attend the Escuela Latinoamericana de Medicina (Latin American School of Medical Sciences, ELACM, Carretera Panamericana Km 3.5, Playa, Havana, tel. 07/210-4644, www.elacm.sld.cu). Courses last six years and graduates are full-fledged doctors.

SPANISH-LANGUAGE COURSES

The Universidad de la Habana (Dirección de Posgrado, Calle J #556, e/ 25 y 27, Vedado, tel. 07/832-4245, www.uh.cu) and provincial universities throughout Cuba offer Spanish-language courses of 20-80 hours (CUC100-300), plus "Spanish and Cuban Culture" courses of 320-480 hours (CUC960-1,392). Courses begin the first Monday of the month, year-round.

The Centro de Idiomas y Computación José Martí (José Martí Language and Computer Center, Calle 90 #531, e/ 5ta B y 5ta C, Miramar, Havana, tel. 07/209-6692, cice@ceniai.inf.cu) offers Spanish-language courses of 20-80 hours (CUC130-330).

Money Transfers

In 2011 President Obama lifted restrictions on how much money Cuban Americans can send to Cuba. And *any* U.S. citizen can now send up to $500 every three months to any Cuban (but no Communist Party member) to "support private economic activity."

Western Union (U.S. tel. 800/325-6000, www.westernunion.com) is licensed to handle wire transfers to Cuba. Senders must fill out an electronic affidavit.

For foreigners, Cuba's **TransCard** (Canada tel. 800/724-5685, www.smart-transfer.com) operates much like a debit card. The user deposits funds into a secure account abroad (you can do so online), then uses that account to withdraw cash at ATMs, banks, and Cadeca, or to pay for goods and services at locations in Cuba.

Costs

Prices rise and fall like a yo-yo, according to the Cuban government's whim. If you use public transport, rent *casas particulares,* and dine on the street and at peso snack bars, you may be able to survive on as little as CUC40 a day (more in Havana). For a modicum of comforts, budget at least CUC75 a day.

TIPPING

Cubans receive slave-rate wages (although fixed living costs are virtually zero). Your waiter or chambermaid probably lives in a slum and is being paid less than CUC1 per day. Waiters expect to be tipped 10 percent, even where a service charge has been added to your bill (waiters and staff see only a small fraction of this, if any). Taxi drivers do not need to be tipped; they're all freelancers and have built their profit into your fare.

Museum guides often follow you around in the hope of soliciting a tip. If you don't welcome the service, say so upfront. Musicians in bars and restaurants will usually hover by your table until tipped, after which they usually move on to the next table.

The arrival en masse of U.S. tourists has changed the tipping scenario, as they tend to *overtip* and to tip where it isn't needed. As a result, taxi fares have skyrocketed.

Communications and Media

Cuba has one of the most restrictive media policies in the world. A recent study by Washington-based advocacy group Freedom House found that more than 90 percent of Cubans had access *solely* to government media.

POSTAL SERVICE

Correos de Cuba (Av. Rancho Boyeros, Havana, tel. 07/879-6824, Mon.-Sat. 8am-6pm) operates the Cuban postal service, which is slow; delivery is never guaranteed. Mail is read by Cuba's censors; avoid politically sensitive comments. *Never* send cash. Post offices (*correos*) are usually open weekdays 10am-5pm and Saturday 8am-3pm, but hours can vary. Most tourist hotels accept mail for delivery.

International airmail (*correo aereo*) averages one month (savvy Cubans usually hand their letters to foreigners to mail outside Cuba). When mailing from Cuba, write the country destination in Spanish: Inglaterra (England, Scotland, and Wales), Francia (France), Italia (Italy), Alemania (Germany), España (Spain), Suiza (Switzerland), and Estados Unidos (United States, often referred to as "EE.UU.").

International postcards, including prepaid ones, cost CUC0.90 (to all destinations); letters cost CUC1.05. Within Cuba, letters cost from 15 centavos (20 grams or less) to 2.05 pesos (up to 500 grams); postcards cost 10 centavos. Stamps are called *sellos* (SAY-yos).

Parcels from Cuba must be *unwrapped* for inspection. It is far better to send packages

Getting Married in Cuba

It's easy to get married in Cuba if you have the correct documents in place. Civil marriages are handled by the **Bufete de Servicios Especializados** (Calle 23 #501, esq. J, Vedado, Havana, tel. 07/832-6813, www.onbc.cu/bes), the "International Lawyer's Office," which has an office in most major cities. The marriage certificate costs CUC525, plus there are other expenses. Foreigners need to produce their birth certificate, proof of marital status if single, and a divorce certificate (if relevant). These need to be translated into Spanish and authenticated by the Cuban consulate in the country in which they were issued. Marriages in Cuba are recognized in the United States.

ESSENTIALS
COMMUNICATIONS AND MEDIA

through an express courier service, although the same regulation applies.

You can receive mail in Havana by having letters and parcels addressed to you using your name as it appears on your passport or other ID for general delivery to: "c/o Espera [your name], Ministerio de Comunicaciones, Avenida Independencia and 19 de Mayo, Habana 6, Cuba." To collect mail, go to the **Correos de Cuba** (Av. Rancho Boyeros, Havana, tel. 07/879-6824, Mon.-Sat. 8am-6pm) for pickup. Consider having incoming mail addressed "Espera [your name] c/o [your embassy]."

Express Mail
DHL Worldwide Express (www.dhl.com) has offices in major cities. The main office is in Havana (1ra Av., esq. 26, Miramar, tel. 07/204-1876). In 2016, President Obama granted **FedEx** (www.fedex.com) permission to open an office, but no office had yet opened at press time.

Cubapost (Calle P #108, Vedado, tel. 07/836-9790) and **Cubapacks** (Calle 22 #4115, e/ 41 y 47, Miramar, tel. 07/204-2742) offer international express mail and parcel service.

Restrictions
Letters and literature can be mailed from the United States without restriction. Gift parcels can be "sent or carried by an authorized traveler" to an individual or religious or educational organization if the domestic retail value does not exceed US$800. Only one parcel per

month is allowed, and contents are limited to food, vitamins, seeds, medicines, medical supplies, clothing, personal hygiene items, computers, software, electronics, and a few other categories. All other parcels are subject to seizure. See http://pe.usps.com/text/imm/ce_017.htm.

TELEPHONE SERVICE
Cuba's modern digital telephone system is the responsibility of the **Empresa de Telecomunicaciones de Cuba** (Etecsa, tel. 07/266-6666 or 118, www.etecsa.cu), headquartered in the Miramar Trade Center in Havana. It has a central office (*telepunto*) with international phone and Internet service in every town (all are open daily 8:30am-7pm). There are still quirks, with some days better than others.

Call 113 for directory inquiries. The national telephone directory is available online at www.pamarillas.cu, and on CD-ROM (Grupo Directorio Telefónico, tel. 07/266-6305). Telephone numbers change often. Trying to determine a correct number can be problematic because many entities have several numbers and rarely publish the same number twice. Most commercial entities have a switchboard (*pizarra*).

Public Phone Booths
Public phone kiosks are ubiquitous. Etecsa operates glass-enclosed telephone kiosks called *micropuntos* (*telecorreos* where they combine postal services). They use phone cards, sold on-site and at tourist hotels and miscellaneous

other outlets. They are inserted into the phone and the cost of the call is automatically deducted from the card's value. If the card expires during your call, you can continue without interruption by pushing button C and inserting a new card.

Propia cards use a number specific to each card that is keyed into the telephone when prompted. Propia cards are for local and national calls (blue, 5 pesos and 10 pesos). **Chip** cards (CUC5, CUC10, and CUC20) are used for international calls.

Some phones still accept 5- and 20-centavo coins, which can only be used for local and national calls. When you hear a short "blip," *immediately* put in another coin to avoid being cut off. Public phones do not accept collect or incoming calls.

International Calls

When calling Cuba from abroad, dial 011 (the international dialing code), then 53 (the Cuba country code), followed by the city code and the number. For direct international calls from Cuba, dial 119, then the country code (for example, 44 for the U.K.), followed by the area code and number. For the international operator, dial 012 (Havana) or 180 (rest of Cuba).

Cost per minute varies depending on time of day and location of the call. At last visit, per-minute rates were: CUC1.40 6pm-6am and CUC1.95 6am-6pm to the United States, Canada, Mexico, Central America, Caribbean, and South America; CUC1.50 to Europe and the rest of the world. Rates are much higher for operator-assisted calls and from tourist hotels, most of which have direct-dial telephones in guest rooms.

Domestic Calls

For local calls in the same area code, simply dial the number you wish to reach. To dial a number outside your area code, dial 0, then wait for a tone before dialing the local city code and the number you wish to reach. For the local operator, dial 0. Local calls in Havana cost approximately 5 centavos (about

a quarter of a cent). Rates for calls beyond Havana range from 30 centavos to 3 pesos and 15 centavos for the first three minutes, depending on zone—tourist hotels and Etecsa booths charge in CUC equivalent.

Cellular Phones

Cell phone use has rocketed, although the cost of use is high at $0.35 cents a minute locally (7am-11pm; the price drops to $0.10 cents 11pm-7am), CUC2.45 per minute to the United States and the Americas, and CUC5.85 to Europe. Most Cubans use their cell phones for SMS texting (CUC0.9 cents local, or $0.60 cents international). Few Cubans answer incoming calls. They note the number of the caller, then call them back on a landline or phone card, which is much cheaper.

Cell phone numbers in Cuba have eight digits, beginning with 5, and omit the provincial area codes.

Cubacel (Calle 28 #510, e/ 5 y 7, Miramar, tel. 05/264-2266 or 07/880-2222, www.cubacel.com, daily 8:30am-7:30pm, Sat. 8am-noon) operates Cuba's cell phone system and has offices in most major cities. It operates two different cell phone networks (TDMA and GSM) and has roaming agreements with several countries, including the United States. In 2009 President Obama permitted U.S. telecommunications companies to do deals with Cuba. If yours is among them, you can bring your cell phone and expect it to function in Cuba. Cubacel can activate most phones.

Since 2011 foreigners can no longer obtain a permanent local line. A local number can now only be obtained in the name of a Cuban resident (cost CUC40). Hence, you need to find a Cuban who doesn't own a cell phone and is willing to open a line on your behalf, but in their own name. Once set up with a line, you then pay in advance for calling credit and are charged the corresponding rates for all local and long-distance calls. You'll have to use your cell phone to keep your line (the grace period is 30-180 days, depending on how much money is in your account).

Foreign visitors *can* obtain SIM cards and/

or rent cell phones (CUC100 deposit, plus CUC10 daily rental—CUC7 for the phone and CUC3 for the line) for the duration of their visit only. In Havana, the only two places where foreigners can get a SIM card or get a cell phone activated are the Cubacel offices at the airport (Terminals 2 and 3) and at the main office in Miramar (Calle 28 #510, e/ 5 y 7, tel. 05/880-2222 or 05/264-2266). You then purchase prepaid cards (CUC10, CUC20, or CUC40, sold at stores and phone centers nationwide) to charge to your account.

The **National Geographic Talk Abroad** cell phone (www.cellularabroad.com/travel-phone.php) can be rented (from $18 weekly) or purchased (from $99) and will function in Cuba with U.S. and U.K. phone numbers and without any setup being required in Cuba. Several other companies offer similar phone service.

ONLINE SERVICE IN CUBA

Etecsa has a monopoly on Internet service, which it offers using prepaid Nauta cards (since December 2016, CUC1.50 per hour for international access; CUC0.25 domestic access) and can be used at any Etecsa office or wherever Internet service is offered. You may need to present your passport, which may be recorded, along with the number of your prepaid card. Assume that all emails are read directly off the server by security personnel.

The U.S. embargo traditionally banned Cuba from accessing international satellite and telecommunications systems. However, service has improved since 2013, when Cuba activated a new fiber-optic cable connected to Jamaica and Venezuela (replacing slow service via a Russian satellite and vastly increasing bandwidth) and opened 118 Etecsa *telepuntos* nationwide. Most towns of any size have since had Wi-Fi installed in public plazas, and Havana now has scores of Wi-Fi zones. All tourist hotels have Wi-Fi service using Etecsa's system. A few hotels have data ports and Wi-Fi in guest rooms; many also have fixed-line Internet stations. A select few hotels

charge their own rates (as high as CUC10 per hour in Havana's Hotel Nacional) and do not accept Nauta cards.

Wi-Fi service is erratic and almost always slow. You'll need lots of patience. Skype is prohibited, but IMO is a popular free video call app preferred by Cubans.

In February 2016, Cuba announced it was initiating residential broadband Internet in parts of Havana, and that cafés and restaurants would also get broadband.

NEWSPAPERS AND MAGAZINES
Before You Go

Take all the reading matter you can with you, as there are no newsagents or newsstands in Cuba. *CubaPlus* (www.cubaplus-magazine.com) is an English-language travel magazine, published in Canada but available in Cuba. Likewise, you can subscribe to *OnCuba* (www.oncubamagazine.com), a glossy monthly magazine distributed on charter aircraft flying between Miami and Cuba. By far the most impressive all-around online magazine is **LaHabana** (www.lahabana.com), covering arts and culture. *Cuba Standard* (www.cubastandard.com) serves investors.

In Cuba

Pre-Castro Cuba had a vibrant media sector, with 58 daily newspapers of differing political hues. The Castro government closed them all down. It's been years since I've seen *any* foreign publications for sale in Cuba. Today domestic media is still almost entirely state controlled. There is no independent press, although things are gradually loosening up under Raúl.

The most important daily—and virtually the sole mouthpiece of international news—is *Granma* (www.granma.cu), the cheaply produced official outlet of the Communist Party (ironically, printed on newssheet imported legally from Alabama). This eight-page rag focuses on denigrating the United States (though that has eased of late) and

Area Codes and Emergency Numbers

	Area Code	Ambulance	Fire	Police
Havana	07	104	105	106
Havana Province	047			
Artemisa	047	36-2597	105	106
San Antonio de los Baños	047	38-2781	105	106
Mayabeque Province	047			
Batabanó	047	58-5335	105	106
Camagüey	032	104	105	106
Ciego de Ávila	033	104	105	106
Cayo Coco	033	104	30-9102	30-8107
Cienfuegos	043	104	105	106
Granma	023	104	105	106
Pilón	023	104	105	59-4493
Guantánamo	021	104	105	106
Holguín	024	104	105	106
Banes	024	80-3798	105	106
Isla de la Juventud	046			
Cayo Largo	046	24-8238	24-8247	39-9406

profiling socialist victories. Until recently, no negatives were reported about domestic affairs, but a forward-thinking editor appointed in 2012 is following a new dictate to permit more realistic and critical coverage, although the paper's international coverage remains heavily distorted. *Granma* is sold on the street but rapidly sells out as many Cubans buy it to resell. A weekly edition published in Spanish, English, and French is sold in hotels. *Habaneros* get their news via *radio bemba*, the fast-moving street gossip or grapevine.

Juventud Rebelde, the evening paper of the Communist Youth League, echoes *Granma*. Similar mouthpieces include the less easily found *Trabajadores* (*Workers*, weekly), *Mujeres* (a monthly magazine for women), and such arts and culture magazines as *Habanera*

(monthly), *Bohemia* (weekly), and, best of all, *Temas* (www.temas.cult.cu).

The daily *Granma* and weekly *Cartelera* newspapers print weather forecasts. Cuban TV newscasts have daily forecasts (in Spanish). The **Instituto de Meteorología** (Meteorological Institute, www.met.inf.cu) provides weather information in Spanish online.

RADIO AND TELEVISION

All broadcast media in Cuba are state controlled.

Television

Most tourist hotel rooms have satellite TVs showing international channels such as HBO, ESPN, CNN, and so on (the Cuban government pirates the signals). No Cuban (except

	Area Code	Ambulance	Fire	Police
Nueva Gerona	046	32-2366	105	106
Las Tunas	031	104	105	106
Matanzas	045			
Cárdenas	045	52-7640	105	106
Jagüey Grande	045	91-3046	105	106
Matanzas	045	28-5023	105	106
Playa Girón	045	98-7364	105	106
Varadero	045	66-2306	105	106
Pinar del Río	048			
Pinar del Río City	048	76-2317	105	106
Viñales			105	106
Sancti Spíritus	041			
Sancti Spíritus	041	32-4462	105	110
Trinidad	041	99-2362	105	106
Santiago de Cuba	022	185, 62-3300	105	106
Villa Clara	042	104		
Caibarién	042	36-3888	105	106
Remedios	042	39-5149	105	106
Santa Clara	042	20-3965	105	106

the Communist elite) is permitted access to satellite TV. Ordinary Cubans must make do with the national TV networks (Canal 6: CubaVisión and Canal 2: Tele Rebelde, plus Canal Educativo and Canal Educativo-Dos, two educational channels) plus state-run Telesur, from Venezuela.

Programming is dominated by dreary reports on socialist progress (Castro speeches take precedence over all other programming) and the daily *mesa redonda* (roundtable), a political "discussion" that is merely a staged denunciation of wicked Uncle Sam. However, Tele Rebelde features selections from CNN España international news coverage. Cuban television also has some very intelligent programming, emphasizing science and culture (often culled from National Geographic, Discovery Channel, etc.), U.S. series such as *First 48 Hours* and *Friends,* foreign comedy (*Mr. Bean* is a favorite), and sports and foreign movies. There are no advertisements, but five-minute slots might inveigh against abortions or exhort Cubans to work hard, while cartoons aim to teach Cuban youth sound morals. Cubans are so addicted to Latin American *telenovelas* (soap operas) that you can walk through Havana when the *novela* is showing and follow the show as you walk.

Radio

Cuba ranked eighth in the world in number of radio stations in 1958. Today it has only nine national radio stations, including Radio Rebelde (640 and 710 AM, and 96.7 FM) and Radio Reloj (950 AM and 101.5 FM), both reporting news, and Radio Progreso (640 AM and 90.3 FM), featuring traditional music.

Radio Taíno (1290 AM and 93.3 FM) caters to tourists with programs in English, French, and Spanish.

There are also provincial and local stations. However, in much of the countryside you can put your car radio onto "scan" and it will just go round and round without ever coming up with a station.

WEIGHTS AND MEASURES

Cuba operates on the metric system. Liquids are sold in liters, fruits and vegetables by the kilo. Distances are given in meters and kilometers. See the chart at the back of the book for metric conversions.

Electricity

Cuba operates on 110-volt AC (60-cycle) nationwide, although a few hotels operate on 220 volts (many have both). Most outlets use U.S. plugs: flat, parallel two-pins, and three rectangular pins. A two-prong adapter is a good idea (take one with you; they're impossible to find in Cuba). Many outlets are faulty and dangerous. Electricity blackouts (*apagones*) are now infrequent. Take a flashlight, spare batteries, and candles plus matches or lighter.

Time

Cuban time is equivalent to U.S. Eastern Standard Time: five hours behind Greenwich mean time, the same as New York and Miami, and three hours ahead of the U.S. West Coast. There is little seasonal variation in dawn. Cuba observes daylight saving time May-October.

CONDUCT AND CUSTOMS

Cubans are respectful and courteous, with a deep sense of integrity. You can ease your way considerably by being courteous and patient. Always greet your host with *"¡Buenos días!"* ("Good morning!") or *"¡Buenas tardes!"* ("Good afternoon!"). And never neglect to say *"gracias"* ("thank you"). Topless sunbathing is tolerated at some tourist resorts, and nude bathing is allowed only on Cayo Largo.

Cubans are extremely hygienic and have a natural prejudice against anyone who ignores personal hygiene.

Smoking is ostensibly prohibited in theaters, stores, buses, taxis, restaurants, and enclosed public areas, but the prohibition is rarely enforced.

Respect the natural environment: Take only photographs, leave only footprints.

Photography

You can take photographs freely (except of military and industrial installations, airports, and officials in uniform). Most museums charge for photography.

Visitors are allowed to bring two cameras plus a video camera. Official permission is needed to bring "professional" camera equipment. Foto Video and Photo Service stores sell instamatic and small digital cameras. However, there are *no* camera stores similar to those found in North America or Europe, and 35mm SLRs, lenses, flash units, filters, and other equipment are unavailable. Bring spare batteries, tapes, and film, which is hard to find. *Snatch-and-grab theft of cameras is a major problem.*

The only camera store in Cuba is in the **Gran Hotel Manzana Kempinski** (Calle San Rafael, e/ Zulueta y Monserrate, Havana, tel), in Havana.

Cubans love to be photographed. However, never assume an automatic right to do so. Ask permission to photograph individuals, and honor any wishing not to be photographed. Cubans often request money for being photographed, as do those Cubans who dress flamboyantly as photo ops: If you don't want to pay, don't take the shot. In markets, it is a courtesy to buy a small trinket from vendors you wish to photograph. *Do* send photographs to anyone you promise to send to.

Several foreigners have been arrested for filming "pornography," which in Cuba includes topless or nude photography.

Business Hours

Bank branches nationwide are open Monday-Saturday 8am-3pm (but 8am-noon only on the last working day of each month). Pharmacies generally open daily 8am-8pm (*turnos permanentes* stay open 24 hours). Post offices are usually open Monday-Saturday 8am-10pm, Sunday 8am-6pm, but hours vary widely. Shops are usually open Monday-Saturday 8:30am-5:30pm, although many remain open later, including all day Sunday. Museum hours vary widely, although most are closed on Monday.

Most banks, businesses, and government offices close during national holidays.

Public Restrooms

Public toilets are few. Many are disgustingly foul. Most hotels and restaurants will let you use their facilities, though most lack toilet paper, which gets stolen. An attendant usually sits outside the door, dispensing pieces of toilet paper. Since 2010, most attendants now pay the state CUC10 for the privilege of cleaning the toilets and collecting tips. CUC0.25 is usually sufficient. Always carry a small packet of toilet tissue with you.

ACCESS FOR TRAVELERS WITH DISABILITIES

Cubans go out of their way to assist travelers with disabilities, although few allowances have been made in infrastructure.

In the United States, the **Society for Accessible Travel & Hospitality** (347 5th Ave. #610, New York, NY 10016, tel. 212/447-7284, www.sath.org) and the **American Foundation for the Blind** (2 Penn Plaza #1102, New York, NY 10001, tel. 212/502-7600 or 800/232-5463, www.afb.org) are good resources, as is Cuba's **Asociación Cubana de Limitados Físicos y Motores** (Cuban Association for Physically & Motor Disabled People, ACLIFIM, Calle 6 #106, e/ 1ra y 3ra, Havana, tel. 07/209-3099, www.aclifim.sld.cu).

TRAVELING WITH CHILDREN

Cubans adore children and will dote on yours. Children under the age of 2 travel free on airlines; children between 2 and 12 are offered discounts. Children under 16 usually stay free with parents at hotels, although an extra-bed rate may be charged. Children under 12 normally get free (or half-price) entry to museums.

Children's items such as diapers (nappies) and baby foods are scarce in Cuba. Bring cotton swabs, diapers, Band-Aids, baby foods, and a small first-aid kit with any necessary medicines for your child. Children's car seats are not offered in rental cars.

The equivalent of the Boy and Girl Scouts and Girl Guides is the **Pioneros José Martí** (Calle F #352, Vedado, Havana, tel. 07/832-5292), which has chapters throughout the country. Having your children interact would be a fascinating education.

MALE TRAVELERS

The average male visitor soon discovers that Cuban women have an open attitude towards sexuality. They are also much more aggressive than foreign men may be used to, displaying little equivocation.

Romantic liaisons require prudence. Petty robbery (your paramour steals your sunglasses or rifles your wallet while you take a shower) is common. Muggings by accomplices are a rare possibility, and high-class prostitutes have been known to rob tourists by drugging their drinks. Several tourists have even been murdered during sexual encounters.

Men in "sensitive" occupations (e.g., journalists) should be aware that the femme fatale who sweeps you off your feet may be in the employ of Cuba's state security.

WOMEN TRAVELERS

Sexual assault of women is almost unheard of. If you welcome the amorous overtures of men, Cuba is heaven. The art of gentle seduction is to Cuban men a kind of national pastime—a sport and a trial of manhood. They will hiss like serpents in appreciation, and call out *piropos*—affectionate and lyrical epithets. Take effusions of love with a grain of salt; while swearing eternal devotion, your Don Juan may conveniently forget to mention he's married. While the affection may be genuine, you are assuredly the moneybags in the relationship. Plenty of Cuban men earn their living giving pleasure to foreign women looking for love beneath the palms or, like their female counterparts, taking advantage of such an opportunity when it arises.

If you're not interested, pretend not to notice advances and avoid eye contact.

Cuba's **Federación de Mujeres Cubanas** (Cuban Women's Federation, Galiano #264, e/ Neptuno y Concordia, Havana, tel. 07/862-4905) is a useful resource. It publishes *Mujeres,* a women's magazine.

STUDENT AND YOUTH TRAVELERS

Foreign students with the **International Student Identity Card** (ISIC) or similar student ID receive discounts to many museums. You can obtain an ISIC at any student union, or in the United States from the **Council on International Educational Exchange** (tel. 207/553-4000, www.ciee.org) and in Canada from **Travel Cuts** (tel. 800/667-2887, www.travelcuts.com).

The **Federación Estudiantil Universitario** (Calle 23, esq. H, Vedado, Havana, tel. 07/832-4646, www.almamater.cu) is Cuba's national student federation.

SENIOR TRAVELERS

Cuba honors senior citizens, who receive discounted entry to museums and other sights. This may apply to foreign seniors in a few instances. A useful resource is the **American Association of Retired Persons** (tel. 888/687-2277, www.aarp.org).

GAY AND LESBIAN TRAVELERS

Cuba—a macho society—is schizophrenic when it comes to homosexuality. Cuba has made strides, much due to the efforts of Raúl Castro's daughter Mariela Castro Espín, director of the **Centro Nacional de Educación Sexual** (Calle 10 #460, Vedado, Havana, tel. 07/832-2528, www.cenesex.org), which has an ongoing campaign to break down macho attitudes and promote acceptance and equal treatment of the LGBT community.

Useful resources include the **International Gay & Lesbian Travel Association** (tel. 954/630-1637, www.iglta.org). **GayCuba** (tel. 5294-2968, www.gaycuba.me) caters to gay travelers to Cuba.

Tourist Information

TOURIST AND INFORMATION BUREAUS

Cuba's **Ministerio de Turismo** (Av. 3ra y F, Vedado, Havana, tel. 07/836-3245 or 07/832-7535, www.cubatravel.cu) is in charge of tourism. It has offices in nine countries, including Canada (1200 Bay St., Suite 305, Toronto, ON M5R 2A5, tel. 416/362-0700, www.gocuba.ca; 2075 rue University, Bureau 460, Montreal, QC H3A 2L1, tel. 514/875-8004) and the United Kingdom (167 High Holborn, London WC1V 6PA, tel. 020/7240-6655, www.travel-2cuba.co.uk). There is no office in the United States; however, the Canadian offices will mail literature to U.S. citizens.

Cuba is a member of the **Caribbean Tourism Organization** (CTO, 80 Broad St., 32nd Floor, New York, NY 10004, tel. 212/635-9530, www.onecaribbean.org), which is a handy information source, and the **Caribbean Hotel Association** (CHA, 2655 LeJeune Rd., Suite 910, Coral Gables, FL

33134, tel. 305/443-3040, www.caribbeanho-telassociation.com). The CTO has an office in the U.K. (22 The Quadrant, Richmond, Surrey TW9 1BP, tel. 0208/948-0057, www.caribbean.co.uk).

Infotur (5ta Av. y 112, Miramar, tel. 07/204-3977, www.infotur.cu), the government tourist information bureau, operates *palacios de turismo* (tourist information booths) in Havana and most major cities and tourist venues nationwide. Every tourist hotel has a *buró de turismo.*

Agencia Cubana de Noticias (Calle 23 #358, esq. J, Vedado, Havana, tel. 07/832-5542, www.acn.cu) dispenses information about virtually every aspect of Cuba but serves primarily as a "news" bureau. The **Oficina Nacional de Estadísticas** (Paseo #60, e/ 3ra y 5ra, Vedado, Havana, tel. 07/830-0053, www.one.cu) provides statistics on Cuba.

MAPS

The best map is National Geographic's waterproof 1:750,000 *Cuba Adventure Map* (http://shop.nationalgeographic.com). A 1:250,000 topographical road map produced by Kartografiai Vallalat, of Hungary, and a similar map by Freytag and Berndt are recommended. Likewise, Cuba's own Ediciones Geo produces a splendid 1:250,000 *La Habana Tourist Map,* plus a 1:20,000 *Ciudad de la Habana* map, sold in Cuba. The superb *Guía de Carreteras* road atlas can be purchased at souvenir outlets.

Resources

Glossary

ache: luck, positive vibe

aduana: customs

agua mala: jellyfish

alfarje: Moorish-inspired ceiling layered with geometric and star patterns

aljibe: well

altos: upstairs unit (in street address)

americano/a: citizen of the Americas (from Alaska to Tierra del Fuego)

animación: entertainment activity involving guests (at hotels)

apagón: electricity blackout

Astro: national bus company

autopista: freeway

azotea: rooftop terrace

babalawo: Santería priest

bagazo: waste from sugarcane processing

bajos: downstairs unit (in street address)

baño: toilet, bathroom

bárbaro: awesome, cool

batido: milkshake

biblioteca: library

bici-taxi: bicycle taxi

bodega: grocery store distributing rations; also Spanish-style inn

bohío: thatched rural homestead

bombo: lottery for U.S. visas

bosque: woodland

botella: hitchhike, graft

buceo: scuba dive

caballería: antiquated land measurement

caballero: sir, respectful address for a male

cabaret espectáculo: Las Vegas-style show

cabildo: colonial-era town council

cacique: Taíno chief

Cadeca: foreign-exchange agency

cajita: boxed meal

calle: street

camarera: maid or waitress

camello: humped mega-bus

camión: truck or crude truck-bus

campesino/a: peasant, country person

campismo: campsite (normally with cabins)

candela: hot (as in a party scene; literally means "flame")

cañonazo: cannon-firing

carne de res: beef

carnet de identidad: ID card that all Cubans must carry at all times

carpeta: reception

carretera: road

carro: automobile

cartelera: cultural calendar

casa de la cultura: "culture house" hosting music and other cultural events

casa de la trova: same as a casa de la cultura

casa particular: licensed room rental in a private home

casco histórico: historic center of a city

cayo: coral cay

CDR: Comité para la Defensa de la Revolución; neighborhood watch committees

cenote: flooded cave

central: sugar mill

ciego: blind

cigarillo: cigarette

cimarrón: runaway slave

circunvalación: ring road around a city

claves: rhythm sticks

coche: horse-drawn taxi

coco-taxi: three-wheeled open-air taxi

cola: line, queue

colectivo: collective taxi that runs along a fixed route like a bus

comemierda: literally "shit-eater"; often used to refer to Communist or MININT officials

compañero/a: companion, used as a revolutionary address for another person

congrí: rice with red beans

coño: slang for female genitalia, equivalent to "damn" (the most utilized cuss word in Cuba)

correo: post or post office

criollo/criolla: Creole, used for Cuban food, or a person born in Cuba during the colonial era

cristianos y moros: rice with black beans

Cuba libre: "free Cuba," or rum and Coke

cuentapropista: self-employed person

custodio: guard (as in parking lots)

daiquiri: rum cocktail served with crushed ice

diente de perro: jagged limestone rock

divisa: U.S. dollars or CUC

edificio: building

efectivo: cash

el último: last person in a queue

embajada: embassy

embalse: reservoir

embori: snitch

encomienda: colonial form of slavery giving landowners usufruct rights to Indian labor

entronque: crossroads

escabeche: ceviche, marinated raw fish

escuela: school

esquina caliente: literally "hot corner"; a place where baseball fans debate the sport

estación: station

fábrica: factory

FAR: Fuerza Revolucionaria Militar, or armed forces

farmacia: pharmacy

faro: lighthouse

ferrocarril: railway

Fidelismo: Cuba's unique style of Communism

Fidelista: a Fidel loyalist

fiesta de quince: girl's 15th birthday party

filin: "feeling" music, usually romantic ballads

finca: farm

flota: Spanish treasure fleet

FMC: Federación de Mujeres Cubanas (Federation of Cuban Women)

fruta bomba: papaya (see *papaya*)

fula: U.S. dollars; also a messy situation

G2: state security agency

gasolinera: gas station

gobernador: colonial-era Spanish governor

golpe: military coup

Granma: yacht that carried Fidel Castro and his guerrilla army from Mexico to Cuba in 1956

gringo/a: person from the United States, but can also apply to any Caucasian

guagua: bus

guaguancó: traditional dance with erotic body movements

guajiro/a: peasant or country bumpkin; also used for a type of traditional country song

guaracha: satirical song

guarapería: place selling *guarapo*

guarapo: fresh-squeezed sugarcane juice

guayabera: pleated, buttoned men's shirt

guayabita: fruit native to Pinar del Río

habanero/a: person from Havana

habano: export-quality cigar

heladería: ice-cream store

iglesia: church

ingenio: colonial-era sugar mill

inmigración: immigration

jaba: plastic bag, as at a supermarket

jefe de sector: Communist *vigilante* in charge of several street blocks

jejénes: minuscule sand fleas

jinetera: female seeking a foreign male for pecuniary or other gain

jinetero: male hustler who hassles tourists

joder: slang for intercourse, but also to mess up

libreta: ration book

luchar: to fight; common term used to describe the difficulty of daily life

M-26-7: "26th of July Movement"; Fidel Castro's underground revolutionary movement named for the date of the attack on the Moncada barracks

machetero: sugarcane cutter/harvester

Mambí: rebels fighting for independence from Spain; sometimes referred to as Mambises

maqueta: scale model

máquina: old Yankee automobile

mausoleo: mausoleum

mediopunto: half-moon stained-glass window

mercado: market

mercado agropecuario: produce market

microbrigadista: brigades of unskilled volunteer labor

MININT: Ministry of the Interior

mirador: lookout point or tower

mogote: limestone monoliths

mojito: rum cocktail served with mint

moneda: coins

moneda nacional: Cuban pesos

Mudejar: Moorish (as in architecture)

muelle: pier, wharf

mulatto/a: a person with both black and white heritage

negro/a: black person

norteamericano/a: U.S. or Canadian citizen

Oriente: eastern provinces of Cuba

orisha: Santería deity

paladar: private restaurant

palenque: thatched structure

palestino: derogatory term for a migrant to Havana from Oriente

papaya: tropical fruit; slang term for vagina

parada: bus stop

parque de diversiones: amusement park

PCC: Partido Comunista de Cuba

pedraplén: causeway connecting offshore islands to the Cuban mainland

peninsular: Spanish-born colonialist in Cuba in pre-independence days

peña: social get-together for cultural enjoyment, such as a literary reading

pesos convertibles: convertible pesos (tourist currency)

piropo: witty or flirtatious comment

pizarra: switchboard

ponchero/a: puncture repair person

presa: dam

prórroga: visa extension

puro: export-quality cigar

quinceañera: girl coming of age

quinta: country house of nobility

quintal: Spanish colonial measure

refresco: "refreshment"; a sugary drink

resolver: to resolve or fix a problem

ropa vieja: shredded beef dish

rumba: a traditional Afro-Cuban dance; also a party involving such

sala: room or gallery

salsa: popular modern dance music

salsero/a: performer of salsa

Santería: a syncretization of the African Yoruba and Catholic religions

santero/a: adherent of Santería

santiagüero/a: person from Santiago de Cuba

sello: postage or similar stamp

sendero: walking trail

servicentro: gasoline station

SIDA: AIDS

son: traditional music as popularized by Buena Vista Social Club

Taíno: the predominant indigenous inhabitants of Cuba at the time of Spanish conquest

taquilla: ticket window

taller: workshop

tarjeta: card, such as a credit card

telenovela: soap opera

telepunto: main telephone exchange

temporada alta/baja: high/low season

terminal de ómnibus: bus station

tienda: shop

tráfico: traffic cop

trago: a shot of rum

tránsito: traffic cop

trova: traditional poetry-based music

UJC: Unión de Jóvenes Comunistas; politically oriented youth Communist group

UNEAC: Unión Nacional de Escritores y Artistas de Cuba; National Union of Cuban Writers and Artists

vaquero: cowboy

vega: patch of land where tobacco is grown

verde: slang for U.S. dollar

Víazul: company offering scheduled tourist bus service

vigilante: community-watch person, on behalf of the Revolution

vitral: stained-glass window

Yoruba: a group of peoples and a pantheistic religion from Nigeria

yuma: slang for the United States

zafra: sugarcane harvest

Cuban Spanish

Learning the basics of Spanish will aid your travels considerably. In key tourist destinations, however, you should be able to get along fine without it. Most larger hotels have bilingual desk staff, and English is widely spoken by the staff of car rental agencies and tour companies. Away from the tourist path, far fewer people speak English. Use that as an excuse to learn some Spanish. Cubans warm quickly to those who make an effort to speak their language.

In its literary form, Cuban Spanish is pure, classical Castilian (the Spanish of Spain). Alas, in its spoken form Cuban Spanish is the most difficult to understand in all of Latin America. Cubans speak more briskly than other Latin Americans, blurring their rapid-fire words together. The diction of Cuba is lazy and unclear. Thought Richard Henry Dana Jr. in 1859: "It strikes me that the tendency here is to enfeeble the language, and take from it the openness of the vowels and the strength of the consonants." The letter "S" is usually swallowed, especially in plurals. Thus, the typical greeting "¿Como estás?" is usually pronounced "como-TAH." (The swallowed S's are apparently accumulated for use in restaurants, where they are released to get the server's attention—"S-s-s-s-s-st!" Because of this, a restaurant with bad service can sound like a pit full of snakes.) The final consonants of words are also often deleted, as are the entire last syllables of words: "If they dropped any more syllables, they would be speechless," suggests author Tom Miller.

Cubanisms to Know

Cubans are long-winded and full of flowery, passionate, rhetorical flourishes. Fidel Castro didn't inherit his penchant for long speeches from dour, taciturn Galicia—it's a purely Cuban characteristic. Cubans also spice up the language with little affectations and teasing endearments—piropos—given and taken among themselves without offense.

Many English (or "American") words have found their way into Cuban diction. Cubans go to béisbol and eat hamburgesas. Like the English, Cubans are clever in their use of words, imbuing their language with double entendres and their own lexicon of similes. Cubans are also great cussers. The two most common cuss words are cojones (slang for male genitalia) and coño (slang for female genitalia), while one of the more common colloquialisms is ojalá, which loosely translated means "I wish" or "If only!" but which most commonly is used to mean "Some hope!"

Formal courtesies are rarely used when greeting someone. Since the Revolution, everyone is a compañero or compañera (señor and señora are considered too bourgeois), although the phrase is disdained by many Cubans as indicating approval of the Communist system. Confusingly, ¡ciao! (used as a long-term goodbye, and spelled "chao" in Cuba) is also used as a greeting in casual passing—the equivalent of "Hi!" You will also be asked ¿Como anda? ("How goes it?"), while younger Cubans prefer ¿Que bola? (the Cuban equivalent of "Wassup?") rather than the traditional ¿Que pasa? ("What's happening?").

Cubans speak to each other directly, no holds barred. Even conversations with strangers are laced with "¡Ay, muchacha!" ("Hey, girl!"), "¡Mira, chica!" ("Look, girl!"), and "¡Hombre!" ("Listen, man!") when one disagrees with the other. Cubans refer to one another in straightforward terms, often playing on their physical or racial characteristics: flaco (skinny), gordo (fatty), negro (black man), china (chinese woman), etc. Cubans do not refer to themselves with a single definition of "white" or "black." There are a zillion gradations of skin color and features, from negro azul y trompudo (blue-black and thick-lipped) and muy negro (very black), for example, to *leche con una gota de café* (milk with a drop of coffee). Whites, too, come in shades. *Un blanco* is a blond or light-haired person with blue, green, or gray eyes. *Un blanquito* is a "white" with dark hair and dark eyes.

Bárbaro is often used to attribute a positive quality to someone, as in *él es un bárbaro* ("he's a great person"). *Está en candela* ("a flame") is its equivalent, but it's more commonly used to describe an alarming or complicated situation (such as "I'm broke!") or someone who's "hot."

Marinovia defines a live-in girlfriend (from *marido*, for spouse, and *novia*, for girlfriend). An *asere* is one's close friend, though this street term is considered a low-class word, especially common with blacks. A *flojo* (literally, "loose guy") is a lounger who pretends to work. Cubans also have no shortage of terms referring to spies, informers, and untrustworthy souls. For example, *embori* refers to an informer in cahoots with the government. *Fronterizo* is a half-mad person. *Chispa* ("spark") is someone with vitality. To become "Cubanized" is to be *aplatanado*.

When Cubans ask home visitors if they want coffee, it is often diplomatic rather than an invitation. Replying *"gracias"* (thanks) usually signifies "thanks for the thought." *"Sí, gracias"* means "yes." Cubans expect you to be explicit.

Spanish Phrasebook

Spanish commonly uses 30 letters—the familiar English 26, plus four straightforward additions: ch, ll, ñ, and rr, which are explained in "Consonants," below.

Christopher Howard's Official Guide to Cuban Spanish is a handy resource.

PRONUNCIATION

Once you learn them, Spanish pronunciation rules—in contrast to English—don't change. Spanish vowels generally sound softer than in English. (*Note:* The capitalized syllables below receive stronger accents.)

Vowels

a like ah, as in "hah": *agua* AH-gooah (water), *pan* PAHN (bread), and *casa* CAH-sah (house)

e like ay, as in "may:" *mesa* MAY-sah (table), *tela* TAY-lah (cloth), and *de* DAY (of, from)

i like ee, as in "need": *diez* dee-AYZ (ten), *comida* ko-MEE-dah (meal), and *fin* FEEN (end)

o like oh, as in "go": *peso* PAY-soh (weight), *ocho* OH-choh (eight), and *poco* POH-koh (a bit)

u like oo, as in "cool": *uno* OO-noh (one), *cuarto* KOOAHR-toh (room), and *usted* oos-TAYD (you); when it follows a "q" the **u** is silent; when it follows an "h" or has an umlaut, it's pronounced like "w"

Consonants

b, d, f, k, l, m, n, p, q, s, t, v, w, x, y, z, and
ch pronounced almost as in English; **h** occurs, but is silent—not pronounced at all

c like k as in "keep": *cuarto* KOOAR-toh (room), Tepic tay-PEEK (capital of Nayarit state); when it precedes "e" or "i," pronounce **c** like s, as in "sit": *cerveza* sayr-VAY-sah (beer), *encima* ayn-SEE-mah (atop)

g like g as in "gift" when it precedes "a," "o," "u," or a consonant: *gato* GAH-toh (cat), *hago* AH-goh (I do, make); otherwise, pronounce **g** like h as in "hat": *giro* HEE-roh (money order), *gente* HAYN-tay (people)

j like h as in "has": *Jueves* HOOAY-vays (Thursday), *mejor* may-HOR (better)

ll like y, as in "yes": *toalla* toh-AH-yah (towel), *ellos* AY-yohs (they, them)

ñ like ny, as in "canyon": *año* AH-nyo (year), *señor* SAY-nyor (Mr., sir)

r is lightly trilled, with tongue at the roof of

your mouth like a very light English d, as in "ready": *pero* PAY-doh (but), *tres* TDAYS (three), *cuatro* KOOAH-tdoh (four)

rr like a Spanish r, but with much more emphasis and trill. Let your tongue flap. Practice with *burro* (donkey), *carretera* (highway), and Carrillo (proper name), then really let go with *ferrocarril* (railroad)

Note: The single small but common exception to all of the above is the pronunciation of Spanish **y** when it's being used as the Spanish word for "and," as in "Ron y Kathy." In such case, pronounce it like the English ee, as in "keep": Ron "ee" Kathy (Ron and Kathy).

Accent

The rule for accent, the relative stress given to syllables within a given word, is straightforward. If a word ends in a vowel, an n, or an s, accent the next-to-last syllable; if not, accent the last syllable.

Pronounce *gracias* GRAH-seeahs (thank you), *orden* OHR-dayn (order), and *carretera* kah-ray-TAY-rah (highway) with stress on the next-to-last syllable.

Otherwise, accent the last syllable: *venir* vay-NEER (to come), *ferrocarril* fay-roh-cah-REEL (railroad), and *edad* ay-DAHD (age).

Exceptions to the accent rule are always marked with an accent sign: (á, é, í, ó, or ú), such as *teléfono* tay-LAY-foh-noh (telephone), *jabón* hah-BON (soap), and *rápido* RAH-pee-doh (rapid).

BASIC AND COURTEOUS EXPRESSIONS

Most Spanish-speaking people consider formalities important. Whenever approaching anyone for information or some other reason, do not forget the appropriate salutation—good morning, good evening, etc. Standing alone, the greeting *hola* (hello) can sound brusque.

Hello. *Hola.*
Good morning. *Buenos días.*
Good afternoon. *Buenas tardes.*
Good evening. *Buenas noches.*
How are you? *¿Cómo está usted?*

Very well, thank you. *Muy bien, gracias.*
Okay; good. *Bien.*
Not okay; bad. *Mal or feo.*
So-so. *Más o menos.*
And you? *¿Y usted?*
Thank you. *Gracias.*
Thank you very much. *Muchas gracias.*
You're very kind. *Muy amable.*
You're welcome. *De nada.*
Goodbye. *Adios.*
See you later. *Hasta luego.*
please *por favor*
yes *sí*
no *no*
I don't know. *No sé.*
Just a moment, please. *Momentito, por favor.*
Excuse me, please (when you're trying to get attention). *Disculpe or Con permiso.*
Excuse me (when you've made a boo-boo). *Lo siento.*
Pleased to meet you. *Mucho gusto.*
How do you say . . . in Spanish? *¿Cómo se dice . . . en español?*
What is your name? *¿Cómo se llama usted?*
Do you speak English? *¿Habla usted inglés?*
Is English spoken here? (Does anyone here speak English?) *¿Se habla inglés?*
I don't speak Spanish well. *No hablo bien el español.*
I don't understand. *No entiendo.*
How do you say . . . in Spanish? *¿Cómo se dice . . . en español?*
My name is . . . *Me llamo . . .*
Would you like . . . *¿Quisiera usted . . .*
Let's go to . . . *Vamos a . . .*

TERMS OF ADDRESS

When in doubt, use the formal *usted* (you) as a form of address.

I *yo*
you (formal) *usted*
you (familiar) *tu*
he/him *él*
she/her *ella*
we/us *nosotros*

you (plural) *ustedes*
they/them *ellos* (all males or mixed gender);
  ellas (all females)
Mr., sir *señor*
Mrs., madam *señora*
miss, young lady *señorita*
wife *esposa*
husband *esposo*
friend *amigo* (male); *amiga* (female)
sweetheart *novio* (male); *novia* (female)
son; daughter *hijo; hija*
brother; sister *hermano; hermana*
father; mother *padre; madre*
grandfather; grandmother *abuelo;*
  abuela

TRANSPORTATION

Where is...? *¿Dónde está...?*
How far is it to...? *¿A cuánto está...?*
from...to... *de...a...*
How many blocks? *¿Cuántas cuadras?*
Where (Which) is the way to...? *¿Dónde*
  está el camino a...?
the bus station *la terminal de autobuses*
the bus stop *la parada de autobuses*
Where is this bus going? *¿Adónde va este*
  autobús?
the taxi stand *la parada de taxis*
the train station *la estación de ferrocarril*
the boat *el barco*
the launch *lancha; tiburonera*
the dock *el muelle*
the airport *el aeropuerto*
I'd like a ticket to... *Quisiera un boleto*
  a...
first (second) class *primera (segunda) clase*
roundtrip *ida y vuelta*
reservation *reservación*
baggage *equipaje*
Stop here, please. *Pare aquí, por favor.*
the entrance *la entrada*
the exit *la salida*
the ticket office *la oficina de boletos*
(very) near; far *(muy) cerca; lejos*
to; toward *a*
by; through *por*
from *de*
the right *la derecha*

the left *la izquierda*
straight ahead *derecho; directo*
in front *en frente*
beside *al lado*
behind *atrás*
the corner *la esquina*
the stoplight *la semáforo*
a turn *una vuelta*
right here *aquí*
somewhere around here *por acá*
right there *allí*
somewhere around there *por allá*
road *el camino*
street; boulevard *calle; bulevar*
block *la cuadra*
highway *carretera*
kilometer *kilómetro*
bridge; toll *puente; cuota*
address *dirección*
north; south *norte; sur*
east; west *oriente (este); poniente (oeste)*

ACCOMMODATIONS

hotel *hotel*
Is there a room? *¿Hay cuarto?*
May I (may we) see it? *¿Puedo (podemos)*
  verlo?
What is the rate? *¿Cuál es el precio?*
Is that your best rate? *¿Es su mejor precio?*
Is there something cheaper? *¿Hay algo*
  más económico?
a single room *un cuarto sencillo*
a double room *un cuarto doble*
double bed *cama matrimonial*
twin beds *camas gemelas*
with private bath *con baño*
hot water *agua caliente*
shower *ducha*
towels *toallas*
soap *jabón*
toilet paper *papel higiénico*
blanket *frazada; manta*
sheets *sábanas*
air-conditioned *aire acondicionado*
fan *abanico; ventilador*
key *llave*
manager *gerente*

FOOD

I'm hungry *Tengo hambre.*
I'm thirsty. *Tengo sed.*
menu *carta; menú*
order *orden*
glass *vaso*
fork *tenedor*
knife *cuchillo*
spoon *cuchara*
napkin *servilleta*
soft drink *refresco*
coffee *café*
tea *té*
drinking water *agua pura; agua potable*
bottled carbonated water *agua mineral*
bottled uncarbonated water *agua sin gas*
beer *cerveza*
wine *vino*
milk *leche*
juice *jugo*
cream *crema*
sugar *azúcar*
cheese *queso*
snack *antojo; botana*
breakfast *desayuno*
lunch *almuerzo*
daily lunch special *comida corrida* (or *el menú del día* depending on region)
dinner *comida* (often eaten in late afternoon); *cena* (a late-night snack)
the check *la cuenta*
eggs *huevos*
bread *pan*
salad *ensalada*
fruit *fruta*
mango *mango*
watermelon *sandía*
papaya *papaya*
banana *plátano*
apple *manzana*
orange *naranja*
lime *limón*
fish *pescado*
shellfish *mariscos*
shrimp *camarones*
meat (without) *(sin) carne*
chicken *pollo*

pork *puerco*
beef; steak *res; bistec*
bacon; ham *tocino; jamón*
fried *frito*
roasted *asada*
barbecue; barbecued *barbacoa; al carbón*

SHOPPING

money *dinero*
money-exchange bureau *casa de cambio*
I would like to exchange traveler's checks. *Quisiera cambiar cheques de viajero.*
What is the exchange rate? *¿Cuál es el tipo de cambio?*
How much is the commission? *¿Cuánto cuesta la comisión?*
Do you accept credit cards? *¿Aceptan tarjetas de crédito?*
money order *giro*
How much does it cost? *¿Cuánto cuesta?*
What is your final price? *¿Cuál es su último precio?*
expensive *caro*
cheap *barato; económico*
more *más*
less *menos*
a little *un poco*
too much *demasiado*

HEALTH

Help me please. *Ayúdeme por favor.*
I am ill. *Estoy enfermo.*
Call a doctor. *Llame un doctor.*
Take me to . . . *Lléveme a . . .*
hospital *hospital; sanatorio*
drugstore *farmacia*
pain *dolor*
fever *fiebre*
headache *dolor de cabeza*
stomach ache *dolor de estómago*
burn *quemadura*
cramp *calambre*
nausea *náusea*
vomiting *vomitar*
medicine *medicina*
antibiotic *antibiótico*
pill; tablet *pastilla*

aspirin *aspirina*
ointment; cream *pomada; crema*
bandage *venda*
cotton *algodón*
sanitary napkins use brand name, e.g.,
  Kotex
birth control pills *pastillas anticonceptivas*
contraceptive foam *espuma
  anticonceptiva*
condoms *preservativos; condones*
toothbrush *cepilla dental*
dental floss *hilo dental*
toothpaste *crema dental*
dentist *dentista*
toothache *dolor de muelas*

POST OFFICE AND COMMUNICATIONS

long-distance telephone *teléfono larga
  distancia*
I would like to call . . . *Quisiera llamar a . . .*
collect *por cobrar*
station to station *a quien contesta*
person to person *persona a persona*
credit card *tarjeta de crédito*
post office *correo*
general delivery *lista de correo*
letter *carta*
stamp *estampilla, timbre*
postcard *tarjeta*
aerogram *aerograma*
air mail *correo aereo*
registered *registrado*
money order *giro*
package; box *paquete; caja*
string; tape *cuerda; cinta*

AT THE BORDER

border *frontera*
customs *aduana*
immigration *migración*
tourist card *tarjeta de turista*
inspection *inspección; revisión*
passport *pasaporte*
profession *profesión*
marital status *estado civil*
single *soltero*
married; divorced *casado; divorciado*

widowed *viudado*
insurance *seguros*
title *título*
driver's license *licencia de manejar*

AT THE GAS STATION

gas station *gasolinera*
gasoline *gasolina*
unleaded *sin plomo*
full, please *lleno, por favor*
tire *llanta*
tire repair shop *vulcanizadora*
air *aire*
water *agua*
oil (change) *aceite (cambio)*
grease *grasa*
My . . . doesn't work. *Mi . . . no sirve.*
battery *batería*
radiator *radiador*
alternator *alternador*
generator *generador*
tow truck *grúa*
repair shop *taller mecánico*
tune-up *afinación*
auto parts store *refaccionería*

VERBS

Verbs are the key to getting along in Spanish.
They employ mostly predictable forms and
come in three classes, which end in *ar, er,* and
ir, respectively:

to buy *comprar*
I buy, you (he, she, it) buys *compro,
  compra*
we buy, you (they) buy *compramos,
  compran*

to eat *comer*
I eat, you (he, she, it) eats *como, come*
we eat, you (they) eat *comemos, comen*

to climb *subir*
I climb, you (he, she, it) climbs *subo,
  sube*
we climb, you (they) climb *subimos,
  suben*

Here are more (with irregularities indicated):

to do or make *hacer* (regular except for *hago,* I do or make)

to go *ir* (very irregular: *voy, va, vamos, van*)

to go (walk) *andar*

to love *amar*

to work *trabajar*

to want *desear, querer*

to need *necesitar*

to read *leer*

to write *escribir*

to repair *reparar*

to stop *parar*

to get off (the bus) *bajar*

to arrive *llegar*

to stay (remain) *quedar*

to stay (lodge) *hospedar*

to leave *salir* (regular except for *salgo,* I leave)

to look at *mirar*

to look for *buscar*

to give *dar* (regular except for *doy,* I give)

to carry *llevar*

to have *tener* (irregular but important: *tengo, tiene, tenemos, tienen*)

to come *venir* (similarly irregular: *vengo, viene, venimos, vienen*)

Spanish has two forms of "to be":

to be *estar* (regular except for *estoy,* I am)
to be *ser* (very irregular: *soy, es, somos, son*)

Use *estar* when speaking of location or a temporary state of being: "I am at home." *"Estoy en casa."* "I'm sick." *"Estoy enfermo."* Use *ser* for a permanent state of being: "I am a doctor." *"Soy doctora."*

NUMBERS
zero *cero*
one *uno*
two *dos*
three *tres*
four *cuatro*
five *cinco*
six *seis*
seven *siete*
eight *ocho*
nine *nueve*
10 *diez*
11 *once*
12 *doce*
13 *trece*
14 *catorce*
15 *quince*
16 *dieciseis*
17 *diecisiete*
18 *dieciocho*
19 *diecinueve*
20 *veinte*
21 *veinte y uno* or *veintiuno*
30 *treinta*
40 *cuarenta*
50 *cincuenta*
60 *sesenta*
70 *setenta*
80 *ochenta*
90 *noventa*
100 *ciento*
101 *ciento y uno* or *cientiuno*
200 *doscientos*
500 *quinientos*
1,000 *mil*
10,000 *diez mil*
100,000 *cien mil*
1,000,000 *millón*
one half *medio*
one third *un tercio*
one fourth *un cuarto*

TIME
What time is it? ¿Qué hora es?
It's one o'clock. Es la una.
It's three in the afternoon. Son las tres de la tarde.
It's 4 a.m. Son las cuatro de la mañana.
six-thirty seis y media
a quarter till eleven un cuarto para las once
a quarter past five las cinco y cuarto
an hour una hora

DAYS AND MONTHS
Monday lunes

Tuesday *martes*	**June** *junio*
Wednesday *miércoles*	**July** *julio*
Thursday *jueves*	**August** *agosto*
Friday *viernes*	**September** *septiembre*
Saturday *sábado*	**October** *octubre*
Sunday *domingo*	**November** *noviembre*
today *hoy*	**December** *diciembre*
tomorrow *mañana*	**a week** *una semana*
yesterday *ayer*	**a month** *un mes*
January *enero*	**after** *después*
February *febrero*	**before** *antes*
March *marzo*	
April *abril*	(Courtesy of Bruce Whipperman, author of
May *mayo*	*Moon Pacific Mexico.*)

Suggested Reading

ART AND CULTURE

Pérez, Louis A. *On Becoming Cuban: Nationality, Identity and Culture.* New York: Harper Perennial, 2001. Seminal and highly readable account of the development of Cuban culture from colonialism through communism.

BIOGRAPHY

Anderson, Jon Lee. *Che Guevara: A Revolutionary Life.* New York: Grove Press, 1997. This definitive biography reveals heretofore unknown details of Che's life and shows the dark side of this revolutionary icon.

Eire, Carlos. *Waiting for Snow in Havana.* New York: Free Press, 2004. An exquisitely told, heart-rending story of an exile's joyous childhood years in Havana on the eve of the Revolution, and the trauma of being put on the Peter Pan airlift, never to see his father again.

Fuentes, Norberto. *Hemingway in Cuba.* Secaucus, NY: Lyle Stuart, 1984. The seminal, lavishly illustrated study of the Nobel Prizewinner's years in Cuba.

Gimbel, Wendy. *Havana Dreams: A Story of Cuba.* London: Virago, 1998. The moving story of Naty Revuelta's tormented love affair with Fidel Castro and the terrible consequences of a relationship as heady as the doomed romanticism of the Revolution.

Hendrickson, Paul. *Hemingway's Boat: Everything He Loved in Life, and Lost.* New York: Vintage Books, 2012. A brilliant meditation on Hemingway in which his beloved *Pilar* serves as anchor.

Neyra, Edward J. *Cuba Lost and Found.* Cincinnati: Clerisy Press, 2009. A Cuban-American's moving tale of leaving Cuba on the Peter Pan airlift and his eventual return to his roots on the island.

Ramonte, Ignacio, ed. *Fidel Castro: My Life.* London: Penguin Books, 2008. In conversation with a fawning interviewer, Fidel tells his fascinating life story and expounds on his philosophy and passions. This often amusing and eyebrow-raising autobiography reveals Castro's astounding erudition, acute grasp of history, unwavering commitment to humanistic ideals, and his delusions and pathological hatred of the United States.

Sánchez, Juan Reinaldo. *The Double Life of Fidel Castro: My 17 Years as a Personal Bodyguard to El Líder Máximo.* New York: St. Martin's Press, 2015. An explosive, jaw-dropping kiss-and-tell.

Stout, Nancy. *One Day in December: Celia Sánchez and the Cuban Revolution.* New York: Monthly Review Press, 2013. A sympathetic and superbly crafted portrait of this fearless revolutionary—a brilliant organizer, recruiter, and Fidel Castro's most precious aide.

Szulc, Tad. *Fidel: A Critical Portrait.* New York: Morrow, 1986. A riveting profile of the astonishing life of this larger-than-life figure.

CIGARS

Habanos, S.A. *The World of the Habano.* Havana: Instituto de Investigaciones del Tabaco, 2012. Beautifully illustrated coffee-table book that tells you all you want to know about tobacco and its metamorphosis into fine cigars. It comes with a CD and ring gauge.

Perelman, Richard B. *Perelman's Pocket Cyclopedia of Havana Cigars.* Los Angeles: Perelman, Pioneer & Co, 1998. More than 160 pages with over 25 color photos, providing a complete list of cigar brands and shapes. Handy four- by six-inch size.

COFFEE-TABLE BOOKS

Baker, Christopher P. *Cuba Classics: A Celebration of Vintage American Automobiles.* Northampton, MA: Interlink Books, 2004. This lavishly illustrated coffee-table book pays homage to Cuba's astonishing wealth of classic American automobiles spanning eight decades. The text traces the long love affair between Cubans and the U.S.

automobile and offers a paean to the owners who keep their weary *cacharros* running.

Barclay, Juliet (photographs by Martin Charles). *Havana: Portrait of a City.* London: Cassell, 1993. A well-researched and abundantly illustrated coffee-table volume especially emphasizing the city's history.

Carley, Rachel. *Cuba: 400 Years of Architectural Legacy.* New York: Whitney Library of Design, 1997. Beautifully illustrated coffee-table book tracing the evolution of architectural styles from colonial days to the Communist aesthetic hiatus and post-Soviet renaissance.

Evans, Walker. *Walker Evans: Cuba.* New York: Getty Publications, 2001. Recorded in 1933, these 60 beautiful black-and-white images capture in stark clarity the misery and hardships of life in the era.

Kenny, Jack. *Cuba.* Ann Arbor, MI: Corazon Press, 2005. Beautiful black-and-white images capture the essence of Cuba and provide an intimate portrait into its soul.

Llanes, Lillian. *Havana Then and Now.* San Diego: Thunder Bay Press, 2004. A delightful collection of images wedding centenary black-and-whites to color photos showing the same locales as they are now.

Moruzzi, Peter. *Havana Before Castro: When Cuba was a Tropical Playground.* Salt Lake City: Gibbs Smith, 2008. This superb book is stuffed with fascinating images and tidbits that recall the heyday of sin and modernism.

GENERAL

Cabrera Infante, Guillermo. *¡Mea Cuba!* New York: Farrar, Straus & Giroux, 1994. An acerbic, indignant, raw, wistful, and brilliant set of essays in which the author pours out his bile at the Castro regime.

Henken, Ted A. *Cuba: A Global Studies Handbook*. Santa Barbara, CA: ABC-CLIO, 2008. A thoroughly insightful compendium spanning everything from history and culture to "Castro as a Charismatic Hero."

Martínez-Fernández, Luis, et al. *Encyclopedia of Cuba: People, History, Culture*. Westport, CT: Greenwood Press, 2004. Comprehensive twin-volume set with chapters arranged by themes, such as history, plastic arts, and sports.

Sánchez, Yoani. *Havana Real: One Woman Fights to Tell the Truth About Cuba*. New York: Melville House, 2009. Sardonic blog posts from "Generation Y" by a leading Cuban dissident paint an unflinching portrait of daily life in Cuba.

Shnookal, Deborah, and Mirta Muñiz, eds. *José Martí Reader*. New York: Ocean Press, 1999. An anthology of writings by one of the most brilliant and impassioned Latin American intellectuals of the 19th century.

HISTORY, ECONOMICS, AND POLITICS

Bardach, Ann Louise. *Cuba Confidential*. New York: Random House, 2002. A brilliant study of the failed politics of poisoned Cuban-U.S. relations, and the grand hypocrisies of the warring factions in Washington, Miami, and Havana.

Bardach, Ann Louise. *Without Fidel*. New York: Scribner, 2009. Bardach reports on Fidel's mystery illness and twilight days, and profiles the new president, Raúl Castro, in raw detail.

Deutschmann, David, and Deborah Shnookal. *Fidel Castro Reader*. Melbourne: Ocean Press, 2007. Twenty of Castro's most important speeches are presented verbatim.

English, T. J. *Havana Nocturne: How the Mob Owned Cuba and then Lost It to the Revolution*. New York: William Morrow, 2008. A fascinating and revealing account of the heyday of Cuba's mobster connections and the sordid Batista era.

Erikson, Daniel. *The Cuba Wars: Fidel Castro, the United States, and the Next Revolution*. New York: Bloomsbury Press, 2008. This seminal and objective work summarizes the U.S.-Cuban relations and "the incestuous relationship between Cuban-Americans and politicians in Washington" in a brilliantly nuanced way.

Frank, Mark. *Cuban Revelations: Behind the Scenes in Havana*. Miami: University Press of Florida, 2013. A U.S. journalist reports on his 25-plus years reporting from Cuba, offering a gripping and nuanced perspective on recent changes and the trajectory ahead.

Gjelten, Tom. *Bacardi and the Long Fight for Cuba*. New York: Viking, 2008. A superb and sweeping distillation of the fortunes of the Bacardi family and corporation and its relations to the epochal transition to Cuban independence, the toppling of the Batista regime, and Castro's Communism.

Gott, Richard. *Cuba: A New History*. New Haven, CT: Yale University Press, 2005. Erudite, entertaining, and concise yet detailed tour de force.

Latell, Brian. *After Fidel: The Inside Story of Castro's Regime and Cuba's Next Leader*. New York: Palgrave Macmillan, 2005. A former senior CIA analyst profiles the personalities of Fidel and Raúl Castro, providing insights into their quixotic, mutually dependent relationship and the motivations that have shaped their antagonistic relationship with the United States.

LeoGrande, William and Peter Kornbluth. *Back Channel to Cuba*. North Carolina: University of North Carolina Press, 2015. A fascinating assessment of secret efforts over decades to normalize relations between Cuba and the USA.

Morais, Fernando. *The Last Soldiers of the Cold War: The Story of the Cuban Five*. New York: Verso, 2015. A fascinating and objective account of how Cuba's intelligence agents infiltrated Cuban-American organizations to thwart terrorism.

Oppenheimer, Andres. *Castro's Final Hour*. New York: Simon and Schuster, 1992. A sobering, in-depth exposé of the uglier side of both Fidel Castro and the state system.

Smith, Wayne. *The Closest of Enemies*. New York: W. W. Norton, 1987. Essential reading, this personal account of the author's years serving as President Carter's man in Havana during the 1970s provides insights into the complexities that haunt U.S. relations with Cuba.

Sweig, Julia E. *Cuba: What Everyone Needs to Know*. Oxford: Oxford University Press, 2009. A reference to Cuba's history and politics, addressed in a clever question and answer format.

Thomas, Hugh. *Cuba: The Pursuit of Freedom, 1726-1969*. New York: Harper and Row, 1971. A seminal work—called a "magisterial conspectus of Cuban history"—tracing the evolution of conditions that eventually engendered the Revolution.

Thomas, Hugh. *The Cuban Revolution*. London: Weidenfeld and Nicolson, 1986. The definitive work on the Revolution, offering a brilliant analysis of all aspects of the country's diverse and tragic history.

Wyden, Peter. *Bay of Pigs: The Untold Story*. New York: Simon and Schuster, 1979. An in-depth and riveting exposé of the CIA's ill-conceived mission to topple Castro.

LITERATURE

Cabrera Infante, Guillermo. *Three Trapped Tigers*. New York: Avon, 1985. A poignant and comic novel that captures the essence of life in Havana before the ascendance of Castro.

García, Cristina. *Dreaming in Cuban*. New York: Ballantine Books, 1992. A poignant and sensual tale of a family divided politically and geographically by the Cuban revolution and the generational fissures that open.

Greene, Graham. *Our Man in Havana*. New York: Penguin, 1971. The story of Wormold, a British vacuum-cleaner salesman in pre-revolutionary Havana. Recruited by British intelligence, Wormold finds little information to pass on, and so invents it. Full of the sensuality and tensions of Batista's last days.

Gutiérrez, Pedro Juan. *Dirty Havana Trilogy*. New York: Farrar, Straus & Giroux, 2001. A bawdy semi-biographical take on the gritty life of Havana's underclass—begging, whoring, escaping hardship through sex and Santería—during the Special Period.

Hemingway, Ernest. *Islands in the Stream*. New York: Harper Collins, 1970. An exciting triptych set in Cuba during the war, it draws on the author's own experience hunting Nazi U-boats.

Hemingway, Ernest. *The Old Man and the Sea*. New York: Scribner's, 1952. The simple yet profound story of an unlucky Cuban angler won the Nobel Prize for Literature.

TRAVEL GUIDES

Lightfoot, Claudia. *Havana: A Cultural and Literary Companion*. Northampton, MA: Interlink Publishing, 2001. The author leads you through Havana past and present using literary quotations and allusions to add dimension to the sites and experiences.

Rodríguez, Eduardo Luis. *The Havana Guide: Modern Architecture 1925-65.* New York: Princeton Architectural Press, 2000. A marvelous guide to individual structures—homes, churches, theaters, government buildings—representing the best of modern architecture (1925-1965) throughout Havana.

TRAVEL LITERATURE

Aschkenas, Lea. *Es Cuba: Life and Love on an Illegal Island.* Emeryville, CA: Seal Press, 2006. Told with gentle compassion for a culture and country, *Es Cuba* reveals how the possibilities and hopes of the heart can surmount obdurate political barriers.

Baker, Christopher P. *Mi Moto Fidel: Motorcycling through Castro's Cuba.* Washington, D.C.: National Geographic's Adventure Press, 2001. Winner of the Lowell Thomas Award Travel Book of the Year, this erotically charged tale of the author's 7,000-mile adventure by motorcycle through Cuba offers a bittersweet look at the last Marxist "utopia."

Cooke, Julia. *The Other Side of Paradise: Life in the New Cuba.* Berkeley, CA: Seal Press, 2014. This exquisite memoir paints a vivid and sympathetic narrative of Cubans whose most common dream is of escaping a sclerotic Communist system.

Corbett, Ben. *This Is Cuba: An Outlaw Culture Survives.* Cambridge, MA: Westview Press, 2002. This first-person account of life in Castro's Cuba is a stinging indictment of the havoc, despair, and restraints wrought by *fidelismo.*

Miller, Tom. *Trading with the Enemy: A Yankee Travels through Castro's Cuba.* New York: Basic Books, 1996. Told by a famous author who lived in Cuba for almost a year, this travelogue is thoughtful, engaging, insightful, compassionate, and told in rich narrative.

Miller, Tom, ed. *Travelers' Tales: Cuba.* San Francisco: Travelers' Tales, 2001. Extracts from the contemporary works of 38 authors provide an at times hilarious, cautionary, and inspiring account of Cuba.

Tattlin, Isadora. *Cuba Diaries: An American Housewife in Havana.* Chapel Hill, NC: Algonquin Books, 2002. A marvelous account of four years in Havana spent raising two children, entertaining her husband's clients (including Fidel), and contending with chronic shortages.

Suggested Viewing

Before Night Falls (2000). A poignant adaptation of Reinaldo Arenas's autobiography, in which the persecuted Cuban novelist recounts his life in Cuba and in exile in the United States. Says film critic Lucas Hilderbrand, "It's an intoxicating, intensely erotic account of sexual discovery and liberation, and a devastating record of the artist's persecution under the Castro regime."

Buena Vista Social Club (1999). An adorable documentary look at the reemergence from obscurity of veteran performers Ruben González, Omara Portuondo, Ibrahim Ferrer, Eliades Ochoa, and Compay Segundo, culminating in their sellout concert at Carnegie Hall.

Death of a Bureaucrat (1966). Tomás Gutiérrez Alea's questioning portrait of the absurdities of the Cuban bureaucratic system and people's propensity to conform to absurd directives that cause misery to others.

El Cuerno de Abundancia (2008). The "Horn of Plenty" is Juan Carlos Tabio's tale of how a million-dollar inheritance upsets an entire town in Cuba's interior.

Fresa y Chocolate (1994). Nominated for an Oscar, Tomás Gutiérrez Alea's classic skit ("Strawberry and Chocolate") about the evolving friendship between a cultured gay man and the ardent revolutionary he attempts to seduce is an indictment of the treatment of homosexuals and liberals in the gray 1970s.

Guantanamera (1997). A road movie with a twist, this rueful romantic comedy by Tomás Gutiérrez Alea and Juan Carlos Tabio begins to unfold after an elderly dame dies from an excess of sexual stimulation. The farce of returning her body to Havana for proper burial provides the vehicle for a comic parody of an overly bureaucratic Cuba.

Los Diosas Rotas (2008). An enthralling, beautifully filmed tale of pimps and prostitutes in contemporary Havana. Nominated for a 2008 Oscar as Best Foreign Film.

Memories of Underdevelopment (1968). Director Tomás Gutiérrez Alea's sensual, wide-ranging masterpiece revolves around an erotically charged, intellectual "playboy" existence in early 1960s Cuba, pinned by the tragedy of the central character's alienation from the "underdeveloped" people around him and his own inability to attain a more fulfilled state.

Miel para Oshún (2003). Humberto Solas's "Honey for Oshún" tells the tale of a Cuban-American who, aided by a taxi driver, embarks on a wild road trip through Cuba to search for the mother he thought had abandoned him as a child.

Paradise Under the Stars (1999). Set around a star-struck woman's dream of singing at the Tropicana nightclub, this buoyantly witty comedy combines exuberant musical numbers, bedroom farce, and some satiric jabs at Cuban machismo.

¡Soy Cuba! (1964). Filmed by Russian director Mikhail Kalatozov, "I Am Cuba" is a brilliant, melodramatic, agitprop black-and-white, anti-American epic to Communist kitsch that exposes the poverty, oppression, and decadence of Batista's Havana.

Suite Habana (2003). The hit of the 25th Havana Film Festival, this emotionally haunting silent documentary records a single day in the life of 10 ordinary Cubans in Havana.

Tomorrow (2006). Alejandro Moya's video-clip style insight into contemporary Cuban reality as revealed by the nation's youthful intelligentsia.

Internet Resources

GENERAL INFORMATION
Cuba Sí
www.cubasi.cu
Generic Cuban government site with sections on travel, culture, news, etc.

Cuba Standard
www.cubastandard.com
Excellent news site focused on economics, business, and politics.

Etecsa
www.etecsa.cu
The website of Cuba's telephone corporation.

Gobierno de la República de Cuba
www.cubagob.cu
Official website of the Cuban government.

Havana Journal
www.havanajournal.com
A news bulletin and forum on everything Cuban related.

Paginas Amarillas
www.paginasamarillas.cu
Online Yellow Pages for commercial entities.

BLOGS
The Cuban Triangle
http://cubantriangle.blogspot.com
Politically focused posts by Phil Peters, of the Lexington Institute.

Generation Y
http://lageneraciony.com
Blog of Yoani Sánchez, Cuba's internationally known dissident, with biting insights into daily life.

CULTURE
Cubarte
www.cubarte.cult.cu
Cuban cultural site.

LaHabana
www.lahabana.com
A superb online magazine covering travel, culture, and the arts.

On Cuba
www.oncubamagazine.com
Excellent magazine spanning culture and travel.

TRAVEL INFORMATION
Christopher P. Baker
www.cubatravelexpert.com
Website of the world's foremost authority on travel and tourism to Cuba.

Infotur
www.infotur.cu
Information on tourist information centers in Havana.

Ministerio de Turismo
www.cubatravel.cu
Portal of Cuba's Ministry of Tourism.

Oficina del Historiador de la Ciudad Habana
www.habananuestra.cu
Spanish-only site (Office of the City Historian) relating to restoration projects, museums, hotels, and sites of interest in Habana Vieja.

U.S. Treasury Department (OFAC)
www.treas.gov/ofac
What you need to know about U.S. law and Cuba, direct from the horse's mouth.

Víazul
www.viazul.com
Website of Cuba's tourist bus company with online reservations.

Index

List of Maps

Acknowledgments

Researching a guidebook is fun, but it's no small task, and this seventh edition could not have been accomplished without the assistance of a coterie of selfless and supportive folk, not least the dozens of *casa particular* and *paladar* owners, Cuban entrepreneurs, and state employees who supported me in their own ways, large and small. They are too many to mention individually.

As always, I am indebted beyond words to my dear friends Jorge Coalla Potts, his wife, Marisel, and their daughter, Jessica. No words can express the devotion I have for this wonderful family, nor the appreciation I feel for their genuine affection, generosity, and support. Likewise, in Trinidad, Julio Muñoz Cocina and his wife, Rosa, continue to offer me the very best of friendship and support. And my time in Cuba in recent years has been blessed by the company of professional violinist and dear friend Ekaterina James Triana, who exemplifies the very best of the upbeat, compassionate, easy-going Cuban persona.

Thanks go to all my friends, acquaintances, and others who kindly forwarded clips and offered insight and tips on Cuba, and especially to those readers who took the trouble to write with recommendations, warnings, and general comments.

I am also extremely grateful for the support of everyone who contributed in ways large or small to the production of the prior editions, helping lay the foundation of this all-new edition.

¡Gracias! too to the countless Cubans who shared insights and shone the light on obscure issues, displayed selfless hospitality, welcomed me into their hearts and homes, and with unequaled verve, virtue, charity, patience, and grace taught me that I, and the world, have much to learn. As always on my lengthy research trips, Cubans everywhere embraced and welcomed me, touching my heart.

This edition I was fortunate to spend the greater part of the past three years in Cuba leading "people-to-people" programs for Lindblad Expeditions and National Geographic Expeditions, etc., as well as my own motorcycle and photography tours. Together these journeys unveiled countless venues I was previously unaware of and introduced me to a pantheon of notable and lesser-known Cubans whose insights have added invaluably to my understanding and knowledge of Cuba.

Yet again, I came away feeling like my friend Stephanie Gervassi-Levin, who on her first visit to Cuba began dancing uncontrollably in a *casa de la trova*. The Cubans formed a line and, "like a diplomat," took her hand, kissed her cheek. As I set out to write the first edition, she implored, "Chris, bring your genuine feeling into your pages. Breathe the innocence and beauty of Cuba without castrating Castro and his revolution." She set me a difficult task.

Ernest Hemingway, who loved Cuba and lived there for the better part of 20 years, once warned novice writer Arnold Samuelson against "a tendency to condemn before you completely understand. You aren't God, and you never judge a man. You present him as he is and you let the reader judge."

Meanwhile, the U.S. invasion has arrived in force. Cuba is changing at a remarkable pace, and not always for the best due to the inevitable fraying of community-based positive values as commercialism, materialism, and individualism take hold. I want to thank all Cubans for their remarkable example, for their gentility, graciousness and generosity. This book is dedicated to them.

Also Available

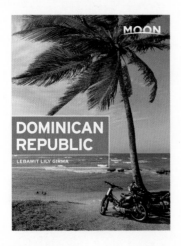

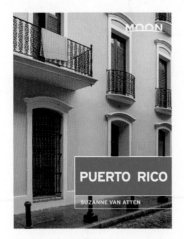

MAP SYMBOLS

	Expressway	○	City/Town	✈	Airport	⛳	Golf Course
	Primary Road	◉	State Capital	✗	Airfield	🅿	Parking Area
	Secondary Road	⦿	National Capital	▲	Mountain	⬢	Archaeological Site
	Unpaved Road	★	Point of Interest	✦	Unique Natural Feature	⛪	Church
	Feature Trail	•	Accommodation				Gas Station
	Other Trail			🐚	Waterfall		
	Ferry	▼	Restaurant/Bar				Glacier
	Pedestrian Walkway	■	Other Location	⚑	Park		Mangrove
	Stairs	Λ	Campground	⊡	Trailhead		Reef
				⛷	Skiing Area		Swamp

CONVERSION TABLES

°C = (°F - 32) / 1.8
°F = (°C x 1.8) + 32
1 inch = 2.54 centimeters (cm)
1 foot = 0.304 meters (m)
1 yard = 0.914 meters
1 mile = 1.6093 kilometers (km)
1 km = 0.6214 miles
1 fathom = 1.8288 m
1 chain = 20.1168 m
1 furlong = 201.168 m
1 acre = 0.4047 hectares
1 sq km = 100 hectares
1 sq mile = 2.59 square km
1 ounce = 28.35 grams
1 pound = 0.4536 kilograms
1 short ton = 0.90718 metric ton
1 short ton = 2,000 pounds
1 long ton = 1.016 metric tons
1 long ton = 2,240 pounds
1 metric ton = 1,000 kilograms
1 quart = 0.94635 liters
1 US gallon = 3.7854 liters
1 Imperial gallon = 4.5459 liters
1 nautical mile = 1.852 km

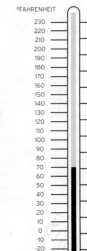

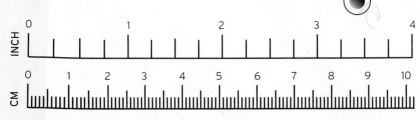

MOON CUBA
Avalon Travel
Hachette Book Group
1700 Fourth Street
Berkeley, CA 94710, USA
www.moon.com

KIRKWOOD

Editor: Sabrina Young
Series Manager: Kathryn Ettinger
Copy Editor: Brett Keener
Production and Graphics Coordinator: Darren Alessi
Cover Design: Faceout Studios, Charles Brock
Interior Design: Domini Dragoone
Moon Logo: Tim McGrath
Map Editor: Mike Morgenfeld
Cartographers: Austin Ehrhardt, Larissa Gatt
Proofreader: Alissa Cyphers
Indexer: Greg Jewett

ISBN-13: 978-1-63121-645-9
Printing History
1st Edition — 1997
7th Edition — January 2018
5 4 3 2 1

Front cover photo: © Christopher P. Baker
Back cover photo: © Sergebelll8 | Dreamstime.com
All interior photos: © Christopher P. Baker

Printed in China by RR Donnelley

Avalon Travel is a division of Hachette Book Group, Inc. Moon and the Moon logo are trademarks of Hachette Book Group, Inc. All other marks and logos depicted are the property of the original owners.

5/11/2018